SPANISH

TRAVEL DICTIONARY

HarperCollins*Publishers*

first published in this edition 1996

©HarperCollins Publishers 1996

ISBN 0 00 471017-7

Typeset by Morton Word Processing Ltd, Scarborough
Printed and bound in Great Britain by
Caledonian International Book Manufacturing Ltd, Glasgow, G64

Contents

Introduction

We are delighted you have decided to buy the **Collins Spanish Travel Dictionary** and hope you will benefit from using it whether you are travelling abroad for pleasure or on business.

This dictionary provides up-to-date coverage of all the Spanish you will need, in a clear and user-friendly layout. The emphasis is on contemporary language, with numerous examples of idiomatic usage which will enable you not only to understand but also to communicate with confidence.

A special feature of the dictionary is the KEYWORD entries which highlight the most frequently-used words in both languages and treat them in depth. In addition, pronunciation is shown throughout in the International Phonetic Alphabet to help you with unfamiliar words.

We hope that you enjoy using the dictionary and that you find it an ideal travelling companion.

Using the Dictionary

The various typefaces, type sizes, symbols, abbreviations and brackets used in this book all convey useful information. Take time to establish what they indicate and this will help you get the most out of your dictionary.

Finding the word you want

The information above the line at the top of each page helps you to locate, quickly and easily, the entry you want to consult. At the outside margin, the first and last entries on that page are shown, separated by an arrow. Information about which side of the dictionary you are using is shown at the inside margin.

On the Spanish-English side, ch, ll and ñ are to be found after the letters C, L and N respectively.

Headwords

The words you look up in a dictionary are called headwords and are printed in **bold** type. The phonetic spelling is given in square brackets immediately after the headword. An explanation of these symbols is given on pages x and xi. Information about the usage or register of certain headwords appears in round brackets, usually abbreviated and in italic eg (*fam*), (*COMM*). A list of all the abbreviations used in the dictionary is given on pages viii-xi.

Where appropriate, words related to headwords are grouped in the same entry in a slightly smaller type than the headword.

> **nación** [...] *nf* nation; **nacional**
> *adj* national; ...

> **reluctance** [...] *n* renuencia;
> **reluctant** *adj* renuente; ...

Common expressions in which the headword appears are shown in smaller bold type.

> **old** [...] *adj* viejo; (*former*) anti-
> guo; **how ~ are you?**

Translations

Headword translations are given in ordinary type and, where more than one meaning or usage exists, these are separated by a semicolon. You will often find bracketed words in italics appearing before the translations. These are called "indicators" and they offer suggested contexts in which the headword might appear or provide synonyms for the headword to guide you to the most appropriate translation.

> **lirón** [...] *nm* (*ZOOL*) dormouse;
> (*fig*) sleepyhead
>
> **erode** [...] *vt* (*GEO*) erosionar;
> (*metal*) corroer, desgastar; (*fig*)
> desgastar

Key words

Special status is given to certain Spanish and English words which are considered "key" words in each language. These words occur very frequently in Spanish or English or have several types of usage (eg **de, haber**). A combination of lozenges and numbers helps you to distinguish different parts of speech and different meanings.

Grammatical information

Parts of speech are given in abbreviated form in italics after the phonetic spellings of headwords (eg *vt, adv, conj*). A lozenge indicates a change in part of speech and different meanings are split into separate categories and numbered accordingly. Genders of Spanish nouns are indicated as follows: *nm* for a masculine and *nf* for a feminine noun. Feminine and irregular plural forms of nouns and adjectives are also shown.

> **Irlanda** [...] *nf* Ireland; **irlandés,**
> **esa** [...] *adj* Irish ◆ *nm/f* Irish-
> man/woman; **los irlandeses** the
> Irish
>
> **luz** [...] (*pl luces*) *nf* light; ...

Abbreviations

adjetivo, locución adjetiva	*adj*	adjective, adjectival phrase
abreviatura	*ab(b)r*	abbreviation
adverbio, locución adverbial	*adv*	adverb, adverbial phrase
administración, lengua administrativa	*ADMIN*	administration
agricultura	*AGR*	agriculture
América Latina	*AM*	Latin America
anatomía	*ANAT*	anatomy
arquitectura	*ARQ, ARCH*	architecture
el automóvil	*AUT(O)*	the motor car and motoring
aviación, viajes aéreos	*AVIAT*	flying, air travel
biología	*BIO(L)*	biology
botánica, flores	*BOT*	botany
inglés británico	*BRIT*	British English
química	*CHEM*	chemistry
comercio, finanzas, banca	*COM(M)*	commerce, finance, banking
informática	*COMPUT*	computers
conjunción	*conj*	conjunction
construcción	*CONSTR*	building
compuesto	*cpd*	compound element
cocina	*CULIN*	cookery
economía	*ECON*	economics
electricidad, electrónica	*ELEC*	electricity, electronics
enseñanza, sistema escolar y universitario	*ESCOL*	schooling, schools and universities
España	*ESP*	Spain
especialmente	*esp*	especially
exclamación, interjección	*excl*	exclamation, interjection
femenino	*f*	feminine
lengua familiar (! vulgar)	*fam(!)*	colloquial usage (! particularly offensive)
ferrocarril	*FERRO*	railways
uso figurado	*fig*	figurative use
fotografía	*FOTO*	photography
(verbo inglés) del cual la partícula es inseparable	*fus*	(phrasal verb) where the particle is inseparable
generalmente	*gen*	generally
geografía, geología	*GEO*	geography, geology
geometría	*GEOM*	geometry
uso familiar (! vulgar)	*inf(!)*	colloquial usage (! particularly offensive)
infinitivo	*infin*	infinitive
informática	*INFORM*	computers
invariable	*inv*	invariable
irregular	*irreg*	irregular
lo jurídico	*JUR*	law
América Latina	*LAM*	Latin America
gramática, lingüística	*LING*	grammar, linguistics

Spanish	Abbreviation	English
masculino	*m*	masculine
matemáticas	*MAT(H)*	mathematics
medicina	*MED*	medical term, medicine
masculino/femenino	*m/f*	masculine/feminine
lo militar, ejército	*MIL*	military matters
música	*MUS*	music
sustantivo, nombre	*n*	noun
navegación, náutica	*NAUT*	sailing, navigation
sustantivo numérico	*num*	numeral noun
complemento	*obj*	(grammatical) object
	o.s.	oneself
peyorativo	*pey, pej*	derogatory, pejorative
fotografía	*PHOT*	photography
fisiología	*PHYSIOL*	physiology
plural	*pl*	plural
política	*POL*	politics
participio de pasado	*pp*	past participle
preposición	*prep*	preposition
pronombre	*pron*	pronoun
psicología, psiquiatría	*PSICO, PSYCH*	psychology, psychiatry
tiempo pasado	*pt*	past tense
química	*QUIM*	chemistry
ferrocarril	*RAIL*	railways
religión, lo eclesiástico	*REL*	religion, church service
	sb	somebody
enseñanza, sistema escolar y universitario	*SCH*	schooling, schools and universities
singular	*sg*	singular
España	*SP*	Spain
	sth	something
sujeto	*su(b)j*	(grammatical) subject
subjuntivo	*subjun*	subjunctive
tauromaquia	*TAUR*	bullfighting
también	*tb*	also
técnica, tecnología	*TEC(H)*	technical term, technology
telecomunicaciones	*TELEC, TEL*	telecommunications
televisión	*TV*	television
imprenta, tipografía	*TIP, TYP*	typography, printing
inglés norteamericano	*US*	American English
verbo	*vb*	verb
verbo intransitivo	*vi*	intransitive verb
verbo pronominal	*vr*	reflexive verb
verbo transitivo	*vt*	transitive verb
zoología, animales	*ZOOL*	zoology
marca registrada	®	registered trademark
indica un equivalente cultural	≈	introduces a cultural equivalent

Spanish Pronunciation

Consonants

b	[b, ß]	**b**oda	see notes on *v* below
		bom**b**a	
		la**b**or	
c	[k]	**c**aja	*c* before *a*, *o* or *u* is pronounced as in *c*at
ce, ci	[θe, θi]	**c**ero	*c* before *e* or *i* is pronounced as in *thin*
		cielo	
ch	[tʃ]	**ch**iste	*ch* is pronounced as *ch* in *ch*air
d	[d, ð]	**d**anés	at the beginning of a phrase or after *l* or *n*, *d* is pronounced as in English. In any other position it is pronounced like *th* in *the*
		ciu**d**a**d**	
g	[g, γ]	**g**afas	*g* before *a*, *o* or *u* is pronounced as in *g*ap, if at the beginning of a phrase or after *n*. In other positions the sound is softened
		pa**g**a	
ge, gi	[xe, xi]	**g**ente	*g* before *e* or *i* is pronounced similar to *ch* in Scottish lo*ch*
		girar	
h		**h**aber	*h* is always silent in Spanish
j	[x]	**j**ugar	*j* is pronounced similar to *ch* in Scottish lo*ch*
ll	[ʎ]	ta**ll**e	*ll* is pronounced like the *lli* in mi*lli*on
ñ	[ɲ]	ni**ñ**o	*ñ* is pronounced like the *ni* in o*ni*on
q	[k]	**q**ue	*q* is pronounced as *k* in *k*ing
r, rr	[r, rr]	quita**r**	*r* is always pronounced in Spanish, unlike the silent *r* in dance*r*. *rr* is trilled, like a Scottish *r*
		ga**rr**a	
s	[s]	quizá**s**	*s* is usually pronounced as in pa**ss**, but before *b*, *d*, *g*, *l*, *m* or *n* it is pronounced as in ro**s**e
		i**s**la	
v	[b, ß]	**v**ía	*v* is pronounced something like *b*. At the beginning of a phrase or after *m* or *n* it is pronounced as *b* in *b*oy. In any other position the sound is softened
		di**v**idir	
z	[θ]	tena**z**	*z* is pronounced as *th* in *th*in.

f, k, l, m, n, p, t and **x** are pronounced as in English.

Vowels

a	[a]	p*a*t*a*	not as long as *a* in f*a*r. When followed by a consonant in the same syllable (i.e. in a closed syllable), as in am*a*nte, the *a* is short, as in b*a*t
e	[e]	m*e*	like *e* in th*e*y. In a closed syllable, as in g*e*nte, the *e* is short as in p*e*t
i	[i]	p*i*no	as in m*ea*n or mach*i*ne
o	[o]	l*o*	as in l*o*cal. In a closed syllable, as in c*o*ntrol, the *o* is short as in c*o*t
u	[u]	l*u*nes	as in r*u*le. It is silent after *q*, and in *gue, gui,* unless marked *güe, güi* e.g. anti*gü*edad, when it is pronounced like *w* in *w*olf

Semivowels

| i, y | [j] | b*i*en
h*i*elo
*y*unta | pronounced like *y* in *y*es |
| u | [w] | h*u*evo
f*u*ente
anti*gü*edad | unstressed *u* between consonant and vowel is pronounced like *w* in *w*ell. See also notes on *u* above |

Diphthongs

ai, ay	[ai]	b*ai*le	as *i* in r*i*de
au	[au]	*au*to	as *ou* in sh*ou*t
ei, ey	[ei]	bu*ey*	as *ey* in gr*ey*
eu	[eu]	de*u*da	both elements pronounced independently [e] + [u]
oi, oy	[oi]	h*oy*	as *oy* in t*oy*

Stress

The rules of stress in Spanish are as follows:

(a) when a word ends in a vowel or in *n* or *s*, the second last syllable is stressed: pat*a*ta, pat*a*tas, c*o*me, c*o*men

(b) when a word ends in a consonant other than *n* or *s*, the stress falls on the last syllable: par*e*d, habl*a*r

(c) when the rules set out in a and b are not applied, an acute accent appears over the stressed vowel: com*ú*n, geograf*í*a, ingl*é*s

In the phonetic transcription, the symbol ['] precedes the syllable on which the stress falls.

ESPAÑOL - INGLÉS
SPANISH - ENGLISH

A a

a [a] (*a*+*el* = *al*) *prep* **1** (*dirección*) to; **fueron ~ Madrid/Grecia** they went to Madrid/Greece; **me voy ~ casa** I'm going home

2 (*distancia*): **está ~ 15 km de aquí** it's 15 kms from here

3 (*posición*): **estar ~ la mesa** to be at table; **al lado de** next to, beside; *ver tb* **puerta**

4 (*tiempo*): **las 10/~ medianoche** at 10/midnight; **~ la mañana siguiente** the following morning; **~ los pocos días** after a few days; **estamos ~ 9 de julio** it's the ninth of July; **~ los 24 años** at the age of 24; **al año/~ la semana** (*AM*) a year/week later

5 (*manera*): **~ la francesa** the French way; **~ caballo** on horseback; **~ oscuras** in the dark

6 (*medio, instrumento*): **~ lápiz** in pencil; **~ mano** by hand; **cocina ~ gas** gas stove

7 (*razón*): **~ 30 ptas el kilo** at 30 pesetas a kilo; **~ más de 50 km/h** at more than 50 kms per hour

8 (*dativo*): **se lo di** → **él** I gave it to him; **vi al policía** I saw the policeman; **se lo compré ~ él** I bought it from him

9 (*tras ciertos verbos*): **voy ~ verle** I'm going to see him; **empezó ~ trabajar** he started working *o* to work

10 (+ *infin*): **al verle, le reconocí inmediatamente** when I saw him I recognized him at once; **el camino ~ recorrer** the distance we (*etc*) have to travel; **¡~ callar!** keep quiet!; **¡~ comer!** let's eat!

abad, esa [a'βað, 'ðesa] *nm/f* abbot/abbess; **~ía** *nf* abbey

abajo [a'βaxo] *adv* (*situación*) (down) below, underneath; (*en edificio*) downstairs; (*dirección*) down, downwards; **el piso de ~** the downstairs flat; **la parte de ~** the lower part; **¡~ el gobierno!** down with the government!; **cuesta/río ~** downhill/downstream; **de arriba ~** from top to bottom; **el ~ firmante** the undersigned; **más ~** lower *o* further down

abalanzarse [aβalan'θarse] *vr*: **~ sobre** *o* **contra** to throw o.s. at

abalorios [aβa'lorjos] *nmpl* (*chucherías*) trinkets

abanderado [aβande'raðo] *nm* standard bearer

abandonado, a [aβando'naðo, a] *adj* derelict; (*desatendido*) abandoned; (*desierto*) deserted; (*descuidado*) neglected

abandonar [aβando'nar] *vt* to leave; (*persona*) to abandon, desert; (*cosa*) to abandon, leave behind; (*descuidar*) to neglect; (*renunciar a*) to give up; (*INFORM*) to quit; **~se** *vr*: **~se a** to abandon o.s. to; **abandono** *nm* (*acto*) desertion, abandonment; (*estado*) abandon, neglect; (*renuncia*) withdrawal, retirement; **ganar por abandono** to win by default

abanicar [aβani'kar] *vt* to fan; **abanico** *nm* fan; (*NAUT*) derrick

abaratar [aβara'tar] *vt* to lower the price of ♦ *vi* to go *o* come down in price; **~se** *vr* to go *o* come down in price

abarcar [aβar'kar] *vt* to include, embrace; (*AM*) to monopolize

abarrotado, a [aβarro'taðo, a] *adj* packed

abarrotar [aβarro'tar] *vt* (*local, estadio, teatro*) to fill, pack

abarrotero, a [aβarro'tero, a] (*AM*) *nm/f* grocer; **abarrotes** *nmpl* (*AM*) groceries, provisions

abastecer [aβaste'θer] *vt*: **~ (de)** to supply (with); **abastecimiento** *nm* supply

abasto [a'βasto] *nm* supply; (*abundancia*)

abundance; **no dar** ~ **a** to be unable to cope with

abatido, a [aβa'tiðo, a] *adj* dejected, downcast

abatimiento [aβati'mjento] *nm* (*depresión*) dejection, depression

abatir [aβa'tir] *vt* (*muro*) to demolish; (*pájaro*) to shoot *o* bring down; (*fig*) to depress; ~**se** *vr* to get depressed; ~**se sobre** to swoop *o* pounce on

abdicación [aβðika'θjon] *nf* abdication

abdicar [aβði'kar] *vi* to abdicate

abdomen [aβ'domen] *nm* abdomen; **abdominales** *nmpl* (*tb: ejercicios abdominales*) sit-ups

abecedario [aβeθe'ðarjo] *nm* alphabet

abedul [aβe'ðul] *nm* birch

abeja [a'βexa] *nf* bee

abejorro [aβe'xorro] *nm* bumblebee

aberración [aβerra'θjon] *nf* aberration

abertura [aβer'tura] *nf* = **apertura**

abeto [a'βeto] *nm* fir

abierto, a [a'βjerto, a] *pp de* **abrir** ♦ *adj* open; (*AM*) generous

abigarrado, a [aβiɣa'rraðo, a] *adj* multicoloured

abismal [aβis'mal] *adj* (*fig*) vast, enormous

abismar [aβis'mar] *vt* to humble, cast down; ~**se** *vr* to sink; ~**se en** (*fig*) to be plunged into

abismo [a'βismo] *nm* abyss

abjurar [aβxu'rar] *vi*: ~ **de** to abjure, forswear

ablandar [aβlan'dar] *vt* to soften ♦ *vi* to get softer; ~**se** *vr* to get softer

abnegación [aβneɣa'θjon] *nf* self-denial

abnegado, a [aβne'ɣaðo, a] *adj* self-sacrificing

abocado, a [aβo'kaðo, a] *adj*: **verse** ~ **al desastre** to be heading for disaster

abochornar [aβotʃor'nar] *vt* to embarrass; ~**se** *vr* to get flustered; (*BOT*) to wilt

abofetear [aβofete'ar] *vt* to slap (in the face)

abogado, a [aβo'ɣaðo, a] *nm/f* lawyer; (*notario*) solicitor; (*en tribunal*) barrister (*BRIT*), attorney (*US*); ~ **defensor** defence lawyer *o* attorney (*US*)

abogar [aβo'ɣar] *vi*: ~ **por** to plead for; (*fig*) to advocate

abolengo [aβo'lengo] *nm* ancestry, lineage

abolición [aβoli'θjon] *nf* abolition

abolir [aβo'lir] *vt* to abolish; (*cancelar*) to cancel

abolladura [aβoʎa'ðura] *nf* dent

abollar [aβo'ʎar] *vt* to dent

abominable [aβomi'naβle] *adj* abominable

abonado, a [aβo'naðo, a] *adj* (*deuda*) paid(-up) ♦ *nm/f* subscriber

abonar [aβo'nar] *vt* (*deuda*) to settle; (*terreno*) to fertilize; (*idea*) to endorse; ~**se** *vr* to subscribe; **abono** *nm* payment; fertilizer;

subscription

abordar [aβor'ðar] *vt* (*barco*) to board; (*asunto*) to broach

aborigen [aβo'rixen] *nm/f* aborigine

aborrecer [aβorre'θer] *vt* to hate, loathe

abortar [aβor'tar] *vi* (*malparir*) to have a miscarriage; (*deliberadamente*) to have an abortion; **aborto** *nm* miscarriage; abortion

abotonar [aβoto'nar] *vt* to button (up), do up

abovedado, a [aβoβe'ðaðo, a] *adj* vaulted, domed

abrasar [aβra'sar] *vt* to burn (up); (*AGR*) to dry up, parch

abrazadera [aβraθa'ðera] *nf* bracket

abrazar [aβra'θar] *vt* to embrace, hug

abrazo [a'βraθo] *nm* embrace, hug; **un** ~ (*en carta*) with best wishes

abrebotellas [aβreβo'teʎas] *nm inv* bottle opener

abrecartas [aβre'kartas] *nm inv* letter opener

abrelatas [aβre'latas] *nm inv* tin (*BRIT*) *o* can opener

abreviar [aβre'βjar] *vt* to abbreviate; (*texto*) to abridge; (*plazo*) to reduce; **abreviatura** *nf* abbreviation

abridor [aβri'ðor] *nm* bottle opener; (*de latas*) tin (*BRIT*) *o* can opener

abrigar [aβri'ɣar] *vt* (*proteger*) to shelter; (*suj: ropa*) to keep warm; (*fig*) to cherish

abrigo [a'βriɣo] *nm* (*prenda*) coat, overcoat; (*lugar protegido*) shelter

abril [a'βril] *nm* April

abrillantar [aβriʎan'tar] *vt* to polish

abrir [a'βrir] *vt* to open (up) ♦ *vi* to open; ~**se** *vr* to open (up); (*extenderse*) to open out; (*cielo*) to clear; ~**se paso** to find *o* force a way through

abrochar [aβro'tʃar] *vt* (*con botones*) to button (up); (*zapato, con broche*) to do up

abrumar [aβru'mar] *vt* to overwhelm; (*sobrecargar*) to weigh down

abrupto, a [a'βrupto, a] *adj* abrupt; (*empinado*) steep

absceso [aβs'θeso] *nm* abscess

absentismo [aβsen'tismo] *nm* absenteeism

absolución [aβsolu'θjon] *nf* (*REL*) absolution; (*JUR*) acquittal

absoluto, a [aβso'luto, a] *adj* absolute; **en** ~ *adv* not at all

absolver [aβsol'βer] *vt* to absolve; (*JUR*) to pardon; (: *acusado*) to acquit

absorbente [aβsor'βente] *adj* absorbent; (*interesante*) absorbing

absorber [aβsor'βer] *vt* to absorb; (*embeber*) to soak up

absorción [aβsor'θjon] *nf* absorption; (*COM*) takeover

absorto, a [aβ'sorto, a] *pp de* **absorber** ♦ *adj* absorbed, engrossed

abstemio, a [aβs'temjo, a] *adj* teetotal

abstención [aßsten'θjon] nf abstention
abstenerse [aßste'nerse] vr: ~ **(de)** to abstain o refrain (from)
abstinencia [aßsti'nenθja] nf abstinence; (ayuno) fasting
abstracción [aßstrak'θjon] nf abstraction
abstracto, a [aß'strakto, a] adj abstract
abstraer [aßstra'er] vt to abstract; ~**se** vr to be o become absorbed
abstraído, a [aßstra'iðo, a] adj absent-minded
absuelto [aß'swelto] pp de absolver
absurdo, a [aß'surðo, a] adj absurd
abuchear [aßutʃe'ar] vt (a actor, orador) to boo
abuelo, a [a'ßwelo, a] nm/f grandfather/mother; ~**s** nmpl grandparents
abulia [a'ßulja] nf apathy
abultado, a [aßul'taðo, a] adj bulky
abultar [aßul'tar] vt to enlarge; (aumentar) to increase; (fig) to exaggerate ♦ vi to be bulky
abundancia [aßun'danθja] nf: **una ~ de** plenty of; **abundante** adj abundant, plentiful
abundar [aßun'dar] vi to abound, be plentiful
aburguesarse [aßurɣe'sarse] vr to become middle-class
aburrido, a [aßu'rriðo, a] adj (hastiado) bored; (que aburre) boring; **aburrimiento** nm boredom, tedium
aburrir [aßu'rrir] vt to bore; ~**se** vr to be bored, get bored
abusar [aßu'sar] vi to go too far; ~ **de** to abuse
abusivo, a [aßu'sißo, a] adj (precio) exorbitant
abuso [a'ßuso] nm abuse
abyecto, a [aß'jekto, a] adj wretched, abject
A.C. abr (= Año de Cristo) A.D.
a/c abr (= al cuidado de) c/o
acá [a'ka] adv (lugar) here; ¿**de cuándo ~?** since when?
acabado, a [aka'ßaðo, a] adj finished, complete; (perfecto) perfect; (agotado) worn out; (fig) masterly ♦ nm finish
acabar [aka'ßar] vt (llevar a su fin) to finish, complete; (consumir) to use up; (rematar) to finish off ♦ vi to finish, end; ~**se** vr to finish, stop; (terminarse) to be over; (agotarse) to run out; ~ **con** to put an end to; ~ **de llegar** to have just arrived; ~ **por hacer** to end (up) by doing; **¡se acabó!** it's all over!; **(¡basta!)** that's enough!
acabóse [aka'ßose] nm: **esto es el ~** this is the last straw
academia [aka'ðemja] nf academy; **académico, a** adj academic
acaecer [akae'θer] vi to happen, occur
acalorado, a [akalo'raðo, a] adj (discusión)

heated
acalorarse [akalo'rarse] vr (fig) to get heated
acallar [aka'ʎar] vt (persona) to silence; (protestas, rumores) to suppress
acampar [akam'par] vi to camp
acantilado [akanti'laðo] nm cliff
acaparar [akapa'rar] vt to monopolize; (acumular) to hoard
acariciar [akari'θjar] vt to caress; (esperanza) to cherish
acarrear [akarre'ar] vt to transport; (fig) to cause, result in
acaso [a'kaso] adv perhaps, maybe ♦ nm chance; (por) si ~ (just) in case
acatamiento [akata'mjento] nm respect; (ley) observance
acatar [aka'tar] vt to respect; (ley) obey
acatarrarse [akata'rrarse] vr to catch a cold
acaudalado, a [akauða'laðo, a] adj well-off
acaudillar [akauði'ʎar] vt to lead, command
acceder [akθe'ðer] vi: ~ **a** (petición etc) to agree to; (tener acceso a) to have access to; (INFORM) to access
accesible [akθe'sißle] adj accessible
acceso [ak'θeso] nm access, entry; (camino) access, approach; (MED) attack, fit
accesorio, a [akθe'sorjo, a] adj, nm accessory
accidentado, a [akθiðen'taðo, a] adj uneven; (montañoso) hilly; (azaroso) eventful ♦ nm/f accident victim
accidental [akθiðen'tal] adj accidental; **accidentarse** vr to have an accident
accidente [akθi'ðente] nm accident; ~**s** nmpl (de terreno) unevenness sg
acción [ak'θjon] nf action; (acto) action, act; (COM) share; (JUR) action, lawsuit; ~ **ordinaria/preferente** ordinary/preference share; **accionar** vt to work, operate; (INFORM) to drive
accionista [akθjo'nista] nm/f shareholder, stockholder
acebo [a'θeßo] nm holly; (árbol) holly tree
acechar [aθe'tʃar] vt to spy on; (aguardar) to lie in wait for; **acecho** nm: **estar al acecho (de)** to lie in wait (for)
aceitar [aθei'tar] vt to oil, lubricate
aceite [a'θeite] nm oil; (de olíva) olive oil; ~**ra** nf oilcan; **aceitoso, a** adj oily
aceituna [aθei'tuna] nf olive
acelerador [aθelera'ðor] nm accelerator
acelerar [aθele'rar] vt to accelerate
acelga [a'θelɣa] nf chard, beet
acento [a'θento] nm accent; (acentuación) stress
acentuar [aθen'twar] vt to accent; to stress; (fig) to accentuate
acepción [aθep'θjon] nf meaning
aceptable [aθep'taßle] adj acceptable

aceptación [aθepta'θjon] *nf* acceptance; (*aprobación*) approval

aceptar [aθep'tar] *vt* to accept; (*aprobar*) to approve

acequia [a'θekja] *nf* irrigation ditch

acera [a'θera] *nf* pavement (*BRIT*), sidewalk (*US*)

acerca [a'θerka]: ~ **de** *prep* about, concerning

acercar [aθer'kar] *vt* to bring *o* move nearer; ~**se** *vr* to approach, come near

acerico [aθe'riko] *nm* pincushion

acero [a'θero] *nm* steel

acérrimo, a [a'θerrimo, a] *adj* (*partidario*) staunch; (*enemigo*) bitter

acertado, a [aθer'taðo, a] *adj* correct; (*apropiado*) apt; (*sensato*) sensible

acertar [aθer'tar] *vt* (*blanco*) to hit; (*solución*) to get right; (*adivinar*) to guess ♦ *vi* to get it right, be right; ~ **a** to manage to; ~ **con** to happen *o* hit on

acertijo [aθer'tixo] *nm* riddle, puzzle

acervo [a'θerßo] *nm* heap; ~ **común** undivided estate

aciago, a [a'θjaɣo, a] *adj* ill-fated, fateful

acicalar [aθika'lar] *vt* to polish; (*persona*) to dress up; ~**se** *vr* to get dressed up

acicate [aθi'kate] *nm* spur

acidez [aθi'ðeθ] *nf* acidity

ácido, a ['aθiðo, a] *adj* sour, acid ♦ *nm* acid

acierto *etc* [a'θjerto] *vb ver* **acertar** ♦ *nm* success; (*buen paso*) wise move; (*solución*) solution; (*habilidad*) skill, ability

aclamación [aklama'θjon] *nf* acclamation; (*aplausos*) applause

aclamar [akla'mar] *vt* to acclaim; (*aplaudir*) to applaud

aclaración [aklara'θjon] *nf* clarification, explanation

aclarar [akla'rar] *vt* to clarify, explain; (*ropa*) to rinse ♦ *vi* to clear up; ~**se** *vr* (*explicarse*) to understand; ~**se la garganta** to clear one's throat

aclaratorio, a [aklara'torjo, a] *adj* explanatory

aclimatación [aklimata'θjon] *nf* acclimatization

aclimatar [aklima'tar] *vt* to acclimatize; ~**se** *vr* to become acclimatized

acné [ak'ne] *nm* acne

acobardar [akoßar'ðar] *vt* to intimidate

acodarse [ako'ðarse] *vr*: ~ **en** to lean on

acogedor, a [akoxe'ðor, a] *adj* welcoming; (*hospitalario*) hospitable

acoger [ako'xer] *vt* to welcome; (*abrigar*) to shelter; ~**se** *vr* to take refuge

acogida [ako'xiða] *nf* reception; refuge

acolchar [akol'tʃar] *vt* to pad; (*fig*) to cushion

acometer [akome'ter] *vt* to attack; (*emprender*) to undertake; **acometida** *nf* at-

tack, assault

acomodado, a [akomo'ðaðo, a] *adj* (*persona*) well-to-do

acomodador, a [akomoða'ðor, a] *nm/f* usher(ette)

acomodar [akomo'ðar] *vt* to adjust; (*alojar*) to accommodate; ~**se** *vr* to conform; (*instalarse*) to install o.s.; (*adaptarse*): ~**se (a)** to adapt (to)

acomodaticio, a [akomoða'tiθjo, a] *adj* (*pey*) accommodating, obliging; (*manejable*) pliable

acompañar [akompa'ɲar] *vt* to accompany; (*documentos*) to enclose

acondicionar [akondiθjo'nar] *vt* to arrange, prepare; (*pelo*) to condition

acongojar [akongo'xar] *vt* to distress, grieve

aconsejar [akonse'xar] *vt* to advise, counsel; ~**se** *vr*: ~**se con** to consult

acontecer [akonte'θer] *vi* to happen, occur; **acontecimiento** *nm* event

acopio [a'kopjo] *nm* store, stock

acoplamiento [akopla'mjento] *nm* coupling, joint; **acoplar** *vt* to fit; (*ELEC*) to connect; (*vagones*) to couple

acorazado, a [akora'θaðo, a] *adj* armour-plated, armoured ♦ *nm* battleship

acordar [akor'ðar] *vt* (*resolver*) to agree, resolve; (*recordar*) to remind; ~**se** *vr* to agree; ~**se (de algo)** to remember (sth); **acorde** *adj* (*MUS*) harmonious; **acorde con** (*medidas etc*) in keeping with ♦ *nm* chord

acordeón [akorðe'on] *nm* accordion

acordonado, a [akorðo'naðo, a] *adj* (*calle*) cordoned-off

acorralar [akorra'lar] *vt* to round up, corral

acortar [akor'tar] *vt* to shorten; (*duración*) to cut short; (*cantidad*) to reduce; ~**se** *vr* to become shorter

acosar [ako'sar] *vt* to pursue relentlessly; (*fig*) to hound, pester

acostar [akos'tar] *vt* (*en cama*) to put to bed; (*en suelo*) to lay down; (*barco*) to bring alongside; ~**se** *vr* to go to bed; to lie down; ~**se con uno** to sleep with sb

acostumbrado, a [akostum'braðo, a] *adj* usual; ~ **a** used to

acostumbrar [akostum'brar] *vt*: ~ **uno a algo** to get sb used to sth ♦ *vi*: ~ **(a) hacer** to be in the habit of doing; ~**se** *vr*: ~**se a** to get used to

acotación [akota'θjon] *nf* marginal note; (*GEO*) elevation mark; (*de límite*) boundary mark; (*TEATRO*) stage direction

ácrata ['akrata] *adj, nm/f* anarchist

acre ['akre] *adj* (*sabor*) sharp, bitter; (*olor*) acrid; (*fig*) biting ♦ *nm* acre

acrecentar [akreθen'tar] *vt* to increase, augment

acreditar [akreði'tar] *vt* (*garantizar*) to vouch for, guarantee; (*autorizar*) to authorize; (dar prueba de) to prove; (COM: abonar) to credit; (embajador) to accredit; ~se vr to become famous

acreedor, a [akree'ðor, a] adj: ~ de worthy of ♦ nm/f creditor

acribillar [akriβi'ʎar] vt: ~ a balazos to riddle with bullets

acrimonia [akri'monja] nf acrimony

acritud [akri'tuð] nf = acrimonia

acróbata [a'kroβata] nm/f acrobat

acta ['akta] nf certificate; (de comisión) minutes pl, record; ~ de nacimiento/de matrimonio birth/marriage certificate; ~ notarial affidavit

actitud [akti'tuð] nf attitude; (postura) posture

activar [akti'ßar] vt to activate; (acelerar) to speed up

actividad [aktiβi'ðað] nf activity

activo, a [ak'tißo, a] adj active; (vivo) lively ♦ nm (COM) assets pl

acto ['akto] nm act, action; (ceremonia) ceremony; (TEATRO) act; en el ~ immediately

actor [ak'tor] nm actor; (JUR) plaintiff ♦ adj: parte ~a prosecution

actriz [ak'triθ] nf actress

actuación [aktwa'θjon] nf action; (comportamiento) conduct, behaviour; (JUR) proceedings pl; (desempeño) performance

actual [ak'twal] adj present(-day), current; ~idad nf present; ~idades nfpl (noticias) news sg; en la ~idad at present; (hoy día) nowadays

actualizar [aktwali'θar] vt to update, modernize

actualmente [aktwal'mente] adv at present; (hoy día) nowadays

actuar [ak'twar] vi (obrar) to work, operate; (actor) to act, perform ♦ vt to work, operate; ~ de to act as

acuarela [akwa'rela] nf watercolour

acuario [a'kwarjo] nm aquarium; (ASTROLOGÍA): A~ Aquarius

acuartelar [akwarte'lar] vt (MIL: disciplinar) to confine to barracks

acuático, a [a'kwatiko, a] adj aquatic

acuciante [aku'θjante] adj urgent

acuciar [aku'θjar] vt to urge on

acuclillarse [akukli'ʎarse] vr to crouch down

acuchillar [akutʃi'ʎar] vt (TEC) to plane (down), smooth

acudir [aku'ðir] vi (asistir) to attend; (ir) to go; ~ a (fig) to turn to; ~ en ayuda de to go to the aid of

acuerdo etc [a'kwerðo] vb ver acordar ♦ nm agreement; ¡de ~! agreed!; de ~ con (persona) in agreement with; (acción, documento) in accordance with; estar de ~ to be agreed, agree

acumular [akumu'lar] vt to accumulate, collect

acuñar [aku'ɲar] vt (moneda) to mint; (frase) to coin

acupuntura [akupun'tura] nf acupuncture

acuoso, a [a'kwoso, a] adj watery

acurrucarse [akurru'karse] vr to crouch; (ovillarse) to curl up

acusación [akusa'θjon] nf accusation

acusar [aku'sar] vt to accuse; (revelar) to reveal; (denunciar) to denounce

acuse [a'kuse] nm: ~ de recibo acknowledgement of receipt

acústica [a'kustika] nf acoustics pl

acústico, a [a'kustiko, a] adj acoustic

achacar [atʃa'kar] vt to attribute

achacoso, a [atʃa'koso, a] adj sickly

achantar [atʃan'tar] (fam) vt to scare, frighten; ~se vr to back down

achaque etc [a'tʃake] vb ver achacar ♦ nm ailment

achicar [atʃi'kar] vt to reduce; (humillar) to humiliate; (NAUT) to bale out

achicoria [atʃi'korja] nf chicory

achicharrar [atʃitʃa'rrar] vt to scorch, burn

adagio [a'ðaxjo] nm adage; (MUS) adagio

adaptación [aðapta'θjon] nf adaptation

adaptador [aðapta'ðor] nm (ELEC) adapter

adaptar [aðap'tar] vt to adapt; (acomodar) to fit

adecuado, a [aðe'kwaðo, a] adj (apto) suitable; (oportuno) appropriate

adecuar [aðe'kwar] vt to adapt; to make suitable

a. de J.C. abr (= antes de Jesucristo) B.C.

adelantado, a [aðelan'taðo, a] adj advanced; (reloj) fast; pagar por ~ to pay in advance

adelantamiento [aðelanta'mjento] nm advance, advancement; (AUTO) overtaking

adelantar [aðelan'tar] vt to move forward; (avanzar) to advance; (acelerar) to speed up; (AUTO) to overtake ♦ vi to go forward, advance; ~se vr to go forward, advance

adelante [aðe'lante] adv forward(s), ahead ♦ excl come in!; de hoy en ~ from now on; más ~ later on; (más allá) further on

adelanto [aðe'lanto] nm advance; (mejora) improvement; (progreso) progress

adelgazar [aðelʏa'θar] vt to thin (down) ♦ vi to get thin; (con régimen) to slim down, lose weight

ademán [aðe'man] nm gesture; ademanes nmpl manners; en ~ de as if to

además [aðe'mas] adv besides; (por otra parte) moreover; (también) also; ~ de besides, in addition to

adentrarse [aðen'trarse] vr: ~ en to go into, get inside; (penetrar) to penetrate (into)

adentro [a'ðentro] adv inside, in; mar ~ out at sea; tierra ~ inland

adepto, a [a'ðepto, a] nm/f supporter

aderezar [aðere'θar] vt (ensalada) to dress;

(comida) to season; **aderezo** *nm* dressing; seasoning

adeudar [aðeu'ðar] *vt* to owe; **~se** *vr* to run into debt

adherirse [aðe'rirse] *vr:* ~ **a** to adhere to; *(partido)* to join

adhesión [aðe'sjon] *nf* adhesion; *(fig)* adherence

adicción [aðik'θjon] *nf* addiction

adición [aði'θjon] *nf* addition

adicto, a [a'ðikto, a] *adj:* ~ **a** addicted to; *(dedicado)* devoted to ♦ *nm/f* supporter, follower; *(toxicómano etc)* addict

adiestrar [aðjes'trar] *vt* to train, teach; *(conducir)* to guide, lead; **~se** *vr* to practise; *(enseñarse)* to train o.s.

adinerado, a [aðine'raðo, a] *adj* wealthy

adiós [a'ðjos] *excl (para despedirse)* goodbye!, cheerio!; *(al pasar)* hello!

aditivo [aði'tiβo] *nm* additive

adivinanza [aðiβi'nanθa] *nf* riddle

adivinar [aðiβi'nar] *vt* to prophesy; *(conjeturar)* to guess; **adivino, a** *nm/f* fortuneteller

adj *abr* (= *adjunto*) encl.

adjetivo [aðxe'tiβo] *nm* adjective

adjudicación [aðxuðika'θjon] *nf* award; adjudication

adjudicar [aðxuði'kar] *vt* to award; **~se** *vr:* **~se algo** to appropriate sth

adjuntar [aðxun'tar] *vt* to attach, enclose; **adjunto, a** *adj* attached, enclosed ♦ *nm/f* assistant

administración [aðministra'θjon] *nf* administration; *(dirección)* management; **administrador, a** *nm/f* administrator; manager(ess)

administrar [aðminis'trar] *vt* to administer; **administrativo, a** *adj* administrative

admirable [aðmi'raβle] *adj* admirable

admiración [aðmira'θjon] *nf* admiration; *(asombro)* wonder; *(LING)* exclamation mark

admirar [aðmi'rar] *vt* to admire; *(extrañar)* to surprise; **~se** *vr* to be surprised

admisible [aðmi'siβle] *adj* admissible

admisión [aðmi'sjon] *nf* admission; *(reconocimiento)* acceptance

admitir [aðmi'tir] *vt* to admit; *(aceptar)* to accept

admonición [aðmoni'θjon] *nf* warning

adobar [aðo'βar] *vt (CULIN)* to season

adobe [a'ðoβe] *nm* adobe, sun-dried brick

adoctrinar [aðoktri'nar] *vt:* ~ **en** to indoctrinate with

adolecer [aðole'θer] *vi:* ~ **de** to suffer from

adolescente [aðoles'θente] *nm/f* adolescent, teenager

adonde [a'ðonðe] *conj* (to) where

adónde [a'ðonðe] *adv* = **dónde**

adopción [aðop'θjon] *nf* adoption

adoptar [aðop'tar] *vt* to adopt

adoptivo, a [aðop'tiβo, a] *adj (padres)* adoptive; *(hijo)* adopted

adoquín [aðo'kin] *nm* paving stone

adorar [aðo'rar] *vt* to adore

adormecer [aðorme'θer] *vt* to put to sleep; **~se** *vr* to become sleepy; *(dormirse)* to fall asleep

adornar [aðor'nar] *vt* to adorn

adorno [a'ðorno] *nm* adornment; *(decoración)* decoration

adosado, a [aðo'saðo, a] *adj:* **casa adosada** semi-detached house

adquiero *etc vb ver* **adquirir**

adquirir [aðki'rir] *vt* to acquire, obtain

adquisición [aðkisi'θjon] *nf* acquisition

adrede [a'ðreðe] *adv* on purpose

adscribir [aðskri'βir] *vt* to appoint

adscrito *pp de* **adscribir**

aduana [a'ðwana] *nf* customs *pl*

aduanero, a [aðwa'nero, a] *adj* customs *cpd* ♦ *nm/f* customs officer

aducir [aðu'θir] *vt* to adduce; *(dar como prueba)* to offer as proof

adueñarse [aðwe'ɲarse] *vr:* ~ **de** to take possession of

adulación [aðula'θjon] *nf* flattery

adular [aðu'lar] *vt* to flatter

adulterar [aðulte'rar] *vt* to adulterate ♦ *vi* to commit adultery

adulterio [aðul'terjo] *nm* adultery

adúltero, a [a'ðultero, a] *adj* adulterous ♦ *nm/f* adulterer/adulteress

adulto, a [a'ðulto, a] *adj, nm/f* adult

adusto, a [a'ðusto, a] *adj* stern; *(austero)* austere

advenedizo, a [aðβene'ðiθo, a] *nm/f* upstart

advenimiento [aðβeni'mjento] *nm* arrival; *(al trono)* accession

adverbio [að'βerβjo] *nm* adverb

adversario, a [aðβer'sarjo, a] *nm/f* adversary

adversidad [aðβersi'ðað] *nf* adversity; *(contratiempo)* setback

adverso, a [að'βerso, a] *adj* adverse

advertencia [aðβer'tenθja] *nf* warning; *(prefacio)* preface, foreword

advertir [aðβer'tir] *vt* to notice; *(avisar):* ~ **a uno de** to warn sb about o of

Adviento [að'βjento] *nm* Advent

advierto *etc vb ver* **advertir**

adyacente [aðja'θente] *adj* adjacent

aéreo, a [a'ereo, a] *adj* aerial

aerobic [ae'roβik] *nm* aerobics *sg*

aerodeslizador [aeroðesliθa'ðor] *nm* hovercraft

aerodeslizante [aeroðesli'θante] *nm* = **aerodeslizador**

aeromozo, a [aero'moθo, a] *(AM) nm/f* air steward(ess)

aeronáutica [aero'nautika] *nf* aeronautics *sg*

aeronave [aero'naðe] nm spaceship
aeroplano [aero'plano] nm aeroplane
aeropuerto [aero'pwerto] nm airport
aerosol [aero'sol] nm aerosol
afabilidad [afaßili'ðað] nf friendliness; **afable** adj affable
afamado, a [afa'maðo, a] adj famous
afán [a'fan] nm hard work; (deseo) desire
afanar [afa'nar] vt to harass; (fam) to pinch; ~se vr: ~se por hacer to strive to do; **afanoso, a** adj (trabajo) hard; (trabajador) industrious
afear [afe'ar] vt to disfigure
afección [afek'θjon] nf (MED) disease
afectación [afekta'θjon] nf affectation; **afectado, a** adj affected
afectar [afek'tar] vt to affect
afectísimo, a [afek'tisimo, a] adj affectionate; ~ suyo yours truly
afectivo, a [afek'tißo, a] adj (problema etc) emotional
afecto [a'fekto] nm affection; **tenerle ~ a uno** to be fond of sb
afectuoso, a [afek'twoso, a] adj affectionate
afeitar [afei'tar] vt to shave; ~se vr to shave
afeminado, a [afemi'naðo, a] adj effeminate
aferrar [afe'rrar] vt to grasp; (barco) to moor ♦ vi to moor
Afganistán [afɣanis'tan] nm Afghanistan
afianzamiento [afjanθa'mjento] nm strengthening; security
afianzar [afjan'θar] vt to strengthen; to secure; ~se vr to become established
afición [afi'θjon] nf fondness, liking; **la ~** the fans pl; **pinto por ~** I paint as a hobby; **aficionado, a** adj keen, enthusiastic; (no profesional) amateur ♦ nm/f enthusiast, fan; amateur; **ser aficionado a algo** to be very keen on o fond of sth
aficionar [afiθjo'nar] vt: ~ **a uno a algo** to make sb like sth; ~se vr: ~se a algo to grow fond of sth
afiche [a'fitʃe] (AM) nm poster
afilado, a [afi'laðo, a] adj sharp
afilar [afi'lar] vt to sharpen
afiliarse [afi'ljarse] vr to affiliate
afín [a'fin] adj (parecido) similar; (conexo) related
afinar [afi'nar] vt (TEC) to refine; (MUS) to tune ♦ vi (tocar) to play in tune; (cantar) to sing in tune
afincarse [afin'karse] vr to settle
afinidad [afini'ðað] nf affinity; (parentesco) relationship; **por ~** by marriage
afirmación [afirma'θjon] nf affirmation
afirmar [afir'mar] vt to affirm, state; (reforzar) to strengthen; **afirmativo, a** adj affirmative
aflicción [aflik'θjon] nf affliction; (dolor) grief

afligir [afli'xir] vt to afflict; (apenar) to distress; ~se vr to grieve
aflojar [aflo'xar] vt to slacken; (desatar) to loosen, undo; (relajar) to relax ♦ vi to drop; (bajar) to go down; ~se vr to relax
aflorar [aflo'rar] vi to come to the surface, emerge
afluente [aflu'ente] adj flowing ♦ nm tributary
afluir [aflu'ir] vi to flow
afmo, a abr (= afectísimo(a) suyo(a)) Yours
afónico, a [a'foniko, a] adj: **estar ~** to have a sore throat; to have lost one's voice
aforo [a'foro] nm (de teatro etc) capacity
afortunado, a [afortu'naðo, a] adj fortunate, lucky
afrancesado, a [afranθe'saðo, a] adj francophile; (pey) Frenchified
afrenta [a'frenta] nf affront, insult; (deshonra) dishonour, shame
África ['afrika] nf Africa; ~ **del Sur** South Africa; ~ **del Norte** North Africa; **africano, a** adj, nm/f African
afrontar [afron'tar] vt to confront; (poner cara a cara) to bring face to face
afuera [a'fwera] adv out, outside; ~s nfpl outskirts
agachar [aɣa'tʃar] vt to bend, bow; ~se vr to stoop, bend
agalla [a'ɣaʎa] nf (ZOOL) gill; ~s nfpl (MED) tonsillitis sg; (ANAT) tonsils; **tener ~s** (fam) to have guts
agarradera [aɣarra'ðera] (AM) nf = agarradero
agarradero [aɣarra'ðero] nm handle; ~s nmpl (fig) pull sg, influence sg
agarrado, a [aɣa'rraðo, a] adj mean, stingy
agarrar [aɣa'rrar] vt to grasp, grab; (AM) to take, catch; (recoger) to pick up ♦ vi (planta) to take root; ~se vr to hold on (tightly)
agarrotar [aɣarro'tar] vt (lío) to tie tightly; (persona) to squeeze tightly; (reo) to garrotte; ~se vr (motor) to seize up; (MED) to stiffen
agasajar [aɣasa'xar] vt to treat well, fête
agazaparse [aɣaθa'parse] vr to crouch down
agencia [a'xenθja] nf agency; ~ **inmobiliaria** estate (BRIT) o real estate (US) agent's (office); ~ **de viajes** travel agency
agenciarse [axen'θjarse] vr to obtain, procure
agenda [a'xenda] nf diary
agente [a'xente] nm/f agent; (de policía) policeman/policewoman; ~ **inmobiliario** estate agent (BRIT), realtor (US); ~ **de seguros** insurance agent
ágil ['axil] adj agile, nimble; **agilidad** nf agility, nimbleness
agilizar [axili'θar] vt (trámites) to speed up

agitación [axita'θjon] *nf* (*de mano etc*) shaking, waving; (*de líquido etc*) stirring; (*fig*) agitation

agitado, a [axi'aðo, a] *adj* hectic; (*viaje*) bumpy

agitar [axi'tar] *vt* to wave, shake; (*líquido*) to stir; (*fig*) to stir up, excite; ~**se** *vr* to get excited; (*inquietarse*) to get worried *o* upset

aglomeración [aɣlomera'θjon] *nf*: ~ **de tráfico/gente** traffic jam/mass of people

aglomerar [aɣlome'rar] *vt* to crowd together; ~**se** *vr* to crowd together

agnóstico, a [aɣ'nostiko, a] *adj, nm/f* agnostic

agobiar [aɣo'ßjar] *vt* to weigh down; (*oprimir*) to oppress; (*cargar*) to burden

agolparse [aɣol'parse] *vr* to crowd together

agonía [aɣo'nia] *nf* death throes *pl*; (*fig*) agony, anguish

agonizante [aɣoni'θante] *adj* dying

agonizar [aɣoni'θar] *vi* (*tb: estar agonizando*) to be dying

agosto [a'ɣosto] *nm* August

agotado, a [aɣo'taðo, a] *adj* (*persona*) exhausted; (*libros*) out of print; (*acabado*) finished; (*COM*) sold out

agotador, a [aɣota'ðor, a] *adj* exhausting

agotamiento [aɣota'mjento] *nm* exhaustion

agotar [aɣo'tar] *vt* to exhaust; (*consumir*) to drain; (*recursos*) to use up, deplete; ~**se** *vr* to be exhausted; (*acabarse*) to run out; (*libro*) to go out of print

agraciado, a [aɣra'θjaðo, a] *adj* (*atractivo*) attractive; (*en sorteo etc*) lucky

agradable [aɣra'ðaßle] *adj* pleasant, nice

agradar [aɣra'ðar] *vt*: **él me agrada** I like him

agradecer [aɣraðe'θer] *vt* to thank; (*favor etc*) to be grateful for; **agradecido, a** *adj* grateful; **¡muy agradecido!** thanks a lot!; **agradecimiento** *nm* thanks *pl*; gratitude

agradezco *etc vb ver* **agradecer**

agrado [a'ɣraðo] *nm*: **ser de tu** *etc* ~ to be to your *etc* liking

agrandar [aɣran'dar] *vt* to enlarge; (*fig*) to exaggerate; ~**se** *vr* to get bigger

agrario, a [a'ɣrarjo, a] *adj* agrarian, land *cpd*; (*política*) agricultural, farming

agravante [aɣra'ßante] *adj* aggravating ♦ *nf*: **con la** ~ **de que** ... with the further difficulty that ...

agravar [aɣra'ßar] *vt* (*pesar sobre*) to make heavier; (*irritar*) to aggravate; ~**se** *vr* to worsen, get worse

agraviar [aɣra'ßjar] *vt* to offend; (*ser injusto con*) to wrong; ~**se** *vr* to take offence; **agravio** *nm* offence; wrong; (*JUR*) grievance

agredir [aɣre'ðir] *vt* to attack

agregado, a [aɣre'ɣaðo, a] *nm/f*: **A~** ≈ teacher (*who is not head of department*) ♦ *nm* aggregate; (*persona*) attaché

agregar [aɣre'ɣar] *vt* to gather; (*añadir*) to add; (*persona*) to appoint

agresión [aɣre'sjon] *nf* aggression

agresivo, a [aɣre'sißo, a] *adj* aggressive

agriar [a'ɣrjar] *vt* to (turn) sour; ~**se** *vr* to turn sour

agrícola [a'ɣrikola] *adj* farming *cpd*, agricultural

agricultor, a [aɣrikul'tor, a] *nm/f* farmer

agricultura [aɣrikul'tura] *nf* agriculture, farming

agridulce [aɣri'ðulθe] *adj* bittersweet; (*CULIN*) sweet and sour

agrietarse [aɣrje'tarse] *vr* to crack; (*piel*) to chap

agrimensor, a [aɣrimen'sor, a] *nm/f* surveyor

agrio, a [a'ɣrjo, a] *adj* bitter

agronomía [aɣrono'mia] *nf* agronomy, agriculture

agropecuario, a [aɣrope'kwarjo, a] *adj* farming *cpd*, agricultural

agrupación [aɣrupa'θjon] *nf* group; (*acto*) grouping

agrupar [aɣru'par] *vt* to group

agua ['aɣwa] *nf* water; (*NAUT*) wake; (*ARQ*) slope of a roof; ~**s** *nfpl* (*de piedra*) water *sg*, sparkle *sg*; (*MED*) water *sg*, urine *sg*; (*NAUT*) waters; ~**s abajo/arriba** downstream/upstream; ~ **bendita/destilada/potable** holy/distilled/drinking water; ~ **caliente** hot water; ~ **corriente** running water; ~ **de colonia** eau de cologne; ~ **mineral (con/sin gas)** (carbonated/uncarbonated) mineral water; ~ **oxigenada** hydrogen peroxide; ~**s jurisdiccionales** territorial waters

aguacate [aɣwa'kate] *nm* avocado (pear)

aguacero [aɣwa'θero] *nm* (heavy) shower, downpour

aguada [a'ɣwaða] *nf* (*AGR*) watering place; (*NAUT*) water supply; (*ARTE*) watercolour

aguado, a [a'ɣwaðo, a] *adj* watery, watered down

aguafiestas [aɣwa'fjestas] *nm/f inv* spoilsport, killjoy

aguanieve [aɣwa'njeße] *nf* sleet

aguantar [aɣwan'tar] *vt* to bear, put up with; (*sostener*) to hold up ♦ *vi* to last; ~**se** *vr* to restrain o.s.; **aguante** *nm* (*paciencia*) patience; (*resistencia*) endurance

aguar [a'ɣwar] *vt* to water down

aguardar [aɣwar'ðar] *vt* to wait for

aguardiente [aɣwar'ðjente] *nm* brandy, liquor

aguarrás [aɣwa'rras] *nm* turpentine

agudeza [aɣu'ðeθa] *nf* sharpness; (*ingenio*) wit

agudizar [aɣuði'θar] *vt* (*crisis*) to make worse; ~**se** *vr* to get worse

agudo, a [a'ɣuðo, a] *adj* sharp; (*voz*) high-pitched, piercing; *(dolor, enfermedad)* acute

agüero [a'ɣwero] *nm*: **buen/mal ~** good/bad omen

aguijón [aɣi'xon] *nm* sting; *(fig)* spur

águila ['aɣila] *nf* eagle; *(fig)* genius

aguileño, a [aɣi'leɲo, a] *adj (nariz)* aquiline; *(rostro)* sharp-featured

aguinaldo [aɣi'naldo] *nm* Christmas box

aguja [a'ɣuxa] *nf* needle; *(de reloj)* hand; *(ARQ)* spire; *(TEC)* firing-pin; **~s** *nfpl* *(ZOOL)* ribs; *(FERRO)* points

agujerear [aɣuxere'ar] *vt* to make holes in

agujero [aɣu'xero] *nm* hole

agujetas [aɣu'xetas] *nfpl* stitch *sg*; *(rigidez)* stiffness *sg*

aguzar [aɣu'θar] *vt* to sharpen; *(fig)* to incite

ahí [a'i] *adv* there; **de ~ que** so that, with the result that; **~ llega** here he comes; **por ~** that way; *(allá)* over there; **200 o por ~** 200 or so

ahijado, a [ai'xaðo, a] *nm/f* godson/daughter

ahínco [a'inko] *nm* earnestness

ahíto, a [a'ito, a] *adj*: **estoy ~** I'm full up

ahogar [ao'ɣar] *vt* to drown; *(asfixiar)* to suffocate, smother; *(fuego)* to put out; **~se** *vr (en el agua)* to drown; *(por asfixia)* to suffocate

ahogo [a'oɣo] *nm* breathlessness; *(fig)* financial difficulty

ahondar [aon'dar] *vt* to deepen, make deeper; *(fig)* to study thoroughly ♦ *vi*: **~ en** to study thoroughly

ahora [a'ora] *adv* now; *(hace poco)* a moment ago, just now; *(dentro de poco)* in a moment; **~ voy** I'm coming; **~ mismo** right now; **~ bien** now then; **por ~** for the present

ahorcar [aor'kar] *vt* to hang; **~se** *vr* to hang o.s.

ahorita [ao'rita] *(fam: esp AM) adv* right now

ahorrar [ao'rrar] *vt (dinero)* to save; *(esfuerzos)* to save, avoid; **ahorro** *nm (acto)* saving; *(frugalidad)* thrift; **ahorros** *nmpl (dinero)* savings

ahuecar [awe'kar] *vt* to hollow (out); *(voz)* to deepen; **~se** *vr* to give o.s. airs

ahumar [au'mar] *vt* to smoke, cure; *(llenar de humo)* to fill with smoke ♦ *vi* to smoke; **~se** *vr* to fill with smoke

ahuyentar [aujen'tar] *vt* to drive off, frighten off; *(fig)* to dispel

airado, a [ai'raðo, a] *adj* angry

airar [ai'rar] *vt* to anger; **~se** *vr* to get angry

aire ['aire] *nm* air; *(viento)* wind; *(corriente)* draught; *(MUS)* tune; **~s** *nmpl*: **darse ~s** to give o.s. airs; **al ~ libre** in the open air; **~ acondicionado** air conditioning; **airearse** *vr (persona)* to go out for a breath of

fresh air; **airoso, a** *adj* windy; draughty; *(fig)* graceful

aislado, a [ais'laðo, a] *adj* isolated; *(incomunicado)* cut-off; *(ELEC)* insulated

aislar [ais'lar] *vt* to isolate; *(ELEC)* to insulate

ajardinado, a [axarði'naðo, a] *adj* landscaped

ajedrez [axe'ðreθ] *nm* chess

ajeno, a [a'xeno, a] *adj (que pertenece a otro)* somebody else's; **~ a** foreign to; **~ de** free from, devoid of

ajetreado, a [axetre'aðo, a] *adj* busy

ajetreo [axe'treo] *nm* bustle

ají [a'xi] *nm* chilli, red pepper; *(salsa)* chilli sauce

ajo ['axo] *nm* garlic

ajuar [a'xwar] *nm* household furnishings *pl*; *(de novia)* trousseau; *(de niño)* layette

ajustado, a [axus'taðo, a] *adj (tornillo)* tight; *(cálculo)* right; *(ropa)* tight(-fitting); *(DEPORTE: resultado)* close

ajustar [axus'tar] *vt (adaptar)* to adjust; *(encajar)* to fit; *(TEC)* to engage; *(IMPRENTA)* to make up; *(apretar)* to tighten; *(concertar)* to agree (on); *(reconciliar)* to reconcile; *(cuentas, deudas)* to settle ♦ *vi* to fit; **~se** *vr*: **~se a** *(precio etc)* to be in keeping with, fit in with; **~ las cuentas a uno** to get even with sb

ajuste [a'xuste] *nm* adjustment; *(COSTURA)* fitting; *(acuerdo)* compromise; *(de cuenta)* settlement

al [al] (= **a + el**) *ver* **a**

ala ['ala] *nf* wing; *(de sombrero)* brim; *(futbolista)* winger

alabanza [ala'ßanθa] *nf* praise

alabar [ala'ßar] *vt* to praise

alacena [ala'θena] *nf* kitchen cupboard *(BRIT)*, kitchen closet *(US)*

alacrán [ala'kran] *nm* scorpion

alado, a [a'laðo, a] *adj* winged

alambique [alam'bike] *nm* still

alambrada [alam'braða] *nf* wire fence; *(red)* wire netting

alambrado [alam'braðo] *nm* = **alambrada**

alambre [a'lambre] *nm* wire; **~ de púas** barbed wire

alameda [ala'meða] *nf (plantío)* poplar grove; *(lugar de paseo)* avenue, boulevard

álamo ['alamo] *nm* poplar; **~ temblón** aspen

alarde [a'larðe] *nm* show, display; **hacer ~ de** to boast of

alargador [alarɣa'ðor] *nm (ELEC)* extension lead

alargar [alar'ɣar] *vt* to lengthen, extend; *(paso)* to hasten; *(brazo)* to stretch out; *(cuerda)* to pay out; *(conversación)* to spin out; **~se** *vr* to get longer

alarido [ala'riðo] *nm* shriek

alarma [a'larma] *nf* alarm

alarmar [alar'mar] *vt* to alarm; **~se** to get alarmed; **alarmante** [alar'mante] *adj* alarming

alba ['alβa] *nf* dawn

albacea [alβa'θea] *nm/f* executor/executrix

albahaca [al'βaka] *nf* basil

Albania [al'βanja] *nf* Albania

albañal [alβa'ɲal] *nm* drain, sewer

albañil [alβa'ɲil] *nm* bricklayer; (*cantero*) mason

albarán [alβa'ran] *nm* (*COM*) delivery note, invoice

albaricoque [alβari'koke] *nm* apricot

albedrío [alβe'ðrio] *nm*: **libre ~** free will

alberca [al'βerka] *nf* reservoir; (*AM*) swimming pool

albergar [alβer'var] *vt* to shelter

albergue *etc* [al'βerxe] *vb ver* **albergar** ♦ *nm* shelter, refuge; **~ juvenil** youth hostel

albóndiga [al'βondiɣa] *nf* meatball

albornoz [alβor'noθ] *nm* (*de los árabes*) burnous; (*para el baño*) bathrobe

alborotar [alβoro'tar] *vi* to make a row ♦ *vt* to agitate, stir up; **~se** *vr* to get excited; (*mar*) to get rough; **alboroto** *nm* row, uproar

alborozar [alβoro'θar] *vt* to gladden; **~se** *vr* to rejoice

alborozo [alβo'roθo] *nm* joy

álbum ['alβum] (*pl* **~s**, **~es**) *nm* album; **~ de recortes** scrapbook

albumen [al'βumen] *nm* egg white, albumen

alcachofa [alka'tʃofa] *nf* artichoke

alcalde, esa [al'kalde, esa] *nm/f* mayor(ess)

alcaldía [alkal'dia] *nf* mayoralty; (*lugar*) mayor's office

alcance *etc* [al'kanθe] *vb ver* **alcanzar** ♦ *nm* reach; (*COM*) adverse balance

alcantarilla [alkanta'riʎa] *nf* (*de aguas cloacales*) sewer; (*en la calle*) gutter

alcanzar [alkan'θar] *vt* (*algo: con la mano, el pie*) to reach; (*alguien: en el camino etc*) to catch up (with); (*autobús*) to catch; (*suj: bala*) to hit, strike ♦ *vi* (*ser suficiente*) to be enough; **~ a hacer** to manage to do

alcaparra [alka'parra] *nf* caper

alcayata [alka'jata] *nf* hook

alcázar [al'kaθar] *nm* fortress; (*NAUT*) quarter-deck

alcoba [al'koβa] *nf* bedroom

alcohol [al'kol] *nm* alcohol; **~ metílico** methylated spirits *pl* (*BRIT*), wood alcohol (*US*); **alcohólico, a** *adj, nm/f* alcoholic

alcoholímetro [alko'limetro] *nm* Breathalyser ® (*BRIT*), drunkometer (*US*)

alcoholismo [alko'lismo] *nm* alcoholism

alcornoque [alkor'noke] *nm* cork tree; (*fam*) idiot

alcurnia [al'kurnja] *nf* lineage

aldaba [al'daβa] *nf* (door) knocker

aldea [al'dea] *nf* village; **~no, a** *adj* village *cpd* ♦ *nm/f* villager

aleación [alea'θjon] *nf* alloy

aleatorio, a [alea'torjo, a] *adj* random

aleccionar [alekθjo'nar] *vt* to instruct; (*adiestrar*) to train

alegación [aleɣa'θjon] *nf* allegation

alegar [ale'ɣar] *vt* to allege; (*JUR*) to plead ♦ *vi* (*AM*) to argue

alegato [ale'ɣato] *nm* (*JUR*) allegation; (*AM*) argument

alegoría [aleɣo'ria] *nf* allegory

alegrar [ale'ɣrar] *vt* (*causar alegría*) to cheer (up); (*fuego*) to poke; (*fiesta*) to liven up; **~se** *vr* (*fam*) to get merry *o* tight; **~se de** to be glad about

alegre [a'leɣre] *adj* happy, cheerful; (*fam*) merry, tight; (*chiste*) risqué, blue; **alegría** *nf* happiness; merriment

alejamiento [alexa'mjento] *nm* removal; (*distancia*) remoteness

alejar [ale'xar] *vt* to remove; (*fig*) to estrange; **~se** *vr* to move away

alemán, ana [ale'man, ana] *adj, nm/f* German ♦ *nm* (*LING*) German

Alemania [ale'manja] *nf*: **~ Occidental/ Oriental** West/East Germany

alentador, a [alenta'ðor, a] *adj* encouraging

alentar [alen'tar] *vt* to encourage

alergia [a'lerxja] *nf* allergy

alero [a'lero] *nm* (*de tejado*) eaves *pl*; (*de carruaje*) mudguard

alerta [a'lerta] *adj, nm* alert

aleta [a'leta] *nf* (*de pez*) fin; (*de ave*) wing; (*de foca, DEPORTE*) flipper; (*AUTO*) mudguard

aletargar [aletar'ɣar] *vt* to make drowsy; (*entumecer*) to make numb; **~se** *vr* to grow drowsy; to become numb

aletear [alete'ar] *vi* to flutter

alevín [ale'βin] *nm* fry, young fish

alevino [ale'βino] *nm* = **alevín**

alevosía [aleβo'sia] *nf* treachery

alfabeto [alfa'βeto] *nm* alphabet

alfalfa [al'falfa] *nf* alfalfa, lucerne

alfarería [alfare'ria] *nf* pottery; (*tienda*) pottery shop; **alfarero, a** *nm/f* potter

alféizar [al'feiðar] *nm* window-sill

alférez [al'fereθ] *nm* (*MIL*) second lieutenant; (*NAUT*) ensign

alfil [al'fil] *nm* (*AJEDREZ*) bishop

alfiler [alfi'ler] *nm* pin; (*broche*) clip; (*pinza*) clothes peg

alfiletero [alfile'tero] *nm* needlecase

alfombra [al'fombra] *nf* carpet; (*más pequeña*) rug; **alfombrar** *vt* to carpet; **alfombrilla** *nf* rug, mat

alforja [al'forxa] *nf* saddlebag

algarabía [alɣara'βia] (*fam*) *nf* gibberish; (*griterío*) hullabaloo

algas ['alɣas] *nfpl* seaweed

álgebra ['alxeβra] *nf* algebra

álgido, a ['alxiðo] *adj* icy, chilly; (*momento*

etc) crucial, decisive

algo ['alɣo] *pron* something; anything ♦ *adv* somewhat, rather; *¿~ más?* anything else?; *(en tienda)* is that all?; *por ~ será* there must be some reason for it

algodón [alɣo'ðon] *nm* cotton; *(planta)* cotton plant; *~ de azúcar* candy floss *(BRIT)*, cotton candy *(US)*; *~ hidrófilo* cotton wool *(BRIT)*, absorbent cotton *(US)*

algodonero, a [alɣoðo'nero, a] *adj* cotton *cpd* ♦ *nm/f* cotton grower ♦ *nm* cotton plant

alguacil [alɣwa'θil] *nm* bailiff; *(TAUR)* mounted official

alguien ['alɣjen] *pron* someone, somebody; *(en frases interrogativas)* anyone, anybody

alguno, a [al'ɣuno, a] *adj (delante de nm: algún)* some; *(después de n)*: **no tiene talento alguno** he has no talent, he doesn't have any talent ♦ *pron (alguien)* someone, somebody; **algún que otro libro** some book or other; **algún día iré** I'll go one *o* some day; **sin interés** ~ without the slightest interest; ~ **que otro** an occasional one; ~**s piensan** some (people) think

alhaja [a'laxa] *nf* jewel; *(tesoro)* precious object, treasure

alhelí [ale'li] *nm* wallflower, stock

aliado, a [a'ljaðo, a] *adj* allied

alianza [a'ljanθa] *nf* alliance; *(anillo)* wedding ring

aliar [a'ljar] *vt* to ally; ~**se** *vr* to form an alliance

alias ['aljas] *adv* alias

alicates [ali'kates] *nmpl* pliers; ~ **de uñas** nail clippers

aliciente [ali'θjente] *nm* incentive; *(atracción)* attraction

alienación [aljena'θjon] *nf* alienation

aliento [a'ljento] *nm* breath; *(respiración)* breathing; **sin** ~ breathless

aligerar [alixe'rar] *vt* to lighten; *(reducir)* to shorten; *(aliviar)* to alleviate; *(mitigar)* to ease; *(paso)* to quicken

alijo [a'lixo] *nm* consignment

alimaña [ali'maɲa] *nf* pest

alimentación [alimenta'θjon] *nf (comida)* food; *(acción)* feeding; *(tienda)* grocer's (shop); **alimentador** *nm*: **alimentador de papel** sheet-feeder

alimentar [alimen'tar] *vt* to feed; *(nutrir)* to nourish; ~**se** *vr* to feed

alimenticio, a [alimen'tiθjo, a] *adj* food *cpd*; *(nutritivo)* nourishing, nutritious

alimento [ali'mento] *nm* food; *(nutrición)* nourishment; ~**s** *nmpl (JUR)* alimony *sg*

alineación [alinea'θjon] *nf* alignment; *(DEPORTE)* line-up

alinear [aline'ar] *vt* to align; ~**se** *vr (DEPORTE)* to line up; ~**se en** to fall in with

aliñar [ali'ɲar] *vt (CULIN)* to season; **aliño** *nm (CULIN)* dressing

alioli [ali'oli] *nm* garlic mayonnaise

alisar [ali'sar] *vt* to smooth

aliso [a'liso] *nm* alder

alistarse [alis'tarse] *vr* to enlist; *(inscribirse)* to enrol

aliviar [ali'βjar] *vt (carga)* to lighten; *(persona)* to relieve; *(dolor)* to relieve, alleviate

alivio [a'liβjo] *nm* alleviation, relief

aljibe [al'xiβe] *nm* cistern

alma ['alma] *nf* soul; *(persona)* person; *(TEC)* core

almacén [alma'θen] *nm (depósito)* warehouse, store; *(MIL)* magazine; *(AM)* shop; **(grandes) almacenes** *nmpl* department store *sg*; **almacenaje** *nm* storage; **almacenaje secundaria** *(INFORM)* backing storage

almacenar [almaθe'nar] *vt* to store, put in storage; *(proveerse)* to stock up with; **almacenero** *nm* warehouseman; *(AM)* shopkeeper

almanaque [alma'nake] *nm* almanac

almeja [al'mexa] *nf* clam

almendra [al'mendra] *nf* almond; **almendro** *nm* almond tree

almíbar [al'miβar] *nm* syrup

almidón [almi'ðon] *nm* starch; **almidonar** *vt* to starch

almirante [almi'rante] *nm* admiral

almirez [almi'reθ] *nm* mortar

almizcle [al'miθkle] *nm* musk

almohada [almo'aða] *nf* pillow; *(funda)* pillowcase; **almohadilla** *nf* cushion; *(TEC)* pad; *(AM)* pincushion

almohadón [almoa'ðon] *nm* large pillow; bolster

almorranas [almo'rranas] *nfpl* piles, haemorrhoids

almorzar [almor'θar] *vt*: ~ **una tortilla** to have an omelette for lunch ♦ *vi* to (have) lunch

almuerzo *etc* [al'mwerθo] *vb ver* **almorzar** ♦ *nm* lunch

alocado, a [alo'kaðo, a] *adj* crazy

alojamiento [aloxa'mjento] *nm* lodging(s) *(pl)*; *(viviendas)* housing

alojar [alo'xar] *vt* to lodge; ~**se** *vr* to lodge, stay

alondra [a'londra] *nf* lark, skylark

alpargata [alpar'ɣata] *nf* rope-soled sandal, espadrille

Alpes ['alpes] *nmpl*: **los** ~ the Alps

alpinismo [alpi'nismo] *nm* mountaineering, climbing; **alpinista** *nm/f* mountaineer, climber

alpiste [al'piste] *nm* birdseed

alquería [alke'ria] *nf* farmhouse

alquilar [alki'lar] *vt (suj: propietario: inmuebles)* to let, rent (out); *(: coche)* to hire out; *(: TV)* to rent (out); *(suj: alquilador: inmuebles, TV)* to rent; *(: coche)* to hire; **"se alquila casa"** "house to let *(BRIT)* o to rent *(US)*"

alquiler [alkiˈler] *nm* renting; letting; hiring; (*arriendo*) rent; hire charge; ~ **de automóviles** car hire; **de** ~ for hire

alquimia [alˈkimja] *nf* alchemy

alquitrán [alkiˈtran] *nm* tar

alrededor [alreðeˈðor] *adv* around, about; ~ **de** around, about; **mirar a su** ~ to look (round) around one; ~**es** *nmpl* surroundings

alta [ˈalta] *nf* (certificate of) discharge; **dar de** ~ to discharge

altanería [altaneˈria] *nf* haughtiness, arrogance; **altanero, a** *adj* arrogant, haughty

altar [alˈtar] *nm* altar

altavoz [altaˈβoθ] *nm* loudspeaker; (*amplificador*) amplifier

alteración [alteraˈθjon] *nf* alteration; (*alboroto*) disturbance

alterar [alteˈrar] *vt* to alter; to disturb; ~**se** *vr* (*persona*) to get upset

altercado [alterˈkaðo] *nm* argument

alternar [alterˈnar] *vt* to alternate ♦ *vi* to alternate; (*turnar*) to take turns; ~**se** *vr* to alternate; to take turns; ~ **con** to mix with; **alternativa** *nf* alternative; (*elección*) choice; **alternativo, a** *adj* alternative; (*alterno*) alternating; **alterno, a** *adj* alternate; (*ELEC*) alternating

Alteza [alˈteθa] *nf* (*tratamiento*) Highness

altibajos [altiˈβaxos] *nmpl* ups and downs

altiplanicie [altiplaˈniθje] *nf* high plateau

altiplano [altiˈplano] *nm* = **altiplanicie**

altisonante [altisoˈnante] *adj* high-flown, high-sounding

altitud [altiˈtuð] *nf* height; (*AVIAT*, *GEO*) altitude

altivez [altiˈβeθ] *nf* haughtiness, arrogance; **altivo, a** *adj* haughty, arrogant

alto, a [ˈalto, a] *adj* high; (*persona*) tall; (*sonido*) high, sharp; (*noble*) high, lofty ♦ *nm* halt; (*MUS*) alto; (*GEO*) hill; (*AM*) pile ♦ *adv* (*de sitio*) high; (*de sonido*) loud, loudly ♦ *excl* halt!; **la pared tiene 2 metros de** ~ the wall is 2 metres high; **en alta mar** on the high seas; **en voz alta** in a loud voice; **las altas horas de la noche** the small o wee hours; **en lo** ~ **de** at the top of; **pasar por** ~ to overlook

altoparlante [altoparˈlante] (*AM*) *nm* loudspeaker

altruismo [altruˈismo] *nm* altruism

altura [alˈtura] *nf* height; (*NAUT*) depth; (*GEO*) latitude; **la pared tiene 1.80 de** ~ the wall is 1 metre 80cm high; **a estas ~s** at this stage; **a estas ~s del año** at this time of the year

alubia [aˈluβja] *nf* French bean, kidney bean

alucinación [aluθinaˈθjon] *nf* hallucination

alucinar [aluθiˈnar] *vi* to hallucinate ♦ *vt* to deceive; (*fascinar*) to fascinate

alud [aˈluð] *nm* avalanche; (*fig*) flood

aludir [aluˈðir] *vi*: ~ **a** to allude to; **darse**

por aludido to take the hint

alumbrado [alumˈbraðo] *nm* lighting; **alumbramiento** *nm* lighting; (*MED*) childbirth, delivery

alumbrar [alumˈbrar] *vt* to light (up) ♦ *vi* (*MED*) to give birth

aluminio [aluˈminjo] *nm* aluminium (*BRIT*), aluminum (*US*)

alumno, a [aˈlumno, a] *nm/f* pupil, student

alunizar [aluniˈθar] *vi* to land on the moon

alusión [aluˈsjon] *nf* allusion

alusivo, a [aluˈsiβo, a] *adj* allusive

aluvión [aluˈβjon] *nm* alluvium; (*fig*) flood

alverja [alˈβerxa] (*AM*) *nf* pea

alza [ˈalθa] *nf* rise; (*MIL*) sight

alzada [alˈθaða] *nf* (*de caballos*) height; (*JUR*) appeal

alzamiento [alθaˈmjento] *nm* (*aumento*) rise, increase; (*acción*) lifting, raising; (*mejor postura*) higher bid; (*rebelión*) rising; (*COM*) fraudulent bankruptcy

alzar [alˈθar] *vt* to lift (up); (*precio, muro*) to raise; (*cuello de abrigo*) to turn up; (*AGR*) to gather in; (*IMPRENTA*) to gather; ~**se** *vr* to get up, rise; (*rebelarse*) to revolt; (*COM*) to go fraudulently bankrupt; (*JUR*) to appeal

allá [aˈʎa] *adv* (*lugar*) there; (*por ahí*) over there; (*tiempo*) then; ~ **abajo** down there; **más** ~ further on; **más** ~ **de** beyond; **¡~ tú!** that's your problem!

allanamiento [aʎanaˈmjento] *nm*: ~ **de morada** burglary

allanar [aʎaˈnar] *vt* to flatten, level (out); (*igualar*) to smooth (out); (*fig*) to subdue; (*JUR*) to burgle, break into; ~**se** *vr* to fall down; ~**se a** to submit to, accept

allegado, a [aʎeˈɣaðo, a] *adj* near, close ♦ *nm/f* relation

allí [aˈʎi] *adv* there; ~ **mismo** right there; **por** ~ over there; (*por ese camino*) that way

ama [ˈama] *nf* lady of the house; (*dueña*) owner; (*institutriz*) governess; (*madre adoptiva*) foster mother; ~ **de casa** housewife; ~ **de llaves** housekeeper

amabilidad [amaβiliˈðað] *nf* kindness; (*simpatía*) niceness; **amable** *adj* kind; nice; **es usted muy amable** that's very kind of you

amaestrado, a [amaesˈtraðo, a] *adj* (*animal: en circo etc*) performing

amaestrar [amaesˈtrar] *vt* to train

amago [aˈmaɣo] *nm* threat; (*gesto*) threatening gesture; (*MED*) symptom

amainar [amaiˈnar] *vi* (*viento*) to die down

amalgama [amalˈɣama] *nf* amalgam; **amalgamar** *vt* to amalgamate; (*combinar*) to combine, mix

amamantar [amamanˈtar] *vt* to suckle, nurse

amanecer [amaneˈθer] *vi* to dawn ♦ *nm* dawn; ~ **afiebrado** to wake up with a fever

amanerado, a [amane'raðo, a] *adj* affected

amansar [aman'sar] *vt* to tame; *(persona)* to subdue; **~se** *vr (persona)* to calm down

amante [a'mante] *adj*: **~ de** fond of ♦ *nm/f* lover

amapola [ama'pola] *nf* poppy

amar [a'mar] *vt* to love

amarar [ama'rar] *vi (avión)* to land (on the sea)

amargado, a [amar'xaðo, a] *adj* bitter

amargar [amar'xar] *vt* to make bitter; *(fig)* to embitter; **~se** *vr* to become embittered

amargo, a [a'marxo, a] *adj* bitter; **amargura** *nf* bitterness

amarillento, a [amari'ʎento, a] *adj* yellowish; *(tez)* sallow; **amarillo, a** *adj, nm* yellow

amarrar [ama'rrar] *vt* to moor; *(sujetar)* to tie up

amarras [a'marras] *nfpl*: **soltar ~** to set sail

amartillar [amarti'ʎar] *vt (fusil)* to cock

amasar [ama'sar] *vt (masa)* to knead; *(mezclar)* to mix, prepare; *(confeccionar)* to concoct; **amasijo** *nm* kneading; mixing; *(fig)* hotchpotch

amateur ['amatur] *nm/f* amateur

amatista [ama'tista] *nf* amethyst

amazona [ama'θona] *nf* horsewoman; **A~s** *nm*: **el A~s** the Amazon

ambages [am'baxes] *nmpl*: **sin ~** in plain language

ámbar ['ambar] *nm* amber

ambición [ambi'θjon] *nf* ambition; **ambicionar** *vt* to aspire to; **ambicioso, a** *adj* ambitious

ambidextro, a [ambi'ðekstro, a] *adj* ambidextrous

ambientación [ambjenta'θjon] *nf (CINE, TEATRO etc)* setting; *(RADIO)* sound effects

ambiente [am'bjente] *nm (tb fig)* atmosphere; *(medio)* environment

ambigüedad [ambixwe'ðað] *nf* ambiguity; **ambiguo, a** *adj* ambiguous

ámbito ['ambito] *nm (campo)* field; *(fig)* scope

ambos, as ['ambos, as] *adj pl, pron pl* both

ambulancia [ambu'lanθja] *nf* ambulance

ambulante [ambu'lante] *adj* travelling *cpd*, itinerant

ambulatorio [ambula'torjo] *nm* state health-service clinic

amedrentar [ameðren'tar] *vt* to scare

amén [a'men] *excl* amen; **~ de** besides

amenaza [ame'naθa] *nf* threat

amenazar [amena'θar] *vt* to threaten ♦ *vi*: **~ con hacer** to threaten to do

amenidad [ameni'ðað] *nf* pleasantness

ameno, a [a'meno, a] *adj* pleasant

América [a'merika] *nf* America; **~ del Norte/del Sur** North/South America; **~ Central/Latina** Central/Latin America;

americana *nf* coat, jacket; *ver tb* **americano**; **americano, a** *adj, nm/f* American

amerizar [ameri'θar] *vi (avión)* to land (on the sea)

ametralladora [ametraʎa'ðora] *nf* machine gun

amianto [a'mjanto] *nm* asbestos

amigable [ami'xaßle] *adj* friendly

amígdala [a'mixðala] *nf* tonsil; **amigdalitis** *nf* tonsillitis

amigo, a [a'mixo, a] *adj* friendly ♦ *nm/f* friend; *(amante)* lover; **ser ~ de algo** to be fond of sth; **ser muy ~s** to be close friends

amilanar [amila'nar] *vt* to scare; **~se** *vr* to get scared

aminorar [amino'rar] *vt* to diminish; *(reducir)* to reduce; **~ la marcha** to slow down

amistad [amis'tað] *nf* friendship; **~es** *nfpl (amigos)* friends; **amistoso, a** *adj* friendly

amnesia [am'nesja] *nf* amnesia

amnistía [amnis'tia] *nf* amnesty

amo ['amo] *nm* owner; *(jefe)* boss

amodorrarse [amoðo'rrarse] *vr* to get sleepy

amolar [amo'lar] *vt (perseguir)* to annoy

amoldar [amol'dar] *vt* to mould; *(adaptar)* to adapt

amonestación [amonesta'θjon] *nf* warning; **amonestaciones** *nfpl (REL)* marriage banns

amonestar [amones'tar] *vt* to warn; *(REL)* to publish the banns of

amontonar [amonto'nar] *vt* to collect, pile up; **~se** *vr* to crowd together; *(acumularse)* to pile up

amor [a'mor] *nm* love; *(amante)* lover; **hacer el ~** to make love; **~ proprio** self-respect

amoratado, a [amora'taðo, a] *adj* purple

amordazar [amorða'θar] *vt* to muzzle; *(fig)* to gag

amorfo, a [a'morfo, a] *adj* amorphous, shapeless

amoroso, a [amo'roso, a] *adj* affectionate, loving

amortajar [amorta'xar] *vt* to shroud

amortiguador [amortigwa'ðor] *nm* shock absorber; *(parachoques)* bumper; **~es** *nmpl (AUTO)* suspension *sg*

amortiguar [amorti'ɣwar] *vt* to deaden; *(ruido)* to muffle; *(color)* to soften

amortización [amortiθa'θjon] *nf (de deuda)* repayment; *(de bono)* redemption

amotinar [amoti'nar] *vt* to stir up, incite (to riot); **~se** *vr* to mutiny

amparar [ampa'rar] *vt* to protect; **~se** *vr* to seek protection; *(de la lluvia etc)* to shelter; **amparo** *nm* help, protection; **al ~ de** under the protection of

amperio [am'perjo] *nm* ampère, amp

ampliación [amplja'θjon] *nf* enlargement; *(extensión)* extension

ampliar [am'pljar] *vt* to enlarge; to extend

amplificación [amplifika'θjon] *nf* enlargement; **amplificador** *nm* amplifier

amplificar [amplifi'kar] *vt* to amplify

amplio, a ['ampljo, a] *adj* spacious; *(de falda etc)* full; *(extenso)* extensive; *(ancho)* wide; **amplitud** *nf* spaciousness; extent; *(fig)* amplitude

ampolla [am'poʎa] *nf* blister; *(MED)* ampoule

ampuloso, a [ampu'loso, a] *adj* bombastic, pompous

amputar [ampu'tar] *vt* to cut off, amputate

amueblar [amwe'βlar] *vt* to furnish

amurallar [amura'ʎar] *vt* to wall up *o* in

anacronismo [anakro'nismo] *nm* anachronism

anadear [anaðe'ar] *vi* to waddle

anales [a'nales] *nmpl* annals

analfabetismo [analfaβe'tismo] *nm* illiteracy; **analfabeto, a** *adj, nm/f* illiterate

analgésico [anal'xesiko] *nm* painkiller, analgesic

análisis [a'nalisis] *nm inv* analysis

analista [ana'lista] *nm/f* (*gen*) analyst

analizar [anali'θar] *vt* to analyse

analogía [analo'xia] *nf* analogy

analógico, a [ana'loxiko, a] *adj* (*INFORM*) analog; *(reloj)* analogue (*BRIT*), analog (*US*)

análogo, a [a'naloxo, a] *adj* analogous, similar

ananá(s) [ana'na(s)] *nm* pineapple

anaquel [ana'kel] *nm* shelf

anarquía [anar'kia] *nf* anarchy; **anarquismo** *nm* anarchism; **anarquista** *nm/f* anarchist

anatomía [anato'mia] *nf* anatomy

anca ['anka] *nf* rump, haunch; **~s** *nfpl* (*fam*) behind *sg*

anciano, a [an'θjano, a] *adj* old, aged ♦ *nm/f* old man/woman; elder

ancla ['ankla] *nf* anchor; **~dero** *nm* anchorage; **anclar** *vi* to (drop) anchor

ancho, a ['antʃo, a] *adj* wide; *(falda)* full; *(fig)* liberal ♦ *nm* width; *(FERRO)* gauge; **ponerse ~** to get conceited; **estar a sus anchas** to be at one's ease

anchoa [an'tʃoa] *nf* anchovy

anchura [an'tʃura] *nf* width; *(extensión)* wideness

andadura [anda'ðura] *nf* gait; *(de caballo)* pace

Andalucía [andalu'θia] *nf* Andalusia; **andaluz, a** *adj, nm/f* Andalusian

andamiaje [anda'mjaxe] *nm* = andamio

andamio [an'damjo] *nm* scaffold(ing)

andar [an'dar] *vt* to go, cover, travel ♦ *vi* to go, walk, travel; *(funcionar)* to go, work; *(estar)* to be ♦ *nm* walk, gait, pace; **~se** *vr* to go away; **~ a pie/a caballo/en bicicleta** to go on foot/on horseback/by bicycle; **~ haciendo algo** to be doing sth; **¡anda!** *(sorpresa)* go on!; **anda por** *o* **en los 40** he's about 40

andariego, a [anda'rjexo, a] *adj* (*itinerante*) wandering

andén [an'den] *nm* (*FERRO*) platform; (*NAUT*) quayside; (*AM: de la calle*) pavement (*BRIT*), sidewalk (*US*)

Andes ['andes] *nmpl:* **los ~** the Andes

Andorra [an'dorra] *nf* Andorra

andrajo [an'draxo] *nm* rag; **~so, a** *adj* ragged

anduve *etc* [an'duße] *vb ver* andar

anécdota [a'nekðota] *nf* anecdote, story

anegar [ane'xar] *vt* to flood; *(ahogar)* to drown; **~se** *vr* to drown; *(hundirse)* to sink

anejo, a [a'nexo, a] *adj, nm* = anexo

anemia [a'nemja] *nf* anaemia

anestesia [anes'tesja] *nf* anaesthesia

anestésico [anes'tesiko] *nm* anaesthetic

anexar [anek'sar] *vt* to annex; *(documento)* to attach; **anexión** *nf* annexation; **anexionamiento** *nm* annexation; **anexo, a** *adj* attached ♦ *nm* annexe

anfibio, a [an'fiβjo, a] *adj* amphibious ♦ *nm* amphibian

anfiteatro [anfite'atro] *nm* amphitheatre; *(TEATRO)* dress circle

anfitrión, ona [anfi'trjon, ona] *nm/f* host(ess)

ángel ['anxel] *nm* angel; **~ de la guarda** guardian angel; **tener ~** to be charming; **angelical** *adj*, **angélico, a** *adj* angelic(al)

angina [an'xina] *nf* (*MED*) inflammation of the throat; **~ de pecho** angina; **tener ~s** to have tonsillitis

anglicano, a [angli'kano, a] *adj, nm/f* Anglican

anglosajón, ona [anglosa'xon, ona] *adj* Anglo-Saxon

angosto, a [an'gosto, a] *adj* narrow

anguila [an'gila] *nf* eel; **~s** *nfpl* (*NAUT*) slipway *sg*

angula [an'gula] *nf* elver, baby eel

ángulo ['angulo] *nm* angle; *(esquina)* corner; *(curva)* bend

angustia [an'gustja] *nf* anguish; **angustiar** *vt* to distress, grieve

anhelar [ane'lar] *vt* to be eager for; *(desear)* to long for, desire ♦ *vi* to pant, gasp; **anhelo** *nm* eagerness; desire

anidar [ani'ðar] *vi* to nest

anillo [a'niʎo] *nm* ring; **~ de boda** wedding ring

animación [anima'θjon] *nf* liveliness; *(vitalidad)* life; *(actividad)* activity; bustle

animado, a [ani'maðo, a] *adj* lively; *(vivaz)* animated; **animador, a** *nm/f* (*TV*) host(ess), compère; *(DEPORTE)* cheerleader

animadversión [animaðßer'sjon] *nf* ill-will, antagonism

animal [ani'mal] *adj* animal; *(fig)* stupid ♦ *nm* animal; *(fig)* fool; *(bestia)* brute

animar [ani'mar] *vt* (*BIO*) to animate, give

life to; (fig) to liven up, brighten up, cheer up; (estimular) to stimulate; ~se vr to cheer up; to feel encouraged; (decidirse) to make up one's mind

ánimo ['animo] nm (alma) soul; (mente) mind; (valentía) courage ♦ excl cheer up!

animoso, a [ani'moso, a] adj brave; (vivo) lively

aniquilar [aniki'lar] vt to annihilate, destroy

anís [a'nis] nm aniseed; (licor) anisette

aniversario [aniβer'sarjo] nm anniversary

anoche [a'notʃe] adv last night; **antes de ~** the night before last

anochecer [anotʃe'θer] vi to get dark ♦ nm nightfall, dark; **al ~** at nightfall

anodino, a [ano'ðino, a] adj dull, anodyne

anomalía [anoma'lia] nf anomaly

anonadado, a [anona'ðaðo, a] adj: **estar/quedar/sentirse ~** to be overwhelmed o amazed

anonimato [anoni'mato] nm anonymity

anónimo, a [a'nonimo, a] adj anonymous; (COM) limited ♦ nm (carta) anonymous letter; (: maliciosa) poison-pen letter

anormal [anor'mal] adj abnormal

anotación [anota'θjon] nf note; annotation

anotar [ano'tar] vt to note down; (comentar) to annotate

anquilosamiento [ankilosa'mjento] nm (fig) paralysis; stagnation

anquilosarse [ankilo'sarse] vr (fig: persona) to get out of touch; (método, costumbres) to go out of date

ansia ['ansja] nf anxiety; (añoranza) yearning; **ansiar** vt to long for

ansiedad [ansje'ðað] nf anxiety

ansioso, a [an'sjoso, a] adj anxious; (anhelante) eager; **~ de** o **por algo** greedy for sth

antagónico, a [anta'ɣoniko, a] adj antagonistic; (opuesto) contrasting; **antagonista** nm/f antagonist

antaño [an'taɲo] adv long ago, formerly

Antártico [an'tartiko] nm: **el ~** the Antarctic

ante ['ante] prep before, in the presence of; (problema etc) faced with ♦ nm (piel) suede; **~ todo** above all

anteanoche [antea'notʃe] adv the night before last

anteayer [antea'jer] adv the day before yesterday

antebrazo [ante'βraθo] nm forearm

antecedente [anteθe'ðente] adj previous ♦ nm antecedent; **~s** nmpl (JUR): **~s penales** criminal record; (procedencia) background

anteceder [anteθe'ðer] vt to precede, go before

antecesor, a [anteθe'sor, a] nm/f predecessor

antedicho, a [ante'ðitʃo, a] adj aforementioned

antelación [antela'θjon] nf: **con ~** in advance

antemano [ante'mano]: **de ~** adv beforehand, in advance

antena [an'tena] nf antenna; (de televisión etc) aerial; **~ parabólica** satellite dish

anteojo [ante'oxo] nm eyeglass; **~s** nmpl (AM) glasses, spectacles

antepasados [antepa'saðos] nmpl ancestors

antepecho [ante'petʃo] nm guardrail, parapet; (repisa) ledge, sill

anteponer [antepo'ner] vt to place in front; (fig) to prefer

anteproyecto [antepro'jekto] nm preliminary sketch; (fig) blueprint

anterior [ante'rjor] adj preceding, previous; **~idad** nf: **con ~idad a** prior to, before

antes ['antes] adv (con prioridad) before ♦ prep: **~ de** before ♦ conj: **~ de ir/de que te vayas** before going/before you go; **~ bien** (but) rather; **dos días ~** two days before o previously; **no quiso venir ~** she didn't want to come any earlier; **tomo el avión ~ que el barco** I take the plane rather than the boat; **~ que yo** before me; **lo ~ posible** as soon as possible; **cuanto ~ mejor** the sooner the better

antiaéreo, a [antia'ereo, a] adj anti-aircraft

antibalas [anti'βalas] adj inv: **chaleco ~** bullet-proof jacket

antibiótico [anti'βjotiko] nm antibiotic

anticiclón [antiθi'klon] nm anticyclone

anticipación [antiθipa'θjon] nf anticipation; **con 10 minutos de ~** 10 minutes early

anticipado, a [antiθi'paðo, a] adj (pago) advance; **por ~** in advance

anticipar [antiθi'par] vt to anticipate; (adelantar) to bring forward; (COM) to advance; **~se** vr: **~se a su época** to be ahead of one's time

anticipo [anti'θipo] nm (COM) advance

anticonceptivo, a [antikonθep'tiβo, a] adj, nm contraceptive

anticongelante [antikonxe'lante] nm antifreeze

anticuado, a [anti'kwaðo, a] adj out-of-date, old-fashioned; (desusado) obsolete

anticuario [anti'kwarjo] nm antique dealer

anticuerpo [anti'kwerpo] nm (MED) antibody

antídoto [an'tiðoto] nm antidote

antiestético, a [anties'tetiko, a] adj unsightly

antifaz [anti'faθ] nm mask; (velo) veil

antigualla [anti'ɣwaʎa] nf antique; (reliquia) relic

antiguamente [antiɣwa'mente] adv formerly; (hace mucho tiempo) long ago

antigüedad [antiɣwe'ðað] nf antiquity; (artículo) antique; (rango) seniority

antiguo, a [an'tiɣwo, a] *adj* old, ancient; (*que fue*) former

antílope [an'tilope] *nm* antelope

Antillas [an'tiʎas] *nfpl*: **las ~** the West Indies

antinatural [antinatu'ral] *adj* unnatural

antipatía [antipa'tia] *nf* antipathy, dislike; **antipático, a** *adj* disagreeable, unpleasant

antirrobo [anti'rroβo] *adj inv* (*alarma etc*) anti-theft

antisemita [antise'mita] *adj* anti-Semitic ♦ *nm/f* anti-Semite

antiséptico, a [anti'septiko, a] *adj* antiseptic ♦ *nm* antiseptic

antítesis [an'titesis] *nf inv* antithesis

antojadizo, a [antoxa'ðiθo, a] *adj* capricious

antojarse [anto'xarse] *vr* (*desear*): **se me antoja comprarlo** I have a mind to buy it; (*pensar*): **se me antoja que** I have a feeling that

antojo [an'toxo] *nm* caprice, whim; (*rosa*) birthmark; (*lunar*) mole

antología [antolo'xia] *nf* anthology

antorcha [an'tortʃa] *nf* torch

antro ['antro] *nm* cavern

antropófago, a [antro'pofaɣo, a] *adj, nm/f* cannibal

antropología [antropolo'xia] *nf* anthropology

anual [a'nwal] *adj* annual; **~idad** *nf* annuity

anuario [a'nwarjo] *nm* yearbook

anudar [anu'ðar] *vt* to knot, tie; (*unir*) to join; **~se** *vr* to get tied up

anulación [anula'θjon] *nf* annulment; (*cancelación*) cancellation

anular [anu'lar] *vt* (*contrato*) to annul, cancel; (*ley*) to revoke, repeal; (*suscripción*) to cancel ♦ *nm* ring finger

anunciación [anunθja'θjon] *nf* announcement; (*REL*): **A~** Annunciation

anunciante [anun'θjante] *nm/f* (*COM*) advertiser

anunciar [anun'θjar] *vt* to announce; (*proclamar*) to proclaim; (*COM*) to advertise

anuncio [a'nunθjo] *nm* announcement; (*señal*) sign; (*COM*) advertisement; (*cartel*) poster

anzuelo [an'θwelo] *nm* hook; (*para pescar*) fish hook

añadidura [aɲaði'ðura] *nf* addition, extra; **por ~** besides, in addition

añadir [aɲa'ðir] *vt* to add

añejo, a [a'ɲexo, a] *adj* old; (*vino*) mellow

añicos [a'ɲikos] *nmpl*: **hacer ~** to smash, shatter

añil [a'ɲil] *nm* (*BOT, color*) indigo

año ['aɲo] *nm* year; **¡Feliz A~ Nuevo!** Happy New Year!; **tener 15 ~s** to be 15 (years old); **los ~s 90** the nineties; **bisiesto/escolar** leap/school year; **el ~**

que viene next year

añoranza [aɲo'ranθa] *nf* nostalgia; (*anhelo*) longing

apabullar [apaβu'ʎar] *vt* (*tb fig*) to crush, squash

apacentar [apaθen'tar] *vt* to pasture, graze

apacible [apa'θiβle] *adj* gentle, mild

apaciguar [apaθi'ɣwar] *vt* to pacify, calm (down)

apadrinar [apaðri'nar] *vt* to sponsor, support; (*REL*) to be godfather to

apagado, a [apa'ɣaðo, a] *adj* (*volcán*) extinct; (*color*) dull; (*voz*) quiet; (*sonido*) muted, muffled; (*persona: apático*) listless; **estar ~** (*fuego, luz*) to be out; (*RADIO, TV etc*) to be off

apagar [apa'ɣar] *vt* to put out; (*ELEC, RADIO, TV*) to turn off; (*sonido*) to silence, muffle; (*sed*) to quench

apagón [apa'ɣon] *nm* blackout; power cut

apalabrar [apala'βrar] *vt* to agree to; (*contratar*) to engage

apalear [apale'ar] *vt* to beat, thrash; (*AGR*) to winnow

apañar [apa'ɲar] *vt* to pick up; (*asir*) to take hold of, grasp; (*reparar*) to mend, patch up; **~se** *vr* to manage, get along

aparador [apara'ðor] *nm* sideboard; (*escaparate*) shop window

aparato [apa'rato] *nm* apparatus; (*máquina*) machine; (*doméstico*) appliance; (*boato*) ostentation; **~ de facsímil** facsimile (machine), fax; **~ digestivo** (*ANAT*) digestive system; **~so, a** *adj* showy, ostentatious

aparcamiento [aparka'mjento] *nm* car park (*BRIT*), parking lot (*US*)

aparcar [apar'kar] *vt, vi* to park

aparear [apare'ar] *vt* (*objetos*) to pair, match; (*animales*) to mate; **~se** *vr* to make a pair; to mate

aparecer [apare'θer] *vi* to appear; **~se** *vr* to appear

aparejado, a [apare'xaðo, a] *adj* fit, suitable; **llevar** *o* **traer ~** to involve; **aparejador, a** *nm/f* (*ARQ*) master builder

aparejo [apa'rexo] *nm* preparation; harness; rigging; (*de poleas*) block and tackle

aparentar [aparen'tar] *vt* (*edad*) to look; (*fingir*): **~ tristeza** to pretend to be sad

aparente [apa'rente] *adj* apparent; (*adecuado*) suitable

aparezco *etc vb ver* **aparecer**

aparición [apari'θjon] *nf* appearance; (*de libro*) publication; (*espectro*) apparition

apariencia [apa'rjenθja] *nf* (outward) appearance; **en ~** outwardly, seemingly

apartado, a [apar'taðo, a] *adj* separate; (*lejano*) remote ♦ *nm* (*tipográfico*) paragraph; **~ (de correos)** post office box

apartamento [aparta'mento] *nm* apartment, flat (*BRIT*)

apartamiento [aparta'mjento] *nm* separation; (*aislamiento*) remoteness, isolation; (*AM*) apartment, flat (*BRIT*)

apartar [apar'tar] *vt* to separate; (*quitar*) to remove; (*MINEROLOGÍA*) to extract; ~**se** *vr* to separate, part; (*irse*) to move away; to keep away

aparte [a'parte] *adv* (*separadamente*) separately; (*además*) besides ♦ *nm* aside; (*tipográfico*) new paragraph

apasionado, a [apasjo'naðo, a] *adj* passionate; biassed, prejudiced

apasionar [apasjo'nar] *vt* to excite; **le apasiona el fútbol** she's crazy about football; ~**se** *vr* to get excited

apatía [apa'tia] *nf* apathy

apático, a [a'patiko, a] *adj* apathetic

apátrida [a'patriða] *adj* stateless

Apdo *abr* (= *Apartado* (*de Correos*)) PO Box

apeadero [apea'ðero] *nm* halt, stop, stopping place

apearse [ape'arse] *vr* (*jinete*) to dismount; (*bajarse*) to get down *o* out; (*AUTO, FERRO*) to get off *o* out

apechugar [apetʃu'xar] *vr:* ~ **con algo** to face up to sth

apedrear [apeðre'ar] *vt* to stone

apegarse [ape'ɣarse] *vr:* ~ **a** to become attached to; **apego** *nm* attachment, devotion

apelación [apela'θjon] *nf* appeal

apelar [ape'lar] *vi* to appeal; ~ **a** (*fig*) to resort to

apelmazarse [apelma'θarse] *vr* (*masa, arroz*) to go hard; (*prenda de tana*) to shrink

apellidar [apeʎi'ðar] *vt* to call, name; ~**se** *vr:* **se apellida Pérez** her (sur)name's Pérez

apellido [ape'ʎiðo] *nm* surname

apenar [ape'nar] *vt* to grieve, trouble; (*AM*: *avergonzar*) to embarrass; ~**se** *vr* to grieve; (*AM*) to be embarrassed

apenas [a'penas] *adv* scarcely, hardly ♦ *conj* as soon as, no sooner

apéndice [a'pendiθe] *nm* appendix; **apendicitis** *nf* appendicitis

aperitivo [aperi'tiβo] *nm* (*bebida*) aperitif; (*comida*) appetizer

apero [a'pero] *nm* (*AGR*) implement; ~**s** *nmpl* farm equipment *sg*

apertura [aper'tura] *nf* opening; (*POL*) liberalization

apesadumbrar [apesaðum'brar] *vt* to grieve, sadden; ~**se** *vr* to distress o.s.

apestar [apes'tar] *vt* to infect ♦ *vi:* ~ **(a)** to stink (of)

apetecer [apete'θer] *vt:* **¿te apetece un café?** do you fancy a (cup of) coffee?; **apetecible** *adj* desirable; (*comida*) appetizing

apetito [ape'tito] *nm* appetite; ~**so, a** *adj* appetizing; (*fig*) tempting

apiadarse [apja'ðarse] *vr:* ~ **de** to take pity on

ápice ['apiθe] *nm* apex; (*fig*) whit, iota

apilar [api'lar] *vt* to pile *o* heap up; ~**se** *vr* to pile up

apiñarse [api'ɲarse] *vr* to crowd *o* press together

apio ['apjo] *nm* celery

apisonadora [apisona'ðora] *nf* (*máquina*) steamroller

aplacar [apla'kar] *vt* to placate; ~**se** *vr* to calm down

aplanar [apla'nar] *vt* to smooth, level; (*allanar*) to roll flat, flatten

aplastante [aplas'tante] *adj* overwhelming; (*lógica*) compelling

aplastar [aplas'tar] *vt* to squash (flat); (*fig*) to crush

aplatanarse [aplata'narse] *vr* to get lethargic

aplaudir [aplau'ðir] *vt* to applaud

aplauso [a'plauso] *nm* applause; (*fig*) approval, acclaim

aplazamiento [aplaθa'mjento] *nm* postponement

aplazar [apla'θar] *vt* to postpone, defer

aplicación [aplika'θjon] *nf* application; (*esfuerzo*) effort

aplicado, a [apli'kaðo, a] *adj* diligent, hard-working

aplicar [apli'kar] *vt* (*ejecutar*) to apply; ~**se** *vr* to apply o.s.

aplique *etc* [a'plike] *vb ver* **aplicar** ♦ *nm* wall light

aplomo [a'plomo] *nm* aplomb, self-assurance

apocado, a [apo'kaðo, a] *adj* timid

apocarse [apo'karse] *vr* to feel small *o* humiliated

apodar [apo'ðar] *vt* to nickname

apoderado [apoðe'raðo] *nm* agent, representative

apoderar [apoðe'rar] *vt* to authorize, empower; (*JUR*) to grant (a) power of attorney to; ~**se** *vr:* ~**se de** to take possession of

apodo [a'poðo] *nm* nickname

apogeo [apo'xeo] *nm* peak, summit

apolillarse [apoli'ʎarse] *vr* to get motheaten

apología [apolo'xia] *nf* eulogy; (*defensa*) defence

apoltronarse [apoltro'narse] *vr* to get lazy

apoplejía [aple'xia] *nf* apoplexy, stroke

apoquinar [apoki'nar] (*fam*) *vt* to fork out, cough up

aporrear [aporre'ar] *vt* to beat (up)

aportar [apor'tar] *vt* to contribute ♦ *vi* to reach port; ~**se** *vr* (*AM*: *llegar*) to arrive, come

aposento [apo'sento] *nm* lodging; (*habitación*) room

aposta [a'posta] *adv* deliberately, on purpose

apostar [apos'tar] *vt* to bet, stake; (*tropas etc*) to station, post ♦ *vi* to bet

apóstol [a'postol] *nm* apostle
apóstrofo [a'postrofo] *nm* apostrophe
apoyar [apo'jar] *vt* to lean, rest; (*fig*) to support, back; ~**se** *vr*: ~**se en** to lean on; **apoyo** *nm* (*gen*) support; backing, help
apreciable [apre'θjaßle] *adj* considerable; (*fig*) esteemed
apreciar [apre'θjar] *vt* to evaluate, assess; (*COM*) to appreciate, value; (*persona*) to respect; (*tamaño*) to gauge, assess; (*detalles*) to notice
aprecio [a'preθjo] *nm* valuation, estimate; (*fig*) appreciation
aprehender [apreen'der] *vt* to apprehend, detain; **aprehensión** *nf* detention, capture
apremiante [apre'mjante] *adj* urgent, pressing
apremiar [apre'mjar] *vt* to compel, force ♦ *vi* to be urgent, press; **apremio** *nm* urgency
aprender [apren'der] *vt, vi* to learn
aprendiz, a [apren'diθ, a] *nm/f* apprentice; (*principiante*) learner; ~ **de conductor** learner driver; ~**aje** *nm* apprenticeship
aprensión [apren'sjon] *nm* apprehension, fear; **aprensivo, a** *adj* apprehensive
apresar [apre'sar] *vt* to seize; (*capturar*) to capture
aprestar [apres'tar] *vt* to prepare, get ready; (*TEC*) to prime, size; ~**se** *vr* to get ready
apresurado, a [apresu'raðo, a] *adj* hurried, hasty; **apresuramiento** *nm* hurry, haste
apresurar [apresu'rar] *vt* to hurry, accelerate; ~**se** *vr* to hurry, make haste
apretado, a [apre'taðo, a] *adj* tight; (*escritura*) cramped
apretar [apre'tar] *vt* to squeeze; (*TEC*) to tighten; (*presionar*) to press together, pack ♦ *vi* to be too tight
apretón [apre'ton] *nm* squeeze; ~ **de manos** handshake
aprieto [a'prjeto] *nm* squeeze; (*dificultad*) difficulty; **estar en un** ~ to be in a fix
aprisa [a'prisa] *adv* quickly, hurriedly
aprisionar [aprisjo'nar] *vt* to imprison
aprobación [aproßa'θjon] *nf* approval
aprobar [apro'ßar] *vt* to approve (of); (*examen, materia*) to pass ♦ *vi* to pass
apropiación [apropja'θjon] *nf* appropriation
apropiado, a [apro'pjaðo, a] *adj* appropriate
apropiarse [apro'pjarse] *vr*: ~ **de** to appropriate
aprovechado, a [aproße'tʃaðo, a] *adj* industrious, hard-working, (*económico*) thrifty; (*pey*) unscrupulous; **aprovechamiento** *nm* use; exploitation
aprovechar [aproße'tʃar] *vt* to use; (*explotar*) to exploit; (*experiencia*) to profit from; (*oferta, oportunidad*) to take advantage of ♦ *vi* to progress, improve; ~**se** *vr*: ~**se de** to

make use of; to take advantage of; **¡que aproveche!** enjoy your meal!
aproximación [aproksima'θjon] *nf* approximation; (*de lotería*) consolation prize; **aproximado, a** *adj* approximate
aproximar [aproksi'mar] *vt* to bring nearer; ~**se** *vr* to come near, approach
apruebo *etc vb ver* **aprobar**
aptitud [apti'tuð] *nf* aptitude
apto, a ['apto, a] *adj* suitable
apuesta [a'pwesta] *nf* bet, wager
apuesto, a [a'pwesto, a] *adj* neat, elegant
apuntador [apunta'ðor] *nm* prompter
apuntalar [apunta'lar] *vt* to prop up
apuntar [apun'tar] *vt* (*con arma*) to aim at; (*con dedo*) to point at *o* to; (*anotar*) to note (down); (*TEATRO*) to prompt; ~**se** *vr* (*DEPORTE: tanto, victoria*) to score; (*ESCOL*) to enrol
apunte [a'punte] *nm* note
apuñalar [apuɲa'lar] *vt* to stab
apurado, a [apu'raðo, a] *adj* needy; (*difícil*) difficult; (*peligroso*) dangerous; (*AM*) hurried, rushed
apurar [apu'rar] *vt* (*agotar*) to drain; (*recursos*) to use up; (*molestar*) to annoy; ~**se** *vr* (*preocuparse*) to worry; (*darse prisa*) to hurry
apuro [a'puro] *nm* (*aprieto*) fix, jam; (*escasez*) want, hardship; (*vergüenza*) embarrassment; (*AM*) haste, urgency
aquejado, a [ake'xaðo, a] *adj*: ~ **de** (*MED*) afflicted by
aquel, aquella [a'kel, a'keʎa] (*pl* **aquellos, as**) *adj* that; (*pl*) those
aquél, aquélla [a'kel, a'keʎa] (*pl* **aquéllos, as**) *pron* that (one); (*pl*) those (ones)
aquello [a'keʎo] *pron* that, that business
aquí [a'ki] *adv* (*lugar*) here; (*tiempo*) now; ~ **arriba** up here; ~ **mismo** right here; ~ **yace** here lies; **de** ~ **a siete días** a week from now
aquietar [akje'tar] *vt* to quieten (down), calm (down)
ara ['ara] *nf*: **en** ~**s de** for the sake of
árabe ['araße] *adj, nm/f* Arab ♦ *nm* (*LING*) Arabic
Arabia [a'raßja] *nf*: ~ **Saudí** *o* **Saudita** Saudi Arabia
arado [a'raðo] *nm* plough
Aragón [ara'ɣon] *nm* Aragon; **aragonés, esa** *adj, nm/f* Aragonese
arancel [aran'θel] *nm* tariff, duty; ~ **de aduanas** customs (duty)
arandela [aran'dela] *nf* (*TEC*) washer
araña [a'raɲa] *nf* (*ZOOL*) spider; (*lámpara*) chandelier
arañar [ara'ɲar] *vt* to scratch
arañazo [ara'ɲaθo] *nm* scratch
arar [a'rar] *vt* to plough, till
arbitraje [arßi'traxe] *nm* arbitration
arbitrar [arßi'trar] *vt* to arbitrate in; (*DE-*

PORTE) to referee ♦ *vi* to arbitrate

arbitrariedad [arßitrarje'ðað] *nf* arbitrariness; (*acto*) arbitrary act; **arbitrario, a** *adj* arbitrary

arbitrio [ar'ßitrjo] *nm* free will; (*JUR*) adjudication, decision

árbitro ['arßitro] *nm* arbitrator; (*DEPORTE*) referee; (*TENIS*) umpire

árbol ['arßol] *nm* (*BOT*) tree; (*NAUT*) mast; (*TEC*) axle, shaft; **arbolado, a** *adj* wooded; (*camino etc*) tree-lined ♦ *nm* woodland

arboleda [arßo'leða] *nf* grove, plantation

arbusto [ar'ßusto] *nm* bush, shrub

arca ['arka] *nf* chest, box

arcada [ar'kaða] *nf* arcade; (*de puente*) arch, span; **~s** *nfpl* (*náuseas*) retching *sg*

arcaico, a [ar'kaiko, a] *adj* archaic

arce ['arθe] *nm* maple tree

arcén [ar'θen] *nm* (*de autopista*) hard shoulder; (*de carretera*) verge

arcilla [ar'θiʎa] *nf* clay

arco ['arko] *nm* arch; (*MAT*) arc; (*MIL*, *MUS*) bow; **~ iris** rainbow

archipiélago [artʃi'pjelaxo] *nm* archipelago

archivador [artʃißa'ðor] *nm* filing cabinet

archivar [artʃi'ßar] *vt* to file (away); **archivo** *nm* file, archive(s) (*pl*)

arder [ar'ðer] *vi* to burn; **estar que arde** (*persona*) to fume

ardid [ar'ðið] *nm* ploy, trick

ardiente [ar'ðjente] *adj* burning, ardent

ardilla [ar'ðiʎa] *nf* squirrel

ardor [ar'ðor] *nm* (*calor*) heat; (*fig*) ardour; **~ de estómago** heartburn

arduo, a ['arðwo, a] *adj* arduous

área ['area] *nf* area; (*DEPORTE*) penalty area

arena [a'rena] *nf* sand; (*de una lucha*) arena; **~ movedizas** quicksand *sg*

arenal [are'nal] *nm* (*arena movediza*) quicksand

arengar [aren'gar] *vt* to harangue

arenisca [are'niska] *nf* sandstone; (*cascajo*) grit

arenoso, a [are'noso, a] *adj* sandy

arenque [a'renke] *nm* herring

arete [a'rete] *nm* earring

argamasa [arxa'masa] *nf* mortar, plaster

Argel [ar'xel] *n* Algiers; **~ia** *nf* Algeria; **argelino, a** *adj*, *nm/f* Algerian

Argentina [arxen'tina] *nf*: **(la) ~** Argentina

argentino, a [arxen'tino, a] *adj* Argentinian; (*de plata*) silvery ♦ *nm/f* Argentinian

argolla [ar'xoʎa] *nf* (*large*) ring

argot [ar'xo] (*pl* **~s**) *nm* slang

argucia [ar'xuθja] *nf* subtlety, sophistry

argüir [ar'xwir] *vt* to deduce; (*discutir*) to argue; (*indicar*) to indicate, imply; (*censurar*) to reproach ♦ *vi* to argue

argumentación [arxumenta'θjon] *nf* (line of) argument

argumentar [arxumen'tar] *vt*, *vi* to argue

argumento [arxu'mento] *nm* argument; (*razonamiento*) reasoning; (*de novela etc*) plot; (*CINE*, *TV*) storyline

aria ['arja] *nf* aria

aridez [ari'ðeθ] *nf* aridity, dryness

árido, a ['ariðo, a] *adj* arid, dry; **~s** *nmpl* (*COM*) dry goods

Aries ['arjes] *nm* Aries

ario, a ['arjo, a] *adj* Aryan

arisco, a [a'risko, a] *adj* surly; (*insociable*) unsociable

aristócrata [aris'tokrata] *nm/f* aristocrat

aritmética [arit'metika] *nf* arithmetic

arma ['arma] *nf* arm; **~s** *nfpl* arms; **~ blanca** blade, knife; (*espada*) sword; **~ de fuego** firearm; **~s cortas** small arms

armada [ar'maða] *nf* armada; (*flota*) fleet

armadillo [arma'ðiʎo] *nm* armadillo

armado, a [ar'maðo, a] *adj* armed; (*TEC*) reinforced

armador [arma'ðor] *nm* (*NAUT*) shipowner

armadura [arma'ðura] *nf* (*MIL*) armour; (*TEC*) framework; (*ZOOL*) skeleton; (*FÍSICA*) armature

armamento [arma'mento] *nm* armament; (*NAUT*) fitting-out

armar [ar'mar] *vt* (*soldado*) to arm; (*máquina*) to assemble; (*navío*) to fit out; **~la**, **~ un lío** to start a row, kick up a fuss

armario [ar'marjo] *nm* wardrobe; (*de cocina*, *baño*) cupboard

armatoste [arma'toste] *nm* (*mueble*) monstrosity; (*máquina*) contraption

armazón [arma'θon] *nf o m* body, chassis; (*de mueble etc*) frame; (*ARQ*) skeleton

armería [arme'ria] *nf* (*museo*) military museum; (*tienda*) gunsmith's

armiño [ar'miɲo] *nm* stoat; (*piel*) ermine

armisticio [armis'tiθjo] *nm* armistice

armonía [armo'nia] *nf* harmony

armónica [ar'monika] *nf* harmonica

armonioso, a [armo'njoso, a] *adj* harmonious

armonizar [armoni'θar] *vt* to harmonize; (*diferencias*) to reconcile ♦ *vi*: **~ con** (*fig*) to be in keeping with; (*colores*) to tone in with, blend

arnés [ar'nes] *nm* armour; **arneses** *nmpl* (*de caballo etc*) harness *sg*

aro ['aro] *nm* ring; (*tejo*) quoit; (*AM: pendiente*) earring

aroma [a'roma] *nm* aroma, scent

aromático, a [aro'matiko, a] *adj* aromatic

arpa ['arpa] *nf* harp

arpía [ar'pia] *nf* shrew

arpillera [arpi'ʎera] *nf* sacking, sackcloth

arpón [ar'pon] *nm* harpoon

arquear [arke'ar] *vt* to arch, bend; **~se** *vr* to arch, bend

arqueología [arkeolo'xia] *nf* archaeology; **arqueólogo, a** *nm/f* archaeologist

arquero [ar'kero] *nm* archer, bowman

arquetipo [arke'tipo] *nm* archetype
arquitecto [arki'tekto] *nm* architect; **arquitectura** *nf* architecture
arrabal [arra'βal] *nm* suburb; (*AM*) slum; **~es** *nmpl* (*afueras*) outskirts
arraigado, a [arrai'ɣaðo, a] *adj* deep-rooted; (*fig*) established
arraigar [arrai'ɣar] *vt* to establish ♦ *vi* to take root; **~se** *vr* to take root; (*persona*) to settle
arrancar [arran'kar] *vt* (*sacar*) to extract, pull out; (*arrebatar*) to snatch (away); (*INFORM*) to boot; (*fig*) to extract ♦ *vi* (*AUTO, máquina*) to start; (*ponerse en marcha*) to get going; **~ de** to stem from
arranque *etc* [a'rranke] *vb ver* **arrancar** ♦ *nm* sudden start; (*AUTO*) start; (*fig*) fit, outburst
arrasar [arra'sar] *vt* (*aplanar*) to level, flatten; (*destruir*) to demolish
arrastrado, a [arras'traðo, a] *adj* poor, wretched; (*AM*) servile
arrastrar [arras'trar] *vt* to drag (along); (*fig*) to drag down, degrade; (*suj: agua, viento*) to carry away ♦ *vi* to drag, trail on the ground; **~se** *vr* to crawl; (*fig*) to grovel; **llevar algo arrastrado** to drag sth along
arrastre [a'rrastre] *nm* drag, dragging
arre ['arre] *excl* gee up!
arrear [arre'ar] *vt* to drive on, urge on ♦ *vi* to hurry along
arrebatado, a [arreβa'taðo, a] *adj* rash, impetuous; (*repentino*) sudden, hasty
arrebatar [arreβa'tar] *vt* to snatch (away), seize; (*fig*) to captivate; **~se** *vr* to get carried away, get excited
arrebato [arre'βato] *nm* fit of rage, fury; (*éxtasis*) rapture
arrecife [arre'θife] *nm* (*tb: ~ de coral*) reef
arredrarse [arre'ðrarse] *vr*: **~ (ante algo)** to be intimidated (by sth)
arreglado, a [arre'ɣlaðo, a] *adj* (*ordenado*) neat, orderly; (*moderado*) moderate, reasonable
arreglar [arre'ɣlar] *vt* (*poner orden*) to tidy up; (*algo roto*) to fix, repair; (*problema*) to solve; **~se** *vr* to reach an understanding; **arreglárselas** (*fam*) to get by, manage
arreglo [a'rreɣlo] *nm* settlement; (*orden*) order; (*acuerdo*) agreement; (*MUS*) arrangement, setting
arrellanarse [arreʎa'narse] *vr*: **~ en** to sit back in/on
arremangar [arreman'gar] *vt* to roll up, turn up; **~se** *vr* to roll up one's sleeves
arremeter [arreme'ter] *vi*: **~ contra** to attack, rush at
arrendamiento [arrenda'mjento] *nm* letting; (*alquilar*) hiring; (*contrato*) lease; (*alquiler*) rent; **arrendar** *vt* to let, lease; to rent; **arrendatario, a** *nm/f* tenant
arreo [a'rreo] *nm* adornment; **~s** *nmpl* (*de*

caballo) harness *sg*, trappings
arrepentimiento [arrepenti'mjento] *nm* regret, repentance
arrepentirse [arrepen'tirse] *vr* to repent; **~ de** to regret
arrestar [arres'tar] *vt* to arrest; (*encarcelar*) to imprison; **arresto** *nm* arrest; (*MIL*) detention; (*audacia*) boldness, daring; **arresto domiciliario** house arrest
arriar [a'rrjar] *vt* (*velas*) to haul down; (*bandera*) to lower, strike; (*cable*) to pay out

────────── PALABRA CLAVE

arriba [a'rriβa] *adv* **1** (*posición*) above; **desde ~** from above; **~ de todo** at the very top, right on top; **Juan está ~** Juan is upstairs; **lo ~ mencionado** the aforementioned

2 (*dirección*): **calle ~** up the street

3: **de ~ abajo** from top to bottom; **mirar a uno de ~ abajo** to look sb up and down

4: **para ~**: **de 5000 pesetas para ~** from 5000 pesetas up(wards)

♦ *adj*: **de ~**: **el piso de ~** the upstairs flat (*BRIT*) *o* apartment; **la parte de ~** the top *o* upper part

♦ *prep*: **~ de** (*AM*) above; **~ de 200 dólares** more than 200 dollars

♦ *excl*: **¡~!** up!; **¡manos ~!** hands up!; **¡~ España!** long live Spain!

arribar [arri'βar] *vi* to put into port; (*llegar*) to arrive
arribista [arri'βista] *nm/f* parvenu(e), upstart
arriendo *etc* [a'rrjendo] *vb ver* **arrendar** ♦ *nm* = **arrendamiento**
arriero [a'rrjero] *nm* muleteer
arriesgado, a [arrjes'ɣaðo, a] *adj* (*peligroso*) risky; (*audaz*) bold, daring
arriesgar [arrjes'ɣar] *vt* to risk; (*poner en peligro*) to endanger; **~se** *vr* to take a risk
arrimar [arri'mar] *vt* (*acercar*) to bring close; (*poner de lado*) to set aside; **~se** *vr* to come close *o* closer; **~se a** to lean on
arrinconar [arrinko'nar] *vt* (*colocar*) to put in a corner; (*enemigo*) to corner; (*fig*) to put on one side; (*abandonar*) to push aside
arrodillarse [arroði'ʎarse] *vr* to kneel (down)
arrogancia [arro'ɣanθja] *nf* arrogance; **arrogante** *adj* arrogant
arrojar [arro'xar] *vt* to throw, hurl; (*humo*) to emit, give out; (*COM*) to yield, produce; **~se** *vr* to throw *o* hurl o.s
arrojo [a'rroxo] *nm* daring
arrollador, a [arroʎa'ðor, a] *adj* overwhelming
arrollar [arro'ʎar] *vt* (*AUTO etc*) to run over, knock down; (*DEPORTE*) to crush

arropar [arro'par] *vt* to cover, wrap up; ~**se** *vr* to wrap o.s. up

arrostrar [arros'trar] *vt* to face (up to); ~**se** *vr*: ~**se con uno** to face up to sb

arroyo [a'rrojo] *nm* stream; (*de la calle*) gutter

arroz [a'rroθ] *nm* rice; ~ **con leche** rice pudding

arruga [a'rruɣa] *nf* fold; (*de cara*) wrinkle; (*de vestido*) crease

arrugar [arru'ɣar] *vt* to fold; to wrinkle; to crease; ~**se** *vr* to get creased

arruinar [arrwi'nar] *vt* to ruin, wreck; ~**se** *vr* to be ruined, go bankrupt

arrullar [arru'ʎar] *vi* to coo ♦ *vt* to lull to sleep

arsenal [arse'nal] *nm* naval dockyard; (*MIL*) arsenal

arsénico [ar'seniko] *nm* arsenic

arte ['arte] (*gen m en sg y siempre f en pl*) *nm* art; (*maña*) skill, guile; ~**s** *nfpl* (*bellas* ~**s**) arts

artefacto [arte'fakto] *nm* appliance; (*ARQUEOLOGÍA*) artefact

arteria [ar'terja] *nf* artery

artesanía [artesa'nia] *nf* craftsmanship; (*artículos*) handicrafts *pl*; **artesano, a** *nm/f* artisan, craftsman/woman

ártico, a ['artiko, a] *adj* Arctic ♦ *nm*: **el Á~** the Arctic

articulación [artikula'θjon] *nf* articulation; (*MED, TEC*) joint; **articulado, a** *adj* articulated; jointed

articular [artiku'lar] *vt* to articulate; to join together

artículo [ar'tikulo] *nm* article; (*cosa*) thing, article; ~**s** *nmpl* (*COM*) goods

artífice [ar'tifiθe] *nm/f* artist, craftsman/woman; (*fig*) architect

artificial [artifi'θjal] *adj* artificial

artificio [arti'fiθjo] *nm* art, skill; (*artesanía*) craftsmanship; (*astucia*) cunning

artilugio [arti'luxjo] *nm* gadget

artillería [artiʎe'ria] *nf* artillery

artillero [arti'ʎero] *nm* artilleryman, gunner

artimaña [arti'maɲa] *nf* trap, snare; (*astucia*) cunning

artista [ar'tista] *nm/f* (*pintor*) artist, painter; (*TEATRO*) artist, artiste; ~ **de cine** film actor/actress; **artístico, a** *adj* artistic

artritis [ar'tritis] *nf* arthritis

arveja [ar'βexa] (*AM*) *nf* pea

arzobispo [arθo'βispo] *nm* archbishop

as [as] *nm* ace

asa ['asa] *nf* handle; (*fig*) lever

asado [a'saðo] *nm* roast (meat); (*AM: barbacoa*) barbecue

asador [asa'ðor] *nm* spit

asadura [asa'ðura] *nf* entrails *pl*, offal

asalariado, a [asala'rjaðo, a] *adj* paid, salaried ♦ *nm/f* wage earner

asaltador, a [asalta'ðor, a] *nm/f* assailant

asaltante [asal'tante] *nm/f* = **asaltador, a**

asaltar [asal'tar] *vt* to attack, assault; (*fig*) to assail; **asalto** *nm* attack, assault; (*DEPORTE*) round

asamblea [asam'blea] *nf* assembly; (*reunión*) meeting

asar [a'sar] *vt* to roast

asbesto [as'βesto] *nm* asbestos

ascendencia [asθen'denθja] *nf* ancestry; (*AM*) ascendancy; **de ~ francesa** of French origin

ascender [asθen'der] *vi* (*subir*) to ascend, rise; (*ser promovido*) to gain promotion ♦ *vt* to promote; ~ **a** to amount to; **ascendiente** *nm* influence ♦ *nm/f* ancestor

ascensión [asθen'sjon] *nf* ascent; (*REL*): **la A~** the Ascension

ascenso [as'θenso] *nm* ascent; (*promoción*) promotion

ascensor [asθen'sor] *nm* lift (*BRIT*), elevator (*US*)

ascético, a [as'θetiko, a] *adj* ascetic

asco ['asko] *nm*: ¡**qué** ~! how revolting *o* disgusting; **el ajo me da** ~ I hate *o* loathe garlic; **estar hecho un** ~ to be filthy

ascua ['askwa] *nf* ember; **estar en** ~**s** to be on tenterhooks

aseado, a [ase'aðo, a] *adj* clean; (*arreglado*) tidy; (*pulcro*) smart

asear [ase'ar] *vt* to clean, wash; to tidy (up)

asediar [ase'ðjar] *vt* (*MIL*) to besiege, lay siege to; (*fig*) to chase, pester; **asedio** *nm* siege; (*COM*) run

asegurado, a [aseɣu'raðo, a] *adj* insured; **asegurador, a** *nm/f* insurer

asegurar [aseɣu'rar] *vt* (*consolidar*) to secure, fasten; (*dar garantía de*) to guarantee; (*preservar*) to safeguard; (*afirmar, dar por cierto*) to assure, affirm; (*tranquilizar*) to reassure; (*tomar un seguro*) to insure; ~**se** *vr* to assure o.s., make sure

asemejarse [aseme'xarse] *vr* to be alike; ~ **a** to be like, resemble

asentado, a [asen'taðo, a] *adj* established, settled

asentar [asen'tar] *vt* (*sentar*) to seat, sit down; (*poner*) to place, establish; (*alisar*) to level, smooth down *o* out; (*anotar*) to note down ♦ *vi* to be suitable, suit

asentir [asen'tir] *vi* to assent, agree; ~ **con la cabeza** to nod (one's head)

aseo [a'seo] *nm* cleanliness; ~**s** *nmpl* (*servicios*) toilet *sg* (*BRIT*), cloakroom *sg* (*BRIT*), restroom *sg* (*US*)

aséptico, a [a'septiko, a] *adj* germ-free, free from infection

asequible [ase'kiβle] *adj* (*precio*) reasonable; (*meta*) attainable; (*persona*) approachable

aserradero [aserra'ðero] *nm* sawmill; **aserrar** *vt* to saw

asesinar [asesi'nar] *vt* to murder; (*POL*) to

assassinate; **asesinato** *nm* murder; assassination

asesino, a [ase'sino, a] *nm/f* murderer, killer; (POL) assassin

asesor, a [ase'sor, a] *nm/f* adviser, consultant

asesorar [aseso'rar] *vt* (JUR) to advise, give legal advice to; (COM) to act as consultant to; ~**se** *vr*: ~**se con** *o* **de** to take advice from, consult; **asesoría** *nf* (cargo) consultancy; (oficina) consultant's office

asestar [ases'tar] *vt* (golpe) to deal, strike; (arma) to aim; (tiro) to fire

asfalto [as'falto] *nm* asphalt

asfixia [as'fiksja] *nf* asphyxia, suffocation

asfixiar [asfik'sjar] *vt* to asphyxiate, suffocate; ~**se** *vr* to be asphyxiated, suffocate

asgo *etc vb ver* **asir**

así [a'si] *adv* (de esta manera) in this way, like this, thus; (aunque) although; (tan pronto como) as soon as; ~ **que** so; ~ **como** as well as; ~ **y todo** even so; ¿**no es ~?** isn't it?, didn't you? *etc*; ~ **de grande** this big

Asia ['asja] *nf* Asia; **asiático, a** *adj, nm/f* Asian, Asiatic

asidero [asi'ðero] *nm* handle

asiduidad [asiðwi'ðað] *nf* assiduousness; **asiduo, a** *adj* assiduous; (frecuente) frequent ♦ *nm/f* regular (customer)

asiento [a'sjento] *nm* (mueble) seat, chair; (de coche, en tribunal etc) seat; (localidad) seat, place; (fundamento) site; ~ **delantero/trasero** front/back seat

asignación [asiɣna'θjon] *nf* (atribución) assignment; (reparto) allocation; (sueldo) salary; ~ (**semanal**) pocket money

asignar [asiɣ'nar] *vt* to assign, allocate

asignatura [asiɣna'tura] *nf* subject; course

asilado, a [asi'laðo, a] *nm/f* inmate; (POL) refugee

asilo [a'silo] *nm* (refugio) asylum, refuge; (establecimiento) home, institution; ~ **político** political asylum

asimilación [asimila'θjon] *nf* assimilation

asimilar [asimi'lar] *vt* to assimilate

asimismo [asi'mismo] *adv* in the same way, likewise

asir [a'sir] *vt* to seize, grasp

asistencia [asis'tenθja] *nf* audience; (MED) attendance; (ayuda) assistance; **asistente** *nm/f* assistant; **los asistentes** those present; **asistente social** social worker

asistido, a [asis'tiðo, a] *adj*: ~ **por ordenador** computer-assisted

asistir [asis'tir] *vt* to assist, help ♦ *vi*: ~ **a** to attend, be present at

asma ['asma] *nf* asthma

asno ['asno] *nm* donkey; (fig) ass

asociación [asoθja'θjon] *nf* association; (COM) partnership; **asociado, a** *adj* associate ♦ *nm/f* associate; (COM) partner

asociar [aso'θjar] *vt* to associate

asolar [aso'lar] *vt* to destroy

asolearse [asole'arse] *vr* to sunbathe

asomar [aso'mar] *vt* to show, stick out ♦ *vi* to appear; ~**se** *vr* to appear, show up; ~ **la cabeza por la ventana** to put one's head out of the window

asombrar [asom'brar] *vt* to amaze, astonish; ~**se** *vr* (sorprenderse) to be amazed; (asustarse) to get a fright; **asombro** *nm* amazement, astonishment; (susto) fright; **asombroso, a** *adj* astonishing, amazing

asomo [a'somo] *nm* hint, sign

aspa ['aspa] *nf* (cruz) cross; (de molino) sail; **en** ~ X-shaped

aspaviento [aspa'ßjento] *nm* exaggerated display of feeling; (fam) fuss

aspecto [as'pekto] *nm* (apariencia) look, appearance; (fig) aspect

aspereza [aspe'reθa] *nf* roughness; (agrura) sourness; (de carácter) surliness; **áspero, a** *adj* rough; bitter, sour; harsh

aspersión [asper'sjon] *nf* sprinkling

aspiración [aspira'θjon] *nf* breath, inhalation; (MUS) short pause; **aspiraciones** *nfpl* (ambiciones) aspirations

aspirador [aspira'ðor] *nm* = **aspiradora**

aspiradora [aspira'ðora] *nf* vacuum cleaner, Hoover ®

aspirante [aspi'rante] *nm/f* (candidato) candidate; (DEPORTE) contender

aspirar [aspi'rar] *vt* to breathe in ♦ *vi*: ~ **a** to aspire to

aspirina [aspi'rina] *nf* aspirin

asquear [aske'ar] *vt* to sicken ♦ *vi* to be sickening; ~**se** *vr* to feel disgusted; **asqueroso, a** *adj* disgusting, sickening

asta ['asta] *nf* lance; (arpón) spear; (mango) shaft, handle; (ZOOL) horn; **a media** ~ at half mast

astado, a [as'taðo, a] *adj* horned ♦ *nm* bull

asterisco [aste'risko] *nm* asterisk

astilla [as'tiʎa] *nf* splinter; (pedacito) chip; ~**s** *nfpl* (leña) firewood *sg*

astillero [asti'ʎero] *nm* shipyard

astringente [astrin'xente] *adj, nm* astringent

astro ['astro] *nm* star

astrología [astrolo'xia] *nf* astrology; **astrólogo, a** *nm/f* astrologer

astronauta [astro'nauta] *nm/f* astronaut

astronave [astro'naße] *nm* spaceship

astronomía [astrono'mia] *nf* astronomy; **astrónomo, a** *nm/f* astronomer

astucia [as'tuθja] *nf* astuteness; (ardid) clever trick; **astuto, a** *adj* astute; (taimado) cunning

asueto [a'sweto] *nm* holiday; (tiempo libre) time off *no pl*

asumir [asu'mir] *vt* to assume

asunción [asun'θjon] *nf* assumption; (REL): **A~** Assumption

asunto [a'sunto] *nm* (*tema*) matter, subject; (*negocio*) business

asustar [asus'tar] *vt* to frighten; ~**se** *vr* to be (*o* become) frightened

atacar [ata'kar] *vt* to attack

atadura [ata'ðura] *nf* bond, tie

atajar [ata'xar] *vt* (*enfermedad, mal*) to stop ♦ *vi* (*persona*) to take a short cut

atajo [a'taxo] *nm* short cut; (*DEPORTE*) tackle

atañer [ata'ɲer] *vi*: ~ **a** to concern

ataque *etc* [a'take] *vb ver* **atacar** ♦ *nm* attack; ~ **cardíaco** heart attack

atar [a'tar] *vt* to tie, tie up

atardecer [atarðe'θer] *vi* to get dark ♦ *nm* evening; (*crepúsculo*) dusk

atareado, a [atare'aðo, a] *adj* busy

atascar [atas'kar] *vt* to clog up; (*obstruir*) to jam; (*fig*) to hinder; ~**se** *vr* to stall; (*cañería*) to get blocked up; **atasco** *nm* obstruction; (*AUTO*) traffic jam

ataúd [ata'uð] *nm* coffin

ataviar [ata'βjar] *vt* to deck, array; ~**se** *vr* to dress up

atavío [ata'βio] *nm* attire, dress; ~**s** *nmpl* finery *sg*

atemorizar [atemori'θar] *vt* to frighten, scare; ~**se** *vr* to get scared

Atenas [a'tenas] *n* Athens

atención [aten'θjon] *nf* attention; (*bondad*) kindness ♦ *excl* (be) careful!, look out!

atender [aten'der] *vt* to attend to, look after ♦ *vi* to pay attention

atenerse [ate'nerse] *vr*: ~ **a** to abide by, adhere to

atentado [aten'taðo] *nm* crime, illegal act; (*asalto*) assault; ~ **contra la vida de uno** attempt on sb's life

atentamente [atenta'mente] *adv*: **Le saluda** ~ Yours faithfully

atentar [aten'tar] *vi*: ~ **a** *o* **contra** to commit an outrage against

atento, a [a'tento, a] *adj* attentive, observant; (*cortés*) polite, thoughtful

atenuante [ate'nwante] *adj* extenuating

atenuar [ate'nwar] *vt* (*disminuir*) to lessen, minimize

ateo, a [a'teo, a] *adj* atheistic ♦ *nm/f* atheist

aterciopelado, a [aterθjope'laðo, a] *adj* velvety

aterido, a [ate'riðo, a] *adj*: ~ **de frío** frozen stiff

aterrador, a [aterra'ðor, a] *adj* frightening

aterrar [ate'rrar] *vt* to frighten; to terrify; ~**se** *vr* to be frightened; to be terrified

aterrizaje [aterri'θaxe] *nm* (*AVIAT*) landing

aterrizar [aterri'θar] *vi* to land

aterrorizar [aterrori'θar] *vt* to terrify

atesorar [ateso'rar] *vt* to hoard, store up

atestado, a [ates'taðo, a] *adj* packed ♦ *nm* (*JUR*) affidavit

atestar [ates'tar] *vt* to pack, stuff; (*JUR*) to attest, testify to

atestiguar [atesti'ɣwar] *vt* to testify to, bear witness to

atiborrar [atiβo'rrar] *vt* to fill, stuff; ~**se** *vr* to stuff o.s

ático ['atiko] *nm* attic; ~ **de lujo** penthouse (flat (*BRIT*) *o* apartment)

atildar [atil'dar] *vt* to criticize; ~**se** *vr* to spruce o.s. up

atinado, a [ati'naðo, a] *adj* (*sensato*) wise; (*correcto*) right, correct

atinar [ati'nar] *vi* (*al disparar*): ~ **al blanco** to hit the target; (*fig*) to be right

atisbar [atis'βar] *vt* to spy on; (*echar una ojeada*) to peep at

atizar [ati'θar] *vt* to poke; (*horno etc*) to stoke; (*fig*) to stir up, rouse

atlántico, a [at'lantiko, a] *adj* Atlantic ♦ *nm*: **el (océano) A~** the Atlantic (Ocean)

atlas ['atlas] *nm* atlas

atleta [at'leta] *nm* athlete; **atlético, a** *adj* athletic; **atletismo** *nm* athletics *sg*

atmósfera [at'mosfera] *nf* atmosphere

atolondramiento [atolondra'mjento] *nm* bewilderment; (*insensatez*) silliness

atolladero [atoʎa'ðero] *nm* (*fig*) jam, fix

atómico, a [a'tomiko, a] *adj* atomic

atomizador [atomiθa'ðor] *nm* atomizer; (*de perfume*) spray

átomo ['atomo] *nm* atom

atónito, a [a'tonito, a] *adj* astonished, amazed

atontado, a [aton'taðo, a] *adj* stunned; (*bobo*) silly, daft

atontar [aton'tar] *vt* to stun; ~**se** *vr* to become confused

atormentar [atormen'tar] *vt* to torture; (*molestar*) to torment; (*acosar*) to plague, harass

atornillar [atorni'ʎar] *vt* to screw on *o* down

atosigar [atosi'ðar] *vt* (*fig*) to harass, pester

atracador, a [atraka'ðor, a] *nm/f* robber

atracar [atra'kar] *vt* (*NAUT*) to moor; (*robar*) to hold up, rob ♦ *vi* to moor; ~**se** *vr*: ~**se (de)** to stuff o.s. (with)

atracción [atrak'θjon] *nf* attraction

atraco [a'trako] *nm* holdup, robbery

atracón [atra'kon] *nm*: **darse** *o* **pegarse un** ~ **(de)** (*fam*) to stuff o.s. (with)

atractivo, a [atrak'tiβo, a] *adj* attractive ♦ *nm* appeal

atraer [atra'er] *vt* to attract

atragantarse [atraɣan'tarse] *vr*: ~ **(con)** to choke (on); **se me ha atragantado el chico** I can't stand the boy

atrancar [atran'kar] *vt* (*puerta*) to bar, bolt

atrapar [atra'par] *vt* to trap; (*resfriado etc*) to catch

atrás [a'tras] *adv* (*movimiento*) back(wards); (*lugar*) behind; (*tiempo*) previously; **ir hacia**

~ to go back(wards); to go to the rear; **estar** ~ to be behind *o* at the back

atrasado, a [atra'saðo, a] *adj* slow; (*pago*) overdue, late; (*país*) backward

atrasar [atra'sar] *vi* to be slow; ~**se** *vr* to remain behind; (*tren*) to be *o* run late; **atraso** *nm* slowness; lateness, delay; (*de país*) backwardness; **atrasos** *nmpl* (COM) arrears

atravesar [atraβe'sar] *vt* (*cruzar*) to cross (over); (*traspasar*) to pierce; to go through; (*poner al través*) to lay *o* put across; ~**se** *vr* to come in between; (*intervenir*) to interfere

atravieso *etc vb ver* **atravesar**

atrayente [atra'jente] *adj* attractive

atreverse [atre'βerse] *vr* to dare; (*insolentarse*) to be insolent; **atrevido, a** *adj* daring; insolent; **atrevimiento** *nm* daring; insolence

atribución [atriβu'θjon] *nf*: **atribuciones** (POL) powers; (ADMIN) responsibilities

atribuir [atriβu'ir] *vt* to attribute; (*funciones*) to confer

atribular [atriβu'lar] *vt* to afflict, distress

atributo [atri'βuto] *nm* attribute

atril [a'tril] *nm* (*para libro*) lectern; (MUS) music stand

atrocidad [atroθi'ðað] *nf* atrocity, outrage

atropellar [atrope'ʎar] *vt* (*derribar*) to knock over *o* down; (*empujar*) to push (aside); (AUTO) to run over, run down; (*agraviar*) to insult; ~**se** *vr* to act hastily; **atropello** *nm* (AUTO) accident; (*empujón*) push; (*agravio*) wrong; (*atrocidad*) outrage

atroz [a'troθ] *adj* atrocious, awful

atto, a *abr* = **atento**

atuendo [a'twendo] *nm* attire

atún [a'tun] *nm* tuna

aturdir [atur'ðir] *vt* to stun; (*de ruido*) to deafen; (*fig*) to dumbfound, bewilder

atusar [atu'sar] *vt* to smooth (down)

audacia [au'ðaθja] *nf* boldness, audacity; **audaz** *adj* bold, audacious

audible [au'ðiβle] *adj* audible

audición [auði'θjon] *nf* hearing; (TEATRO) audition

audiencia [au'ðjenθja] *nf* audience; **A~** (JUR) High Court

audífono [au'ðifono] *nm* (*para sordos*) hearing aid

auditor [auði'tor] *nm* (JUR) judge advocate; (COM) auditor

auditorio [auði'torjo] *nm* audience; (*sala*) auditorium

auge [auxe] *nm* boom; (*clímax*) climax

augurar [auɣu'rar] *vt* to predict; (*presagiar*) to portend

augurio [au'ɣurjo] *nm* omen

aula ['aula] *nf* classroom; (*en universidad etc*) lecture room

aullar [au'ʎar] *vi* to howl, yell

aullido [au'ʎiðo] *nm* howl, yell

aumentar [aumen'tar] *vt* to increase; (*precios*) to put up; (*producción*) to step up; (*con microscopio, anteojos*) to magnify ♦ *vi* to increase, be on the increase; ~**se** *vr* to increase, be on the increase; **aumento** *nm* increase; rise

aun [a'un] *adv* even; ~ **así** even so; ~ **más** even *o* yet more

aún [a'un] *adv*: ~ **está aquí** he's still here; ~ **no lo sabemos** we don't know yet; **¿no ha venido ~?** hasn't she come yet?

aunque [a'unke] *conj* though, although, even though

aúpa [a'upa] *excl* come on!

aureola [aure'ola] *nf* halo

auricular [auriku'lar] *nm* (TEL) earpiece, receiver; ~**es** *nmpl* (*para escuchar música etc*) headphones

aurora [au'rora] *nf* dawn

auscultar [auskul'tar] *vt* (MED: *pecho*) to listen to, sound

ausencia [au'senθja] *nf* absence

ausentarse [ausen'tarse] *vr* to go away; (*por poco tiempo*) to go out

ausente [au'sente] *adj* absent

auspicios [aus'piθjos] *nmpl* auspices; (*protección*) protection *sg*

austeridad [austeri'ðað] *nf* austerity; **austero, a** *adj* austere

austral [aus'tral] *adj* southern ♦ *nm* monetary unit of Argentina

Australia [aus'tralja] *nf* Australia; **australiano, a** *adj, nm/f* Australian

Austria ['austrja] *nf* Austria; **austríaco, a** *adj, nm/f* Austrian

auténtico, a [au'tentiko, a] *adj* authentic

auto ['auto] *nm* edict, decree; (: *orden*) writ; (AUTO) car; ~**s** *nmpl* (JUR) proceedings; (: *acta*) court record *sg*

autoadhesivo [autoaðe'siβo] *adj* self-adhesive; (*sobre*) self-sealing

autobiografía [autoβjovra'fia] *nf* autobiography

autobús [auto'βus] *nm* bus

autocar [auto'kar] *nm* coach (BRIT), (passenger) bus (US)

autóctono, a [au'toktono, a] *adj* native, indigenous

autodefensa [autoðe'fensa] *nf* self-defence

autodeterminación [autoðetermina'θjon] *nf* self-determination

autodidacto, a [autoði'ðakto, a] *adj* self-taught

autoescuela [autoes'kwela] *nf* driving school

autógrafo [au'toɣrafo] *nm* autograph

automación [automa'θjon] *nf* = **automatización**

autómata [au'tomata] *nm* automaton

automático, a [auto'matiko, a] *adj* automatic ♦ *nm* press stud

automatización [automatiθa'θjon] *nf* auto-

mation
automotor, triz [automo'tor, 'triθ] *adj*
self-propelled ♦ *nm* diesel train
automóvil [auto'moβil] *nm* (motor) car
(*BRIT*), automobile (*US*); **automovilismo**
nm (*actividad*) motoring; (*DEPORTE*) motor
racing; **automovilista** *nm/f* motorist, driver; **automovilístico, a** *adj* (*industria*) motor *cpd*
autonomía [autono'mia] *nf* autonomy; **autónomo, a** (*ESP*) *adj* (*POL*) autonomous;
autonómico, a (*ESP*) *adj* (*POL*) autonomous
autopista [auto'pista] *nf* motorway (*BRIT*),
freeway (*US*); **~ de peaje** toll road (*BRIT*),
turnpike road (*US*)
autopsia [au'topsja] *nf* autopsy, postmor-
tem
autor, a [au'tor, a] *nm/f* author
autoridad [autori'ðað] *nf* authority; **autoritario, a** *adj* authoritarian
autorización [autoriθa'θjon] *nf* authori-
zation; **autorizado, a** *adj* authorized;
(*aprobado*) approved
autorizar [autori'θar] *vt* to authorize; (*aprobar*) to approve
autorretrato [autorre'trato] *nm* self-portrait
autoservicio [autoser'βiθjo] *nm* (*tienda*)
self-service shop (*BRIT*) o store (*US*); (*restaurante*) self-service restaurant
autostop [auto'stop] *nm* hitch-hiking; **hacer ~** to hitch-hike; **~ista** *nm/f* hitch-hiker
autosuficiencia [autosufi'θjenθja] *nf* self-
sufficiency
autovía [auto'βia] *nf* ≈ A-road (*BRIT*), dual
carriageway (*BRIT*), ≈ state highway (*US*)
auxiliar [auksi'ljar] *vt* to help ♦ *nm/f* assistant; **auxilio** *nm* assistance, help; **primeros
auxilios** first aid *sg*
Av *abr* (= *Avenida*) Av(e).
aval [a'βal] *nm* guarantee; (*persona*) guarantor
avalancha [aβa'lantʃa] *nf* avalanche
avance [a'βanθe] *nm* advance; (*pago*) advance payment; (*CINE*) trailer
avanzar [aβan'θar] *vt, vi* to advance
avaricia [aβa'riθja] *nf* avarice, greed; **avari-
cioso, a** *adj* avaricious, greedy
avaro, a [a'βaro, a] *adj* miserly, mean ♦
nm/f miser
avasallar [aβasa'ʎar] *vt* to subdue, subjugate
Avda *abr* (= *Avenida*) Av(e).
ave [a'βe] *nf* bird; **~ de rapiña** bird of prey
avecinarse [aβeθi'narse] *vr* (*tormenta, fig*)
to be on the way
avellana [aβe'ʎana] *nf* hazelnut; **avellano**
nm hazel tree
avemaría [aβema'ria] *nm* Hail Mary, Ave
Maria
avena [a'βena] *nf* oats *pl*
avenida [aβe'niða] *nf* (*calle*) avenue

avenir [aβe'nir] *vt* to reconcile; **~se** *vr* to
come to an agreement, reach a compromise
aventajado, a [aβenta'xaðo, a] *adj* outstanding
aventajar [aβenta'xar] *vt* (*sobrepasar*) to
surpass, outstrip
aventar [aβen'tar] *vt* to fan, blow; (*grano*)
to winnow
aventura [aβen'tura] *nf* adventure; **aventu-
rado, a** *adj* risky; **aventurero, a** *adj* adventurous
avergonzar [aβerɣon'θar] *vt* to shame;
(*desconcertar*) to embarrass; **~se** *vr* to be
ashamed; to be embarrassed
avería [aβe'ria] *nf* (*TEC*) breakdown, fault
averiado, a [aβe'rjaðo, a] *adj* broken
down; **"~"** "out of order"
averiguación [aβeriɣwa'θjon] *nf* investigation; (*descubrimiento*) ascertainment
averiguar [aβeri'ɣwar] *vt* to investigate;
(*descubrir*) to find out, ascertain
aversión [aβer'sjon] *nf* aversion, dislike
avestruz [aβes'truθ] *nm* ostrich
aviación [aβja'θjon] *nf* aviation; (*fuerzas
aéreas*) air force
aviador, a [aβja'ðor, a] *nm/f* aviator,
airman/woman
avicultura [aβikul'tura] *nf* poultry farming
avidez [aβi'ðeθ] *nf* avidity, eagerness; **ávido, a** *adj* avid, eager
avinagrado, a [aβina'ɣraðo, a] *adj* sour,
acid
avío [a'βio] *nm* preparation; **~s** *nmpl*
(*equipamiento*) gear *sg*, kit *sg*
avión [a'βjon] *nm* aeroplane; (*ave*) martin;
~ de reacción jet (plane)
avioneta [aβjo'neta] *nf* light aircraft
avisar [aβi'sar] *vt* (*advertir*) to warn, notify;
(*informar*) to tell; (*aconsejar*) to advise,
counsel; **aviso** *nm* warning; (*noticia*) notice
avispa [a'βispa] *nf* wasp
avispado, a [aβis'paðo, a] *adj* sharp, clever
avispero [aβis'pero] *nm* wasp's nest
avispón [aβis'pon] *nm* hornet
avistar [aβis'tar] *vt* to sight, spot
avituallar [aβitwa'ʎar] *vt* to supply with
food
avivar [aβi'βar] *vt* to strengthen, intensify;
~se *vr* to revive, acquire new life
axila [ak'sila] *nf* armpit
axioma [ak'sjoma] *nm* axiom
ay [ai] *excl* (*dolor*) ow!, ouch!; (*aflicción*)
oh!, oh dear!; **¡~ de mí!** poor me!
aya ['aja] *nf* governess; (*niñera*) nanny
ayer [a'jer] *adv, nm* yesterday; **antes de ~**
the day before yesterday
ayote [a'jote] *nm* (*AM*) pumpkin
ayuda [a'juða] *nf* help, assistance ♦ *nm*
page; **ayudante, a** *nm/f* assistant, helper;
(*ESCOL*) assistant; (*MIL*) adjutant
ayudar [aju'ðar] *vt* to help, assist
ayunar [aju'nar] *vi* to fast; **ayunas** *nfpl*: **es-**

tar en ayunas (no haber comido) to be fasting; (ignorar) to be in the dark; **ayuno** nm fast; fasting

ayuntamiento [ajunta'mjento] nm (consejo) town (o city) council; (edificio) town (o city) hall

azabache [aθa'βatʃe] nm jet

azada [a'θaða] nf hoe

azafata [aθa'fata] nf air stewardess

azafrán [aθa'fran] nm saffron

azahar [aθa'ar] nm orange/lemon blossom

azar [a'θar] nm (casualidad) chance, fate; (desgracia) misfortune, accident; **por ~** by chance; **al ~** at random

azoramiento [aθora'mjento] nm alarm; (confusión) confusion

azorar [aθo'rar] vt to alarm; **~se** vr to get alarmed

Azores [a'θores] nfpl: **las ~** the Azores

azotar [aθo'tar] vt to whip, beat; (pegar) to spank; **azote** nm (látigo) whip; (latigazo) lash, stroke; (en las nalgas) spank; (calamidad) calamity

azotea [aθo'tea] nf (flat) roof

azteca [aθ'teka] adj, nm/f Aztec

azúcar [a'θukar] nm sugar; **azucarado, a** adj sugary, sweet

azucarero, a [aθuka'rero, a] adj sugar cpd ♦ nm sugar bowl

azucena [aθu'θena] nf white lily

azufre [a'θufre] nm sulphur

azul [a'θul] adj, nm blue; **~ marino** navy blue

azulejo [aθu'lexo] nm tile

azuzar [aθu'θar] vt to incite, egg on

B b

B.A. abr (= Buenos Aires) B.A.

baba ['baβa] nf spittle, saliva; **babear** vi to drool, slaver

babero [ba'βero] nm bib

babor [ba'βor] nm port (side)

baboso, a [ba'βoso, a] (AM: fam) adj silly

baca ['baka] nf (AUTO) luggage o roof rack

bacalao [baka'lao] nm cod(fish)

bacteria [bak'terja] nf bacterium, germ

báculo ['bakulo] nm stick, staff

bache ['batʃe] nm pothole, rut; (fig) bad patch

bagaje [ba'ɣaxe] nm baggage, luggage

Bahama [ba'ama]: **las (Islas) ~** nfpl the Bahamas

bahía [ba'ia] nf bay

bailar [bai'lar] vt, vi to dance; **~ín, ina** nm/f (ballet) dancer; **baile** nm dance; (formal) ball

baja ['baxa] nf drop, fall; (MIL) casualty; **dar de ~** (soldado) to discharge; (empleado) to dismiss

bajada [ba'xaða] nf descent; (camino) slope; (de aguas) ebb

bajar [ba'xar] vi to go down, come down; (temperatura, precios) to drop, fall ♦ vt (cabeza) to bow; (escalera) to go down, come down; (precio, voz) to lower; (llevar abajo) to take down; **~se** vr (de coche) to get out; (de autobús, tren) to get off; **~ de** (coche) to get out of; (autobús, tren) to get off

bajeza [ba'xeθa] nf baseness no pl; (una ~) vile deed

bajío [ba'xio] nm shoal, sandbank; (AM) lowlands pl

bajo, a ['baxo, a] adj (mueble, número, precio) low; (piso) ground; (de estatura) small, short; (color) pale; (sonido) faint, soft, low; (voz: en tono) deep; (metal) base; (humilde) low, humble ♦ adv (hablar) softly, quietly; (volar) low ♦ prep under, below, underneath ♦ nm (MUS) bass; **~ la lluvia** in the rain

bajón [ba'xon] nm fall, drop

bala ['bala] nf bullet

balance [ba'lanθe] nm (COM) balance; (: libro) balance sheet; (: cuenta general) stocktaking

balancear [balanθe'ar] vt to balance ♦ vi to swing (to and fro); (vacilar) to hesitate; **~se** vr to swing (to and fro); to hesitate; **balanceo** nm swinging

balanza [ba'lanθa] nf scales pl, balance; (ASTROLOGÍA): **B~** Libra; **~ comercial** balance of trade; **~ de pagos** balance of payments

balar [ba'lar] vi to bleat

balaustrada [balaus'traða] nf balustrade; (pasamanos) banisters pl

balazo [ba'laθo] nm (golpe) shot; (herida) bullet wound

balbucear [balβuθe'ar] vi, vt to stammer, stutter; **balbuceo** nm stammering, stuttering

balbucir [balβu'θir] vi, vt to stammer, stutter

balcón [bal'kon] nm balcony

balde ['balde] nm bucket, pail; **de ~** (for) free, for nothing; **en ~** in vain

baldío, a [bal'dio, a] adj uncultivated; (terreno) waste ♦ nm waste land

baldosa [bal'dosa] nf (azulejo) floor tile; (grande) flagstone; **baldosin** nm (small) tile

Baleares [bale'ares] nfpl: **las (Islas) ~** the Balearic Islands

balido [ba'liðo] nm bleat, bleating

balín [ba'lin] nm pellet; **balines** nmpl buckshot *sg*

baliza [ba'liθa] *nf* (*AVIAT*) beacon; (*NAUT*) buoy

balneario, a [balne'arjo, a] *adj*: **estación balnearia** (bathing) resort ♦ *nm* spa, health resort

balón [ba'lon] *nm* ball

baloncesto [balon'θesto] *nm* basketball

balonmano [balom'mano] *nm* handball

balonvolea [balombo'lea] *nm* volleyball

balsa ['balsa] *nf* raft; (*BOT*) balsa wood

bálsamo ['balsamo] *nm* balsam, balm

baluarte [ba'lwarte] *nm* bastion, bulwark

ballena [ba'ʎena] *nf* whale

ballesta [ba'ʎesta] *nf* crossbow; (*AUTO*) spring

ballet [ba'le] (*pl* **~s**) *nm* ballet

bambolear [bambole'ar] *vi* to swing, sway; (*silla*) to wobble; **~se** *vr* to swing, sway; to wobble; **bamboleo** *nm* swinging, swaying; wobbling

bambú [bam'bu] *nm* bamboo

banana [ba'nana] (*AM*) *nf* banana; **banano** (*AM*) *nm* banana tree

banca ['banka] *nf* (*asiento*) bench; (*COM*) banking

bancario, a [ban'karjo, a] *adj* banking *cpd*, bank *cpd*

bancarrota [banka'rrota] *nf* bankruptcy; **hacer ~** to go bankrupt

banco ['banko] *nm* bench; (*ESCOL*) desk; (*COM*) bank; (*GEO*) stratum; **~ de crédito/ de ahorros** credit/savings bank; **~ de arena** sandbank; **~ de datos** databank; **~ de hielo** iceberg

banda ['banda] *nf* band; (*pandilla*) gang; (*NAUT*) side, edge; **la B~ Oriental** Uruguay; **~ sonora** soundtrack

bandada [ban'daða] *nf* (*de pájaros*) flock; (*de peces*) shoal

bandazo [ban'daθo] *nm*: **dar ~s** to sway from side to side

bandeja [ban'dexa] *nf* tray

bandera [ban'dera] *nf* (*de tela*) flag; (*estandarte*) banner

banderilla [bande'riʎa] *nf* banderilla

banderín [bande'rin] *nm* pennant, small flag

bandido [ban'diðo] *nm* bandit

bando ['bando] *nm* (*edicto*) edict, proclamation; (*facción*) faction; **los ~s** (*REL*) the banns

bandolera [bando'lera] *nf*: **llevar en ~** to wear across one's chest

bandolero [bando'lero] *nm* bandit, brigand

Bangladesh [baeŋglə'deʃ] *nm* Bangladesh

banquero [ban'kero] *nm* banker

banqueta [ban'keta] *nf* stool; (*AM: en la calle*) pavement (*BRIT*), sidewalk (*US*)

banquete [ban'kete] *nm* banquet; (*para convidados*) formal dinner

banquillo [ban'kiʎo] *nm* (*JUR*) dock, pris-

oner's bench; (*banco*) bench; (*para los pies*) footstool

bañador [baɲa'ðor] *nm* swimming costume (*BRIT*), bathing suit (*US*)

bañar [ba'ɲar] *vt* to bath, bathe; (*objeto*) to dip; (*de barniz*) to coat; **~se** *vr* (*en el mar*) to bathe, swim; (*en la bañera*) to have a bath

bañera [ba'ɲera] *nf* bath(tub)

bañero, a [ba'ɲero, a] *nm/f* lifeguard

bañista [ba'ɲista] *nm/f* bather

baño ['baɲo] *nm* (*en bañera*) bath; (*en río*) dip, swim; (*cuarto*) bathroom; (*bañera*) bath(tub); (*capa*) coating

baqueta [ba'keta] *nf* (*MUS*) drumstick

bar [bar] *nm* bar

barahúnda [bara'unda] *nf* uproar, hubbub

baraja [ba'raxa] *nf* pack (of cards); **barajar** *vt* (*naipes*) to shuffle; (*fig*) to jumble up

baranda [ba'randa] *nf* = **barandilla**

barandilla [baran'diʎa] *nf* rail, railing

baratija [bara'tixa] *nf* trinket

baratillo [bara'tiʎo] *nm* (*tienda*) junkshop; (*subasta*) bargain sale; (*conjunto de cosas*) secondhand goods *pl*

barato, a ['ba'rato, a] *adj* cheap ♦ *adv* cheap, cheaply

baraúnda [bara'unda] *nf* = **barahúnda**

barba ['barβa] *nf* (*mentón*) chin; (*pelo*) beard

barbacoa [barβa'koa] *nf* (*parrilla*) barbecue; (*carne*) barbecued meat

barbaridad [barβari'ðað] *nf* barbarity; (*acto*) barbarism; (*atrocidad*) outrage; **una ~** (*fam*) loads; **¡qué ~!** (*fam*) how awful!

barbarie [bar'βarje] *nf* barbarism, savagery; (*crueldad*) barbarity

barbarismo [barβa'rismo] *nm* = **barbarie**

bárbaro, a ['barβaro, a] *adj* barbarous, cruel; (*grosero*) rough, uncouth ♦ *nm/f* barbarian ♦ *adv*: **lo pasamos ~** (*fam*) we had a great time; **¡qué ~!** (*fam*) how marvellous!; **un éxito ~** (*fam*) a terrific success; **es un tipo ~** (*fam*) he's a great bloke

barbecho [bar'βetʃo] *nm* fallow land

barbero [bar'βero] *nm* barber, hairdresser

barbilampiño [barβilam'piɲo] *adj* cleanshaven, smooth-faced; (*fig*) inexperienced

barbilla [bar'βiʎa] *nf* chin, tip of the chin

barbo ['barβo] *nm*: **~ de mar** red mullet

barbotear [barβote'ar] *vt, vi* to mutter, mumble

barbudo, a [bar'βuðo, a] *adj* bearded

barca ['barka] *nf* (small) boat; **~ pesquera** fishing boat; **~ de pasaje** ferry; **~za** *nf* barge; **~za de desembarco** landing craft

Barcelona [barθe'lona] *n* Barcelona

barcelonés, esa [barθelo'nes, esa] *adj* of o from Barcelona

barco ['barko] *nm* boat; (*buque*) ship; **~ de carga** cargo boat; **~ de vela** sailing ship

baremo [ba'remo] *nm* (*MAT, fig*) scale

barítono [ba'ritono] *nm* baritone
barman ['barman] *nm* barman
Barna. *abr* = Barcelona
barniz [bar'niθ] *nm* varnish; (*en la loza*) glaze; (*fig*) veneer; ~**ar** *vt* to varnish; (*loza*) to glaze
barómetro [ba'rometro] *nm* barometer
barquero [bar'kero] *nm* boatman
barquillo [bar'kiʎo] *nm* cone, cornet
barra ['barra] *nf* bar, rod; (*de un bar, café*) bar; (*de pan*) French stick; (*palanca*) lever; ~ **de carmín** *o* **de labios** lipstick; ~ **libra** free bar
barraca [ba'rraka] *nf* hut, cabin
barranco [ba'rranko] *nm* ravine; (*fig*) difficulty
barrena [ba'rrena] *nf* drill; **barrenar** *vt* to drill (through), bore; **barreno** *nm* large drill
barrer [ba'rrer] *vt* to sweep; (*quitar*) to sweep away
barrera [ba'rrera] *nf* barrier
barriada [ba'rrjaða] *nf* quarter, district
barricada [barri'kaða] *nf* barricade
barrida [ba'rriða] *nf* sweep, sweeping
barrido [ba'rriðo] *nm* = **barrida**
barriga [ba'rriɣa] *nf* belly; (*panza*) paunch; **barrigón, ona** *adj* potbellied; **barrigudo, a** *adj* potbellied
barril [ba'rril] *nm* barrel, cask
barrio ['barrjo] *nm* (*vecindad*) area, neighborhood (*US*); (*en las afueras*) suburb; ~ **chino** red-light district
barro ['barro] *nm* (*lodo*) mud; (*objetos*) earthenware; (*MED*) pimple
barroco, a [ba'rroko, a] *adj, nm* baroque
barrote [ba'rrote] *nm* (*de ventana*) bar
barruntar [barrun'tar] *vt* (*conjeturar*) to guess; (*presentir*) to suspect; **barrunto** *nm* guess; suspicion
bartola [bar'tola]: **a la** ~ *adv*: **tirarse a la** ~ to take it easy, be lazy
bártulos ['bartulos] *nmpl* things, belongings
barullo [ba'ruʎo] *nm* row, uproar
basar [ba'sar] *vt* to base; ~**se** *vr*: ~**se en** to be based on
basca ['baska] *nf* nausea
báscula ['baskula] *nf* (platform) scales
base ['base] *nf* base; **a** ~ **de** on the basis of; (*mediante*) by means of; ~ **de datos** (*INFORM*) database
básico, a ['basiko, a] *adj* basic
basílica [ba'silika] *nf* basilica

────────── **PALABRA CLAVE**

bastante [bas'tante] *adj* **1** (*suficiente*) enough; ~ **dinero** enough *o* sufficient money; ~**s libros** enough books
2 (*valor intensivo*): ~ **gente** quite a lot of people; **tener** ~ **calor** to be rather hot
♦ *adv*: ~ **bueno/malo** quite good/rather

bad; ~ **rico** pretty rich; **(lo)** ~ **inteligente (como) para hacer algo** clever enough *o* sufficiently clever to do sth
└──────────────────

bastar [bas'tar] *vi* to be enough *o* sufficient; ~**se** *vr* to be self-sufficient; ~ **para** to be enough to; ¡**basta!** (that's) enough!
bastardilla [bastar'ðiʎa] *nf* italics
bastardo, a [bas'tarðo, a] *adj, nm/f* bastard
bastidor [basti'ðor] *nm* frame; (*de coche*) chassis; (*TEATRO*) wing; **entre** ~**es** (*fig*) behind the scenes
basto, a ['basto, a] *adj* coarse, rough; ~**s** *nmpl* (*NAIPES*) ≈ clubs
bastón [bas'ton] *nm* stick, staff; (*para pasear*) walking stick
bastoncillo [baston'θiʎo] *nm* cotton bud
bastos ['bastos] *nmpl* (*NAIPES*) clubs
basura [ba'sura] *nf* rubbish (*BRIT*), garbage (*US*)
basurero [basu'rero] *nm* (*hombre*) dustman (*BRIT*), garbage man (*US*); (*lugar*) dump; (*cubo*) (rubbish) bin (*BRIT*), trash can (*US*)
bata ['bata] *nf* (*gen*) dressing gown; (*cubretodo*) smock, overall; (*MED, TEC etc*) lab(oratory) coat
batalla [ba'taʎa] *nf* battle; **de** ~ (*fig*) for everyday use
batallar [bata'ʎar] *vi* to fight
batallón [bata'ʎon] *nm* battalion
batata [ba'tata] *nf* (*AM*) sweet potato
batería [bate'ria] *nf* battery; (*MUS*) drums; ~ **de cocina** kitchen utensils
batido, a [ba'tiðo, a] *adj* (*camino*) beaten, well-trodden ♦ *nm* (*CULIN*): ~ **(de leche)** milk shake
batidora [bati'ðora] *nf* beater, mixer; ~ **eléctrica** food mixer, blender
batir [ba'tir] *vt* to beat, strike; (*vencer*) to beat, defeat; (*revolver*) to beat, mix; ~**se** *vr* to fight; ~ **palmas** to clap, applaud
batuta [ba'tuta] *nf* baton; **llevar la** ~ (*fig*) to be the boss, be in charge
baúl [ba'ul] *nm* trunk; (*AUTO*) boot (*BRIT*), trunk (*US*)
bautismo [bau'tismo] *nm* baptism, christening
bautizar [bauti'θar] *vt* to baptize, christen; (*fam: diluir*) to water down; **bautizo** *nm* baptism, christening
baya ['baja] *nf* berry
bayeta [ba'jeta] *nf* floorcloth
bayo, a ['bajo, a] *adj* bay
bayoneta [bajo'neta] *nf* bayonet
baza ['baθa] *nf* trick; **meter** ~ to butt in
bazar [ba'θar] *nm* bazaar
bazofia [ba'θofja] *nf* pigswill (*BRIT*), hogwash (*US*); (*libro etc*) trash
beato, a [be'ato, a] *adj* blessed; (*piadoso*) pious
bebé [be'ße] (*pl* ~**s**) *nm* baby
bebedero [beße'ðero] *nm* (*para animales*)

drinking trough

bebedor, a [beße'ðor, a] *adj* hard-drinking

beber [be'ßer] *vt, vi* to drink

bebida [be'ßiða] *nf* drink; **bebido, a** *adj* drunk

beca ['beka] *nf* grant, scholarship

becario, a [be'karjo, a] *nm/f* scholarship holder, grant holder

bedel [be'ðel] *nm* (*ESCOL*) janitor; (*UNIV*) porter

béisbol ['beisßol] *nm* (*DEPORTE*) baseball

belén [be'len] *nm* (*de navidad*) nativity scene, crib; B~ Bethlehem

belga ['belɣa] *adj, nm/f* Belgian

Bélgica ['belxika] *nf* Belgium

bélico, a ['beliko, a] *adj* (*actitud*) warlike; **belicoso, a** *adj* (*guerrero*) warlike; (*agresivo*) aggressive, bellicose

beligerante [belive'rante] *adj* belligerent

belleza [be'ʎeθa] *nf* beauty

bello, a ['beʎo, a] *adj* beautiful, lovely; Bellas Artes Fine Art

bellota [be'ʎota] *nf* acorn

bemol [be'mol] *nm* (*MUS*) flat; **esto tiene ~es** (*fam*) this is a tough one

bencina [ben'θina] (*AM*) *nf* (*gasolina*) petrol (*BRIT*), gasoline (*US*)

bendecir [bende'θir] *vt* to bless

bendición [bendi'θjon] *nf* blessing

bendito, a [ben'dito, a] *pp de* **bendecir** ♦ *adj* holy; (*afortunado*) lucky; (*feliz*) happy; (*sencillo*) simple ♦ *nm/f* simple soul

beneficencia [benefi'θenθja] *nf* charity

beneficiar [benefi'θjar] *vt* to benefit, be of benefit to; **~se** *vr* to benefit, profit; **~io, a** *nm/f* beneficiary

beneficio [bene'fiθjo] *nm* (*bien*) benefit, advantage; (*ganancia*) profit, gain; **~so, a** *adj* beneficial

benéfico, a [be'nefiko, a] *adj* charitable

beneplácito [bene'plaθito] *nm* approval, consent

benevolencia [beneßo'lenθja] *nf* benevolence, kindness; **benévolo, a** *adj* benevolent, kind

benigno, a [be'niɣno, a] *adj* kind; (*suave*) mild; (*MED: tumor*) benign, non-malignant

berberecho [berße'retʃo] *nm* (*ZOOL, CULIN*) cockle

berenjena [beren'xena] *nf* aubergine (*BRIT*), eggplant (*US*)

Berlín [ber'lin] *n* Berlin; **berlinés, esa** *adj* of o from Berlin ♦ *nm/f* Berliner

bermudas [ber'muðas] *nfpl* Bermuda shorts

berrear [berre'ar] *vt* to bellow, low

berrido [be'rriðo] *nm* bellow(ing)

berrinche [be'rrintʃe] (*fam*) *nm* temper, tantrum

berro ['berro] *nm* watercress

berza ['berθa] *nf* cabbage

besamel [besa'mel] *nf* (*CULIN*) white sauce, bechamel sauce

besar [be'sar] *vt* to kiss; (*fig: tocar*) to graze; **~se** *vr* to kiss (one another); **beso** *nm* kiss

bestia ['bestja] *nf* beast, animal; (*fig*) idiot; ~ **de carga** beast of burden

bestial [bes'tjal] *adj* bestial; (*fam*) terrific; **~idad** *nf* bestiality; (*fam*) stupidity

besugo [be'suɣo] *nm* sea bream; (*fam*) idiot

besuquear [besuke'ar] *vt* to cover with kisses; **~se** *vr* to kiss and cuddle

betún [be'tun] *nm* shoe polish; (*QUÍMICA*) bitumen

biberón [biße'ron] *nm* feeding bottle

Biblia ['bißlja] *nf* Bible

bibliografía [bißljoxra'fia] *nf* bibliography

biblioteca [bißljo'teka] *nf* library; (*mueble*) bookshelves; ~ **de consulta** reference library; **~rio, a** *nm/f* librarian

BIC [bik] *nf abr* (*ESP*: = *Brigada de Investigación Criminal*) ≈ CBI (*BRIT*), FBI (*US*)

bicarbonato [bikarßo'nato] *nm* bicarbonate

bici ['biθi] (*fam*) *nf* bike

bicicleta [biθi'kleta] *nf* bicycle, cycle; **ir en** ~ to cycle

bicho ['bitʃo] *nm* (*animal*) small animal; (*sabandija*) bug, insect; (*TAUR*) bull

bidé [bi'ðe] (*pl* **~s**) *nm* bidet

bidón [bi'ðon] *nm* (*de aceite*) drum; (*de gasolina*) can

──── PALABRA CLAVE

bien [bjen] *nm* **1** (*bienestar*) good; **te lo digo por tu** ~ I'm telling you for your own good; **el** ~ **y el mal** good and evil
2 (*posesión*): **~es** goods; **~es de consumo** consumer goods; **~es inmuebles** *o* **raíces/~es muebles** real estate *sg*/personal property *sg*
♦ *adv* **1** (*de manera satisfactoria, correcta etc*) well; **trabaja/come** ~ she works/eats well; **contestó** ~ he answered correctly; **me siento** ~ I feel fine; **no me siento** ~ I don't feel very well; **se está** ~ **aquí** it's nice here
2 (*frases*): **hiciste** ~ **en llamarme** you were right to call me
3 (*valor intensivo*) very; **un cuarto** ~ **caliente** a nice warm room; ~ **se ve que ...** it's quite clear that ...
4: **estar** ~: **estoy muy** ~ **aquí** I feel very happy here; **está** ~ **que vengan** it's all right for them to come; **¡está** ~**! lo haré** oh all right, I'll do it
5 (*de buena gana*): **yo** ~ **que iría pero ...** I'd gladly go but ...
♦ *excl*: **¡**~**!** (*aprobación*) O.K.!; **¡muy** ~**!** well done!
♦ *adj inv* (*matiz despectivo*): **niño** ~ rich kid; **gente** ~ posh people
♦ *conj* **1**: ~ ... ~: ~ **en coche** ~ **en tren**

either by car or by train

2: no ~ (esp AM): no ~ **llegue te llamaré** as soon as I arrive I'll call you

3: si ~ even though; ver tb **más**

bienal [bje'nal] adj biennial

bienaventurado, a [bjenaßentu'raðo, a] adj (feliz) happy, fortunate

bienestar [bjenes'tar] nm well-being, welfare

bienhechor, a [bjene'tʃor, a] adj beneficent ♦ nm/f benefactor/benefactress

bienvenida [bjembe'niða] nf welcome; **dar la ~ a uno** to welcome sb

bienvenido [bjembe'niðo] excl welcome!

bife ['bife] (AM) nm steak

bifurcación [bifurka'θjon] nf fork

bifurcarse [bifur'karse] vr (camino, carretera, río) to fork

bigamia [bi'xamja] nf bigamy; **bígamo, a** adj bigamous ♦ nm/f bigamist

bigote [bi'yote] nm moustache; **bigotudo, a** adj with a big moustache

bikini [bi'kini] nm bikini; (CULIN) toasted ham and cheese sandwich

bilbaíno, a [bilßa'ino, a] adj from o of Bilbao

bilingüe [bi'lingwe] adj bilingual

billar [bi'ʎar] nm billiards sg; (lugar) billiard hall; (mini-casino) amusement arcade; ~ **americano** pool

billete [bi'ʎete] nm ticket; (de banco) (bank)note (BRIT), bill (US); (carta) note; ~ **sencillo**, ~ **de ida solamente** single (BRIT) o one-way (US) ticket; ~ **de ida y vuelta** return (BRIT) o round-trip (US) ticket; ~ **de 20 libras** £20 note

billetera [biʎe'tera] nf wallet

billetero [biʎe'tero] nm = **billetera**

billón [bi'ʎon] nm billion

bimensual [bimen'swal] adj twice monthly

bimotor [bimo'tor] adj twin-engined ♦ nm twin-engined plane

bingo ['bingo] nm bingo

biodegradable [bioðexra'ðaßle] adj biodegradable

biografía [bjoxra'fia] nf biography; **biógrafo, a** nm/f biographer

biología [bjolo'xia] nf biology; **biológico, a** adj biological; **biólogo, a** nm/f biologist

biombo ['bjombo] nm (folding) screen

biopsia [bi'opsja] nf biopsy

biquini [bi'kini] nm bikini

birlar [bir'lar] (fam) vt to pinch

Birmania [bir'manja] nf Burma

birria ['birrja] nf: **ser una ~** (película, libro) to be rubbish

bis [bis] excl encore! ♦ adv: **viven en el 27 ~** they live at 27a

bisabuelo, a [bisa'ßwelo, a] nm/f great-grandfather/mother

bisagra [bi'saxra] nf hinge

bisbisar [bisßi'sar] vt to mutter, mumble

bisbisear [bisßise'ar] vt = **bisbisar**

bisiesto [bi'sjesto] adj: **año ~** leap year

bisnieto, a [bis'njeto, a] nm/f great-grandson/daughter

bisonte [bi'sonte] nm bison

bisté [bis'te] nm = **bistec**

bistec [bis'tek] nm steak

bisturí [bistu'ri] nm scalpel

bisutería [bisute'ria] nf imitation o costume jewellery

bit [bit] nm (INFORM) bit

bizco, a ['biθko, a] adj cross-eyed

bizcocho [biθ'kotʃo] nm (CULIN) sponge cake

bizquear [biθke'ar] vi to squint

blanca ['blanka] nf (MUS) minim; **estar sin ~** to be broke; ver tb **blanco**

blanco, a ['blanko, a] adj white ♦ nm/f white man/woman, white ♦ nm (color) white; (en texto) blank; (MIL, fig) target; **en ~** blank; **noche en ~** sleepless night

blancura [blan'kura] nf whiteness

blandir [blan'dir] vt to brandish

blando, a ['blando, a] adj soft; (tierno) tender, gentle; (carácter) mild; (fam) cowardly; **blandura** nf softness; tenderness; mildness

blanquear [blanke'ar] vt to whiten; (fachada) to whitewash; (paño) to bleach ♦ vi to turn white; **blanquecino, a** adj whitish

blasfemar [blasfe'mar] vi to blaspheme, curse; **blasfemia** nf blasphemy

blasón [bla'son] nm coat of arms; (fig) honour; **blasonar** vt to emblazon ♦ vi to boast, brag

bledo ['bleðo] nm: **me importa un ~** I couldn't care less

blindado, a [blin'daðo, a] adj (MIL) armour-plated; (antibala) bullet-proof; **coche** (ESP) o **carro** (AM) ~ armoured car

blindaje [blin'daxe] nm armour, armour-plating

bloc [blok] (pl ~s) nm writing pad

bloque ['bloke] nm block; (POL) bloc; ~ **de cilindros** cylinder block

bloquear [bloke'ar] vt to blockade; **bloqueo** nm blockade; (COM) freezing, blocking

blusa ['blusa] nf blouse

boato [bo'ato] nm show, ostentation

bobada [bo'ßaða] nf foolish action; foolish statement; **decir ~s** to talk nonsense

bobería [boße'ria] nf = **bobada**

bobina [bo'ßina] nf (TEC) bobbin; (FOTO) spool; (ELEC) coil

bobo, a ['boßo, a] adj (tonto) daft, silly; (cándido) naïve ♦ nm/f fool, idiot ♦ nm (TEATRO) clown, funny man

boca ['boka] nf mouth; (de crustáceo) pincer; (de cañón) muzzle; (entrada) mouth, entrance; ~**s** nfpl (de río) mouth sg; ~ **abajo/arriba** face down/up; **se me hace**

agua la ~ my mouth is watering
bocacalle [boka'kaʎe] nf (entrance to a) street; **la primera ~** the first turning o street
bocadillo [boka'ðiʎo] nm sandwich
bocado [bo'kaðo] nm mouthful, bite; (de caballo) bridle; (de **Adán** Adam's apple
bocajarro [boka'xarro]: **a ~** adv (disparar, preguntar) point-blank
bocanada [boka'naða] nf (de vino) mouthful, swallow; (de aire) gust, puff
bocata [bo'kata] (fam) nm sarnie
bocazas [bo'kaθas] (fam) nm inv bigmouth
boceto [bo'θeto] nm sketch, outline
bocina [bo'θina] nf (MUS) trumpet; (AUTO) horn; (para hablar) megaphone
bochorno [bo'tʃorno] nm (vergüenza) embarrassment; (calor): **hace ~** it's very muggy; **~so, a** adj muggy; embarrassing
boda ['boða] nf (tb: **~s**) wedding, marriage; (fiesta) wedding reception; **~s de plata/de oro** silver/golden wedding
bodega [bo'ðeɣa] nf (de vino) (wine) cellar; (depósito) storeroom; (de barco) hold
bodegón [boðe'ɣon] nm (ARTE) still life
bofe ['bofe] nm (tb: **~s: de res**) lights
bofetada [bofe'taða] nf slap (in the face)
bofetón [bofe'ton] nm = **bofetada**
boga ['boɣa] nf: **en ~** (fig) in vogue
bogar [bo'ɣar] vi (remar) to row; (navegar) to sail
Bogotá [boɣo'ta] n Bogotá
bohemio, a [bo'emjo, a] adj, nm/f Bohemian
boicot [boi'kot] (pl **~s**) nm boycott; **~ear** vt to boycott; **~eo** nm boycott
boina ['boina] nf beret
bola ['bola] nf ball; (canica) marble; (NAIPES) (grand) slam; (betún) shoe polish; (mentira) tale, story; **~s** (AM) nfpl bolas sg; **~ de billar** billiard ball; **~ de nieve** snowball
bolchevique [boltʃe'ßike] adj, nm/f Bolshevik
boleadoras [bolea'ðoras] (AM) nfpl bolas sg
bolera [bo'lera] nf skittle o bowling alley
boleta [bo'leta] (AM) nf (billete) ticket; (permiso) pass, permit
boletería [bolete'ria] (AM) nf ticket office
boletín [bole'tin] nm bulletin; (periódico) journal, review; **~ de noticias** news bulletin
boleto [bo'leto] nm ticket
boli ['boli] (fam) nm Biro ®, pen
boliche [bo'litʃe] nm (bola) jack; (juego) bowls sg; (lugar) bowling alley
bolígrafo [bo'liɣrafo] nm ball-point pen, Biro ®
bolívar [bo'lißar] nm monetary unit of Venezuela
Bolivia [bo'lißja] nf Bolivia; **boliviano, a**

adj, nm/f Bolivian
bolo ['bolo] nm skittle; (píldora) (large) pill; (juego de) **~s** nmpl skittles sg
bolsa ['bolsa] nf (cartera) purse; (saco) bag; (AM) pocket; (ANAT) cavity, sac; (COM) stock exchange; (MINERÍA) pocket; **de ~** pocket cpd; **~ de agua caliente** hot water bottle; **~ de aire** air pocket; **~ de papel** paper bag; **~ de plástico** plastic bag
bolsillo [bol'siʎo] nm pocket; (cartera) purse; **de ~** pocket(-size)
bolsista [bol'sista] nm/f stockbroker
bolso ['bolso] nm (bolsa) bag; (de mujer) handbag
bollo ['boʎo] nm (pan) roll; (bulto) bump, lump; (abolladura) dent
bomba ['bomba] nf (MIL) bomb; (TEC) pump ♦ (fam) adj: **noticia ~** bombshell ♦ (fam) adv: **pasarlo ~** to have a great time; **~ atómica/de humo/de retardo** atomic/smoke/time bomb; **~ de gasolina** petrol pump
bombardear [bombarðe'ar] vt to bombard; (MIL) to bomb; **bombardeo** nm bombardment; bombing
bombardero [bombar'ðero] nm bomber
bombear [bombe'ar] vt (agua) to pump (out o up); (MIL) to bomb; **~se** vr to warp
bombero [bom'bero] nm fireman
bombilla [bom'biʎa] (ESP) nf (light) bulb
bombín [bom'bin] nm bowler hat
bombo ['bombo] nm (MUS) bass drum; (TEC) drum
bombón [bom'bon] nm chocolate
bombona [bom'bona] nf (de butano, oxígeno) cylinder
bonachón, ona [bona'tʃon, ona] adj good-natured, easy-going
bonanza [bo'nanθa] nf (NAUT) fair weather; (fig) bonanza; (MINERÍA) rich pocket o vein
bondad [bon'dað] nf goodness, kindness; **tenga la ~ de** (please) be good enough to; **~oso, a** adj good, kind
bonificación [bonifika'θjon] nf bonus
bonito, a [bo'nito, a] adj pretty; (agradable) nice ♦ nm (atún) tuna (fish)
bono ['bono] nm voucher; (FINANZAS) bond
bonobús [bono'ßus] (ESP) nm bus pass
boquerón [boke'ron] nm (pez) (kind of) anchovy; (agujero) large hole
boquete [bo'kete] nm gap, hole
boquiabierto, a [bokia'ßjerto, a] adj: **quedar ~** to be amazed o flabbergasted
boquilla [bo'kiʎa] nf (para riego) nozzle; (para cigarro) cigarette holder; (MUS) mouthpiece
borbotón [borßo'ton] nm: **salir a borbotones** to gush out
borda ['borða] nf (NAUT) (ship's) rail; **tirar algo/caerse por la ~** to throw sth/fall

overboard
bordado [bor'ðaðo] *nm* embroidery
bordar [bor'ðar] *vt* to embroider
borde ['borðe] *nm* edge, border; *(de camino etc)* side; *(en la costura)* hem; **al ~ de** *(fig)* on the verge o brink of; **ser ~** *(ESP: fam)* to be a pain (in the neck); **~ar** *vt* to border
bordillo [bor'ðiʎo] *nm* kerb *(BRIT)*, curb *(US)*
bordo ['borðo] *nm* *(NAUT)* side; **a ~** on board
borinqueño, a [borin'keɲo, a] *adj, nm/f* Puerto Rican
borla ['borla] *nf* *(adorno)* tassel
borra ['borra] *nf* *(pelusa)* fluff; *(sedimento)* sediment
borrachera [borra'tʃera] *nf* *(ebriedad)* drunkenness; *(orgía)* spree, binge
borracho, a [bo'rratʃo, a] *adj* drunk ♦ *nm/f* *(que bebe mucho)* drunkard, drunk; *(temporalmente)* drunk, drunk man/woman
borrador [borra'ðor] *nm* *(escritura)* first draft, rough sketch; *(cuaderno)* scribbling pad; *(goma)* rubber, eraser
borrar [bo'rrar] *vt* to erase, rub out
borrasca [bo'rraska] *nf* storm
borrico, a [bo'rriko, a] *nm/f* donkey/she-donkey; *(fig)* stupid man/woman
borrón [bo'rron] *nm* *(mancha)* stain
borroso, a [bo'rroso, a] *adj* vague, unclear; *(escritura)* illegible
bosque ['boske] *nm* wood; *(grande)* forest
bosquejar [boske'xar] *vt* to sketch; **bosquejo** *nm* sketch
bostezar [boste'θar] *vi* to yawn; **bostezo** *nm* yawn
bota ['bota] *nf* *(calzado)* boot; *(saco)* leather wine bottle; **~s de agua**, **~ de goma** Wellingtons
botánica [bo'tanika] *nf* *(ciencia)* botany; *ver tb* **botánico**
botánico, a [bo'taniko, a] *adj* botanical ♦ *nm/f* botanist
botar [bo'tar] *vt* to throw, hurl; *(NAUT)* to launch; *(fam)* to throw out ♦ *vi* to bounce
bote ['bote] *nm* *(salto)* bounce; *(golpe)* thrust; *(vasija)* tin, can; *(embarcación)* boat; **de ~ en ~** packed, jammed full; **~ de la basura** *(AM)* dustbin *(BRIT)*, trashcan *(US)*; **~ salvavidas** lifeboat
botella [bo'teʎa] *nf* bottle; **botellín** *nm* small bottle
botica [bo'tika] *nf* chemist's (shop) *(BRIT)*, pharmacy; **~rio, a** *nm/f* chemist *(BRIT)*, pharmacist
botijo [bo'tixo] *nm* (earthenware) jug
botín [bo'tin] *nm* *(calzado)* half boot; *(polaina)* spat; *(MIL)* booty
botiquín [boti'kin] *nm* *(armario)* medicine cabinet; *(portátil)* first-aid kit
botón [bo'ton] *nm* button; *(BOT)* bud; *(de*

florete) tip; **~ de oro** buttercup
botones [bo'tones] *nm inv* bellboy *(BRIT)*, bellhop *(US)*
bóveda ['boβeða] *nf* *(ARQ)* vault
boxeador [boksea'ðor] *nm* boxer
boxear [bokse'ar] *vi* to box
boxeo [bok'seo] *nm* boxing
boya ['boja] *nf* *(NAUT)* buoy; *(flotador)* float
boyante [bo'jante] *adj* prosperous
bozal [bo'θal] *nm* *(de caballo)* halter; *(de perro)* muzzle
bracear [braθe'ar] *vi* *(agitar los brazos)* to wave one's arms
bracero [bra'θero] *nm* labourer; *(en el campo)* farmhand
braga ['braɣa] *nf* *(cuerda)* sling, rope; *(de bebé)* nappy *(BRIT)*, diaper *(US)*; **~s** *nfpl* *(de mujer)* panties, knickers *(BRIT)*
bragueta [bra'ɣeta] *nf* fly, flies *pl*
braille [breil] *nm* braille
bramar [bra'mar] *vi* to bellow, roar; **bramido** *nm* bellow, roar
brasa ['brasa] *nf* live o hot coal
brasero [bra'sero] *nm* brazier
Brasil [bra'sil] *nm*: **(el) ~** Brazil; **brasileño, a** *adj, nm/f* Brazilian
bravata [bra'βata] *nf* boast
braveza [bra'βeθa] *nf* *(valor)* bravery; *(ferocidad)* ferocity
bravío, a [bra'βio, a] *adj* wild; *(feroz)* fierce
bravo, a ['braβo, a] *adj* *(valiente)* brave; *(bueno)* fine, splendid; *(feroz)* ferocious; *(salvaje)* wild; *(mar etc)* rough, stormy ♦ *excl* bravo!; **bravura** *nf* bravery; ferocity; *(pey)* boast
braza ['braθa] *nf* fathom; **nadar a la ~** to swim (the) breast-stroke
brazada [bra'θaða] *nf* stroke
brazado [bra'θaðo] *nm* armful
brazalete [braθa'lete] *nm* *(pulsera)* bracelet; *(banda)* armband
brazo ['braθo] *nm* arm; *(ZOOL)* foreleg; *(BOT)* limb, branch; **luchar a ~ partido** to fight hand-to-hand; **ir cogidos del ~** to walk arm in arm
brea ['brea] *nf* pitch, tar
brebaje [bre'βaxe] *nm* potion
brecha ['bretʃa] *nf* *(hoyo, vacío)* gap, opening; *(MIL, fig)* breach
brega ['breɣa] *nf* *(lucha)* struggle; *(trabajo)* hard work
breve ['breβe] *adj* short, brief ♦ *nf* *(MUS)* breve; **~dad** *nf* brevity, shortness
brezo ['breθo] *nm* heather
bribón, ona [bri'βon, ona] *adj* idle, lazy ♦ *nm/f* *(vagabundo)* vagabond; *(pícaro)* rascal, rogue
bricolaje [briko'laxe] *nm* do-it-yourself, DIY
brida ['briða] *nf* bridle, rein; *(TEC)* clamp; **a toda ~** at top speed
bridge [britʃ] *nm* bridge

brigada [bri'βaða] *nf* (*unidad*) brigade; (*trabajadores*) squad, gang ♦ *nm* ≈ staff-sergeant, sergeant-major

brillante [bri'ʎante] *adj* brilliant ♦ *nm* diamond

brillar [bri'ʎar] *vi* (*tb fig*) to shine; (*joyas*) to sparkle

brillo ['briʎo] *nm* shine; (*brillantez*) brilliance; (*fig*) splendour; **sacar ~ a** to polish

brincar [brin'kar] *vi* to skip about, hop about, jump about; **está que brinca** he's hopping mad

brinco ['brinko] *nm* jump, leap

brindar [brin'dar] *vi*: **~ a** *o* **por** to drink (a toast) to ♦ *vt* to offer, present

brindis ['brindis] *nm inv* toast; (*TAUR*) (ceremony of) dedication

brío ['brio] *nm* spirit, dash; **brioso, a** *adj* spirited, dashing

brisa ['brisa] *nf* breeze

británico, a [bri'taniko, a] *adj* British ♦ *nm/f* Briton, British person

brizna ['briθna] *nf* (*de hierba, paja*) blade; (*de tabaco*) leaf

broca ['broka] *nf* (*TEC*) drill, bit

brocal [bro'kal] *nm* rim

brocha ['brotʃa] *nf* (large) paintbrush; **~ de afeitar** shaving brush

broche ['brotʃe] *nm* brooch

broma ['broma] *nf* joke; **en ~** in fun, as a joke; **~ pesada** practical joke; **bromear** *vi* to joke

bromista [bro'mista] *adj* fond of joking ♦ *nm/f* joker, wag

bronca ['bronka] *nf* row; **echar una ~ a uno** to tick sb off

bronce ['bronθe] *nm* bronze; **~ado, a** *adj* bronze; (*por el sol*) tanned ♦ *nm* (sun)tan; (*TEC*) bronzing

bronceador [bronθea'ðor] *nm* suntan lotion

broncearse [bronθe'arse] *vr* to get a suntan

bronco, a ['bronko, a] *adj* (*manera*) rude, surly; (*voz*) harsh

bronquio ['bronkjo] *nm* (*ANAT*) bronchial tube

bronquitis [bron'kitis] *nf inv* bronchitis

brotar [bro'tar] *vi* (*BOT*) to sprout; (*aguas*) to gush (forth); (*MED*) to break out

brote ['brote] *nm* (*BOT*) shoot; (*MED, fig*) outbreak

bruces ['bruθes]: **de ~** *adv*: **caer** *o* **dar de ~** to fall headlong, fall flat

bruja ['bruxa] *nf* witch; **brujería** *nf* witchcraft

brujo ['bruxo] *nm* wizard, magician

brújula ['bruxula] *nf* compass

bruma ['bruma] *nf* mist; **brumoso, a** *adj* misty

bruñir [bru'ɲir] *vt* to polish

brusco, a ['brusko, a] *adj* (*súbito*) sudden; (*áspero*) brusque

Bruselas [bru'selas] *n* Brussels

brutal [bru'tal] *adj* brutal

brutalidad [brutali'ðað] *nf* brutality

bruto, a ['bruto, a] *adj* (*idiota*) stupid; (*bestial*) brutish; (*peso*) gross; **en ~** raw, unworked

Bs.As. *abr* (= *Buenos Aires*) B.A.

bucal [bu'kal] *adj* oral; **por vía ~** orally

bucear [buθe'ar] *vi* to dive ♦ *vt* to explore; **buceo** *nm* diving; (*fig*) investigation

bucle ['bukle] *nm* curl

budismo [bu'ðismo] *nm* Buddhism

buen [bwen] *adj m ver* **bueno**

buenamente [bwena'mente] *adv* (*fácilmente*) easily; (*voluntariamente*) willingly

buenaventura [bwenaβen'tura] *nf* (*suerte*) good luck; (*adivinación*) fortune

---
PALABRA CLAVE

bueno, a ['bweno, a] (*antes de nmsg*: **buen**) *adj* **1** (*excelente etc*) good; **es un libro ~** *o* **es un buen libro** it's a good book; **hace ~, hace buen tiempo** the weather is fine, it's fine; **el ~ de Paco** good old Paco; **fue muy ~ conmigo** he was very nice *o* kind to me

2 (*apropiado*): **ser ~ para** to be good for; **creo que vamos por buen camino** I think we're on the right track

3 (*irónico*): **le di un buen rapapolvo** I gave him a good *o* real ticking off; **¡buen conductor estás hecho!** some *o* a fine driver you are!; **¡estaría ~ que ...!** a fine thing it would be if ...!

4 (*atractivo, sabroso*): **está ~ este bizcocho** this sponge is delicious; **Carmen está muy buena** Carmen is looking good

5 (*saludos*): **¡buen día!, ¡~s días!** (good) morning!; **¡buenas (tardes)!** (good) afternoon!; (*más tarde*) (good) evening!; **¡buenas noches!** good night!

6 (*otras locuciones*): **estar de buenas** to be in a good mood; **por las buenas** *o* **por las malas** by hook or by crook; **de buenas a primeras** all of a sudden

♦ *excl*: **¡~!** all right!; **~, ¿y qué?** well, so what?

Buenos Aires *nm* Buenos Aires

buey [bwei] *nm* ox

búfalo ['bufalo] *nm* buffalo

bufanda [bu'fanda] *nf* scarf

bufar [bu'far] *vi* to snort

bufete [bu'fete] *nm* (*despacho de abogado*) lawyer's office

buffer ['bufer] *nm* (*INFORM*) buffer

bufón [bu'fon] *nm* clown

buhardilla [buar'ðiʎa] *nf* (*desván*) attic

búho ['buo] *nm* owl; (*fig*) hermit, recluse

buhonero [buo'nero] *nm* pedlar

buitre ['bwitre] *nm* vulture

bujía [bu'xia] *nf* (*vela*) candle; (*ELEC*) candle (power); (*AUTO*) spark plug
bula ['bula] *nf* (*papal*) bull
bulbo ['bulβo] *nm* bulb
bulevar [bule'βar] *nm* boulevard
Bulgaria [bul'γarja] *nf* Bulgaria; **búlgaro, a** *adj, nm/f* Bulgarian
bulto ['bulto] *nm* (*paquete*) package; (*fardo*) bundle; (*tamaño*) size, bulkiness, (*MED*) swelling, lump; (*silueta*) vague shape; (*estatua*) bust, statue
bulla ['buʎa] *nf* (*ruido*) uproar; (*de gente*) crowd
bullicio [bu'ʎiθjo] *nm* (*ruido*) uproar; (*movimiento*) bustle
bullir [bu'ʎir] *vi* (*hervir*) to boil; (*burbujear*) to bubble; (*mover*) to move, stir
buñuelo [bu'ɲwelo] *nm* ≈ doughnut (*BRIT*), ≈ donut (*US*); (*fruta de sartén*) fritter
BUP [bup] *nm abr* (*ESP*: = *Bachillerato Unificado Polivalente*) *secondary education and leaving certificate for 14–17 age group*
buque ['buke] *nm* ship, vessel
burbuja [bur'βuxa] *nf* bubble; **burbujear** *vi* to bubble
burdel [bur'ðel] *nm* brothel
burdo, a ['burðo, a] *adj* coarse, rough
burgués, esa [bur'γes, esa] *adj* middle-class, bourgeois; **burguesía** *nf* middle class, bourgeoisie
burla ['burla] *nf* (*mofa*) gibe; (*broma*) joke; (*engaño*) trick
burladero [burla'ðero] *nm* (bullfighter's) refuge
burlar [bur'lar] *vt* (*engañar*) to deceive; (*seducir*) to seduce ♦ *vi* to joke; **~se** *vr* to joke; **~se** to make fun of
burlesco, a [bur'lesko, a] *adj* burlesque
burlón, ona [bur'lon, ona] *adj* mocking
burocracia [buro'kraθja] *nf* civil service; (*pey*) bureaucracy
burócrata [bu'rokrata] *nm/f* civil servant; (*pey*) bureaucrat
burrada [bu'rraða] *nf*: **decir/soltar ~s** to talk nonsense; **hacer ~s** to act stupid; **una ~ a** (hell of a) lot
burro, a ['burro] *nm/f* donkey/she-donkey; (*fig*) ass, idiot
bursátil [bur'satil] *adj* stock-exchange *cpd*
bus [bus] *nm* bus
busca ['buska] *nf* search, hunt ♦ *nm* (*TEL*) bleeper; **en ~ de** in search of
buscar [bus'kar] *vt* to look for, search for, seek ♦ *vi* to look, search, seek; **se busca secretaria** secretary wanted
busque *etc vb ver* **buscar**
búsqueda ['buskeða] *nf* = **busca** *nf*
busto ['busto] *nm* (*ANAT, ARTE*) bust
butaca [bu'taka] *nf* armchair; (*de cine, teatro*) stall, seat
butano [bu'tano] *nm* butane (gas)

buzo ['buθo] *nm* diver
buzón [bu'θon] *nm* (*en puerta*) letter box; (*en la calle*) pillar box

C c

C. *abr* (= *centígrado*) C; (= *compañía*) Co.
c. *abr* (= *capítulo*) ch.
C/ *abr* (= *calle*) St
c.a. *abr* (= *corriente alterna*) AC
cabal [ka'βal] *adj* (*exacto*) exact; (*correcto*) right, proper; (*acabado*) finished, complete; **~es** *nmpl*: **estar en sus ~es** to be in one's right mind
cábalas ['kaβalas] *nfpl*: **hacer ~** to guess
cabalgar [kaβal'γero] *vt, vi* to ride
cabalgata [kaβal'γata] *nf* procession
caballa [ka'βaʎa] *nf* mackerel
caballeresco, a [kaβaʎe'resko, a] *adj* noble, chivalrous
caballería [kaβaʎe'ria] *nf* mount; (*MIL*) cavalry
caballeriza [kaβaʎe'riθa] *nf* stable; **caballerizo** *nm* groom, stableman
caballero [kaβa'ʎero] *nm* (*hombre galante*) gentleman; (*de la orden de caballería*) knight; (*trato directo*) sir
caballerosidad [kaβaʎerosi'ðað] *nf* chivalry
caballete [kaβa'ʎete] *nm* (*ARTE*) easel; (*TEC*) trestle
caballito [kaβa'ʎito] *nm* (*caballo pequeño*) small horse, pony; **~s** *nmpl* (*en verbena*) roundabout, merry-go-round
caballo [ka'βaʎo] *nm* horse; (*AJEDREZ*) knight; (*NAIPES*) queen; **ir en ~** to ride; **~ de vapor** o **de fuerza** horsepower; **~ carreras** racehorse
cabaña [ka'βaɲa] *nf* (*casita*) hut, cabin
cabaré [kaβa're] (*pl* **~s**) *nm* cabaret
cabaret [kaβa're] (*pl* **~s**) *nm* cabaret
cabecear [kaβeθe'ar] *vt, vi* to nod
cabecera [kaβe'θera] *nf* (*de*) head; (*de distrito*) chief town; (*IMPRENTA*) headline
cabecilla [kaβe'θiʎa] *nm* ringleader
cabellera [kaβe'ʎera] *nf* (head of) hair; (*de cometa*) tail
cabello [ka'βeʎo] *nm* (*tb*: **~s**) hair
caber [ka'βer] *vi* (*entrar*) to fit, go; **caben 3 más** there's room for 3 more
cabestrillo [kaβes'triʎo] *nm* sling
cabestro [ka'βestro] *nm* halter
cabeza [ka'βeθa] *nf* head; (*POL*) chief,

leader; ~**da** *nf* (*golpe*) butt; **dar** ~**das** to nod off; **cabezón, ona** *adj* (*vino*) heady; (*fam: persona*) pig-headed

cabida [ka'βiða] *nf* space

cabildo [ka'βildo] *nm* (*de iglesia*) chapter; (*POL*) town council

cabina [ka'βina] *nf* cabin; (*de camión*) cab; ~ **telefónica** telephone box (*BRIT*) o booth

cabizbajo, a [kaβiθ'βaxo, a] *adj* crestfallen, dejected

cable ['kaβle] *nm* cable

cabo ['kaβo] *nm* (*de objeto*) end, extremity; (*MIL*) corporal; (*NAUT*) rope, cable; (*GEO*) cape; **al ~ de 3 días** after 3 days

cabra ['kaβra] *nf* goat

cabré *etc vb ver* **caber**

cabrear [kaβre'ar] (*fam*) *vt* to bug; ~**se** *vr* (*enfadarse*) to fly off the handle

cabrío, a [ka'βrio, a] *adj* goatish; **macho** ~ (he-)goat, billy goat

cabriola [ka'βrjola] *nf* caper

cabritilla [kaβri'tiʎa] *nf* kid, kidskin

cabrito [ka'βrito] *nm* kid

cabrón [ka'βron] *nm* cuckold; (*fam!*) bastard (*!*)

caca ['kaka] (*fam*) *nf* shit; (*usado para/por niños*) pooh

cacahuete [kaka'wete] (*ESP*) *nm* peanut

cacao [ka'kao] *nm* cocoa; (*BOT*) cacao

cacarear [kakare'ar] *vi* (*persona*) to boast; (*gallina*) to crow

cacería [kaθe'ria] *nf* hunt

cacerola [kaθe'rola] *nf* pan, saucepan

cacique [ka'θike] *nm* chief, local ruler; (*POL*) local party boss; **caciquismo** *nm* system of control by the local boss

caco ['kako] *nm* pickpocket

cacto ['kakto] *nm* cactus

cactus ['kaktus] *nm inv* cactus

cachalote [katʃa'lote] *nm* (*ZOOL*) sperm whale

cacharro [ka'tʃarro] *nm* earthenware pot; ~**s** *nmpl* pots and pans

cachear [katʃe'ar] *vt* to search, frisk

cachemir [katʃe'mir] *nm* cashmere

cacheo [ka'tʃeo] *nm* searching, frisking

cachete [ka'tʃete] *nm* (*ANAT*) cheek; (*bofetada*) slap (in the face)

cachiporra [katʃi'porra] *nf* truncheon

cachivache [katʃi'βatʃe] *nm* (*trasto*) piece of junk; ~**s** *nmpl* junk *sg*

cacho ['katʃo] *nm* (small) bit; (*AM: cuerno*) horn

cachondeo [katʃon'deo] (*fam*) *nm* farce, joke

cachondo, a [ka'tʃondo, a] *adj* (*ZOOL*) on heat; (*fam*) sexy; (*gracioso*) funny

cachorro, a [ka'tʃorro, a] *nm/f* (*perro*) pup, puppy; (*león*) cub

cada ['kaða] *adj inv* each; (*antes de número*) every; ~ **día** each day, every day; ~ **dos días** every other day; ~ **uno/a** each one,

every one; ~ **vez más/menos** more and more/less and less; **uno de** ~ **diez** one out of every ten

cadalso [ka'ðalso] *nm* scaffold

cadáver [ka'ðaβer] *nm* (dead) body, corpse

cadena [ka'ðena] *nf* chain; (*TV*) channel; **trabajo en** ~ assembly line work; ~ **perpetua** (*JUR*) life imprisonment

cadencia [ka'ðenθja] *nf* rhythm

cadera [ka'ðera] *nf* hip

cadete [ka'ðete] *nm* cadet

caducar [kaðu'kar] *vi* to expire; **caduco, a** *adj* expired; (*persona*) very old

C.A.E. *abr* (= *cóbrese al entregar*) C.O.D.

caer [ka'er] *vi* to fall (down); ~**se** *vr* to fall (down); **me cae bien/mal** I get on well with him/I can't stand him; ~ **en la cuenta** to catch on; **su cumpleaños cae en viernes** her birthday falls on a Friday

café [ka'fe] (*pl* ~**s**) *nm* (*bebida, planta*) coffee; (*lugar*) café ♦ *adj* (*color*) brown; ~ **con leche** white coffee; ~ **solo** black coffee

cafetera [kafe'tera] *nf* coffee pot

cafetería [kafete'ria] *nf* (*gen*) café

cafetero, a [kafe'tero, a] *adj* coffee *cpd*; **ser muy** ~ to be a coffee addict

cagar [ka'ɣar] (*fam!*) *vt* to shit (*!*); to bungle, mess up ♦ *vi* to have a shit (*!*)

caída [ka'iða] *nf* fall; (*declive*) slope; (*disminución*) fall, drop

caído, a [ka'iðo, a] *adj* drooping

caiga *etc vb ver* **caer**

caimán [kai'man] *nm* alligator

caja ['kaxa] *nf* box; (*para reloj*) case; (*de ascensor*) shaft; (*COM*) cashbox; (*donde se hacen los pagos*) cashdesk; (*: en supermercado*) checkout, till; ~ **de ahorros** savings bank; ~ **de cambios** gearbox; ~ **fuerte, ~ de caudales** safe, strongbox

cajero, a [ka'xero, a] *nm/f* cashier; ~ **automático** cash dispenser

cajetilla [kaxe'tiʎa] *nf* (*de cigarrillos*) packet

cajón [ka'xon] *nm* big box; (*de mueble*) drawer

cal [kal] *nf* lime

cala ['kala] *nf* (*GEO*) cove, inlet; (*de barco*) hold

calabacín [kalaβa'θin] *nm* (*BOT*) baby marrow; (*: más pequeño*) courgette (*BRIT*), zucchini (*US*)

calabaza [kala'βaθa] *nf* (*BOT*) pumpkin

calabozo [kala'βoθo] *nm* (*cárcel*) prison; (*celda*) cell

calada [ka'laða] *nf* (*de cigarrillo*) puff

calado, a [ka'laðo, a] *adj* (*prenda*) lace *cpd* ♦ *nm* (*NAUT*) draught

calamar [kala'mar] *nm* squid *no pl*

calambre [ka'lambre] *nm* (*tb*: ~**s**) cramp

calamidad [kalami'ðað] *nf* calamity, disaster

calar [ka'lar] *vt* to soak, drench; (*penetrar*) to pierce, penetrate; (*comprender*) to see through; (*vela*) to lower; ~**se** *vr* (*AUTO*) to stall; ~**se las gafas** to stick one's glasses on

calavera [kala'ßera] *nf* skull

calcañal [kalka'ɲal] *nm* = **calcañar**

calcañar [kalka'ɲar] *nm* heel

calcaño [kal'kaɲo] *nm* = **calcañar**

calcar [kal'kar] *vt* (*reproducir*) to trace; (*imitar*) to copy

calcetín [kalθe'tin] *nm* sock

calcinar [kalθi'nar] *vt* to burn, blacken

calcio ['kalθjo] *nm* calcium

calco ['kalko] *nm* tracing

calcomanía [kalkoma'nia] *nf* transfer

calculador, a [kalkula'ðor, a] *adj* (*persona*) calculating

calculadora [kalkula'ðora] *nf* calculator

calcular [kalku'lar] *vt* (*MAT*) to calculate, compute; ~ **que** ... to reckon that ...; **cálculo** *nm* calculation

caldear [kalde'ar] *vt* to warm (up), heat (up)

caldera [kal'dera] *nf* boiler

calderilla [kalde'riʎa] *nf* (*moneda*) small change

caldero [kal'dero] *nm* small boiler

caldo ['kaldo] *nm* stock; (*consomé*) consommé

calefacción [kalefak'θjon] *nf* heating; ~ **central** central heating

calendario [kalen'darjo] *nm* calendar

calentador [kalenta'ðor] *nm* heater

calentamiento [kalenta'mjento] *nm* (*DEPORTE*) warm-up

calentar [kalen'tar] *vt* to heat (up); ~**se** *vr* to heat up, warm up; (*fig: discusión etc*) to get heated

calentura [kalen'tura] *nf* (*MED*) fever, (high) temperature

calibrar [kali'ßrar] *vt* to gauge, measure; **calibre** *nm* (*de cañón*) calibre, bore; (*diámetro*) diameter; (*fig*) calibre

calidad [kali'ðað] *nf* quality; **de** ~ quality *cpd*; **en** ~ **de** in the capacity of, as

cálido, a ['kaliðo, a] *adj* hot; (*fig*) warm

caliente *etc* [ka'ljente] *vb ver* **calentar** ♦ *adj* hot; (*fig*) fiery; (*disputa*) heated; (*fam: cachondo*) randy

calificación [kalifika'θjon] *nf* qualification; (*de alumno*) grade, mark

calificar [kalifi'kar] *vt* to qualify; (*alumno*) to grade, mark; ~ **de** to describe as

calima [ka'lima] *nf* (*cerca del mar*) mist

cáliz ['kaliθ] *nm* chalice

caliza [ka'liθa] *nf* limestone

calizo, a [ka'liθo, a] *adj* lime *cpd*

calma ['kalma] *nf* calm; (*pachorra*) slowness

calmante [kal'mante] *nm* sedative, tranquillizer

calmar [kal'mar] *vt* to calm, calm down ♦ *vi* (*tempestad*) to abate; (*mente etc*) to become calm

calmoso, a [kal'moso, a] *adj* calm, quiet

calor [ka'lor] *nm* heat; (~ *agradable*) warmth; **hace** ~ it's hot; **tener** ~ to be hot

caloría [kalo'ria] *nf* calorie

calumnia [ka'lumnja] *nf* calumny, slander; **calumnioso, a** *adj* slanderous

caluroso, a [kalu'roso, a] *adj* hot; (*sin exceso*) warm; (*fig*) enthusiastic

calva ['kalßa] *nf* bald patch; (*en bosque*) clearing

calvario [kal'ßarjo] *nm* stations *pl* of the cross

calvicie [kal'ßiθje] *nf* baldness

calvo, a ['kalßo, a] *adj* bald; (*terreno*) bare, barren; (*tejido*) threadbare

calza ['kalθa] *nf* wedge, chock

calzada [kal'θaða] *nf* roadway, highway

calzado, a [kal'θaðo, a] *adj* shod ♦ *nm* footwear

calzador [kalθa'ðor] *nm* shoehorn

calzar [kal'θar] *vt* (*zapatos etc*) to wear; (*un mueble*) to put a wedge under; ~**se los zapatos** to put on one's shoes; **¿qué (número) calza?** what size do you take?

calzón [kal'θon] *nm* (*tb: calzones nmpl*) shorts; (*AM: de hombre*) pants; (: *de mujer*) panties

calzoncillos [kalθon'θiʎos] *nmpl* underpants

callado, a [ka'ʎaðo, a] *adj* quiet

callar [ka'ʎar] *vt* (*asunto delicado*) to keep quiet about, say nothing about; (*persona, opinión*) to silence ♦ *vi* to keep quiet, be silent; ~**se** *vr* to keep quiet, be silent; **¡cállate!** be quiet!, shut up!

calle ['kaʎe] *nf* street; (*DEPORTE*) lane; ~ **arriba/abajo** up/down the street; ~ **de un solo sentido** one-way street

calleja [ka'ʎexa] *nf* alley, narrow street; **callejear** *vi* to wander (about) the streets; **callejero, a** *adj* street *cpd* ♦ *nm* street map; **callejón** *nm* alley, passage; **callejón sin salida** cul-de-sac; **callejuela** *nf* side-street, alley

callista [ka'ʎista] *nm/f* chiropodist

callo ['kaʎo] *nm* callus; (*en el pie*) corn; ~**s** *nmpl* (*CULIN*) tripe *sg*; ~**so, a** *adj* horny, rough

cama ['kama] *nf* bed; (*GEO*) stratum; ~ **individual/de matrimonio** single/double bed

camada [ka'maða] *nf* litter; (*de personas*) gang, band

camafeo [kama'feo] *nm* cameo

camaleón [kamale'on] *nm* (*ZOOL*) chameleon

cámara ['kamara] *nf* chamber; (*habitación*) room; (*sala*) hall; (*CINE*) camera; (*fotográfica*) camera; ~ **de aire** inner tube; ~ **de comercio** chamber of commerce; ~ **frigorífica** cold-storage room

camarada [kama'raða] *nm* comrade, companion

camarera [kama'rera] *nf* (*en restaurante*) waitress; (*en casa, hotel*) maid

camarero [kama'rero] *nm* waiter

camarilla [kama'riʎa] *nf* (*clan*) clique; (*POL*) lobby

camarón [kama'ron] *nm* shrimp

camarote [kama'rote] *nm* cabin

cambiable [kam'bjaßle] *adj* (*variable*) changeable, variable; (*intercambiable*) interchangeable

cambiante [kam'bjante] *adj* variable

cambiar [kam'bjar] *vt* to change; (*dinero*) to exchange ♦ *vi* to change; **~se** *vr* (*mudarse*) to move; (*de ropa*) to change; **~ de idea** to change one's mind; **~ de ropa** to change (one's clothes)

cambiazo [kam'bjaθo] *nm*: **dar el ~ a uno** to swindle sb

cambio ['kambjo] *nm* change; (*trueque*) exchange; (*COM*) rate of exchange; (*oficina*) bureau de change; (*dinero menudo*) small change; **en ~** on the other hand; (*en lugar de*) instead; **~ de divisas** foreign exchange; **~ de velocidades** gear lever; **~ de vía** points *pl*

camelar [kame'lar] *vt* (*con mujer*) to flirt with; (*persuadir*) to cajole

camello [ka'meʎo] *nm* camel; (*fam: traficante*) pusher

camerino [kame'rino] *nm* (*TEATRO*) dressing room

camilla [ka'miʎa] *nf* (*MED*) stretcher

caminante [kami'nante] *nm/f* traveller

caminar [kami'nar] *vi* (*marchar*) to walk, go; (*viajar*) to travel, journey ♦ *vt* (*recorrer*) to cover, travel

caminata [kami'nata] *nf* long walk; (*por el campo*) hike

camino [ka'mino] *nm* way, road; (*sendero*) track; **a medio ~** halfway (there); **en el ~** on the way, en route; **~ de** on the way to; **~ particular** private road

camión [ka'mjon] *nm* lorry (*BRIT*), truck (*US*); **~ cisterna** tanker; **camionero, a** *nm/f* lorry o truck driver

camioneta [kamjo'neta] *nf* van, light truck

camisa [ka'misa] *nf* shirt; (*BOT*) skin; **~ de fuerza** straitjacket; **camisería** *nf* outfitter's (shop)

camiseta [kami'seta] *nf* (*prenda*) tee-shirt; (*: ropa interior*) vest; (*de deportista*) top

camisón [kami'son] *nm* nightdress, nightgown

camorra [ka'morra] *nf*: **armar o buscar ~** to look for trouble, kick up a fuss

campamento [kampa'mento] *nm* camp

campana [kam'pana] *nf* bell; **~ de cristal** bell jar; **~da** *nf* peal; **~rio** *nm* belfry

campanilla [kampa'niʎa] *nf* small bell

campaña [kam'paɲa] *nf* (*MIL, POL*) campaign

campechano, a [kampe'tʃano, a] *adj* (*franco*) open

campeón, ona [kampe'on, ona] *nm/f* champion; **campeonato** *nm* championship

campesino, a [kampe'sino, a] *adj* country *cpd*, rural; (*gente*) peasant *cpd* ♦ *nm/f* countryman/woman; (*agricultor*) farmer

campestre [kam'pestre] *adj* country *cpd*, rural

camping ['kampin] (*pl* ~s) *nm* camping; (*lugar*) campsite; **ir de o hacer ~** to go camping

campo ['kampo] *nm* (*fuera de la ciudad*) country, countryside; (*AGR, ELEC*) field; (*de fútbol*) pitch; (*de golf*) course; (*MIL*) camp; **~ de batalla** battlefield; **~ de deportes** sports ground, playing field

camposanto [kampo'santo] *nm* cemetery

camuflaje [kamu'flaxe] *nm* camouflage

cana ['kana] *nf* white o grey hair; **tener ~s** to be going grey

Canadá [kana'ða] *nm* Canada; **canadiense** *adj, nm/f* Canadian ♦ *nf* fur-lined jacket

canal [ka'nal] *nm* canal; (*GEO*) channel, strait; (*de televisión*) channel; (*de tejado*) gutter; **~ de Panamá** Panama Canal; **~izar** *vt* to channel

canalón [kana'lon] *nm* (*conducto vertical*) drainpipe; (*del tejado*) gutter

canalla [ka'naʎa] *nf* rabble, mob ♦ *nm* swine

canapé [kana'pe] (*pl* ~s) *nm* sofa, settee; (*CULIN*) canapé

Canarias [ka'narjas] *nfpl*: (**las Islas**) **~** the Canary Islands, the Canaries

canario, a [ka'narjo, a] *adj, nm/f* (native) of the Canary Isles ♦ *nm* (*ZOOL*) canary

canasta [ka'nasta] *nf* (round) basket; **canastilla** *nf* small basket; (*de niño*) layette

canasto [ka'nasto] *nm* large basket

cancela [kan'θela] *nf* gate

cancelación [kanθela'θjon] *nf* cancellation

cancelar [kanθe'lar] *vt* to cancel; (*una deuda*) to write off

cáncer ['kanθer] *nm* (*MED*) cancer; (*ASTROLOGÍA*): **C~** Cancer

canciller [kanθi'ʎer] *nm* chancellor

canción [kan'θjon] *nf* song; **~ de cuna** lullaby; **cancionero** *nm* song book

cancha ['kantʃa] *nf* (*de baloncesto, tenis etc*) court; (*AM: de fútbol*) pitch

candado [kan'daðo] *nm* padlock

candente [kan'dente] *adj* red-hot; (*fig: tema*) burning

candidato, a [kandi'ðato, a] *nm/f* candidate

candidez [kandi'ðeθ] *nf* (*sencillez*) simplicity; (*simpleza*) naiveté; **cándido, a** *adj* simple; naive

candil [kan'dil] *nm* oil lamp; **~ejas** *nfpl* (*TEATRO*) footlights

candor [kan'dor] *nm* (*sinceridad*) frankness;

(inocencia) innocence

canela [ka'nela] *nf* cinnamon

cangrejo [kan'grexo] *nm* crab

canguro [kan'guro] *nm* kangaroo; **hacer de ~** to babysit

caníbal [ka'niβal] *adj, nm/f* cannibal

canica [ka'nika] *nf* marble

canijo, a [ka'nixo, a] *adj* frail, sickly

canino, a [ka'nino, a] *adj* canine ♦ *nm* canine (tooth)

canjear [kanxe'ar] *vt* to exchange

cano, a ['kano, a] *adj* grey-haired, white-haired

canoa [ka'noa] *nf* canoe

canon [ka'non] *nm* canon; *(pensión)* rent; *(COM)* tax

canónigo [ka'noniɣo] *nm* canon

canonizar [kanoni'θar] *vt* to canonize

canoso, a [ka'noso, a] *adj* grey-haired

cansado, a [kan'saðo, a] *adj* tired, weary; *(tedioso)* tedious, boring

cansancio [kan'sanθjo] *nm* tiredness, fatigue

cansar [kan'sar] *vt (fatigar)* to tire, tire out; *(aburrir)* to bore; *(fastidiar)* to bother; **~se** *vr* to tire, get tired; *(aburrirse)* to get bored

cantábrico, a [kan'taβriko, a] *adj* Cantabrian; **mar C~** Bay of Biscay

cantante [kan'tante] *adj* singing ♦ *nm/f* singer

cantar [kan'tar] *vt* to sing ♦ *vi* to sing; *(insecto)* to chirp; *(rechinar)* to squeak ♦ *nm (acción)* singing; *(canción)* song; *(poema)* poem

cántara ['kantara] *nf* large pitcher

cántaro ['kantaro] *nm* pitcher, jug; **llover a ~s** to rain cats and dogs

cante ['kante] *nm:* **~ jondo** flamenco singing

cantera [kan'tera] *nf* quarry

cantidad [kanti'ðað] *nf* quantity, amount

cantilena [kanti'lena] *nf* = **cantinela**

cantimplora [kantim'plora] *nf (frasco)* water bottle, canteen

cantina [kan'tina] *nf* canteen; *(de estación)* buffet

cantinela [kanti'nela] *nf* ballad, song

canto ['kanto] *nm* singing; *(canción)* song; *(borde)* edge, rim; *(de un cuchillo)* back; **~ rodado** boulder

cantor, a [kan'tor, a] *nm/f* singer

canturrear [kanturre'ar] *vi* to sing softly

canuto [ka'nuto] *nm (tubo)* small tube; *(fam: droga)* joint

caña ['kana] *nf (BOT: tallo)* stem, stalk; *(carrizo)* reed; *(vaso)* tumbler; *(de cerveza)* glass of beer; *(ANAT)* shinbone; **~ de azúcar** sugar cane; **~ de pescar** fishing rod

cañada [ka'naða] *nf (entre dos montañas)* gully, ravine; *(camino)* cattle track

cáñamo ['kanamo] *nm* hemp

cañería [kane'ria] *nf (tubo)* pipe

caño ['kano] *nm (tubo)* tube, pipe; *(de albañal)* sewer; *(MUS)* pipe; *(de fuente)* jet

cañón [ka'non] *nm (MIL)* cannon; *(de fusil)* barrel; *(GEO)* canyon, gorge

caoba [ka'oβa] *nf* mahogany

caos ['kaos] *nm* chaos

cap. *abr* (= *capítulo*) ch

capa ['kapa] *nf* cloak, cape; *(GEO)* layer, stratum; **so ~ de** under the pretext of; **~ de ozono** ozone layer

capacidad [kapaθi'ðað] *nf (medida)* capacity; *(aptitud)* capacity, ability

capacitar [kapaθi'tar] *vt:* **~ a algn para (hacer)** to enable sb to (do)

capar [ka'par] *vt* to castrate, geld

caparazón [kapara'θon] *nm* shell

capataz [kapa'taθ] *nm* foreman

capaz [ka'paθ] *adj* able, capable; *(amplio)* capacious, roomy

capcioso, a [kap'θjoso, a] *adj* wily, deceitful

capellán [kape'ʎan] *nm* chaplain; *(sacerdote)* priest

caperuza [kape'ruθa] *nf* hood

capicúa [kapi'kua] *adj inv (número, fecha)* reversible

capilla [ka'piʎa] *nf* chapel

capital [kapi'tal] *adj* capital ♦ *nm (COM)* capital ♦ *nf (ciudad)* capital; **~ social** share o authorized capital

capitalismo [kapita'lismo] *nm* capitalism; **capitalista** *adj, nm/f* capitalist

capitán [kapi'tan] *nm* captain

capitanear [kapitane'ar] *vt* to captain

capitulación [kapitula'θjon] *nf (rendición)* capitulation, surrender; *(acuerdo)* agreement, pact; **capitulaciones (matrimoniales)** *nfpl* marriage contract *sg*

capitular [kapitu'lar] *vi* to come to terms, make an agreement

capítulo [ka'pitulo] *nm* chapter

capó [ka'po] *nm (AUTO)* bonnet

capón [ka'pon] *nm (gallo)* capon

capota [ka'pota] *nf (de mujer)* bonnet; *(AUTO)* hood *(BRIT)*, top *(US)*

capote [ka'pote] *nm (abrigo: de militar)* greatcoat; (: *de torero)* cloak

Capricornio [kapri'kornjo] *nm* Capricorn

capricho [ka'pritʃo] *nm* whim, caprice; **~so, a** *adj* capricious

cápsula ['kapsula] *nf* capsule

captar [kap'tar] *vt (comprender)* to understand; *(RADIO)* to pick up; *(atención, apoyo)* to attract

captura [kap'tura] *nf* capture; *(JUR)* arrest; **capturar** *vt* to capture; to arrest

capucha [ka'putʃa] *nf* hood, cowl

capullo [ka'puʎo] *nm (BOT)* bud; *(ZOOL)* cocoon; *(fam)* idiot

caqui ['kaki] *nm* khaki

cara ['kara] *nf (ANAT, de moneda)* face; *(aspecto)* appearance; *(de disco)* side; *(fig)* boldness; ~ **a facing; de** ~ opposite, facing; **dar la** ~ to face the consequences; *¿*~ **o cruz?** heads or tails?; **¡qué** ~ **(más dura)!** what a nerve!

carabina [kara'βina] *nf* carbine, rifle; (*persona*) chaperone

Caracas [ka'rakas] *n* Caracas

caracol [kara'kol] *nm* (*ZOOL*) snail; (*concha*) (sea) shell

carácter [ka'rakter] (*pl* **caracteres**) *nm* character; **tener buen/mal** ~ to be good natured/bad tempered

característica [karakte'ristika] *nf* characteristic

característico, a [karakte'ristiko, a] *adj* characteristic

caracterizar [karakteri'θar] *vt* (*distinguir*) to characterize, typify; (*honrar*) to confer (a) distinction on

caradura [kara'ðura] *nm/f*: **es un** ~ he's got a nerve

carajillo [kara'xiʎo] *nm* coffee with a dash of brandy

carajo [ka'raxo] (*fam!*) *nm*: ¡~! shit! (*!*)

caramba [ka'ramba] *excl* good gracious!

carámbano [ka'rambano] *nm* icicle

caramelo [kara'melo] *nm* (*dulce*) sweet; (*azúcar fundida*) caramel

caravana [kara'βana] *nf* caravan; (*fig*) group; (*AUTO*) tailback

carbón [kar'βon] *nm* coal; **papel** ~ carbon paper; **carboncillo** *nm* (*ARTE*) charcoal; **carbonero, a** *nm/f* coal merchant; **carbonilla** [-'niʎa] *nf* coal dust

carbonizar [karβoni'θar] *vt* to carbonize; (*quemar*) to char

carbono [kar'βono] *nm* carbon

carburador [karβura'ðor] *nm* carburettor

carburante [karβu'rante] *nm* (*para motor*) fuel

carcajada [karka'xaða] *nf* (loud) laugh, guffaw

cárcel ['karθel] *nf* prison, jail; (*TEC*) clamp; **carcelero, a** *adj* prison *cpd* ♦ *nm/f* warder

carcoma [kar'koma] *nf* woodworm

carcomer [karko'mer] *vt* to bore into, eat into; (*fig*) to undermine; ~**se** *vr* to become worm-eaten; (*fig*) to decay

cardar [kar'ðar] *vt* (*pelo*) to backcomb

cardenal [karðe'nal] *nm* (*REL*) cardinal; (*MED*) bruise

cardíaco, a [kar'ðiako, a] *adj* cardiac, heart *cpd*

cardinal [karði'nal] *adj* cardinal

cardo ['karðo] *nm* thistle

carearse [kare'arse] *vr* to come face to face, meet

carecer [kare'θer] *vi*: ~ **de** to lack, be in need of

carencia [ka'renθja] *nf* lack; (*escasez*) shortage; (*MED*) deficiency

carente [ka'rente] *adj*: ~ **de** lacking in, devoid of

carestía [kares'tia] *nf* (*escasez*) scarcity, shortage; (*COM*) high cost

careta [ka'reta] *nf* mask

carga ['karɣa] *nf* (*peso, ELEC*) load; (*de barco*) cargo, freight; (*MIL*) charge; (*obligación, responsabilidad*) duty, obligation

cargado, a [kar'ɣaðo, a] *adj* loaded; (*ELEC*) live; (*café, té*) strong; (*cielo*) overcast

cargamento [karɣa'mento] *nm* (*acción*) loading; (*mercancías*) load, cargo

cargar [kar'ɣar] *vt* (*barco, arma*) to load; (*ELEC*) to charge; (*COM: algo en cuenta*) to charge; (*INFORM*) to load ♦ *vi* (*MIL: enemigo*) to charge; (*AUTO*) to load (up); (*inclinarse*) to lean; ~ **con** to pick up, carry away; (*peso, fig*) to shoulder, bear; ~**se** (*fam*) *vr* (*estropear*) to break; (*matar*) to bump off

cargo ['karɣo] *nm* (*puesto*) post, office; (*responsabilidad*) duty, obligation; (*fig*) weight, burden; (*JUR*) charge; **hacerse** ~ **de** to take charge of *o* responsibility for

carguero [kar'ɣero] *nm* freighter, cargo boat; (*avión*) freight plane

Caribe [ka'riβe] *nm*: **el** ~ the Caribbean; **del** ~ Caribbean

caribeño, a [kari'βeɲo, a] *adj* Caribbean

caricatura [karika'tura] *nf* caricature

caricia [ka'riθja] *nf* caress

caridad [kari'ðað] *nf* charity

caries ['karjes] *nf inv* (*MED*) tooth decay

cariño [ka'riɲo] *nm* affection, love; (*caricia*) caress; (*en carta*) love ...; **tener** ~ **a** to be fond of; ~**so, a** *adj* affectionate

carisma [ka'risma] *nm* charisma

caritativo, a [karita'tiβo, a] *adj* charitable

cariz [ka'riθ] *nm*: **tener** *o* **tomar buen/mal** ~ to look good/bad

carmesí [karme'si] *adj, nm* crimson

carmín [kar'min] *nm* lipstick

carnal [kar'nal] *adj* carnal; **primo** ~ first cousin

carnaval [karna'βal] *nm* carnival

carne ['karne] *nf* flesh; (*CULIN*) meat; ~ **de cerdo/cordero/ternera/vaca** pork/lamb/veal/beef; ~ **de gallina** (*fig*): **se me pone la** ~ **de gallina sólo verlo** I get the creeps just seeing it

carné [kar'ne] (*pl* ~**s**) *nm*: ~ **de conducir** driving licence (*BRIT*), driver's license (*US*); ~ **de identidad** identity card

carnero [kar'nero] *nm* sheep, ram; (*carne*) mutton

carnet [kar'ne] (*pl* ~**s**) *nm* = **carné**

carnicería [karniθe'ria] *nf* butcher's (shop); (*fig: matanza*) carnage, slaughter

carnicero, a [karni'θero, a] *adj* carnivorous ♦ *nm/f* (*tb fig*) butcher; (*carnívoro*) carnivore

carnívoro, a [kar'niβoro, a] *adj* carnivorous

carnoso, a [kar'noso, a] *adj* beefy, fat
caro, a ['karo, a] *adj* dear; (*COM*) dear, expensive ♦ *adv* dear, dearly
carpa ['karpa] *nf* (*pez*) carp; (*de circo*) big top; (*AM: de camping*) tent
carpeta [kar'peta] *nf* folder, file
carpintería [karpinte'ria] *nf* carpentry, joinery; **carpintero** *nm* carpenter
carraspear [karraspe'ar] *vi* to clear one's throat
carraspera [karras'pera] *nf* hoarseness
carrera [ka'rrera] *nf* (*acción*) run(ning); (*espacio recorrido*) run; (*certamen*) race; (*trayecto*) course; (*profesión*) career; (*ESCOL*) course
carreta [ka'rreta] *nf* wagon, cart
carrete [ka'rrete] *nm* reel, spool; (*TEC*) coil
carretera [karre'tera] *nf* (main) road, highway; ~ **de circunvalación** ring road; ~ **nacional** ≈ A road (*BRIT*), ≈ state highway (*US*)
carretilla [karre'tiʎa] *nf* trolley; (*AGR*) (wheel)barrow
carril [ka'rril] *nm* furrow; (*de autopista*) lane; (*FERRO*) rail
carrillo [ka'rriʎo] *nm* (*ANAT*) cheek; (*TEC*) pulley
carro ['karro] *nm* cart, wagon; (*MIL*) tank; (*AM: coche*) car
carrocería [karroθe'ria] *nf* bodywork, coachwork
carroña [ka'rroɲa] *nf* carrion *no pl*
carroza [ka'rroθa] *nf* (*carruaje*) coach
carrusel [karru'sel] *nm* merry-go-round, roundabout
carta ['karta] *nf* letter; (*CULIN*) menu; (*naipe*) card; (*mapa*) map; (*JUR*) document; ~ **de ajuste** (*TV*) test card; ~ **de crédito** credit card; ~ **certificada** registered letter; ~ **marítima** chart; ~ **verde** (*AUTO*) green card
cartabón [karta'βon] *nm* set square
cartel [kar'tel] *nm* (*anuncio*) poster, placard; (*ESCOL*) wall chart; (*COM*) cartel; ~**era** *nf* hoarding, billboard; (*en periódico etc*) entertainments guide; **"en ~era"** "showing"
cartera [kar'tera] *nf* (*de bolsillo*) wallet; (*de colegial, cobrador*) satchel; (*de señora*) handbag; (*para documentos*) briefcase; (*COM*) portfolio; **ocupa la ~ de Agricultura** she is Minister of Agriculture
carterista [karte'rista] *nm/f* pickpocket
cartero [kar'tero] *nm* postman
cartilla [kar'tiʎa] *nf* primer, first reading book; ~ **de ahorros** savings book
cartón [kar'ton] *nm* cardboard; ~ **piedra** papier-mâché
cartucho [kar'tutʃo] *nm* (*MIL*) cartridge
cartulina [kartu'lina] *nf* card
casa ['kasa] *nf* house; (*hogar*) home; (*edificio*) building; (*COM*) firm, company; **en ~** at home; ~ **consistorial** town hall; ~ **de**

huéspedes boarding house; ~ **de socorro** first aid post
casado, a [ka'saðo, a] *adj* married ♦ *nm/f* married man/woman
casamiento [kasa'mjento] *nm* marriage, wedding
casar [ka'sar] *vt* to marry; (*JUR*) to quash, annul; ~**se** *vr* to marry, get married
cascabel [kaska'βel] *nm* (small) bell
cascada [kas'kaða] *nf* waterfall
cascanueces [kaska'nweθes] *nm inv* nutcrackers *pl*
cascar [kas'kar] *vt* to crack, split, break (open); ~**se** *vr* to crack, split, break (open)
cáscara ['kaskara] *nf* (*de huevo, fruta seca*) shell; (*de fruta*) skin; (*de limón*) peel
casco ['kasko] *nm* (*de bombero, soldado*) helmet; (*NAUT: de barco*) hull; (*ZOOL: de caballo*) hoof; (*botella*) empty bottle; (*de ciudad*): **el ~ antiguo** the old part; **el ~ urbano** the town centre
cascote [kas'kote] *nm* rubble
caserío [kase'rio] *nm* hamlet; (*casa*) country house
casero, a [ka'sero, a] *adj* (*pan etc*) homemade ♦ *nm/f* (*propietario*) landlord/lady; (*COM*) house agent; **ser muy ~** to be home-loving; **"comida casera"** "home cooking"
caseta [ka'seta] *nf* hut; (*para bañista*) cubicle; (*de feria*) stall
casete [ka'sete] *nm o f* cassette
casi ['kasi] *adv* almost, nearly; ~ **nada** hardly anything; ~ **nunca** hardly ever, almost never; ~ **te caes** you almost fell
casilla [ka'siʎa] *nf* (*casita*) hut, cabin; (*TEATRO*) box office; (*AJEDREZ*) square; (*para cartas*) pigeonhole; **casillero** *nm* (*para cartas*) pigeonholes *pl*
casino [ka'sino] *nm* club; (*de juego*) casino
caso ['kaso] *nm* case; **en ~ de ...** in case of ...; **en ~ de que ...** in case ...; **el ~ es que** the fact is that; **en ese ~** in that case; **hacer ~ a** to pay attention to; **hacer o venir al ~** to be relevant
caspa ['kaspa] *nf* dandruff
cassette [ka'sete] *nm o f* = **casete**
casta ['kasta] *nf* caste; (*raza*) breed; (*linaje*) lineage
castaña [kas'taɲa] *nf* chestnut
castañetear [kastaɲete'ar] *vi* (*dientes*) to chatter
castaño, a [kas'taɲo, a] *adj* chestnut(-coloured), brown ♦ *nm* chestnut tree
castañuelas [kasta'ɲwelas] *nfpl* castanets
castellano, a [kaste'ʎano, a] *adj, nm/f* Castilian ♦ *nm* (*LING*) Castilian, Spanish
castidad [kasti'ðað] *nf* chastity, purity
castigar [kasti'var] *vt* to punish; (*DEPORTE*) to penalize; (*afligir*) to afflict; **castigo** *nm* punishment; (*DEPORTE*) penalty
Castilla [kas'tiʎa] *nf* Castile

castillo [kas'tiʎo] nm castle

castizo, a [kas'tiθo, a] adj (LING) pure; (de buena casta) purebred, pedigree

casto, a ['kasto, a] adj chaste, pure

castor [kas'tor] nm beaver

castrar [kas'trar] vt to castrate

castrense [kas'trense] adj (disciplina, vida) military

casual [ka'swal] adj chance, accidental; ~**idad** nf chance, accident; (combinación de circunstancias) coincidence; **¡qué ~idad!** what a coincidence!

cataclismo [kata'klismo] nm cataclysm

catador, a [kata'ðor, a] nm/f wine taster

catalán, ana [kata'lan, ana] adj, nm/f Catalan ♦ nm (LING) Catalan

catalizador [kataliθa'ðor] nm catalyst; (AUT) catalytic convertor

catalogar [katalo'ɣar] vt to catalogue; ~ **a algn(de)** (fig) to categorize sb(as)

catálogo [ka'taloɣo] nm catalogue

Cataluña [kata'luɲa] nf Catalonia

catar [ka'tar] vt to taste, sample

catarata [kata'rata] nf (GEO) waterfall; (MED) cataract

catarro [ka'tarro] nm catarrh; (constipado) cold

catástrofe [ka'tastrofe] nf catastrophe

catear [kate'ar] (fam) vt (examen, alumno) to fail

cátedra ['kateðra] nf (UNIV) chair, professorship

catedral [kate'ðral] nf cathedral

catedrático, a [kate'ðratiko, a] nm/f professor

categoría [kateɣo'ria] nf category; (rango) rank, standing; (calidad) quality; **de ~** (hotel) top-class

categórico, a [kate'ɣoriko, a] adj categorical

cateto, a ['kateto, a] (pey) nm/f peasant

catolicismo [katoli'θismo] nm Catholicism

católico, a [ka'toliko, a] adj, nm/f Catholic

catorce [ka'torθe] num fourteen

cauce ['kauθe] nm (de río) riverbed; (fig) channel

caución [kau'θjon] nf bail; **caucionar** vt (JUR) to bail, go bail for

caucho ['kautʃo] nm rubber; (AM: llanta) tyre

caudal [kau'ðal] nm (de río) volume, flow; (fortuna) wealth; (abundancia) abundance; ~**oso, a** adj (río) large; (persona) wealthy, rich

caudillo [kau'ðiʎo] nm leader, chief

causa ['kausa] nf cause; (razón) reason; (JUR) lawsuit, case; **a ~ de** because of

causar [kau'sa] vt to cause

cautela [kau'tela] nf caution, cautiousness; **cauteloso, a** adj cautious, wary

cautivar [kauti'ßar] vt to capture; (fig) to captivate

cautiverio [kauti'ßerjo] nm captivity

cautividad [kautißi'ðað] nf = **cautiverio**

cautivo, a [kau'tißo, a] adj, nm/f captive

cauto, a ['kauto, a] adj cautious, careful

cava ['kaßa] nm champagne-type wine

cavar [ka'ßar] vt to dig

caverna [ka'ßerna] nf cave, cavern

cavidad [kaßi'ðað] nf cavity

cavilar [kaßi'lar] vt to ponder

cayado [ka'jaðo] nm (de pastor) crook; (de obispo) crozier

cayendo etc vb ver **caer**

caza ['kaθa] nf (acción: gen) hunting; (: con fusil) shooting; (una ~) hunt, chase; (animales) game ♦ nm (AVIAT) fighter

cazador, a [kaθa'ðor, a] nm/f hunter; **cazadora** nf jacket

cazar [ka'θar] vt to hunt; (perseguir) to chase; (prender) to catch

cazo ['kaθo] nm saucepan

cazuela [ka'θwela] nf (vasija) pan; (guisado) casserole

CD abbr (= compact disc) CD

CD-ROM abbr m CD-ROM

cebada [θe'ßaða] nf barley

cebar [θe'ßar] vt (animal) to fatten (up); (anzuelo) to bait; (MIL, TEC) to prime

cebo ['θeßo] nm (para animales) feed, food; (para peces, fig) bait; (de arma) charge

cebolla [θe'ßoʎa] nf onion; **cebollín** nm spring onion

cebra ['θeßra] nf zebra

cecear [θeθe'ar] vi to lisp; **ceceo** nm lisp

ceder [θe'ðer] vt to hand over, give up, part with ♦ vi (renunciar) to give in, yield; (disminuir) to diminish, decline; (romperse) to give way

cedro ['θeðro] nm cedar

cédula ['θeðula] nf certificate, document

CE nf abr (= Comunidad Europea) EC

cegar [θe'ɣar] vt to blind; (tubería etc) to block up, stop up ♦ vi to go blind; ~**se** vr: ~**se (de)** to be blinded (by)

ceguera [θe'ɣera] nf blindness

CEI abbr (= Confederación de Estados Independientes) CIS

ceja ['θexa] nf eyebrow

cejar [θe'xar] vi (fig) to back down

celada [θe'laða] nf ambush, trap

celador, a [θela'ðor, a] nm/f (de edificio) watchman; (de museo etc) attendant

celda ['θelda] nf cell

celebración [θeleßra'θjon] nf celebration

celebrar [θele'ßrar] vt to celebrate; (alabar) to praise ♦ vi to be glad; ~**se** vr to occur, take place

célebre ['θelebre] adj famous

celebridad [θeleßri'ðað] nf fame; (persona) celebrity

celeste [θe'leste] adj sky-blue; celestial, heavenly

celestial [θeles'tjal] adj celestial, heavenly

celibato [θeli'βato] *nm* celibacy
célibe ['θeliβe] *adj, nm/f* celibate
celo[1] ['θelo] *nm* zeal; (*REL*) fervour; (*ZOOL*): **en ~** on heat; **~s** *nmpl* (*envidia*) jealousy *sg*; **tener ~s** to be jealous
celo[2] ['θelo] ® *nm* Sellotape ®
celofán [θelo'fan] *nm* cellophane
celoso, a [θe'loso, a] *adj* (*envidioso*) jealous; (*trabajador*) zealous; (*desconfiado*) suspicious
celta ['θelta] *adj* Celtic ♦ *nm/f* Celt
célula ['θelula] *nf* cell; **~ solar** solar cell
celulitis [θelu'litis] *nf* cellulite
celuloide [θelu'loiðe] *nm* celluloid
cementerio [θemen'terjo] *nm* cemetery, graveyard
cemento [θe'mento] *nm* cement; (*hormigón*) concrete; (*AM: cola*) glue
cena ['θena] *nf* evening meal, dinner
cenagal [θena'ɣal] *nm* bog, quagmire
cenar [θe'nar] *vt* to have for dinner ♦ *vi* to have dinner
cenicero [θeni'θero] *nm* ashtray
cenit [θe'nit] *nm* zenith
ceniza [θe'niθa] *nf* ash, ashes *pl*
censo ['θenso] *nm* census; **~ electoral** electoral roll
censura [θen'sura] *nf* (*POL*) censorship; (*moral*) censure, criticism
censurar [θensu'rar] *vt* (*idea*) to censure; (*cortar: película*) to censor
centella [θen'teʎa] *nf* spark
centellear [θenteʎe'ar] *vi* (*metal*) to gleam; (*estrella*) to twinkle; (*fig*) to sparkle
centenar [θente'nar] *nm* hundred
centenario, a [θente'narjo, a] *adj* centenary; hundred-year-old ♦ *nm* centenary
centeno [θen'teno] *nm* (*BOT*) rye
centésimo, a [θen'tesimo, a] *adj* hundredth
centígrado [θen'tiɣraðo] *adj* centigrade
centímetro [θen'timetro] *nm* centimetre (*BRIT*), centimeter (*US*)
céntimo ['θentimo] *nm* cent
centinela [θenti'nela] *nm* sentry, guard
centollo [θen'toʎo] *nm* spider crab
central [θen'tral] *adj* central ♦ *nf* head office; (*TEC*) plant; (*TEL*) exchange; **~ eléctrica** power station; **~ nuclear** nuclear power station
centralizar [θentrali'θar] *vt* to centralize
centrar [θen'trar] *vt* to centre
céntrico, a ['θentriko, a] *adj* central
centrifugar [θentrifu'ɣar] *vt* to spin-dry
centrista [θen'trista] *adj* centre *cpd*
centro ['θentro] *nm* centre; **~ comercial** shopping centre; **~ juvenil** youth club
centroamericano, a [θentroameri'kano, a] *adj, nm/f* Central American
ceñido, a [θe'niðo, a] *adj* (*chaqueta, pantalón*) tight(-fitting)
ceñir [θe'nir] *vt* (*rodear*) to encircle, surround; (*ajustar*) to fit (tightly); (*apretar*) to tighten
ceño [θe'no] *nm* frown, scowl; **fruncir el ~** to frown, knit one's brow
CEOE *nf abr* (*ESP*: = *Confederación Española de Organizaciones Empresariales*) ≈ CBI (*BRIT*), employers' organization
cepillar [θepi'ʎar] *vt* to brush; (*madera*) to plane (down)
cepillo [θe'piʎo] *nm* brush; (*para madera*) plane; **~ de dientes** toothbrush
cera ['θera] *nf* wax
cerámica [θe'ramika] *nf* pottery; (*arte*) ceramics
cerca ['θerka] *nf* fence ♦ *adv* near, nearby, close ♦ *nm*: **~s** foreground *sg*; **~ de** near, close to
cercanía [θerka'nia] *nf* nearness, closeness; **~s** *nfpl* (*afueras*) outskirts, suburbs
cercano, a [θer'kano, a] *adj* close, near
cercar [θer'kar] *vt* to fence in; (*rodear*) to surround
cerciorar [θerθjo'rar] *vt* (*asegurar*) to assure; **~se** *vr* (*descubrir*) to find out; (*asegurarse*) to make sure
cerco ['θerko] *nm* (*AGR*) enclosure; (*AM*) fence; (*MIL*) siege
cerdo, a ['θerðo, a] *nm/f* pig/sow
cereal [θere'al] *nm* cereal; **~es** *nmpl* cereals, grain *sg*
cerebro [θe'reβro] *nm* brain; (*fig*) brains *pl*
ceremonia [θere'monja] *nf* ceremony; **ceremonial** *adj, nm* ceremonial; **ceremonioso, a** *adj* ceremonious; (*cumplido*) formal
cereza [θe'reθa] *nf* cherry
cerilla [θe'riʎa] *nf* (*fósforo*) match
cernerse [θer'nerse] *vr* to hover
cero ['θero] *nm* nothing, zero
cerrado, a [θe'rraðo, a] *adj* closed, shut; (*con llave*) locked; (*tiempo*) cloudy, overcast; (*curva*) sharp; (*acento*) thick, broad
cerradura [θerra'ðura] *nf* (*acción*) closing; (*mecanismo*) lock
cerrajero [θerra'xero] *nm* locksmith
cerrar [θe'rrar] *vt* to close, shut; (*paso, carretera*) to close; (*grifo*) to turn off; (*cuenta, negocio*) to close ♦ *vi* to close, shut; (*la noche*) to come down; **~se** *vr* to close, shut; **~ con llave** to lock; **~ un trato** to strike a bargain
cerro ['θerro] *nm* hill
cerrojo [θe'rroxo] *nm* (*herramienta*) bolt; (*de puerta*) latch
certamen [θer'tamen] *nm* competition, contest
certero, a [θer'tero, a] *adj* (*gen*) accurate
certeza [θer'teθa] *nf* certainty
certidumbre [θerti'ðumbre] *nf* = **certeza**
certificado [θertifi'kaðo] *nm* certificate
certificar [θertifi'kar] *vt* (*asegurar, atestar*) to certify
cervatillo [θerβa'tiʎo] *nm* fawn

cervecería [θerßeθe'ria] *nf (fábrica)* brewery; *(bar)* public house, pub

cerveza [θer'ßeθa] *nf* beer

cesante [θe'sante] *adj* redundant

cesantía [θesan'tia] *nf* unemployment

cesar [θe'sar] *vi* to cease, stop ♦ *vt (funcionario)* to remove from office

cesárea [θe'sarea] *nf (MED)* Caesarean operation *o* section

cese ['θese] *nm (de trabajo)* dismissal; *(de pago)* suspension

césped ['θespeð] *nm* grass, lawn

cesta ['θesta] *nf* basket

cesto ['θesto] *nm (large)* basket, hamper

cetro ['θetro] *nm* sceptre

cfr *abr (= confróntese)* cf.

ch... *see under letter CH, after C*

Cía *abr (= compañía)* Co.

cianuro [θja'nuro] *nm* cyanide

cicatriz [θika'triθ] *nf* scar; **~arse** *vr* to heal (up), form a scar

ciclismo [θi'klismo] *nm* cycling

ciclista [θi'lista] *adj* cycle *cpd* ♦ *nm/f* cyclist

ciclo ['θiklo] *nm* cycle

ciclón [θi'klon] *nm* cyclone

ciego, a ['θjeγo, a] *adj* blind ♦ *nm/f* blind man/woman

cielo ['θjelo] *nm* sky; *(REL)* heaven; **¡~s!** good heavens!

ciempiés [θjem'pjes] *nm inv* centipede

cien [θjen] *num ver* **ciento**

ciénaga ['θjenaγa] *nf* marsh, swamp

ciencia ['θjenθja] *nf* science; **~s** *nfpl (ESCOL)* science *sg*; **~-ficción** *nf* science fiction

cieno ['θjeno] *nm* mud, mire

científico, a [θjen'tifiko, a] *adj* scientific ♦ *nm/f* scientist

ciento ['θjento] *(tb: cien)* *num* hundred; **pagar al 10 por ~** to pay at 10 per cent

cierne ['θjerne] *nm*: **en ~** in blossom

cierre *etc* ['θjerre] *vb ver* **cerrar** ♦ *nm* closing, shutting; *(con llave)* locking; **~ de cremallera** zip (fastener)

cierro *etc vb ver* **cerrar**

cierto, a ['θjerto, a] *adj* sure, certain; *(un tal)* a certain; *(correcto)* right, correct; **~ hombre** a certain man; **ciertas personas** certain *o* some people; **sí, es ~** yes, that's correct

ciervo ['θjerßo] *nm (ZOOL)* deer; (: *macho)* stag

cierzo ['θjerθo] *nm* north wind

cifra ['θifra] *nf* number, numeral; *(cantidad)* number, quantity; *(secreta)* code

cifrar [θi'frar] *vt* to code, write in code; *(resumir)* to abridge

cigala [θi'γala] *nf* Norway lobster

cigarra [θi'γarra] *nf* cicada

cigarrera [θiγa'rrera] *nf* cigar case

cigarrillo [θiγa'rriʎo] *nm* cigarette

cigarro [θi'γarro] *nm* cigarette; *(puro)* cigar

cigüeña [θi'γweɲa] *nf* stork

cilíndrico, a [θi'lindriko, a] *adj* cylindrical

cilindro [θi'lindro] *nm* cylinder

cima ['θima] *nf (de montaña)* top, peak; *(de árbol)* top; *(fig)* height

cimbrarse [θim'brarse] *vr* to sway

cimbrear [θimbre'ar] *vt* = **cimbrar**

cimentar [θimen'tar] *vt* to lay the foundations of; *(fig: fundar)* to found

cimiento [θi'mjento] *nm* foundation

cinc [θink] *nm* zinc

cincel [θin'θel] *nm* chisel; **~ar** *vt* to chisel

cinco ['θinko] *num* five

cincuenta [θin'kwenta] *num* fifty

cine ['θine] *nm* cinema

cineasta [θine'asta] *nm/f (director de cine)* film director

cinematográfico, a [θinemato'γrafiko, a] *adj* cine-, film *cpd*

cínico, a ['θiniko, a] *adj* cynical ♦ *nm/f* cynic

cinismo [θi'nismo] *nm* cynicism

cinta ['θinta] *nf* band, strip; *(de tela)* ribbon; *(película)* reel; *(de máquina de escribir)* ribbon; **~ adhesiva** sticky tape; **~ de vídeo** videotape; **~ magnetofónica** tape; **~ métrica** tape measure

cinto ['θinto] *nm* belt

cintura [θin'tura] *nf* waist

cinturón [θintu'ron] *nm* belt; **~ de seguridad** safety belt

ciprés [θi'pres] *nm* cypress (tree)

circo ['θirko] *nm* circus

circuito [θir'kwito] *nm* circuit

circulación [θirkula'θjon] *nf* circulation; *(AUTO)* traffic

circular [θirku'lar] *adj, nf* circular ♦ *vi, vt* to circulate ♦ *vi (AUTO)* to drive; **"circule por la derecha"** "keep (to the) right"

círculo ['θirkulo] *nm* circle; **~ vicioso** vicious circle

circuncidar [θirkunθi'dar] *vt* to circumcise

circundar [θirkun'dar] *vt* to surround

circunferencia [θirkunfe'renθja] *nf* circumference

circunscribir [θirkunskri'ßir] *vt* to circumscribe; **~se** *vr* to be limited

circunscripción [θirkunskrip'θjon] *nf* division; *(POL)* constituency

circunspecto, a [θirkuns'pekto, a] *adj* circumspect, cautious

circunstancia [θirkuns'tanθja] *nf* circumstance

cirio ['θirjo] *nm (wax)* candle

ciruela [θi'rwela] *nf* plum; **~ pasa** prune

cirugía [θiru'xia] *nf* surgery; **~ estética** *o* **plástica** plastic surgery

cirujano [θiru'xano] *nm* surgeon

cisne ['θisne] *nm* swan

cisterna [θis'terna] *nf* cistern, tank

cita ['θita] *nf* appointment, meeting; *(de novios)* date; *(referencia)* quotation

citación [θita'θjon] nf (JUR) summons sg
citar [θi'tar] vt (gen) to make an appointment with; (JUR) to summons; (un autor, texto) to quote; ~**se** vr: **se citaron en el cine** they arranged to meet at the cinema
cítricos ['θitrikos] nmpl citrus fruit(s)
ciudad [θju'ðað] nf town; (más grande) city; ~**anía** nf citizenship; ~**ano, a** nm/f citizen
cívico, a ['θiβiko, a] adj civic
civil [θi'βil] adj civil ♦ nm (guardia) policeman
civilización [θiβiliθa'θjon] nf civilization
civilizar [θiβili'θar] vt to civilize
civismo [θi'βismo] nm public spirit
cizaña [θi'θaɲa] nf (fig) discord
cl. abr (= centilitro) cl.
clamar [kla'mar] vt to clamour for, cry out for ♦ vi to cry out, clamour
clamor [kla'mor] nm (grito) cry, shout; (fig) clamour, protest
clandestino, a [klandes'tino, a] adj clandestine; (POL) underground
clara ['klara] nf (de huevo) egg white
claraboya [klara'βoja] nf skylight
clarear [klare'ar] vi (el día) to dawn; (el cielo) to clear up, brighten up; ~**se** vr to be transparent
clarete [kla'rete] nm rosé (wine)
claridad [klari'ðað] nf (del día) brightness; (de estilo) clarity
clarificar [klarifi'kar] vt to clarify
clarín [kla'rin] nm bugle
clarinete [klari'nete] nm clarinet
clarividencia [klariβi'ðenθja] nf clairvoyance; (fig) far-sightedness
claro, a ['klaro, a] adj clear; (luminoso) bright; (color) light; (evidente) clear, evident; (poco espeso) thin ♦ nm (en bosque) clearing ♦ adv clearly ♦ excl (tb: ~ **que sí**) of course!
clase ['klase] nf class; ~ **alta/media/obrera** upper/middle/working class; ~**s particulares** private lessons, private tuition
clásico, a ['klasiko, a] adj classical; (fig) classic
clasificación [klasifika'θjon] nf classification; (DEPORTE) league (table)
clasificar [klasifi'kar] vt to classify
claudicar [klauði'kar] vi (fig) to back down
claustro ['klaustro] nm cloister
cláusula ['klausula] nf clause
clausura [klau'sura] nf closing, closure; **clausurar** vt (congreso etc) to bring to a close
clavar [kla'βar] vt (clavo) to hammer in; (cuchillo) to stick, thrust; (tablas etc) to nail (together)
clave ['klaβe] nf key; (MUS) clef
clavel [kla'βel] nm carnation
clavícula [kla'βikula] nf collar bone
clavija [kla'βixa] nf peg, dowel, pin; (ELEC) plug

clavo ['klaβo] nm (de metal) nail; (BOT) clove
claxon ['klakson] (pl ~**s**) nm horn
clemencia [kle'menθja] nf mercy, clemency
cleptómano, a [klep'tomano, a] nm/f kleptomaniac
clerical [kleri'kal] adj clerical
clérigo ['klerixo] nm priest
clero ['klero] nm clergy
cliché [kli'tʃe] nm cliché; (FOTO) negative
cliente, a ['kljente, a] nm/f client, customer
clientela [kljen'tela] nf clientele, customers pl
clima ['klima] nm climate
climatizado, a [klimati'θaðo, a] adj air-conditioned
clímax ['klimaks] nm inv climax
clínica ['klinika] nf clinic; (particular) private hospital
clip [klip] (pl ~**s**) nm paper clip
clítoris ['klitoris] nm inv (ANAT) clitoris
cloaca [klo'aka] nf sewer
cloro ['kloro] nm chlorine
club [klub] (pl ~**s** o ~**es**) nm club; ~ **de jóvenes** youth club
cm abr (= centímetro, centímetros) cm
C.N.T. (ESP) abr = Confederación Nacional de Trabajo
coacción [koak'θjon] nf coercion, compulsion; **coaccionar** vt to compel
coagular [koaɣu'lar] vt (leche, sangre) to clot; ~**se** vr to clot; **coágulo** nm clot
coalición [koali'θjon] nf coalition
coartada [koar'taða] nf alibi
coartar [koar'tar] vt to limit, restrict
coba ['koβa] nf: **dar** ~ **a uno** to soft-soap sb
cobarde [ko'βarðe] adj cowardly ♦ nm coward; **cobardía** nf cowardice
cobaya [ko'βaja] nf guinea pig
cobertizo [koβer'tiθo] nm shelter
cobertura [koβer'tura] nf cover
cobija [ko'βixa] (AM) nf blanket
cobijar [koβi'xar] vt (cubrir) to cover; (abrigar) to shelter; **cobijo** nm shelter
cobra ['koβra] nf cobra
cobrador, a [koβra'ðor, a] nm/f (de autobús) conductor/conductress; (de impuestos, gas) collector
cobrar [ko'βrar] vt (cheque) to cash; (sueldo) to collect, draw; (objeto) to recover; (precio) to charge; (deuda) to collect ♦ vi to draw one's pay; ~**se** vr to recover, get well; **cóbrese al entregar** cash on delivery
cobre ['koβre] nm copper; ~**s** nmpl (MUS) brass instruments
cobro ['koβro] nm (de cheque) cashing; (pago) payment; **presentar al** ~ to cash
Coca-Cola ['koka'kola] ® nf Coca-Cola ®
cocaína [koka'ina] nf cocaine
cocción [kok'θjon] nf (CULIN) cooking; (: el hervir) boiling

cocear [koθe'ar] vi to kick
cocer [ko'θer] vt, vi to cook; (en agua) to boil; (en horno) to bake
cocido [ko'θiðo] nm stew
cocina [ko'θina] nf kitchen; (aparato) cooker, stove; (acto) cookery; ~ **eléctrica/de gas** electric/gas cooker; ~ **francesa** French cuisine; **cocinar** vt, vi to cook
cocinero, a [koθi'nero, a] nm/f cook
coco ['koko] nm coconut; ~**tero** nm coconut palm
cocodrilo [koko'ðrilo] nm crocodile
cóctel ['koktel] nm cocktail
coche ['kotʃe] nm (AUTO) car (BRIT), automobile (US); (de tren, de caballos) coach, carriage; (para niños) pram (BRIT), baby carriage (US); **ir en** ~ to drive; ~ **celular** Black María, prison van; ~ **de bomberos** fire engine; ~ **fúnebre** hearse; **coche-cama** (pl **coches-cama**) nm (FERRO) sleeping car, sleeper
cochera [ko'tʃera] nf garage; (de autobuses, trenes) depot
coche restaurante (pl **coches restaurante**) nm (FERRO) dining car, diner
cochino, a [ko'tʃino, a] adj filthy, dirty ♦ nm/f pig
codazo [ko'ðaθo] nm: **dar un** ~ **a uno** to nudge sb
codicia [ko'ðiθja] nf greed; (fig) lust; **codiciar** vt to covet; **codicioso, a** adj covetous
código ['koðiɣo] nm code; ~ **de barras** bar code; ~ **civil** common law; ~ **de (la) circulación** highway code; ~ **postale** postcode
codillo [ko'ðiʎo] nm (ZOOL) knee; (TEC) elbow (joint)
codo ['koðo] nm (ANAT, de tubo) elbow; (ZOOL) knee
codorniz [koðor'niθ] nf quail
coerción [koer'θjon] nf coercion
coetáneo, a [koe'taneo, a] adj, nm/f contemporary
coexistir [koe(k)sis'tir] vi to coexist
cofradía [kofra'ðia] nf brotherhood, fraternity
cofre ['kofre] nm (de joyas) case; (de dinero) chest
coger [ko'xer] (ESP) vt to take (hold of); (objeto caído) to pick up; (frutas) to pick, harvest; (resfriado, ladrón, pelota) to catch ♦ vi: ~ **por el buen camino** to take the right road; ~**se** vr (el dedo) to catch; ~**se a algo** to get hold of sth
cogollo [ko'ɣoʎo] nm (de lechuga) heart
cogote [ko'ɣote] nm back o nape of the neck
cohabitar [koaβi'tar] vi to live together, cohabit
cohecho [ko'etʃo] nm (acción) bribery; (soborno) bribe
coherente [koe'rente] adj coherent
cohesión [koe'sjon] nm cohesion

cohete [ko'ete] nm rocket
cohibido, a [koi'βiðo, a] adj (PSICO) inhibited; (tímido) shy
cohibir [koi'βir] vt to restrain, restrict
coincidencia [koinθi'ðenθja] nf coincidence
coincidir [koinθi'ðir] vi (en idea) to coincide, agree; (en lugar) to coincide
coito ['koito] nm intercourse, coitus
coja etc vb ver **coger**
cojear [koxe'ar] vi (persona) to limp, hobble; (mueble) to wobble, rock
cojera [ko'xera] nf lameness; (andar cojo) limp
cojín [ko'xin] nm cushion; **cojinete** nm small cushion, pad; (TEC) ball bearing
cojo, a etc [ko'xoxo, a] vb ver **coger** ♦ adj (que no puede andar) lame, crippled; (mueble) wobbly ♦ nm/f lame person, cripple
cojón [ko'xon] (fam) nm: **¡cojones!** shit! (!); **cojonudo, a** (fam) adj great, fantastic
col [kol] nf cabbage; ~**es de Bruselas** Brussels sprouts
cola ['kola] nf tail; (de gente) queue; (lugar) end, last place; (para pegar) glue, gum; **hacer** ~ to queue (up)
colaborador, a [kolaβora'ðor, a] nm/f collaborator
colaborar [kolaβo'rar] vi to collaborate
colada [ko'laða] nf: **hacer la** ~ to do the washing
colador [kola'ðor] nm (de té) strainer; (para verduras etc) colander
colapso [ko'lapso] nm collapse; ~ **nervioso** nervous breakdown
colar [ko'lar] vt (líquido) to strain off; (metal) to cast ♦ vi to ooze, seep (through); ~**se** vr to jump the queue; ~**se en** to get into without paying; (fiesta) to gatecrash
colateral [kolate'ral] nm collateral
colcha ['koltʃa] nf bedspread
colchón [kol'tʃon] nm mattress; ~ **inflable** o **neumático** air bed, air mattress
colchoneta [koltʃo'neta] nf (en gimnasio) mattress
colear [kole'ar] vi (perro) to wag its tail
colección [kolek'θjon] nf collection; **coleccionar** vt to collect; **coleccionista** nm/f collector
colecta [ko'lekta] nf collection
colectivo, a [kolek'tiβo, a] adj collective, joint ♦ nm (AM) (small) bus
colector [kolek'tor] nm collector; (sumidero) sewer
colega [ko'leɣa] nm/f colleague
colegial, a [kole'xjal, a] nm/f schoolboy/girl
colegio [ko'lexjo] nm college; (escuela) school; (de abogados etc) association; ~ **electoral** polling station; ~ **mayor** hall of residence
colegir [kole'xir] vt (juntar) to collect, gather; (deducir) to infer, conclude

cólera ['kolera] *nf* (*ira*) anger; (*MED*) cholera; **colérico, a** [ko'leriko, a] *adj* irascible, bad-tempered

colesterol [koleste'rol] *nm* cholesterol

coleta [ko'leta] *nf* pigtail

colgante [kol'vante] *adj* hanging ♦ *nm* (*joya*) pendant

colgar [kol'var] *vt* to hang (up); (*ropa*) to hang out ♦ *vi* to hang; (*teléfono*) to hang up

cólico ['koliko] *nm* colic

coliflor [koli'flor] *nf* cauliflower

colilla [ko'liʎa] *nf* cigarette end, butt

colina [ko'lina] *nf* hill

colindante [kolin'dante] *adj* adjacent, neighbouring

colisión [koli'sjon] *nf* collision; ~ **de frente** head-on crash

colmado, a [kol'maðo, a] *adj* full

colmar [kol'mar] *vt* to fill to the brim; (*fig*) to fulfil, realize

colmena [kol'mena] *nf* beehive

colmillo [kol'miʎo] *nm* (*diente*) eye tooth; (*de elefante*) tusk; (*de perro*) fang

colmo ['kolmo] *nm* height, summit; ¡es el ~! it's the limit!

colocación [koloka'θjon] *nf* (*acto*) placing; (*empleo*) job, position; (*situación*) place, position

colocar [kolo'kar] *vt* to place, put, position; (*dinero*) to invest; (*poner en empleo*) to find a job for; ~**se** *vr* to get a job

Colombia [ko'lombja] *nf* Colombia; **colombiano, a** [kolom'bjano, a] *adj, nm/f* Colombian

colonia [ko'lonja] *nf* colony; (*de casas*) housing estate; (*agua de* ~) cologne

colonización [koloniθa'θjon] *nf* colonization; **colonizador, a** [koloniθa'ðor, a] *adj* colonizing ♦ *nm/f* colonist, settler

colonizar [koloni'θar] *vt* to colonize

coloquio [ko'lokjo] *nm* conversation; (*congreso*) conference

color [ko'lor] *nm* colour

colorado, a [kolo'raðo, a] *adj* (*rojo*) red; (*LAM*: *chiste*) rude

colorante [kolo'rante] *nm* colouring

colorear [kolore'ar] *vt* to colour

colorete [kolo'rete] *nm* blusher

colorido [kolo'riðo] *nm* colouring

columna [ko'lumna] *nf* column; (*pilar*) pillar; (*apoyo*) support

columpiar [kolum'pjar] *vt* to swing; ~**se** *vr* to swing; **columpio** *nm* swing

collar [ko'ʎar] *nm* necklace; (*de perro*) collar

coma ['koma] *nf* comma ♦ *nm* (*MED*) coma

comadre [ko'maðre] *nf* (*madrina*) godmother; (*vecina*) neighbour; (*chismosa*) gossip; **comadrona** *nf* midwife

comandancia [koman'danθja] *nf* command

comandante [koman'dante] *nm* commandant

comarca [ko'marka] *nf* region

comba ['komba] *nf* (*curva*) curve; (*cuerda*) skipping rope; **saltar a la** ~ to skip

combar [kom'bar] *vt* to bend, curve

combate [kom'bate] *nm* fight; (*fig*) battle; **combatiente** *nm* combatant

combatir [komba'tir] *vt* to fight, combat

combinación [kombina'θjon] *nf* combination; (*QUÍMICA*) compound; (*bebida*) cocktail; (*plan*) scheme, setup; (*prenda*) slip

combinar [kombi'nar] *vt* to combine

combustible [kombus'tiβle] *nm* fuel

combustión [kombus'tjon] *nf* combustion

comedia [ko'meðja] *nf* comedy; (*TEATRO*) play, drama

comediante [kome'ðjante] *nm/f* (comic) actor/actress

comedido, a [kome'ðiðo, a] *adj* moderate

comedor, a [kome'ðor, a] *nm/f* (*persona*) glutton ♦ *nm* (*habitación*) dining room; (*restaurante*) restaurant; (*cantina*) canteen

comensal [komen'sal] *nm/f* fellow guest (*o* diner)

comentar [komen'tar] *vt* to comment on; (*fam*) to discuss

comentario [komen'tarjo] *nm* comment, remark; (*literario*) commentary; ~**s** *nmpl* (*chismes*) gossip *sg*

comentarista [komenta'rista] *nm/f* commentator

comenzar [komen'θar] *vt, vi* to begin, start, commence; ~ **a hacer algo** to begin *o* start doing sth

comer [ko'mer] *vt* to eat; (*DAMAS, AJEDREZ*) to take, capture ♦ *vi* to eat; (*almorzar*) to have lunch; ~**se** *vr* to eat up

comercial [komer'θjal] *adj* commercial; (*relativo al negocio*) business *cpd*; **comercializar** *vt* (*producto*) to market; (*pey*) to commercialize

comerciante [komer'θjante] *nm/f* trader, merchant

comerciar [komer'θjar] *vi* to trade, do business

comercio [ko'merθjo] *nm* commerce, trade; (*negocio*) business; (*fig*) dealings *pl*

comestible [komes'tiβle] *adj* eatable, edible; ~**s** *nmpl* food *sg*, foodstuffs

cometa [ko'meta] *nm* comet ♦ *nf* kite

cometer [kome'ter] *vt* to commit

cometido [kome'tiðo] *nm* (*misión*) task, assignment; (*deber*) commitment

comezón [kome'θon] *nf* itch, itching

cómic ['komik] *nm* (*historieta*) comic

comicios [ko'miθjos] *nmpl* elections

cómico, a ['komiko, a] *adj* comic(al) ♦ *nm/f* comedian; (*de teatro*) (comic) actor/actress

comida [ko'miða] *nf* (*alimento*) food; (*almuerzo, cena*) meal; (*de mediodía*) lunch

comidilla [komi'ðiʎa] *nf*: **ser la** ~ **de la ciudad** to be the talk of the town

comienzo etc [ko'mjenθo] *vb ver* **comenzar**
♦ *nm* beginning, start

comilona [komi'lona] (*fam*) *nf* blow-out

comillas [ko'miʎas] *nfpl* quotation marks

comino [ko'mino] *nm*: **(no) me importa un ~** I don't give a damn

comisaría [komisa'ria] *nf* (*de policía*) police station; (*MIL*) commissariat

comisario [komi'sarjo] *nm* (*MIL etc*) commissary; (*POL*) commissar

comisión [komi'sjon] *nf* commission

comité [komi'te] (*pl ~s*) *nm* committee

comitiva [komi'tiβa] *nf* retinue

como ['komo] *adv* as; (*tal ~*) like; (*aproximadamente*) about, approximately ♦ *conj* (*ya que, puesto que*) as, since; (*en cuanto*) as soon as; **¡~ no!** of course!; **~ no lo haga hoy** unless he does it today; **~ si** as if; **es tan alto ~ ancho** it is as high as it is wide

cómo ['komo] *adv* how?, why? ♦ *excl* what?, I beg your pardon? ♦ *nm*: **el ~ y el porqué** the whys and wherefores

cómoda ['komoða] *nf* chest of drawers

comodidad [komoði'ðað] *nf* comfort; **venga a su ~** come at your convenience

comodín [komo'ðin] *nm* joker

cómodo, a ['komoðo, a] *adj* comfortable; (*práctico, de fácil uso*) convenient

compact disc *nm* compact disk player

compacto, a [kom'pakto, a] *adj* compact

compadecer [kompaðe'θer] *vt* to pity, be sorry for; **~se** *vr*: **~se de** to pity, be *o* feel sorry for

compadre [kom'paðre] *nm* (*padrino*) godfather; (*amigo*) friend, pal

compañero, a [kompa'ɲero, a] *nm/f* companion; (*novio*) boy/girlfriend; **~ de clase** classmate

compañía [kompa'ɲia] *nf* company

comparación [kompara'θjon] *nf* comparison; **en ~ con** in comparison with

comparar [kompa'rar] *vt* to compare

comparativo, a [kompara'tiβo, a] *adj* comparative

comparecer [kompare'θer] *vi* to appear (in court)

comparsa [kom'parsa] *nm/f* (*TEATRO*) extra

compartimiento [komparti'mjento] *nm* (*FERRO*) compartment

compartir [kompar'tir] *vt* to share; (*dinero, comida etc*) to divide (up), share (out)

compás [kom'pas] *nm* (*MUS*) beat, rhythm; (*MAT*) compasses *pl*; (*NAUT etc*) compass

compasión [kompa'sjon] *nf* compassion, pity

compasivo, a [kompa'siβo, a] *adj* compassionate

compatibilidad [kompatiβili'ðað] *nf* compatibility

compatible [kompa'tiβle] *adj* compatible

compatriota [kompa'trjota] *nm/f* compatriot, fellow countryman/woman

compenetrarse [kompene'trarse] *vr* (*persona*) to see eye to eye

compendiar [kompen'djar] *vt* to summarize; (*libro*) to abridge; **compendio** *nm* summary; abridgement

compensación [kompensa'θjon] *nf* compensation

compensar [kompen'sar] *vt* to compensate

competencia [kompe'tenθja] *nf* (*incumbencia*) domain, field; (*JUR, habilidad*) competence; (*rivalidad*) competition

competente [kompe'tente] *adj* (*JUR, persona*) competent; (*conveniente*) suitable

competición [kompeti'θjon] *nf* competition

competir [kompe'tir] *vi* to compete

compilar [kompi'lar] *vt* to compile

complacencia [kompla'θenθja] *nf* (*placer*) pleasure; (*tolerancia excesiva*) complacency

complacer [kompla'θer] *vt* to please; **~se** *vr* to be pleased

complaciente [kompla'θjente] *adj* kind, obliging, helpful

complejo, a [kom'plexo, a] *adj, nm* complex

complementario, a [komplemen'tarjo, a] *adj* complementary

completar [komple'tar] *vt* to complete

completo, a [kom'pleto, a] *adj* complete; (*perfecto*) perfect; (*lleno*) full ♦ *nm* full complement

complicado, a [kompli'kaðo, a] *adj* complicated; **estar ~ en** to be mixed up in

complicar [kompli'kar] *vt* to complicate

cómplice ['kompliθe] *nm/f* accomplice

complot [kom'plo(t)] (*pl ~s*) *nm* plot; (*conspiración*) conspiracy

componer [kompo'ner] *vt* to make up, put together; (*MUS, LITERATURA, IMPRENTA*) to compose; (*algo roto*) to mend, repair; (*arreglar*) to arrange; **~se** *vr*: **~se de** to consist of; **componérselas para hacer algo** to manage to do sth

comportamiento [komporta'mjento] *nm* behaviour, conduct

comportarse [kompor'tarse] *vr* to behave

composición [komposi'θjon] *nf* composition

compositor, a [komposi'tor, a] *nm/f* composer

compostura [kompos'tura] *nf* (*composición*) composition; (*reparación*) mending, repair; (*acuerdo*) agreement; (*actitud*) composure

compra ['kompra] *nf* purchase; **~s** *nfpl* purchases, shopping *sg*; **ir de ~s** to go shopping; **comprador, a** *nm/f* buyer, purchaser

comprar [kom'prar] *vt* to buy, purchase

comprender [kompren'der] *vt* to understand; (*incluir*) to comprise, include

comprensión [kompren'sjon] *nf* understanding; *(totalidad)* comprehensiveness; **comprensivo, a** *adj* comprehensive; *(actitud)* understanding

compresa [kom'presa] *nf*: ~ **higiénica** sanitary towel *(BRIT)* o napkin *(US)*

comprimido, a [kompri'miðo, a] *adj* compressed ♦ *nm (MED)* pill, tablet

comprimir [kompri'mir] *vt* to compress; *(fig)* to control

comprobante [kompro'ßante] *nm* proof; *(COM)* voucher; ~ **de recibo** receipt

comprobar [kompro'ßar] *vt* to check; *(probar)* to prove; *(TEC)* to check, test

comprometer [komprome'ter] *vt* to compromise; *(exponer)* to endanger; ~**se** *vr* to compromise o.s.; *(involucrarse)* to get involved

compromiso [kompro'miso] *nm (obligación)* obligation; *(cometido)* commitment; *(convenio)* agreement; *(dificultad)* awkward situation

compuesto, a [kom'pwesto, a] *adj*: ~ **de** composed of, made up of ♦ *nm* compound

computador [komputa'ðor] *nm* computer; ~ **central** mainframe computer; ~ **personal** personal computer

computadora [komputa'ðora] *nf* = **computador**

cómputo ['komputo] *nm* calculation

comulgar [komul'var] *vi* to receive communion

común [ko'mun] *adj* common ♦ *nm*: **el** ~ the community

comunicación [komunika'θjon] *nf* communication; *(informe)* report

comunicado [komuni'kaðo] *nm* announcement; ~ **de prensa** press release

comunicar [komuni'kar] *vt, vi* to communicate; ~**se** *vr* to communicate; **está comunicando** *(TEL)* the line's engaged *(BRIT)* o busy *(US)*; **comunicativo, a** *adj* communicative

comunidad [komuni'ðað] *nf* community; ~ **autónoma** *(POL)* autonomous region; **C~ Económica Europea** European Economic Community

comunión [komu'njon] *nf* communion

comunismo [komu'nismo] *nm* communism; **comunista** *adj, nm/f* communist

──────── *PALABRA CLAVE*

con [kon] *prep* **1** *(medio, compañía)* with; **comer** ~ **cuchara** to eat with a spoon; **pasear** ~ **uno** to go for a walk with sb

2 *(a pesar de)*: ~ **todo, merece nuestros respetos** all the same, he deserves our respect

3 *(para* ~*)*: **es muy bueno para** ~ **los niños** he's very good with (the) children

4 *(+ infin)*: ~ **llegar tan tarde se quedó sin comer** by arriving so late he missed out on eating

♦ *conj*: ~ **que**: **será suficiente** ~ **que le escribas** it will be sufficient if you write to her

──────────────

conato [ko'nato] *nm* attempt; ~ **de robo** attempted robbery

concebir [konθe'ßir] *vt, vi* to conceive

conceder [konθe'ðer] *vt* to concede

concejal, a [konθe'xal, a] *nm/f* town councillor

concentración [konθentra'θjon] *nf* concentration

concentrar [konθen'trar] *vt* to concentrate; ~**se** *vr* to concentrate

concepción [konθep'θjon] *nf* conception

concepto [kon'θepto] *nm* concept

concernir [konθer'nir] *vi* to concern; **en lo que concierne a ...** *(cosa)* as far as ... is concerned; **en lo que a mí concierne** as far as I'm concerned

concertar [konθer'tar] *vt (MUS)* to harmonize; *(acordar: precio)* to agree; (: *tratado)* to conclude; *(trato)* to arrange, fix up; *(combinar: esfuerzos)* to coordinate; *(reconciliar: personas)* to reconcile ♦ *vi* to harmonize, be in tune

concesión [konθe'sjon] *nf* concession

concesionario [konθesjo'narjo] *nm* (licensed) dealer, agent

conciencia [kon'θjenθja] *nf* conscience; **tener/tomar** ~ **de** to be/become aware of; **tener la** ~ **limpia/tranquila** to have a clear conscience

concienciar [konθjen'θjar] *vt* to make aware; ~**se** *vr* to become aware

concienzudo, a [konθjen'θuðo, a] *adj* conscientious

concierto *etc* [kon'θjerto] *vb ver* **concertar** ♦ *nm* concert; *(obra)* concerto

conciliar [konθi'ljar] *vt* to reconcile

concilio [kon'θiljo] *nm* council

conciso, a [kon'θiso, a] *adj* concise

conciudadano, a [konθjuða'ðano, a] *nm/f* fellow citizen

concluir [konklu'ir] *vt, vi* to conclude; ~**se** *vr* to conclude

conclusión [konklu'sjon] *nf* conclusion

concluyente [konklu'jente] *adj (prueba, información)* conclusive

concordar [konkor'ðar] *vt* to reconcile ♦ *vi* to agree, tally

concordia [kon'korðja] *nf* harmony

concretar [konkre'tar] *vt* to make concrete, make more specific; ~**se** *vr* to become more definite

concreto, a [kon'kreto, a] *adj, nm (AM)* concrete; **en** ~ *(en resumen)* to sum up; *(específicamente)* specifically; **no hay nada en** ~ there's nothing definite

concurrencia [konku'rrenθja] *nf* turnout

concurrido, a [konku'rriðo, a] *adj (calle)* busy; *(local, reunión)* crowded

concurrir [konku'rrir] *vi (juntarse: ríos)* to meet, come together; *(: personas)* to gather, meet

concursante [konkur'sante] *nm/f* competitor

concurso [kon'kurso] *nm (de público)* crowd; *(ESCOL, DEPORTE, competencia)* competition; *(ayuda)* help, cooperation

concha ['kontʃa] *nf* shell

condal [kon'dal] *adj*: **la Ciudad C~** Barcelona

conde ['konde] *nm* count

condecoración [kondekora'θjon] *nf (MIL)* medal

condecorar [kondeko'rar] *vt (MIL)* to decorate

condena [kon'dena] *nf* sentence

condenación [kondena'θjon] *nf* condemnation; *(REL)* damnation

condenar [konde'nar] *vt* to condemn; *(JUR)* to convict; **~se** *vr (JUR)* to confess (one's guilt); *(REL)* to be damned

condensar [konden'sar] *vt* to condense

condesa [kon'desa] *nf* countess

condescender [kondesθen'der] *vi* to acquiesce, comply

condición [kondi'θjon] *nf* condition; **condicional** *adj* conditional

condicionar [kondiθjo'nar] *vt (acondicionar)* to condition; **~ algo a** to make sth conditional on

condimento [kondi'mento] *nm* seasoning

condolerse [kondo'lerse] *vr* to sympathize

condón [kon'don] *nm* condom

conducir [kondu'θir] *vt* to take, convey; *(AUTO)* to drive ♦ *vi* to drive; *(fig)* to lead; **~se** *vr* to behave

conducta [kon'dukta] *nf* conduct, behaviour

conducto [kon'dukto] *nm* pipe, tube; *(fig)* channel

conductor, a [konduk'tor, a] *adj* leading, guiding ♦ *nm (FÍSICA)* conductor; *(de vehículo)* driver

conduje *etc vb ver* **conducir**

conduzco *etc vb ver* **conducir**

conectado, a [konek'taðo, a] *adj (INFORM)* on-line

conectar [konek'tar] *vt* to connect (up); *(enchufar)* plug in

conejillo [kone'xiλo] *nm*: **~ de Indias** *(ZOOL)* guinea pig

conejo [ko'nexo] *nm* rabbit

conexión [konek'sjon] *nf* connection

confección [confe(k)'θjon] *nf* preparation; *(industria)* clothing industry

confeccionar [konfekθjo'nar] *vt* to make (up)

confederación [konfeðera'θjon] *nf* confederation

conferencia [konfe'renθja] *nf* conference; *(lección)* lecture; *(TEL)* call

conferir [konfe'rir] *vt* to award

confesar [konfe'sar] *vt* to confess, admit

confesión [konfe'sjon] *nf* confession

confesionario [konfesjo'narjo] *nm* confessional

confeti [kon'feti] *nm* confetti

confiado, a [kon'fjaðo, a] *adj (crédulo)* trusting; *(seguro)* confident; *(presumido)* conceited, vain

confianza [kon'fjanθa] *nf* trust; *(aliento, confidencia)* confidence; *(familiaridad)* intimacy, familiarity; *(pey)* vanity, conceit

confiar [kon'fjar] *vt* to entrust ♦ *vi* to trust

confidencia [konfi'ðenθja] *nf* confidence

confidencial [konfiðen'θjal] *adj* confidential

confidente [konfi'ðente] *nm/f* confidant/e; *(policial)* informer

configurar [konfiyu'rar] *vt* to shape, form

confín [kon'fin] *nm* limit; **confines** *nmpl* confines, limits

confinar [konfi'nar] *vi* to confine; *(desterrar)* to banish

confirmar [konfir'mar] *vt* to confirm

confiscar [konfis'kar] *vt* to confiscate

confite [kon'fite] *nm* sweet *(BRIT)*, candy *(US)*

confitería [konfite'ria] *nf* confectionery; *(tienda)* confectioner's (shop)

confitura [konfi'tura] *nf* jam

conflictivo, a [konflik'tiβo, a] *adj (asunto, propuesta)* controversial; *(país, situación)* troubled

conflicto [kon'flikto] *nm* conflict; *(fig)* clash

confluir [kon'flwir] *vi (ríos)* to meet; *(gente)* to gather

conformar [konfor'mar] *vt* to shape, fashion ♦ *vi* to agree; **~se** *vr* to conform; *(resignarse)* to resign o.s

conforme [kon'forme] *adj (correspondiente)*: **~ con** in line with; *(de acuerdo)*: **estar ~s (con algo)** to be in agreement (with sth) ♦ *adv* as ♦ *excl* agreed! ♦ *prep*: **~ a** in accordance with; **quedarse ~ (con algo)** to be satisfied (with sth)

conformidad [konformi'ðað] *nf (semejanza)* similarity; *(acuerdo)* agreement; *(resignación)* resignation; **conformista** *adj, nm/f* conformist

confortable [konfor'taβle] *adj* comfortable

confortar [konfor'tar] *vt* to comfort

confrontar [konfron'tar] *vt* to confront; *(dos personas)* to bring face to face; *(cotejar)* to compare ♦ *vi* to border

confundir [konfun'dir] *vt (borrar)* to blur; *(equivocar)* to mistake, confuse; *(mezclar)* to mix; *(turbar)* to confuse; **~se** *vr (hacerse borroso)* to become blurred; *(turbarse)* to get confused; *(equivocarse)* to make a mistake; *(mezclarse)* to mix

confusión [konfu'sjon] *nf* confusion

confuso, a [kon'fuso, a] adj confused

congelado, a [konxe'laðo, a] adj frozen; ~s nmpl frozen food(s); **congelador** nm (aparato) freezer, deep freeze; **congeladora** nf freezer, deep freeze

congelar [konxe'lar] vt to freeze; ~se vr (sangre, grasa) to congeal

congeniar [konxe'njar] vi to get on (BRIT) o along (US) well

congestión [konxes'tjon] nf congestion

congestionar [konxestjo'nar] vt to congest; ~se vr: **se le congestionó la cara** his face became flushed

congoja [kon'goxa] nf distress, grief

congraciarse [kongra'θjarse] vr to ingratiate o.s.

congratular [kongratu'lar] vt to congratulate

congregación [kongreɣa'θjon] nf congregation

congregar [kongre'ɣar] vt to gather together; ~se vr to gather together

congresista [kongre'sista] nm/f delegate, congressman/woman

congreso [kon'greso] nm congress

conjetura [konxe'tura] nf guess; **conjeturar** vt to guess

conjugar [konxu'ɣar] vt to combine, fit together; (LING) to conjugate

conjunción [konxun'θjon] nf conjunction

conjunto, a [kon'xunto, a] adj joint, united ♦ nm whole; (MUS) band; **en** ~ as a whole

conjurar [konxu'rar] vt (REL) to exorcise; (fig) to ward off ♦ vi to plot

conmemoración [konmemora'θjon] nf commemoration

conmemorar [konmemo'rar] vt to commemorate

conmigo [kon'miɣo] pron with me

conminar [konmi'nar] vt to threaten

conmoción [konmo'θjon] nf shock; (fig) upheaval; ~ **cerebral** (MED) concussion

conmovedor, a [konmoβe'ðor, a] adj touching, moving; (emocionante) exciting

conmover [konmo'βer] vt to shake, disturb; (fig) to move

conmutador [konmuta'ðor] nm switch; (AM: TEL: centralita) switchboard; (: central) telephone exchange

cono ['kono] nm cone

conocedor, a [konoθe'ðor, a] adj expert, knowledgeable ♦ nm/f expert

conocer [kono'θer] vt to know; (por primera vez) to meet, get to know; (entender) to know about; (reconocer) to recognize; ~se vr (una persona) to know o.s.; (dos personas) to (get to) know each other

conocido, a [kono'θiðo, a] adj (well-) known ♦ nm/f acquaintance

conocimiento [konoθi'mjento] nm knowledge; (MED) consciousness; ~s nmpl (personas) acquaintances; (saber) knowledge sg

conozco etc vb ver **conocer**

conque ['konke] conj and so, so then

conquista [kon'kista] nf conquest; **conquistador, a** adj conquering ♦ nm conqueror

conquistar [konkis'tar] vt to conquer

consagrar [konsa'ɣrar] vt (REL) to consecrate; (fig) to devote

consciente [kons'θjente] adj conscious

consecución [konseku'θjon] nf acquisition; (de fin) attainment

consecuencia [konse'kwenθja] nf consequence, outcome; (firmeza) consistency

consecuente [konse'kwente] adj consistent

consecutivo, a [konseku'tiβo, a] adj consecutive

conseguir [konse'ɣir] vt to get, obtain; (sus fines) to attain

consejero, a [konse'xero, a] nm/f adviser, consultant; (POL) councillor

consejo [kon'sexo] nm advice; (POL) council; ~ **de administración** (COM) board of directors; ~ **de guerra** court martial; ~ **de ministros** cabinet meeting

consenso [kon'senso] nm consensus

consentimiento [konsenti'mjento] nm consent

consentir [konsen'tir] vt (permitir, tolerar) to consent to; (mimar) to pamper, spoil; (aguantar) to put up with ♦ vi to agree, consent; ~ **que uno haga algo** to allow sb to do sth

conserje [kon'serxe] nm caretaker; (portero) porter

conservación [konserβa'θjon] nf conservation; (de alimentos, vida) preservation

conservador, a [konserβa'ðor, a] adj (POL) conservative ♦ nm/f conservative

conservante [konser'βante] nm preservative

conservar [konser'βar] vt to conserve, keep; (alimentos, vida) to preserve; ~se vr to survive

conservas [kon'serβas] nfpl canned food(s) (pl)

conservatorio [konserβa'torjo] nm (MUS) conservatoire, conservatory

considerable [konsiðe'raβle] adj considerable

consideración [konsiðera'θjon] nf consideration; (estimación) respect

considerado, a [konsiðe'raðo, a] adj (atento) considerate; (respetado) respected

considerar [konsiðe'rar] vt to consider

consigna [kon'siɣna] nf (orden) order, instruction; (para equipajes) left-luggage office

consigo etc [kon'siɣo] vb ver **conseguir** ♦ pron (m) with him; (f) with her; (Vd) with you; (reflexivo) with o.s.

consiguiendo etc vb ver **conseguir**

consiguiente [konsi'ɣjente] adj consequent; **por** ~ and so, therefore, conse-

quently
consistente [konsis'tente] *adj* consistent; (*sólido*) solid, firm; (*válido*) sound
consistir [konsis'tir] *vi*: ~ **en** (*componerse de*) to consist of; (*ser resultado de*) to be due to
consolación [konsola'θjon] *nf* consolation
consolar [konso'lar] *vt* to console
consolidar [konsoli'ðar] *vt* to consolidate
consomé [konso'me] (*pl* ~s) *nm* consommé, clear soup
consonante [konso'nante] *adj* consonant, harmonious ♦ *nf* consonant
consorcio [kon'sorθjo] *nm* consortium
conspiración [konspira'θjon] *nf* conspiracy
conspirador, a [konspira'ðor, a] *nm/f* conspirator
conspirar [konspi'rar] *vi* to conspire
constancia [kon'stanθja] *nf* constancy; **dejar** ~ **de** to put on record
constante [kons'tante] *adj, nf* constant
constar [kons'tar] *vi* (*evidenciarse*) to be clear *o* evident; ~ **de** to consist of
constatar [konsta'tar] *vt* (*controlar*) to check; (*observar*) to note
consternación [konsterna'θjon] *nf* consternation
constipado, a [konsti'paðo, a] *adj*: **estar** ~ to have a cold ♦ *nm* cold
constitución [konstitu'θjon] *nf* constitution; **constitucional** *adj* constitutional
constituir [konstitu'ir] *vt* (*formar, componer*) to constitute, make up; (*fundar, erigir, ordenar*) to constitute, establish
constituyente [konstitu'jente] *adj* constituent
constreñir [konstre'ɲir] *vt* (*restringir*) to restrict
construcción [konstruk'θjon] *nf* construction, building
constructor, a [konstruk'tor, a] *nm/f* builder
construir [konstru'ir] *vt* to build, construct
construyendo *etc vb ver* **construir**
consuelo [kon'swelo] *nm* consolation, solace
cónsul ['konsul] *nm* consul; **consulado** *nm* consulate
consulta [kon'sulta] *nf* consultation; (*MED*): **horas de** ~ surgery hours
consultar [konsul'tar] *vt* to consult
consultorio [konsul'torjo] *nm* (*MED*) surgery
consumar [konsu'mar] *vt* to complete, carry out; (*crimen*) to commit; (*sentencia*) to carry out
consumición [konsumi'θjon] *nf* consumption; (*bebida*) drink; (*comida*) food; ~ **mínima** cover charge
consumidor, a [konsumi'ðor, a] *nm/f* consumer
consumir [konsu'mir] *vt* to consume; ~**se**

vr to be consumed; (*persona*) to waste away
consumismo [konsu'mismo] *nm* consumerism
consumo [kon'sumo] *nm* consumption
contabilidad [kontaßili'ðað] *nf* accounting, book-keeping; (*profesión*) accountancy; **contable** *nm/f* accountant
contacto [kon'takto] *nm* contact; (*AUTO*) ignition
contado, a [kon'taðo, a] *adj*: ~**s** (*escasos*) numbered, scarce, few ♦ *nm*: **pagar al** ~ to pay (in) cash
contador [konta'ðor] *nm* (*aparato*) meter; (*AM*: *contante*) accountant
contagiar [konta'xjar] *vt* (*enfermedad*) to pass on, transmit; (*persona*) to infect; ~**se** *vr* to become infected
contagio [kon'taxjo] *nm* infection; **contagioso, a** *adj* infectious; (*fig*) catching
contaminación [kontamina'θjon] *nf* contamination; (*polución*) pollution
contaminar [kontami'nar] *vt* to contaminate; (*aire, agua*) to pollute
contante [kon'tante] *adj*: **dinero** ~ (**y sonante**) cash
contar [kon'tar] *vt* (*páginas, dinero*) to count; (*anécdota, chiste etc*) to tell ♦ *vi* to count; ~ **con** to rely on, count on
contemplación [kontempla'θjon] *nf* contemplation
contemplar [kontem'plar] *vt* to contemplate; (*mirar*) to look at
contemporáneo, a [kontempo'raneo, a] *adj, nm/f* contemporary
contendiente [konten'djente] *nm/f* contestant
contenedor [kontene'ðor] *nm* container
contener [konte'ner] *vt* to contain, hold; (*retener*) to hold back, contain; ~**se** *vr* to control *o* restrain o.s.
contenido, a [konte'niðo, a] *adj* (*moderado*) restrained; (*risa etc*) suppressed ♦ *nm* contents *pl*, content
contentar [konten'tar] *vt* (*satisfacer*) to satisfy; (*complacer*) to please; ~**se** *vr* to be satisfied
contento, a [kon'tento, a] *adj* contented, content; (*alegre*) pleased; (*feliz*) happy
contestación [kontesta'θjon] *nf* answer, reply
contestador [kontesta'ðor] *nm*: ~ **automático** answering machine
contestar [kontes'tar] *vt* to answer, reply; (*JUR*) to corroborate, confirm
contexto [kon'te(k)sto] *nm* context
contienda [kon'tjenda] *nf* contest
contigo [kon'tixo] *pron* with you
contiguo, a [kon'tixwo, a] *adj* (*de al lado*) next; (*vecino*) adjacent, adjoining
continente [konti'nente] *adj, nm* continent
contingencia [kontin'xenθja] *nf* con-

tingency; (*riesgo*) risk; **contingente** *adj, nm* contingent

continuación [kontinwa'θjon] *nf* continuation; **a ~** then, next

continuar [konti'nwar] *vt* to continue, go on with ♦ *vi* to continue, go on; **~ hablando** to continue talking *o* to talk

continuidad [kontinwi'ðað] *nf* continuity

continuo, a [kon'tinwo, a] *adj* (*sin interrupción*) continuous; (*acción perseverante*) continual

contorno [kon'torno] *nm* outline; (*GEO*) contour; **~s** *nmpl* neighbourhood *sg*, surrounding area *sg*

contorsión [kontor'sjon] *nf* contortion

contra ['kontra] *prep, ad* against ♦ *nm inv* con ♦ *nf*: **la C~** (*de Nicaragua*) the Contras *pl*

contraataque [kontraa'take] *nm* counterattack

contrabajo [kontra'βaxo] *nm* double bass

contrabandista [kontraβan'dista] *nm/f* smuggler

contrabando [kontra'βando] *nm* (*acción*) smuggling; (*mercancías*) contraband

contracción [kontrak'θjon] *nf* contraction

contracorriente [kontrako'rrjente]: **(a) ~** *adv* against the current

contrachapado [kontratʃa'paðo] *nm* plywood

contradecir [kontraðe'θir] *vt* to contradict

contradicción [kontraðik'θjon] *nf* contradiction

contradictorio, a [kontraðik'torjo, a] *adj* contradictory

contraer [kontra'er] *vt* to contract; (*limitar*) to restrict; **~se** *vr* to contract; (*limitarse*) to limit o.s.

contraluz [kontra'luθ] *nf*: **a ~** against the light

contramaestre [kontrama'estre] *nm* foreman

contrapartida [kontrapar'tiða] *nf*: **como ~ (de)** in return (for)

contrapelo [kontra'pelo]: **a ~** *adv* the wrong way

contrapesar [kontrape'sar] *vt* to counterbalance; (*fig*) to offset; **contrapeso** *nm* counterweight

contraportada [kontrapor'taða] *nf* (*de revista*) back cover

contraproducente [kontraproðu'θente] *adj* counterproductive

contrariar [kontra'rjar] *vt* (*oponerse*) to oppose; (*poner obstáculo*) to impede; (*enfadar*) to vex

contrariedad [kontrarje'ðað] *nf* (*oposición*) opposition; (*obstáculo*) obstacle, setback; (*disgusto*) vexation, annoyance

contrario, a [kon'trarjo, a] *adj* contrary; (*persona*) opposed; (*sentido, lado*) opposite ♦ *nm/f* enemy, adversary; (*DEPORTE*) oppo-

nent; **al/por el ~** on the contrary; **de lo ~** otherwise

contrarrestar [kontrarres'tar] *vt* to counteract

contrasentido [kontrasen'tiðo] *nm*: **es un ~ que él ...** it doesn't make sense for him to ...

contraseña [kontra'seɲa] *nf* (*INFORM*) password

contrastar [kontras'tar] *vt* to resist ♦ *vi* to contrast

contraste [kon'traste] *nm* contrast

contratar [kontra'tar] *vt* (*firmar un acuerdo para*) to contract for; (*empleados, obreros*) to hire, engage; **~se** *vr* to sign on

contratiempo [kontra'tjempo] *nm* setback

contratista [kontra'tista] *nm/f* contractor

contrato [kon'trato] *nm* contract

contravenir [kontraβe'nir] *vi*: **~ a** to contravene, violate

contraventana [kontraβen'tana] *nf* shutter

contribución [kontriβu'θjon] *nf* (*municipal etc*) tax; (*ayuda*) contribution

contribuir [kontriβu'ir] *vt, vi* to contribute; (*COM*) to pay (in taxes)

contribuyente [kontriβu'jente] *nm/f* (*COM*) taxpayer; (*que ayuda*) contributor

contrincante [kontrin'kante] *nm* opponent

control [kon'trol] *nm* control; (*inspección*) inspection, check; **~ador, a** *nm/f* controller; **~ador aéreo** air-traffic controller

controlar [kontro'lar] *vt* to control; (*inspeccionar*) to inspect, check

controversia [kontro'βersja] *nf* controversy

contundente [kontun'dente] *adj* (*instrumento*) blunt; (*argumento, derrota*) overwhelming

contusión [kontu'sjon] *nf* bruise

convalecencia [kombale'θenθja] *nf* convalescence

convalecer [kombale'θer] *vi* to convalesce, get better

convaleciente [kombale'θjente] *adj, nm/f* convalescent

convalidar [kombali'ðar] *vt* (*título*) to recognize

convencer [komben'θer] *vt* to convince; (*persuadir*) to persuade

convencimiento [kombenθi'mjento] *nm* (*acción*) convincing; (*persuasión*) persuasion; (*certidumbre*) conviction

convención [komben'θjon] *nf* convention

conveniencia [kombe'njenθja] *nf* suitability; (*conformidad*) agreement; (*utilidad, provecho*) usefulness; **~s** *nfpl* (*convenciones*) conventions; (*COM*) property *sg*

conveniente [kombe'njente] *adj* suitable; (*útil*) useful

convenio [kom'benjo] *nm* agreement, treaty

convenir [kombe'nir] *vi* (*estar de acuerdo*) to agree; (*ser conveniente*) to suit, be suitable

convento [kom'bento] *nm* convent
convenza *etc vb ver* **convencer**
converger [komber'xer] *vi* to converge
convergir [komber'xir] *vi* = **converger**
conversación [kombersa'θjon] *nf* conversation
conversar [komber'sar] *vi* to talk, converse
conversión [komber'sjon] *nf* conversion
convertir [komber'tir] *vt* to convert
convicción [kombik'θjon] *nf* conviction
convicto, a [kom'bikto, a] *adj* convicted, found guilty; (*condenado*) condemned
convidado, a [kombi'ðaðo, a] *nm/f* guest
convidar [kombi'ðar] *vt* to invite
convincente [kombin'θente] *adj* convincing
convite [kom'bite] *nm* invitation; (*banquete*) banquet
convivencia [kombi'βenθja] *nf* coexistence, living together
convivir [kombi'βir] *vi* to live together
convocar [kombo'kar] *vt* to summon, call (together)
convocatoria [komboka'torja] *nf* (*de oposiciones, elecciones*) notice; (*de huelga*) call
convulsión [kombul'sjon] *nf* convulsion
conyugal [konju'ɣal] *adj* conjugal; **cónyuge** ['konjuxe] *nm/f* spouse
coñac [ko'ɲa(k)] (*pl* ~**s**) *nm* cognac, brandy
coño ['koɲo] (*fam!*) *excl* (*enfado*) shit! (*!*); (*sorpresa*) bloody hell! (*!*)
cooperación [koopera'θjon] *nf* cooperation
cooperar [koope'rar] *vi* to cooperate
cooperativa [koopera'tiβa] *nf* cooperative
coordinadora [koorðina'ðora] *nf* (*comité*) coordinating committee
coordinar [koorði'nar] *vt* to coordinate
copa ['kopa] *nf* cup; (*vaso*) glass; (*bebida*): (**tomar una**) ~ (to have a) drink; (*de árbol*) top; (*de sombrero*) crown; ~**s** *nfpl* (*NAIPES*) ≈ hearts
copia ['kopja] *nf* copy; ~ **de respaldo** *o* **seguridad** (*INFORM*) back-up copy; **copiar** *vt* to copy
copioso, a [ko'pjoso, a] *adj* copious, plentiful
copla ['kopla] *nf* verse; (*canción*) (popular) song
copo ['kopo] *nm*: ~ **de nieve** snowflake; ~**s de maíz** cornflakes
copropietarios [kopropje'tarjos] *nmpl* joint owners
coqueta [ko'keta] *adj* flirtatious, coquettish; **coquetear** *vi* to flirt
coraje [ko'raxe] *nm* courage; (*ánimo*) spirit; (*ira*) anger
coral [ko'ral] *adj* choral ♦ *nf* (*MUS*) choir ♦ *nm* (*ZOOL*) coral
coraza [ko'raθa] *nf* (*armadura*) armour; (*blindaje*) armour-plating
corazón [kora'θon] *nm* heart
corazonada [koraθo'naða] *nf* impulse; (*presentimiento*) hunch
corbata [kor'βata] *nf* tie
corchete [kor'tʃete] *nm* catch, clasp
corcho ['kortʃo] *nm* cork; (*PESCA*) float
cordel [kor'ðel] *nm* cord, line
cordero [kor'ðero] *nm* lamb
cordial [kor'ðjal] *adj* cordial; ~**idad** *nf* warmth, cordiality
cordillera [korði'ʎera] *nf* range (of mountains)
Córdoba ['korðoβa] *n* Cordova
cordón [kor'ðon] *nm* (*cuerda*) cord, string; (*de zapatos*) lace; (*MIL etc*) cordon
cordura [kor'ðura] *nf*: **con** ~ (*obrar, hablar*) sensibly
corneta [kor'neta] *nf* bugle
cornisa [kor'nisa] *nf* (*ARQ*) cornice
coro ['koro] *nm* chorus; (*conjunto de cantores*) choir
corona [ko'rona] *nf* crown; (*de flores*) garland; ~**ción** *nf* coronation; **coronar** *vt* to crown
coronel [koro'nel] *nm* colonel
coronilla [koro'niʎa] *nf* (*ANAT*) crown (of the head)
corporación [korpora'θjon] *nf* corporation
corporal [korpo'ral] *adj* corporal, bodily
corpulento, a [korpu'lento, a] *adj* (*persona*) heavily-built
corral [ko'rral] *nm* farmyard
correa [ko'rrea] *nf* strap; (*cinturón*) belt; (*de perro*) lead, leash
corrección [korrek'θjon] *nf* correction; (*reprensión*) rebuke; **correccional** *nm* reformatory
correcto, a [ko'rrekto, a] *adj* correct; (*persona*) well-mannered
corredizo, a [korre'ðiθo, a] *adj* (*puerta etc*) sliding
corredor, a [korre'ðor, a] *adj* running ♦ *nm* (*pasillo*) corridor; (*balcón corrido*) gallery; (*COM*) agent, broker ♦ *nm/f* (*DEPORTE*) runner
corregir [korre'xir] *vt* (*error*) to correct; (*amonestar, reprender*) to rebuke, reprimand; ~**se** *vr* to reform
correo [ko'rreo] *nm* post, mail; (*persona*) courier; **C**~**s** *nmpl* Post Office *sg*; ~ **aéreo** airmail
correr [ko'rrer] *vt* to run; (*viajar*) to cover, travel; (*cortinas*) to draw; (*cerrojo*) to shoot ♦ *vi* to run; (*líquido*) to run, flow; ~**se** *vr* to slide, move; (*colores*) to run
correspondencia [korrespon'denθja] *nf* correspondence; (*FERRO*) connection
corresponder [korrespon'der] *vi* to correspond; (*convenir*) to be suitable; (*pertenecer*) to belong; (*tocar*) to concern; ~**se** *vr* (*por escrito*) to correspond; (*amarse*) to love one another
correspondiente [korrespon'djente] *adj* corresponding

corresponsal [korrespon'sal] *nm/f* correspondent

corrida [ko'rriða] *nf (de toros)* bullfight

corrido, a [ko'rriðo, a] *adj (avergonzado)* abashed; **3 noches corridas** 3 nights running; **un kilo ~ a** good kilo

corriente [ko'rrjente] *adj (agua)* running; *(fig)* flowing; *(dinero etc)* current; *(común)* ordinary, normal ♦ *nf* current ♦ *nm* current month; **~ eléctrica** electric current

corrija *etc vb ver* **corregir**

corrillo [ko'rriʎo] *nm* ring, circle (of people); *(fig)* clique

corro ['korro] *nm* ring, circle of people

corroborar [korroβo'rar] *vt* to corroborate

corroer [korro'er] *vt* to corrode; *(GEO)* to erode

corromper [korrom'per] *vt (madera)* to rot; *(fig)* to corrupt

corrosivo, a [korro'siβo, a] *adj* corrosive

corrupción [korrup'θjon] *nf* rot, decay; *(fig)* corruption

corsé [kor'se] *nm* corset

cortacésped [korta'θespeð] *nm* lawn mower

cortado, a [kor'taðo, a] *adj (gen)* cut; *(leche)* sour; *(confuso)* confused; *(desconcertado)* embarrassed ♦ *nm* coffee (with a little milk)

cortar [kor'tar] *vt* to cut; *(suministro)* to cut off; *(un pasaje)* to cut out ♦ *vi* to cut; **~se** *vr (turbarse)* to become embarrassed; *(leche)* to turn, curdle; **~se el pelo** to have one's hair cut

cortauñas [korta'uɲas] *nm inv* nail clippers *pl*

corte ['korte] *nm* cut, cutting; *(de tela)* piece, length ♦ *nf:* **las C~s** the Spanish Parliament; **~ y confección** dressmaking; **~ de luz** power cut

cortejar [korte'xar] *vt* to court

cortejo [kor'texo] *nm* entourage; **~ fúnebre** funeral procession

cortés [kor'tes] *adj* courteous, polite

cortesía [korte'sia] *nf* courtesy

corteza [kor'teθa] *nf (de árbol)* bark; *(de pan)* crust

cortina [kor'tina] *nf* curtain

corto, a ['korto, a] *adj (breve)* short; *(tímido)* bashful; **~ de luces** not very bright; **~ de vista** short-sighted; **estar ~ de fondos** to be short of funds; **~circuito** *nm* short circuit; **~metraje** *nm (CINE)* short

cosa ['kosa] *nf* thing; *(asunto)* affair; **~ de** about; **eso es ~ mía** that's my business

coscorrón [kosko'rron] *nm* bump on the head

cosecha [ko'setʃa] *nf (AGR)* harvest; *(de vino)* vintage

cosechar [kose'tʃar] *vt* to harvest, gather (in)

coser [ko'ser] *vt* to sew

cosmético, a [kos'metiko, a] *adj, nm* cosmetic

cosquillas [kos'kiʎas] *nfpl:* **hacer ~** to tickle; **tener ~** to be ticklish

costa ['kosta] *nf (GEO)* coast; **C~ Brava** Costa Brava; **C~ Cantábrica** Cantabrian Coast; **C~ del Sol** Costa del Sol; **a toda ~** at any price

costado [kos'taðo] *nm* side

costar [kos'tar] *vt (valer)* to cost; *(necesitar)* to require, need; **me cuesta hablarle** I find it hard to talk to him

Costa Rica *nf* Costa Rica; **costarricense** *adj, nm/f* Costa Rican; **costarriqueño, a** *adj, nm/f* Costa Rican

coste ['koste] *nm* = **costo**

costear [koste'ar] *vt* to pay for

costero, a [kos'tero, a] *adj (pueblecito, camino)* coastal

costilla [kos'tiʎa] *nf* rib; *(CULIN)* cutlet

costo ['kosto] *nm* cost, price; **~ de la vida** cost of living; **~so, a** *adj* costly, expensive

costra ['kostra] *nf (corteza)* crust; *(MED)* scab

costumbre [kos'tumbre] *nf* custom, habit

costura [kos'tura] *nf* sewing, needlework; *(zurcido)* seam

costurera [kostu'rera] *nf* dressmaker

costurero [kostu'rero] *nm* sewing box *o* case

cotejar [kote'xar] *vt* to compare

cotidiano, a [koti'ðjano, a] *adj* daily, day to day

cotilla [ko'tiʎa] *nm/f (fam)* gossip; **cotillear** *vi* to gossip

cotización [kotiθa'θjon] *nf (COM)* quotation, price; *(de club)* dues *pl*

cotizar [koti'θar] *vt (COM)* to quote, price; **~se** *vr:* **~se a** to sell at, fetch; *(BOLSA)* to stand at, be quoted at

coto ['koto] *nm (terreno cercado)* enclosure; *(de caza)* reserve

cotorra [ko'torra] *nf* parrot

COU [kou] *nm abr* (= *Curso de Orientación Universitaria*) *1 year course leading to final school-leaving certificate and university entrance examinations*

coyote [ko'jote] *nm* coyote, prairie wolf

coyuntura [kojun'tura] *nf (ANAT)* joint; *(fig)* juncture, occasion

crack *nm (droga)* crack

coz [koθ] *nf* kick

cráneo ['kraneo] *nm* skull, cranium

cráter ['krater] *nm* crater

creación [krea'θjon] *nf* creation

creador, a [krea'ðor, a] *adj* creative ♦ *nm/f* creator

crear [kre'ar] *vt* to create, make

crecer [kre'θer] *vi* to grow; *(precio)* to rise

creces ['kreθes]: **con ~** *adv* amply, fully

crecido, a [kre'θiðo, a] *adj (persona, planta)* full-grown; *(cantidad)* large

creciente [kre'θjente] *adj* growing; *(cantidad)* increasing; *(luna)* crescent ♦ *nm* crescent

crecimiento [kreθi'mjento] *nm* growth; *(aumento)* increase

credenciales [kreðen'θjales] *nfpl* credentials

crédito ['kreðito] *nm* credit

credo ['kreðo] *nm* creed

crédulo, a ['kreðulo, a] *adj* credulous

creencia [kre'enθja] *nf* belief

creer [kre'er] *vt, vi* to think, believe; ~**se** *vr* to believe o.s. (to be); ~ **en** to believe in; ¡ya lo creo! I should think so!

creíble [kre'iβle] *adj* credible, believable

creído, a [kre'iðo, a] *adj* (*engreído*) conceited

crema ['krema] *nf* cream; *(natillas)* custard; ~ **pastelera** (confectioner's) custard

cremallera [krema'ʎera] *nf* zip (fastener)

crematorio [krema'torjo] *nm* (*tb:* horno ~) crematorium

crepitar [krepi'tar] *vi* to crackle

crepúsculo [kre'puskulo] *nm* twilight, dusk

crespo, a ['krespo, a] *adj* (*pelo*) curly

cresta ['kresta] *nf* (*GEO, ZOOL*) crest

creyendo *vb ver* **creer**

creyente [kre'jente] *nm/f* believer

creyó *etc vb ver* **creer**

crezco *etc vb ver* **crecer**

cría *etc* ['kria] *vb ver* **criar** ♦ *nf* (*de animales*) rearing, breeding; (*animal*) young; *ver tb* **crío**

criadero [kria'ðero] *nm* nursery; *(ZOOL)* breeding place

criado, a [kri'aðo, a] *nm* servant ♦ *nf* servant, maid

criador [kria'ðor] *nm* breeder

crianza [kri'anθa] *nf* rearing, breeding; *(fig)* breeding

criar [kri'ar] *vt* (*amamantar*) to suckle, feed; (*educar*) to bring up; (*producir*) to grow, produce; (*animales*) to breed

criatura [kria'tura] *nf* creature; (*niño*) baby, (small) child

criba ['kriβa] *nf* sieve; **cribar** *vt* to sieve

crimen ['krimen] *nm* crime

criminal [krimi'nal] *adj, nm/f* criminal

crin [krin] *nf* (*tb:* ~es *nfpl*) mane

crío, a ['krio, a] *(fam) nm/f* (*niño*) kid

crisis ['krisis] *nf inv* crisis; ~ **nerviosa** nervous breakdown

crispar [kris'par] *vt* (*músculo*) to tense (up); (*nervios*) to set on edge

cristal [kris'tal] *nm* crystal; (*de ventana*) glass, pane; (*lente*) lens; ~**ino, a** *adj* crystalline; (*fig*) clear ♦ *nm* lens (of the eye); ~**izar** *vt, vi* to crystallize

cristiandad [kristjan'daθ] *nf* Christendom

cristianismo [kristja'nismo] *nm* Christianity

cristiano, a [kris'tjano, a] *adj, nm/f* Christian

Cristo ['kristo] *nm* Christ; (*crucifijo*) crucifix

criterio [kri'terjo] *nm* criterion; (*juicio*) judgement

crítica ['kritika] *nf* criticism; *ver tb* **crítico**

criticar [kriti'kar] *vt* to criticize

crítico, a ['kritiko, a] *adj* critical ♦ *nm/f* critic

Croacia *nf* Croatia

croar [kro'ar] *vi* to croak

croqueta [kro'keta] *nf* (*CULIN*) croquette

cromo ['kromo] *nm* chrome

crónica ['kronika] *nf* chronicle, account

crónico, a ['kroniko, a] *adj* chronic

cronómetro [kro'nometro] *nm* (*DEPORTE*) stopwatch

cruce *etc* ['kruθe] *vb ver* **cruzar** ♦ *nm* crossing; *(de carreteras)* crossroads

crucificar [kruθifi'kar] *vt* to crucify

crucifijo [kruθi'fixo] *nm* crucifix

crucigrama [kruθi'xrama] *nm* crossword (puzzle)

crudo, a ['kruðo, a] *adj* raw; *(no maduro)* unripe; *(petróleo)* crude; *(rudo, cruel)* cruel ♦ *nm* crude (oil)

cruel [krwel] *adj* cruel; ~**dad** *nf* cruelty

crujido [kru'xiðo] *nm* (*de madera etc*) creak

crujiente [kru'xjente] *adj* (*galleta etc*) crunchy

crujir [kru'xir] *vi* (*madera etc*) to creak; (*dedos*) to crack; (*dientes*) to grind; (*nieve, arena*) to crunch

cruz [kruθ] *nf* cross; (*de moneda*) tails *sg*; ~ **gamada** swastika

cruzada [kru'θaða] *nf* crusade

cruzado, a [kru'θaðo, a] *adj* crossed ♦ *nm* crusader

cruzar [kru'θar] *vt* to cross; ~**se** *vr* (*líneas etc*) to cross; (*personas*) to pass each other

Cruz Roja *nf* Red Cross

cuaderno [kwa'ðerno] *nm* notebook; (*de escuela*) exercise book; (*NAUT*) logbook

cuadra ['kwaðra] *nf* (*caballeriza*) stable; (*AM*) block

cuadrado, a [kwa'ðraðo, a] *adj* square ♦ *nm* (*MAT*) square

cuadrar [kwa'ðrar] *vt* to square ♦ *vi*: ~ **con** to square with, tally with; ~**se** *vr* (*soldado*) to stand to attention

cuadrilátero [kwaðri'latero] *nm* (*DEPORTE*) boxing ring; (*GEOM*) quadrilateral

cuadrilla [kwa'ðriʎa] *nf* party, group

cuadro ['kwaðro] *nm* square; (*ARTE*) painting; (*TEATRO*) scene; (*diagrama*) chart; (*DEPORTE, MED*) team; (*POL*) executive; **tela a** ~**s** checked (*BRIT*) o chequered (*US*) material

cuádruple ['kwaðruple] *adj* quadruple

cuádruplo, a ['kwaðruplo, a] *adj* quadruple

cuajar [kwa'xar] *vt* to thicken; (*leche*) to curdle; (*sangre*) to congeal; (*adornar*) to adorn; (*CULIN*) to set; ~**se** *vr* to curdle; to

what's the date?; **Señor no sé** ~**s** Mr. So-
and-So

cuajo ['kwaxo] *nm*: **de** ~ (*arrancar*) by the
roots; (*cortar*) completely

cuarenta [kwa'renta] *num* forty

cual [kwal] *adv* like, as ♦ *pron*: **el** ~ *etc*
which; (*persona: sujeto*) who; (: *objeto*)
whom ♦ *adj* such as; **cada** ~ each one; **tal**
~ just as it is

cuarentena [kwaren'tena] *nf* quarantine

cuaresma [kwa'resma] *nf* Lent

cuál [kwal] *pron interr* which (one)

cuarta ['kwarta] *nf* (*MAT*) quarter, fourth;
(*palmo*) span

cualesquier(a) [kwales'kjer(a)] *pl de* **cual-
quier(a)**

cualidad [kwali'ðað] *nf* quality

cuartear [kwarte'ar] *vt* to quarter; (*dividir*)
to divide up; ~**se** *vr* to crack, split

cualquier [kwal'kjer] *adj ver* **cualquiera**

cualquiera [kwal'kjera] (*pl* **cualesquiera**)
adj (*delante de nm y f:* **cualquier**) any ♦
pron anybody; **un coche** ~ **servirá** any car
will do; **no es un hombre** ~ he isn't just
anybody; **cualquier día/libro** any day/book;
eso ~ **lo sabe hacer** anybody can do that;
es un ~ he's a nobody

cuartel [kwar'tel] *nm* (*de ciudad*) quarter,
district; (*MIL*) barracks *pl*; ~ **general** headquarters *pl*

cuarteto [kwar'teto] *nm* quartet

cuarto, a ['kwarto, a] *adj* fourth ♦ *nm*
(*MAT*) quarter, fourth; (*habitación*) room; ~
de baño bathroom; ~ **de estar** living
room; ~ **de hora** quarter (of an) hour; ~
de kilo quarter kilo

cuando ['kwando] *adv* when; (*aún si*) if,
even if ♦ *conj* (*puesto que*) since ♦ *prep*:
yo, ~ **niño ...** when I was a child ...; ~ **no
sea así** even if it is not so; ~ **más** at (the)
most; ~ **menos** at least; ~ **no** if not, otherwise; **de** ~ **en** ~ from time to time

cuatro ['kwatro] *num* four

cuba ['kuβa] *nf* cask, barrel

Cuba ['kuβa] *nf* Cuba; **cubano, a** *adj, nm/f*
Cuban

cuándo ['kwando] *adv* when; **¿desde** ~?,
¿de ~ **acá?** since when?

cúbico, a ['kuβiko, a] *adj* cubic

cuantía [kwan'tia] *nf* (*importe: de pérdidas,
deuda, daños*) extent

cubierta [ku'βjerta] *nf* cover, covering;
(*neumático*) tyre; (*NAUT*) deck

cuantioso, a [kwan'tjoso, a] *adj* substantial

cubierto, a [ku'βjerto, a] *pp de* **cubrir** ♦
adj covered ♦ *nm* cover; (*en la mesa*) place;
~**s** *nmpl* cutlery *sg*; **a** ~ **de** covered with *o*
in

PALABRA CLAVE

cubil [ku'βil] *nm* den; ~**ete** *nm* (*en juegos*)
cup

cubito [ku'βito] *nm*: ~ **de hielo** ice-cube

cuanto, a ['kwanto, a] *adj* **1** (*todo*): **tiene
todo** ~ **desea** he's got everything he
wants; **le daremos** ~**s ejemplares necesite**
we'll give him as many copies as *o* all the
copies he needs; ~**s hombres la ven** all
the men who see her

cubo ['kuβo] *nm* cube; (*balde*) bucket, tub;
(*TEC*) drum

cubrecama [kuβre'kama] *nm* bedspread

2: **unos** ~**s**: **había unos** ~**s periodistas**
there were (quite) a few journalists

cubrir [ku'βrir] *vt* to cover; ~**se** *vr* (*cielo*) to
become overcast

3 (+ *más*): ~ **más vino bebes peor te sen-
tirás** the more wine you drink the worse
you'll feel

cucaracha [kuka'ratʃa] *nf* cockroach

cuclillas [ku'kliʎas] *nfpl*: **en** ~ squatting

♦ *pron*: **tiene** ~ **desea** he has everything
he wants; **tome** ~/~**s quiera** take as
much/many as you want

cuco, a ['kuko, a] *adj* pretty; (*astuto*) sharp
♦ *nm* cuckoo

♦ *adv*: **en** ~: **en** ~ **profesor** as a teacher;
en ~ **a mí** as for me; *ver tb* **antes**

cucurucho [kuku'rutʃo] *nm* cornet

♦ *conj* **1**: ~ **más gana menos gasta** the
more he earns the less he spends; ~ **más
joven se es más se es confiado** the
younger you are the more trusting you are

cuchara [ku'tʃara] *nf* spoon; (*TEC*) scoop;
~**da** *nf* spoonful; ~**dita** *nf* teaspoonful

cucharilla [kutʃa'riʎa] *nf* teaspoon

cucharón [kutʃa'ron] *nm* ladle

2: **en** ~: **en** ~ **llegue/llegué** as soon as I
arrive/arrived

cuchichear [kutʃitʃe'ar] *vi* to whisper

cuchilla [ku'tʃiʎa] *nf* (large) knife; (*de arma
blanca*) blade; ~ **de afeitar** razor blade

cuchillo [ku'tʃiʎo] *nm* knife

cuánto, a ['kwanto, a] *adj* (*exclamación*)
what a lot of; (*interr: sg*) how much?; (: *pl*)
how many? ♦ *pron, adv* how; (*interr: sg*)
how much?; (: *pl*) how many?; **¡cuánta
gente!** what a lot of people!; **¿**~ **cuesta?**
how much does it cost?; **¿a** ~**s estamos?**

cuchitril [kutʃi'tril] *nm* hovel; (*habitación
etc*) pigsty

cuello ['kweʎo] *nm* (*ANAT*) neck; (*de vestido, camisa*) collar

cuenca ['kwenka] *nf* (*ANAT*) eye socket;
(*GEO*) bowl, deep valley

cuenco ['kwenko] *nm* bowl

cuenta *etc* ['kwenta] *vb ver* **contar** ♦ *nf*
(*cálculo*) count, counting; (*en café, restaurante*) bill; (*COM*) account; (*de collar*) bead;
(*fig*) account; **a fin de** ~**s** in the end; **caer
en la** ~ to catch on; **darse** ~ **de** to realize;

tener en ~ to bear in mind; **echar** ~**s** to take stock; ~ **corriente/de ahorros** current/savings account; ~ **atrás** count-down; **~kilómetros** *nm inv* ≈ milometer; *(de velocidad)* speedometer

cuento *etc* ['kwento] *vb ver* **contar ♦** *nm* story

cuerda ['kwerða] *nf* rope; *(hilo)* string; *(de reloj)* spring; **dar ~ a un reloj** to wind up a clock; ~ **floja** tightrope

cuerdo, a ['kwerðo, a] *adj* sane; *(prudente)* wise, sensible

cuerno ['kwerno] *nm* horn

cuero ['kwero] *nm* (*ZOOL*) skin, hide; *(TEC)* leather; **en ~s** stark naked; ~ **cabelludo** scalp

cuerpo ['kwerpo] *nm* body

cuervo ['kwerßo] *nm* crow

cuesta *etc* ['kwesta] *vb ver* **costar ♦** *nf* slope; *(en camino etc)* hill; ~ **arriba/abajo** uphill/downhill; **a ~s** on one's back

cueste *etc vb ver* **costar**

cuestión [kwes'tjon] *nf* matter, question, is-sue; *(riña)* quarrel, dispute

cueva ['kweßa] *nf* cave

cuidado [kwi'ðaðo] *nm* care, carefulness; *(preocupación)* care, worry **♦** *excl* careful!, look out!

cuidadoso, a [kwiða'ðoso, a] *adj* careful; *(preocupado)* anxious

cuidar [kwi'ðar] *vt* (*MED*) to care for; *(ocu-parse de)* to take care of, look after **♦** *vi*: ~ **de** to take care of, look after; **~se** *vr* to look after o.s.; **~se de hacer algo** to take care to do sth

culata [ku'lata] *nf* (*de fusil*) butt

culebra [ku'leßra] *nf* snake

culebrón [kule'ßron] *(fam) nm* (*TV*) soap-opera

culinario, a [kuli'narjo, a] *adj* culinary, cooking *cpd*

culminación [kulmina'θjon] *nf* culmination

culo ['kulo] *nm* bottom, backside; *(de vaso, botella)* bottom

culpa ['kulpa] *nf* fault; (*JUR*) guilt; **por ~ de** because of, through; **tener la ~ (de)** ~ to be to blame (for); **~bilidad** *nf* guilt; **~ble** *adj* guilty **♦** *nm/f* culprit

culpar [kul'par] *vt* to blame; *(acusar)* to ac-cuse

cultivar [kulti'ßar] *vt* to cultivate

cultivo [kul'tißo] *nm* (*acto*) cultivation; *(plantas)* crop

culto, a ['kulto, a] *adj (cultivado)* culti-vated; *(que tiene cultura)* cultured, educated **♦** *nm (homenaje)* worship; *(religión)* cult

cultura [kul'tura] *nf* culture

culturismo [kultu'rismo] *nm* body-building

cumbre ['kumbre] *nf* summit, top

cumpleaños [kumple'aɲos] *nm inv* birth-day

cumplido, a [kum'pliðo, a] *adj* complete,

perfect; *(abundante)* plentiful; *(cortés)* courteous **♦** *nm* compliment; **visita de ~** courtesy call

cumplidor, a [kumpli'ðor, a] *adj* reliable

cumplimentar [kumplimen'tar] *vt* to con-gratulate

cumplimiento [kumpli'mjento] *nm (de un deber)* fulfilment; *(acabamiento)* completion

cumplir [kum'plir] *vt (orden)* to carry out, obey; *(promesa)* to carry out, fulfil; *(conde-na)* to serve; *(años)* to reach, attain **♦** *vi*: ~ **con** *(deberes)* to carry out, fulfil; **~se** *vr (plazo)* to expire; **hoy cumple dieciocho años** he is eighteen today

cúmulo ['kumulo] *nm* heap

cuna ['kuna] *nf* cradle, cot

cundir [kun'dir] *vi (noticia, rumor, pánico)* to spread; *(rendir)* to go a long way

cuneta [ku'neta] *nf* ditch

cuña ['kuɲa] *nf* wedge

cuñado, a [ku'ɲaðo, a] *nm/f* brother/sister-in-law

cuota ['kwota] *nf (parte proporcional)* share; *(cotización)* fee, dues *pl*

cupe *etc vb ver* **caber**

cupiera *etc vb ver* **caber**

cupo ['kupo] *vb ver* **caber ♦** *nm* quota

cupón [ku'pon] *nm* coupon

cúpula ['kupula] *nf* dome

cura ['kura] *nf (curación)* cure; *(método cu-rativo)* treatment **♦** *nm* priest

curación [kura'θjon] *nf* cure; *(acción)* cur-ing

curandero, a [kuran'dero, a] *nm/f* quack

curar [ku'rar] *vt* (*MED: herida*) to treat, dress; *(: enfermo)* to cure; *(CULIN)* to cure, salt; *(cuero)* to tan **♦** *vi* to get well, recover; **~se** *vr* to get well, recover

curiosear [kurjose'ar] *vt* to glance at, look over **♦** *vi* to look round, wander round; *(explorar)* to poke about

curiosidad [kurjosi'ðað] *nf* curiosity

curioso, a [ku'rjoso, a] *adj* curious **♦** *nm/f* bystander, onlooker

currante [ku'rrante] *(fam) nm/f* worker

currar [ku'rrar] *(fam) vi* to work

currelar [kurre'lar] *(fam) vi* to work

currículo [ku'rrikulo] = **curriculum**

curriculum [ku'rrikulum] *nm* curriculum vitae

curro ['kurro] *(fam) nm* work, job

cursi ['kursi] *(fam) adj* pretentious; *(amane-rado)* affected

cursillo [kur'siʎo] *nm* short course

cursiva [kur'sißa] *nf* italics *pl*

curso ['kurso] *nm* course; **en ~** *(año)* cur-rent; *(proceso)* going on, under way

cursor [kur'sor] *nm (INFORM)* cursor

curtido, a [kur'tiðo, a] *adj (cara etc)* weather-beaten; *(fig: persona)* experienced

curtir [kur'tir] *vt (cuero etc)* to tan

curva ['kurßa] *nf* curve, bend

curvo, a ['kurβo, a] *adj* (*gen*) curved; (*torcido*) bent

cúspide ['kuspiðe] *nf* (*GEO*) peak; (*fig*) top

custodia [kus'toðja] *nf* safekeeping; custody; **custodiar** *vt* (*conservar*) to take care of; (*vigilar*) to guard

cutícula [ku'tikula] *nf* cuticle

cutis ['kutis] *nm inv* skin, complexion

cutre ['kutre] (*fam*) *adj* (*lugar*) grotty; (*persona*) naff

cuyo, a ['kujo, a] *pron* (*de quien*) whose; (*de que*) whose, of which; **en ~ caso** in which case

C.V. *abr* (= *caballos de vapor*) H.P.

——— CH ch

chabacano, a [tʃaβa'kano, a] *adj* vulgar, coarse

chabola [tʃa'βola] *nf* shack; **~s** *nfpl* shanty town *sg*

chacal [tʃa'kal] *nm* jackal

chacra ['tʃakra] (*AM*) *nf* smallholding

chacha ['tʃatʃa] (*fam*) *nf* maid

cháchara ['tʃatʃara] *nf* chatter; **estar de ~** to chatter away

chafar [tʃa'far] *vt* (*aplastar*) to crush; (*arruinar*) to ruin

chal [tʃal] *nm* shawl

chalado, a [tʃa'laðo, a] (*fam*) *adj* crazy

chalé [tʃa'le] (*pl* **~s**) *nm* villa; ≈ detached house

chaleco [tʃa'leko] *nm* waistcoat, vest (*US*); **~ salvavidas** life jacket

chalet [tʃa'le] (*pl* **~s**) *nm* = **chalé**

champán [tʃam'pan] *nm* champagne

champaña [tʃam'paɲa] *nm* = **champán**

champiñón [tʃampi'ɲon] *nm* mushroom

champú [tʃam'pu] (*pl* **champúes, champús**) *nm* shampoo

chamuscar [tʃamus'kar] *vt* to scorch, sear, singe

chance ['tʃanθe] (*AM*) *nm* chance

chancho, a ['tʃantʃo, a] (*AM*) *nm/f* pig

chanchullo [tʃan'tʃuʎo] (*fam*) *nm* fiddle

chandal [tʃan'dal] *nm* tracksuit

chantaje [tʃan'taxe] *nm* blackmail

chapa ['tʃapa] *nf* (*de metal*) plate, sheet; (*de madera*) board, panel; (*AM: AUTO*) number (*BRIT*) o license (*US*) plate

chaparrón [tʃapa'rron] *nm* downpour, cloudburst

chapotear [tʃapote'ar] *vi* to splash about

chapucero, a [tʃapu'θero, a] *adj* rough, crude ♦ *nm/f* bungler

chapurrear [tʃapurre'ar] *vt* (*idioma*) to speak badly

chapuza [tʃa'puθa] *nf* botched job

chapuzón [tʃapu'θon] *nm*: **darse un ~** to go for a dip

chaqueta [tʃa'keta] *nf* jacket

chaquetón [tʃake'ton] *nm* long jacket

charca ['tʃarka] *nf* pond, pool

charco ['tʃarko] *nm* pool, puddle

charcutería [tʃarkute'ria] *nf* (*tienda*) shop selling chiefly pork meat products; (*productos*) cooked pork meats *pl*

charla ['tʃarla] *nf* talk, chat; (*conferencia*) lecture

charlar [tʃar'lar] *vi* to talk, chat

charlatán, ana [tʃarla'tan, ana] *nm/f* chatterbox; (*estafador*) trickster

charol [tʃa'rol] *nm* varnish; (*cuero*) patent leather

chascarrillo [tʃaska'rriʎo] (*fam*) *nm* funny story

chasco ['tʃasko] *nm* (*broma*) trick, joke; (*desengaño*) disappointment

chasis ['tʃasis] *nm inv* chassis

chasquear [tʃaske'ar] *vt* (*látigo*) to crack; (*lengua*) to click; **chasquido** *nm* crack; click

chatarra [tʃa'tarra] *nf* scrap (metal)

chato, a ['tʃato, a] *adj* flat; (*nariz*) snub

chaval, a [tʃa'βal, a] *nm/f* kid, lad/lass

checo(e)slovaco, a [tʃeko(e)slo'βako, a] *adj, nm/f* Czech, Czechoslovak

Checo(e)slovaquia [tʃeko(e)slo'βakja] *nf* Czechoslovakia

cheque ['tʃeke] *nm* cheque (*BRIT*), check (*US*); **~ de viajero** traveller's cheque (*BRIT*), traveler's check (*US*)

chequeo [tʃe'keo] *nm* (*MED*) check-up; (*AUTO*) service

chequera [tʃe'kera] (*AM*) *nf* chequebook (*BRIT*), checkbook (*US*)

chicano, a [tʃi'kano, a] *adj, nm/f* Chicano

chicle ['tʃikle] *nm* chewing gum

chico, a ['tʃiko, a] *adj* small, little ♦ *nm/f* (*niño*) child; (*muchacho*) boy/girl

chícharo ['tʃitʃaro] (*AM*) *nm* pea

chichón [tʃi'tʃon] *nm* bump, lump

chiflado, a [tʃi'flaðo, a] *adj* crazy

chiflar [tʃi'flar] *vt* to hiss, boo

chile ['tʃile] *nm* chilli pepper

Chile ['tʃile] *nm* Chile; **chileno, a** *adj, nm/f* Chilean

chillar [tʃi'ʎar] *vi* (*persona*) to yell, scream; (*animal salvaje*) to howl; (*cerdo*) to squeal; (*puerta*) to creak

chillido [tʃi'ʎiðo] *nm* (*de persona*) yell, scream; (*de animal*) howl; (*de frenos*) screech(ing)

chillón, ona [tʃi'ʎon, ona] *adj* (*niño*) noisy; (*color*) loud, gaudy

chimenea [tʃime'nea] *nf* chimney; (*hogar*) fireplace

China ['tʃina] *nf*: **(la)** ~ China

chinche ['tʃintʃe] *nf* (*insecto*) (bed)bug; (*TEC*) drawing pin (*BRIT*), thumbtack (*US*) ♦ *nm/f* nuisance, pest

chincheta [tʃin'tʃeta] *nf* drawing pin (*BRIT*), thumbtack (*US*)

chino, a ['tʃino, a] *adj, nm/f* Chinese ♦ *nm* (*LING*) Chinese

chipirón [tʃipi'ron] *nm* (*ZOOL, CULIN*) squid

Chipre ['tʃipre] *nf* Cyprus; **chipriota** *adj, nm/f* Cypriot

chiquillo, a [tʃi'kiʎo, a] *nm/f* (*fam*) kid

chiringuito [tʃirin'ɣito] *nm* small open-air bar

chiripa [tʃi'ripa] *nf* fluke

chirriar [tʃi'rrjar] *vi* (*goznes etc*) to creak, squeak; (*pájaros*) to chirp, sing

chirrido [tʃi'rriðo] *nm* creak(ing), squeak(ing); (*de pájaro*) chirp(ing)

chis [tʃis] *excl* sh!

chisme ['tʃisme] *nm* (*habladurías*) piece of gossip; (*fam: objeto*) thingummyjig

chismoso, a [tʃis'moso, a] *adj* gossiping ♦ *nm/f* gossip

chispa ['tʃispa] *nf* spark; (*fig*) sparkle; (*ingenio*) wit; (*fam*) drunkenness

chispear [tʃispe'ar] *vi* to spark; (*lloviznar*) to drizzle

chisporrotear [tʃisporrote'ar] *vi* (*fuego*) to throw out sparks; (*leña*) to crackle; (*aceite*) to hiss, splutter

chiste ['tʃiste] *nm* joke, funny story

chistoso, a [tʃis'toso, a] *adj* (*gracioso*) funny, amusing; (*bromista*) witty

chivo, a ['tʃiβo, a] *nm/f* (billy-/nanny-)goat; ~ **expiatorio** scapegoat

chocante [tʃo'kante] *adj* startling; (*extraño*) odd; (*ofensivo*) shocking

chocar [tʃo'kar] *vi* (*coches etc*) to collide, crash ♦ *vt* to shock; (*sorprender*) to startle; ~ **con** to collide with; (*fig*) to run into, run up against; **¡chócala!** (*fam*) put it there!

chocolate [tʃoko'late] *adj, nm* chocolate; **chocolatina** *nf* chocolate

chochear [tʃotʃe'ar] *vi* to dodder, be senile

chocho, a ['tʃotʃo, a] *adj* doddering, senile; (*fig*) soft, doting

chofer [tʃo'fer] *nm* = **chófer**

chófer ['tʃofer] *nm* driver

chollo [tʃoʎo] (*fam*) *nm* bargain, snip

choque *etc* ['tʃoke] *vb ver* **chocar** ♦ *nm* (*impacto*) impact; (*golpe*) jolt; (*AUTO*) crash; (*fig*) conflict; ~ **frontal** head-on collision

chorizo [tʃo'riθo] *nm* hard pork sausage, (type of) salami

chorrear [tʃorre'ar] *vi* to gush (out), spout (out); (*gotear*) to drip, trickle

chorro ['tʃorro] *nm* jet; (*fig*) stream

choza ['tʃoθa] *nf* hut, shack

chubasco [tʃu'βasko] *nm* squall

chubasquero [tʃuβas'kero] *nm* lightweight raincoat

chuchería [tʃutʃe'ria] *nf* trinket

chuleta [tʃu'leta] *nf* chop, cutlet

chulo ['tʃulo] *nm* (*pícaro*) rascal; (*rufián*) pimp

chupar [tʃu'par] *vt* to suck; (*absorber*) to absorb; ~**se** *vr* to grow thin

chupete [tʃu'pete] *nm* dummy (*BRIT*), pacifier (*US*)

churro, a ['tʃurro, a] *adj* coarse ♦ *nm* (type of) fritter

chusma ['tʃusma] *nf* rabble, mob

chutar [tʃu'tar] *vi* (*DEPORTE*) to shoot (at goal)

D d

D. *abr* (= *Don*) Esq.

Da. *abr* = **Doña**

dádiva ['daðiβa] *nf* (*donación*) donation; (*regalo*) gift; **dadivoso, a** *adj* generous

dado, a ['daðo, a] *pp de* **dar** ♦ *nm* die; ~**s** *nmpl* dice; ~ **que** given that

daltónico, a [dal'toniko, a] *adj* colour-blind

dama ['dama] *nf* (*gen*) lady; (*AJEDREZ*) queen; ~**s** *nfpl* (*juego*) draughts *sg*

damnificar [damnifi'kar] *vt* to harm; (*persona*) to injure

danés, esa [da'nes, esa] *adj* Danish ♦ *nm/f* Dane

danzar [dan'θar] *vt, vi* to dance

dañar [da'ɲar] *vt* (*objeto*) to damage; (*persona*) to hurt; ~**se** *vr* (*objeto*) to get damaged

dañino, a [da'ɲino, a] *adj* harmful

daño ['daɲo] *nm* (*a un objeto*) damage; (*a una persona*) harm, injury; ~**s y perjuicios** (*JUR*) damages; **hacer** ~ **a** to damage; (*persona*) to hurt, injure; **hacerse** ~ to hurt o.s.

── PALABRA CLAVE

dar [dar] *vt* **1** (*gen*) to give; (*obra de teatro*) to put on; (*film*) to show; (*fiesta*) to hold; ~ **algo a uno** to give sb sth o sth to sb; ~ **de beber a uno** to give sb a drink

2 (*producir: intereses*) to yield; (*fruta*) to produce

3 (*locuciones* + *n*): **da gusto escucharle** it's

a pleasure to listen to him; *ver tb paseo y otros sustantivos*

4 (*+ n:* = *perifrasis de verbo*): **me da pena/asco** it frightens/sickens me

5 (*considerar*): ~ **algo por descontado/ entendido** to take sth for granted/as read; ~ **algo por concluido** to consider sth finished

6 (*hora*): **el reloj dio las 6** the clock struck 6 (o'clock)

7: me da lo mismo it's all the same to me; *ver tb igual, más*

♦ *vi* **1:** ~ **con: dimos con él dos horas más tarde** we came across him two hours later; **al final di con la solución** I eventually came up with the answer

2: ~ **en:** ~ **en** (*blanco, suelo*) to hit; **el sol me da en la cara** the sun is shining (right) on my face

3: ~ **de sí** (*zapatos etc*) to stretch, give

♦ ~**se** *vr* **1:** ~**se por vencido** to give up

2 (*ocurrir*): **se han dado muchos casos** there have been a lot of cases

3: ~**se a: se ha dado a la bebida** he's taken to drinking

4: se me dan bien/mal las ciencias I'm good/bad at science

5: dárselas de: se las da de experto he fancies himself *o* poses as an expert

dardo ['darðo] *nm* dart
dársena ['darsena] *nf* dock
datar [da'tar] *vi:* ~ **de** to date from
dátil ['datil] *nm* date
dato ['dato] *nm* fact, piece of information
DC *abbr m* (= *disco compacto*) CD
dcha. *abr* (= *derecha*) r.h.
d. de J.C. *abr* (= *después de Jesucristo*) A.D.

── PALABRA CLAVE ──

de [de] *prep* (*de+ el* = *del*) **1** (*posesión*): of; **la casa** ~ **Isabel/mis padres** Isabel's/my parents' house; **es** ~ **ellos** it's theirs

2 (*origen, distancia, con números*) from; **soy** ~ **Gijón** I'm from Gijón; ~ **8 a 20** from 8 to 20; **salir del cine** to go out of *o* leave the cinema; ~ **... en ...** from ... to ...; ~ **2 en 2** 2 by 2, 2 at a time

3 (*valor descriptivo*): **una copa** ~ **vino** a glass of wine; **la mesa** ~ **la cocina** the kitchen table; **un billete** ~ **1000 pesetas** a 1000 peseta note; **un niño** ~ **tres años** a three-year-old (child); **una máquina** ~ **coser** a sewing machine; **ir vestido** ~ **gris** to be dressed in grey; **la niña del vestido azul** the girl in the blue dress; **trabaja** ~ **profesora** she works as a teacher; ~ **lado** sideways; ~ **atrás/delante** rear/front

4 (*hora, tiempo*): **a las 8** ~ **la mañana** at 8 o'clock in the morning; ~ **día/noche** by

day/night; ~ **hoy en ocho días** a week from now; ~ **niño era gordo** as a child he was fat

5 (*comparaciones*): **más/menos** ~ **cien personas** more/less than a hundred people; **el más caro** ~ **la tienda** the most expensive in the shop; **menos/más** ~ **lo pensado** less/more than expected

6 (*causa*): **del calor** from the heat; ~ **puro tonto** out of sheer stupidity

7 (*tema*): about; **clases** ~ **inglés** English classes; **¿sabes algo** ~ **él?** do you know anything about him?; **un libro** ~ **física** a physics book

8 (*adj + de + infin*): **fácil** ~ **entender** easy to understand

9 (*oraciones pasivas*): **fue respetado** ~ **todos** he was loved by all

10 (*condicional + infin*) if; ~ **ser posible** if possible; ~ **no terminarlo hoy** if I *etc* don't finish it today

dé *vb ver* **dar**
deambular [deambu'lar] *vi* to stroll, wander
debajo [de'βaxo] *adv* underneath; ~ **de** below, under; **por** ~ **de** beneath
debate [de'βate] *nm* debate; **debatir** *vt* to debate
deber [de'βer] *nm* duty ♦ *vt* to owe ♦ *vi:* **debe (de)** it must, it should; ~**es** *nmpl* (*ESCOL*) homework; **debo hacerlo** I must do it; **debe de ir** he should go; ~**se** *vr:* ~**se a** to be owing *o* due to
debido, a [de'βiðo, a] *adj* proper, just; ~ **a** due to, because of
débil ['deβil] *adj* (*persona, carácter*) weak; (*luz*) dim; **debilidad** *nf* weakness; dimness
debilitar [deβili'tar] *vt* to weaken; ~**se** *vr* to grow weak
debutar [deβu'tar] *vi* to make one's debut
década ['dekaða] *nf* decade
decadencia [deka'ðenθja] *nf* (*estado*) decadence; (*proceso*) decline, decay
decaer [deka'er] *vi* (*declinar*) to decline; (*debilitarse*) to weaken
decaído, a [deka'iðo, a] *adj:* **estar** ~ (*abatido*) to be down
decaimiento [dekai'mjento] *nm* (*declinación*) decline; (*desaliento*) discouragement; (*MED: estado débil*) weakness
decano, a [de'kano, a] *nm/f* (*de universidad etc*) dean
decapitar [dekapi'tar] *vt* to behead
decena [de'θena] *nf:* **una** ~ ten (or so)
decencia [de'θenθja] *nf* (*modestia*) modesty; (*honestidad*) respectability
decente [de'θente] *adj* (*correcto*) seemly, proper; (*honesto*) respectable
decepción [deθep'θjon] *nf* disappointment
decepcionar [deθepθjo'nar] *vt* to disappoint

decidir [deθi'ðir] vt (*persuadir*) to convince, persuade; (*resolver*) to decide ♦ vi to decide; ~se vr: ~se a to make up one's mind to

décimo, a ['deθimo, a] adj tenth ♦ nm tenth

decir [de'θir] vt (*expresar*) to say; (*contar*) to tell; (*hablar*) to speak ♦ nm saying; ~se vr: se dice que it is said that; ~ para o entre sí to say to o.s.; querer ~ to mean; ¡dígame! (*TEL*) hello!; (*en tienda*) can I help you?

decisión [deθi'sjon] nf (*resolución*) decision; (*firmeza*) decisiveness

decisivo, a [deθi'siβo, a] adj decisive

declamar [dekla'mar] vt, vi to declaim

declaración [deklara'θjon] nf (*manifestación*) statement; (*explicación*) explanation; ~ de ingresos o de la renta o fiscal income-tax return

declarar [dekla'rar] vt to declare ♦ vi to declare; (*JUR*) to testify; ~se vr to propose

declinar [dekli'nar] vt (*gen*) to decline; (*JUR*) to reject ♦ vi (*el día*) to draw to a close

declive [de'kliβe] nm (*cuesta*) slope; (*fig*) decline

decodificador [dekoðifika'ðor] nm decoder

decolorarse [dekolo'rarse] vr to become discoloured

decoración [dekora'θjon] nf decoration

decorado [deko'raðo] nm (*CINE, TEATRO*) scenery, set

decorar [deko'rar] vt to decorate; **decorativo, a** adj ornamental, decorative

decoro [de'koro] nm (*respeto*) respect; (*dignidad*) decency; (*recato*) propriety; ~so, a adj (*decente*) decent; (*modesto*) modest; (*digno*) proper

decrecer [dekre'θer] vi to decrease, diminish

decrépito, a [de'krepito, a] adj decrepit

decretar [dekre'tar] vt to decree; **decreto** nm decree

dedal [de'ðal] nm thimble

dedicación [deðika'θjon] nf dedication

dedicar [deði'kar] vt (*libro*) to dedicate; (*tiempo, dinero*) to devote; (*palabras: decir, consagrar*) to dedicate, devote; **dedicatoria** nf (*de libro*) dedication

dedo ['deðo] nm finger; ~ (**del pie**) toe; ~ pulgar thumb; ~ índice index finger; ~ mayor o cordial middle finger; ~ anular ring finger; ~ meñique little finger; hacer ~ (*fam*) to hitch (a lift)

deducción [deðuk'θjon] nf deduction

deducir [deðu'θir] vt (*concluir*) to deduce, infer; (*COM*) to deduct

defecto [de'fekto] nm defect, flaw; **defectuoso, a** adj defective, faulty

defender [defen'der] vt to defend

defensa [de'fensa] nf defence ♦ nm (*DE-*

PORTE*) defender, back; **defensiva nf: a la ~ on the defensive; **defensivo, a** adj defensive

defensor, a [defen'sor, a] adj defending ♦ nm/f (*abogado* ~) defending counsel; (*protector*) protector

deficiencia [defi'θjenθja] nf deficiency

deficiente [defi'θjente] adj (*defectuoso*) defective; ~ en lacking o deficient in; ser un ~ mental to be mentally handicapped

déficit ['defiθit] (*pl* ~s) nm deficit

definición [defini'θjon] nf definition

definir [defi'nir] vt (*determinar*) to determine, establish; (*decidir*) to define; (*aclarar*) to clarify; **definitivo, a** adj definitive; **en definitiva** definitively; (*en resumen*) in short

deformación [deforma'θjon] nf (*alteración*) deformation; (*RADIO etc*) distortion

deformar [defor'mar] vt (*gen*) to deform; ~se vr to become deformed; **deforme** adj (*informe*) deformed; (*feo*) ugly; (*malhecho*) misshapen

defraudar [defrau'ðar] vt (*decepcionar*) to disappoint; (*estafar*) to cheat; to defraud

defunción [defun'θjon] nf death, demise

degeneración [dexenera'θjon] nf (*de las células*) degeneration; (*moral*) degeneracy

degenerar [dexene'rar] vi to degenerate

degollar [dexo'ʎar] vt to behead; (*fig*) to slaughter

degradar [deɣra'ðar] vt to debase, degrade; ~se vr to demean o.s

degustación [deɣusta'θjon] nf sampling, tasting

deificar [deifi'kar] vt (*persona*) to deify

dejadez [dexa'ðeθ] nf (*negligencia*) neglect; (*descuido*) untidiness, carelessness

dejar [de'xar] vt to leave; (*permitir*) to allow, let; (*abandonar*) to abandon, forsake; (*beneficios*) to produce, yield ♦ vi: ~ de (*parar*) to stop; (*no hacer*) to fail to; **no dejes de comprar un billete** make sure you buy a ticket; ~ a un lado to leave o set aside

dejo ['dexo] nm (*LING*) accent

del [del] (= **de** + **el**) ver **de**

delantal [delan'tal] nm apron

delante [de'lante] adv in front, (*enfrente*) opposite; (*adelante*) ahead; ~ de in front of, before

delantera [delan'tera] nf (*de vestido, casa etc*) front part; (*DEPORTE*) forward line; **llevar la ~ (a uno)** to be ahead (of sb)

delantero, a [delan'tero, a] adj front ♦ nm (*DEPORTE*) forward, striker

delatar [dela'tar] vt to inform on o against, betray; **delator, a** nm/f informer

delegación [deleɣa'θjon] nf (*acción, delegados*) delegation; (*COM: oficina*) office, branch; ~ de policía police station

delegado, a [dele'ɣaðo, a] nm/f delegate;

(COM) agent

delegar [dele'ɣar] vt to delegate

deletrear [deletre'ar] vt to spell (out)

deleznable [deleθ'naβle] adj brittle; (excusa, idea) feeble

delfín [del'fin] nm dolphin

delgadez [delɣa'ðeθ] nf thinness, slimness

delgado, a [del'ɣaðo, a] adj thin; (persona) slim, thin; (tierra) poor; (tela etc) light, delicate

deliberación [deliβera'θjon] nf deliberation

deliberar [deliβe'rar] vt to debate, discuss

delicadeza [delika'ðeθa] nf (gen) delicacy; (refinamiento, sutileza) refinement

delicado, a [deli'kaðo, a] adj (gen) delicate; (sensible) sensitive; (quisquilloso) touchy

delicia [de'liθja] nf delight

delicioso, a [deli'θjoso, a] adj (gracioso) delightful; (exquisito) delicious

delimitar [delimi'tar] vt (funciones, responsabilidades) to define

delincuencia [delin'kwenθja] nf delinquency; **delincuente** nm/f delinquent; (criminal) criminal

delineante [deline'ante] nm/f draughtsman/woman

delinear [deline'ar] vt (dibujo) to draw; (fig, contornos) to outline

delinquir [delin'kir] vi to commit an offence

delirante [deli'rante] adj delirious

delirar [deli'rar] vi to be delirious, rave

delirio [de'lirjo] nm (MED) delirium; (palabras insensatas) ravings pl

delito [de'lito] nm (gen) crime; (infracción) offence

delta ['delta] nm delta

demacrado, a [dema'kraðo, a] adj: **estar ~** to look pale and drawn, be wasted away

demagogo, a [dema'ɣoɣo, a] nm/f demagogue

demanda [de'manda] nf (pedido, COM) demand; (petición) request; (JUR) action, lawsuit

demandante [deman'dante] nm/f claimant

demandar [deman'dar] vt (gen) to demand; (JUR) to sue, file a lawsuit against

demarcación [demarka'θjon] nf (de terreno) demarcation

demás [de'mas] adj: **los ~ niños** the other children, the remaining children ♦ pron: **los/las ~** the others, the rest (of them); **lo ~** the rest (of it)

demasía [dema'sia] nf (exceso) excess, surplus; **comer en ~** to eat to excess

demasiado, a [dema'sjaðo, a] adj: **~ vino** too much wine; **~s libros** too many books ♦ adv (antes de adj, adv) too; **¡esto es ~!** that's the limit!; **hace ~ calor** it's too hot; **~ despacio** too slowly; **~s** too many

demencia [de'menθja] nf (locura) madness;

demente nm/f lunatic ♦ adj mad, insane

democracia [demo'kraθja] nf democracy

demócrata [de'mokrata] nm/f democrat; **democrático, a** adj democratic

demoler [demo'ler] vt to demolish; **demolición** nf demolition

demonio [de'monjo] nm devil, demon; **¡~s!** hell!, damn!; **¿cómo ~s?** how the hell?

demora [de'mora] nf delay; **demorar** vt (retardar) to delay, hold back; (detener) to hold up ♦ vi to linger, stay on; **~se** vr to be delayed

demos vb ver **dar**

demostración [demostra'θjon] nf (MAT) proof; (de afecto) show, display

demostrar [demos'trar] vt (probar) to prove; (mostrar) to show; (manifestar) to demonstrate

demudado, a [demu'ðaðo, a] adj (rostro) pale

den vb ver **dar**

denegar [dene'ɣar] vt (rechazar) to refuse; (JUR) to reject

denigrar [deni'ɣrar] vt (desacreditar, infamar) to denigrate; (injuriar) to insult

denominación [denomina'θjon] nf (clase) denomination

denotar [deno'tar] vt (indicar) to indicate; (significar) to denote

densidad [densi'ðað] nf (FÍSICA) density; (fig) thickness

denso, a ['denso, a] adj (apretado) solid; (espeso, pastoso) thick; (fig) heavy

dentadura [denta'ðura] nf (set of) teeth pl; **~ postiza** false teeth pl

dentera [den'tera] nf (sensación desagradable) the shivers pl

dentífrico, a [den'tifriko, a] adj dental ♦ nm toothpaste

dentista [den'tista] nm/f dentist

dentro ['dentro] adv inside ♦ prep: **~ de** in, inside, within; **por ~** (on the) inside; **mirar por ~** to look inside; **~ de tres meses** within three months

denuncia [de'nunθja] nf (delación) denunciation; (acusación) accusation; (de accidente) report; **denunciar** vt to report; (delatar) to inform on o against

departamento [departa'mento] nm (sección administrativa) department, section; (AM: apartamento) flat (BRIT), apartment

dependencia [depen'denθja] nf dependence; (POL) dependency; (COM) office, section

depender [depen'der] vi: **~ de** to depend on

dependienta [depen'djenta] nf saleswoman, shop assistant

dependiente [depen'djente] adj dependent ♦ nm salesman, shop assistant

depilar [depi'lar] vt (con cera) to wax; (ce-

jas) to pluck; **depilatorio** *nm* hair remover
deplorable [deplo'raßle] *adj* deplorable
deplorar [deplo'rar] *vt* to deplore
deponer [depo'ner] *vt* to lay down ♦ *vi*
(*JUR*) to give evidence; (*declarar*) to make a
statement
deportar [depor'tar] *vt* to deport
deporte [de'porte] *nm* sport; **hacer ~** to
play sports; **deportista** *adj* sports *cpd* ♦
nm/f sportsman/woman; **deportivo, a** *adj*
(*club, periódico*) sports *cpd* ♦ *nm* sports car
depositante [deposi'tante] *nm/f* depositor
depositar [deposi'tar] *vt* (*dinero*) to deposit; (*mercancías*) to put away, store; (*persona*) to confide; **~se** *vr* to settle; **~io, a**
nm/f trustee
depósito [de'posito] *nm* (*gen*) deposit; (*almacén*) warehouse, store; (*de agua, gasolina
etc*) tank; **~ de cadáveres** mortuary
depreciar [depre'θjar] *vt* to depreciate, reduce the value of; **~se** *vr* to depreciate,
lose value
depredador, a [depreða'ðor, a] *adj* predatory ♦ *nm* predator
depresión [depre'sjon] *nf* depression
deprimido, a [depri'miðo, a] *adj* depressed
deprimir [depri'mir] *vt* to depress; **~se** *vr*
(*persona*) to become depressed
deprisa [de'prisa] *adv* quickly, hurriedly
depuración [depura'θjon] *nf* purification;
(*POL*) purge
depurar [depu'rar] *vt* to purify; (*purgar*) to
purge
derecha [de'retʃa] *nf* right(-hand) side;
(*POL*) right; **a la ~** (*estar*) on the right; (*torcer etc*) (to the) right
derecho, a [de'retʃo, a] *adj* right, right-
hand ♦ *nm* (*privilegio*) right; (*lado*) right(-
hand) side; (*leyes*) law ♦ *adv* straight, directly; **~s** *nmpl* (*de aduana*) duty *sg*; (*de
autor*) royalties; **tener ~ a** to have a right
to
deriva [de'rißa] *nf*: **ir** *o* **estar a la ~** to
drift, be adrift
derivado [deri'ßaðo] *nm* (*COM*) by-product
derivar [deri'ßar] *vt* to derive; (*desviar*) to
direct ♦ *vi* to derive, be derived; (*NAUT*) to
drift; **~se** *vr* to derive, be derived; to drift
derramamiento [derrama'mjento] *nm* (*dispersión*) spilling; **~ de sangre** bloodshed
derramar [derra'mar] *vt* to spill; (*verter*) to
pour out; (*esparcir*) to scatter; **~se** *vr* to
pour out; **~ lágrimas** to weep
derrame [de'rrame] *nm* (*de líquido*) spilling; (*de sangre*) shedding; (*de tubo etc*)
overflow; (*pérdida*) leakage; (*MED*) discharge; (*declive*) slope
derredor [derre'ðor] *adv*: **al** *o* **en ~ de**
around, about
derretido, a [derre'tiðo, a] *adj* melted;
(*metal*) molten
derretir [derre'tir] *vt* (*gen*) to melt; (*nieve*)

to thaw; (*fig*) to squander; **~se** *vr* to melt
derribar [derri'ßar] *vt* to knock down;
(*construcción*) to demolish; (*persona, gobierno, político*) to bring down
derrocar [derro'kar] *vt* (*gobierno*) to bring
down, overthrow
derrochar [derro'tʃar] *vt* to squander; **derroche** *nm* (*despilfarro*) waste, squandering
derrota [de'rrota] *nf* (*NAUT*) course; (*MIL,
DEPORTE etc*) defeat, rout; **derrotar** *vt*
(*gen*) to defeat; **derrotero** *nm* (*rumbo*)
course
derruir [derru'ir] *vt* (*edificio*) to demolish
derrumbar [derrum'bar] *vt* (*edificio*) to
knock down; **~se** *vr* to collapse
derruyendo *etc vb ver* **derruir**
des *vb ver* **dar**
desabotonar [desaßoto'nar] *vt* to unbutton, undo ♦ *vi* (*flores*) to bloom; **~se** *vr* to
come undone
desabrido, a [desa'ßriðo, a] *adj* (*comida*)
insipid, tasteless; (*persona*) rude, surly; (*respuesta*) sharp; (*tiempo*) unpleasant
desabrochar [desaßro'tʃar] *vt* (*botones,
broches*) to undo, unfasten; **~se** *vr* (*ropa
etc*) to come undone
desacato [desa'kato] *nm* (*falta de respeto*)
disrespect; (*JUR*) contempt
desacertado, a [desaθer'taðo, a] *adj* (*equivocado*) mistaken; (*inoportuno*) unwise
desacierto [desa'θjerto] *nm* mistake, error
desaconsejado, a [desakonse'xaðo, a] *adj*
ill-advised
desaconsejar [desakonse'xar] *vt* to advise
against
desacreditar [desakreði'tar] *vt* (*desprestigiar*) to discredit, bring into disrepute;
(*denigrar*) to run down
desacuerdo [desa'kwerðo] *nm* (*conflicto*)
disagreement, discord; (*error*) error, blunder
desafiar [desa'fjar] *vt* (*retar*) to challenge;
(*enfrentarse a*) to defy
desafilado, a [desafi'laðo, a] *adj* blunt
desafinado, a [desafi'naðo, a] *adj*: **estar ~**
to be out of tune
desafinar [desafi'nar] *vi* (*al cantar*) to be *o*
go out of tune
desafío *etc* [desa'fio] *vb ver* **desafiar** ♦ *nm*
(*reto*) challenge; (*combate*) duel; (*resistencia*) defiance
desaforado, a [desafo'raðo, a] *adj* (*grito*)
ear-splitting; (*comportamiento*) outrageous
desafortunadamente [desafortunaða-
'mente] *adv* unfortunately
desafortunado, a [desafortu'naðo, a] *adj*
(*desgraciado*) unfortunate, unlucky
desagradable [desaɣra'ðaßle] *adj* (*fastidioso, enojoso*) unpleasant; (*irritante*) disagreeable
desagradar [desaɣra'ðar] *vi* (*disgustar*) to
displease; (*molestar*) to bother
desagradecido, a [desaɣraðe'θiðo, a] *adj*

ungrateful

desagrado [desa'ɣɾaðo] nm (disgusto) displeasure; (contrariedad) dissatisfaction

desagraviar [desaɣɾa'βjar] vt to make amends to

desagüe [des'aɣwe] nm (de un líquido) drainage; (cañería) drainpipe; (salida) outlet, drain

desaguisado, a [desaɣi'saðo, a] adj illegal ♦ nm outrage

desahogado, a [desao'ɣaðo, a] adj (holgado) comfortable; (espacioso) roomy, large

desahogar [desao'ɣar] vt (aliviar) to ease, relieve; (ira) to vent; ~se vr (relajarse) to relax; (desfogarse) to let off steam

desahogo [desa'oɣo] nm (alivio) relief; (comodidad) comfort, ease

desahuciar [desau'θjar] vt (enfermo) to give up hope for; (inquilino) to evict; **desahucio** nm eviction

desairar [desai'rar] vt (menospreciar) to slight, snub; (cosa) to disregard

desaire [des'aire] nm (menosprecio) slight; (falta de garbo) unattractiveness

desajustar [desaxus'tar] vt (desarreglar) to disarrange; (desconcertar) to throw off balance; ~se vr to get out of order; (aflojarse) to loosen

desajuste [desa'xuste] nm (de máquina) disorder; (situación) imbalance

desalentador, a [desalenta'ðor, a] adj discouraging

desalentar [desalen'tar] vt (desanimar) to discourage

desaliento etc [desa'ljento] vb ver **desalentar** ♦ nm discouragement

desaliño [desa'liɲo] nm (negligencia) slovenliness

desalmado, a [desal'maðo, a] adj (cruel) cruel, heartless

desalojar [desalo'xar] vt (expulsar, echar) to eject; (abandonar) to move out of ♦ vi to move out

desamor [desa'mor] nm (frialdad) indifference; (odio) dislike

desamparado, a [desampa'raðo, a] adj (persona) helpless; (lugar: expuesto) exposed; (desierto) deserted

desamparar [desampa'rar] vt (abandonar) to desert, abandon; (JUR) to leave defenceless; (barco) to abandon

desandar [desan'dar] vt: ~ lo andado o el camino to retrace one's steps

desangrar [desan'grar] vt to bleed; (fig: persona) to bleed dry; ~se vr to lose a lot of blood

desanimado, a [desani'maðo, a] adj (persona) downhearted; (espectáculo, fiesta) dull

desanimar [desani'mar] vt (desalentar) to discourage; (deprimir) to depress; ~se vr to lose heart

desapacible [desapa'θiβle] adj (gen) unpleasant

desaparecer [desapare'θer] vi (gen) to disappear; (el sol, la luz) to vanish; **desaparecido, a** adj missing; **desaparecidos** nmpl (en accidente) people missing; **desaparición** nf disappearance

desapasionado, a [desapasjo'naðo, a] adj dispassionate, impartial

desapego [desa'peɣo] nm (frialdad) coolness; (distancia) detachment

desapercibido, a [desaperθi'βiðo, a] adj (desprevenido) unprepared; **pasar** ~ to go unnoticed

desaprensivo, a [desapren'siβo, a] adj unscrupulous

desaprobar [desapro'βar] vt (reprobar) to disapprove of; (condenar) to condemn; (no consentir) to reject

desaprovechado, a [desaproβe'tʃaðo, a] adj (oportunidad, tiempo) wasted; (estudiante) slack

desaprovechar [desaproβe'tʃar] vt to waste

desarmar [desar'mar] vt (MIL, fig) to disarm; (TEC) to take apart, dismantle; **desarme** nm disarmament

desarraigar [desarrai'ɣar] vt to uproot; **desarraigo** nm uprooting

desarreglar [desarre'ɣlar] vt (desordenar) to disarrange; (trastocar) to upset, disturb

desarreglo [desa'rreɣlo] nm (de casa, persona) untidiness; (desorden) disorder

desarrollar [desarro'ʎar] vt (gen) to develop; (extender) to unfold; ~se vr to develop; (extenderse) to open (out); (FOTO) to develop; **desarrollo** nm development

desarticular [desartiku'lar] vt (hueso) to dislocate; (objeto) to take apart; (fig) to break up

desasir [desa'sir] vt to loosen; ~se vr to extricate o.s.; ~se de to let go, give up

desasosegar [desasose'ɣar] vt (inquietar) to disturb, make uneasy; ~se vr to become uneasy

desasosiego etc [desaso'sjeɣo] vb ver **desasosegar** ♦ nm (intranquilidad) uneasiness, restlessness; (ansiedad) anxiety

desastrado, a [desas'traðo, a] adj (desaliñado) shabby; (sucio) dirty

desastre [de'sastre] nm disaster; **desastroso, a** adj disastrous

desatado, a [desa'taðo, a] adj (desligado) untied; (violento) violent, wild

desatar [desa'tar] vt (nudo) to untie; (paquete) to undo; (separar) to detach; ~se vr (zapatos) to come untied; (tormenta) to break

desatascar [desatas'kar] vt (cañería) to unblock, clear

desatender [desaten'der] vt (no prestar atención a) to disregard; (abandonar) to neglect

desatento, a [desa'tento, a] adj (distraído) inattentive; (descortés) discourteous

desatinado, a [desati'naðo, a] adj foolish, silly; **desatino** nm (idiotez) foolishness, folly; (error) blunder

desatornillar [desatorni'ʎar] vt to unscrew

desatrancar [desatran'kar] vt (puerta) to unbolt; (cañería) to clear, unblock

desautorizado, a [desautori'θaðo, a] adj unauthorized

desautorizar [desautori'θar] vt (oficial) to deprive of authority; (informe) to deny

desavenencia [desaβe'nenθja] nf (desacuerdo) disagreement; (discrepancia) quarrel

desayunar [desaju'nar] vi to have breakfast ♦ vt to have for breakfast; **desayuno** nm breakfast

desazón [desa'θon] nf (angustia) anxiety; (fig) annoyance

desazonar [desaθo'nar] vt (fig) to annoy, upset; ~**se** vr (enojarse) to be annoyed; (preocuparse) to worry, be anxious

desbandarse [desβan'darse] vr (MIL) to disband; (fig) to flee in disorder

desbarajuste [desβara'xuste] nm confusion, disorder

desbaratar [desβara'tar] vt (deshacer, destruir) to ruin

desbloquear [desβloke'ar] vt (negociaciones, tráfico) to get going again; (COM: cuenta) to unfreeze

desbocado, a [desβo'kaðo, a] adj (caballo) runaway

desbordar [desβor'ðar] vt (sobrepasar) to go beyond; (exceder) to exceed ♦ vi (río) to overflow; (entusiasmo) to erupt; ~**se** vr to overflow; to erupt

descabalgar [deskaβal'ɣar] vi to dismount

descabellado, a [deskaβe'ʎaðo, a] adj (disparatado) wild, crazy

descafeinado, a [deskafei'naðo, a] adj decaffeinated ♦ nm decaffeinated coffee

descalabro [deska'laβro] nm blow; (desgracia) misfortune

descalificar [deskalifi'kar] vt to disqualify; (desacreditar) to discredit

descalzar [deskal'θar] vt (zapato) to take off; **descalzo, a** adj barefoot(ed); (fig) destitute

descambiar [deskam'bjar] vt to exchange

descaminado, a [deskami'naðo, a] adj (equivocado) on the wrong road; (fig) misguided

descampado [deskam'paðo] nm open space

descansado, a [deskan'saðo, a] adj (gen) rested; (que tranquiliza) restful

descansar [deskan'sar] vt (gen) to rest ♦ vi to rest, have a rest; (echarse) to lie down

descansillo [deskan'siʎo] nm (de escalera) landing

descanso [des'kanso] nm (reposo) rest; (alivio) relief; (pausa) break; (DEPORTE) interval, half time

descapotable [deskapo'taβle] nm (tb: coche ~) convertible

descarado, a [deska'raðo, a] adj shameless; (insolente) cheeky

descarga [des'karɣa] nf (ARQ, ELEC, MIL) discharge; (NAUT) unloading

descargar [deskar'ɣar] vt to unload; (golpe) to let fly; ~**se** vr to unburden o.s.; **descargo** nm (COM) receipt; (JUR) evidence

descarnado, a [deskar'naðo, a] adj scrawny; (fig) bare

descaro [des'karo] nm nerve

descarriar [deska'rrjar] vt (descaminar) to misdirect; (fig) to lead astray; ~**se** vr (perderse) to lose one's way; (separarse) to stray; (pervertirse) to err, go astray

descarrilamiento [deskarrila'mjento] nm (de tren) derailment

descarrilar [deskarri'lar] vi to be derailed

descartar [deskar'tar] vt (rechazar) to reject; (eliminar) to rule out; ~**se** vr (NAIPES) to discard; ~**se de** to shirk

descascarillado, a [deskaskari'ʎaðo, a] adj (paredes) peeling

descendencia [desθen'denθja] nf (origen) origin, descent; (hijos) offspring

descender [desθen'der] vt (bajar: escalera) to go down ♦ vi to descend; (temperatura, nivel) to fall, drop; ~ **de** to be descended from

descendiente [desθen'djente] nm/f descendant

descenso [des'θenso] nm descent; (de temperatura) drop

descifrar [desθi'frar] vt to decipher; (mensaje) to decode

descolgar [deskol'ɣar] vt (bajar) to take down; (teléfono) to pick up; ~**se** vr to let o.s. down

descolorido, a [deskolo'riðo, a] adj faded; (pálido) pale

descompasado, a [deskompa'saðo, a] adj (sin proporción) out of all proportion; (excesivo) excessive

descomponer [deskompo'ner] vt (desordenar) to disarrange, disturb; (TEC) to put out of order; (dividir) to break down (into parts); (fig) to provoke; ~**se** vr (corromperse) to rot, decompose; (el tiempo) to change (for the worse); (TEC) to break down

descomposición [deskomposi'θjon] nf (gen) breakdown; (de fruta etc) decomposition; ~ **de vientre** stomach upset, diarrhoea

descompostura [deskompos'tura] nf (TEC) breakdown; (desorganización) disorganization; (desorden) untidiness

descompuesto, a [deskom'pwesto, a] *adj*
(*corrompido*) decomposed; (*roto*) broken
descomunal [deskomu'nal] *adj* (*enorme*)
huge
desconcertado, a [deskonθer'taðo, a] *adj*
disconcerted, bewildered
desconcertar [deskonθer'tar] *vt* (*confundir*)
to baffle; (*incomodar*) to upset, put out;
~**se** *vr* (*turbarse*) to be upset
desconcierto *etc* [deskon'θjerto] *vb ver*
desconcertar ♦ *nm* (*gen*) disorder; (*desorientación*) uncertainty; (*inquietud*) uneasiness
desconchado, a [deskon'tʃaðo, a] *adj*
(*pintura*) peeling
desconectar [deskonek'tar] *vt* to disconnect
desconfianza [deskon'fjanθa] *nf* distrust
desconfiar [deskon'fjar] *vi* to be distrustful;
~ **de** to distrust, suspect
descongelar [deskonxe'lar] *vt* to defrost;
(*COM, POL*) to unfreeze
descongestionar [deskonxestjo'nar] *vt* (*cabeza, tráfico*) to clear
desconocer [deskono'θer] *vt* (*ignorar*) not
to know, be ignorant of; (*no aceptar*) to
deny; (*repudiar*) to disown
desconocido, a [deskono'θiðo, a] *adj* unknown ♦ *nm/f* stranger
desconocimiento [deskonoθi'mjento] *nm*
(*falta de conocimientos*) ignorance; (*repudio*)
disregard
desconsiderado, a [deskonsiðe'raðo, a]
adj inconsiderate; (*insensible*) thoughtless
desconsolar [deskonso'lar] *vt* to distress;
~**se** *vr* to despair
desconsuelo *etc* [deskon'swelo] *vb ver*
desconsolar ♦ *nm* (*tristeza*) distress; (*desesperación*) despair
descontado, a [deskon'taðo, a] *adj*: **dar
por** ~ (**que**) to take (it) for granted (that)
descontar [deskon'tar] *vt* (*deducir*) to take
away, deduct; (*rebajar*) to discount
descontento, a [deskon'tento, a] *adj* dis-
satisfied ♦ *nm* dissatisfaction, discontent
descorazonar [deskoraθo'nar] *vt* to discourage, dishearten
descorchar [deskor'tʃar] *vt* to uncork
descorrer [desko'rrer] *vt* (*cortinas, cerrojo*)
to draw back
descortés [deskor'tes] *adj* (*mal educado*)
discourteous; (*grosero*) rude
descoser [desko'ser] *vt* to unstitch; ~**se** *vr*
to come apart (at the seams)
descosido, a [desko'siðo, a] *adj* (*COS-
TURA*) unstitched; (*desordenado*) disjointed
descrédito [des'kreðito] *nm* discredit
descreído, a [deskre'iðo, a] *adj* (*incrédulo*)
incredulous; (*falto de fe*) unbelieving
descremado, a [deskre'maðo, a] *adj*
skimmed
describir [deskri'βir] *vt* to describe; **des-**

cripción [deskrip'θjon] *nf* description
descrito [des'krito] *pp de* **describir**
descuartizar [deskwarti'θar] *vt* (*animal*) to
cut up
descubierto, a [desku'βjerto, a] *pp de*
descubrir ♦ *adj* uncovered, bare; (*persona*)
bareheaded ♦ *nm* (*bancario*) overdraft; **al** ~
in the open
descubrimiento [deskuβri'mjento] *nm*
(*hallazgo*) discovery; (*revelación*) revelation
descubrir [desku'βrir] *vt* to discover, find;
(*inaugurar*) to unveil; (*vislumbrar*) to detect;
(*revelar*) to reveal, show; (*destapar*) to uncover; ~**se** *vr* to reveal o.s.; (*quitarse sombrero*) to take off one's hat; (*confesar*) to
confess
descuento *etc* [des'kwento] *vb ver* **descontar** ♦ *nm* discount
descuidado, a [deskwi'ðaðo, a] *adj* (*sin
cuidado*) careless; (*desordenado*) untidy; (*olvidadizo*) forgetful; (*dejado*) neglected; (*desprevenido*) unprepared
descuidar [deskwi'ðar] *vt* (*dejar*) to neglect;
(*olvidar*) to overlook ♦ *vi* (*distraerse*) to be
careless; (*estar desaliñado*) to let o.s. go;
(*desprevenirse*) to drop one's guard; ~**se** *vr*
to be careless; (*no let o.s. go*; to drop one's
guard; **¡descuida!** don't worry!; **descuido**
nm (*dejadez*) carelessness; (*olvido*) negligence

―――――― PALABRA CLAVE

desde ['desðe] *prep* **1** (*lugar*) from; ~ **Burgos hasta mi casa hay 30 km** it's 30 kms
from Burgos to my house
2 (*posición*): **hablaba** ~ **el balcón** she was
speaking from the balcony
3 (*tiempo: + ad, n*): ~ **ahora** from now on;
~ **la boda** since the wedding; ~ **niño** since
I *etc* was a child; ~ **3 años atrás** since 3
years ago
4 (*tiempo: + vb*) since; for; **nos conocemos**
~ **1978/** ~ **hace 20 años** we've known
each other since 1978/for 20 years; **no le
veo** ~ **1983/**~ **hace 5 años** I haven't seen
him since 1983/for 5 years
5 (*gama*): ~ **los más lujosos hasta los
más económicos** from the most luxurious
to the most reasonably priced
6: ~ **luego (que no)** of course (not)
♦ *conj*: ~ **que**: ~ **que recuerdo** for as long
as I can remember; ~ **que llegó no ha salido** he hasn't been out since he arrived

desdecirse [desðe'θirse] *vr* to retract; ~ **de**
to go back on
desdén [des'ðen] *nm* scorn
desdeñar [desðe'ɲar] *vt* (*despreciar*) to
scorn
desdicha [des'ðitʃa] *nf* (*desgracia*) misfortune; (*infelicidad*) unhappiness; **desdicha-**

do, a adj (*sin suerte*) unlucky; (*infeliz*) unhappy

desdoblar [desðo'ßlar] vt (*extender*) to spread out; (*desplegar*) to unfold

desear [dese'ar] vt to want, desire, wish for

desecar [dese'kar] vt to dry up; ~**se** vr to dry up

desechar [dese't∫ar] vt (*basura*) to throw out o away; (*ideas*) to reject, discard; **desechos** nmpl rubbish sg, waste sg

desembalar [desemba'lar] vt to unpack

desembarazado, a [desembara'θaðo, a] adj (*libre*) clear, free; (*desenvuelto*) free and easy

desembarazar [desembara'θar] vt (*desocupar*) to clear; (*desenredar*) to free; ~**se** vr: ~**se de** to free o.s. of, get rid of

desembarcar [desembar'kar] vt (*mercancías etc*) to unload ♦ vi to disembark; ~**se** vr to disembark

desembocadura [desemboka'ðura] nf (*de río*) mouth; (*de calle*) opening

desembocar [desembo'kar] vi to flow into; (*fig*) to result in

desembolso [desem'bolso] nm payment

desembragar [desembra'var] vi to declutch

desembrollar [desembro'ʎar] vt (*madeja*) to unravel; (*asunto, malentendido*) to sort out

desemejanza [deseme'xanθa] nf dissimilarity

desempaquetar [desempake'tar] vt (*regalo*) to unwrap; (*mercancía*) to unpack

desempatar [desempa'tar] vt to replay, hold a play-off; **desempate** nm (*FÚTBOL*) replay, play-off; (*TENIS*) tie-break(er)

desempeñar [desempe'ɲar] vt (*cargo*) to hold; (*papel*) to perform; (*lo empeñado*) to redeem; ~**se** vr to get out of debt; ~ **un papel** (*fig*) to play (a role)

desempeño [desem'peɲo] nm redeeming; (*de cargo*) occupation

desempleado, a [desemple'aðo, a] nm/f unemployed person; **desempleo** nm unemployment

desempolvar [desempol'ßar] vt (*muebles etc*) to dust; (*lo olvidado*) to revive

desencadenar [desenkaðe'nar] vt to unchain; (*ira*) to unleash; ~**se** vr to break loose; (*tormenta*) to burst; (*guerra*) to break out

desencajar [desenka'xar] vt (*hueso*) to dislocate; (*mecanismo, pieza*) to disconnect, disengage

desencanto [desen'kanto] nm disillusionment

desenchufar [desent∫u'far] vt to unplug

desenfadado, a [desenfa'ðaðo, a] adj (*desenvuelto*) uninhibited; (*descarado*) forward; **desenfado** nm (*libertad*) freedom; (*comportamiento*) free and easy manner; (*descaro*) forwardness

desenfocado, a [desenfo'kaðo, a] adj (*FOTO*) out of focus

desenfrenado, a [desenfre'naðo, a] adj (*descontrolado*) uncontrolled; (*inmoderado*) unbridled; **desenfreno** nm (*vicio*) wildness; (*de las pasiones*) lack of self-control

desenganchar [desengan't∫ar] vt (*gen*) to unhook; (*FERRO*) to uncouple

desengañar [desenga'ɲar] vt to disillusion; ~**se** vr to become disillusioned; **desengaño** nm disillusionment; (*decepción*) disappointment

desenlace [desen'laθe] nm outcome

desenmarañar [desenmara'ɲar] vt (*fig*) to unravel

desenmascarar [desenmaska'rar] vt to unmask

desenredar [desenre'ðar] vt (*pelo*) to untangle; (*problema*) to sort out

desenroscar [desenros'kar] vt to unscrew

desentenderse [desenten'derse] vr: ~ **de** to pretend not to know about; (*apartarse*) to have nothing to do with

desenterrar [desente'rrar] vt to exhume; (*tesoro, fig*) to unearth, dig up

desentonar [desento'nar] vi (*MUS*) to sing (o play) out of tune; (*color*) to clash

desentrañar [desentra'ɲar] vt (*misterio*) to unravel

desentumecer [desentume'θer] vt (*pierna etc*) to stretch; (*DEPORTE*) to loosen up

desenvoltura [desenßol'tura] nf (*libertad, gracia*) ease; (*descaro*) free and easy manner

desenvolver [desenßol'ßer] vt (*paquete*) to unwrap; (*fig*) to develop; ~**se** vr (*desarrollarse*) to unfold, develop; (*arreglárselas*) to cope

deseo [de'seo] nm desire, wish; ~**so, a** adj: **estar** ~**so de** to be anxious to

desequilibrado, a [desekili'ßraðo, a] adj unbalanced

desertar [deser'tar] vi to desert

desértico, a [de'sertiko, a] adj desert cpd

desesperación [desespera'θjon] nf (*impaciencia*) desperation, despair; (*irritación*) fury

desesperar [desespe'rar] vt to drive to despair; (*exasperar*) to drive to distraction ♦ vi: ~ **de** to despair of; ~**se** vr to despair, lose hope

desestabilizar [desestaßili'θar] vt to destabilize

desestimar [desesti'mar] vt (*menospreciar*) to have a low opinion of; (*rechazar*) to reject

desfachatez [desfat∫a'teθ] nf (*insolencia*) impudence; (*descaro*) rudeness

desfalco [des'falko] nm embezzlement

desfallecer [desfaʎe'θer] vi (*perder las fuerzas*) to become weak; (*desvanecerse*) to faint

desfasado, a [desfa'saðo, a] *adj* (*anticuado*) old-fashioned; **desfase** *nm* (*diferencia*) gap

desfavorable [desfaβo'raβle] *adj* unfavourable

desfigurar [desfiɣu'rar] *vt* (*cara*) to disfigure; (*cuerpo*) to deform

desfiladero [desfila'ðero] *nm* gorge

desfilar [desfi'lar] *vi* to parade; **desfile** *nm* procession

desfogarse [desfo'ɣarse] *vr* (*fig*) to let off steam

desgajar [desɣa'xar] *vt* (*arrancar*) to tear off; (*romper*) to break off; **~se** *vr* to come off

desgana [des'ɣana] *nf* (*falta de apetito*) loss of appetite; (*renuencia*) unwillingness; **~do, a** *adj*: **estar ~do** (*sin apetito*) to have no appetite; (*sin entusiasmo*) to have lost interest

desgarrador, a [desɣarra'ðor, a] *adj* (*fig*) heartrending

desgarrar [desɣa'rrar] *vt* to tear (up); (*fig*) to shatter; **desgarro** *nm* (*en tela*) tear; (*aflicción*) grief; (*descaro*) impudence

desgastar [desɣas'tar] *vt* (*deteriorar*) to wear away *o* down; (*estropear*) to spoil; **~se** *vr* to get worn out; **desgaste** *nm* wear (and tear)

desglosar [desɣlo'sar] *vt* (*factura*) to break down

desgracia [des'ɣraθja] *nf* misfortune; (*accidente*) accident; (*vergüenza*) disgrace; (*contratiempo*) setback; **por ~** unfortunately

desgraciado, a [desɣra'θjaðo, a] *adj* (*sin suerte*) unlucky, unfortunate; (*miserable*) wretched; (*infeliz*) miserable

desgravación [desɣraβa'θjon] *nf* (*COM*): **~ fiscal** tax relief

desgravar [desɣra'βar] *vt* (*impuestos*) to reduce the tax *o* duty on

desgreñado, a [desɣre'ɲaðo, a] *adj* dishevelled

deshabitado, a [desaβi'taðo, a] *adj* uninhabited

deshacer [desa'θer] *vt* (*casa*) to break up; (*TEC*) to take apart; (*enemigo*) to defeat; (*diluir*) to melt; (*contrato*) to break; (*intriga*) to solve; **~se** *vr* (*disolverse*) to melt; (*despedazarse*) to come apart *o* undone; **~se de** to get rid of; **~se en lágrimas** to burst into tears

desharrapado, a [desarra'paðo, a] *adj* (*persona*) shabby

deshecho, a [des'etʃo, a] *adj* undone; (*roto*) smashed; (*persona*): **estar ~** to be shattered

desheredar [desere'ðar] *vt* to disinherit

deshidratar [desiðra'tar] *vt* to dehydrate

deshielo [des'jelo] *nm* thaw

deshonesto, a [deso'nesto, a] *adj* indecent

deshonra [des'onra] *nf* (*deshonor*) dishonour; (*vergüenza*) shame

deshora [des'ora]: **a ~** *adv* at the wrong time

deshuesar [deswe'sar] *vt* (*carne*) to bone; (*fruta*) to stone

desierto, a [de'sjerto, a] *adj* (*casa, calle, negocio*) deserted ♦ *nm* desert

designar [desiɣ'nar] *vt* (*nombrar*) to designate; (*indicar*) to fix

designio [de'siɣnjo] *nm* plan

desigual [desi'ɣwal] *adj* (*terreno*) uneven; (*lucha etc*) unequal

desilusión [desilu'sjon] *nf* disillusionment; (*decepción*) disappointment; **desilusionar** *vt* to disillusion; to disappoint; **desilusionarse** *vr* to become disillusioned

desinfectar [desinfek'tar] *vt* to disinfect

desinflar [desin'flar] *vt* to deflate

desintegración [desinteɣra'θjon] *nf* disintegration

desinterés [desinte'res] *nm* (*objetividad*) disinterestedness; (*altruismo*) unselfishness

desintoxicarse [desintoksi'karse] *vr* (*drogadicto*) to undergo detoxification

desistir [desis'tir] *vi* (*renunciar*) to stop, desist

desleal [desle'al] *adj* (*infiel*) disloyal; (*COM: competencia*) unfair; **~tad** *nf* disloyalty

desleír [desle'ir] *vt* (*líquido*) to dilute; (*sólido*) to dissolve

deslenguado, a [deslen'gwaðo, a] *adj* (*grosero*) foul-mouthed

desligar [desli'ɣar] *vt* (*desatar*) to untie, undo; (*separar*) to separate; **~se** *vr* (*de un compromiso*) to extricate o.s.

desliz [des'liθ] *nm* (*fig*) lapse; **~ar** *vt* to slip, slide

deslucido, a [deslu'θiðo, a] *adj* dull; (*torpe*) awkward, graceless; (*deslustrado*) tarnished

deslumbrar [deslum'brar] *vt* to dazzle

desmadrarse [desma'ðrarse] (*fam*) *vr* (*descontrolarse*) to run wild; (*divertirse*) to let one's hair down

desmán [des'man] *nm* (*exceso*) outrage; (*abuso de poder*) abuse

desmandarse [desman'darse] *vr* (*portarse mal*) to behave badly; (*excederse*) to get out of hand; (*caballo*) to bolt

desmantelar [desmante'lar] *vt* (*deshacer*) to dismantle; (*casa*) to strip

desmaquillador [desmakiʎa'ðor] *nm* make-up remover

desmayado, a [desma'jaðo, a] *adj* (*sin sentido*) unconscious; (*carácter*) dull; (*débil*) faint, weak

desmayar [desma'jar] *vi* to lose heart; **~se** *vr* (*MED*) to faint; **desmayo** *nm* (*MED: acto*) faint; (*: estado*) unconsciousness; (*depresión*) dejection

desmedido, a [desme'ðiðo, a] *adj* excessive

desmejorar [desmexo'rar] vt (dañar) to impair, spoil; (MED) to weaken

desmembrar [desmem'brar] vt (MED) to dismember; (fig) to separate

desmemoriado, a [desmemo'rjaðo, a] adj forgetful

desmentir [desmen'tir] vt (contradecir) to contradict; (refutar) to deny ♦ vi: ~ de to refute; ~se vr to contradict o.s.

desmenuzar [desmenu'θar] vt (deshacer) to crumble; (carne) to chop; (examinar) to examine closely

desmerecer [desmere'θer] vt to be unworthy of ♦ vi (deteriorarse) to deteriorate

desmesurado, a [desmesu'raðo, a] adj disproportionate

desmontable [desmon'taßle] adj (que se quita: pieza) detachable; (que sa pueda plegar etc) collapsible, folding

desmontar [desmon'tar] vt (deshacer) to dismantle; (tierra) to level ♦ vi to dismount

desmoralizar [desmorali'θar] vt to demoralize

desmoronar [desmoro'nar] vt to wear away, erode; ~se vr (edificio, dique) to fall into disrepair; (economía) to decline

desnatado, a [desna'taðo, a] adj skimmed

desnivel [desni'ßel] nm (de terreno) unevenness

desnudar [desnu'ðar] vt (desvestir) to undress; (despojar) to strip; ~se vr (desvestirse) to get undressed; **desnudo, a** adj naked ♦ nm/f nude; **desnudo de** devoid o bereft of

desnutrición [desnutri'θjon] nf malnutrition; **desnutrido, a** adj undernourished

desobedecer [desoßeðe'θer] vt, vi to disobey; **desobediencia** nf disobedience

desocupado, a [desoku'paðo, a] adj at leisure; (desempleado) unemployed; (deshabitado) empty, vacant

desocupar [desoku'par] vt to vacate

desodorante [desoðo'rante] nm deodorant

desolación [desola'θjon] nf (lugar) desolation; (fig) grief

desolar [deso'lar] vt to ruin, lay waste

desorbitado, a [desorßi'taðo, a] adj (excesivo: ambición) boundless; (deseos) excessive; (: precio) exorbitant

desorden [des'orðen] nm confusion; (político) disorder, unrest

desorganizar [desorɣani'θar] vt (desordenar) to disorganize; **desorganización** nf (de persona) disorganization; (en empresa, oficina) disorder, chaos

desorientar [desorjen'tar] vt (extraviar) to mislead; (confundir, desconcertar) to confuse; ~se vr (perderse) to lose one's way

despabilado, a [despaßi'laðo, a] adj (despierto) wide-awake; (fig) alert, sharp

despabilar [despaßi'lar] vt (el ingenio) to

sharpen ♦ vi to wake up; (fig) to get a move on; ~se vr to wake up; to get a move on

despacio [des'paθjo] adv slowly

despachar [despa'tʃar] vt (negocio) to do, complete; (enviar) to send, dispatch; (vender) to sell, deal in; (billete) to issue; (mandar ir) to send away

despacho [des'patʃo] nm (oficina) office; (de paquetes) dispatch; (venta) sale; (comunicación) message

desparpajo [despar'paxo] nm self-confidence; (pey) nerve

desparramar [desparra'mar] vt (esparcir) to scatter; (líquido) to spill

despavorido, a [despaßo'riðo, a] adj terrified

despectivo, a [despek'tißo, a] adj (despreciativo) derogatory; (LING) pejorative

despecho [des'petʃo] nm spite; **a ~ de** in spite of

despedazar [despeða'θar] vt to tear to pieces

despedida [despe'ðiða] nf (adiós) farewell; (de obrero) sacking

despedir [despe'ðir] vt (visita) to see off, show out; (empleado) to dismiss; (inquilino) to evict; (objeto) to hurl; (olor etc) to give out o off; ~se vr: ~se de to say goodbye to

despegar [despe'ɣar] vt to unstick ♦ vi (avión) to take off; ~se vr to come loose, come unstuck; **despego** nm detachment

despegue etc [des'peɣe] vb ver **despegar** ♦ nm takeoff

despeinado, a [despei'naðo, a] adj dishevelled, unkempt

despejado, a [despe'xaðo, a] adj (lugar) clear, free; (cielo) clear; (persona) wide-awake, bright

despejar [despe'xar] vt (gen) to clear; (misterio) to clear up ♦ vi (el tiempo) to clear; ~se vr (tiempo, cielo) to clear (up); (misterio) to become clearer; (cabeza) to clear

despellejar [despeʎe'xar] vt (animal) to skin

despensa [des'pensa] nf larder

despeñadero [despeɲa'ðero] nm (GEO) cliff, precipice

despeñarse [despe'ɲarse] vr to hurl o.s. down; (coche) to tumble over

desperdicio [desper'ðiθjo] nm (despilfarro) squandering; ~s nmpl (basura) rubbish sg (BRIT), garbage sg (US); (residuos) waste sg

desperdigarse [desperði'xarse] vr (rebaño, familia) to scatter, spread out; (granos de arroz, semillas) to scatter

desperezarse [despere'θarse] vr to stretch

desperfecto [desper'fekto] nm (deterioro) slight damage; (defecto) flaw, imperfection

despertador [desperta'ðor] nm alarm clock

despertar [desper'tar] nm awakening ♦ vt

(*persona*) to wake up; (*recuerdos*) to revive; (*sentimiento*) to arouse ♦ *vi* to awaken, wake up; ~**se** *vr* to awaken, wake up

despiadado, a [despja'ðaðo, a] *adj* (*ataque*) merciless; (*persona*) heartless

despido *etc* [des'piðo] *vb ver* **despedir** ♦ *nm* dismissal, sacking

despierto, a *etc* [des'pjerto, a] *vb ver* **despertar** ♦ *adj* (*fig*) sharp, alert

despilfarro [despil'farro] *nm* (*derroche*) squandering; (*lujo desmedido*) extravagance

despistar [despis'tar] *vt* to throw off the track *o* scent; (*fig*) to mislead, confuse; ~**se** *vr* to take the wrong road; (*fig*) to become confused

despiste [des'piste] *nm* absent-mindedness; **un ~** a mistake, slip

desplazamiento [desplaθa'mjento] *nm* displacement

desplazar [despla'θar] *vt* to move; (*NAUT*) to displace; (*INFORM*) to scroll; (*fig*) to oust; ~**se** *vr* (*persona*) to travel

desplegar [desple'yar] *vt* (*tela, papel*) to unfold, open out; (*bandera*) to unfurl; **despliegue** *etc* [des'pleγe] *vb ver* **desplegar** ♦ *nm* display

desplomarse [desplo'marse] *vr* (*edificio, gobierno, persona*) to collapse

desplumar [desplu'mar] *vt* (*ave*) to pluck; (*fam: estafar*) to fleece

despoblado, a [despo'βlaðo, a] *adj* (*sin habitantes*) uninhabited ∘

despojar [despo'xar] *vt* (*alguien: de sus bienes*) to divest of, deprive of; (*casa*) to strip, leave bare; (*alguien: de su cargo*) to strip of

despojo [des'poxo] *nm* (*acto*) plundering; (*objetos*) plunder, loot; ~**s** *nmpl* (*de ave, res*) offal *sg*

desposado, a [despo'saðo, a] *adj, nm/f* newly-wed

desposar [despo'sar] *vt* to marry; ~**se** *vr* to get married

desposeer [despose'er] *vt*: ~ **a uno de** (*puesto, autoridad*) to strip sb of

déspota ['despota] *nm/f* despot

despreciar [despre'θjar] *vt* (*desdeñar*) to despise, scorn; (*afrentar*) to slight; **desprecio** *nm* scorn, contempt; slight

desprender [despren'der] *vt* (*broche*) to unfasten; (*olor*) to give off; ~**se** *vr* (*botón: caerse*) to fall off; (*broche*) to come unfastened; (*olor, perfume*) to be given off; ~**se de algo que ...** to draw from sth that ...

desprendimiento [desprendi'mjento] *nm* (*gen*) loosening; (*generosidad*) disinterestedness; (*indiferencia*) detachment; (*de gas*) leak; (*de tierra, rocas*) landslide

despreocupado, a [despreoku'paðo, a] *adj* (*sin preocupación*) unworried, nonchalant; (*negligente*) careless

despreocuparse [despreoku'parse] *vr* not to worry; ~ **de** to have no interest in

desprestigiar [despresti'xjar] *vt* (*criticar*) to run down; (*desacreditar*) to discredit

desprevenido, a [despreße'niðo, a] *adj* (*no preparado*) unprepared, unready

desproporcionado, a [desproporθjo'naðo, a] *adj* disproportionate, out of proportion

desprovisto, a [despro'βisto, a] *adj*: ~ **de** devoid of

después [des'pwes] *adv* afterwards, later; (*próximo paso*) next; ~ **de comer** after lunch; **un año ~** a year later; ~ **se debatió el tema** next the matter was discussed; ~ **de corregido el texto** after the text had been corrected; ~ **de todo** after all

desquiciado, a [deski'θjaðo, a] *adj* deranged

desquite [des'kite] *nm* (*satisfacción*) satisfaction; (*venganza*) revenge

destacar [desta'kar] *vt* to emphasize, point up; (*MIL*) to detach, detail ♦ *vi* (*resaltarse*) to stand out; (*persona*) to be outstanding *o* exceptional; ~**se** *vr* to stand out; to be outstanding *o* exceptional

destajo [des'taxo] *nm*: **trabajar a ~** to do piecework

destapar [desta'par] *vt* (*botella*) to open; (*cacerola*) to take the lid off; (*descubrir*) to uncover; ~**se** *vr* (*revelarse*) to reveal one's true character

destartalado, a [destarta'laðo, a] *adj* (*desordenado*) untidy; (*ruinoso*) tumbledown

destello [des'teʎo] *nm* (*de estrella*) twinkle; (*de faro*) signal light

destemplado, a [destem'plaðo, a] *adj* (*MUS*) out of tune; (*voz*) harsh; (*MED*) out of sorts; (*tiempo*) unpleasant, nasty

desteñir [deste'ɲir] *vt* to fade ♦ *vi* to fade; ~**se** *vr* to fade; **esta tela no destiñe** this fabric will not run

desternillarse [desterni'ʎarse] *vr*: ~ **de risa** to split one's sides laughing

desterrar [deste'rrar] *vt* (*exilar*) to exile; (*fig*) to banish, dismiss

destiempo [des'tjempo]: **a ~** *adv* out of turn

destierro *etc* [des'tjerro] *vb ver* **desterrar** ♦ *nm* exile

destilar [desti'lar] *vt* to distil; **destilería** *nf* distillery

destinar [desti'nar] *vt* (*funcionario*) to appoint, assign; (*fondos*): ~ **(a)** to set aside (for)

destinatario, a [destina'tarjo, a] *nm/f* addressee

destino [des'tino] *nm* (*suerte*) destiny; (*de avión, viajero*) destination

destituir [destitu'ir] *vt* to dismiss

destornillador [destorniʎa'ðor] *nm* screwdriver

destornillar [destorni'ʎar] *vt* (*tornillo*) to

unscrew; ~**se** vr to unscrew

destreza [des'treθa] nf (habilidad) skill; (maña) dexterity

destrozar [destro'θar] vt (romper) to smash, break (up); (estropear) to ruin; (nervios) to shatter

destrozo [des'troθo] nm (acción) destruction; (desastre) smashing; ~**s** nmpl (pedazos) pieces; (daños) havoc sg

destrucción [destruk'θjon] nf destruction

destruir [destru'ir] vt to destroy

desuso [des'uso] nm disuse; **caer en** ~ to become obsolete

desvalido, a [desßa'liðo, a] adj (desprotegido) destitute; (sin fuerzas) helpless

desvalijar [desßali'xar] vt (persona) to rob; (casa, tienda) to burgle; (coche) to break into

desván [des'ßan] nm attic

desvanecer [desßane'θer] vt (disipar) to dispel; (borrar) to blur; ~**se** vr (humo etc) to vanish, disappear; (color) to fade; (recuerdo, sonido) to fade away; (MED) to pass out; (duda) to be dispelled

desvanecimiento [desßaneθi'mjento] nm (desaparición) disappearance; (de colores) fading; (evaporación) evaporation; (MED) fainting fit

desvariar [desßa'rjar] vi (enfermo) to be delirious; **desvarío** nm delirium

desvelar [desße'lar] vt to keep awake; ~**se** vr (no poder dormir) to stay awake; (vigilar) to be vigilant o watchful

desvelos [des'ßelos] nmpl worrying sg

desvencijado, a [desßenθi'xaðo, a] adj (silla) rickety; (máquina) broken-down

desventaja [desßen'taxa] nf disadvantage

desventura [desßen'tura] nf misfortune

desvergonzado, a [desßerxon'θaðo, a] adj shameless

desvergüenza [desßer'xwenθa] nf (descaro) shamelessness; (insolencia) impudence; (mala conducta) effrontery

desvestir [desßes'tir] vt to undress; ~**se** vr to undress

desviación [desßja'θjon] nf deviation; (AUTO) diversion, detour

desviar [des'ßjar] vt to turn aside; (río) to alter the course of; (navío) to divert, reroute; (conversación) to sidetrack; ~**se** vr (apartarse del camino) to turn aside; (: barco) to go off course

desvío etc [des'ßio] vb ver **desviar** ♦ nm (desviación) detour, diversion; (fig) indifference

desvirtuar [desßir'twar] vt to spoil; ~**se** vr to spoil

desvivirse [desßi'ßirse] vr: ~ **por** (anhelar) to long for, crave for; (hacer lo posible por) to do one's utmost for

detallar [deta'ʎar] vt to detail

detalle [de'taʎe] nm detail; (fig) gesture, to-

ken; **al** ~ in detail; (COM) retail

detallista [deta'ʎista] nm/f retailer

detective [detek'tiße] nm/f detective

detener [dete'ner] vt (gen) to stop; (JUR) to arrest; (objeto) to keep; ~**se** vr to stop; (demorarse): ~**se en** to delay over, linger over

detenidamente [deteniða'mente] adv (minuciosamente) carefully; (extensamente) at great length

detenido, a [dete'niðo, a] adj (arrestado) under arrest; (minucioso) detailed ♦ nm/f person under arrest, prisoner

detenimiento [deteni'mjento] nm: **con** ~ thoroughly; (observar, considerar) carefully

detergente [deter'xente] nm detergent

deteriorar [deterjo'rar] vt to spoil, damage; ~**se** vr to deteriorate; **deterioro** nm deterioration

determinación [determina'θjon] nf (empeño) determination; (decisión) decision; **determinado, a** adj specific

determinar [determi'nar] vt (plazo) to fix; (precio) to settle; ~**se** vr to decide

detestar [detes'tar] vt to detest

detractor, a [detrak'tor, a] nm/f slanderer, libeller

detrás [de'tras] adv behind; (atrás) at the back; ~ **de** behind

detrimento [detri'mento] nm: **en** ~ **de** to the detriment of

deuda ['deuða] nf (condición) indebtedness, debt; (cantidad) debt

devaluación [deßalwa'θjon] nf devaluation

devastar [deßas'tar] vt (destruir) to devastate

devoción [deßo'θjon] nf devotion

devolución [deßolu'θjon] nf (reenvío) return, sending back; (reembolso) repayment; (JUR) devolution

devolver [deßol'ßer] vt to return; (lo extraviado, lo prestado) to give back; (carta al correo) to send back; (COM) to repay, refund; (lo prestado) to give back ♦ vi (vomitar) to be sick

devorar [deßo'rar] vt to devour

devoto, a [de'ßoto, a] adj devout ♦ nm/f admirer

devuelto pp de **devolver**

devuelva etc vb ver **devolver**

di vb ver **dar; decir**

día ['dia] nm day; ¿**qué** ~ **es?** what's the date?; **estar/poner al** ~ to be/keep up to date; **el** ~ **de hoy/de mañana** today/tomorrow; **al** ~ **siguiente** (on) the following day; **vivir al** ~ to live from hand to mouth; **de** ~ by day, in daylight; **en pleno** ~ in full daylight; **D~ de Reyes** Epiphany; ~ **festivo** (ESP) o **feriado** (AM) holiday; ~ **libre** day off

diabetes [dja'ßetes] nf diabetes

diablo ['djaßlo] nm devil; **diablura** nf

prank
diadema [dja'ðema] *nf* tiara
diafragma [dja'fraɣma] *nm* diaphragm
diagnosis [djaɣ'nosis] *nf inv* diagnosis
diagnóstico [diaɣ'nostiko] *nm* = diagnosis
diagonal [djaɣo'nal] *adj* diagonal
diagrama [dja'ɣrama] *nm* diagram; ~ **de flujo** flowchart
dial ['djal] *nm* dial
dialecto [dja'lekto] *nm* dialect
dialogar [djalo'xar] *vi:* ~ **con** (*POL*) to hold talks with
diálogo ['djaloxo] *nm* dialogue
diamante [dja'mante] *nm* diamond
diana ['djana] *nf* (*MIL*) reveille; (*de blanco*) centre, bull's-eye
diapositiva [djaposi'tißa] *nf* (*FOTO*) slide, transparency
diario, a ['djarjo, a] *adj* daily ♦ *nm* newspaper; **a** ~ daily; **de** ~ everyday
diarrea [dja'rrea] *nf* diarrhoea
dibujar [dißu'xar] *vt* to draw, sketch; **dibujo** *nm* drawing; **dibujos animados** cartoons
diccionario [dikθjo'narjo] *nm* dictionary
dice *etc vb ver* **decir**
diciembre [di'θjembre] *nm* December
dictado [dik'taðo] *nm* dictation
dictador [dikta'ðor] *nm* dictator; **dictadura** *nf* dictatorship
dictamen [dik'tamen] *nm* (*opinión*) opinion; (*juicio*) judgment; (*informe*) report
dictar [dik'tar] *vt* (*carta*) to dictate; (*JUR: sentencia*) to pronounce; (*decreto*) to issue; (*AM: clase*) to give
dicho, a ['ditʃo, a] *pp de* **decir** ♦ *adj:* **en** ~**s países** in the aforementioned countries ♦ *nm* saying
dichoso, a [di'tʃoso, a] *adj* happy
didáctico, a [di'ðaktiko, a] *adj* educational
diecinueve [djeθi'nweße] *num* nineteen
dieciocho [djeθi'otʃo] *num* eighteen
dieciséis [djeθi'seis] *num* sixteen
diecisiete [djeθi'sjete] *num* seventeen
diente ['djente] *nm* (*ANAT, TEC*) tooth; (*ZOOL*) fang; (: *de elefante*) tusk; (*de ajo*) clove; **hablar entre** ~**s** to mutter, mumble
diera *etc vb ver* **dar**
diesel ['disel] *adj:* **motor** ~ diesel engine
diestro, a ['djestro, a] *adj* (*derecho*) right; (*hábil*) skilful
dieta ['djeta] *nf* diet; **diétetico, a** *adj* diet (*atr*), dietary
diez [djeθ] *num* ten
diezmar [djeθ'mar] *vt* (*población*) to decimate
difamar [difa'mar] *vt* (*JUR: hablando*) to slander; (: *por escrito*) to libel
diferencia [dife'renθja] *nf* difference; **diferenciar** *vt* to differentiate between ♦ *vi* to differ; **diferenciarse** *vr* to differ, be different; (*distinguirse*) to distinguish o.s.
diferente [dife'rente] *adj* different

diferido [dife'riðo] *nm:* **en** ~ (*TV etc*) recorded
difícil [di'fiθil] *adj* difficult
dificultad [difikul'taθ] *nf* difficulty; (*problema*) trouble; (*objeción*) objection
dificultar [difikul'tar] *vt* (*complicar*) to complicate, make difficult; (*estorbar*) to obstruct
difteria [dif'terja] *nf* diphtheria
difundir [difun'dir] *vt* (*calor, luz*) to diffuse; (*RADIO, TV*) to broadcast; ~ **una noticia** to spread a piece of news; ~**se** *vr* to spread (out)
difunto, a [di'funto, a] *adj* dead, deceased ♦ *nm/f* deceased (person)
difusión [difu'sjon] *nf* (*RADIO, TV*) broadcasting
diga *etc vb ver* **decir**
digerir [dixe'rir] *vt* to digest; (*fig*) to absorb; **digestión** *nf* digestion; **digestivo, a** *adj* digestive
digital [dixi'tal] *adj* (*INFORM*) digital
dignarse [diɣ'narse] *vr* to deign to
dignatario [diɣna'tarjo, a] *nm/f* dignitary
dignidad [diɣni'ðað] *nf* dignity
digno, a ['diɣno, a] *adj* worthy
digo *etc vb ver* **decir**
dije *etc vb ver* **decir**
dilapidar [dilapi'ðar] *vt* (*dinero, herencia*) to squander, waste
dilatar [dila'tar] *vt* (*cuerpo*) to dilate; (*prolongar*) to prolong; (*aplazar*) to delay
dilema [di'lema] *nm* dilemma
diligencia [dili'xenθja] *nf* diligence; (*ocupación*) errand, job; ~**s** *nfpl* (*JUR*) formalities; **diligente** *adj* diligent
diluir [dilu'ir] *vt* to dilute
diluvio [di'lußjo] *nm* deluge, flood
dimensión [dimen'sjon] *nf* dimension
diminuto, a [dimi'nuto, a] *adj* tiny, diminutive
dimitir [dimi'tir] *vi* to resign
dimos *vb ver* **dar**
Dinamarca [dina'marka] *nf* Denmark
dinámico, a [di'namiko, a] *adj* dynamic
dinamita [dina'mita] *nf* dynamite
dínamo ['dinamo] *nf* dynamo
dineral [dine'ral] *nm* large sum of money, fortune
dinero [di'nero] *nm* money; ~ **contante,** ~ **efectivo** (ready) cash; ~ **suelto** (loose) change
dio *vb ver* **dar**
dios [djos] *nm* god; **¡D~ mío!** (oh,) my God!
diosa ['djosa] *nf* goddess
diploma [di'ploma] *nm* diploma
diplomacia [diplo'maθja] *nf* diplomacy; (*fig*) tact
diplomado, a [diplo'maðo, a] *adj* qualified
diplomático, a [diplo'matiko, a] *adj* diplo-

matic ♦ nm/f diplomat
diputación [diputa'θjon] nf (tb: ~ provincial) ≈ county council
diputado, a [dipu'taðo, a] nm/f delegate; (POL) ≈ member of parliament (BRIT), ≈ representative (US)
dique ['dike] nm dyke
diré etc vb ver **decir**
dirección [direk'θjon] nf direction; (señas) address; (AUTO) steering; (gerencia) management; (POL) leadership; ~ única/prohibida one-way street/no entry
directa [di'rekta] nf (AUT) top gear
directiva [direk'tiβa] nf (DEP, tb: junta ~) board of directors
directo, a [di'rekto, a] adj direct; (RADIO, TV) live; **transmitir en** ~ to broadcast live
director, a [direk'tor, a] adj leading ♦ nm/f director; (ESCOL) head(teacher) (BRIT), principal (US); (gerente) manager(ess); (PRENSA) editor; ~ **de cine** film director; ~ **general** managing director
dirigente [diri'xente] nm/f (POL) leader
dirigir [diri'xir] vt to direct; (carta) to address; (obra de teatro, film) to direct; (MUS) to conduct; (comercio) to manage; ~**se** vr: ~**se a** to go towards, make one's way towards; (hablar con) to speak to
dirija etc vb ver **dirigir**
discernir [disθer'nir] vt (distinguir, discriminar) to discern
disciplina [disθi'plina] nf discipline
discípulo, a [dis'θipulo, a] nm/f disciple
disco ['disko] nm disc; (DEPORTE) discus; (TEL) dial; (AUTO: semáforo) light; (MUS) record; (INFORM): ~ **flexible/rígido** floppy/hard disk; ~ **compacto/de larga duración** compact disc/long-playing record; ~ **de freno** brake disc
disconforme [diskon'forme] adj differing; **estar** ~ (**con**) to be in disagreement (with)
discordia [dis'korðja] nf discord
discoteca [disko'teka] nf disco(theque)
discreción [diskre'θjon] nf discretion; (reserva) prudence; **comer a** ~ to eat as much as one wishes; **discrecional** adj (facultativo) discretionary
discrepancia [diskre'panθja] nf (diferencia) discrepancy; (desacuerdo) disagreement
discreto, a [dis'kreto, a] adj (diplomático) discreet; (sensato) sensible; (reservado) quiet; (sobrio) sober
discriminación [diskrimina'θjon] nf discrimination
disculpa [dis'kulpa] nf excuse; (pedir perdón) apology; **pedir** ~**s a/por** to apologize to/for; **disculpar** vt to excuse, pardon; **disculparse** vr to excuse o.s.; to apologize
discurrir [disku'rrir] vi (pensar, reflexionar) to think, meditate; (recorrer) to roam, wander; (el tiempo) to pass, go by
discurso [dis'kurso] nm speech

discusión [disku'sjon] nf (diálogo) discussion; (riña) argument
discutir [disku'tir] vt (debatir) to discuss; (pelear) to argue about; (contradecir) to argue against ♦ vi to discuss; (disputar) to argue
disecar [dise'kar] vt (conservar: animal) to stuff; (: planta) to dry
diseminar [disemi'nar] vt to disseminate, spread
diseño [di'seɲo] nm design; (ARTE) drawing
disfraz [dis'fraθ] nm (máscara) disguise; (excusa) pretext; ~**ar** vt to disguise; ~**arse** vr: ~**arse de** to disguise o.s. as
disfrutar [disfru'tar] vt to enjoy ♦ vi to enjoy o.s.; ~ **de** to enjoy, possess
disgregarse [disɣre'varse] vr (muchedumbre) to disperse
disgustar [disɣus'tar] vt (no gustar) to displease; (contrariar, enojar) to annoy, upset; ~**se** vr to be annoyed; (dos personas) to fall out
disgusto [dis'ɣusto] nm (repugnancia) disgust; (contrariedad) annoyance; (tristeza) grief; (riña) quarrel; (avería) misfortune
disidente [disi'ðente] nm dissident
disimular [disimu'lar] vt (ocultar) to hide, conceal ♦ vi to dissemble
disipar [disi'par] vt to dispel; (fortuna) to squander; ~**se** vr (nubes) to vanish; (indisciplinarse) to dissipate
dislocarse [dislo'karse] vr (articulación) to sprain, dislocate
disminución [disminu'θjon] nf decrease, reduction
disminuir [disminu'ir] vt to decrease, diminish
disociarse [diso'θjarse] vr: ~ (**de**) to dissociate o.s. (from)
disolver [disol'βer] vt (gen) to dissolve; ~**se** vr to dissolve; (COM) to go into liquidation
dispar [dis'par] adj different
disparar [dispa'rar] vt, vi to shoot, fire
disparate [dispa'rate] nm (tontería) foolish remark; (error) blunder; **decir** ~**s** to talk nonsense
disparo [dis'paro] nm shot
dispensar [dispen'sar] vt to dispense; (disculpar) to excuse
dispersar [disper'sar] vt to disperse; ~**se** vr to scatter
disponer [dispo'ner] vt (arreglar) to arrange; (ordenar) to put in order; (preparar) to prepare, get ready ♦ vi: ~ **de** to have, own; ~**se** vr: ~**se a o para hacer** to prepare to do
disponible [dispo'niβle] adj available
disposición [disposi'θjon] nf arrangement, disposition; (aptitud) aptitude; (INFORM) layout; **a la** ~ **de** at the disposal of; ~ **de**

animo state of mind

dispositivo [disposi'tiβo] *nm* device, mechanism

dispuesto, a [dis'pwesto, a] *pp de* **disponer** ♦ *adj*. (*arreglado*) arranged; (*preparado*) disposed

disputar [dispu'tar] *vt* (*discutir*) to dispute, question; (*contender*) to contend for ♦ *vi* to argue

disquete [dis'kete] *nm* floppy disk, diskette

distancia [dis'tanθja] *nf* distance

distanciar [distan'θjar] *vt* to space out; ~**se** *vr* to become estranged

distante [dis'tante] *adj* distant

distar [dis'tar] *vi*: **dista 5km de aquí** it is 5km from here

diste *vb ver* **dar**

disteis ['disteis] *vb ver* **dar**

distension [disten'sjon] *nf* (*en las relaciones*) relaxation; (*POL*) détente; (*muscular*) strain

distinción [distin'θjon] *nf* distinction; (*elegancia*) elegance; (*honor*) honour

distinguido, a [distin'giðo, a] *adj* distinguished

distinguir [distin'gir] *vt* to distinguish; (*escoger*) to single out; ~**se** *vr* to be distinguished

distintivo [distin'tiβo] *nm* badge; (*fig*) characteristic

distinto, a [dis'tinto, a] *adj* different; (*claro*) clear

distracción [distrak'θjon] *nf* distraction; (*pasatiempo*) hobby, pastime; (*olvido*) absent-mindedness, distraction

distraer [distra'er] *vt* (*atención*) to distract; (*divertir*) to amuse;. (*fondos*) to embezzle; ~**se** *vr* (*entretenerse*) to amuse o.s; (*perder la concentración*) to allow one's attention to wander

distraído, a [distra'iðo, a] *adj* (*gen*) absent-minded; (*entretenido*) amusing

distribuidor, a [distriβui'ðor, a] *nm/f* distributor; (*AUT*) distributor; **distribuidora** *nf* (*COM*) dealer, agent; (*CINE*) distributor

distribuir [distriβu'ir] *vt* to distribute

distrito [dis'trito] *nm* (*sector, territorio*) region; (*barrio*) district

disturbio [dis'turβjo] *nm* disturbance; (*desorden*) riot

disuadir [diswa'ðir] *vt* to dissuade

disuelto [di'swelto] *pp de* **disolver**

disyuntiva [disjun'tiβa] *nf* dilemma

DIU *nm abr* (= *dispositivo intrauterino*) IUD

diurno, a ['djurno, a] *adj* day *cpd*

divagar [diβa'var] *vi* (*desviarse*) to digress

diván [di'βan] *nm* divan

divergencia [diβer'xenθja] *nf* divergence

diversidad [diβersi'ðað] *nf* diversity, variety

diversificar [diβersifi'kar] *vt* to diversify

diversión [diβer'sjon] *nf* (*gen*) entertainment; (*actividad*) hobby, pastime

diverso, a [di'βerso, a] *adj* diverse; ~**s** *nmpl* sundries; ~**s libros** several books

divertido, a [diβer'tiðo, a] *adj* (*chiste*) amusing; (*fiesta etc*) enjoyable

divertir [diβer'tir] *vt* (*entretener, recrear*) to amuse; ~**se** *vr* (*pasarlo bien*) to have a good time; (*distraerse*) to amuse o.s

dividir [diβi'ðir] *vt* (*gen*) to divide; (*separar*) to separate; (*distribuir*) to distribute, share out

divierta *etc vb ver* **divertir**

dividendo [diβi'ðendo] *nm* (*COM*): ~**s** *nmpl* dividends

divino, a [di'βino, a] *adj* divine

divirtiendo *etc vb ver* **divertir**

divisa [di'βisa] *nf* (*emblema, moneda*) emblem, badge; ~**s** *nfpl* foreign exchange *sg*

divisar [diβi'sar] *vt* to make out, distinguish

división [diβi'sjon] *nf* (*gen*) division; (*de partido*) split; (*de país*) partition

divorciar [diβor'θjar] *vt* to divorce; ~**se** *vr* to get divorced; **divorcio** *nm* divorce

divulgar [diβul'var] *vt* (*desparramar*) to spread; (*hacer circular*) to divulge, circulate; ~**se** *vr* to leak out

DNI (*ESP*) *nm abr* (= *Documento Nacional de Identidad*) national identity card

Dña. *abr* (= *doña*) Mrs

do [do] *nm* (*MUS*) do, C

dobladillo [doβla'ðiʎo] *nm* (*de vestido*) hem; (*de pantalón: vuelta*) turn-up (*BRIT*), cuff (*US*)

doblar [do'βlar] *vt* to double; (*papel*) to fold; (*caño*) to bend; (*la esquina*) to turn, go round; (*film*) to dub ♦ *vi* to turn; (*campana*) to toll; ~**se** *vr* (*plegarse*) to fold (up), crease; (*encorvarse*) to bend

doble ['doβle] *adj* double; (*de dos aspectos*) dual; (*fig*) two-faced ♦ *nm* double ♦ *nm/f* (*TEATRO*) double, stand-in; ~**s** *nmpl* (*DEPORTE*) doubles *sg*; **con sentido** ~ with a double meaning

doblegar [doβle'var] *vt* to fold, crease; ~**se** *vr* to yield

doblez [do'βleθ] *nm* fold, hem ♦ *nf* insincerity, duplicity

doce ['doθe] *num* twelve; ~**na** *nf* dozen

docente [do'θente] *adj*: **centro/personal** ~ teaching establishment/staff

dócil ['doθil] *adj* (*pasivo*) docile; (*obediente*) obedient

docto, a ['dokto, a] *adj*: ~ **en** instructed in

doctor, a [dok'tor, a] *nm/f* doctor

doctorado [dokto'raðo] *nm* doctorate

doctrina [dok'trina] *nf* doctrine, teaching

documentación [dokumenta'θjon] *nf* documentation, papers *pl*

documental [dokumen'tal] *adj, nm* documentary

documento [doku'mento] *nm* (*certificado*) document; ~ **national de identidad** identity card

dólar ['dolar] *nm* dollar

doler [do'ler] *vt, vi* to hurt; (*fig*) to grieve; **~se** *vr* (*de su situación*) to grieve, feel sorry; (*de las desgracias ajenas*) to sympathize; **me duele el brazo** my arm hurts

dolor [do'lor] *nm* pain; (*fig*) grief, sorrow; **~ de cabeza** headache; **~ de estómago** stomachache

domar [do'mar] *vt* to tame

domesticar [domesti'kar] *vt* = **domar**

doméstico, a [do'mestiko, a] *adj* (*vida, servicio*) home; (*tareas*) household; (*animal*) tame, pet

domiciliación [domiθilia'θjon] *nf*: **~ de pagos** (*COM*) standing order

domicilio [domi'θiljo] *nm* home; **~ particular** private residence; **~ social** (*COM*) head office; **sin ~ fijo** of no fixed abode

dominante [domi'nante] *adj* dominant; (*persona*) domineering

dominar [domi'nar] *vt* (*gen*) to dominate; (*idiomas*) to be fluent in ♦ *vi* to dominate, prevail; **~se** *vr* to control o.s.

domingo [do'mingo] *nm* Sunday

dominio [do'minjo] *nm* (*tierras*) domain; (*autoridad*) power, authority; (*de las pasiones*) grip, hold; (*de idiomas*) command

don [don] *nm* (*talento*) gift; **~ Juan Gómez** Mr Juan Gómez *o* Juan Gómez Esq

donaire [do'naire] *nm* charm

donar [do'nar] *vt* to donate

donativo [dona'tiβo] *nm* donation

doncella [don'θeʎa] *nf* (*criada*) maid

donde ['donde] *adv* where ♦ *prep*: **el coche está allí ~ el farol** the car is over there by the lamppost *o* where the lamppost is; **por ~** through which; **en ~** where, in which

dónde ['donde] *adv interrogativo* where?; **¿a ~ vas?** where are you going (to)?; **¿de ~ vienes?** where have you come from?; **¿por ~?** where?, whereabouts?

dondequiera [donde'kjera] *adv* anywhere; **por ~** everywhere, all over the place ♦ *conj*: **~ que** wherever

doña ['doɲa] *nf*: **~ Alicia** Alicia; **~ Victoria Benito** Mrs Victoria Benito

dorado, a [do'raðo, a] *adj* (*color*) golden; (*TEC*) gilt

dormir [dor'mir] *vt*: **~ la siesta por la tarde** to have an afternoon nap ♦ *vi* to sleep; **~se** *vr* to fall asleep

dormitar [dormi'tar] *vi* to doze

dormitorio [dormi'torjo] *nm* bedroom; **~ común** dormitory

dorsal [dor'sal] *nm* (*DEPORTE*) number

dorso ['dorso] *nm* (*de mano*) back; (*de hoja*) other side

dos [dos] *num* two

dosis ['dosis] *nf inv* dose, dosage

dotado, a [do'taðo, a] *adj* gifted; **~ de** endowed with

dotar [do'tar] *vt* to endow; **dote** *nf* dowry;

dotes *nfpl* (*talentos*) gifts

doy *vb ver* **dar**

dragaminas [draɣa'minas] *nm* minesweeper

dragar [dra'ɣar] *vt* (*río*) to dredge; (*minas*) to sweep

drama ['drama] *nm* drama

dramaturgo [drama'turɣo] *nm* dramatist, playwright

drástico, a ['drastiko, a] *adj* drastic

drenaje [dre'naxe] *nm* drainage

droga ['droɣa] *nf* drug

drogadicto, a [droɣa'ðikto, a] *nm/f* drug addict

droguería [droɣe'ria] *nf* hardware shop (*BRIT*) *o* store (*US*)

ducha ['dutʃa] *nf* (*baño*) shower; (*MED*) douche; **ducharse** *vr* to take a shower

duda ['duða] *nf* doubt; **dudar** *vt, vi* to doubt; **dudoso, a** [du'ðoso, a] *adj* (*incierto*) hesitant; (*sospechoso*) doubtful

duela *etc vb ver* **doler**

duelo ['dwelo] *vb ver* **doler** ♦ *nm* (*combate*) duel; (*luto*) mourning

duende ['dwende] *nm* imp, goblin

dueño, a ['dweɲo, a] *nm/f* (*propietario*) owner; (*de pensión, taberna*) landlord/lady; (*empresario*) employer

duermo *etc vb ver* **dormir**

dulce ['dulθe] *adj* sweet ♦ *adv* gently, softly ♦ *nm* sweet

dulzura [dul'θura] *nf* sweetness; (*ternura*) gentleness

duna ['duna] *nf* (*GEO*) dune

dúo ['duo] *nm* duet

duplicar [dupli'kar] *vt* (*hacer el doble de*) to duplicate; **~se** *vr* to double

duque ['duke] *nm* duke; **~sa** *nf* duchess

duración [dura'θjon] *nf* (*de película, disco etc*) length; (*de pila etc*) life; (*curso: de acontecimientos etc*) duration

duradero, a [dura'ðero, a] *adj* (*tela etc*) hard-wearing; (*fe, paz*) lasting

durante [du'rante] *prep* during

durar [du'rar] *vi* (*permanecer*) to last; (*recuerdo*) to remain

durazno [du'raθno] (*AM*) *nm* (*fruta*) peach; (*árbol*) peach tree

durex ['dureks] (*AM*) *nm* (*tira adhesiva*) Sellotape ® (*BRIT*), Scotch tape ® (*US*)

dureza [du'reθa] *nf* (*calidad*) hardness

duro, a ['duro, a] *adj* hard; (*carácter*) tough ♦ *adv* hard ♦ *nm* (*moneda*) five peseta coin *o* piece

E e

e [e] *conj* and

E *abr* (= *este*) E

ebanista [eßa'nista] *nm/f* cabinetmaker

ébano ['eßano] *nm* ebony

ebrio, a ['eßrjo, a] *adj* drunk

ebullición [eßuʎi'θjon] *nf* boiling

eccema [ek'θema] *nf* (*MED*) eczema

eclesiástico, a [ekle'sjastiko, a] *adj* ecclesiastical

eclipse [e'klipse] *nm* eclipse

eco ['eko] *nm* echo; **tener ~** to catch on

ecología [ekolo'ɣia] *nf* ecology; **ecologista** *adj* ecological, environmental ♦ *nm/f* environmentalist

economato [ekono'mato] *nm* cooperative store

economía [ekono'mia] *nf* (*sistema*) economy; (*cualidad*) thrift

económico, a [eko'nomiko, a] *adj* (*barato*) cheap, economical; (*persona*) thrifty; (*COM*: *año etc*) financial; (: *situación*) economic

economista [ekono'mista] *nm/f* economist

ECU [eku] *nm* ECU

ecuador [ekwa'ðor] *nm* equator; (**el**) **E~** Ecuador

ecuánime [e'kwanime] *adj* (*carácter*) level-headed; (*estado*) calm

ecuatoriano, a [ekwato'rjano, a] *adj, nm/f* Ecuadorian

ecuestre [e'kwestre] *adj* equestrian

eczema [ek'θema] *nm* = **eccema**

echar [e'tʃar] *vt* to throw; (*agua, vino*) to pour (out); (*empleado*: *despedir*) to fire, sack; (*hojas*) to sprout; (*cartas*) to post; (*humo*) to emit, give out ♦ *vi*: **~ a correr/llorar** to run off/burst into tears; **~se** *vr* to lie down; **~ llave a** to lock (up); **~ abajo** (*gobierno*) to overthrow; (*edificio*) to demolish; **~ mano a** to lay hands on; **~ una mano a uno** (*ayudar*) to give sb a hand; **~ de menos** to miss

edad [e'ðað] *nf* age; **¿qué ~ tienes?** how old are you?; **tiene ocho años de ~** he is eight (years old); **de ~ mediana/avanzada** middle-aged/advanced in years; **la E~ Media** the Middle Ages

edición [eði'θjon] *nf* (*acto*) publication; (*ejemplar*) edition

edicto [e'ðikto] *nm* edict, proclamation

edificio [eði'fiθjo] *nm* building; (*fig*) edifice, structure

Edimburgo [eðim'burɣo] *nm* Edinburgh

editar [eði'tar] *vt* (*publicar*) to publish; (*preparar textos*) to edit

editor, a [eði'tor, a] *nm/f* (*que publica*) publisher; (*redactor*) editor ♦ *adj*: **casa ~a** publishing house, publisher; **~ial** *adj* editorial ♦ *nm* leading article, editorial; **casa ~ial** publishing house, publisher

edredón [eðre'ðon] *nm* duvet

educación [eðuka'θjon] *nf* education; (*crianza*) upbringing; (*modales*) (good) manners *pl*

educar [eðu'kar] *vt* to educate; (*criar*) to bring up; (*voz*) to train

EE. UU. *nmpl abr* (= *Estados Unidos*) US(A)

efectista [efek'tista] *adj* sensationalist

efectivamente [efektißa'mente] *adv* (*como respuesta*) exactly, precisely; (*verdaderamente*) really; (*de hecho*) in fact

efectivo, a [efek'tißo, a] *adj* effective; (*real*) actual, real ♦ *nm*: **pagar en ~** to pay (in) cash; **hacer ~ un cheque** to cash a cheque

efecto [e'fekto] *nm* effect, result; **~s** *nmpl* (*~s personales*) effects; (*bienes*) goods; (*COM*) assets; **en ~** in fact; (*respuesta*) exactly, indeed; **~ invernadero** greenhouse effect

efectuar [efek'twar] *vt* to carry out; (*viaje*) to make

eficacia [efi'kaθja] *nf* (*de persona*) efficiency; (*de medicamento etc*) effectiveness

eficaz [efi'kaθ] *adj* (*persona*) efficient; (*acción*) effective

eficiente [efi'θjente] *adj* efficient

efusivo, a [efu'sißo, a] *adj* effusive; **mis más efusivas gracias** my warmest thanks

EGB (*ESP*) *nf abr* (*ESCOL*) = *Educación General Básica*

egipcio, a [e'xipθjo, a] *adj, nm/f* Egyptian

Egipto [e'xipto] *nm* Egypt

egoísmo [eɣo'ismo] *nm* egoism

egoísta [eɣo'ista] *adj* egoistical, selfish ♦ *nm/f* egoist

egregio, a [e'ɣrexjo, a] *adj* eminent, distinguished

Eire ['eire] *nm* Eire

ej. *abr* (= *ejemplo*) eg

eje ['exe] *nm* (*GEO, MAT*) axis; (*de rueda*) axle; (*de máquina*) shaft, spindle

ejecución [exeku'θjon] *nf* execution; (*cumplimiento*) fulfilment; (*actuación*) performance; (*JUR*: *embargo de deudor*) attachment

ejecutar [exeku'tar] *vt* to execute, carry out; (*matar*) to execute; (*cumplir*) to fulfil; (*MUS*) to perform; (*JUR*: *embargar*) to attach, distrain (on)

ejecutivo, a [exeku'tißo, a] *adj* executive; **el (poder) ~** the executive (power)

ejemplar [exem'plar] *adj* exemplary ♦ *nm*

example; (*ZOOL*) specimen; (*de libro*) copy; (*de periódico*) number, issue

ejemplo [e'xemplo] *nm* example; **por ~** for example

ejercer [exer'θer] *vt* (*influencia*) to exert; (*un oficio*) to practise ♦ *vi* (*practicar*): **~ (de)** to practise (as); (*tener oficio*) to hold office

ejercicio [exer'θiθjo] *nm* exercise; (*período*) tenure; **~ comercial** financial year

ejército [e'xerθito] *nm* army; **entrar en el ~** to join the army, join up

ejote [e'xote] (*AM*) *nm* green bean

PALABRA CLAVE

el [el] (*f* **la**, *pl* **los, las**, *neutro* **lo**) *art def* **1** the; **el libro/la mesa/los estudiantes** the book/table/students

2 (*con n abstracto: no se traduce*): **el amor/la juventud** love/youth

3 (*posesión: se traduce a menudo por adj posesivo*): **romperse el brazo** to break one's arm; **levantó la mano** he put his hand up; **se puso el sombrero** she put her hat on

4 (*valor descriptivo*): **tener la boca grande/los ojos azules** to have a big mouth/blue eyes

5 (*con días*) on; **me iré el viernes** I'll leave on Friday; **los domingos suelo ir a nadar** on Sundays I generally go swimming

6 (*lo + adj*): **lo difícil/caro** what is difficult/expensive; (= *cuán*): **no se da cuenta de lo pesado que es** he doesn't realise how boring he is

♦ *pron demos* **1**: **mi libro y el de usted** my book and yours; **las de Pepe son mejores** Pepe's are better; **no la(s) blanca(s) sino la(s) gris(es)** not the white one(s) but the grey one(s)

2: **lo de**: **lo de ayer** what happened yesterday; **lo de las facturas** that business about the invoices

♦ *pron relativo*: **el que** *etc* **1** (*indef*): **el (los) que quiera(n) que se vaya(n)** anyone who wants to can leave; **llévese el que más le guste** take the one you like best

2 (*def*): **el que compré ayer** the one I bought yesterday; **los que se van** those who leave

3: **lo que**: **lo que pienso yo/más me gusta** what I think/like most

♦ *conj*: **el que**: **el que lo diga** the fact that he says so; **el que sea tan vago me molesta** his being so lazy really bothers me

♦ *excl*: **¡el susto que me diste!** what a fright you gave me!

♦ *pron personal* **1** (*persona: m*) him; (: *f*) her; (: *pl*) them; **lo/las veo** I can see him/them

2 (*animal, cosa: sg*) it; (: *pl*) them; **lo** (*o* **la**)

veo I can see it; **los** (*o* **las**) **veo** I can see them

3: **lo** (*como sustituto de frase*): **no lo sabía** I didn't know; **ya lo entiendo** I understand now

---

él [el] *pron* (*persona*) he; (*cosa*) it; (*después de prep: persona*) him; (: *cosa*) it; **de ~** his

elaborar [elaβo'rar] *vt* (*producto*) to make, manufacture; (*preparar*) to prepare; (*madera, metal etc*) to work; (*proyecto etc*) to work on *o* out

elasticidad [elastiθi'ðað] *nf* elasticity

elástico, a [e'lastiko, a] *adj* elastic; (*flexible*) flexible ♦ *nm* elastic; (*un ~*) elastic band

elección [elek'θjon] *nf* election; (*selección*) choice, selection

electorado [elekto'raðo] *nm* electorate, voters *pl*

electricidad [elektriθi'ðað] *nf* electricity

electricista [elektri'θista] *nm/f* electrician

eléctrico, a [e'lektriko, a] *adj* electric

electro... [elektro] *prefijo* electro...; **~cardiograma** *nm* electrocardiogram; **~cutar** *vt* to electrocute; **~do** *nm* electrode; **~domésticos** *nmpl* (electrical) household appliances; **~magnético, a** *adj* electromagnetic

electrónica [elek'tronika] *nf* electronics *sg*

electrónico, a [elek'troniko, a] *adj* electronic

electrotecnia [elektro'teknja] *nf* electrical engineering; **electrotécnico, a** *nm/f* electrical engineer

elefante [ele'fante] *nm* elephant

elegancia [ele'ɣanθja] *nf* elegance, grace; (*estilo*) stylishness

elegante [ele'ɣante] *adj* elegant, graceful; (*estiloso*) stylish, fashionable

elegía [ele'xia] *nf* elegy

elegir [ele'xir] *vt* (*escoger*) to choose, select; (*optar*) to opt for; (*presidente*) to elect

elemental [elemen'tal] *adj* (*claro, obvio*) elementary; (*fundamental*) elemental, fundamental

elemento [ele'mento] *nm* element; (*fig*) ingredient; **~s** *nmpl* elements, rudiments

elenco [e'lenko] *nm* (*TEATRO, CINE*) cast

elepé [ele'pe] (*pl*: **elepés**) *nm* L.P.

elevación [eleβa'θjon] *nf* elevation; (*acto*) raising, lifting; (*de precios*) rise; (*GEO etc*) height, altitude; (*de persona*) nobleness

elevar [ele'βar] *vt* to raise, lift (up); (*precio*) to put up; **~se** *vr* (*edificio*) to rise; (*precios*) to go up; (*transportarse, enajenarse*) to get carried away

eligiendo *etc vb ver* **elegir**

elija *etc vb ver* **elegir**

eliminar [elimi'nar] *vt* to eliminate, remove

eliminatoria [elimina'torja] *nf* heat, preliminary (round)

elite [e'lite] *nf* elite
elocuencia [elo'kwenθja] *nf* eloquence
elogiar [elo'xjar] *vt* to praise, eulogize; **elogio** *nm* praise
elote [e'lote] (*AM*) *nm* corn on the cob
eludir [elu'ðir] *vt* (*evitar*) to avoid, evade; (*escapar*) to escape, elude
ella ['eʎa] *pron* (*persona*) she; (*cosa*) it; (*después de prep*: *persona*) her; (: *cosa*) it; **de ~** hers
ellas ['eʎas] *pron* (*personas y cosas*) they; (*después de prep*) them; **de ~** theirs
ello ['eʎo] *pron* it
ellos ['eʎos] *pron* they; (*después de prep*) them; **de ~** theirs
emanar [ema'nar] *vi*: **~ de** to emanate from, come from; (*derivar de*) to originate in
emancipar [emanθi'par] *vt* to emancipate; **~se** *vr* to become emancipated, free o.s.
embadurnar [embaður'nar] *vt* to smear
embajada [emba'xaða] *nf* embassy
embajador, a [embaxa'ðor, a] *nm/f* ambassador/ambassadress
embalaje [emba'laxe] *nm* packing
embalar [emba'lar] *vt* (*envolver*) to parcel, wrap (up); (*envasar*) to package; **~se** *vr* to go fast
embalsamar [embalsa'mar] *vt* to embalm
embalse [em'balse] *nm* (*presa*) dam; (*lago*) reservoir
embarazada [embara'θaða] *adj* pregnant ♦ *nf* pregnant woman
embarazar [embara'θar] *vt* to obstruct, hamper; **~se** *vr* (*aturdirse*) to become embarrassed; (*confundirse*) to get into a mess
embarazo [emba'raθo] *nm* (*de mujer*) pregnancy; (*impedimento*) obstacle, obstruction; (*timidez*) embarrassment; **embarazoso, a** *adj* awkward, embarrassing
embarcación [embarka'θjon] *nf* (*barco*) boat, craft; (*acto*) embarkation, boarding
embarcadero [embarka'ðero] *nm* pier, landing stage
embarcar [embar'kar] *vt* (*cargamento*) to ship, stow; (*persona*) to embark, put on board; **~se** *vr* to embark, go on board
embargar [embar'xar] *vt* (*JUR*) to seize, impound
embargo [em'barɣo] *nm* (*JUR*) seizure; (*COM, POL*) embargo
embargue [em'barɣe] *etc vb ver* **embargar**
embarque *etc* [em'barke] *vb ver* **embarcar** ♦ *nm* shipment, loading
embaucar [embau'kar] *vt* to trick, fool
embeber [embe'ßer] *vt* (*absorber*) to absorb, soak up; (*empapar*) to saturate ♦ *vi* to shrink; **~se** *vr*: **~se en un libro** to be engrossed o absorbed in a book
embellecer [embeʎe'θer] *vt* to embellish, beautify
embestida [embes'tiða] *nf* attack, on-

slaught; (*carga*) charge
embestir [embes'tir] *vt* to attack, assault; to charge, attack ♦ *vi* to attack
emblema [em'blema] *nm* emblem
embobado, a [embo'ßaðo, a] *adj* (*atontado*) stunned, bewildered
embolia [em'bolja] *nf* (*MED*) clot
émbolo ['embolo] *nm* (*AUTO*) piston
embolsar [embol'sar] *vt* to pocket, put in one's pocket
emborrachar [emborra'tʃar] *vt* to make drunk, intoxicate; **~se** *vr* to get drunk
emboscada [embos'kaða] *nf* (*celada*) ambush
embotar [embo'tar] *vt* to blunt, dull; **~se** *vr* (*adormecerse*) to go numb
embotellamiento [emboteʎa'mjento] *nm* (*AUTO*) traffic jam
embotellar [embote'ʎar] *vt* to bottle; **~se** *vr* (*circulación*) to get into a jam
embozo [em'boθo] *nm* (*de sábana*) turndown
embrague [em'braɣe] *nm* (*tb: pedal de ~*) clutch
embriagar [embrja'xar] *vt* (*emborrachar*) to make drunk; (*alegrar*) to delight; **~se** *vr* (*emborracharse*) to get drunk
embriaguez [embrja'xeθ] *nf* (*borrachera*) drunkenness
embrión [em'brjon] *nm* embryo
embrollar [embro'ʎar] *vt* (*el asunto*) to confuse, complicate; (*persona*) to involve, embroil; **~se** *vr* (*confundirse*) to get into a muddle o mess
embrollo [em'broʎo] *nm* (*enredo*) muddle, confusion; (*aprieto*) fix, jam
embrujado, a [embru'xado, a] *adj* bewitched; **casa embrujada** haunted house
embrutecer [embrute'θer] *vt* (*atontar*) to stupefy; **~se** *vr* to be stupefied
embudo [em'buðo] *nm* funnel
embuste [em'buste] *nm* trick; (*mentira*) lie; (*hum*) fib; **~ro, a** *adj* lying, deceitful ♦ *nm/f* (*tramposo*) cheat; (*mentiroso*) liar; (*humorístico*) fibber
embutido [embu'tiðo] *nm* (*CULIN*) sausage; (*TEC*) inlay
embutir [embu'tir] *vt* (*TEC*) to inlay; (*llenar*) to pack tight, cram
emergencia [emer'xenθja] *nf* emergency; (*surgimiento*) emergence
emerger [emer'xer] *vi* to emerge, appear
emigración [emixra'θjon] *nf* emigration; (*de pájaros*) migration
emigrar [emi'xrar] *vi* (*personas*) to emigrate; (*pájaros*) to migrate
eminencia [emi'nenθja] *nf* eminence; **eminente** *adj* eminent, distinguished; (*elevado*) high
emisario [emi'sarjo] *nm* emissary
emisión [emi'sjon] *nf* (*acto*) emission; (*COM etc*) issue; (*RADIO, TV*: *acto*) broadcasting;

(: *programa*) broadcast, programme (*BRIT*), program (*US*)

emisora [emi'sora] *nf* radio *o* broadcasting station

emitir [emi'tir] *vt* (*olor etc*) to emit, give off; (*moneda etc*) to issue; (*opinión*) to express; (*RADIO*) to broadcast

emoción [emo'θjon] *nf* emotion; (*excitación*) excitement; (*sentimiento*) feeling

emocionante [emoθjo'nante] *adj* (*excitante*) exciting, thrilling

emocionar [emoθjo'nar] *vt* (*excitar*) to excite, thrill; (*conmover*) to move, touch; (*impresionar*) to impress

emotivo, a [emo'tiβo, a] *adj* emotional

empacar [empa'kar] *vt* (*gen*) to pack; (*en caja*) to bale, crate

empacho [em'patʃo] *nm* (*MED*) indigestion; (*fig*) embarrassment

empadronarse [empaðro'narse] *vr* (*POL: como elector*) to register

empalagoso, a [empala'ɣoso, a] *adj* cloying; (*fig*) tiresome

empalizada [empali'θaða] *nf* (*valla*) fence

empalmar [empal'mar] *vt* to join, connect ♦ *vi* (*dos caminos*) to meet, join; **empalme** *nm* joint, connection; junction; (*de trenes*) connection

empanada [empa'naða] *nf* pie, pasty

empantanarse [empanta'narse] *vr* to get swamped; (*fig*) to get bogged down

empañarse [empa'ɲarse] *vr* (*cristales etc*) to steam up

empapar [empa'par] *vt* (*mojar*) to soak, saturate; (*absorber*) to soak up, absorb; **~se** *vr*. **~se de** to soak up

empapelar [empape'lar] *vt* (*paredes*) to paper

empaquetar [empake'tar] *vt* to pack, parcel up

emparedado [empare'ðaðo] *nm* sandwich

empastar [empas'tar] *vt* (*embadurnar*) to paste; (*diente*) to fill

empaste [em'paste] *nm* (*de diente*) filling

empatar [empa'tar] *vi* to draw, tie; **empate** *nm* draw, tie

empecé *etc vb ver* **empezar**

empedernido, a [empeðer'niðo, a] *adj* hard, heartless; (*fijado*) hardened, inveterate

empedrado, a [empe'ðraðo, a] *adj* paved ♦ *nm* paving

empeine [em'peine] *nm* (*de pie, zapato*) instep

empellón [empe'ʎon] *nm* push, shove

empeñado, a [empe'ɲaðo, a] *adj* (*persona*) pawned

empeñar [empe'ɲar] *vt* (*objeto*) to pawn, pledge; (*persona*) to compel; **~se** *vr* (*obligarse*) to bind o.s., pledge o.s.; (*endeudarse*) to get into debt; **~se en** to be set on, be determined to

empeño [em'peɲo] *nm* (*determinación, in-*

sistencia) determination, insistence; (*cosa prendada*) pledge; **casa de ~s** pawnshop

empeorar [empeo'rar] *vt* to make worse, worsen ♦ *vi* to get worse, deteriorate

empequeñecer [empekeɲe'θer] *vt* to dwarf; (*fig*) to belittle

emperador [empera'ðor] *nm* emperor; **emperatriz** *nf* empress

empezar [empe'θar] *vt, vi* to begin, start

empiece *etc vb ver* **empezar**

empiezo *etc vb ver* **empezar**

empinar [empi'nar] *vt* to raise; **~se** *vr* (*persona*) to stand on tiptoe; (*animal*) to rear up; (*camino*) to climb steeply

empírico, a [em'piriko, a] *adj* empirical

emplasto [em'plasto] *nm* (*MED*) plaster

emplazamiento [emplaθa'mjento] *nm* site, location; (*JUR*) summons

emplazar [empla'θar] *vt* (*ubicar*) to site, place, locate; (*JUR*) to summons; (*convocar*) to summon

empleado, a [emple'aðo, a] *nm/f* (*gen*) employee; (*de banco etc*) clerk

emplear [emple'ar] *vt* (*usar*) to use, employ; (*dar trabajo a*) to employ; **~se** *vr* (*conseguir trabajo*) to be employed; (*ocuparse*) to occupy o.s.

empleo [em'pleo] *nm* (*puesto*) job; (*puestos: colectivamente*) employment; (*uso*) use, employment

empobrecer [empoβre'θer] *vt* to impoverish; **~se** *vr* to become poor *o* impoverished

empolvarse [empol'βarse] *vr* to powder one's face

empollar [empo'ʎar] (*fam*) *vt, vi* to swot (up); **empollón, ona** (*fam*) *nm/f* swot

emporio [em'porjo] *nm* emporium, trading centre; (*AM: gran almacén*) department store

empotrado, a [empo'traðo, a] *adj* (*armario etc*) built-in

emprender [empren'der] *vt* (*empezar*) to begin, embark on; (*acometer*) to tackle, take on

empresa [em'presa] *nf* (*de espíritu etc*) enterprise; (*COM*) company, firm; **~rio, a** *nm/f* (*COM*) manager

empréstito [em'prestito] *nm* (*public*) loan

empujar [empu'xar] *vt* to push, shove; **empuje** *nm* thrust; (*presión*) pressure; (*fig*) vigour, drive

empujón [empu'xon] *nm* push, shove

empuñar [empu'ɲar] *vt* (*asir*) to grasp, take (firm) hold of

emular [emu'lar] *vt* to emulate; (*rivalizar*) to rival

PALABRA CLAVE

en [en] *prep* **1** (*posición*) in; (: *sobre*) on; **está ~ el cajón** it's in the drawer; **~ Argentina/La Paz** in Argentina/La Paz; **~**

la oficina/el colegio at the office/school;
está ~ el suelo/quinto piso it's on the
floor/the fifth floor
2 (*dirección*) into; **entró ~ el aula** she
went into the classroom; **meter algo ~ el
bolso** to put sth into one's bag
3 (*tiempo*) in; on; **~ 1605/3 semanas/
invierno** in 1605/3 weeks/winter; **~ (el
mes de) enero** in (the month of) January;
~ aquella ocasión/época on that
occasion/at that time
4 (*precio*) for; **lo vendió ~ 20 dólares** he
sold it for 20 dollars
5 (*diferencia*) by; **reducir/aumentar ~ una
tercera parte/20 por ciento** to reduce/
increase by a third/20 per cent
6 (*manera*): **~ avión/autobús** by plane/
bus; **escrito ~ inglés** written in English
7 (*después de vb que indica gastar etc*) on;
han cobrado demasiado ~ dietas ·they've
charged too much to expenses; **se le va la
mitad del sueldo ~ comida** he spends half
his salary on food
8 (*tema, ocupación*): **experto ~ la materia**
expert on the subject; **trabaja ~ la construcción** he works in the building industry
9 (*adj* + ~ + *infin*): **lento ~ reaccionar**
slow to react

enaguas [e'nawas] *nfpl* petticoat *sg*, underskirt *sg*
enajenación [enaxena'θjon] *nf* (*fig: distracción*) absent-mindedness; (: *embelesa-
miento*) rapture, trance
enajenamiento [enaxena'mjento] *nm* = **enajenación**
enajenar [enaxe'nar] *vt* to alienate; (*fig*) to
carry away
enamorado, a [enamo'raðo, a] *adj* in love
♦ *nm/f* lover
enamorar [enamo'rar] *vt* to win the love
of; **~se** *vr*: **~se de alguien** to fall in love
with sb
enano, a [e'nano, a] *adj* tiny ♦ *nm/f* dwarf
enardecer [enarðe'θer] *vt* (*pasiones*) to fire,
inflame; (*persona*) to fill with enthusiasm;
~se *vr*: **~se por** to get excited about; (*entusiasmarse*) to get enthusiastic about
encabezamiento [enkaβeθa'mjento] *nm*
(*de carta*) heading; (*de periódico*) headline;
(*preámbulo*) foreword, preface
encabezar [enkaβe'θar] *vt* (*movimiento, revolución*) to lead, head; (*lista*) to head, be
at the top of; (*carta*) to put a heading to;
(*libro*) to entitle
encadenar [enkaðe'nar] *vt* to chain (together); (*poner grilletes a*) to shackle
encajar [enka'xar] *vt* (*ajustar*): **~ (en)** to fit
(into); (*fam: golpe*) to give, deal; (*entro-
meter*) to insert ♦ *vi* to fit (well); (*fig: corresponder a*) to match; **~se** *vr*: **~se en un sillón** to squeeze into a chair

encaje [en'kaxe] *nm* (*labor*) lace
encalar [enka'lar] *vt* (*pared*) to whitewash
encallar [enka'ʎar] *vi* (*NAUT*) to run
aground
encaminar [enkami'nar] *vt* to direct, send;
~se a *vr*: **~se a** to set out for
encandilar [enkandi'lar] *vt* to dazzle
encantado, a [enkan'taðo, a] *adj* (*hechizado*) bewitched; (*muy contento*) delighted;
¡**~!** how do you do, pleased to meet you
encantador, a [enkanta'ðor, a] *adj* charming, lovely ♦ *nm/f* magician, enchanter/
enchantress
encantar [enkan'tar] *vt* to charm, delight;
(*hechizar*) to bewitch, cast a spell on; **encanto** *nm* (*magia*) spell, charm; (*fig*)
charm, delight
encarcelar [enkarθe'lar] *vt* to imprison, jail
encarecer [enkare'θer] *vt* to put up the
price of ♦ *vi* to get dearer; **~se** *vr* to get
dearer
encarecimiento [enkareθi'mjento] *nm*
price increase
encargado, a [enkar'ɣaðo, a] *adj* in charge
♦ *nm/f* agent, representative; (*responsable*)
person in charge
encargar [enkar'ɣar] *vt* to entrust; (*recomendar*) to urge, recommend; **~se** *vr*: **~se
de** to look after, take charge of
encargo [en'karɣo] *nm* (*pedido*) assignment, job; (*responsabilidad*) responsibility;
(*recomendación*) recommendation; (*COM*)
order
encariñarse [enkari'narse] *vr*: **~ con** to
grow fond of, get attached to
encarnación [enkarna'θjon] *nf* incarnation,
embodiment
encarnizado, a [enkarni'θaðo, a] *adj*
(*lucha*) bloody, fierce
encarrilar [enkarri'lar] *vt* (*tren*) to put back
on the rails; (*fig*) to correct, put on the
right track
encasillar [enkasi'ʎar] *vt* (*tb fig*) to pigeonhole; (*actor*) to typecast
encasquetar [enkaske'tar] *vt* (*gorro, sombrero*) to pull on, stick on; **~se** *vr* to pull
on, stick on
encauzar [enkau'θar] *vt* to channel
encendedor [enθende'ðor] *nm* lighter
encender [enθen'der] *vt* (*con fuego*) to
light; (*incendiar*) to set fire to; (*luz, radio*) to
put on, switch on; (*avivar: pasiones*) to inflame; **~se** *vr* to catch fire; (*excitarse*) to
get excited; (*de cólera*) to flare up; (*el rostro*) to blush
encendido [enθen'diðo] *nm* (*AUTO*) ignition
encerado [enθe'raðo] *nm* (*ESCOL*) blackboard
encerar [enθe'rar] *vt* (*suelo*) to wax, polish
encerrar [enθe'rrar] *vt* (*confinar*) to shut in,
shut up; (*comprender, incluir*) to include,

contain

encía [en'θia] *nf* gum

encienda *etc vb ver* **encender**

encierro *etc* [en'θjerro] *vb ver* **encerrar** ♦ *nm* shutting in, shutting up; (*calabozo*) prison

encima [en'θima] *adv* (*sobre*) above, over; (*además*) besides; ~ **de** (*en*) on, on top of; (*sobre*) above, over; (*además de*) besides, on top of; **por** ~ **de** over; ¿**llevas dinero** ~? have you (got) any money on you?; **se me vino** ~ it took me by surprise

encinta [en'θinta] *adj* pregnant

enclenque [en'klenke] *adj* weak, sickly

encoger [enko'xer] *vt* to shrink, contract; (*fig: asustar*) to scare; ~**se** *vr* to shrink, contract; (*fig*) to cringe; ~**se de hombros** to shrug one's shoulders

encolar [enko'lar] *vt* (*engomar*) to glue, paste; (*pegar*) to stick down

encolerizar [enkoleri'θar] *vt* to anger, provoke; ~**se** *vr* to get angry

encomendar [enkomen'dar] *vt* to entrust, commend; ~**se** *vr*: ~**se a** to put one's trust in

encomiar [enko'mjar] *vt* to praise, pay tribute to

encomienda *etc* [enko'mjenda] *vb ver* **encomendar** ♦ *nf* (*encargo*) charge, commission; (*elogio*) tribute; ~ **postal** (*AM*) parcel post

encontrado, a [enkon'traðo, a] *adj* (*contrario*) contrary, conflicting; (*hostil*) hostile

encontrar [enkon'trar] *vt* (*hallar*) to find; (*inesperadamente*) to meet, run into; ~**se** *vr* to meet (each other); (*situarse*) to be (situated); (*entrar en conflicto*) to crash, collide; ~**se con** to meet; ~**se bien (de salud)** to feel well

encorvar [enkor'βar] *vt* to curve, (*inclinar*) to bend (down); ~**se** *vr* to bend down, bend over

encrespar [enkres'par] *vt* (*cabellos*) to curl; (*fig*) to anger, irritate; ~**se** *vr* (*el mar*) to get rough; (*fig*) to get cross, get irritated

encrucijada [enkruθi'xaða] *nf* crossroads *sg*; (*empalme*) junction

encuadernación [enkwaðerna'θjon] *nf* binding

encuadernador, a [enkwaðerna'ðor, a] *nm/f* bookbinder

encuadrar [enkwa'ðrar] *vt* (*retrato*) to frame; (*ajustar*) to fit, insert; (*encerrar*) to contain

encubrir [enku'βrir] *vt* (*ocultar*) to hide, conceal; (*criminal*) to harbour, shelter

encuentro *etc* [en'kwentro] *vb ver* **encontrar** ♦ *nm* (*de personas*) meeting; (*AUTO etc*) collision, crash; (*DEPORTE*) match, game; (*MIL*) encounter

encuesta [en'kwesta] *nf* inquiry, investigation; (*sondeo*) (public) opinion poll; ~

judicial post mortem

encumbrar [enkum'brar] *vt* (*persona*) to exalt; ~**se** *vr* (*fig*) to become conceited

encharcado, a [entʃar'kaðo, a] *adj* (*terreno*) flooded

encharcarse [entʃar'karse] *vr* to get flooded

enchufado, a [entʃu'faðo, a] (*fam*) *nm/f* well-connected person

enchufar [entʃu'far] *vt* (*ELEC*) to plug in; (*TEC*) to connect, fit together; **enchufe** *nm* (*ELEC: clavija*) plug; (: *toma*) socket; (*de dos tubos*) joint, connection; (*fam: influencia*) contact, connection; (: *puesto*) cushy job

endeble [en'deβle] *adj* (*argumento, excusa, persona*) weak

endémico, a [en'demiko, a] *adj* (*MED*) endemic; (*fig*) rife, chronic

endemoniado, a [endemo'njaðo, a] *adj* possessed (of the devil); (*travieso*) devilish

enderezar [endere'θar] *vt* (*poner derecho*) to straighten (out); (: *verticalmente*) to set upright; (*fig*) to straighten *o* sort out; (*dirigir*) to direct; ~**se** *vr* (*persona sentada*) to straighten up

endeudarse [endeu'ðarse] *vr* to get into debt

endiablado, a [endja'βlaðo, a] *adj* devilish, diabolical; (*travieso*) mischievous

endilgar [endil'var] (*fam*) *vt*: ~**le algo a uno** to lumber sb with sth; ~**le un sermón a uno** to lecture sb

endiñar [endi'ɲar] (*fam*) *vt* (*bofetón*) to land, belt

endosar [endo'sar] *vt* (*cheque etc*) to endorse

endulzar [endul'θar] *vt* to sweeten; (*suavizar*) to soften

endurecer [endure'θer] *vt* to harden; ~**se** *vr* to harden, grow hard

enema [e'nema] *nm* (*MED*) enema

enemigo, a [ene'miɣo, a] *adj* enemy, hostile ♦ *nm/f* enemy

enemistad [enemis'tað] *nf* enmity

enemistar [enemis'tar] *vt* to make enemies of, cause a rift between; ~**se** *vr* to become enemies; (*amigos*) to fall out

energía [ener'xia] *nf* (*vigor*) energy, drive; (*empuje*) push; (*TEC, ELEC*) energy, power; ~ **eolica** wind power; ~ **solar** solar energy/power

enérgico, a [e'nerxiko, a] *adj* (*gen*) energetic; (*voz, modales*) forceful

energúmeno, a [ener'vumeno, a] (*fam*) *nm/f* (*fig*) madman/woman

enero [e'nero] *nm* January

enfadado, a [enfa'ðaðo, a] *adj* angry, annoyed

enfadar [enfa'ðar] *vt* to anger, annoy; ~**se** *vr* to get angry *o* annoyed

enfado [en'faðo] *nm* (*enojo*) anger, annoyance; (*disgusto*) trouble, bother

énfasis ['enfasis] *nm* emphasis, stress

enfático, a [en'fatiko, a] *adj* emphatic

enfermar [enfer'mar] *vt* to make ill ♦ *vi* to fall ill, be taken ill

enfermedad [enferme'ðað] *nf* illness; ~ **venérea** venereal disease

enfermera [enfer'mera] *nf* nurse

enfermería [enferme'ria] *nf* infirmary; (*de colegio etc*) sick bay

enfermero [enfer'mero] *nm* (male) nurse

enfermizo, a [enfer'miθo, a] *adj* (*persona*) sickly, unhealthy; (*fig*) unhealthy

enfermo, a [en'fermo, a] *adj* ill, sick ♦ *nm/f* invalid, sick person; (*en hospital*) patient

enflaquecer [enflake'θer] *vt* (*adelgazar*) to make thin; (*debilitar*) to weaken

enfocar [enfo'kar] *vt* (*foto etc*) to focus; (*problema etc*) to consider, look at

enfoque *etc* [en'foke] *vb ver* **enfocar** ♦ *nm* focus.

enfrascarse [enfras'karse] *vr*: ~ **en algo** to bury o.s. in sth

enfrentar [enfren'tar] *vt* (*peligro*) to face (up to), confront; (*oponer*) to bring face to face; ~**se** *vr* (*dos personas*) to face o confront each other; (*DEPORTE: dos equipos*) to meet; ~**se a** o **con** to face up to, confront

enfrente [en'frente] *adv* opposite; **la casa de** ~ the house opposite, the house across the street; ~ **de** opposite, facing

enfriamiento [enfria'mjento] *nm* chilling, refrigeration; (*MED*) cold, chill

enfriar [enfri'ar] *vt* (*alimentos*) to cool, chill; (*algo caliente*) to cool down; (*habitación*) to air, freshen; ~**se** *vr* to cool down; (*MED*) to catch a chill; (*amistad*) to cool

enfurecer [enfure'θer] *vt* to enrage, madden; ~**se** *vr* to become furious, fly into a rage; (*mar*) to get rough

engalanar [engala'nar] *vt* (*adornar*) to adorn; (*ciudad*) to decorate; ~**se** *vr* to get dressed up

enganchar [engan't∫ar] *vt* to hook; (*ropa*) to hang up; (*dos vagones*) to hitch up; (*TEC*) to couple, connect; (*MIL*) to recruit; (*fam: persona*) to rope in; ~**se** *vr* (*MIL*) to enlist, join up

enganche [en'gant∫e] *nm* hook; (*TEC*) coupling, connection; (*acto*) hooking (up); (*MIL*) recruitment, enlistment; (*AM: depósito*) deposit

engañar [enga'ɲar] *vt* to deceive; (*estafar*) to cheat, swindle; ~**se** *vr* (*equivocarse*) to be wrong; (*disimular la verdad*) to deceive o.s.

engaño [en'gaɲo] *nm* deceit; (*estafa*) trick, swindle; (*error*) mistake, misunderstanding; (*ilusión*) delusion; ~**so, a** *adj* (*tramposo*) crooked; (*mentiroso*) dishonest, deceitful; (*aspecto*) deceptive; (*consejo*) misleading

engarzar [engar'θar] *vt* (*joya*) to set, mount; (*fig*) to link, connect

engatusar [engatu'sar] (*fam*) *vt* to coax

engendrar [enxen'drar] *vt* to breed; (*procrear*) to beget; (*fig*) to cause, produce; **engendro** [en'xendro] *nm* (*BIO*) foetus; (*fig*) monstrosity; (*idea*) brainchild

englobar [englo'ßar] *vt* (*incluir*) to include, comprise

engordar [engor'ðar] *vt* to fatten ♦ *vi* to get fat, put on weight

engorroso, a [engo'rroso, a] *adj* bothersome, trying

engranaje [engra'naxe] *nm* (*AUTO*) gear

engrandecer [engrande'θer] *vt* to enlarge, magnify; (*alabar*) to praise, speak highly of; (*exagerar*) to exaggerate

engrasar [engra'sar] *vt* (*TEC: poner grasa*) to grease; (: *lubricar*) to lubricate, oil; (*manchar*) to make greasy

engreído, a [engre'iðo, a] *adj* vain, conceited

engrosar [engro'sar] *vt* (*ensanchar*) to enlarge; (*aumentar*) to increase; (*hinchar*) to swell

enhebrar [ene'ßrar] *vt* to thread

enhorabuena [enora'ßwena] *excl*: ¡~! congratulations! ♦ *nf*: **dar la** ~ **a** to congratulate

enigma [e'niɣma] *nm* enigma; (*problema*) puzzle; (*misterio*) mystery

enjabonar [enxaßo'nar] *vt* to soap; (*fam: adular*) to soft-soap; (: *regañar*) to tick off

enjambre [en'xambre] *nm* swarm

enjaular [enxau'lar] *vt* to (put in a) cage; (*fam*) to jail, lock up

enjuagar [enxwa'ɣar] *vt* (*ropa*) to rinse (out)

enjuague *etc* [en'xwaɣe] *vb ver* **enjuagar** ♦ *nm* (*MED*) mouthwash; (*de ropa*) rinse, rinsing

enjugar [enxu'ɣar] *vt* to wipe (off); (*lágrimas*) to dry; (*déficit*) to wipe out

enjuiciar [enxwi'θjar] *vt* (*JUR: procesar*) to prosecute, try; (*fig*) to judge

enjuto, a [en'xuto, a] *adj* dry, dried up; (*fig*) lean, skinny

enlace [en'laθe] *nm* link, connection; (*relación*) relationship; (*tb:* ~ **matrimonial**) marriage; (*de carretera, trenes*) connection; ~ **sindical** shop steward

enlatado, a [enla'taðo, a] *adj* (*comida, productos*) tinned, canned

enlazar [enla'θar] *vt* (*unir con lazos*) to bind together; (*atar*) to tie; (*conectar*) to link, connect; (*AM*) to lasso

enlodar [enlo'ðar] *vt* to cover in mud; (*fig: manchar*) to stain; (: *rebajar*) to debase

enloquecer [enloke'θer] *vt* to drive mad ♦ *vi* to go mad; ~**se** *vr* to go mad

enlutado, a [enlu'taðo, a] *adj* (*persona*) in mourning

enmarañar [enmara'ɲar] vt (enredar) to tangle (up), entangle; (complicar) to complicate; (confundir) to confuse; ~se vr (enredarse) to become entangled; (confundirse) to get confused

enmarcar [enmar'kar] vt (cuadro) to frame

enmascarar [enmaska'rar] vt to mask; ~se vr to put on a mask

enmendar [enmen'dar] vt to emend, correct; (constitución etc) to amend; (comportamiento) to reform; ~se vr to reform, mend one's ways; **enmienda** nf correction; amendment; reform

enmohecerse [enmoe'θerse] vr (metal) to rust, go rusty; (muro, plantas) to get mouldy

enmudecer [enmuðe'θer] vi (perder el habla) to fall silent; (guardar silencio) to remain silent; ~se vr to fall silent; to remain silent

ennegrecer [enneɣre'θer] vt (poner negro) to blacken; (oscurecer) to darken; ~se vr to turn black; (oscurecerse) to get dark, darken

ennoblecer [ennoβle'θer] vt to ennoble

enojar [eno'xar] vt (encolerizar) to anger; (disgustar) to annoy, upset; ~se vr to get angry; to get annoyed

enojo [e'noxo] nm (cólera) anger; (irritación) annoyance; ~so, a adj annoying

enorgullecerse [enorɣuʎe'θerse] vr to be proud; ~ de to pride o.s. on, be proud of

enorme [e'norme] adj enormous, huge; (fig) monstrous; **enormidad** nf hugeness, immensity

enrarecido, a [enrare'θiðo, a] adj (atmósfera, aire) rarefied

enredadera [enreða'ðera] nf (BOT) creeper, climbing plant

enredar [enre'ðar] vt (cables, hilos etc) to tangle (up), entangle; (situación) to complicate, confuse; (meter cizaña) to sow discord among o between; (implicar) to embroil, implicate; ~se vr to get entangled, get tangled (up); (situación) to get complicated; (persona) to get embroiled; (AM: fam) to meddle

enredo [en'reðo] nm (maraña) tangle; (confusión) mix-up, confusion; (intriga) intrigue

enrejado [enre'xaðo] nm fence, railings pl

enrevesado, a [enreβe'saðo, a] adj (asunto) complicated, involved

enriquecer [enrike'θer] vt to make rich, enrich; ~se vr to get rich

enrojecer [enroxe'θer] vt to redden ♦ vi (persona) to blush; ~se vr to blush

enrolar [enro'lar] vt (MIL) to enlist; (reclutar) to recruit; ~se vr (MIL) to join up; (afiliarse) to enrol

enrollar [enro'ʎar] vt to roll (up), wind (up)

enroscar [enros'kar] vt (torcer, doblar) to coil (round), wind; (tornillo, rosca) to screw in; ~se vr to coil, wind

ensalada [ensa'laða] nf salad; **ensaladilla (rusa)** nf Russian salad

ensalzar [ensal'θar] vt (alabar) to praise, extol; (exaltar) to exalt

ensambladura [ensambla'ðura] nf assembly; (TEC) joint

ensamblaje [ensam'blaxe] nm = ensambla- dura

ensanchar [ensan'tʃar] vt (hacer más ancho) to widen; (agrandar) to enlarge, expand; (COSTURA) to let out; ~se vr to get wider, expand; (pey) to give o.s. airs; **ensanche** nm (de calle) widening; (de negocio) expansion

ensangrentar [ensangren'tar] vt to stain with blood

ensañar [ensa'ɲar] vt to enrage; ~se vr: ~se con to treat brutally

ensartar [ensar'tar] vt (cuentas, perlas etc) to string (together)

ensayar [ensa'jar] vt to test, try (out); (TEATRO) to rehearse

ensayista [ensa'jista] nm/f essayist

ensayo [en'sajo] nm test, trial; (QUÍMICA) experiment; (TEATRO) rehearsal; (DEPORTE) try; (ESCOL, LITERATURA) essay

ensenada [ense'naða] nf inlet, cove

enseñanza [ense'ɲanθa] nf (educación) education; (acción) teaching; (doctrina) teaching, doctrine

enseñar [ense'ɲar] vt (educar) to teach; (instruir) to teach, instruct; (mostrar, señalar) to show

enseres [en'seres] nmpl belongings

ensillar [ensi'ʎar] vt to saddle (up)

ensimismarse [ensimis'marse] vr (abstraerse) to become lost in thought; (estar absorto) to be lost in thought; (AM) to become conceited

ensombrecer [ensombre'θer] vt to darken, cast a shadow over; (fig) to overshadow, put in the shade

ensordecer [ensorðe'θer] vt to deafen ♦ vi to go deaf

ensortijado, a [ensorti'xaðo, a] adj (pelo) curly

ensuciar [ensu'θjar] vt (manchar) to dirty, soil; (fig) to defile; ~se vr to get dirty; (niño) to wet o.s.

ensueño [en'sweɲo] nm (sueño) dream, fantasy; (ilusión) illusion; (soñando despierto) daydream

entablar [enta'βlar] vt (recubrir) to board (up); (AJEDREZ, DAMAS) to set up; (conversación) to strike up; (JUR) to file ♦ vi to draw

entablillar [entaβli'ʎar] vt (MED) to (put in a) splint

entallar [enta'ʎar] vt (traje) to tailor ♦ vi: el traje entalla bien the suit fits well

ente ['ente] *nm (organización)* body, organization; *(fam: persona)* odd character

entender [enten'der] *vt (comprender)* to understand; *(darse cuenta)* to realize; *(querer decir)* to mean ♦ *vi* to understand; *(creer)* to think, believe; **~se** *vr (comprenderse)* to be understood; *(2 personas)* to get on together; *(ponerse de acuerdo)* to agree, reach an agreement; **~ de** to know all about; **~ algo de** to know a little about; **~ en** to deal with, have to do with; **~se mal** *(2 personas)* to get on badly

entendido, a [enten'diðo, a] *adj (comprendido)* understood; *(hábil)* skilled; *(inteligente)* knowledgeable ♦ *nm/f (experto)* expert ♦ *excl* agreed!; **entendimiento** *nm (comprensión)* understanding; *(inteligencia)* mind, intellect; *(juicio)* judgement

enterado, a [ente'raðo, a] *adj* well-informed; **estar ~ de** to know about, be aware of

enteramente [entera'mente] *adv* entirely, completely

enterar [ente'rar] *vt (informar)* to inform, tell; **~se** *vr* to find out, get to know

entereza [ente'reθa] *nf (totalidad)* entirety; *(fig: carácter)* strength of mind; *(: honradez)* integrity

enternecer [enterne'θer] *vt (ablandar)* to soften; *(apiadar)* to touch, move; **~se** *vr* to be touched, be moved

entero, a [en'tero, a] *adj (total)* whole, entire; *(fig: recto)* honest; *(: firme)* firm, resolute ♦ *nm (COM: punto)* point; *(AM: pago)* payment

enterrador [enterra'ðor] *nm* gravedigger

enterrar [ente'rrar] *vt* to bury

entibiar [enti'βjar] *vt (enfriar)* to cool; *(calentar)* to warm; **~se** *vr (fig)* to cool

entidad [enti'ðað] *nf (empresa)* firm, company; *(organismo)* body; *(sociedad)* society; *(FILOSOFÍA)* entity

entiendo *etc vb ver* **entender**

entierro [en'tjerro] *nm (acción)* burial; *(funeral)* funeral

entomología [entomolo'xia] *nf* entomology

entonación [entona'θjon] *nf (LING)* intonation; *(fig)* conceit

entonar [ento'nar] *vt (canción)* to intone; *(colores)* to tone; *(MED)* to tone up ♦ *vi* to be in tune; **~se** *vr (engreírse)* to give o.s. airs

entonces [en'tonθes] *adv* then, at that time; **desde ~** since then; **en aquel ~** at that time; **(pues) ~** and so

entornar [entor'nar] *vt (puerta, ventana)* to half close, leave ajar; *(los ojos)* to screw up

entorpecer [entorpe'θer] *vt (entendimiento)* to dull; *(impedir)* to obstruct, hinder; *(: tránsito)* to slow down, delay

entrada [en'traða] *nf (acción)* entry, access; *(sitio)* entrance, way in; *(INFORM)* input;

(COM) receipts *pl*, takings *pl*; *(CULIN)* starter; *(DEPORTE)* innings *sg*; *(TEATRO)* house, audience; *(para el cine etc)* ticket; *(COM)*: **~s y salidas** income and expenditure; *(TEC)*: **~ de aire** air intake *o* inlet; **de ~** from the outset

entrado, a [en'traðo, a] *adj*: **~ en años** elderly; **una vez ~ el verano** in the summer(time), when summer comes

entramparse [entram'parse] *vr* to get into debt

entrante [en'trante] *adj* next, coming; **mes/año ~** next month/year

entraña [en'trana] *nf (fig: centro)* heart, core; *(raíz)* root; **~s** *nfpl (ANAT)* entrails; *(fig)* heart *sg*; **sin ~s** *(fig)* heartless; **entrañable** *adj* close, intimate; **entrañar** *vt* to entail

entrar [en'trar] *vt (introducir)* to bring in; *(INFORM)* to input ♦ *vi (meterse)* to go in, come in, enter; *(comenzar)*: **~ diciendo** to begin by saying; **hacer ~** to show in; **no me entra** I can't get the hang of it

entre ['entre] *prep (dos)* between; *(más de dos)* among(st)

entreabrir [entrea'βrir] *vt* to half-open, open halfway

entrecejo [entre'θexo] *nm*: **fruncir el ~** to frown

entrecortado, a [entrekor'taðo, a] *adj (respiración)* difficult; *(habla)* faltering

entredicho [entre'ðitʃo] *nm (JUR)* injunction; **poner en ~** to cast doubt on; **estar en ~** to be banned

entrega [en'treɣa] *nf (de mercancías)* delivery; *(de novela etc)* instalment

entregar [entre'ɣar] *vt (dar)* to hand (over), deliver; **~se** *vr (rendirse)* to surrender, give in, submit; *(dedicarse)* to devote o.s.

entrelazar [entrela'θar] *vt* to entwine

entremeses [entre'meses] *nmpl* hors d'œuvres

entremeter [entreme'ter] *vt* to insert, put in; **~se** *vr* to meddle, interfere; **entremetido, a** *adj* meddling, interfering

entremezclar [entremeθ'klar] *vt* to intermingle; **~se** *vr* to intermingle

entrenador, a [entrena'ðor, a] *nm/f* trainer, coach

entrenarse [entre'narse] *vr* to train

entrepierna [entre'pjerna] *nf* crotch

entresacar [entresa'kar] *vt* to pick out, select

entresuelo [entre'swelo] *nm* mezzanine

entretanto [entre'tanto] *adv* meanwhile, meantime

entretejer [entrete'xer] *vt* to interweave

entretener [entrete'ner] *vt (divertir)* to entertain, amuse; *(detener)* to hold up, delay; *(mantener)* to maintain; **~se** *vr (divertirse)* to amuse o.s.; *(retrasarse)* to delay, linger; **entretenido, a** *adj* entertaining, amusing;

entretenimiento *nm* entertainment, amusement; (*mantenimiento*) upkeep, maintenance

entrever [entre'ßer] *vt* to glimpse, catch a glimpse of

entrevista [entre'ßista] *nf* interview; **entrevistar** *vt* to interview; **entrevistarse** *vr* to have an interview

entristecer [entriste'θer] *vt* to sadden, grieve; ~**se** *vr* to grow sad

entrometerse [entrome'terse] *vr*: ~ (**en**) to interfere (in *o* with)

entroncar [entron'kar] *vi* to be connected *o* related

entumecer [entume'θer] *vt* to numb, benumb; ~**se** *vr* (*por el frío*) to go *o* become numb; **entumecido, a** *adj* numb, stiff

enturbiar [entur'ßjar] *vt* (*el agua*) to make cloudy; (*fig*) to confuse; ~**se** *vr* (*oscurecerse*) to become cloudy; (*fig*) to get confused, become obscure

entusiasmar [entusjas'mar] *vt* to excite, fill with enthusiasm; (*gustar mucho*) to delight; ~**se** *vr*: ~**se con** *o* **por** to get enthusiastic *o* excited about

entusiasmo [entu'sjasmo] *nm* enthusiasm; (*excitación*) excitement

entusiasta [entu'sjasta] *adj* enthusiastic ♦ *nm/f* enthusiast

enumerar [enume'rar] *vt* to enumerate

enunciación [enunθja'θjon] *nf* enunciation

enunciado [enun'θjaðo] *nm* enunciation; (*declaración*) declaration, statement

envainar [embai'nar] *vt* to sheathe

envalentonar [embalento'nar] *vt* to give courage to; ~**se** *vr* (*pey: jactarse*) to boast, brag

envanecer [embane'θer] *vt* to make conceited; ~**se** *vr* to grow conceited

envasar [emba'sar] *vt* (*empaquetar*) to pack, wrap; (*enfrascar*) to bottle; (*enlatar*) to can; (*embolsar*) to pocket

envase [em'base] *nm* (*en paquete*) packing, wrapping; (*en botella*) bottling; (*en lata*) canning; (*recipiente*) container; (*paquete*) package; (*botella*) bottle; (*lata*) tin (*BRIT*), can

envejecer [embexe'θer] *vt* to make old, age ♦ *vi* (*volverse viejo*) to grow old; (*parecer viejo*) to age; ~**se** *vr* to grow old; to age

envenenar [embene'nar] *vt* to poison; (*fig*) to embitter

envergadura [emberva'ðura] *nf* (*fig*) scope, compass

envés [em'bes] *nm* (*de tela*) back, wrong side

enviar [em'bjar] *vt* to send

enviciarse [embi'θjarse] *vr*: ~ (**con**) to get addicted (to)

envidia [em'biðja] *nf* envy; **tener** ~ **a** to envy, be jealous of; **envidiar** *vt* (*desear*) to envy; (*tener celos de*) to be jealous of

envío [em'bio] *nm* (*acción*) sending; (*de mercancías*) consignment; (*de dinero*) remittance

enviudar [embju'ðar] *vi* to be widowed

envoltura [embol'tura] *nf* (*cobertura*) cover; (*embalaje*) wrapper, wrapping; **envoltorio** *nm* package

envolver [embol'ßer] *vt* to wrap (up); (*cubrir*) to cover; (*enemigo*) to surround; (*implicar*) to involve, implicate

envuelto [em'bwelto] *pp de* **envolver**

enyesar [enje'sar] *vt* (*pared*) to plaster; (*MED*) to put in plaster

enzarzarse [enθar'θarse] *vr*: ~ **en** (*en pelea*) to get mixed up in; (*en disputa*) to get involved in

épica ['epika] *nf* epic

épico, a ['epiko, a] *adj* epic

epidemia [epi'ðemja] *nf* epidemic

epilepsia [epi'lepsja] *nf* epilepsy

epílogo [e'piloxo] *nm* epilogue

episodio [epi'soðjo] *nm* episode

epístola [e'pistola] *nf* epistle

época ['epoka] *nf* period, time; (*HISTORIA*) age, epoch; **hacer** ~ to be epoch-making

equidad [eki'ðað] *nf* equity

equilibrar [ekili'ßrar] *vt* to balance; **equilibrio** *nm* balance, equilibrium; **equilibrista** *nm/f* (*funámbulo*) tightrope walker; (*acróbata*) acrobat

equipaje [eki'paxe] *nm* luggage; (*avíos*) equipment, kit; ~ **de mano** hand luggage

equipar [eki'par] *vt* (*proveer*) to equip

equipararse [ekipa'rarse] *vr*: ~ **con** to be on a level with

equipo [e'kipo] *nm* (*conjunto de cosas*) equipment; (*DEPORTE*) team; (*de obreros*) shift

equis ['ekis] *nf inv* (the letter) X

equitación [ekita'θjon] *nf* (*acto*) riding; (*arte*) horsemanship

equitativo, a [ekita'tißo, a] *adj* equitable, fair

equivalente [ekißa'lente] *adj, nm* equivalent

equivaler [ekißa'ler] *vi* to be equivalent *o* equal

equivocación [ekißoka'θjon] *nf* mistake, error

equivocado, a [ekißo'kaðo, a] *adj* wrong, mistaken

equivocarse [ekißo'karse] *vr* to be wrong, make a mistake; ~ **de camino** to take the wrong road

equívoco, a [e'kißoko, a] *adj* (*dudoso*) suspect; (*ambiguo*) ambiguous ♦ *nm* ambiguity; (*malentendido*) misunderstanding

era ['era] *vb ver* **ser** ♦ *nf* era, age

erais *vb ver* **ser**

éramos *vb ver* **ser**

eran *vb ver* **ser**

erario [e'rarjo] *nm* exchequer (*BRIT*),

treasury
erección [erek'θjon] *nf* erection
eras *vb ver* **ser**
eres *vb ver* **ser**
erguir [er'xir] *vt* to raise, lift; (*poner derecho*) to straighten; ~**se** *vr* to straighten up
erigir [eri'xir] *vt* to erect, build; ~**se** *vr*: ~**se en** to set o.s. up as
erizarse [eri'θarse] *vr* (*pelo: de perro*) to bristle; (: *de persona*) to stand on end
erizo [e'riθo] *nm* (*ZOOL*) hedgehog; ~ **de mar** sea-urchin
ermita [er'mita] *nf* hermitage
ermitaño, a [ermi'taɲo, a] *nm/f* hermit
erosion [ero'sjon] *nf* erosion
erosionar [erosjo'nar] *vt* to erode
erótico, a [e'rotiko, a] *adj* erotic; **erotismo** *nm* eroticism
erradicar [erraði'kar] *vt* to eradicate
errante [e'rrante] *adj* wandering, errant
errar [e'rrar] *vi* (*vagar*) to wander, roam; (*equivocarse*) to be mistaken ♦ *vt*: ~ **el camino** to take the wrong road; ~ **el tiro** to miss
erróneo, a [e'rroneo, a] *adj* (*equivocado*) wrong, mistaken; (*falso*) false, untrue
error [e'rror] *nm* error, mistake; (*INFORM*) bug; ~ **de imprenta** misprint
eructar [eruk'tar] *vt* to belch, burp
erudito, a [eru'ðito, a] *adj* erudite, learned
erupción [erup'θjon] *nf* eruption; (*MED*) rash
es *vb ver* **ser**
esa ['esa] (*pl* **esas**) *adj demos ver* **ese**
ésa ['esa] (*pl* **ésas**) *pron ver* **ése**
esbelto, a [es'βelto, a] *adj* slim, slender
esbozo [es'βoθo] *nm* sketch, outline
escabeche [eska'βetʃe] *nm* brine; (*de aceitunas etc*) pickle; **en** ~ pickled
escabroso, a [eska'βroso, a] *adj* (*accidentado*) rough, uneven; (*fig*) tough, difficult; (: *atrevido*) risqué
escabullirse [eskaβu'ʎirse] *vr* to slip away, to clear out
escafandra [eska'fandra] *nf* (*buzo*) diving suit; (~ *espacial*) space suit
escala [es'kala] *nf* (*proporción, MUS*) scale; (*de mano*) ladder; (*AVIAT*) stopover; **hacer** ~ **en** to stop *o* call in at
escalafón [eskala'fon] *nm* (*escala de salarios*) salary scale, wage scale
escalar [eska'lar] *vt* to climb, scale
escalera [eska'lera] *nf* stairs *pl*, staircase; (*escala*) ladder; (*NAIPES*) run; ~ **mecánica** escalator; ~ **de caracol** spiral staircase
escalfar [eskal'far] *vt* (*huevos*) to poach
escalinata [eskali'nata] *nf* staircase
escalofriante [eskalo'frjante] *adj* chilling
escalofrío [eskalo'frio] *nm* (*MED*) chill; ~**s** *nmpl* (*fig*) shivers
escalón [eska'lon] *nm* step, stair; (*de escalera*) rung

escalope [eska'lope] *nm* (*CULIN*) escalope
escama [es'kama] *nf* (*de pez, serpiente*) scale; (*de jabón*) flake; (*fig*) resentment
escamar [eska'mar] *vt* (*fig*) to make wary *o* suspicious
escamotear [eskamote'ar] *vt* (*robar*) to lift, swipe; (*hacer desaparecer*) to make disappear
escampar [eskam'par] *vb impers* to stop raining
escandalizar [eskandali'θar] *vt* to scandalize, shock; ~**se** *vr* to be shocked; (*ofenderse*) to be offended
escándalo [es'kandalo] *nm* scandal; (*alboroto, tumulto*) row, uproar; **escandaloso, a** *adj* scandalous, shocking
escandinavo, a [eskandi'naβo, a] *adj, nm/f* Scandinavian
escaño [es'kaɲo] *nm* bench; (*POL*) seat
escapar [eska'par] *vi* (*gen*) to escape, run away; (*DEPORTE*) to break away; ~**se** *vr* to escape, get away; (*agua, gas*) to leak (out)
escaparate [eskapa'rate] *nm* shop window
escape [es'kape] *nm* (*de agua, gas*) leak; (*de motor*) exhaust; (*de persona*) escape
escarabajo [eskara'βaxo] *nm* beetle
escaramuza [eskara'muθa] *nf* skirmish; (*fig*) brush
escarbar [eskar'βar] *vt* (*gallina*) to scratch; (*fig*) to inquire into, investigate
escarceos [eskar'θeos] *nmpl* (*fig*): **en mis** ~ **con la política** ... in my dealings with politics ...; ~ **amorosos** love affairs
escarcha [es'kartʃa] *nf* frost
escarchado, a [eskar'tʃaðo, a] *adj* (*CULIN: fruta*) crystallized
escarlata [eskar'lata] *adj inv* scarlet; **escarlatina** *nf* scarlet fever
escarmentar [eskarmen'tar] *vt* to punish severely ♦ *vi* to learn one's lesson
escarmiento *etc* [eskar'mjento] *vb ver* **escarmentar** ♦ *nm* (*ejemplo*) lesson; (*castigo*) punishment
escarnio [es'karnjo] *nm* mockery; (*injuria*) insult
escarola [eska'rola] *nf* endive
escarpado, a [eskar'paðo, a] *adj* (*pendiente*) sheer, steep; (*rocas*) craggy
escasear [eskase'ar] *vi* to be scarce
escasez [eska'seθ] *nf* (*falta*) shortage, scarcity; (*pobreza*) poverty
escaso, a [es'kaso, a] *adj* (*poco*) scarce; (*raro*) rare; (*ralo*) thin, sparse; (*limitado*) limited
escatimar [eskati'mar] *vt* (*limitar*) to skimp (on), be sparing with
escayola [eska'jola] *nf* plaster
escena [es'θena] *nf* scene
escenario [esθe'narjo] *nm* (*TEATRO*) stage; (*CINE*) set; (*fig*) scene; **escenografía** *nf* set design
escepticismo [esθepti'θismo] *nm* scepti-

cism; **escéptico, a** adj sceptical ♦ nm/f sceptic

escisión [esθi'sjon] nf (de partido, secta) split

esclarecer [esklare'θer] vt (iluminar) to light up, illuminate; (misterio, problema) to shed light on

esclavitud [esklaβi'tuð] nf slavery

esclavizar [esklaβi'θar] vt to enslave

esclavo, a [es'klaβo, a] nm/f slave

esclusa [es'klusa] nf (de canal) lock; (compuerta) floodgate

escoba [es'koβa] nf broom

escocer [esko'θer] vi to burn, sting; ~**se** vr to chafe, get chafed

escocés, esa [esko'θes, esa] adj Scottish ♦ nm/f Scotsman/woman, Scot

Escocia [es'koθja] nf Scotland

escoger [esko'xer] vt to choose, pick, select; **escogido, a** adj chosen, selected; (calidad) choice, select

escolar [esko'lar] adj school cpd ♦ nm/f schoolboy/girl, pupil

escolta [es'kolta] nf escort; **escoltar** vt to escort

escollo [es'koλo] nm reef

escombros [es'kombros] nmpl (basura) rubbish sg; (restos) debris sg

esconder [eskon'der] vt to hide, conceal; ~**se** vr to hide; **escondidas** (AM) nfpl: **a** ~ secretly; **escondite** nm hiding place; (juego) hide-and-seek; **escondrijo** nm hiding place, hideout

escopeta [esko'peta] nf shotgun

escoria [es'korja] nf (de alto horno) slag; (fig) scum, dregs pl

Escorpio [es'korpjo] nm Scorpio

escorpión [eskor'pjon] nm scorpion

escotado, a [esko'taðo, a] adj low-cut

escote [es'kote] nm (de vestido) low neck; **pagar a** ~ to share the expenses

escotilla [esko'tiλa] nf (NAUT) hatch(way)

escozor [esko'θor] nm (dolor) sting(ing)

escribir [eskri'βir] vt, vi to write; ~ **a máquina** to type; ¿**cómo se escribe?** how do you spell it?

escrito, a [es'krito, a] pp de **escribir** ♦ nm (documento) document; (manuscrito) text, manuscript; **por** ~ in writing

escritor, a [eskri'tor, a] nm/f writer

escritorio [eskri'torjo] nm desk; (oficina) office

escritura [eskri'tura] nf (acción) writing; (caligrafía) (hand)writing; (JUR: documento) deed

escrúpulo [es'krupulo] nm scruple; (minuciosidad) scrupulousness; **escrupuloso, a** adj scrupulous

escrutar [eskru'tar] vt to scrutinize, examine; (votos) to count

escrutinio [eskru'tinjo] nm (examen atento) scrutiny; (POL: recuento de votos) count(ing)

escuadra [es'kwaðra] nf (MIL etc) squad; (NAUT) squadron; (de coches etc) fleet; **escuadrilla** nf (de aviones) squadron; (AM: de obreros) gang

escuadrón [eskwa'ðron] nm squadron

escuálido, a [es'kwaliðo, a] adj skinny, scraggy; (sucio) squalid

escuchar [esku'tʃar] vt to listen to ♦ vi to listen

escudilla [esku'ðiλa] nf bowl, basin

escudo [es'kuðo] nm shield

escudriñar [eskuðri'ɲar] vt (examinar) to investigate, scrutinize; (mirar de lejos) to scan

escuela [es'kwela] nf school; ~ **de artes y oficios** (ESP) ≈ technical college; ~ **normal** teacher training college

escueto, a [es'kweto, a] adj plain; (estilo) simple

escuincle [es'kwinkle] (AM: fam) nm/f kid

esculpir [eskul'pir] vt to sculpt; (grabar) to engrave; (tallar) to carve; **escultor, a** nm/f sculptor/tress; **escultura** nf sculpture

escupidera [eskupi'ðera] nf spittoon

escupir [esku'pir] vt, vi to spit (out)

escurreplatos [eskurre'platos] nm inv plate rack

escurridizo, a [eskurri'ðiθo, a] adj slippery

escurridor [eskurri'ðor] nm colander

escurrir [esku'rrir] vt (ropa) to wring out; (verduras, platos) to drain ♦ vi (líquidos) to drip; ~**se** vr (secarse) to drain; (resbalarse) to slip, slide; (escaparse) to slip away

ese ['ese] (f **esa**, pl **esos**, **esas**) adj demos (sg) that; (pl) those

ése ['ese] (f **ésa**, pl **ésos**, **ésas**) pron (sg) that (one); (pl) those (ones); ~ ... **éste** ... the former ... the latter ...; **no me vengas con ésas** don't give me any more of that nonsense

esencia [e'senθja] nf essence; **esencial** adj essential

esfera [es'fera] nf sphere; (de reloj) face; **esférico, a** adj spherical

esforzarse [esfor'θarse] vr to exert o.s., make an effort

esfuerzo etc [es'fwerθo] vb ver **esforzar** ♦ nm effort

esfumarse [esfu'marse] vr (apoyo, esperanzas) to fade away

esgrima [es'rrima] nf fencing

esgrimir [esrri'mir] vt (arma) to brandish; (argumento) to use

esguince [es'ɣinθe] nm (MED) sprain

eslabón [esla'βon] nm link

esmaltar [esmal'tar] vt to enamel; **esmalte** nm enamel; **esmalte de uñas** nail varnish o polish

esmerado, a [esme'raðo, a] adj careful, neat

esmeralda [esme'ralda] nf emerald

esmerarse [esme'rarse] vr (aplicarse) to take great pains, exercise great care; (afanarse) to work hard

esmero [es'mero] nm (great) care

esnob [es'nob] (pl ~s) adj (persona) snobbish; (coche etc) posh ♦ nm/f snob; ~ismo nm snobbery

eso ['eso] pron that, that thing o matter; ~ de su coche that business about his car; ~ de ir al cine all that about going to the cinema; a ~ de las cinco at about five o'clock; en ~ thereupon, at that point; ~ es that's it; ¡~ sí que es vida! now that is really living!; por ~ te lo dije that's why I told you; y ~ que llovía in spite of the fact it was raining

esófago [e'sofaxo] nm (ANAT) oesophagus

esos ['esos] adj demos ver **ese**

ésos ['esos] pron ver **ése**

espabilar etc [espaβi'lar] = **despabilar** etc

espacial [espa'θjal] adj (del espacio) space cpd

espaciar [espa'θjar] vt to space (out)

espacio [es'paθjo] nm space; (MUS) interval; (RADIO, TV) programme (BRIT), program (US); **el ~** space; ~**so, a** adj spacious, roomy

espada [es'paða] nf sword; ~**s** nfpl (NAIPES) spades

espaguetis [espa'ɣetis] nmpl spaghetti sg

espalda [es'palda] nf (gen) back; ~**s** nfpl (hombros) shoulders; **a ~s de uno** behind sb's back; **tenderse de ~s** to lie (down) on one's back; **volver la ~ a alguien** to coldshoulder sb

espantadizo, a [espanta'ðiθo, a] adj timid, easily frightened

espantajo [espan'taxo] nm = **espantapájaros**

espantapájaros [espanta'paxaros] nm inv scarecrow

espantar [espan'tar] vt (asustar) to frighten, scare; (ahuyentar) to frighten off; (asombrar) to horrify, appal; ~**se** vr to get frightened o scared; to be appalled

espanto [es'panto] nm (susto) fright; (terror) terror; (asombro) astonishment; ~**so, a** adj frightening; terrifying; astonishing

España [es'paɲa] nf Spain; **español, a** adj Spanish ♦ nm/f Spaniard ♦ nm (LING) Spanish

esparadrapo [espara'ðrapo] nm (sticking) plaster (BRIT), adhesive tape (US)

esparcimiento [esparθi'mjento] nm (dispersión) spreading; (derramamiento) scattering; (fig) cheerfulness

esparcir [espar'θir] vt to spread; (derramar) to scatter; ~**se** vr to spread (out); to scatter; (divertirse) to enjoy o.s.

espárrago [es'parraxo] nm asparagus

esparto [es'parto] nm esparto (grass)

espasmo [es'pasmo] nm spasm

espátula [es'patula] nf spatula

especia [es'peθja] nf spice

especial [espe'θjal] adj special; ~**idad** nf speciality (BRIT), specialty (US)

especie [es'peθje] nf (BIO) species; (clase) kind, sort; **en ~** in kind

especificar [espeθifi'kar] vt to specify; **específico, a** adj specific

espécimen [es'peθimen] (pl **especímenes**) nm specimen

espectáculo [espek'takulo] nm (gen) spectacle; (TEATRO etc) show

espectador, a [espekta'ðor, a] nm/f spectator

espectro [es'pektro] nm ghost; (fig) spectre

especular [espeku'lar] vt, vi to speculate

espejismo [espe'xismo] nm mirage

espejo [es'pexo] nm mirror; (fig) model; ~ **retrovisor** rear-view mirror

espeluznante [espeluθ'nante] adj horrifying, hair-raising

espera [es'pera] nf (pausa, intervalo) wait; (JUR: plazo) respite; **en ~ de** waiting for; (con expectativa) expecting

esperanza [espe'ranθa] nf (confianza) hope; (expectativa) expectation; **hay pocas ~s de que venga** there is little prospect of his coming

esperar [espe'rar] vt (aguardar) to wait for; (tener expectativa de) to expect; (desear) to hope for ♦ vi to wait; to expect; to hope

esperma [es'perma] nf sperm

espesar [espe'sar] vt to thicken; ~**se** vr to thicken, get thicker

espeso, a [es'peso, a] adj thick; **espesor** nm thickness

espía [es'pia] nm/f spy; **espiar** vt (observar) to spy on ♦ vi: ~ **para** to spy for

espiga [es'piɣa] nf (BOT: de trigo etc) ear

espigón [espi'ɣon] nm (BOT) ear; (NAUT) breakwater

espina [es'pina] nf thorn; (de pez) bone; ~ **dorsal** (ANAT) spine

espinaca [espi'naka] nf spinach

espinazo [espi'naθo] nm spine, backbone

espinilla [espi'niʎa] nf (ANAT: tibia) shin(bone); (grano) blackhead

espino [es'pino] nm hawthorn

espinoso, a [espi'noso, a] adj (planta) thorny, prickly; (fig) difficult

espionaje [espjo'naxe] nm spying, espionage

espiral [espi'ral] adj, nf spiral

espirar [espi'rar] vt to breathe out, exhale

espiritista [espiri'tista] adj, nm/f spiritualist

espíritu [es'piritu] nm spirit; **espiritual** adj spiritual

espita [es'pita] nf tap

espléndido, a [es'plendiðo, a] adj (magnífico) magnificent, splendid; (generoso) generous

esplendor [esplen'dor] nm splendour

espolear [espole'ar] *vt* to spur on
espoleta [espo'leta] *nf* (*de bomba*) fuse
espolón [espo'lon] *nm* sea wall
espolvorear [espolβore'ar] *vt* to dust, sprinkle
esponja [es'ponxa] *nf* sponge; (*fig*) sponger; **esponjoso, a** *adj* spongy
espontaneidad [espontanei'ðað] *nf* spontaneity; **espontáneo, a** *adj* spontaneous
esposa [es'posa] *nf* wife; **~s** *nfpl* handcuffs; **esposar** *vt* to handcuff
esposo [es'poso] *nm* husband
espuela [es'pwela] *nf* spur
espuma [es'puma] *nf* foam; (*de cerveza*) froth, head; (*de jabón*) lather; **espumadera** *nf* (*utensilio*) skimmer; **espumoso, a** *adj* frothy, foamy; (*vino*) sparkling
esqueje [es'kexe] *nm* (*de planta*) cutting
esqueleto [eske'leto] *nm* skeleton
esquema [es'kema] *nm* (*diagrama*) diagram; (*dibujo*) plan; (*plan*) scheme; (*FILOSOFÍA*) schema
esquí [es'ki] (*pl* **~s**) *nm* (*objeto*) ski; (*DEPORTE*) skiing; **~ acuático** water-skiing; **esquiar** *vi* to ski
esquilar [eski'lar] *vt* to shear
esquimal [eski'mal] *adj, nm/f* Eskimo
esquina [es'kina] *nf* corner
esquinazo [eski'naθo] *nm*: **dar ~ a algn** to give sb the slip
esquirol [eski'rol] *nm* blackleg
esquivar [eski'βar] *vt* to avoid; (*evadir*) to dodge, elude
esquivo, a [es'kiβo, a] *adj* evasive; (*tímido*) reserved; (*huraño*) unsociable
esta ['esta] *adj demos ver* **este²**
ésta ['esta] *pron ver* **éste**
está *vb ver* **estar**
estabilidad [estaβili'ðað] *nf* stability; **estable** *adj* stable
establecer [estaβle'θer] *vt* to establish; **~se** *vr* to establish o.s.; (*echar raíces*) to settle (down); **establecimiento** *nm* establishment
establo [es'taβlo] *nm* (*AGR*) stable
estaca [es'taka] *nf* stake, post; (*de tienda de campaña*) peg
estacada [esta'kaða] *nf* (*cerca*) fence, fencing; (*palenque*) stockade
estación [esta'θjon] *nf* station; (*del año*) season; **~ de autobuses** bus station; **~ balnearia** seaside resort; **~ de servicio** service station
estacionamiento [estaθjona'mjento] *nm* (*AUTO*) parking; (*MIL*) stationing
estacionar [estaθjo'nar] *vt* (*AUTO*) to park; (*MIL*) to station; **~io, a** *adj* stationary; (*COM: mercado*) slack
estadio [es'taðjo] *nm* (*fase*) stage, phase; (*DEPORTE*) stadium
estadista [esta'ðista] *nm* (*POL*) statesman; (*ESTADÍSTICA*) statistician

estadística [esta'ðistika] *nf* figure, statistic; (*ciencia*) statistics *sg*
estado [es'taðo] *nm* (*POL: condición*) state; **~ de ánimo** state of mind; **~ de cuenta** bank statement; **~ de sitio** state of siege; **~ civil** marital status; **~ mayor** staff; **estar en ~** to be pregnant; **(los) E~s Unidos** *nmpl* the United States (of America) *sg*
estadounidense [estaðouni'ðense] *adj* United States *cpd*, American ♦ *nm/f* American
estafa [es'tafa] *nf* swindle, trick; **estafar** *vt* to swindle, defraud
estafeta [esta'feta] *nf* (*oficina de correos*) post office; **~ diplomática** diplomatic bag
estáis *vb ver* **estar**
estallar [esta'ʎar] *vi* to burst; (*bomba*) to explode, go off; (*epidemia, guerra, rebelión*) to break out; **~ en llanto** to burst into tears; **estallido** *nm* explosion; (*fig*) outbreak
estampa [es'tampa] *nf* (*impresión, imprenta*) print, engraving; (*imagen, figura: de persona*) appearance
estampado, a [estam'paðo, a] *adj* printed ♦ *nm* (*impresión: acción*) printing; (*: efecto*) print; (*marca*) stamping
estampar [estam'par] *vt* (*imprimir*) to print; (*marcar*) to stamp; (*metal*) to engrave; (*poner sello en*) to stamp; (*fig*) to stamp, imprint
estampida [estam'piða] *nf* stampede
estampido [estam'piðo] *nm* bang, report
estampilla [estam'piʎa] *nf* stamp
están *vb ver* **estar**
estancado, a [estan'kaðo, a] *adj* stagnant
estancar [estan'kar] *vt* (*aguas*) to hold up, hold back; (*COM*) to monopolize; (*fig*) to block, hold up; **~se** *vr* to stagnate
estancia [es'tanθja] *nf* (*permanencia*) stay; (*sala*) room; (*AM*) farm, ranch; **estanciero** (*AM*) farmer, rancher
estanco, a [es'tanko, a] *adj* watertight ♦ *nm* tobacconist's (shop), cigar store (*US*)
estándar [es'tandar] *adj, nm* standard; **estandarizar** *vt* to standardize
estandarte [estan'darte] *nm* banner, standard
estanque [es'tanke] *nm* (*lago*) pool, pond; (*AGR*) reservoir
estanquero, a [estan'kero, a] *nm/f* tobacconist
estante [es'tante] *nm* (*armario*) rack, stand; (*biblioteca*) bookcase; (*anaquel*) shelf; (*AM*) prop; **estantería** *nf* shelving, shelves *pl*
estaño [es'taɲo] *nm* tin

───────── *PALABRA CLAVE*

estar [es'tar] *vi* **1** (*posición*) to be; **está en la plaza** it's in the square; **¿está Juan?** is Juan in?; **estamos a 30 km de Junín** we're

30 kms from Junín
2 (+ *adj: estado*) to be; ~ **enfermo** to be ill; **está muy elegante** he's looking very smart; **¿cómo estás?** how are you keeping?
3 (+ *gerundio*) to be; **estoy leyendo** I'm reading
4 (*uso pasivo*): **está condenado a muerte** he's been condemned to death; **está envasado en ...** it's packed in ...
5 (*con fechas*): **¿a cuántos estamos?** what's the date today?; **estamos a 5 de mayo** it's the 5th of May
6 (*locuciones*): **¿estamos?** (*¿de acuerdo?*) okay?; (*¿listo?*) ready?; **¡ya está bien!** that's enough!
7. ~ **de**: ~ **de vacaciones/viaje** to be on holiday/away *o* on a trip; **está de camarero** he's working as a waiter
8. ~ **para**: **está para salir** he's about to leave; **no estoy para bromas** I'm not in the mood for jokes
9. ~ **por** (*propuesta etc*) to be in favour of; (*persona etc*) to support, side with; **está por limpiar** it still has to be cleaned
10: ~ **sin**: ~ **sin dinero** to have no money; **está sin terminar** it isn't finished yet
♦ **~se** *vr*: **se estuvo en la cama toda la tarde** he stayed in bed all afternoon

estas ['estas] *adj demos ver* **este**[2]
éstas ['estas] *pron ver* **éste**
estatal [esta'tal] *adj state cpd*
estático, a [es'tatiko, a] *adj static*
estatua [es'tatwa] *nf statue*
estatura [esta'tura] *nf stature, height*
estatuto [esta'tuto] *nm* (*JUR*) statute; (*de ciudad*) bye-law; (*de comité*) rule
este[1] ['este] *nm east*
este[2] ['este] (*f* **esta**, *pl* **estos, estas**) *adj demos* (*sg*) this; (*pl*) these
éste ['este] (*f* **ésta**, *pl* **éstos, éstas**) *pron* (*sg*) this (one); (*pl*) these (ones); **ése ... ~ ...** the former ... the latter ....
esté *etc vb ver* **estar**
estela [es'tela] *nf wash*; (*fig*) trail
estelar [este'lar] *adj* (*ASTRO*) stellar; (*actuación, reparto*) star (*atr*)
estén *etc vb ver* **estar**
estenografía [estenoɣra'fia] *nf shorthand* (*BRIT*), stenography (*US*)
estepa [es'tepa] *nf* (*GEO*) steppe
estera [es'tera] *nf mat(ting)*
estéreo [es'tereo] *adj inv, nm stereo*; **estereotipo** *nm stereotype*
estéril [es'teril] *adj sterile, barren*; (*fig*) vain, futile; **esterilizar** *vt* to sterilize
esterlina [ester'lina] *adj*: **libra ~** pound sterling
estés *etc vb ver* **estar**
estética [es'tetika] *nf aesthetics sg*
estético, a [es'tetiko, a] *adj aesthetic*

estibador [estiβa'ðor] *nm stevedore, docker*
estiércol [es'tjerkol] *nm dung, manure*
estigma [es'tixma] *nm stigma*
estilarse [esti'larse] *vr* to be in fashion
estilo [es'tilo] *nm style*; (*TEC*) stylus; (*NATACIÓN*) stroke; **algo por el ~** something along those lines
estima [es'tima] *nf esteem, respect*
estimación [estima'θjon] *nf* (*evaluación*) estimation; (*aprecio, afecto*) esteem, regard
estimar [esti'mar] *vt* (*evaluar*) to estimate; (*valorar*) to value; (*apreciar*) to esteem, respect; (*pensar, considerar*) to think, reckon
estimulante [estimu'lante] *adj stimulating* ♦ *nm stimulant*
estimular [estimu'lar] *vt* to stimulate; (*excitar*) to excite
estímulo [es'timulo] *nm stimulus*; (*ánimo*) encouragement
estío [es'tio] *nm summer*
estipulación [estipula'θjon] *nf stipulation, condition*
estipular [estipu'lar] *vt* to stipulate
estirado, a [esti'raðo, a] *adj* (*tenso*) (stretched *o* drawn) tight; (*fig: persona*) stiff, pompous
estirar [esti'rar] *vt* to stretch; (*dinero, suma etc*) to stretch out; **~se** *vr* to stretch
estirón [esti'ron] *nm pull, tug*; (*crecimiento*) spurt, sudden growth; **dar un ~** (*niño*) to shoot up
estirpe [es'tirpe] *nf stock, lineage*
estival [esti'βal] *adj summer cpd*
esto ['esto] *pron this, this thing o matter*; **~ de la boda** this business about the wedding
Estocolmo [esto'kolmo] *nm Stockholm*
estofado [esto'faðo] *nm* (*CULIN*) stew
estofar [esto'far] *vt* (*CULIN*) to stew
estómago [es'tomaɣo] *nm stomach*; **tener ~** to be thick-skinned
estorbar [estor'βar] *vt* to hinder, obstruct; (*fig*) to bother, disturb ♦ *vi* to be in the way; **estorbo** *nm* (*molestia*) bother, nuisance; (*obstáculo*) hindrance, obstacle
estornudar [estornu'ðar] *vi* to sneeze
estos ['estos] *adj demos ver* **este**[2]
éstos ['estos] *pron ver* **éste**
estoy *vb ver* **estar**
estrado [es'traðo] *nm platform*
estrafalario, a [estrafa'larjo, a] *adj odd, eccentric*; (*desarreglado*) slovenly, sloppy
estrago [es'traɣo] *nm ruin, destruction*; **hacer ~s en** to wreak havoc among
estragón [estra'ɣon] *nm tarragon*
estrambótico, a [estram'botiko, a] *adj* (*persona*) eccentric; (*peinado, ropa*) outlandish
estrangulador, a [estrangula'ðor, a] *nm/f strangler* ♦ *nm* (*TEC*) throttle; (*AUTO*) choke
estrangular [estrangu'lar] *vt* (*persona*) to

strangle; (*MED*) to strangulate

estraperlo [estra'perlo] *nm* black market

estratagema [estrata'xema] *nf* (*MIL*) stratagem; (*astucia*) cunning

estrategia [estra'texja] *nf* strategy; **estratégico, a** *adj* strategic

estrato [es'trato] *nm* stratum, layer

estrechamente [es'tretʃamente] *adv* (*íntimamente*) closely, intimately; (*pobremente*: *vivir*) poorly

estrechar [estre'tʃar] *vt* (*reducir*) to narrow; (*COSTURA*) to take in; (*persona*) to hug, embrace; ~**se** *vr* (*reducirse*) to narrow, grow narrow; (*2 personas*) to embrace; ~ **la mano** to shake hands

estrechez [estre'tʃeθ] *nf* narrowness; (*de ropa*) tightness; (*intimidad*) intimacy; (*COM*) want *o* shortage of money; **estrecheces** *nfpl* (*dificultades económicas*) financial difficulties

estrecho, a [es'tretʃo, a] *adj* narrow; (*apretado*) tight; (*íntimo*) close, intimate; (*miserable*) mean ♦ *nm* strait; ~ **de miras** narrow-minded

estrella [es'treʎa] *nf* star; ~ **de mar** (*ZOOL*) starfish; ~ **fugaz** shooting star; **estrellado, a** *adj* (*forma*) star-shaped; (*cielo*) starry

estrellar [estre'ʎar] *vt* (*hacer añicos*) to smash (to pieces); (*huevos*) to fry; ~**se** *vr* to smash; (*chocarse*) to crash; (*fracasar*) to fail

estremecer [estreme'θer] *vt* to shake; ~**se** *vr* to shake, tremble; **estremecimiento** *nm* (*temblor*) trembling, shaking

estrenar [estre'nar] *vt* (*vestido*) to wear for the first time; (*casa*) to move into; (*película, obra de teatro*) to première; ~**se** *vr* (*persona*) to make one's début; **estreno** *nm* (*primer uso*) first use; (*CINE etc*) première

estreñido, a [estre'ɲiðo, a] *adj* constipated

estreñimiento [estreɲi'mjento] *nm* constipation

estrépito [es'trepito] *nm* noise, racket; (*fig*) fuss; **estrepitoso, a** *adj* noisy; (*fiesta*) rowdy

estría [es'tria] *nf* groove

estribación [estriβa'θjon] *nf* (*GEO*) spur, foothill

estribar [estri'βar] *vi*: ~ **en** to rest on, be supported by

estribillo [estri'βiʎo] *nm* (*LITERATURA*) refrain; (*MUS*) chorus

estribo [es'triβo] *nm* (*de jinete*) stirrup; (*de coche, tren*) step; (*de puente*) support; (*GEO*) spur; **perder los** ~**s** to fly off the handle

estribor [estri'βor] *nm* (*NAUT*) starboard

estricto, a [es'trikto, a] *adj* (*riguroso*) strict; (*severo*) severe

estridente [estri'ðente] *adj* (*color*) loud; (*voz*) raucous

estropajo [estro'paxo] *nm* scourer

estropear [estrope'ar] *vt* (*arruinar*) to spoil; (*dañar*) to damage; ~**se** *vr* (*objeto*) to get damaged; (*la piel etc*) to be ruined

estructura [estruk'tura] *nf* structure

estruendo [es'trwendo] *nm* (*ruido*) racket, din; (*fig*: *alboroto*) uproar, turmoil

estrujar [estru'xar] *vt* (*apretar*) to squeeze; (*aplastar*) to crush; (*fig*) to drain, bleed

estuario [es'twarjo] *nm* estuary

estuche [es'tutʃe] *nm* box, case

estudiante [estu'ðjante] *nm/f* student; **estudiantil** *adj* student *cpd*

estudiar [estu'ðjar] *vt* to study

estudio [es'tuðjo] *nm* study; (*CINE, ARTE, RADIO*) studio; ~**s** *nmpl* studies; (*erudición*) learning *sg*; ~**so, a** *adj* studious

estufa [es'tufa] *nf* heater, fire

estupefaciente [estupefa'θjente] *nm* drug, narcotic

estupefacto, a [estupe'fakto, a] *adj* speechless, thunderstruck

estupendo, a [estu'pendo, a] *adj* wonderful, terrific; (*fam*) great; ¡~! that's great!, fantastic!

estupidez [estupi'ðeθ] *nf* (*torpeza*) stupidity; (*acto*) stupid thing (to do)

estúpido, a [es'tupiðo, a] *adj* stupid, silly

estupor [estu'por] *nm* stupor; (*fig*) astonishment, amazement

estupro [es'tupro] *nm* rape

estuve *etc vb ver* **estar**

esvástica [es'βastika] *nf* swastika

ETA ['eta] (*ESP*) *nf abr* (= *Euskadi ta Askatasuna*) ETA

etapa [e'tapa] *nf* (*de viaje*) stage; (*DEPORTE*) leg; (*parada*) stopping place; (*fig*) stage, phase

etarra [e'tarra] *nm/f* member of ETA

etc. *abr* (= *etcétera*) etc

etcétera [et'θetera] *adv* etcetera

eternidad [eterni'ðað] *nf* eternity; **eterno, a** *adj* eternal, everlasting

ética ['etika] *nf* ethics *pl*

ético, a ['etiko, a] *adj* ethical

etiqueta [eti'keta] *nf* (*modales*) etiquette; (*rótulo*) label, tag

Eucaristía [eukaris'tia] *nf* Eucharist

eufemismo [eufe'mismo] *nm* euphemism

euforia [eu'forja] *nf* euphoria

eunuco [eu'nuko] *nm* eunuch

eurodiputado, a [eurodipu'taðo, a] *nm/f* Euro MP

Europa [eu'ropa] *nf* Europe; **europeo, a** *adj, nm/f* European

Euskadi [eus'kaði] *nm* the Basque Country *o* Provinces *pl*

euskera [eus'kera] *nm* (*LING*) Basque

evacuación [eβakwa'θjon] *nf* evacuation

evacuar [eβa'kwar] *vt* to evacuate

evadir [eβa'ðir] *vt* to evade, avoid; ~**se** *vr* to escape

evaluar [eβa'lwar] *vt* to evaluate

evangelio [eßan'xeljo] *nm* gospel
evaporar [eßapo'rar] *vt* to evaporate; ~**se**
vr to vanish
evasión [eßa'sjon] *nf* escape, flight; *(fig)*
evasion; ~ **de capitales** flight of capital
evasiva [eßa'sißa] *nf (pretexto)* excuse
evasivo, a [eßa'sißo, a] *adj* evasive, non-
committal
evento [e'ßento] *nm* event
eventual [eßen'twal] *adj* possible, conditional (upon circumstances); *(trabajador)*
casual, temporary
evidencia [eßi'ðenθja] *nf* evidence, proof;
evidenciar *vt (hacer patente)* to make evident; *(probar)* to prove, show; **evidenciarse**
vr to be evident
evidente [eßi'ðente] *adj* obvious, clear, evident
evitar [eßi'tar] *vt (evadir)* to avoid; *(impedir)* to prevent
evocar [eßo'kar] *vt* to evoke, call forth
evolución [eßolu'θjon] *nf (desarrollo)* evolution, development; *(cambio)* change;
(MIL) manoeuvre; **evolucionar** *vi* to
evolve; to manoeuvre
ex [eks] *adj* ex-; **el ~ ministro** the former
minister, the ex-minister
exacerbar [eksaθer'ßar] *vt* to irritate, annoy
exactamente [eksakta'mente] *adv* exactly
exactitud [eksakti'tuð] *nf* exactness; *(precisión)* accuracy; *(puntualidad)* punctuality;
exacto, a *adj* exact; accurate; punctual;
¡**exacto!** exactly!
exageración [eksaxera'θjon] *nf* exaggeration
exagerar [eksaxe'rar] *vt, vi* to exaggerate
exaltado, a [eksal'taðo, a] *adj (apasionado)*
over-excited, worked-up; *(exagerado)* extreme
exaltar [eksal'tar] *vt* to exalt, glorify; ~**se**
vr (excitarse) to get excited *o* worked-up
examen [ek'samen] *nm* examination
examinar [eksami'nar] *vt* to examine; ~**se**
vr to be examined, take an examination
exasperar [eksaspe'rar] *vt* to exasperate;
~**se** *vr* to get exasperated, lose patience
Exca. *abr* = **Excelencia**
excavadora [ekskaßa'ðora] *nf* excavator
excavar [ekska'ßar] *vt* to excavate
excedencia [eksðe'ðenθja] *nf*: **estar en ~**
to be on leave; **pedir** *o* **solicitar la ~** to
ask for leave
excedente [ɛksθe'ðente] *adj, nm* excess,
surplus
exceder [eksθe'ðer] *vt* to exceed, surpass;
~**se** *vr (extralimitarse)* to go too far; *(sobre-
pasarse)* to excel o.s.
excelencia [eksθe'lenθja] *nf* excellence; **E~**
Excellency; **excelente** *adj* excellent
excentricidad [eksθentriθi'ðað] *nf* eccentricity; **excéntrico, a** *adj, nm/f* eccentric
excepción [eksθep'θjon] *nf* exception; **ex-**

cepcional *adj* exceptional
excepto [eks'θepto] *adv* excepting, except
(for)
exceptuar [eksθep'twar] *vt* to except, exclude
excesivo, a [eksθe'sißo, a] *adj* excessive
exceso [eks'θeso] *nm (gen)* excess; *(COM)*
surplus; ~ **de equipaje/peso** excess
luggage/weight
excitación [eksθita'θjon] *nf (sensación)* excitement; *(acción)* excitation
excitado, a [eksθi'taðo, a] *adj* excited;
(emociones) aroused
excitar [eksθi'tar] *vt* to excite; *(incitar)* to
urge; ~**se** *vr* to get excited
exclamación [eksklama'θjon] *nf* exclamation
exclamar [ekskla'mar] *vi* to exclaim.
excluir [eksklu'ir] *vt* to exclude; *(dejar
fuera)* to shut out; *(descartar)* to reject; **ex-
clusión** *nf* exclusion
exclusiva [eksklu'sißa] *nf (PRENSA)* exclusive, scoop; *(COM)* sole right
exclusivo, a [eksklu'sißo, a] *adj* exclusive;
derecho ~ sole *o* exclusive right
Excmo. *abr* = **excelentísimo**
excomulgar [ekskomul'yar] *vt (REL)* to excommunicate
excomunión [ekskomu'njon] *nf* excommu-
nication
excursión [ekskur'sjon] *nf* excursion, outing; **excursionista** *nm/f (turista)* sightseer
excusa [eks'kusa] *nf* excuse; *(disculpa)*
apology
excusar [eksku'sar] *vt* to excuse; *(evitar)* to
avoid, prevent; ~**se** *vr (disculparse)* to
apologize
exento, a [ek'sento, a] *adj* exempt
exequias [ek'sekjas] *nfpl* funeral rites
exhalar [eksa'lar] *vt* to exhale, breathe out;
(olor etc) to give off; *(suspiro)* to breathe,
heave
exhaustivo, a [eksaus'tißo, a] *adj (análisis)*
thorough; *(estudio)* exhaustive
exhausto, a [ek'sausto, a] *adj* exhausted
exhibición [eksißi'θjon] *nf* exhibition, display, show
exhibir [eksi'ßir] *vt* to exhibit, display,
show
exhortar [eksor'tar] *vt*: ~ **a** to exhort to
exigencia [eksi'xenθja] *nf* demand, requirement; **exigente** *adj* demanding
exigir [eksi'xir] *vt (gen)* to demand, require;
~ **el pago** to demand payment
exiliado, a [eksi'ljaðo, a] *adj* exiled ♦ *nm/f*
exile
exilio [ek'siljo] *nm* exile
eximir [eksi'mir] *vt* to exempt
existencia [eksis'tenθja] *nf* existence; ~**s**
nfpl stock(s) *(pl)*
existir [eksis'tir] *vi* to exist, be
éxito ['eksito] *nm (resultado)* result, out-

come; (*triunfo*) success; (*MUS etc*) hit; **te-ner** ~ to be successful

exonerar [eksone'rar] *vt* to exonerate; ~ **de una obligación** to free from an obligation

exorbitante [eksorßi'tante] *adj* (*precio*) exorbitant; (*cantidad*) excessive

exorcizar [eksorθi'θar] *vt* to exorcize

exótico, a [ek'sotiko, a] *adj* exotic

expandir [ekspan'dir] *vt* to expand

expansión [ekspan'sjon] *nf* expansion

expansivo, a [ekspan'sißo, a] *adj*: **onda** ~**a** shock wave

expatriarse [ekspa'trjarse] *vr* to emigrate; (*POL*) to go into exile

expectativa [ekspekta'tißa] *nf* (*espera*) expectation; (*perspectiva*) prospect

expedición [ekspeði'θjon] *nf* (*excursión*) expedition

expediente [ekspe'ðjente] *nm* expedient; (*JUR: procedimiento*) action, proceedings *pl*; (: *papeles*) dossier, file, record

expedir [ekspe'ðir] *vt* (*despachar*) to send, forward; (*pasaporte*) to issue

expendedor, a [ekspende'ðor, a] *nm/f* (*vendedor*) dealer

expensas [eks'pensas] *nfpl*: **a** ~ **de** at the expense of

experiencia [ekspe'rjenθja] *nf* experience

experimentado, a [eksperimen'taðo, a] *adj* experienced

experimentar [eksperimen'tar] *vt* (*en laboratorio*) to experiment with; (*probar*) to test, try out; (*notar, observar*) to experience; (*deterioro, pérdida*) to suffer; **experimento** *nm* experiment

experto, a [eks'perto, a] *adj* expert, skilled ♦ *nm/f* expert

expiar [ekspi'ar] *vt* to atone for

expirar [ekspi'rar] *vi* to expire

explanada [ekspla'naða] *nf* (*llano*) plain

explayarse [ekspla'jarse] *vr* (*en discurso*) to speak at length; ~ **con uno** to confide in sb

explicación [eksplika'θjon] *nf* explanation

explicar [ekspli'kar] *vt* to explain; ~**se** *vr* to explain (o.s.)

explícito, a [eks'pliθito, a] *adj* explicit

explique *etc vb ver* **explicar**

explorador, a [eksplora'ðor, a] *nm/f* (*pionero*) explorer; (*MIL*) scout ♦ *nm* (*MED*) probe; (*TEC*) (*radar*) scanner

explorar [eksplo'rar] *vt* to explore; (*MED*) to probe; (*radar*) to scan

explosión [eksplo'sjon] *nf* explosion; **explosivo, a** *adj* explosive

explotación [eksplota'θjon] *nf* exploitation; (*de planta etc*) running

explotar [eksplo'tar] *vt* to exploit; to run, operate ♦ *vi* to explode

exponer [ekspo'ner] *vt* to expose; (*cuadro*) to display; (*vida*) to risk; (*idea*) to explain; ~**se** *vr*: ~**se a (hacer) algo** to run the risk

of (doing) sth

exportación [eksporta'θjon] *nf* (*acción*) export; (*mercancías*) exports *pl*

exportar [ekspor'tar] *vt* to export

exposición [eksposi'θjon] *nf* (*gen*) exposure; (*de arte*) show, exhibition; (*explicación*) explanation; (*narración*) account, statement

expresamente [ekspresa'mente] *adv* (*decir*) clearly; (*a propósito*) expressly

expresar [ekspre'sar] *vt* to express; **expresión** *nf* expression

expresivo, a [ekspre'sißo, a] *adj* (*persona, gesto, palabras*) expressive; (*cariñoso*) affectionate

expreso, a [eks'preso, a] *pp de* **expresar** ♦ *adj* (*explícito*) express; (*claro*) specific, clear; (*tren*) fast ♦ *adv*: **mandar** ~ to send by express (delivery)

express [eks'pres] (*AM*) *adv*: **enviar algo** ~ to send sth special delivery

exprimidor [eksprimi'ðor] *nm* squeezer

exprimir [ekspri'mir] *vt* (*fruta*) to squeeze; (*zumo*) to squeeze out

expropiar [ekspro'pjar] *vt* to expropriate

expuesto, a [eks'pwesto, a] *pp de* **exponer** ♦ *adj* exposed; (*cuadro etc*) on show, on display

expulsar [ekspul'sar] *vt* (*echar*) to eject, throw out; (*alumno*) to expel; (*despedir*) to sack, fire; (*DEPORTE*) to send off; **expulsión** *nf* expulsion; sending-off

exquisito, a [ekski'sito, a] *adj* exquisite; (*comida*) delicious

éxtasis ['ekstasis] *nm* ecstasy

extender [eksten'der] *vt* to extend; (*los brazos*) to stretch out, hold out; (*mapa, tela*) to spread (out), open (out); (*mantequilla*) to spread; (*certificado*) to issue; (*cheque, recibo*) to make out; (*documento*) to draw up; ~**se** *vr* (*gen*) to extend; (*persona: en el suelo*) to stretch out; (*epidemia*) to spread; **extendido, a** *adj* (*abierto*) spread out, open; (*brazos*) outstretched; (*costumbre*) widespread; (*pey*) rife

extensión [eksten'sjon] *nf* (*de terreno, mar*) expanse, stretch; (*de tiempo*) length, duration; (*TEL*) extension; **en toda la** ~ **de la palabra** in every sense of the word

extenso, a [eks'tenso, a] *adj* extensive

extenuar [ekste'nwar] *vt* (*debilitar*) to weaken

exterior [ekste'rjor] *adj* (*de fuera*) external; (*afuera*) outside, exterior; (*apariencia*) outward; (*deuda, relaciones*) foreign ♦ *nm* (*gen*) exterior, outside; (*aspecto*) outward appearance; (*DEPORTE*) wing(er); (*países extranjeros*) abroad; **en el** ~ abroad; **al** ~ outwardly, on the surface

exterminar [ekstermi'nar] *vt* to exterminate; **exterminio** *nm* extermination

externo, a [eks'terno, a] *adj* (*exterior*) external, outside; *(superficial)* outward ♦ *nm/f* day pupil

extinguir [ekstin'gir] *vt (fuego)* to extinguish, put out; *(raza, población)* to wipe out; **~se** *vr (fuego)* to go out; *(BIO)* to die out, become extinct

extinto, a [eks'tinto, a] *adj* extinct

extintor [ekstin'tor] *nm* (fire) extinguisher

extirpar [ekstir'par] *vt (MED)* to remove (surgically)

extorsión [ekstor'sjon] *nf (FIN, JUR)* blackmail; *(molestia)* inconvenience

extra ['ekstra] *adj inv (tiempo)* extra; *(chocolate, vino)* good-quality ♦ *nm/f* extra ♦ *nm* extra; *(bono)* bonus

extracción [ekstrak'θjon] *nf* extraction; *(en lotería)* draw

extracto [eks'trakto] *nm* extract

extradición [ekstraði'θjon] *nf* extradition

extraer [ekstra'er] *vt* to extract, take out

extraescolar [ekstraesko'lar] *adj*: **actividad ~** extracurricular activity

extralimitarse [ekstralimi'tarse] *vr* to go too far

extranjero, a [ekstran'xero, a] *adj* foreign ♦ *nm/f* foreigner ♦ *nm* foreign countries *pl*; **en el ~** abroad

extrañar [ekstra'ɲar] *vt (sorprender)* to find strange o odd; *(echar de menos)* to miss; **~se** *vr (sorprenderse)* to be amazed, be surprised; *(distanciarse)* to become estranged, grow apart

extrañeza [ekstra'ɲeθa] *nf (rareza)* strangeness, oddness; *(asombro)* amazement, surprise

extraño, a [eks'traɲo, a] *adj (extranjero)* foreign; *(raro, sorprendente)* strange, odd

extraordinario, a [ekstraorði'narjo, a] *adj* extraordinary; *(edición, número)* special ♦ *nm (de periódico)* special edition; **horas extraordinarias** overtime *sg*

extrarradio [ekstra'rraðjo] *nm* poor suburban area

extravagancia [ekstraβa'ɣanθja] *nf* oddness, outlandishness; **extravagante** *adj (excéntrico)* eccentric; *(estrafalario)* outlandish

extraviado, a [ekstra'βjaðo, a] *adj* lost, missing

extraviar [ekstra'βjar] *vt (persona: desorientar)* to mislead, misdirect; *(perder)* to lose, misplace; **~se** *vr* to lose one's way, get lost; **extravío** *nm* loss; *(fig)* deviation

extremar [ekstre'mar] *vt* to carry to extremes; **~se** *vr* to do one's utmost, make every effort

extremaunción [ekstremaun'θjon] *nf* extreme unction

extremidad [ekstremi'ðað] *nf (punta)* extremity; *(fila)* edge; **~es** *nfpl (ANAT)* extremities

extremo, a [eks'tremo, a] *adj* extreme; *(úl-*

timo) last ♦ *nm* end; *(límite, grado sumo)* extreme; **en último ~** as a last resort

extrovertido, a [ekstroβer'tiðo, a] *adj, nm/f* extrovert

exuberancia [eksuβe'ranθja] *nf* exuberance; **exuberante** *adj* exuberant; *(fig)* luxuriant, lush

eyacular [ejaku'lar] *vt, vi* to ejaculate

F f

f.a.b. *abr (= franco a bordo)* f.o.b.

fábrica ['faβrika] *nf* factory; **marca de ~** trademark; **precio de ~** factory price

fabricación [faβrika'θjon] *nf (manufactura)* manufacture; *(producción)* production; **de ~ casera** home-made; **~ en serie** mass production

fabricante [faβri'kante] *nm/f* manufacturer

fabricar [faβri'kar] *vt (manufacturar)* to manufacture, make; *(construir)* to build; *(cuento)* to fabricate, devise

fábula ['faβula] *nf (cuento)* fable; *(chisme)* rumour; *(mentira)* fib

fabuloso, a [faβu'loso, a] *adj (oportunidad, tiempo)* fabulous, great

facción [fak'θjon] *nf (POL)* faction; **facciones** *nfpl (del rostro)* features

faceta [fa'θeta] *nf* facet

fácil ['faθil] *adj (simple)* easy; *(probable)* likely

facilidad [faθili'ðað] *nf (capacidad)* ease; *(sencillez)* simplicity; *(de palabra)* fluency; **~es** *nfpl* facilities

facilitar [faθili'tar] *vt (hacer fácil)* to make easy; *(proporcionar)* to provide

fácilmente ['faθilmente] *adv* easily

facsímil [fak'simil] *nm* facsimile, fax

factible [fak'tiβle] *adj* feasible

factor [fak'tor] *nm* factor

factura [fak'tura] *nf (cuenta)* bill; *(hechura)* manufacture; **facturar** *vt (COM)* to invoice, charge for; *(equipaje)* to register *(BRIT)*, check *(US)*

facultad [fakul'tað] *nf (aptitud, ESCOL etc)* faculty; *(poder)* power

facha ['fatʃa] *(fam) nf (aspecto)* look; *(cara)* face

fachada [fa'tʃaða] *nf (ARQ)* façade, front

faena [fa'ena] *nf (trabajo)* work; *(quehacer)* task, job

faisán [fai'san] *nm* pheasant

faja ['faxa] *nf (para la cintura)* sash; *(de mu-*

jer) corset; (_de tierra_) strip

fajo ['faxo] _nm_ (_de papeles_) bundle; (_de billetes_) wad

falacia [fa'laθja] _nf_ fallacy

falda ['falda] _nf_ (_prenda de vestir_) skirt

falo ['falo] _nm_ phallus

falsedad [false'ðað] _nf_ falseness; (_hipocresía_) hypocrisy; (_mentira_) falsehood

falsificar [falsifi'kar] _vt_ (_firma etc_) to forge; (_voto etc_) to rig; (_moneda_) to counterfeit

falso, a ['falso, a] _adj_ false; (_erróneo_) mistaken; (_documento, moneda etc_) fake; **en ~** falsely

falta ['falta] _nf_ (_defecto_) fault, flaw; (_privación_) lack, want; (_ausencia_) absence; (_carencia_) shortage; (_equivocación_) mistake; (_DEPORTE_) foul; **echar en ~** to miss; **hacer ~** hacer algo to be necessary to do sth; **me hace ~ una pluma** I need a pen; **~ de educación** bad manners _pl_

faltar [fal'tar] _vi_ (_escasear_) to be lacking, be wanting; (_ausentarse_) to be absent, be missing; **faltan 2 horas para llegar** there are 2 hours to go till arrival; **~ al respeto a uno** to be disrespectful to sb; **¡no faltaba más!** that's the last straw!

falto, a ['falto, a] _adj_ (_desposeído_) deficient, lacking; (_necesitado_) poor, wretched

falla ['faʎa] _nf_ (_defecto_) fault, flaw

fallar [fa'ʎar] _vt_ (_JUR_) to pronounce sentence on ♦ _vi_ (_memoria_) to fail; (_motor_) to miss

fallecer [faʎe'θer] _vi_ to pass away, die; **fallecimiento** _nm_ decease, demise

fallido, a [fa'ʎiðo, a] _adj_ (_gen_) frustrated, unsuccessful

fallo ['faʎo] _nm_ (_JUR_) verdict, ruling; (_fracaso_) failure; **~ cardíaco** heart failure

fama ['fama] _nf_ (_renombre_) fame; (_reputación_) reputation

famélico, a [fa'meliko, a] _adj_ starving

familia [fa'milja] _nf_ family; **~ política** in-laws _pl_

familiar [fami'ljar] _adj_ (_relativo a la familia_) family _cpd_; (_conocido, informal_) familiar ♦ _nm_ relative, relation; **~idad** _nf_ (_gen_) familiarity; (_informalidad_) homeless; **~izarse** _vr_: **~izarse con** to familiarize o.s. with

famoso, a [fa'moso, a] _adj_ (_renombrado_) famous

fanático, a [fa'natiko, a] _adj_ fanatical ♦ _nm/f_ fanatic; (_CINE, DEPORTE_) fan; **fanatismo** _nm_ fanaticism

fanfarrón, ona [fanfa'rron, ona] _adj_ boastful; (_pey_) showy

fango ['fango] _nm_ mud; **~so, a** _adj_ muddy

fantasía [fanta'sia] _nf_ fantasy, imagination; **joyas de ~** imitation jewellery _sg_

fantasma [fan'tasma] _nm_ (_espectro_) ghost, apparition; (_presumido_) show-off

fantástico, a [fan'tastiko, a] _adj_ fantastic

farmacéutico, a [farma'θeutiko, a] _adj_

pharmaceutical ♦ _nm/f_ chemist (_BRIT_), pharmacist

farmacia [far'maθja] _nf_ chemist's (shop) (_BRIT_), pharmacy; **~ de turno** duty chemist; **~ de guardia** all-night chemist

fármaco ['farmako] _nm_ drug

faro ['faro] _nm_ (_NAUT: torre_) lighthouse; (_AUTO_) headlamp; (_foco_) floodlight; **~s antiniebla** fog lamps; **~s delanteros/traseros** headlights/rear lights

farol [fa'rol] _nm_ lantern, lamp

farola [fa'rola] _nf_ street lamp (_BRIT_) _o_ light (_US_)

farsa ['farsa] _nf_ (_gen_) farce

farsante [far'sante] _nm/f_ fraud, fake

fascículo [fas'θikulo] _nm_ (_de revista_) part, instalment

fascinar [fasθi'nar] _vt_ (_gen_) to fascinate

fascismo [fas'θismo] _nm_ fascism; **fascista** _adj, nm/f_ fascist

fase ['fase] _nf_ phase

fastidiar [fasti'ðjar] _vt_ (_disgustar_) to annoy, bother; (_estropear_) to spoil; **~se** _vr_ (_disgustarse_) to get annoyed _o_ cross; **¡que se fastidie!** (_fam_) he'll just have to put up with it!

fastidio [fas'tiðjo] _nm_ (_disgusto_) annoyance; **~so, a** _adj_ (_molesto_) annoying

fastuoso, a [fas'twoso, a] _adj_ (_banquete, boda_) lavish; (_acto_) pompous

fatal [fa'tal] _adj_ (_gen_) fatal; (_desgraciado_) ill-fated; (_fam: malo, pésimo_) awful; **~idad** _nf_ (_destino_) fate; (_mala suerte_) misfortune

fatiga [fa'tiɣa] _nf_ (_cansancio_) fatigue, weariness

fatigar [fati'ɣar] _vt_ to tire, weary; **~se** _vr_ to get tired

fatigoso, a [fati'ɣoso, a] _adj_ (_cansador_) tiring

fatuo, a ['fatwo, a] _adj_ (_vano_) fatuous; (_presuntuoso_) conceited

fauces ['fauθes] _nfpl_ jaws, mouth _sg_

favor [fa'ßor] _nm_ favour; **estar a ~ de** to be in favour of; **haga el ~ de...** would you be so good as to..., kindly...; **por ~** please; **~able** _adj_ favourable

favorecer [faßore'θer] _vt_ to favour; (_vestido etc_) to become, flatter; **este peinado le favorece** this hairstyle suits him

favorito, a [faßo'rito, a] _adj, nm/f_ favourite

faz [faθ] _nf_ face; **la ~ de la tierra** the face of the earth

fe [fe] _nf_ (_REL_) faith; (_confianza_) belief; (_documento_) certificate; **prestar ~ a** to believe, credit; **actuar con buena/mala ~** to act in good/bad faith; **dar ~ de** to bear witness to

fealdad [feal'dað] _nf_ ugliness

febril [fe'ßril] _adj_ (_fig: actividad_) hectic; (_mente, mirada_) feverish

febrero [fe'ßrero] _nm_ February

fecundar [fekun'dar] _vt_ (_generar_) to fertilize, make fertile; **fecundo, a** adj (*fértil*) fertile; (*fig*) prolific; (*productivo*) productive

fecha ['fetʃa] nf date; ~ **de caducidad** (*de producto alimenticio*) sell-by date; (*de contrato etc*) expiry date; **con ~ adelantada** postdated; **en ~ próxima** soon; **hasta la ~** to date, so far; **poner ~** to date; **fechar** vt to date

federación [feðera'θjon] nf federation

federal [feðe'ral] adj federal

felicidad [feliθi'ðað] nf (*satisfacción, contento*) happiness; ~**es** nfpl (*felicitaciones*) best wishes, congratulations

felicitación [feliθita'θjon] nf: **¡felicitaciones!** congratulations!

felicitar [feliθi'tar] vt to congratulate

feligrés, esa [feli'ɣres, esa] nm/f parishioner

feliz [fe'liθ] adj (*contento*) happy; (*afortunado*) lucky

felpudo [fel'puðo] nm doormat

femenino, a [feme'nino, a] adj, nm feminine

feminista [femi'nista] adj, nm/f feminist

fenómeno [fe'nomeno] nm phenomenon; (*fig*) freak, accident ♦ adj great ♦ excl great!, marvellous!; **fenomenal** adj = **fenómeno**

feo, a ['feo, a] adj (*gen*) ugly; (*desagradable*) bad, nasty

féretro ['feretro] nm (*ataúd*) coffin; (*sarcófago*) bier

feria ['ferja] nf (*gen*) fair; (*descanso*) holiday, rest day; (AM: *mercado*) village market; (: *cambio*) loose o small change

fermentar [fermen'tar] vi to ferment

ferocidad [feroθi'ðað] nf fierceness, ferocity

feroz [fe'roθ] adj (*cruel*) cruel; (*salvaje*) fierce

férreo, a ['ferreo, a] adj iron

ferretería [ferrete'ria] nf (*tienda*) ironmonger's (shop) (BRIT), hardware store

ferrocarril [ferroka'rril] nm railway

ferroviario, a [ferro'βjarjo, a] adj rail cpd

fértil ['fertil] adj (*productivo*) fertile; (*rico*) rich; **fertilidad** nf (*gen*) fertility; (*productividad*) fruitfulness

ferviente [fer'βjente] adj fervent

fervor [fer'βor] nm fervour; ~**oso, a** adj fervent

festejar [feste'xar] vt (*celebrar*) to celebrate; **festejo** nm celebration; **festejos** nmpl (*fiestas*) festivals

festín [fes'tin] nm feast, banquet

festival [festi'βal] nm festival

festividad [festiβi'ðað] nf festivity

festivo, a [fes'tiβo, a] adj (*de fiesta*) festive; (*fig*) witty; (CINE, LITERATURA) humorous; **día ~** holiday

fétido, a ['fetiðo, a] adj (*hediondo*) foul-smelling

feto ['feto] nm foetus

fiable ['fjaβle] adj (*persona*) trustworthy; (*máquina*) reliable

fiador, a [fia'ðor, a] nm/f (JUR) surety, guarantor; (COM) backer; **salir ~ por uno** to stand bail for sb

fiambre ['fjambre] nm cold meat

fianza ['fianθa] nf surety; (JUR): **libertad bajo ~** release on bail

fiar [fi'ar] vt (*salir garante de*) to guarantee; (*vender a crédito*) to sell on credit; (*secreto*): ~ **a** to confide (to) ♦ vi to trust; ~**se** vr to trust (in), rely on; ~**se de uno** to rely on sb

fibra ['fiβra] nf fibre; ~ **óptica** optical fibre

ficción [fik'θjon] nf fiction

ficticio, a [fik'tiθjo, a] adj (*imaginario*) fictitious; (*falso*) fabricated

ficha ['fitʃa] nf (TEL) token; (*en juegos*) counter, marker; (*tarjeta*) (index) card; **fichar** vt (*archivar*) to file, index; (DEPORTE) to sign; **estar fichado** to have a record; **fichero** nm box file; (INFORM) file

fidelidad [fiðeli'ðað] nf (*lealtad*) fidelity, loyalty; **alta ~** high fidelity, hi-fi

fideos [fi'ðeos] nmpl noodles

fiebre ['fjeβre] nf (MED) fever; (*fig*) fever, excitement; ~ **amarilla/del heno** yellow/hay fever; ~ **palúdica** malaria; **tener ~** to have a temperature

fiel [fjel] adj (*leal*) faithful, loyal; (*fiable*) reliable; (*exacto*) accurate, faithful ♦ nm: **los ~es** the faithful

fieltro ['fjeltro] nm felt

fiera ['fjera] nf (*animal feroz*) wild animal o beast; (*fig*) dragon; *ver tb* **fiero**

fiero, a ['fjero, a] adj (*cruel*) cruel; (*feroz*) fierce; (*duro*) harsh ♦ nm/f (*fig*) fiend

fiesta ['fjesta] nf party; (*de pueblo*) festival; (*vacaciones*) ~ **s** holiday sg; (REL): ~ **de guardar** day of obligation

figura [fi'ɣura] nf (*gen*) figure; (*forma, imagen*) shape, form; (NAIPES) face card

figurar [fiɣu'rar] vt (*representar*) to represent; (*fingir*) to figure ♦ vi to figure; ~**se** vr (*imaginarse*) to imagine; (*suponer*) to suppose

fijador [fixa'ðor] nm (FOTO etc) fixative; (*de pelo*) gel

fijar [fi'xar] vt (*gen*) to fix; (*estampilla*) to affix, stick (on); (*fig*) to settle (on), decide; ~**se en** to notice

fijo, a ['fixo, a] adj (*gen*) fixed; (*firme*) firm; (*permanente*) permanent ♦ adv: **mirar ~** to stare

fila ['fila] nf row; (MIL) rank; (*cadena*) line; **ponerse en ~** to line up, get into line

filántropo, a [fi'lantropo, a] nm/f philanthropist

filatelia [fila'telja] nf philately, stamp collecting

filete [fi'lete] nm (*carne*) fillet steak; (*pescado*) fillet

filiación [filja'θjon] nf (POL) affiliation
filial [fi'ljal] adj filial ♦ nf subsidiary
Filipinas [fili'pinas] nfpl: **las ~** the Philippines; **filipino, a** adj, nm/f Philippine
filmar [fil'mar] vt to film, shoot
filo ['filo] nm (gen) edge; **sacar ~ a** to sharpen; **al ~ del mediodía** at about midday; **de doble ~** double-edged
filón [fi'lon] nm (MINERÍA) vein, lode; (fig) goldmine
filosofía [filoso'fia] nf philosophy; **filósofo, a** nm/f philosopher
filtrar [fil'trar] vt, vi to filter, strain; **~se** vr to filter; (fig: dinero) to dwindle; **filtro** nm (TEC, utensilio) filter
fin [fin] nm end; (objetivo) aim, purpose; **al ~ y al cabo** when all's said and done; **a ~ de** in order to; **por ~** finally; **en ~** in short; **~ de semana** weekend
final [fi'nal] adj final ♦ nm end, conclusion ♦ nf final; (propósito) purpose, intention; **~ista** nm/f finalist; **~izar** vt to end, finish; (INFORM) to log out o off ♦ vi to end, come to an end
financiar [finan'θjar] vt to finance; **financiero, a** adj financial ♦ nm/f financier
finca ['finka] nf (bien inmueble) property, land; (casa de campo) country house; (AM) farm
fingir [fin'xir] vt (simular) to simulate, feign; (pretextar) to sham, fake ♦ vi (aparentar) to pretend; **~se** vr to pretend to be
finlandés, esa [finlan'des, esa] adj Finnish ♦ nm/f Finn ♦ nm (LING) Finnish
Finlandia [fin'landja] nf Finland
fino, a ['fino, a] adj fine; (delgado) slender; (de buenas maneras) polite, refined; (jerez) fino, dry
firma ['firma] nf signature; (COM) firm, company
firmamento [firma'mento] nm firmament
firmar [fir'mar] vt to sign
firme ['firme] adj firm; (estable) stable; (sólido) solid; (constante) steady; (decidido) resolute ♦ nm road (surface); **~mente** adv firmly; **~za** nf firmness; (constancia) steadiness; (solidez) solidity
fiscal [fis'kal] adj fiscal ♦ nm/f public prosecutor; **año ~** tax o fiscal year
fisco ['fisko] nm (hacienda) treasury, exchequer (BRIT)
fisgar [fis'xar] vt to pry into
fisgonear [fisxone'ar] vt to poke one's nose into ♦ vi to pry, spy
física ['fisika] nf physics sg; ver tb **físico**
físico, a ['fisiko, a] adj physical ♦ nm physique ♦ nm/f physicist
fisura [fi'sura] nf crack; (MED) (hairline) fracture
flac(c)ido, a ['fla(k)θiðo, a] adj flabby
flaco, a ['flako, a] adj (muy delgado) skinny, thin; (débil) weak, feeble

flagrante [fla'xrante] adj flagrant
flamante [fla'mante] (fam) adj brilliant; (nuevo) brand-new
flamenco, a [fla'menko, a] adj (de Flandes) Flemish; (baile, música) flamenco ♦ nm (baile, música) flamenco
flan [flan] nm creme caramel
flaqueza [fla'keθa] nf (delgadez) thinness, leanness; (fig) weakness
flash [flaʃ] (pl ~s o ~es) nm (FOTO) flash
flauta ['flauta] nf (MUS) flute
fleco ['fleko] nm fringe
flecha ['fletʃa] nf arrow
flechazo [fle'tʃaθo] nm love at first sight
flema ['flema] nm phlegm
flequillo [fle'kiʎo] nm (pelo) fringe
flete ['flete] nm (carga) freight; (alquiler) charter; (precio) freightage
flexible [flek'sißle] adj flexible
flexo ['flekso] nm adjustable table-lamp
flojera [flo'xera] (AM: fam) nf: **me da ~** I can't be bothered
flojo, a ['floxo, a] adj (gen) loose; (sin fuerzas) limp; (débil) weak
flor [flor] nf flower; (piropo) compliment; **a ~ de** on the surface of; **~ecer** vi (BOT) to flower, bloom; (fig) to flourish; **~eciente** adj (BOT) in flower, flowering; (fig) thriving; **~ero** nm vase; **~istería** nf florist's (shop)
flota ['flota] nf fleet
flotador [flota'ðor] nm (gen) float; (para nadar) rubber ring
flotar [flo'tar] vi (gen) to float; **flote** nm: **a flote** afloat; **salir a flote** (fig) to get back on one's feet
fluctuar [fluk'twar] vi (oscilar) to fluctuate
fluidez [flui'ðeθ] nf fluidity; (fig) fluency
flúido, a ['fluiðo, a] adj, nm fluid
fluir [flu'ir] vi to flow
flujo ['fluxo] nm flow; **~ y reflujo** ebb and flow; **~ de sangre** (MED) loss of blood
fluvial [fluß'jal] adj (navegación, cuenca) fluvial, river cpd
foca ['foka] nf seal
foco ['foko] nm focus; (ELEC) floodlight; (AM) (light) bulb
fofo, a ['fofo, a] adj soft, spongy; (carnes) flabby
fogata [fo'xata] nf bonfire
fogón [fo'xon] nm (de cocina) ring, burner
fogoso, a [fo'xoso, a] adj spirited
folio ['foljo] nm folio, page
follaje [fo'ʎaxe] nm foliage
folletín [foʎe'tin] nm newspaper serial
folleto [fo'ʎeto] nm (POL) pamphlet
follón [fo'ʎon] (fam) nm (lío) mess; (conmoción) fuss; **armar un ~** to kick up a row
fomentar [fomen'tar] vt (MED) to foment; **fomento** nm (promoción) promotion
fonda ['fonda] nf inn
fondear [fonde'ar] vt to search

fondo ['fondo] *nm* (*de mar*) bottom; (*de coche, sala*) back; (*ARTE etc*) background; (*reserva*) fund; **~s** *nmpl* (*COM*) funds, resources; **una investigación a ~** a thorough investigation; **en el ~** at bottom, deep down

fontanería [fontane'ria] *nf* plumbing; **fontanero, a** *nm/f* plumber

footing ['futɪn] *nm* jogging; **hacer ~** to jog, go jogging

foráneo, a [fo'raneo, a] *adj* foreign

forastero, a [foras'tero, a] *nm/f* stranger

forcejear [forθexe'ar] *vi* (*luchar*) to struggle

forense [fo'rense] *nm/f* pathologist

forjar [for'xar] *vt* to forge

forma ['forma] *nf* (*figura*) form, shape; (*molde*) mould, pattern; (*MED*) fitness; (*método*) way, means; **las ~s** the conventions; **estar en ~** to be fit

formación [forma'θjon] *nf* (*gen*) formation; (*educación*) education; **~ profesional** vocational training

formal [for'mal] *adj* (*gen*) formal; (*fig: persona*) serious; (: *de fiar*) reliable; **~idad** *nf* formality; seriousness; **~izar** *vt* (*JUR*) to formalize; (*situación*) to put in order, regularize; **~izarse** *vr* (*situación*) to be put in order, be regularized

formar [for'mar] *vt* (*componer*) to form, shape; (*constituir*) to make up, constitute; (*ESCOL*) to train, educate; **~se** *vr* (*ESCOL*) to be trained, educated; (*cobrar forma*) to form, take form; (*desarrollarse*) to develop

formatear [formate'ar] *vt* to format

formativo, a [forma'tiβo, a] *adj* (*lecturas, años*) formative

formato [for'mato] *nm* format

formidable [formi'ðaβle] *adj* (*temible*) formidable; (*asombroso*) tremendous

fórmula ['formula] *nf* formula

formular [formu'lar] *vt* (*queja*) to make, lodge; (*petición*) to draw up; (*pregunta*) to pose

formulario [formu'larjo] *nm* form

fornido, a [for'niðo, a] *adj* well-built

forrar [fo'rrar] *vt* (*abrigo*) to line; (*libro*) to cover; **forro** *nm* (*de cuaderno*) cover; (*COSTURA*) lining; (*de sillón*) upholstery

fortalecer [fortale'θer] *vt* to strengthen

fortaleza [forta'leθa] *nf* (*MIL*) fortress, stronghold; (*fuerza*) strength; (*determinación*) resolution

fortuito, a [for'twito, a] *adj* accidental

fortuna [for'tuna] *nf* (*suerte*) fortune, (good) luck; (*riqueza*) fortune, wealth

forzar [for'θar] *vt* (*puerta*) to force (open); (*compeler*) to compel

forzoso, a [for'θoso, a] *adj* necessary

fosa ['fosa] *nf* (*sepultura*) grave; (*en tierra*) pit; (*MED*) cavity; **~s nasales** nostrils

fósforo ['fosforo] *nm* (*QUÍMICA*) phosphorus; (*AM*) match

foso ['foso] *nm* ditch; (*TEATRO*) pit; (*AUTO*): **~ de reconocimiento** inspection pit

foto ['foto] *nf* photo, snap(shot); **sacar una ~** to take a photo o picture

fotocopia [foto'kopja] *nf* photocopy; **fotocopiadora** *nf* photocopier; **fotocopiar** *vt* to photocopy

fotografía [fotoɤra'fia] *nf* (*ARTE*) photography; (*una ~*) photograph; **fotografiar** *vt* to photograph

fotógrafo, a [fo'toɤrafo, a] *nm/f* photographer

fracasar [fraka'sar] *vi* (*gen*) to fail

fracaso [fra'kaso] *nm* (*desgracia, revés*) failure

fracción [frak'θjon] *nf* fraction; (*POL*) faction; **fraccionamiento** (*AM*) *nm* housing estate

fractura [frak'tura] *nf* fracture, break

fragancia [fra'ɤanθja] *nf* (*olor*) fragrance, perfume

frágil ['fraxil] *adj* (*débil*) fragile; (*COM*) breakable

fragmento [fraɤ'mento] *nm* (*pedazo*) fragment

fragua ['fraɤwa] *nf* forge; **fraguar** *vt* to forge; (*fig*) to concoct ♦ *vi* to harden

fraile ['fraile] *nm* (*REL*) friar; (: *monje*) monk

frambuesa [fram'bwesa] *nf* raspberry

francés, esa [fran'θes, esa] *adj* French ♦ *nm/f* Frenchman/woman ♦ *nm* (*LING*) French

Francia ['franθja] *nf* France

franco, a ['franko, a] *adj* (*cándido*) frank, open; (*COM: exento*) free ♦ *nm* (*moneda*) franc; **francamente** *adv* (*hablar, decir*) frankly; (*realmente*) really

francotirador, a [frankotira'ðor, a] *nm/f* sniper

franela [fra'nela] *nf* flannel

franja ['franxa] *nf* fringe

franquear [franke'ar] *vt* (*camino*) to clear; (*carta, paquete postal*) to frank, stamp; (*obstáculo*) to overcome

franqueo [fran'keo] *nm* postage

franqueza [fran'keθa] *nf* (*candor*) frankness

frasco ['frasko] *nm* bottle, flask; **~ al vacío** (vacuum) flask

frase ['frase] *nf* sentence; **~ hecha** set phrase; (*pey*) stock phrase

fraterno, a [fra'terno, a] *adj* brotherly, fraternal

fraude ['frauðe] *nm* (*cualidad*) dishonesty; (*acto*) fraud; **fraudulento, a** *adj* fraudulent

frazada [fra'saða] (*AM*) *nf* blanket

frecuencia [fre'kwenθja] *nf* frequency; **con ~** frequently, often

frecuentar [frekwen'tar] *vt* to frequent

fregadero [freɤa'ðero] *nm* (kitchen) sink

fregar [fre'ɤar] *vt* (*frotar*) to scrub; (*platos*)

to wash (up); (*AM*) to annoy

fregona [fre'ɣona] *nf* (*utensilio*) mop; (*pey: sirvienta*) skivvy

freír [fre'ir] *vt* to fry

frenar [fre'nar] *vt* to brake; (*fig*) to check

frenazo [fre'naθo] *nm*: **dar un ~** to brake sharply

frenesí [frene'si] *nm* frenzy; **frenético, a** *adj* frantic

freno ['freno] *nm* (*TEC, AUTO*) brake; (*de cabalgadura*) bit; (*fig*) check

frente ['frente] *nm* (*ARQ, POL*) front; (*de objeto*) front part ♦ *nf* forehead, brow; **~ a** in front of; (*en situación opuesta de*) opposite; **al ~ de** (*fig*) at the head of; **chocar de ~** to crash head-on; **hacer ~ a** to face up to

fresa ['fresa] (*ESP*) *nf* strawberry

fresco, a ['fresko, a] *adj* (*nuevo*) fresh; (*frío*) cool; (*descarado*) cheeky ♦ *nm* (*aire*) fresh air; (*ARTE*) fresco; (*AM: jugo*) fruit drink ♦ *nm/f* (*fam*): **ser un(a) ~** to have a nerve; **tomar el ~** to get some fresh air; **frescura** *nf* freshness; (*descaro*) cheek, nerve; (*calma*) calmness

frialdad [frial'dað] *nf* (*gen*) coldness; (*indiferencia*) indifference

fricción [frik'θjon] *nf* (*gen*) friction; (*acto*) rub(bing); (*MED*) massage

frigidez [frixi'ðeθ] *nf* frigidity

frigorífico [friɣo'rifiko] *nm* refrigerator

frijol [fri'xol] *nm* kidney bean

frío, a *etc* ['frio, a] *vb ver* **freír** ♦ *adj* cold; (*indiferente*) indifferent ♦ *nm* cold; indifference; **hace ~** it's cold; **tener ~** to be cold

frito, a ['frito, a] *adj* fried; **me trae ~ ese hombre** I'm sick and tired of that man; **fritos** *nmpl* fried food

frívolo, a ['friβolo, a] *adj* frivolous

frontal [fron'tal] *adj* frontal; **choque ~** head-on collision

frontera [fron'tera] *nf* frontier; **fronterizo, a** *adj* frontier *cpd*; (*contiguo*) bordering

frontón [fron'ton] *nm* (*DEPORTE: cancha*) pelota court; (: *juego*) pelota

frotar [fro'tar] *vt* to rub; **~se** *vr*: **~se las manos** to rub one's hands

fructífero, a [fruk'tifero, a] *adj* fruitful

frugal [fru'ɣal] *adj* frugal

fruncir [frun'θir] *vt* to pucker; (*COSTURA*) to pleat; **~ el ceño** to knit one's brow

frustrar [frus'trar] *vt* to frustrate

fruta ['fruta] *nf* fruit; **frutería** *nf* fruit shop; **frutero, a** *adj* fruit *cpd* ♦ *nm/f* fruiterer ♦ *nm* fruit bowl

frutilla [fru'tiʎa] (*AM*) *nf* strawberry

fruto ['fruto] *nm* fruit; (*fig: resultado*) result; (: *utilidad*) benefit; **~s secos** nuts; (*pasas etc*) dried fruit *sg*

fue *vb ver* **ser**; **ir**

fuego ['fweɣo] *nm* (*gen*) fire; **a ~ lento** on a low flame *o* gas; **¿tienes ~?** have you

(got) a light?; **~s artificiales** *o* **de artificio** fireworks

fuente ['fwente] *nf* fountain; (*manantial, fig*) spring; (*origen*) source; (*plato*) large dish

fuera *etc* ['fwera] *vb ver* **ser, ir** ♦ *adv* out(side); (*en otra parte*) away; (*excepto, salvo*) except, save ♦ *prep*: **~ de** outside; (*fig*) besides; **~ de sí** beside o.s.; **por ~** (on the) outside

fuerte ['fwerte] *adj* strong; (*golpe*) hard; (*ruido*) loud; (*comida*) rich; (*lluvia*) heavy; (*dolor*) intense ♦ *adv* strongly; hard; loud(ly)

fuerza *etc* ['fwerθa] *vb ver* **forzar** ♦ *nf* (*fortaleza*) strength; (*TEC, ELEC*) power; (*coacción*) force; (*MIL: tb*: **~s**) forces *pl*; **a ~ de** by dint of; **cobrar ~s** to recover one's strength; **tener ~s para** to have the strength to; **a la ~** forcibly, by force; **por ~** of necessity; **~ de voluntad** willpower

fuga ['fuɣa] *nf* (*huida*) flight, escape; (*de gas etc*) leak

fugarse [fu'ɣarse] *vr* to flee, escape

fugaz [fu'ɣaθ] *adj* fleeting

fugitivo, a [fuxi'tiβo, a] *adj, nm/f* fugitive

fui *vb ver* **ser**; **ir**

fulano, a [fu'lano, a] *nm/f* so-and-so, what's-his-name/what's-her-name

fulminante [fulmi'mante] *adj* (*fig: mirada*) fierce; (*MED: enfermedad, ataque*) sudden; (*fam: éxito, golpe*) sudden

fumador, a [fuma'ðor, a] *nm/f* smoker

fumar [fu'mar] *vt, vi* to smoke; **~se** *vr* (*disipar*) to squander; **~ en pipa** to smoke a pipe

función [fun'θjon] *nf* function; (*de puesto*) duties *pl*; (*espectáculo*) show; **entrar en funciones** to take up one's duties

funcionar [funθjo'nar] *vi* (*gen*) to function; (*máquina*) to work; **"no funciona"** "out of order"

funcionario, a [funθjo'narjo, a] *nm/f* official; (*público*) civil servant

funda ['funda] *nf* (*gen*) cover; (*de almohada*) pillowcase

fundación [funda'θjon] *nf* foundation

fundamental [fundamen'tal] *adj* fundamental, basic

fundamentar [fundamen'tar] *vt* (*poner base*) to lay the foundations of; (*establecer*) to found; (*fig*) to base; **fundamento** *nm* (*base*) foundation

fundar [fun'dar] *vt* to found; **~se** *vr*: **~se en** to be founded on

fundición [fundi'θjon] *nf* fusing; (*fábrica*) foundry

fundir [fun'dir] *vt* (*gen*) to fuse; (*metal*) to smelt, melt down; (*nieve etc*) to melt; (*COM*) to merge; (*estatua*) to cast; **~se** *vr* (*colores etc*) to merge, blend; (*unirse*) to fuse together; (*ELEC: fusible, lámpara etc*) to fuse, blow; (*nieve etc*) to melt

fúnebre ['funeβre] adj funeral cpd, funereal
funeral [fune'ral] nm funeral; **funeraria** nf undertaker's
funesto, a [fu'nesto, a] adj (día) ill-fated; (decisión) fatal
furgón [fur'γon] nm wagon; **furgoneta** nf (AUTO, COM) (transit) van (BRIT), pick-up (truck) (US)
furia ['furja] nf (ira) fury; (violencia) violence; **furibundo, a** adj furious; **furioso, a** adj (iracundo) furious; (violento) violent; **furor** nm (cólera) rage
furtivo, a [fur'tiβo, a] adj furtive ♦ nm poacher
fusible [fu'siβle] nm fuse
fusil [fu'sil] nm rifle; **~ar** vt to shoot
fusión [fu'sjon] nf (gen) melting; (unión) fusion; (COM) merger
fusta ['fusta] nf (látigo) riding crop
fútbol ['futβol] nm football; **futbolista** nm footballer
fútil ['futil] adj trifling
futuro, a [fu'turo, a] adj, nm future

G g

gabardina [gaβar'ðina] nf raincoat, gabardine
gabinete [gaβi'nete] nm (POL) cabinet; (estudio) study; (de abogados etc) office
gaceta [ga'θeta] nf gazette
gachas ['gatʃas] nfpl porridge sg
gafas ['gafas] nfpl glasses; **~ de sol** sunglasses
gafe ['gafe] nm jinx
gaita ['gaita] nf bagpipes pl
gajes ['gaxes] nmpl: **los ~ del oficio** occupational hazards
gajo ['gaxo] nm (de naranja) segment
gala ['gala] nf (traje de etiqueta) full dress; (fig: lo mejor) cream, flower; **~s** nfpl (ropa) finery sg; **estar de ~** to be in one's best clothes; **hacer ~ de** to display, show off
galante [ga'lante] adj gallant; **galantear** vt (hacer la corte a) to court, woo; **galantería** nf (caballerosidad) gallantry; (cumplido) politeness; (comentario) compliment
galápago [ga'lapaγo] nm (ZOOL) turtle
galaxia [ga'laksja] nf galaxy
galera [ga'lera] nf (nave) galley; (carro) wagon; (IMPRENTA) galley
galería [gale'ria] nf (gen) gallery; (balcón) veranda(h); (pasillo) corridor

Gales ['gales] nm (tb: País de ~) Wales; **galés, esa** adj Welsh ♦ nm/f Welshman/woman ♦ nm (LING) Welsh
galgo, a ['galγo, a] nm/f greyhound
galimatías [galima'tias] nmpl (lenguaje) gibberish sg, nonsense sg
galón [ga'lon] nm (MIL) stripe; (COSTURA) braid; (medida) gallon
galopar [galo'par] vi to gallop
gallardía [gaʎar'ðia] nf (galantería) dash; (valor) bravery; (elegancia) elegance
gallego, a [ga'ʎeγo, a] adj, nm/f Galician
galleta [ga'ʎeta] nf biscuit (BRIT), cookie (US)
gallina [ga'ʎina] nf hen ♦ nm/f (fam: cobarde) chicken; **gallinero** nm henhouse; (TEATRO) top gallery
gallo ['gaʎo] nm cock, rooster
gama ['gama] nf (fig) range
gamba ['gamba] nf prawn (BRIT), shrimp (US)
gamberro, a [gam'berro, a] nm/f hooligan, lout
gamuza [ga'muθa] nf chamois
gana ['gana] nf (deseo) desire, wish; (apetito) appetite; (voluntad) will; (añoranza) longing; **de buena ~** willingly; **de mala ~** reluctantly; **me da ~s de** I feel like, I want to; **no me da la ~** I don't feel like it; **tener ~s de** to feel like
ganadería [ganaðe'ria] nf (ganado) livestock; (ganado vacuno) cattle pl; (cría, comercio) cattle raising
ganado [ga'naðo] nm livestock; **~ lanar** sheep pl; **~ mayor** cattle pl; **~ porcino** pigs pl
ganador, a [gana'ðor, a] adj winning ♦ nm/f winner
ganancia [ga'nanθja] nf (lo ganado) gain; (aumento) increase; (beneficio) profit; **~s** nfpl (ingresos) earnings; (beneficios) profit sg, winnings
ganar [ga'nar] vt (obtener) to get, obtain; (sacar ventaja) to gain; (salario etc) to earn; (DEPORTE, premio) to win; (derrotar a) to beat; (alcanzar) to reach ♦ vi (DEPORTE) to win; **~se** vr: **~se la vida** to earn one's living
ganchillo [gan'tʃiʎo] nm crochet
gancho ['gantʃo] nm (gen) hook; (colgador) hanger
gandul, a [gan'dul, a] adj, nm/f good-for-nothing, layabout
ganga ['ganga] nf (cosa buena y barata) bargain; (buena situación) cushy job
gangrena [gan'grena] nf gangrene
gansada [gan'saða] (fam) nf stupid thing to do
ganso, a ['ganso, a] nm/f (ZOOL) goose; (fam) idiot
ganzúa [gan'θua] nf skeleton key
garabatear [garaβate'ar] vi, vt (al escribir)

to scribble, scrawl
garabato [gara'ßato] *nm* (*escritura*) scrawl, scribble
garaje [ga'raxe] *nm* garage
garante [ga'rante] *adj* responsible ♦ *nm/f* guarantor
garantía [garan'tia] *nf* guarantee
garantizar [garanti'θar] *vt* (*hacerse responsable de*) to vouch for; (*asegurar*) to guarantee
garbanzo [gar'ßanθo] *nm* chickpea (*BRIT*), garbanzo (*US*)
garbo ['garßo] *nm* grace, elegance
garfio ['garfjo] *nm* grappling iron
garganta [gar'ɣanta] *nf* (*ANAT*) throat; (*de botella*) neck; **gargantilla** *nf* necklace
gárgaras ['garɣaras] *nfpl:* **hacer ~** to gargle
garita [ga'rita] *nf* cabin, hut; (*MIL*) sentry box
garra ['garra] *nf* (*de gato, TEC*) claw; (*de ave*) talon; (*fam*) hand, paw
garrafa [ga'rrafa] *nf* carafe, decanter
garrapata [garra'pata] *nf* tick
garrote [ga'rrote] *nm* (*palo*) stick; (*porra*) cudgel; (*suplicio*) garrotte
garza ['garθa] *nf* heron
gas [gas] *nm* gas
gasa ['gasa] *nf* gauze
gaseosa [gase'osa] *nf* lemonade
gaseoso, a [gase'oso, a] *adj* gassy, fizzy
gasoil [ga'soil] *nm* diesel (oil)
gasóleo [ga'soleo] *nm* = **gasoil**
gasolina [gaso'lina] *nf* petrol, gas(oline) (*US*); **gasolinera** *nf* petrol (*BRIT*) o gas (*US*) station
gastado, a [gas'taðo, a] *adj* (*rendido*) spent; (*raído*) worn out; (*usado: frase etc*) trite
gastar [gas'tar] *vt* (*dinero, tiempo*) to spend; (*fuerzas*) to use up; (*desperdiciar*) to waste; (*llevar*) to wear; **~se** *vr* to wear out; (*estropearse*) to waste; **~ en** to spend on; **~ bromas** to crack jokes; **¿qué número gastas?** what size (shoe) do you take?
gastronomía [gastrono'mia] *nf* gastronomy
gasto ['gasto] *nm* (*desembolso*) expenditure, spending; (*consumo, uso*) use; **~s** *nmpl* (*desembolsos*) expenses; (*cargos*) charges, costs
gatear [gate'ar] *vi* (*andar a gatas*) to go on all fours
gatillo [ga'tiʎo] *nm* (*de arma de fuego*) trigger; (*de dentista*) forceps
gato, a ['gato, a] *nm/f* cat ♦ *nm* (*TEC*) jack; **andar a gatas** to go on all fours
gaviota [ga'ßjota] *nf* seagull
gay [ge] *adj inv* gay, homosexual
gazpacho [gaθ'patʃo] *nm* gazpacho
gel [xel] *nm* (*tb:* **~ de baño/ducha**) gel
gelatina [xela'tina] *nf* jelly; (*polvos etc*) gelatine
gema ['xema] *nf* gem

gemelo, a [xe'melo, a] *adj, nm/f* twin; **~s** *nmpl* (*de camisa*) cufflinks; **~s de campo** field glasses, binoculars
gemido [xe'miðo] *nm* (*quejido*) moan, groan; (*aullido*) howl
Géminis ['xeminis] *nm* Gemini
gemir [xe'mir] *vi* (*quejarse*) to moan, groan; (*aullar*) to howl
generación [xenera'θjon] *nf* generation
general [xene'ral] *adj* general ♦ *nm* general; **por lo** o **en ~** in general; **G~itat** *nf* Catalan parliament; **~izar** *vt* to generalize; **~izarse** *vr* to become generalized, spread; **~mente** *adv* generally
generar [xene'rar] *vt* to generate
género ['xenero] *nm* (*clase*) kind, sort; (*tipo*) type; (*BIO*) genus; (*LING*) gender; (*COM*) material; **~ humano** human race
generosidad [xenerosi'ðað] *nf* generosity; **generoso, a** *adj* generous
genial [xe'njal] *adj* inspired; (*idea*) brilliant; (*afable*) genial
genio ['xenjo] *nm* (*carácter*) nature, disposition; (*humor*) temper; (*facultad creadora*) genius; **de mal ~** bad-tempered
genital [xeni'tal] *adj* genital; **genitales** *nmpl* genitals
gente ['xente] *nf* (*personas*) people *pl*; (*raza*) race; (*nación*) nation; (*parientes*) relatives *pl*
gentil [xen'til] *adj* (*elegante*) graceful; (*encantador*) charming; **~eza** *nf* grace; charm; (*cortesía*) courtesy
gentío [xen'tio] *nm* crowd, throng
genuino, a [xe'nwino, a] *adj* genuine
geografía [xeoɣra'fia] *nf* geography
geología [xeolo'xia] *nf* geology
geometría [xeome'tria] *nf* geometry
gerencia [xe'renθja] *nf* management; **gerente** *nm/f* (*supervisor*) manager; (*jefe*) director
geriatría [xeria'tria] *nf* (*MED*) geriatrics *sg*
germen ['xermen] *nm* germ
germinar [xermi'nar] *vi* to germinate
gesticular [xestiku'lar] *vi* to gesticulate; (*hacer muecas*) to grimace; **gesticulación** *nf* gesticulation; (*mueca*) grimace
gestión [xes'tjon] *nf* management; (*diligencia, acción*) negotiation; **gestionar** *vt* (*lograr*) to try to arrange; (*llevar*) to manage
gesto ['xesto] *nm* (*mueca*) grimace; (*ademán*) gesture
Gibraltar [xißral'tar] *nm* Gibraltar; **gibraltareño, a** *adj, nm/f* Gibraltarian
gigante [xi'ɣante] *adj, nm/f* giant; **gigantesco, a** *adj* gigantic
gilipollas [xili'poʎas] (*fam*) *adj inv* daft ♦ *nm/f inv* wally
gimnasia [xim'nasja] *nf* gymnastics *pl*; **gimnasio** *nm* gymnasium; **gimnasta** *nm/f* gymnast
gimotear [ximote'ar] *vi* to whine, whimper

ginebra [xi'neβra] *nf* gin
ginecólogo, a [xine'koloɣo, a] *nm/f* gynaecologist
gira ['xira] *nf* tour, trip
girar [xi'rar] *vt* (*dar la vuelta*) to turn (around); (: *rápidamente*) to spin; (*COM: giro postal*) to draw; (*comerciar: letra de cambio*) to issue ♦ *vi* to turn (round); (*rápido*) to spin; (*COM*) to draw
girasol [xira'sol] *nm* sunflower
giratorio, a [xira'torjo, a] *adj* (*gen*) revolving; (*puente*) swing
giro ['xiro] *nm* (*movimiento*) turn, revolution; (*LING*) expression; (*COM*) draft; ~ **bancario/postal** bank giro/postal order
gis [xis] (*AM*) *nm* chalk
gitano, a [xi'tano, a] *adj, nm/f* gypsy
glacial [gla'θjal] *adj* icy, freezing
glaciar [gla'θjar] *nm* glacier
glándula ['glandula] *nf* gland
global [glo'βal] *adj* global
globo ['gloβo] *nm* (*esfera*) globe, sphere; (*aerostato, juguete*) balloon
glóbulo ['gloβulo] *nm* globule; (*ANAT*) corpuscle
gloria ['glorja] *nf* glory
glorieta [glo'rjeta] *nf* (*de jardín*) bower, arbour; (*plazoleta*) roundabout (*BRIT*), traffic circle (*US*)
glorificar [glorifi'kar] *vt* (*enaltecer*) to glorify, praise
glorioso, a [glo'rjoso, a] *adj* glorious
glosa ['glosa] *nf* comment
glosario [glo'sarjo] *nm* glossary
glotón, ona [glo'ton, ona] *adj* gluttonous, greedy ♦ *nm/f* glutton
glucosa [glu'kosa] *nf* glucose
gobernador, a [goβerna'ðor, a] *adj* governing ♦ *nm/f* governor; **gobernante** *adj* governing
gobernar [goβer'nar] *vt* (*dirigir*) to guide, direct; (*POL*) to rule, govern ♦ *vi* to govern; (*NAUT*) to steer
gobierno *etc* [go'βjerno] *vb ver* **gobernar** ♦ *nm* (*POL*) government; (*dirección*) guidance, direction; (*NAUT*) steering
goce *etc* ['goθe] *vb ver* **gozar** ♦ *nm* enjoyment
gol [gol] *nm* goal
golf [golf] *nm* golf
golfa ['golfa] (*fam*) *nf* (*mujer*) slut, whore
golfo, a ['golfo, a] *nm* (*GEO*) gulf ♦ *nm/f* (*fam: niño*) urchin; (*gamberro*) lout
golondrina [golon'drina] *nf* swallow
golosina [golo'sina] *nf* titbit; (*dulce*) sweet; **goloso, a** *adj* sweet-toothed
golpe ['golpe] *nm* blow; (*de puño*) punch; (*de mano*) smack; (*de remo*) stroke; (*fig: choque*) clash; **no dar** ~ to be bone idle; **de un** ~ with one blow; **de** ~ suddenly; **~ (de estado)** coup (d'état); **golpear** *vt, vi* to strike, knock; (*asestar*) to beat; (*de puño*)

to punch; (*golpetear*) to tap
goma ['goma] *nf* (*caucho*) rubber; (*elástico*) elastic; (*una* ~) elastic band; ~ **espuma** foam rubber; ~ **de pegar** gum, glue
gordo, a ['gorðo, a] *adj* (*gen*) fat; (*persona*) plump; (*fam*) enormous; **el (premio)** ~ (*en lotería*) first prize; **gordura** *nf* fat; (*corpulencia*) fatness, stoutness
gorila [go'rila] *nm* gorilla
gorjear [gorxe'ar] *vi* to twitter, chirp
gorra ['gorra] *nf* cap; (*de niño*) bonnet; (*militar*) bearskin; **entrar de** ~ (*fam*) to gatecrash; **ir de** ~ to sponge
gorrión [go'rrjon] *nm* sparrow
gorro ['gorro] *nm* (*gen*) cap; (*de niño, mujer*) bonnet
gorrón, ona [go'rron, ona] *nm/f* scrounger; **gorronear** (*fam*) to scrounge
gota ['gota] *nf* (*gen*) drop; (*de sudor*) bead; (*MED*) gout; **gotear** *vi* to drip; (*lloviznar*) to drizzle; **gotera** *nf* leak
gozar [go'θar] *vi* to enjoy o.s.; ~ **de** (*disfrutar*) to enjoy; (*poseer*) to possess
gozne ['goθne] *nm* hinge
gozo ['goθo] *nm* (*alegría*) joy; (*placer*) pleasure
gr. *abr* (= *gramo, gramos*) g
grabación [graβa'θjon] *nf* recording
grabado [gra'βaðo] *nm* print, engraving
grabadora [graβa'ðora] *nf* tape-recorder
grabar [gra'βar] *vt* to engrave; (*discos, cintas*) to record
gracia ['graθja] *nf* (*encanto*) grace, gracefulness; (*humor*) humour, wit; **¡(muchas)** ~**s!** thanks (very much)!; ~**s a** thanks to; **tener** ~ (*chiste etc*) to be funny; **no me hace** ~ I am not keen; **gracioso, a** *adj* (*divertido*) funny, amusing; (*cómico*) comical ♦ *nm/f* (*TEATRO*) comic character
grada ['graða] *nf* (*de escalera*) step; (*de anfiteatro*) tier, row; ~**s** *nfpl* (*DEPORTE: de estadio*) terraces
gradación [graða'θjon] *nf* gradation
gradería [graðe'ria] *nf* (*gradas*) (flight of) steps *pl*; (*de anfiteatro*) tiers *pl*, rows *pl*; (*DEPORTE: de estadio*) terraces *pl*; ~ **cubierta** covered stand
grado ['graðo] *nm* degree; (*de aceite, vino*) grade; (*grada*) step; (*MIL*) rank; **de buen** ~ willingly
graduación [graðwa'θjon] *nf* (*del alcohol*) proof, strength; (*ESCOL*) graduation; (*MIL*) rank
gradual [gra'ðwal] *adj* gradual
graduar [gra'ðwar] *vt* (*gen*) to graduate; (*MIL*) to commission; ~**se** *vr* to graduate; ~**se la vista** to have one's eyes tested
gráfica ['grafika] *nf* graph
gráfico, a ['grafiko, a] *adj* graphic ♦ *nm* diagram; ~**s** *nmpl* (*INFORM*) graphics
grajo ['graxo] *nm* rook
Gral *abr* (= *General*) Gen.

gramática [gra'matika] nf grammar
gramo ['gramo] nm gramme (BRIT), gram (US)
gran [gran] adj ver **grande**
grana ['grana] nf (BOT) seedling; (color, tela) scarlet
granada [gra'naða] nf pomegranate; (MIL) grenade
granate [gra'nate] adj (color) deep red
Gran Bretaña [-bre'taɲa] nf Great Britain
grande ['grande] (antes de nmsg: **gran**) adj (de tamaño) big, large; (alto) tall; (distinguido) great; (impresionante) grand ♦ nm grandee; **grandeza** nf greatness
grandioso, a [gran'djoso, a] adj magnificent, grand
granel [gra'nel]: **a ~** adv (COM) in bulk
granero [gra'nero] nm granary, barn
granito [gra'nito] nm (AGR) small grain; (roca) granite
granizado [grani'θaðo] nm iced drink
granizar [grani'θar] vi to hail; **granizo** nm hail
granja ['granxa] nf (gen) farm; **granjear** vt to win, gain; **granjearse** vr to win, gain; **granjero, a** nm/f farmer
grano ['grano] nm grain; (semilla) seed; (baya) berry; (MED) pimple, spot; **~s** nmpl (cereales) cereals
granuja [gra'nuxa] nm/f rogue; (golfillo) urchin
grapa ['grapa] nf staple; (TEC) clamp; **grapadora** nf stapler
grasa ['grasa] nf (gen) grease; (de cocina) fat, lard; (sebo) suet; (mugre) filth; **grasiento, a** adj greasy; (de aceite) oily; **graso, a** adj (leche, queso, carne) fatty; (pelo, piel) greasy
gratificación [gratifika'θjon] nf (propina) tip; (bono) bonus; (recompensa) reward
gratificar [gratifi'kar] vt to tip; to reward
gratis ['gratis] adv free
gratitud [grati'tuð] nf gratitude
grato, a ['grato, a] adj (agradable) pleasant, agreeable; (bienvenido) welcome
gratuito, a [gra'twito, a] adj (gratis) free; (sin razón) gratuitous
gravamen [gra'ßamen] nm (carga) burden; (impuesto) tax
gravar [gra'ßar] vt to burden; (COM) to tax
grave ['graße] adj heavy; (serio) grave, serious; **~dad** nf gravity
gravilla [gra'ßiʎa] nf gravel
gravitar [graßi'tar] vi to gravitate; **~ sobre** to rest on
graznar [graθ'nar] vi (cuervo) to squawk; (pato) to quack; (hablar ronco) to croak
Grecia ['greθja] nf Greece
gremio ['gremjo] nm (asociación) trade, industry
greña ['greɲa] nf (cabellos) shock of hair; (maraña) tangle

gresca ['greska] nf uproar
griego, a ['grjeɣo, a] adj, nm/f Greek
grieta ['grjeta] nf crack
grifo ['grifo] nm tap; (AM: AUTO) petrol (BRIT) o gas (US) station
grilletes [gri'ʎetes] nmpl fetters
grillo ['griʎo] nm (ZOOL) cricket; (BOT) shoot
gripe ['gripe] nf flu, influenza
gris [gris] adj (color) grey
gritar [gri'tar] vt, vi to shout, yell; **grito** nm shout, yell; (de horror) scream
grosella [gro'seʎa] nf (red)currant; **~ negra** blackcurrant
grosería [grose'ria] nf (actitud) rudeness; (comentario) vulgar comment; **grosero, a** adj (poco cortés) rude, bad-mannered; (ordinario) vulgar, crude
grosor [gro'sor] nm thickness
grotesco, a [gro'tesko, a] adj grotesque
grúa ['grua] nf (TEC) crane; (de petróleo) derrick
grueso, a ['grweso, a] adj thick; (persona) stout ♦ nm bulk; **el ~ de** the bulk of
grulla ['gruʎa] nf crane
grumo ['grumo] nm clot, lump
gruñido [gru'ɲiðo] nm grunt; (fig) grumble
gruñir [gru'ɲir] vi (animal) to growl; (fam) to grumble
grupa ['grupa] nf (ZOOL) rump
grupo ['grupo] nm group; (TEC) unit, set
gruta ['gruta] nf grotto
guadaña [gwa'ðaɲa] nf scythe
guagua ['gwa'ɣwa] (AM) nf (niño) baby; (bus) bus
guante ['gwante] nm glove
guapo, a ['gwapo, a] adj good-looking, attractive; (elegante) smart
guarda ['gwarða] nm/f (persona) guard, keeper ♦ nf (acto) guarding; (custodia) custody; **~bosques** nm inv gamekeeper; **~costas** nm inv coastguard vessel ♦ nm/f guardian, protector; **~espaldas** nm/f inv bodyguard; **~meta** nm/f goalkeeper; **guardar** vt (gen) to keep; (vigilar) to guard, watch over; (dinero: ahorrar) to save; **guardarse** vr (preservarse) to protect o.s.; (evitar) to avoid; **guardar cama** to stay in bed; **~rropa** nm (armario) wardrobe; (en establecimiento público) cloakroom
guardería [gwarðe'ria] nf nursery
guardia ['gwarðja] nf (MIL) guard; (cuidado) care, custody ♦ nm/f guard; (policía) policeman/woman; **estar de ~** to be on guard; **montar ~** to mount guard; **G~ Civil** Civil Guard; **G~ Nacional** National Guard
guardián, ana [gwar'ðjan, ana] nm/f (gen) guardian, keeper
guarecer [gware'θer] vt (proteger) to protect; (abrigar) to shelter; **~se** vr to take refuge
guarida [gwa'riða] nf (de animal) den, lair;

(*refugio*) refuge

guarnecer [gwarne'θer] *vt* (*equipar*) to provide; (*adornar*) to adorn; (*TEC*) to reinforce; **guarnición** *nf* (*de vestimenta*) trimming; (*de piedra*) mount; (*CULIN*) garnish; (*arneses*) harness; (*MIL*) garrison

guarro, a ['gwarro, a] *nm/f* pig

guasa ['gwasa] *nf* joke; **guasón, ona** *adj* witty; (*bromista*) joking ♦ *nm/f* wit; joker

Guatemala [gwate'mala] *nf* Guatemala

gubernativo, a [gußerna'tißo, a] *adj* governmental

guerra ['gerra] *nf* war; (*pelea*) struggle; ~ **civil** civil war; ~ **fría** cold war; **dar** ~ **to** annoy; **guerrear** *vi* to wage war; **guerrero, a** *adj* fighting; (*carácter*) warlike ♦ *nm/f* warrior

guerrilla [ge'rriʎa] *nf* guerrilla warfare; (*tropas*) guerrilla band *o* group

guía *etc* ['gia] *vb ver* **guiar** ♦ *nm/f* (*persona*) guide ♦ *nf* (*libro*) guidebook; G~ Girl Guide; ~ **de ferrocarriles** railway timetable; ~ **telefónica** telephone directory

guiar [gi'ar] *vt* to guide, direct; (*AUTO*) to steer; ~**se** *vr*: ~**se por** to be guided by

guijarro [gi'xarro] *nm* pebble

guillotina [giʎo'tina] *nf* guillotine

guinda ['ginda] *nf* morello cherry

guindilla [gin'diʎa] *nf* chilli pepper

guiñapo [gi'ɲapo] *nm* (*harapo*) rag; (*persona*) reprobate, rogue

guiñar [gi'ɲar] *vt* to wink

guión [gi'on] *nm* (*LING*) hyphen, dash; (*CINE*) script; **guionista** *nm/f* scriptwriter

guiri ['giri] (*pey*) *nm/f* foreigner

guirnalda [gir'nalda] *nf* garland

guisado [gi'saðo] *nm* stew

guisante [gi'sante] *nm* pea

guisar [gi'sar] *vt, vi* to cook; **guiso** *nm* cooked dish

guitarra [gi'tarra] *nf* guitar

gula ['gula] *nf* gluttony, greed

gusano [gu'sano] *nm* maggot; (*lombriz*) earthworm

gustar [gus'tar] *vt* to taste, sample ♦ *vi* to please, be pleasing; ~ **de algo** to like *o* enjoy sth; **me gustan las uvas** I like grapes; **le gusta nadar** she likes *o* enjoys swimming

gusto ['gusto] *nm* (*sentido, sabor*) taste; (*placer*) pleasure; **tiene** ~ **a menta** it tastes of mint; **tener buen** ~ to have good taste; **sentirse a** ~ to feel at ease; **mucho** ~ (*en conocerle*) pleased to meet you; **el** ~ **es mío** the pleasure is mine; **con** ~ willingly, gladly; ~**so, a** *adj* (*sabroso*) tasty; (*agradable*) pleasant

H h

ha *vb ver* **haber**

haba ['aßa] *nf* bean

Habana [a'ßana] *nf*: **la** ~ Havana

habano [a'ßano] *nm* Havana cigar

habéis *vb ver* **haber**

──────── *PALABRA CLAVE*

haber [a'ßer] *vb aux* **1** (*tiempos compuestos*) to have; **había comido** I have/had eaten; **antes/después de** ~**lo visto** before seeing/after seeing *o* having seen it

2: ¡~**lo dicho antes!** you should have said so before!

3: ~ **de**: **he de hacerlo** I have to do it; **ha de llegar mañana** it should arrive tomorrow

♦ *vb impers* **1** (*existencia: sg*) there is; (*: pl*) there are; **hay un hermano/dos hermanos** there is one brother/there are two brothers; ¿**cuánto hay de aquí a Sucre?** how far is it from here to Sucre?

2 (*obligación*): **hay que hacer algo** something must be done; **hay que apuntarlo para acordarse** you have to write it down to remember

3: ¡**hay que ver!** well I never!

4: ¡**no hay de** *o* **por** (*AM*) **qué!** don't mention it!, not at all!

5: ¿**qué hay?** (¿*qué pasa?*) what's up?, what's the matter?; (¿*qué tal?*) how's it going?

♦ ~**se** *vr*: **habérselas con uno** to have it out with sb

♦ *vt*: **he aquí unas sugerencias** here are some suggestions; **no hay cintas blancas pero sí las hay rojas** there aren't any white ribbons but there are some red ones

♦ *nm* (*en cuenta*) credit side; ~**es** *nmpl* assets; ¿**cuánto tengo en el** ~? how much do I have in my account?; **tiene varias novelas en su** ~ he has several novels to his credit

habichuela [aßi'tʃwela] *nf* kidney bean

hábil ['aßil] *adj* (*listo*) clever, smart; (*capaz*) fit, capable; (*experto*) expert; **día** ~ working day; **habilidad** *nf* (*gen*) skill, ability; (*inteligencia*) cleverness

habilitar [aßili'tar] *vt* (*capacitar*) to enable;

(*dar instrumentos*) to equip; (*financiar*) to finance

hábilmente [aßil'mente] *adv* skilfully, expertly

habitación [aßita'θjon] *nf* (*cuarto*) room; (*casa*) dwelling, abode; (*BIO: morada*) habitat; ~ **sencilla** o **individual** single room; ~ **doble** o **de matrimonio** double room

habitante [aßi'tante] *nm/f* inhabitant

habitar [aßi'tar] *vt* (*residir en*) to inhabit; (*ocupar*) to occupy ♦ *vi* to live

hábito ['aßito] *nm* habit

habitual [aßi'twal] *adj* usual

habituar [aßi'twar] *vt* to accustom; ~**se** *vr*: ~**se a** to get used to

habla ['aßla] *nf* (*capacidad de hablar*) speech; (*idioma*) language; (*dialecto*) dialect; **perder el** ~ to become speechless; **de** ~ **francesa** French-speaking; **estar al** ~ to be in contact; (*TEL*) to be on the line; **¡González al** ~! (*TEL*) González speaking!

hablador, a [aßla'ðor, a] *adj* talkative ♦ *nm/f* chatterbox

habladuría [aßlaðu'ria] *nf* rumour; ~**s** *nfpl* gossip *sg*

hablante [a'ßlante] *adj* speaking ♦ *nm/f* speaker

hablar [a'ßlar] *vt* to speak, talk ♦ *vi* to speak; ~**se** *vr* to speak to each other; ~ **con** to speak to; ~ **de** to speak of o about; "**se habla inglés**" "English spoken here"; **¡ni** ~! it's out of the question!

habré *etc vb ver* **haber**

hacendado [asen'daðo] (*AM*) *nm* large landowner

hacendoso, a [aθen'doso, a] *adj* industrious

PALABRA CLAVE

hacer [a'θer] *vt* **1** (*fabricar, producir*) to make; (*construir*) to build; ~ **una película/un ruido** to make a film/noise; **el guisado lo hice yo** I made o cooked the stew

2 (*ejecutar: trabajo etc*) to do; ~ **la colada** to do the washing; ~ **la comida** to do the cooking; **¿qué haces?** what are you doing?; ~ **el malo** o **el papel del malo** (*TEATRO*) to play the villain

3 (*estudios, algunos deportes*) to do; ~ **español/económicas** to do o study Spanish/economics; ~ **yoga/gimnasia** to do yoga/go to gym

4 (*transformar, incidir en*): **esto lo hará más difícil** this will make it more difficult; **salir te hará sentir mejor** going out will make you feel better

5 (*cálculo*): **2 y 2 hacen 4** 2 and 2 make 4; **éste hace 100** this one makes 100

6 (+ *sub*): **esto hará que ganemos** this will make us win; **harás que no quiera venir** you'll stop him wanting to come

7 (*como sustituto de vb*) to do; **él bebió y yo hice lo mismo** he drank and I did likewise

8: no hace más que criticar all he does is criticize

♦ *vb semi-aux*: ~ + *infin* **1** (*directo*): **les hice venir** I made o had them come; ~ **trabajar a los demás** to get others to work

2 (*por intermedio de otros*): ~ **reparar algo** to get sth repaired

♦ *vi* **1: haz como que no lo sabes** act as if you don't know

2 (*ser apropiado*): **si os hace** if it's alright with you

3. ~ **de:** ~ **de madre para uno** to be like a mother to sb; (*TEATRO*): ~ **de Otelo** to play Othello

♦ *vb impers* **1: hace calor/frío** it's hot/cold; *ver tb* **bueno; sol; tiempo**

2 (*tiempo*): **hace 3 años** 3 years ago; **hace un mes que voy/no voy** I've been going/I haven't been for a month

3: ¿cómo has hecho para llegar tan rápido? how did you manage to get here so quickly?

♦ ~**se** *vr* **1** (*volverse*) to become; **se hicieron amigos** they became friends

2 (*acostumbrarse*): ~**se a** to get used to

3: se hace con huevos y leche it's made out of eggs and milk; **eso no se hace** that's not done

4 (*obtener*): ~**se de** o **con algo** to get hold of sth

5 (*fingirse*): ~**se el sueco** to turn a deaf ear

---

hacia ['aθja] *prep* (*en dirección de*) towards; (*cerca de*) near; (*actitud*) towards; ~ **arriba/abajo** up(wards)/down(wards); ~ **mediodía** about noon

hacienda [a'θjenda] *nf* (*propiedad*) property; (*finca*) farm; (*AM*) ranch; ~ **pública** public finance; (**Ministerio de**) **H~** Exchequer (*BRIT*), Treasury Department (*US*)

hacha ['atʃa] *nf* axe; (*antorcha*) torch

hachís [a'tʃis] *nm* hashish

hada ['aða] *nf* fairy

hago *etc vb ver* **hacer**

Haití [ai'ti] *nm* Haiti

halagar [ala'ɣar] *vt* (*lisonjear*) to flatter

halago [a'laɣo] *nm* (*adulación*) flattery; **halagüeño, a** *adj* flattering

halcón [al'kon] *nm* falcon, hawk

halterofilia [altero'filja] *nf* weightlifting

hallar [a'ʎar] *vt* (*gen*) to find; (*descubrir*) to discover; (*toparse con*) to run into; ~**se** *vr* to be (situated); **hallazgo** *nm* discovery; (*cosa*) find

hamaca [a'maka] *nf* hammock

hambre ['ambre] *nf* hunger; (*carencia*) famine; (*fig*) longing; **tener** ~ to be hungry; **hambriento, a** *adj* hungry, starving

hamburguesa [ambur'ɣesa] *nf* hamburger
han *vb ver* **haber**
haragán, ana [ara'ɣan, ana] *adj, nm/f* good-for-nothing
harapiento, a [ara'pjento, a] *adj* tattered, in rags
harapos [a'rapos] *nmpl* rags
haré *etc vb ver* **hacer**
harina [a'rina] *nf* flour
hartar [ar'tar] *vt* to satiate, glut; (*fig*) to tire, sicken; ~**se** *vr* (*de comida*) to fill o.s., gorge o.s.; (*cansarse*) to get fed up (*de* with); **hartazgo** *nm* surfeit, glut; **harto, a** *adj* (*lleno*) full; (*cansado*) fed up ♦ *adv* (*bastante*) enough; (*muy*) very; **estar harto de** to be fed up with
has *vb ver* **haber**
hasta ['asta] *adv* even ♦ *prep* (*alcanzando a*) as far as; up to; down to; (*de tiempo: a tal hora*) till, until; (*antes de*) before ♦ *conj*: ~ **que** until; ~ **luego/el sábado** see you soon/on Saturday
hastiar [as'tjar] *vt* (*gen*) to weary; (*aburrir*) to bore; ~**se** *vr*: ~**se de** to get fed up with; **hastío** *nm* weariness; boredom
hatillo [a'tiʎo] *nm* belongings *pl*, kit; (*montón*) bundle, heap
hay *vb ver* **haber**
Haya ['aja] *nf*: **la** ~ The Hague
haya *etc* ['aja] *vb ver* **haber** ♦ *nf* beech tree
haz [aθ] *vb ver* **hacer** ♦ *nm* bundle, bunch; (*rayo: de luz*) beam
hazaña [a'θaɲa] *nf* feat, exploit
hazmerreír [aθmerre'ir] *nm inv* laughing stock
he *vb ver* **haber**
hebilla [e'βiʎa] *nf* buckle, clasp
hebra ['eβra] *nf* thread; (*BOT: fibra*) fibre, grain
hebreo, a [e'βreo, a] *adj, nm/f* Hebrew ♦ *nm* (*LING*) Hebrew
hectárea [ek'tarea] *nf* hectare
hechizar [etʃi'θar] *vt* to cast a spell on, bewitch
hechizo [e'tʃiθo] *nm* witchcraft, magic; (*acto de magía*) spell, charm
hecho, a ['etʃo, a] *pp de* **hacer** ♦ *adj* complete; (*maduro*) mature; (*COSTURA*) ready-to-wear ♦ *nm* deed, act; (*dato*) fact; (*cuestión*) matter; (*suceso*) event ♦ *excl* agreed!, done!; ¡**bien** ~! well done!; **de** ~ in fact, as a matter of fact
hechura [e'tʃura] *nf* making, creation; (*producto*) product; (*forma*) form, shape; (*de persona*) build; (*TEC*) craftsmanship
heder [e'ðer] *vi* to stink, smell; (*fig*) to be unbearable
hediondo, a [e'ðjondo, a] *adj* stinking
hedor [e'ðor] *nm* stench
helada [e'laða] *nf* frost
heladera [ela'ðera] (*AM*) *nf* (*refrigerador*) refrigerator

helado, a [e'laðo, a] *adj* frozen; (*glacial*) icy; (*fig*) chilly, cold ♦ *nm* ice cream
helar [e'lar] *vt* to freeze, ice (up); (*dejar atónito*) to amaze; (*desalentar*) to discourage ♦ *vi* to freeze; ~**se** *vr* to freeze
helecho [e'letʃo] *nm* fern
hélice ['eliθe] *nf* spiral; (*TEC*) propeller
helicóptero [eli'koptero] *nm* helicopter
hembra ['embra] *nf* (*BOT, ZOOL*) female; (*mujer*) woman; (*TEC*) nut
hemorragia [emo'rraxja] *nf* haemorrhage
hemorroides [emo'rroiðes] *nfpl* haemorrhoids, piles
hemos *vb ver* **haber**
hendidura [endi'ðura] *nf* crack, split; (*GEO*) fissure
heno ['eno] *nm* hay
herbicida [erβi'θiða] *nm* weedkiller
heredad [ere'ðað] *nf* landed property; (*granja*) farm
heredar [ere'ðar] *vt* to inherit; **heredero, a** *nm/f* heir(ess)
hereje [e'rexe] *nm/f* heretic
herencia [e'renθja] *nf* inheritance
herida [e'riða] *nf* wound, injury; *ver tb* **herido**
herido, a [e'riðo, a] *adj* injured, wounded ♦ *nm/f* casualty
herir [e'rir] *vt* to wound, injure; (*fig*) to offend
hermanastro, a [erma'nastro, a] *nm/f* stepbrother/sister
hermandad [erman'dað] *nf* brotherhood
hermano, a [er'mano, a] *nm/f* brother/sister; ~ **gemelo** twin brother; ~ **político** brother-in-law; **hermana política** sister-in-law
hermético, a [er'metiko, a] *adj* hermetic; (*fig*) watertight
hermoso, a [er'moso, a] *adj* beautiful, lovely; (*estupendo*) splendid; (*guapo*) handsome; **hermosura** *nf* beauty
hernia ['ernja] *nf* hernia
héroe ['eroe] *nm* hero
heroína [ero'ina] *nf* (*mujer*) heroine; (*droga*) heroin
heroísmo [ero'ismo] *nm* heroism
herradura [erra'ðura] *nf* horseshoe
herramienta [erra'mjenta] *nf* tool
herrero [e'rrero] *nm* blacksmith
herrumbre [e'rrumbre] *nf* rust
hervidero [erβi'ðero] *nm* (*fig*) swarm; (*POL etc*) hotbed
hervir [er'βir] *vi* to boil; (*burbujear*) to bubble; (*fig*): ~ **de** to teem with; ~ **a fuego lento** to simmer; **hervor** *nm* boiling; (*fig*) ardour, fervour
heterosexual [eterosek'swal] *adj* heterosexual
hice *etc vb ver* **hacer**
hidratante [iðra'tante] *adj*: **crema** ~ moisturizing cream, moisturizer; **hidratar** *vt*

(*piel*) to moisturize; **hidrato** *nm*: **hidratos de carbono** carbohydrates

hidráulica [i'ðraulika] *nf* hydraulics *sg*

hidráulico, a [i'ðrauliko, a] *adj* hydraulic

hidro... [iðro] *prefijo* hydro..., water-...; **~eléctrico, a** *adj* hydroelectric; **~fobia** *nf* hydrophobia, rabies; **hidrógeno** *nm* hydrogen

hiedra ['jeðra] *nf* ivy

hiel [jel] *nf* gall, bile; (*fig*) bitterness

hiela *etc vb ver* helar

hielo ['jelo] *nm* (*gen*) ice; (*escarcha*) frost; (*fig*) coldness, reserve

hiena ['jena] *nf* hyena

hierba ['jerßa] *nf* (*pasto*) grass; (*CULIN, MED*: *planta*) herb; **mala ~** weed; (*fig*) evil influence; **~buena** *nf* mint

hierro ['jerro] *nm* (*metal*) iron; (*objeto*) iron object

hígado ['iyaðo] *nm* liver

higiene [i'xjene] *nf* hygiene; **higiénico, a** *adj* hygienic

higo ['iyo] *nm* fig; **higuera** *nf* fig tree

hijastro, a [i'xastro, a] *nm/f* stepson/ daughter

hijo, a ['ixo, a] *nm/f* son/daughter, child; **~s** *nmpl* children, sons and daughters; **~ de papá/mamá** daddy's/mummy's boy; **~ de puta** (*fam!*) bastard (*!*), son of a bitch (*!*)

hilar [i'lar] *vt* to spin; **~ fino** to split hairs

hilera [i'lera] *nf* row, file

hilo ['ilo] *nm* thread; (*BOT*) fibre; (*metal*) wire; (*de agua*) trickle, thin stream; (*de luz*) beam, ray

hilvanar [ilßa'nar] *vt* (*COSTURA*) to tack (*BRIT*), baste (*US*); (*fig*) to do hurriedly

himno ['imno] *nm* hymn; **~ nacional** national anthem

hincapié [inka'pje] *nm*: **hacer ~ en** to emphasize

hincar [in'kar] *vt* to drive (in), thrust (in); **~se** *vr*: **~se de rodillas** to kneel down

hincha ['intʃa] (*fam*) *nm/f* fan

hinchado, a [in'tʃaðo, a] *adj* (*gen*) swollen; (*persona*) pompous

hinchar [in'tʃar] *vt* (*gen*) to swell; (*inflar*) to blow up, inflate; (*fig*) to exaggerate; **~se** *vr* (*inflarse*) to swell up; (*fam*: *llenarse*) to stuff o.s.; **hinchazón** *nf* (*MED*) swelling; (*altivez*) arrogance

hinojo [i'noxo] *nm* fennel

hipermercado [ipermer'kaðo] *nm* hypermarket, superstore

hípico, a ['ipiko, a] *adj* horse *cpd*

hipnotismo [ipno'tismo] *nm* hypnotism; **hipnotizar** *vt* to hypnotize

hipo ['ipo] *nm* hiccups *pl*

hipocresía [ipokre'sia] *nf* hypocrisy; **hipócrita** *adj* hypocritical ♦ *nm/f* hypocrite

hipódromo [i'poðromo] *nm* racetrack

hipopótamo [ipo'potamo] *nm* hippopotamus

hipoteca [ipo'teka] *nf* mortgage

hipótesis [i'potesis] *nf inv* hypothesis

hiriente [i'rjente] *adj* offensive, wounding

hispánico, a [is'paniko, a] *adj* Hispanic

hispano, a [is'pano, a] *adj* Hispanic, Spanish, Hispano- ♦ *nm/f* Spaniard; **H~américa** *nf* Latin America; **~americano, a** *adj, nm/f* Latin American

histeria [is'terja] *nf* hysteria

historia [is'torja] *nf* history; (*cuento*) story, tale; **~s** *nfpl* (*chismes*) gossip *sg*; **dejarse de ~s** to come to the point; **pasar a la ~** to go down in history; **~dor, a** *nm/f* historian; **historial** *nm* (*profesional*) curriculum vitae, C.V.; (*MED*) case history; **histórico, a** *adj* historical; (*fig*) historic

historieta [isto'rjeta] *nf* tale, anecdote; (*dibujos*) comic strip

hito ['ito] *nm* (*fig*) landmark; (*objetivo*) goal, target

hizo *vb ver* hacer

Hnos *abr* (= *Hermanos*) Bros.

hocico [o'θiko] *nm* snout; (*fig*) grimace

hockey ['xoki] *nm* hockey; **~ sobre hielo** ice hockey

hogar [o'yar] *nm* fireplace, hearth; (*casa*) home; (*vida familiar*) home life; **~eño, a** *adj* home *cpd*; (*persona*) home-loving

hoguera [o'yera] *nf* (*gen*) bonfire

hoja ['oxa] *nf* (*gen*) leaf; (*de flor*) petal; (*de papel*) sheet; (*página*) page; **~ de afeitar** razor blade

hojalata [oxa'lata] *nf* tin(plate)

hojaldre [o'xaldre] *nm* (*CULIN*) puff pastry

hojear [oxe'ar] *vt* to leaf through, turn the pages of

hola ['ola] *excl* hello!

Holanda [o'landa] *nf* Holland; **holandés, esa** *adj* Dutch ♦ *nm/f* Dutchman/woman ♦ *nm* (*LING*) Dutch

holgado, a [ol'yaðo, a] *adj* loose, baggy; (*rico*) well-to-do

holgar [ol'yar] *vi* (*descansar*) to rest; (*sobrar*) to be superfluous; **huelga decir que** it goes without saying that

holgazán, ana [olya'θan, ana] *adj* idle, lazy ♦ *nm/f* loafer

holgura [ol'yura] *nf* looseness, bagginess; (*TEC*) play, free movement; (*vida*) comfortable living, luxury

hollín [o'ʎin] *nm* soot

hombre ['ombre] *nm* (*gen*) man; (*raza humana*): **el ~** man(kind); (*uno*) man ♦ *excl*: **¡sí ~!** (*claro*) of course!; (*para énfasis*) man, old boy; **~ de negocios** businessman; **~ de pro** honest man; **~-rana** frogman

hombrera [om'brera] *nf* shoulder strap

hombro ['ombro] *nm* shoulder

hombruno, a [om'bruno, a] *adj* mannish

homenaje [ome'naxe] *nm* (*gen*) homage; (*tributo*) tribute

homicida [omi'θiða] *adj* homicidal ♦ *nm/f* murderer; **homicidio** *nm* murder, homicide

homologar [omolo'ɣar] *vt* (COM: *productos, tamaños*) to standardize; **homólogo, a** *nm/f*: **su** etc **homólogo** his etc counterpart *o* opposite number

homosexual [omosek'swal] *adj*, *nm/f* homosexual

hondo, a ['ondo, a] *adj* deep; **lo** ~ the depth(s) (*pl*), the bottom; **~nada** *nf* hollow, depression; (*cañón*) ravine; (GEO) lowland

Honduras [on'duras] *nf* Honduras

hondureño, a [ondu'reɲo, a] *adj*, *nm/f* Honduran

honestidad [onesti'ðað] *nf* purity, chastity; (*decencia*) decency; **honesto, a** *adj* chaste; decent, honest; (*justo*) just

hongo ['ongo] *nm* (BOT: gen) fungus; (: *comestible*) mushroom; (: *venenoso*) toadstool

honor [o'nor] *nm* (gen) honour; (*gloria*) glory; **en** ~ **a la verdad** to be fair; **~able** *adj* honourable

honorario, a [ono'rarjo, a] *adj* honorary; **~s** *nmpl* fees

honra ['onra] *nf* (gen) honour; (*renombre*) good name; **~dez** *nf* honesty; (*de persona*) integrity; **~do, a** *adj* honest, upright

honrar [on'rar] *vt* to honour; **~se** *vr*: **~se con algo/de hacer algo** to be honoured by sth/to do sth

honroso, a [on'roso, a] *adj* (*honrado*) honourable; (*respetado*) respectable

hora ['ora] *nf* (*una* ~) hour; (*tiempo*) time; **¿qué** ~ **es?** what time is it?; **¿a qué** ~? at what time?; **media** ~ half an hour; **a la** ~ **de recreo** at playtime; **a primera** ~ first thing (in the morning); **a última** ~ at the last moment; **a altas** ~**s** in the small hours; **¡a buena** ~! about time, too!; **dar la** ~ to strike the hour; **~s de oficina/de trabajo** office/working hours; **~s de visita** visiting times; **~s extras** *o* **extraordinarias** overtime *pl*; **~s punta** rush hours

horadar [ora'ðar] *vt* to drill, bore

horario, a [o'rarjo, a] *adj* hourly, hour *cpd* ♦ *nm* timetable; ~ **comercial** business hours *pl*

horca ['orka] *nf* gallows *sg*

horcajadas [orka'xaðas]: **a** ~ *adv* astride

horchata [or'tʃata] *nf* cold drink made from tiger nuts and water, tiger nut milk

horizontal [oriθon'tal] *adj* horizontal

horizonte [ori'θonte] *nm* horizon

horma ['orma] *nf* mould

hormiga [or'miɣa] *nf* ant; **~s** *nfpl* (MED) pins and needles

hormigón [ormi'ɣon] *nm* concrete; ~ **armado/pretensado** reinforced/prestressed concrete

hormigueo [ormi'ɣeo] *nm* (*comezón*) itch; (*fig*) uneasiness

hormona [or'mona] *nf* hormone

hornada [or'naða] *nf* batch (of loaves *etc*)

hornillo [or'niʎo] *nm* (*cocina*) portable stove

horno ['orno] *nm* (CULIN) oven; (TEC) furnace; **alto** ~ blast furnace

horóscopo [o'roskopo] *nm* horoscope

horquilla [or'kiʎa] *nf* hairpin; (AGR) pitchfork

horrendo, a [o'rrendo, a] *adj* horrendous, frightful

horrible [o'rrißle] *adj* horrible, dreadful

horripilante [orripi'lante] *adj* hair-raising, horrifying

horror [o'rror] *nm* horror, dread; (*atrocidad*) atrocity; **¡qué** ~! (*fam*) how awful!; **~izar** *vt* to horrify, frighten; **~izarse** *vr* to be horrified; **~oso, a** *adj* horrifying, ghastly

hortaliza [orta'liθa] *nf* vegetable

hortelano, a [orte'lano, a] *nm/f* (market) gardener

hortera [or'tera] (*fam*) *adj* tacky

hosco, a ['osko, a] *adj* dark; (*persona*) sullen, gloomy

hospedar [ospe'ðar] *vt* to put up; **~se** *vr* to stay, lodge

hospital [ospi'tal] *nm* hospital

hospitalario, a [ospita'larjo, a] *adj* (*acogedor*) hospitable; **hospitalidad** *nf* hospitality

hostal [os'tal] *nm* small hotel

hostelería [ostele'ria] *nf* hotel business *o* trade

hostia ['ostja] *nf* (REL) host, consecrated wafer; (*fam: golpe*) whack, punch ♦ *excl* (*fam!*): **¡~s!** damn!

hostigar [osti'ɣar] *vt* to whip; (*fig*) to harass, pester

hostil [os'til] *adj* hostile; **~idad** *nf* hostility

hotel [o'tel] *nm* hotel; **~ero, a** *adj* hotel *cpd* ♦ *nm/f* hotelier

hoy [oi] *adv* (*este día*) today; (*la actualidad*) now(adays) ♦ *nm* present time; ~ **(en) día** now(adays)

hoyo ['ojo] *nm* hole, pit; **hoyuelo** *nm* dimple

hoz [oθ] *nf* sickle

hube etc *vb ver* **haber**

hucha ['utʃa] *nf* money box

hueco, a ['weko, a] *adj* (*vacío*) hollow, empty; (*resonante*) booming ♦ *nm* hollow, cavity

huelga etc ['welɣa] *vb ver* **holgar** ♦ *nf* strike; **declararse en** ~ to go on strike, come out on strike; ~ **de hambre** hunger strike

huelguista [wel'ɣista] *nm/f* striker

huelo etc *vb ver* **oler**

huella ['weʎa] *nf* (*acto de pisar, pisada*) tread(ing); (*marca del paso*) footprint, footstep; (: *de animal, máquina*) track; ~ **digital** fingerprint

huérfano, a ['werfano, a] *adj* orphan(ed) ♦

nm/f orphan

huerta ['werta] *nf* market garden; (*en Murcia y Valencia*) irrigated region

huerto ['werto] *nm* kitchen garden; (*de árboles frutales*) orchard

hueso ['weso] *nm* (*ANAT*) bone; (*de fruta*) stone

huésped, a ['wespeð, a] *nm/f* (*invitado*) guest; (*habitante*) resident; (*anfitrión*) host(ess)

huesudo, a [we'suðo, a] *adj* bony, big-boned

huevera [we'ßera] *nf* eggcup

huevo ['weßo] *nm* egg; **~ duro/escalfado/frito** (*ESP*) *o* **estrellado** (*AM*)/**pasado por agua** hard-boiled/poached/fried/soft-boiled egg; **~s revueltos** scrambled eggs

huida [u'iða] *nf* escape, flight

huidizo, a [ui'ðiθo, a] *adj* (*tímido*) shy; (*pasajero*) fleeting

huir ['u'ir] *vi* (*escapar*) to flee, escape; (*evadir*) to avoid; **~se** *vr* (*escaparse*) to escape

hule ['ule] *nm* (*encerado*) oilskin

humanidad [umani'ðað] *nf* (*género humano*) man(kind); (*cualidad*) humanity

humanitario, a [umani'tarjo, a] *adj* humanitarian

humano, a [u'mano, a] *adj* (*gen*) human; (*humanitario*) humane ♦ *nm* human; **ser ~** human being

humareda [uma'reða] *nf* cloud of smoke

humedad [ume'ðað] *nf* (*del clima*) humidity; (*de pared etc*) dampness; **a prueba de ~** damp-proof; **humedecer** *vt* to moisten, wet; **humedecerse** *vr* to get wet

húmedo, a ['umeðo, a] *adj* (*mojado*) damp, wet; (*tiempo etc*) humid

humildad [umil'dað] *nf* humility, humbleness; **humilde** *adj* humble, modest

humillación [umiʎa'θjon] *nf* humiliation; **humillante** *adj* humiliating

humillar [umi'ʎar] *vt* to humiliate; **~se** *vr* to humble o.s., grovel

humo ['umo] *nm* (*de fuego*) smoke; (*gas nocivo*) fumes *pl*; (*vapor*) steam, vapour; **~s** *nmpl* (*fig*) conceit *sg*

humor [u'mor] *nm* (*disposición*) mood, temper; (*lo que divierte*) humour; **de buen/mal ~** in a good/bad mood; **~ista** *nm/f* comic; **~ístico, a** *adj* funny, humorous

hundimiento [undi'mjento] *nm* (*gen*) sinking; (*colapso*) collapse

hundir [un'dir] *vt* to sink; (*edificio, plan*) to ruin, destroy; **~se** *vr* to sink, collapse

húngaro, a ['ungaro, a] *adj*, *nm/f* Hungarian

Hungría [un'gria] *nf* Hungary

huracán [ura'kan] *nm* hurricane

huraño, a [u'raɲo, a] *adj* shy; (*antisocial*) unsociable

hurgar [ur'xar] *vt* to poke, jab; (*remover*) to stir (up); **~se** *vr*: **~se (las narices)** to pick

one's nose

hurón, ona [u'ron, ona] *nm* (*ZOOL*) ferret

hurtadillas [urta'ðiʎas]: **a ~** *adv* stealthily, on the sly

hurtar [ur'tar] *vt* to steal; **hurto** *nm* theft, stealing

husmear [usme'ar] *vt* (*oler*) to sniff out, scent; (*fam*) to pry into ♦ *vi* to smell bad

huyo *etc vb ver* **huir**

I i

iba *etc vb ver* **ir**

ibérico, a [i'ßeriko, a] *adj* Iberian

iberoamericano, a [ißeroameri'kano, a] *adj*, *nm/f* Latin American

Ibiza [i'ßiθa] *nf* Ibiza

iceberg [iθe'ßer] *nm* iceberg

ícono ['ikono] *nm* ikon, icon

iconoclasta [ikono'klasta] *adj* iconoclastic ♦ *nm/f* iconoclast

ictericia [ikte'riθja] *nf* jaundice

ida ['iða] *nf* going, departure; **~ y vuelta** round trip, return

idea [i'ðea] *nf* idea; **no tengo la menor ~** I haven't a clue

ideal [iðe'al] *adj*, *nm* ideal; **~ista** *nm/f* idealist; **~izar** *vt* to idealize

idear [iðe'ar] *vt* to think up; (*aparato*) to invent; (*viaje*) to plan

ídem ['iðem] *pron* ditto

idéntico, a [i'ðentiko, a] *adj* identical

identidad [iðenti'ðað] *nf* identity

identificación [iðentifika'θjon] *nf* identification

identificar [iðentifi'kar] *vt* to identify; **~se** *vr*: **~se con** to identify with

ideología [iðeolo'xia] *nf* ideology

idilio [i'ðiljo] *nm* love-affair

idioma [i'ðjoma] *nm* (*gen*) language

idiota [i'ðjota] *adj* idiotic ♦ *nm/f* idiot; **idiotez** *nf* idiocy

ídolo ['iðolo] *nm* (*tb: fig*) idol

idóneo, a [i'ðoneo, a] *adj* suitable

iglesia [i'ɣlesja] *nf* church

ignominia [iɣno'minja] *nf* ignominy

ignorancia [iɣno'ranθja] *nf* ignorance; **ignorante** *adj* ignorant, uninformed ♦ *nm/f* ignoramus

ignorar [iɣno'rar] *vt* not to know, be ignorant of; (*no hacer caso a*) to ignore

igual [i'ɣwal] *adj* (*gen*) equal; (*similar*) like, similar; (*mismo*) (the) same; (*constante*)

constant; (*temperatura*) even ♦ *nm/f* equal;
~ que like, the same as; **me da** *o* **es ~** I
don't care; **son ~es** they're the same; **al ~
que** *prep, conj* like, just like

igualada [iɣwa'laða] *nf* equaliser

igualar [iɣwa'lar] *vt* (*gen*) to equalize, make
equal; (*allanar, nivelar*) to level (off), even
(out); **~se** *vr* (*platos de balanza*) to balance
out

igualdad [iɣwal'daθ] *nf* equality; (*similaridad*) sameness; (*uniformidad*) uniformity

igualmente [iɣwal'mente] *adv* equally;
(*también*) also, likewise ♦ *excl* the same to
you!

ikurriña [iku'rriɲa] *nf* Basque flag

ilegal [ile'ɣal] *adj* illegal

ilegítimo, a [ile'xitimo, a] *adj* illegitimate

ileso, a [i'leso, a] *adj* unhurt

ilícito, a [i'liθito] *adj* illicit

ilimitado, a [ilimi'taðo, a] *adj* unlimited

ilógico, a [i'loxiko, a] *adj* illogical

iluminación [ilumina'θjon] *nf* illumination;
(*alumbrado*) lighting

iluminar [ilumi'nar] *vt* to illuminate, light
(up); (*fig*) to enlighten

ilusión [ilu'sjon] *nf* illusion; (*quimera*) delusion; (*esperanza*) hope; **hacerse ilusiones**
to build up one's hopes; **ilusionado, a** *adj*
excited; **ilusionar** *vi*: **le ilusiona ir de vacaciones** he's looking forward to going on
holiday; **ilusionarse** *vr*: **ilusionarse (con)** to
get excited about

ilusionista [ilusjo'nista] *nm/f* conjurer

iluso, a [i'luso, a] *adj* easily deceived ♦
nm/f dreamer

ilusorio, a [ilu'sorjo, a] *adj* (*de ilusión*) illusory, deceptive; (*esperanza*) vain

ilustración [ilustra'θjon] *nf* illustration; (*saber*) learning, erudition; **la l~** the Enlightenment; **ilustrado, a** *adj* illustrated;
learned

ilustrar [ilus'trar] *vt* to illustrate; (*instruir*)
to instruct; (*explicar*) to explain, make
clear; **~se** *vr* to acquire knowledge

ilustre [i'lustre] *adj* famous, illustrious

imagen [i'maxen] *nf* (*gen*) image; (*dibujo*)
picture

imaginación [imaxina'θjon] *nf* imagination

imaginar [imaxi'nar] *vt* (*gen*) to imagine;
(*idear*) to think up; (*suponer*) to suppose;
~se *vr* to imagine; **~io, a** *adj* imaginary;
imaginativo, a *adj* imaginative

imán [i'man] *nm* magnet

imbécil [im'beθil] *nm/f* imbecile, idiot

imitación [imita'θjon] *nf* imitation

imitar [imi'tar] *vt* to imitate; (*parodiar, remedar*) to mimic, ape

impaciencia [impa'θjenθja] *nf* impatience;
impaciente *adj* impatient; (*nervioso*) anxious

impacto [im'pakto] *nm* impact

impar [im'par] *adj* odd

imparcial [impar'θjal] *adj* impartial, fair

impartir [impar'tir] *vt* to impart, give

impasible [impa'sißle] *adj* impassive

impávido, a [im'paßiðo, a] *adj* fearless, intrepid

impecable [impe'kaßle] *adj* impeccable

impedimento [impeði'mento] *nm* impediment, obstacle

impedir [impe'ðir] *vt* (*obstruir*) to impede,
obstruct; (*estorbar*) to prevent

impenetrable [impene'traßle] *adj* impenetrable; (*fig*) incomprehensible

imperar [impe'rar] *vi* (*reinar*) to rule, reign;
(*fig*) to prevail, reign; (*precio*) to be current

imperativo, a [impera'tißo, a] *adj* (*persona*) imperious; (*urgente, LING*) imperative

imperceptible [imperθep'tißle] *adj* imperceptible

imperdible [imper'ðißle] *nm* safety pin

imperdonable [imperðo'naßle] *adj* unforgivable, inexcusable

imperfección [imperfek'θjon] *nf* imperfection

imperfecto, a [imper'fekto, a] *adj* imperfect

imperial [impe'rjal] *adj* imperial; **~ismo**
nm imperialism

imperio [im'perjo] *nm* empire; (*autoridad*)
rule, authority; (*fig*) pride, haughtiness;
~so, a *adj* imperious; (*urgente*) urgent;
(*imperativo*) imperative

impermeable [imperme'aßle] *adj* (*a prueba
de agua*) waterproof ♦ *nm* raincoat, mac
(*BRIT*)

impersonal [imperso'nal] *adj* impersonal

impertinencia [imperti'nenθja] *nf* impertinence; **impertinente** *adj* impertinent

imperturbable [impertur'ßaßle] *adj* imperturbable

ímpetu ['impetu] *nm* (*impulso*) impetus, impulse; (*impetuosidad*) impetuosity; (*violencia*) violence

impetuoso, a [impe'twoso, a] *adj* impetuous; (*río*) rushing; (*acto*) hasty

impío, a [im'pio, a] *adj* impious, ungodly

implacable [impla'kaßle] *adj* implacable

implantar [implan'tar] *vt* to introduce

implicar [impli'kar] *vt* to involve; (*entrañar*)
to imply

implícito, a [im'pliθito, a] *adj* (*tácito*) implicit; (*sobreentendido*) implied

implorar [implo'rar] *vt* to beg, implore

imponente [impo'nente] *adj* (*impresionante*) impressive, imposing; (*solemne*)
grand

imponer [impo'ner] *vt* (*gen*) to impose;
(*exigir*) to exact; **~se** *vr* to assert o.s.; (*prevalecer*) to prevail; **imponible** *adj* (*COM*)
taxable

impopular [impopu'lar] *adj* unpopular

importación [importa'θjon] *nf* (*acto*) importing; (*mercancías*) imports *pl*

importancia [impor'tanθja] nf importance; (*valor*) value, significance; (*extensión*) size, magnitude; **importante** adj important; valuable, significant

importar [impor'tar] vt (*del extranjero*) to import; (*costar*) to amount to ♦ vi to be important, matter; **me importa un rábano** I couldn't care less; **no importa** it doesn't matter; **¿le importa que fume?** do you mind if I smoke?

importe [im'porte] nm (*total*) amount; (*valor*) value

importunar [importu'nar] vt to bother, pester

imposibilidad [imposiβili'ðað] nf impossibility; **imposibilitar** vt to make impossible, prevent

imposible [impo'siβle] adj (*gen*) impossible; (*insoportable*) unbearable, intolerable

imposición [imposi'θjon] nf imposition; (*COM: impuesto*) tax; (*: inversión*) deposit

impostor, a [impos'tor, a] nm/f impostor

impotencia [impo'tenθja] nf impotence; **impotente** adj impotent

impracticable [imprakti'kaβle] adj (*irrealizable*) impracticable; (*intransitable*) impassable

impreciso, a [impre'θiso, a] adj imprecise, vague

impregnar [impreɣ'nar] vt to impregnate; ~se vr to become impregnated

imprenta [im'prenta] nf (*acto*) printing; (*aparato*) press; (*casa*) printer's; (*letra*) print

imprescindible [impresθin'diβle] adj essential, vital

impresión [impre'sjon] nf (*gen*) impression; (*IMPRENTA*) printing; (*edición*) edition; (*FOTO*) print; (*marca*) imprint; ~ **digital** fingerprint

impresionable [impresjo'naβle] adj (*sensible*) impressionable

impresionante [impresjo'nante] adj impressive; (*tremendo*) tremendous; (*maravilloso*) great, marvellous

impresionar [impresjo'nar] vt (*conmover*) to move; (*afectar*) to impress, strike; (*película fotográfica*) to expose; ~se vr to be impressed; (*conmoverse*) to be moved

impreso, a [im'preso, a] pp de **imprimir** ♦ adj printed; ~**s** nmpl printed matter; **impresora** nf printer

imprevisto, a [impre'βisto, a] adj (*gen*) unforeseen; (*inesperado*) unexpected

imprimir [impri'mir] vt to imprint, impress, stamp; (*textos*) to print; (*INFORM*) to output, print out

improbable [impro'βaβle] adj improbable; (*inverosímil*) unlikely

improcedente [improθe'ðente] adj inappropriate

improductivo, a [improðuk'tiβo, a] adj unproductive

improperio [impro'perjo] nm insult

impropio, a [im'propjo, a] adj improper

improvisado, a [improβi'saðo, a] adj improvised

improvisar [improβi'sar] vt to improvise

improviso, a [impro'βiso, a] adj: **de ~** unexpectedly, suddenly

imprudencia [impru'ðenθja] nf imprudence; (*indiscreción*) indiscretion; (*descuido*) carelessness; **imprudente** adj unwise, imprudent; (*indiscreto*) indiscreet

impúdico, a [im'puðiko, a] adj shameless; (*lujurioso*) lecherous

impudor [impu'ðor] nm shamelessness; (*lujuria*) lechery

impuesto, a [im'pwesto, a] adj imposed ♦ nm tax; ~ **sobre el valor añadido** value added tax

impugnar [impuɣ'nar] vt to oppose, contest; (*refutar*) to refute, impugn

impulsar [impul'sar] vt = **impeler**

impulsivo, a [impul'siβo, a] adj impulsive; **impulso** nm impulse; (*fuerza, empuje*) thrust, drive; (*fig: sentimiento*) urge, impulse

impune [im'pune] adj unpunished

impureza [impu'reθa] nf impurity; (*fig*) lewdness; **impuro, a** adj impure; lewd

imputar [impu'tar] vt: ~ **a** to attribute to

inacabable [inaka'βaβle] adj (*infinito*) endless; (*interminable*) interminable

inaccesible [inakθe'siβle] adj inaccessible

inacción [inak'θjon] nf inactivity

inaceptable [inaθep'taβle] adj unacceptable

inactividad [inaktiβi'ðað] nf inactivity; (*COM*) dullness; **inactivo, a** adj inactive

inadecuado, a [inaðe'kwaðo, a] adj (*insuficiente*) inadequate; (*inapto*) unsuitable

inadmisible [inaðmi'siβle] adj inadmissible

inadvertido, a [inaðβer'tiðo, a] adj (*no visto*) unnoticed

inagotable [inaɣo'taβle] adj inexhaustible

inaguantable [inaɣwan'taβle] adj unbearable

inalterable [inalte'raβle] adj immutable, unchangeable

inanición [inani'θjon] nf starvation

inanimado, a [inani'maðo, a] adj inanimate

inapreciable [inapre'ðjaβle] adj (*cantidad, diferencia*) imperceptible; (*ayuda, servicio*) invaluable

inaudito, a [inau'ðito, a] adj unheard-of

inauguración [inauɣura'θjon] nf inauguration; opening

inaugurar [inauɣu'rar] vt to inaugurate; (*exposición*) to open

I.N.B. (*ESP*) abr (= *Instituto Nacional de Bachillerato*) ≈ comprehensive school (*BRIT*), ≈ high school (*US*)

inca ['inka] nm/f Inca

incalculable [inkalku'laβle] adj incalculable

incandescente [inkandes'θente] *adj* incandescent

incansable [inkan'saβle] *adj* tireless, untiring

incapacidad [inkapaθi'ðað] *nf* incapacity; *(incompetencia)* incompetence; ~ **física/mental** physical/mental disability

incapacitar [inkapaθi'tar] *vt (inhabilitar)* to incapacitate, render unfit; *(descalificar)* to disqualify

incapaz [inka'paθ] *adj* incapable

incautación [inkauta'θjon] *nf* confiscation

incautarse [inkau'tarse] *vr:* ~ **de** to seize, confiscate

incauto, a [in'kauto, a] *adj (imprudente)* incautious, unwary

incendiar [inθen'djar] *vt* to set fire to; *(fig)* to inflame; ~**se** *vr* to catch fire; ~**io, a** *adj* incendiary

incendio [in'θendjo] *nm* fire

incentivo [inθen'tiβo] *nm* incentive

incertidumbre [inθerti'ðumbre] *nf (inseguridad)* uncertainty; *(duda)* doubt

incesante [inθe'sante] *adj* incessant

incesto [in'θesto] *nm* incest

incidencia [inθi'ðenθja] *nf (MAT)* incidence

incidente [inθi'ðente] *nm* incident

incidir [inθi'ðir] *vi (influir)* to influence; *(afectar)* to affect; ~ **en un error** to fall into error

incienso [in'θjenso] *nm* incense

incierto, a [in'θjerto, a] *adj* uncertain

incineración [inθinera'θjon] *nf* incineration; *(de cadáveres)* cremation

incinerar [inθine'rar] *vt* to burn; *(cadáveres)* to cremate

incipiente [inθi'pjente] *adj* incipient

incisión [inθi'sjon] *nf* incision

incisivo, a [inθi'siβo, a] *adj* sharp, cutting; *(fig)* incisive

incitar [inθi'tar] *vt* to incite, rouse

inclemencia [inkle'menθja] *nf (severidad)* harshness, severity; *(del tiempo)* inclemency

inclinación [inklina'θjon] *nf (gen)* inclination; *(de tierras)* slope, incline; *(de cabeza)* nod, bow; *(fig)* leaning, bent

inclinar [inkli'nar] *vt* to incline; *(cabeza)* to nod, bow ♦ *vi* to lean, slope; ~**se** *vr* to bow; *(encorvarse)* to stoop; ~**se a** *(parecerse a)* to take after, resemble; ~**se ante** to bow down to; **me inclino a pensar que** I'm inclined to think that

incluir [inklu'ir] *vt* to include; *(incorporar)* to incorporate; *(meter)* to enclose

inclusive [inklu'siβe] *adv* inclusive ♦ *prep* including

incluso, a [in'kluso, a] *adj* included ♦ *adv* inclusively; *(hasta)* even

incógnita [in'koɣnita] *nf (MAT)* unknown quantity

incógnito [in'koɣnito] *nm:* **de** ~ incognito

incoherente [inkoe'rente] *adj* incoherent

incoloro, a [inko'loro, a] *adj* colourless

incólume [in'kolume] *adj (gen)* safe; *(indemne)* unhurt, unharmed

incomodar [inkomo'ðar] *vt* to inconvenience; *(molestar)* to bother, trouble; *(fastidiar)* to annoy; ~**se** *vr* to put o.s. out; *(fastidiarse)* to get annoyed

incomodidad [inkomoði'ðað] *nf* inconvenience; *(fastidio, enojo)* annoyance; *(de vivienda)* discomfort

incómodo, a [in'komoðo, a] *adj (inconfortable)* uncomfortable; *(molesto)* annoying; *(inconveniente)* inconvenient

incomparable [inkompa'raβle] *adj* incomparable

incompatible [inkompa'tiβle] *adj* incompatible

incompetencia [inkompe'tenθja] *nf* incompetence; **incompetente** *adj* incompetent

incompleto, a [inkom'pleto, a] *adj* incomplete, unfinished

incomprensible [inkompren'siβle] *adj* incomprehensible

incomunicado, a [inkomuni'kaðo, a] *adj (aislado)* cut off, isolated; *(confinado)* in solitary confinement

inconcebible [inkonθe'βiβle] *adj* inconceivable

incondicional [inkondi'θjonal] *adj* unconditional; *(apoyo)* wholehearted; *(partidario)* staunch

inconexo, a [inko'nekso, a] *adj (gen)* unconnected; *(desunido)* disconnected

inconfundible [inkonfun'diβle] *adj* unmistakable

incongruente [inkon'ɡwente] *adj* incongruous

inconsciencia [inkons'θjenθja] *nf* unconsciousness; *(fig)* thoughtlessness; **inconsciente** *adj* unconscious; thoughtless

inconsecuente [inkonse'kwente] *adj* inconsistent

inconsiderado, a [inkonsiðe'raðo, a] *adj* inconsiderate

inconsistente [inkonsis'tente] *adj* weak; *(tela)* flimsy

inconstancia [inkon'stanθja] *nf* inconstancy; *(inestabilidad)* unsteadiness; **inconstante** *adj* inconstant

incontable [inkon'taβle] *adj* countless, innumerable

incontestable [inkontes'taβle] *adj* unanswerable; *(innegable)* undeniable

incontinencia [inkonti'nenθja] *nf* incontinence

inconveniencia [inkombe'njenθja] *nf* unsuitability, inappropriateness; *(descortesía)* impoliteness; **inconveniente** *adj* unsuitable; impolite ♦ *nm* obstacle; *(desventaja)* disadvantage; **el inconveniente es que ...** the trouble is that ...

incordiar [inkor'ðjar] *(fam) vt* to bug, annoy

incorporación [inkorpora'θjon] *nf* incorporation

incorporar [inkorpo'rar] *vt* to incorporate; **~se** *vr* to sit up

incorrección [inkorrek'θjon] *nf* (*gen*) incorrectness, inaccuracy; (*descortesía*) bad-mannered behaviour; **incorrecto, a** *adj* (*gen*) incorrect, wrong; (*comportamiento*) bad-mannered

incorregible [inkorre'xiβle] *adj* incorrigible

incredulidad [inkreðuli'ðað] *nf* incredulity; (*escepticismo*) scepticism; **incrédulo, a** *adj* incredulous, unbelieving; sceptical

increíble [inkre'iβle] *adj* incredible

incremento [inkre'mento] *nm* increment; (*aumento*) rise, increase

increpar [inkre'par] *vt* to reprimand

incruento, a [in'krwento, a] *adj* bloodless

incrustar [inkrus'tar] *vt* to incrust; (*piedras: en joya*) to inlay

incubar [inku'βar] *vt* to incubate; (*fig*) to hatch

inculcar [inkul'kar] *vt* to inculcate

inculpar [inkul'par] *vt* (*acusar*) to accuse; (*achacar, atribuir*) to charge, blame

inculto, a [in'kulto, a] *adj* (*persona*) uneducated; (*grosero*) uncouth ♦ *nm/f* ignoramus

incumplimiento [inkumpli'mjento] *nm* non-fulfilment; **~ de contrato** breach of contract

incurrir [inku'rrir] *vi*: **~ en** to incur; (*crimen*) to commit; **~ en un error** to make a mistake

indagación [indaɣa'θjon] *nf* investigation; (*búsqueda*) search; (*JUR*) inquest

indagar [inda'ɣar] *vt* to investigate; to search; (*averiguar*) to ascertain

indecente [inde'θente] *adj* indecent, improper; (*lascivo*) obscene

indecible [inde'θiβle] *adj* unspeakable; (*indescriptible*) indescribable

indeciso, a [inde'θiso, a] *adj* (*por decidir*) undecided; (*vacilante*) hesitant

indefenso, a [inde'fenso, a] *adj* defenceless

indefinido, a [indefi'niðo, a] *adj* indefinite; (*vago*) vague, undefined

indeleble [inde'leβle] *adj* indelible

indemne [in'demne] *adj* (*objeto*) undamaged; (*persona*) unharmed, unhurt

indemnizar [indemni'θar] *vt* to indemnify; (*compensar*) to compensate

independencia [indepen'denθja] *nf* independence

independiente [indepen'djente] *adj* (*libre*) independent; (*autónomo*) self-sufficient

indeterminado, a [indetermi'naðo, a] *adj* indefinite; (*desconocido*) indeterminate

India ['indja] *nf*: **la ~** India

indicación [indika'θjon] *nf* indication; (*señal*) sign; (*sugerencia*) suggestion, hint

indicado, a [indi'kaðo, a] *adj* (*momento,*

método) right; (*tratamiento*) appropriate; (*solución*) likely

indicador [indika'ðor] *nm* indicator; (*TEC*) gauge, meter

indicar [indi'kar] *vt* (*mostrar*) to indicate, show; (*termómetro etc*) to read, register; (*señalar*) to point to

índice ['indiθe] *nm* index; (*catálogo*) catalogue; (*ANAT*) index finger, forefinger

indicio [in'diθjo] *nm* indication, sign; (*en pesquisa etc*) clue

indiferencia [indife'renθja] *nf* indifference; (*apatía*) apathy; **indiferente** *adj* indifferent

indígena [in'dixena] *adj* indigenous, native ♦ *nm/f* native

indigencia [indi'xenθja] *nf* poverty, need

indigestión [indixes'tjon] *nf* indigestion

indigesto, a [indi'xesto, a] *adj* undigested; (*indigestible*) indigestible; (*fig*) turgid

indignación [indixna'θjon] *nf* indignation

indignar [indix'nar] *vt* to anger, make indignant; **~se** *vr*: **~se por** to get indignant about

indigno, a [in'dixno, a] *adj* (*despreciable*) low, contemptible; (*inmerecido*) unworthy

indio, a ['indjo, a] *adj, nm/f* Indian

indirecta [indi'rekta] *nf* insinuation, innuendo; (*sugerencia*) hint

indirecto, a [indi'rekto, a] *adj* indirect

indiscreción [indiskre'θjon] *nf* (*imprudencia*) indiscretion; (*irreflexión*) tactlessness; (*acto*) gaffe, faux pas

indiscreto, a [indis'kreto, a] *adj* indiscreet

indiscriminado, a [indiskrimi'naðo, a] *adj* indiscriminate

indiscutible [indisku'tiβle] *adj* indisputable, unquestionable

indispensable [indispen'saβle] *adj* indispensable, essential

indisponer [indispo'ner] *vt* to spoil, upset; (*salud*) to make ill; **~se** *vr* to fall ill; **~se con uno** to fall out with sb

indisposición [indisposi'θjon] *nf* indisposition

indispuesto, a [indis'pwesto, a] *adj* (*enfermo*) unwell, indisposed

indistinto, a [indis'tinto, a] *adj* indistinct; (*vago*) vague

individual [indiβi'ðwal] *adj* individual; (*habitación*) single ♦ *nm* (*DEPORTE*) singles *sg*

individuo, a [indi'βiðwo, a] *adj, nm* individual

índole ['indole] *nf* (*naturaleza*) nature; (*clase*) sort, kind

indolencia [indo'lenθja] *nf* indolence, laziness

indómito, a [in'domito, a] *adj* indomitable

inducir [indu'θir] *vt* to induce; (*inferir*) to infer; (*persuadir*) to persuade

indudable [indu'ðaβle] *adj* undoubted; (*incuestionable*) unquestionable

indulgencia [indul'xenθja] *nf* indulgence

indultar [indul'tar] *vt* (*perdonar*) to pardon, reprieve; (*librar de pago*) to exempt; **indulto** *nm* pardon; exemption

industria [in'dustrja] *nf* industry; (*habilidad*) skill; **industrial** *adj* industrial ♦ *nm* industrialist

inédito, a [in'eðito, a] *adj* (*texto*) unpublished; (*nuevo*) new

inefable [ine'faßle] *adj* ineffable, indescribable

ineficaz [inefi'kaθ] *adj* (*inútil*) ineffective; (*ineficiente*) inefficient

ineludible [inelu'ðißle] *adj* inescapable, unavoidable

ineptitud [inepti'tuð] *nf* ineptitude, incompetence; **inepto, a** *adj* inept, incompetent

inequívoco, a [ine'kißoko, a] *adj* unequivocal; (*inconfundible*) unmistakable

inercia [in'erθja] *nf* inertia; (*pasividad*) passivity

inerme [in'erme] *adj* (*sin armas*) unarmed; (*indefenso*) defenceless

inerte [in'erte] *adj* inert; (*inmóvil*) motionless

inesperado, a [inespe'raðo, a] *adj* unexpected, unforeseen

inestable [ines'taßle] *adj* unstable

inevitable [ineßi'taßle] *adj* inevitable

inexactitud [ineksakti'tuð] *nf* inaccuracy; **inexacto, a** *adj* inaccurate; (*falso*) untrue

inexperto, a [inek'sperto, a] *adj* (*novato*) inexperienced

infalible [infa'lißle] *adj* infallible; (*plan*) foolproof

infame [in'fame] *adj* infamous; (*horrible*) dreadful; **infamia** *nf* infamy; (*deshonra*) disgrace

infancia [in'fanθja] *nf* infancy, childhood

infantería [infante'ria] *nf* infantry

infantil [infan'til] *adj* (*pueril, aniñado*) infantile; (*cándido*) childlike; (*literatura, ropa etc*) children's

infarto [in'farto] *nm* (*tb:* ~ *de miocardio*) heart attack

infatigable [infati'vaßle] *adj* tireless, untiring

infección [infek'θjon] *nf* infection; **infeccioso, a** *adj* infectious

infectar [infek'tar] *vt* to infect; ~**se** *vr* to become infected

infeliz [infe'liθ] *adj* unhappy, wretched ♦ *nm/f* wretch

inferior [infe'rjor] *adj* inferior; (*situación*) lower ♦ *nm/f* inferior, subordinate

inferir [infe'rir] *vt* (*deducir*) to infer, deduce; (*causar*) to cause

infestar [infes'tar] *vt* to infest

infidelidad [infiðeli'ðað] *nf* (*gen*) infidelity, unfaithfulness

infiel [in'fjel] *adj* unfaithful, disloyal; (*erróneo*) inaccurate ♦ *nm/f* infidel, unbeliever

infierno [in'fjerno] *nm* hell

infiltrarse [infil'trarse] *vr:* ~ **en** to infiltrate in(to); (*persona*) to work one's way in(to)

ínfimo, a ['infimo, a] *adj* (*más bajo*) lowest; (*despreciable*) vile, mean

infinidad [infini'ðað] *nf* infinity; (*abundancia*) great quantity

infinito, a [infi'nito, a] *adj, nm* infinite

inflación [infla'θjon] *nf* (*hinchazón*) swelling; (*monetaria*) inflation; (*fig*) conceit; **inflacionario, a** *adj* inflationary

inflamar [infla'mar] *vt* (*MED, fig*) to inflame; ~**se** *vr* to catch fire; to become inflamed

inflar [in'flar] *vt* (*hinchar*) to inflate, blow up; (*fig*) to exaggerate; ~**se** *vr* to swell (up); (*fig*) to get conceited

inflexible [inflek'sißle] *adj* inflexible; (*fig*) unbending

infligir [infli'xir] *vt* to inflict

influencia [influ'enθja] *nf* influence; **influenciar** *vt* to influence

influir [influ'ir] *vt* to influence

influjo [in'fluxo] *nm* influence

influya *etc vb ver* **influir**

influyente [influ'jente] *adj* influential

información [informa'θjon] *nf* information; (*noticias*) news *sg*; (*JUR*) inquiry; I~ (*oficina*) Information Office; (*mostrador*) Information Desk; (*TEL*) Directory Enquiries

informal [infor'mal] *adj* (*gen*) informal

informar [infor'mar] *vt* (*gen*) to inform; (*revelar*) to reveal, make known ♦ *vi* (*JUR*) to plead; (*denunciar*) to inform; (*dar cuenta de*) to report on; ~**se** *vr* to find out; ~**se de** to inquire into

informática [infor'matika] *nf* computer science, information technology

informe [in'forme] *adj* shapeless ♦ *nm* report

infortunio [infor'tunjo] *nm* misfortune

infracción [infrak'θjon] *nf* infraction, infringement

infranqueable [infranke'aßle] *adj* impassable; (*fig*) insurmountable

infringir [infrin'xir] *vt* to infringe, contravene

infructuoso, a [infruk'twoso, a] *adj* fruitless, unsuccessful

infundado, a [infun'daðo, a] *adj* groundless, unfounded

infundir [infun'dir] *vt* to infuse, instil

infusión [infu'sjon] *nf* infusion; ~ **de manzanilla** camomile tea

ingeniar [inxe'njar] *vt* to think up, devise; ~**se** *vr:* ~**se para** to manage to

ingeniería [inxenje'ria] *nf* engineering; ~ **genética** genetic engineering; **ingeniero, a** *nm/f* engineer; **ingeniero de caminos/de sonido** civil engineer/sound engineer

ingenio [in'xenjo] *nm* (*talento*) talent; (*agudeza*) wit; (*habilidad*) ingenuity, inventiveness; (*TEC*): ~ **azucarero** sugar refinery

ingenioso, a [inxe'njoso, a] *adj* ingenious, clever; (*divertido*) witty

ingenuidad [inxenwi'ðað] *nf* ingenuousness; (*sencillez*) simplicity; **ingenuo, a** *adj* ingenuous

ingerir [inxe'rir] *vt* to ingest; (*tragar*) to swallow; (*consumir*) to consume

Inglaterra [ingla'terra] *nf* England

ingle ['ingle] *nf* groin

inglés, esa [in'gles, esa] *adj* English ♦ *nm/f* Englishman/woman ♦ *nm* (*LING*) English

ingratitud [ingrati'tuð] *nf* ingratitude; **ingrato, a** *adj* (*gen*) ungrateful

ingrediente [ingre'ðjente] *nm* ingredient

ingresar [ingre'sar] *vt* (*dinero*) to deposit ♦ *vi* to come in; ~ **en un club** to join a club; ~ **en el hospital** to go into hospital

ingreso [in'greso] *nm* (*entrada*) entry; (: *en hospital etc*) admission; ~**s** *nmpl* (*dinero*) income *sg*; (: *COM*) takings *pl*

inhabitable [inaβi'taβle] *adj* uninhabitable

inhalar [ina'lar] *vt* to inhale

inherente [ine'rente] *adj* inherent

inhibir [ini'βir] *vt* to inhibit; (*REL*) to restrain

inhóspito, a [i'nospito, a] *adj* (*región, paisaje*) inhospitable

inhumano, a [inu'mano, a] *adj* inhuman

INI ['ini] (*ESP*) *nm abr* (= *Instituto Nacional de Industria*) ≈ NEB (*BRIT*)

inicial [ini'θjal] *adj, nf* initial

iniciar [ini'θjar] *vt* (*persona*) to initiate; (*empezar*) to begin, commence; (*conversación*) to start up

iniciativa [iniθja'tiβa] *nf* initiative; **la** ~ **privada** private enterprise

ininterrumpido, a [ininterrum'piðo, a] *adj* uninterrupted

injerencia [inxe'renθja] *nf* interference

injertar [inxer'tar] *vt* to graft; **injerto** *nm* graft

injuria [in'xurja] *nf* (*agravio, ofensa*) offence; (*insulto*) insult; **injuriar** *vt* to insult; **injurioso, a** *adj* offensive; insulting

injusticia [inxus'tiθja] *nf* injustice

injusto, a [in'xusto, a] *adj* unjust, unfair

inmadurez [inmaðu'reθ] *nf* immaturity

inmediaciones [inmeðja'θjones] *nfpl* neighbourhood *sg*, environs

inmediato, a [inme'ðjato, a] *adj* immediate; (*contiguo*) adjoining; (*rápido*) prompt; (*próximo*) neighbouring, next; **de** ~ immediately

inmejorable [inmexo'raβle] *adj* unsurpassable; (*precio*) unbeatable

inmenso, a [in'menso, a] *adj* immense, huge

inmerecido, a [inmere'θiðo, a] *adj* undeserved

inmigración [inmiɣra'θjon] *nf* immigration

inmiscuirse [inmisku'irse] *vr* to interfere, meddle

inmobiliaria [inmoβi'ljarja] *nf* estate agency

inmobiliario, a [inmoβi'ljarjo, a] *adj* real-estate *cpd*, property *cpd*

inmolar [inmo'lar] *vt* to immolate, sacrifice

inmoral [inmo'ral] *adj* immoral

inmortal [inmor'tal] *adj* immortal; ~**izar** *vt* to immortalize

inmóvil [in'moβil] *adj* immobile

inmueble [in'mweβle] *adj*: **bienes** ~**s** real estate, landed property ♦ *nm* property

inmundicia [inmun'diθja] *nf* filth; **inmundo, a** *adj* filthy

inmune [in'mune] *adj*: ~ **(a)** (*MED*) immune (to)

inmunidad [inmuni'ðað] *nf* immunity

inmutarse [inmu'tarse] *vr* to turn pale; **no se inmutó** he didn't turn a hair

innato, a [in'nato, a] *adj* innate

innecesario, a [inneθe'sarjo, a] *adj* unnecessary

innoble [in'noβle] *adj* ignoble

innovación [innoβa'θjon] *nf* innovation

innovar [inno'βar] *vt* to introduce

inocencia [ino'θenθja] *nf* innocence

inocentada [inoθen'taða] *nf* practical joke

inocente [ino'θente] *adj* (*ingenuo*) naive, innocent; (*inculpable*) innocent; (*sin malicia*) harmless ♦ *nm/f* simpleton

inodoro [ino'ðoro] *nm* toilet, lavatory (*BRIT*)

inofensivo, a [inofen'siβo, a] *adj* inoffensive, harmless

inolvidable [inolβi'ðaβle] *adj* unforgettable

inopinado, a [inopi'naðo, a] *adj* unexpected

inoportuno, a [inopor'tuno, a] *adj* untimely; (*molesto*) inconvenient

inoxidable [inoksi'ðaβle] *adj*: **acero** ~ stainless steel

inquebrantable [inkeβran'taβle] *adj* unbreakable

inquietar [inkje'tar] *vt* to worry, trouble; ~**se** *vr* to worry, get upset; **inquieto, a** *adj* anxious, worried; **inquietud** *nf* anxiety, worry

inquilino, a [inki'lino, a] *nm/f* tenant

inquirir [inki'rir] *vt* to enquire into, investigate

insaciable [insa'θjaβle] *adj* insatiable

insalubre [insa'luβre] *adj* unhealthy

inscribir [inskri'βir] *vt* to inscribe; ~ **a uno en** (*lista*) to put sb on; (*censo*) to register sb on

inscripción [inskrip'θjon] *nf* inscription; (*ESCOL etc*) enrolment; (*censo*) registration

insecticida [insekti'θiða] *nm* insecticide

insecto [in'sekto] *nm* insect

inseguridad [inseɣuri'ðað] *nf* insecurity

inseguro, a [inse'ɣuro, a] *adj* insecure; (*inconstante*) unsteady; (*incierto*) uncertain

insensato, a [insen'sato, a] *adj* foolish, stupid

insensibilidad [insensiβili'ðað] *nf* (*gen*) insensitivity; (*dureza de corazón*) callousness

insensible [insen'siβle] *adj* (*gen*) insensitive; (*movimiento*) imperceptible; (*sin sentido*) numb

insertar [inser'tar] *vt* to insert

inservible [inser'ßißle] *adj* useless

insidioso, a [insi'ðjoso, a] *adj* insidious

insignia [in'siɣnja] *nf* (*señal distintiva*) badge; (*estandarte*) flag

insignificante [insiɣnifi'kante] *adj* insignificant

insinuar [insi'nwar] *vt* to insinuate, imply; ~**se** *vr*: ~**se con uno** to ingratiate o.s. with sb

insípido, a [in'sipiðo, a] *adj* insipid

insistencia [insis'tenθja] *nf* insistence

insistir [insis'tir] *vi* to insist; ~ **en algo** to insist on sth; (*enfatizar*) to stress sth

insolación [insola'θjon] *nf* (*MED*) sunstroke

insolencia [inso'lenθja] *nf* insolence; **insolente** *adj* insolent

insólito, a [in'solito, a] *adj* unusual

insoluble [inso'lußle] *adj* insoluble

insolvencia [insol'ßenθja] *nf* insolvency

insomnio [in'somnjo] *nm* insomnia

insondable [inson'daßle] *adj* bottomless; (*fig*) impenetrable

insonorizado, a [insonori'θaðo, a] *adj* (*cuarto etc*) soundproof

insoportable [insopor'taßle] *adj* unbearable

insospechado, a [insospe'tʃaðo, a] *adj* (*inesperado*) unexpected

inspección [inspek'θjon] *nf* inspection, check; **inspeccionar** *vt* (*examinar*) to inspect, examine; (*controlar*) to check

inspector, a [inspek'tor, a] *nm/f* inspector

inspiración [inspira'θjon] *nf* inspiration

inspirar [inspi'rar] *vt* to inspire; (*MED*) to inhale; ~**se** *vr*: ~**se en** to be inspired by

instalación [instala'θjon] *nf* (*equipo*) fittings *pl*, equipment; ~ **eléctrica** wiring

instalar [insta'lar] *vt* (*establecer*) to instal; (*erguir*) to set up, erect; ~**se** *vr* to establish o.s.; (*en una vivienda*) to move into

instancia [ins'tanθja] *nf* (*JUR*) petition; (*ruego*) request; **en última** ~ as a last resort

instantánea [instan'tanea] *nf* snap(shot)

instantáneo, a [instan'taneo, a] *adj* instantaneous; **café** ~ instant coffee

instante [ins'tante] *nm* instant, moment

instar [ins'tar] *vt* to press, urge

instaurar [instau'rar] *vt* (*costumbre*) to establish; (*normas, sistema*) to bring in, introduce; (*gobierno*) to instal

instigar [insti'ɣar] *vt* to instigate

instinto [ins'tinto] *nm* instinct; **por** ~ instinctively

institución [institu'θjon] *nf* institution, establishment

instituir [institu'ir] *vt* to establish; (*fundar*) to found; **instituto** *nm* (*gen*) institute; **Instituto Nacional de Enseñanza** (*ESP*) ≈ comprehensive (*BRIT*) o high (*US*) school

institutriz [institu'triθ] *nf* governess

instrucción [instruk'θjon] *nf* instruction

instructivo, a [instruk'tiβo, a] *adj* instructive

instruir [instru'ir] *vt* (*gen*) to instruct; (*enseñar*) to teach, educate

instrumento [instru'mento] *nm* (*gen*) instrument; (*herramienta*) tool, implement

insubordinarse [insuβorði'narse] *vr* to rebel

insuficiencia [insufi'θjenθja] *nf* (*carencia*) lack; (*inadecuación*) inadequacy; **insuficiente** *adj* (*gen*) insufficient; (*ESCOL: calificación*) unsatisfactory

insufrible [insu'frißle] *adj* insufferable

insular [insu'lar] *adj* insular

insultar [insul'tar] *vt* to insult; **insulto** *nm* insult

insuperable [insupe'raßle] *adj* (*excelente*) unsurpassable; (*problema etc*) insurmountable

insurgente [insur'xente] *adj, nm/f* insurgent

insurrección [insurrek'θjon] *nf* insurrection, rebellion

intacto, a [in'takto, a] *adj* intact

intachable [inta'tʃaßle] *adj* irreproachable

integral [inte'ɣral] *adj* integral; (*completo*) complete; **pan** ~ wholemeal (*BRIT*) o wholewheat (*US*) bread

integrar [inte'ɣrar] *vt* to make up, compose; (*MAT, fig*) to integrate

integridad [inteɣri'ðað] *nf* wholeness; (*carácter*) integrity; **íntegro, a** *adj* whole, entire; (*honrado*) honest

intelectual [intelek'twal] *adj, nm/f* intellectual

inteligencia [inteli'xenθja] *nf* intelligence; (*ingenio*) ability; **inteligente** *adj* intelligent

inteligible [inteli'xißle] *adj* intelligible

intemperie [intem'perje] *nf*: **a la** ~ out in the open, exposed to the elements

intempestivo, a [intempes'tiβo, a] *adj* untimely

intención [inten'θjon] *nf* (*gen*) intention, purpose; **con segundas intenciones** maliciously; **con** ~ deliberately

intencionado, a [intenθjo'naðo, a] *adj* deliberate; **bien/mal** ~ well-meaning/ill-disposed, hostile

intensidad [intensi'ðað] *nf* (*gen*) intensity; (*ELEC, TEC*) strength; **llover con** ~ to rain hard

intenso, a [in'tenso, a] *adj* intense; (*sentimiento*) profound, deep

intentar [inten'tar] *vt* (*tratar*) to try, attempt; **intento** *nm* (*intención*) intention, purpose; (*tentativa*) attempt

interactivo, a [interak'tiβo, a] *adj* (*IN-FORM*) interactive

intercalar [interka'lar] *vt* to insert

intercambio [inter'kambjo] *nm* exchange, swap

interceder [interθe'ðer] *vi* to intercede

interceptar [interθep'tar] *vt* to intercept

intercesión [interθe'sjon] *nf* intercession

interés [inte'res] *nm* (*gen*) interest; (*parte*) share, part; (*pey*) self-interest; **intereses creados** vested interests

interesado, a [intere'saðo, a] *adj* interested; (*prejuiciado*) prejudiced; (*pey*) mercenary, self-seeking

interesante [intere'sante] *adj* interesting

interesar [intere'sar] *vt, vi* to interest, be of interest to; **~se** *vr:* **~se en o por** to take an interest in

interface [inter'faθe] *nm* (*INFORM*) interface

interfase [inter'fase] *nm* = **interface**

interferir [interfe'rir] *vt* to interfere with; (*TEL*) to jam ♦ *vi* to interfere

interfono [inter'fono] *nm* intercom

interino, a [inte'rino, a] *adj* temporary ♦ *nm/f* temporary holder of a post; (*MED*) locum; (*ESCOL*) supply teacher

interior [inte'rjor] *adj* inner, inside; (*COM*) domestic, internal ♦ *nm* interior, inside; (*fig*) soul, mind; **Ministerio del I~** ≈ Home Office (*BRIT*), ≈ Department of the Interior (*US*)

interjección [interxek'θjon] *nf* interjection

interlocutor, a [interloku'tor, a] *nm/f* speaker

intermediario, a [interme'ðjarjo, a] *nm/f* intermediary

intermedio, a [inter'meðjo, a] *adj* intermediate ♦ *nm* interval

interminable [intermi'naβle] *adj* endless

intermitente [intermi'tente] *adj* intermittent ♦ *nm* (*AUTO*) indicator

internacional [internaθjo'nal] *adj* international

internado [inter'naðo] *nm* boarding school

internar [inter'nar] *vt* to intern; (*en un manicomio*) to commit; **~se** *vr* (*penetrar*) to penetrate

interno, a [in'terno, a] *adj* internal, interior; (*POL etc*) domestic ♦ *nm/f* (*alumno*) boarder

interponer [interpo'ner] *vt* to interpose, put in; **~se** *vr* to intervene

interpretación [interpreta'θjon] *nf* interpretation

interpretar [interpre'tar] *vt* to interpret; (*TEATRO, MUS*) to perform, play; **intérprete** *nm/f* (*LING*) interpreter, translator; (*MUS, TEATRO*) performer, artist(e)

interrogación [interroɣa'θjon] *nf* interrogation; (*LING: tb: signo de* ~) question mark

interrogar [interro'ɣar] *vt* to interrogate, question

interrumpir [interrum'pir] *vt* to interrupt

interrupción [interrup'θjon] *nf* interruption

interruptor [interrup'tor] *nm* (*ELEC*) switch

intersección [intersek'θjon] *nf* intersection

interurbano, a [interur'βano, a] *adj:* **llamada interurbana** long-distance call

intervalo [inter'βalo] *nm* interval; (*descanso*) break; **a ~s** at intervals, every now and then

intervenir [interβe'nir] *vt* (*controlar*) to control, supervise; (*MED*) to operate on ♦ *vi* (*participar*) to take part, participate; (*mediar*) to intervene

interventor, a [interβen'tor, a] *nm/f* inspector; (*COM*) auditor

interviú [inter'βju] *nf* interview

intestino [intes'tino] *nm* intestine

intimar [inti'mar] *vi* to become friendly

intimidad [intimi'ðað] *nf* intimacy; (*familiaridad*) familiarity; (*vida privada*) private life; (*JUR*) privacy

íntimo, a ['intimo, a] *adj* intimate

intolerable [intole'raβle] *adj* intolerable, unbearable

intoxicación [intoksika'θjon] *nf* poisoning

intranquilizarse [intrankili'θarse] *vr* to get worried o anxious; **intranquilo, a** *adj* worried

intransigente [intransi'xente] *adj* intransigent

intransitable [intransi'taβle] *adj* impassable

intrépido, a [in'trepiðo, a] *adj* intrepid

intriga [in'triɣa] *nf* intrigue; (*plan*) plot; **intrigar** *vt, vi* to intrigue

intrincado, a [intrin'kaðo, a] *adj* intricate

intrínseco, a [in'trinseko, a] *adj* intrinsic

introducción [introðuk'θjon] *nf* introduction

introducir [introðu'θir] *vt* (*gen*) to introduce; (*moneda etc*) to insert; (*INFORM*) to input, enter

intromisión [intromi'sjon] *nf* interference, meddling

introvertido, a [introβer'tiðo, a] *adj, nm/f* introvert

intruso, a [in'truso, a] *adj* intrusive ♦ *nm/f* intruder

intuición [intwi'θjon] *nf* intuition

inundación [inunda'θjon] *nf* flood(ing); **inundar** *vt* to flood; (*fig*) to swamp, inundate

inusitado, a [inusi'taðo, a] *adj* unusual, rare

inútil [in'util] *adj* useless; (*esfuerzo*) vain, fruitless; **inutilidad** *nf* uselessness

inutilizar [inutili'θar] *vt* to make o render useless; **~se** *vr* to become useless

invadir [imba'ðir] *vt* to invade

inválido, a [im'baliðo, a] *adj* invalid ♦ *nm/f* invalid

invariable [imba'rjaβle] *adj* invariable

invasión [imba'sjon] *nf* invasion
invasor, a [imba'sor, a] *adj* invading ◊ *nm/f* invader
invención [imben'θjon] *nf* invention
inventar [imben'tar] *vt* to invent
inventario [imben'tarjo] *nm* inventory
inventiva [imben'tiβa] *nf* inventiveness
invento [im'bento] *nm* invention
inventor, a [imben'tor, a] *nm/f* inventor
invernadero [imberna'ðero] *nm* greenhouse
inverosímil [imbero'simil] *adj* implausible
inversión [imber'sjon] *nf* (COM) investment
inverso, a [im'berso, a] *adj* inverse, opposite; **en el orden ~** in reverse order; **a la inversa** inversely, the other way round
inversor, a [imber'sor, a] *nm/f* (COM) investor
invertir [imber'tir] *vt* (COM) to invest; (*volcar*) to turn upside down; (*tiempo etc*) to spend
investigación [imbestiva'θjon] *nf* investigation; (ESCOL) research; **~ de mercado** market research
investigar [imbesti'var] *vt* to investigate; (ESCOL) to do research into
invierno [im'bjerno] *nm* winter
invisible [imbi'siβle] *adj* invisible
invitado, a [imbi'taðo, a] *nm/f* guest
invitar [imbi'tar] *vt* to invite; (*incitar*) to entice; (*pagar*) to buy, pay for
invocar [imbo'kar] *vt* to invoke, call on
involucrar [imbolu'krar] *vt*: **~** to involve in; **~se** *vr* (*persona*): **~ en** to get mixed up in
involuntario, a [imbolun'tarjo, a] *adj* (*movimiento, gesto*) involuntary; (*error*) unintentional
inyección [injek'θjon] *nf* injection
inyectar [injek'tar] *vt* to inject

─────── *PALABRA CLAVE*

ir [ir] *vi* **1** to go; (*a pie*) to walk; (*viajar*) to travel; **~ caminando** to walk; **fui en tren** I went *o* travelled by train; **¡(ahora) voy!** (I'm just) coming!
2: **~ (a) por**: **~ (a) por el médico** to fetch the doctor
3 (*progresar: persona, cosa*) to go; **el trabajo va muy bien** work is going very well; **¿cómo te va?** how are things going?; **me va muy bien** I'm getting on very well; **le fue fatal** it went awfully badly for him
4 (*funcionar*): **el coche no va muy bien** the car isn't running very well
5: **te va estupendamente ese color** that colour suits you fantastically well
6 (*locuciones*): **¿vino? – ¡que va!** did he come? – of course not!; **vamos, no llores** come on, don't cry; **¡vaya coche!** what a car!, that's some car!

7: **no vaya a ser: tienes que correr, no vaya a ser que pierdas el tren** you'll have to run so as not to miss the train
8 (+ *pp*): **iba vestido muy bien** he was very well dressed
9: **no me etc va ni me viene** I *etc* don't care
◊ *vb aux* **1**: **~ a: voy/iba a hacerlo hoy** I am/was going to do it today
2 (+ *gerundio*): **iba anocheciendo** it was getting dark; **todo se me iba aclarando** everything was gradually becoming clearer to me
3 (+ *pp = pasivo*): **van vendidos 300 ejemplares** 300 copies have been sold so far
◊ **~se** *vr* **1**: **¿por dónde se va al zoológico?** which is the way to the zoo?
2 (*marcharse*) to leave; **ya se habrán ido** they must already have left *o* gone

ira ['ira] *nf* anger, rage
iracundo, a [ira'kundo, a] *adj* irascible
Irak [i'rak] *nm* = **Iraq**
Irán [i'ran] *nm* Iran; **iraní** *adj, nm/f* Iranian
Iraq [i'rak] *nm* Iraq; **iraquí** *adj, nm/f* Iraqui
iris ['iris] *nm inv* (*tb:* **arco ~**) rainbow; (ANAT) iris
Irlanda [ir'landa] *nf* Ireland; **irlandés, esa** *adj* Irish ◊ *nm/f* Irishman/woman; **los irlandeses** the Irish
ironía [iro'nia] *nf* irony; **irónico, a** *adj* ironic(al)
irreal [irre'al] *adj* unreal
irrecuperable [irrekupe'raβle] *adj* irrecoverable, irretrievable
irreflexión [irreflek'sjon] *nf* thoughtlessness
irregular [irrevu'lar] *adj* (*gen*) irregular; (*situación*) abnormal
irremediable [irreme'ðjaβle] *adj* irremediable; (*vicio*) incurable
irreparable [irrepa'raβle] *adj* (*daños*) irreparable; (*pérdida*) irrecoverable
irresoluto, a [irreso'luto, a] *adj* irresolute, hesitant
irrespetuoso, a [irrespe'twoso, a] *adj* disrespectful
irresponsable [irrespon'saβle] *adj* irresponsible
irreversible [irreβer'siβle] *adj* irreversible
irrigar [irri'var] *vt* to irrigate
irrisorio, a [irri'sorjo, a] *adj* derisory, ridiculous
irritar [irri'tar] *vt* to irritate, annoy
irrupción [irrup'θjon] *nf* irruption; (*invasión*) invasion
isla ['isla] *nf* island
islandés, esa [islan'des, esa] *adj* Icelandic ◊ *nm/f* Icelander
Islandia [is'landja] *nf* Iceland
isleño, a [is'leno, a] *adj* island *cpd* ◊ *nm/f* islander

Israel [isra'el] *nm* Israel; **israelí** *adj, nm/f* Israeli

istmo ['istmo] *nm* isthmus

Italia [i'talja] *nf* Italy; **italiano, a** *adj, nm/f* Italian

itinerario [itine'rarjo] *nm* itinerary, route

IVA ['iβa] *nm abr* (= *impuesto sobre el valor añadido*) VAT

izar [i'θar] *vt* to hoist

izdo, a *abr* (= *izquierdo, a*) l.

izquierda [iθ'kjerða] *nf* left; (*POL*) left (wing); **a la ~** (*estar*) on the left; (*torcer etc*) (to the) left

izquierdista [iθkjer'ðista] *nm/f* left-winger, leftist

izquierdo, a [iθ'kjerðo, a] *adj* left

J j

jabalí [xaβa'li] *nm* wild boar

jabalina [xaβa'lina] *nf* javelin

jabón [xa'βon] *nm* soap; **jabonar** *vt* to soap

jaca ['xaka] *nf* pony

jacinto [xa'θinto] *nm* hyacinth

jactarse [xak'tarse] *vr* to boast, brag

jadear [xaðe'ar] *vi* to pant, gasp for breath; **jadeo** *nm* panting, gasping

jaguar [xa'ɣwar] *nm* jaguar

jalea [xa'lea] *nf* jelly

jaleo [xa'leo] *nm* racket, uproar; **armar un ~** to kick up a racket

jalón [xa'lon] (*AM*) *nm* tug

Jamaica [xa'maika] *nf* Jamaica

jamás [xa'mas] *adv* never; (*interrogación*) ever

jamón [xa'mon] *nm* ham; **~ dulce, ~ de York** cooked ham; **~ serrano** cured ham

Japón [xa'pon] *nm*: **el ~** Japan; **japonés, esa** *adj, nm/f* Japanese ♦ *nm* (*LING*) Japanese

jaque ['xake] *nm*: **~ mate** checkmate

jaqueca [xa'keka] *nf* (very bad) headache, migraine

jarabe [xa'raβe] *nm* syrup

jarcia ['xarθja] *nf* (*NAUT*) ropes *pl*, rigging

jardín [xar'ðin] *nm* garden; **~ de (la) infancia** (*ESP*) **o de niños** (*AM*) nursery (school); **jardinería** *nf* gardening; **jardinero, a** *nm/f* gardener

jarra ['xarra] *nf* jar; (*jarro*) jug

jarro ['xarro] *nm* jug

jaula ['xaula] *nf* cage

jauría [xau'ria] *nf* pack of hounds

J. C. *abr* (= *Jesucristo*) J.C.

jefa ['xefa] *nf ver* **jefe**

jefatura [xefa'tura] *nf*: **~ de policía** police headquarters *sg*

jefe, a ['xefe, a] *nm/f* (*gen*) chief, head; (*patrón*) boss; **~ de cocina** chef; **~ de estación** stationmaster; **~ de estado** head of state

jengibre [xen'xiβre] *nm* ginger

jeque ['xeke] *nm* sheik

jerarquía [xerar'kia] *nf* (*orden*) hierarchy; (*rango*) rank; **jerárquico, a** *adj* hierarchic(al)

jerez [xe'reθ] *nm* sherry

jerga ['xerɣa] *nf* (*tela*) coarse cloth; (*lenguaje*) jargon

jeringa [xe'ringa] *nf* syringe; (*AM*) annoyance, bother; **~ de engrase** grease gun; **jeringar** (*AM*) *vt* to annoy, bother

jeroglífico [xero'ɣlifiko] *nm* hieroglyphic

jersey [xer'sei] (*pl* **~s**) *nm* jersey, pullover, jumper

Jerusalén [xerusa'len] *n* Jerusalem

Jesucristo [xesu'kristo] *nm* Jesus Christ

jesuita [xe'swita] *adj, nm* Jesuit

Jesús [xe'sus] *nm* Jesus; **¡~!** good heavens!; (*al estornudar*) bless you!

jinete, a [xi'nete, a] *nm/f* horseman/woman, rider

jipijapa [xipi'xapa] (*AM*) *nm* straw hat

jirafa [xi'rafa] *nf* giraffe

jirón [xi'ron] *nm* rag, shred

jocoso, a [xo'koso, a] *adj* humorous, jocular

jofaina [xo'faina] *nf* washbasin

jornada [xor'naða] *nf* (*viaje de un día*) day's journey; (*camino o viaje entero*) journey; (*día de trabajo*) working day

jornal [xor'nal] *nm* (day's) wage; **~ero** *nm* (day) labourer

joroba [xo'roβa] *nf* hump, hunched back; **~do, a** *adj* hunchbacked ♦ *nm/f* hunchback

jota ['xota] *nf* (the letter) J; (*danza*) Aragonese dance; (*fam*) jot, iota; **no saber ni ~** to have no idea

joven ['xoβen] (*pl* **jóvenes**) *adj* young ♦ *nm* young man, youth ♦ *nf* young woman, girl

jovial [xo'βjal] *adj* cheerful, jolly

joya ['xoja] *nf* jewel, gem; (*fig: persona*) gem; **joyería** *nf* (*joyas*) jewellery; (*tienda*) jeweller's (shop); **joyero** *nm* (*persona*) jeweller; (*caja*) jewel case

juanete [xwa'nete] *nm* (*del pie*) bunion

jubilación [xuβila'θjon] *nf* (*retiro*) retirement

jubilado, a [xuβi'laðo, a] *adj* retired ♦ *nm/f* pensioner (*BRIT*), senior citizen

jubilar [xuβi'lar] *vt* to pension off, retire; (*fam*) to discard; **~se** *vr* to retire

júbilo ['xuβilo] *nm* joy, rejoicing; **jubiloso,**

a adj jubilant

judía [xuˈðia] nf (CULIN) bean; ~ **verde** French bean; ver tb **judío**

judicial [xuðiˈθjal] adj judicial

judío, a [xuˈðio, a] adj Jewish ♦ nm/f Jew(ess)

judo [ˈjuðo] nm judo

juego etc [ˈxweɣo] vb ver **jugar** ♦ nm (gen) play; (pasatiempo, partido) game; (en casino) gambling; (conjunto) set; **fuera de ~** (DEPORTE: persona) offside; (: pelota) out of play; **J~s Olímpicos** Olympic Games

juerga [ˈxwerɣa] nf binge; (fiesta) party; **ir de ~** to go out on a binge

jueves [ˈxweβes] nm inv Thursday

juez [xweθ] nm/f judge; ~ **de línea** linesman; ~ **de salida** starter

jugada [xuˈɣaða] nf play; **buena ~** good move/shot/stroke etc

jugador, a [xuɣaˈðor, a] nm/f player; (en casino) gambler

jugar [xuˈɣar] vt, vi to play; (en casino) to gamble; (apostar) to bet; ~ **al fútbol** to play football

juglar [xuˈɣlar] nm minstrel

jugo [ˈxuɣo] nm (BOT) juice; (fig) essence, substance; ~ **de fruta** (AM) fruit juice; ~**so, a** adj juicy; (fig) substantial, important

juguete [xuˈɣete] nm toy; ~**ar** vi to play; ~**ría** nf toyshop

juguetón, ona [xuɣeˈton, ona] adj playful

juicio [ˈxwiθjo] nm judgement; (razón) sanity, reason; (opinión) opinion; **estar fuera de ~** to be out of one's mind; ~**so, a** adj wise, sensible

julio [ˈxuljo] nm July

junco [ˈxunko] nm rush, reed

jungla [ˈxuŋgla] nf jungle

junio [ˈxunjo] nm June

junta [ˈxunta] nf (asamblea) meeting, assembly; (comité, consejo) board, council, committee; (articulación) joint

juntar [xunˈtar] vt to join, unite; (maquinaria) to assemble, put together; (dinero) to collect; ~**se** vr to join, meet; (reunirse: personas) to meet, assemble; (arrimarse) to approach, draw closer; ~**se con uno** to join sb

junto, a [ˈxunto, a] adj joined; (unido) united; (anexo) near, close; (contiguo, próximo) next, adjacent ♦ adv: **todo ~** all at once; ~**s** together; ~ **a** near (to), next to

jurado [xuˈraðo] nm (JUR: individuo) juror; (: grupo) jury; (de concurso: grupo) panel (of judges); (: individuo) member of a panel

juramento [xuraˈmento] nm oath; (maldición) oath, curse; **prestar ~** to take the oath; **tomar ~ a** to swear in, administer the oath to

jurar [xuˈrar] vt, vi to swear; ~ **en falso** to commit perjury; **jurárselas a uno** to have it

in for sb

jurídico, a [xuˈriðiko, a] adj legal

jurisdicción [xurisðikˈθjon] nf (poder, autoridad) jurisdiction; (territorio) district

jurisprudencia [xurispruˈðenθja] nf jurisprudence

jurista [xuˈrista] nm/f jurist

justamente [xustaˈmente] adv justly, fairly; (precisamente) just, exactly

justicia [xusˈtiθja] nf justice; (equidad) fairness, justice; **justiciero, a** adj just, righteous

justificación [xustifikaˈθjon] nf justification; **justificar** vt to justify

justo, a [ˈxusto, a] adj (equitativo) just, fair, right; (preciso) exact, correct; (ajustado) tight ♦ adv (precisamente) exactly, precisely; (AM: apenas a tiempo) just in time

juvenil [xuβeˈnil] adj youthful

juventud [xuβenˈtuð] nf (adolescencia) youth; (jóvenes) young people pl

juzgado [xuθˈɣaðo] nm tribunal; (JUR) court

juzgar [xuθˈɣar] vt to judge; **a ~ por ...** to judge by ..., judging by ...

K k

kg abr (= kilogramo) kg

kilo [ˈkilo] nm kilo ♦ pref: ~**gramo** nm kilogramme; ~**metraje** nm distance in kilometres, ≈ mileage; **kilómetro** nm kilometre; ~**vatio** nm kilowatt

kiosco [ˈkjosko] nm = **quiosco**

km abr (= kilómetro) km

kv abr (= kilovatio) kw

L l

l abr (= litro) l

la [la] art def the ♦ pron her; (Ud.) you; (cosa) it ♦ nm (MUS) la; ~ **del sombrero rojo** the girl in the red hat; tb ver **el**

laberinto [laβeˈrinto] nm labyrinth

labia ['laβja] nf fluency; (pey) glib tongue
labio ['laβjo] nm lip
labor [la'βor] nf labour; (AGR) farm work; (tarea) job, task; (COSTURA) needlework; **~able** adj (AGR) workable; **día ~able** working day; **~al** adj (accidente) at work; (jornada) working
laboratorio [laβora'torjo] nm laboratory
laborioso, a [laβo'rjoso, a] adj (persona) hard-working; (trabajo) tough
laborista [laβo'rista] adj: **Partido L~** Labour Party
labrado, a [la'βraðo, a] adj worked; (madera) carved; (metal) wrought ♦ nm (AGR) cultivated field
labrador, a [laβra'ðor, a] adj farming cpd ♦ nm/f farmer
labranza [la'βranθa] nf (AGR) cultivation
labrar [la'βrar] vt (gen) to work; (madera etc) to carve; (fig) to cause, bring about
labriego, a [la'βrjeɣo, a] nm/f peasant
laca ['laka] nf lacquer
lacayo [la'kajo] nm lackey
lacio, a ['laθjo, a] adj (pelo) lank, straight
lacónico, a [la'koniko, a] adj laconic
lacra ['lakra] nf (fig) blot; **lacrar** vt (cerrar) to seal (with sealing wax); **lacre** nm sealing wax
lactancia [lak'tanθja] nf lactation
lactar [lak'tar] vt, vi to suckle
lácteo, a [a 'lakteo, a] adj: **productos ~s** dairy products
ladear [laðe'ar] vt to tip, tilt ♦ vi to tilt; **~se** vr to lean
ladera [la'ðera] nf slope
lado ['laðo] nm (gen) side; (fig) protection; (MIL) flank; **al ~ de** beside; **poner de ~** to put on its side; **poner a un ~** to put aside; **por todos ~s** on all sides, all round (BRIT)
ladrar [la'ðrar] vi to bark; **ladrido** nm bark, barking
ladrillo [la'ðriʎo] nm (gen) brick; (azulejo) tile
ladrón, ona [la'ðron, ona] nm/f thief
lagartija [laɣar'tixa] nf (ZOOL) (small) lizard
lagarto [la'ɣarto] nm (ZOOL) lizard
lago ['laɣo] nm lake
lágrima ['laɣrima] nf tear
laguna [la'ɣuna] nf (lago) lagoon; (hueco) gap
laico, a ['laiko, a] adj lay
lamentable [lamen'taβle] adj lamentable, regrettable; (miserable) pitiful
lamentar [lamen'tar] vt (sentir) to regret; (deplorar) to lament; **lo lamento mucho** I'm very sorry; **~se** vr to lament; **lamento** nm lament
lamer [la'mer] vt to lick
lámina ['lamina] nf (plancha delgada) sheet; (para estampar, estampa) plate
lámpara ['lampara] nf lamp; **~ de**

alcohol/gas spirit/gas lamp; **~ de pie** standard lamp
lamparón [lampa'ron] nm grease spot
lampiño [lam'piɲo] adj clean-shaven
lana ['lana] nf wool
lance etc ['lanθe] vb ver **lanzar** ♦ nm (golpe) stroke; (suceso) event, incident
lancha ['lantʃa] nf launch; **~ de pesca** fishing boat; **~ salvavidas/torpedera** lifeboat/torpedo boat
langosta [lan'gosta] nf (crustáceo) lobster; (: de río) crayfish; **langostino** nm Dublin Bay prawn; (: de río) crayfish
languidecer [langiðe'θer] vi to languish; **languidez** nf langour; **lánguido, a** adj (gen) languid; (sin energía) listless
lanilla [la'niʎa] nf nap
lanza ['lanθa] nf (arma) lance, spear
lanzamiento [lanθa'mjento] nm (gen) throwing; (NAUT, COM) launch, launching; **~ de peso** putting the shot
lanzar [lan'θar] vt (gen) to throw; (DEPORTE: pelota) to bowl; (NAUT, COM) to launch; (JUR) to evict; **~se** vr to throw o.s.
lapa ['lapa] nf limpet
lapicero [lapi'θero] nm propelling (BRIT) o mechanical (US) pencil; (AM: boligrafo) Biro ®
lápida ['lapiða] nf stone; **~ mortuoria** headstone; **~ conmemorativa** memorial stone; **lapidario, a** adj, nm lapidary
lápiz ['lapiθ] nm pencil; **~ de color** coloured pencil; **~ de labios** lipstick
lapón, ona [la'pon, ona] nm/f Laplander, Lapp
lapso ['lapso] nm (de tiempo) interval; (error) error
lapsus ['lapsus] nm inv error, mistake
largar [lar'ɣar] vt (soltar) to release; (aflojar) to loosen; (lanzar) to launch; (fam) to let fly; (velas) to unfurl; (AM) to throw; **~se** vr (fam) to beat it; **~se a** (AM) to start to
largo, a ['larɣo, a] adj (longitud) long; (tiempo) lengthy; (fig) generous ♦ nm length; (MÚS) largo; **dos años ~s** two long years; **tiene 9 metros de ~** it is 9 metres long; **a lo ~ de** along; (tiempo) all through, throughout; **~metraje** nm feature film
laringe [la'rinxe] nf larynx; **laringitis** nf laryngitis
larva ['larβa] nf larva
las [las] art def the ♦ pron them; **~ que cantan** the ones/women/girls who sing; tb ver **el**
lascivo, a [las'θiβo, a] adj lewd
láser ['laser] nm laser
lástima ['lastima] nf (pena) pity; **dar ~** to be pitiful; **es una ~ que** it's a pity that; **¡qué ~!** what a pity!; **ella está hecha una ~** she looks pitiful
lastimar [lasti'mar] vt (herir) to wound; (ofender) to offend; **~se** vr to hurt o.s.; **las-**

timero, a adj pitiful, pathetic
lastre ['lastre] nm (TEC, NAUT) ballast; (fig) dead weight
lata ['lata] nf (metal) tin; (caja) tin (BRIT), can; (fam) nuisance; **en ~** tinned (BRIT), canned; **dar (la) ~** to be a nuisance
latente [la'tente] adj latent
lateral [late'ral] adj side cpd, lateral ♦ nm (TEATRO) wings
latido [la'tiðo] nm (del corazón) beat
latifundio [lati'fundjo] nm large estate; **latifundista** nm/f owner of a large estate
latigazo [lati'yaθo] nm (golpe) lash; (sonido) crack
látigo ['latiyo] nm whip
latín [la'tin] nm Latin
latino, a [la'tino, a] adj Latin; **~americano, a** adj, nm/f Latin-American
latir [la'tir] vi (corazón, pulso) to beat
latitud [lati'tuð] nf (GEO) latitude
latón [la'ton] nm brass
latoso, a [la'toso, a] adj (molesto) annoying; (aburrido) boring
laúd [la'uð] nm lute
laurel [lau'rel] nm (BOT) laurel; (CULIN) bay
lava ['laβa] nf lava
lavabo [la'βaβo] nm (jofaina) washbasin; (tb: ~s) toilet
lavado [la'βaðo] nm washing; (de ropa) laundry; (ARTE) wash; **~ de cerebro** brainwashing; **~ en seco** dry-cleaning
lavadora [laβa'ðora] nf washing machine
lavanda [la'βanda] nf lavender
lavandería [laβande'ria] nf laundry; **~ automática** launderette
lavaplatos [laβa'platos] nm inv dishwasher
lavar [la'βar] vt to wash; (borrar) to wipe away; **~se** vr to wash o.s.; **~se las manos** to wash one's hands; **~ y marcar** (pelo) to shampoo and set; **~ en seco** to dry-clean
lavavajillas [laβaβa'xiʎas] nm inv dishwasher
laxante [lak'sante] nm laxative
lazada [la'θaða] nf bow
lazarillo [laθa'riʎo] nm: **perro ~** guide dog
lazo ['laθo] nm knot; (lazada) bow; (para animales) lasso; (trampa) snare; (vínculo) tie
le [le] pron (directo) him (o her); (: usted) you; (indirecto) to him (o her o it); (: usted) to you
leal [le'al] adj loyal; **~tad** nf loyalty
lección [lek'θjon] nf lesson
lector, a [lek'tor, a] nm/f reader
lectura [lek'tura] nf reading
leche ['letʃe] nf milk; **tiene mala ~** (fam!) he's a swine (!); **~ condensada/en polvo** condensed/powdered milk; **~ desnatada** skimmed milk; **~ra** nf (vendedora) milkmaid; (recipiente) (milk) churn; (AM) cow; **~ro, a** adj dairy
lecho ['letʃo] nm (cama, de río) bed; (GEO) layer

lechón [le'tʃon] nm sucking (BRIT) o suckling (US) pig
lechoso, a [le'tʃoso, a] adj milky
lechuga [le'tʃuɣa] nf lettuce
lechuza [le'tʃuθa] nf owl
leer [le'er] vt to read
legado [le'ɣaðo] nm (don) bequest; (herencia) legacy; (enviado) legate
legajo [le'ɣaxo] nm file
legal [le'ɣal] adj (gen) legal; (persona) trustworthy; **~idad** nf legality; **~izar** vt to legalize; (documento) to authenticate
legaña [le'ɣaɲa] nf sleep (in eyes)
legar [le'ɣar] vt to bequeath, leave
legendario, a [lexen'darjo, a] adj legendary
legión [le'xjon] nf legion; **legionario, a** adj legionary ♦ nm legionnaire
legislación [lexisla'θjon] nf legislation
legislar [lexis'lar] vi to legislate
legislatura [lexisla'tura] nf (POL) period of office
legitimar [lexiti'mar] vt to legitimize; **legítimo, a** adj (genuino) authentic; (legal) legitimate
lego, a ['leɣo, a] adj (REL) secular; (ignorante) ignorant ♦ nm layman
legua ['leɣwa] nf league
legumbres [le'ɣumbres] nfpl pulses
leído, a [le'iðo, a] adj well-read
lejanía [lexa'nia] nf distance; **lejano, a** adj far-off; (en el tiempo) distant; (fig) remote
lejía [le'xia] nf bleach
lejos ['lexos] adv far, far away; **a lo ~** in the distance; **de o desde ~** from afar; **de ~** far from
lelo, a ['lelo, a] adj silly ♦ nm/f idiot
lema ['lema] nm motto; (POL) slogan
lencería [lenθe'ria] nf linen, drapery
lengua ['leŋgwa] nf tongue; (LING) language; **morderse la ~** to hold one's tongue
lenguado [leŋ'gwaðo] nm sole
lenguaje [leŋ'gwaxe] nm language
lengüeta [leŋ'gweta] nf (ANAT) epiglottis; (zapatos, MUS) tongue
lente ['lente] nf lens; (lupa) magnifying glass; **~s** nfpl (gafas) glasses; **~s de contacto** contact lenses
lenteja [len'texa] nf lentil; **lentejuela** nf sequin
lentilla [len'tiʎa] nf contact lens
lentitud [lenti'tuð] nf slowness; **con ~** slowly
lento, a ['lento, a] adj slow
leña ['leɲa] nf firewood; **~dor, a** nm/f woodcutter
leño ['leɲo] nm (trozo de árbol) log; (madera) timber; (fig) blockhead
Leo ['leo] nm Leo
león [le'on] nm lion; **~ marino** sea lion
leopardo [leo'parðo] nm leopard
leotardos [leo'tarðos] nmpl tights
lepra ['lepra] nf leprosy; **leproso, a** nm/f

leper
lerdo, a ['lerðo, a] *adj* (*lento*) slow; (*patoso*) clumsy
les [les] *pron* (*directo*) them; (: *ustedes*) you; (*indirecto*) to them; (: *ustedes*) to you
lesbiana [les'βjana] *adj, nf* lesbian
lesión [le'sjon] *nf* wound, lesion; (*DE-PORTE*) injury; **lesionado, a** *adj* injured ♦ *nm/f* injured person
letal [le'tal] *adj* lethal
letania [leta'nia] *nf* litany
letargo [le'tarχo] *nm* lethargy
letra ['letra] *nf* letter; (*escritura*) handwriting; (*MUS*) lyrics *pl*; ~ **de cambio** bill of exchange; ~ **de imprenta** print; ~**do, a** *adj* learned; (*fam*) pedantic ♦ *nm* lawyer; **letrero** *nm* (*cartel*) sign; (*etiqueta*) label
letrina [le'trina] *nf* latrine
leucemia [leu'θemja] *nf* leukaemia
levadizo [leβa'ðiθo] *adj*: **puente** ~ drawbridge
levadura [leβa'ðura] *nf* (*para el pan*) yeast; (*de la cerveza*) brewer's yeast
levantamiento [leβanta'mjento] *nm* raising, lifting; (*rebelión*) revolt, uprising; ~ **de pesos** weight-lifting
levantar [leβan'tar] *vt* (*gen*) to raise; (*del suelo*) to pick up; (*hacia arriba*) to lift (up); (*plan*) to make, draw up; (*mesa*) to clear; (*campamento*) to strike; (*fig*) to cheer up, hearten; ~**se** *vr* to get up; (*enderezarse*) to straighten up; (*rebelarse*) to rebel; ~ **el ánimo** to cheer up
levante [le'βante] *nm* east coast; **el L~** region of Spain extending from Castellón to Murcia
levar [le'βar] *vt* to weigh anchor
leve ['leβe] *adj* light; (*fig*) trivial; ~**dad** *nf* lightness
levita [le'βita] *nf* frock coat
léxico ['leksiko] *nm* (*vocabulario*) vocabulary
ley [lei] *nf* (*gen*) law; (*metal*) standard
leyenda [le'jenda] *nf* legend
leyó *etc vb ver* **leer**
liar [li'ar] *vt* to tie (up); (*unir*) to bind; (*envolver*) to wrap (up); (*enredar*) to confuse; (*cigarrillo*) to roll; ~**se** *vr* (*fam*) to get involved; ~**se a palos** to get involved in a fight
Líbano ['liβano] *nm*: **el** ~ (the) Lebanon
libelo [li'βelo] *nm* satire, lampoon; (*JUR*) petition
libélula [li'βelula] *nf* dragonfly
liberación [liβera'θjon] *nf* liberation; (*de la cárcel*) release
liberal [liβe'ral] *adj, nm/f* liberal; ~**idad** *nf* liberality, generosity
liberar [liβe'rar] *vt* to liberate
libertad [liβer'tað] *nf* liberty, freedom; ~ **de culto/de prensa/de comercio** freedom of worship/of the press/of trade; ~ **condicio-**

nal probation; ~ **bajo palabra** parole; ~ **bajo fianza** bail
libertar [liβer'tar] *vt* (*preso*) to set free; (*de una obligación*) to release; (*eximir*) to exempt
libertino, a [liβer'tino, a] *adj* permissive ♦ *nm/f* permissive person
libra ['liβra] *nf* pound; (*ASTROLOGÍA*): **L~** Libra; ~ **esterlina** pound sterling
libramiento [liβra'mjento] *nm* rescue; (*COM*) delivery
libranza [li'βranθa] *nf* (*COM*) draft; (*letra de cambio*) bill of exchange
librar [li'βrar] *vt* (*de peligro*) to save; (*batalla*) to wage, fight; (*de impuestos*) to exempt; (*cheque*) to make out; (*JUR*) to exempt; ~**se** *vr*: ~**se de** to escape from, free o.s. from
libre ['liβre] *adj* free; (*lugar*) unoccupied; (*asiento*) vacant; (*de deudas*) free of debts; ~ **de impuestos** free of tax; **tiro** ~ free kick; **los 100 metros** ~ the 100 metres free-style (race); **al aire** ~ in the open air
librería [liβre'ria] *nf* (*tienda*) bookshop; **librero, a** *nm/f* bookseller
libreta [li'βreta] *nf* notebook; ~ **de ahorros** savings book
libro ['liβro] *nm* book; ~ **de bolsillo** paperback; ~ **de caja** cashbook; ~ **de cheques** chequebook (*BRIT*), checkbook (*US*); ~ **de texto** textbook
Lic. *abr* = **licenciado, a**
licencia [li'θenθja] *nf* (*gen*) licence; (*permiso*) permission; ~ **por enfermedad/con goce de sueldo** sick leave/paid leave; ~ **de caza** game licence; ~**do, a** *adj* licensed ♦ *nm/f* graduate; **licenciar** *vt* (*empleado*) to dismiss; (*permitir*) to permit, allow; (*soldado*) to discharge; (*estudiante*) to confer a degree upon; **licenciarse** *vr*: **licenciarse en letras** to graduate in arts
licencioso, a [liθen'θjoso, a] *adj* licentious
licitar [liθi'tar] *vt* to bid for; (*AM*) to sell by auction
lícito, a ['liθito, a] *adj* (*legal*) lawful; (*justo*) fair, just; (*permisible*) permissible
licor [li'kor] *nm* spirits *pl* (*BRIT*), liquor (*US*); (*de frutas etc*) liqueur
licuadora [likwa'ðora] *nf* blender
licuar [li'kwar] *vt* to liquidize
lid [lið] *nf* combat; (*fig*) controversy
líder ['liðer] *nm/f* leader; **liderato** *nm* leadership; **liderazgo** *nm* leadership
lidia ['liðja] *nf* bullfighting; (*una* ~) bullfight; **toros de** ~ fighting bulls; **lidiar** *vt, vi* to fight
liebre ['ljeβre] *nf* hare
lienzo ['ljenθo] *nm* linen; (*ARTE*) canvas; (*ARQ*) wall
liga ['liχa] *nf* (*de medias*) garter, suspender; (*AM: gomita*) rubber band; (*confederación*) league

ligadura [liva'ðura] *nf* bond, tie; *(MED, MUS)* ligature

ligamento [liva'mento] *nm (ANAT)* ligament; *(atadura)* tie; *(unión)* bond

ligar [li'var] *vt (atar)* to tie; *(unir)* to join; *(MED)* to bind up; *(MUS)* to slur ♦ *vi* to mix, blend; *(fam)*: **(él) liga mucho** he pulls a lot of women; **~se** *vr* to commit o.s.

ligereza [lixe're θa] *nf* lightness; *(rapidez)* swiftness; *(agilidad)* agility; *(superficialidad)* flippancy

ligero, a [li'xero, a] *adj (de peso)* light; *(tela)* thin; *(rápido)* swift, quick; *(ágil)* agile, nimble; *(de importancia)* slight; *(de carácter)* flippant, superficial ♦ *adv*: **a la ligera** superficially

liguero [li'vero] *nm* suspender *(BRIT)* o garter *(US)* belt

lija ['lixa] *nf (ZOOL)* dogfish; *(tb: papel de ~)* sandpaper

lila ['lila] *nf* lilac

lima ['lima] *nf* file; *(BOT)* lime; **~ de uñas** nailfile; **limar** *vt* to file

limitación [limita'θjon] *nf* limitation, limit; **~ de velocidad** speed limit

limitar [limi'tar] *vt* to limit; *(reducir)* to reduce, cut down ♦ *vi*: **~ con** to border on; **~se** *vr*: **~se a** to limit o.s. to

límite ['limite] *nm (gen)* limit; *(fin)* end; *(frontera)* border; **~ de velocidad** speed limit

limítrofe [li'mitrofe] *adj* bordering, neighbouring

limón [li'mon] *nm* lemon ♦ *adj*: **amarillo ~** lemon-yellow; **limonada** *nf* lemonade

limosna [li'mosna] *nf* alms *pl*; **vivir de ~** to live on charity

limpiaparabrisas [limpjapara'ßrisas] *nm inv* windscreen *(BRIT)* o windshield *(US)* wiper

limpiar [lim'pjar] *vt* to clean; *(con trapo)* to wipe; *(quitar)* to wipe away; *(zapatos)* to shine, polish; *(fig)* to clean up

limpieza [lim'pjeθa] *nf (estado)* cleanliness; *(acto)* cleaning; (: *de las calles)* cleansing; (: *de zapatos)* polishing; *(habilidad)* skill; *(fig: POLICÍA)* clean-up; *(pureza)* purity; *(MIL)*: **operación de ~** mopping-up operation; **~ en seco** dry cleaning

limpio, a ['limpjo, a] *adj* clean; *(moralmente)* pure; *(COM)* clear, net; *(fam)* honest ♦ *adv*: **jugar ~** to play fair; **pasar a ~** *(ESP)* o **en ~** *(AM)* to make a clean copy

linaje [li'naxe] *nm* lineage, family

lince ['linθe] *nm* lynx

linchar [lin'tʃar] *vt* to lynch

lindar [lin'dar] *vi* to adjoin; **~ con** to border on; **linde** *nm* o *f* boundary; **lindero, a** *adj* adjoining ♦ *nm* boundary

lindo, a ['lindo, a] *adj* pretty, lovely ♦ *adv*: **nos divertimos de lo ~** we had a marvellous time; **canta muy ~** *(AM)* he sings beautifully

línea ['linea] *nf (gen)* line; **en ~** *(INFORM)* on line; **~ aérea** airline; **~ de meta** goal line; **~ de carrera** finishing line; **~ recta** straight line

lingote [lin'gote] *nm* ingot

lingüista [lin'gwista] *nm/f* linguist; **lingüística** *nf* linguistics *sg*

linimento [lini'mento] *nm* liniment

lino ['lino] *nm* linen; *(BOT)* flax

linóleo [li'noleo] *nm* lino, linoleum

linterna [lin'terna] *nf* lantern, lamp; **~ eléctrica** o **a pilas** torch *(BRIT)*, flashlight *(US)*

lío ['lio] *nm* bundle; *(fam)* fuss; *(desorden)* muddle, mess; **armar un ~** to make a fuss

liquen ['liken] *nm* lichen

liquidación [likiða'θjon] *nf* liquidation; **venta de ~** clearance sale

liquidar [liki'ðar] *vt (mercancías)* to liquidate; *(deudas)* to pay off; *(empresa)* to wind up

líquido, a ['likiðo, a] *adj* liquid; *(ganancia)* net ♦ *nm* liquid; **~ imponible** net taxable income

lira ['lira] *nf (MUS)* lyre; *(moneda)* lira

lírico, a ['liriko, a] *adj* lyrical

lirio ['lirjo] *nm (BOT)* iris

lirón [li'ron] *nm (ZOOL)* dormouse; *(fig)* sleepyhead

Lisboa [lis'ßoa] *n* Lisbon

lisiado, a [li'sjaðo, a] *adj* injured ♦ *nm/f* cripple

lisiar [li'sjar] *vt* to maim; **~se** *vr* to injure o.s

liso, a ['liso, a] *adj (terreno)* flat; *(cabello)* straight; *(superficie)* even; *(tela)* plain

lisonja [li'sonxa] *nf* flattery; **lisonjear** *vt* to flatter; *(fig)* to please

lista ['lista] *nf* list; *(de alumnos)* school register; *(de libros)* catalogue; *(de platos)* menu; *(de precios)* price list; **pasar ~** to call the roll; **~ de correos** poste restante; **~ de espera** waiting list; **tela a ~s** striped material

listo, a ['listo, a] *adj (perspicaz)* smart, clever; *(preparado)* ready

listón [lis'ton] *nm (tela)* ribbon; *(de madera, metal)* strip

litera [li'tera] *nf (en barco, tren)* berth; *(en dormitorio)* bunk, bunk bed

literal [lite'ral] *adj* literal

literario, a [lite'rarjo, a] *adj* literary

literato, a [lite'rato, a] *adj* literary ♦ *nm/f* writer

literatura [litera'tura] *nf* literature

litigar [liti'var] *vt* to fight ♦ *vi (JUR)* to go to law; *(fig)* to dispute, argue

litigio [li'tixjo] *nm (JUR)* lawsuit; *(fig)*: **en ~ con** in dispute with

litografía [litovra'fia] *nf* lithography; *(una ~)* lithograph

litoral [lito'ral] *adj* coastal ♦ *nm* coast, seaboard

litro ['litro] *nm* litre

liviano, a [li'βjano, a] *adj* (*persona*) fickle; (*cosa, objeto*) trivial

lívido, a ['liβiðo, a] *adj* livid

ll... *see under letter* LL, *after* L

lo [lo] *art def*: ~ **bello** the beautiful, what is beautiful, that which is beautiful ♦ *pron* (*persona*) him; (*cosa*) it; *tb ver* **el**

loable [lo'aβle] *adj* praiseworthy; **loar** *vt* to praise

lobato [lo'βato] *nm* (*ZOOL*) wolf cub; **L~** Cub Scout

lobo ['loβo] *nm* wolf; ~ **de mar** (*fig*) sea dog; ~ **marino** seal

lóbrego, a ['loβreyo, a] *adj* dark; (*fig*) gloomy

lóbulo ['loβulo] *nm* lobe

local [lo'kal] *adj* local ♦ *nm* place, site; (*oficinas*) premises *pl*; **~idad** *nf* (*barrio*) locality; (*lugar*) location; (*TEATRO*) seat, ticket; **~izar** *vt* (*ubicar*) to locate, find; (*restringir*) to localize; (*situar*) to place

loción [lo'θjon] *nf* lotion

loco, a ['loko, a] *adj* mad ♦ *nm/f* lunatic, mad person

locomoción [lokomo'θjon] *nf* locomotion

locomotora [lokomo'tora] *nf* engine, locomotive

locuaz [lo'kwaθ] *adj* loquacious

locución [loku'θjon] *nf* expression

locura [lo'kura] *nf* madness; (*acto*) crazy act

locutor, a [loku'tor, a] *nm/f* (*RADIO*) announcer; (*comentarista*) commentator; (*TV*) newsreader

locutorio [loku'torjo] *nm* (*en telefónica*) telephone booth

lodo ['loðo] *nm* mud

lógica ['loxika] *nf* logic

lógico, a ['loxiko, a] *adj* logical

logística [lo'xistika] *nf* logistics *sg*

logotipo [loðo'tipo] *nm* logo

logrado, a [lo'ðraðo, a] *adj* (*interpretación, reproducción*) polished, excellent

lograr [lo'ɣrar] *vt* to achieve; (*obtener*) to get, obtain; ~ **hacer** to manage to do; ~ **que uno venga** to manage to get sb to come

logro ['loɣro] *nm* achievement, success

loma ['loma] *nf* hillock, (*BRIT*), small hill

lombriz [lom'briθ] *nf* worm

lomo ['lomo] *nm* (*de animal*) back; (*CULIN: de cerdo*) pork loin; (: *de vaca*) rib steak; (*de libro*) spine

lona ['lona] *nf* canvas

loncha ['lontʃa] *nf* = **lonja**

lonche ['lontʃe] (*AM*) *nm* lunch; **~ría** (*AM*) *nf* snack bar, diner (*US*)

Londres ['londres] *n* London

longaniza [longa'niθa] *nf* pork sausage

longitud [lonxi'tuð] *nf* length; (*GEO*) longitude; **tener 3 metros de** ~ to be 3 metres long; ~ **de onda** wavelength

lonja ['lonxa] *nf* slice; (*de tocino*) rasher; ~ **de pescado** fish market

loro ['loro] *nm* parrot

los [los] *art def* the ♦ *pron* them; (*ustedes*) you; **mis libros y** ~ **de Ud** my books and yours; *tb ver* **el**

losa ['losa] *nf* stone; ~ **sepulcral** gravestone

lote ['lote] *nm* portion, (*COM*) lot

lotería [lote'ria] *nf* lottery; (*juego*) lotto

loza ['loθa] *nf* crockery

lozanía [loθa'nia] *nf* (*lujo*) luxuriance; **lozano, a** *adj* luxuriant; (*animado*) lively

lubricante [luβri'kante] *nm* lubricant

lubricar [luβri'kar] *vt* to lubricate

lucidez [luθi'ðeθ] *nf* lucidity

lúcido, a ['luθiðo, a] *adj* (*persona*) lucid; (*mente*) logical; (*idea*) crystal-clear

luciérnaga [lu'θjernaɣa] *nf* glow-worm

lucir [lu'θir] *vt* to illuminate, light (up); (*ostentar*) to show off ♦ *vi* (*brillar*) to shine; **~se** *vr* (*irónico*) to make a fool of o.s.

lucro ['lukro] *nm* profit, gain

lucha ['lutʃa] *nf* fight, struggle; ~ **de clases** class struggle; ~ **libre** wrestling; **luchar** *vi* to fight

lúdico, a ['ludiko, a] *adj* (*aspecto, actividad*) play *atr*

luego ['lweɣo] *adv* (*después*) next; (*más tarde*) later, afterwards

lugar [lu'ɣar] *nm* place; (*sitio*) spot; **en** ~ **de** instead of; **hacer** ~ to make room; **fuera de** ~ out of place; **tener** ~ to take place; ~ **común** commonplace

lugareño, a [luɣa'reno, a] *adj* village *cpd* ♦ *nm/f* villager

lugarteniente [luɣarte'njente] *nm* deputy

lúgubre ['luɣuβre] *adj* mournful

lujo ['luxo] *nm* luxury; (*fig*) profusion, abundance; **~so, a** *adj* luxurious

lujuria [lu'xurja] *nf* lust

lumbre ['lumbre] *nf* (*gen*) light

lumbrera [lum'brera] *nf* luminary

luminoso, a [lumi'noso, a] *adj* luminous, shining

luna ['luna] *nf* moon; (*de un espejo*) glass; (*de gafas*) lens; (*fig*) crescent; ~ **llena/ nueva** full/new moon; **estar en la** ~ to have one's head in the clouds; ~ **de miel** honeymoon

lunar [lu'nar] *adj* lunar ♦ *nm* (*ANAT*) mole; **tela a ~es** spotted material

lunes ['lunes] *nm inv* Monday

lupa ['lupa] *nf* magnifying glass

lustrar [lus'trar] *vt* (*mueble*) to polish; (*zapatos*) to shine; **lustre** *nm* polish; (*fig*) lustre; **dar lustre a** to polish; **lustroso, a** *adj* shining

luto ['luto] *nm* mourning; (*congoja*) grief, sorrow; **llevar el** *o* **vestirse de** ~ to be in mourning

Luxemburgo [luksem'burɣo] nm Luxembourg

luz [luθ] (pl **luces**) nf light; **dar a ~ un niño** to give birth to a child; **sacar a la ~** to bring to light; **dar o encender** (ESP) o **prender** (AM)/**apagar la ~** to switch the light on/off; **a todas luces** by any reckoning; **hacer la ~ sobre** to shed light on; **tener pocas luces** to be dim o stupid; **~ roja/verde** red/green light; **~ de freno** brake light; **luces de tráfico** traffic lights; **traje de luces** bullfighter's costume

LL ll

llaga ['ʎaɣa] nf wound

llama ['ʎama] nf flame; (ZOOL) llama

llamada [ʎa'maða] nf call; **~ al orden** call to order; **~ a pie de página** reference note

llamamiento [ʎama'mjento] nm call

llamar [ʎa'mar] vt to call; (atención) to attract ♦ vi (por teléfono) to telephone; (a la puerta) to knock (o ring); (por señas) to beckon; (MIL) to call up; **~se** vr to be called, be named; **¿cómo se llama usted?** what's your name?

llamarada [ʎama'raða] nf (llamas) blaze; (rubor) flush; (fig) flare-up

llamativo, a [ʎama'tiβo, a] adj showy; (color) loud

llamear [ʎame'ar] vi to blaze

llano, a ['ʎano, a] adj (superficie) flat; (persona) straightforward; (estilo) clear ♦ nm plain, flat ground

llanta ['ʎanta] nf (wheel) rim; (AM): **~ (de goma)** tyre; (: cámara) inner (tube)

llanto ['ʎanto] nm weeping

llanura [ʎa'nura] nf plain

llave ['ʎaβe] nf key; (del agua) tap; (MECÁNICA) spanner; (de la luz) switch; (MUS) key; **~ inglesa** monkey wrench; **~ maestra** master key; **~ de contacto** (AUTO) ignition key; **~ de paso** stopcock; **echar ~ a** to lock up; **~ro** nm keyring

llegada [ʎe'ɣaða] nf arrival

llegar [ʎe'ɣar] vi to arrive; (alcanzar) to reach; (bastar) to be enough; **~se** vr: **~se a** to approach; **~ a** to manage to, succeed in; **~ a saber** to find out; **~ a ser** to become; **~ a las manos de** to come into the hands of

llenar [ʎe'nar] vt to fill; (espacio) to cover; (formulario) to fill in o up; (fig) to heap

lleno, a ['ʎeno, a] adj full, filled; (repleto) full up ♦ nm (abundancia) abundance; (TEATRO) full house; **dar de ~ contra un muro** to hit a wall head-on

llevadero, a [ʎeβa'ðero, a] adj bearable, tolerable

llevar [ʎe'βar] vt to take; (ropa) to wear; (cargar) to carry; (quitar) to take away; (en coche) to drive; (transportar) to transport; (traer: dinero) to carry; (conducir) to lead; (MAT) to carry ♦ vi (suj: camino etc): **~ a** to lead to; **~se** vr to carry off, take away; **llevamos dos días aquí** we have been here for two days; **él me lleva 2 años** he's 2 years older than me; (COM): **~ los libros** to keep the books; **~se bien** to get on well (together)

llorar [ʎo'rar] vt, vi to cry, weep; **~ de risa** to cry with laughter

lloriquear [ʎorike'ar] vi to snivel, whimper

lloro ['ʎoro] nm crying, weeping; **llorón, ona** adj tearful ♦ nm/f cry-baby; **~so, a** adj (gen) weeping, tearful; (triste) sad, sorrowful

llover [ʎo'βer] vi to rain

llovizna [ʎo'βiθna] nf drizzle; **lloviznar** vi to drizzle

llueve etc vb ver **llover**

lluvia ['ʎuβja] nf rain; **~ radioactiva** (radioactive) fallout; **lluvioso, a** adj rainy

M m

m abr (= metro) m; (= minuto) m

macarrones [maka'rrones] nmpl macaroni sg

macedonia [maθe'ðonja] nf: **~ de frutas** fruit salad

macerar [maθe'rar] vt to macerate

maceta [ma'θeta] nf (de flores) pot of flowers; (para plantas) flowerpot

macizo, a [ma'θiθo, a] adj (grande) massive; (fuerte, sólido) solid ♦ nm mass, chunk

machacar [matʃa'kar] vt to crush, pound ♦ vi (insistir) to go on, keep on

machete [ma'tʃete] (AM) nm machete, (large) knife

machismo [ma'tʃismo] nm male chauvinism; **machista** adj, nm sexist

macho ['matʃo] adj male; (fig) virile ♦ nm male; (fig) he-man

madeja [ma'ðexa] nf (de lana) skein, hank;

(de pelo) mass, mop

madera [ma'ðera] nf wood; (fig) nature, character; **una ~** a piece of wood

madero [ma'ðero] nm beam; (fig) ship

madrastra [ma'ðrastra] nf stepmother

madre ['maðre] adj mother cpd; (AM) tremendous ♦ nf mother; (de vino etc) dregs pl; **~ política/soltera** mother-in-law/ unmarried mother

Madrid [ma'ðrið] n Madrid

madriguera [maðri'xera] nf burrow

madrileño, a [maðri'leɲo, a] adj of o from Madrid ♦ nm/f native of Madrid

madrina [ma'ðrina] nf godmother; (ARQ) prop, shore; (TEC) brace; **~ de boda** bridesmaid

madrugada [maðru'xaða] nf early morning; (alba) dawn, daybreak

madrugador, a [maðruxa'ðor, a] adj early-rising

madrugar [maðru'xar] vi to get up early; (fig) to get ahead

madurar [maðu'rar] vt, vi (fruta) to ripen; (fig) to mature; **madurez** nf ripeness; maturity; **maduro, a** adj ripe; mature

maestra [ma'estra] nf ver maestro

maestría [maes'tria] nf mastery; (habilidad) skill, expertise

maestro, a [ma'estro, a] adj masterly; (perito) skilled, expert; (principal) main; (educado) trained ♦ nm/f master/mistress; (profesor) teacher ♦ nm (autoridad) authority; (MUS) maestro; (AM) skilled workman; **~ albañil** master mason

magia ['maxja] nf magic; **mágico, a** adj magic(al) ♦ nm/f magician

magisterio [maxis'terjo] nm (enseñanza) teaching; (profesión) teaching profession; (maestros) teachers pl

magistrado [maxis'traðo] nm magistrate

magistral [maxis'tral] adj magisterial; (fig) masterly

magnánimo, a [max'nanimo, a] adj magnanimous

magnate [max'nate] nm magnate, tycoon

magnético, a [max'netiko, a] adj magnetic; **magnetizar** vt to magnetize

magnetofón [maxneto'fon] nm tape recorder; **magnetofónico, a** adj: **cinta magnetofónica** recording tape

magnetófono [maxne'tofono] nm = **magnetofón**

magnífico, a [max'nifiko, a] adj splendid, magnificent

magnitud [maxni'tuð] nf magnitude

mago, a ['maxo, a] nm/f magician; **los Reyes M~s** the Magi, the Three Wise Men

magro, a ['maxro, a] adj (persona) thin, lean; (carne) lean

maguey [ma'xei] nm agave

magullar [maxu'ʎar] vt (amoratar) to bruise; (dañar) to damage; (fam: golpear) to

bash, beat

mahometano, a [maome'tano, a] adj Mohammedan

mahonesa [mao'nesa] nf = **mayonesa**

maíz [ma'iθ] nm maize (BRIT), corn (US); sweet corn

majadero, a [maxa'ðero, a] adj silly, stupid

majestad [maxes'taθ] nf majesty; **majestuoso, a** adj majestic

majo, a ['maxo, a] adj nice; (guapo) attractive, good-looking; (elegante) smart

mal [mal] adv badly; (equivocadamente) wrongly; (con dificultad) with difficulty ♦ adj = **malo** ♦ nm evil; (desgracia) misfortune; (daño) harm, damage; (MED) illness; **~ que bien** rightly or wrongly; **ir de ~ en peor** to get worse and worse

mala ['mala] nf spell of bad luck; **estar de ~s** to be in a bad mood; ver tb **malo**

malabarismo [malaβa'rismo] nm juggling; **malabarista** nm/f juggler

malaria [ma'larja] nf malaria

malcriado, a [mal'krjaðo, a] adj (consentido) spoiled

maldad [mal'daθ] nf evil, wickedness

maldecir [malde'θir] vt to curse ♦ vi: **~ de** to speak ill of

maldición [maldi'θjon] nf curse

maldito, a [mal'dito, a] adj (condenado) damned; (perverso) wicked; **¡~ sea!** damn it!

maleante [male'ante] adj wicked ♦ nm/f criminal, crook

maledicencia [maleði'θenθja] nf slander, scandal

maleducado, a [maleðu'kaðo, a] adj bad-mannered, rude

malentendido [malenten'diðo] nm misunderstanding

malestar [males'tar] nm (gen) discomfort; (fig: inquietud) uneasiness; (POL) unrest

maleta [ma'leta] nf case, suitcase; (AUTO) boot (BRIT), trunk (US); **hacer la ~s** to pack; **maletera** (AM) nf = **maletero**; **maletero** nm (AUTO) boot (BRIT), trunk (US); **maletín** nm small case, bag

malévolo, a [ma'leβolo, a] adj malicious, spiteful

maleza [ma'leθa] nf (hierbas malas) weeds pl; (arbustos) thicket

malgastar [malxas'tar] vt (tiempo, dinero) to waste; (salud) to ruin

malhechor, a [male'tʃor, a] nm/f delinquent

malhumorado, a [malumo'raðo, a] adj bad-tempered

malicia [ma'liθja] nf (maldad) wickedness; (astucia) slyness, guile; (mala intención) malice, spite; (carácter travieso) mischievousness; **malicioso, a** adj wicked, evil; sly, crafty; malicious, spiteful; mischievous

maligno, a [ma'liɣno, a] adj evil; (ma-

lévolo) malicious; (*MED*) malignant

malo, a ['malo, a] *adj* bad; (*falso*) false ♦ *nm/f* villain; **estar ~ to be ill**

malograr [malo'ɤrar] *vt* to spoil; (*plan*) to upset; (*ocasión*) to waste; **~se** *vr* (*plan etc*) to fail, come to grief; (*persona*) to die before one's time

malparado, a [malpa'raðo, a] *adj*: **salir ~ to come off badly**

malpensado, a [malpen'saðo, a] *adj* (*persona*) nasty

malsano, a [mal'sano, a] *adj* unhealthy

Malta ['malta] *nf* Malta

malteada [malte'aða] (*AM*) *nf* milk shake

maltratar [maltra'tar] *vt* to ill-treat, mistreat

maltrecho, a [mal'tretʃo, a] *adj* battered, damaged

malvado, a [mal'βaðo, a] *adj* evil, villainous

malversar [malβer'sar] *vt* to embezzle, misappropriate

Malvinas [mal'βinas]: **Islas ~** *nfpl* Falkland Islands

malvivir [malβi'βir] *vi* to live poorly

malla ['maʎa] *nf* mesh; (*de baño*) swimsuit; (*de ballet, gimnasia*) leotard; **~s** *nfpl* tights; **~ de alambre** wire mesh

Mallorca [ma'ʎorka] *nf* Majorca

mama ['mama] *nf* (*de animal*) teat; (*de mujer*) breast

mamá [ma'ma] (*pl* **~s**) (*fam*) *nf* mum, mummy

mamar [ma'mar] *vt* (*pecho*) to suck; (*fig*) to absorb, assimilate ♦ *vi* to suck

mamarracho [mama'rratʃo] *nm* sight, mess

mamífero [ma'mifero] *nm* mammal

mampara [mam'para] *nf* (*entre habitaciones*) partition; (*biombo*) screen

mampostería [mamposte'ria] *nf* masonry

manada [ma'naða] *nf* (*ZOOL*) herd; (*: de leones*) pride; (*: de lobos*) pack

Managua [ma'naɤwa] *n* Managua

manantial [manan'tjal] *nm* spring; (*fuente*) fountain; (*fig*) source

manar [ma'nar] *vt* to run with, flow with ♦ *vi* to run, flow; (*abundar*) to abound

manco, a ['manko, a] *adj* (*de un brazo*) one-armed; (*de una mano*) one-handed; (*fig*) defective, faulty

mancomunar [mankomu'nar] *vt* to unite, bring together; (*recursos*) to pool; (*JUR*) to make jointly responsible; **mancomunidad** *nf* union, association; (*comunidad*) community; (*JUR*) joint responsibility

mancha ['mantʃa] *nf* stain, mark; (*ZOOL*) patch; (*boceto*) sketch, outline; **manchar** *vt* (*gen*) to stain, mark; (*ensuciar*) to soil, dirty

manchego, a [man'tʃeɤo, a] *adj* of o from La Mancha

mandamiento [manda'mjento] *nm* (*orden*) order, command; (*REL*) commandment; **~ judicial** warrant

mandar [man'dar] *vt* (*ordenar*) to order; (*dirigir*) to lead, command; (*enviar*) to send; (*pedir*) to order, ask for ♦ *vi* to be in charge; (*pey*) to be bossy; **¿mande?** pardon?, excuse me?; **~ hacer un traje** to have a suit made

mandarina [manda'rina] *nf* (*fruta*) tangerine, mandarin (orange)

mandatario, a [manda'tarjo, a] *nm/f* (*representante*) agent; **primer ~** head of state

mandato [man'dato] *nm* (*orden*) order; (*INFORM*) command; (*POL*: *período*) term of office; (*: territorio*) mandate; **~ judicial** (search) warrant

mandíbula [man'diβula] *nf* jaw

mandil [man'dil] *nm* (*delantal*) apron

mando ['mando] *nm* (*MIL*) command; (*de país*) rule; (*el primer lugar*) lead; (*POL*) term of office; (*TEC*) control; **~ a la izquierda** left-hand drive

mandón, ona [man'don, ona] *adj* bossy, domineering

manejable [mane'xaβle] *adj* manageable

manejar [mane'xar] *vt* to manage; (*máquina*) to work, operate; (*caballo etc*) to handle; (*casa*) to run, manage; (*AM*: *AUTO*) to drive; **~se** *vr* (*comportarse*) to act, behave; (*arreglárselas*) to manage; **manejo** *nm* management; handling; running; driving; (*facilidad de trato*) ease, confidence; **manejos** *nmpl* (*intrigas*) intrigues

manera [ma'nera] *nf* way, manner, fashion; **~s** *nfpl* (*modales*) manners; **su ~ de ser** the way he is; (*aire*) his manner; **de ninguna ~** no way, by no means; **de otra ~** otherwise; **de todas ~s** at any rate; **no hay ~ de persuadirle** there's no way of convincing him

manga ['manga] *nf* (*de camisa*) sleeve; (*de riego*) hose

mangar [man'gar] (*fam*) *vt* to pinch, nick

mango ['mango] *nm* handle; (*BOT*) mango

mangonear [mangone'ar] *vi* (*meterse*) to meddle, interfere; (*ser mandón*) to boss people about

manguera [man'gera] *nf* (*de riego*) hose; (*tubo*) pipe

manía [ma'nia] *nf* (*MED*) mania; (*fig*: *moda*) rage, craze; (*disgusto*) dislike; (*malicia*) spite; **maníaco, a** *adj* maniac(al) ♦ *nm/f* maniac

maniatar [manja'tar] *vt* to tie the hands of

maniático, a [ma'njatiko, a] *adj* maniac(al) ♦ *nm/f* maniac

manicomio [mani'komjo] *nm* mental hospital (*BRIT*), insane asylum (*US*)

manifestación [manifesta'θjon] *nf* (*declaración*) statement, declaration; (*de emoción*) show, display; (*POL*: *desfile*) demonstration; (*: concentración*) mass meeting

manifestar [manifes'tar] vt to show, manifest; (declarar) to state, declare; **manifiesto, a** adj clear, manifest ♦ nm manifesto

manija [ma'nixa] nf handle

manillar [mani'ʎar] nm (de bicicleta) handlebars pl

maniobra [ma'njoβra] nf manœuvring; (manejo) handling; (fig) manœuvre; (estratagema) stratagem; ~s nfpl (MIL) manœuvres; **maniobrar** vt to manœuvre; (manejar) to handle

manipulación [manipula'θjon] nf manipulation

manipular [manipu'lar] vt to manipulate; (manejar) to handle

maniquí [mani'ki] nm dummy ♦ nm/f model

manirroto, a [mani'rroto, a] adj lavish, extravagant ♦ nm/f spendthrift

manivela [mani'βela] nf crank

manjar [man'xar] nm (tasty) dish

mano ['mano] nf hand; (ZOOL) foot, paw; (de pintura) coat; (serie) lot, series; a ~ by hand; a ~ **derecha/izquierda** on the right(-hand side)/left(-hand side); **de primera** ~ (at) first hand; **de segunda** ~ (at) second hand; **robo a** ~ **armada** armed robbery; ~ **de obra** labour, manpower; **estrechar la** ~ **a uno** to shake sb's hand

manojo [ma'noxo] nm handful, bunch; ~ **de llaves** bunch of keys

manopla [ma'nopla] nf (guante) glove; (paño) face cloth

manoseado, a [manose'aðo, a] adj well-worn

manosear [manose'ar] vt (tocar) to handle, touch; (desordenar) to mess up, rumple; (insistir en) to overwork; (AM) to caress, fondle

manotazo [mano'taðo] nm slap, smack

mansalva [man'salβa]: **a** ~ adv indiscriminately

mansedumbre [manse'ðumbre] nf gentleness, meekness

mansión [man'sjon] nf mansion

manso, a ['manso, a] adj gentle, mild; (animal) tame

manta ['manta] nf blanket; (AM: poncho) poncho

manteca [man'teka] nf fat; (AM) butter; ~ **de cacahuete/cacao** peanut/cocoa butter; ~ **de cerdo** lard

mantecado [mante'kaðo] (AM) nm ice cream

mantel [man'tel] nm tablecloth

mantendré etc vb ver **mantener**

mantener [mante'ner] vt to support, maintain; (alimentar) to sustain; (conservar) to keep; (TEC) to maintain, service; ~**se** vr (seguir de pie) to be still standing; (no ceder) to hold one's ground; (subsistir) to sustain o.s., keep going; **mantenimiento**

nm maintenance; sustenance; (sustento) support

mantequilla [mante'kiʎa] nf butter

mantilla [man'tiʎa] nf mantilla; ~**s** nfpl (de bebé) baby clothes

manto ['manto] nm (capa) cloak; (de ceremonia) robe, gown

mantuve etc vb ver **mantener**

manual [ma'nwal] adj manual ♦ nm manual, handbook

manufactura [manufak'tura] nf manufacture; (fábrica) factory; **manufacturado, a** adj (producto) manufactured

manuscrito, a [manus'krito, a] adj handwritten ♦ nm manuscript

manutención [manuten'θjon] nf maintenance; (sustento) support

manzana [man'θana] nf apple; (ARQ) block (of houses)

manzanilla [manθa'niʎa] nf (planta) camomile; (infusión) camomile tea

manzano [man'θano] nm apple tree

maña ['maɲa] nf (gen) skill, dexterity; (pey) guile; (costumbre) habit; (destreza) trick, knack

mañana [ma'ɲana] adv tomorrow ♦ nm future ♦ nf morning; **de o por la** ~ **in the** morning; ¡hasta ~! I see you tomorrow!; ~ **por la** ~ tomorrow morning

mañoso, a [ma'ɲoso, a] adj (hábil) skilful; (astuto) smart, clever

mapa ['mapa] nm map

maqueta [ma'keta] nf (scale) model

maquillaje [maki'ʎaxe] nm make-up; (acto) making up

maquillar [maki'ʎar] vt to make up; ~**se** vr to put on (some) make-up

máquina ['makina] nf machine; (de tren) locomotive, engine; (FOTO) camera; (AM: coche) car; (fig) machinery; (: proyecto) plan, project; **escrito a** ~ typewritten; **de escribir** typewriter; ~ **de coser/lavar** sewing/washing machine

maquinación [makina'θjon] nf machination, plot

maquinal [maki'nal] adj (fig) mechanical, automatic

maquinaria [maki'narja] nf (máquinas) machinery; (mecanismo) mechanism, works pl

maquinilla [maki'niʎa] nf: ~ **de afeitar** razor

maquinista [maki'nista] nm/f (de tren) engine driver; (TEC) operator; (NAUT) engineer

mar [mar] nm o f sea; ~ **adentro** o **afuera** out at sea; **en alta** ~ on the high seas; **la** ~ **de** (fam) lots of; **el M~ Negro/Báltico** the Black/Baltic Sea

maraña [ma'raɲa] nf (maleza) thicket; (confusión) tangle

maravilla [mara'βiʎa] nf marvel, wonder;

(*BOT*) marigold; **maravillar** *vt* to astonish, amaze; **maravillarse** *vr* to be astonished, be amazed; **maravilloso, a** *adj* wonderful, marvellous

marca ['marka] *nf* (*gen*) mark; (*sello*) stamp; (*COM*) make, brand; **de** ~ excellent, outstanding; ~ **de fábrica** trademark; ~ **registrada** registered trademark

marcado, a [mar'kaðo, a] *adj* marked, strong

marcador [marka'ðor] *nm* (*DEPORTE*) scoreboard; (: *persona*) scorer

marcar [mar'kar] *vt* (*gen*) to mark; (*número de teléfono*) to dial; (*gol*) to score; (*números*) to record, keep a tally of; (*pelo*) to set ♦ *vi* (*DEPORTE*) to score; (*TEL*) to dial

marcial [mar'θjal] *adj* martial, military

marciano, a [mar'θjano, a] *adj, nm/f* Martian

marco ['marko] *nm* frame; (*DEPORTE*) goal posts *pl*; (*moneda*) mark; (*fig*) framework; ~ **de chimenea** mantelpiece

marcha ['martʃa] *nf* march; (*TEC*) running, working; (*AUTO*) gear; (*velocidad*) speed; (*fig*) progress; (*dirección*) course; **poner en** ~ to put into gear; (*fig*) to set in motion, get going; **dar** ~ **atrás** to reverse, put into reverse; **estar en** ~ to be under way, be in motion

marchar [mar'tʃar] *vi* (*ir*) to go; (*funcionar*) to work, go; ~**se** *vr* to go (away), leave

marchitar [martʃi'tar] *vt* to wither, dry up; ~**se** *vr* (*BOT*) to wither; (*fig*) to fade away; **marchito, a** *adj* withered, faded; (*fig*) in decline

marea [ma'rea] *nf* tide; (*llovizna*) drizzle

marear [mare'ar] *vt* (*fig*) to annoy, upset; (*MED*): ~ **a uno** to make sb feel sick; ~**se** *vr* (*tener náuseas*) to feel sick; (*desvanecerse*) to feel faint; (*aturdirse*) to feel dizzy; (*fam: emborracharse*) to get tipsy

maremoto [mare'moto] *nm* tidal wave

mareo [ma'reo] *nm* (*náusea*) sick feeling; (*en viaje*) travel sickness; (*aturdimiento*) dizziness; (*fam: lata*) nuisance

marfil [mar'fil] *nm* ivory

margarina [marɣa'rina] *nf* margarine

margarita [marɣa'rita] *nf* (*BOT*) daisy; (*rueda*) ~ daisywheel

margen ['marxen] *nm* (*borde*) edge, border; (*fig*) margin, space ♦ *nf* (*de río etc*) bank; **dar** ~ **para** to give an opportunity for; **mantenerse al** ~ to keep out (of things)

marginar [marxi'nar] *vt* (*grupo, individuo: socialmente*) to marginalize, ostracize

marica [ma'rika] (*fam*) *nm* sissy

maricón [mari'kon] (*fam*) *nm* queer

marido [ma'riðo] *nm* husband

mariguana [mari'ɣwana], **marihuana** [mari'wana] *nf* marijuana, cannabis

marina [ma'rina] *nf* navy; ~ **mercante** merchant navy

marinero, a [mari'nero, a] *adj* sea *cpd*; (*barco*) seaworthy ♦ *nm* sailor, seaman

marino, a [ma'rino, a] *adj* sea *cpd*, marine ♦ *nm* sailor

marioneta [marjo'neta] *nf* puppet

mariposa [mari'posa] *nf* butterfly

mariquita [mari'kita] *nf* ladybird (*BRIT*), ladybug (*US*)

mariscos [ma'riskos] *nmpl* shellfish *inv*, seafood(s)

marítimo, a [ma'ritimo, a] *adj* sea *cpd*, maritime

mármol ['marmol] *nm* marble

marqués, esa [mar'kes, esa] *nm/f* marquis/marchioness

marrón [ma'rron] *adj* brown

marroquí [marro'ki] *adj, nm/f* Moroccan ♦ *nm* Morocco (leather)

Marruecos [ma'rrwekos] *nm* Morocco

martes ['martes] *nm inv* Tuesday

martillo [mar'tiʎo] *nm* hammer; ~ **neumático** pneumatic drill (*BRIT*), jackhammer

mártir ['martir] *nm/f* martyr; **martirio** *nm* martyrdom; (*fig*) torture, torment

Marxismo [mark'sismo] *nm* Marxism; **marxista** *adj, nm/f* Marxist

marzo ['marθo] *nm* March

mas [mas] *conj* but

PALABRA CLAVE

más [mas] *adj, adv* **1**: ~ **(que, de)** (*compar*) more (than), ...+er (than); ~ **grande/inteligente** bigger/more intelligent; **trabaja** ~ **(que yo)** he works more (than me); *ver tb* **cada**

2 (*superl*): **el** ~ **the** most, ...+est; **el** ~ **grande/inteligente (de)** the biggest/most intelligent (in)

3 (*negativo*): **no tengo** ~ **dinero** I haven't got any more money; **no viene** ~ **por aquí** he doesn't come round here any more

4 (*adicional*): **no le veo** ~ **solución que** ... I see no other solution than to ...; **¿quién** ~**?** anybody else?

5 (+ *adj: valor intensivo*): **¡qué perro** ~ **sucio!** what a filthy dog!; **¡es** ~ **tonto!** he's so stupid!

6 (*locuciones*): ~ **o menos** more or less; **los** ~ **most** people; **es** ~ furthermore; ~ **bien** rather; **¡qué** ~ **da!** what does it matter!; *ver tb* **no**

7: **por** ~: **por** ~ **que te esfuerces** no matter how hard you try; **por** ~ **que quisiera** ... much as I should like to ...

8: **de** ~: **veo que aquí estoy de** ~ I can see I'm not needed here; **tenemos uno de** ~ we've got one extra

♦ *prep*: **2** ~ **2 son 4** 2 and *o* plus 2 are 4

♦ *nm inv*: **este trabajo tiene sus** ~ **y sus menos** this job's got its good points and its bad points

masa ['masa] *nf* (*mezcla*) dough; (*volumen*) volume; mass; (*FÍSICA*) mass; **en ~ en** masse; **las ~s** (*POL*) the masses

masacre [ma'sakre] *nf* massacre

masaje [ma'saxe] *nm* massage

máscara ['maskara] *nf* (*gen*) mask ♦ *nm/f* masked person; **mascarilla** *nf* (*de belleza, MED*) mask

masculino, a [masku'lino, a] *adj* masculine; (*BIO*) male

masificación [masifika'θjon] *nf* overcrowding

masivo, a [ma'sißo, a] *adj* (*en masa*) mass

masón [ma'son] *nm* (free)mason

masoquista [maso'kista] *nm/f* masochist

masticar [masti'kar] *vt* to chew; (*fig*) to ponder

mástil ['mastil] *nm* (*de navío*) mast; (*de guitarra*) neck

mastín [mas'tin] *nm* mastiff

masturbación [masturßa'θjon] *nf* masturbation

masturbarse [mastur'ßarse] *vr* to masturbate

mata ['mata] *nf* (*arbusto*) bush, shrub; (*de hierba*) tuft

matadero [mata'ðero] *nm* slaughterhouse, abattoir

matador, a [mata'ðor, a] *adj* killing ♦ *nm/f* killer ♦ *nm* (*TAUR*) matador, bullfighter

matamoscas [mata'moskas] *nm inv* (*palo*) fly swat

matanza [ma'tanθa] *nf* slaughter

matar [ma'tar] *vt, vi* to kill; **~se** *vr* (*suicidarse*) to kill o.s., commit suicide; (*morir*) to o get killed; **~ el hambre** to stave off hunger

matasellos [mata'seʎos] *nm inv* postmark

mate ['mate] *adj* (*sin brillo*: *color*) dull, matt ♦ *nm* (*en ajedrez*) (check)mate; (*AM*: *hierba*) maté; (: *vasija*) gourd

matemáticas [mate'matikas] *nfpl* mathematics; **matemático, a** *adj* mathematical ♦ *nm/f* mathematician

materia [ma'terja] *nf* (*gen*) matter; (*TEC*) material; (*ESCOL*) subject; **en ~ de** on the subject of; **~ prima** raw material; **material** *adj* material; (*dolor*) physical ♦ *nm* material; (*TEC*) equipment; **materialismo** *nm* materialism; **materialista** *adj* materialist(ic); **materialmente** *adv* materially; (*fig*) absolutely

maternal [mater'nal] *adj* motherly, maternal

maternidad [materni'ðað] *nf* motherhood, maternity; **materno, a** *adj* maternal; (*lengua*) mother *cpd*

matinal [mati'nal] *adj* morning *cpd*

matiz [ma'tiθ] *nm* shade; **~ar** *vt* (*variar*) to vary; (*ARTE*) to blend; **~ar de** to tinge with

matón [ma'ton] *nm* bully

matorral [mato'rral] *nm* thicket

matraca [ma'traka] *nf* rattle

matrícula [ma'trikula] *nf* (*registro*) register; (*AUTO*) registration number; (: *placa*) number plate; **matricular** *vt* to register, enrol

matrimonial [matrimo'njal] *adj* matrimonial

matrimonio [matri'monjo] *nm* (*pareja*) (marrid) couple; (*unión*) marriage

matriz [ma'triθ] *nf* (*ANAT*) womb; (*TEC*) mould; **casa ~** (*COM*) head office

matrona [ma'trona] *nf* (*persona de edad*) matron

maullar [mau'ʎar] *vi* to mew, miaow

maxilar [maksi'lar] *nm* jaw(bone)

máxima ['maksima] *nf* maxim

máxime ['maksime] *adv* especially

máximo, a ['maksimo, a] *adj* maximum; (*más alto*) highest; (*más grande*) greatest ♦ *nm* maximum

mayo ['majo] *nm* May

mayonesa [majo'nesa] *nf* mayonnaise

mayor [ma'jor] *adj* main, chief; (*adulto*) adult; (*de edad avanzada*) elderly; (*MUS*) major; (*compar*: *de tamaño*) bigger; (: *de edad*) older; (*superl*: *de tamaño*) biggest; (: *de edad*) oldest ♦ *nm* chief, boss; (*adulto*) adult; **al por ~** wholesale; **~ de edad** adult; **~es** *nmpl* (*antepasados*) ancestors

mayoral [majo'ral] *nm* foreman

mayordomo [major'ðomo] *nm* butler

mayoría [majo'ria] *nf* majority, greater part

mayorista [majo'rista] *nm/f* wholesaler

mayoritario, a [majori'tarjo, a] *adj* majority *cpd*

mayúscula [ma'juskula] *nf* capital letter

mayúsculo, a [ma'juskulo, a] *adj* (*fig*) big, tremendous

mazapán [maθa'pan] *nm* marzipan

mazo ['maθo] *nm* (*martillo*) mallet; (*de flores*) bunch; (*DEPORTE*) bat

me [me] *pron* (*directo*) me; (*indirecto*) (to) me; (*reflexivo*) (to) myself; **¡dámelo!** give it to me!

mear [me'ar] (*fam*) *vi* to pee, piss

mecánica [me'kanika] *nf* (*ESCOL*) mechanics *sg*; (*mecanismo*) mechanism; *ver tb* **mecánico**

mecánico, a [me'kaniko, a] *adj* mechanical ♦ *nm/f* mechanic

mecanismo [meka'nismo] *nm* mechanism; (*marcha*) gear

mecanografía [mekanoʸra'fia] *nf* typewriting; **mecanógrafo, a** *nm/f* typist

mecate [me'kate] (*AM*) *nm* rope

mecedora [meθe'ðora] *nf* rocking chair

mecer [me'θer] *vt* (*cuna*) to rock; **~se** *vr* to rock; (*ramo*) to sway

mecha ['metʃa] *nf* (*de vela*) wick; (*de bomba*) fuse

mechero [me'tʃero] *nm* (*cigarette*) lighter

mechón [me'tʃon] nm (gen) tuft; (manojo) bundle; (de pelo) lock

medalla [me'ðaʎa] nf medal

media ['meðja] nf (ESP) stocking; (AM) sock; (promedio) average

mediado, a [me'ðjaðo, a] adj half-full; (trabajo) half-completed; **a ~s de** in the middle of, halfway through

mediano, a [me'ðjano, a] adj (regular) medium, average; (mediocre) mediocre

medianoche [meðja'notʃe] nf midnight

mediante [me'ðjante] adv by (means of), through

mediar [me'ðjar] vi (interceder) to mediate, intervene

medicación [meðika'θjon] nf medication, treatment

medicamento [meðika'mento] nm medicine, drug

medicina [meði'θina] nf medicine

medición [meði'θjon] nf measurement

médico, a ['meðiko, a] adj medical ♦ nm/f doctor

medida [me'ðiða] nf measure; (medición) measurement; (prudencia) moderation, prudence; **en cierta/gran ~** up to a point/to a great extent; **un traje a la ~** made-to-measure suit; **~ de cuello** collar size; **a ~ de** in proportion to; (de acuerdo con) in keeping with; **a ~ que** (conforme) as

medio, a ['meðjo, a] adj half (a); (punto) mid, middle; (promedio) average ♦ adv half ♦ nm (centro) middle, centre; (promedio) average; (método) means, way; (ambiente) environment; **~s** nmpl means, resources; **~ litro** half a litre; **las tres y media** half past three; **M~ Oriente** Middle East; **a ~ terminar** half finished; **pagar a medias** to share the cost; **~ ambiental** adj (política, efectos) environmental

mediocre [me'ðjokre] adj middling, average; (pey) mediocre

mediodía [meðjo'ðia] nm midday, noon

medir [me'ðir] vt, vi (gen) to measure

meditar [meði'tar] vt to ponder, think over, meditate on; (planear) to think out

mediterráneo, a [meðite'rraneo, a] adj Mediterranean ♦ nm: **el M~** the Mediterranean (Sea)

médula ['meðula] nf (ANAT) marrow; **~ espinal** spinal cord

medusa [me'ðusa] (ESP) nf jellyfish

megafonía [meðafo'nia] nf public address system, PA system; **megáfono** nm megaphone

megalómano, a [meɣa'lomano, a] nm/f megalomaniac

mejicano, a [mexi'kano, a] adj, nm/f Mexican

Méjico ['mexiko] nm Mexico

mejilla [me'xiʎa] nf cheek

mejillón [mexi'ʎon] nm mussel

mejor [me'xor] adj, adv (compar) better; (superl) best; **a lo ~** probably; (quizá) maybe; **~ dicho** rather; **tanto ~** so much the better

mejora [me'xora] nf improvement; **mejorar** vt to improve, make better ♦ vi to improve, get better; **mejorarse** vr to improve, get better

melancólico, a [melan'koliko, a] adj (triste) sad, melancholy; (soñador) dreamy

melena [me'lena] nf (de persona) long hair; (ZOOL) mane

melocotón [meloko'ton] (ESP) nm peach

melodía [melo'ðia] nf melody, tune

melodrama [melo'ðrama] nm melodrama; **melodramático, a** adj melodramatic

melón [me'lon] nm melon

mellizo, a [me'ʎiθo, a] adj, nm/f twin; **~s** nmpl (AM) cufflinks

membrete [mem'brete] nm letterhead

membrillo [mem'briʎo] nm quince; **carne de ~** quince jelly

memorable [memo'raßle] adj memorable

memorándum [memo'randum] (pl ~s) nm (libro) notebook; (comunicación) memorandum

memoria [me'morja] nf (gen) memory; **~s** nfpl (de autor) memoirs; **~ intermedia** (INFORM) buffer; **memorizar** vt to memorize

menaje [me'naxe] nm: **~ de cocina** kitchenware

mencionar [menθjo'nar] vt to mention

mendigar [mendi'ɣar] vt to beg (for)

mendigo, a [men'diɣo, a] nm/f beggar

mendrugo [men'druɣo] nm crust

menear [mene'ar] vt to move; (fig) to handle; **~se** vr to shake; (balancearse) to sway; (moverse) to move; (fig) to get a move on

menester [menes'ter] nm (necesidad) necessity; **~es** nmpl (deberes) duties; **es ~** it is necessary

menestra [me'nestra] nf: **~ de verduras** vegetable stew

menguante [men'gwante] adj decreasing, diminishing

menguar [men'gwar] vt to lessen, diminish; (fig) to discredit ♦ vi to diminish, decrease; (fig) to decline

menopausia [meno'pausja] nf menopause

menor [me'nor] adj (más pequeño: compar) smaller; (: superl) smallest; (más joven: compar) younger; (: superl) youngest; (MUS) minor ♦ nm/f (joven) young person, juvenile; **no tengo la ~ idea** I haven't the faintest idea; **al por ~** retail; **~ de edad** person under age

Menorca [me'norka] nf Minorca

─────── **PALABRA CLAVE**

menos [menos] adj 1: **~ (que, de)** (compar:

cantidad) less (than); (: *número*) fewer (than); **con ~ entusiasmo** with less enthusiasm; **~ gente** fewer people; *ver tb* **cada**
2 (*superl*): **es el que ~ culpa tiene** he is the least to blame
♦ *adv* **1** (*compar*): **~ (que, de)** less (than); **me gusta ~ que el otro** I like it less than the other one
2 (*superl*): **es el ~ listo (de su clase)** he's the least bright in his class; **de todas ellas es la que ~ me agrada** out of all of them she's the one I like least; **(por) lo ~** at the (very) least
3 (*locuciones*): **no quiero verle y ~ visitarle** I don't want to see him let alone visit him; **tenemos 7 de ~** we're seven short
♦ *prep* except; (*cifras*) minus; **todos ~ él** everyone except him; **5 ~ 2** 5 minus 2
♦ *conj*: **a ~ que: a ~ que venga mañana** unless he comes tomorrow

menospreciar [menospre'θjar] *vt* to underrate, undervalue; (*despreciar*) to scorn, despise

mensaje [men'saxe] *nm* message; **~ro, a** *nm/f* messenger

menstruación [menstrua'θjon] *nf* menstruation

menstruar [mens'trwar] *vi* to menstruate

mensual [men'swal] *adj* monthly; **1000 ptas ~es** 1000 ptas a month; **~idad** *nf* (*salario*) monthly salary; (*COM*) monthly payment, monthly instalment

menta ['menta] *nf* mint

mental [men'tal] *adj* mental; **~idad** *nf* mentality; **~izar** *vt* (*opinión publica*) to convince; (*padres*) to prepare (mentally); **~izarse** *vr*: **~izarse (de)** to get used to the idea (of)

mentar [men'tar] *vt* to mention, name

mente ['mente] *nf* mind

mentir [men'tir] *vi* to lie

mentira [men'tira] *nf* (*una ~*) lie; (*acto*) lying; (*invención*) fiction; **parece ~ que ...** it seems incredible that ..., I can't believe that ...

mentiroso, a [menti'roso, a] *adj* lying ♦ *nm/f* liar

menú [me'nu] (*pl* **~s**) *nm* menu; (*AM*) set meal

menudo, a [me'nuðo, a] *adj* (*pequeño*) small, tiny; (*sin importancia*) petty, insignificant; **¡~ negocio!** (*fam*) some deal!; **a ~** often, frequently

meñique [me'ɲike] *nm* little finger

meollo [me'ɲoʎo] *nm* (*fig*) core

mercaderías [merkaðe'rias] *nfpl* goods, merchandise *sg*

mercado [mer'kaðo] *nm* market; **M~ Común** Common Market

mercancía [merkan'θia] *nf* commodity; **~s** *nfpl* goods, merchandise *sg*

mercantil [merkan'til] *adj* mercantile, commercial

mercenario, a [merθe'narjo, a] *adj*, *nm* mercenary

mercería [merθe'ria] *nf* haberdashery (*BRIT*), notions (*US*); (*tienda*) haberdasher's (*BRIT*), notions store (*US*); (*AM*) drapery

mercurio [mer'kurjo] *nm* mercury

merecer [mere'θer] *vt* to deserve, merit ♦ *vi* to be deserving, be worthy; **merece la pena** it's worthwhile; **merecido, a** *adj* (well) deserved; **llevar su merecido** to get one's deserts

merendar [meren'dar] *vt* to have for tea ♦ *vi* to have tea; (*en el campo*) to have a picnic

merengue [me'renge] *nm* meringue

meridiano [meri'ðjano] *nm* (*GEO*) meridian

merienda [me'rjenda] *nf* (light) tea, afternoon snack; (*de campo*) picnic

mérito ['merito] *nm* merit; (*valor*) worth, value

merluza [mer'luθa] *nf* hake

merma ['merma] *nf* decrease; (*pérdida*) wastage; **mermar** *vt* to reduce, lessen ♦ *vi* to decrease, dwindle

mermelada [merme'laða] *nf* jam

mero, a ['mero, a] *adj* mere; (*AM: fam*) very

merodear [meroðe'ar] *vi*: **~ por** to prowl about

mes [mes] *nm* month; (*salario*) month's pay

mesa ['mesa] *nf* table; (*de trabajo*) desk; (*GEO*) plateau; (*ARQ*) landing; **~ directiva** board; **~ redonda** (*reunión*) round table; **poner/quitar la ~** to lay/clear the table; **mesero, a** (*AM*) *nm/f* waiter/waitress

meseta [me'seta] *nf* (*GEO*) meseta, tableland; (*ARQ*) landing

mesilla [me'siʎa] *nf*: **~ (de noche)** bedside table

mesón [me'son] *nm* inn

mestizo, a [mes'tiθo, a] *adj* half-caste, of mixed race; (*ZOOL*) crossbred ♦ *nm/f* half-caste

mesura [me'sura] *nf* (*moderación*) moderation, restraint; (*cortesía*) courtesy

meta ['meta] *nf* goal; (*de carrera*) finish

metabolismo [metaßo'lismo] *nm* (*BIO*) metabolism

metáfora [me'tafora] *nf* metaphor

metal [me'tal] *nm* (*materia*) metal; (*MUS*) brass; **metálico, a** *adj* metallic; (*de metal*) metal ♦ *nm* (*dinero contante*) cash

metalurgia [meta'lurxja] *nf* metallurgy

meteoro [mete'oro] *nm* meteor; **~logia** *nf* meteorology

meter [me'ter] *vt* (*colocar*) to put, place; (*introducir*) to put in, insert; (*involucrar*) to involve; (*causar*) to make, cause; **~se** *vr*: **~se en** to go into, enter; (*fig*) to interfere in, meddle in; **~se a** to start; **~se a escri-**

tor to become a writer; ~**se con uno** to provoke sb, pick a quarrel with sb

meticuloso, a [metiku'loso, a] *adj* meticulous, thorough

metódico, a [me'toðiko, a] *adj* methodical

método ['metoðo] *nm* method

metralleta [metra'ʎeta] *nf* sub-machine-gun

métrico, a ['metriko, a] *adj* metric

metro ['metro] *nm* metre; (*tren*) underground (*BRIT*), subway (*US*)

México ['mexiko] *nm* Mexico; **Ciudad de ~** Mexico City

mezcla ['meθkla] *nf* mixture; **mezclar** *vt* to mix (up); **mezclarse** *vr* to mix, mingle; **mezclarse en** to get mixed up in, get involved in

mezquino, a [meθ'kino, a] *adj* (*cicatero*) mean

mezquita [meθ'kita] *nf* mosque

mg. *abr* (= *miligramo*) mg

mi [mi] *adj pos* my ♦ *nm* (*MUS*) E

mí [mi] *pron* me; myself

mía ['mia] *pron ver* **mío**

miaja ['mjaxa] *nf* crumb

micro ['mikro] (*AM*) *nm* minibus

microbio [mi'kroβjo] *nm* microbe

micrófono [mi'krofono] *nm* microphone

microondas [mikro'ondas] *nm inv* (*tb: horno ~*) microwave (oven)

microordenador [mikro(o)rðena'ðor] *nm* microcomputer

microscopio [mikro'skopjo] *nm* microscope

michelín [mitʃe'lin] (*fam*) *nm* (*de grasa*) spare tyre

miedo ['mjeðo] *nm* fear; (*nerviosismo*) apprehension, nervousness; **tener ~** to be afraid; **de ~** wonderful, marvellous; **hace un frío de ~** (*fam*) it's terribly cold; **~so, a** *adj* fearful, timid

miel [mjel] *nf* honey

miembro ['mjembro] *nm* limb; (*socio*) member; **~ viril** penis

mientras ['mjentras] *conj* while; (*duración*) as long as ♦ *adv* meanwhile; **~ tanto** meanwhile; **~ más tiene, más quiere** the more he has, the more he wants

miércoles ['mjerkoles] *nm inv* Wednesday

mierda ['mjerða] (*fam!*) *nf* shit (*!*)

miga ['miɣa] *nf* crumb; (*fig: meollo*) essence; **hacer buenas ~s** (*fam*) to get on well

migración [miɣra'θjon] *nf* migration

mil [mil] *num* thousand; **dos ~ libras** two thousand pounds

milagro [mi'laɣro] *nm* miracle; **~so, a** *adj* miraculous

milésima [mi'lesima] *nf* (*de segundo*) thousandth

mili ['mili] (*fam*) *nf*: **hacer la ~** to do one's military service

milicia [mi'liθja] *nf* militia; (*servicio militar*) military service

milímetro [mi'limetro] *nm* millimetre

militante [mili'tante] *adj* militant

militar [mili'tar] *adj* military ♦ *nm/f* soldier ♦ *vi* to serve in the army; (*fig*) to be a member of a party

milla ['miʎa] *nf* mile

millar [mi'ʎar] *nm* thousand

millón [mi'ʎon] *num* million; **millonario, a** *nm/f* millionaire

mimar [mi'mar] *vt* (*gen*) to spoil, pamper

mimbre ['mimbre] *nm* wicker

mímica ['mimika] *nf* (*para comunicarse*) sign language; (*imitación*) mimicry

mimo ['mimo] *nm* (*caricia*) caress; (*de niño*) spoiling; (*TEATRO*) mime; (: *actor*) mime artist

mina ['mina] *nf* mine; **minar** *vt* to mine; (*fig*) to undermine

mineral [mine'ral] *adj* mineral ♦ *nm* (*GEO*) mineral; (*mena*) ore

minero, a [mi'nero, a] *adj* mining *cpd* ♦ *nm/f* miner

miniatura [minja'tura] *adj inv*, *nf* miniature

minifalda [mini'falda] *nf* miniskirt

mínimo, a ['minimo, a] *adj*, *nm* minimum

minino, a [mi'nino, a] (*fam*) *nm/f* puss, pussy

ministerio [minis'terjo] *nm* Ministry; **M~ de Hacienda/del Exterior** Treasury (*BRIT*), Treasury Department (*US*)/Foreign Office (*BRIT*), State Department (*US*)

ministro, a [mi'nistro, a] *nm/f* minister

minoría [mino'ria] *nf* minority

minucioso, a [minu'θjoso, a] *adj* thorough, meticulous; (*prolijo*) very detailed

minúscula [mi'nuskula] *nf* small letter

minúsculo, a [mi'nuskulo, a] *adj* tiny, minute

minusválido, a [minus'βaliðo, a] *adj* (physically) handicapped ♦ *nm/f* (physically) handicapped person

minuta [mi'nuta] *nf* (*de comida*) menu

minutero [minu'tero] *nm* minute hand

minuto [mi'nuto] *nm* minute

mío, a ['mio, a] *pron*: **el ~/la mía** mine; **un amigo ~** a friend of mine; **lo ~** what is mine

miope [mi'ope] *adj* short-sighted

mira ['mira] *nf* (*de arma*) sight(s) (*pl*); (*fig*) aim, intention

mirada [mi'raða] *nf* look, glance; (*expresión*) look, expression; **clavar la ~ en** to stare at; **echar una ~ a** to glance at

mirado, a [mi'raðo, a] *adj* (*sensato*) sensible; (*considerado*) considerate; **bien/mal ~** well/not well thought of; **bien ~** all things considered

mirador [mira'ðor] *nm* viewpoint, vantage point

mirar [mi'rar] *vt* to look at; (*observar*) to

watch; (*considerar*) to consider, think over; (*vigilar, cuidar*) to watch, look after ♦ *vi* to look; (*ARQ*) to face; ~**se** *vr* (*dos personas*) to look at each other; ~ **bien/mal** to think highly of/have a poor opinion of; ~**se al espejo** to look at o.s. in the mirror

mirilla [mi'riʎa] *nf* (*agujero*) spyhole, peephole

mirlo ['mirlo] *nm* blackbird

misa ['misa] *nf* (*REL*) mass

miserable [mise'raßle] *adj* (*avaro*) mean, stingy; (*nimio*) miserable, paltry; (*lugar*) squalid; (*fam*) vile, despicable ♦ *nm/f* (*malvado*) rogue

miseria [mi'serja] *nf* misery; (*pobreza*) poverty; (*tacañería*) meanness, stinginess; (*condiciones*) squalor; **una ~** a pittance

misericordia [miseri'korðja] *nf* (*compasión*) compassion, pity; (*piedad*) mercy

misil [mi'sil] *nm* missile

misión [mi'sjon] *nf* mission; **misionero, a** *nm/f* missionary

mismo, a ['mismo, a] *adj* (*semejante*) same; (*después de pron*) -self; (*para énfasis*) very ♦ *adv*: **aquí/hoy ~** right here/this very day; **ahora ~** right now ♦ *conj*: **lo ~ que** just like, just as; **el ~ traje** the same suit; **en ese ~ momento** at that very moment; **vino el ~ Ministro** the minister himself came; **yo ~ lo vi** I saw it myself; **lo ~** the same (thing); **da lo ~** it's all the same; **quedamos en las mismas** we're no further forward; **por lo ~** for the same reason

misterio [mis'terjo] *nm* (*gen*) mystery; (*lo secreto*) secrecy; ~**so, a** *adj* mysterious

mitad [mi'tað] *nf* (*medio*) half; (*centro*) middle; **a ~ de precio** (at) half-price; **en o a ~ del camino** halfway along the road; **cortar por la ~** to cut through the middle

mitigar [miti'ɣar] *vt* to mitigate; (*dolor*) to ease; (*sed*) to quench

mitin ['mitin] (*pl* **mítines**) *nm* meeting

mito ['mito] *nm* myth

mixto, a ['miksto, a] *adj* mixed

ml. *abr* (= *mililitro*) ml

mm. *abr* (= *milímetro*) mm

mobiliario [moßi'ljarjo] *nm* furniture

moción [mo'θjon] *nf* motion

moco ['moko] *nm* mucus; ~**s** *nmpl* (*fam*) snot; **quitarse los ~s de la nariz** (*fam*) to wipe one's nose

mochila [mo'tʃila] *nf* rucksack (*BRIT*), back-pack

moda ['moða] *nf* fashion; (*estilo*) style; **a la o de ~** in fashion, fashionable; **pasado de ~** out of fashion

modales [mo'ðales] *nmpl* manners

modalidad [moðali'ðað] *nf* kind, variety

modelar [moðe'lar] *vt* to model

modelo [mo'ðelo] *adj inv, nm/f* model

módem ['moðem] *nm* (*INFORM*) modem

moderado, a [moðe'raðo, a] *adj* moderate

moderar [moðe'rar] *vt* to moderate; (*violencia*) to restrain, control; (*velocidad*) to reduce; ~**se** *vr* to restrain o.s., control o.s.

modernizar [moðerni'θar] *vt* to modernize

moderno, a [mo'ðerno, a] *adj* modern; (*actual*) present-day

modestia [mo'ðestja] *nf* modesty; **modesto, a** *adj* modest

módico, a ['moðiko, a] *adj* moderate, reasonable

modificar [moðifi'kar] *vt* to modify

modisto, a [mo'ðisto, a] *nm/f* dressmaker

modo ['moðo] *nm* (*manera, forma*) way, manner; (*MUS*) mode; ~**s** *nmpl* manners; **de ningún ~** in no way; **de todos ~s** at any rate; ~ **de empleo** directions *pl* (for use)

modorra [mo'ðorra] *nf* drowsiness

mofa ['mofa] *nf*: **hacer ~ de** to mock; **mofarse** *vr*: **mofarse de** to mock, scoff at

mogollón [moɣo'ʎon] (*fam*) *adv* (*gustar, beber*) a hell of a lot

moho ['moo] *nm* (*BOT*) mould, mildew; (*en metal*) rust; ~**so, a** *adj* mouldy; rusty

mojar [mo'xar] *vt* to wet; (*humedecer*) to damp(en), moisten; (*calar*) to soak; ~**se** *vr* to get wet

mojón [mo'xon] *nm* boundary stone

molde ['molde] *nm* mould; (*COSTURA*) pattern; (*fig*) model; ~**ar** *vt* to mould

mole ['mole] *nf* mass, bulk; (*edificio*) pile

moler [mo'ler] *vt* to grind, crush; (*cansar*) to tire out, exhaust

molestar [moles'tar] *vt* to bother; (*fastidiar*) to annoy; (*incomodar*) to inconvenience, put out ♦ *vi* to be a nuisance; ~**se** *vr* to bother; (*incomodarse*) to go to trouble; (*ofenderse*) to take offence

molestia [mo'lestja] *nf* bother, trouble; (*incomodidad*) inconvenience; (*MED*) discomfort; **es una ~** it's a nuisance; **molesto, a** *adj* (*que fastidia*) annoying; (*incómodo*) inconvenient; (*inquieto*) uncomfortable, ill at ease; (*enfadado*) annoyed

molido, a [mo'liðo, a] *adj*: **estar ~** (*fig*) to be exhausted *o* dead beat

molinillo [moli'niʎo] *nm*: ~ **de carne/café** mincer/coffee grinder

molino [mo'lino] *nm* (*edificio*) mill; (*máquina*) grinder

momentáneo, a [momen'taneo, a] *adj* momentary

momento [mo'mento] *nm* (*gen*) moment; (*TEC*) momentum; **de ~** at the moment, for the moment

momia ['momja] *nf* mummy

monarca [mo'narka] *nm/f* monarch, ruler; **monarquía** *nf* monarchy; **monárquico, a** *nm/f* royalist, monarchist

monasterio [monas'terjo] *nm* monastery

mondar [mon'dar] *vt* (*limpiar*) to clean; (*pelar*) to peel; ~**se** *vr*: ~**se de risa** (*fam*) to split one's sides laughing

moneda [mo'neða] *nf* (*tipo de dinero*) currency, money; (*pieza*) coin; **una ~ de 5 pesetas** a 5 peseta piece; **monedero** *nm* purse; **monetario, a** *adj* monetary, financial

monitor, a [moni'tor, a] *nm/f* instructor, coach ♦ *nm* (*TV*) set; (*INFORM*) monitor

monja ['monxa] *nf* nun

monje ['monxe] *nm* monk

mono, a ['mono, a] *adj* (*bonito*) lovely, pretty; (*gracioso*) nice, charming ♦ *nm/f* monkey, ape ♦ *nm* dungarees *pl*; (*overoles*) overalls *pl*

monopatín [monopa'tin] *nm* skateboard

monopolio [mono'poljo] *nm* monopoly; **monopolizar** *vt* to monopolize

monotonía [monoto'nia] *nf* (*sonido*) monotone; (*fig*) monotony

monótono, a [mo'notono, a] *adj* monotonous

monstruo ['monstrwo] *nm* monster ♦ *adj inv* fantastic; **~so, a** *adj* monstrous

montaje [mon'taxe] *nm* assembly; (*TEATRO*) décor; (*CINE*) montage

montaña [mon'taɲa] *nf* (*monte*) mountain; (*sierra*) mountains *pl*, mountainous area; (*AM: selva*) forest; **~ rusa** roller coaster; **montañero, a** *nm/f* mountaineer ♦ *nm/f* highlander; **montañismo** *nm* mountaineering

montar [mon'tar] *vt* (*subir a*) to mount, get on; (*TEC*) to assemble, put together; (*negocio*) to set up; (*arma*) to cock; (*colocar*) to lift on to; (*CULIN*) to beat ♦ *vi* to mount, get on; (*sobresalir*) to overlap; **~ en cólera** to get angry; **~ a caballo** to ride, go horseriding

monte ['monte] *nm* (*montaña*) mountain; (*bosque*) woodland; (*área sin cultivar*) wild area, wild country; **M~ de Piedad** pawnshop

monto ['monto] *nm* total, amount

montón [mon'ton] *nm* heap, pile; (*fig*): **un ~ de** heaps of, lots of

monumento [monu'mento] *nm* monument

monzón [mon'θon] *nm* monsoon

moño ['moɲo] *nm* bun

moqueta [mo'keta] *nf* fitted carpet

mora ['mora] *nf* blackberry; *ver tb* **moro**

morada [mo'raða] *nf* (*casa*) dwelling, abode

morado, a [mo'raðo, a] *adj* purple, violet ♦ *nm* bruise

moral [mo'ral] *adj* moral ♦ *nf* (*ética*) ethics *pl*; (*moralidad*) morals *pl*, morality; (*ánimo*) morale

moraleja [mora'lexa] *nf* moral

moralidad [morali'ðað] *nf* morals *pl*, morality

morboso, a [mor'βoso, a] *adj* morbid

morcilla [mor'θiʎa] *nf* blood sausage, ≈ black pudding (*BRIT*)

mordaz [mor'ðaθ] *adj* (*crítica*) biting, scathing

mordaza [mor'ðaθa] *nf* (*para la boca*) gag; (*TEC*) clamp

morder [mor'ðer] *vt* to bite; (*mordisquear*) to nibble; (*fig: consumir*) to eat away, eat into; **mordisco** *nm* bite

moreno, a [mo'reno, a] *adj* (*color*) (dark) brown; (*de tez*) dark; (*de pelo ~*) dark-haired; (*negro*) black

morfina [mor'fina] *nf* morphine

moribundo, a [mori'βundo, a] *adj* dying

morir [mo'rir] *vi* to die; (*fuego*) to die down; (*luz*) to go out; **~se** *vr* to die; (*fig*) to be dying; **fue muerto en un accidente** he was killed in an accident; **~se por algo** to be dying for sth

moro, a ['moro, a] *adj* Moorish ♦ *nm/f* Moor

moroso, a [mo'roso, a] *nm/f* (*COM*) bad debtor, defaulter

morral [mo'rral] *nm* haversack

morro ['morro] *nm* (*ZOOL*) snout, nose; (*AUTO, AVIAT*) nose

morsa ['morsa] *nf* walrus

mortaja [mor'taxa] *nf* shroud

mortal [mor'tal] *adj* mortal; (*golpe*) deadly; **~idad** *nf* mortality

mortero [mor'tero] *nm* mortar

mortífero, a [mor'tifero, a] *adj* deadly, lethal

mortificar [mortifi'kar] *vt* to mortify

mosca ['moska] *nf* fly

Moscú [mos'ku] *n* Moscow

mosquearse [moske'arse] (*fam*) *vr* (*enojarse*) to get cross; (*ofenderse*) to take offence

mosquitero [moski'tero] *nm* mosquito net

mosquito [mos'kito] *nm* mosquito

mostaza [mos'taθa] *nf* mustard

mostrador [mostra'ðor] *nm* (*de tienda*) counter; (*de café*) bar

mostrar [mos'trar] *vt* to show; (*exhibir*) to display, exhibit; (*explicar*) to explain; **~se** *vr*: **~se amable** to be kind; to prove to be kind; **no se muestra muy inteligente** he doesn't seem (to be) very intelligent

mota ['mota] *nf* speck, tiny piece; (*en diseño*) dot

mote ['mote] *nm* (*apodo*) nickname

motín [mo'tin] *nm* (*del pueblo*) revolt, rising; (*del ejército*) mutiny

motivar [moti'βar] *vt* (*causar*) to cause, motivate; (*explicar*) to explain, justify; **motivo** *nm* motive, reason

moto ['moto] (*fam*) *nf* = **motocicleta**

motocicleta [motoθi'kleta] *nf* motorbike (*BRIT*), motorcycle

motor [mo'tor] *nm* motor, engine; **~ a chorro** *o* **de reacción/de explosión** jet engine/internal combustion engine

motora [mo'tora] *nf* motorboat

movedizo, a [moβe'ðiθo, a] *adj (inseguro)* unsteady; *(fig)* unsettled, changeable; *(persona)* fickle

mover [mo'βer] *vt* to move; *(cabeza)* to shake; *(accionar)* to drive; *(fig)* to cause, provoke; **~se** *vr* to move; *(fig)* to get a move on

móvil ['moβil] *adj* mobile; *(pieza de máquina)* moving; *(mueble)* movable ♦ *nm* motive; **movilidad** *nf* mobility; **movilizar** *vt* to mobilize

movimiento [moβi'mjento] *nm* movement; *(TEC)* motion; *(actividad)* activity

mozo, a ['moθo, a] *adj (joven)* young ♦ *nm/f (joven)* youth, young man/girl; *(camarero)* waiter; *(camarera)* waitress

muchacho, a [mu'tʃatʃo, a] *nm/f (niño)* boy/girl; *(criado)* servant; *(criada)* maid

muchedumbre [mutʃe'ðumbre] *nf* crowd

┌─────── *PALABRA CLAVE*

mucho, a ['mutʃo, a] *adj* **1** *(cantidad)* a lot of, much; *(número)* lots of, a lot of, many; **~ dinero** a lot of money; **hace ~ calor** it's very hot; **muchas amigas** lots *o* a lot of friends

2 *(sg: grande)*: **ésta es mucha casa para él** this house is much too big for him

♦ *pron*: **tengo ~ que hacer** I've got a lot to do; **~s dicen que ...** a lot of people say that ...; *ver tb* **tener**

♦ *adv* **1**: **me gusta ~** I like it a lot; **lo siento ~** I'm very sorry; **come ~** he eats a lot; **¿te vas a quedar ~?** are you going to be staying long?

2 *(respuesta)* very; **¿estás cansado? – ¡~!** are you tired? – very!

3 *(locuciones)*: **como ~** at (the) most; **con ~**: **el mejor con ~** by far the best; **ni ~ menos**: **no es rico ni ~ menos** he's far from being rich

4: **por ~ que**: **por ~ que le creas** no matter how *o* however much you believe her

└───────────────────────

muda ['muða] *nf* change of clothes

mudanza [mu'ðanθa] *nf (cambio)* change; *(de casa)* move

mudar [mu'ðar] *vt* to change; *(ZOOL)* to shed ♦ *vi* to change; **~se** *vr (la ropa)* to change; **~se de casa** to move house

mudo, a ['muðo, a] *adj* dumb; *(callado, CINE)* silent

mueble ['mweβle] *nm* piece of furniture; **~s** *nmpl* furniture *sg*

mueca ['mweka] *nf* face, grimace; **hacer ~s a** to make faces at

muela ['mwela] *nf (diente)* tooth; *(: de atrás)* molar

muelle ['mweʎe] *nm* spring; *(NAUT)* wharf; *(malecón)* pier

muero *etc vb ver* **morir**

muerte ['mwerte] *nf* death; *(homicidio)* murder; **dar ~ a** to kill

muerto, a ['mwerto, a] *pp de* **morir** ♦ *adj* dead; *(color)* dull ♦ *nm/f* dead man/woman; *(difunto)* deceased; *(cadáver)* corpse; **estar ~ de cansancio** to be dead tired

muestra ['mwestra] *nf (señal)* indication, sign; *(demostración)* demonstration; *(prueba)* proof; *(estadística)* sample; *(modelo)* model, pattern; *(testimonio)* token

muestreo [mwes'treo] *nm* sample, sampling

muestro *etc vb ver* **mostrar**

muevo *etc vb ver* **mover**

mugir [mu'xir] *vi (vaca)* to moo

mugre ['muxre] *nf* dirt, filth; **mugriento, a** *adj* dirty, filthy

mujer [mu'xer] *nf* woman; *(esposa)* wife; **~iego** *nm* womanizer

mula ['mula] *nf* mule

mulato, a [mu'lato, a] *adj, nm/f* mulatto

muleta [mu'leta] *nf (para andar)* crutch; *(TAUROMAQUIA)* stick with red cape attached

multa ['multa] *nf* fine; **poner una ~ a** to fine; **multar** *vt* to fine

multicopista [multiko'pista] *nm* duplicator

multinacional [multinaθjo'nal] *nf (COM)* multinational

múltiple ['multiple] *adj* multiple; *(pl)* many, numerous

multiplicar [multipli'kar] *vt (MAT)* to multiply; *(fig)* to increase; **~se** *vr (BIO)* to multiply; *(fig)* to be everywhere at once

multitud [multi'tuð] *nf (muchedumbre)* crowd; **~ de cosas** lot of

mullido, a [mu'ʎiðo, a] *adj (cama)* soft; *(hierba)* soft, springy

mundano, a [mun'dano, a] *adj* worldly; *(de moda)* fashionable

mundial [mun'djal] *adj* world-wide, universal; *(guerra, récord)* world *cpd*

mundo ['mundo] *nm* world; **todo el ~** everybody; **tener ~** to be experienced, know one's way around

munición [muni'θjon] *nf (MIL: provisiones)* stores *pl*, supplies *pl*; *(: balas)* ammunition

municipal [muniθi'pal] *adj* municipal, local

municipio [muni'θipjo] *nm (ayuntamiento)* town council, corporation; *(territorio administrativo)* town, municipality

muñeca [mu'ɲeka] *nf (ANAT)* wrist; *(juguete)* doll

muñeco [mu'ɲeko] *nm (figura)* figure; *(marioneta)* puppet; *(fig)* puppet, pawn

mural [mu'ral] *adj* mural, wall *cpd* ♦ *nm* mural

muralla [mu'raʎa] *nf (city)* wall(s) *(pl)*

murciélago [mur'θjelaxo] *nm* bat

murmullo [mur'muʎo] *nm* murmur(ing); *(cuchicheo)* whispering; *(de arroyo)* murmur, rippling

murmuración [murmura'θjon] *nf* gossip;
  murmurar *vi* to murmur, whisper; (*criticar*)
  to criticize; (*cotillear*) to gossip

muro [='muro] *nm* wall

muscular [musku'lar] *adj* muscular

músculo ['muskulo] *nm* muscle

museo [mu'seo] *nm* museum

musgo ['musɣo] *nm* moss

música ['musika] *nf* music; *ver tb* **músico**

músico, a ['musiko, a] *adj* musical ♦ *nm/f*
  musician

musitar [musi'tar] *vt*, *vi* to mutter, mumble

muslo ['muslo] *nm* thigh

mustio, a ['mustjo, a] *adj* (*persona*) depressed, gloomy; (*planta*) faded, withered

musulmán, ana [musul'man, ana] *nm/f*
  Moslem

mutación [muta'θjon] *nf* (*BIO*) mutation; (:
  cambio) (sudden) change

mutilar [muti'lar] *vt* to mutilate; (*a una per-*
  sona) to maim

mutismo [mu'tismo] *nm* (*de persona*) un-
  communicativeness; (*de autoridades*) silence

mutuamente [mutwa'mente] *adv* mutually

mutuo, a ['mutwo, a] *adj* mutual

muy [mwi] *adv* very; (*demasiado*) too; M~
  Señor mío Dear Sir; ~ de noche very late
  at night; eso es ~ de él that's just like him

N n

ñ *see under letter* **Ñ**, *after* **N**

N *abr* (= *norte*) N

nabo ['naβo] *nm* turnip

nácar ['nakar] *nm* mother-of-pearl

nacer [na'θer] *vi* to be born; (*de huevo*) to
  hatch; (*vegetal*) to sprout; (*río*) to rise; nací
  en Barcelona I was born in Barcelona; na-
  ció una sospecha en su mente a suspicion formed in her mind; **nacido, a** *adj*
  born; **recién nacido** newborn; **naciente**
  adj new, emerging; (*sol*) rising; **nacimiento**
  nm birth; (*fig*) birth, origin; (*de Navidad*)
  Nativity; (*linaje*) descent, family; (*de río*)
  source

nación [na'θjon] *nf* nation; **nacional** *adj*
  national; **nacionalismo** *nm* nationalism;
  nacionalista *nm/f* nationalist; **nacionalizar** *vt* to nationalize; **nacionalizarse** *vr*
  (*persona*) to become naturalized

nada ['naða] *pron* nothing ♦ *adv* not at all,
  in no way; **no decir** ~ to say nothing, not
  to say anything; ~ **más** nothing else; de ~

don't mention it

nadador, a [naða'ðor, a] *nm/f* swimmer

nadar [na'ðar] *vi* to swim

nadie ['naðje] *pron* nobody, no-one; ~ habló nobody spoke; no había ~ there was
  nobody there, there wasn't anybody there

nado ['naðo]: a ~ *adv*: pasar a ~ to swim
  across

nafta ['nafta] (*AM*) *nf* petrol (*BRIT*), gas (*US*)

naipe ['naipe] *nm* (playing) card; ~s *nmpl*
  cards

nalgas ['nalɣas] *nfpl* buttocks

nana ['nana] *nf* lullaby

naranja [na'ranxa] *adj inv*, *nf* orange; media
  ~ (*fam*) better half; **naranjada** *nf* orange-
  ade; **naranjo** *nm* orange tree

narciso [nar'θiso] *nm* narcissus

narcótico, a [nar'kotiko, a] *adj, nm* narcotic; **narcotizar** *vt* to drug; **narcotráfico**
  nm drug trafficking *o* running

nardo ['narðo] *nm* lily

narigón, ona, [nari'ɣon, ona] *adj* big-
  nosed

narigudo, a [narɪ'ɣuðo, a] *adj* = **narigón**

nariz [na'riθ] *nf* nose; narices *nfpl* nostrils;
  delante de las narices de uno under one's
  (very) nose

narración [narra'θjon] *nf* narration; **narra-
  dor, a** *nm/f* narrator

narrar [na'rrar] *vt* to narrate, recount; **na-
  rrativa** *nf* narrative, story

nata ['nata] *nf* cream

natación [nata'θjon] *nf* swimming

natal [na'tal] *adj*: ciudad ~ home town;
  ~idad *nf* birth rate

natillas [na'tiʎas] *nfpl* custard *sg*

nativo, a [na'tiβo, a] *adj, nm/f* native

nato, a ['nato, a] *adj* born; un músico ~ a
  born musician

natural [natu'ral] *adj* natural; (*fruta etc*)
  fresh ♦ *nm/f* native ♦ *nm* (*disposición*) nature

naturaleza [natura'leθa] *nf* nature; (*género*)
  nature, kind; ~ muerta still life

naturalidad [naturali'ðað] *nf* naturalness

naturalmente [natural'mente] *adv* (*de
  modo natural*) in a natural way; ¡~! of
  course!

naufragar [naufra'ɣar] *vi* to sink; **naufragio** *nm* shipwreck; **náufrago, a** *nm/f* castaway, shipwrecked person

nauseabundo, a [nausea'βundo, a] *adj*
  nauseating, sickening

náuseas ['nauseas] *nfpl* nausea; me da ~ it
  makes me feel sick

náutico, a ['nautiko, a] *adj* nautical

navaja [na'βaxa] *nf* (*cortaplumas*) clasp
  knife (*BRIT*), penknife; (*de barbero, peluquero*) razor

naval [na'βal] *adj* (*MIL*: combat, escuela) naval

Navarra [na'βarra] *n* Navarre

nave ['naβe] *nf* (*barco*) ship, vessel; (*ARQ*) nave; ~ **espacial** spaceship

navegación [naβeɣa'θjon] *nf* navigation; (*viaje*) sea journey; ~ **aérea** air traffic; ~ **costera** coastal shipping; **navegante** *nm/f* navigator; **navegar** *vi* (*barco*) to sail; (*avión*) to fly ♦ *vt* to sail; to fly; (*dirigir el rumbo*) to navigate

navidad [naβi'ðað] *nf* Christmas; ~**es** *nfpl* Christmas time; **navideño, a** *adj* Christmas *cpd*

navío [na'βio] *nm* ship

nazca *etc vb ver* **nacer**

nazi ['naθi] *adj, nm/f* Nazi

NE *abr* (= *nor(d)este*) NE

neblina [ne'βlina] *nf* mist

nebuloso, a [neβu'loso, a] *adj* foggy; (*calinoso*) misty; (*indefinido*) nebulous, vague ♦ *nf* nebula

necedad [neθe'ðað] *nf* foolishness; (*una* ~) foolish act

necesario, a [neθe'sarjo, a] *adj* necessary

neceser [neθe'ser] *nm* toilet bag; (*bolsa grande*) holdall

necesidad [neθesi'ðað] *nf* need; (*lo inevitable*) necessity; (*miseria*) poverty, need; **en caso de** ~ in case of need *o* emergency; **hacer sus** ~**es** to relieve o.s

necesitado, a [neθesi'tado, a] *adj* needy, poor; ~ **de** in need of

necesitar [neθesi'tar] *vt* to need, require ♦ *vi*: ~ **de** to have need of

necio, a ['neθjo, a] *adj* foolish

necrópolis [ne'kropolis] *nf inv* cemetery

nectarina [nekta'rina] *nf* nectarine

nefasto, a [ne'fasto, a] *adj* ill-fated, unlucky

negación [neɣa'θjon] *nf* negation; (*rechazo*) refusal, denial

negar [ne'ɣar] *vt* (*renegar, rechazar*) to refuse; (*prohibir*) to refuse, deny; (*desmentir*) to deny; ~**se** *vr*: ~**se a** to refuse to

negativa [neɣa'tiβa] *nf* negative; (*rechazo*) refusal, denial

negativo, a [neɣa'tiβo, a] *adj, nm* negative

negligencia [neɣli'xenθja] *nf* negligence; **negligente** *adj* negligent

negociable [neɣo'θjaβle] *adj* (*COM*) negotiable

negociado [neɣo'θjaðo] *nm* department, section

negociante [neɣo'θjante] *nm/f* businessman/woman

negociar [neɣo'θjar] *vt, vi* to negotiate; ~ **en** to deal in, trade in

negocio [ne'ɣoθjo] *nm* (*COM*) business; (*asunto*) affair, business; (*operación comercial*) deal, transaction; (*AM*) firm; (*lugar*) place of business; **los** ~**s** business *sg*; **hacer** ~ to do business

negra ['neɣra] *nf* (*MUS*) crotchet; *ver tb* **negro**

negro, a ['neɣro, a] *adj* black; (*suerte*) awful ♦ *nm* black ♦ *nm/f* Negro/Negress, Black

nene, a ['nene, a] *nm/f* baby, small child

nenúfar [ne'nufar] *nm* water lily

neologismo [neolo'xismo] *nm* neologism

neón [ne'on] *nm*: **luces/lámpara de** ~ neon lights/lamp

neoyorquino, a [neojor'kino, a] *adj* (of) New York

nepotismo [nepo'tismo] *nm* nepotism

nervio ['nerβjo] *nm* (*ANAT*) nerve; (: *tendón*) tendon; (*fig*) vigour; **nerviosismo** *nm* nervousness, nerves *pl*; ~**so, a** *adj* nervous

neto, a ['neto, a] *adj* clear; (*limpio*) clean; (*COM*) net

neumático, a [neu'matiko, a] *adj* pneumatic ♦ *nm* (*ESP*) tyre (*BRIT*), tire (*US*); ~ **de recambio** spare tyre

neurasténico, a [neuras'teniko, a] *adj* (*fig*) hysterical

neurólogo, a [neu'roloɣo, a] *nm/f* neurologist

neurona [neu'rona] *nf* (*ANAT*) nerve cell

neutral [neu'tral] *adj* neutral; ~**izar** *vt* to neutralize; (*contrarrestar*) to counteract

neutro, a ['neutro, a] *adj* (*BIO, LING*) neuter

neutrón [neu'tron] *nm* neutron

nevada [ne'βaða] *nf* snowstorm; (*caída de nieve*) snowfall

nevar [ne'βar] *vi* to snow

nevera [ne'βera] (*ESP*) *nf* refrigerator (*BRIT*), icebox (*US*)

nevería [neβe'ria] (*AM*) *nf* ice-cream parlour

nexo ['nekso] *nm* link, connection

ni [ni] *conj* nor, neither; (*tb*: ~ **siquiera**) not ... even; ~ **que** not even if; ~ **blanco** ~ **negro** neither white nor black

Nicaragua [nika'raɣwa] *nf* Nicaragua; **nicaragüense** *adj, nm/f* Nicaraguan

nicotina [niko'tina] *nf* nicotine

nicho ['nitʃo] *nm* niche

nido ['niðo] *nm* nest; (*fig*) hiding place

niebla ['njeβla] *nf* fog; (*neblina*) mist

niego *etc vb ver* **negar**

nieto, a ['njeto, a] *nm/f* grandson/daughter; ~**s** *nmpl* grandchildren

nieve *etc* ['njeβe] *vb ver* **nevar** ♦ *nf* snow; (*AM*) icecream

nimiedad [nimje'ðað] *nf* small-mindedness; (*trivialidad*) triviality

nimio, a ['nimjo, a] *adj* trivial, insignificant

ninfa ['ninfa] *nf* nymph

ninfómana [nin'fomana] *nf* nymphomaniac

ningún [nin'gun] *adj ver* **ninguno**

ninguno, a [nin'guno, a] *adj* (*delante de nm*: **ningún**) no ♦ *pron* (*nadie*) nobody; (*ni uno*) none, not one; (*ni uno ni otro*) neither; **de ninguna manera** by no means, not at all

niña ['niɲa] *nf* (*ANAT*) pupil; *ver tb* **niño**

niñera '[ni'ɲera] *nf* nursemaid, nanny; **niñería** *nf* childish act

niñez [ni'ɲeθ] *nf* (*infancia*) childhood; (*infancia*) infancy

niño, a ['niɲo, a] *adj* (*joven*) young; (*inmaduro*) immature ♦ *nm/f* child, boy/girl

nipón, ona [ni'pon, ona] *adj*, *nm/f* Japanese

níquel ['nikel] *nm* nickel; **niquelar** *vt* (*TEC*) to nickel-plate

níspero [ni'spero] *nm* medlar

nitidez [niti'ðeθ] *nf* (*claridad*) clarity; (: *de atmósfera*) brightness; (: *de imagen*) sharpness; **nítido, a** *adj* clear; sharp

nitrato [ni'trato] *nm* nitrate

nitrógeno [ni'troxeno] *nm* nitrogen

nitroglicerina [nitroxliθe'rina] *nf* nitroglycerine

nivel [ni'ßel] *nm* (*GEO*) level; (*norma*) level, standard; (*altura*) height; ~ **de aceite** oil level; ~ **de aire** spirit level; ~ **de vida** standard of living; **~ar** *vt* to level out; (*fig*) to even up; (*COM*) to balance

NN. UU. *nfpl abr* (= *Naciones Unidas*) UN *sg*

no [no] *adv* no; not; (*con verbo*) not ♦ *excl* no!; ~ **tengo nada** I don't have anything, I have nothing; ~ **es el mío** it's not mine; **ahora** ~ not now; **¿~ lo sabes?** don't you know?; ~ **mucho** not much; ~ **bien termine, lo entregaré** as soon as I finish I'll hand it over; ~ **más: ayer** ~ **más** just yesterday; **¡pase** ~ **más!** come in!; **¡a que ~ lo sabes!** I bet you don't know!; **¡cómo ~!** of course!; **los países** ~ **alineados** the non-aligned countries; **la** ~ **intervención** non-intervention

noble ['noßle] *adj*, *nm/f* noble; **~za** *nf* nobility

noción [no'θjon] *nf* notion

nocivo, a [no'θiβo, a] *adj* harmful

noctámbulo, a [nok'tambulo, a] *nm/f* sleepwalker

nocturno, a [nok'turno, a] *adj* (*de la noche*) nocturnal, night *cpd*; (*de la tarde*) evening *cpd* ♦ *nm* nocturne

noche ['notʃe] *nf* night, night-time; (*la tarde*) evening; (*fig*) darkness; **de** ~, **por la** ~ at night

nochebuena [notʃe'ßwena] *nf* Christmas Eve

nochevieja [notʃe'ßjexa] *nf* New Year's Eve

nodriza [no'ðriθa] *nf* wet nurse; **buque** *o* **nave** ~ supply ship

nogal [no'val] *nm* walnut tree

nómada ['nomaða] *adj* nomadic ♦ *nm/f* nomad

nombramiento [nombra'mjento] *nm* naming; (*a un empleo*) appointment

nombrar [nom'brar] *vt* (*designar*) to name; (*mencionar*) to mention; (*dar puesto a*) to appoint

nombre ['nombre] *nm* name; (*sustantivo*) noun; (*fama*) renown; ~ **y apellidos** name in full; ~ **común/propio** common/proper noun; ~ **de pila/de soltera** Christian/maiden name; **poner** ~ **a** to call, name

nomenclatura [nomenkla'tura] *nf* nomenclature

nomeolvides [nomeol'ßiðes] *nm inv* forget-me-not

nómina ['nomina] *nf* (*lista*) list; (*COM*) payroll

nominal [nomi'nal] *adj* nominal

nominar [nomi'nar] *vt* to nominate

nominativo, a [nomina'tißo, a] *adj* (*COM*): **cheque** ~ **a X** cheque made out to X

nono, a ['nono, a] *adj* ninth

nordeste [nor'ðeste] *adj* north-east, north-eastern, north-easterly ♦ *nm* north-east

nórdico, a ['norðiko, a] *adj* (*del norte*) northern, northerly; (*escandinavo*) Nordic

noreste [no'reste] *adj*, *nm* = **nordeste**

noria ['norja] *nf* (*AGR*) waterwheel; (*de carnaval*) big (*BRIT*) *o* Ferris (*US*) wheel

norma ['norma] *nf* rule (of thumb)

normal [nor'mal] *adj* (*corriente*) normal; (*habitual*) usual, natural; (**gasolina**) ~ two-star petrol; **~idad** *nf* normality; **restablecer la ~idad** to restore order; **~izar** *vt* (*reglamentar*) to normalize; (*TEC*) to standardize; **~izarse** *vr* to return to normal

normando, a [nor'mando, a] *adj*, *nm/f* Norman

normativa [norma'tißa] *nf* (set of) rules

noroeste [noro'este] *adj* north-west, north-western, north-westerly ♦ *nm* north-west

norte ['norte] *adj* north, northern, northerly ♦ *nm* north; (*fig*) guide

norteamericano, a [norteameri'kano, a] *adj*, *nm/f* (North) American

Noruega [no'rweɣa] *nf* Norway

noruego, a [no'rweɣo, a] *adj*, *nm/f* Norwegian

nos [nos] *pron* (*directo*) us; (*indirecto*) us; to us; for us; from us; (*reflexivo*) (to) ourselves; (*recíproco*) (to) each other; ~ **levantamos a las 7** we get up at 7

nosotros, as [no'sotros, as] *pron* (*sujeto*) we; (*después de prep*) us

nostalgia [nos'talxja] *nf* nostalgia

nota ['nota] *nf* note; (*ESCOL*) mark

notable [no'taßle] *adj* notable; (*ESCOL*) outstanding ♦ *nm/f* notable

notar [no'tar] *vt* to notice, note; **~se** *vr* to be obvious; **se nota que ...** one observes that ...

notarial [nota'rjal] *adj*: **acta** ~ affidavit

notario [no'tarjo] *nm* notary

noticia [no'tiθja] *nf* (*información*) piece of news; **las ~s** the news *sg*; **tener ~s de alguien** to hear from sb

noticiero [noti'θjero] (AM) nm news bulletin

notificación [notifika'θjon] nf notification; **notificar** vt to notify, inform

notoriedad [notorje'ðað] nf fame, renown; **notorio, a** adj (público) well-known; (evidente) obvious

novato, a [no'ßato, a] adj inexperienced ♦ nm/f beginner, novice

novecientos, as [noße'θjentos, as] num nine hundred

novedad [noße'ðað] nf (calidad de nuevo) newness; (noticia) piece of news; (cambio) change, (new) development

novel [no'ßel] adj new; (inexperto) inexperienced ♦ nm/f beginner

novela [no'ßela] nf novel

novelero, a [noße'lero, a] adj highly imaginative

noveno, a [no'ßeno, a] adj ninth

noventa [no'ßenta] num ninety

novia ['noßja] nf ver novio

noviazgo [no'ßjaθvo] nm engagement

novicio, a [no'ßiθjo, a] nm/f novice

noviembre [no'ßjembre] nm November

novillada [noßi'ʎaða] nf (TAUROMAQUIA) bullfight with young bulls; **novillero** nm novice bullfighter; **novillo** nm young bull, bullock; **hacer novillos** (fam) to play truant

novio, a ['noßjo, a] nm/f boyfriend/girlfriend; (prometido) fiancé/fiancée; (recién casado) bridegroom/bride; **los ~s** the newly-weds

nubarrón [nußa'rron] nm storm cloud

nube ['nuße] nf cloud

nublado, a [nu'ßlaðo, a] adj cloudy ♦ nm storm cloud; **nublar** vt (oscurecer) to darken; (confundir) to cloud; **nublarse** vr to grow dark

nubosidad [nußosi'ðað] nf cloudiness; **había mucha ~** it was very cloudy

nuca ['nuka] nf nape of the neck

nuclear [nukle'ar] adj nuclear

núcleo ['nukleo] nm (centro) core; (FÍSICA) nucleus

nudillo [nu'ðiʎo] nm knuckle

nudista [nu'ðista] adj (playa) nudist

nudo ['nuðo] nm knot; (unión) bond; (de problema) crux; **~so, a** adj knotty

nuera ['nwera] nf daughter-in-law

nuestro, a ['nwestro, a] adj pos our ♦ pron ours; **~ padre** our father; **un amigo ~** a friend of ours; **es el ~** it's ours

nueva ['nweßa] nf piece of news

nuevamente [nweßa'mente] adv (otra vez) again; (de nuevo) anew

Nueva York [-jɔrk] n New York

Nueva Zelandia [-θe'landja] nf New Zealand

nueve ['nweße] num nine

nuevo, a ['nweßo, a] adj (gen) new; **de ~** again

nuez [nweθ] nf (fruto) nut; (del nogal) walnut; **~ de Adán** Adam's apple; **~ moscada** nutmeg

nulidad [nuli'ðað] nf (incapacidad) incompetence; (abolición) nullity

nulo, a ['nulo, a] adj (inepto, torpe) useless; (inválido) (null and) void; (DEPORTE) drawn, tied

núm. abr (= número) no

numeración [numera'θjon] nf (cifras) numbers pl; (arábiga, romana etc) numerals pl

numeral [nume'ral] nm numeral

numerar [nume'rar] vt to number

número ['numero] nm (gen) number; (tamaño: de zapato) size; (ejemplar: de diario) number, issue; **sin ~** numberless, unnumbered; **~ de matrícula/de teléfono** registration/telephone number; **~ atrasado** back number

numeroso, a [nume'roso, a] adj numerous

nunca ['nunka] adv (jamás) never; **~ lo pensé** I never thought it; **no viene ~** he never comes; **~ más** never again; **más que ~** more than ever

nuncio ['nunθjo] nm (REL) nuncio

nupcias ['nupθjas] nfpl wedding sg, nuptials

nutria ['nutrja] nf otter

nutrición [nutri'θjon] nf nutrition

nutrido, a [nu'triðo, a] adj (alimentado) nourished; (fig: grande) large; (abundante) abundant

nutrir [nu'trir] vt (alimentar) to nourish; (dar de comer) to feed; (fig) to strengthen; **nutritivo, a** adj nourishing, nutritious

nylon [ni'lon] nm nylon

Ñ ñ

ñato, a ['ɲato, a] (AM) adj snub-nosed

ñoñería [ɲoɲe'ria] nf insipidness

ñoño, a ['ɲoɲo, a] adj (AM: tonto) silly, stupid; (soso) insipid; (persona) spineless

O o

o [o] *conj* or

O *abr* (= *oeste*) W

o/ *abr* (= *orden*) o.

oasis [o'asis] *nm inv* oasis

obcecar [oβθe'kar] *vt* to blind

obcecarse [oβθe'karse] *vr* to get/become stubborn

obedecer [oβeðe'θer] *vt* to obey; **obediencia** *nf* obedience; **obediente** *adj* obedient

obertura [oβer'tura] *nf* overture

obesidad [oβesi'ðað] *nf* obesity; **obeso, a** *adj* obese

obispo [o'βispo] *nm* bishop

objeción [oβxe'θjon] *nf* objection; **poner objeciones** to raise objections

objetar [oβxe'tar] *vt, vi* to object

objetivo, a [oβxe'tiβo, a] *adj, nm* objective

objeto [oβ'xeto] *nm* (*cosa*) object; (*fin*) aim

objetor, a [oβxe'tor, a] *nm/f* objector

oblicuo, a [o'βlikwo, a] *adj* oblique; (*mirada*) sidelong

obligación [oβliɣa'θjon] *nf* obligation; (*COM*) bond

obligar [oβli'ɣar] *vt* to force; **~se** *vr* to bind o.s.; **obligatorio, a** *adj* compulsory, obligatory

oboe [o'βoe] *nm* oboe

obra ['oβra] *nf* work; (*hechura*) piece of work; (*ARQ*) construction, building; (*TEATRO*) play; ~ **maestra** masterpiece; **~s públicas** public works; **por ~ de** thanks to (the efforts of); **obrar** *vt* to work; (*tener efecto*) to have an effect on ♦ *vi* to act, behave; (*tener efecto*) to have an effect; **la carta obra en su poder** the letter is in his/her possession

obrero, a [o'βrero, a] *adj* (*clase*) working; (*movimiento*) labour *cpd*; **clase obrera** working class ♦ *nm/f* (*gen*) worker; (*sin oficio*) labourer

obscenidad [oβsθeni'ðað] *nf* obscenity; **obsceno, a** *adj* obscene

obscu... = **oscu...**

obsequiar [oβse'kjar] *vt* (*ofrecer*) to present with; (*agasajar*) to make a fuss of, lavish attention on; **obsequio** *nm* (*regalo*) gift; (*cortesía*) courtesy, attention

observación [oβserβa'θjon] *nf* observation; (*reflexión*) remark

observador, a [oβserβa'ðor, a] *nm/f* ob-

server

observar [oβser'βar] *vt* to observe; (*anotar*) to notice; **~se** *vr* to keep to, observe

obsesión [oβse'sjon] *nf* obsession; **obsesionar** *vt* to obsess; **obsesivo, a** *adj* obsessive

obsoleto, a [oβso'leto, a] *adj* (*máquina, técnica*) obsolete

obstaculizar [oβstakuli'θar] *vt* (*dificultar*) to hinder, hamper

obstáculo [oβs'takulo] *nm* (*gen*) obstacle; (*impedimento*) hindrance, drawback

obstante [oβs'tante]: **no ~** *adv* nevertheless ♦ *prep* in spite of

obstinado, a [oβsti'naðo, a] *adj* (*gen*) obstinate, stubborn

obstinarse [oβsti'narse] *vr* to be obstinate; **~ en** to persist in

obstrucción [oβstruk'θjon] *nf* obstruction; **obstruir** *vt* to obstruct

obtener [oβte'ner] *vt* (*conseguir*) to obtain; (*ganar*) to gain

obturador [oβtura'ðor] *nm* (*FOTO*) shutter

obtuso, a [oβ'tuso, a] *adj* (*filo*) blunt; (*MAT, fig*) obtuse

obvio, a ['oββjo, a] *adj* obvious

ocasión [oka'sjon] *nf* (*oportunidad*) opportunity, chance; (*momento*) occasion, time; (*causa*) cause; **de ~** secondhand; **ocasionar** *vt* to cause

ocaso [o'kaso] *nm* (*fig*) decline

occidente [okθi'ðente] *nm* west

OCDE *nf abr* (= *Organización de Cooperación y Desarrollo Económico*) OECD

océano [o'θeano] *nm* ocean; **el ~ Índico** the Indian Ocean

ocio ['oθjo] *nm* (*tiempo*) leisure; (*pey*) idleness; **~so, a** *adj* (*inactivo*) idle; (*inútil*) useless

octanaje [okta'naxe] *nm*: **de alto ~** high octane; **octano** *nm* octane

octavilla [okta'viʎa] *nf* leaflet, pamphlet

octavo, a [ok'taβo, a] *adj* eighth

octogenario, a [oktoxe'narjo, a] *adj* octogenarian

octubre [ok'tuβre] *nm* October

ocular [oku'lar] *adj* ocular, eye *cpd*; **testigo ~** eyewitness

oculista [oku'lista] *nm/f* oculist

ocultar [okul'tar] *vt* (*esconder*) to hide; (*callar*) to conceal; **oculto, a** *adj* hidden; (*fig*) secret

ocupación [okupa'θjon] *nf* occupation

ocupado, a [oku'paðo, a] *adj* (*persona*) busy; (*plaza*) occupied, taken; (*teléfono*) engaged; **ocupar** *vt* (*gen*) to occupy; **ocuparse** *vr*: **ocuparse de** *o* **en** (*gen*) to concern o.s. with; (*cuidar*) to look after

ocurrencia [oku'rrenθja] *nf* (*suceso*) incident, event; (*idea*) bright idea

ocurrir [oku'rrir] *vi* to happen; **~se** *vr*: **se me ocurrió que ...** it occurred to me that ...

ochenta [o'tʃenta] *num* eighty

ocho ['otʃo] *num* eight; ~ **días** a week

odiar [o'ðjar] *vt* to hate; **odio** *nm* (*gen*) hate, hatred; (*disgusto*) dislike; **odioso, a** *adj* (*gen*) hateful; (*malo*) nasty

odontólogo, a [oðon'tolovo, a] *nm/f* dentist, dental surgeon

OEA *nf abr* (= *Organización de Estados Americanos*) OAS

oeste [o'este] *nm* west; **una película del** ~ a western

ofender [ofen'der] *vt* (*agraviar*) to offend; (*insultar*) to insult; ~**se** *vr* to take offence; **ofensa** *nf* offence; **ofensiva** *nf* offensive; **ofensivo, a** *adj* (*insultante*) insulting; (*MIL*) offensive

oferta [o'ferta] *nf* offer; (*propuesta*) proposal; **la** ~ **y la demanda** supply and demand; **artículos en** ~ goods on offer

oficial [ofi'θjal] *adj* official ♦ *nm* official; (*MIL*) officer

oficina [ofi'θina] *nf* office; ~ **de correos** post office; ~ **de turismo** tourist office; **oficinista** *nm/f* clerk

oficio [o'fiθjo] *nm* (*profesión*) profession; (*puesto*) post; (*REL*) service; **ser del** ~ to be an old hand; **tener mucho** ~ to have a lot of experience; ~ **de difuntos** funeral service; **de** ~ officially

oficioso, a [ofi'θjoso, a] *adj* (*pey*) officious; (*no oficial*) unofficial, informal

ofimática [ofi'matika] *nf* office automation

ofrecer [ofre'θer] *vt* (*dar*) to offer; (*proponer*) to propose; ~**se** *vr* (*persona*) to offer o.s., volunteer; (*situación*) to present itself; **¿qué se le ofrece?, ¿se le ofrece algo?** what can I do for you?, can I get you anything?

ofrecimiento [ofreθi'mjento] *nm* offer, offering

ofrendar [ofren'dar] *vt* to offer, contribute

oftalmólogo, a [oftal'molovo, a] *nm/f* ophthalmologist

ofuscación [ofuska'θjon] *nf* (*fig*) bewilderment

ofuscar [ofus'kar] *vt* (*confundir*) to bewilder; (*enceguecer*) to dazzle, blind

oída [o'ixal] *nf*: **de** ~**s** by hearsay

oído [ɔ'iðo] *nm* (*ANAT*) ear; (*sentido*) hearing

oigo *etc vb ver* **oír**

oír [o'ir] *vt* (*gen*) to hear; (*atender a*) to listen to; **¡oiga!** listen!; ~ **misa** to attend mass

OIT *nf abr* (= *Organización Internacional del Trabajo*) ILO

ojal [o'xal] *nm* buttonhole

ojalá [oxa'la] *excl* if only (it were so)!, some hope! ♦ *conj* if only ...!, would that ...!; ~ **que venga hoy** I hope he comes today

ojeada [oxe'aða] *nf* glance

ojera [o'xera] *nf*: **tener** ~**s** to have bags under one's eyes

ojeriza [oxe'riθa] *nf* ill-will

ojeroso, a [oxe'roso, a] *adj* haggard

ojo ['oxo] *nm* eye; (*de puente*) span; (*de cerradura*) keyhole ♦ *excl* careful!; **tener** ~ **para** to have an eye for; ~ **de buey** porthole

ola ['ola] *nf* wave

olé [o'le] *excl* bravo!, olé!

oleada [ole'aða] *nf* big wave, swell; (*fig*) wave

oleaje [ole'axe] *nm* swell

óleo ['oleo] *nm* oil; **oleoducto** *nm* (oil) pipeline

oler [o'ler] *vt* (*gen*) to smell; (*inquirir*) to pry into; (*fig: sospechar*) to sniff out ♦ *vi* to smell; ~ **a** to smell of

olfatear [olfate'ar] *vt* to smell; (*fig: sospechar*) to sniff out; (*inquirir*) to pry into; **olfato** *nm* sense of smell

oligarquía [olixar'kia] *nf* oligarchy

olimpíada [olim'piaða] *nf*: **las O**~**s** the Olympics

oliva [o'lißa] *nf* (*aceituna*) olive; **aceite de** ~ olive oil; **olivo** *nm* olive tree

olmo ['olmo] *nm* elm (tree)

olor [o'lor] *nm* smell; ~**oso, a** *adj* scented

olvidadizo, a [olßiða'ðiθo, a] *adj* (*desmemoriado*) forgetful; (*distraído*) absentminded

olvidar [olßi'ðar] *vt* to forget; (*omitir*) to omit; ~**se** *vr* (*fig*) to forget o.s.; **se me olvidó** I forgot

olvido [ol'ßiðo] *nm* oblivion; (*despiste*) forgetfulness

olla ['oʎa] *nf* pan; (*comida*) stew; ~ **a presión** *o* **exprés** pressure cooker; ~ **podrida** type of Spanish stew

ombligo [om'blivo] *nm* navel

omisión [omi'sjon] *nf* (*abstención*) omission; (*descuido*) neglect

omiso, a [o'miso, a] *adj*: **hacer caso** ~ **de** to ignore, pass over

omitir [omi'tir] *vt* to omit

omnipotente [omnipo'tente] *adj* omnipotent

omnívoro, a [om'nißoro, a] *adj* omnivorous

omóplato [o'moplato] *nm* shoulder blade

OMS *nf abr* (= *Organización Mundial de la Salud*) WHO

once ['onθe] *num* eleven; ~**s** (*AM*) *nfpl* tea break

onda ['onda] *nf* wave; ~ **corta/larga/media** short/long/medium wave; **ondear** *vt*, *vi* to wave; (*tener ondas*) to be wavy; (*agua*) to ripple; **ondearse** *vr* to swing, sway

ondulación [ondula'θjon] *nf* undulation; **ondulado, a** *adj* wavy ♦ *nm* wave

ondular [ondu'lar] *vt* (*el pelo*) to wave ♦ *vi* to undulate; ~**se** *vr* to undulate

ONU ['onu] *nf abr* (= *Organización de las Naciones Unidas*) UNO

opaco, a [o'pako, a] *adj* opaque; (*fig*) dull

opción [op'θjon] *nf* (*gen*) option; (*derecho*) right, option

OPEP ['opep] *nf abr* (= *Organización de Países Exportadores de Petróleo*) OPEC

ópera ['opera] *nf* opera; ~ **bufa** *o* **cómica** comic opera

operación [opera'θjon] *nf* (*gen*) operation; (*COM*) transaction, deal

operador, a [opera'ðor, a] *nm/f* operator; (*CINE: proyección*) projectionist; (: *rodaje*) cameraman

operar [ope'rar] *vt* (*producir*) to produce, bring about; (*MED*) to operate on ♦ *vi* (*COM*) to operate, deal; ~**se** *vr* to occur; (*MED*) to have an operation

opereta [ope'reta] *nf* operetta

opinar [opi'nar] *vt* (*estimar*) to think ♦ *vi* (*enjuiciar*) to give one's opinion; **opinión** *nf* (*creencia*) belief; (*criterio*) opinion

opio ['opjo] *nm* opium

oponente [opo'nente] *nm/f* opponent

oponer [opo'ner] *vt* (*resistencia*) to put up, offer; (*negativa*) to raise; ~**se** *vr* (*objetar*) to object; (*estar frente a frente*) to be opposed; (*dos personas*) to oppose each other; ~ A **a** B to set A against B; **me opongo a pensar que** ... I refuse to believe *o* think that ...

oportunidad [oportuni'ðað] *nf* (*ocasión*) opportunity; (*posibilidad*) chance

oportunismo [oportu'nismo] *nm* opportunism; **oportunista** *nm/f* opportunist

oportuno, a [opor'tuno, a] *adj* (*en su tiempo*) opportune, timely; (*respuesta*) suitable; **en el momento** ~ at the right moment

oposición [oposi'θjon] *nf* opposition; **oposiciones** *nfpl* (*ESCOL*) public examinations

opositor, a [oposi'tor, a] *nm/f* (*adversario*) opponent; (*candidato*): ~ (**a**) candidate (for)

opresión [opre'sjon] *nf* oppression; **opresivo, a** *adj* oppressive; **opresor, a** *nm/f* oppressor

oprimir [opri'mir] *vt* to squeeze; (*fig*) to oppress

optar [op'tar] *vi* (*elegir*) to choose; ~ **a** *o* **por** to opt for; **optativo, a** *adj* optional

óptico, a ['optiko, a] *adj* optic(al) ♦ *nm/f* optician; **óptica** *nf* optician's (shop); **desde esta óptica** from this point of view

optimismo [opti'mismo] *nm* optimism; **optimista** *nm/f* optimist

óptimo, a ['optimo, a] *adj* (*el mejor*) very best

opuesto, a [o'pwesto, a] *adj* (*contrario*) opposite; (*antagónico*) opposing

opulencia [opu'lenθja] *nf* opulence; **opulento, a** *adj* opulent

oración [ora'θjon] *nf* (*discurso*) speech; (*REL*) prayer; (*LING*) sentence

orador, a [ora'ðor, a] *nm/f* (*conferenciante*) speaker, orator

oral [o'ral] *adj* oral

orangután [orangu'tan] *nm* orang-utan

orar [o'rar] *vi* (*REL*) to pray

oratoria [ora'torja] *nf* oratory

órbita ['orßita] *nf* orbit

orden ['orðen] *nm* (*gen*) order ♦ *nf* (*gen*) order; (*INFORM*) command; ~ **del día** agenda; **de primer** ~ first-rate; **en** ~ **de prioridad** in order of priority

ordenado, a [orðe'naðo, a] *adj* (*metódico*) methodical; (*arreglado*) orderly

ordenador [orðena'ðor] *nm* computer; ~ **central** mainframe computer

ordenanza [orðe'nanθa] *nf* ordinance

ordenar [orðe'nar] *vt* (*mandar*) to order; (*poner orden*) to put in order, arrange; ~**se** *vr* (*REL*) to be ordained

ordeñar [orðe'nar] *vt* to milk

ordinario, a [orði'narjo, a] *adj* (*común*) ordinary, usual; (*vulgar*) vulgar, common

orégano [o'reɣano] *nm* oregano

oreja [o'rexa] *nf* ear; (*MECÁNICA*) lug, flange

orfanato [orfa'nato] *nm* orphanage

orfandad [orfan'dað] *nf* orphanhood

orfebrería [orfeßre'ria] *nf* gold/silver work

orgánico, a [or'ɣaniko, a] *adj* organic

organigrama [orɣani'xrama] *nm* flow chart

organismo [orɣa'nismo] *nm* (*BIO*) organism; (*POL*) organization

organización [orɣaniθa'θjon] *nf* organization; **organizar** *vt* to organize

órgano ['orɣano] *nm* organ

orgasmo [or'ɣasmo] *nm* orgasm

orgía [or'xia] *nf* orgy

orgullo [or'ɣuʎo] *nm* (*altanería*) pride; (*autorespeto*) self-respect; **orgulloso, a** *adj* (*gen*) proud; (*altanero*) haughty

orientación [orjenta'θjon] *nf* (*posición*) position; (*dirección*) direction

orientar [orjen'tar] *vt* (*situar*) to orientate; (*señalar*) to point; (*dirigir*) to direct; (*guiar*) to guide; ~**se** *vr* to get one's bearings; (*decidirse*) to decide on a course of action

oriente [o'rjente] *nm* east; **Cercano/Medio/Lejano** O~ Near/Middle/Far East

origen [o'rixen] *nm* origin; (*nacimiento*) lineage, birth

original [orixi'nal] *adj* (*nuevo*) original; (*extraño*) odd, strange; ~**idad** *nf* originality

originar [orixi'nar] *vt* to start, cause; ~**se** *vr* to originate; ~**io, a** *adj* (*nativo*) native; (*primordial*) original

orilla [o'riʎa] *nf* (*borde*) border; (*de río*) bank; (*de bosque, tela*) edge; (*de mar*) shore

orina [o'rina] *nf* urine; **orinal** *nm* (*chamber*) pot; **orinar** *vi* to urinate; **orinarse** *vr* to wet o.s.; **orines** *nmpl* urine

oriundo, a [o'rjundo, a] *adj*: ~ **de** native of

ornitología [ornitolo'xia] *nf* ornithology, bird-watching

oro ['oro] *nm* gold; **~s** *nmpl* (*NAIPES*) hearts

oropel [oro'pel] *nm* tinsel

orquesta [or'kesta] *nf* orchestra; **~ de cámara/sinfónica** chamber/symphony orchestra

orquídea [or'kiðea] *nf* orchid

ortiga [or'tiɣa] *nf* nettle

ortodoxo, a [orto'ðokso, a] *adj* orthodox

ortografía [ortoɣra'fia] *nf* spelling

ortopedia [orto'peðja] *nf* orthopaedics *sg*; **ortopédico, a** *adj* orthopaedic

oruga [o'ruɣa] *nf* caterpillar

orzuelo [or'θwelo] *nm* (*MED*) stye

os [os] *pron* (*gen*) you; (*a vosotros*) to you

osa [o'sa] *nf* (she-)bear; **O~ Mayor/Menor** Great/Little Bear

osadía [osa'ðia] *nf* daring

osar [o'sar] *vi* to dare

oscilación [osθila'θjon] *nf* (*movimiento*) oscillation; (*fluctuación*) fluctuation; (*vacilación*) hesitation; (*columpio*) swinging, movement to and fro

oscilar [osθi'lar] *vi* to oscillate; to fluctuate; to hesitate

oscurecer [oskure'θer] *vt* to darken ♦ *vi* to grow dark; **~se** *vr* to grow *o* get dark

oscuridad [oskuri'ðað] *nf* obscurity; (*tinieblas*) darkness

oscuro, a [os'kuro, a] *adj* dark; (*fig*) obscure; **a oscuras** in the dark

óseo, a ['oseo, a] *adj* bony

oso ['oso] *nm* bear; **~ de peluche** teddy bear; **~ hormiguero** anteater

ostensible [osten'siβle] *adj* obvious

ostentación [ostenta'θjon] *nf* (*gen*) ostentation; (*acto*) display

ostentar [osten'tar] *vt* (*gen*) to show; (*pey*) to flaunt, show off; (*poseer*) to have, possess

ostra ['ostra] *nf* oyster

OTAN ['otan] *nf abr* (= *Organización del Tratado del Atlántico Norte*) NATO

otear [ote'ar] *vt* to observe; (*fig*) to look into

otitis [o'titis] *nf* earache

otoñal [oto'ɲal] *adj* autumnal

otoño [o'toɲo] *nm* autumn

otorgar [otor'ɣar] *vt* (*conceder*) to concede; (*dar*) to grant

otorrino, a [oto'rrino, a] *nm/f* ear, nose and throat specialist

otorrinolaringólogo, a [otorrinolarin'goloɣo, a] *nm/f* = **otorrino**

───────── *PALABRA CLAVE*

otro, a ['otro, a] *adj* **1** (*distinto: sg*) another; (: *pl*) other; **con ~s amigos** with other *o* different friends

2 (*adicional*): **tráigame ~ café (más)**, **por favor** can I have another coffee please; **~s 10 días más** another ten days

♦ *pron* **1**: **el ~** the other one; **(los) ~s** (the) others; **de ~** somebody else's; **que lo haga ~** let somebody else do it

2 (*recíproco*): **se odian (la) una a (la) otra** they hate one another *o* each other

3: **~ tanto**: **comer ~ tanto** to eat the same *o* as much again; **recibió una decena de telegramas y otras tantas llamadas** he got about ten telegrams and as many calls

───────────────────

ovación [oβa'θjon] *nf* ovation

oval [o'βal] *adj* oval; **~ado, a** *adj* oval; **óvalo** *nm* oval

ovario [o'βarjo] *nm* (*ANAT*) ovary

oveja [o'βexa] *nf* sheep

overol [oβe'rol] (*AM*) *nm* overalls *pl*

ovillo [o'βiʎo] *nm* (*de lana*) ball of wool; **hacerse un ~** to curl up

OVNI ['oβni] *nm abr* (= *objeto volante no identificado*) UFO

ovulación [oβula'θjon] *nf* ovulation; **óvulo** *nm* ovum

oxidación [oksiða'θjon] *nf* rusting

oxidar [oksi'ðar] *vt* to rust; **~se** *vr* to go rusty

óxido ['oksiðo] *nm* oxide

oxigenado, a [oksixe'naðo, a] *adj* (*QUÍMICA*) oxygenated; (*pelo*) bleached

oxígeno [ok'sixeno] *nm* oxygen

oyente [o'jente] *nm/f* listener, hearer

oyes *etc vb ver* **oír**

ozono [o'θono] *nm* ozone

P p

P *abr* (= *padre*) Fr.

pabellón [paβe'ʎon] *nm* bell tent; (*ARQ*) pavilion; (*de hospital etc*) block, section; (*bandera*) flag

pacer [pa'θer] *vi* to graze

paciencia [pa'θjenθja] *nf* patience

paciente [pa'θjente] *adj, nm/f* patient

pacificación [paθifika'θjon] *nf* pacification

pacificar [paθifi'kar] *vt* to pacify; (*tranquilizar*) to calm

pacífico, a [pa'θifiko, a] *adj* (*persona*) peaceable; (*existencia*) peaceful; **el (océano) P~** the Pacific (Ocean)

pacifismo [paθi'fismo] *nm* pacifism; **pacifista** *nm/f* pacifist

pacotilla [pako'tiʎa] nf: **de ~** (actor, escritor) third-rate; (mueble etc) cheap

pactar [pak'tar] vt to agree to o on ♦ vi to come to an agreement

pacto ['pakto] nm (tratado) pact; (acuerdo) agreement

padecer [paðe'θer] vt (sufrir) to suffer; (soportar) to endure, put up with; (engaño, error) to be a victim of; **padecimiento** nm suffering

padrastro [pa'ðrastro] nm stepfather

padre ['paðre] nm father ♦ adj (fam): **un éxito ~** a tremendous success; **~s** nmpl parents

padrino [pa'ðrino] nm (REL) godfather; (tb: **~ de boda**) best man; (fig) sponsor, patron; **~s** nmpl godparents

padrón [pa'ðron] nm (censo) census, roll; (de socios) register

paella [pa'eʎa] nf paella, dish of rice with meat, shellfish etc

paga ['paɣa] nf (pago) payment; (sueldo) pay, wages pl

pagadero, a [paɣa'ðero, a] adj payable; **~ a plazos** payable in instalments

pagano, a [pa'ɣano, a] adj, nm/f pagan, heathen

pagar [pa'ɣar] vt to pay; (las compras, crimen) to pay for; (fig: favor) to repay ♦ vi to pay; **~ al contado/a plazos** to pay (in) cash/in instalments

pagaré [paɣa're] nm I.O.U.

página ['paxina] nf page

pago ['paɣo] nm (dinero) payment; (fig) return; **estar ~** to be even o quits; **~ anticipado/a cuenta/contra reembolso/en especie** advance payment/payment on account/cash on delivery/payment in kind

pág(s). abr (= página(s)) p(p).

pague etc vb ver **pagar**

país [pa'is] nm (gen) country; (región) land; **los P~es Bajos** the Low Countries; **el P~ Vasco** the Basque Country

paisaje [pai'saxe] nm countryside, scenery

paisano, a [pai'sano, a] adj of the same country ♦ nm/f (compatriota) fellow countryman/woman; **vestir de ~** (soldado) to be in civvies; (guardia) to be in plain clothes

paja ['paxa] nf straw; (fig) rubbish (BRIT), trash (US)

pajarita [paxa'rita] nf (corbata) bow tie

pájaro ['paxaro] nm bird; **~ carpintero** woodpecker

pajita [pa'xita] nf (drinking) straw

pala ['pala] nf spade, shovel; (raqueta etc) bat; (: de tenis) racquet; (CULIN) slice; **~ matamoscas** fly swat

palabra [pa'laβra] nf word; (facultad) (power of) speech; (derecho de hablar) right to speak; **tomar la ~** (en mitin) to take the floor

palabrota [pala'βrota] nf swearword

palacio [pa'laθjo] nm palace; (mansión) mansion, large house; **~ de justicia** courthouse; **~ municipal** town/city hall

paladar [pala'ðar] nm palate; **paladear** vt to taste

palanca [pa'lanka] nf lever; (fig) pull, influence

palangana [palan'gana] nf washbasin

palco ['palko] nm box

Palestina [pales'tina] nf Palestine; **palestino, a** nm/f Palestinian

paleta [pa'leta] nf (de pintor) palette; (de albañil) trowel; (de ping-pong) bat; (AM) ice lolly

paleto, a [pa'leto, a] (fam, pey) nm/f yokel

paliar [pa'ljar] vt (mitigar) to mitigate, alleviate; **paliativo** nm palliative

palidecer [paliðe'θer] vi to turn pale; **palidez** nf paleness; **pálido, a** adj pale

palillo [pa'liʎo] nm small stick; (mondadientes) toothpick; (para comer) chopstick

paliza [pa'liθa] nf beating, thrashing

palma ['palma] nf (ANAT) palm; (árbol) palm tree; **batir o dar ~s** to clap, applaud; **~da** nf slap; **~das** nfpl clapping sg, applause sg

palmar [pal'mar] (fam) vi (tb: **~la**) to die, kick the bucket

palmear [palme'ar] vi to clap

palmera [pal'mera] nf (BOT) palm tree

palmo ['palmo] nm (medida) span; (fig) small amount; **~ a ~** inch by inch

palmotear [palmote'ar] vi to clap, applaud

palo ['palo] nm stick; (poste) post; (de tienda de campaña) pole; (mango) handle, shaft; (golpe) blow, hit; (de golf) club; (de béisbol) bat; (NAUT) mast; (NAIPES) suit

paloma [pa'loma] nf dove, pigeon

palomilla [palo'miʎa] nf moth; (TEC: tuerca) wing nut; (: hierro) angle iron

palomitas [palo'mitas] nfpl popcorn sg

palpar [pal'par] vt to touch, feel

palpitación [palpita'θjon] nf palpitation

palpitante [palpi'tante] adj palpitating; (fig) burning

palpitar [palpi'tar] vi to palpitate; (latir) to beat

palta ['palta] (AM) nf avocado (pear)

paludismo [palu'ðismo] nm malaria

pamela [pa'mela] nf picture hat, sun hat

pampa ['pampa] (AM) nf pampas, prairie

pan [pan] nm bread; (una barra) loaf; **~ integral** wholemeal (BRIT) o wholewheat (US) bread; **~ rallado** breadcrumbs pl

pana ['pana] nf corduroy

panadería [panaðe'ria] nf baker's (shop); **panadero, a** nm/f baker

Panamá [pana'ma] nm Panama; **panameño, a** adj Panamanian

pancarta [pan'karta] nf placard, banner

panda ['panda] nm (ZOOL) panda

pandereta [pande'reta] *nf* tambourine
pandilla [pan'diʎa] *nf* set, group; (*de criminales*) gang; (*pey: camarilla*) clique
panecillo [pane'θiʎo] *nm* (bread) roll
panel [pa'nel] *nm* panel; ~ **solar** solar panel
panfleto [pan'fleto] *nm* pamphlet
pánico ['paniko] *nm* panic
panorama [pano'rama] *nm* panorama; (*vista*) view
pantalón [panta'lon] *nm* trousers; **pantalones** *nmpl* trousers
pantalla [pan'taʎa] *nf* (*de cine*) screen; (*de lámpara*) lampshade
pantano [pan'tano] *nm* (*ciénaga*) marsh, swamp; (*depósito: de agua*) reservoir; (*fig*) jam, difficulty
panteón [pante'on] *nm*: ~ **familiar** family tomb
pantera [pan'tera] *nf* panther
pantomima [panto'mima] *nf* pantomime
pantorrilla [panto'rriʎa] *nf* calf (of the leg)
pantufla [pan'tufla] *nf* slipper
panza ['panθa] *nf* belly, paunch
pañal [pa'nal] *nm* nappy (*BRIT*), diaper (*US*); ~**es** *nmpl* (*fig*) early stages, infancy *sg*
paño ['paɲo] *nm* (*tela*) cloth; (*pedazo de tela*) (piece of) cloth; (*trapo*) duster, rag; ~ **higiénico** sanitary towel; ~**s menores** underclothes
pantis [pan'tis] *nmpl* tights
pañuelo [pa'ɲwelo] *nm* handkerchief, hanky (*fam*); (*para la cabeza*) (head)scarf
papa ['papa] *nm*: **el P**~ the Pope ♦ (*AM*) *nf* potato
papá [pa'pa] (*pl* ~**s**) (*fam*) *nm* dad(dy), pa (*US*)
papada [pa'paða] *nf* (*ANAT*) double chin
papagayo [papa'ɣajo] *nm* parrot
papanatas [papa'natas] (*fam*) *nm inv* simpleton
paparrucha [papa'rrutʃa] *nf* piece of nonsense
papaya [pa'paja] *nf* papaya
papel [pa'pel] *nm* paper; (*hoja de* ~) sheet of paper; (*TEATRO, fig*) role; ~ **de calco/carbón/de cartas** tracing paper/carbon paper/stationery; ~ **de envolver/pintado** wrapping paper/wallpaper; ~ **de aluminio/higiénico** aluminium (*BRIT*) o aluminum (*US*) foil/toilet paper; ~ **de estaño** o **plata** tinfoil; ~ **de lija** sandpaper; ~ **moneda** paper money; ~ **secante** blotting paper
papeleo [pape'leo] *nm* red tape
papelera [pape'lera] *nf* wastepaper basket; (*escritorio*) desk
papelería [papele'ria] *nf* stationer's (shop)
papeleta [pape'leta] *nf* (*pedazo de papel*) slip of paper; (*POL*) ballot paper; (*ESCOL*) report

paperas [pa'peras] *nfpl* mumps *sg*
papilla [pa'piʎa] *nf* (*para niños*) baby food
paquete [pa'kete] *nm* (*de cigarrillos etc*) packet; (*CORREOS etc*) parcel; (*AM*) package tour; (: *fam*) nuisance, bore
par [par] *adj* (*igual*) like, equal; (*MAT*) even ♦ *nm* equal; (*de guantes*) pair; (*de veces*) couple; (*POL*) peer; (*GOLF, COM*) par; **abrir de** ~ **en** ~ to open wide
para ['para] *prep* for; **no es** ~ **comer** it's not for eating; **decir** ~ **sí** to say to o.s.; *¿~ qué lo quieres?* what do you want it for?; **se casaron** ~ **separarse otra vez** they married only to separate again; **lo tendré** ~ **mañana** I'll have it (for) tomorrow; **ir** ~ **casa** to go home, head for home; ~ **profesor es muy estúpido** he's very stupid for a teacher; *¿quién es usted* ~ *gritar así?* who are you to shout like that?; **tengo bastante** ~ **vivir** I have enough to live on; **ver** *tb* **con**
parabién [para'βjen] *nm* congratulations *pl*
parábola [pa'raβola] *nf* parable; (*MAT*) parabola; **parabólica** *nf* (*tb*: *antena* ~) satellite dish
parabrisas [para'βrisas] *nm inv* windscreen (*BRIT*), windshield (*US*)
paracaídas [paraka'iðas] *nm inv* parachute; **paracaidista** *nm/f* parachutist; (*MIL*) paratrooper
parachoques [para'tʃokes] *nm inv* (*AUTO*) bumper; (*MECÁNICA etc*) shock absorber
parada [pa'raða] *nf* stop; (*acto*) stopping; (*de industria*) shutdown, stoppage; (*lugar*) stopping place; ~ **de autobús** bus stop
paradero [para'ðero] *nm* stopping-place; (*situación*) whereabouts
parado, a [pa'raðo, a] *adj* (*persona*) motionless, standing still; (*fábrica*) closed, at a standstill; (*coche*) stopped; (*AM*) standing (up); (*sin empleo*) unemployed, idle
paradoja [para'ðoxa] *nf* paradox
parador [para'ðor] *nm* parador, state-run hotel
paráfrasis [pa'rafrasis] *nf inv* paraphrase
paraguas [pa'raɣwas] *nm inv* umbrella
Paraguay [para'ɣwai] *nm*: **el** ~ Paraguay; **paraguayo, a** *adj, nm/f* Paraguayan
paraíso [para'iso] *nm* paradise, heaven
paraje [pa'raxe] *nm* place, spot
paralelo [para'lelo, a] *adj* parallel
parálisis [pa'ralisis] *nf inv* paralysis; **paralítico, a** *adj, nm/f* paralytic
paralizar [parali'θar] *vt* to paralyse; ~**se** *vr* to become paralysed; (*fig*) to come to a standstill
paramilitar [paramili'tar] *adj* paramilitary
páramo ['paramo] *nm* bleak plateau
parangón [paran'gon] *nm*: **sin** ~ incomparable
paranoico, a [para'noiko, a] *nm/f* paranoiac

parapléjico, a [para'plexiko, a] *adj, nm/f* paraplegic

parar [pa'rar] *vt* to stop; (*golpe*) to ward off ♦ *vi* to stop; **~se** *vr* to stop; (*AM*) to stand up; **ha parado de llover** it has stopped raining; **van a ~ en la comisaría** they're going to end up in the police station; **~se en** to pay attention to

pararrayos [para'rrajos] *nm inv* lightning conductor

parásito, a [pa'rasito, a] *nm/f* parasite

parcela [par'θela] *nf* plot, piece of ground

parcial [par'θjal] *adj* (*pago*) part-; (*eclipse*) partial; (*JUR*) prejudiced, biased; (*POL*) partisan; **~idad** *nf* (*prejuicio*) prejudice, bias

parco, a ['parko, a] *adj* (*moderado*) moderate

parche ['partʃe] *nm* (*gen*) patch

pardillo, a [par'ðiʎo, a] (*pey*) *adj* yokel

parecer [pare'θer] *nm* (*opinión*) opinion, view; (*aspecto*) looks *pl* ♦ *vi* (*tener apariencia*) to seem, look; (*asemejarse*) to look o seem like; (*aparecer, llegar*) to appear; **~se** *vr* to look alike, resemble each other; **~se a** to look like, resemble; **según o a lo que parece** evidently, apparently; **me parece que** I think (that), it seems to me that

parecido, a [pare'θiðo, a] *adj* similar ♦ *nm* similarity, likeness, resemblance; **bien ~** good-looking, nice-looking

pared [pa'reð] *nf* wall

pareja [pa'rexa] *nf* (*par*) pair; (*dos personas*) couple; (*otro: de un par*) other one (of a pair); (*persona*) partner

parentela [paren'tela] *nf* relations *pl*

parentesco [paren'tesko] *nm* relationship

paréntesis [pa'rentesis] *nm inv* parenthesis; (*digresión*) digression; (*en escrito*) bracket

parezco *etc vb ver* **parecer**

pariente, a [pa'rjente, a] *nm/f* relative, relation

parir [pa'rir] *vt* to give birth to ♦ *vi* (*mujer*) to give birth, have a baby

París [pa'ris] *n* Paris

parking ['parkin] *nm* car park (*BRIT*), parking lot (*US*)

parlamentar [parlamen'tar] *vi* (*negociar*) to parley

parlamentario, a [parlamen'tarjo, a] *adj* parliamentary ♦ *nm/f* member of parliament

parlamento [parla'mento] *nm* (*POL*) parliament

parlanchín, ina [parlan'tʃin, ina] *adj* indiscreet ♦ *nm/f* chatterbox

paro ['paro] *nm* (*huelga*) stoppage (of work), strike; (*desempleo*) unemployment; **subsidio de ~** unemployment benefit; **hay ~ en la industria** work in the industry is at a standstill

parodia [pa'roðja] *nf* parody; **parodiar** *vt* to parody

parpadear [parpaðe'ar] *vi* (*ojos*) to blink;

(*luz*) to flicker

párpado ['parpaðo] *nm* eyelid

parque ['parke] *nm* (*lugar verde*) park; **~ de atracciones/infantil/zoológico** fairground/playground/zoo

parquímetro [par'kimetro] *nm* parking meter

parra ['parra] *nf* (*grape*)vine

párrafo ['parrafo] *nm* paragraph; **echar un ~** (*fam*) to have a chat

parranda [pa'rranda] (*fam*) *nf* spree, binge

parrilla [pa'rriʎa] *nf* (*CULIN*) grill; (*de coche*) grille; (**carne a la ~**) barbecue; **~da** *nf* barbecue

párroco ['parroko] *nm* parish priest

parroquia [pa'rrokja] *nf* parish; (*iglesia*) parish church; (*COM*) clientele, customers *pl*; **~no, a** *nm/f* parishioner; client, customer

parsimonia [parsi'monja] *nf* calmness, level-headedness

parte ['parte] *nm* message; (*informe*) report ♦ *nf* part; (*lado, cara*) side; (*de reparto*) share; (*JUR*) party; **en alguna ~ de Europa** somewhere in Europe; **en/por todas ~s** everywhere; **en gran ~** to a large extent; **la mayor ~ de los españoles** most Spaniards; **de un tiempo a esta ~** for some time past; **de ~ de alguien** on sb's behalf; **¿de ~ de quién?** (*TEL*) who is speaking?; **por ~ de** on the part of; **yo por mi ~** I for my part; **por otra ~** on the other hand; **dar ~** to inform; **tomar ~** to take part

partición [parti'θjon] *nf* division, sharing-out; (*POL*) partition

participación [partiθipa'θjon] *nf* (*acto*) participation, taking part; (*parte, COM*) share; (*de lotería*) shared prize; (*aviso*) notice, notification

participante [partiθi'pante] *nm/f* participant

participar [partiθi'par] *vt* to notify, inform ♦ *vi* to take part, participate

partícipe [par'tiθipe] *nm/f* participant

particular [partiku'lar] *adj* (*especial*) particular, special; (*individual, personal*) private, personal ♦ *nm* (*punto, asunto*) particular, point; (*individuo*) individual; **tiene coche ~** he has a car of his own; **~izar** *vt* to distinguish; (*especificar*) to specify; (*detallar*) to give details about

partida [par'tiða] *nf* (*salida*) departure; (*COM*) entry, item; (*juego*) game; (*grupo de personas*) band, group; **mala ~** dirty trick; **~ de nacimiento / matrimonio / defunción** birth/marriage/death certificate

partidario, a [parti'ðarjo, a] *adj* partisan ♦ *nm/f* supporter, follower

partido [par'tiðo] *nm* (*POL*) party; (*DEPORTE: encuentro*) game, match; (: *equipo*) team; (*apoyo*) support; **sacar ~ de** to profit o benefit from; **tomar ~** to take sides

partir [par'tir] vt (*dividir*) to split, divide; (*compartir, distribuir*) to share (out), distribute; (*romper*) to break open, split open; (*rebanada*) to cut (off) ♦ vi (*ponerse en camino*) to set off o out; (*comenzar*) to start (off o out); ~**se** vr to crack o split o break (in two etc); **a** ~ **de** (starting) from

partitura [parti'tura] nf (*MUS*) score

parto ['parto] nm birth; (*fig*) product, creation; **estar de** ~ to be in labour

parvulario [parβu'larjo] nm nursery school, kindergarten

pasa ['pasa] nf raisin; ~ **de Corinto/de Esmirna** currant/sultana

pasada [pa'saða] nf passing, passage; **de** ~ in passing, incidentally; **una mala** ~ a dirty trick

pasadizo [pasa'ðiθo] nm (*pasillo*) passage, corridor; (*callejuela*) alley

pasado, a [pa'saðo, a] adj past; (*malo: comida, fruta*) bad; (*muy cocido*) overdone; (*anticuado*) out of date ♦ nm past; ~ **mañana** the day after tomorrow; **el mes** ~ last month

pasador [pasa'ðor] nm (*gen*) bolt; (*de pelo*) hair slide; (*horquilla*) grip

pasaje [pa'saxe] nm passage; (*pago de viaje*) fare; (*los pasajeros*) passengers pl; (*pasillo*) passageway

pasajero, a [pasa'xero, a] adj passing; (*situación, estado*) temporary; (*amor, enfermedad*) brief ♦ nm/f passenger

pasamanos [pasa'manos] nm inv (hand)rail; (*de escalera*) banisters pl

pasamontañas [pasamon'taɲas] nm inv balaclava helmet

pasaporte [pasa'porte] nm passport

pasar [pa'sar] vt to pass; (*tiempo*) to spend; (*desgracias*) to suffer, endure; (*noticia*) to give, pass on; (*río*) to cross; (*barrera*) to pass through; (*falta*) to overlook, tolerate; (*contrincante*) to surpass, do better than; (*coche*) to overtake; (*CINE*) to show; (*enfermedad*) to give, infect with ♦ vi (*gen*) to pass; (*terminarse*) to be over; (*ocurrir*) to happen; ~**se** vr (*flores*) to fade; (*comida*) to go bad o off; (*fig*) to overdo it, go too far; ~ **de** to go beyond, exceed; ~ **por** (*AM*) to fetch; ~**lo bien/mal** to have a good/bad time; **¡pase!** come in!; **hacer** ~ to show in; ~**se al enemigo** to go over to the enemy; **se me pasó** I forgot; **no se le pasa nada** he misses nothing; **pase lo que pase** come what may

pasarela [pasa'rela] nf footbridge; (*en barco*) gangway

pasatiempo [pasa'tjempo] nm pastime, hobby

Pascua ['paskwa] nf: ~ **(de Resurrección)** Easter; ~ **de Navidad** Christmas; ~**s** nfpl Christmas (time); **¡felices** ~**s!** Merry Christmas!

pase ['pase] nm pass; (*CINE*) performance, showing

pasear [pase'ar] vt to take for a walk; (*exhibir*) to parade, show off ♦ vi to walk, go for a walk; ~**se** vr to walk, go for a walk; ~ **en coche** to go for a drive; **paseo** nm (*avenida*) avenue; (*distancia corta*) walk, stroll; **dar un** o **ir de paseo** to go for a walk

pasillo [pa'siʎo] nm passage, corridor

pasión [pa'sjon] nf passion

pasivo, a [pa'siβo, a] adj passive; (*inactivo*) inactive ♦ nm (*COM*) liabilities pl, debts pl; (*LING*) passive

pasmar [pas'mar] vt (*asombrar*) to amaze, astonish; **pasmo** nm amazement, astonishment; (*resfriado*) chill; (*fig*) wonder, marvel; **pasmoso, a** adj amazing, astonishing

paso, a ['paso, a] adj dried ♦ nm step; (*modo de andar*) walk; (*huella*) footprint; (*rapidez*) speed, pace, rate; (*camino accesible*) way through, passage; (*cruce*) crossing; (*pasaje*) passing, passage; (*GEO*) pass; (*estrecho*) strait; ~ **a nivel** (*FERRO*) level-crossing; ~ **de peatones** pedestrian crossing; **a ese** ~ (*fig*) at that rate; **salir al** ~ **de** o **a** to waylay; **estar de** ~ to be passing through; ~ **elevado** flyover; **prohibido el** ~ no entry; **ceda el** ~ give way

pasota [pa'sota] (*fam*) adj, nm/f ≈ dropout; **ser un (tipo)** ~ to be a bit of a dropout; (*ser indiferente*) not to care about anything

pasta ['pasta] nf paste; (*CULIN: masa*) dough; (: *de bizcochos etc*) pastry; (*fam*) dough; ~**s** nfpl (*bizcochos*) pastries, small cakes; (*fideos, espaguetis etc*) pasta; ~ **de dientes** o **dentífrica** toothpaste

pastar [pas'tar] vt, vi to graze

pastel [pas'tel] nm (*dulce*) cake; ~ **de carne** meat pie; (*ARTE*) pastel; ~**ería** nf cake shop

pasteurizado, a [pasteuri'θaðo, a] adj pasteurized

pastilla [pas'tiʎa] nf (*de jabón, chocolate*) bar; (*píldora*) tablet, pill

pasto ['pasto] nm (*hierba*) grass; (*lugar*) pasture, field

pastor, a [pas'tor, a] nm/f shepherd/ess ♦ nm (*REL*) clergyman, pastor; ~ **alemán** Alsatian

pata ['pata] nf (*pierna*) leg; (*pie*) foot; (*de muebles*) leg; ~**s arriba** upside down; **metedura de** ~ (*fam*) gaffe; **meter la** ~ (*fam*) to put one's foot in it; (*TEC*): ~ **de cabra** crowbar; **tener buena/mala** ~ to be lucky/unlucky; ~**da** nf kick; (*en el suelo*) stamp

patalear [patale'ar] vi (*en el suelo*) to stamp one's feet

patata [pa'tata] nf potato; ~**s fritas** o **a la española** chips, French fries; ~**s fritas** (*de bolsa*) crisps

paté [pa'te] nm pâté

patear [pate'ar] vt (*pisar*) to stamp on, trample (on); (*pegar con el pie*) to kick ♦ vi to stamp (with rage), stamp one's feet

patentar [paten'tar] vt to patent

patente [pa'tente] adj obvious, evident; (COM) patent ♦ nf patent

paternal [pater'nal] adj fatherly, paternal; **paterno, a** adj paternal

patético, a [pa'tetiko, a] adj pathetic, moving

patilla [pa'tiʎa] nf (*de gafas*) side(piece)

patillas [pa'tiʎas] nfpl sideburns

patín [pa'tin] nm skate; (*de trineo*) runner; **patinaje** nm skating; **patinar** vi to skate; (*resbalarse*) to skid, slip; (*fam*) to slip up, blunder

patio ['patjo] nm (*de casa*) patio, courtyard; ~ **de recreo** playground

pato ['pato] nm duck; **pagar el** ~ (*fam*) to take the blame, carry the can

patológico, a [pato'loxiko, a] adj pathological

patoso, a [pa'toso, a] (*fam*) adj clumsy

patraña [pa'traɲa] nf story, fib

patria ['patrja] nf native land, mother country

patrimonio [patri'monjo] nm inheritance; (*fig*) heritage

patriota [pa'trjota] nm/f patriot; **patriotismo** nm patriotism

patrocinar [patroθi'nar] vt to sponsor; (*apoyar*) to back, support; **patrocinio** nm sponsorship; backing, support

patrón, ona [pa'tron, ona] nm/f (*jefe*) boss, chief, master/mistress; (*propietario*) landlord/lady; (REL) patron saint ♦ nm (TEC, COSTURA) pattern

patronal [patro'nal] adj: **la clase** ~ management

patronato [patro'nato] nm sponsorship; (*acto*) patronage; (*fundación benéfica*) trust, foundation

patrulla [pa'truʎa] nf patrol

pausa ['pausa] nf pause, break

pausado, a [pau'saðo, a] adj slow, deliberate

pauta ['pauta] nf line, guide line

pavimento [paβi'mento] nm (*con losas*) pavement, paving

pavo ['paβo] nm turkey; ~ **real** peacock

pavor [pa'βor] nm dread, terror

payaso, a [pa'jaso, a] nm/f clown

payo, a ['pajo] nm/f (*para gitanos*) non-gipsy

paz [paθ] nf peace; (*tranquilidad*) peacefulness, tranquillity; **hacer las paces** to make peace; (*fig*) to make up

P.D. abr (= *posdata*) P.S., p.s.

peaje [pe'axe] nm toll

peatón [pea'ton] nm pedestrian

peca ['peka] nf freckle

pecado [pe'kaðo] nm sin; **pecador, a** adj sinful ♦ nm/f sinner

pecaminoso, a [pekami'noso, a] adj sinful

pecar [pe'kar] vi (REL) to sin; (*fig*): **peca de generoso** he is generous to a fault

peculiar [peku'ljar] adj special, peculiar; (*característico*) typical, characteristic; ~**idad** nf peculiarity; special feature, characteristic

pecho ['petʃo] nm (ANAT) chest; (*de mujer*) breast(s) (*pl*), bosom; (*fig: corazón*) heart, breast; (: *valor*) courage, spirit; **dar el** ~ **a** to breast-feed; **tomar algo a** ~ to take sth to heart

pechuga [pe'tʃuɣa] nf breast

pedal [pe'ðal] nm pedal; ~**ear** vi to pedal

pedante [pe'ðante] adj pedantic ♦ nm/f pedant; ~**ría** nf pedantry

pedazo [pe'ðaθo] nm piece, bit; **hacerse** ~**s** (*romperse*) to smash, shatter

pedernal [peðer'nal] nm flint

pediatra [pe'ðjatra] nm/f paediatrician

pedido [pe'ðiðo] nm (COM: *mandado*) order; (*petición*) request

pedir [pe'ðir] vt to ask for, request; (*comida, COM: mandar*) to order; (*exigir: precio*) to ask; (*necesitar*) to need, demand, require ♦ vi to ask; **me pidió que cerrara la puerta** he asked me to shut the door; **¿cuánto piden por el coche?** how much are they asking for the car?

pedo ['peðo] (*fam!*) nm fart

pega ['peɣa] nf snag; **poner** ~**s (a)** to complain (about)

pegadizo, a [peɣa'ðiθo, a] adj (MUS) catchy

pegajoso, a [peɣa'xoso, a] adj sticky, adhesive

pegamento [peɣa'mento] nm gum, glue

pegar [pe'ɣar] vt (*papel, sellos*) to stick (on); (*cartel*) to stick up; (*coser*) to sew (on); (*unir: partes*) to join, fix together; (MED) to give, infect with; (*dar: golpe*) to give, deal ♦ vi (*adherirse*) to stick, adhere; (*ir juntos: colores*) to match, go together; (*golpear*) to hit; (*quemar: el sol*) to strike hot, burn (*fig*); ~**se** vr (*gen*) to stick; (*dos personas*) to hit each other, fight; (*fam*): ~ **un grito** to let out a yell; ~ **un salto** to jump (with fright); ~ **en** to touch; ~**se un tiro** to shoot o.s.

pegatina [peɣa'tina] nf sticker

pegote [pe'ɣote] nm (*fig*) mess; (*fam, pey*) eyesore, sight

peinado [pei'naðo] nm (*en peluquería*) hairdo; (*estilo*) hair style

peinar [pei'nar] vt to comb; (*hacer estilo*) to style; ~**se** vr to comb one's hair

peine ['peine] nm comb; ~**ta** nf ornamental comb

p.ej. abr (= *por ejemplo*) e.g.

Pekín [pe'kin] n Pekin(g)

pelado, a [pe'laðo, a] adj (*fruta, patata etc*)

peeled; (*cabeza*) shorn; (*campo, fig*) bare; (*fam: sin dinero*) broke

pelaje [pe'laxe] *nm* (*ZOOL*) fur, coat; (*fig*) appearance

pelar [pe'lar] *vt* (*fruta, patatas etc*) to peel; (*cortar el pelo a*) to cut the hair of; (*quitar la piel: animal*) to skin; ~**se** *vr* (*la piel*) to peel off; **voy a ~me** I'm going to get my hair cut

peldaño [pel'daɲo] *nm* step

pelea [pe'lea] *nf* (*lucha*) fight; (*discusión*) quarrel, row

peleado, a [pele'aðo, a] *adj:* **estar ~ (con uno)** to have fallen out (with sb)

pelear [pele'ar] *vi* to fight; ~**se** *vr* to fight; (*reñirse*) to fall out, quarrel

peletería [pelete'ria] *nf* furrier's, fur shop

pelícano [pe'likano] *nm* pelican

película [pe'likula] *nf* film; (*cobertura ligera*) thin covering; (*FOTO: rollo*) roll o reel of film

peligro [pe'liɣro] *nm* danger; (*riesgo*) risk; **correr ~ de** to run the risk of; ~**so, a** *adj* dangerous; risky

pelirrojo, a [peli'rroxo, a] *adj* red-haired, red-headed ♦ *nm/f* redhead

pelma ['pelma] (*fam*) *nm/f* pain (in the neck)

pelmazo [pel'maθo] (*fam*) *nm* = **pelma**

pelo ['pelo] *nm* (*cabellos*) hair; (*de barba, bigote*) whisker; (*de animal: pellejo*) hair, fur, coat; **al ~** just right; **venir al ~** to be exactly what one needs; **un hombre de ~ en pecho** a brave man; **por los ~s** by the skin of one's teeth; **no tener ~s en la lengua** to be outspoken, not mince words; **tomar el ~ a uno** to pull sb's leg

pelota [pe'lota] *nf* ball; (*fam: cabeza*) nut; **en ~** stark naked; **hacer la ~ (a uno)** (*fam*) to creep (to sb); ~ **vasca** pelota

pelotari [pelo'tari] *nm* pelota player

pelotón [pelo'ton] *nm* (*MIL*) squad, detachment

peluca [pe'luka] *nf* wig

peluche [pe'lutʃe] *nm:* **oso/muñeco de ~** teddy bear/soft toy

peludo, a [pe'luðo, a] *adj* hairy, shaggy

peluquería [peluke'ria] *nf* hairdresser's; (*para hombres*) barber's (shop); **peluquero, a** *nm/f* hairdresser; barber

pelusa [pe'lusa] *nf* (*BOT*) down; (*COSTURA*) fluff

pellejo [pe'ʎexo] *nm* (*de animal*) skin, hide

pellizcar [peʎiθ'kar] *vt* to pinch, nip

pena ['pena] *nf* (*congoja*) grief, sadness; (*remordimiento*) regret; (*dificultad*) trouble; (*dolor*) pain; (*JUR*) sentence; **merecer o valer la ~** to be worthwhile; **a duras ~s** with great difficulty; ~ **de muerte** death penalty; ~ **pecuniaria** fine; **¡qué ~!** what a shame!

penal [pe'nal] *adj* penal ♦ *nm* (*cárcel*) prison

penalidad [penali'ðað] *nf* (*problema, dificultad*) trouble, hardship; (*JUR*) penalty, punishment; ~**es** *nfpl* trouble, hardship

penalti [pe'nalti] (*pl* ~**s** *o* ~**es**) *nm* penalty (kick)

penalty [pe'nalti] (*pl* ~**s** *o* ~**es**) *nm* = **penalti**

penar [pe'nar] *vt* to penalize; (*castigar*) to punish ♦ *vi* to suffer

pendiente [pen'djente] *adj* pending, unsettled ♦ *nm* earring ♦ *nf* hill, slope

pene ['pene] *nm* penis

penetración [penetra'θjon] *nf* (*acto*) penetration; (*agudeza*) sharpness, insight

penetrante [pene'trante] *adj* (*herida*) deep; (*persona, arma*) sharp; (*sonido*) penetrating, piercing; (*mirada*) searching; (*viento, ironía*) biting

penetrar [pene'trar] *vt* to penetrate, pierce; (*entender*) to grasp ♦ *vi* to penetrate, go in; (*entrar*) to enter, go in; (*líquido*) to soak in; (*fig*) to pierce

penicilina [peniθi'lina] *nf* penicillin

península [pe'ninsula] *nf* peninsula; **peninsular** *adj* peninsular

penique [pe'nike] *nm* penny

penitencia [peni'tenθja] *nf* (*remordimiento*) penitence; (*castigo*) penance

penoso, a [pe'noso, a] *adj* (*difícil*) arduous, difficult

pensador, a [pensa'ðor, a] *nm/f* thinker

pensamiento [pensa'mjento] *nm* thought; (*mente*) mind; (*idea*) idea

pensar [pen'sar] *vt* to think; (*considerar*) to think over, think out; (*proponerse*) to intend, plan; (*imaginarse*) to think up, invent ♦ *vi* to think; ~ **en** to aim at, aspire to; **pensativo, a** *adj* thoughtful, pensive

pensión [pen'sjon] *nf* (*casa*) boarding o guest house; (*dinero*) pension; (*cama y comida*) board and lodging; ~ **completa** full board; **pensionista** *nm/f* (*jubilado*) (old-age) pensioner; (*huésped*) lodger

penúltimo, a [pe'nultimo, a] *adj* penultimate, last but one

penumbra [pe'numbra] *nf* half-light

penuria [pe'nurja] *nf* shortage, want

peña ['peɲa] *nf* (*roca*) rock; (*cuesta*) cliff, crag; (*grupo*) group, circle; (*AM: club*) folk club

peñasco [pe'ɲasko] *nm* large rock, boulder

peñón [pe'ɲon] *nm* wall of rock; **el P~** the Rock (of Gibraltar)

peón [pe'on] *nm* labourer; (*AM*) farm labourer, farmhand; (*AJEDREZ*) pawn

peonza [pe'onθa] *nf* spinning top

peor [pe'or] *adj* (*comparativo*) worse; (*superlativo*) worst ♦ *adv* worse; worst; **de mal en ~** from bad to worse

pepinillo [pepi'niʎo] *nm* gherkin

pepino [pe'pino] *nm* cucumber; **(no) me importa un ~** I don't care one bit

pepita [pe'pita] *nf* (*BOT*) pip; (*MINERÍA*) nugget

pequeñez [peke'ɲeθ] *nf* smallness, littleness; (*trivialidad*) trifle, triviality

pequeño, a [pe'keɲo, a] *adj* small, little

pera ['pera] *nf* pear; **peral** *nm* pear tree

percance [per'kanθe] *nm* setback, misfortune

percatarse [perka'tarse] *vr*: ~ **de** to notice, take note of

percepción [perθep'θjon] *nf* (*vista*) perception; (*idea*) notion, idea

perceptible [perθep'tiβle] *adj* perceptible, noticeable; (*COM*) payable, receivable

percibir [perθi'βir] *vt* to perceive, notice; (*COM*) to earn, get

percusión [perku'sjon] *nf* percussion

percha ['pertʃa] *nf* (*ganchos*) coat hooks *pl*; (*colgador*) coat hanger; (*de ave*) perch

perdedor, a [perðe'ðor, a] *adj* losing ♦ *nm/f* loser

perder [per'ðer] *vt* to lose; (*tiempo, palabras*) to waste; (*opportunidad*) to lose, miss; (*tren*) to miss ♦ *vi* to lose; ~**se** *vr* (*extraviarse*) to get lost; (*desaparecer*) to disappear, be lost to view; (*arruinarse*) to be ruined; **echar a** ~ (*comida*) to spoil, ruin; (*oportunidad*) to waste

perdición [perði'θjon] *nf* perdition, ruin

pérdida ['perðiða] *nf* loss; (*de tiempo*) waste; ~**s** *nfpl* (*COM*) losses

perdido, a [per'ðiðo, a] *adj* lost

perdiz [per'ðiθ] *nf* partridge

perdón [per'ðon] *nm* (*disculpa*) pardon, forgiveness; (*clemencia*) mercy; ¡~! sorry!, I beg your pardon!; **perdonar** *vt* to pardon, forgive; (*la vida*) to spare; (*excusar*) to exempt, excuse; ¡**perdone (usted)**! sorry!, I beg your pardon!

perdurable [perðu'raβle] *adj* lasting; (*eterno*) everlasting

perdurar [perðu'rar] *vi* (*resistir*) to last, endure; (*seguir existiendo*) to stand, still exist

perecedero, a [pereθe'ðero, a] *adj* (*COM etc*) perishable

perecer [pere'θer] *vi* (*morir*) to perish, die; (*objeto*) to shatter

peregrinación [pereðrina'θjon] *nf* (*REL*) pilgrimage

peregrino, a [pere'ðrino, a] *adj* (*idea*) strange, absurd ♦ *nm/f* pilgrim

perejil [pere'xil] *nm* parsley

perenne [pe'renne] *adj* everlasting, perennial

perentorio, a [peren'torjo, a] *adj* (*urgente*) urgent, peremptory; (*fijo*) set, fixed

pereza [pe'reθa] *nf* laziness, idleness; **perezoso, a** *adj* lazy, idle

perfección [perfek'θjon] *nf* perfection; **perfeccionar** *vt* to perfect; (*mejorar*) to improve; (*acabar*) to complete, finish

perfectamente [perfekta'mente] *adv* perfectly

perfecto, a [per'fekto, a] *adj* perfect; (*terminado*) complete, finished

perfidia [per'fiðja] *nf* perfidy, treachery

perfil [per'fil] *nm* profile; (*contorno*) silhouette, outline; (*ARQ*) (cross) section; ~**es** *nmpl* features; (*fig*) social graces; ~**ar** *vt* (*trazar*) to outline; (*fig*) to shape, give character to

perforación [perfora'θjon] *nf* perforation; (*con taladro*) drilling; **perforadora** *nf* punch

perforar [perfo'rar] *vt* to perforate; (*agujero*) to drill, bore; (*papel*) to punch a hole in ♦ *vi* to drill, bore

perfume [per'fume] *nm* perfume, scent

pericia [pe'riθja] *nf* skill, expertise

periferia [peri'ferja] *nf* periphery; (*de ciudad*) outskirts *pl*

periférico [peri'feriko] (*AM*) *nm* ring road (*BRIT*), beltway (*US*)

perímetro [pe'rimetro] *nm* perimeter

periódico, a [pe'rjoðiko, a] *adj* periodic(al) ♦ *nm* newspaper

periodismo [perjo'ðismo] *nm* journalism; **periodista** *nm/f* journalist

periodo [pe'rjoðo] *nm* period

período [pe'rioðo] *nm* = **periodo**

periquito [peri'kito] *nm* budgerigar, budgie

perito, a [pe'rito, a] *adj* (*experto*) expert; (*diestro*) skilled, skilful ♦ *nm/f* expert; skilled worker; (*técnico*) technician

perjudicar [perxuði'kar] *vt* (*gen*) to damage, harm; **perjudicial** *adj* damaging, harmful; (*en detrimento*) detrimental; **perjuicio** *nm* damage, harm

perjurar [perxu'rar] *vi* to commit perjury

perla ['perla] *nf* pearl; **me viene de** ~ it suits me fine

permanecer [permane'θer] *vi* (*quedarse*) to stay, remain; (*seguir*) to continue to be

permanencia [perma'nenθja] *nf* permanence; (*estancia*) stay

permanente [perma'nente] *adj* permanent, constant ♦ *nf* perm

permisible [permi'siβle] *adj* permissible, allowable

permisivo, a [permi'siβo, a] *adj* permissive

permiso [per'miso] *nm* permission; (*licencia*) permit, licence; **con** ~ excuse me; **estar de** ~ (*MIL*) to be on leave; ~ **de conducir** driving licence (*BRIT*), driver's license (*US*)

permitir [permi'tir] *vt* to permit, allow

pernera [per'nera] *nf* trouser leg

pernicioso, a [perni'θjoso, a] *adj* (*maligno, MED*) pernicious; (*persona*) wicked

pero ['pero] *conj* but; (*aún*) yet ♦ *nm* (*defecto*) flaw, defect; (*reparo*) objection

perpendicular [perpendiku'lar] *adj* perpendicular

perpetrar [perpe'trar] *vt* to perpetrate

perpetuar [perpe'twar] *vt* to perpetuate; **perpetuo, a** *adj* perpetual

perplejo, a [per'plexo, a] *adj* perplexed, bewildered

perra ['perra] *nf* (*ZOOL*) bitch; (*fam: dinero*) money; **estar sin una** ~ to be flat broke

perrera ['pe'rrera] *nf* kennel

perro ['perro] *nm* dog

persa ['persa] *adj*, *nm/f* Persian

persecución [perseku'θjon] *nf* pursuit, chase; (*REL, POL*) persecution

perseguir [perse'vir] *vt* to pursue, hunt; (*cortejar*) to chase after; (*molestar*) to pester, annoy; (*REL, POL*) to persecute

perseverante [perseße'rante] *adj* persevering, persistent

perseverar [perseße'rar] *vi* to persevere, persistent; ~ **en** to persevere in, persist with

persiana [per'sjana] *nf* (Venetian) blind

persignarse [persix'narse] *vr* to cross o.s.

persistente [persis'tente] *adj* persistent

persistir [persis'tir] *vi* to persist

persona [per'sona] *nf* person; ~ **mayor** elderly person; **10** ~s 10 people

personaje [perso'naxe] *nm* important person, celebrity; (*TEATRO etc*) character

personal [perso'nal] *adj* (*particular*) personal; (*para una persona*) single, for one person ♦ *nm* personnel, staff; ~**idad** *nf* personality

personarse [perso'narse] *vr* to appear in person

personificar [personifi'kar] *vt* to personify

perspectiva [perspek'tißa] *nf* perspective; (*vista, panorama*) view, panorama; (*posibilidad futura*) outlook, prospect

perspicacia [perspi'kaθja] *nf* (*fig*) discernment, perspicacity

perspicaz [perspi'kaθ] *adj* shrewd

persuadir [perswa'ðir] *vt* (*gen*) to persuade; (*convencer*) to convince; ~**se** *vr* to become convinced; **persuasión** *nf* persuasion; **persuasivo, a** *adj* persuasive; convincing

pertenecer [pertene'θer] *vi* to belong; (*fig*) to concern; **perteneciente** *adj*: **perteneciente a** belonging to; **pertenencia** *nf* ownership; **pertenencias** *nfpl* (*bienes*) possessions, property *sg*

pertenezca *etc vb ver* **pertenecer**

pértiga ['pertixa] *nf*: **salto de** ~ pole vault

pertinaz [perti'naθ] *adj* (*persistente*) persistent; (*terco*) obstinate

pertinente [perti'nente] *adj* relevant, pertinent; (*apropiado*) appropriate; ~ **a** concerning, relevant to

perturbación [perturßa'θjon] *nf* (*POL*) disturbance; (*MED*) upset, disturbance

perturbado, a [pertur'ßaðo, a] *adj* mentally unbalanced

perturbador, a [perturßa'ðor, a] *adj* perturbing, disturbing; (*subversivo*) subversive

perturbar [pertur'ßar] *vt* (*el orden*) to disturb; (*MED*) to upset, disturb; (*mentalmente*) to perturb

Perú [pe'ru] *nm*: **el** ~ Peru; **peruano, a** *adj*, *nm/f* Peruvian

perversión [perßer'sjon] *nf* perversion; **perverso, a** *adj* perverse; (*depravado*) depraved

pervertido, a [perßer'tiðo, a] *adj* perverted ♦ *nm/f* pervert

pervertir [perßer'tir] *vt* to pervert, corrupt

pesa ['pesa] *nf* weight; (*DEPORTE*) shot

pesadez [pesa'ðeθ] *nf* (*peso*) heaviness; (*lentitud*) slowness; (*aburrimiento*) tediousness

pesadilla [pesa'ðiʎa] *nf* nightmare, bad dream

pesado, a [pe'saðo, a] *adj* heavy; (*lento*) slow; (*difícil, duro*) tough, hard; (*aburrido*) boring, tedious; (*tiempo*) sultry

pesadumbre [pesa'ðumbre] *nf* grief, sorrow

pésame ['pesame] *nm* expression of condolence, message of sympathy; **dar el** ~ to express one's condolences

pesar [pe'sar] *vt* to weigh ♦ *vi* to weigh; (*ser pesado*) to weigh a lot, be heavy; (*fig: opinión*) to carry weight; **no pesa mucho** it doesn't weigh much ♦ *nm* (*arrepentimiento*) regret; (*pena*) grief, sorrow; **a** ~ **de** *o* **pese a (que)** in spite of, despite

pesca ['peska] *nf* (*acto*) fishing; (*lo pescado*) catch; **ir de** ~ to go fishing

pescadería [peskaðe'ria] *nf* fish shop, fishmonger's (*BRIT*)

pescadilla [peska'ðiʎa] *nf* (*pez*) whiting

pescado [pes'kaðo] *nm* fish

pescador, a [peska'ðor, a] *nm/f* fisherman/woman

pescar [pes'kar] *vt* (*tomar*) to catch; (*intentar tomar*) to fish for; (*conseguir: trabajo*) to manage to get ♦ *vi* to fish, go fishing

pescuezo [pes'kweθo] *nm* (*ZOOL*) neck

pesebre [pe'seßre] *nm* manger

peseta [pe'seta] *nf* peseta

pesimista [pesi'mista] *adj* pessimistic ♦ *nm/f* pessimist

pésimo, a ['pesimo, a] *adj* awful, dreadful

peso ['peso] *nm* weight; (*balanza*) scales *pl*; (*moneda*) peso; ~ **bruto/neto** gross/net weight; **vender a** ~ to sell by weight

pesquero, a [pes'kero, a] *adj* fishing *cpd*

pesquisa [pes'kisa] *nf* inquiry, investigation

pestaña [pes'tana] *nf* (*ANAT*) eyelash; (*borde*) rim; **pestañear** *vi* to blink

peste ['peste] *nf* plague; (*mal olor*) stink, stench

pesticida [pesti'θiða] *nm* pesticide

pestilencia [pesti'lenθja] *nf* (*mal olor*) stink, stench

pestillo [pes'tiʎo] *nm* (*cerrojo*) bolt; (*picaporte*) doorhandle

petaca [pe'taka] nf (de cigarros) cigarette case; (de pipa) tobacco pouch; (AM: maleta) suitcase

pétalo ['petalo] nm petal

petardo [pe'tardo] nm firework, firecracker

petición [peti'θjon] nf (pedido) request, plea; (memorial) petition; (JUR) plea

petrificar [petrifi'kar] vt to petrify

petróleo [pe'troleo] nm oil, petroleum; **petrolero, a** adj petroleum cpd ♦ nm (COM: persona) oil man; (buque) (oil) tanker

peyorativo, a [pejora'tiβo, a] adj pejorative

pez [peθ] nm fish

pezón [pe'θon] nm teat, nipple

pezuña [pe'θuɲa] nf hoof

piadoso, a [pja'ðoso, a] adj (devoto) pious, devout; (misericordioso) kind, merciful

pianista [pja'nista] nm/f pianist

piano ['pjano] nm piano

piar [pjar] vi to cheep

pibe, a ['piβe, a] (AM) nm/f boy/girl

picadero [pika'ðero] nm riding school

picadillo [pika'ðiʎo] nm mince, minced meat

picado, a [pi'kaðo, a] adj pricked, punctured; (CULIN) minced, chopped; (mar) choppy; (diente) bad; (tabaco) cut; (enfadado) cross

picador [pika'ðor] nm (TAUR) picador; (minero) faceworker

picadura [pika'ðura] nf (pinchazo) puncture; (de abeja) sting; (de mosquito) bite; (tabaco picado) cut tobacco

picante [pi'kante] adj hot; (comentario) racy, spicy

picaporte [pika'porte] nm (manija) doorhandle; (pestillo) latch

picar [pi'kar] vt (agujerear, perforar) to prick, puncture; (abeja) to sting; (mosquito, serpiente) to bite; (CULIN) to mince, chop; (incitar) to incite, goad; (dañar, irritar) to annoy, bother; (quemar: lengua) to burn, sting ♦ vi (pez) to bite, take the bait; (sol) to burn, scorch; (abeja, MED) to sting; (mosquito) to bite; ~se vr (agriarse) to turn sour, go off; (ofenderse) to take offence

picardía [pikar'ðia] nf villainy; (astucia) slyness, craftiness; (una ~) dirty trick; (palabra) rude/bad word o expression

pícaro, a ['pikaro, a] adj (malicioso) villainous; (travieso) mischievous ♦ nm (astuto) crafty sort; (sinvergüenza) rascal, scoundrel

pico ['piko] nm (de ave) beak; (punta) sharp point; (TEC) pick, pickaxe; (GEO) peak, summit; **y ~** and a bit

picotear [pikote'ar] vt to peck ♦ vi to nibble, pick

picudo, a [pi'kuðo, a] adj pointed, with a point

pichón [pi'tʃon] nm young pigeon

pidió etc vb ver **pedir**

pido etc vb ver **pedir**

pie [pje] (pl ~s) nm foot; (fig: motivo) motive, basis; (: fundamento) foothold; **ir a ~** to go on foot, walk; **estar de ~** to be standing (up); **ponerse de ~** to stand up; **de ~s a cabeza** from top to bottom; **al ~ de la letra** (citar) literally, verbatim; (copiar) exactly, word for word; **en ~ de guerra** on a war footing; **dar ~ a** to give cause for; **hacer ~** (en el agua) to touch (the) bottom

piedad [pje'ðað] nf (lástima) pity, compassion; (clemencia) mercy; (devoción) piety, devotion

piedra ['pjeðra] nf stone; (roca) rock; (de mechero) flint; (METEOROLOGÍA) hailstone

piel [pjel] nf (ANAT) skin; (ZOOL) skin, hide, fur; (cuero) leather; (BOT) skin, peel

pienso etc vb ver **pensar**

pierdo etc vb ver **perder**

pierna ['pjerna] nf leg

pieza ['pjeθa] nf piece; (habitación) room; ~ **de recambio** o **repuesto** spare (part)

pigmeo, a [piɣ'meo, a] adj, nm/f pigmy

pijama [pi'xama] nm pyjamas pl

pila ['pila] nf (ELEC) battery; (montón) heap, pile; (lavabo) sink

píldora ['pildora] nf pill; **la ~ (anticonceptiva)** the (contraceptive) pill

pileta [pi'leta] nf basin, bowl; (AM) swimming pool

piloto [pi'loto] nm pilot; (de aparato) (pilot) light; (AUTO: luz) tail o rear light; (: conductor) driver

pillaje [pi'ʎaxe] nm pillage, plunder

pillar [pi'ʎar] vt (saquear) to pillage, plunder; (fam: coger) to catch; (: agarrar) to grasp, seize; (: entender) to grasp, catch on to; ~se vr: ~se un dedo con la puerta to catch one's finger in the door

pillo, a ['piʎo, a] adj villainous; (astuto) sly, crafty ♦ nm/f rascal, rogue, scoundrel

pimentón [pimen'ton] nm paprika

pimienta [pi'mjenta] nf pepper

pimiento [pi'mjento] nm pepper, pimiento

pinacoteca [pinako'teka] nf art gallery

pinar [pi'nar] nm pine forest (BRIT), pine grove (US)

pincel [pin'θel] nm paintbrush

pinchadiscos [pintʃa'ðiskos] nm/f inv disc-jockey, DJ

pinchar [pin'tʃar] vt (perforar) to prick, pierce; (neumático) to puncture; (fig) to prod

pinchazo [pin'tʃaθo] nm (perforación) prick; (de neumático) puncture; (fig) prod

pincho ['pintʃo] nm (punta) point; (aguijón) spike; (CULIN) savoury (snack); ~ **moruno** shish kebab; ~ **de tortilla** small slice of omelette

ping-pong ['pin'pon] nm table tennis

pingüino [pin'gwino] nm penguin

pino ['pino] nm pine (tree)

pinta ['pinta] nf spot; (de líquidos) spot, drop; (aspecto) appearance, look(s) (pl); ~do, a adj spotted; (de muchos colores) colourful; ~das nfpl graffiti sg

pintar [pin'tar] vt to paint ♦ vi to paint; (fam) to count, be important; ~se vr to put on make-up

pintor, a [pin'tor, a] nm/f painter

pintoresco, a [pinto'resko, a] adj picturesque

pintura [pin'tura] nf painting; ~ a la acuarela watercolour; ~ al óleo oil painting

pinza ['pinθa] nf (ZOOL) claw; (para colgar ropa) clothes peg; (TEC) pincers pl; ~s nfpl (para depilar etc) tweezers pl

piña ['piɲa] nf (fruto del pino) pine cone; (fruta) pineapple; (fig) group

piñón [pi'ɲon] nm (fruto) pine nut; (TEC) pinion

pío, a ['pio, a] adj (devoto) pious, devout; (misericordioso) merciful

piojo ['pioxo] nm louse

pionero, a [pjo'nero, a] adj pioneering ♦ nm/f pioneer

pipa ['pipa] nf pipe; ~s nfpl (BOT) (edible) sunflower seeds

pipí [pi'pi] (fam) nm: hacer ~ to have a wee(-wee) (BRIT), have to go (wee-wee) (US)

pique ['pike] nm (resentimiento) pique, resentment; (rivalidad) rivalry, competition; irse a ~ to sink; (esperanza, familia) to be ruined

piqueta [pi'keta] nf pick(axe)

piquete [pi'kete] nm (agujerito) small hole; (MIL) squad, party; (de obreros) picket

piragua [pi'raɣwa] nf canoe; **piragüismo** nm canoeing

pirámide [pi'ramiðe] nf pyramid

pirata [pi'rata] adj, nm pirate ♦ nm/f: ~ informático/a hacker

Pirineo(s) [piri'neo(s)] nm(pl) Pyrenees pl

pirómano, a [pi'romano, a] nm/f (MED, JUR) arsonist

piropo [pi'ropo] nm compliment, (piece of) flattery

pirueta [pi'rweta] nf pirouette

pis [pis] (fam) nm pee, piss; hacer ~ to have a pee; (para niños) to wee-wee

pisada [pi'saða] nf (paso) footstep; (huella) footprint

pisar [pi'sar] vt (caminar sobre) to walk on, tread on; (apretar con el pie) to press; (fig) to trample on, walk all over ♦ vi to tread, step, walk

piscina [pis'θina] nf swimming pool

Piscis ['pisθis] nm Pisces

piso ['piso] nm (suelo, planta) floor; (apartamento) flat (BRIT), apartment; primer ~ (ESP) first floor; (AM) ground floor

pisotear [pisote'ar] vt to trample (on o underfoot)

pista ['pista] nf track, trail; (indicio) clue; ~ de aterrizaje runway; ~ de baile dance floor; ~ de hielo ice rink; ~ de tenis tennis court

pistola [pis'tola] nf pistol; (TEC) spray-gun; **pistolero, a** nm/f gunman/woman, gangster

pistón [pis'ton] nm (TEC) piston; (MUS) key

pitar [pi'tar] vt (silbato) to blow; (rechiflar) to whistle at, boo ♦ vi to whistle; (AUTO) to sound o toot one's horn; (AM) to smoke

pitillo [pi'tiʎo] nm cigarette

pito ['pito] nm whistle; (de coche) horn

pitón [pi'ton] nm (ZOOL) python

pitonisa [pito'nisa] nf fortune-teller

pitorreo [pito'rreo] nm joke; estar de ~ to be joking

pizarra [pi'θarra] nf (piedra) slate; (encerado) blackboard

pizca ['piθka] nf pinch, spot; (fig) spot, speck; ni ~ not a bit

placa ['plaka] nf plate; (distintivo) badge, insignia; ~ de matrícula number plate

placentero, a [plaθen'tero, a] adj pleasant, agreeable

placer [pla'θer] nm pleasure ♦ vt to please

plácido, a ['plaθiðo, a] adj placid

plaga ['plaɣa] nf pest; (MED) plague; (abundancia) abundance; **plagar** vt to infest, plague; (llenar) to fill

plagio ['plaxjo] nm plagiarism

plan [plan] nm (esquema, proyecto) plan; (idea, intento) idea, intention; tener ~ (fam) to have a date; tener un ~ (fam) to have an affair; en ~ económico (fam) on the cheap; vamos en ~ de turismo we're going as tourists; si te pones en ese ~ ... if that's your attitude ...

plana ['plana] nf sheet (of paper), page; (TEC) trowel; en primera ~ on the front page; ~ mayor staff

plancha ['plantʃa] nf (para planchar) iron; (rótulo) plate, sheet; (NAUT) gangway; a la ~ (CULIN) grilled; ~do nm ironing; **planchar** vt to iron ♦ vi to do the ironing

planeador [planea'ðor] nm glider

planear [plane'ar] vt to plan ♦ vi to glide

planeta [pla'neta] nm planet

planicie [pla'niθje] nf plain

planificación [planifika'θjon] nf planning; ~ familiar family planning

plano, a ['plano, a] adj flat, level, even ♦ nm (MAT, TEC, AVIAT) plane; (FOTO) shot; (ARQ) plan; (GEO) map; (de ciudad) map, street plan; primer ~ close-up; caer de ~ to fall flat

planta ['planta] nf (BOT, TEC) plant; (ANAT) sole of the foot, foot; (piso) floor; (AM: personal) staff; ~ baja ground floor

plantación [planta'θjon] nf (AGR) plantation; (acto) planting

plantar [plan'tar] *vt* (*BOT*) to plant; (*levantar*) to erect, set up; **~se** *vr* to stand firm; **~ a uno en la calle** to throw sb out; **dejar plantado a uno** (*fam*) to stand sb up

plantear [plante'ar] *vt* (*problema*) to pose; (*dificultad*) to raise

plantilla [plan'tiʎa] *nf* (*de zapato*) insole; (*personal*) personnel; **ser de ~** to be on the staff

plantón [plan'ton] *nm* (*MIL*) guard, sentry; (*fam*) long wait; **dar (un) ~ a uno** to stand sb up

plasmar [plas'mar] *vt* (*dar forma*) to mould, shape; (*representar*) to represent ♦ *vi*: **~ en** to take the form of

plasta ['plasta] (*fam*) *adj inv* boring ♦ *nmf* bore

Plasticina [plasti'θina] ® *nf* Plasticine ®

plástico, a ['plastiko, a] *adj* plastic ♦ *nm* plastic

Plastilina [plasti'lina] ® *nf* Plasticine ®

plata ['plata] *nf* (*metal*) silver; (*cosas hechas de ~*) silverware; (*AM*) cash, dough; **hablar en ~** to speak bluntly *o* frankly

plataforma [plata'forma] *nf* platform; **~ de lanzamiento/perforación** launch(ing) pad/drilling rig

plátano ['platano] *nm* (*fruta*) banana; (*árbol*) plane tree; banana tree

platea [pla'tea] *nf* (*TEATRO*) pit

plateado, a [plate'aðo, a] *adj* silver; (*TEC*) silver-plated

plática ['platika] *nf* talk, chat; **platicar** *vi* to talk, chat

platillo [pla'tiʎo] *nm* saucer; **~s** *nmpl* (*MUS*) cymbals; **~ volador** *o* **volante** flying saucer

platino [pla'tino] *nm* platinum; **~s** *nmpl* (*AUTO*) contact points

plato ['plato] *nm* plate, dish; (*parte de comida*) course; (*comida*) dish; **~ combinado** set main course (*served on one plate*); **~ fuerte** main course; **primer ~** first course

playa ['plaja] *nf* beach; (*costa*) seaside; **~ de estacionamiento** (*AM*) car park

playera [pla'jera] *nf* (*AM: camiseta*) T-shirt; **~s** *nfpl* (*zapatos*) (slip-on) canvas shoes

plaza ['plaθa] *nf* square; (*mercado*) market(place); (*sitio*) room, space; (*en vehículo*) seat, place; (*colocación*) post, job; **~ de toros** bullring

plazo ['plaθo] *nm* (*lapso de tiempo*) time, period; (*fecha de vencimiento*) expiry date; (*pago parcial*) instalment; **a corto/largo ~** short-/long-term; **comprar algo a ~s** to buy sth on hire purchase (*Brit*) *o* on time (*US*)

plazoleta [plaθo'leta] *nf* small square

pleamar [plea'mar] *nf* high tide

plebe ['pleβe] *nf*: **la ~** the common people *pl*, the masses *pl*; (*pey*) the plebs *pl*; **~yo, a** *adj* plebeian; (*pey*) coarse, common

plebiscito [pleβis'θito] *nm* plebiscite

plegable [ple'βaβle] *adj* pliable; (*silla*) folding

plegar [ple'xar] *vt* (*doblar*) to fold, bend; (*COSTURA*) to pleat; **~se** *vr* to yield, submit

pleito ['pleito] *nm* (*JUR*) lawsuit, case; (*fig*) dispute, feud

plenilunio [pleni'lunjo] *nm* full moon

plenitud [pleni'tuð] *nf* plenitude, fullness; (*abundancia*) abundance

pleno, a ['pleno, a] *adj* full; (*completo*) complete ♦ *nm* plenum; **en ~ día** in broad daylight; **en ~ verano** at the height of summer; **en plena cara** full in the face

pleuresía [pleure'sia] *nf* pleurisy

pliego *etc* ['pljexo] *vb ver* **plegar** ♦ *nm* (*hoja*) sheet (of paper); (*carta*) sealed letter/document; **~ de condiciones** details *pl*, specifications *pl*

pliegue *etc* ['pljexe] *vb ver* **plegar** ♦ *nm* fold, crease; (*de vestido*) pleat

plomero [plo'mero] *nm* (*AM*) plumber

plomo ['plomo] *nm* (*metal*) lead; (*ELEC*) fuse; **sin ~** unleaded

pluma ['pluma] *nf* feather; (*para escribir*): (**estilográfica**) ink pen; **~ fuente** (*AM*) fountain pen

plumero [plu'mero] *nm* (*quitapolvos*) feather duster

plumón [plu'mon] *nm* (*AM: fino*) felt-tip pen; (: *ancho*) marker

plural [plu'ral] *adj* plural; **~idad** *nf* plurality; **una ~idad de votos** a majority of votes

pluriempleo [pluriem'pleo] *nm* having more than one job

plus [plus] *nm* bonus; **~valía** *nf* (*COM*) appreciation

población [poβla'θjon] *nf* population; (*pueblo, ciudad*) town, city

poblado, a [po'βlaðo, a] *adj* inhabited ♦ *nm* (*aldea*) village; (*pueblo*) (small) town; **densamente ~** densely populated

poblador, a [poβla'ðor, a] *nm/f* settler, colonist

poblar [po'βlar] *vt* (*colonizar*) to colonize; (*fundar*) to found; (*habitar*) to inhabit

pobre ['poβre] *adj* poor ♦ *nmf* poor person; **~za** *nf* poverty

pocilga [po'θilxa] *nf* pigsty

pócima ['poθima] *nf* = **poción**

─────── PALABRA CLAVE ───────

poco, a ['poko, a] *adj* **1** (*sg*) little, not much; **~ tiempo** little *o* not much time; **de ~ interés** of little interest, not very interesting; **poca cosa** not much

2 (*pl*) few, not many; **unos ~s** a few, some; **~s niños comen lo que les conviene** few children eat what they should

♦ adv 1 little, not much; cuesta ~ it doesn't cost much

2 (+ adj.: = negativo, antónimo): ~ amable/inteligente not very nice/intelligent

3: por ~ me caigo I almost fell

4: a ~: a ~ de haberse casado shortly after getting married

5: ~ a ~ little by little

♦ nm a little, a bit; un ~ triste/de dinero a little sad/money

podar [po'ðar] vt to prune

─── PALABRA CLAVE

poder [po'ðer] vi 1 (capacidad) can, be able to; **no puedo hacerlo** I can't do it, I'm unable to do it

2 (permiso) can, may, be allowed to; **¿se puede?** may I (o we)?; **puedes irte ahora** you may go now; **no se puede fumar en este hospital** smoking is not allowed in this hospital

3 (posibilidad) may, might, could; **puede llegar mañana** he may o might arrive tomorrow; **pudiste haberte hecho daño** you might o could have hurt yourself; **¡podías habérmelo dicho antes!** you might have told me before!

4: **puede ser: puede ser** perhaps; **puede ser que lo sepa Tomás** Tomás may o might know

5: **¡no puedo más!** I've had enough!; **no pude menos que dejarlo** I couldn't help but leave it; **es tonto a más no ~** he's as stupid as they come

6: ~ **con: no puedo con este crío** this kid's too much for me

♦ nm power; ~ **adquisitivo** purchasing power; **detentar** o **ocupar** o **estar en el ~** to be in power

poderoso, a [poðe'roso, a] adj (político, país) powerful

podio ['poðjo] nm (DEPORTE) podium

podium ['poðjum] = **podio**

podrido, a [po'ðriðo, a] adj rotten, bad; (fig) rotten, corrupt

podrir [po'ðrir] = **pudrir**

poema [po'ema] nm poem

poesía [poe'sia] nf poetry

poeta [po'eta] nm/f poet; **poético, a** adj poetic(al)

poetisa [poe'tisa] nf (woman) poet

póker ['poker] nm poker

polaco, a [po'lako, a] adj Polish ♦ nm/f Pole

polar [po'lar] adj polar; ~**idad** nf polarity; ~**izarse** vr to polarize

polea [po'lea] nf pulley

polémica [po'lemika] nf polemics sg; (una

~) controversy, polemic

polen ['polen] nm pollen

policía [poli'θia] nm/f policeman/woman ♦ nf police; ~**co**, a adj police cpd; **novela policíaca** detective story; **policial** adj police cpd

polideportivo [poliðepor'tiβo] nm sports centre o complex

polietileno [polieti'leno] nm polythene (BRIT), polyethylene (US)

poligamia [poli'xamja] nf polygamy

polilla [po'liʎa] nf moth

polio ['poljo] nf polio

política [po'litika] nf politics sg; (económica, agraria etc) policy; ver tb **político**

político, a [po'litiko, a] adj political; (discreto) tactful; (de familia) -in-law ♦ nm/f politician; **padre** ~ father-in-law

póliza ['poliθa] nf certificate, voucher; (impuesto) tax stamp; ~ **de seguros** insurance policy

polizón [poli'θon] nm (en barco etc) stowaway

polo ['polo] nm (GEO, ELEC) pole; (helado) ice lolly; (DEPORTE) polo; (suéter) polo-neck; ~ **Norte/Sur** North/South Pole

Polonia [po'lonja] nf Poland

poltrona [pol'trona] nf easy chair

polución [polu'θjon] nf pollution

polvera [pol'βera] nf powder compact

polvo ['polβo] nm dust; (QUÍMICA, CULIN, MED) powder; ~**s** nmpl (maquillage) powder sg; ~ **de talco** talcum powder; **estar hecho** ~ (fam) to be worn out o exhausted

pólvora ['polβora] nf gunpowder; (fuegos artificiales) fireworks pl

polvoriento, a [polβo'rjento, a] adj (superficie) dusty; (sustancia) powdery

pollera [po'ʎera] nf (AM) skirt

pollería [poʎe'ria] nf poulterer's (shop)

pollo ['poʎo] nm chicken

pomada [po'maða] nf (MED) cream, ointment

pomelo [po'melo] nm grapefruit

pómez ['pomeθ] nf: **piedra** ~ pumice stone

pomo ['pomo] nm doorknob

pompa ['pompa] nf (burbuja) bubble; (bomba) pump; (esplendor) pomp, splendour; **pomposo, a** adj splendid, magnificent; (pey) pompous

pómulo ['pomulo] nm cheekbone

pon [pon] vb ver **poner**

ponche ['pontʃe] nm punch

poncho ['pontʃo] nm (AM) poncho

ponderar [ponde'rar] vt (considerar) to weigh up, consider; (elogiar) to praise highly, speak in praise of

pondré etc vb ver **poner**

─── PALABRA CLAVE

poner [po'ner] vt 1 (colocar) to put; (tele-

grama) to send; (*obra de teatro*) to put on; (*película*) to show; **ponlo más fuerte** turn it up; **¿qué ponen en el Excelsior?** what's on at the Excelsior?

2 (*tienda*) to open; (*instalar: gas etc*) to put in; (*radio, TV*) to switch *o* turn on

3 (*suponer*): **pongamos que ...** let's suppose that ...

4 (*contribuir*): **el gobierno ha puesto otro millón** the government has contributed another million

5 (*TELEC*): **póngame con el Sr. López** can you put me through to Mr. López?

6: **~ de**: **le han puesto de director general** they've appointed him general manager

7 (+ *adj*) to make; **me estás poniendo nerviosa** you're making me nervous

8 (*dar nombre*): **al hijo le pusieron Diego** they called their son Diego

♦ *vi* (*gallina*) to lay

♦ **~se** *vr* **1** (*colocarse*): **se puso a mi lado** he came and stood beside me; **tú pónte en esa silla** you go and sit on that chair

2 (*vestido, cosméticos*) to put on; **¿por qué no te pones el vestido nuevo?** why don't you put on *o* wear your new dress?

3 (+ *adj*) to turn; to get, become; **se puso muy serio** he got very serious; **después de lavarla la tela se puso azul** after washing it the material turned blue

4: **~se a**: **se puso a llorar** he started to cry; **tienes que ~te a estudiar** you must get down to studying

5: **~se bien con uno** to make it up with sb; **~se a mal con uno** to get on the wrong side of sb

pongo *etc vb ver* **poner**

poniente [po'njente] *nm* (*occidente*) west; (*viento*) west wind

pontífice [pon'tifiθe] *nm* pope, pontiff

popa ['popa] *nf* stern

popular [popu'lar] *adj* popular; (*cultura*) of the people, folk *cpd*; **~idad** *nf* popularity; **~izarse** *vr* to become popular

──────── *PALABRA CLAVE*

por [por] *prep* **1** (*objetivo*) for; **luchar ~ la patria** to fight for one's country

2 (+ *infin*): **~ no llegar tarde** so as not to arrive late; **~ citar unos ejemplos** to give a few examples

3 (*causa*) out of, because of; **~ escasez de fondos** through *o* for lack of funds

4 (*tiempo*): **~ la mañana/noche** in the morning/at night; **se queda ~ una semana** she's staying (for) a week

5 (*lugar*): **pasar ~ Madrid** to pass through Madrid; **ir a Guayaquil ~** Quito to go to Guayaquil via Quito; **caminar ~ la calle** to walk along the street; *ver tb* **todo**

6 (*cambio, precio*): **te doy uno nuevo ~ el que tienes** I'll give you a new one (in return) for the one you've got

7 (*valor distributivo*): **550 pesetas ~ hora/cabeza** 550 pesetas an *o* per hour/a *o* per head

8 (*modo, medio*) by; **~ correo/avión** by post/air; **día ~ día** day by day; **entrar ~ la entrada principal** to go in through the main entrance

9: **10 ~ 10 son 100** 10 by 10 is 100

10 (*en lugar de*): **vino él ~ su jefe** he came instead of his boss

11: **~ mí que revienten** as far as I'm concerned they can drop dead

12: **¿~ qué?** why?; **¿~ qué no?** why not?

porcelana [porθe'lana] *nf* porcelain; (*china*) china

porcentaje [porθen'taxe] *nm* percentage

porción [por'θjon] *nf* (*parte*) portion, share; (*cantidad*) quantity, amount

pordiosero, a [porðjo'sero, a] *nm/f* beggar

porfiar [por'fjar] *vi* to persist, insist; (*disputar*) to argue stubbornly

pormenor [porme'nor] *nm* detail, particular

pornografía [pornoɣra'fia] *nf* pornography

poro ['poro] *nm* pore; **~so, a** *adj* porous

porque ['porke] *conj* (*a causa de*) because; (*ya que*) since; (*con el fin de*) so that, in order that

porqué [por'ke] *nm* reason, cause

porquería [porke'ria] *nf* (*suciedad*) filth, dirt; (*acción*) dirty trick; (*objeto*) small thing, trifle; (*fig*) rubbish

porra ['porra] *nf* (*arma*) stick, club

porrazo [po'rraθo] *nm* blow, bump

porro ['porro] *nm* (*droga*) joint (*fam*)

porrón [po'rron] *nm* glass wine jar with a long spout

portaaviones [porta'(a)βjones] *nm inv* aircraft carrier

portada [por'taða] *nf* (*de revista*) cover

portador, a [porta'ðor, a] *nm/f* carrier, bearer; (*COM*) bearer, payee

portaequipajes [portaeki'paxes] *nm inv* (*AUTO: maletero*) boot; (*: baca*) luggage rack

portal [por'tal] *nm* (*entrada*) vestibule, hall; (*portada*) porch, doorway; (*puerta de entrada*) main door; (*DEPORTE*) goal

portamaletas [portama'letas] *nm inv* (*AUTO: maletero*) boot; (*: baca*) roof rack

portarse [por'tarse] *vr* to behave, conduct o.s.

portátil [por'tatil] *adj* portable

portavoz [porta'βoθ] *nm/f* (*persona*) spokesman/woman

portazo [por'taθo] *nm*: **dar un ~** to slam the door

porte ['porte] *nm* (*COM*) transport; (*precio*) transport charges *pl*

portento [por'tento] *nm* marvel, wonder; **~so, a** *adj* marvellous, extraordinary

porteño, a [por'teɲo, a] *adj* of o from Buenos Aires

portería [porte'ria] *nf* (*oficina*) porter's office; (*gol*) goal

portero, a [por'tero, a] *nm/f* porter; (*conserje*) caretaker; (*ujier*) doorman; (*DEPORTE*) goalkeeper; **~ automático** intercom

pórtico ['portiko] *nm* (*patio*) portico, porch; (*fig*) gateway; (*arcada*) arcade

portorriqueño, a [portorri'keɲo, a] *adj* Puerto Rican

Portugal [portu'ɣal] *nm* Portugal; **portugués, esa** *adj, nm/f* Portuguese ♦ *nm* (*LING*) Portuguese

porvenir [porβe'nir] *nm* future

pos [pos] *prep*: **en ~ de** after, in pursuit of

posada [po'saða] *nf* (*refugio*) shelter, lodging; (*mesón*) guest house; **dar ~ a** to give shelter to, take in

posaderas [posa'ðeras] *nfpl* backside *sg*, buttocks

posar [po'sar] *vt* (*en el suelo*) to lay down, put down; (*la mano*) to place, put gently ♦ *vi* to sit, pose; **~se** *vr* to settle; (*pájaro*) to perch; (*avión*) to land, come down

posdata [pos'ðata] *nf* postscript

pose ['pose] *nf* pose

poseedor, a [posee'ðor, a] *nm/f* owner, possessor; (*de récord, puesto*) holder

poseer [pose'er] *vt* to possess, own; (*ventaja*) to enjoy; (*récord, puesto*) to hold

posesión [pose'sjon] *nf* possession; **posesionarse** *vr*: **posesionarse de** to take possession of, take over

posesivo, a [pose'siβo, a] *adj* possessive

posibilidad [posiβili'ðað] *nf* possibility; (*oportunidad*) chance; **posibilitar** *vt* to make possible; (*hacer realizable*) to make feasible

posible [po'siβle] *adj* possible; (*realizable*) feasible; **de ser ~** if possible; **en lo ~** as far as possible

posición [posi'θjon] *nf* position; (*rango social*) status

positivo, a [posi'tiβo, a] *adj* positive

poso ['poso] *nm* sediment; (*heces*) dregs *pl*

posponer [pospo'ner] *vt* to put behind/below; (*aplazar*) to postpone

posta ['posta] *nf*: **a ~** deliberately, on purpose

postal [pos'tal] *adj* postal ♦ *nf* postcard

poste ['poste] *nm* (*de telégrafos etc*) post, pole; (*columna*) pillar

póster ['poster] (*pl* **pósteres, pósters**) *nm* poster

postergar [poster'ɣar] *vt* to postpone, delay

posteridad [posteri'ðað] *nf* posterity

posterior [poste'rjor] *adj* back, rear; (*si-*

guiente) following, subsequent; (*más tarde*) later; **~idad** *nf*: **con ~idad** later, subsequently

postizo, a [pos'tiθo, a] *adj* false, artificial ♦ *nm* hairpiece

postor, a [pos'tor, a] *nm/f* bidder

postre ['postre] *nm* sweet, dessert

postrero, a [pos'trero, a] *adj* (*delante de nmsg*: **postrer**) *adj* (*último*) last; (*que viene detrás*) rear

postulado [postu'laðo] *nm* postulate

póstumo, a ['postumo, a] *adj* posthumous

postura [pos'tura] *nf* (*del cuerpo*) posture, position; (*fig*) attitude, position

potable [po'taβle] *adj* drinkable; **agua ~** drinking water

potaje [po'taxe] *nm* thick vegetable soup

pote ['pote] *nm* pot, jar

potencia [po'tenθja] *nf* power

potencial [poten'θjal] *adj, nm* potential

potenciar [poten'θjar] *vt* to boost

potente [po'tente] *adj* powerful

potro, a ['potro, a] *nm/f* (*ZOOL*) colt/filly ♦ *nm* (*de gimnasia*) vaulting horse

pozo ['poθo] *nm* well; (*de río*) deep pool; (*de mina*) shaft

P.P. *abr* (= *porte pagado*) CP

práctica ['praktika] *nf* practice; (*método*) method; (*arte, capacidad*) skill; **en la ~** in practice

practicable [prakti'kaβle] *adj* practicable; (*camino*) passable

practicante [prakti'kante] *nm/f* (*MED*: ayudante de doctor) medical assistant; (: enfermero) male nurse; (*quien practica algo*) practitioner ♦ *adj* practising

practicar [prakti'kar] *vt* to practise; (*DEPORTE*) to go in for (*BRIT*) o out for (*US*), play; (*realizar*) to carry out, perform

práctico, a ['praktiko, a] *adj* practical; (*instruido*: persona) skilled, expert

practique *etc vb ver* **practicar**

pradera [pra'ðera] *nf* meadow; (*US etc*) prairie

prado ['praðo] *nm* (*campo*) meadow, field; (*pastizal*) pasture

Praga ['praɣa] *n* Prague

pragmático, a [praɣ'matiko, a] *adj* pragmatic

preámbulo [pre'ambulo] *nm* preamble, introduction

precario, a [pre'karjo, a] *adj* precarious

precaución [prekau'θjon] *nf* (*medida preventiva*) preventive measure, precaution; (*prudencia*) caution, wariness

precaver [preka'βer] *vt* to guard against; (*impedir*) to forestall; **~se** *vr*: **~se de** o **contra algo** (be on one's) guard against sth; **precavido, a** *adj* cautious, wary

precedente [preθe'ðente] *adj* preceding; (*anterior*) former ♦ *nm* precedent

preceder [preθe'ðer] *vt, vi* to precede, go

before, come before

precepto [pre'θepto] *nm* precept

preciado, a [pre'θjaðo, a] *adj (estimado)* esteemed, valuable

preciarse [pre'θjarse] *vr* to boast; **~se** to pride o.s. on, boast of being

precinto [pre'θinto] *nm (tb: ~ de garantía)* seal

precio ['preθjo] *nm* price; *(costo)* cost; *(valor)* value, worth; *(de viaje)* fare; **~ al contado/de coste/de oportunidad** cash/cost/bargain price; **~ al detalle** o **al por menor** retail price; **~ tope** top price

preciosidad [preθjosi'ðað] *nf (valor)* (high) value, (great) worth; *(encanto)* charm; *(cosa bonita)* beautiful thing; **es una ~** it's lovely, it's really beautiful

precioso, a [pre'θjoso, a] *adj* precious; *(de mucho valor)* valuable; *(fam)* lovely, beautiful

precipicio [preθi'piθjo] *nm* cliff, precipice; *(fig)* abyss

precipitación [preθipita'θjon] *nf* haste; *(lluvia)* rainfall

precipitado, a [preθipi'taðo, a] *adj (conducta)* hasty, rash; *(salida)* hasty, sudden

precipitar [preθipi'tar] *vt (arrojar)* to hurl down, throw; *(apresurar)* to hasten; *(acelerar)* to speed up, accelerate; **~se** *vr* to throw o.s.; *(apresurarse)* to rush; *(actuar sin pensar)* to act rashly

precisamente [preθisa'mente] *adv* precisely; *(exactamente)* precisely, exactly

precisar [preθi'sar] *vt (necesitar)* to need, require; *(fijar)* to determine exactly, fix; *(especificar)* to specify

precisión [preθi'sjon] *nf (exactitud)* precision

preciso, a [pre'θiso, a] *adj (exacto)* precise; *(necesario)* necessary, essential

preconcebido, a [prekonθe'βiðo, a] *adj* preconceived

precoz [pre'koθ] *adj (persona)* precocious; *(calvicie etc)* premature

precursor, a [prekur'sor, a] *nm/f* predecessor, forerunner

predecir [preðe'θir] *vt* to predict, forecast

predestinado, a [preðesti'naðo, a] *adj* predestined

predicar [preði'kar] *vt, vi* to preach

predicción [preðik'θjon] *nf* prediction

predilecto, a [preði'lekto, a] *adj* favourite

predisponer [preðispo'ner] *vt* to predispose; *(pey)* to prejudice; **predisposición** *nf* inclination; prejudice, bias

predominante [preðomi'nante] *adj* predominant

predominar [preðomi'nar] *vt* to dominate ♦ *vi* to predominate; *(prevalecer)* to prevail; **predominio** *nm* predominance; prevalence

preescolar [preeskolar] *adj* preschool

prefabricado, a [prefaβri'kaðo, a] *adj* pre-

fabricated

prefacio [pre'faθjo] *nm* preface

preferencia [prefe'renθja] *nf* preference; **de ~** preferably, for preference

preferible [prefe'riβle] *adj* preferable

preferir [prefe'rir] *vt* to prefer

prefiero *etc vb ver* **preferir**

pregonar [preɣo'nar] *vt* to proclaim, announce

pregunta [pre'ɣunta] *nf* question; **hacer una ~** to ask o put (forth *(US)*) a question

preguntar [preɣun'tar] *vt* to ask; *(cuestionar)* to question ♦ *vi* to ask; **~se** *vr* to wonder; **~ por alguien** to ask for sb

preguntón, ona [preɣun'ton, ona] *adj* inquisitive

prehistórico, a [preis'toriko, a] *adj* prehistoric

prejuicio [pre'xwiθjo] *nm (acto)* prejudgement; *(idea preconcebida)* preconception; *(parcialidad)* prejudice, bias

preliminar [pretimi'nar] *adj* preliminary

preludio [pre'luðjo] *nm* prelude

prematuro, a [prema'turo, a] *adj* premature

premeditación [premeðita'θjon] *nf* premeditation

premeditar [premeði'tar] *vt* to premeditate

premiar [pre'mjar] *vt* to reward; *(en un concurso)* to give a prize to

premio ['premjo] *nm* reward; prize; *(COM)* premium

premonición [premoni'θjon] *nf* premonition

prenatal [prena'tal] *adj* antenatal, prenatal

prenda ['prenda] *nf (ropa)* garment, article of clothing; *(garantía)* pledge; **~s** *nfpl (talentos)* talents, gifts

prendedor [prende'ðor] *nm* brooch

prender [pren'der] *vt (captar)* to catch, capture; *(detener)* to arrest; *(COSTURA)* to pin, attach; *(sujetar)* to fasten ♦ *vi* to catch; *(arraigar)* to take root; **~se** *vr (encenderse)* to catch fire

prendido, a [pren'diðo, a] *(AM) adj (luz etc)* on

prensa ['prensa] *nf* press; **la P~** the press; **prensar** *vt* to press

preñado, a [pre'ɲaðo, a] *adj (ZOOL)* pregnant; **~ de** pregnant with, full of

preocupación [preokupa'θjon] *nf* worry, concern; *(ansiedad)* anxiety

preocupado, a [preoku'paðo, a] *adj* worried, concerned; *(ansioso)* anxious

preocupar [preoku'par] *vt* to worry; **~se** *vr* to worry; **~se de algo** *(hacerse cargo)* to take care of sth

preparación [prepara'θjon] *nf (acto)* preparation; *(estado)* readiness; *(entrenamiento)* training

preparado, a [prepa'raðo, a] *adj (dispuesto)* prepared; *(CULIN)* ready (to serve)

♦ *nm* preparation

preparar [prepa'rar] *vt (disponer)* to prepare, get ready; *(TEC: tratar)* to prepare, process; *(entrenar)* to teach, train; **~se** *vr:* **~se a** *o* **para** to prepare to *o* for, get ready to *o* for; **preparativo, a** *adj* preparatory, preliminary; **preparativos** *nmpl* preparations; **preparatoria** *(AM)* *nf* sixth-form college *(BRIT)*, senior high school *(US)*

prerrogativa [prerroγa'tiβa] *nf* prerogative, privilege

presa ['presa] *nf (cosa apresada)* catch; *(víctima)* victim; *(de animal)* prey; *(de agua)* dam

presagiar [presa'xjar] *vt* to presage, forebode; **presagio** *nm* omen

prescindir [presθin'dir] *vi:* **~ de** *(privarse de)* to do without, go without; *(descartar)* to dispense with

prescribir [preskri'βir] *vt* to prescribe; **prescripción** *nf* prescription

presencia [pre'senθja] *nf* presence; **presencial** *adj:* **testigo presencial** eyewitness; **presenciar** *vt* to be present at; *(asistir a)* to attend; *(ver)* to see, witness

presentación [presenta'θjon] *nf* presentation; *(introducción)* introduction

presentador, a [presenta'ðor, a] *nm/f* presenter, compère

presentar [presen'tar] *vt* to present; *(ofrecer)* to offer; *(mostrar)* to show, display; *(a una persona)* to introduce; **~se** *vr (llegar inesperadamente)* to appear, turn up; *(ofrecerse como candidato)* to run, stand; *(aparecer)* to show, appear; *(solicitar empleo)* to apply

presente [pre'sente] *adj* present ♦ *nm* present; **hacer ~** to state, declare; **tener ~** to remember, bear in mind

presentimiento [presenti'mjento] *nm* premonition, presentiment

presentir [presen'tir] *vt* to have a premonition of

preservación [preserβa'θjon] *nf* protection, preservation

preservar [preser'βar] *vt* to protect, serve; **preservativo** *nm* sheath, condom

presidencia [presi'ðenθja] *nf* presidency; *(de comité)* chairmanship

presidente [presi'ðente] *nm/f* president; *(de comité)* chairman/woman

presidiario [presi'ðjarjo] *nm* convict

presidio [pre'siðjo] *nm* prison, penitentiary

presidir [presi'ðir] *vt (dirigir)* to preside at, preside over; *(: comité)* to take the chair at; *(dominar)* to dominate, rule ♦ *vi* to preside; to take the chair

presión [pre'sjon] *nf* pressure; **presionar** *vt* to press; *(fig)* to press, put pressure on ♦ *vi:* **presionar para** to press for

preso, a ['preso, a] *nm/f* prisoner; **tomar** *o* **llevar ~ a uno** to arrest sb, take sb pris-

oner

prestaciones [presta'θjones] *nfpl (TEC, AUT)* features

prestado, a [pres'taðo, a] *adj* on loan; **pedir ~** to borrow

prestamista [presta'mista] *nm/f* moneylender

préstamo ['prestamo] *nm* loan; **~ hipotecario** mortgage

prestar [pres'tar] *vt* to lend, loan; *(atención)* to pay; *(ayuda)* to give

presteza [pres'teθa] *nf* speed, promptness

prestigio [pres'tixjo] *nm* prestige; **~so, a** *adj (honorable)* prestigious; *(famoso, renombrado)* renowned, famous

presumido, a [presu'miðo, a] *adj (persona)* vain

presumir [presu'mir] *vt* to presume ♦ *vi (tener aires)* to be conceited; **según cabe ~** as may be presumed, presumably; **presunción** *nf* presumption; **presunto, a** *adj (supuesto)* supposed, presumed; *(así llamado)* so-called; **presuntuoso, a** *adj* conceited, presumptuous

presuponer [presupo'ner] *vt* to presuppose

presupuesto [presu'pwesto] *pp de* **presuponer** ♦ *nm (FINANZAS)* budget; *(estimación: de costo)* estimate

pretencioso, a [preten'θjoso, a] *adj* pretentious

pretender [preten'der] *vt (intentar)* to try to, seek to; *(reivindicar)* to claim; *(buscar)* to seek, try for; *(cortejar)* to woo, court; **~ que** to expect that; **pretendiente** *nm/f (candidato)* candidate, applicant; *(amante)* suitor; **pretensión** *nf (aspiración)* aspiration; *(reivindicación)* claim; *(orgullo)* pretension

pretexto [pre'teksto] *nm* pretext; *(excusa)* excuse

prevalecer [preβale'θer] *vi* to prevail

prevención [preβen'θjon] *nf (preparación)* preparation; *(estado)* preparedness, readiness; *(el evitar)* prevention; *(previsión)* foresight, forethought; *(precaución)* precaution

prevenido, a [preβe'niðo, a] *adj* prepared, ready; *(cauteloso)* cautious

prevenir [preβe'nir] *vt (impedir)* to prevent; *(prever)* to foresee, anticipate; *(predisponer)* to prejudice, bias; *(avisar)* to warn; *(preparar)* to prepare, get ready; **~se** *vr* to get ready, prepare; **~se contra** to take precautions against; **preventivo, a** *adj* preventive, precautionary

prever [pre'βer] *vt* to foresee

previo, a ['preβjo, a] *adj (anterior)* previous; *(preliminar)* preliminary ♦ *prep:* **~ acuerdo de los otros** subject to the agreement of the others

previsión [preβi'sjon] *nf (perspicacia)* foresight; *(predicción)* forecast; **previsto, a** *adj* anticipated, forecast

prima ['prima] *nf* (*COM*) bonus; ~ **de segu-ro** insurance premium; *ver tb* **primo**

primacía [prima'θia] *nf* primacy

primario, a [pri'marjo, a] *adj* primary

primavera [prima'βera] *nf* spring(-time)

primera [pri'mera] *nf* (*AUTO*) first gear; (*FERRO*: *tb*: ~ *clase*) first class; **de** ~ (*fam*) first-class, first-rate

primero, a [pri'mero, a] (*delante de nmsg*: **primer**) *adj* first; (*principal*) prime ♦ *adv* first; (*más bien*) sooner, rather; **primera plana** front page

primicia [pri'miθja] *nf* (*PRENSA*) (*tb*: ~ *in-formativa*) scoop

primitivo, a [primi'tiβo, a] *adj* primitive; (*original*) original

primo, a ['primo, a] *adj* prime ♦ *nm/f* cousin; (*fam*) fool, idiot; ~ **hermano** first cousin; **materias primas** raw materials

primogénito, a [primo'xenito, a] *adj* first-born

primordial [primor'ðjal] *adj* basic, funda-mental

primoroso, a [primo'roso, a] *adj* exquisite, delicate

princesa [prin'θesa] *nf* princess

principal [prinθi'pal] *adj* principal, main ♦ *nm* (*jefe*) chief, principal

príncipe ['prinθipe] *nm* prince

principiante [prinθi'pjante] *nm/f* beginner

principio [prin'θipjo] *nm* (*comienzo*) begin-ning, start; (*origen*) origin; (*primera etapa*) rudiment, basic idea; (*moral*) principle; **a** ~**s de** at the beginning of

pringoso, a [prin'yoso, a] *adj* (*grasiento*) greasy; (*pegajoso*) sticky

pringue ['pringe] *nm* (*grasa*) grease, fat, dripping

prioridad [priori'ðað] *nf* priority

prisa ['prisa] *nf* (*apresuramiento*) hurry, haste; (*rapidez*) speed; (*urgencia*) (sense of) urgency; **a o de** ~ quickly; **correr** ~ to be urgent; **darse** ~ to hurry up; **estar de o te-ner** ~ to be in a hurry

prisión [pri'sjon] *nf* (*cárcel*) prison; (*período de cárcel*) imprisonment; **prisionero, a** *nm/f* prisoner

prismáticos [pris'matikos] *nmpl* binoculars

privación [priβa'θjon] *nf* deprivation; (*falta*) want, privation

privado, a [pri'βaðo, a] *adj* private

privar [pri'βar] *vt* to deprive; **privativo, a** *adj* exclusive

privilegiado, a [priβile'xjaðo, a] *adj* privi-leged; (*memoria*) very good

privilegiar [priβile'xjar] *vt* to grant a privi-lege to; (*favorecer*) to favour

privilegio [priβi'lexjo] *nm* privilege; (*conce-sión*) concession

pro [pro] *nm o f* profit, advantage ♦ *prep*: **asociación** ~ **ciegos** association for the blind ♦ *prefijo*: ~ **soviético/americano** pro-Soviet/American; **en** ~ **de** on behalf of, for; **los** ~**s y los contras** the pros and cons

proa ['proa] *nf* bow, prow; **de** ~ bow *cpd*, fore

probabilidad [proβaβili'ðað] *nf* probability, likelihood; (*oportunidad*, *posibilidad*) chance, prospect; **probable** *adj* probable, likely

probador [proβa'ðor] *nm* (*en tienda*) fitting room

probar [pro'βar] *vt* (*demostrar*) to prove; (*someter a prueba*) to test, try out; (*ropa*) to try on; (*comida*) to taste ♦ *vi* to try; ~**se un traje** to try on a suit

probeta [pro'βeta] *nf* test tube

problema [pro'βlema] *nm* problem

procedente [proθe'ðente] *adj* (*razonable*) reasonable; (*conforme a derecho*) proper, fitting; ~ **de** coming from, originating in

proceder [proθe'ðer] *vi* (*avanzar*) to pro-ceed; (*actuar*) to act; (*ser correcto*) to be right (and proper), be fitting ♦ *nm* (*compor-tamiento*) behaviour, conduct; ~ **de** to come from, originate in; **procedimiento** *nm* procedure; (*proceso*) process; (*método*) means *pl*, method

procesado, a [proθe'saðo, a] *nm/f* accused

procesador [proθesa'ðor] *nm*: ~ **de textos** word processor

procesar [proθe'sar] *vt* to try, put on trial

procesión [proθe'sjon] *nf* procession

proceso [pro'θeso] *nm* process; (*JUR*) trial; (*lapso*) course (of time)

proclamar [prokla'mar] *vt* to proclaim

procreación [prokrea'θjon] *nf* procreation

procrear [prokre'ar] *vt, vi* to procreate

procurador, a [prokura'ðor, a] *nm/f* attor-ney

procurar [proku'rar] *vt* (*intentar*) to try, en-deavour; (*conseguir*) to get, obtain; (*asegu-rar*) to secure; (*producir*) to produce

prodigio [pro'ðixjo] *nm* prodigy; (*milagro*) wonder, marvel; ~**so, a** *adj* prodigious, marvellous

pródigo, a ['proðiyo, a] *adj*: **hijo** ~ prodi-gal son

producción [proðuk'θjon] *nf* (*gen*) produc-tion; (*producto*) product; ~ **en serie** mass production

producir [proðu'θir] *vt* to produce; (*causar*) to cause, bring about; ~**se** *vr* (*cambio*) to come about; (*accidente*) to take place; (*pro-blema etc*) to arise; (*hacerse*) to be pro-duced, be made; (*estallar*) to break out

productividad [proðuktiβi'ðað] *nf* produc-tivity; **productivo, a** *adj* productive; (*pro-vechoso*) profitable

producto [pro'ðukto] *nm* product; (*produc-ción*) production

productor, a [proðuk'tor, a] *adj* produc-tive, producing ♦ *nm/f* producer

proeza [pro'eθa] *nf* exploit, feat
profanar [profa'nar] *vt* to desecrate, profane; **profano, a** *adj* profane ♦ *nm/f* layman/woman
profecía [profe'θia] *nf* prophecy
proferir [profe'rir] *vt* (*palabra, sonido*) to utter; (*injuria*) to hurl, let fly
profesar [profe'sar] *vt* (*practicar*) to practise
profesión [profe'sjon] *nf* profession; **profesional** *adj* professional
profesor, a [profe'sor, a] *nm/f* teacher; **~ado** *nm* teaching profession
profeta [pro'feta] *nm/f* prophet; **profetizar** *vt, vi* to prophesy
prófugo, a [ˈprofuxo, a] *nm/f* fugitive; (*MIL: desertor*) deserter
profundidad [profundi'ðað] *nf* depth; **profundizar** *vt* (*fig*): **profundizar en** to go deeply into; **profundo, a** *adj* deep; (*misterio, pensador*) profound
profusión [profu'sjon] *nf* (*abundancia*) profusion; (*prodigalidad*) extravagance
progenitor [proxeni'tor] *nm* ancestor; **~es** *nmpl* (*padres*) parents
programa [pro'ɣrama] *nm* programme (*BRIT*), program (*US*); **~ción** *nf* programming; **~dor, a** *nm/f* programmer; **programar** *vt* to program
progresar [proɣre'sar] *vi* to progress, make progress; **progresista** *adj, nm/f* progressive; **progresivo, a** *adj* progressive; (*gradual*) gradual; (*continuo*) continuous; **progreso** *nm* progress
prohibición [proiβi'θjon] *nf* prohibition, ban
prohibir [proi'βir] *vt* to prohibit, ban, forbid; **se prohíbe fumar, prohibido fumar** no smoking
prójimo, a [ˈproximo, a] *nm/f* fellow man; (*vecino*) neighbour
proletariado [proleta'rjaðo] *nm* proletariat
proletario, a [prole'tarjo, a] *adj, nm/f* proletarian
proliferación [prolifera'θjon] *nf* proliferation
proliferar [prolife'rar] *vi* to proliferate; **prolífico, a** *adj* prolific
prólogo [ˈproloxo] *nm* prologue
prolongación [prolonga'θjon] *nf* extension; **prolongado, a** *adj* (*largo*) long; (*alargado*) lengthy
prolongar [prolon'xar] *vt* to extend; (*reunión etc*) to prolong; (*calle, tubo*) to extend
promedio [pro'meðjo] *nm* average; (*de distancia*) middle, mid-point
promesa [pro'mesa] *nf* promise
prometer [prome'ter] *vt* to promise ♦ *vi* to show promise; **~se** *vr* (*novios*) to get engaged; **prometido, a** *adj* promised; engaged ♦ *nm/f* fiancé/fiancée
prominente [promi'nente] *adj* prominent
promiscuo, a [pro'miskwo, a] *adj* promiscuous

promoción [promo'θjon] *nf* promotion
promotor [promo'tor] *nm* promoter; (*instigador*) instigator
promover [promo'βer] *vt* to promote; (*causar*) to cause; (*instigar*) to instigate, stir up
promulgar [promul'xar] *vt* to promulgate; (*fig*) to proclaim
pronombre [pro'nombre] *nm* pronoun
pronosticar [pronosti'kar] *vt* to predict, foretell, forecast; **pronóstico** *nm* prediction, forecast; **pronóstico del tiempo** weather forecast
pronto, a [ˈpronto, a] *adj* (*rápido*) prompt, quick; (*preparado*) ready ♦ *adv* quickly, promptly; (*en seguida*) at once, right away; (*dentro de poco*) soon; (*temprano*) early ♦ *nm*: **tener ~s de enojo** to be quick-tempered; **al ~** at first; **de ~** suddenly; **por lo ~** meanwhile, for the present
pronunciación [pronunθja'θjon] *nf* pronunciation
pronunciar [pronun'θjar] *vt* to pronounce; (*discurso*) to make, deliver; **~se** *vr* to revolt, rebel; (*declararse*) to declare o.s.
propagación [propaxa'θjon] *nf* propagation
propaganda [propa'xanda] *nf* (*política*) propaganda; (*comercial*) advertising
propagar [propa'xar] *vt* to propagate
propensión [propen'sjon] *nf* inclination, propensity; **propenso, a** *adj* inclined to; **ser propenso a** to be inclined to, have a tendency to
propicio, a [pro'piθjo, a] *adj* favourable, propitious
propiedad [propje'ðað] *nf* property; (*posesión*) possession, ownership; **~ particular** private property
propietario, a [propje'tarjo, a] *nm/f* owner, proprietor
propina [pro'pina] *nf* tip
propio, a [ˈpropjo, a] *adj* own, of one's own; (*característico*) characteristic, typical; (*debido*) proper; (*mismo*) selfsame, very; **el ~ ministro** the minister himself; **¿tienes casa propia?** have you a house of your own?
proponer [propo'ner] *vt* to propose, put forward; (*problema*) to pose; **~se** *vr* to propose, intend
proporción [propor'θjon] *nf* proportion; (*MAT*) ratio; **proporciones** *nfpl* (*dimensiones*) dimensions; (*fig*) size *sg*; **proporcionado, a** *adj* proportionate; (*regular*) medium, middling; (*justo*) just right; **proporcionar** *vt* (*dar*) to give, supply, provide
proposición [proposi'θjon] *nf* proposition; (*propuesta*) proposal
propósito [pro'posito] *nm* purpose; (*intento*) aim, intention ♦ *adv*: **a ~** by the way, incidentally; (*a posta*) on purpose, deliberately; **a ~ de** about, with regard to

propuesta [pro'pwesta] *vb ver* **proponer** ♦ *nf* proposal

propulsar [propul'sar] *vt* to drive, propel; *(fig)* to promote, encourage; **propulsión** *nf* propulsion; **propulsión a chorro** *o* **por reacción** jet propulsion

prórroga ['prorroɣa] *nf* extension; *(JUR)* stay; *(COM)* deferment; *(DEPORTE)* extra time; **prorrogar** *vt (período)* to extend; *(decisión)* to defer, postpone

prorrumpir [prorrum'pir] *vi* to burst forth, break out

prosa ['prosa] *nf* prose

proscrito, a [pro'skrito, a] *adj (prohibido, desterrado)* banned

proseguir [prose'ɣir] *vt* to continue, carry on ♦ *vi* to continue, go on

prospección [prospek'θjon] *nf* exploration; *(del oro)* prospecting

prospecto [pros'pekto] *nm* prospectus

prosperar [prospe'rar] *vi* to prosper, thrive, flourish; **prosperidad** *nf* prosperity; *(éxito)* success; **próspero, a** *adj* prosperous, flourishing; *(que tiene éxito)* successful

prostíbulo [pros'tiβulo] *nm* brothel (*BRIT*), house of prostitution (*US*)

prostitución [prostitu'θjon] *nf* prostitution

prostituir [prosti'twir] *vt* to prostitute; **~se** *vr* to prostitute o.s., become a prostitute

prostituta [prosti'tuta] *nf* prostitute

protagonista [protaɣo'nista] *nm/f* protagonist

protagonizar [protaɣoni'θar] *vt* to take the chief rôle in

protección [protek'θjon] *nf* protection

protector, a [protek'tor, a] *adj* protective, protecting ♦ *nm/f* protector

proteger [prote'xer] *vt* to protect; **protegido, a** *nm/f* protégé/protégée

proteína [prote'ina] *nf* protein

protesta [pro'testa] *nf* protest; *(declaración)* protestation

protestante [protes'tante] *adj* Protestant

protestar [protes'tar] *vt* to protest, declare; *(fe)* to protest ♦ *vi* to protest

protocolo [proto'kolo] *nm* protocol

prototipo [proto'tipo] *nm* prototype

prov. *abr* (= *provincia*) prov

provecho [pro'βetʃo] *nm* advantage, benefit; *(FINANZAS)* profit; **¡buen ~!** bon appétit!; **en ~ de** to the benefit of; **sacar ~ de** to benefit from, profit by

proveer [proβe'er] *vt* to provide, supply ♦ *vi*: **~ a** to provide for

provenir [proβe'nir] *vi*: **~ de** to come from, stem from

proverbio [pro'βerβjo] *nm* proverb

providencia [proβi'ðenθja] *nf* providence; *(previsión)* foresight

provincia [pro'βinθja] *nf* province; **~no, a** *adj* provincial; *(del campo)* country *cpd*

provisión [proβi'sjon] *nf* provision; *(abas-*

tecimiento) provision, supply; *(medida)* measure, step

provisional [proβisjo'nal] *adj* provisional

provocación [proβoka'θjon] *nf* provocation

provocar [proβo'kar] *vt* to provoke; *(alentar)* to tempt, invite; *(causar)* to bring about, lead to; *(promover)* to promote; *(estimular)* to rouse, stimulate; **¿te provoca un café?** (*AM*) would you like a coffee?; **provocativo, a** *adj* provocative

próximamente [proksima'mente] *adv* shortly, soon

proximidad [proksimi'ðað] *nf* closeness, proximity; **próximo, a** *adj* near, close; *(vecino)* neighbouring; *(siguiente)* next

proyectar [projek'tar] *vt (objeto)* to hurl, throw; *(luz)* to cast, shed; *(CINE)* to screen, show; *(planear)* to plan

proyectil [projek'til] *nm* projectile, missile

proyecto [pro'jekto] *nm* plan; *(estimación de costo)* detailed estimate

proyector [projek'tor] *nm (CINE)* projector

prudencia [pru'ðenθja] *nf (sabiduría)* wisdom; *(cuidado)* care; **prudente** *adj* sensible, wise; *(conductor)* careful

prueba *etc* ['prweβa] *vb ver* **probar** ♦ *nf* proof; *(ensayo)* test, trial; *(degustación)* tasting, sampling; *(de ropa)* fitting; **a ~ on** trial; **a ~ de** proof against; **a ~ de agua/fuego** waterproof/fireproof; **someter a ~** to put to the test

prurito [pru'rito] *nm* itch; *(de bebé)* nappy (*BRIT*) *o* diaper (*US*) rash

psico... [siko] *prefijo* psycho...; **~análisis** *nm inv* psychoanalysis; **~logía** *nf* psychology; **~lógico, a** *adj* psychological; **psicólogo, a** *nm/f* psychologist; **psicópata** *nm/f* psychopath; **~sis** *nf inv* psychosis

psiquiatra [si'kjatra] *nm/f* psychiatrist; **psiquiátrico, a** *adj* psychiatric

psíquico, a ['sikiko, a] *adj* psychic(al)

PSOE [pe'soe] *nm abr* = **Partido Socialista Obrero Español**

pta(s) *abr* = **peseta(s)**

pts *abr* = **pesetas**

púa ['pua] *nf* sharp point; *(BOT, ZOOL)* prickle, spine; *(para guitarra)* plectrum (*BRIT*), pick (*US*); **alambre de ~** barbed wire

pubertad [puβer'tað] *nf* puberty

publicación [puβlika'θjon] *nf* publication

publicar [puβli'kar] *vt (editar)* to publish; *(hacer público)* to publicize; *(divulgar)* to make public, divulge

publicidad [puβliθi'ðað] *nf* publicity; *(COM: propaganda)* advertising; **publicitario, a** *adj* publicity *cpd*; advertising *cpd*

público, a ['puβliko, a] *adj* public ♦ *nm* public; *(TEATRO etc)* audience

puchero [pu'tʃero] *nm (CULIN: guiso)* stew; *(: olla)* cooking pot; **hacer ~s** to pout

pude *etc vb ver* **poder**

púdico, a ['puðiko, a] *adj* modest
pudiente [pu'ðjente] *adj* (*rico*) wealthy, well-to-do
pudiera *etc vb ver* **poder**
pudor [pu'ðor] *nm* modesty
pudrir [pu'ðrir] *vt* to rot; (*fam*) to upset, annoy; **~se** *vr* to rot, decay
pueblo ['pweßlo] *nm* people; (*nación*) nation; (*aldea*) village
puedo *etc vb ver* **poder**
puente ['pwente] *nm* bridge; **hacer ~** (*inf*) to take an extra day off work between 2 public holidays; to take a long weekend; **~ aéreo** shuttle service; **~ colgante** suspension bridge
puerco, a ['pwerko, a] *nm/f* pig/sow ♦ *adj* (*sucio*) dirty, filthy; (*obsceno*) disgusting; **~ de mar** porpoise; **~ marino** dolphin
pueril [pwe'ril] *adj* childish
puerro ['pwerro] *nm* leek
puerta ['pwerta] *nf* door; (*de jardín*) gate; (*portal*) doorway; (*fig*) gateway; (*portería*) goal; **a la ~** at the door; **a ~ cerrada** behind closed doors; **~ giratoria** revolving door
puerto ['pwerto] *nm* port; (*paso*) pass; (*fig*) haven, refuge
Puerto Rico [pwerto'riko] *nm* Puerto Rico; **puertorriqueño, a** *adj, nm/f* Puerto Rican
pues [pwes] *adv* (*entonces*) then; (*bueno*) well, well then; (*así que*) so ♦ *conj* (*ya que*) since; **¡~!** (*sí*) yes!, certainly!
puesta ['pwesta] *nf* (*apuesta*) bet, stake; **~ en marcha** starting; **~ del sol** sunset
puesto, a ['pwesto, a] *pp de* **poner** ♦ *adj*: **tener algo ~** to have sth on, be wearing sth ♦ *nm* (*lugar, posición*) place; (*trabajo*) post, job; (*COM*) stall ♦ *conj*: **~ que** since, as
púgil ['puxil] *nm* boxer
pugna ['puxna] *nf* battle, conflict; **pugnar** *vi* (*luchar*) to struggle, fight; (*pelear*) to fight
pujar [pu'xar] *vi* (*en subasta*) to bid; (*esforzarse*) to struggle, strain
pulcro, a ['pulkro, a] *adj* neat, tidy; (*bello*) exquisite
pulga ['pulxa] *nf* flea
pulgada [pul'xaða] *nf* inch
pulgar [pul'xar] *nm* thumb
pulir [pu'lir] *vt* to polish; (*alisar*) to smooth; (*fig*) to polish up, touch up
pulmón [pul'mon] *nm* lung; **pulmonía** *nf* pneumonia
pulpa ['pulpa] *nf* pulp; (*de fruta*) flesh, soft part
pulpería [pulpe'ria] (*AM*) *nf* (*tienda*) small grocery store
púlpito ['pulpito] *nm* pulpit
pulpo ['pulpo] *nm* octopus
pulsación [pulsa'θjon] *nf* beat, pulsation; (*ANAT*) throb(bing)
pulsar [pul'sar] *vt* (*tecla*) to touch, tap;

(*MUS*) to play; (*botón*) to press, push ♦ *vi* to pulsate; (*latir*) to beat, throb; (*MED*): **~ a uno** to take sb's pulse
pulsera [pul'sera] *nf* bracelet
pulso ['pulso] *nm* (*ANAT*) pulse; (: *muñeca*) wrist; (*fuerza*) strength; (*firmeza*) steadiness, steady hand; (*tacto*) tact, good sense
pulverizador [pulßeriθa'ðor] *nm* spray, spray gun
pulverizar [pulßeri'θar] *vt* to pulverize; (*líquido*) to spray
pulla ['puʎa] *nf* cutting remark; (*expresión grosera*) obscene remark
puna ['puna] (*AM*) *nf* mountain sickness
punitivo, a [puni'tißo, a] *adj* punitive
punta ['punta] *nf* point, tip; (*extremidad*) end; (*fig*) touch, trace; **horas ~s** peak hours, rush hours; **sacar ~ a** to sharpen; **estar de ~** to be edgy
puntada [pun'taða] *nf* (*COSTURA*) stitch
puntal [pun'tal] *nm* prop, support
puntapié [punta'pje] *nm* kick
puntear [punte'ar] *vt* to tick, mark
puntería [punte'ria] *nf* (*de arma*) aim, aiming; (*destreza*) marksmanship
puntero, a [pun'tero, a] *adj* leading ♦ *nm* (*palo*) pointer
puntiagudo, a [puntja'xuðo, a] *adj* sharp, pointed
puntilla [pun'tiʎa] *nf* (*encaje*) lace edging o trim; (*andar*) **de ~s** (to walk) on tiptoe
punto ['punto] *nm* (*gen*) point; (*señal diminuta*) spot, dot; (*COSTURA, MED*) stitch; (*lugar*) spot, place; (*momento*) point, moment; **a ~** ready; **estar a ~ de** to be on the point of o about to; **en ~** on the dot; **~ muerto** dead centre; (*AUTO*) neutral (gear); **~ final** full stop (*BRIT*), period (*US*); **~ y coma** semicolon; **~ de interrogación** question mark; **~ de vista** point of view, viewpoint; **hacer ~** (*tejer*) to knit
puntuación [puntwa'θjon] *nf* punctuation; (*puntos: en examen*) mark(s) (*pl*); (: *DEPORTE*) score
puntual [pun'twal] *adj* (*a tiempo*) punctual; (*exacto*) exact, accurate; (*seguro*) reliable; **~idad** *nf* punctuality; exactness, accuracy; reliability; **~izar** *vt* to fix, specify
puntuar [pun'twar] *vi* (*DEPORTE*) to score, count
punzada [pun'θaða] *nf* (*de dolor*) twinge
punzante [pun'θante] *adj* (*dolor*) shooting, sharp; (*herramienta*) sharp; **punzar** *vt* to prick, pierce ♦ *vi* to shoot, stab
puñado [pu'ɲaðo] *nm* handful
puñal [pu'ɲal] *nm* dagger; **~ada** *nf* stab
puñetazo [puɲe'taθo] *nm* punch
puño ['puɲo] *nm* (*ANAT*) fist; (*cantidad*) fistful, handful; (*COSTURA*) cuff; (*de herramienta*) handle
pupila [pu'pila] *nf* pupil
pupitre [pu'pitre] *nm* desk

puré [pu're] *nm* puree; (*sopa*) (thick) soup; **~ de patatas** mashed potatoes

pureza [pu'reθa] *nf* purity

purga ['purɣa] *nf* purge; **purgante** *adj, nm* purgative; **purgar** *vt* to purge

purgatorio [purɣa'torjo] *nm* purgatory

purificar [purifi'kar] *vt* to purify; (*refinar*) to refine

puritano, a [puri'tano, a] *adj* (*actitud*) puritanical; (*iglesia, tradición*) puritan ♦ *nm/f* puritan

puro, a ['puro, a] *adj* pure; (*cielo*) clear; (*verdad*) simple, plain ♦ *adv*: **de ~ cansado** out of sheer tiredness ♦ *nm* cigar

púrpura ['purpura] *nf* purple; **purpúreo, a** *adj* purple

pus [pus] *nm* pus

puse *etc vb ver* **poner**

pusiera *etc vb ver* **poner**

pústula ['pustula] *nf* pimple, sore

puta ['puta] *nf* whore, prostitute

putrefacción [putrefak'θjon] *nf* rotting, putrefaction

pútrido, a ['putriðo, a] *adj* rotten

PVP *abr* (*ESP*: = *precio venta al público*) RRP

──────── *Q q*

──────── PALABRA CLAVE

que [ke] *conj* **1** (*con oración subordinada: muchas veces no se traduce*) that; **dijo ~ vendría** he said (that) he would come; **espero ~ lo encuentres** I hope (that) you find it; *ver tb* **el**

2 (*en oración independiente*): ¡**~ entre!** send him in; ¡**~ se mejore tu padre!** I hope your father gets better

3 (*enfático*): ¿**me quieres? – ¡~ sí!** do you love me? – of course!

4 (*consecutivo: muchas veces no se traduce*) that; **es tan grande ~ no lo puedo levantar** it's so big (that) I can't lift it

5 (*comparaciones*) than; **yo ~ tú/él** if I were you/him; *ver tb* **más; menos; mismo**

6 (*valor disyuntivo*): **~ le guste o no** whether he likes it or not; **~ venga o ~ no venga** whether he comes or not

7 (*porque*): **no puedo, ~ tengo ~ quedarme en casa** I can't, I've got to stay in

♦ *pron* **1** (*cosa*) that, which; (+ *prep*)

which; **el sombrero ~ te compraste** the hat (that *o* which) you bought; **la cama en ~ dormí** the bed (that *o* which) I slept in

2 (*persona: suj*) that, who; (: *objeto*) that, whom; **el amigo ~ me acompañó al museo** the friend that *o* who went to the museum with me: **la chica ~ invité** the girl (that *o* whom) I invited

qué [ke] *adj* what?, which? ♦ *pron* what?; ¡**~ divertido!** how funny!; ¿**~ edad tienes?** how old are you?; ¿**de ~ me hablas?** what are you saying to me?; ¿**~ tal?** how are you?, how are things?; ¿**~ hay (de nuevo)?** what's new?

quebrada [ke'βraða] *nf* ravine; *ver tb* **quebrado**

quebradizo, a [keβra'ðiθo, a] *adj* fragile; (*persona*) frail

quebrado, a [ke'βraðo, a] *adj* (*roto*) broken ♦ *nm/f* bankrupt ♦ *nm* (*MAT*) fraction

quebrantar [keβran'tar] *vt* (*infringir*) to violate, transgress; **~se** *vr* (*persona*) to fail in health

quebranto [ke'βranto] *nm* damage, harm; (*decaimiento*) exhaustion; (*dolor*) grief, pain

quebrar [ke'βrar] *vt* to break, smash ♦ *vi* to go bankrupt; **~se** *vr* to break, get broken; (*MED*) to be ruptured

quedar [ke'ðar] *vi* to stay, remain; (*encontrarse: sitio*) to be; (*restar*) to remain, be left; **~se** *vr* to remain, stay (behind); **~se (con) algo** to keep sth; **~ en** (*acordar*) to agree on/to; **~ en nada** to come to nothing; **~ por hacer** to be still to be done; **~ ciego/mudo** to be left blind/dumb; **no te queda bien ese vestido** that dress doesn't suit you; **eso queda muy lejos** that's a long way (away); **quedamos a las seis** we agreed to meet at six

quedo, a ['keðo, a] *adj* still ♦ *adv* softly, gently

quehacer [kea'θer] *nm* task, job; **~es** (*domésticos*) *nmpl* household chores

queja ['kexa] *nf* complaint; **quejarse** *vr* (*enfermo*) to moan, groan; (*protestar*) to complain; **quejarse de que** to complain (about the fact) that; **quejido** *nm* moan

quemado, a [ke'maðo, a] *adj* burnt

quemadura [kema'ðura] *nf* burn, scald

quemar [ke'mar] *vt* to burn; (*fig: malgastar*) to burn up, squander ♦ *vi* to be burning hot; **~se** *vr* (*consumirse*) to burn (up); (*del sol*) to get sunburnt

quemarropa [kema'rropa]: **a ~** *adv* point-blank

quemazón [kema'θon] *nf* burn; (*calor*) intense heat; (*sensación*) itch

quepo *etc vb ver* **caber**

querella [ke'reʎa] *nf* (*JUR*) charge; (*disputa*) dispute; **~se** *vr* (*JUR*) to file a complaint

┌─────────── *PALABRA CLAVE*

querer [ke'rer] *vt* **1** *(desear)* to want; **quiero más dinero** I want more money; **quisiera** *o* **querría un té** I'd like a tea; **sin ~** unintentionally; **quiero ayudar/que vayas** I want to help/you to go
2 *(preguntas: para pedir algo)*: **¿quiere abrir la ventana?** could you open the window?; **¿quieres echarme una mano?** can you give me a hand?
3 *(amar)* to love; *(tener cariño a)* to be fond of; **quiere mucho a sus hijos** he's very fond of his children
4 *(requerir)*: **esta planta quiere más luz** this plant needs more light
5: **le pedí que me dejara ir pero no quiso** I asked him to let me go but he refused

querido, a [ke'riðo, a] *adj* dear ♦ *nm/f* darling; *(amante)* lover
queso ['keso] *nm* cheese; **~ crema** cream cheese
quicio ['kiθjo] *nm* hinge; **sacar a uno de ~** to get on sb's nerves
quiebra ['kjeβra] *nf* break, split; *(COM)* bankruptcy; *(ECON)* slump
quiebro ['kjeβro] *nm* *(del cuerpo)* swerve
quien [kjen] *pron* who; **hay ~ piensa que** there are those who think that; **no hay ~ lo haga** no-one will do it
quién [kjen] *pron* who, whom; **¿~ es?** who's there?
quienquiera [kjen'kjera] *(pl* **quienesquiera)** *pron* whoever
quiero *etc vb ver* **querer**
quieto, a ['kjeto, a] *adj* still; *(carácter)* placid; **quietud** *nf* stillness
quilate [ki'late] *nm* carat
quilla ['kiʎa] *nf* keel
quimera [ki'mera] *nf* chimera; **quimérico, a** *adj* fantastic
químico, a ['kimiko, a] *adj* chemical ♦ *nm/f* chemist ♦ *nf* chemistry
quincalla [kin'kaʎa] *nf* hardware, ironmongery *(BRIT)*
quince ['kinθe] *num* fifteen; **~ días** a fortnight; **~añero, a** *nm/f* teenager; **~na** *nf* fortnight; *(pago)* fortnightly pay; **~nal** *adj* fortnightly
quiniela [ki'njela] *nf* football pools *pl*; **~s** *nfpl* *(impreso)* pools coupon *sg*
quinientos, as [ki'njentos, as] *adj, num* five hundred
quinina [ki'nina] *nf* quinine
quinqui ['kinki] *nm* delinquent
quinto, a ['kinto, a] *adj* fifth ♦ *nf* country house; *(MIL)* call-up, draft
quiosco ['kjosko] *nm* *(de música)* bandstand; *(de periódicos)* news stand
quirófano [ki'rofano] *nm* operating theatre

quirúrgico, a [ki'rurxiko, a] *adj* surgical
quise *etc vb ver* **querer**
quisiera *etc vb ver* **querer**
quisquilloso, a [kiski'ʎoso, a] *adj* *(susceptible)* touchy; *(meticuloso)* pernickety
quiste ['kiste] *nm* cyst
quitaesmalte [kitaes'malte] *nm* nail-polish remover
quitamanchas [kita'mantʃas] *nm inv* stain remover
quitanieves [kita'njeßes] *nm inv* snowplough *(BRIT)*, snowplow *(US)*
quitar [ki'tar] *vt* to remove, take away; *(ropa)* to take off; *(dolor)* to relieve; **¡quita de ahí!** get away!; **~se** *vr* to withdraw; *(ropa)* to take off; **se quitó el sombrero** he took off his hat
quitasol [kita'sol] *nm* sunshade *(BRIT)*, parasol
quite ['kite] *nm* *(esgrima)* parry; *(evasión)* dodge
Quito ['kito] *n* Quito
quizá(s) [ki'θa(s)] *adv* perhaps, maybe

─────────── *R r*

rábano ['raßano] *nm* radish; **me importa un ~** I don't give a damn
rabia ['raßja] *nf* *(MED)* rabies *sg*; *(fig: ira)* fury, rage; **rabiar** *vi* to have rabies; to rage, be furious; **rabiar por algo** to long for sth
rabieta [ra'ßjeta] *nf* tantrum, fit of temper
rabino [ra'ßino] *nm* rabbi
rabioso, a [ra'ßjoso, a] *adj* rabid; *(fig)* furious
rabo ['raßo] *nm* tail
racial [ra'θjal] *adj* racial, race *cpd*
racimo [ra'θimo] *nm* bunch
raciocinio [raθjo'θinjo] *nm* reason
ración [ra'θjon] *nf* portion; **raciones** *nfpl* rations
racional [raθjo'nal] *adj* *(razonable)* reasonable; *(lógico)* rational; **~izar** *vt* to rationalize
racionar [raθjo'nar] *vt* to ration (out)
racismo [ra'θismo] *nm* racialism, racism; **racista** *adj, nm/f* racist
racha ['ratʃa] *nf* gust of wind: **buena/mala ~** *(fig)* spell of good/bad luck
radar [ra'ðar] *nm* radar
radiactivo, a [raðjak'tißo, a] *adj* = **radioactivo**
radiador [raðja'ðor] *nm* radiator

radiante [ra'ðjante] adj radiant
radical [raði'kal] adj, nm/f radical
radicar [raði'kar] vi to take root; ~ **en** to lie o consist in; ~**se** vr to establish o.s., put down (one's) roots
radio ['raðjo] nf radio; (aparato) radio (set) ♦ nm (MAT) radius; (QUÍMICA) radium; ~**actividad** nf radioactivity; ~**activo, a** adj radioactive; ~**difusión** nf broadcasting; ~**emisora** nf transmitter, radio station; ~**escucha** nm/f listener; ~**grafía** nf X-ray; ~**grafiar** vt to X-ray; ~**terapia** nf radiotherapy; ~**yente** nm/f listener
ráfaga ['rafaβa] nf gust; (de luz) flash; (de tiros) burst
raído, a [ra'iðo, a] adj (ropa) threadbare
raigambre [rai'γambre] nf (BOT) roots pl; (fig) tradition
raíz [ra'iθ] nf root; ~ **cuadrada** square root; **a** ~ **de** as a result of
raja ['raxa] nf (de melón etc) slice; (grieta) crack; **rajar** vt to split; (fam) to slash; **rajarse** vr to split, crack; **rajarse de** to back out of
rajatabla [raxa'taβla]: **a** ~ adv (estrictamente) strictly, to the letter
rallador [raλa'ðor] nm grater
rallar [ra'λar] vt to grate
RAM [ram] nf abr (= memoria de acceso aleatorio) RAM
rama ['rama] nf branch; ~**je** nm branches pl, foliage; **ramal** nm (de cuerda) strand; (FERRO) branch line (BRIT); (AUTO) branch (road) (BRIT)
rambla ['rambla] nf (avenida) avenue
ramera [ra'mera] nf whore
ramificación [ramifika'θjon] nf ramification
ramificarse [ramifi'karse] vr to branch out
ramillete [rami'λete] nm bouquet
ramo ['ramo] nm branch; (sección) department, section
rampa ['rampa] nf ramp
ramplón, ona [ram'plon, ona] adj uncouth, coarse
rana ['rana] nf frog; **salto de** ~ leapfrog
rancio, a ['ranθjo, a] adj (comestibles) rancid; (vino) aged, mellow; (fig) ancient
ranchero [ran'tʃero] nm (AM) rancher; smallholder
rancho ['rantʃo] nm grub (fam); (AM: grande) ranch; (: pequeño) small farm
rango ['rango] nm rank, standing
ranura [ra'nura] nf groove; (de teléfono etc) slot
rapar [ra'par] vt to shave; (los cabellos) to crop
rapaz [ra'paθ] (nf: **rapaza**) nm/f young boy/girl ♦ adj (ZOOL) predatory
rape ['rape] nm quick shave; (pez) angler fish; **al** ~ cropped
rapé [ra'pe] nm snuff
rapidez [rapi'ðeθ] nf speed, rapidity; **rápi-**

do, a adj fast, quick ♦ adv quickly ♦ nm (FERRO) express; **rápidos** nmpl rapids
rapiña [ra'piɲa] nm robbery; **ave de** ~ bird of prey
raptar [rap'tar] vt to kidnap; **rapto** nm kidnapping; (impulso) sudden impulse; (éxtasis) ecstasy, rapture
raqueta [ra'keta] nf racquet
raquítico, a [ra'kitiko, a] adj stunted; (fig) poor, inadequate; **raquitismo** nm rickets sg
rareza [ra'reθa] nf rarity; (fig) eccentricity
raro, a ['raro, a] adj (poco común) rare; (extraño) odd, strange; (excepcional) remarkable
ras [ras] nm: **a** ~ **de** level with; **a** ~ **de tierra** at ground level
rasar [ra'sar] vt (igualar) to level
rascacielos [raska'θjelos] nm inv skyscraper
rascar [ras'kar] vt (con las uñas etc) to scratch; (raspar) to scrape; ~**se** vr to scratch (o.s.)
rasgar [ras'γar] vt to tear, rip (up)
rasgo ['rasγo] nm (con pluma) stroke; ~**s** nmpl (facciones) features, characteristics; **a grandes** ~**s** in outline, broadly
rasguñar [rasγu'ɲar] vt to scratch; **rasguño** nm scratch
raso, a ['raso, a] adj (liso) flat, level; (a baja altura) very low ♦ nm satin; **cielo** ~ clear sky
raspadura [raspa'ðura] nf (acto) scrape, scraping; (marca) scratch; ~**s** nfpl (de papel etc) scrapings
raspar [ras'par] vt to scrape; (arañar) to scratch; (limar) to file
rastra ['rastra] nf (AGR) rake; **a** ~**s** by dragging; (fig) unwillingly
rastreador [rastrea'ðor] nm tracker; ~ **de minas** minesweeper
rastrear [rastre'ar] vt (seguir) to track
rastrero, a [ras'trero, a] adj (BOT, ZOOL) creeping; (fig) despicable, mean
rastrillo [ras'triλo] nm rake
rastro ['rastro] nm (AGR) rake; (pista) track, trail; (vestigio) trace; **el R~** the Madrid fleamarket
rastrojo [ras'troxo] nm stubble
rasurador [rasura'ðor] (AM) nm electric shaver
rasuradora [rasura'ðora] (AM) nf = **rasurador**
rasurarse [rasu'rarse] vr to shave
rata ['rata] nf rat
ratear [rate'ar] vt (robar) to steal
ratero, a [ra'tero, a] adj light-fingered ♦ nm/f (carterista) pickpocket; (AM: de casas) burglar
ratificar [ratifi'kar] vt to ratify
rato ['rato] nm while, short time; **a** ~**s** from time to time; **hay para** ~ there's still a long way to go; **al poco** ~ soon afterwards;

pasar el ~ to kill time; **pasar un buen/ mal ~** to have a good/rough time

ratón [ra'ton] *nm* mouse; **ratonera** *nf* mousetrap

raudal [rau'ðal] *nm* torrent; **a ~es** in abundance

raya ['raja] *nf* line; *(marca)* scratch; *(en tela)* stripe; *(de pelo)* parting; *(límite)* boundary; *(pez)* ray; *(puntuación)* dash; **a ~s** striped; **pasarse de la ~** to go too far: **tener a ~** to keep in check; **rayar** *vt* to line; to scratch; *(subrayar)* to underline ♦ *vi:* **rayar en** *o* **con** to border on

rayo ['rajo] *nm (del sol)* ray, beam; *(de luz)* shaft; *(en una tormenta)* (flash of) lightning; **~s X** X-rays

raza ['raθa] *nf* race; **~ humana** human race

razón [ra'θon] *nf* reason; *(justicia)* right, justice; *(razonamiento)* reasoning; *(motivo)* reason, motive; *(MAT)* ratio; **a ~ de 10 cada día** at the rate of 10 a day; **"~: ..."** "inquiries to ..."; **en ~ de** with regard to; **dar ~ a uno** to agree that sb is right; **tener ~** to be right; **~ directa/inversa** direct/ inverse proportion; **~ de ser** raison d'être; **razonable** *adj* reasonable; *(justo, moderado)* fair; **razonamiento** *nm (juicio)* judgement; *(argumento)* reasoning; **razonar** *vt, vi* to reason, argue

reacción [reak'θjon] *nf* reaction; **avión a ~** jet plane; **~ en cadena** chain reaction; **reaccionar** *vi* to react; **reaccionario, a** *adj* reactionary

reacio, a [re'aθjo, a] *adj* stubborn

reactivar [reakti'ßar] *vt* to revitalize

reactor [reak'tor] *nm* reactor

readaptación [reaðapta'θjon] *nf:* **~ profesional** industrial retraining

reajuste [rea'xuste] *nm* readjustment

real [re'al] *adj* real; *(del rey, fig)* royal

realce [re'alθe] *nm (TEC)* embossing; *(lustre, fig)* splendour; *(ARTE)* highlight; **poner de ~** to emphasize

realidad [reali'ðað] *nf* reality, fact; *(verdad)* truth

realista [rea'lista] *nm/f* realist

realización [realiθa'θjon] *nf* fulfilment; *(COM)* selling up *(BRIT)*, conversion into money *(US)*

realizador, a [realiθa'ðor, a] *nm/f (TV etc)* producer

realizar [reali'θar] *vt (objetivo)* to achieve; *(plan)* to carry out; *(viaje)* to make, undertake; *(COM)* to sell up *(BRIT)*, convert into money *(US)*; **~se** *vr* to come about, come true

realmente [real'mente] *adv* really, actually

realquilar [realki'lar] *vt (subarrendar)* to sublet

realzar [real'θar] *vt (TEC)* to raise; *(embellecer)* to enhance; *(acentuar)* to highlight

reanimar [reani'mar] *vt* to revive; *(alentar)*

to encourage; **~se** *vr* to revive

reanudar [reanu'ðar] *vt (renovar)* to renew; *(historia, viaje)* to resume

reaparición [reapari'θjon] *nf* reappearance

rearme [re'arme] *nm* rearmament

rebaja [re'ßaxa] *nf (COM)* reduction; (: *descuento)* discount; **~s** *nfpl (COM)* sale; **rebajar** *vt (bajar)* to lower; *(reducir)* to reduce; *(disminuir)* to lessen; *(humillar)* to humble

rebanada [reßa'naða] *nf* slice

rebañar [reßa'nar] *vt (comida)* to scrape up; *(plato)* to scrape clean

rebaño [re'ßano] *nm* herd; *(de ovejas)* flock

rebasar [reßa'sar] *vt (tb: ~ de)* to exceed

rebatir [reßa'tir] *vt* to refute

rebeca [re'ßeka] *nf* cardigan

rebelarse [reße'larse] *vr* to rebel, revolt

rebelde [re'ßelde] *adj* rebellious; *(niño)* unruly ♦ *nm/f* rebel; **rebeldía** *nf* rebelliousness; *(desobediencia)* disobedience

rebelión [reße'ljon] *nf* rebellion

reblandecer [reßlande'θer] *vt* to soften

rebobinar [reßoßi'nar] *vt (cinta, película de video)* to rewind

rebosante [reßo'sante] *adj* overflowing

rebosar [reßo'sar] *vi (líquido, recipiente)* to overflow; *(abundar)* to abound, be plentiful

rebotar [reßo'tar] *vt* to bounce; *(rechazar)* to repel ♦ *vi (pelota)* to bounce; *(bala)* to ricochet; **rebote** *nm* rebound; **de rebote** on the rebound

rebozado, a [reßo'θaðo, a] *adj* fried in batter *o* breadcrumbs

rebozar [reßo'θar] *vt* to wrap up; *(CULIN)* to fry in batter *o* breadcrumbs

rebuscado, a [reßus'kaðo, a] *adj (amanerado)* affected; *(palabra)* recherché; *(idea)* far-fetched

rebuscar [reßus'kar] *vi:* **~ (en/por)** to search carefully (in/for)

rebuznar [reßuθ'nar] *vi* to bray

recabar [reka'ßar] *vt (obtener)* to manage to get

recado [re'kaðo] *nm* message; **tomar un ~** *(TEL)* to take a message

recaer [reka'er] *vi* to relapse; **~ en** to fall to *o* on; *(criminal etc)* to fall back into, relapse into; **recaída** *nf* relapse

recalcar [rekal'kar] *vt (fig)* to stress, emphasize

recalcitrante [rekalθi'trante] *adj* recalcitrant

recalentar [rekalen'tar] *vt (volver a calentar)* to reheat; *(calentar demasiado)* to overheat

recámara [re'kamara] *(AM) nf* bedroom

recambio [re'kambjo] *nm* spare; *(de pluma)* refill

recapacitar [rekapaθi'tar] *vi* to reflect

recargado, a [rekar'xaðo, a] *adj* overloaded

recargar [rekar'xar] *vt* to overload; *(batería)*

to recharge; **recargo** nm surcharge; (aumento) increase

recatado, a [reka'taðo, a] adj (modesto) modest, demure; (prudente) cautious

recato [re'kato] nm (modestia) modesty, demureness; (cautela) caution

recaudación [rekauða'θjon] nf (acción) collection; (cantidad) takings pl; (en deporte) gate; **recaudador, a** nm/f tax collector

recelar [reθe'lar] vt: ~ **que** (sospechar) to suspect that; (temer) to fear that ♦ vi: ~ **de** to distrust; **recelo** nm distrust, suspicion; **receloso, a** adj distrustful, suspicious

recepción [reθep'θjon] nf reception; **recepcionista** nm/f receptionist

receptáculo [reθep'takulo] nm receptacle

receptivo, a [reθep'tiβo, a] adj receptive

receptor, a [reθep'tor, a] nm/f recipient ♦ nm (TEL) receiver

recesión [reθe'sjon] nf (COM) recession

receta [re'θeta] nf (CULIN) recipe; (MED) prescription

recibidor, a [reθiβi'ðor, a] nm entrance hall

recibimiento [reθiβi'mjento] nm reception, welcome

recibir [reθi'βir] vt to receive; (dar la bienvenida) to welcome ♦ vi to entertain; ~**se** vr: ~**se de** to qualify as; **recibo** nm receipt

reciclar [reθi'klar] vt to recycle

recién [re'θjen] adv recently, newly; **los ~ casados** the newly-weds; **el ~ llegado** the newcomer; **el ~ nacido** the newborn child

reciente [re'θjente] adj recent; (fresco) fresh; ~**mente** adv recently

recinto [re'θinto] nm enclosure; (área) area, place

recio, a ['reθjo, a] adj strong, tough; (voz) loud ♦ adv hard; loud(ly)

recipiente [reθi'pjente] nm receptacle

reciprocidad [reθiproθi'ðað] nf reciprocity; **recíproco, a** adj reciprocal

recital [reθi'tal] nm (MUS) recital; (LITERATURA) reading

recitar [reθi'tar] vt to recite

reclamación [reklama'θjon] nf claim, demand; (queja) complaint

reclamar [rekla'mar] vt to claim, demand ♦ vi: ~ **contra** to complain about; ~ **a uno en justicia** to take sb to court; **reclamo** nm (anuncio) advertisement; (tentación) attraction

reclinar [rekli'nar] vt to recline, lean; ~**se** vr to lean back

recluir [reklu'ir] vt to intern, confine

reclusión [reklu'sjon] nf (prisión) prison; (refugio) seclusion; ~ **perpetua** life imprisonment

recluta [re'kluta] nm/f recruit ♦ nf recruitment; **reclutar** vt (datos) to collect; (dinero) to collect up

reclutamiento [rekluta'mjento] nm recruitment

recobrar [reko'βrar] vt (salud) to recover; (rescatar) to get back; ~**se** vr to recover

recodo [re'koðo] nm (de río, camino) bend

recoger [reko'xer] vt to collect; (AGR) to harvest; (levantar) to pick up; (juntar) to gather; (pasar a buscar) to come for, get; (dar asilo) to give shelter to; (faldas) to gather up; (pelo) to put up; ~**se** vr (retirarse) to retire; **recogido, a** adj (lugar) quiet, secluded; (pequeño) small ♦ nf (CORREOS) collection; (AGR) harvest

recolección [rekolek'θjon] nf (AGR) harvesting; (colecta) collection

recomendación [rekomenda'θjon] nf (sugerencia) suggestion, recommendation; (referencia) reference

recomendar [rekomen'dar] vt to suggest, recommend; (confiar) to entrust

recompensa [rekom'pensa] nf reward, recompense; **recompensar** vt to reward, recompense

recomponer [rekompo'ner] vt to mend

reconciliación [rekonθilja'θjon] nf reconciliation

reconciliar [rekonθi'ljar] vt to reconcile; ~**se** vr to become reconciled

recóndito, a [re'kondito, a] adj (lugar) hidden, secret

reconfortar [rekonfor'tar] vt to comfort

reconocer [rekono'θer] vt to recognize; (registrar) to search; (MED) to examine; **reconocido, a** adj recognized; (agradecido) grateful; **reconocimiento** nm recognition; search; examination; gratitude; (confesión) admission

reconquista [rekon'kista] nf reconquest; **la R~** the Reconquest (of Spain)

reconstituyente [rekonstitu'jente] nm tonic

reconstruir [rekonstru'ir] vt to reconstruct

reconversión [rekonßer'sjon] nf: ~ **industrial** industrial rationalization

recopilación [rekopila'θjon] nf (resumen) summary; (compilación) compilation; **recopilar** vt to compile

récord ['rekorð] (pl ~**s**) adj inv, nm record

recordar [rekor'ðar] vt (acordarse de) to remember; (acordar a otro) to remind ♦ vi to remember

recorrer [reko'rrer] vt (país) to cross, travel through; (distancia) to cover; (registrar) to search; (repasar) to look over; **recorrido** nm run, journey; **tren de largo recorrido** main-line train

recortado, a [rekor'taðo, a] adj uneven, irregular

recortar [rekor'tar] vt to cut out; **recorte** nm (acción, de prensa) cutting; (de telas, chapas) trimming

recostado, a [rekos'taðo, a] adj leaning; **estar ~** to be lying down

recostar [rekos'tar] *vt* to lean; **~se** *vr* to lie down

recoveco [reko'βeko] *nm* (*de camino, río etc*) bend; (*en casa*) cubby hole

recreación [rekrea'θjon] *nf* recreation

recrear [rekre'ar] *vt* (*entretener*) to entertain; (*volver a crear*) to recreate; **recreativo, a** *adj* recreational; **recreo** *nm* recreation; (*ESCOL*) break, playtime

recriminar [rekrimi'nar] *vt* to reproach ♦ *vi* to recriminate; **~se** *vr* to reproach each other

recrudecer [rekruðe'θer] *vt, vi* to worsen; **~se** *vr* to worsen

recrudecimiento [rekruðeθi'mjento] *nm* upsurge

recta ['rekta] *nf* straight line

rectángulo, a [rek'tangulo, a] *adj* rectangular ♦ *nm* rectangle

rectificar [rektifi'kar] *vt* to rectify; (*volverse recto*) to straighten ♦ *vi* to correct o.s.

rectitud [rekti'tuð] *nf* straightness; (*fig*) rectitude

recto, a ['rekto, a] *adj* straight; (*persona*) honest, upright ♦ *nm* rectum

rector, a [rek'tor, a] *adj* governing

recuadro [re'kwaðro] *nm* box; (*TIPOGRAFÍA*) inset

recubrir [reku'βrir] *vt*: **~ (con)** (*pintura, crema*) to cover (with)

recuento [re'kwento] *nm* inventory; **hacer el ~ de** to count *o* reckon up

recuerdo [re'kwerðo] *nm* souvenir; **~s** *nmpl* (*memorias*) memories; **¡~s a tu madre!** give my regards to your mother!

recular [reku'lar] *vi* to back down

recuperable [rekupe'raβle] *adj* recoverable

recuperación [rekupera'θjon] *nf* recovery

recuperar [rekupe'rar] *vt* to recover; (*tiempo*) to make up; **~se** *vr* to recuperate

recurrir [reku'rrir] *vi* (*JUR*) to appeal; **~ a** to resort to; (*persona*) to turn to; **recurso** *nm* resort; (*medios*) means *pl*, resources *pl*; (*JUR*) appeal

recusar [reku'sar] *vt* to reject, refuse

rechazar [retʃa'θar] *vt* to repel, drive back; (*idea*) to reject; (*oferta*) to turn down

rechazo [re'tʃaθo] *nm* (*de fusil*) recoil; (*rebote*) rebound; (*negación*) rebuff

rechifla [re'tʃifla] *nf* hissing, booing; (*fig*) derision

rechinar [retʃi'nar] *vi* to creak; (*dientes*) to grind

rechistar [retʃis'tar] *vi*: **sin ~** without a murmur

rechoncho, a [re'tʃontʃo, a] (*fam*) *adj* thickset (*BRIT*), heavy-set (*US*)

rechupete [retʃu'pete] (*LAM*): **de ~** (*comida*) delicious, scrumptious

red [reð] *nf* net, mesh; (*FERRO etc*) network; (*trampa*) trap

redacción [reðak'θjon] *nf* (*acción*) editing; (*personal*) editorial staff; (*ESCOL*) essay, composition

redactar [reðak'tar] *vt* to draw up, draft; (*periódico*) to edit

redactor, a [reðak'tor, a] *nm/f* editor

redada [re'ðaða] *nf*: **~ policial** police raid, round-up

rededor [reðe'ðor] *nm*: **al** *o* **en ~** around, round about

redención [reðen'θjon] *nf* redemption

redicho, a [re'ðitʃo, a] *adj* affected

redil [re'ðil] *nm* sheepfold

redimir [reði'mir] *vt* to redeem

rédito ['reðito] *nm* interest, yield

redoblar [reðo'βlar] *vt* to redouble ♦ *vi* (*tambor*) to play a roll on the drums

redomado, a [reðo'maðo, a] *adj* (*astuto*) sly, crafty; (*perfecto*) utter

redonda [re'ðonda] *nf*: **a la ~** around, round about

redondear [reðonde'ar] *vt* to round, round off

redondel [reðon'del] *nm* (*círculo*) circle; (*TAUR*) bullring, arena; (*AUTO*) roundabout

redondo, a [re'ðondo, a] *adj* (*circular*) round; (*completo*) complete

reducción [reðuk'θjon] *nf* reduction

reducido, a [reðu'θiðo, a] *adj* reduced; (*limitado*) limited; (*pequeño*) small

reducir [reðu'θir] *vt* to reduce; to limit; **~se** *vr* to diminish

redundancia [reðun'danθja] *nf* redundancy

reembolsar [re(e)mbol'sar] *vt* (*persona*) to reimburse; (*dinero*) to repay, pay back; (*depósito*) to refund; **reembolso** *nm* reimbursement; refund

reemplazar [re(e)mpla'θar] *vt* to replace; **reemplazo** *nm* replacement; **de reemplazo** (*MIL*) reserve

reencuentro [re(e)n'kwentro] *nm* reunion

referencia [refe'renθja] *nf* reference; **con ~ a** with reference to

referéndum [refe'rendum] (*pl* **~s**) *nm* referendum

referente [refe'rente] *adj*: **~ a** concerning, relating to

referir [refe'rir] *vt* (*contar*) to tell, recount; (*relacionar*) to refer, relate; **~se** *vr*: **~se a** to refer to

refilón [refi'lon]: **de ~** *adv* obliquely

refinado, a [refi'naðo, a] *adj* refined

refinamiento [refina'mjento] *nm* refinement

refinar [refi'nar] *vt* to refine; **refinería** *nf* refinery

reflejar [refle'xar] *vt* to reflect; **reflejo, a** *adj* reflected; (*movimiento*) reflex ♦ *nm* reflection; (*ANAT*) reflex

reflexión [reflek'sjon] *nf* reflection; **reflexionar** *vt* to reflect on ♦ *vi* to reflect; (*detenerse*) to pause (to think)

reflexivo, a [reflek'siβo, a] *adj* thoughtful;

(*LING*) reflexive

reflujo [re'fluxo] *nm* ebb

reforma [re'forma] *nf* reform; (*ARQ etc*) repair; ~ **agraria** agrarian reform

reformar [refor'mar] *vt* to reform; (*modificar*) to change, alter; (*ARQ*) to repair; ~**se** *vr* to mend one's ways

reformatorio [reforma'torjo] *nm* reformatory

reforzar [refor'θar] *vt* to strengthen; (*ARQ*) to reinforce; (*fig*) to encourage

refractario, a [refrak'tarjo, a] *adj* (*TEC*) heat-resistant

refrán [re'fran] *nm* proverb, saying

refregar [refre'ɣar] *vt* to scrub

refrenar [refre'nar] *vt* to check, restrain

refrendar [refren'dar] *vt* (*firma*) to endorse, countersign; (*ley*) to approve

refrescante [refres'kante] *adj* refreshing, cooling

refrescar [refres'kar] *vt* to refresh ♦ *vi* to cool down; ~**se** *vr* to get cooler; (*tomar aire fresco*) to go out for a breath of fresh air; (*beber*) to have a drink

refresco [re'fresko] *nm* soft drink, cool drink; "~**s**" "refreshments"

refriega [re'frjeɣa] *nf* scuffle, brawl

refrigeración [refrixera'θjon] *nf* refrigeration; (*de sala*) air-conditioning

refrigerador [refrixera'ðor] *nm* refrigerator (*BRIT*), icebox (*US*)

refrigeradora [refrixera'ðora] *nf* = **refrigerador**

refrigerar [refrixe'rar] *vt* to refrigerate; (*sala*) to air-condition

refuerzo [re'fwerθo] *nm* reinforcement; (*TEC*) support

refugiado, a [refu'xjaðo, a] *nm/f* refugee

refugiarse [refu'xjarse] *vr* to take refuge, shelter

refugio [re'fuxjo] *nm* refuge; (*protección*) shelter

refulgir [reful'xir] *vi* to shine, be dazzling

refunfuñar [refunfu'ɲar] *vi* to grunt, growl; (*quejarse*) to grumble

refutar [refu'tar] *vt* to refute

regadera [reɣa'ðera] *nf* watering can

regadío [reɣa'ðio] *nm* irrigated land

regalado, a [reɣa'laðo, a] *adj* comfortable, luxurious; (*gratis*) free, for nothing

regalar [reɣa'lar] *vt* (*dar*) to give (as a present); (*entregar*) to give away; (*mimar*) to pamper, make a fuss of

regalía [reɣa'lia] *nf* privilege, prerogative; (*COM*) bonus; (*de autor*) royalty

regaliz [reɣa'liθ] *nm* liquorice

regalo [re'ɣalo] *nm* (*obsequio*) gift, present; (*gusto*) pleasure; (*comodidad*) comfort

regañadientes [reɣaɲa'ðjentes]: **a** ~ *adv* reluctantly

regañar [reɣa'ɲar] *vt* to scold ♦ *vi* to grumble; **regañón, ona** *adj* nagging

regar [re'ɣar] *vt* to water, irrigate; (*fig*) to scatter, sprinkle

regatear [reɣate'ar] *vt* (*COM*) to bargain over; (*escatimar*) to be mean with ♦ *vi* to bargain, haggle; (*DEPORTE*) to dribble; **regateo** *nm* bargaining; dribbling; (*del cuerpo*) swerve, dodge

regazo [re'ɣaθo] *nm* lap

regeneración [rexenera'θjon] *nf* regeneration

regenerar [rexene'rar] *vt* to regenerate

regentar [rexen'tar] *vt* to direct, manage; **regente** (*COM*) manager; (*POL*) regent

régimen ['reximen] (*pl* **regímenes**) *nm* regime; (*MED*) diet

regimiento [rexi'mjento] *nm* regiment

regio, a ['rexjo, a] *adj* royal, regal; (*fig: suntuoso*) splendid; (*AM: fam*) great, terrific

región [re'xjon] *nf* region; **regionalista** *nm/f* regionalist

regir [re'xir] *vt* to govern, rule; (*dirigir*) to manage, run ♦ *vi* to apply, be in force

registrador [rexistra'ðor] *nm* registrar, recorder

registrar [rexis'trar] *vt* (*buscar*) to search; (: *en cajón*) to look through; (*inspeccionar*) to inspect; (*anotar*) to register, record; (*INFORM*) to log; ~**se** *vr* to register; (*ocurrir*) to happen

registro [re'xistro] *nm* (*acto*) registration; (*MUS, libro*) register; (*inspección*) inspection, search; ~ **civil** registry office

regla ['reɣla] *nf* (*ley*) rule, regulation; (*de medir*) ruler, rule; (*MED: período*) period

reglamentación [reɣlamenta'θjon] *nf* (*acto*) regulation; (*lista*) rules *pl*

reglamentar [reɣlamen'tar] *vt* to regulate; **reglamentario, a** *adj* statutory; **reglamento** *nm* rules *pl*, regulations *pl*

regocijarse [reɣoθi'xarse] *vr*: ~ **de** to rejoice at, be happy about; **regocijo** *nm* joy, happiness

regodearse [reɣoðe'arse] *vr* to be glad, be delighted; **regodeo** *nm* delight

regresar [reɣre'sar] *vi* to come back, go back, return; **regresivo, a** *adj* backward; (*fig*) regressive; **regreso** *nm* return

reguero [re'ɣero] *nm* (*de sangre etc*) trickle; (*de humo*) trail

regulador [reɣula'ðor] *nm* regulator; (*de radio etc*) knob, control

regular [reɣu'lar] *adj* regular; (*normal*) normal, usual; (*común*) ordinary; (*organizado*) regular, orderly; (*mediano*) average; (*fam*) not bad, so-so ♦ *adv* so-so, alright ♦ *vt* (*controlar*) to control, regulate; (*TEC*) to adjust; **por lo** ~ as a rule; ~**idad** *nf* regularity; ~**izar** *vt* to regularize

regusto [re'ɣusto] *nm* aftertaste

rehabilitación [reaβilita'θjon] *nf* rehabilitation; (*ARQ*) restoration

rehabilitar [reaβili'tar] *vt* to rehabilitate;

(ARQ) to restore; (reintegrar) to reinstate

rehacer [rea'θer] vt (reparar) to mend, repair; (volver a hacer) to redo, repeat; ~se vr (MED) to recover

rehén [re'en] nm hostage

rehuir [reu'ir] vt to avoid, shun

rehusar [reu'sar] vt, vi to refuse

reina ['reina] nf queen; ~do nm reign

reinante [rei'nante] adj (fig) prevailing

reinar [rei'nar] vi to reign

reincidir [reinθi'ðir] vi to relapse

reincorporarse [reinkorpo'rarse] vr: ~ a to rejoin

reino ['reino] nm kingdom; **el R~ Unido** the United Kingdom

reintegrar [reinte'vrar] vt (reconstituir) to reconstruct; (persona) to reinstate; (dinero) to refund, pay back; ~se vr: ~se a to return to

reír [re'ir] vi to laugh; ~se vr to laugh; ~se **de** to laugh at

reiterar [reite'rar] vt to reiterate

reivindicación [reißindika'θjon] nf (demanda) claim, demand; (justificación) vindication

reivindicar [reißindi'kar] vt to claim

reja ['rexa] nf (de ventana) grille, bars pl; (en la calle) grating

rejilla [re'xiʎa] nf grating, grille; (muebles) wickerwork; (de ventilación) vent; (de coche etc) luggage rack

rejoneador [rexonea'ðor] nm mounted bullfighter

rejuvenecer [rexußene'θer] vt, vi to rejuvenate

relación [rela'θjon] nf relation, relationship; (MAT) ratio; (narración) report; **relaciones públicas** public relations; **con ~ a, en ~ con** in relation to; **relacionar** vt to relate, connect; **relacionarse** vr to be connected, be linked

relajación [relaxa'θjon] nf relaxation

relajado, a [rela'xaðo, a] adj (disoluto) loose; (cómodo) relaxed; (MED) ruptured

relajar [rela'xar] vt to relax; ~se vr to relax

relamerse [rela'merse] vr to lick one's lips

relamido, a [rela'miðo, a] adj (pulcro) overdressed; (afectado) affected

relámpago [re'lampavo] nm flash of lightning; **visita/huelga ~** lightning visit/strike; **relampaguear** vi to flash

relatar [rela'tar] vt to tell, relate

relativo, a [rela'tißo, a] adj relative; **en lo ~ a** concerning

relato [re'lato] nm (narración) story, tale

relegar [rele'var] vt to relegate

relevante [rele'ßante] adj eminent, outstanding

relevar [rele'ßar] vt (sustituir) to relieve; ~se vr to relay; **~ a uno de un cargo** to relieve sb of his post

relevo [re'leßo] nm relief; **carrera de ~s** re-

lay race

relieve [re'ljeße] nm (ARTE, TEC) relief; (fig) prominence, importance; **bajo ~** basrelief

religión [reli'xjon] nf religion; **religioso, a** adj religious ♦ nm/f monk/nun

relinchar [relin'tʃar] vi to neigh; **relincho** nm neigh; (acto) neighing

reliquia [re'likja] nf relic; **~ de familia** heirloom

reloj [re'lo(x)] nm clock; **~ (de pulsera)** wristwatch; **~ despertador** alarm (clock); **poner el ~** to set one's watch (o the clock); **~ero, a** nm/f clockmaker; watchmaker

reluciente [relu'θjente] adj brilliant, shining

relucir [relu'θir] vi to shine; (fig) to excel

relumbrar [relum'brar] vi to dazzle, shine brilliantly

rellano [re'ʎano] nm (ARQ) landing

rellenar [reʎe'nar] vt (llenar) to fill up; (CULIN) to stuff; (COSTURA) to pad; **relleno, a** adj full up; stuffed ♦ nm stuffing; (de tapicería) padding

remachar [rema'tʃar] vt to rivet; (fig) to hammer home, drive home; **remache** nm rivet

remanente [rema'nente] nm remainder; (COM) balance; (de producto) surplus

remangar [reman'gar] vt to roll up

remanso [re'manso] nm pool

remar [re'mar] vi to row

rematado, a [rema'taðo, a] adj complete, utter

rematar [rema'tar] vt to finish off; (COM) to sell off cheap ♦ vi to end, finish off; (DEPORTE) to shoot

remate [re'mate] nm end, finish; (punta) tip; (DEPORTE) shot; (ARQ) top; (COM) auction sale; **de o para ~** to crown it all (BRIT), to top it off

remedar [reme'ðar] vt to imitate

remediar [reme'ðjar] vt to remedy; (subsanar) to make good, repair; (evitar) to avoid

remedio [re'meðjo] nm remedy; (alivio) relief, help; (JUR) recourse, remedy; **poner ~ a** to correct, stop; **no tener más ~** to have no alternative; **¡qué ~!** there's no choice!; **sin ~** hopeless

remedo [re'meðo] nm imitation; (pey) parody

remendar [remen'dar] vt to repair; (con parche) to patch

remesa [ʀe'mesa] nf remittance; (COM) shipment

remiendo [re'mjendo] nm mend; (con parche) patch; (cosido) darn

remilgado, a [remil'vaðo, a] adj prim; (afectado) affected

remilgo [re'milvo] nm primness; (afectación) affectation

reminiscencia [reminis'θenθja] nf remi-

niscence
remiso, a [re'miso, a] *adj* slack, slow
remite [re'mite] *nm (en sobre)* name and
address of sender
remitir [remi'tir] *vt* to remit, send ♦ *vi* to
slacken; *(en carta)*: **remite: X sender: X;
remitente** *nm/f* sender
remo ['remo] *nm (de barco)* oar; *(DEPORTE)*
rowing
remojar [remo'xar] *vt* to steep, soak; *(galleta etc)* to dip, dunk
remojo [re'moxo] *nm*: **dejar la ropa en ~**
to leave clothes to soak
remolacha [remo'latʃa] *nf* beet, beetroot
remolcador [remolka'ðor] *nm (NAUT)* tug;
(AUTO) breakdown lorry
remolcar [remol'kar] *vt* to tow
remolino [remo'lino] *nm* eddy; *(de agua)*
whirlpool; *(de viento)* whirlwind; *(de gente)*
crowd
remolque [re'molke] *nm* tow, towing;
(cuerda) towrope; **llevar a ~** to tow
remontar [remon'tar] *vt* to mend; **~se** *vr*
to soar; **~se a** *(COM)* to amount to; **~ el
vuelo** to soar
remorder [remor'ðer] *vt* to distress, disturb; **~le la conciencia a uno** to have a
guilty conscience; **remordimiento** *nm* remorse
remoto, a [re'moto, a] *adj* remote
remover [remo'ßer] *vt* to stir; *(tierra)* to
turn over; *(objetos)* to move round
remozar [remo'θar] *vt (ARQ)* to refurbish
remuneración [remunera'θjon] *nf* remu-
neration
remunerar [remune'rar] *vt* to remunerate;
(premiar) to reward
renacer [rena'θer] *vi* to be reborn; *(fig)* to
revive; **renacimiento** *nm* rebirth; **el Renacimiento** the Renaissance
renacuajo [rena'kwaxo] *nm (ZOOL)* tadpole
renal [re'nal] *adj* renal, kidney *cpd*
rencilla [ren'θiʎa] *nf* quarrel
rencor [ren'kor] *nm* rancour, bitterness;
~oso, a *adj* spiteful
rendición [rendi'θjon] *nf* surrender
rendido, a [ren'diðo, a] *adj (sumiso)* submissive; *(cansado)* worn-out, exhausted
rendija [ren'dixa] *nf (hendedura)* crack, cleft
rendimiento [rendi'mjento] *nm (producción)* output; *(TEC, COM)* efficiency
rendir [ren'dir] *vt (vencer)* to defeat; *(producir)* to produce; *(dar beneficio)* to yield;
(agotar) to exhaust ♦ *vi* to pay; **~se** *vr
(someterse)* to surrender; *(cansarse)* to wear
o.s. out; **~ homenaje o culto a** to pay
homage to
renegar [rene'xar] *vi (renunciar)* to renounce; *(blasfemar)* to blaspheme; *(quejarse)* to complain
RENFE ['renfe] *nf abr* (= *Red Nacional de
los Ferrocarriles Españoles*) ≈ BR *(BRIT)*

renglón [ren'glon] *nm (línea)* line; *(COM)*
item, article; **a ~ seguido** immediately
after
renombrado, a [renom'braðo, a] *adj* renowned
renombre [re'nombre] *nm* renown
renovación [renoßa'θjon] *nf (de contrato)*
renewal; *(ARQ)* renovation
renovar [reno'ßar] *vt* to renew; *(ARQ)* to
renovate
renta ['renta] *nf (ingresos)* income; *(beneficio)* profit; *(alquiler)* rent; **~ vitalicia** annuity; **rentable** *adj* profitable; **rentar** *vt* to
produce, yield
renuncia [re'nunθja] *nf* resignation
renunciar [renun'θjar] *vt* to renounce; *(tabaco, alcohol etc)*: **~ a** to give up; *(oferta,
oportunidad)* to turn down; *(puesto)* to resign ♦ *vi* to resign
reñido, a [re'niðo, a] *adj (batalla)* bitter,
hard-fought; **estar ~ con uno** to be on bad
terms with sb
reñir [re'nir] *vt (regañar)* to scold ♦ *vi (estar
peleado)* to quarrel, fall out; *(combatir)* to
fight
reo ['reo] *nm/f* culprit, offender; **~ de
muerte** prisoner condemned to death
reojo [re'oxo]: **de ~** *adv* out of the corner
of one's eye
reparación [repara'θjon] *nf (acto)* mending,
repairing; *(TEC)* repair; *(fig)* amends, repa-
ration
reparar [repa'rar] *vt* to repair; *(fig)* to make
amends for; *(observar)* to observe ♦ *vi*: **~
en** *(darse cuenta de)* to notice; *(prestar
atención a)* to pay attention to
reparo [re'paro] *nm (advertencia)* observation; *(duda)* doubt; *(dificultad)* difficulty;
poner ~s (a) to raise objections (to)
repartición [reparti'θjon] *nf* distribution;
(división) division; **repartidor, a** *nm/f* distributor
repartir [repar'tir] *vt* to distribute, share
out; *(CORREOS)* to deliver; **reparto** *nm* distribution; delivery; *(TEATRO, CINE)* cast;
(AM: urbanización) housing estate *(BRIT)*,
real estate development *(US)*
repasar [repa'sar] *vt (ESCOL)* to revise;
(MECÁNICA) to check, overhaul; *(COS-
TURA)* to mend; **repaso** *nm* revision; overhaul, checkup; mending
repatriar [repa'trjar] *vt* to repatriate
repecho [re'petʃo] *nm* steep incline
repelente [repe'lente] *adj* repellent, repulsive
repeler [repe'ler] *vt* to repel
repensar [repen'sar] *vt* to reconsider
repente [re'pente] *nm*: **de ~** suddenly; **~
de ira** fit of anger
repentino, a [repen'tino, a] *adj* sudden
repercusión [reperku'sjon] *nf* repercussion
repercutir [reperku'tir] *vi (objeto)* to re-

bound; (*sonido*) to echo; ~ **en** (*fig*) to have repercussions on
repertorio [reper'torjo] *nm* list; (*TEATRO*) repertoire
repetición [repeti'θjon] *nf* repetition
repetir [repe'tir] *vt* to repeat; (*plato*) to have a second helping of ◊ *vi* to repeat; (*sabor*) to come back; ~**se** *vr* (*volver sobre un tema*) to repeat o.s.
repetitivo, a [repeti'tißo, a] *adj* repetitive, repetitious
repicar [repi'kar] *vt* (*campanas*) to ring
repique [re'pike] *nm* pealing, ringing; ~**teo** *nm* pealing; (*de tambor*) drumming
repisa [re'pisa] *nf* ledge, shelf; (*de ventana*) windowsill; ~ **de chimenea** mantelpiece
repito *etc vb ver* **repetir**
replantearse [replante'arse] *vr*: ~ **un problema** to reconsider a problem
replegarse [reple'xarse] *vr* to fall back, retreat
repleto, a [re'pleto, a] *adj* replete, full up
réplica ['replika] *nf* answer; (*ARTE*) replica
replicar [repli'kar] *vi* to answer; (*objetar*) to argue, answer back
repliegue [re'pljexe] *nm* (*MIL*) withdrawal
repoblación [repoßla'θjon] *nf* repopulation; (*de río*) restocking; ~ **forestal** reafforestation
repoblar [repo'ßlar] *vt* to repopulate; (*con árboles*) to reafforest
repollo [re'poʎo] *nm* cabbage
reponer [repo'ner] *vt* to replace, put back; (*TEATRO*) to revive; ~**se** *vr* to recover; ~ **que** to reply that
reportaje [repor'taxe] *nm* report, article
reportero, a [repor'tero, a] *nm/f* reporter
reposacabezas [reposaka'ßeθas] *nm inv* headrest
reposado, a [repo'saðo, a] *adj* (*descansado*) restful; (*tranquilo*) calm
reposar [repo'sar] *vi* to rest, repose
reposición [reposi'θjon] *nf* replacement; (*CINE*) remake
reposo [re'poso] *nm* rest
repostar [repos'tar] *vt* to replenish; (*AUTO*) to fill up (with petrol (*BRIT*) o gasoline (*US*))
repostería [reposte'ria] *nf* confectioner's (shop); **repostero, a** *nm/f* confectioner
reprender [repren'der] *vt* to reprimand
represa [re'presa] *nf* dam; (*lago artificial*) lake, pool
represalia [repre'salja] *nf* reprisal
representación [representa'θjon] *nf* representation; (*TEATRO*) performance; **representante** *nm/f* representative; performer
representar [represen'tar] *vt* to represent; (*TEATRO*) to perform; (*edad*) to look; ~**se** *vr* to imagine; **representativo, a** *adj* representative
represión [repre'sjon] *nf* repression

reprimenda [repri'menda] *nf* reprimand, rebuke
reprimir [repri'mir] *vt* to repress
reprobar [repro'ßar] *vt* to censure, reprove
reprochar [repro'tʃar] *vt* to reproach; **reproche** *nm* reproach
reproducción [reproðuk'θjon] *nf* reproduction
reproducir [reproðu'θir] *vt* to reproduce; ~**se** *vr* to breed; (*situación*) to recur
reproductor, a [reproðuc'tor, a] *adj* reproductive
reptil [rep'til] *nm* reptile
república [re'pußlika] *nf* republic; **republicano, a** *adj*, *nm/f* republican
repudiar [repu'ðjar] *vt* to repudiate; (*fe*) to renounce
repuesto [re'pwesto] *nm* (*pieza de recambio*) spare (part); (*abastecimiento*) supply; **rueda de** ~ spare wheel
repugnancia [repux'nanθja] *nf* repugnance; **repugnante** *adj* repugnant, repulsive
repugnar [repux'nar] *vt* to disgust
repulsa [re'pulsa] *nf* rebuff
repulsión [repul'sjon] *nf* repulsion, aversion; **repulsivo, a** *adj* repulsive
reputación [reputa'θjon] *nf* reputation
reputar [repu'tar] *vt* to consider, deem
requemado, a [reke'maðo, a] *adj* (*quemado*) scorched; (*bronceado*) tanned
requerimiento [rekeri'mjento] *nm* request; (*JUR*) summons
requerir [reke'rir] *vt* (*pedir*) to ask, request; (*exigir*) to require; (*llamar*) to send for, summon
requesón [reke'son] *nm* cottage cheese
requete... [re'kete] *prefijo* extremely
réquiem ['rekjem] (*pl* ~**s**) *nm* requiem
requisito [reki'sito] *nm* requirement, requisite
res [res] *nf* beast, animal
resaca [re'saka] *nf* (*en el mar*) undertow, undercurrent; (*fig*) backlash; (*fam*) hangover
resaltar [resal'tar] *vi* to project, stick out; (*fig*) to stand out
resarcir [resar'θir] *vt* to compensate; ~**se** *vr* to make up for
resbaladizo, a [resßala'ðiθo, a] *adj* slippery
resbalar [resßa'lar] *vi* to slip, slide; (*fig*) to slip (up); ~**se** *vr* to slip, slide; to slip (up); **resbalón** *nm* (*acción*) slip
rescatar [reska'tar] *vt* (*salvar*) to save, rescue; (*objeto*) to get back, recover; (*cautivos*) to ransom
rescate [res'kate] *nm* rescue; (*de objeto*) recovery; **pagar un** ~ to pay a ransom
rescindir [resθin'dir] *vt* to rescind
rescisión [resθi'sjon] *nf* cancellation
rescoldo [res'koldo] *nm* embers *pl*
resecar [rese'kar] *vt* to dry thoroughly;

(*MED*) to cut out, remove; ~**se** *vr* to dry up
reseco, a [re'seko, a] *adj* very dry; (*fig*) skinny
resentido, a [resen'tiðo, a] *adj* resentful
resentimiento [resenti'mjento] *nm* resentment, bitterness
resentirse [resen'tirse] *vr* (*debilitarse: persona*) to suffer; ~ **de** (*consecuencias*) to feel the effects of; ~ **de** (*o por*) **algo** to resent sth, be bitter about sth
reseña [re'seɲa] *nf* (*cuenta*) account; (*informe*) report; (*LITERATURA*) review
reseñar [rese'ɲar] *vt* to describe; (*LITERATURA*) to review
reserva [re'serßa] *nf* reserve; (*reservación*) reservation; **a** ~ **de que ... unless ...; con toda** ~ in strictest confidence
reservado, a [reser'ßaðo, a] *adj* reserved; (*retraído*) cold, distant ♦ *nm* private room
reservar [reser'ßar] *vt* (*guardar*) to keep; (*habitación, entrada*) to reserve; ~**se** *vr* to save o.s.; (*callar*) to keep to o.s.
resfriado [resfri'aðo] *nm* cold; **resfriarse** *vr* to cool; (*MED*) to catch (a) cold
resguardar [resɣwar'ðar] *vt* to protect, shield; ~**se** *vr*: ~**se de** to guard against; **resguardo** *nm* defence; (*vale*) voucher; (*recibo*) receipt, slip
residencia [resi'ðenθja] *nf* residence; ~**l** (*urbanización*) housing estate
residente [resi'ðente] *adj, nm/f* resident
residir [resi'ðir] *vi* to reside, live; ~ **en** to reside in, lie in
residuo [re'siðwo] *nm* residue
resignación [resiɣna'θjon] *nf* resignation; **resignarse** *vr*: **resignarse a** *o* **con** to resign o.s. to, be resigned to
resina [re'sina] *nf* resin
resistencia [resis'tenθja] *nf* (*dureza*) endurance, strength; (*oposición, ELEC*) resistance; **resistente** *adj* strong, hardy; resistant
resistir [resis'tir] *vt* (*soportar*) to bear; (*oponerse a*) to resist, oppose; (*aguantar*) to put up with ♦ *vi* to resist; (*aguantar*) to last, endure; ~**se** *vr*: ~**se a** to refuse to, resist
resolución [resolu'θjon] *nf* resolution; (*decisión*) decision; **resoluto, a** *adj* resolute
resolver [resol'ßer] *vt* to resolve; (*solucionar*) to solve, resolve; (*decidir*) to decide, settle; ~**se** *vr* to make up one's mind
resollar [reso'ʎar] *vi* to breathe noisily, wheeze
resonancia [reso'nanθja] *nf* (*del sonido*) resonance; (*repercusión*) repercussion
resonar [reso'nar] *vi* to ring, echo
resoplar [reso'plar] *vi* to snort; **resoplido** *nm* heavy breathing
resorte [re'sorte] *nm* spring; (*fig*) lever
respaldar [respal'dar] *vt* to back (up), support; ~**se** *vr* to lean back; ~**se con** *o* **en** (*fig*) to take one's stand on; **respaldo** *nm* (*de sillón*) back; (*fig*) support, backing

respectivo, a [respek'tißo, a] *adj* respective; **en lo** ~ **a** with regard to
respecto [res'pekto] *nm*: **al** ~ on this matter; **con** ~ **a**, ~ **de** with regard to, in relation to
respetable [respe'taßle] *adj* respectable
respetar [respe'tar] *vt* to respect; **respeto** *nm* respect; (*acatamiento*) deference; **respetos** *nmpl* respects; **respetuoso, a** *adj* respectful
respingo [res'pingo] *nm* start, jump
respiración [respira'θjon] *nf* breathing; (*MED*) respiration; (*ventilación*) ventilation
respirar [respi'rar] *vi* to breathe; **respiratorio, a** *adj* respiratory; **respiro** *nm* breathing; (*fig: descanso*) respite
resplandecer [resplande'θer] *vi* to shine; **resplandeciente** *adj* resplendent, shining; **resplandor** *nm* brilliance, brightness; (*de luz, fuego*) blaze
responder [respon'der] *vt* to answer ♦ *vi* to answer; (*fig*) to respond; (*pey*) to answer back; ~ **de** *o* **por** to answer for; **respondón, ona** *adj* cheeky
responsabilidad [responsaßili'ðað] *nf* responsibility
responsabilizarse [responsaßili'θarse] *vr* to make o.s. responsible, take charge
responsable [respon'saßle] *adj* responsible
respuesta [res'pwesta] *nf* answer, reply
resquebrajar [reskeßra'xar] *vt* to crack, split; ~**se** *vr* to crack, split
resquemor [reske'mor] *nm* resentment
resquicio [res'kiθjo] *nm* chink; (*hendedura*) crack ·
resta ['resta] *nf* (*MAT*) remainder
restablecer [restaßle'θer] *vt* to re-establish, restore; ~**se** *vr* to recover
restallar [resta'ʎar] *vi* to crack
restante [res'tante] *adj* remaining; **lo** ~ the remainder
restar [res'tar] *vt* (*MAT*) to subtract; (*fig*) to take away ♦ *vi* to remain, be left
restauración [restaura'θjon] *nf* restoration
restaurante [restau'rante] *nm* restaurant
restaurar [restau'rar] *vt* to restore
restitución [restitu'θjon] *nf* return, restitution
restituir [restitu'ir] *vt* (*devolver*) to return, give back; (*rehabilitar*) to restore
resto ['resto] *nm* (*residuo*) rest, remainder; (*apuesta*) stake; ~**s** *nmpl* remains
restregar [restre'ɣar] *vt* to scrub, rub
restricción [restrik'θjon] *nf* restriction
restrictivo, a [restrik'tißo, a] *adj* restrictive
restringir [restrin'xir] *vt* to restrict, limit
resucitar [resuθi'tar] *vt, vi* to resuscitate, revive
resuelto, a [re'swelto, a] *pp de* **resolver** ♦ *adj* resolute, determined
resuello [re'sweʎo] *nm* (*aliento*) breath; **estar sin** ~ to be breathless

resultado [resul'taðo] *nm* result; (*conclusión*) outcome; **resultante** *adj* resulting, resultant

resultar [resul'tar] *vi* (*ser*) to be; (*llegar a ser*) to turn out to be; (*salir bien*) to turn out well; (*COM*) to amount to; ~ **de** to stem from; **me resulta difícil hacerlo** it's difficult for me to do it

resumen [re'sumen] (*pl* **resúmenes**) *nm* summary, résumé; **en** ~ in short

resumir [resu'mir] *vt* to sum up; (*cortar*) to abridge, cut down; (*condensar*) to summarize

resurgir [resur'xir] *vi* (*reaparecer*) to reappear

resurrección [resurre(k)'θjon] *nf* resurrection

retablo [re'taβlo] *nm* altarpiece

retaguardia [reta'ywarðja] *nf* rearguard

retahíla [reta'ila] *nf* series, string

retal [re'tal] *nm* remnant

retar [re'tar] *vt* to challenge; (*desafiar*) to defy, dare

retardar [retar'ðar] *vt* (*demorar*) to delay; (*hacer más lento*) to slow down; (*retener*) to hold back

retazo [re'taθo] *nm* snippet (*BRIT*), fragment

retener [rete'ner] *vt* (*intereses*) to withhold

reticente [reti'θente] *adj* (*tono*) insinuating; (*postura*) reluctant; **ser** ~ **a hacer algo** to be reluctant *o* unwilling to do sth

retina [re'tina] *nf* retina

retintín [retin'tin] *nm* jangle, jingle

retirada [reti'raða] *nf* (*MIL*, *refugio*) retreat; (*de dinero*) withdrawal; (*de embajador*) recall; **retirado, a** *adj* (*lugar*) remote; (*vida*) quiet; (*jubilado*) retired

retirar [reti'rar] *vt* to withdraw; (*quitar*) to remove; (*jubilar*) to retire, pension off; **~se** *vr* to retreat, withdraw; to retire; (*acostarse*) to retire, go to bed; **retiro** *nm* retreat; retirement; (*pago*) pension

reto ['reto] *nm* dare, challenge

retocar [reto'kar] *vt* (*fotografía*) to touch up, retouch

retoño [re'toɲo] *nm* sprout, shoot; (*fig*) offspring, child

retoque [re'toke] *nm* retouching

retorcer [retor'θer] *vt* to twist; (*manos, lavado*) to wring; **~se** *vr* to become twisted; (*mover el cuerpo*) to writhe

retorcido, a [retor'θiðo, a] *adj* (*persona*) devious

retórica [re'torika] *nf* rhetoric; (*pey*) affectedness; **retórico, a** *adj* rhetorical

retornar [retor'nar] *vt* to return, give back ♦ *vi* to return, go/come back; **retorno** *nm* return

retortijón [retorti'xon] *nm* twist, twisting

retozar [reto'θar] *vi* (*juguetear*) to frolic, romp; (*saltar*) to gambol; **retozón, ona** *adj* playful

retracción [retrak'θjon] *nf* retraction

retractarse [retrak'tarse] *vr* to retract; **me retracto** I take that back

retraerse [retra'erse] *vr* to retreat, withdraw; **retraído, a** *adj* shy, retiring; **retraimiento** *nm* retirement; (*timidez*) shyness

retransmisión [retransmi'sjon] *nf* repeat (broadcast)

retransmitir [retransmi'tir] *vt* (*mensaje*) to relay; (*TV etc*) to repeat, retransmit; (: *en vivo*) to broadcast live

retrasado, a [retra'saðo, a] *adj* late; (*MED*) mentally retarded; (*país etc*) backward, underdeveloped

retrasar [retra'sar] *vt* (*demorar*) to postpone, put off; (*retardar*) to slow down ♦ *vi* (*atrasarse*) to be late; (*reloj*) to be slow; (*producción*) to fall (away); (*quedarse atrás*) to lag behind; **~se** *vr* to be late; to be slow; to fall away; to lag behind

retraso [re'traso] *nm* (*demora*) delay; (*lentitud*) slowness; (*tardanza*) lateness; (*atraso*) backwardness; **~s** (*FINANZAS*) *nmpl* arrears; **llegar con** ~ to arrive late; ~ **mental** mental deficiency

retratar [retra'tar] *vt* (*ARTE*) to paint the portrait of; (*fotografiar*) to photograph; (*fig*) to depict, describe; **~se** *vr* to have one's portrait painted; to have one's photograph taken; **retrato** *nm* portrait; (*fig*) likeness; **retrato-robot** *nm* identikit picture

retreta [re'treta] *nf* retreat

retrete [re'trete] *nm* toilet

retribución [retriβu'θjon] *nf* (*recompensa*) reward; (*pago*) pay, payment

retribuir [retri'βwir] *vt* (*recompensar*) to reward; (*pagar*) to pay

retro... ['retro] *prefijo* retro...

retroactivo, a [retroak'tiβo, a] *adj* retroactive, retrospective

retroceder [retroθe'ðer] *vi* (*echarse atrás*) to move back(wards); (*fig*) to back down

retroceso [retro'θeso] *nm* backward movement; (*MED*) relapse; (*fig*) backing down

retrógrado, a [re'troyraðo, a] *adj* retrograde, retrogressive; (*POL*) reactionary

retropropulsión [retropropul'sjon] *nf* jet propulsion

retrospectivo, a [retrospek'tiβo, a] *adj* retrospective

retrovisor [retroβi'sor] *nm* (*tb*: *espejo* ~) rear-view mirror

retumbar [retum'bar] *vi* to echo, resound

reuma ['reuma] *nm* rheumatism

reumatismo [reuma'tismo] *nm* = **reuma**

reunificar [reunifi'kar] *vt* to reunify

reunión [reu'njon] *nf* (*asamblea*) meeting; (*fiesta*) party

reunir [reu'nir] *vt* (*juntar*) to reunite, join (together); (*recoger*) to gather (together); (*personas*) to get together; (*cualidades*) to combine; **~se** vr (personas: en asamblea) to meet, gather

revalidar [reβali'ðar] vt (ratificar) to confirm, ratify

revalorizar [reβalori'θar] vt to revalue, re-assess

revancha [re'βantʃa] nf revenge

revelación [reβela'θjon] nf revelation

revelado [reβe'laðo] nm developing

revelar [reβe'lar] vt to reveal; (FOTO) to develop

reventa [re'βenta] nf (de entradas: para concierto) touting

reventar [reβen'tar] vt to burst, explode

reventón [reβen'ton] nm (AUTO) blow-out (BRIT), flat (US)

reverberación [reβerβera'θjon] nf reverberation

reverberar [reβerβe'rar] vi to reverberate

reverencia [reβe'renθja] nf reverence; **reverenciar** vt to revere

reverendo, a [reβe'rendo, a] adj reverend

reverente [reβe'rente] adj reverent

reversible [reβer'siβle] adj (prenda) reversible

reverso [re'βerso] nm back, other side; (de moneda) reverse

revertir [reβer'tir] vi to revert

revés [re'βes] nm back, wrong side; (fig) reverse, setback; (DEPORTE) backhand; **al ~** the wrong way round; (de arriba abajo) upside down; (ropa) inside out; **volver algo al ~** to turn sth round; (ropa) to turn sth inside out

revestir [reβes'tir] vt (poner) to put on; (cubrir) to cover, coat; **~ con** o **de** to invest with

revisar [reβi'sar] vt (examinar) to check; (texto etc) to revise; **revisión** nf revision

revisor, a [reβi'sor, a] nm/f inspector; (FERRO) ticket collector

revista [re'βista] nf magazine, review; (TEATRO) revue; (inspección) inspection; **pasar ~ a** to review, inspect

revivir [reβi'βir] vi to revive

revocación [reβoka'θjon] nf repeal

revocar [reβo'kar] vt to revoke

revolcarse [reβol'karse] vr to roll about

revolotear [reβolote'ar] vi to flutter

revoltijo [reβol'tixo] nm mess, jumble

revoltoso, a [reβol'toso, a] adj (travieso) naughty, unruly

revolución [reβolu'θjon] nf revolution; **revolucionar** vt to revolutionize; **revolucionario, a** adj, nm/f revolutionary

revolver [reβol'βer] vt (desordenar) to disturb, mess up; (mover) to move about; (POL) to stir up ♦ vi: **~ en** to go through, rummage (about) in; **~se** vr (volver contra) to turn on o against

revólver [re'βolβer] nm revolver

revuelo [re'βwelo] nm fluttering; (fig) commotion

revuelta [re'βwelta] nf (motín) revolt; (agitación) commotion

revuelto, a [re'βwelto, a] pp de **revolver** ♦ adj (mezclado) mixed-up, in disorder

revulsivo [reβul'siβo] nm enema

rey [rei] nm king; **Día de R~es** Twelfth Night

reyerta [re'jerta] nf quarrel, brawl

rezagado, a [reθa'xaðo, a] nm/f straggler

rezagar [reθa'xar] vt (dejar atrás) to leave behind; (retrasar) to delay, postpone

rezar [re'θar] vi to pray; **~ con** (fam) to concern, have to do with; **rezo** nm prayer

rezongar [reθon'gar] vi to grumble

rezumar [reθu'mar] vt to ooze

ría ['ria] nf estuary

riada [ri'aða] nf flood

ribera [ri'βera] nf (de río) bank; (: área) riverside

ribete [ri'βete] nm (de vestido) border; (fig) addition; **~ar** vt to edge, border

ricino [ri'θino] nm: **aceite de ~** castor oil

rico, a ['riko, a] adj rich; (adinerado) wealthy, rich; (lujoso) luxurious; (comida) delicious; (niño) lovely, cute ♦ nm/f rich person

rictus ['riktus] nm (mueca) sneer, grin

ridiculez [riðiku'leθ] nf absurdity

ridiculizar [riðikuli'θar] vt to ridicule

ridículo, a [ri'ðikulo, a] adj ridiculous; **hacer el ~** to make a fool of o.s.; **poner a uno en ~** to make a fool of sb

riego ['rjexo] nm (aspersión) watering; (irrigación) irrigation

riel [rjel] nm rail

rienda ['rjenda] nf rein; **dar ~ suelta a** to give free rein to

riesgo ['rjesxo] nm risk; **correr el ~ de** to run the risk of

rifa ['rifa] nf (lotería) raffle; **rifar** vt to raffle

rifle ['rifle] nm rifle

rigidez [rixi'ðeθ] nf rigidity, stiffness; (fig) strictness; **rígido, a** adj rigid, stiff; strict, inflexible

rigor [ri'xor] nm strictness, rigour; (inclemencia) harshness; **de ~** de rigueur, essential; **riguroso, a** adj rigorous; harsh; (severo) severe

rimar [ri'mar] vi to rhyme

rimbombante [rimbom'bante] adj (fig) pompous

rímel ['rimel] nm mascara

rímmel ['rimel] nm = **rímel**

rincón [rin'kon] nm corner (inside)

rinoceronte [rinoθe'ronte] nm rhinoceros

riña ['riɲa] nf (disputa) argument; (pelea) brawl

riñón [ri'ɲon] nm kidney; **tener riñones** to have guts

río etc ['rio] vb ver **reír** ♦ nm river; (fig) torrent, stream; **~ abajo/arriba** downstream/

upstream; ~ **de la Plata** River Plate
rioja [ri'oxa] *nm* (*vino*) rioja (wine)
rioplatense [riopla'tense] *adj* of o from the
  River Plate region
riqueza [ri'keθa] *nf* wealth, riches *pl*; (*cualidad*) richness
risa ['risa] *nf* laughter; (*una* ~) laugh; ¡qué
  ~! what a laugh!
risco ['risko] *nm* crag, cliff
risible [ri'siβle] *adj* ludicrous, laughable
risotada [riso'taða] *nf* guffaw, loud laugh
ristra ['ristra] *nf* string
risueño, a [ri'sweɲo, a] *adj* (*sonriente*)
  smiling; (*contento*) cheerful
ritmo ['ritmo] *nm* rhythm; **a ~ lento**
  slowly; **trabajar a ~ lento** to go slow
rito ['rito] *nm* rite
ritual [ri'twal] *adj, nm* ritual
rival [ri'βal] *adj, nm/f* rival; ~**idad** *nf* rivalry; ~**izar** *vi*: ~**izar con** to rival, vie with
rizado, a [ri'θaðo, a] *adj* curly ♦ *nm* curls
  pl
rizar [ri'θar] *vt* to curl; ~**se** *vr* (*pelo*) to
  curl; (*agua*) to ripple; **rizo** *nm* curl; ripple
RNE *nf abr* = **Radio Nacional de España**
robar [ro'βar] *vt* to rob; (*objeto*) to steal;
  (*casa etc*) to break into; (*NAIPES*) to draw
roble ['roβle] *nm* oak; ~**dal** *nm* = **robledo**;
  ~**do** *nm* oakwood
robo ['roβo] *nm* robbery, theft
robot [ro'βot] *nm* robot; ~ (**de cocina**)
  food processor
robustecer [roβuste'θer] *vt* to strengthen
robusto, a [ro'βusto, a] *adj* robust, strong
roca ['roka] *nf* rock
roce ['roθe] *nm* (*caricia*) brush; (*TEC*) friction; (*en la piel*) graze; **tener ~ con** to be
  in close contact with
rociar [ro'θjar] *vt* to spray
rocín [ro'θin] *nm* nag, hack
rocío [ro'θio] *nm* dew
rocoso, a [ro'koso, a] *adj* rocky
rodado, a [ro'ðaðo, a] *adj* (*con ruedas*)
  wheeled
rodaja [ro'ðaxa] *nf* (*raja*) slice
rodaje [ro'ðaxe] *nm* (*CINE*) shooting,
  filming; (*AUTO*): **en ~** running in
rodar [ro'ðar] *vt* (*vehículo*) to wheel
  (along); (*escalera*) to roll down; (*viajar por*)
  to travel (over) ♦ *vi* to roll; (*coche*) to go,
  run; (*CINE*) to shoot, film
rodear [roðe'ar] *vt* to surround ♦ *vi* to go
  round; ~**se** *vr*: ~**se de amigos** to surround
  o.s. with friends
rodeo [ro'ðeo] *nm* (*ruta indirecta*) detour;
  (*evasión*) evasion; (*AM*) rodeo; **hablar sin**
  ~**s** to come to the point, speak plainly
rodilla [ro'ðiʎa] *nf* knee; **de** ~**s** kneeling;
  ponerse de ~**s** to kneel (down)
rodillo [ro'ðiʎo] *nm* roller; (*CULIN*) rolling-
  pin
roedor, a [roe'ðor, a] *adj* gnawing ♦ *nm*

rodent
roer [ro'er] *vt* (*masticar*) to gnaw; (*corroer,
  fig*) to corrode
rogar [ro'ɣar] *vt, vi* (*pedir*) to ask for; (*suplicar*) to beg, plead; **se ruega no fumar**
  please do not smoke
rojizo, a [ro'xiθo, a] *adj* reddish
rojo, a ['roxo, a] *adj, nm* red; **al ~ vivo**
  red-hot
rol [rol] *nm* list, roll; (*AM: papel*) role
rollizo, a [ro'ʎiθo, a] *adj* (*objeto*) cylindrical; (*persona*) plump
rollo ['roʎo] *nm* roll; (*de cuerda*) coil; (*madera*) log; (*fam*) bore; ¡qué ~! what a
  carry-on!
ROM [rom] *nf abr* (= *memoria de sólo lectura*) ROM
Roma ['roma] *n* Rome
romance [ro'manθe] *nm* (*idioma castellano*)
  Romance language; (*LITERATURA*) ballad;
  hablar en ~ to speak plainly
romanticismo [romanti'θismo] *nm* romanticism
romántico, a [ro'mantiko, a] *adj* romantic
rombo ['rombo] *nm* (*GEOM*) rhombus
romería [rome'ria] *nf* (*REL*) pilgrimage; (*excursión*) trip, outing
romero, a [ro'mero, a] *nm/f* pilgrim ♦ *nm*
  rosemary
romo, a ['romo, a] *adj* blunt; (*fig*) dull
rompecabezas [rompeka'βeθas] *nm inv*
  riddle, puzzle; (*juego*) jigsaw (puzzle)
rompeolas [rompe'olas] *nm inv* breakwater
romper [rom'per] *vt* to break; (*hacer pedazos*) to smash; (*papel, tela etc*) to tear, rip ♦
  vi (*olas*) to break; (*sol, diente*) to break
  through; ~ **un contrato** to break a contract; ~ **a** (*empezar a*) to start (suddenly)
  to; ~ **a llorar** to burst into tears; ~ **con
  uno** to fall out with sb
rompimiento [rompi'mjento] *nm* (*acto*)
  breaking; (*fig*) break; (*quiebra*) crack
ron [ron] *nm* rum
roncar [ron'kar] *vi* to snore
ronco, a ['ronko, a] *adj* (*afónico*) hoarse;
  (*áspero*) raucous
ronda ['ronda] *nf* (*gen*) round; (*patrulla*) patrol; **rondar** *vt* to patrol ♦ *vi* to patrol; (*fig*)
  to prowl round
ronquido [ron'kiðo] *nm* snore, snoring
ronronear [ronrone'ar] *vi* to purr; **ronroneo** *nm* purr
roña ['roɲa] *nf* (*VETERINARIA*) mange;
  (*mugre*) dirt, grime; (*óxido*) rust
roñoso, a [ro'ɲoso, a] *adj* (*mugriento*)
  filthy; (*tacaño*) mean
ropa ['ropa] *nf* clothes *pl*, clothing; ~ **blanca** linen; ~ **de cama** bed linen; ~ **interior**
  underwear; ~ **para lavar** washing; ~**je** *nm*
  gown, robes *pl*
ropero [ro'pero] *nm* linen cupboard; (*guardarropa*) wardrobe

rosa ['rosa] adj pink ♦ nf rose; (ANAT) red birthmark; ~ **de los vientos** the compass

rosado, a [ro'saðo, a] adj pink ♦ nm rosé

rosal [ro'sal] nm rosebush

rosario [ro'sarjo] nm (REL) rosary; **rezar el** ~ to say the rosary

rosca ['roska] nf (de tornillo) thread; (de humo) coil, spiral; (pan, postre) ring-shaped roll/pastry

rosetón [rose'ton] nm rosette; (ARQ) rose window

rosquilla [ros'kiʎa] nf doughnut-shaped fritter

rostro ['rostro] nm (cara) face

rotación [rota'θjon] nf rotation; ~ **de cultivos** crop rotation

rotativo, a [rota'tiβo, a] adj rotary

roto, a ['roto, a] pp de **romper** ♦ adj broken

rótula ['rotula] nf kneecap; (TEC) ball-and-socket joint

rotulador [rotula'ðor] nm felt-tip pen

rotular [rotu'lar] vt (carta, documento) to head, entitle; (objeto) to label; **rótulo** nm heading, title; label; (letrero) sign

rotundamente [rotunda'mente] adv (negar) flatly; (responder, afirmar) emphatically; **rotundo, a** adj round; (enfático) emphatic

rotura [ro'tura] nf (rompimiento) breaking; (MED) fracture

roturar [rotu'rar] vt to plough

rozadura [roθa'ðura] nf abrasion, graze

rozar [ro'θar] vt (frotar) to rub; (arañar) to scratch; (tocar ligeramente) to shave, touch lightly; ~**se** vr to rub (together); ~**se con** (fam) to rub shoulders with

rte. abr (= remite, remitente) sender

RTVE nf abr = **Radiotelevisión Española**

rubí [ru'βi] nm ruby; (de reloj) jewel

rubio, a ['ruβjo, a] adj fair-haired, blond(e) ♦ nm/f blond/blonde; **tabaco** ~ Virginia tobacco

rubor [ru'βor] nm (sonrojo) blush; (timidez) bashfulness; ~**izarse** vr to blush

rúbrica ['ruβrika] nf (título) title, heading; (de la firma) flourish; **rubricar** vt (firmar) to sign with a flourish; (concluir) to sign and seal

rudeza [ru'ðeθa] nf (tosquedad) coarseness; (sencillez) simplicity

rudimentario, a [ruðimen'tarjo, a] adj (conocimientos, noción) rudimentary; **rudimento** nm rudiment

rudo, a ['ruðo, a] adj (sin pulir) unpolished; (grosero) coarse; (violento) violent; (sencillo) simple

rueda ['rweða] nf wheel; (círculo) ring, circle; (rodaja) slice, round; ~ **delantera/trasera/de repuesto** front/back/spare wheel; ~ **de prensa** press conference

ruedo ['rweðo] nm (contorno) edge, border; (de vestido) hem; (círculo) circle; (TAUR) arena, bullring

ruego etc ['rweɣo] vb ver **rogar** ♦ nm request

rufián [ru'fjan] nm scoundrel

rugby ['ruɣβi] nm rugby

rugido [ru'xiðo] nm roar

rugir [ru'xir] vi to roar

rugoso, a [ru'ɣoso, a] adj (arrugado) wrinkled; (áspero) rough; (desigual) ridged

ruido ['rwiðo] nm noise; (sonido) sound; (alboroto) racket, row; (escándalo) commotion, rumpus; ~**so, a** adj noisy, loud; (fig) sensational

ruin [rwin] adj contemptible, mean

ruina ['rwina] nf ruin; (colapso) collapse; (de persona) ruin, downfall

ruindad [rwin'dað] nf lowness, meanness; (acto) low o mean act

ruinoso, a [rwi'noso, a] adj ruinous; (destartalado) dilapidated, tumbledown; (COM) disastrous

ruiseñor [rwise'ɲor] nm nightingale

ruleta [ru'leta] nf roulette

rulo ['rulo] nm (para el pelo) curler

Rumania [ru'manja] nf Rumania

rumba ['rumba] nf rumba

rumbo ['rumbo] nm (ruta) route, direction; (ángulo de dirección) course, bearing; (fig) course of events: **ir con** ~ **a** to be heading for

rumboso, a [rum'boso, a] adj (generoso) generous

rumiante [ru'mjante] nm ruminant

rumiar [ru'mjar] vt to chew; (fig) to chew over ♦ vi to chew the cud

rumor [ru'mor] nm (ruido sordo) low sound; (murmuración) murmur, buzz

rumorearse vr: **se rumorea que** it is rumoured that

runrún [run'run] nm (voces) murmur, sound of voices; (fig) rumour

rupestre [ru'pestre] adj rock cpd

ruptura [rup'tura] nf rupture

rural [ru'ral] adj rural

Rusia ['rusja] nf Russia; **ruso, a** adj, nm/f Russian

rústica ['rustika] nf: **libro en** ~ paperback (book); ver tb **rústico**

rústico, a ['rustiko, a] adj rustic; (ordinario) coarse, uncouth ♦ nm/f yokel

ruta ['ruta] nf route

rutina [ru'tina] nf routine; ~**rio, a** adj routine

S s

S *abr* (= *santo, a*) St; (= *sur*) S
s. *abr* (= *siglo*) C.; (= *siguiente*) foll
S.A. *abr* (= *Sociedad Anónima*) Ltd. (*BRIT*), Inc. (*US*)
sábado ['saβaðo] *nm* Saturday
sábana ['saβana] *nf* sheet
sabandija [saβan'dixa] *nf* bug, insect
sabañón [saβa'ɲon] *nm* chilblain
saber [sa'βer] *vt* to know; (*llegar a conocer*) to find out, learn; (*tener capacidad de*) to know how to ♦ *vi:* ~ **a** to taste of, taste like ♦ *nm* knowledge, learning; **a** ~ namely; **¿sabes conducir/nadar?** can you drive/swim?; **¿sabes francés?** do you speak French?; ~ **de memoria** to know by heart; **hacer** ~ **algo a uno** to inform sb of sth, let sb know sth
sabiduría [saβiðu'ria] *nf* (*conocimientos*) wisdom; (*instrucción*) learning
sabiendas [sa'βjendas]: **a** ~ *adv* knowingly
sabio, a ['saβjo,a] *adj* (*docto*) learned; (*prudente*) wise, sensible
sabor [sa'βor] *nm* taste, flavour; ~**ear** *vt* to taste, savour; (*fig*) to relish
sabotaje [saβo'taxe] *nm* sabotage
saboteador, a [saβotea'ðor, a] *nm/f* saboteur
sabotear [saβote'ar] *vt* to sabotage
sabré *etc vb ver* **saber**
sabroso, a [sa'βroso, a] *adj* tasty; (*fig: fam*) racy, salty
sacacorchos [saka'kortʃos] *nm inv* corkscrew
sacapuntas [saka'puntas] *nm inv* pencil sharpener
sacar [sa'kar] *vt* to take out; (*fig: extraer*) to get (out); (*quitar*) to remove, get out; (*hacer salir*) to bring out; (*conclusión*) to draw; (*novela etc*) to publish, bring out; (*ropa*) to take off; (*obra*) to make; (*premio*) to receive; (*entradas*) to get; (*TENIS*) to serve; ~ **adelante** (*niño*) to bring up; (*negocio*) to carry on, go on with; ~ **a uno a bailar** to get sb up to dance; ~ **una foto** to take a photo; ~ **la lengua** to stick out one's tongue; ~ **buenas/malas notas** to get good/bad marks
sacarina [saka'rina] *nf* saccharin(e)
sacerdote [saθer'ðote] *nm* priest
saciar [sa'θjar] *vt* (*hambre, sed*) to satisfy;

~**se** *vr* (*de comida*) to get full up; **comer hasta** ~**se** to eat one's fill
saco ['sako] *nm* bag; (*grande*) sack; (*su contenido*) bagful; (*AM*) jacket; ~ **de dormir** sleeping bag
sacramento [sakra'mento] *nm* sacrament
sacrificar [sakrifi'kar] *vt* to sacrifice; **sacrificio** *nm* sacrifice
sacrilegio [sakri'lexjo] *nm* sacrilege; **sacrílego, a** *adj* sacrilegious
sacristía [sakris'tia] *nf* sacristy
sacro, a ['sakro, a] *adj* sacred
sacudida [saku'ðiða] *nf* (*agitación*) shake, shaking; (*sacudimiento*) jolt, bump; ~ **eléctrica** electric shock
sacudir [saku'ðir] *vt* to shake; (*golpear*) to hit
sádico, a ['saðiko, a] *adj* sadistic ♦ *nm/f* sadist; **sadismo** *nm* sadism
saeta [sa'eta] *nf* (*flecha*) arrow
sagacidad [saɣaθi'ðað] *nf* shrewdness, cleverness; **sagaz** *adj* shrewd, clever
sagitario [saxi'tarjo] *nm* Sagittarius
sagrado, a [sa'ɣraðo, a] *adj* sacred, holy
Sáhara ['saara] *nm:* **el** ~ **the** Sahara (desert)
sal [sal] *vb ver* **salir** ♦ *nf* salt
sala ['sala] *nf* (*cuarto grande*) large room; (~ **de estar**) living room; (*TEATRO*) house, auditorium; (*de hospital*) ward; ~ **de apelación** court; ~ **de espera** waiting room; ~ **de estar** living room; ~ **de fiestas** dance hall
salado, a [sa'laðo, a] *adj* salty; (*fig*) witty, amusing; **agua salada** salt water
salar [sa'lar] *vt* to salt, add salt to
salarial [sala'rjal] *adj* (*aumento, revisión*) wage *cpd*, salary *cpd*
salario [sa'larjo] *nm* wage, pay
salchicha [sal'tʃitʃa] *nf* (*pork*) sausage; **salchichón** *nm* (*salami-type*) sausage
saldar [sal'dar] *vt* to pay; (*vender*) to sell off; (*fig*) to settle, resolve; **saldo** *nm* (*pago*) settlement; (*de una cuenta*) balance; (*lo restante*) remnant(s) (*pl*), remainder; ~**s** *nmpl* (*en tienda*) sale
saldré *etc vb ver* **salir**
salero [sa'lero] *nm* salt cellar
salgo *etc vb ver* **salir**
salida [sa'liða] *nf* (*puerta etc*) exit, way out; (*acto*) leaving, going out; (*de tren, ʻAVIAT*) departure; (*TEC*) output, production; (*fig*) way out; (*COM*) opening; (*GEO, válvula*) outlet; (*de gas*) leak; **calle sin** ~ cul-de-sac; ~ **de incendios** fire escape
saliente [sa'ljente] *adj* (*ARQ*) projecting; (*sol*) rising; (*fig*) outstanding

PALABRA CLAVE

salir [sa'lir] *vi* **1** (*partir: tb:* ~ **de**) to leave; **Juan ha salido** Juan is out; **salió de la co-**

cina he came out of the kitchen
2 (*aparecer*) to appear; (*disco, libro*) to come out; **anoche salió en la tele** she appeared o was on TV last night; **salió en todos los periódicos** it was in all the papers
3 (*resultar*): **la muchacha nos salió muy trabajadora** the girl turned out to be a very hard worker; **la comida te ha salido exquisita** the food was delicious; **sale muy caro** it's very expensive
4: ~**le a uno algo: la entrevista que hice me salió bien/mal** the interview I did went o turned out well/badly
5: ~ **adelante: no sé como haré para ~ adelante** I don't know how I'll get by
♦ ~**se** *vr* (*líquido*) to spill; (*animal*) to escape

saliva [sa'liβa] *nf* saliva
salmo ['salmo] *nm* psalm
salmón [sal'mon] *nm* salmon
salmuera [sal'mwera] *nf* pickle, brine
salón [sa'lon] *nm* (*de casa*) living room, lounge; (*muebles*) lounge suite; ~ **de belleza** beauty parlour; ~ **de baile** dance hall
salpicadero [salpika'ðero] *nm* (*AUTO*) dashboard
salpicar [salpi'kar] *vt* (*rociar*) to sprinkle, spatter; (*esparcir*) to scatter
salsa ['salsa] *nf* sauce; (*con carne asada*) gravy; (*fig*) spice
saltamontes [salta'montes] *nm inv* grasshopper
saltar [sal'tar] *vt* to jump (over), leap (over); (*dejar de lado*) to skip, miss out ♦ *vi* to jump, leap; (*pelota*) to bounce; (*al aire*) to fly up; (*quebrarse*) to break; (*al agua*) to dive; (*fig*) to explode, blow up
salto ['salto] *nm* jump, leap; (*al agua*) dive; ~ **de agua** waterfall; ~ **de altura** high jump
saltón, ona [sal'ton, ona] *adj* (*ojos*) bulging, popping; (*dientes*) protruding
salud [sa'luð] *nf* health; **¡(a su) ~!** cheers!, good health!; ~**able** *adj* (*de buena ~*) healthy; (*provechoso*) good, beneficial
saludar [salu'ðar] *vt* to greet; (*MIL*) to salute; **saludo** *nm* greeting; **"saludos"** (*en carta*) "best wishes", "regards"
salva ['salβa] *nf*: ~ **de aplausos** ovation
salvación [salβa'θjon] *nf* salvation; (*rescate*) rescue
salvado [sal'βaðo] *nm* bran
salvaguardar [salβaɣwar'ðar] *vt* to safeguard
salvajada [salβa'xaða] *nf* (*una ~*) atrocity
salvaje [sal'βaxe] *adj* wild; (*tribu*) savage; **salvajismo** *nm* savagery
salvamento [salβa'mento] *nm* rescue
salvar [sal'βar] *vt* (*rescatar*) to save, rescue; (*resolver*) to overcome, resolve; (*cubrir distancias*) to cover, travel; (*hacer excep-*

ción) to except, exclude; (*un barco*) to salvage
salvavidas [salβa'βiðas] *adj inv*: **bote/ chaleco/cinturón** ~ lifeboat/life jacket/life belt
salvo, a ['salβo, a] *adj* safe ♦ *adv* except (for), save; **a** ~ out of danger; ~ **que** unless; ~**conducto** *nm* safe-conduct
san [san] *adj* saint; **S**~ **Juan** St. John
sanar [sa'nar] *vt* (*herida*) to heal; (*persona*) to cure ♦ *vi* (*persona*) to get well, recover; (*herida*) to heal
sanatorio [sana'torjo] *nm* sanatorium
sanción [san'θjon] *nf* sanction; **sancionar** *vt* to sanction
sandalia [san'dalja] *nf* sandal
sandez [san'deθ] *nf* foolishness
sandía [san'dia] *nf* watermelon
sandwich ['sandwitʃ] (*pl* ~**s**, ~**es**) *nm* sandwich
saneamiento [sanea'mjento] *nm* sanitation
sanear [sane'ar] *vt* (*terreno*) to drain
sangrar [san'grar] *vt, vi* to bleed; **sangre** *nf* blood
sangría [san'gria] *nf* sangria, *sweetened drink of red wine with fruit*
sangriento, a [san'grjento, a] *adj* bloody
sanguijuela [sangi'xwela] *nf* (*ZOOL, fig*) leech
sanguinario, a [sangi'narjo, a] *adj* bloodthirsty
sanguíneo, a [san'gineo, a] *adj* blood *cpd*
sanidad [sani'ðað] *nf* sanitation; (*calidad de sano*) health, healthiness; ~ **pública** public health
sanitario, a [sani'tarjo, a] *adj* sanitary; (*de la salud*) health; ~**s** *nmpl* toilets (*BRIT*), washroom (*US*)
sano, a ['sano, a] *adj* healthy; (*sin daños*) sound; (*comida*) wholesome; (*entero*) whole, intact; ~ **y salvo** safe and sound
Santiago [san'tjaɣo] *nm*: ~ (**de Chile**) Santiago
santiamén [santja'men] *nm*: **en un** ~ in no time at all
santidad [santi'ðað] *nf* holiness, sanctity
santiguarse [santi'ɣwarse] *vr* to make the sign of the cross
santo, a ['santo, a] *adj* holy; (*fig*) wonderful, miraculous ♦ *nm/f* saint ♦ *nm* saint's day; ~ **y seña** password
santuario [san'twarjo] *nm* sanctuary, shrine
saña ['saɲa] *nf* rage, fury
sapo ['sapo] *nm* toad
saque ['sake] *nm* (*TENIS*) service, serve; (*FÚTBOL*) throw-in; ~ **de esquina** corner (kick)
saquear [sake'ar] *vt* (*MIL*) to sack; (*robar*) to loot, plunder; (*fig*) to ransack; **saqueo** *nm* sacking; looting, plundering; ransacking
sarampión [saram'pjon] *nm* measles *sg*
sarcasmo [sar'kasmo] *nm* sarcasm; **sarcás-**

tico, a adj sarcastic

sardina [sar'ðina] nf sardine

sargento [sar'xento] nm sergeant

sarmiento [sar'mjento] nm (BOT) vine shoot

sarna ['sarna] nf itch; (MED) scabies

sarpullido [sarpu'ʎiðo] nm (MED) rash

sarro ['sarro] nm (en dientes) tartar, plaque

sartén [sar'ten] nf frying pan

sastre ['sastre] nm tailor; **~ría** nf (arte) tailoring; (tienda) tailor's (shop)

Satanás [sata'nas] nm Satan

satélite [sa'telite] nm satellite

sátira ['satira] nf satire

satisfacción [satisfak'θjon] nf satisfaction

satisfacer [satisfa'θer] vt to satisfy; (gastos) to meet; (pérdida) to make good; **~se** vr to satisfy o.s., be satisfied; (vengarse) to take revenge; **satisfecho, a** adj satisfied; (contento) content(ed), happy; (tb: satisfecho de sí mismo) self-satisfied, smug

saturar [satu'rar] vt to saturate

sauce ['sauθe] nm willow; **~ llorón** weeping willow

sauna ['sauna] nf sauna

savia ['saßja] nf sap

saxofón [sakso'fon] nm saxophone

sazonar [saθo'nar] vt to ripen; (CULIN) to flavour, season

——— PALABRA CLAVE

se [se] pron **1** (reflexivo: sg: m) himself; (: f) herself; (: pl) themselves; (: cosa) itself; (: de Vd) yourself; (: de Vds) yourselves; **~ está preparando** she's preparing herself; para usos léxicos del pron ver el vb en cuestión, p.ej. **arrepentirse**

2 (con complemento indirecto) to him; to her; to them; to it; to you; **a usted ~ lo dije ayer** I told you yesterday; **~ compró un sombrero** he bought himself a hat; **~ rompió la pierna** he broke his leg

3 (uso recíproco) each other, one another; **~ miraron (el uno al otro)** they looked at each other o one another

4 (en oraciones pasivas): **se han vendido muchos libros** a lot of books have been sold

5 (impers): **~ dice que** people say that, it is said that; **allí ~ come muy bien** the food there is very good, you can eat very well there

---

SE abr (= sudeste) SE

sé vb ver **saber**; **ser**

sea etc vb ver **ser**

sebo ['seßo] nm fat, grease

secador [seka'ðor] nm: **~ de pelo** hairdryer

secadora [seka'ðora] nf (ELEC) tumble dryer

secar [se'kar] vt to dry; **~se** vr to dry (off); (río, planta) to dry up

sección [sek'θjon] nf section

seco, a ['seko, a] adj dry; (carácter) cold; (respuesta) sharp, curt; **habrá pan a secas** there will be just bread; **decir algo a secas** to say sth curtly; **parar en ~** to stop dead

secretaría [sekreta'ria] nf secretariat

secretario, a [sekre'tarjo, a] nm/f secretary

secreto, a [se'kreto, a] adj secret; (persona) secretive ♦ nm secret; (calidad) secrecy

secta ['sekta] nf sect; **~rio, a** adj sectarian

sector [sek'tor] nm sector

secuela [se'kwela] nf consequence

secuencia [se'kwenθja] nf sequence

secuestrar [sekwes'trar] vt to kidnap; (bienes) to seize, confiscate; **secuestro** nm kidnapping; seizure, confiscation

secular [seku'lar] adj secular

secundar [sekun'dar] vt to second, support

secundario, a [sekun'darjo, a] adj secondary

sed [seð] nf thirst; **tener ~** to be thirsty

seda ['seða] nf silk

sedal [se'ðal] nm fishing line

sedante [se'ðante] nm sedative

sede ['seðe] nf (de gobierno) seat; (de compañía) headquarters pl; **Santa S~** Holy See

sedentario, a [seðen'tarjo, a] adj sedentary

sediento, a [se'ðjento, a] adj thirsty

sedimento [seði'mento] nm sediment

sedoso, a [se'ðoso, a] adj silky, silken

seducción [seðuk'θjon] nf seduction

seducir [seðu'θir] vt to seduce; (sobornar) to bribe; (cautivar) to charm, fascinate; (atraer) to attract; **seductor, a** adj seductive; charming, fascinating; attractive; (engañoso) deceptive, misleading ♦ nm/f seducer

segar [se'ɣar] vt (mies) to reap, cut; (hierba) to mow, cut

seglar [se'ɣlar] adj secular, lay

segregación [seɣreɣa'θjon] nf segregation. **~ racial** racial segregation

segregar [seɣre'ɣar] vt to segregate, separate

seguida [se'ɣiða] nf: **en ~** at once, right away

seguido, a [se'ɣiðo, a] adj (continuo) continuous, unbroken; (recto) straight ♦ adv (directo) straight (on); (después) after; (AM: a menudo) often; **~s** consecutive, successive; **5 días ~s** 5 days running, 5 days in a row

seguimiento [seɣi'mjento] nm chase, pursuit; (continuación) continuation

seguir [se'ɣir] vt to follow; (venir después) to follow on, come after; (proseguir) to continue; (perseguir) to chase, pursue ♦ vi (gen) to follow; (continuar) to continue, carry o go on; **~se** vr to follow; **sigo sin comprender** I still don't understand; **sigue**

lloviendo it's still raining

según [se'ɣun] *prep* according to ♦ *adv*: ¿**irás?** – ~ are you going? – it all depends ♦ *conj* as; ~ **caminamos** while we walk

segunda [se'ɣunda] *nf* double meaning; (*tb*: ~ *clase*) second class; (*tb*: ~ *marcha*) second (gear)

segundo, a [se'ɣundo, a] *adj* second ♦ *nm* second; **de segunda mano** second-hand; **segunda enseñanza** secondary education

seguramente [seɣura'mente] *adv* surely; (*con certeza*) for sure, with certainty

seguridad [seɣuri'ðað] *nf* safety; (*del estado, de casa etc*) security; (*certidumbre*) certainty; (*confianza*) confidence; (*estabilidad*) stability; ~ **social** social security

seguro, a [se'ɣuro, a] *adj* (*cierto*) sure, certain; (*fiel*) trustworthy; (*libre del peligro*) safe; (*bien defendido, firme*) secure ♦ *adv* for sure, certainly ♦ *nm* (*COM*) insurance; ~ **contra terceros/a todo riesgo** third party/comprehensive insurance; ~**s sociales** social security *sg*

seis [seis] *num* six

seísmo [se'ismo] *nm* tremor, earthquake

selección [selek'θjon] *nf* selection; **seleccionar** *vt* to pick, choose, select

selectividad [selektiβi'ðað] (*ESP*) *nf* university entrance examination

selecto, a [se'lekto, a] *adj* select, choice; (*escogido*) selected

selva ['selβa] *nf* (*bosque*) forest, woods *pl*; (*jungla*) jungle

sellar [se'ʎar] *vt* (*documento oficial*) to seal; (*pasaporte, visado*) to stamp

sello ['seʎo] *nm* stamp; (*precinto*) seal

semáforo [se'maforo] *nm* (*AUTO*) traffic lights *pl*; (*FERRO*) signal

semana [se'mana] *nf* week; **entre** ~ during the week; **S~ Santa** Holy Week; **semanal** *adj* weekly

semblante [sem'blante] *nm* face; (*fig*) look

sembrar [sem'brar] *vt* to sow; (*objetos*) to sprinkle, scatter about; (*noticias etc*) to spread

semejante [seme'xante] *adj* (*parecido*) similar ♦ *nm* fellow man, fellow creature; ~**s** alike, similar; **nunca hizo cosa** ~ he never did any such thing; **semejanza** *nf* similarity, resemblance

semejar [seme'xar] *vi* to seem like, resemble; ~**se** *vr* to look alike, be similar

semen ['semen] *nm* semen; ~**tal** *nm* stud

semestral [semes'tral] *adj* half-yearly, bi-annual

semicírculo [semi'θirkulo] *nm* semicircle

semifinal [semifi'nal] *nf* semifinal

semilla [se'miʎa] *nf* seed

seminario [semi'narjo] *nm* (*REL*) seminary; (*ESCOL*) seminar

sémola ['semola] *nf* semolina

sempiterno, a [sempi'terno, a] *adj* everlasting

Sena ['sena] *nm*: **el** ~ the (river) Seine

senado [se'naðo] *nm* senate; **senador, a** *nm/f* senator

sencillez [senθi'ʎeθ] *nf* simplicity; (*de persona*) naturalness; **sencillo, a** *adj* simple; natural, unaffected

senda ['senda] *nf* path, track

sendero [sen'dero] *nm* path, track

sendos, as ['sendos, as] *adj pl*: **les dio** ~ **golpes** he hit both of them

senil [se'nil] *adj* senile

seno ['seno] *nm* (*ANAT*) bosom, bust; (*fig*) bosom; ~**s** breasts

sensación [sensa'θjon] *nf* sensation; (*sentido*) sense; (*sentimiento*) feeling; **sensacional** *adj* sensational

sensato, a [sen'sato, a] *adj* sensible

sensible [sen'sible] *adj* sensitive; (*apreciable*) perceptible, appreciable; (*pérdida*) considerable; ~**ro, a** *adj* sentimental

sensitivo, a [sensi'tiβo, a] *adj* sense *cpd*

sensorial [senso'rjal] *adj* sensory

sensual [sen'swal] *adj* sensual

sentada [sen'taða] *nf* sitting; (*protesta*) sit-in

sentado, a [sen'taðo, a] *adj* (*establecido*) settled; (*carácter*) sensible; **estar** ~ to sit, be sitting (down); **dar por** ~ to take for granted, assume

sentar [sen'tar] *vt* to sit, seat; (*fig*) to establish ♦ *vi* (*vestido*) to suit; (*alimento*): ~ **bien/mal a** to agree/disagree with; ~**se** *vr* (*persona*) to sit, sit down; (*el tiempo*) to settle (down); (*los depósitos*) to settle

sentencia [sen'tenθja] *nf* (*máxima*) maxim, saying; (*JUR*) sentence; **sentenciar** *vt* to sentence

sentido, a [sen'tiðo, a] *adj* (*pérdida*) regrettable; (*carácter*) sensitive ♦ *nm* sense; (*sentimiento*) feeling; (*significado*) sense, meaning; (*dirección*) direction; **mi más** ~ **pésame** my deepest sympathy; ~ **del humor** sense of humour; ~ **único** one-way (street); **tener** ~ to make sense

sentimental [sentimen'tal] *adj* sentimental; **vida** ~ love life

sentimiento [senti'mjento] *nm* (*emoción*) feeling, emotion; (*sentido*) sense; (*pesar*) regret, sorrow

sentir [sen'tir] *vt* to feel; (*percibir*) to perceive, sense; (*lamentar*) to regret, be sorry for ♦ *vi* (*tener la sensación*) to feel; (*lamentarse*) to feel sorry ♦ *nm* opinion, judgement; ~**se bien/mal** to feel well/ill; **lo siento** I'm sorry

seña ['seɲa] *nf* sign; (*MIL*) password; ~**s** *nfpl* (*dirección*) address *sg*; ~**s personales** personal description *sg*

señal [se'ɲal] *nf* sign; (*síntoma*) symptom; (*FERRO, TELEC*) signal; (*marca*) mark;

(COM) deposit; **en ~ de** as a token of, as a sign of; **~ar** vt to mark; (indicar) to point out, indicate; (fijar) to fix, settle

señor [se'ɲor] nm (hombre) man; (caballero) gentleman; (dueño) owner, master; (trato: antes de nombre propio) Mr; (: hablando directamente) sir; **muy ~ mío** Dear Sir; **el ~ alcalde/presidente** the mayor/president

señora [se'ɲora] nf (dama) lady; (trato: antes de nombre propio) Mrs; (: hablando directamente) madam; (esposa) wife; **Nuestra S~** Our Lady

señorita [seɲo'rita] nf (con nombre y/o apellido) Miss; (mujer joven) young lady

señorito [seɲo'rito] nm young gentleman; (pey) rich kid

señuelo [se'ɲwelo] nm decoy

sepa etc vb ver **saber**

separación [separa'θjon] nf separation; (división) division; (distancia) gap

separar [sepa'rar] vt to separate; (dividir) to divide; **~se** vr (parte) to come away; (partes) to come apart; (persona) to leave, go away; (matrimonio) to separate; **separatismo** nm separatism

sepia ['sepja] nf cuttlefish

septiembre [sep'tjembre] nm September

séptimo, a ['septimo, a] adj, nm seventh

sepulcral [sepul'kral] adj (fig: silencio, atmósfera) deadly; **sepulcro** nm tomb, grave

sepultar [sepul'tar] vt to bury; **sepultura** nf (acto) burial; (tumba) grave, tomb

sequedad [seke'ðað] nf dryness; (fig) brusqueness, curtness

sequía [se'kia] nf drought

séquito ['sekito] nm (de rey etc) retinue; (POL) followers pl

―――――― **PALABRA CLAVE** ――――――

ser [ser] vi **1** (descripción) to be; **es médica/muy alta** she's a doctor/very tall; **la familia es de Cuzco** his (o her etc) family is from Cuzco; **soy Ana** (TELEC) Ana speaking o here

2 (propiedad): **es de Joaquín** it's Joaquín's, it belongs to Joaquín

3 (horas, fechas, números): **es la una** it's one o'clock; **son las seis y media** it's half-past six; **es el 1 de junio** it's the first of June; **somos/son seis** there are six of us/them

4 (en oraciones pasivas): **ha sido descubierto ya** it's already been discovered

5: **es de esperar que ...** it is to be hoped o I etc hope that ...

6 (locuciones con sub): **o sea** that is to say; **sea él sea su hermana** either him or his sister

7: **a no ~ por él ...** but for him ...

8: **a no ~ que: a no ~ que tenga uno ya** unless he's got one already

♦ nm being; **~ humano** human being

serenarse [sere'narse] vr to calm down

sereno, a [se'reno, a] adj (persona) calm, unruffled; (el tiempo) fine, settled; (ambiente) calm, peaceful ♦ nm night watchman

serial [se'rjal] nm serial

serie ['serje] nf series; (cadena) sequence, succession; **fuera de ~** out of order; (fig) special, out of the ordinary; **fabricación en ~** mass production

seriedad [serje'ðað] nf seriousness; (formalidad) reliability; (de crisis) gravity, seriousness; **serio, a** adj serious; reliable, dependable; grave, serious; **en serio** adv seriously

sermón [ser'mon] nm (REL) sermon

serpentear [serpente'ar] vi to wriggle; (camino, río) to wind, snake

serpentina [serpen'tina] nf streamer

serpiente [ser'pjente] nf snake; **~ boa** boa constrictor; **~ de cascabel** rattlesnake

serranía [serra'nia] nf mountainous area

serrar [se'rrar] vt = **aserrar**

serrín [se'rrin] nm = **aserrín**

serrucho [se'rrutʃo] nm saw

servicio [ser'βiθjo] nm service; **~s** nmpl toilet(s); **~ incluido** service charge included; **~ militar** military service

servidumbre [serβi'ðumbre] nf (sujeción) servitude; (criados) servants pl, staff

servil [ser'βil] adj servile

servilleta [serβi'ʎeta] nf serviette, napkin

servir [ser'βir] vt to serve ♦ vi to serve; (tener utilidad) to be of use, be useful; **~se** vr to serve o help o.s.; **~se de algo** to make use of sth, use sth; **sírvase pasar** please come in

sesenta [se'senta] num sixty

sesgo ['sesɣo] nm slant; (fig) slant, twist

sesión [se'sjon] nf (POL) session, sitting; (CINE) showing

seso ['seso] nm brain; **sesudo, a** adj sensible, wise

seta ['seta] nf mushroom; **~ venenosa** toadstool

setecientos, as [sete'θjentos, as] adj, num seven hundred

setenta [se'tenta] num seventy

seudónimo [seu'ðonimo] nm pseudonym

severidad [seβeri'ðað] nf severity; **severo, a** adj severe

Sevilla [se'βiʎa] n Seville; **sevillano, a** adj of o from Seville ♦ nm/f native o inhabitant of Seville

sexo ['sekso] nm sex

sexto, a ['seksto, a] adj, nm sixth

sexual [sek'swal] adj sexual; **vida ~** sex life

si [si] conj if; **me pregunto ~ ...** I wonder if o whether ....

sí [si] adv yes ♦ nm consent ♦ pron (uso im-

personal) oneself; *(sg: m)* himself; *(: f)* herself; *(: de cosa)* itself; *(de usted)* yourself; *(pl)* themselves; *(de ustedes)* yourselves; *(recíproco)* each other; **él no quiere pero yo ~** he doesn't want to but I do; **ella ~ vendrá** she will certainly come, she is sure to come; **claro que ~** of course; **creo que ~** I think so

siamés, esa [sja'mes, esa] *adj, nm/f* Siamese

SIDA ['siða] *nm abr* (= *Síndrome de Inmunodeficiencia Adquirida*) AIDS

siderúrgico, a [siðe'rurxico, a] *adj* iron and steel *cpd*

sidra ['siðra] *nf* cider

siembra ['sjembra] *nf* sowing

siempre ['sjempre] *adv* always; *(todo el tiempo)* all the time; **~ que** *(cada vez)* whenever; *(dado que)* provided that; **como ~** as usual; **para ~** for ever

sien [sjen] *nf* temple

siento *etc vb ver* **sentar; sentir**

sierra ['sjerra] *nf (TEC)* saw; *(cadena de montañas)* mountain range

siervo, a [sjerßo, a] *nm/f* slave

siesta ['sjesta] *nf* siesta, nap; **echar la ~** to have an afternoon nap *o* a siesta

siete ['sjete] *num* seven

sífilis ['sifilis] *nf* syphilis

sifón [si'fon] *nm* syphon; **whisky con ~** whisky and soda

sigilo [si'xilo] *nm* secrecy, discretion; *(al moverse)* stealth

sigla ['siɣla] *nf* abbreviation; acronym

siglo ['siɣlo] *nm* century; *(fig)* age

significación [siɣnifika'θjon] *nf* significance

significado [siɣnifi'kaðo] *nm* significance; *(de palabra etc)* meaning

significar [siɣnifi'kar] *vt* to mean, signify; *(notificar)* to make known, express; **significativo, a** *adj* significant

signo ['siɣno] *nm* sign; **~ de admiración** *o* **exclamación** exclamation mark; **~ de interrogación** question mark

sigo *etc vb ver* **seguir**

siguiente [si'ɣjente] *adj* next, following

siguió *etc vb ver* **seguir**

sílaba ['silaßa] *nf* syllable

silbar [sil'ßar] *vt, vi* to whistle; **silbato** *nm* whistle; **silbido** *nm* whistle, whistling

silenciador [silenθja'ðor] *nm* silencer

silenciar [silen'θjar] *vt (persona)* to silence; *(escándalo)* to hush up; **silencio** *nm* silence, quiet; **silencioso, a** *adj* silent, quiet

silicio [si'liθjo] *nm* silicon

silueta [si'lweta] *nf* silhouette; *(de edificio)* outline; *(figura)* figure

silvestre [sil'ßestre] *adj (BOT)* wild; *(fig)* rustic, rural

silla ['siʎa] *nf (asiento)* chair; *(tb:* **~ de montar)** saddle; **~ de ruedas** wheelchair

sillón [si'ʎon] *nm* armchair, easy chair

simbólico, a [sim'boliko, a] *adj* symbolic(al)

simbolizar [simboli'θar] *vt* to symbolize

símbolo ['simbolo] *nm* symbol

simetría [sime'tria] *nf* symmetry

simiente [si'mjente] *nf* seed

similar [simi'lar] *adj* similar

simio ['simjo] *nm* ape

simpatía [simpa'tia] *nf* liking; *(afecto)* affection; *(amabilidad)* kindness; *(solidaridad)* mutual support, solidarity; **simpático, a** *adj* nice, pleasant; kind

simpatizante [simpati'θante] *nm/f* sympathizer

simpatizar [simpati'θar] *vi:* **~ con** to get on well with

simple ['simple] *adj* simple; *(elemental)* simple, easy; *(mero)* mere; *(puro)* pure, sheer ♦ *nm/f* simpleton; **~za** *nf* simpleness; *(necedad)* silly thing; **simplificar** *vt* to simplify

simposio [sim'posjo] *nm* symposium

simular [simu'lar] *vt* to simulate

simultáneo, a [simul'taneo, a] *adj* simultaneous

sin [sin] *prep* without; **la ropa está ~ lavar** the clothes are unwashed; **~ que** without; **~ embargo** however, still

sinagoga [sina'ɣoɣa] *nf* synagogue

sinceridad [sinθeri'ðað] *nf* sincerity; **sincero, a** *adj* sincere

sincronizar [sinkroni'θar] *vt* to synchronize

sindical [sindi'kal] *adj* union *cpd,* trade-union *cpd;* **~ista** *adj, nm/f* trade-unionist

sindicato [sindi'kato] *nm (de trabajadores)* trade(s) union; *(de negociantes)* syndicate

síndrome [si'nðrome] *nm (MED)* syndrome; **~ de abstinencia** *(MED)* withdrawal symptoms *cpd*

sinfín [sin'fin] *nm:* **un ~ de** a great many, no end of

sinfonía [sinfo'nia] *nf* symphony

singular [singu'lar] *adj* singular; *(fig)* outstanding, exceptional; *(pey)* peculiar, odd; **~idad** *nf* singularity, peculiarity; **~izarse** *vr* to distinguish o.s., stand out

siniestro, a [si'njestro, a] *adj* left; *(fig)* sinister ♦ *nm (accidente)* accident

sinnúmero [sin'numero] *nm =* **sinfín**

sino ['sino] *nm* fate, destiny ♦ *conj (pero)* but; *(salvo)* except, save

sinónimo, a [si'nonimo, a] *adj* synonymous ♦ *nm* synonym

síntesis ['sintesis] *nf* synthesis; **sintético, a** *adj* synthetic

sintetizar [sinteti'θar] *vt* to synthesize

sintió *vb ver* **sentir**

síntoma ['sintoma] *nm* symptom

sintonía [sinto'nia] *nf (RADIO, MUS: de programa)* tuning; **sintonizar** *vt (RADIO: emisora)* to tune (in)

sinvergüenza [simber'xwenθa] *nm/f* rogue, scoundrel; **¡es un ~!** he's got a nerve!

sionismo [sjo'nismo] *nm* Zionism

siquiera [si'kjera] *conj* even if, even though ♦ *adv* at least; **ni** ~ not even

sirena [si'rena] *nf* siren

Siria ['sirja] *nf* Syria

sirviente, a [sir'βjente, a] *nm/f* servant

sirvo *etc vb ver* **servir**

sisear [sise'ar] *vt, vi* to hiss

sistema [sis'tema] *nm* system; (*método*) method; **sistemático, a** *adj* systematic

sitiar [si'tjar] *vt* to besiege, lay siege to

sitio ['sitjo] *nm* (*lugar*) place; (*espacio*) room, space; (*MIL*) siege

situación [sitwa'θjon] *nf* situation, position; (*estatus*) position, standing

situado, a [situ'aðo] *adj* situated, placed

situar [si'twar] *vt* to place, put; (*edificio*) to locate, situate

slip [slip] *nm* pants *pl*, briefs *pl*

smoking ['smokin, es'mokin] (*pl* ~s) *nm* dinner jacket (*BRIT*), tuxedo (*US*)

snob [es'nob] = **esnob**

SO *abr* (= *suroeste*) SW

sobaco [so'βako] *nm* armpit

sobar [so'βar] *vt* (*ropa*) to rumple; (*libro*) to dirty (with one's fingers); (*comida*) to play around with

soberanía [soβera'nia] *nf* sovereignty; **soberano, a** *adj* sovereign; (*fig*) supreme ♦ *nm/f* sovereign

soberbia [so'βerβja] *nf* pride; haughtiness, arrogance; magnificence

soberbio, a [so'βerβjo, a] *adj* (*orgulloso*) proud; (*altivo*) haughty, arrogant; (*fig*) magnificent, superb

sobornar [soβor'nar] *vt* to bribe; **soborno** *nm* bribe

sobra ['soβra] *nf* excess, surplus; ~s *nfpl* left-overs, scraps; **de** ~ surplus, extra; **tengo de** ~ I've more than enough; ~**do, a** *adj* (*más que suficiente*) more than enough; (*superfluo*) excessive ♦ *adv* too, exceedingly; **sobrante** *adj* remaining, extra ♦ *nm* surplus, remainder

sobrar [so'βrar] *vt* to exceed, surpass ♦ *vi* (*tener de más*) to be more than enough; (*quedar*) to remain, be left (over)

sobrasada [soβra'saða] *nf* pork sausage spread

sobre ['soβre] *prep* (*gen*) on; (*encima*) on (top of); (*por encima de, arriba de*) over, above; (*más que*) more than; (*además*) in addition to, besides; (*alrededor de*) about ♦ *nm* envelope; ~ **todo** above all

sobrecama [soβre'kama] *nf* bedspread

sobrecargar [soβrekar'γar] *vt* (*camión*) to overload; (*COM*) to surcharge

sobredosis [soβre'ðosis] *nf inv* overdose

sobreentender [soβre(e)nten'der] *vt* (*adivinar*) to deduce, infer; ~**se** *vr*: **se sobreentiende que ...** it is implied that ...

sobrehumano, a [soβreu'mano, a] *adj* superhuman

sobrellevar [soβreʎe'βar] *vt* (*fig*) to bear, endure

sobremesa [soβre'mesa] *nf*: **durante la** ~ after dinner; **ordenador de** ~ desktop computer

sobrenatural [soβrenatu'ral] *adj* supernatural

sobrenombre [soβre'nombre] *nm* nickname

sobrepasar [soβrepa'sar] *vt* to exceed, surpass

sobreponer [soβrepo'ner] *vt* (*poner encima*) to put on top; (*añadir*) to add; ~**se** *vr*: ~**se a** to overcome

sobresaliente [soβresa'ljente] *adj* projecting; (*fig*) outstanding, excellent

sobresalir [soβresa'lir] *vi* to project, jut out; (*fig*) to stand out, excel

sobresaltar [soβresal'tar] *vt* (*asustar*) to scare, frighten; (*sobrecoger*) to startle; **sobresalto** *nm* (*movimiento*) start; (*susto*) scare; (*turbación*) sudden shock

sobretodo [soβre'toðo] *nm* overcoat

sobrevenir [soβreβe'nir] *vi* (*ocurrir*) to happen (unexpectedly); (*resultar*) to follow, ensue

sobreviviente [soβreβi'βjente] *adj* surviving ♦ *nm/f* survivor

sobrevivir [soβreβi'βir] *vi* to survive

sobrevolar [soβreβo'lar] *vt* to fly over

sobriedad [soβrje'ðað] *nf* sobriety, soberness; (*moderación*) moderation, restraint

sobrino, a [so'βrino, a] *nm/f* nephew/niece

sobrio, a ['soβrjo, a] *adj* (*moderado*) moderate, restrained

socarrón, ona [soka'rron, ona] *adj* (*sarcástico*) sarcastic, ironic(al)

socavar [soka'βar] *vt* (*tb fig*) to undermine

socavón [soka'βon] *nm* (*hoyo*) hole

sociable [so'θjaβle] *adj* (*persona*) sociable, friendly; (*animal*) social

social [so'θjal] *adj* social; (*COM*) company *cpd*

socialdemócrata [soθjalde'mokrata] *nm/f* social democrat

socialista [soθja'lista] *adj, nm/f* socialist

socializar [soθjali'θar] *vt* to socialize

sociedad [soθje'ðað] *nf* society; (*COM*) company; ~ **anónima** limited company; ~ **de consumo** consumer society

socio, a ['soθjo, a] *nm/f* (*miembro*) member; (*COM*) partner

sociología [soθjolo'xia] *nf* sociology; **sociólogo, a** *nm/f* sociologist

socorrer [soko'rrer] *vt* to help; **socorrista** *nm/f* first aider; (*en piscina, playa*) lifeguard; **socorro** *nm* (*ayuda*) help, aid; (*MIL*) relief; **¡socorro!** help!

soda ['soða] *nf* (*sosa*) soda; (*bebida*) soda (water)

sofá [so'fa] (*pl* ~s) *nm* sofa, settee; ~-

cama *nm* studio couch; sofa bed

sofisticación [sofistika'θjon] *nf* sophistication

sofocar [sofo'kar] *vt* to suffocate; *(apagar)* to smother, put out; **~se** *vr* to suffocate; *(fig)* to blush, feel embarrassed; **sofoco** *nm* suffocation; embarrassment

sofreír [sofre'ir] *vt* (*CULIN*) to fry lightly

soga ['soɣa] *nf* rope

sois *vb ver* **ser**

soja ['soxa] *nf* soya

sojuzgar [soxuθ'ɣar] *vt* to subdue, rule despotically

sol [sol] *nm* sun; *(luz)* sunshine, sunlight; **hace ~** it is sunny

solamente [sola'mente] *adv* only, just

solapa [so'lapa] *nf* (*de chaqueta*) lapel; (*de libro*) jacket

solapado, a [sola'paðo, a] *adj* (*intenciones*) underhand; (*gestos, movimiento*) sly

solar [so'lar] *adj* solar, sun *cpd*

solaz [so'laθ] *nm* recreation, relaxation; **~ar** *vt* (*divertir*) to amuse

soldada [sol'daða] *nf* pay

soldado [sol'daðo] *nm* soldier; **~ raso** private

soldador [solda'ðor] *nm* soldering iron; (*persona*) welder

soldar [sol'dar] *vt* to solder, weld; (*unir*) to join, unite

soleado, a [sole'aðo, a] *adj* sunny

soledad [sole'ðað] *nf* solitude; (*estado infeliz*) loneliness

solemne [so'lemne] *adj* solemn; **solemnidad** *nf* solemnity

soler [so'ler] *vi* to be in the habit of, be accustomed to; **suele salir a las ocho** she usually goes out at 8 o'clock

solfeo [sol'feo] *nm* solfa

solicitar [soliθi'tar] *vt* (*permiso*) to ask for, seek; (*puesto*) to apply for; (*votos*) to canvass for; (*atención*) to attract; (*persona*) to pursue, chase after

solícito, a [so'liθito, a] *adj* (*diligente*) diligent; (*cuidadoso*) careful; **solicitud** *nf* (*calidad*) great care; (*petición*) request; (*a un puesto*) application

solidaridad [soliðari'ðað] *nf* solidarity; **solidario, a** *adj* (*participación*) joint, common; (*compromiso*) mutually binding

solidez [soli'ðeθ] *nf* solidity; **sólido, a** *adj* solid

soliloquio [soli'lokjo] *nm* soliloquy

solista [so'lista] *nm/f* soloist

solitario, a [soli'tarjo, a] *adj* (*persona*) lonely, solitary; (*lugar*) lonely, desolate ♦ *nm/f* (*reclusa*) recluse; (*en la sociedad*) loner ♦ *nm* solitaire

solo, a [a ['solo, a] *adj* (*único*) single, sole; (*sin compañía*) alone; (*solitario*) lonely; **hay una sola dificultad** there is just one difficulty; **a solas** alone, by oneself

sólo ['solo] *adv* only, just

solomillo [solo'miʎo] *nm* sirloin

soltar [sol'tar] *vt* (*dejar ir*) to let go of; (*desprender*) to unfasten, loosen; (*librar*) to release, set free; (*risa etc*) to let out

soltero, a [sol'tero, a] *adj* single, unmarried ♦ *nm/f* bachelor/single woman; **solterón, ona** *nm/f* old bachelor/spinster

soltura [sol'tura] *nf* looseness, slackness; (*de los miembros*) agility, ease of movement; (*en el hablar*) fluency, ease

soluble [so'luβle] *adj* (*QUÍMICA*) soluble; (*problema*) solvable; **~ en agua** soluble in water

solución [solu'θjon] *nf* solution; **solucionar** *vt* (*problema*) to solve; (*asunto*) to settle, resolve

solventar [solβen'tar] *vt* (*pagar*) to settle, pay; (*resolver*) to resolve; **solvente** *adj* (*ECON: empresa, persona*) solvent

sollozar [soʎo'θar] *vi* to sob; **sollozo** *nm* sob

sombra ['sombra] *nf* shadow; (*como protección*) shade; **~s** *nfpl* (*oscuridad*) darkness *sg*, shadows; **tener buena/mala ~** to be lucky/unlucky

sombrero [som'brero] *nm* hat

sombrilla [som'briʎa] *nf* parasol, sunshade

sombrío, a [som'brio, a] *adj* (*oscuro*) dark; (*fig*) sombre, sad; (*persona*) gloomy

somero, a [so'mero, a] *adj* superficial

someter [some'ter] *vt* (*país*) to conquer; (*persona*) to subject to one's will; (*informe*) to present, submit; **~se** *vr* to give in, yield, submit; **~ a** to subject to

somier [so'mjer] (*pl* **somiers**) *n* spring mattress

somnífero [som'nifero] *nm* sleeping pill

somnolencia [somno'lenθja] *nf* sleepiness, drowsiness

somos *vb ver* **ser**

son [son] *vb ver* **ser** ♦ *nm* sound; **en ~ de broma** as a joke

sonajero [sona'xero] *nm* (baby's) rattle

sonambulismo [sonambu'lismo] *nm* sleepwalking; **sonámbulo, a** *nm/f* sleepwalker

sonar [so'nar] *vt* to ring ♦ *vi* to sound; (*hacer ruido*) to make a noise; (*pronunciarse*) to be sounded, be pronounced; (*ser conocido*) to sound familiar; (*campana*) to ring; (*reloj*) to strike, chime; **~se** *vr*: **~se (las narices)** to blow one's nose; **me suena ese nombre** that name rings a bell

sonda ['sonda] *nf* (*NAUT*) sounding; (*TEC*) bore, drill; (*MED*) probe

sondear [sonde'ar] *vt* to sound; to bore (into), drill; to probe, sound; (*fig*) to sound out; **sondeo** *nm* sounding; boring, drilling; (*fig*) poll, enquiry

sónico, a [so'niko, a] *adj* sonic, sound *cpd*

sonido [so'niðo] *nm* sound

sonoro, a [so'noro, a] *adj* sonorous; (*reso-*

nante) loud, resonant

sonreír [sonre'ir] *vi* to smile; ~**se** *vr* to smile; **sonriente** *adj* smiling; **sonrisa** *nf* smile

sonrojarse [sonro'xarse] *vr* to blush, go red; **sonrojo** *nm* blush

sonsacar [son'sakar] *vt* to coax

soñador, a [soɲa'ðor, a] *nm/f* dreamer

soñar [so'ɲar] *vt, vi* to dream; ~ **con** to dream about *o* of

soñoliento, a [soɲo'ljento, a] *adj* sleepy, drowsy

sopa ['sopa] *nf* soup

sopesar [sope'sar] *vt* to consider, weigh up

soplar [so'plar] *vt* (*polvo*) to blow away, blow off; (*inflar*) to blow up; (*vela*) to blow out ♦ *vi* to blow; **soplo** *nm* blow, puff; (*de viento*) puff, gust

soplón, ona [so'plon, ona] (*fam*), *nm/f* (*niño*) telltale; (*de policía*) grass (*fam*)

sopor [so'por] *nm* drowsiness

soporífero [sopo'rifero] *nm* sleeping pill

soportable [sopor'taβle] *adj* bearable

soportar [sopor'tar] *vt* to bear, carry; (*fig*) to bear, put up with; **soporte** *nm* support; (*fig*) pillar, support

soprano [so'prano] *nf* soprano

sorber [sor'βer] *vt* (*chupar*) to sip; (*inhalar*) to inhale; (*tragar*) to swallow (up); (*absorber*) to soak up, absorb

sorbete [sor'βete] *nm* iced fruit drink

sorbo ['sorβo] *nm* (*trago: grande*) gulp, swallow; (: *pequeño*) sip

sordera [sor'ðera] *nf* deafness

sórdido, a ['sorðiðo, a] *adj* dirty, squalid

sordo, a ['sorðo, a] *adj* (*persona*) deaf ♦ *nm/f* deaf person; ~**mudo, a** *adj* deaf and dumb

sorna ['sorna] *nf* sarcastic tone

soroche [so'rotʃe] (*AM*) *nm* mountain sickness

sorprendente [sorpren'dente] *adj* surprising

sorprender [sorpren'der] *vt* to surprise; **sorpresa** *nf* surprise

sortear [sorte'ar] *vt* to draw lots for; (*rifar*) to raffle; (*dificultad*) to avoid; **sorteo** *nm* (*en lotería*) draw; (*rifa*) raffle

sortija [sor'tixa] *nf* ring; (*rizo*) ringlet, curl

sosegado, a [sose'γaðo, a] *adj* quiet, calm

sosegar [sose'γar] *vt* to quieten, calm; (*el ánimo*) to reassure ♦ *vi* to rest; **sosiego** *nm* quiet(ness), calm(ness)

soslayo [sos'lajo]: **de** ~ *adv* obliquely, sideways

soso, a ['soso, a] *adj* (*CULIN*) tasteless; (*fig*) dull, uninteresting

sospecha [sos'petʃa] *nf* suspicion; **sospechar** *vt* to suspect; **sospechoso, a** *adj* suspicious; (*testimonio, opinión*) suspect ♦ *nm/f* suspect

sostén [sos'ten] *nm* (*apoyo*) support; (*suje-*

tador) bra; (*alimentación*) sustenance, food

sostener [soste'ner] *vt* to support; (*mantener*) to keep up, maintain; (*alimentar*) to sustain, keep going; ~**se** *vr* to support o.s.; (*seguir*) to continue, remain; **sostenido, a** *adj* continuous, sustained; (*prolongado*) prolonged

sotana [so'tana] *nf* (*REL*) cassock

sótano ['sotano] *nm* basement

soviético, a [so'βjetiko, a] *adj* Soviet; **los** ~**s** the Soviets

soy *vb ver* **ser**

Sr. *abr* (= *Señor*) Mr

Sra. *abr* (= *Señora*) Mrs

S.R.C. *abr* (= *se ruega contestación*) R.S.V.P.

Sres. *abr* (= *Señores*) Messrs

Srta. *abr* (= *Señorita*) Miss

Sta. *abr* (= *Santa*) St

status ['status, e'status] *nm inv* status

Sto. *abr* (= *Santo*) St

su [su] *pron* (*de él*) his; (*de ella*) her; (*de una cosa*) its; (*de ellos, ellas*) their; (*de usted, ustedes*) your

suave ['swaβe] *adj* gentle; (*superficie*) smooth; (*trabajo*) easy; (*música, voz*) soft, sweet; **suavidad** *nf* gentleness; smoothness; softness, sweetness; **suavizar** *vt* to soften; (*quitar la aspereza*) to smooth (out)

subalimentado, a [suβalimen'taðo, a] *adj* undernourished

subasta [su'βasta] *nf* auction; **subastar** *vt* to auction (off)

subcampeón, ona [suβkampe'on, ona] *nm/f* runner-up

subconsciente [suβkon'sθjente] *adj, nm* subconscious

subdesarrollado, a [suβðesarro'ʎaðo, a] *adj* underdeveloped

subdesarrollo [suβðesa'rroʎo] *nm* under-development

subdirector, a [suβðirek'tor, a] *nm/f* assistant director

súbdito, a ['suβðito, a] *nm/f* subject

subestimar [suβesti'mar] *vt* to underestimate, underrate

subida [su'βiða] *nf* (*de montaña etc*) ascent, climb; (*de precio*) rise, increase; (*pendiente*) slope, hill

subir [su'βir] *vt* (*objeto*) to raise, lift up; (*cuesta, calle*) to go up; (*colina, montaña*) to climb; (*precio*) to raise, put up ♦ *vi* to go up, come up; (*a un coche*) to get in; (*a un autobús, tren o avión*) to get on, board; (*precio*) to rise, go up; (*río, marea*) to rise; ~**se** *vr* to get up, climb

súbito, a ['suβito, a] *adj* (*repentino*) sudden; (*imprevisto*) unexpected

subjetivo, a [suβxe'tiβo, a] *adj* subjective

sublevación [suβleβa'θjon] *nf* revolt, rising

sublevar [suβle'βar] *vt* to rouse to revolt; ~**se** *vr* to revolt, rise

sublime [su'βlime] *adj* sublime
submarino, a [suβma'rino, a] *adj* underwater ∮ *nm* submarine
subnormal [suβnor'mal] *adj* subnormal ∮ *nm/f* subnormal person
subordinado, a [suβorði'naðo, a] *adj, nm/f* subordinate
subrayar [suβra'jar] *vt* to underline
subsanar [suβsa'nar] *vt* (*reparar*) to make good; (*perdonar*) to excuse; (*sobreponerse a*) to overcome
subscribir [suβskri'βir] *vt* = **suscribir**
subsidio [suβ'siðjo] *nm* (*ayuda*) aid, financial help; (*subvención*) subsidy, grant; (*de enfermedad, paro etc*) benefit, allowance
subsistencia [suβsis'tenθja] *nf* subsistence
subsistir [suβsis'tir] *vi* to subsist; (*vivir*) to live; (*sobrevivir*) to survive, endure
subterráneo, a [suβte'rraneo, a] *adj* underground, subterranean ∮ *nm* underpass, underground passage
subtítulo [suβ'titulo] *nm* (*CINE*) subtitle
suburbano, a [suβur'βano, a] *adj* suburban
suburbio [su'βurβjo] *nm* (*barrio*) slum quarter; (*afueras*) suburbs *pl*
subvención [suβßen'θjon] *nf* (*ECON*) subsidy, grant; **subvencionar** *vt* to subsidize
subversión [suβßer'sjon] *nf* subversion; **subversivo, a** *adj* subversive
subyugar [suβju'yar] *vt* (*país*) to subjugate, subdue; (*enemigo*) to overpower; (*voluntad*) to dominate
succión [suk'θjon] *nf* suction
sucedáneo, a [suθe'ðaneo, a] *adj* substitute ∮ *nm* substitute (food)
suceder [suθe'ðer] *vt, vi* to happen; (*seguir*) to succeed, follow; **lo que sucede es que ... the fact is that ...; **sucesión** *nf* succession; (*serie*) sequence, series
sucesivamente [suθesiβa'mente] *adv*: **y así ~** and so on
sucesivo, a [suθe'siβo, a] *adj* successive, following; **en lo ~** in future, from now on
suceso [su'θeso] *nm* (*hecho*) event, happening; (*incidente*) incident
suciedad [suθje'ðað] *nf* (*estado*) dirtiness; (*mugre*) dirt, filth
sucinto, a [su'θinto, a] *adj* (*conciso*) succinct, concise
sucio, a ['suθjo, a] *adj* dirty
suculento, a [suku'lento, a] *adj* succulent
sucumbir [sukum'bir] *vi* to succumb
sucursal [sukur'sal] *nf* branch (office)
Sudáfrica [suð'afrika] *nf* South Africa
Sudamérica [suða'merika] *nf* South America; **sudamericano, a** *adj, nm/f* South American
sudar [su'ðar] *vt, vi* to sweat
sudeste [su'ðeste] *nm* south-east
sudoeste [suðo'este] *nm* south-west
sudor [su'ðor] *nm* sweat; **~oso, a** *adj* sweaty, sweating

Suecia ['sweθja] *nf* Sweden; **sueco, a** *adj* Swedish ∮ *nm/f* Swede
suegro, a ['sweɣro, a] *nm/f* father-/mother-in-law
suela ['swela] *nf* sole
sueldo ['sweldo] *nm* pay, wage(s) (*pl*)
suele *etc vb ver* **soler**
suelo ['swelo] *nm* (*tierra*) ground; (*de casa*) floor
suelto, a ['swelto, a] *adj* loose; (*libre*) free; (*separado*) detached; (*ágil*) quick, agile; (*corriente*) fluent, flowing ∮ *nm* (*loose*) change, small change
sueño *etc* ['sweɲo] *vb ver* **soñar** ∮ *nm* sleep; (*somnolencia*) sleepiness, drowsiness; (*lo soñado, fig*) dream; **tener ~** to be sleepy
suero ['swero] *nm* (*MED*) serum; (*de leche*) whey
suerte ['swerte] *nf* (*fortuna*) luck; (*azar*) chance; (*destino*) fate, destiny; (*condición*) lot; (*género*) sort, kind; **tener ~** to be lucky; **de otra ~** otherwise, if not; **de ~ que** so that, in such a way that
suéter ['sweter] *nm* sweater
suficiente [sufi'θjente] *adj* enough, sufficient ∮ *nm* (*ESCOL*) pass
sufragio [su'fraxjo] *nm* (*voto*) vote; (*derecho de voto*) suffrage
sufrido, a [su'friðo, a] *adj* (*persona*) tough; (*paciente*) long-suffering, patient
sufrimiento [sufri'mjento] *nm* (*dolor*) suffering
sufrir [su'frir] *vt* (*padecer*) to suffer; (*soportar*) to bear, put up with; (*apoyar*) to hold up, support ∮ *vi* to suffer
sugerencia [suxe'renθja] *nf* suggestion
sugerir [suxe'rir] *vt* to suggest; (*sutilmente*) to hint
sugestión [suxes'tjon] *nf* suggestion; (*sutil*) hint; **sugestionar** *vt* to influence
sugestivo, a [suxes'tiβo, a] *adj* stimulating; (*fascinante*) fascinating
suicida [sui'θiða] *adj* suicidal ∮ *nm/f* suicidal person; (*muerto*) suicide, person who has committed suicide; **suicidarse** *vr* to commit suicide, kill o.s.; **suicidio** *nm* suicide
Suiza ['swiθa] *nf* Switzerland; **suizo, a** *adj, nm/f* Swiss
sujeción [suxe'θjon] *nf* subjection
sujetador [suxeta'ðor] *nm* fastener, clip; (*sostén*) bra
sujetar [suxe'tar] *vt* (*fijar*) to fasten; (*detener*) to hold down; (*fig*) to subject, subjugate; **~se** *vr* to subject o.s.; **sujeto, a** *adj* fastened, secure ∮ *nm* subject; (*individuo*) individual; **sujeto a** subject to
suma ['suma] *nf* (*cantidad*) total, sum; (*de dinero*) sum; (*acto*) adding (up), addition; **en ~** in short
sumamente [suma'mente] *adv* extremely,

exceedingly

sumar [su'mar] *vt* to add (up); (*reunir*) to collect, gather ♦ *vi* to add up

sumario, a [su'marjo, a] *adj* brief, concise ♦ *nm* summary

sumergir [sumer'xir] *vt* to submerge; (*hundir*) to sink; (*bañar*) to immerse, dip

suministrar [suminis'trar] *vt* to supply, provide; **suministro** *nm* supply; (*acto*) supplying, providing

sumir [su'mir] *vt* to sink, submerge; (*fig*) to plunge

sumisión [sumi'sjon] *nf* (*acto*) submission; (*calidad*) submissiveness, docility; **sumiso, a** *adj* submissive, docile

sumo, a ['sumo, a] *adj* great, extreme; (*mayor*) highest, supreme

suntuoso, a [sun'twoso, a] *adj* sumptuous, magnificent

supe *etc vb ver* **saber**

supeditar [supeði'tar] *vt*: ~ **algo a algo** to subordinate sth to sth

súper ['super] *nf* (*gasolina*) three-star (petrol)

super... [super] *prefijo* super..., over...; **~bueno** *adj* great, fantastic

superar [supe'rar] *vt* (*sobreponerse a*) to overcome; (*rebasar*) to surpass, do better than; (*pasar*) to go beyond; **~se** *vr* to excel o.s.

superávit [supe'raßit] *nm inv* surplus

superficial [superfi'θjal] *adj* superficial; (*medida*) surface *cpd*, of the surface

superficie [super'fiθje] *nf* surface; (*área*) area

superfluo, a [su'perflwo, a] *adj* superfluous

superior [supe'rjor] *adj* (*piso, clase*) upper; (*temperatura, número, nivel*) higher; (*mejor: calidad, producto*) superior, better ♦ *nm/f* superior; **~idad** *nf* superiority

supermercado [supermer'kaðo] *nm* supermarket

superponer [superpo'ner] *vt* to superimpose

supersónico, a [super'soniko, a] *adj* supersonic

superstición [supersti'θjon] *nf* superstition; **supersticioso, a** *adj* superstitious

supervisar [superßi'sar] *vt* to supervise

supervivencia [superßi'ßenθja] *nf* survival

superviviente [superßi'ßjente] *adj* surviving

supiera *etc vb ver* **saber**

suplantar [suplan'tar] *vt* (*persona*) to supplant; (*documento etc*) to falsify

suplemento [suple'mento] *nm* supplement

suplente [su'plente] *adj, nm/f* substitute

supletorio, a [suple'torjo, a] *adj* supplementary ♦ *nm* supplement; **mesa supletoria** spare table

súplica ['suplika] *nf* request; (*JUR*) petition

suplicar [supli'kar] *vt* (*cosa*) to beg (for), plead for; (*persona*) to beg, plead with

suplicio [su'pliθjo] *nm* torture

suplir [su'plir] *vt* (*compensar*) to make good, make up for; (*reemplazar*) to replace, substitute ♦ *vi*: ~ **a** to take the place of, substitute for

supo *etc vb ver* **saber**

suponer [supo'ner] *vt* to suppose ♦ *vi* to have authority; **suposición** *nf* supposition

supremacía [suprema'θia] *nf* supremacy

supremo, a [su'premo, a] *adj* supreme

supresión [supre'sjon] *nf* suppression; (*de derecho*) abolition; (*de dificultad*) removal; (*de palabra etc*) deletion; (*de restricción*) cancellation, lifting

suprimir [supri'mir] *vt* to suppress; (*derecho, costumbre*) to abolish; (*dificultad*) to remove; (*palabra etc*) to delete; (*restricción*) to cancel, lift

supuesto, a [su'pwesto, a] *pp de* **suponer** ♦ *adj* (*hipotético*) supposed; (*falso*) false ♦ *nm* assumption, hypothesis; ~ **que** since; **por** ~ of course

sur [sur] *nm* south

surcar [sur'kar] *vt* to plough; (*superficie*) to cut, score; **surco** *nm* (*en metal, disco*) groove; (*AGR*) furrow

surgir [sur'xir] *vi* to arise, emerge; (*dificultad*) to come up, crop up

surtido, a [sur'tiðo, a] *adj* mixed, assorted ♦ *nm* (*selección*) selection, assortment; (*abastecimiento*) supply, stock

surtir [sur'tir] *vt* to supply, provide ♦ *vi* to spout, spurt

susceptible [susθep'tißle] *adj* susceptible; (*sensible*) sensitive; ~ **de** capable of

suscitar [susθi'tar] *vt* to cause, provoke; (*interés, sospechas*) to arouse

suscribir [suskri'ßir] *vt* (*firmar*) to sign; (*respaldar*) to subscribe to, endorse; **~se** *vr* to subscribe; **suscripción** *nf* subscription

susodicho, a [suso'ðitʃo, a] *adj* abovementioned

suspender [suspen'der] *vt* (*objeto*) to hang (up), suspend; (*trabajo*) to stop, suspend; (*ESCOL*) to fail; **suspensión** *nf* suspension; (*fig*) stoppage, suspension

suspenso, a [sus'penso, a] *adj* hanging, suspended; (*ESCOL*) failed ♦ *nm*: **quedar** o **estar en** ~ to be pending

suspicacia [suspi'kaθja] *nf* suspicion, mistrust; **suspicaz** *adj* suspicious, distrustful

suspirar [suspi'rar] *vi* to sigh; **suspiro** *nm* sigh

sustancia [sus'tanθja] *nf* substance

sustentar [susten'tar] *vt* (*alimentar*) to sustain, nourish; (*objeto*) to hold up, support; (*idea, teoría*) to maintain, uphold; (*fig*) to sustain, keep going; **sustento** *nm* support; (*alimento*) sustenance, food

sustituir [sustitu'ir] *vt* to substitute, replace; **sustituto, a** *nm/f* substitute, replacement

susto ['susto] *nm* fright, scare
sustraer [sustra'er] *vt* to remove, take away; (*MAT*) to subtract
susurrar [susu'rrar] *vi* to whisper; **susurro** *nm* whisper
sutil [su'til] *adj* (*aroma, diferencia*) subtle; (*tenue*) thin; (*inteligencia, persona*) sharp; **~eza** *nf* subtlety; thinness
suyo, a ['sujo, a] (*con artículo o después del verbo* **ser**) *adj* (*de él*) his; (*de ella*) hers; (*de ellos, ellas*) theirs; (*de Ud, Uds*) yours; **un amigo ~** a friend of his (*o* hers *o* theirs *o* yours)

T t

tabacalera [taβaka'lera] *nf*: **T~** Spanish state tobacco monopoly
tabaco [ta'βako] *nm* tobacco; (*fam*) cigarettes *pl*
taberna [ta'βerna] *nf* bar, pub (*BRIT*); **tabernero, a** *nm/f* (*encargado*) publican; (*camarero*) barman/maid
tabique [ta'βike] *nm* partition (wall)
tabla ['taβla] *nf* (*de madera*) plank; (*estante*) shelf; (*de vestido*) pleat; (*ARTE*) panel; **~s** *nfpl*: **estar** *o* **quedar en ~s** to draw; **~do** *nm* (*plataforma*) platform; (*TEATRO*) stage
tablao [ta'βlao] *nm* (*tb:* **~ flamenco**) flamenco show
tablero [ta'βlero] *nm* (*de madera*) plank, board; (*de ajedrez, damas*) board; (*AUTO*) dashboard; **~ de anuncios** notice (*BRIT*) *o* bulletin (*US*) board
tableta [ta'βleta] *nf* (*MED*) tablet; (*de chocolate*) bar
tablón [ta'βlon] *nm* (*de suelo*) plank; (*de techo*) beam; **~ de anuncios** notice board (*BRIT*), bulletin board (*US*)
tabú [ta'βu] *nm* taboo
tabular [taβu'lar] *vt* to tabulate
taburete [taβu'rete] *nm* stool
tacaño, a [ta'kaɲo, a] *adj* (*avaro*) mean
tácito, a ['taθito, a] *adj* tacit
taciturno, a [taθi'turno, a] *adj* (*callado*) silent; (*malhumorado*) sullen
taco ['tako] *nm* (*BILLAR*) cue; (*libro de billetes*) book; (*AM: de zapato*) heel; (*tarugo*) peg; (*palabrota*) swear word
tacón [ta'kon] *nm* heel; **de ~ alto** high-heeled; **taconeo** *nm* (*heel*) stamping
táctica ['taktika] *nf* tactics *pl*
táctico, a ['taktiko, a] *adj* tactical

tacto ['takto] *nm* touch; (*fig*) tact
tacha ['tatʃa] *nf* flaw; (*TEC*) stud; **tachar** *vt* (*borrar*) to cross out; **tachar de** to accuse of
tafetán [tafe'tan] *nm* taffeta
tafilete [tafi'lete] *nm* morocco leather
tahona [ta'ona] *nf* (*panadería*) bakery
taimado, a [tai'maðo, a] *adj* (*astuto*) sly
taita ['taita] (*fam*) *nm* dad, daddy
tajada [ta'xaða] *nf* slice
tajante [ta'xante] *adj* sharp
tajo ['taxo] *nm* (*corte*) cut; (*GEO*) cleft
tal [tal] *adj* such; **~ vez** perhaps ♦ *pron* (*persona*) someone, such a one; (*cosa*) something, such a thing; **~ como** such as; **~ para cual** tit for tat; (*dos iguales*) two·of a kind ♦ *adv*: **~ como** (*igual*) just as; **~ cual** (*como es*) just as it is; **¿qué ~?** how are things?; **¿qué ~ te gusta?** how do you like it? ♦ *conj*: **con ~ de que** provided that
taladrar [tala'ðrar] *vt* to drill; **taladro** *nm* drill; (*hoyo*) drill hole
talante [ta'lante] *nm* (*humor*) mood; (*voluntad*) will, willingness
talar [ta'lar] *vt* to fell, cut down; (*devastar*) to devastate
talco ['talko] *nm* (*polvos*) talcum powder
talego [ta'leɣo] *nm* sack
talento [ta'lento] *nm* talent; (*capacidad*) ability
TALGO ['talɣo] (*ESP*) *nm abr* (= *tren articulado ligero Goicoechea-Oriol*) ≈ HST (*BRIT*)
talismán [talis'man] *nm* talisman
talón [ta'lon] *nm* (*ANAT*) heel; (*COM*) counterfoil; (*cheque*) cheque (*BRIT*), check (*US*)
talonario [talo'narjo] *nm* (*de cheques*) chequebook (*BRIT*), checkbook (*US*); (*de billetes*) book of tickets; (*de recibos*) receipt book
talla ['taʎa] *nf* (*estatura, fig, MED*) height, stature; (*palo*) measuring rod; (*ARTE*) carving; (*medida*) size
tallado, a [ta'ʎaðo, a] *adj* carved ♦ *nm* carving
tallar [ta'ʎar] *vt* (*madera*) to carve; (*metal etc*) to engrave; (*medir*) to measure
tallarines [taʎa'rines] *nmpl* noodles
talle ['taʎe] *nm* (*ANAT*) waist; (*fig*) appearance
taller [ta'ʎer] *nm* (*TEC*) workshop; (*de artista*) studio
tallo ['taʎo] *nm* (*de planta*) stem; (*de hierba*) blade; (*brote*) shoot
tamaño, a [ta'maɲo, a] *adj* (*tan grande*) such a big; (*tan pequeño*) such a small ♦ *nm* size; **de ~ natural** full-size
tamarindo [tama'rindo] *nm* tamarind
tambalearse [tambale'arse] *vr* (*persona*) to stagger; (*vehículo*) to sway
también [tam'bjen] *adv* (*igualmente*) also, too, as well; (*además*) besides
tambor [tam'bor] *nm* drum; (*ANAT*) ear-

drum; ~ **del freno** brake drum

tamiz [ta'miθ] *nm* sieve; ~**ar** *vt* to sieve

tampoco [tam'poko] *adv* nor, neither; **yo ~ lo compré** I didn't buy it either

tampón [tam'pon] *nm* tampon

tan [tan] *adv* so; ~ **es así que ...** so much so that ....

tanda ['tanda] *nf* (*gen*) series; (*turno*) shift

tangente [tan'xente] *nf* tangent

Tánger ['tanxer] *n* Tangier(s)

tangible [tan'xiβle] *adj* tangible

tanque ['tanke] *nm* (*cisterna, MIL*) tank; (*AUTO*) tanker

tantear [tante'ar] *vt* (*calcular*) to reckon (up); (*medir*) to take the measure of; (*probar*) to test, try out; (*tomar la medida: persona*) to take the measurements of; (*situación*) to weigh up; (*persona: opinión*) to sound out ♦ *vi* (*DEPORTE*) to score; **tanteo** *nm* (*cálculo*) (rough) calculation; (*prueba*) test, trial; (*DEPORTE*) scoring

tanto, a ['tanto, a] *adj* (*cantidad*) so much, as much; ~**s** so many, as many; **20 y ~s** 20-odd ♦ *adv* (*cantidad*) so much, as much; (*tiempo*) so long, as long ♦ *conj*: **en ~ que** while; **hasta ~ (que)** until such time as ♦ *nm* (*suma*) certain amount; (*proporción*) so much; (*punto*) point; (*gol*) goal; **un ~ perezoso** somewhat lazy ♦ *pron*: **cada uno paga ~** each one pays so much; ~ **tú como yo** both you and I; ~ **como eso** it's not as bad as that; ~ **más ... cuanto que** it's all the more ... because; ~ **mejor/peor** so much the better/the worse; ~ **si viene como si va** whether he comes or whether he goes; ~ **es así que** so much so that; **por o por lo ~** therefore; **me he vuelto ronco de o con ~ hablar** I have become hoarse with so much talking; **a ~ s de agosto** on such and such a day in August

tapa ['tapa] *nf* (*de caja, olla*) lid; (*de botella*) top; (*de libro*) cover; (*comida*) snack

tapadera [tapa'ðera] *nf* lid, cover

tapar [ta'par] *vt* (*cubrir*) to cover; (*envolver*) to wrap o cover up; (*la vista*) to obstruct; (*persona, falta*) to conceal; (*AM*) to fill; ~**se** *vr* to wrap o.s. up

taparrabo [tapa'rraβo] *nm* loincloth

tapete [ta'pete] *nm* table cover

tapia ['tapja] *nf* (*garden*) wall; **tapiar** *vt* to wall in

tapicería [tapiθe'ria] *nf* tapestry; (*para muebles*) upholstery; (*tienda*) upholsterer's (shop)

tapiz [ta'piθ] *nm* (*alfombra*) carpet; (*tela tejida*) tapestry; ~**ar** *vt* (*muebles*) to upholster

tapón [ta'pon] *nm* (*corcho*) stopper; (*TEC*) plug; ~ **de rosca** screw-top

taquigrafía [takiγra'fia] *nf* shorthand; **taquígrafo, a** *nm/f* shorthand writer, stenographer

taquilla [ta'kiʎa] *nf* (*donde se compra*) booking office; (*suma recogida*) takings *pl*; **taquillero, a** *adj*: **función taquillera** box office success ♦ *nm/f* ticket clerk

tara ['tara] *nf* (*defecto*) defect; (*COM*) tare

tarántula [ta'rantula] *nf* tarantula

tararear [tarare'ar] *vi* to hum

tardanza [tar'ðanθa] *nf* (*demora*) delay

tardar [tar'ðar] *vi* (*tomar tiempo*) to take a long time; (*llegar tarde*) to be late; (*demorar*) to delay; **¿tarda mucho el tren?** does the train take (very) long?; **a más ~** at the latest; **no tardes en venir** come soon

tarde ['tarðe] *adv* late ♦ *nf* (*de día*) afternoon; (*al anochecer*) evening; **de ~ en ~** from time to time; **¡buenas ~s!** good afternoon!; **a o por la ~** in the afternoon; in the evening

tardío, a [tar'ðio, a] *adj* (*retrasado*) late; (*lento*) slow (to arrive)

tarea [ta'rea] *nf* task; (*faena*) chore; (*ESCOL*) homework

tarifa [ta'rifa] *nf* (*lista de precios*) price list; (*precio*) tariff

tarima [ta'rima] *nf* (*plataforma*) platform

tarjeta [tar'xeta] *nf* card; ~ **postal/de crédito/de Navidad** postcard/credit card/Christmas card

tarro ['tarro] *nm* jar, pot

tarta ['tarta] *nf* (*pastel*) cake; (*torta*) tart

tartamudear [tartamuðe'ar] *vi* to stammer; **tartamudo, a** *adj* stammering ♦ *nm/f* stammerer

tártaro, a ['tartaro, a] *adj*: **salsa tártara** tartare sauce

tasa ['tasa] *nf* (*precio*) (fixed) price, rate; (*valoración*) valuation; (*medida, norma*) measure, standard; ~ **de cambio/interés** exchange/interest rate; ~**ción** *nf* valuation; ~**dor, a** *nm/f* valuer

tasar [ta'sar] *vt* (*arreglar el precio*) to fix a price for; (*valorar*) to value, assess

tasca ['taska] *nf* (*fam*) pub

tatarabuelo, a [tatara'βwelo, a] *nm/f* great-great-grandfather/mother

tatuaje [ta'twaxe] *nm* (*dibujo*) tattoo; (*acto*) tattooing

tatuar [ta'twar] *vt* to tattoo

taurino, a [tau'rino, a] *adj* bullfighting *cpd*

Tauro ['tauro] *nm* Taurus

tauromaquia [tauro'makja] *nf* tauromachy, (art of) bullfighting

taxi ['taksi] *nm* taxi

taxista [tak'sista] *nm/f* taxi driver

taza ['taθa] *nf* cup; (*de retrete*) bowl; ~ **para café** coffee cup; **tazón** *nm* (*taza grande*) mug, large cup; (*de fuente*) basin

te [te] *pron* (*complemento de objeto*) you; (*complemento indirecto*) (to) you; (*reflexivo*) (to) yourself; **¿~ duele mucho el brazo?** does your arm hurt a lot?; ~ **equivocas** you're wrong; **¡cálma~!** calm down!

té [te] *nm* tea

tea ['tea] *nf* torch
teatral [tea'tral] *adj* theatre *cpd*; (*fig*) theatrical
teatro [te'atro] *nm* theatre; (*LITERATURA*) plays *pl*, drama
tebeo [te'βeo] *nm* comic
tecla ['tekla] *nf* key; ~**do** *nm* keyboard; **teclear** *vi* (*MUS*) to strum; (*con los dedos*) to tap ♦ *vt* (*INFORM*) to key in
técnica ['teknika] *nf* technique; (*arte, oficio*) craft, *ver tb* **técnico**
técnico, a ['tekniko, a] *adj* technical ♦ *nm/f* technician; (*experto*) expert
tecnócrata [tek'nokrata] *nm/f* technocrat
tecnología [teknolo'xia] *nf* technology; **tecnológico, a** *adj* technological
techo ['tetʃo] *nm* (*externo*) roof; (*interno*) ceiling; ~ **corredizo** sunroof
tedio ['teðjo] *nm* boredom, tedium; ~**so, a** *adj* boring, tedious
teja ['texa] *nf* (*azulejo*) tile; (*BOT*) lime (tree); ~**do** *nm* (tiled) roof
tejemaneje [texema'nexe] *nm* (*lío*) fuss; (*intriga*) intrigue
tejer [te'xer] *vt* to weave; (*hacer punto*) to knit; (*fig*) to fabricate; **tejido** *nm* (*tela*) material, fabric; (*telaraña*) web; (*ANAT*) tissue
tel [tel] *abr* (= *teléfono*) tel
tela ['tela] *nf* (*tejido*) material; (*telaraña*) web; (*en líquido*) skin; **telar** *nm* (*máquina*) loom; **telares** *nmpl* (*fábrica*) textile mill *sg*
telaraña [tela'raɲa] *nf* cobweb
tele ['tele] (*fam*) *nf* telly (*BRIT*), tube (*US*)
tele... ['tele] *pref* tele...; ~**comunicación** *nf* telecommunication; ~**control** *nm* remote control; ~**diario** *nm* television news; ~**difusión** *nf* (*television*) broadcast; ~**dirigido, a** *adj* remote-controlled
teléf *abr* (= *teléfono*) tel
teleférico [tele'feriko] *nm* (*tren*) cable-railway; (*de esquí*) ski-lift
telefonear [telefone'ar] *vi* to telephone
telefónico, a [tele'foniko, a] *adj* telephone *cpd*
telefonillo [telefo'niʎo] *nm* (*de puerta*) intercom
telefonista [telefo'nista] *nm/f* telephonist
teléfono [te'lefono] *nm* (tele)phone; **estar hablando al** ~ to be on the phone; **llamar a uno por** ~ to ring sb (up) *o* phone sb (up); ~ **móvil** car phone; ~ **portátil** mobile phone
telegrafía [televra'fia] *nf* telegraphy
telégrafo [te'levrafo] *nm* telegraph
telegrama [tele'vrama] *nm* telegram
tele: ~**impresor** *nm* teleprinter (*BRIT*), teletype (*US*); ~**objetivo** *nm* telephoto lens; ~**patía** *nf* telepathy; ~**pático, a** *adj* telepathic; ~**scópico, a** *adj* telescopic; ~**scopio** *nm* telescope; ~**silla** *nf* chairlift; ~**spectador, a** *nm/f* viewer; ~**squí** *nm* ski-lift; ~**tarjeta** *nf* phonecard; ~**tipo** *nm*

teletype
televidente [teleβi'ðente] *nm/f* viewer
televisar [teleβi'sar] *vt* to televise
televisión [teleβi'sjon] *nf* television; ~ **en colores** colour television
televisor [teleβi'sor] *nm* television set
télex ['teleks] *nm inv* telex
telón [te'lon] *nm* curtain; ~ **de acero** (*POL*) iron curtain; ~ **de fondo** backcloth, background
tema ['tema] *nm* (*asunto*) subject, topic; (*MUS*) theme ♦ *nf* (*obsesión*) obsession; **temática** *nf* (*social, histórica, artística*) range of topics; **temático, a** *adj* thematic
temblar [tem'blar] *vi* to shake, tremble; (*de frío*) to shiver; **temblón, ona** *adj* shaking; **temblor** *nm* trembling; (*de tierra*) earthquake; **tembloroso, a** *adj* trembling
temer [te'mer] *vt* to fear ♦ *vi* to be afraid; **temo que llegue tarde** I am afraid he may be late
temerario, a [teme'rarjo, a] *adj* (*descuidado*) reckless; (*irreflexivo*) hasty; **temeridad** *nf* (*imprudencia*) rashness; (*audacia*) boldness
temeroso, a [teme'roso, a] *adj* (*miedoso*) fearful; (*que inspira temor*) frightful
temible [te'miβle] *adj* fearsome
temor [te'mor] *nm* (*miedo*) fear; (*duda*) suspicion
témpano ['tempano] *nm*: ~ **de hielo** ice-floe
temperamento [tempera'mento] *nm* temperament
temperatura [tempera'tura] *nf* temperature
tempestad [tempes'tað] *nf* storm; **tempestuoso, a** *adj* stormy
templado, a [tem'plaðo, a] *adj* (*moderado*) moderate; (*: en el comer*) frugal; (*: en el beber*) abstemious; (*agua*) lukewarm; (*clima*) mild; (*MUS*) well-tuned; **templanza** *nf* moderation; abstemiousness; mildness
templar [tem'plar] *vt* (*moderar*) to moderate; (*furia*) to restrain; (*calor*) to reduce; (*afinar*) to tune (up); (*acero*) to temper; (*tuerca*) to tighten up; **temple** *nm* (*ajuste*) tempering; (*afinación*) tuning; (*clima*) temperature; (*pintura*) tempera
templo ['templo] *nm* (*iglesia*) church; (*pagano etc*) temple
temporada [tempo'raða] *nf* time, period; (*estación*) season
temporal [tempo'ral] *adj* (*no permanente*) temporary; (*REL*) temporal ♦ *nm* storm
tempranero, a [tempra'nero, a] *adj* (*BOT*) early; (*persona*) early-rising
temprano, a [tem'prano, a] *adj* early; (*demasiado pronto*) too soon, too early
ten *vb ver* **tener**
tenaces [te'naθes] *adj pl ver* **tenaz**
tenacidad [tenaθi'ðað] *nf* tenacity; (*dureza*) toughness; (*terquedad*) stubbornness

tenacillas [tena'θiʎas] *nfpl* tongs; (*para el pelo*) curling tongs (*BRIT*) *o* iron *sg* (*US*); (*MED*) forceps

tenaz [te'naθ] *adj* (*material*) tough; (*persona*) tenacious; (*creencia, resistencia*) stubborn

tenaza(s) [te'naθa(s)] *nf(pl)* (*MED*) forceps; (*TEC*) pliers; (*ZOOL*) pincers

tendedero [tende'ðero] *nm* (*para ropa*) drying place; (*cuerda*) clothes line

tendencia [ten'denθja] *nf* tendency; (*proceso*) trend; **tener ~ a** to tend to, have a tendency to; **tendencioso, a** *adj* tendentious

tender [ten'der] *vt* (*extender*) to spread out; (*colgar*) to hang out; (*vía férrea, cable*) to lay; (*estirar*) to stretch ♦ *vi*: **~ a** to tend to, have a tendency towards; **~se** *vr* to lie down; **~ la cama/la mesa** (*AM*) to make the bed/lay (*BRIT*) *o* set (*US*) the table

tenderete [tende'rete] *nm* (*puesto*) stall; (*exposición*) display of goods

tendero, a [ten'dero, a] *nm/f* shopkeeper

tendido, a [ten'diðo, a] *adj* (*acostado*) lying down, flat; (*colgado*) hanging ♦ *nm* (*TAUR*) front rows of seats; **a galope ~** flat out

tendón [ten'don] *nm* tendon

tendré *etc vb ver* **tener**

tenebroso, a [tene'βroso, a] *adj* (*oscuro*) dark; (*fig*) gloomy; (*complot*) sinister

tenedor [tene'ðor] *nm* (*CULIN*) fork; (*poseedor*) holder; **~ de libros** book-keeper

teneduría [teneðu'ria] *nf* keeping; **~ de libros** book-keeping

tenencia [te'nenθja] *nf* (*de casa*) tenancy; (*de oficio*) tenure; (*de propiedad*) possession

---

PALABRA CLAVE

tener [te'ner] *vt* **1** (*poseer, gen*) to have; (*en la mano*) to hold; **¿tienes un boli?** have you got a pen?; **va a ~ un niño** she's going to have a baby; **¡ten** (*o* **tenga**)!, **¡aquí tienes** (*o* **tiene**)! here you are!

2 (*edad, medidas*) to be; **tiene 7 años** she's 7 (years old); **tiene 15 cm de largo** it's 15 cm long; *ver* **calor; hambre** *etc*

3 (*considerar*): **lo tengo por brillante** I consider him to be brilliant; **~ en mucho a uno** to think very highly of sb

4 (+ *pp*: = *pretérito*): **tengo terminada ya la mitad del trabajo** I've done half the work already

5: **~ que hacer algo** to have to do sth; **tengo que acabar este trabajo hoy** I have to finish this job today

6: **¿qué tienes, estás enfermo?** what's the matter with you, are you ill?

♦ **~se** *vr* **1**: **~se en pie** to stand up

2: **~se por** to think o.s.; **se tiene por muy listo** he thinks himself very clever

tengo *etc vb ver* **tener**

tenia ['tenja] *nf* tapeworm

teniente [te'njente] *nm* (*rango*) lieutenant; (*ayudante*) deputy

tenis ['tenis] *nm* tennis; **~ de mesa** table tennis; **~ta** *nm/f* tennis player

tenor [te'nor] *nm* (*sentido*) meaning; (*MUS*) tenor; **a ~ de** on the lines of

tensar [ten'sar] *vt* to tauten; (*arco*) to draw

tensión [ten'sjon] *nf* tension; (*TEC*) stress; (*MED*): **~ arterial** blood pressure; **tener la ~ alta** to have high blood pressure

tenso, a ['tenso, a] *adj* tense

tentación [tenta'θjon] *nf* temptation

tentáculo [ten'takulo] *nm* tentacle

tentador, a [tenta'ðor, a] *adj* tempting ♦ *nm/f* tempter/temptress

tentar [ten'tar] *vt* (*tocar*) to touch, feel; (*seducir*) to tempt; (*atraer*) to attract; **tentativa** *nf* attempt; **tentativa de asesinato** attempted murder

tentempié [tentem'pje] (*fam*) *nm* snack

tenue ['tenwe] *adj* (*delgado*) thin, slender; (*neblina*) light; (*lazo, vínculo*) slight

teñir [te'ɲir] *vt* to dye; (*fig*) to tinge; **~se** *vr* to dye; **~se el pelo** to dye one's hair

teología [teolo'xia] *nf* theology

teorema [teo'rema] *nm* theorem

teoría [teo'ria] *nf* theory; **en ~** in theory; **teóricamente** *adv* theoretically; **teórico, a** *adj* theoretic(al) ♦ *nm/f* theoretician, theorist; **teorizar** *vi* to theorize

terapéutico, a [tera'peutiko, a] *adj* therapeutic

terapia [te'rapja] *nf* therapy

tercer [ter'θer] *adj ver* **tercero**

tercermundista [terθermun'dista] *adj* Third World *cpd*

tercero, a [ter'θero, a] *adj* (*delante de nmsg*: **tercer**) third ♦ *nm* (*JUR*) third party

terceto [ter'θeto] *nm* trio

terciado, a [ter'θjaðo, a] *adj* slanting

terciar [ter'θjar] *vt* (*llevar*) to wear (across the shoulder) ♦ *vi* (*participar*) to take part; (*hacer de árbitro*) to mediate; **~se** *vr* to come up; **~io, a** *adj* tertiary

tercio ['terθjo] *nm* third

terciopelo [terθjo'pelo] *nm* velvet

terco, a ['terko, a] *adj* obstinate

tergal [ter'val] ® *nm* type of polyester

tergiversar [terxiβer'sar] *vt* to distort

termal [ter'mal] *adj* thermal

termas ['termas] *nfpl* hot springs

térmico, a [ter'miko, a] *adj* thermal

terminación [termina'θjon] *nf* (*final*) end; (*conclusión*) conclusion, ending

terminal [termi'nal] *adj, nm, nf* terminal

terminante [termi'nante] *adj* (*final*) final, definitive; (*tajante*) categorical; **~mente** *adv*: **~mente prohibido** strictly forbidden

terminar [termi'nar] *vt* (*completar*) to complete, finish; (*concluir*) to end ♦ *vi* (*llegar a su fin*) to end; (*parar*) to stop; (*acabar*) to finish; ~**se** *vr* to come to an end; ~ **por hacer algo** to end up (by) doing sth

término ['termino] *nm* end, conclusion; (*parada*) terminus; (*límite*) boundary; ~ **medio** average; (*fig*) middle way; **en último** ~ (*a fin de cuentas*) in the last analysis; (*como último recurso*) as a last resort; **en ~s de** in terms of

terminología [terminolo'xia] *nf* terminology

termodinámico, a [termoδi'namiko, a] *adj* thermodynamic

termómetro [ter'mometro] *nm* thermometer

termonuclear [termonukle'ar] *adj* thermonuclear

termo(s) ['termo(s)] ® *nm* Thermos (flask) ®

termostato [termo'stato] *nm* thermostat

ternero, a [ter'nero, a] *nm/f* (*animal*) calf ♦ *nf* (*carne*) veal

ternura [ter'nura] *nf* (*trato*) tenderness; (*palabra*) endearment; (*cariño*) fondness

terquedad [terke'δaδ] *nf* obstinacy; (*dureza*) harshness

terrado [te'rraδo] *nm* terrace

terraplén [terra'plen] *nm* (*AGR*) terrace; (*cuesta*) slope

terrateniente [terrate'njente] *nm/f* landowner

terraza [te'rraθa] *nf* (*balcón*) balcony; (*techo*) (flat) roof; (*AGR*) terrace

terremoto [terre'moto] *nm* earthquake

terrenal [terre'nal] *adj* earthly

terreno [te'rreno] *nm* (*tierra*) land; (*parcela*) plot; (*suelo*) soil; (*fig*) field; **un** ~ a piece of land

terrestre [te'rrestre] *adj* terrestrial; (*ruta*) land *cpd*

terrible [te'rriβle] *adj* terrible, awful

territorio [terri'torjo] *nm* territory

terrón [te'rron] *nm* (*de azúcar*) lump; (*de tierra*) clod, lump

terror [te'rror] *nm* terror; ~**ífico, a** *adj* terrifying; ~**ista** *adj, nm/f* terrorist

terruño [te'rruɲo] *nm* (*parcela*) plot; (*fig*) native soil

terso, a ['terso, a] *adj* (*liso*) smooth; (*pulido*) polished; **tersura** *nf* smoothness

tertulia [ter'tulja] *nf* (*reunión informal*) social gathering; (*grupo*) group, circle

tesis ['tesis] *nf inv* thesis

tesón [te'son] *nm* (*firmeza*) firmness; (*tenacidad*) tenacity

tesorero, a [teso'rero, a] *nm/f* treasurer

tesoro [te'soro] *nm* treasure; (*COM, POL*) treasury

testaferro [testa'ferro] *nm* figurehead

testamentaría [testamenta'ria] *nf* execution of a will

testamentario, a [testamen'tarjo, a] *adj* testamentary ♦ *nm/f* executor/executrix

testamento [testa'mento] *nm* will

testar [tes'tar] *vi* to make a will

testarudo, a [testa'ruδo, a] *adj* stubborn

testículo [tes'tikulo] *nm* testicle

testificar [testifi'kar] *vt* to testify; (*fig*) to attest ♦ *vi* to give evidence

testigo [tes'tixo] *nm/f* witness; ~ **de cargo/descargo** witness for the prosecution/defence; ~ **ocular** eye witness

testimoniar [testimo'njar] *vt* to testify to; (*fig*) to show; **testimonio** *nm* testimony

teta ['teta] *nf* (*de biberón*) teat; (*ANAT: pezón*) nipple; (: *fam*) breast

tétanos ['tetanos] *nm* tetanus

tetera [te'tera] *nf* teapot

tétrico, a ['tetriko, a] *adj* gloomy, dismal

textil [teks'til] *adj* textile

texto ['teksto] *nm* text; **textual** *adj* textual

textura [teks'tura] *nf* (*de tejido*) texture

tez [teθ] *nf* (*cutis*) complexion; (*color*) colouring

ti [ti] *pron* you; (*reflexivo*) yourself

tía ['tia] *nf* (*pariente*) aunt; (*fam*) chick, bird

tibieza [ti'βjeθa] *nf* (*temperatura*) tepidness; (*fig*) coolness; **tibio, a** *adj* lukewarm

tiburón [tiβu'ron] *nm* shark

tic [tik] *nm* (*ruido*) click; (*de reloj*) tick; (*MED*): ~ **nervioso** nervous tic

tictac [tik'tak] *nm* (*de reloj*) tick tock

tiempo ['tjempo] *nm* time; (*época, período*) age, period; (*METEOROLOGÍA*) weather; (*LING*) tense; (*DEPORTE*) half; **a** ~ in time; **a un** ~ **al mismo** ~ at the same time; **al poco** ~ very soon (after); **se quedó poco** ~ he didn't stay very long; **hace poco** ~ not long ago; **mucho** ~ a long time; **de** ~ **en** ~ from time to time; **hace buen/mal** ~ the weather is fine/bad; **estar a** ~ to be in time; **hace** ~ some time ago; **hacer** ~ to while away the time; **motor de 2** ~**s** two-stroke engine; **primer** ~ first half

tienda ['tjenda] *nf* shop, store; ~ **(de campaña)** tent

tienes *etc vb ver* **tener**

tienta *etc* ['tjenta] *vb ver* **tentar** ♦ *nf*: **andar a** ~**s** to grope one's way along

tiento ['tjento] *vb ver* **tentar** ♦ *nm* (*tacto*) touch; (*precaución*) wariness

tierno, a ['tjerno, a] *adj* (*blando*) tender; (*fresco*) fresh; (*amable*) sweet

tierra ['tjerra] *nf* earth; (*suelo*) soil; (*mundo*) earth, world; (*país*) country, land; ~ **adentro** inland

tieso, a ['tjeso, a] *adj* (*rígido*) rigid; (*duro*) stiff; (*fam: orgulloso*) conceited

tiesto ['tjesto] *nm* flowerpot

tifoidea [tifoi'δea] *nf* typhoid

tifón [ti'fon] *nm* typhoon

tifus ['tifus] *nm* typhus

tigre ['tixre] *nm* tiger

tijera [ti'xera] *nf* scissors *pl*; (*ZOOL*) claw; ~**s** *nfpl* scissors; (*para plantas*) shears

tijereta [tixe'reta] nf earwig
tijeretear [tixerete'ar] vt to snip
tildar [til'dar] vt: ~ **de** to brand as
tilde ['tilde] nf (TIP) tilde
tilín [ti'lin] nm tinkle
tilo ['tilo] nm lime tree
timar [ti'mar] vt (robar) to steal; (estafar) to swindle
timbal [tim'bal] nm small drum
timbrar [tim'brar] vt to stamp
timbre ['timbre] nm (sello) stamp; (campanilla) bell; (tono) timbre; (COM) stamp duty
timidez [timi'ðeθ] nf shyness; **tímido, a** adj shy
timo ['timo] nm swindle
timón [ti'mon] nm helm, rudder; **timonel** nm helmsman
tímpano ['timpano] nm (ANAT) eardrum; (MUS) small drum
tina ['tina] nf tub; (baño) bath(tub); **tinaja** nf large jar
tinglado [tin'glaðo] nm (cobertizo) shed; (fig: truco) trick; (intriga) intrigue
tinieblas [ti'njeßlas] nfpl darkness sg; (sombras) shadows
tino ['tino] nm (habilidad) skill; (juicio) insight
tinta ['tinta] nf ink; (TEC) dye; (ARTE) colour
tinte ['tinte] nm (acto) dyeing
tintero [tin'tero] nm inkwell
tintinear [tintine'ar] vt to tinkle
tinto, a ['tinto, a] adj (teñido) dyed ♦ nm red wine
tintorería [tintore'ria] nf dry cleaner's
tintura [tin'tura] nf (acto) dyeing; (QUÍMICA) dye; (farmacéutico) tincture
tío ['tio] nm (pariente) uncle; (fam: individuo) bloke (BRIT), guy
tiovivo [tio'ßißo] nm merry-go-round
típico, a ['tipiko, a] adj typical
tipo ['tipo] nm (clase) type, kind; (norma) norm; (patrón) pattern; (hombre) fellow; (ANAT: de hombre) build; (: de mujer) figure; (IMPRENTA) type; ~ **bancario/de descuento/de interés/de cambio** bank/discount/interest/exchange rate
tipografía [tipoɣra'fia] nf (tipo) printing cpd; (lugar) printing press; **tipográfico, a** adj printing cpd
tíquet ['tiket] (pl ~s) nm ticket; (en tienda) cash slip
tiquismiquis [tikis'mikis] nm inv fussy person ♦ nmpl (querellas) squabbling sg; (escrúpulos) silly scruples
tira ['tira] nf strip; (fig) abundance; ~ **y afloja** give and take
tirabuzón [tiraßu'θon] nm (rizo) curl
tirachinas [tira'tʃinas] nm inv catapult
tirada [ti'raða] nf (acto) cast, throw; (distancia) distance; (serie) series; (TIP) printing, edition; **de una** ~ at one go

tiradero [tira'ðero] nm rubbish dump
tirado, a [ti'raðo, a] adj (barato) dirt-cheap; (fam: fácil) very easy
tirador [tira'ðor] nm (mango) handle
tiranía [tira'nia] nf tyranny; **tirano, a** adj tyrannical ♦ nm/f tyrant
tirante [ti'rante] adj (cuerda etc) tight, taut; (relaciones) strained ♦ nm (ARQ) brace; (TEC) stay; (correa) shoulder strap; ~**s** nmpl (de pantalón) braces (BRIT), suspenders (US); **tirantez** nf tightness; (fig) tension
tirar [ti'rar] vt to throw; (dejar caer) to drop; (volcar) to upset; (derribar) to knock down o over; (jalar) to pull; (desechar) to throw out o away; (disipar) to squander; (imprimir) to print; (dar: golpe) to deal ♦ vi (disparar) to shoot; (jalar) to pull; (fig) to draw; (fam: andar) to go; (tender a, buscar realizar) to tend to; (DEPORTE) to shoot; ~**se** vr to throw o.s.; (fig) to cheapen o.s.; ~ **abajo** to bring down, destroy; **tira más a su padre** he takes more after his father; **ir tirando** to manage; **a todo** ~ at the most
tirita [ti'rita] nf (sticking) plaster (BRIT), bandaid (US)
tiritar [tiri'tar] vi to shiver
tiro ['tiro] nm (lanzamiento) throw; (disparo) shot; (disparar) shooting; (DEPORTE) shot; (GOLF, TENIS) drive; (alcance) range; (golpe) blow; (engaño) hoax; ~ **al blanco** target practice; **caballo de** ~ cart-horse; **andar de** ~**s largos** to be all dressed up; **al** ~ (AM) at once
tirón [ti'ron] nm (sacudida) pull, tug; **de un** ~ in one go, all at once
tiroteo [tiro'teo] nm exchange of shots, shooting
tísico, a ['tisiko, a] adj consumptive
tisis ['tisis] nf inv consumption, tuberculosis
títere ['titere] nm puppet
titiritero [a] [titiri'tero, a] nm/f puppeteer
titubeante [tituße'ante] adj (inestable) shaky, tottering; (farfullante) stammering; (dudoso) hesitant
titubear [tituße'ar] vi to stagger; to stammer; (fig) to hesitate; **titubeo** nm staggering; stammering; hesitation
titulado, a [titu'laðo, a] adj (libro) entitled; (persona) titled
titular [titu'lar] adj titular ♦ nm/f occupant ♦ nm headline ♦ vt to title; ~**se** vr to be entitled; **título** nm title; (de diario) headline; (certificado) professional qualification; (universitario) (university) degree; (fig) right; **a título de** in the capacity of
tiza [ti'θa] nf chalk
tiznar [tiθ'nar] vt to blacken; (fig) to tarnish
tizo ['tiθo] nm brand
tizón [ti'θon] nm brand; (fig) stain
toalla [to'aʎa] nf towel
tobillo [to'ßiʎo] nm ankle
tobogán [toßo'ɣan] nm toboggan; (montaña

rusa) roller-coaster; (*resbaladilla*) chute, slide

toca ['toka] *nf* headdress

tocadiscos [toka'ðiskos] *nm inv* record player

tocado, a [to'kaðo, a] *adj* (*fam*) touched ♦ *nm* headdress

tocador [toka'ðor] *nm* (*mueble*) dressing table; (*cuarto*) boudoir; (*fam*) ladies' toilet (*BRIT*) o room (*US*)

tocante [to'kante]: ~ **a** *prep* with regard to

tocar [to'kar] *vt* to touch; (*MUS*) to play; (*topar con*) to run into, strike; (*referirse a*) to allude to; (*padecer*) to suffer ♦ *vi* (*a la puerta*) to knock (on o at the door); (*ser de turno*) to fall to, be the turn of; (*ser hora*) to be due; (*barco, avión*) to call at; (*atañer*) to concern; ~**se** *vr* (*cubrirse la cabeza*) to cover one's head; (*tener contacto*) to touch (each other); **por lo que a mí me toca** as far as I am concerned

tocayo, a [to'kajo, a] *nm/f* namesake

tocino [to'θino] *nm* bacon

todavía [toða'βia] *adv* (*aun*) even; (*aún*) still, yet; ~ **más** yet more; ~ **no** not yet

┌─────── *PALABRA CLAVE*

todo, a ['toðo, a] *adj* **1** (*con artículo sg*) all; **toda la carne** all the meat; **toda la noche** all night, the whole night; ~ **el libro** the whole book; **toda una botella** a whole bottle; **lo contrario** quite the opposite; **está toda sucia** she's all dirty; **por ~ el país** throughout the whole country

2 (*con artículo pl*) all; every; ~**s los libros** all the books; **todas las noches** every night; ~**s los que quieran salir** all those who want to leave

♦ *pron* **1** everything, all; ~**s** everyone, everybody; **lo sabemos** ~ we know everything; ~**s querían más tiempo** everybody o everyone wanted more time; **nos marchamos** ~**s** all of us left

2: **con** ~: **con** ~ **él me sigue gustando** even so I still like him

♦ *adv* all; **vaya** ~ **seguido** keep straight on o ahead

♦ *nm*: **como un** ~ as a whole; **del** ~: **no me agrada del** ~ I don't entirely like it

└────────────

todopoderoso, a [toðopoðe'roso, a] *adj* all powerful; (*REL*) almighty

toga ['toɣa] *nf* toga; (*ESCOL*) gown

Tokio ['tokjo] *n* Tokyo

toldo ['toldo] *nm* (*para el sol*) sunshade (*BRIT*), parasol; (*tienda*) marquee

tolerancia [tole'ranθja] *nf* tolerance; **tolerante** *adj* (*sociedad*) liberal; (*persona*) open-minded

tolerar [tole'rar] *vt* to tolerate; (*resistir*) to endure

toma ['toma] *nf* (*acto*) taking; (*MED*) dose; ~ (**de corriente**) socket

tomar [to'mar] *vt* to take; (*aspecto*) to take on; (*beber*) to drink ♦ *vi* to take; (*AM*) to drink; ~**se** *vr* to take; ~**se por** to consider o.s. to be; ~ **a bien/a mal** to take well/badly; ~ **en serio** to take seriously; ~ **el pelo a alguien** to pull sb's leg; ~**la con uno** to pick a quarrel with sb

tomate [to'mate] *nm* tomato

tomavistas [toma'βistas] *nm inv* movie camera

tomillo [to'miʎo] *nm* thyme

tomo ['tomo] *nm* (*libro*) volume

ton [ton] *abr* = **tonada** ♦ *nm*: **sin** ~ **ni son** without rhyme or reason

tonada [to'naða] *nf* tune

tonalidad [tonali'ðað] *nf* tone

tonel [to'nel] *nm* barrel

tonelada [tone'laða] *nf* ton; **tonelaje** *nm* tonnage

tónica ['tonika] *nf* (*MUS*) tonic; (*fig*) keynote

tónico, a ['toniko, a] *adj* tonic ♦ *nm* (*MED*) tonic

tonificar [tonifi'kar] *vt* to tone up

tono ['tono] *nm* tone; **fuera de** ~ inappropriate; **darse** ~ to put on airs

tontería [tonte'ria] *nf* (*estupidez*) foolishness; (*cosa*) stupid thing; (*acto*) foolish act; ~**s** *nfpl* (*disparates*) rubbish *sg*, nonsense *sg*

tonto, a ['tonto, a] *adj* stupid, silly ♦ *nm/f* fool; (*payaso*) clown

topar [to'par] *vt* (*tropezar*) to bump into; (*encontrar*) to find, come across; (*ZOOL*) to butt ♦ *vi*: ~ **contra** o **en** to run into; ~ **con** to run up against

tope ['tope] *adj* maximum ♦ *nm* (*fin*) end; (*límite*) limit; (*FERRO*) buffer; (*AUTO*) bumper; **al** ~ end to end

tópico, a ['topiko, a] *adj* topical ♦ *nm* platitude

topo ['topo] *nm* (*ZOOL*) mole; (*fig*) blunderer

topografía [topoɣra'fia] *nf* topography; **topógrafo, a** *nm/f* topographer

toque *etc* ['toke] *vb ver* **tocar** ♦ *nm* touch; (*MUS*) beat; (*de campana*) peal; (*fig*) crux; **dar un** ~ **a** to test; ~ **de queda** curfew; ~**tear** *vt* to handle

toqué *vb ver* **tocar**

toquilla [to'kiʎa] *nf* (*pañuelo*) headscarf; (*chal*) shawl

tórax ['toraks] *nm* thorax

torbellino [torbe'ʎino] *nm* whirlwind; (*fig*) whirl

torcedura [torθe'ðura] *nf* twist; (*MED*) sprain

torcer [tor'θer] *vt* to twist; (*la esquina*) to turn; (*MED*) to sprain ♦ *vi* (*desviar*) to turn off; ~**se** *vr* (*ladearse*) to bend; (*desviarse*) to go astray; (*fracasar*) to go wrong; **torcido, a** *adj* twisted; (*fig*) crooked ♦ *nm* curl

tordo, a ['torðo, a] *adj* dappled ♦ *nm* thrush

torear [tore'ar] *vt* (*fig: evadir*) to avoid; (*jugar con*) to tease ♦ *vi* to fight bulls; **toreo** *nm* bullfighting; **torero, a** *nm/f* bullfighter

tormenta [tor'menta] *nf* storm; (*fig: confusión*) turmoil

tormento [tor'mento] *nm* torture; (*fig*) anguish

tornar [tor'nar] *vt* (*devolver*) to return, give back; (*transformar*) to transform ♦ *vi* to go back; **~se** *vr* (*ponerse*) to become

tornasolado, a [tornaso'laðo, a] *adj* (*brillante*) iridescent; (*reluciente*) shimmering

torneo [tor'neo] *nm* tournament

tornillo [tor'niʎo] *nm* screw

torniquete [torni'kete] *nm* (*puerta*) turnstile; (*MED*) tourniquet

torno ['torno] *nm* (*TEC*) winch; (*tambor*) drum; **en ~ (a)** round, about

toro ['toro] *nm* bull; (*fam*) he-man; **los ~s** bullfighting

toronja [to'ronxa] *nf* grapefruit

torpe ['torpe] *adj* (*poco hábil*) clumsy, awkward, (*necio*) dim; (*lento*) slow

torpedo [tor'peðo] *nm* torpedo

torpeza [tor'peθa] *nf* (*falta de agilidad*) clumsiness; (*lentitud*) slowness; (*error*) mistake

torre ['torre] *nf* tower; (*de petróleo*) derrick

torrefacto, a [torre'fakto, a] *adj* roasted

torrente [to'rrente] *nm* torrent

tórrido, a ['torriðo, a] *adj* torrid

torrija [to'rrixa] *nf* French toast

torsión [tor'sjon] *nf* twisting

torso ['torso] *nm* torso

torta ['torta] *nf* cake; (*fam*) slap

tortícolis [tor'tikolis] *nm inv* stiff neck

tortilla [tor'tiʎa] *nf* omelette; (*AM*) maize pancake; **~ francesa/española** plain/potato omelette

tórtola ['tortola] *nf* turtledove

tortuga [tor'tuxa] *nf* tortoise

tortuoso, a [tor'twoso, a] *adj* winding

tortura [tor'tura] *nf* torture; **torturar** *vt* to torture

tos [tos] *nf* cough; **~ ferina** whooping cough

tosco, a ['tosko, a] *adj* coarse

toser [to'ser] *vi* to cough

tostada [tos'taða] *nf* piece of toast; **tostado, a** *adj* toasted; (*por el sol*) dark brown; (*piel*) tanned

tostador [tosta'ðor] *nm* toaster

tostar [tos'tar] *vt* to toast; (*café*) to roast; (*persona*) to tan; **~se** *vr* to get brown

total [to'tal] *adj* total ♦ *adv* in short; (*al fin y al cabo*) when all is said and done ♦ *nm* total; **~ que** to cut (*BRIT*) *o* make (*US*) a long story short

totalidad [totali'ðað] *nf* whole

totalitario, a [totali'tarjo, a] *adj* totalitarian

tóxico, a ['toksiko, a] *adj* toxic ♦ *nm* poison; **toxicómano, a** *nm/f* drug addict

toxina [to'ksina] *nf* toxin

tozudo, a [to'θuðo, a] *adj* obstinate

traba ['traβa] *nf* bond, tie; (*cadena*) shackle

trabajador, a [traβaxa'ðor, a] *adj* hardworking ♦ *nm/f* worker

trabajar [traβa'xar] *vt* to work; (*AGR*) to till; (*empeñarse en*) to work at; (*empujar: persona*) to push; (*convencer*) to persuade ♦ *vi* to work; (*esforzarse*) to strive; **trabajo** *nm* work; (*tarea*) task; (*POL*) labour; (*fig*) effort; **tomarse el trabajo de** to take the trouble to; **trabajo por turno/a destajo** shift work/piecework; **trabajoso, a** *adj* hard

trabalenguas [traβa'lengwas] *nm inv* tongue twister

trabar [tra'βar] *vt* (*juntar*) to join, unite; (*atar*) to tie down, fetter; (*agarrar*) to seize; (*amistad*) to strike up; **~se** *vr* to become entangled; **trabársele a uno la lengua** to be tongue-tied

tracción [trak'θjon] *nf* traction; **~ delantera/trasera** front-wheel/rear-wheel drive

tractor [trak'tor] *nm* tractor

tradición [traði'θjon] *nf* tradition; **tradicional** *adj* traditional

traducción [traðuk'θjon] *nf* translation

traducir [traðu'θir] *vt* to translate; **traductor, a** *nm/f* translator

traer [tra'er] *vt* to bring; (*llevar*) to carry; (*ropa*) to wear; (*incluir*) to carry; (*fig*) to cause; **~se** *vr:* **~se algo** to be up to sth

traficar [trafi'kar] *vi* to trade

tráfico ['trafiko] *nm* (*COM*) trade; (*AUTO*) traffic

tragaluz [traxa'luθ] *nm* skylight

tragaperras [traxa'perras] *nm o f inv* slot machine

tragar [tra'xar] *vt* to swallow; (*devorar*) to devour, bolt down; **~se** *vr* to swallow

tragedia [tra'xeðja] *nf* tragedy; **trágico, a** *adj* tragic

trago ['traxo] *nm* (*líquido*) drink; (*bocado*) gulp; (*fam: de bebida*) swig; (*desgracia*) blow

traición [trai'θjon] *nf* treachery; (*JUR*) treason; (*una ~*) act of treachery; **traicionar** *vt* to betray

traicionero, a [traiθjo'nero, a] *adj* treacherous

traidor, a [trai'ðor, a] *adj* treacherous ♦ *nm/f* traitor

traigo *etc vb ver* **traer**

traje ['traxe] *vb ver* **traer** ♦ *nm* (*de hombre*) suit; (*de mujer*) dress; (*vestido típico*) costume; **~ de baño** swimsuit; **~ de luces** bullfighter's costume

trajera etc vb ver **traer**

trajín [tra'xin] nm haulage; (fam: movimiento) bustle; **trajinar** vt (llevar) to carry, transport ♦ vi (moverse) to bustle about; (viajar) to travel around

trama ['trama] nf (intriga) plot; (de tejido) weft (BRIT), woof (US); **tramar** vt to plot; (TEC) to weave

tramitar [trami'tar] vt (asunto) to transact; (negociar) to negotiate; (manejar) to handle

trámite ['tramite] nm (paso) step; (JUR) transaction; ~s nmpl (burocracia) procedure sg; (JUR) proceedings

tramo ['tramo] nm (de tierra) plot; (de escalera) flight; (de vía) section

tramoya [tra'moja] nf (TEATRO) piece of stage machinery; (fig) scheme; **tramoyista** nm/f scene shifter; (paz) trickster

trampa ['trampa] nf trap; (en el suelo) trapdoor; (engaño) trick; (fam) fiddle; **trampear** vt, vi to cheat

trampolín [trampo'lin] nm trampoline; (de piscina etc) diving board

tramposo, a [tram'poso, a] adj crooked, cheating ♦ nm/f crook, cheat

tranca ['tranka] nf (palo) stick; (de puerta, ventana) bar; **trancar** vt to bar

trance ['tranθe] nm (momento difícil) difficult moment o juncture; (estado hipnotizado) trance

tranco ['tranko] nm stride

tranquilidad [trankili'ðað] nf (calma) calmness, stillness; (paz) peacefulness

tranquilizar [trankili'θar] vt (calmar) to calm (down); (asegurar) to reassure; ~se vr to calm down; **tranquilo, a** adj (calmado) calm; (apacible) peaceful; (mar) calm; (mente) untroubled

transacción [transak'θjon] nf transaction

transbordador [transβorða'ðor] nm ferry

transbordar [transβor'ðar] vt to transfer; **transbordo** nm transfer; **hacer transbordo** to change (trains)

transcurrir [transku'rrir] vi (tiempo) to pass; (hecho) to turn out

transcurso [trans'kurso] nm: ~ **del tiempo** lapse (of time)

transeúnte [transe'unte] adj transient ♦ nm/f passer-by

transferencia [transfe'renθja] nf transference; (COM) transfer

transferir [transfe'rir] vt to transfer

transformador [transforma'ðor] nm (ELEC) transformer

transformar [transfor'mar] vt to transform; (convertir) to convert

tránsfuga ['transfuɣa] nm/f (MIL) deserter; (POL) turncoat

transfusión [transfu'sjon] nf transfusion

transición [transi'θjon] nf transition

transigir [transi'xir] vi to compromise, make concessions

transistor [transis'tor] nm transistor

transitar [transi'tar] vi to go (from place to place); **tránsito** nm transit; (AUTO) traffic; **transitorio, a** adj transitory

transmisión [transmi'sjon] nf (TEC) transmission; (transferencia) transfer; ~ **en directo/exterior** live/outside broadcast

transmitir [transmi'tir] vt to transmit; (RADIO, TV) to broadcast

transparencia [transpa'renθja] nf transparency; (claridad) clearness, clarity; (foto) slide

transparentar [transparen'tar] vt to reveal ♦ vi to be transparent; **transparente** adj transparent; (claro) clear; (ligero) diaphanous

transpirar [transpi'rar] vi to perspire; (fig) to transpire

transportar [transpor'tar] vt to transport; (llevar) to carry; **transporte** nm transport; (COM) haulage

transversal [transβer'sal] adj transverse, cross

tranvía [tram'bia] nm tram

trapecio [tra'peθjo] nm trapeze; **trapecista** nm/f trapeze artist

trapero, a [tra'pero, a] nm/f ragman

trapicheo [trapi'tʃeo] (fam) nm scheme, fiddle

trapo ['trapo] nm (tela) rag; (de cocina) cloth; **poner un** ~ (o por) to dust

tráquea ['trakea] nf windpipe

traqueteo [trake'teo] nm (golpeteo) rattling

tras [tras] prep (detrás) behind; (después) after

trasatlántico [trasat'lantiko] nm (barco) (cabin) cruiser

trascendencia [trasθen'denθja] nf (importancia) importance; (FILOSOFÍA) transcendence

trascendental [trasθenden'tal] adj important; (FILOSOFÍA) transcendental

trascender [trasθen'der] vi (noticias) to come out; (suceso) to have a wide effect

trasero, a [tra'sero, a] adj back, rear ♦ nm (ANAT) bottom

trasfondo [tras'fondo] nm background

trasgredir [trasɣre'ðir] vt to contravene

trashumante [trasu'mante] adj (animales) migrating

trasladar [trasla'ðar] vt to move; (persona) to transfer; (postergar) to postpone; (copiar) to copy; ~se vr (mudarse) to move; **traslado** nm (mudanza) move, removal

traslucir [traslu'θir] vt to show; ~se vr to be translucent; (fig) to be revealed

trasluz [tras'luθ] nm reflected light; **al** ~ against o up to the light

trasnochador, a [trasnotʃa'ðor, a] nm/f night owl

trasnochar [trasno'tʃar] vi (acostarse tarde) to stay up late; (no dormir) to have a sleepless night

traspapelar [traspape'lar] *vt* (*document, carta*) to mislay, misplace

traspasar [traspa'sar] *vt* (*suj: bala etc*) to pierce, go through; (*propiedad*) to sell, transfer; (*calle*) to cross over; (*límites*) to go beyond; (*ley*) to break; **traspaso** *nm* (*venta*) transfer, sale

traspié [tras'pje] *nm* (*tropezón*) trip; (*fig*) blunder

trasplantar [trasplan'tar] *vt* to transplant

traste ['traste] *nm* (*MUS*) fret; **dar al ~ con algo** to ruin sth

trastero [tras'tero] *nm* storage room

trastienda [tras'tjenda] *nf* back of shop

trasto ['trasto] (*pey*) *nm* (*cosa*) piece of junk; (*persona*) dead loss

trastornado, a [trastor'naðo, a] *adj* (*loco*) mad, crazy

trastornar [trastor'nar] *vt* to overturn, upset; (*fig: ideas*) to confuse; (: *nervios*) to shatter; (: *persona*) to drive crazy; **~se** *vr* (*volverse loco*) to go mad *o* crazy; **trastorno** *nm* (*acto*) overturning; (*confusión*) confusion

tratable [tra'taβle] *adj* friendly

tratado [tra'taðo] *nm* (*POL*) treaty; (*COM*) agreement

tratamiento [trata'mjento] *nm* treatment; **~ de textos** (*INFORM*) word processing *cpd*

tratar [tra'tar] *vt* (*ocuparse de*) to treat; (*manejar, TEC*) to handle; (*MED*) to treat; (*dirigirse a: persona*) to address ♦ *vi*: **~ de** (*hablar sobre*) to deal with, be about; (*intentar*) to try to; **~se** *vr* to treat each other; **~ con** (*COM*) to trade in; (*negociar*) to negotiate with; (*tener contactos*) to have dealings with; **¿de qué se trata?** what's it about?; **trato** *nm* dealings *pl*; (*relaciones*) relationship; (*comportamiento*) manner; (*COM*) agreement; (*título*) (form of) address

trauma ['trauma] *nm* trauma

través [tra'βes] *nm* (*fig*) reverse; **al ~** across, crossways; **a ~ de** across; (*sobre*) over; (*por*) through

travesaño [traβe'saɲo] *nm* (*ARQ*) crossbeam; (*DEPORTE*) crossbar

travesía [traβe'sia] *nf* (*calle*) cross-street; (*NAUT*) crossing

travesura [traβe'sura] *nf* (*broma*) prank; (*ingenio*) wit

traviesa [tra'βjesa] *nf* (*ARQ*) crossbeam

travieso, a [tra'βjeso, a] *adj* (*niño*) naughty

trayecto [tra'jekto] *nm* (*ruta*) road, way; (*viaje*) journey; (*tramo*) stretch; (*curso*) course; **~ria** *nf* trajectory; (*fig*) path

traza ['traθa] *nf* (*aspecto*) looks *pl*; (*señal*) sign; **~do, a** *adj*: **bien ~do** shapely, well-formed ♦ *nm* (*ARQ*) plan, design; (*fig*) outline

trazar [tra'θar] *vt* (*ARQ*) to plan; (*ARTE*) to

sketch; (*fig*) to trace; (*plan*) to follow; **trazo** *nm* (*línea*) line; (*bosquejo*) sketch

trébol ['treβol] *nm* (*BOT*) clover

trece ['treθe] *num* thirteen

trecho ['tretʃo] *nm* (*distancia*) distance; (*de tiempo*) while; (*fam*) piece; **de ~ en ~** at intervals

tregua ['treɣwa] *nf* (*MIL*) truce; (*fig*) lull

treinta ['treinta] *num* thirty

tremendo, a [tre'mendo, a] *adj* (*terrible*) terrible; (*imponente: cosa*) imposing; (*fam: fabuloso*) tremendous

trémulo, a ['tremulo, a] *adj* quivering

tren [tren] *nm* train; **~ de aterrizaje** undercarriage

trenza ['trenθa] *nf* (*de pelo*) plait (*BRIT*), braid (*US*); **trenzar** *vt* (*pelo*) to plait, braid; **trenzarse** *vr* (*AM*) to become involved

trepadora [trepa'ðora] *nf* (*BOT*) climber

trepar [tre'par] *vt, vi* to climb

trepidante [trepi'ðante] *adj* (*acción*) fast; (*ritmo*) hectic

trepidar [trepi'ðar] *vi* to shake, vibrate

tres [tres] *num* three

tresillo [tre'siʎo] *nm* three-piece suite; (*MUS*) triplet

treta ['treta] *nf* (*COM etc*) gimmick; (*fig*) trick

triángulo ['trjangulo] *nm* triangle

tribu ['triβu] *nf* tribe

tribuna [tri'βuna] *nf* (*plataforma*) platform; (*DEPORTE*) (grand)stand; (*fig*) public speaking

tribunal [triβu'nal] *nm* (*JUR*) court; (*comisión, fig*) tribunal

tributar [triβu'tar] *vt* (*gen*) to pay; **tributo** *nm* (*COM*) tax

tricotar [triko'tar] *vi* to knit

trigal [tri'ɣal] *nm* wheat field

trigo ['triɣo] *nm* wheat

trigueño, a [tri'ɣeɲo, a] *adj* (*pelo*) corn-coloured; (*piel*) olive-skinned

trillado, a [tri'ʎaðo, a] *adj* threshed; (*fig*) trite, hackneyed; **trilladora** *nf* threshing machine

trillar [tri'ʎar] *vt* (*AGR*) to thresh

trimestral [trimes'tral] *adj* quarterly; (*ESCOL*) termly

trimestre [tri'mestre] *nm* (*ESCOL*) term

trinar [tri'nar] *vi* (*pájaros*) to sing; (*rabiar*) to fume, be angry

trincar [trin'kar] *vt* (*atar*) to tie up; (*inmovilizar*) to pinion

trinchar [trin'tʃar] *vt* to carve

trinchera [trin'tʃera] *nf* (*fosa*) trench

trineo [tri'neo] *nm* sledge

trinidad [trini'ðað] *nf* trio; (*REL*): **la T~** the Trinity

trino ['trino] *nm* trill

tripa ['tripa] *nf* (*ANAT*) intestine; (*fam: tb: ~s*) insides *pl*

triple ['triple] *adj* triple

triplicado, a [tripli'kaðo, a] *adj*: **por ~** in triplicate

tripulación [tripula'θjon] *nf* crew

tripulante [tripu'lante] *nm/f* crewman/woman

tripular [tripu'lar] *vt* (*barco*) to man; (*AUTO*) to drive

triquiñuela [triki'ɲwela] *nf* trick

tris [tris] *nm inv* crack; **en un ~** in an instant

triste ['triste] *adj* (*afligido*) sad; (*sombrío*) melancholy, gloomy; (*lamentable*) sorry, miserable; **~za** *nf* (*aflicción*) sadness; (*melancolía*) melancholy

triturar [tritu'rar] *vt* (*moler*) to grind; (*mascar*) to chew

triunfar [trjun'far] *vi* (*tener éxito*) to triumph; (*ganar*) to win; **triunfo** *nm* triumph

trivial [tri'βjal] *adj* trivial; **~izar** *vt* to minimize, play down

triza ['triθa] *nf*: **hacer ~s** to smash to bits; (*papel*) to tear to shreds

trocar [tro'kar] *vt* to exchange

trocear [troθe'ar] *vt* (*carne, manzana*) to cut up, cut into pieces

trocha ['trotʃa] *nf* short cut

troche ['trotʃe]: **a ~ y moche** *adv* helter-skelter, pell-mell

trofeo [tro'feo] *nm* (*premio*) trophy; (*éxito*) success

tromba ['tromba] *nf* whirlwind

trombón [trom'bon] *nm* trombone

trombosis [trom'bosis] *nf inv* thrombosis

trompa ['trompa] *nf* horn; (*trompo*) humming top; (*hocico*) snout; (*fam*): **cogerse una ~** to get tight

trompazo [trom'paθo] *nm* bump, bang

trompeta [trom'peta] *nf* trumpet; (*clarín*) bugle

trompicón [trompi'kon]: **a ~es** *adv* in fits and starts

trompo ['trompo] *nm* spinning top

trompón [trom'pon] *nm* bump

tronar [tro'nar] *vt* (*AM*) to shoot ♦ *vi* to thunder; (*fig*) to rage

tronco ['tronko] *nm* (*de árbol, ANAT*) trunk

tronchar [tron'tʃar] *vt* (*árbol*) to chop down; (*fig: vida*) to cut short; (*: esperanza*) to shatter; (*persona*) to tire out; **~se** *vr* to fall down

tronera [tro'nera] *nf* (*MIL*) loophole; (*ARQ*) small window

trono ['trono] *nm* throne

tropa ['tropa] *nf* (*MIL*) troop; (*soldados*) soldiers *pl*

tropel [tro'pel] *nm* (*muchedumbre*) crowd

tropezar [trope'θar] *vi* to trip, stumble; (*fig*) to slip up; **~ con** to run into; (*topar con*) to bump into; **tropezón** *nm* trip; (*fig*) blunder

tropical [tropi'kal] *adj* tropical

trópico ['tropiko] *nm* tropic

tropiezo [tro'pjeθo] *vb ver* **tropezar** ♦ *nm* (*error*) slip, blunder; (*desgracia*) misfortune; (*obstáculo*) snag

trotamundos [trota'mundos] *nm inv* globetrotter

trotar [tro'tar] *vi* to trot; **trote** *nm* trot; (*fam*) travelling; **de mucho trote** hard-wearing

trozo ['troθo] *nm* bit, piece

truco ['truko] *nm* (*habilidad*) knack; (*engaño*) trick

trucha ['trutʃa] *nf* trout

trueno ['trweno] *nm* thunder; (*estampido*) bang

trueque *etc* ['trweke] *vb ver* **trocar** ♦ *nm* exchange; (*COM*) barter

trufa ['trufa] *nf* (*BOT*) truffle

truhán, ana [tru'an, ana] *nm/f* rogue

truncar [trun'kar] *vt* (*cortar*) to truncate; (*fig: la vida etc*) to cut short; (*: el desarrollo*) to stunt

tu [tu] *adj* your

tú [tu] *pron* you

tubérculo [tu'βerkulo] *nm* (*BOT*) tuber

tuberculosis [tußerku'losis] *nf inv* tuberculosis

tubería [tuße'ria] *nf* pipes *pl*; (*conducto*) pipeline

tubo ['tußo] *nm* tube, pipe; **~ de ensayo** test tube; **~ de escape** exhaust (pipe)

tuerca ['twerka] *nf* nut

tuerto, a ['twerto, a] *adj* blind in one eye ♦ *nm/f* one-eyed person

tuerza *etc vb ver* **torcer**

tuétano ['twetano] *nm* marrow; (*BOT*) pith

tufo ['tufo] *nm* vapour; (*fig: pey*) stench

tugurio [tu'vurio] *nm* slum

tul [tul] *nm* tulle

tulipán [tuli'pan] *nm* tulip

tullido, a [tu'ʎiðo, a] *adj* crippled

tumba ['tumba] *nf* (*sepultura*) tomb

tumbar [tum'bar] *vt* to knock down; **~se** *vr* (*echarse*) to lie down; (*extenderse*) to stretch out

tumbo ['tumbo] *nm* (*caída*) fall; (*de vehículo*) jolt

tumbona [tum'bona] *nf* (*butaca*) easy chair; (*de playa*) deckchair (*BRIT*), beach chair (*US*)

tumor [tu'mor] *nm* tumour

tumulto [tu'multo] *nm* turmoil

tuna ['tuna] *nf* (*BOT*) prickly pear; (*MUS*) student music group; *ver tb* **tuno**

tunante [tu'nante] *nm/f* rascal

tunda ['tunda] *nf* (*golpeo*) beating

túnel ['tunel] *nm* tunnel

Túnez ['tuneθ] *nm* Tunisia; (*ciudad*) Tunis

tuno, a ['tuno, a] *nm/f* (*fam*) rogue ♦ *nm* member of student music group

tuntún [tun'tun]: **al ~** *adv* thoughtlessly

tupido, a [tu'piðo, a] *adj* (*denso*) dense; (*tela*) close-woven; (*fig*) dim

turba ['turßa] nf crowd

turbación [turßa'θjon] nf (molestia) disturbance; (preocupación) worry; **turbado, a** adj (molesto) disturbed; (preocupado) worried

turbante [tur'ßante] nm turban

turbar [tur'ßar] vt (molestar) to disturb; (incomodar) to upset; ~**se** vr to be disturbed

turbina [tur'ßina] nf turbine

turbio, a ['turßjo, a] adj cloudy; (tema etc) confused ♦ adv indistinctly

turbulencia [turßu'lenθja] nf turbulence; (fig) restlessness; **turbulento, a** adj turbulent; (fig: intranquilo) restless; (: ruidoso) noisy

turco, a ['turko, a] adj Turkish ♦ nm/f Turk

turismo [tu'rismo] nm tourism; (coche) saloon car; **turista** nm/f tourist; **turístico, a** adj tourist cpd

turnar [tur'nar] vi to take (it in) turns; ~**se** vr to take (it in) turns; **turno** nm (INDUSTRIA) shift; (oportunidad, orden de prioridad) opportunity; (juegos etc) turn

turquesa [tur'kesa] nf turquoise

Turquía [tur'kia] nf Turkey

turrón [tu'rron] nm (dulce) nougat

tutear [tute'ar] vt to address as familiar "tú"; ~**se** vr to be on familiar terms

tutela [tu'tela] nf (legal) guardianship; (instrucción) guidance; **tutelar** adj tutelary ♦ vt to protect

tutor, a [tu'tor, a] nm/f (legal) guardian; (ESCOL) tutor

tuve etc vb ver **tener**

tuviera etc vb ver **tener**

tuyo, a ['tujo, a] adj yours, of yours ♦ pron yours; **un amigo** ~ a friend of yours; **los** ~**s** (fam) your relations, your family

TV ['te'ße] nf abr (= televisión) TV

TVE nf abr = **Televisión Española**

U u

u [u] conj or

ubicar [ußi'kar] vt to place, situate; (: fig) to install in a post; (AM: encontrar) to find; ~**se** vr to lie, be located

ubre ['ußre] nf udder

Ud(s) abr = **usted(es)**

ufanarse [ufa'narse] vr to boast; ~ **de** to pride o.s. on; **ufano, a** adj (arrogante) arrogant; (presumido) conceited

UGT nf abr = **Unión General de Trabaja-**

dores

ujier [u'xjer] nm usher; (portero) doorkeeper

úlcera ['ulθera] nf ulcer

ulcerar [ulθe'rar] vt to make sore; ~**se** vr to ulcerate

ulterior [ulte'rjor] adj (más allá) farther, further; (subsecuente, siguiente) subsequent

últimamente ['ultimamente] adv (recientemente) lately, recently

ultimar [ulti'mar] vt to finish; (finalizar) to finalize; (AM: rematar) to finish off

ultimátum [ulti'matum] (pl ~**s**) ultimatum

último, a ['ultimo, a] adj last; (más reciente) latest, most recent; (más bajo) bottom; (más alto) top; (fig) final, extreme; **en las últimas** on one's last legs; **por ~** finally

ultra ['ultra] adj ultra ♦ nm/f extreme right-winger

ultrajar [ultra'xar] vt (escandalizar) to outrage; (insultar) to insult, abuse; **ultraje** nm outrage; insult

ultramar [ultra'mar] nm: **de** o **en ~** abroad, overseas

ultramarinos [ultrama'rinos] nmpl groceries; **tienda de ~** grocer's (shop)

ultranza [ul'tranθa]: **a ~** adv (a todo trance) at all costs; (completo) outright

ultrasónico, a [ultra'soniko, a] adj ultrasonic

ultratumba [ultra'tumba] nf: **la vida de ~** the next life

ulular [ulu'lar] vi to howl; (búho) to hoot

umbral [um'bral] nm (gen) threshold

umbrío, a [um'brio, a] adj shady

PALABRA CLAVE

un, una [un, 'una] art indef a; (antes de vocal) an; **una mujer/naranja** a woman/an orange

♦ adj: **unos** (o **unas**): **hay unos regalos para ti** there are some presents for you; **hay unas cervezas en la nevera** there are some beers in the fridge

---

unánime [u'nanime] adj unanimous; **unanimidad** nf unanimity

undécimo, a [un'deθimo, a] adj eleventh

ungir [un'xir] vt to rub with ointment; (REL) to anoint

ungüento [un'gwento] nm ointment; (fig) salve, balm

únicamente ['unikamente] adv solely, only

único, a ['uniko, a] adj only, sole; (sin par) unique

unidad [uni'ðað] nf unity; (COM, TEC etc) unit

unido, a [u'niðo, a] adj joined, linked; (fig) united

unificar [unifi'kar] vt to unite, unify

uniformar [unifor'mar] vt to make uniform, level up; (persona) to put into uniform

uniforme [uni'forme] *adj* uniform, equal; *(superficie)* even ♦ *nm* uniform; **uniformidad** *nf* uniformity; *(llaneza)* levelness, evenness

unilateral [unilate'ral] *adj* unilateral

unión [u'njon] *nf* union; *(acto)* uniting, joining; *(calidad)* unity; *(TEC)* joint; *(fig)* closeness, togetherness; **la U~ Soviética** the Soviet Union

unir [u'nir] *vt* (*juntar*) to join, unite; (*atar*) to tie, fasten; (*combinar*) to combine; **~se** *vr* to join together, unite; (*empresas*) to merge

unísono [u'nisono] *nm*: **al ~** in unison

universal [uniβer'sal] *adj* universal; (*mundial*) world *cpd*

universidad [uniβersi'ðað] *nf* university

universitario, a [uniβersi'tarjo, a] *adj* university *cpd* ♦ *nm/f* (*profesor*) lecturer; (*estudiante*) (university) student; (*graduado*) graduate

universo [uni'βerso] *nm* universe

─────── PALABRA CLAVE ───────

uno, a ['uno, a] *adj* one; **es todo ~** it's all one and the same; **~s pocos** a few; **~s cien** about a hundred
♦ *pron* **1** one; **quiero ~ solo** I only want one; **~ de ellos** one of them
2 (*alguien*) somebody, someone; **conozco a ~ que se te parece** I know somebody *o* someone who looks like you; **~ mismo** oneself; **~s querían quedarse** some (people) wanted to stay
3: **(los) ~s ... (los) otros ...** some ... others; each other, one another; **una y otra son muy agradables** they're both very nice
♦ *nf* one; **es la una** it's one o'clock
♦ *nm* (number) one

─────────────────────────────

untar [un'tar] *vt* to rub; (*engrasar*) to grease, oil; (*fig*) to bribe

uña ['uɲa] *nf* (*ANAT*) nail; (*garra*) claw; (*casco*) hoof; (*arrancaclavos*) claw

uranio [u'ranjo] *nm* uranium

urbanidad [urβani'ðað] *nf* courtesy, politeness

urbanismo [urβa'nismo] *nm* town planning

urbanización [urβaniθa'θjon] *nf* (*barrio, colonia*) housing estate

urbanizar [urβani'θar] *vt* (*zona*) to develop, urbanize

urbano, a [ur'βano, a] *adj* (*de ciudad*) urban; (*cortés*) courteous, polite

urbe ['urβe] *nf* large city

urdimbre [ur'ðimbre] *nf* (*de tejido*) warp; (*intriga*) intrigue

urdir [ur'ðir] *vt* to warp; (*fig*) to plot, contrive

urgencia [ur'xenθja] *nf* urgency; (*prisa*) haste, rush; (*emergencia*) emergency; **servicios de ~** emergency services; **urgente** *adj* urgent

urgir [ur'xir] *vi* to be urgent; **me urge** I'm in a hurry for it

urinario, a [uri'narjo, a] *adj* urinary ♦ *nm* urinal

urna ['urna] *nf* urn; (*POL*) ballot box

urraca [u'rraka] *nf* magpie

URSS *nf*: **la ~** the USSR

Uruguay [uru'ɣwai] *nm*: **el ~** Uruguay; **uruguayo, a** *adj*, *nm/f* Uruguayan

usado, a [u'saðo, a] *adj* used; (*ropa etc*) worn

usanza [u'sanθa] *nf* custom, usage

usar [u'sar] *vt* to use; (*ropa*) to wear; (*tener costumbre*) to be in the habit of; **~se** *vr* to be used; **uso** *nm* use; wear; (*costumbre*) usage, custom; (*moda*) fashion; **al uso** in keeping with custom; **al uso de** in the style of

usted [us'teð] *pron* (*sg*) you *sg*; (*pl*): **~es** you *pl*

usual [u'swal] *adj* usual

usuario, a [usu'arjo, a] *nm/f* user

usufructo [usu'frukto] *nm* use

usura [u'sura] *nf* usury; **usurero, a** *nm/f* usurer

usurpar [usur'par] *vt* to usurp

utensilio [uten'siljo] *nm* tool; (*CULIN*) utensil

útero ['utero] *nm* uterus, womb

útil ['util] *adj* useful ♦ *nm* tool; **utilidad** *nf* usefulness; (*COM*) profit; **utilizar** *vt* to use, utilize

utopía [uto'pia] *nf* Utopia; **utópico, a** *adj* Utopian

uva ['uβa] *nf* grape

V v

V *abr* (= *voltio*) V

va *vb ver* **ir**

vaca ['baka] *nf* (*animal*) cow; **carne de ~** beef

vacaciones [baka'θjones] *nfpl* holidays

vacante [ba'kante] *adj* vacant, empty ♦ *nf* vacancy

vaciar [ba'θjar] *vt* to empty out; (*ahuecar*) to hollow out; (*moldear*) to cast ♦ *vi* (*río*): **~ (en)** to flow (into); **~se** *vr* to empty

vacilación [baθila'θjon] *nf* hesitation

vacilante [baθi'lante] *adj* unsteady; (*habla*) faltering; (*fig*) hesitant

vacilar [baθi'lar] *vi* to be unsteady; (*al hablar*) to falter; (*fig*) to hesitate, waver; (*memoria*) to fail

vacío, a [ba'θio, a] *adj* empty; (*puesto*) vacant; (*desocupado*) idle; (*vano*) vain ♦ *nm* emptiness; (*FÍSICA*) vacuum; (*un ~*) (empty) space

vacuna [ba'kuna] *nf* vaccine; **vacunar** *vt* to vaccinate

vacuno, a [ba'kuno, a] *adj* cow *cpd*; **ganado ~** cattle

vacuo, a ['bakwo, a] *adj* empty

vadear [baðe'ar] *vt* (*río*) to ford; **vado** *nm* ford

vagabundo, a [baɣa'βundo, a] *adj* wandering; (*pey*) vagrant ♦ *nm* tramp

vagamente [baɣa'mente] *adv* vaguely

vagancia [ba'ɣanθja] *nf* (*pereza*) idleness, laziness

vagar [ba'ɣar] *vi* to wander; (*no hacer nada*) to idle

vagina [ba'xina] *nf* vagina

vago, a ['baɣo, a] *adj* vague; (*perezoso*) lazy; (*ambulante*) wandering ♦ *nm/f* (*vagabundo*) tramp; (*flojo*) lazybones *sg*, idler

vagón [ba'ɣon] *nm* (*FERRO: de pasajeros*) carriage; (: *de mercancías*) wagon

vaguedad [baɣe'ðað] *nf* vagueness

vaho ['bao] *nm* (*vapor*) vapour, steam; (*respiración*) breath

vaina ['baina] *nf* sheath

vainilla [bai'niʎa] *nf* vanilla

vainita [bai'nita] (*AM*) *nf* green *o* French bean

vais *vb ver* **ir**

vaivén [bai'βen] *nm* to-and-fro movement; (*de tránsito*) coming and going; **vaivenes** *nmpl* (*fig*) ups and downs

vajilla [ba'xiʎa] *nf* crockery, dishes *pl*; **lavar la ~** to do the washing-up (*BRIT*), wash the dishes (*US*)

valdré *etc vb ver* **valer**

vale ['bale] *nm* voucher; (*recibo*) receipt; (*pagaré*) IOU

valedero, a [bale'ðero, a] *adj* valid

valenciano, a [balen'θjano, a] *adj* Valenciano

valentía [balen'tia] *nf* courage, bravery; (*acción*) heroic deed

valer [ba'ler] *vt* to be worth; (*MAT*) to equal; (*costar*) to cost ♦ *vi* (*ser útil*) to be useful; (*ser válido*) to be valid; **~se** *vr* to defend o.s.; **~se de** to make use of, take advantage of; **~ la pena** to be worthwhile; **¿vale?** (*ESP*) OK?

valeroso, a [bale'roso, a] *adj* brave, valiant

valgo *etc vb ver* **valer**

valía [ba'lia] *nf* worth, value

validar [bali'ðar] *vt* to validate; **validez** *nf* validity; **válido, a** *adj* valid

valiente [ba'ljente] *adj* brave, valiant ♦ *nm* hero

valioso, a [ba'ljoso, a] *adj* valuable; (*rico*) wealthy

valor [ba'lor] *nm* value, worth; (*precio*) price; (*valentía*) valour, courage; (*importancia*) importance; **~es** *nmpl* (*COM*) securities; **~ar** *vt* to value

vals [bals] *nm inv* waltz

válvula ['balβula] *nf* valve

valla ['baʎa] *nf* fence; (*DEPORTE*) hurdle; (*fig*) barrier; **~ publicitaria** hoarding; **vallar** *vt* to fence in

valle ['baʎe] *nm* valley

vamos *vb ver* **ir**

vampiro, resa [bam'piro, 'resa] *nm/f* vampire

van *vb ver* **ir**

vanagloriarse [banaɣlo'rjarse] *vr* to boast

vandalismo [banda'lismo] *nm* vandalism; **vándalo, a** *nm/f* vandal

vanguardia [ban'gwardja] *nf* vanguard; (*ARTE etc*) avant-garde

vanidad [bani'ðað] *nf* vanity; **vanidoso, a** *adj* vain, conceited

vano, a ['bano, a] *adj* (*irreal*) unreal, vain; (*inútil*) useless; (*persona*) vain, conceited; (*frívolo*) frivolous

vapor [ba'por] *nm* vapour; (*vaho*) steam; **al ~** (*CULIN*) steamed; **~izador** *nm* atomizer; **~izar** *vt* to vaporize; **~oso, a** *adj* vaporous

vapulear [bapule'ar] *vt* to beat, thrash

vaquero, a [ba'kero, a] *adj* cattle *cpd* ♦ *nm* cowboy; **~s** *nmpl* (*pantalones*) jeans

vaquilla [ba'kiʎa] *nf* (*ZOOL*) heifer

vara ['bara] *nf* stick; (*TEC*) rod; **~ mágica** magic wand

variable [ba'rjaβle] *adj, nf* variable

variación [baria'θjon] *nf* variation

variar [bar'jar] *vt* to vary; (*modificar*) to modify; (*cambiar de posición*) to switch around ♦ *vi* to vary

varices [ba'riθes] *nfpl* varicose veins

variedad [barje'ðað] *nf* variety

varilla [ba'riʎa] *nf* stick; (*BOT*) twig; (*TEC*) rod; (*de rueda*) spoke

vario, a ['barjo, a] *adj* varied; **~s** various, several

varita [ba'rita] *nf*: **~ mágica** magic wand

varón [ba'ron] *nm* male, man; **varonil** *adj* manly, virile

Varsovia [bar'soβja] *n* Warsaw

vas *vb ver* **ir**

vasco, a ['basko, a] *adj, nm/f* Basque

vascongado, a [baskon'gaðo, a] *adj* Basque; **las Vascongadas** the Basque Country

vascuence [bas'kwenθe] *adj* = **vascongado**

vaselina [base'lina] *nf* Vaseline ®

vasija [ba'sixa] *nf* container, vessel

vaso ['baso] *nm* glass, tumbler; (*ANAT*) vessel

vástago ['bastaɣo] *nm* (*BOT*) shoot; (*TEC*) rod; (*fig*) offspring

vasto, a ['basto, a] *adj* vast, huge
Vaticano [bati'kano] *nm*: **el ~** the Vatican
vaticinio [bati'θinjo] *nm* prophecy
vatio ['batjo] *nm (ELEC)* watt
vaya *etc vb ver* **ir**
Vd(s) *abr* = **usted(es)**
ve *vb ver* **ir**; **ver**
vecindad [beθin'daθ] *nf* neighbourhood; *(habitantes)* residents *pl*
vecindario [beθin'darjo] *nm* neighbourhood; residents *pl*
vecino, a [be'θino, a] *adj* neighbouring ♦ *nm/f* neighbour; *(residente)* resident
veda ['beθa] *nf* prohibition
vedado [be'θaθo] *nm* preserve
vedar [be'θar] *vt (prohibir)* to ban, prohibit; *(impedir)* to stop, prevent
vegetación [bexeta'θjon] *nf* vegetation
vegetariano, a [bexeta'rjano, a] *adj, nm/f* vegetarian
vegetal [bexe'tal] *adj, nm* vegetable
vehemencia [be(e)'menθja] *nf (insistencia)* vehemence; *(pasión)* passion; *(fervor)* fervour; *(violencia)* violence; **vehemente** *adj* vehement; passionate; fervent
vehículo [be'ikulo] *nm* vehicle; *(MED)* carrier
veía *etc vb ver* **ver**
veinte ['beinte] *num* twenty
vejación [bexa'θjon] *nf* vexation; *(humillación)* humiliation
vejar [be'xar] *vt (irritar)* to annoy, vex; *(humillar)* to humiliate
vejez [be'xeθ] *nf* old age
vejiga [be'xiɣa] *nf (ANAT)* bladder
vela ['bela] *nf (de cera)* candle; *(NAUT)* sail; *(insomnio)* sleeplessness; *(vigilia)* vigil; *(MIL)* sentry duty; **estar a dos ~s** *(fam)* to be skint
velado, a [be'laθo, a] *adj* veiled; *(sonido)* muffled; *(FOTO)* blurred ♦ *nf* soirée
velar [be'lar] *vt (vigilar)* to keep watch over ♦ *vi* to stay awake; **~ por** to watch over, look after
velatorio [bela'torjo] *nm (funeral)* wake
veleidad [belei'θaθ] *nf (ligereza)* fickleness; *(capricho)* whim
velero [be'lero] *nm (NAUT)* sailing ship; *(AVIAT)* glider
veleta [be'leta] *nf* weather vane
veliz [be'lis] *(AM) nm* suitcase
velo ['belo] *nm* veil
velocidad [beloθi'θaθ] *nf* speed; *(TEC, AUTO)* gear
velocímetro [belo'θimetro] *nm* speedometer
veloz [be'loθ] *adj* fast
vello ['beʎo] *nm* down, fuzz
ven *vb ver* **venir**
vena ['bena] *nf* vein
venado [be'naθo] *nm* deer
vencedor, a [benθe'θor, a] *adj* victorious ♦

nm/f victor, winner
vencer [ben'θer] *vt (dominar)* to defeat, beat; *(derrotar)* to vanquish; *(superar, controlar)* to overcome, master ♦ *vi (triunfar)* to win (through), triumph; *(plazo)* to expire; **vencido, a** *adj (derrotado)* defeated, beaten; *(COM)* due ♦ *adv*: **pagar vencido** to pay in arrears; **vencimiento** *nm (COM)* maturity
venda ['benda] *nf* bandage; **~je** *nm* bandage, dressing; **vendar** *vt* to bandage; **vendar los ojos** to blindfold
vendaval [benda'βal] *nm (viento)* gale
vendedor, a [bende'θor, a] *nm/f* seller
vender [ben'der] *vt* to sell; **~ al contado/al por mayor/al por menor** to sell for cash/ wholesale/retail
vendimia [ben'dimja] *nf* grape harvest
vendré *etc vb ver* **venir**
veneno [be'neno] *nm* poison; *(de serpiente)* venom; **~so, a** *adj* poisonous; venomous
venerable [bene'raβle] *adj* venerable; **venerar** *vt (respetar)* to revere; *(adorar)* to worship
venéreo, a [be'nereo, a] *adj*: **enfermedad venérea** venereal disease
venezolano, a [beneθo'lano, a] *adj* Venezuelan
Venezuela [bene'θwela] *nf* Venezuela
venganza [ben'ganθa] *nf* vengeance, revenge; **vengar** *vt* to avenge; **vengarse** *vr* to take revenge; **vengativo, a** *adj (persona)* vindictive
vengo *etc vb ver* **venir**
venia ['benja] *nf (perdón)* pardon; *(permiso)* consent
venial [be'njal] *adj* venial
venida [be'niθa] *nf (llegada)* arrival; *(regreso)* return
venidero, a [beni'θero, a] *adj* coming, future
venir [be'nir] *vi* to come; *(llegar)* to arrive; *(ocurrir)* to happen; *(fig)*: **~ de** to stem from; **~ bien/mal** to be suitable/ unsuitable; **el año que viene** next year; **~se abajo** to collapse
venta ['benta] *nf (COM)* sale; **~ a plazos** hire purchase; **~ al contado/al por mayor/al por menor** *o* **al detalle** cash sale/wholesale/retail; **~ con derecho a retorno** sale or return; **"en ~"** "for sale"
ventaja [ben'taxa] *nf* advantage; **ventajoso, a** *adj* advantageous
ventana [ben'tana] *nf* window; **ventanilla** *nf (de taquilla)* window *(of booking office etc)*
ventilación [bentila'θjon] *nf* ventilation; *(corriente)* draught; **ventilar** *vt* to ventilate; *(para secar)* to put out to dry; *(fig)* to air, discuss
ventisca [ben'tiska] *nf* blizzard; *(nieve amontonada)* snowdrift

ventrílocuo, a [ben'trilokwo, a] *nm/f* ventriloquist

ventura [ben'tura] *nf* (*felicidad*) happiness; (*buena suerte*) luck; (*destino*) fortune; **a la (buena) ~** at random; **venturoso, a** *adj* happy; (*afortunado*) lucky, fortunate

veo *etc vb ver* **ver**

ver [ber] *vt* to see; (*mirar*) to look at, watch; (*entender*) to understand; (*investigar*) to look into; ♦ *vi* to see; to understand; **~se** *vr* (*encontrarse*) to meet; (*dejarse ~*) to be seen; (*hallarse: en un apuro*) to find o.s., be ♦ *nm* looks *pl*, appearance; **a ~** let's see; **dejarse ~** to become apparent; **no tener nada que ~ con** to have nothing to do with; **a mi modo de ~** as I see it

vera ['bera] *nf* edge, verge; (*de río*) bank

veracidad [beraθi'ðað] *nf* truthfulness

veranear [berane'ar] *vi* to spend the summer; **veraneo** *nm* summer holiday; **veraniego, a** *adj* summer *cpd*

verano [be'rano] *nm* summer

veras ['beras] *nfpl* truth *sg*; **de ~** really, truly

veraz [be'raθ] *adj* truthful

verbal [ber'ßal] *adj* verbal

verbena [ber'ßena] *nf* (*fiesta*) fair; (*baile*) open-air dance

verbo ['berßo] *nm* verb; **~so, a** *adj* verbose

verdad [ber'ðað] *nf* truth; (*fiabilidad*) reliability; **de ~** real, proper; **a decir ~** to tell the truth; **~ero, a** *adj* (*veraz*) true, truthful; (*fiable*) reliable; (*fig*) real

verde ['berðe] *adj* green; (*chiste*) blue, dirty ♦ *nm* green; **viejo ~** dirty old man; **~ar** *vi* to turn green; **verdor** *nm* (*lo ~*) greenness; (*BOT*) verdure

verdugo [ber'ðuɣo] *nm* executioner

verdulero, a [berðu'lero, a] *nm/f* greengrocer

verduras [ber'ðuras] *nfpl* (*CULIN*) greens

vereda [be'reða] *nf* path; (*AM*) pavement (*BRIT*), sidewalk (*US*)

veredicto [bere'ðikto] *nm* verdict

vergonzoso, a [berɣon'θoso, a] *adj* shameful; (*tímido*) timid, bashful

vergüenza [ber'ɣwenθa] *nf* shame, sense of shame; (*timidez*) bashfulness; (*pudor*) modesty; **me da ~** I'm ashamed

verídico, a [be'riðiko, a] *adj* true, truthful

verificar [berifi'kar] *vt* to check; (*corroborar*) to verify; (*llevar a cabo*) to carry out; **~se** *vr* to occur, happen

verja ['berxa] *nf* (*cancela*) iron gate; (*FERRO*) line; (*fig*) iron railings *pl*; (*de ventana*) grille

vermut [ber'mut] (*pl* **~s**) *nm* vermouth

verosímil [bero'simil] *adj* likely, probable; (*relato*) credible

verruga [be'rruɣa] *nf* wart

versado, a [ber'saðo, a] *adj*: **~ en** versed in

versátil [ber'satil] *adj* versatile

versión [ber'sjon] *nf* version

verso ['berso] *nm* verse; **un ~** a line of poetry

vértebra ['berteßra] *nf* vertebra

verter [ber'ter] *vt* (*líquido: adrede*) to empty, pour (out); (: *sin querer*) to spill; (*basura*) to dump ♦ *vi* to flow

vertical [berti'kal] *adj* vertical

vértice ['bertiθe] *nm* vertex, apex

vertiente [ber'tjente] *nf* slope; (*fig*) aspect

vertiginoso, a [bertixi'noso, a] *adj* giddy, dizzy

vértigo ['bertiɣo] *nm* vertigo; (*mareo*) dizziness

vesícula [be'sikula] *nf* blister

vespertino, a [besper'tino, a] *adj* evening *cpd*

vestíbulo [bes'tiβulo] *nm* hall; (*de teatro*) foyer

vestido [bes'tiðo] *pp de* **vestir**; **~ de azul/ marinero** dressed in blue/as a sailor ♦ *nm* (*ropa*) clothes *pl*, clothing; (*de mujer*) dress, frock

vestigio [bes'tixjo] *nm* (*huella*) trace; **~s** *nmpl* (*restos*) remains

vestimenta [besti'menta] *nf* clothing

vestir [bes'tir] *vt* (*poner: ropa*) to put on; (*llevar: ropa*) to wear; (*proveer de ropa a*) to clothe; (*suj: sastre*) to make clothes for ♦ *vi* to dress; (*vérse bien*) to look good; **~se** *vr* to get dressed, dress o.s.

vestuario [bes'twarjo] *nm* clothes *pl*, wardrobe; (*TEATRO: cuarto*) dressing room; (*DEPORTE*) changing room

veta ['beta] *nf* (*vena*) vein, seam; (*en carne*) streak; (*de madera*) grain

vetar [be'tar] *vt* to veto

veterano, a [bete'rano, a] *adj, nm* veteran

veterinaria [beteri'narja] *nf* veterinary science; *ver tb* **veterinario**

veterinario, a [beteri'narjo, a] *nm/f* vet(erinary surgeon)

veto ['beto] *nm* veto

vetusto, a [be'tusto, a] *adj* ancient

vez [beθ] *nf* time; (*turno*) turn; **a la ~ que** at the same time as; **a su ~** in its turn; **otra ~** again; **una ~** once; **de una ~** in one go; **de una ~ para siempre** once and for all; **en ~ de** instead of; **a o algunas veces** sometimes; **una y otra ~** repeatedly; **de ~ en cuando** from time to time; **7 veces 9** 7 times 9; **hacer las veces de** to stand in for; **tal ~** perhaps

vía ['bia] *nf* track, route; (*FERRO*) line; (*fig*) way; (*ANAT*) passage, tube ♦ *prep* via, by way of; **por ~ judicial** by legal means; **por ~ oficial** through official channels; **en ~s de** in the process of; **~ aérea** airway; **V~ Láctea** Milky Way; **~ pública** public road *o* thoroughfare

viable ['bjaßle] *adj* (*solución, plan, alternativa*) feasible

viaducto [bja'ðukto] *nm* viaduct
viajante [bja'xante] *nm* commercial traveller
viajar [bja'xar] *vi* to travel; **viaje** *nm* journey; (*gira*) tour; (*NAUT*) voyage; **estar de viaje** to be on a journey; **viaje de ida y vuelta** round trip; **viaje de novios** honeymoon; **viajero, a** *adj* travelling; (*ZOOL*) migratory ♦ *nm/f* (*quien viaja*) traveller; (*pasajero*) passenger
vial [bjal] *adj* road *cpd*, traffic *cpd*
víbora ['bißora] *nf* viper; (*AM*) poisonous snake
vibración [bißra'θjon] *nf* vibration
vibrar [bi'ßrar] *vt*, *vi* to vibrate
vicario [bi'karjo] *nm* curate
vicepresidente [biθepresi'ðente] *nm/f* vice-president
viceversa [biθe'ßersa] *adv* vice versa
viciado, a [bi'θjaðo, a] *adj* (*corrompido*) corrupt; (*contaminado*) foul, contaminated; **viciar** *vt* (*pervertir*) to pervert; (*JUR*) to nullify; (*estropear*) to spoil; **viciarse** *vr* to become corrupted
vicio [bi'θjo] *nm* vice; (*mala costumbre*) bad habit; **~so, a** *adj* (*muy malo*) vicious; (*corrompido*) depraved ♦ *nm/f* depraved person
vicisitud [biθisi'tuð] *nf* vicissitude
víctima ['biktima] *nf* victim
victoria [bik'torja] *nf* victory; **victorioso, a** *adj* victorious
vicuña [bi'kuɲa] *nf* vicuna
vid [bið] *nf* vine
vida ['biða] *nf* (*gen*) life; (*duración*) lifetime; **de por ~** for life; **en la/mi ~** never; **estar con ~** to be still alive; **ganarse la ~** to earn one's living
vídeo ['biðeo] *nm* video ♦ *adj inv*: **película ~** video film; **~cámara** *nf* camcorder; **~club** *nm* video club
vidriero, a [bi'ðrjero, a] *nm/f* glazier ♦ *nf* (*ventana*) stained-glass window; (*AM*: *de tienda*) shop window; (*puerta*) glass door
vidrio ['biðrjo] *nm* glass
vieira ['bjeira] *nf* scallop
viejo, a ['bjexo, a] *adj* old ♦ *nm/f* old man/woman; **hacerse ~** to get old
Viena ['bjena] *n* Vienna
vienes *etc vb ver* **venir**
vienés, esa [bje'nes, esa] *adj* Viennese
viento ['bjento] *nm* wind; **hacer ~** to be windy
vientre ['bjentre] *nm* belly; (*matriz*) womb
viernes ['bjernes] *nm inv* Friday; **V~ Santo** Good Friday
Vietnam [bjet'nam] *nm*: **el ~** Vietnam; **vietnamita** *adj* Vietnamese
viga ['biɣa] *nf* beam, rafter; (*de metal*) girder
vigencia [bi'xenθja] *nf* validity; **estar en ~** to be in force; **vigente** *adj* valid, in force;

(*imperante*) prevailing
vigésimo, a [bi'xesimo, a] *adj* twentieth
vigía [bi'xia] *nm* look-out ♦ *nf* (*atalaya*) watchtower; (*acción*) watching
vigilancia [bixi'lanθja] *nf*: **tener a uno bajo ~** to keep watch on sb
vigilar [bixi'lar] *vt* to watch over ♦ *vi* (*gen*) to be vigilant; (*hacer guardia*) to keep watch; **~ por** to take care of
vigilia [vi'xilja] *nf* wakefulness, being awake; (*REL*) fast
vigor [bi'ɣor] *nm* vigour, vitality; **en ~** in force; **entrar/poner en ~** to come/put into effect; **~oso, a** *adj* vigorous
VIH *nm abr de* **virus de la inmunodeficiencia humana** HIV; **~ positivo/negativo** HIV-positive/-negative
vil [bil] *adj* vile, low; **~eza** *nf* vileness; (*acto*) base deed
vilipendiar [bilipen'djar] *vt* to vilify, revile
vilo ['bilo]: **en ~** *adv* in the air, suspended; (*fig*) on tenterhooks, in suspense
villa ['biʎa] *nf* (*casa*) villa; (*pueblo*) small town; (*municipalidad*) municipality; **~ miseria** (*AM*) shantytown
villancico [biʎan'θiko] *nm* (Christmas) carol
villorrio [bi'ʎorrjo] (*AM*) *nm* shantytown
vinagre [bi'naɣre] *nm* vinegar
vinagreta [bina'ɣreta] *nf* vinaigrette, French dressing
vinatero, a [bina'tero, a] *adj* wine *cpd* ♦ *nm* wine merchant
vinculación [binkula'θjon] *nf* (*lazo*) link, bond; (*acción*) linking
vincular [binku'lar] *vt* to link, bind; **vínculo** *nm* link, bond
vine *etc vb ver* **venir**
vinicultura [binikul'tura] *nf* wine growing
viniera *etc vb ver* **venir**
vino ['bino] *vb ver* **venir** ♦ *nm* wine; **~ blanco/tinto** white/red wine
viña ['biɲa] *nf* vineyard; **viñedo** *nm* vineyard
viola ['bjola] *nf* viola
violación [bjola'θjon] *nf* violation; (*estupro*): **~ (sexual)** rape
violar [bjo'lar] *vt* to violate; (*cometer estupro*) to rape
violencia [bjo'lenθja] *nf* (*fuerza*) violence, force; (*embarazo*) embarrassment; (*acto injusto*) unjust act; **violentar** *vt* to force; (*casa*) to break into; (*agredir*) to assault; (*violar*) to violate; **violento, a** *adj* violent; (*furioso*) furious; (*situación*) embarrassing; (*acto*) forced, unnatural
violeta [bjo'leta] *nf* violet
violín [bjo'lin] *nm* violin
violón [bjo'lon] *nm* double bass
viraje [bi'raxe] *nm* turn; (*de vehículo*) swerve; (*de carretera*) bend; (*fig*) change of direction; **virar** *vi* to change direction

virgen ['birxen] *adj, nf* virgin
Virgo ['birγo] *nm* Virgo
viril [bi'ril] *adj* virile; **~idad** *nf* virility
virtud [bir'tuð] *nf* virtue; **en ~ de** by virtue of; **virtuoso, a** *adj* virtuous ♦ *nm/f* virtuoso
viruela [bi'rwela] *nf* smallpox; **~s** *nfpl* (*granos*) pockmarks
virulento, a [biru'lento, a] *adj* virulent
virus ['birus] *nm inv* virus
visa ['bisa] (*AM*) *nf* = visado
visado [bi'saðo] *nm* visa
víscera ['bisθera] *nf* (*ANAT, ZOOL*) gut, bowel; **~s** *nfpl* entrails
visceral [bisθe'ral] *adj* (*odio*) intense; **reacción ~** gut reaction
viscoso, a [bis'koso, a] *adj* viscous
visera [bi'sera] *nf* visor
visibilidad [bisiβili'ðað] *nf* visibility; **visible** *adj* visible; (*fig*) obvious
visillos [bi'siʎos] *nmpl* lace curtains
visión [bi'sjon] *nf* (*ANAT*) vision, (eye)sight; (*fantasía*) vision, fantasy
visita [bi'sita] *nf* call, visit; (*persona*) visitor; **hacer una ~** to pay a visit
visitar [bisi'tar] *vt* to visit, call on
vislumbrar [bislum'brar] *vt* to glimpse, catch a glimpse of; **vislumbre** *nf* glimpse; (*centelleo*) gleam; (*idea vaga*) glimmer
viso ['biso] *nm* (*del metal*) glint, gleam; (*de tela*) sheen; (*aspecto*) appearance
visón [bi'son] *nm* mink
visor [bi'sor] *nm* (*FOTO*) viewfinder
víspera ['bispera] *nf*: **la ~ de ...** the day before ...
vista ['bista] *nf* sight, vision; (*capacidad de ver*) (eye)sight; (*mirada*) look(s) (*pl*) ♦ *nm* customs officer; **a primera ~** at first glance; **hacer la ~ gorda** to turn a blind eye; **volver la ~** to look back; **está a la ~ que** it's obvious that; **en ~ de** in view of; **en ~ de que** in view of the fact that; **¡hasta la ~!** so long!, see you!; **con ~s a** with a view to; **~zo** *nm* glance; **dar o echar un ~zo a** to glance at
visto, a ['bisto, a] *pp de* **ver** ♦ *vb ver tb* **vestir** ♦ *adj* seen; (*considerado*) considered ♦ *nm*: **~ bueno** approval; **"~ bueno"** "approved"; **por lo ~** apparently; **está ~ que** it's clear that; **está bien/mal ~** it's acceptable/unacceptable; **~ que** since, considering that
vistoso, a [bis'toso, a] *adj* colourful
visual [bi'swal] *adj* visual
vital [bi'tal] *adj* life *cpd*, living *cpd*; (*fig*) vital; (*persona*) lively, vivacious; **~icio, a** *adj* for life; **~idad** *nf* (*de persona, negocio*) energy; (*de ciudad*) liveliness
vitamina [bita'mina] *nf* vitamin
viticultor, a [bitikul'tor, a] *nm/f* wine grower; **viticultura** *nf* wine growing
vitorear [bitore'ar] *vt* to cheer, acclaim

vítores ['bitores] *nmpl* cheers
vitrina [bi'trina] *nf* show case; (*AM*) shop window
vituperio [bitu'perjo] *nm* (*condena*) condemnation; (*censura*) censure; (*insulto*) insult
viudez *nf* widowhood
viudo, a ['bjuðo, a] *nm/f* widower/widow
viva ['biβa] *excl* hurrah!: **¡~ el rey!** long live the king!
vivacidad [biβaθi'ðað] *nf* (*vigor*) vigour; (*vida*) liveliness
vivaracho, a [biβa'ratʃo, a] *adj* jaunty, lively; (*ojos*) bright, twinkling
vivaz [bi'βaθ] *adj* lively
víveres ['biβeres] *nmpl* provisions
vivero [bi'βero] *nm* (*para plantas*) nursery; (*para peces*) fish farm; (*fig*) hotbed
viveza [bi'βeθa] *nf* liveliness; (*agudeza: mental*) sharpness
vivienda [bi'βjenda] *nf* housing; (*una ~*) house; (*piso*) flat (*BRIT*), apartment (*US*)
viviente [bi'βjente] *adj* living
vivir [bi'βir] *vt, vi* to live ♦ *nm* life, living
vivo, a ['biβo, a] *adj* living, alive; (*fig: descripción*) vivid; (*persona: astuto*) smart, clever; **en ~** (*transmisión etc*) live
vocablo [bo'kaβlo] *nm* (*palabra*) word; (*término*) term
vocabulario [bokaβu'larjo] *nm* vocabulary
vocación [boka'θjon] *nf* vocation; **vocacional** (*AM*) *nf* ≈ technical college
vocal [bo'kal] *adj* vocal ♦ *nf* vowel; **~izar** *vt* to vocalize
vocear [boθe'ar] *vt* (*para vender*) to cry; (*aclamar*) to acclaim; (*fig*) to proclaim ♦ *vi* to yell; **vocerío** *nm* shouting
vocero [bo'θero] *nm/f* spokesman/woman
voces ['boθes] *pl de* **voz**
vociferar [boθife'rar] *vt* to shout ♦ *vi* to yell
vodka ['boðka] *nm o f* vodka
vol *abr* = **volumen**
volador, a [bola'ðor, a] *adj* flying
volandas [bo'landas]: **en ~** *adv* in the air; (*fig*) swiftly
volante [bo'lante] *adj* flying ♦ *nm* (*de coche*) steering wheel; (*de reloj*) balance
volar [bo'lar] *vt* (*edificio*) to blow up ♦ *vi* to fly
volátil [bo'latil] *adj* volatile
volcán [bol'kan] *nm* volcano; **~ico, a** *adj* volcanic
volcar [bol'kar] *vt* to upset, overturn; (*tumbar, derribar*) to knock over; (*vaciar*) to empty out ♦ *vi* to overturn; **~se** *vr* to tip over
voleíbol [bolei'βol] *nm* volleyball
volqué *etc vb ver* **volcar**
voltaje [bol'taxe] *nm* voltage
voltear [bolte'ar] *vt* to turn over; (*volcar*) to turn upside down

voltereta [bolte'reta] nf somersault
voltio ['boltjo] nm volt
voluble [bo'luβle] adj fickle
volumen [bo'lumen] (pl **volúmenes**) nm volume; **voluminoso, a** adj voluminous; (enorme) massive
voluntad [bolun'tað] nf will; (resolución) willpower; (deseo) desire, wish
voluntario, a [bolun'tarjo, a] adj voluntary ♦ nm/f volunteer
voluntarioso, a [bolunta'rjoso, a] adj headstrong
voluptuoso, a [bolup'twoso, a] adj voluptuous
volver [bol'βer] vt (gen) to turn; (dar vuelta a) to turn (over); (voltear) to turn round, turn upside down; (poner al revés) to turn inside out; (devolver) to return ♦ vi to return, go back, come back; **~se** vr to turn round; ~ **la espalda** to turn one's back; ~ **triste** etc **a uno** to make sb sad etc; ~ **a hacer** to do again; ~ **en sí** to come to; **~se insoportable/muy caro** to get o become unbearable/very expensive; **~se loco** to go mad
vomitar [bomi'tar] vt, vi to vomit; **vómito** nm (acto) vomiting; (resultado) vomit
voraz [bo'raθ] adj voracious
vos [bos] (AM) pron you
vosotros, as [bo'sotros, as] pron you; (reflexivo): **entre/para** ~ among/for yourselves
votación [bota'θjon] nf (acto) voting; (voto) vote
votar [bo'tar] vi to vote; **voto** nm vote; (promesa) vow; **votos** (good) wishes
voy vb ver **ir**
voz [boθ] nf voice; (grito) shout; (chisme) rumour; (LING) word; **dar voces** to shout, yell; **a media** ~ in a low voice; **a** ~ **en cuello** o **en grito** at the top of one's voice; **de viva** ~ verbally; **en** ~ **alta** aloud; ~ **de mando** command
vuelco ['bwelko] vb ver **volcar** ♦ nm spill, overturning
vuelo ['bwelo] vb ver **volar** ♦ nm flight; (encaje) lace, frill; **coger al** ~ to catch in flight; ~ **charter/regular** charter/scheduled flight; ~ **libre** (DEPORTE) hang-gliding
vuelque etc vb ver **volcar**
vuelta ['bwelta] nf (gen) turn; (curva) bend, curve; (regreso) return; (revolución) revolution; (circuito) lap; (de papel, tela) reverse; (cambio) change; **a la** ~ on one's return; **a** ~ **de correo** by return of post; **dar** ~s (suj: cabeza) to spin; **dar** ~s **a una idea** to turn over an idea (in one's head); **estar de** ~ to be back; **dar una** ~ to go for a walk; (en coche) to go for a drive; ~ **ciclista** (DEPORTE) (cycle) tour
vuelto pp de **volver**
vuelvo etc vb ver **volver**

vuestro, a ['bwestro, a] adj your; **un amigo** ~ a friend of yours ♦ pron: **el** ~/**la vuestra, los ~s/las vuestras** yours
vulgar [bul'xar] adj (ordinario) vulgar; (común) common; **~idad** nf commonness; (acto) vulgarity; (expresión) coarse expression; **~idades** nfpl (banalidades) banalities; **~izar** vt to popularize
vulgo ['bulxo] nm common people
vulnerable [bulne'raβle] adj vulnerable
vulnerar [bulne'rar] vt (ley, acuerdo) to violate, breach; (derechos, intimidad) to violate; (reputación) to damage

W w

Walkman [wak'man] ® (MUS) Walkman ®
wáter ['bater] nm toilet
whisky ['wiski] nm whisky, whiskey

X x

xenofobia [kseno'foβja] nf xenophobia
xilófono [ksi'lofono] nm xylophone

Y y

y [i] conj and
ya [ja] adv (gen) already; (ahora) now; (en seguida) at once; (pronto) soon ♦ excl all right! ♦ conj (ahora que) now that; ~ **lo sé** I know; ~ **que** since
yacer [ja'θer] vi to lie

yacimiento [jaθi'mjento] *nm* deposit
yanqui ['janki] *adj, nm/f* Yankee
yate ['jate] *nm* yacht
yazco *etc vb ver* **yacer**
yedra ['jeðra] *nf* ivy
yegua ['jeɣwa] *nf* mare
yema ['jema] *nf* (*del huevo*) yoke; (*BOT*) leaf bud; (*fig*) best part; ~ **del dedo** finger-tip
yergo *etc vb ver* **erguir**
yermo, a ['jermo, a] *adj* (*despoblado*) uninhabited; (*estéril, fig*) barren ♦ *nm* wasteland
yerno ['jerno] *nm* son-in-law
yerro *etc vb ver* **errar**
yerto, a ['jerto, a] *adj* stiff
yeso ['jeso] *nm* (*GEO*) gypsum; (*ARQ*) plaster
yo ['jo] *pron* I; **soy** ~ it's me, it is I
yodo ['joðo] *nm* iodine
yoga ['joɣa] *nm* yoga
yogur(t) [jo'ɣur(t)] *nm* yoghurt
yugo ['juɣo] *nm* yoke
Yugoslavia [juɣos'laβja] *nf* Yugoslavia
yugular [juɣu'lar] *adj* jugular
yunque ['junke] *nm* anvil
yunta ['junta] *nf* yoke; **yuntero** *nm* ploughman
yute ['jute] *nm* jute
yuxtaponer [jukstapo'ner] *vt* to juxtapose; **yuxtaposición** *nf* juxtaposition

Z z

zafar [θa'far] *vt* (*soltar*) to untie; (*superficie*) to clear; ~**se** *vr* (*escaparse*) to escape; (*TEC*) to slip off
zafio, a ['θafjo, a] *adj* coarse
zafiro [θa'firo] *nm* sapphire
zaga ['θaɣa] *nf:* **a la** ~ behind, in the rear
zaguán [θa'xwan] *nm* hallway
zaherir [θae'rir] *vt* (*criticar*) to criticize
zaino, a ['θaino, a] *adj* (*color de caballo*) chestnut
zalamería [θalame'ria] *nf* flattery; **zalamero, a** *adj* flattering; (*relamido*) suave
zamarra [θa'marra] *nf* (*piel*) sheepskin; (*chaqueta*) sheepskin jacket
zambullirse [θambu'ʎirse] *vr* to dive; (*ocultarse*) to hide o.s.

zampar [θam'par] *vt* to gobble down ♦ *vi* gobble (up)
zanahoria [θana'orja] *nf* carrot
zancada [θan'kaða] *nf* stride
zancadilla [θanka'ðiʎa] *nf* trip; (*fig*) stratagem
zanco ['θanko] *nm* stilt
zancudo, a [θan'kuðo, a] *adj* long-legged ♦ *nm* (*AM*) mosquito
zángano ['θangano] *nm* drone
zanja ['θanxa] *nf* ditch; **zanjar** *vt* (*superar*) to surmount; (*resolver*) to resolve
zapata [θa'pata] *nf* half-boot; (*MECÁNICA*) shoe
zapatear [θapate'ar] *vi* to tap with one's feet
zapatería [θapate'ria] *nf* (*oficio*) shoe-making; (*tienda*) shoe shop; (*fábrica*) shoe factory; **zapatero, a** *nm/f* shoemaker
zapatilla [θapa'tiʎa] *nf* slipper; ~ **de deporte** training shoe
zapato [θa'pato] *nm* shoe
zar [θar] *nm* tsar, czar
zarandear [θarande'ar] (*fam*) *vt* to shake vigorously
zarpa ['θarpa] *nf* (*garra*) claw
zarpar [θar'par] *vi* to weigh anchor
zarza ['θarθa] *nf* (*BOT*) bramble; **zarzal** *nm* (*matorral*) bramble patch
zarzamora [θarθa'mora] *nf* blackberry
zarzuela [θar'θwela] *nf* Spanish light opera
zigzag [θiɣ'θaɣ] *nm* zigzag; **zigzaguear** *vi* to zigzag
zinc [θink] *nm* zinc
zócalo ['θokalo] *nm* (*ARQ*) plinth, base
zodíaco [θo'ðiako] *nm* (*ASTRO*) zodiac
zona ['θona] *nf* zone; ~ **fronteriza** border area
zoo ['θoo] *nm* zoo
zoología [θoolo'xia] *nf* zoology; **zoológico, a** *adj* zoological ♦ *nm* (*tb: parque* ~) zoo; **zoólogo, a** *nm/f* zoologist
zoom [θum] *nm* zoom lens
zopilote [θopi'lote] (*AM*) *nm* buzzard
zoquete [θo'kete] *nm* (*madera*) block; (*fam*) blockhead
zorro, a ['θorro, a] *adj* crafty ♦ *nm/f* fox/vixen
zozobra [θo'θoβra] *nf* (*fig*) anxiety; **zozobrar** *vi* (*hundirse*) to capsize; (*fig*) to fail
zueco ['θweko] *nm* clog
zumbar [θum'bar] *vt* (*golpear*) to hit ♦ *vi* to buzz; **zumbido** *nm* buzzing
zumo ['θumo] *nm* juice
zurcir [θur'θir] *vt* (*coser*) to darn
zurdo, a ['θurðo, a] *adj* (*mano*) left; (*persona*) left-handed
zurrar [θu'rrar] (*fam*) *vt* to wallop
zurrón [θu'rron] *nm* pouch

ENGLISH-SPANISH
INGLÉS-ESPAÑOL

─── A a ───

A [eɪ] n (MUS) la m

a [ə] indef art (before vowel or silent h: an) **1** un(a); ~ **book** un libro; **an apple** una manzana; **she's** ~ **doctor** (ella) es médica **2** (instead of the number "one") un(a); ~ **year ago** hace un año; ~ **hundred/ thousand** etc **pounds** cien/mil etc libras **3** (in expressing ratios, prices etc): **3** ~ **day/week** 3 al día/a la semana; **10 km an hour** 10 km por hora; **£5** ~ **person** £5 por persona; **30p** ~ **kilo** 30p el kilo

A.A. n abbr (= Automobile Association: BRIT) ≈ RACE m (SP); (= Alcoholics Anonymous) Alcohólicos Anónimos
A.A.A. (US) n abbr (= American Automobile Association) ≈ RACE m (SP)
aback [ə'bæk] adv: **to be taken** ~ quedar desconcertado
abandon [ə'bændən] vt abandonar; (give up) renunciar a ♦ n abandono; (wild behaviour): **with** ~ sin reparos
abate [ə'beɪt] vi (storm) amainar; (anger) aplacarse; (terror) disminuir
abattoir ['æbətwɑ:*] (BRIT) n matadero
abbey ['æbɪ] n abadía
abbot ['æbət] vt see aid
abbreviation [ə'bri:vɪ'eɪʃən] n (short form) abreviatura
abdicate ['æbdɪkeɪt] vt renunciar a ♦ vi abdicar; **abdication** [-'keɪʃən] n renuncia; (of monarch) abdicación f
abdomen ['æbdəmən] n abdomen m
abduct [æb'dʌkt] vt raptar, secuestrar
abet [ə'bɛt] vt see aid
abeyance [ə'beɪəns] n: **in** ~ (law) en desuso; (matter) en suspenso
abhor [əb'hɔ:*] vt aborrecer, abominar (de)
abide [ə'baɪd] vt: **I can't** ~ **it/him** no lo/le puedo ver; ~ **by** vt fus atenerse a

ability [ə'bɪlɪtɪ] n habilidad f, capacidad f; (talent) talento
abject ['æbdʒɛkt] adj (poverty) miserable; (apology) rastrero
ablaze [ə'bleɪz] adj en llamas, ardiendo
able ['eɪbl] adj capaz; (skilled) hábil; **to be** ~ **to do sth** poder hacer algo; ~**-bodied** adj sano; **ably** adv hábilmente
abnormal [æb'nɔ:məl] adj anormal
aboard [ə'bɔ:d] adv a bordo ♦ prep a bordo de
abode [ə'bəud] n: **of no fixed** ~ sin domicilio fijo
abolish [ə'bɔlɪʃ] vt suprimir, abolir; **abolition** [æbə'lɪʃən] n supresión f, abolición f
aborigine [æbə'rɪdʒɪnɪ] n aborigen m/f
abort [ə'bɔ:t] vt, vi abortar; ~**ion** [ə'bɔ:ʃən] n aborto; **to have an** ~**ion** abortar, hacerse abortar; ~**ive** adj malogrado
abound [ə'baund] vi: **to** ~ (**in** or **with**) abundar (de or en)

about [ə'baut] adv **1** (approximately) más o menos, aproximadamente; ~ **a hundred/ thousand** etc unos(unas) cien/mil etc; **it takes** ~ **10 hours** se tarda unas or más o menos 10 horas; **at** ~ **2 o'clock** sobre las dos; **I've just** ~ **finished** casi he terminado **2** (referring to place) por todas partes; **to leave things lying** ~ dejar las cosas (tiradas) por ahí; **to run** ~ correr por todas partes; **to walk** ~ pasearse, ir y venir **3**: **to be** ~ **to do sth** estar a punto de hacer algo

♦ prep **1** (relating to) de, sobre, acerca de; **a book** ~ **London** un libro sobre or acerca de Londres; **what is it** ~? ¿de qué se trata?, ¿qué pasa?; **we talked** ~ **it** hablamos de eso or ello; **what** or **how** ~ **doing this?** ¿qué tal si hacemos esto? **2** (referring to place) por; **to walk** ~ **the** town caminar por la ciudad

above [ə'bʌv] *adv* encima, por encima, arriba ♦ *prep* encima de; (*greater than: in number*) más de; (: *in rank*) superior a; **mentioned** ~ susodicho; ~ **all** sobre todo; ~ **board** *adj* legítimo

abrasive [ə'breɪzɪv] *adj* abrasivo; (*manner*) brusco

abreast [ə'brest] *adv* de frente; **to keep** ~ **of** (*fig*) mantenerse al corriente de

abridge [ə'brɪdʒ] *vt* abreviar

abroad [ə'brɔːd] *adv* (*to be*) en el extranjero; (*to go*) al extranjero

abrupt [ə'brʌpt] *adj* (*sudden*) brusco; (*curt*) áspero

abruptly [ə'brʌptlɪ] *adv* (*leave*) repentinamente; (*speak*) bruscamente

abscess ['æbsɪs] *n* absceso

abscond [əb'skɒnd] *vi* (*thief*): **to** ~ **with** fugarse con; (*prisoner*): **to** ~ **(from)** escaparse (de)

absence ['æbsəns] *n* ausencia

absent ['æbsənt] *adj* ausente; ~**ee** [-'tiː] *n* ausente *m/f*; ~**-minded** *adj* distraído

absolute ['æbsəluːt] *adj* absoluto; ~**ly** [-'luːtlɪ] *adv* (*totally*) totalmente; (*certainly!*) ¡por supuesto (que sí)!

absolve [əb'zɒlv] *vt*: **to** ~ **sb (from)** absolver a alguien (de)

absorb [əb'zɔːb] *vt* absorber; **to be** ~**ed in a book** estar absorto en un libro; ~**ent cotton** (*US*) *n* algodón *m* hidrófilo; ~**ing** *adj* absorbente

absorption [əb'zɔːpʃən] *n* absorción *f*

abstain [əb'steɪn] *vi*: **to** ~ **(from)** abstenerse (de)

abstinence ['æbstɪnəns] *n* abstinencia

abstract ['æbstrækt] *adj* abstracto

absurd [əb'sɜːd] *adj* absurdo

abundance [ə'bʌndəns] *n* abundancia

abuse [*n* ə'bjuːs, *vb* ə'bjuːz] *n* (*insults*) insultos *mpl*, injurias *fpl*; (*ill-treatment*) malos tratos *mpl*; (*misuse*) abuso ♦ *vt* insultar; maltratar; abusar de; **abusive** *adj* ofensivo

abysmal [ə'bɪzməl] *adj* pésimo; (*failure*) garrafal; (*ignorance*) supino

abyss [ə'bɪs] *n* abismo

AC *abbr* (= *alternating current*) corriente *f* alterna

academic [ækə'demɪk] *adj* académico, universitario; (*pej: issue*) puramente teórico ♦ *n* estudioso/a; profesor(a) *m/f* universitario/a

academy [ə'kædəmɪ] *n* (*learned body*) academia; (*school*) instituto, colegio; ~ **of music** conservatorio

accelerate [æk'sɛləreɪt] *vt, vi* acelerar; **accelerator** (*BRIT*) *n* acelerador *m*

accent ['æksent] *n* acento; (*fig*) énfasis *m*

accept [ək'sept] *vt* aceptar; (*responsibility, blame*) admitir; ~**able** *adj* aceptable;

~**ance** *n* aceptación *f*

access ['ækses] *n* acceso; **to have** ~ **to** tener libre acceso a; ~**ible** [-'sesəbl] *adj* (*place, person*) accesible; (*knowledge etc*) asequible

accessory [æk'sesərɪ] *n* accesorio; (*LAW*): ~ **to** cómplice de

accident ['æksɪdənt] *n* accidente *m*; (*chance event*) casualidad *f*; **by** ~ (*unintentionally*) sin querer; (*by chance*) por casualidad; ~**al** [-'dentl] *adj* accidental, fortuito; ~**ally** [-'dentəlɪ] *adv* sin querer; por casualidad; ~**prone** *adj* propenso a los accidentes

acclaim [ə'kleɪm] *vt* aclamar, aplaudir ♦ *n* aclamación *f*, aplausos *mpl*

acclimate [ə'klaɪmət] (*US*) *vt* = **acclimatize**

acclimatize [ə'klaɪmətaɪz] (*BRIT*) *vt*: **to become** ~**d** aclimatarse

accolade ['ækəleɪd] *n* premio

accommodate [ə'kɒmədeɪt] *vt* (*subj: person*) alojar, hospedar; (: *car, hotel etc*) tener cabida para; (*oblige, help*) complacer; **accommodating** *adj* servicial, complaciente

accommodation [əkɒmə'deɪʃən] *n* (*US* **accommodations** *npl*) alojamiento

accompaniment [ə'kʌmpənɪmənt] *n* (*MUS*) acompañamiento

accompany [ə'kʌmpənɪ] *vt* acompañar

accomplice [ə'kʌmplɪs] *n* cómplice *m/f*

accomplish [ə'kʌmplɪʃ] *vt* (*finish*) concluir; (*achieve*) lograr; ~**ed** *adj* experto, hábil; ~**ment** *n* (*skill: gen pl*) talento; (*completion*) realización *f*

accord [ə'kɔːd] *n* acuerdo ♦ *vt* conceder; **of his own** ~ espontáneamente; ~**ance** *n*: **in** ~**ance with** de acuerdo con; ~**ing**: ~**ing to** *prep* según; (*in accordance with*) conforme a; ~**ingly** *adv* (*appropriately*) de acuerdo con esto; (*as a result*) en consecuencia

accordion [ə'kɔːdɪən] *n* acordeón *m*

accost [ə'kɒst] *vt* abordar, dirigirse a

account [ə'kaunt] *n* (*COMM*) cuenta; (*report*) informe *m*; ~**s** *npl* (*COMM*) cuentas *fpl*; **of no** ~ de ninguna importancia; **on** ~ a cuenta; **on no** ~ bajo ningún concepto; **on** ~ **of** a causa de, por motivo de; **to take into** ~, **take** ~ **of** tener en cuenta; ~ **for** *vt fus* (*explain*) explicar; (*represent*) representar; ~**able** *adj*: ~**able to** responsable (ante)

accountancy [ə'kauntənsɪ] *n* contabilidad *f*

accountant [ə'kauntənt] *n* contable *m/f*, contador(a) *m/f*

account number *n* (*at bank etc*) número de cuenta

accredited [ə'kredɪtɪd] *adj* (*agent etc*) autorizado

accrued interest [ə'kruːd-] *n* interés *m* acumulado

accumulate [ə'kjuːmjuleɪt] *vt* acumular ♦ *vi* acumularse

accuracy ['ækjʊrəsı] n (of total) exactitud f; (of description etc) precisión f

accurate ['ækjʊrɪt] adj (total) exacto; (description) preciso; (person) cuidadoso; (device) de precisión; **~ly** adv con precisión

accusation [ækjuːˈzeɪʃən] n acusación f

accuse [əˈkjuːz] vt: to ~ sb (of sth) acusar a uno (de algo); **~d** n (LAW) acusado/a

accustom [əˈkʌstəm] vt acostumbrar; **~ed** adj: ~ed to acostumbrado a

ace [eɪs] n as m

ache [eɪk] n dolor m ♦ vi doler; **my head ~s** me duele la cabeza

achieve [əˈtʃiːv] vt (aim, result) alcanzar; (success) lograr, conseguir; **~ment** n (completion) realización f; (success) éxito

acid ['æsɪd] adj ácido; (taste) agrio ♦ n (CHEM, inf: LSD) ácido; ~ **rain** n lluvia ácida

acknowledge [əkˈnɒlɪdʒ] vt (letter: also: ~ receipt of) acusar recibo de; (fact, situation, person) reconocer; **~ment** n acuse m de recibo

acne ['æknɪ] n acné m

acorn ['eɪkɔːn] n bellota

acoustic [əˈkuːstɪk] adj acústico; **~s** n, npl acústica sg

acquaint [əˈkweɪnt] vt: to ~ sb with sth (inform) poner a uno al corriente de algo; **to be ~ed with** conocer; **~ance** n (person) conocido/a; (with person, subject) conocimiento

acquiesce [ækwɪˈɛs] vi: to ~ (to) consentir (en)

acquire [əˈkwaɪə*] vt adquirir; **acquisition** [ækwɪˈzɪʃən] n adquisición f

acquit [əˈkwɪt] vt absolver, exculpar; to ~ o.s. well salir con éxito

acre ['eɪkə*] n acre m

acrid ['ækrɪd] adj acre

acrimonious [ækrɪˈməʊnɪəs] adj (remark) mordaz; (argument) reñido

acrobat ['ækrəbæt] n acróbata m/f

acronym ['ækrənɪm] n siglas fpl

across [əˈkrɒs] prep (on the other side of) al otro lado de, del otro lado de; (crosswise) a través de ♦ adv de un lado a otro, de una parte a otra; a través; (measurement): **the road is 10m ~** la carretera tiene 10m de ancho; **to run/swim ~** atravesar corriendo/nadando; **~ from** enfrente de

acrylic [əˈkrɪlɪk] adj acrílico ♦ n acrílica

act [ækt] n acto, acción f; (of play) acto; (in music hall etc) número; (LAW) decreto, ley f ♦ vi (behave) comportarse; (have effect: drug, chemical) hacer efecto; (THEATRE) actuar; (pretend) fingir; (take action) obrar ♦ vt (part) hacer el papel de; **in the ~ of: to catch sb in the ~ of ...** pillar a uno en el momento en que ...; **to ~** as actuar or hacer de; **~ing** adj suplente ♦ n (activity) actuación f; (profession) profesión f de actor

action ['ækʃən] n acción f, acto; (MIL) acción f, batalla; (LAW) proceso, demanda; **out of ~** (person) fuera de combate; (thing) estropeado; **to take ~** tomar medidas; **~ replay** n (TV) repetición f

activate ['æktɪveɪt] vt activar

active ['æktɪv] adj activo, enérgico; (volcano) en actividad; **~ly** adv (participate) activamente; (discourage, dislike) enérgicamente; **activist** n activista m/f; **activity** [-'tɪvɪtɪ] n actividad f

actor ['æktə*] n actor m

actress ['æktrɪs] n actriz f

actual ['æktjuəl] adj verdadero, real; (emphatic use) propiamente dicho; **~ly** adv realmente, en realidad; (even) incluso

acumen ['ækjumən] n perspicacia

acute [əˈkjuːt] adj agudo

ad [æd] n abbr = advertisement

A.D. adv abbr (= anno Domini) A.C

adamant ['ædəmənt] adj firme, inflexible

adapt [əˈdæpt] vt adaptar ♦ vi: to ~ (to) adaptarse (a), ajustarse (a); **~able** adj adaptable; **~er** or **~or** n (ELEC) adaptador m

add [æd] vt añadir, agregar; (figures: also: ~ up) sumar ♦ vi: to ~ to (increase) aumentar, acrecentar; **it doesn't ~ up** (fig) no tiene sentido

adder ['ædə*] n víbora

addict ['ædɪkt] n adicto/a; (enthusiast) entusiasta m/f; **~ed** [əˈdɪktɪd] adj: to be ~ed to ser adicto a; (football etc) ser fanático de; **~ion** [əˈdɪkʃən] n (to drugs etc) adicción f; **~ive** [əˈdɪktɪv] adj que causa adicción

addition [əˈdɪʃən] n (adding up) adición f; (thing added) añadidura, añadido; **in ~** además, por añadidura; **in ~ to** además de; **~al** adj adicional

additive ['ædɪtɪv] n aditivo

address [əˈdrɛs] n dirección f, señas fpl; (speech) discurso ♦ vt (letter) dirigir; (speak to) dirigirse a, dirigir la palabra a; (problem) tratar

adept ['ædɛpt] adj: ~ **at** experto or hábil en

adequate ['ædɪkwɪt] adj (satisfactory) adecuado; (enough) suficiente

adhere [ədˈhɪə*] vi: to ~ to (stick to) pegarse a; (fig: abide by) observar; (: belief etc) ser partidario de

adhesive [ədˈhiːzɪv] n adhesivo; ~ **tape** n (BRIT) cinta adhesiva; (US: MED) esparadrapo

ad hoc [ædˈhɒk] adj ad hoc

adjacent [əˈdʒeɪsənt] adj: ~ **to** contiguo a, inmediato a

adjective ['ædʒɛktɪv] n adjetivo

adjoining [əˈdʒɔɪnɪŋ] adj contiguo, vecino

adjourn [əˈdʒɜːn] vt aplazar ♦ vi suspenderse

adjudicate [əˈdʒuːdɪkeɪt] vi sentenciar

adjust [əˈdʒʌst] vt (change) modificar; (cloth-

ing) arreglar; (*machine*) ajustar ♦ *vi*: **to ~ (to)** adaptarse (a); **~able** *adj* ajustable; **~ment** *n* adaptación *f*; (*to machine, prices*) ajuste *m*

ad-lib [æd'lɪb] *vt, vi* improvisar; **ad lib** *adv* de forma improvisada

administer [əd'mɪnɪstə*] *vt* administrar; **administration** [-'treɪʃən] *n* (*management*) administración *f*; (*government*) gobierno; **administrative** [-trətɪv] *adj* administrativo

admiral ['ædmərəl] *n* almirante *m*; **A~ty** (*BRIT*) *n* Ministerio de Marina, Almirantazgo

admiration [ædmə'reɪʃən] *n* admiración *f*

admire [əd'maɪə*] *vt* admirar; **~r** *n* (*fan*) admirador(a) *m/f*

admission [əd'mɪʃən] *n* (*to university, club*) ingreso; (*entry fee*) entrada; (*confession*) confesión *f*

admit [əd'mɪt] *vt* (*confess*) confesar; (*permit to enter*) dejar entrar, dar entrada a; (*to club, organization*) admitir; (*accept: defeat*) reconocer; **to be ~ted to hospital** ingresar en el hospital; **~ to** *vt fus* confesarse culpable de; **~tance** *n* entrada; **~tedly** *adv* es cierto *or* verdad que

admonish [əd'mɒnɪʃ] *vt* amonestar

ad nauseam [æd'nɔːsɪæm] *adv* hasta el cansancio

ado [ə'duː] *n*: **without (any) more ~** sin más (ni más)

adolescent [ædəu'lɛsnt] *adj, n* adolescente *m/f*

adopt [ə'dɒpt] *vt* adoptar; **~ed** *adj* adoptivo; **~ive** *adj* adoptivo; **~ion** [ə'dɒpʃən] *n* adopción *f*

adore [ə'dɔː*] *vt* adorar

Adriatic [eɪdrɪ'ætɪk] *n*: **the ~ (Sea)** el (Mar) Adriático

adrift [ə'drɪft] *adv* a la deriva

adult ['ædʌlt] *n* adulto/a ♦ *adj* (*grown-up*) adulto; (*for adults*) para adultos

adultery [ə'dʌltərɪ] *n* adulterio

advance [əd'vɑːns] *n* (*progress*) adelanto, progreso; (*money*) anticipo, préstamo; (*MIL*) avance *m* ♦ *adj*: **~ booking** venta anticipada; **~ notice, ~ warning** previo aviso ♦ *vt* (*money*) anticipar; (*theory, idea*) proponer (para la discusión) ♦ *vi* avanzar, adelantarse; **to make ~s (to sb)** hacer proposiciones a (alguien); **in ~** por adelantado; **~d** *adj* avanzado; (*SCOL: studies*) adelantado; **~ment** *n* progreso; (*in job*) ascenso

advantage [əd'vɑːntɪdʒ] *n* (*also TENNIS*) ventaja; **to take ~ of** (*person*) aprovecharse de; (*opportunity*) aprovechar; **~ous** [ædvən'teɪdʒəs] *adj*: **~ous (to)** ventajoso (para)

Advent ['ædvənt] *n* (*REL*) Adviento

adventure [əd'vɛntʃə*] *n* aventura; **adventurous** [-tʃərəs] *adj* atrevido; aventurero

adverb ['ædvəːb] *n* adverbio

adverse ['ædvəːs] *adj* adverso, contrario

adversity [əd'vəːsɪtɪ] *n* infortunio

advert ['ædvəːt] (*BRIT*) *n abbr* = **advertisement**

advertise ['ædvətaɪz] *vi* (*in newspaper etc*) anunciar, hacer publicidad; **to ~ for** (*staff, accommodation etc*) buscar por medio de anuncios ♦ *vt* anunciar; **~ment** [əd'vəːtɪsmənt] *n* (*COMM*) anuncio; **~r** *n* anunciante *m/f*; **advertising** *n* publicidad *f*, anuncios *mpl*; (*industry*) industria publicitaria

advice [əd'vaɪs] *n* consejo, consejos *mpl*; (*notification*) aviso; **a piece of ~** un consejo; **to take legal ~** consultar con un abogado

advisable [əd'vaɪzəbl] *adj* aconsejable, conveniente

advise [əd'vaɪz] *vt* aconsejar; (*inform*): **to ~ sb of sth** informar a uno de algo; **to ~ sb against sth/doing sth** desaconsejar algo a uno/aconsejar a uno que no haga algo; **~dly** [əd'vaɪzɪdlɪ] *adv* (*deliberately*) deliberadamente; **~r** *n* = **advisor**; **advisor** *n* consejero/a, (*consultant*) asesor/a *m/f*; **advisory** *adj* consultivo

advocate ['ædvəkeɪt] *vt* abogar por ♦ *n* [-kɪt] (*lawyer*) abogado/a; (*supporter*): **~ of** defensor(a) *m/f* de

Aegean [iː'dʒiːən] *n*: **the ~ (Sea)** el (Mar) Egeo

aerial ['ɛərɪəl] *n* antena ♦ *adj* aéreo

aerobics [ɛə'rəubɪks] *n* aerobic *m*

aeroplane ['ɛərəpleɪn] (*BRIT*) *n* avión *m*

aerosol ['ɛərəsɒl] *n* aerosol *m*

aesthetic [iːs'θɛtɪk] *adj* estético

afar [ə'fɑː*] *adv*: **from ~** desde lejos

affair [ə'fɛə*] *n* asunto; (*also: love ~*) aventura (amorosa)

affect [ə'fɛkt] *vt* (*influence*) afectar, influir en; (*afflict, concern*) afectar; (*move*) conmover; **~ed** *adj* afectado

affection [ə'fɛkʃən] *n* afecto, cariño; **~ate** *adj* afectuoso, cariñoso

affiliated [əfɪlɪ'eɪtd] *adj* afiliado

affinity [ə'fɪnɪtɪ] *n* (*bond, rapport*): **to feel an ~ with** sentirse identificado con; (*resemblance*) afinidad *f*

afflict [ə'flɪkt] *vt* afligir

affluence ['æfluəns] *n* opulencia, riqueza

affluent ['æfluənt] *adj* (*wealthy*) acomodado; **the ~ society** la sociedad opulenta

afford [ə'fɔːd] *vt* (*provide*) proporcionar; **can we ~ (to buy) it?** ¿tenemos bastante dinero para comprarlo?

Afghanistan [æf'gænɪstæn] *n* Afganistán *m*

afield [ə'fiːld] *adv*: **far ~** muy lejos

afloat [ə'fləut] *adv* (*floating*) a flote

afoot [ə'fut] *adv*: **there is something ~** algo se está tramando

afraid [ə'freɪd] *adj*: **to be ~ of** (*person*) tener miedo a; (*thing*) tener miedo de; **to be**

~ **to** tener miedo de, temer; **I am ~ that** me temo que; **I am ~ not/so** lo siento, pero no/es así

afresh [ə'freʃ] *adv* de nuevo, otra vez

Africa ['æfrɪkə] *n* África; **~n** *adj*, *n* africano/a *m/f*

aft [ɑːft] *adv* (*to be*) en popa; (*to go*) a popa

after ['ɑːftə*] *prep* (*time*) después de; (*place, order*) detrás de, tras ♦ *adv* después ♦ *conj* después (de) que; **what/who are you ~?** ¿qué/a quién busca usted?; ~ **having done/he left** después de haber hecho/ después de que se marchó; **to name sb ~ sb** llamar a uno por uno; **it's twenty ~ eight** (*US*) son las ocho y veinte; **to ask ~ sb** preguntar por alguien; ~ **all** después de todo, al fin y al cabo; ~ **you!** ¡pase usted!; **~effects** *npl* consecuencias *fpl*, efectos *mpl*; **~math** *n* consecuencias *fpl*, resultados *mpl*; **~noon** *n* tarde *f*; **~s** (*inf*) *n* (*dessert*) postre *m*; **~-sales service** (*BRIT*) *n* servicio de asistencia pos-venta; **~-shave (lotion)** *n* aftershave *m*; **~thought** *n* ocurrencia (tardía); **~wards** (*US* **~ward**) *adv* después, más tarde

again [ə'gɛn] *adv* otra vez, de nuevo; **to do sth ~** volver a hacer algo; ~ **and ~** una y otra vez

against [ə'gɛnst] *prep* (*in opposition to*) en contra de; (*leaning on, touching*) contra, junto a

age [eɪdʒ] *n* edad *f*; (*period*) época ♦ *vi* envejecer(se) ♦ *vt* envejecer; **she is 20 years of ~** tiene 20 años; **to come of ~** llegar a la mayoría de edad; **it's been ~s since I saw you** hace siglos que no te veo; **~d 10** de 10 años de edad; **the ~d** ['eɪdʒɪd] *npl* los ancianos; ~ **group** *n*: **to be in the same ~ group** tener la misma edad; ~ **limit** *n* edad *f* mínima (*or* máxima)

agency ['eɪdʒənsɪ] *n* agencia

agenda [ə'dʒɛndə] *n* orden *m* del día

agent ['eɪdʒənt] *n* agente *m/f*; (*COMM: holding concession*) representante *m/f*, delegado/a; (*CHEM, fig*) agente *m*

aggravate ['ægrəveɪt] *vt* (*situation*) agravar; (*person*) irritar

aggregate ['ægrɪgeɪt] *n* conjunto

aggressive [ə'grɛsɪv] *adj* (*belligerent*) agresivo; (*assertive*) enérgico

aggrieved [ə'griːvd] *adj* ofendido, agraviado

aghast [ə'gɑːst] *adj* horrorizado

agile ['ædʒaɪl] *adj* ágil

agitate ['ædʒɪteɪt] *vt* (*trouble*) inquietar ♦ *vi*: **to ~ for/against** hacer campaña pro *or* en favor de/en contra de; **agitator** *n* agitador(a) *m/f*

AGM *n abbr* (= *annual general meeting*) asamblea anual

ago [ə'gəu] *adv*: **2 days ~** hace 2 días; **not long ~** hace poco; **how long ~?** ¿hace

cuánto tiempo?

agog [ə'gɔg] *adj* (*eager*) ansioso; (*excited*) emocionado

agonizing ['ægənaɪzɪŋ] *adj* (*pain*) atroz; (*decision, wait*) angustioso

agony ['ægənɪ] *n* (*pain*) dolor *m* agudo; (*distress*) angustia; **to be in ~** retorcerse de dolor

agree [ə'griː] *vt* (*price, date*) acordar, quedar en ♦ *vi* (*have same opinion*): **to ~ (with/that)** estar de acuerdo (con/que); (*correspond*) coincidir, concordar; (*consent*) acceder; **to ~ with** (*subj: person*) estar de acuerdo con, ponerse de acuerdo con; (: *food*) sentar bien a; (*LING*) concordar con; **to ~ to sth/to do sth** consentir en algo/ aceptar hacer algo; **to ~ that** (*admit*) estar de acuerdo en que; **~able** *adj* (*sensation*) agradable; (*person*) simpático; (*willing*) de acuerdo, conforme; **~d** *adj* (*time, place*) convenido; **~ment** *n* acuerdo; (*contract*) contrato; **in ~ment** de acuerdo, conforme

agricultural [ægrɪ'kʌltʃərəl] *adj* agrícola

agriculture ['ægrɪkʌltʃə*] *n* agricultura

aground [ə'graund] *adv*: **to run ~** (*NAUT*) encallar, embarrancar

ahead [ə'hɛd] *adv* (*in front*) delante; (*into the future*): **she had no time to think ~** no tenía tiempo de hacer planes para el futuro; ~ **of** delante de; (*in advance of*) antes de; ~ **of time** antes de la hora; **go right** *or* **straight ~** (*direction*) siga adelante; (*permission*) hazlo (*or* hágalo)

aid [eɪd] *n* ayuda, auxilio; (*device*) aparato ♦ *vt* ayudar, auxiliar; **in ~ of** a beneficio de; **to ~ and abet** (*LAW*) ser cómplice de

aide [eɪd] *n* (*person, also*: *MIL*) ayudante *m/f*

AIDS [eɪdz] *n abbr* (= *acquired immune deficiency syndrome*) SIDA *m*

ailing ['eɪlɪŋ] *adj* (*person*) enfermizo; (*economy*) debilitado

ailment ['eɪlmənt] *n* enfermedad *f*, achaque *m*

aim [eɪm] *vt* (*gun, camera*) apuntar; (*missile, remark*) dirigir; (*blow*) asestar ♦ *vi* (*also: take ~*) apuntar ♦ *n* (*in shooting: skill*) puntería; (*objective*) propósito, meta; **to ~ at** (*with weapon*) apuntar a; (*objective*) aspirar a, pretender; **to ~ to do** tener la intención de hacer; **~less** *adj* sin propósito, sin objeto

ain't [eɪnt] (*inf*) = **am not**; **aren't**; **isn't**

air [ɛə*] *n* aire *m*; (*appearance*) aspecto ♦ *vt* (*room*) ventilar; (*clothes, ideas*) airear ♦ *cpd* aéreo; **to throw sth into the ~** (*ball etc*) lanzar algo al aire; **by ~** (*travel*) en avión; **to be on the ~** (*RADIO, TV*) estar en antena; ~ **bed** (*BRIT*) *n* colchón *m* neumático; **~borne** *adj* (*in the air*) en el aire; **~-conditioned** *adj* climatizado; ~ **conditioning** *n* aire acondicionado; **~craft** *n inv* avión *m*; **~craft carrier** *n* porta(a)viones *m inv*; **~field** *n* campo de aviación; **~ force** *n* fuerzas *fpl* aéreas, aviación *f*; **~ freshener** *n* ambientador *m*; **~gun** *n* escopeta de aire comprimido; **~ hostess** (*BRIT*) *n* azafata; **~ letter** (*BRIT*) *n* carta aérea; **~lift** *n* puente *m* aéreo; **~line** *n* línea aérea; **~liner** *n* avión *m* de pasajeros; **~mail** *n*: **by ~mail** por avión; **~plane** (*US*) *n* avión *m*; **~port** *n* aeropuerto; **~ raid** *n* ataque *m* aéreo; **~sick** *adj*: **to be ~sick** marearse (en avión); **~ space** *n* espacio aéreo; **~ terminal** *n* terminal *f*; **~tight** *adj* hermético; **~-traffic controller** *n* controlador(a) *m/f* aéreo/a; **~y** *adj* (*room*) bien ventilado; (*fig: manner*) desenfadado

aisle [aɪl] *n* (*of church*) nave *f*; (*of theatre, supermarket*) pasillo

ajar [əˈdʒɑː*] *adj* entreabierto

akin [əˈkɪn] *adj*: **~ to** parecido a

alacrity [əˈlækrɪtɪ] *n* presteza

alarm [əˈlɑːm] *n* (*in shop, bank*) alarma; (*anxiety*) inquietud *f* ♦ *vt* asustar, inquietar; **~ call** *n* (*in hotel etc*) alarma; **~ clock** *n* despertador *m*

alas [əˈlæs] *adv* desgraciadamente

albeit [ɔːlˈbiːɪt] *conj* aunque

album [ˈælbəm] *n* álbum *m*; (*L.P.*) elepé *m*

alcohol [ˈælkəhɒl] *n* alcohol *m*; **~ic** [-ˈhɒlɪk] *adj*, *n* alcohólico/a *m/f*

alcove [ˈælkəʊv] *n* nicho, hueco

ale [eɪl] *n* cerveza

alert [əˈlɜːt] *adj* (*attentive*) atento; (*to danger, opportunity*) alerta ♦ *n* alerta *m*, alarma ♦ *vt* poner sobre aviso; **to be on the ~** (*also MIL*) estar alerta *or* sobre aviso

algebra [ˈældʒɪbrə] *n* álgebra

Algeria [ælˈdʒɪərɪə] *n* Argelia

alias [ˈeɪlɪəs] *adv* alias, conocido por ♦ *n* (*of criminal*) apodo; (*of writer*) seudónimo

alibi [ˈælɪbaɪ] *n* coartada

alien [ˈeɪlɪən] *n* (*foreigner*) extranjero/a; (*extraterrestrial*) extraterrestre *m/f* ♦ *adj*: **~ to** ajeno a; **~ate** *vt* enajenar, alejar

alight [əˈlaɪt] *adj* ardiendo, (*eyes*) brillante ♦ *vi* (*person*) apearse, bajar; (*bird*) posarse

align [əˈlaɪn] *vt* alinear

alike [əˈlaɪk] *adj* semejantes, iguales ♦ *adv* igualmente, del mismo modo; **to look ~** parecerse

alimony [ˈælɪmənɪ] *n* manutención *f*

alive [əˈlaɪv] *adj* vivo; (*lively*) alegre

— *KEYWORD* —

all [ɔːl] *adj* (*sg*) todo/a; (*pl*) todos/as; **~ day** todo el día; **~ night** toda la noche; **~ men** todos los hombres; **~ five came** vinieron los cinco; **~ the books** todos los libros; **~ his life** toda su vida

♦ *pron* **1** todo; **I ate it ~, I ate ~ of it** me lo comí todo; **~ of us went** fuimos todos;

~ the boys went fueron todos los chicos; **is that ~?** ¿eso es todo?, ¿algo más?; (*in shop*) ¿algo más?, ¿alguna cosa más?

2 (*in phrases*): **above ~** sobre todo; por encima de todo; **after ~** después de todo; **at ~**: **not at ~** (*in answer to question*) en absoluto; (*in answer to thanks*) ¡de nada!, ¡no hay de qué!; **I'm not at ~ tired** no estoy nada cansado/a; **anything at ~ will do** cualquier cosa viene bien; **~ in ~** a fin de cuentas

♦ *adv*: **~ alone** completamente solo/a; **it's not as hard as ~ that** no es tan difícil como lo pintas; **~ the more/the better** tanto más/mejor; **~ but** casi; **the score is 2 ~** están empatados a 2

allay [əˈleɪ] *vt* (*fears*) aquietar

all clear *n* (*after attack etc*) fin *m* de la alerta; (*fig*) luz *f* verde

allegation [ælɪˈɡeɪʃən] *n* alegato

allege [əˈledʒ] *vt* pretender; **~dly** [əˈledʒɪdlɪ] *adv* supuestamente, según se afirma

allegiance [əˈliːdʒəns] *n* lealtad *f*

allergy [ˈælədʒɪ] *n* alergia

alleviate [əˈliːvɪeɪt] *vt* aliviar

alley [ˈælɪ] *n* callejuela

alliance [əˈlaɪəns] *n* alianza

allied [ˈælaɪd] *adj* aliado

alligator [ˈælɪɡeɪtə*] *n* (*ZOOL*) caimán *m*

all-in (*BRIT*) *adj*, *adv* (*charge*) todo incluido; **~ wrestling** *n* lucha libre

all-night *adj* (*café, shop*) abierto toda la noche; (*party*) que dura toda la noche

allocate [ˈæləkeɪt] *vt* (*money etc*) asignar

allot [əˈlɒt] *vt* asignar; **~ment** *n* ración *f*; (*garden*) parcela

all-out *adj* (*effort etc*) supremo; **all out** *adv* con todas las fuerzas

allow [əˈlaʊ] *vt* permitir, dejar; (*a claim*) admitir; (*sum, time etc*) dar, conceder; (*concede*): **to ~ that** reconocer que; **to ~ sb to do** permitir a alguien hacer; **he is ~ed to ... se le permite ...; ~ for** *vt fus* tener en cuenta; **~ance** *n* subvención *f*; (*welfare payment*) subsidio, pensión *f*; (*pocket money*) dinero de bolsillo; (*tax ~*) desgravación *f*; **to make ~ances for** (*person*) disculpar a; (*thing*) tener en cuenta

alloy [ˈælɔɪ] *n* mezcla

all: **~ right** *adv* bien; (*as answer*) ¡conforme!, ¡está bien!; **~-rounder** *n*: **he's a good ~-rounder** se le da bien todo; **~-time** *adj* (*record*) de todos los tiempos

allude [əˈluːd] *vi*: **to ~ to** aludir a

alluring [əˈljʊərɪŋ] *adj* atractivo, tentador(a)

allusion [əˈluːʒən] *n* referencia, alusión *f*

ally [ˈælaɪ] *n* aliado/a ♦ *vt*: **to ~ o.s. with** aliarse con

almighty [ɔːlˈmaɪtɪ] *adj* todopoderoso; (*row etc*) imponente

almond ['ɑːmənd] *n* almendra
almost ['ɔːlməʊst] *adv* casi
alms [ɑːmz] *npl* limosna
aloft [ə'lɒft] *adv* arriba
alone [ə'ləʊn] *adj, adv* solo; **to leave sb ~** dejar a uno en paz; **to leave sth ~** no tocar algo, dejar algo sin tocar; **let ~ ... y** mucho menos ...
along [ə'lɒŋ] *prep* a lo largo de, por ♦ *adv*: **is he coming ~ with us?** ¿viene con nosotros?; **he was limping ~** iba cojeando; **~ with** junto con; **all ~** (*all the time*) desde el principio; **~side** *prep* al lado de ♦ *adv* al lado
aloof [ə'luːf] *adj* reservado ♦ *adv*: **to stand ~** mantenerse apartado
aloud [ə'laʊd] *adv* en voz alta
alphabet ['ælfəbɛt] *n* alfabeto
Alps [ælps] *npl*: **the ~** los Alpes
already [ɔːl'rɛdɪ] *adv* ya
alright [ɔːl'raɪt] (*BRIT*) *adv* = **all right**
Alsatian [æl'seɪʃən] *n* (*dog*) pastor *m* alemán
also ['ɔːlsəʊ] *adv* también, además
altar ['ɔltə*] *n* altar *m*
alter ['ɔltə*] *vt* cambiar, modificar ♦ *vi* cambiar
alteration [ɔltə'reɪʃən] *n* cambio; (*to clothes*) arreglo; (*to building*) arreglos *mpl*
alternate [*adj* ɔl'tɔːnɪt, *vb* 'ɔltɔːneɪt] *adj* (*actions etc*) alternativo; (*events*) alterno; (*US*) = **alternative** ♦ *vi*: **to ~ (with)** alternar (con); **on ~ days** un día sí y otro no; **alternating current** [-neɪtɪŋ] *n* corriente *f* alterna
alternative [ɔl tɔːnətɪv] *adj* alternativo ♦ *n* alternativa; **~ly** *adv*: **~ly one could ...** por otra parte se podría ....
although [ɔːl'ðəʊ] *conj* aunque
altitude ['æltɪtjuːd] *n* altura
alto ['æltəʊ] *n* (*female*) contralto *f*; (*male*) alto
altogether [ɔːltə'gɛðə*] *adv* completamente, del todo; (*on the whole*) en total, en conjunto
aluminium [æljuˈmɪnɪəm] (*BRIT*) *n* aluminio
aluminum [ə'luːmɪnəm] (*US*) *n* = **aluminium**
always ['ɔːlweɪz] *adv* siempre
Alzheimer's (disease) ['æltshaɪməz-] *n* enfermedad *f* de Alzheimer
am [æm] *vb see* **be**
a.m. *adv abbr* (= *ante meridiem*) de la mañana
amalgamate [ə'mælgəmeɪt] *vi* amalgamarse ♦ *vt* amalgamar, unir
amass [ə'mæs] *vt* amontonar, acumular
amateur ['æmətə*] *n* aficionado/a, amateur *m/f*; **~ish** *adj* inexperto, superficial
amaze [ə'meɪz] *vt* asombrar, pasmar; **to be ~d (at)** quedar pasmado (de); **~ment** *n*

asombro, sorpresa; **amazing** *adj* extraordinario; (*fantastic*) increíble
Amazon ['æməzən] *n* (*GEO*) Amazonas *m*
ambassador [æm'bæsədə*] *n* embajador(a) *m/f*
amber ['æmbə*] *n* ámbar *m*; **at ~** (*BRIT: AUT*) en el amarillo
ambiguity [æmbɪ'gjuɪtɪ] *n* ambigüedad *f*
ambiguous [æm'bɪgjuəs] *adj* ambiguo
ambition [æm'bɪʃən] *n* ambición *f*; **ambitious** [-ʃəs] *adj* ambicioso
amble ['æmbl] *vi* (*gen*: **~ along**) deambular, andar sin prisa
ambulance ['æmbjuləns] *n* ambulancia
ambush ['æmbʊʃ] *n* emboscada ♦ *vt* tender una emboscada a
amenable [ə'miːnəbl] *adj*: **to be ~ to** dejarse influir por
amend [ə'mɛnd] *vt* enmendar; **to make ~s** dar cumplida satisfacción; **~ment** *n* enmienda
amenities [ə'miːnɪtɪz] *npl* comodidades *fpl*
America [ə'mɛrɪkə] *n* (*USA*) Estados *mpl* Unidos; **~n** *adj*, *n* norteamericano/a *m/f*, estadounidense *m/f*
amiable ['eɪmɪəbl] *adj* amable, simpático
amicable ['æmɪkəbl] *adj* amistoso, amigable
amid(st) [ə'mɪd(st)] *prep* entre, en medio de
amiss [ə'mɪs] *adv*: **to take sth ~** tomar algo a mal; **there's something ~** pasa algo
ammonia [ə'məʊnɪə] *n* amoníaco
ammunition [æmjuˈnɪʃən] *n* municiones *fpl*
amnesty ['æmnɪstɪ] *n* amnistía
amok [ə'mɒk] *adv*: **to run ~** enloquecerse, desbocarse
among(st) [ə'mʌŋ(st)] *prep* entre, en medio de
amorous ['æmərəs] *adj* amoroso
amount [ə'maʊnt] *n* (*gen*) cantidad *f*; (*of bill etc*) suma, importe *m* ♦ *vi*: **to ~ to** sumar; (*be same as*) equivaler a, significar
amp(ère) ['æmp(ɛə*)] *n* amperio
amphibious [æm'fɪbɪəs] *adj* anfibio
amphitheatre ['æmfɪθɪətə*] (*US* **amphitheater**) *n* anfiteatro
ample ['æmpl] *adj* (*large*) grande; (*abundant*) abundante; (*enough*) bastante, suficiente
amplifier ['æmplɪfaɪə*] *n* amplificador *m*
amputate ['æmpjuteɪt] *vt* amputar
amuse [ə'mjuːz] *vt* divertir; (*distract*) distraer, entretener; **~ment** *n* diversión *f*; (*pastime*) pasatiempo; (*laughter*) risa; **~ment arcade** *n* salón *m* de juegos
an [æn] *indef art see* **a**
anaemia [ə'niːmɪə] *n* (*US* **anemia**) anemia
anaemic [-mɪk] (*US* **anemic**) *adj* anémico; (*fig*) soso, insípido
anaesthetic [ænɪs'θetɪk] *n* (*US* **anesthetic**) anestesia; **anaesthetist** [æ'niːsθɪtɪst] (*US*

anesthetist) *n* anestesista *m/f*
analog(ue) ['ænɔlɔg] *adj* (*computer, watch*) analógico
analogy [ɔ'nælɔdʒɪ] *n* analogía
analyse ['ænɔlaɪz] (*US* analyze) *vt* analizar; **analyses** [ɔ'nælɔsɪːz] *npl* of **analysis**; **analysis** [ɔ'nælɔsɪs] (*pl* **analyses**) *n* análisis *m inv*; **analyst** [-lɪst] *n* (*political ~, psycho~*) analista *m/f*; **analytic(al)** [-'lɪtɪk(ɔl)] *adj* analítico
analyze ['ænɔlaɪz] (*US*) *vt* = **analyse**
anarchist ['ænɔkɪst] *n* anarquista *m/f*
anarchy ['ænɔkɪ] *n* anarquía
anatomy [ɔ'nætɔmɪ] *n* anatomía
ancestor ['ænsɪstɔ*] *n* antepasado
anchor ['æŋkɔ*] *n* ancla, áncora ♦ *vi* (*also: to drop ~*) anclar ♦ *vt* anclar; **to weigh ~** levar anclas
anchovy ['æntʃɔvɪ] *n* anchoa
ancient ['eɪnʃɔnt] *adj* antiguo
ancillary [æn'sɪlɔrɪ] *adj* auxiliar
and [ænd] *conj* y; (*before i-, hi- + consonant*) e; **men ~ women** hombres y mujeres; **father ~ son** padre e hijo; **trees ~ grass** árboles y hierba; **~ so on** etcétera, y así sucesivamente; **try ~ come** procura venir; **he talked ~ talked** habló sin parar; **better ~ better** cada vez mejor
Andes ['ændiːz] *npl*: **the ~** los Andes
anemia *etc* [ɔ'niːmɪɔ] (*US*) = **anaemia** *etc*
anesthetic *etc* [ænɪs'θetɪk] (*US*) = **anaesthetic** *etc*
anew [ɔ'njuː] *adv* de nuevo, otra vez
angel ['eɪndʒɔl] *n* ángel *m*
anger ['æŋgɔ*] *n* cólera
angina [æn'dʒaɪnɔ] *n* angina (del pecho)
angle ['æŋgl] *n* ángulo; **from their ~** desde su punto de vista
angler ['æŋglɔ*] *n* pescador(a) *m/f* (de caña)
Anglican ['æŋglɪkɔn] *adj, n* anglicano/a *m/f*
angling ['æŋglɪŋ] *n* pesca con caña
Anglo... ['æŋglɔu] *prefix* anglo...
angrily ['æŋgrɪlɪ] *adv* coléricamente, airadamente
angry ['æŋgrɪ] *adj* enfadado, airado; (*wound*) inflamado; **to be ~ with sb/at sth** estar enfadado con alguien/por algo; **to get ~** enfadarse, enojarse
anguish ['æŋgwɪʃ] *n* (*physical*) tormentos *mpl*; (*mental*) angustia
angular ['æŋgjulɔ*] *adj* (*shape*) angular; (*features*) anguloso
animal ['ænɪmɔl] *n* animal *m*; (*pej: person*) bestia ♦ *adj* animal
animate ['ænɪmɪt] *adj* vivo; **~d** [-meɪtɪd] *adj* animado
animosity [ænɪ'mɔsɪtɪ] *n* animosidad *f*, rencor *m*
aniseed ['ænɪsiːd] *n* anís *m*
ankle ['æŋkl] *n* tobillo *m*; **~ sock** *n* calcetín *m* corto

annex [*n* 'æneks, *vb* æ'neks] *n* (*also: BRIT: annexe*) (*building*) edificio anexo ♦ *vt* (*territory*) anexionar
annihilate [ɔ'naɪɔleɪt] *vt* aniquilar
anniversary [ænɪ'vɜːsɔrɪ] *n* aniversario
announce [ɔ'nauns] *vt* anunciar; **~ment** *n* anuncio; (*official*) declaración *f*; **~r** *n* (*RADIO*) locutor(a) *m/f*; (*TV*) presentador(a) *m/f*
annoy [ɔ'nɔɪ] *vt* molestar, fastidiar; **don't get ~ed!** ¡no se enfade!; **~ance** *n* enojo; **~ing** *adj* molesto, fastidioso; (*person*) pesado
annual ['ænjuɔl] *adj* anual ♦ *n* (*BOT*) anual *m*; (*book*) anuario; **~ly** *adv* anualmente, cada año
annul [ɔ'nʌl] *vt* anular
annum ['ænɔm] *n* see **per**
anomaly [ɔ'nɔmɔlɪ] *n* anomalía
anonymous [ɔ'nɔnɪmɔs] *adj* anónimo
anorak ['ænɔræk] *n* anorak *m*
another [ɔ'nʌðɔ*] *adj* (*one more, a different one*) otro ♦ *pron* otro; see **one**
answer ['ɑːnsɔ*] *n* contestación *f*, respuesta; (*to problem*) solución *f* ♦ *vi* contestar, responder ♦ *vt* (*reply to*) contestar a, responder a; (*problem*) resolver; (*prayer*) escuchar; **in ~ to your letter** contestando *or* en contestación a su carta; **to ~ the phone** contestar *or* coger el teléfono; **to ~ the bell** *or* **the door** acudir a la puerta; **~ back** *vi* replicar, ser respondón/ona; **~ for** *vt fus* responder de *or* por; **~ to** *vt fus* (*description*) corresponder a; **~able** *adj*: **~able to sb for sth** responsable ante uno de algo; **~ing machine** *n* contestador *m* automático
ant [ænt] *n* hormiga
antagonism [æn'tægɔnɪzm] *n* antagonismo, hostilidad *f*
antagonize [æn'tægɔnaɪz] *vt* provocar la enemistad de
Antarctic [ænt'ɑːktɪk] *n*: **the ~** el Antártico
antelope ['æntɪlɔup] *n* antílope *m*
antenatal ['æntɪ'neɪtl] *adj* antenatal, prenatal; **~ clinic** *n* clínica prenatal
antenna [æn'tenɔ] (*pl* **~e**) *n* antena
anthem ['ænθɔm] *n*: **national ~** himno nacional
anthology [æn'θɔlɔdʒɪ] *n* antología
anthropology [ænθrɔ'pɔlɔdʒɪ] *n* antropología
anti... [ænti] *prefix* anti...; **~aircraft** [-'ɛɔkrɑːft] *adj* antiaéreo; **~biotic** [-baɪ'ɔtɪk] *n* antibiótico; **~body** ['æntɪbɔdɪ] *n* anticuerpo
anticipate [æn'tɪsɪpeɪt] *vt* prever; (*expect*) esperar, contar con; (*look forward to*) esperar con ilusión; (*do first*) anticiparse a, adelantarse a; **anticipation** [-'peɪʃɔn] *n* (*expectation*) previsión *f*; (*eagerness*) ilusión *f*, expectación *f*

anticlimax [æntɪ'klaɪmæks] *n* decepción *f*
anticlockwise [æntɪ'klɔkwaɪz] (*BRIT*) *adv*
en dirección contraria a la de las agujas
del reloj
antics ['æntɪks] *npl* gracias *fpl*
anticyclone [æntɪ'saɪkləʊn] *n* anticiclón *m*
antidote ['æntɪdəʊt] *n* antídoto
antifreeze ['æntɪfriːz] *n* anticongelante *m*
antihistamine [æntɪ'hɪstəmiːn] *n* antihista-
mínico
antipathy [æn'tɪpəθɪ] *n* (*between people*)
antipatía; (*to person, thing*) aversión *f*
antiquated ['æntɪkweɪtɪd] *adj* anticuado
antique [æn'tiːk] *n* antigüedad *f* ♦ *adj* antiguo; ~ **dealer** *n* anticuario/a; ~ **shop** *n*
tienda de antigüedades
antiquity [æn'tɪkwɪtɪ] *n* antigüedad *f*
anti-Semitism [æntɪ'sɛmɪtɪzm] *n* antisemi-
tismo
antiseptic [æntɪ'sɛptɪk] *adj*, *n* antiséptico
antlers ['æntləz] *npl* cuernas *fpl*, cornamen-
ta *sg*
anus ['eɪnəs] *n* ano
anvil ['ænvɪl] *n* yunque *m*
anxiety [æŋ'zaɪətɪ] *n* inquietud *f*; (*MED*) ansiedad *f*; ~ **to do** deseo de hacer
anxious ['æŋkʃəs] *adj* inquieto, preocupado; (*worrying*) preocupante; (*keen*): **to be ~
to do** tener muchas ganas de hacer

─────────── *KEYWORD* ───────────

any ['enɪ] *adj* **1** (*in questions etc*) algún/
alguna; **have you ~ butter/children?** ¿tienes mantequilla/hijos?; **if there are ~ tickets left** si quedan billetes, si queda algún
billete
2 (*with negative*): **I haven't ~ money/
books** no tengo dinero/libros
3 (*no matter which*) cualquier; ~ **excuse
will do** valdrá *or* servirá cualquier excusa;
choose ~ book you like escoge el libro
que quieras; ~ **teacher you ask will tell
you** cualquier profesor al que preguntes te
lo dirá
4 (*in phrases*): **in ~ case** de todas formas,
en cualquier caso; ~ **day now** cualquier
día (de estos); **at ~ moment** en cualquier
momento, de un momento a otro; **at ~
rate** en todo caso; ~ **time: come (at) ~
time** ven cuando quieras; **he might come
(at) ~ time** podría llegar de un momento a
otro
♦ *pron* **1** (*in questions etc*): **have you got
~?** ¿tienes alguno(s)/a(s)?; **can ~ of you
sing?** ¿sabéis/saben cantar alguno de
vosotros/ustedes?
2 (*with negative*): **I haven't ~ (of them)** no
tengo ninguno
3 (*no matter which one(s)*): **take ~ of those
books (you like)** toma cualquier libro que
quieras de ésos
♦ *adv* **1** (*in questions etc*): **do you want ~**

more soup/sandwiches? ¿quieres más
sopa/bocadillos?; **are you feeling ~ better?** ¿te sientes algo mejor?
2 (*with negative*): **I can't hear him ~ more**
ya no le oigo; **don't wait ~ longer** no es-
peres más

─────────────────────────────

anybody ['enɪbɔdɪ] *pron* cualquiera; (*in interrogative sentences*) alguien; (*in negative
sentences*): **I don't see ~** no veo a nadie; **if
~ should phone ...** si llama alguien ....
anyhow ['enɪhaʊ] *adv* (*at any rate*) de todos modos, de todas formas; (*haphazard*):
do it ~ you like hazlo como quieras; **she
leaves things just ~** deja las cosas como
quiera *or* de cualquier modo; **I shall go ~**
de todos modos iré
anyone ['enɪwʌn] *pron* = **anybody**
anything ['enɪθɪŋ] *pron* (*in questions etc*)
algo, alguna cosa; (*with negative*) nada; **can
you see ~?** ¿ves algo?; **if ~ happens to
me ...** si algo me ocurre ...; (*no matter
what*): **you can say ~ you like** puedes decir lo que quieras; ~ **will do** vale todo *or*
cualquier cosa; **he'll eat ~** come de todo
or lo que sea
anyway ['enɪweɪ] *adv* (*at any rate*) de todos
modos, de todas formas; **I shall go ~** iré
de todos modos; (*besides*): **~, I couldn't
come even if I wanted to** además, no podría venir aunque quisiera; **why are you
phoning, ~?** ¿entonces, por qué llamas?,
¿por qué llamas, pues?
anywhere ['enɪweə*] *adv* (*in questions etc*):
can you see him ~? ¿le ves por algún
lado?; **are you going ~?** ¿vas a algún sitio?; (*with negative*): **I can't see him ~** no
le veo por ninguna parte; ~ **in the world**
(*no matter where*) en cualquier parte (del
mundo); **put the books down ~** deja los
libros donde quieras
apart [ə'pɑːt] *adv* (*aside*) aparte; (*situation*):
~ **(from)** separado (de); (*movement*): **to
pull ~** separar; **10 miles ~** separados por
10 millas; **to take ~** desmontar; ~ **from**
prep aparte de
apartheid [ə'pɑːteɪt] *n* apartheid *m*
apartment [ə'pɑːtmənt] *n* (*US*) piso (*SP*),
departamento (*AM*), apartamento; (*room*)
cuarto; ~ **building** (*US*) *n* edificio de
apartamentos
apathetic [æpə'θɛtɪk] *adj* apático, indiferente
apathy ['æpəθɪ] *n* apatía, indiferencia
ape [eɪp] *n* mono ♦ *vt* imitar, remedar
aperitif [ə'perɪtɪf] *n* aperitivo
aperture ['æpətʃjʊə*] *n* rendija, resquicio;
(*PHOT*) abertura
apex ['eɪpɛks] *n* ápice *m*; (*fig*) cumbre *f*
apiece [ə'piːs] *adv* cada uno
aplomb [ə'plɔm] *n* aplomo
apologetic [əpɔlə'dʒɛtɪk] *adj* de disculpa;

(*person*) arrepentido

apologize [ə'pɒlədʒaɪz] *vi*: **to ~ (for sth to sb)** disculparse (con alguien de algo)

apology [ə'pɒlədʒɪ] *n* disculpa, excusa

apostrophe [ə'pɒstrəfɪ] *n* apóstrofo *m*

appal [ə'pɔːl] *vt* horrorizar, espantar; **~ling** *adj* espantoso; (*awful*) pésimo

apparatus [æpə'reɪtəs] *n* (*equipment*) equipo; (*organization*) aparato; (*in gymnasium*) aparatos *mpl*

apparel [ə'pærl] (*US*) *n* ropa

apparent [ə'pærənt] *adj* aparente; (*obvious*) evidente; **~ly** *adv* por lo visto, al parecer

appeal [ə'piːl] *vi* (*LAW*) apelar ♦ *n* (*LAW*) apelación *f*; (*request*) llamamiento; (*plea*) petición *f*; (*charm*) atractivo; **to ~ for** reclamar; **to ~ to** (*be attractive to*) atraer; **it doesn't ~ to me** no me atrae, no me llama la atención; **~ing** *adj* (*attractive*) atractivo

appear [ə'pɪə*] *vi* aparecer, presentarse; (*LAW*) comparecer; (*publication*) salir (a luz), publicarse; (*seem*) parecer; **to ~ on TV/in "Hamlet"** salir por la tele/hacer un papel en "Hamlet"; **it would ~ that** parecería que; **~ance** *n* aparición *f*; (*look*) apariencia, aspecto

appease [ə'piːz] *vt* (*pacify*) apaciguar; (*satisfy*) satisfacer

appendices [ə'pendɪsiːz] *npl of* appendix

appendicitis [əpendɪ'saɪtɪs] *n* apendicitis *f*

appendix [ə'pendɪks] (*pl* **appendices**) *n* apéndice *m*

appetite ['æpɪtaɪt] *n* apetito; (*fig*) deseo, anhelo

appetizer ['æpɪtaɪzə*] *n* (*drink*) aperitivo; (*food*) tapas *fpl* (*SP*)

appetizing ['æpɪtaɪzɪŋ] *adj* apetitoso

applaud [ə'plɔːd] *vt, vi* aplaudir

applause [ə'plɔːz] *n* aplausos *mpl*

apple ['æpl] *n* manzana; **~ tree** *n* manzano

appliance [ə'plaɪəns] *n* aparato

applicable [ə'plɪkəbl] *adj* (*relevant*): **to be ~ (to)** referirse (a)

applicant ['æplɪkənt] *n* candidato/a; solicitante *m/f*

application [æplɪ'keɪʃən] *n* aplicación *f*; (*for a job etc*) solicitud *f*, petición *f*; **~ form** *n* solicitud *f*

applied [ə'plaɪd] *adj* aplicado

apply [ə'plaɪ] *vt* (*paint etc*) poner; (*law etc*: *put into practice*) poner en vigor ♦ *vi*: **to ~ to** (*ask*) dirigirse a; (*be applicable*) ser aplicable a; **to ~ for** (*permit, grant, job*) solicitar; **to ~ o.s. to** aplicarse a, dedicarse a

appoint [ə'pɔɪnt] *vt* (*to post*) nombrar; **~ed** *adj*: **at the ~ed time** a la hora señalada; **~ment** *n* (*with client*) cita; (*act*) nombramiento; (*post*) puesto; (*at hairdresser etc*): **to have an ~ment** tener hora; **to make an ~ment (with sb)** citarse (con uno)

appraisal [ə'preɪzl] *n* valoración *f*

appreciable [ə'priːʃəbl] *adj* sensible

appreciate [ə'priːʃɪeɪt] *vt* apreciar, tener en mucho; (*be grateful for*) agradecer; (*be aware of*) comprender ♦ *vi* (*COMM*) aumentar(se) en valor; **appreciation** [-'eɪʃən] *n* apreciación *f*; (*gratitude*) reconocimiento, agradecimiento; (*COMM*) aumento en valor

appreciative [ə'priːʃɪətɪv] *adj* apreciativo; (*comment*) agradecido

apprehend [æprɪ'hend] *vt* detener

apprehension [æprɪ'henʃən] *n* (*fear*) aprensión *f*; **apprehensive** [-'hensɪv] *adj* aprensivo

apprentice [ə'prentɪs] *n* aprendiz/a *m/f*; **~ship** *n* aprendizaje *m*

approach [ə'prəʊtʃ] *vi* acercarse ♦ *vt* acercarse a; (*ask, apply to*) dirigirse a; (*situation, problem*) abordar ♦ *n* acercamiento; (*access*) acceso; (*to problem, situation*): **~ (to)** actitud *f* (ante); **~able** *adj* (*person*) abordable; (*place*) accesible

appropriate [*adj* ə'prəʊprɪɪt, *vb* ə'prəʊprɪeɪt] *adj* apropiado, conveniente ♦ *vt* (*take*) apropiarse de

approval [ə'pruːvəl] *n* aprobación *f*, visto bueno; (*permission*) consentimiento; **on ~** (*COMM*) a prueba

approve [ə'pruːv] *vt* aprobar; **~ of** *vt fus* (*thing*) aprobar; (*person*): **they don't ~ of her** (ella) no les parece bien

approximate [ə'prɒksɪmɪt] *adj* aproximado; **~ly** *adv* aproximadamente, más o menos

apricot ['eɪprɪkɒt] *n* albaricoque *m* (*SP*), damasco (*AM*)

April ['eɪprəl] *n* abril *m*; **~ Fools' Day** *n* el primero de abril; ≈ día *m* de los Inocentes (*28 December*)

apron ['eɪprən] *n* delantal *m*

apt [æpt] *adj* acertado, apropiado; (*likely*): **~ to do** propenso a hacer

aquarium [ə'kwɛərɪəm] *n* acuario

Aquarius [ə'kwɛərɪəs] *n* Acuario

aqueduct ['ækwɪdʌkt] *n* acueducto

Arab ['ærəb] *adj, n* árabe *m/f*

Arabian [ə'reɪbɪən] *adj* árabe

Arabic ['ærəbɪk] *adj* árabe; (*numerals*) arábigo ♦ *n* árabe *m*

arable ['ærəbl] *adj* cultivable

Aragon ['ærəgən] *n* Aragón *m*

arbitrary ['ɑːbɪtrərɪ] *adj* arbitrario

arbitration [ɑːbɪ'treɪʃən] *n* arbitraje *m*

arcade [ɑː'keɪd] *n* (*round a square*) soportales *mpl*; (*shopping mall*) galería comercial

arch [ɑːtʃ] *n* arco; (*of foot*) arco del pie ♦ *vt* arquear

archaeologist [ɑːkɪ'ɒlədʒɪst] (*US* **archeologist**) *n* arqueólogo/a

archaeology [ɑːkɪ'ɒlədʒɪ] (*US* **archeology**) *n* arqueología

archaic [ɑː'keɪɪk] *adj* arcaico

archbishop [ɑːtʃ'bɪʃəp] *n* arzobispo

archenemy *n* enemigo jurado

archeology etc [ɑːkɪˈɔlədʒɪ] (US) = **archaeology** etc

archery ['ɑːtʃərɪ] n tiro al arco

archipelago [ɑːkɪˈpelɪgəu] n archipiélago

architect ['ɑːkɪtɛkt] n arquitecto/a; **~ural** [-'tɛktʃərəl] adj arquitectónico; **~ure** n arquitectura

archives ['ɑːkaɪvz] npl archivo

Arctic ['ɑːktɪk] adj ártico ♦ n: the ~ el Ártico

ardent ['ɑːdənt] adj ardiente, apasionado

arduous ['ɑːdjuəs] adj (task) arduo; (journey) agotador(a)

are [ɑː*] vb see be

area ['ɛərɪə] n área, región f; (part of place) zona; (MATH etc) área, superficie f; (in room: e.g. dining ~) parte f; (of knowledge, experience) campo

arena [əˈriːnə] n estadio; (of circus) pista

aren't [ɑːnt] = are not

Argentina [ɑːdʒənˈtiːnə] n Argentina; **Argentinian** [-'tɪnɪən] adj, n argentino/a m/f

arguably ['ɑːgjuəblɪ] adv posiblemente

argue ['ɑːgjuː] vi (quarrel) discutir, pelearse; (reason) razonar, argumentar; **to ~ that** sostener que

argument ['ɑːgjumənt] n discusión f, pelea; (reasons) argumento; **~ative** [-'mɛntətɪv] adj discutidor(a)

Aries ['ɛərɪz] n Aries m

arise [əˈraɪz] (pt arose, pp arisen) vi surgir, presentarse

arisen [əˈrɪzn] pp of arise

aristocrat ['ærɪstəkræt] n aristócrata m/f

arithmetic [əˈrɪθmətɪk] n aritmética

ark [ɑːk] n: Noah's A~ el Arca f de Noé

arm [ɑːm] n brazo ♦ vt armar; **~s** npl armas fpl; **~ in ~** cogidos del brazo

armaments ['ɑːməmənts] npl armamento

armchair ['ɑːmtʃɛə*] n sillón m, butaca

armed [ɑːmd] adj armado; **~ robbery** n robo a mano armada

armour ['ɑːmə*] (US armor) n armadura; (MIL: tanks) blindaje m; **~ed car** n coche (SP) m or carro (AM) blindado

armpit ['ɑːmpɪt] n sobaco, axila

armrest ['ɑːmrɛst] n apoyabrazos m inv

army ['ɑːmɪ] n ejército; (fig) multitud f

aroma [əˈrəumə] n aroma m, fragancia

arose [əˈrəuz] pt of arise

around [əˈraund] adv alrededor; (in the area): **there is no one else ~** no hay nadie más por aquí ♦ prep alrededor de

arouse [əˈrauz] vt despertar; (anger) provocar

arrange [əˈreɪndʒ] vt arreglar, ordenar; (organize) organizar; **to ~ to do sth** quedar en hacer algo; **~ment** n arreglo; (agreement) acuerdo; **~ments** npl (preparations) preparativos mpl

array [əˈreɪ] n: **~ of** (things) serie f de; (people) conjunto de

arrears [əˈrɪəz] npl atrasos mpl; **to be in ~ with one's rent** estar retrasado en el pago del alquiler

arrest [əˈrɛst] vt detener; (sb's attention) llamar ♦ n detención f; **under ~** detenido

arrival [əˈraɪvəl] n llegada; **new ~** recién llegado/a; (baby) recién nacido

arrive [əˈraɪv] vi llegar; (baby) nacer

arrogant ['ærəgənt] adj arrogante

arrow ['ærəu] n flecha

arse [ɑːs] (BRIT: inf!) n culo, trasero

arsenal ['ɑːsɪnl] n arsenal m

arson ['ɑːsn] n incendio premeditado

art [ɑːt] n arte m; (skill) destreza; **A~s** npl (SCOL) Letras fpl

artery ['ɑːtərɪ] n arteria

artful ['ɑːtful] adj astuto

art gallery n pinacoteca; (saleroom) galería de arte

arthritis [ɑːˈθraɪtɪs] n artritis f

artichoke ['ɑːtɪtʃəuk] n alcachofa; **Jerusalem ~** aguaturma

article ['ɑːtɪkl] n artículo; (BRIT: LAW: training): **~s** npl contrato de aprendizaje; **~ of clothing** prenda de vestir

articulate [adj ɑːˈtɪkjulɪt, vb ɑːˈtɪkjuleɪt] adj claro, bien expresado ♦ vt expresar; **~d lorry** (BRIT) n trailer m

artificial [ɑːtɪˈfɪʃl] adj artificial; (affected) afectado

artillery [ɑːˈtɪlərɪ] n artillería

artisan ['ɑːtɪzæn] n artesano

artist ['ɑːtɪst] n artista m/f; (MUS) intérprete m/f; **~ic** [ɑːˈtɪstɪk] adj artístico; **~ry** n arte m, habilidad f (artística)

art school n escuela de bellas artes

––––––––– KEYWORD

as [æz] conj **1** (referring to time) cuando, mientras; a medida que; **~ the years went by** con el paso de los años; **he came in ~ I was leaving** entró cuando me marchaba; **~ from tomorrow** desde or a partir de mañana

2 (in comparisons): **~ big ~** tan grande como; **twice ~ big ~** el doble de grande que; **~ much money/many books ~** tanto dinero/tantos libros como; **~ soon ~** en cuanto

3 (since, because) como, ya que; **he left early ~** he had to be home by 10 se fue temprano como tenía que estar en casa a las 10

4 (referring to manner, way): **do ~ you wish** haz lo que quieras; **~ she said** como dijo; **he gave it to me ~ a present** me lo dio de regalo

5 (in the capacity of): **he works ~ a barman** trabaja de barman; **~ chairman of the company, he ...** como presidente de la compañía, ...

6 (concerning): **~ for or to that** por or en

lo que respecta a eso
7: ~ **if** or **though** como si; **he looked** ~ **if he was ill** parecía como si estuviera enfermo, tenía aspecto de enfermo; see also **long; such; well**

a.s.a.p. abbr (= as soon as possible) cuanto antes

asbestos [æz'bestəs] n asbesto, amianto

ascend [ə'send] vt subir; (throne) ascender or subir a; **~ancy** n ascendiente m, dominio

ascent [ə'sent] n subida; (slope) cuesta, pendiente f

ascertain [æsə'teɪn] vt averiguar

ascribe [ə'skraɪb] vt: **to ~ sth to** atribuir algo a

ash [æʃ] n ceniza; (tree) fresno

ashamed [ə'feɪmd] adj avergonzado, apenado (AM); **to be ~ of** avergonzarse de

ashen [æʃn] adj pálido

ashore [ə'ʃɔː*] adv en tierra; (swim etc) a tierra

ashtray ['æʃtreɪ] n cenicero

Ash Wednesday n miércoles m de Ceniza

Asia ['eɪʃə] n Asia; **~n** adj, n asiático/a m/f

aside [ə'saɪd] adv a un lado ♦ n aparte m

ask [ɑːsk] vt (question) preguntar; (invite) invitar; **to ~ sb sth/to do sth** preguntar algo a alguien/pedir a alguien que haga algo; **to ~ sb about sth** preguntar algo a alguien; **to ~ (sb) a question** hacer una pregunta (a alguien); **to ~ sb out to dinner** invitar a cenar a uno; **~ after** vt fus preguntar por; **~ for** vt fus pedir; (trouble) buscar

askance [ə'skɑːns] adv: **to look ~ at sb/ sth** mirar con recelo a uno/mirar algo con recelo

askew [ə'skjuː] adv torcido, ladeado

asking price n precio inicial

asleep [ə'sliːp] adj dormido; **to fall ~** dormirse, quedarse dormido

asparagus [əs'pærəgəs] n (plant) espárrago; (food) espárragos mpl

aspect ['æspekt] n aspecto, apariencia; (direction in which a building etc faces) orientación f

aspersions [əs'pɜːʃənz] npl: **to cast ~ on** difamar a, calumniar a

asphyxiation [æsfɪksɪ'eɪʃən] n asfixia

aspirations [æspə'reɪʃənz] npl ambición f

aspire [əs'paɪə*] vi: **to ~ to** aspirar a, ambicionar

aspirin ['æsprɪn] n aspirina

ass [æs] n asno, burro; (inf: idiot) imbécil m/f, (US: inf!) culo, trasero

assailant [ə'seɪlənt] n asaltador(a) m/f, agresor(a) m/f

assassin [ə'sæsɪn] n asesino/a; **~ate** vt asesinar; **~ation** [-'neɪʃən] n asesinato

assault [ə'sɔːlt] n asalto; (LAW) agresión f ♦ vt asaltar, atacar; (sexually) violar

assemble [ə'sembl] vt reunir, juntar; (TECH) montar ♦ vi reunirse, juntarse

assembly [ə'semblɪ] n reunión f, asamblea; (parliament) parlamento; (construction) montaje m; **~ line** n cadena de montaje

assent [ə'sent] n asentimiento, aprobación f

assert [ə'sɜːt] vt afirmar; (authority) hacer valer; **~ion** [-ʃən] n afirmación f

assess [ə'ses] vt valorar, calcular; (tax, damages) fijar; (for tax) gravar; **~ment** n valoración f; (for tax) gravamen m; **~or** n asesor(a) m/f

asset ['æset] n ventaja; **~s** npl (COMM) activo; (property, funds) fondos mpl

assign [ə'saɪn] vt: **to ~ (to)** (date) fijar (para); (task) asignar (a); (resources) destinar (a); **~ment** n tarea

assist [ə'sɪst] vt ayudar; **~ance** n ayuda, auxilio; **~ant** n ayudante m/f; (BRIT: also: shop ~ant) dependiente/a m/f

associate [adj, n ə'səʊʃɪɪt, vb ə'səʊʃɪeɪt] adj asociado ♦ n (at work) colega m/f ♦ vt asociar; (ideas) relacionar ♦ vi: **to ~ with sb** tratar con alguien

association [əsəʊsɪ'eɪʃən] n asociación f

assorted [ə'sɔːtɪd] adj surtido, variado

assortment [ə'sɔːtmənt] n (of shapes, colours) surtido; (of books) colección f; (of people) mezcla

assume [ə'sjuːm] vt suponer; (responsibilities) asumir; (attitude) adoptar, tomar; **~d name** n nombre m falso

assumption [ə'sʌmpʃən] n suposición f, presunción f; (of power etc) toma

assurance [ə'ʃʊərəns] n garantía, promesa; (confidence) confianza, aplomo; (insurance) seguro

assure [ə'ʃʊə*] vt asegurar

asthma ['æsmə] n asma

astonish [ə'stɒnɪʃ] vt asombrar, pasmar; **~ment** n asombro, sorpresa

astound [ə'staʊnd] vt asombrar, pasmar

astray [ə'streɪ] adv: **to go ~** extraviarse; **to lead ~** (morally) llevar por mal camino

astride [ə'straɪd] prep a caballo or horcajadas sobre

astrology [æs'trɒlədʒɪ] n astrología

astronaut ['æstrənɔːt] n astronauta m/f

astronomy [əs'trɒnəmɪ] n astronomía

astute [əs'tjuːt] adj astuto

asylum [ə'saɪləm] n (refuge) asilo; (mental hospital) manicomio

────── **KEYWORD** ──────

at [æt] prep **1** (referring to position) en; (direction) a; ~ **the top** en lo alto; ~ **home/ school** en casa/la escuela; **to look ~ sth/ sb** mirar algo/a uno
2 (referring to time): ~ **4 o'clock** a las 4; ~ **night** por la noche; ~ **Christmas** en Navi-

dad; ~ **times** a veces
3 (*referring to rates, speed etc*): ~ **£1 a kilo**
a una libra el kilo; **two** ~ **a time** de dos
en dos; ~ **50 km/h** a 50 km/h
4 (*referring to manner*): ~ **a stroke** de un
golpe; ~ **peace** en paz
5 (*referring to activity*): **to be** ~ **work** estar
trabajando; (*in the office etc*) estar en el trabajo; **to play** ~ **cowboys** jugar a los vaqueros; **to be good** ~ **sth** ser bueno en
algo
6 (*referring to cause*): **shocked/surprised/
annoyed** ~ **sth** asombrado/sorprendido/
fastidiado por algo; **I went** ~ **his suggestion** fui a instancias suyas

ate [eɪt] *pt of* **eat**
atheist ['eɪθɪɪst] *n* ateo/a
Athens ['æθɪnz] *n* Atenas
athlete ['æθliːt] *n* atleta *m/f*
athletic [æθ'lɛtɪk] *adj* atlético; ~**s** *n* atletismo
Atlantic [ət'læntɪk] *adj* atlántico ♦ *n*: **the** ~
(Ocean) el (Océano) Atlántico
atlas ['ætləs] *n* atlas *m*
atmosphere ['ætməsfɪə*] *n* atmósfera; (*of
place*) ambiente *m*
atom ['ætəm] *n* átomo; ~**ic** [ə'tɔmɪk] *adj*
atómico; ~**(ic) bomb** *n* bomba atómica;
~**izer** ['ætəmaɪzə*] *n* atomizador *m*
atone [ə'təʊn] *vi*: **to** ~ **for** expiar
atrocious [ə'trəʊʃəs] *adj* atroz
attach [ə'tætʃ] *vt* (*fasten*) atar; (*join*) unir,
sujetar; (*document, letter*) adjuntar; (*importance etc*) dar, conceder; **to be** ~**ed to sb/
sth** (*to like*) tener cariño a a alguien/algo
attaché [ə'tæʃeɪ] *n* agregado/a; ~ **case** *n*
maletín *m*
attachment [ə'tætʃmənt] *n* (*tool*) accesorio;
(*love*): ~ **(to)** apego (a)
attack [ə'tæk] *vt* (*MIL*) atacar; (*subj: criminal*) agredir, asaltar; (*criticize*) criticar; (*task*)
emprender ♦ *n* ataque *m*, asalto; (*on sb's
life*) atentado; (*fig: criticism*) crítica; (*of illness*) ataque *m*; **heart** ~ infarto (de miocardio); ~**er** *n* agresor/a *m/f*, asaltante *m/f*
attain [ə'teɪn] *vt* (*also*: ~ **to**) alcanzar;
(*achieve*) lograr, conseguir; ~**ments** *npl* lo-
gros *mpl*
attempt [ə'tɛmpt] *n* tentativa, intento; (*attack*) atentado ♦ *vt* intentar; ~**ed** *adj*:
burglary/murder/suicide tentativa *or* intento de robo/asesinato/suicidio
attend [ə'tɛnd] *vt* asistir a; (*patient*) atender; ~ **to** *vt fus* ocuparse de; (*customer,
patient*) atender a; ~**ance** *n* asistencia, presencia; (*people present*) concurrencia; ~**ant**
n ayudante *m/f*, (*in garage etc*) encargado/a
♦ *adj* (*dangers*) concomitante
attention [ə'tɛnʃən] *n* atención *f*, (*care*)
atenciones *fpl* ♦ *excl* (*MIL*) ¡firme(s)!; **for
the** ~ **of ...** (*ADMIN*) atención ....

attentive [ə'tɛntɪv] *adj* atento
attest [ə'tɛst] *vi*: **to** ~ **to** demostrar; (*LAW:
confirm*) dar fe de
attic ['ætɪk] *n* desván *m*
attitude ['ætɪtjuːd] *n* actitud *f*, (*disposition*)
disposición *f*
attorney [ə'tɜːnɪ] *n* (*lawyer*) abogado/a;
A~ General *n* (*BRIT*) ≈ Presidente *m* del
Consejo del Poder Judicial (*SP*); (*US*) ≈
ministro de justicia
attract [ə'trækt] *vt* atraer; (*sb's attention*)
llamar; ~**ion** [ə'trækʃən] *n* encanto; (*gen pl:
amusements*) diversiones *fpl*; (*PHYSICS*)
atracción *f*, (*fig: towards sb, sth*) atractivo;
~**ive** *adj* guapo; (*interesting*) atrayente
attribute [*n* 'ætrɪbjuːt, *vb* ə'trɪbjuːt] *n* atributo ♦ *vt*: **to** ~ **sth to** atribuir algo a
attrition [ə'trɪʃən] *n*: **war of** ~ guerra de
agotamiento
aubergine ['əʊbəʒiːn] (*BRIT*) *n* berenjena;
(*colour*) morado
auburn ['ɔːbən] *adj* color castaño rojizo
auction ['ɔːkʃən] *n* (*also: sale by* ~) subasta
♦ *vt* subastar; ~**eer** [-'nɪə*] *n* subastador(a)
m/f
audacity [ɔː'dæsɪtɪ] *n* audacia, atrevimiento; (*pej*) descaro
audible ['ɔːdɪbl] *adj* audible, que se puede
oír
audience ['ɔːdɪəns] *n* público; (*RADIO*) ra-
dioescuchas *mpl*; (*TV*) telespectadores *mpl*;
(*interview*) audiencia
audio-typist [ɔːdɪəʊ'taɪpɪst] *n*
mecanógrafo/a de dictáfono
audio-visual [ɔːdɪəʊ'vɪzjuəl] *adj* audiovisual; ~ **aid** *n* ayuda audiovisual
audit ['ɔːdɪt] *vt* revisar, intervenir
audition [ɔː'dɪʃən] *n* audición *f*
auditor ['ɔːdɪtə*] *n* interventor(a) *m/f*, cen-
sor(a) *m/f* de cuentas
augment [ɔːg'mɛnt] *vt* aumentar
augur ['ɔːgə*] *vi*: **it** ~**s well** es un buen augurio
August ['ɔːgəst] *n* agosto
aunt [ɑːnt] *n* tía; ~**ie** *n diminutive of* **aunt**;
~**y** *n diminutive of* **aunt**
au pair ['əʊ'pɛə*] *n* (*also:* ~ **girl**) (chica) *f*
au pair
auspices ['ɔːspɪsɪz] *npl*: **under the** ~ **of**
bajo los auspicios de
auspicious [ɔːs'pɪʃəs] *adj* propicio, de
buen augurio
austerity [ə'stɛrɪtɪ] *n* austeridad *f*
Australia [əs'treɪlɪə] *n* Australia; ~**n** *adj, n*
australiano/a *m/f*
Austria ['ɔstrɪə] *n* Austria; ~**n** *adj, n*
austríaco/a *m/f*
authentic [ɔː'θɛntɪk] *adj* auténtico
author ['ɔːθə*] *n* autor(a) *m/f*
authoritarian [ɔːθɔrɪ'tɛərɪən] *adj* autoritario
authoritative [ɔː'θɔrɪtətɪv] *adj* autorizado;
(*manner*) autoritario

authority [ɔːˈθɔrɪtɪ] n autoridad f; (official permission) autorización f; **the authorities** npl las autoridades

authorize [ˈɔːθəraɪz] vt autorizar

auto [ˈɔːtəu] (US) n coche m (SP), carro (AM), automóvil m

autobiography [ɔːtəbaɪˈɔɡrəfɪ] n autobiografía

autograph [ˈɔːtəɡruːf] n autógrafo ♦ vt (photo etc) dedicar; (programme) firmar

automated [ˈɔːtəmeɪtɪd] adj automatizado

automatic [ɔːtəˈmætɪk] adj automático ♦ n (gun) pistola automática; (car) coche m automático; **~ally** adv automáticamente

automation [ɔːtəˈmeɪʃən] n reconversión f

automaton [ɔːˈtɔmətən] (pl **automata**) n autómata m/f

automobile [ˈɔːtəməbiːl] (US) n coche m (SP), carro (AM), automóvil m

autonomy [ɔːˈtɔnəmɪ] n autonomía

autopsy [ˈɔːtɔpsɪ] n autopsia

autumn [ˈɔːtəm] n otoño

auxiliary [ɔːgˈzɪlɪərɪ] adj, n auxiliar m/f

avail [əˈveɪl] vt: **to ~ o.s. of** aprovechar(se) de ♦ n: **to no ~** en vano, sin resultado

available [əˈveɪləbl] adj disponible; (unoccupied) libre; (person: unattached) soltero y sin compromiso

avalanche [ˈævəlɑːnʃ] n alud m, avalancha

avant-garde [ˈævæŋˈgɑːd] adj de vanguardia

Ave. abbr = **avenue**

avenge [əˈvɛndʒ] vt vengar

avenue [ˈævənjuː] n avenida; (fig) camino

average [ˈævərɪdʒ] n promedio, término medio ♦ adj medio, de término medio; (ordinary) regular, corriente ♦ vt sacar un promedio de; **on ~** por regla general; **~ out** vi: **to ~ out at** salir en un promedio de

averse [əˈvɜːs] adj: **to be ~ to sth/doing** sentir aversión or antipatía por algo/por hacer

avert [əˈvɜːt] vt prevenir; (blow) desviar; (one's eyes) apartar

aviary [ˈeɪvɪərɪ] n pajarera, avería

avid [ˈævɪd] adj ávido, ansioso

avocado [ævəˈkɑːdəu] n (also: BRIT: ~ pear) aguacate m (SP), palta (AM)

avoid [əˈvɔɪd] vt evitar, eludir

await [əˈweɪt] vt esperar, aguardar

awake [əˈweɪk] (pt **awoke**, pp **awoken** or **awaked**) adj despierto ♦ vt despertar ♦ vi despertarse; **to be ~** estar despierto; **~ning** n el despertar

award [əˈwɔːd] n premio; (LAW: damages) indemnización f ♦ vt otorgar, conceder; (LAW: damages) adjudicar

aware [əˈwɛə*] adj: **~ (of)** consciente (de); **to become ~ of/that** (realize) darse cuenta de/de que; (learn) enterarse de/de que; **~ness** n conciencia; (knowledge) conocimiento

awash [əˈwɔʃ] adj: **~ with** (also fig) inundado de

away [əˈweɪ] adv fuera; (movement): **she went ~** se marchó; (far ~) lejos; **two kilometres ~** a dos kilómetros de distancia; **two hours ~ by car** a dos horas en coche; **the holiday was two weeks ~** faltaban dos semanas para las vacaciones; **he's ~ for a week** estará ausente una semana; **to take ~ (from)** quitar (a); (subtract) substraer (de); **to work/pedal ~** seguir trabajando/pedaleando; **to fade ~** (colour) desvanecerse; (sound) apagarse; **~ game** n (SPORT) partido de fuera

awe [ɔː] n admiración f respetuosa; **~-inspiring** adj imponente; **~some** adj imponente

awful [ˈɔːfəl] adj horroroso; (quantity): **an ~ lot (of)** cantidad (de); **~ly** adv (very) terriblemente

awhile [əˈwaɪl] adv (durante) un rato, algún tiempo

awkward [ˈɔːkwəd] adj desmañado, torpe; (shape) incómodo; (embarrassing) delicado, difícil

awning [ˈɔːnɪŋ] n (of tent, caravan, shop) toldo

awoke [əˈwəuk] pt of **awake**

awoken [əˈwəukən] pp of **awake**

awry [əˈraɪ] adv: **to be ~** estar descolocado or mal puesto; **to go ~** salir mal, fracasar

axe [æks] (US **ax**) n hacha ♦ vt (project) cortar; (jobs) reducir

axes [ˈæksiːz] npl of **axis**

axis [ˈæksɪs] (pl **axes**) n eje m

axle [ˈæksl] n eje m, árbol m

ay(e) [aɪ] excl sí

B b

B [biː] n (MUS) si m

B.A. abbr = **Bachelor of Arts**

babble [ˈbæbl] vi barbotear; (brook) murmurar

baby [ˈbeɪbɪ] n bebé m/f; (US: inf: darling) mi amor; **~ carriage** (US) n cochecito; **~-sit** vi hacer de canguro; **~-sitter** n canguro/a

bachelor [ˈbætʃələ*] n soltero; **B~ of Arts/Science** licenciado/a en Filosofía y Letras/Ciencias

back [bæk] n (of person) espalda; (of animal) lomo; (of hand) dorso; (as opposed to *front*) parte f de atrás; (*of chair*) respaldo; (*of page*) reverso; (*of book*) final m; (*of crowd*): **the ones at the ~** los del fondo; (*FOOTBALL*) defensa m ♦ vt (*candidate*: *also*: ~ up) respaldar, apoyar; (*horse: at races*) apostar a; (*car*) dar marcha atrás a or con ♦ vi (*car etc*) ir (or salir or entrar) marcha atrás ♦ adj (*payment, rent*) atrasado; (*seats, wheels*) de atrás ♦ adv (*not forward*) (hacia) atrás; (*returned*): **he's ~** está de vuelta, ha vuelto; **he ran ~** volvió corriendo; (*restitution*): **throw the ball ~** devuelve la pelota; **can I have it ~?** ¿me lo devuelve?; (*again*): **he called ~** llamó de nuevo; **~ down** vi echarse atrás; **~ out** vi (*of promise*) volverse atrás; **~ up** vt (*person*) apoyar, respaldar; (*theory*) defender; (*COMPUT*) hacer una copia preventiva or de reserva; **~bencher** (*BRIT*) n miembro del parlamento sin cargo relevante; **~bone** n columna vertebral; **~-cloth** n telón m de fondo; **~date** vt (*pay rise*) dar efecto retroactivo a; (*letter*) poner fecha atrasada a; **~drop** n = **~-cloth**; **~fire** vi (*AUT*) petardear; (*plans*) fallar, salir mal; **~ground** n fondo; (*of events*) antecedentes mpl; (*basic knowledge*) bases fpl; (*experience*) conocimientos mpl, educación f; **family ~ground** origen m, antecedentes mpl; **~hand** n (*TENNIS*: *also*: **~hand stroke**) revés m; **~hander** (*BRIT*) n (*bribe*) soborno; **~ing** n (*fig*) apoyo, respaldo; **~lash** n reacción f; **~log** n: **~log of work** trabajo atrasado; **~ number** n (*of magazine etc*) número atrasado; **~pack** n mochila; **~ pay** n pago atrasado; **~side** (*inf*) n trasero, culo; **~stage** adv entre bastidores; **~stroke** n espalda; **~up** adj suplementario; (*COMPUT*) de reserva ♦ n (*support*) apoyo; (*also*: **~up file**) copia preventiva or de reserva; **~ward** adj (*person, country*) atrasado; **~wards** adv hacia atrás; (*read a list*) al revés; (*fall*) de espaldas; **~water** n (*fig*) lugar m atrasado or apartado; **~yard** n traspatio

bacon [ˈbeɪkən] n tocino, beicon m

bad [bæd] adj malo; (*mistake, accident*) grave; (*food*) podrido, pasado; **his ~ leg** su pierna lisiada; **to go ~** (*food*) pasarse

bade [bæd, beɪd] pt of **bid**

badge [bædʒ] n insignia; (*policeman's*) chapa, placa

badger [ˈbædʒə*] n tejón m

badly [ˈbædlɪ] adv mal; **to reflect ~ on sb** influir negativamente en la reputación de uno; **~ wounded** gravemente herido; **he needs it ~** le hace gran falta; **to be ~ off** (*for money*) andar mal de dinero

badminton [ˈbædmɪntən] n bádminton m

bad-tempered adj de mal genio or carácter; (*temporarily*) de mal humor

baffle [ˈbæfl] vt desconcertar, confundir

bag [bæg] n bolsa, (*handbag*) bolso; (*satchel*) mochila; (*case*) maleta; **~s of** (*inf*) un montón de; **~gage** n equipaje m; **~gy** adj amplio; **~pipes** npl gaita

Bahamas [bəˈhɑːməz] npl: **the ~** las Islas Bahamas

bail [beɪl] n fianza ♦ vt (*prisoner: gen: grant ~ to*) poner en libertad bajo fianza; (*boat: also*: ~ out) achicar; **on ~** (*prisoner*) bajo fianza; **to ~ sb out** obtener la libertad de uno bajo fianza; *see also* **bale**

bailiff [ˈbeɪlɪf] n alguacil m

bait [beɪt] n cebo ♦ vt poner cebo en; (*tease*) tomar el pelo a

bake [beɪk] vt cocer (al horno) ♦ vi cocerse; **~d beans** npl judías fpl en salsa de tomate; **~r** n panadero; **~ry** n panadería; (*for cakes*) pastelería; **baking** n (*act*) amasar m; (*batch*) hornada; **baking powder** n levadura (en polvo)

balance [ˈbæləns] n equilibrio; (*COMM: sum*) balance m; (*remainder*) resto; (*scales*) balanza ♦ vt equilibrar; (*budget*) nivelar; (*account*) saldar; (*make equal*) equilibrar; **~ of trade/payments** balanza de comercio/pagos; **~d** adj (*personality, diet*) equilibrado; (*report*) objetivo; **~ sheet** n balance m

balcony [ˈbælkənɪ] n (*open*) balcón m; (*closed*) galería; (*in theatre*) anfiteatro

bald [bɔːld] adj calvo; (*tyre*) liso

bale [beɪl] n (*AGR*) paca, fardo; (*of papers etc*) fajo; **~ out** vi lanzarse en paracaídas

Balearics [bælɪˈærɪks] npl: **the ~** las Baleares

ball [bɔːl] n pelota; (*football*) balón m; (*of wool, string*) ovillo; (*dance*) baile m; **to play ~** (*fig*) cooperar

ballast [ˈbæləst] n lastre m

ball bearings npl cojinetes mpl de bolas

ballerina [bæləˈriːnə] n bailarina

ballet [ˈbæleɪ] n ballet m; **~ dancer** n bailarín/ina m/f

ballistics [bəˈlɪstɪks] n balística

balloon [bəˈluːn] n globo

ballot [ˈbælət] n votación f; **~ paper** n papeleta (para votar)

ball-point (pen) [ˈbɔːlpɔɪnt-] n bolígrafo

ballroom [ˈbɔːlrum] n salón m de baile

balm [bɑːm] n bálsamo

Baltic [ˈbɔːltɪk] n: **the ~ (Sea)** el (Mar) Báltico

balustrade [ˈbæləstreɪd] n barandilla

ban [bæn] n prohibición f, proscripción f ♦ vt prohibir, proscribir

banal [bəˈnɑːl] adj banal, vulgar

banana [bəˈnɑːnə] n plátano (*SP*), banana (*AM*)

band [bænd] n grupo; (*strip*) faja, tira; (*stripe*) lista; (*MUS: jazz*) orquesta; (: *rock*) grupo; (: *MIL*) banda; **~ together** vi juntarse, asociarse

bandage [ˈbændɪdʒ] n venda, vendaje m ♦ vt vendar

Bandaid ['bændeɪd] ® (US) n tirita

bandit ['bændɪt] n bandido

bandwagon ['bændwægən] n: **to jump on the ~** subirse al carro

bandy ['bændɪ] vt (jokes, insults) cambiar

bandy-legged ['bændɪ'lɛgd] adj estevado

bang [bæŋ] n (of gun, exhaust) estallido, detonación f; (of door) portazo; (blow) golpe m ♦ vt (door) cerrar de golpe; (one's head) golpear ♦ vi estallar; (door) cerrar de golpe

Bangladesh [bɑːŋglə'dɛʃ] n Bangladesh m

bangs [bæŋz] (US) npl flequillo

banish ['bænɪʃ] vt desterrar

banister(s) ['bænɪstə(z)] n(pl) barandilla, pasamanos m inv

bank [bæŋk] n (COMM) banco; (of river, lake) ribera, orilla; (of earth) terraplén m ♦ vi (AVIAT) ladearse; **~ on** vt fus contar con; **~ account** n cuenta de banco; **~ card** n tarjeta bancaria; **~er** n banquero; **~er's card** (BRIT) n = **~ card**; **B~ holiday** (BRIT) n día m festivo; **~ing** n banca; **~note** n billete m de banco; **~ rate** n tipo de interés bancario

bankrupt ['bæŋkrʌpt] adj quebrado, insolvente; **to go ~** hacer bancarrota; **to be ~** estar en quiebra; **~cy** n quiebra

bank statement n balance m or detalle m de cuenta

banner ['bænə*] n pancarta

banns [bænz] npl amonestaciones fpl

banquet ['bæŋkwɪt] n banquete m

baptism ['bæptɪzəm] n bautismo; (act) bautizo

baptize [bæp'taɪz] vt bautizar

bar [bɑː*] n (pub) bar m; (counter) mostrador m; (rod) barra; (of window, cage) reja; (of soap) pastilla; (of chocolate) tableta; (fig: hindrance) obstáculo; (prohibition) prohibición f; (MUS) barra ♦ vt (road) obstruir; (person) excluir; (activity) prohibir; **behind ~s** entre rejas; **the B~** (LAW) la abogacía; **~ none** sin excepción

barbaric [bɑː'bærɪk] adj bárbaro

barbecue ['bɑːbɪkjuː] n barbacoa

barbed wire ['bɑːbd-] n alambre m de púas

barber ['bɑːbə*] n peluquero, barbero

bar code n código de barras

bare [bɛə*] adj desnudo; (trees) sin hojas; (necessities etc) básico ♦ vt desnudar; (teeth) enseñar; **~back** adv a pelo, sin silla; **~faced** adj descarado; **~foot** adj, adv descalzo; **~ly** adv apenas

bargain ['bɑːgɪn] n pacto, negocio; (good buy) ganga ♦ vi negociar; (haggle) regatear; **into the ~** además, por añadidura; **~ for** vt fus: **he got more than he ~ed for** le resultó peor de lo que esperaba

barge [bɑːdʒ] n in vi irrumpir; (interrupt: conversation) interrumpir

bark [bɑːk] n (of tree) corteza; (of dog) la-

drido ♦ vi ladrar

barley ['bɑːlɪ] n cebada; **~ sugar** n azúcar m cande

barmaid ['bɑːmeɪd] n camarera

barman ['bɑːmən] n camarero, barman m

barn [bɑːn] n granero

barometer [bə'rɒmɪtə*] n barómetro

baron ['bærən] n barón m; (press ~ etc) magnate m; **~ess** n baronesa

barracks ['bærəks] npl cuartel m

barrage ['bærɑːʒ] n (MIL) descarga, bombardeo; (dam) presa; (of criticism) lluvia, aluvión m

barrel ['bærəl] n barril m; (of gun) cañón m

barren ['bærən] adj estéril

barricade [bærɪ'keɪd] n barricada ♦ vt cerrar con barricadas; **to ~ o.s. (in)** hacerse fuerte (en)

barrier ['bærɪə*] n barrera

barring ['bɑːrɪŋ] prep excepto, salvo

barrister ['bærɪstə*] (BRIT) n abogado/a

barrow ['bærəu] n (cart) carretilla (de mano)

bartender ['bɑːtɛndə*] (US) n camarero, barman m

barter ['bɑːtə*] vt: **to ~ sth for sth** trocar algo por algo

base [beɪs] n base f ♦ vt: **to ~ sth on** basar or fundar algo en ♦ adj bajo, infame

baseball ['beɪsbɔːl] n béisbol m

basement ['beɪsmənt] n sótano

bases¹ ['beɪsiːz] npl of **basis**

bases² ['beɪsɪz] npl of **base**

bash [bæʃ] (inf) vt golpear

bashful ['bæʃful] adj tímido, vergonzoso

basic ['beɪsɪk] adj básico; **~ally** adv fundamentalmente, en el fondo; (simply) sencillamente; **~s** npl: **the ~s** los fundamentos

basil ['bæzl] n albahaca

basin ['beɪsn] n cuenco, tazón m; (GEO) cuenca; (also: wash~) lavabo

basis ['beɪsɪs] (pl **bases**) n base f; **on a part-time/trial ~** a tiempo parcial/a prueba

bask [bɑːsk] vi: **to ~ in the sun** tomar el sol

basket ['bɑːskɪt] n cesta, cesto; canasta; **~ball** n baloncesto

Basque [bæsk] adj, n vasco/a m/f; **~ Country** n Euskadi m, País m Vasco

bass [beɪs] n (MUS: instrument) bajo; (double ~) contrabajo; (singer) bajo

bassoon [bə'suːn] n fagot m

bastard ['bɑːstəd] n bastardo; (inf!) hijo de puta (!)

bastion ['bæstɪən] n baluarte m

bat [bæt] n (ZOOL) murciélago; (for ball games) palo; (BRIT: for table tennis) pala ♦ vt: **he didn't ~ an eyelid** ni pestañeó

batch [bætʃ] n (of bread) hornada; (of letters etc) lote m

bated ['beɪtɪd] adj: **with ~ breath** sin respirar

bath [bɑːθ, *pl* bɑːðz] *n* (*action*) baño; (~*tub*) baño (*SP*), bañera (*SP*), tina (*AM*) ♦ *vt* bañar; **to have a ~** bañarse, tomar un baño; *see also* **baths**

bathe [beɪð] *vi* bañarse ♦ *vt* (*wound*) lavar; **~r** *n* bañista *m/f*

bathing ['beɪðɪŋ] *n* el bañarse; **~ cap** *n* gorro de baño; **~ costume** (*US* = **suit**) *n* traje *m* de baño

bath: **~robe** *n* (*man's*) batín *m*; (*woman's*) bata; **~room** *n* (cuarto de) baño; **~s** [bɑːðz] *npl* (*also*: *swimming* ~s) piscina; **~ towel** *n* toalla de baño

baton ['bætən] *n* (*MUS*) batuta; (*ATHLETICS*) testigo; (*weapon*) porra

batter ['bætə*] *vt* maltratar; (*subj*: *rain etc*) azotar ♦ *n* masa (para rebozar); **~ed** *adj* (*hat, pan*) estropeado

battery ['bætərɪ] *n* (*AUT*) batería; (*of torch*) pila

battle ['bætl] *n* batalla; (*fig*) lucha ♦ *vi* luchar; **~ship** *n* acorazado

bawdy ['bɔːdɪ] *adj* (*joke*) verde

bawl [bɔːl] *vi* chillar, gritar; (*child*) berrear

bay [beɪ] *n* (*GEO*) bahía; **B~ of Biscay** ≈ mar Cantábrico; **to hold sb at ~** mantener a alguien a raya; **~ leaf** *n* hoja de laurel

bay window *n* ventana salediza

bazaar [bə'zɑː*] *n* bazar *m*; (*fete*) venta con fines benéficos

B. & B. *n abbr* (= *bed and breakfast*) cama y desayuno

BBC *n abbr* (= *British Broadcasting Corporation*) cadena de radio y televisión estatal británica

B.C. *adv abbr* (= *before Christ*) a. de C

──────── KEYWORD ────────

be [biː] (*pt* **was, were**, *pp* **been**) *aux vb* **1** (*with present participle: forming continuous tenses*): **what are you doing?** ¿qué estás haciendo?, ¿qué haces?; **they're coming tomorrow** vienen mañana; **I've been waiting for you for hours** llevo horas esperándote

2 (*with pp: forming passives*) ser (*but often replaced by active or reflective constructions*); **to ~ murdered** ser asesinado; **the box had been opened** habían abierto la caja; **the thief was nowhere to ~ seen** no se veía al ladrón por ninguna parte

3 (*in tag questions*): **it was fun, wasn't it?** fue divertido, ¿no? *or* ¿verdad?; **he's good-looking, isn't he?** es guapo, ¿no te parece?; **she's back again, is she?** entonces, ¿ha vuelto?

4 (*+ to + infin*): **the house is to ~ sold** (*necessity*) hay que vender la casa; (*future*) van a vender la casa; **he's not to open it** no tiene que abrirlo

♦ *vb + complement* **1** (*with n or num complement, but see also* **3, 4, 5** *and impers vb below*) ser; **he's a doctor** es médico; **2 and 2 are 4** 2 y 2 son 4

2 (*with adj complement: expressing permanent or inherent quality*) ser; (: *expressing state seen as temporary or reversible*) estar; **I'm English** soy inglés/esa; **she's tall/pretty** es alta/bonita; **he's young** es joven; **~ careful/good/quiet** ten cuidado/pórtate bien/cállate; **I'm tired** estoy cansado/a; **it's dirty** está sucio/a

3 (*of health*) estar; **how are you?** ¿cómo estás?; **he's very ill** está muy enfermo; **I'm better now** ya estoy mejor

4 (*of age*) tener; **how old are you?** ¿cuántos años tienes?; **I'm sixteen (years old)** tengo dieciséis años

5 (*cost*) costar; ser; **how much was the meal?** ¿cuánto fue *or* costó la comida?; **that'll ~ £5.75, please** son £5.75, por favor; **this shirt is £17** esta camisa cuesta £17

♦ *vi* **1** (*exist, occur etc*) existir, haber; **the best singer that ever was** el mejor cantante que existió jamás; **is there a God?** ¿hay un Dios?, ¿existe Dios?; **~ that as it may** sea como sea; **so ~ it** así sea

2 (*referring to place*) estar; **I won't ~ here tomorrow** no estaré aquí mañana

3 (*referring to movement*): **where have you been?** ¿dónde has estado?

♦ *impers vb* **1** (*referring to time*): **it's 5 o'clock** son las 5; **it's the 28th of April** estamos a 28 de abril

2 (*referring to distance*): **it's 10 km to the village** el pueblo está a 10 km

3 (*referring to the weather*): **it's too hot/cold** hace demasiado calor/frío; **it's windy today** hace viento hoy

4 (*emphatic*): **it's me** soy yo; **it was Maria who paid the bill** fue María la que pagó la cuenta

──────────────────

beach [biːtʃ] *n* playa ♦ *vt* varar

beacon ['biːkən] *n* (*lighthouse*) faro; (*marker*) guía

bead [biːd] *n* cuenta; (*of sweat etc*) gota

beak [biːk] *n* pico

beaker ['biːkə*] *n* vaso de plástico

beam [biːm] *n* (*ARCH*) viga, travesaño; (*of light*) rayo, haz *m* de luz ♦ *vi* brillar; (*smile*) sonreír

bean [biːn] *n* judía; **runner/broad ~** habichuela/haba; **coffee ~** grano de café; **~sprouts** *npl* brotes *mpl* de soja

bear [bɛə*] (*pt* **bore**, *pp* **borne**) *n* oso ♦ *vt* (*weight etc*) llevar; (*cost*) pagar; (*responsibility*) tener; (*endure*) soportar, aguantar; (*children*) parir, tener; (*fruit*) dar ♦ *vi*: **to ~ right/left** torcer a la derecha/izquierda; **~ out** (*suspicions*) corroborar, confirmar; (*person*) dar la razón a; **~ up** *vi* (*remain* *cheerful*) mantenerse animado

beard [bɪəd] *n* barba; **~ed** *adj* con barba, barbudo

bearer ['bɛərə*] *n* portador(a) *m/f*

bearing ['bɛərɪŋ] *n* porte *m*, comportamiento; (*connection*) relación *f*; **~s** *npl* (*also: ball ~s*) cojinetes *mpl* a bolas; **to take a ~** tomar marcaciones; **to find one's ~s** orientarse

beast [biːst] *n* bestia; (*inf*) bruto, salvaje *m*; **~ly** (*inf*) *adj* horrible

beat [biːt] (*pt* beat, *pp* beaten) *n* (*of heart*) latido; (*MUS*) ritmo, compás *m*; (*of policeman*) ronda ♦ *vt* pegar, golpear; (*eggs*) batir; (*defeat: opponent*) vencer, derrotar; (: *record*) sobrepasar ♦ *vi* (*heart*) latir; (*drum*) redoblar; (*rain, wind*) azotar; **off the ~en track** aislado; **to ~ it** (*inf*) largarse; **~ off** *vt* rechazar; **~ up** *vt* (*attack*) dar una paliza a; **~ing** *n* paliza

beautiful ['bjuːtɪful] *adj* precioso, hermoso, bello; **~ly** *adv* maravillosamente

beauty ['bjuːtɪ] *n* belleza; **~ salon** *n* salón *m* de belleza; **~ spot** *n* (*TOURISM*) lugar *m* pintoresco

beaver ['biːvə*] *n* castor *m*

became [bɪ'keɪm] *pt* of become

because [bɪ'kɔz] *conj* porque; **~ of** debido a, a causa de

beck [bek] *n*: **to be at the ~ and call of** estar a disposición de

beckon ['bekən] *vt* (*also: ~ to*) llamar con señas

become [bɪ'kʌm] (*irreg: like come*) *vt* (*suit*) favorecer, sentar bien a ♦ *vi* (+*n*) hacerse, llegar a ser; (+*adj*) ponerse, volverse; **to ~ fat** engordar

becoming [bɪ'kʌmɪŋ] *adj* (*behaviour*) decoroso; (*clothes*) favorecedor(a)

bed [bed] *n* cama; (*of flowers*) macizo; (*of coal, clay*) capa; (*of river*) lecho; (*of sea*) fondo; **to go to ~** acostarse; **~ and breakfast** *n* (*place*) pensión *f*; (*terms*) cama y desayuno; **~clothes** *npl* ropa de cama; **~ding** *n* ropa de cama

bedlam ['bedləm] *n* desbarajuste *m*

bedraggled [bɪ'dræɡld] *adj* (*untidy: person*) desastrado; (*clothes, hair*) desordenado

bed: **~ridden** *adj* postrado (en cama); **~room** *n* dormitorio; **~side** *n*: **at the ~side of** a la cabecera de; **~sit(ter)** (*BRIT*) *n* estudio (*SP*), suite *m* (*AM*); **~spread** *n* cubrecama *m*, colcha; **~time** *n* hora de acostarse

bee [biː] *n* abeja

beech [biːtʃ] *n* haya

beef [biːf] *n* carne *f* de vaca; **roast ~** rosbif *m*; **~burger** *n* hamburguesa; **B~eater** *n* alabardero de la Torre de Londres

beehive ['biːhaɪv] *n* colmena

beeline ['biːlaɪn] *n*: **to make a ~ for** ir derecho a

been [biːn] *pp* of be

beer [bɪə*] *n* cerveza

beet [biːt] (*US*) *n* (*also: red ~*) remolacha

beetle ['biːtl] *n* escarabajo

beetroot ['biːtruːt] (*BRIT*) *n* remolacha

before [bɪ'fɔː*] *prep* (*of time*) antes de; (*of space*) delante de ♦ *conj* antes (de) que ♦ *adv* antes, anteriormente; delante, adelante; **~ going** antes de marcharse; **~ she goes** antes de que se vaya; **the week ~** la semana anterior; **I've never seen it ~** no lo he visto nunca; **~hand** *adv* de antemano, con anticipación

beg [beɡ] *vi* pedir limosna ♦ *vt* pedir, rogar; (*entreat*) suplicar; **to ~ sb to do sth** rogar a uno que haga algo; *see also* pardon

began [bɪ'ɡæn] *pt* of begin

beggar ['beɡə*] *n* mendigo/a *m/f*

begin [bɪ'ɡɪn] (*pt* began, *pp* begun) *vt*, *vi* empezar, comenzar; **to ~ doing** *or* **to do sth** empezar a hacer algo; **~ner** *n* principiante *m/f*; **~ning** *n* principio, comienzo

begun [bɪ'ɡʌn] *pp* of begin

behalf [bɪ'hɑːf] *n*: **on ~ of** en nombre de, por; (*for benefit of*) en beneficio de; **on my/his ~** por mí/él

behave [bɪ'heɪv] *vi* (*person*) portarse, comportarse; (*well: also: ~ o.s.*) portarse bien; **behaviour** (*US* **behavior**) *n* comportamiento, conducta

behead [bɪ'hed] *vt* decapitar

beheld [bɪ'held] *pt, pp* of behold

behind [bɪ'haɪnd] *prep* detrás de; (*supporting*): **to be ~ sb** apoyar a alguien; (*lower in rank etc*) estar por detrás de ♦ *adv* detrás, por detrás, atrás ♦ *n* trasero; **to be ~ (schedule)** ir retrasado; **~ the scenes** (*fig*) entre bastidores

behold [bɪ'həuld] (*irreg: like hold*) *vt* contemplar

beige [beɪʒ] *adj* color beige

being [biːɪŋ] *n* ser *m*; (*existence*): **in ~** existente; **to come into ~** aparecer

belated [bɪ'leɪtɪd] *adj* atrasado, tardío

belch [beltʃ] *vi* eructar ♦ *vt* (*gen: ~ out: smoke etc*) arrojar

belfry ['belfrɪ] *n* campanario

Belgian ['beldʒən] *adj, n* belga *m/f*

Belgium ['beldʒəm] *n* Bélgica

belie [bɪ'laɪ] *vt* desmentir, contradecir

belief [bɪ'liːf] *n* opinión *f*; (*faith*) fe *f*

believe [bɪ'liːv] *vt, vi* creer; **to ~ in** creer en; **~r** *n* partidario/a; (*REL*) creyente *m/f*, fiel *m/f*

belittle [bɪ'lɪtl] *vt* quitar importancia a

bell [bel] *n* campana; (*small*) campanilla; (*on door*) timbre *m*

belligerent [bɪ'lɪdʒərənt] *adj* agresivo

bellow ['beləu] *vi* bramar; (*person*) rugir; **~s** *npl* fuelle *m*

belly ['belɪ] *n* barriga, panza

belong [bɪ'lɒŋ] *vi*: **to ~ to** pertenecer a;

(*club etc*) ser socio de; **this book ~s here** este libro va aquí; **~ings** *npl* pertenencias *fpl*

beloved [bɪ'lʌvɪd] *adj* querido/a

below [bɪ'ləu] *prep* bajo, debajo de; (*less than*) inferior a ◊ *adv* abajo, (por) debajo; **see ~** véase más abajo

belt [bɛlt] *n* cinturón *m*; (*TECH*) correa, cinta ◊ *vt* (*thrash*) pegar con correa; **~way** (*US*) *n* (*AUT*) carretera de circunvalación

bemused [bɪ'mju:zd] *adj* aturdido

bench [bɛntʃ] *n* banco; (*BRIT: POL*): **the Government/Opposition ~es** (los asientos de) los miembros del Gobierno/de la Oposición; **the B~** (*LAW: judges*) magistratura

bend [bɛnd] (*pt, pp* bent) *vt* doblar ◊ *vi* inclinarse ◊ *n* (*BRIT: in road, river*) curva; (*in pipe*) codo; **~ down** *vi* inclinarse, doblarse; **~ over** *vi* inclinarse

beneath [bɪ'ni:θ] *prep* bajo, debajo de; (*unworthy of*) indigno de ◊ *adv* abajo, (por) debajo

benefactor ['bɛnɪfæktə*] *n* bienhechor *m*

beneficial [bɛnɪ'fɪʃəl] *adj* beneficioso

benefit ['bɛnɪfɪt] *n* beneficio; (*allowance of money*) subsidio ◊ *vt* beneficiar ◊ *vi*: **he'll ~ from it** le sacará provecho

benevolent [bɪ'nɛvələnt] *adj* (*person*) benévolo

benign [bɪ'naɪn] *adj* benigno; (*smile*) afable

bent [bɛnt] *pt, pp of* bend ◊ *n* inclinación *f* ◊ *adj*: **to be ~ on** estar empeñado en

bequest [bɪ'kwɛst] *n* legado

bereaved [bɪ'ri:vd] *npl*: **the ~** los íntimos de una persona afligidos por su muerte

beret ['bɛreɪ] *n* boina

Berlin [bə:'lɪn] *n* Berlín

berm [bə:m] (*US*) *n* (*AUT*) arcén *m*

Bermuda [bə:'mju:də] *n* las Bermudas

berry ['bɛrɪ] *n* baya

berserk [bə'sə:k] *adj*: **to go ~** perder los estribos

berth [bə:θ] *n* (*bed*) litera; (*cabin*) camarote *m*; (*for ship*) amarradero ◊ *vi* atracar, amarrar

beseech [bɪ'si:tʃ] (*pt, pp* besought) *vt* suplicar

beset [bɪ'sɛt] (*pt, pp* beset) *vt* (*person*) acosar

beside [bɪ'saɪd] *prep* junto a, al lado de; **to be ~ o.s. with anger** estar fuera de sí; **that's ~ the point** eso no tiene nada que ver

besides [bɪ'saɪdz] *adv* además ◊ *prep* además de

besiege [bɪ'si:dʒ] *vt* sitiar; (*fig*) asediar

besought [bɪ'sɔ:t] *pt, pp of* beseech

best [bɛst] *adj* (el/la) mejor ◊ *adv* (lo) mejor; **the ~ part of** (*quantity*) la mayor parte de; **at ~** en el mejor de los casos; **to make the ~ of sth** sacar el mejor partido de algo; **to do one's ~** hacer todo lo posible; **to the ~ of my knowledge** que yo sepa; **to the ~ of my ability** como mejor puedo; **~ man** *n* padrino de boda

bestow [bɪ'stəu] *vt* (*title*) otorgar

bestseller ['bɛst'sɛlə*] *n* éxito de librería, bestseller *m*

bet [bɛt] (*pt, pp* bet *or* betted) *n* apuesta ◊ *vt*: **to ~ money on** apostar dinero por; **to ~ sb sth** apostar algo a uno ◊ *vi* apostar

betray [bɪ'treɪ] *vt* traicionar; (*trust*) faltar a; **~al** *n* traición *f*

better ['bɛtə*] *adj, adv* mejor ◊ *vt* superar ◊ *n*: **to get the ~ of sb** quedar por encima de alguien; **you had ~ do it** más vale que lo hagas; **he thought ~ of it** cambió de parecer; **to get ~** (*MED*) mejorar(se); **~ off** *adj* mejor; (*wealthier*) más acomodado

betting ['bɛtɪŋ] *n* juego, el apostar; **~ shop** (*BRIT*) *n* agencia de apuestas

between [bɪ'twi:n] *prep* entre ◊ *adv* (*time*) mientras tanto; (*place*) en medio

beverage ['bɛvərɪdʒ] *n* bebida

beware [bɪ'wɛə*] *vi*: **to ~ (of)** tener cuidado (con); **"~ of the dog"** "perro peligroso"

bewildered [bɪ'wɪldəd] *adj* aturdido, perplejo

bewitching [bɪ'wɪtʃɪŋ] *adj* hechicero, encantador(a)

beyond [bɪ'jɔnd] *prep* más allá de; (*past: understanding*) fuera de; (*after: date*) después de, más allá de; (*above*) superior a ◊ *adv* (*in space*) más allá; (*in time*) posteriormente; **~ doubt** fuera de toda duda; **~ repair** irreparable

bias ['baɪəs] *n* (*prejudice*) prejuicio, pasión *f*; (*preference*) predisposición *f*; **~(s)ed** *adj* parcial

bib [bɪb] *n* babero

Bible ['baɪbl] *n* Biblia

bicarbonate of soda [baɪ'kɑ:bənɪt-] *n* bicarbonato sódico

bicker ['bɪkə*] *vi* pelearse

bicycle ['baɪsɪkl] *n* bicicleta

bid [bɪd] (*pt* bade *or* bid, *pp* bidden *or* bid) *n* oferta, postura; (*in tender*) licitación *f*; (*attempt*) tentativa, conato ◊ *vi* hacer una oferta ◊ *vt* (*offer*) ofrecer; **to ~ sb good day** dar a uno los buenos días; **~der** *n*: **the highest ~der** el mejor postor; **~ding** *n* (*at auction*) ofertas *fpl*

bide [baɪd] *vt*: **to ~ one's time** esperar el momento adecuado

bifocals [baɪ'fəuklz] *npl* gafas *fpl* (*SP*) or anteojos *mpl* (*AM*) bifocales

big [bɪg] *adj* grande; (*brother, sister*) mayor

bigheaded ['bɪg'hɛdɪd] *adj* engreído

bigot ['bɪgət] *n* fanático/a, intolerante *m/f*; **~ed** *adj* fanático, intolerante; **~ry** *n* fanatismo, intolerancia

big top *n* (*at circus*) carpa

bike [baɪk] *n* bici *f*

bikini [bɪ'kiːnɪ] n bikini m
bile [baɪl] n bilis f
bilingual [baɪ'lɪŋgwəl] adj bilingüe
bill [bɪl] n cuenta; (invoice) factura; (POL) proyecto de ley; (US: banknote) billete m; (of bird) pico; (of show) programa m; "**post no ~s**" "prohibido fijar carteles"; **to fit** or **fill the ~** (fig) cumplir con los requisitos; **~board** (US) n cartelera
billet ['bɪlɪt] n alojamiento
billfold ['bɪlfəuld] (US) n cartera
billiards ['bɪljədz] n billar m
billion ['bɪljən] n (BRIT) billón m (millón de millones); (US) mil millones
bin [bɪn] n (for rubbish) cubo (SP) or bote m (AM) de la basura; (container) recipiente m
bind [baɪnd] (pt, pp bound) vt atar; (book) encuadernar; (oblige) obligar ♦ n (inf: nuisance) lata; **~ing** adj (contract) obligatorio
binge [bɪndʒ] (inf) n: **tc go on a ~** ir de juerga
bingo ['bɪŋgəu] n bingo m
binoculars [bɪ'nɔkjuləz] npl prismáticos mpl
bio... [baɪə'] prefix: **~chemistry** n bioquímica; **~graphy** [baɪ'ɔgrəfɪ] n biografía; **~logical** adj biológico; **~logy** [baɪ'ɔlədʒɪ] n biología
birch [bəːtʃ] n (tree) abedul m
bird [bəːd] n ave f, pájaro; (BRIT: inf: girl) chica; **~'s eye view** n (aerial view) vista de pájaro; (overview) visión f de conjunto; **~ watcher** n ornitólogo/a
Biro ['baɪrəu] ® n bolígrafo
birth [bəːθ] n nacimiento; **to give ~ to** parir, dar a luz; **~ certificate** n partida de nacimiento; **~ control** n (policy) control m de natalidad; (methods) métodos mpl anticonceptivos; **~day** n cumpleaños m inv ♦ cpd (cake, card etc) de cumpleaños; **~place** n lugar m de nacimiento; **~ rate** n (tasa de) natalidad f
biscuit ['bɪskɪt] (BRIT) n galleta, bizcocho (AM)
bisect [baɪ'sɛkt] vt bisecar
bishop ['bɪʃəp] n obispo; (CHESS) alfil m
bit [bɪt] pt of **bite** ♦ n trozo, pedazo, pedacito; (COMPUT) bit m, bitio; (for horse) freno, bocado; **a ~ of** un poco de; **a ~ mad** un poco loco; **by ~** poco a poco
bitch [bɪtʃ] n perra; (inf!: woman) zorra (!)
bite [baɪt] (pt **bit**, pp **bitten**) vt, vi morder; (insect etc) picar ♦ n (insect ~) picadura; (mouthful) bocado; **to ~ one's nails** comerse las uñas; **let's have a ~ (to eat)** (inf) vamos a comer algo
bitter ['bɪtə*] adj amargo; (wind) cortante, penetrante; (battle) encarnizado ♦ n (BRIT: beer) cerveza típica británica a base de lúpulos; **~ness** n lo amargo, amargura; (anger) rencor m

bizarre [bɪ'zɑː*] adj raro, extraño
blab [blæb] (inf) vi soplar
black [blæk] adj negro; (tea, coffee) solo ♦ n color m negro; (person): **B~** negro/a ♦ vt (BRIT: INDUSTRY) boicotear; **to give sb a ~ eye** ponerle a uno el ojo morado; **~ and blue** (bruised) amoratado; **to be in the ~** (bank account) estar en números negros; **~berry** n zarzamora; **~bird** n mirlo; **~board** n pizarra; **~ coffee** n café m solo; **~currant** n grosella negra; **~en** (fig) desacreditar; **~ ice** n hielo invisible en la carretera; **~leg** (BRIT) n esquirol m, rompehuelgas m inv; **~list** n lista negra; **~mail** n chantaje m ♦ vt chantajear; **~ market** n mercado negro; **~out** n (MIL) oscurecimiento; (power cut) apagón m; (TV, RADIO) interrupción f de programas; (fainting) desvanecimiento; **B~ Sea** n: **the B~ Sea** el Mar Negro; **~ sheep** n (fig) oveja negra; **~smith** n herrero; **~ spot** n (AUT) lugar m peligroso; (for unemployment etc) punto negro
bladder ['blædə*] n vejiga
blade [bleɪd] n hoja; (of propeller) paleta; **a ~ of grass** una brizna de hierba
blame [bleɪm] n culpa ♦ vt: **to ~ sb for sth** echar a uno la culpa de algo; **to be to ~** tener la culpa de; **~less** adj inocente
bland [blænd] adj (music, taste) soso
blank [blæŋk] adj en blanco; (look) sin expresión ♦ n (of memory): **my mind is a ~** no puedo recordar nada; (on form) blanco, espacio en blanco; (cartridge) cartucho sin bala or de fogueo; **~ cheque** n cheque m en blanco
blanket ['blæŋkɪt] n manta (SP), cobija (AM); (of snow) capa; (of fog) manto
blare [blɛə*] vi sonar estrepitosamente
blasé ['blɑːzeɪ] adj hastiado
blasphemy ['blæsfɪmɪ] n blasfemia
blast [blɑːst] n (of wind) ráfaga, soplo; (of explosive) explosión f ♦ vt (blow up) volar; **~-off** n (SPACE) lanzamiento
blatant ['bleɪtənt] adj descarado
blaze [bleɪz] n (fire) fuego; (fig: of colour) despliegue m; (: of glory) esplendor m ♦ vi arder en llamas; (fig) brillar ♦ vt: **to ~ a trail** (fig) abrir (un) camino; **in a ~ of publicity** con gran publicidad
blazer ['bleɪzə*] n chaqueta de uniforme de colegial o de socio de club
bleach [bliːtʃ] n (also: household ~) lejía ♦ vt blanquear; **~ed** adj (hair) teñido (de rubio); **~ers** (US) npl (SPORT) gradas fpl al sol
bleak [bliːk] adj (countryside) desierto; (prospect) poco prometedor(a); (weather) crudo; (smile) triste
bleary-eyed ['blɪərɪ'aɪd] adj: **to be ~** tener ojos de cansado
bleat [bliːt] vi balar

bleed [bliːd] (*pt, pp* **bled**) *vt, vi* sangrar; **my nose is ~ing** me está sangrando la nariz

bleeper ['bliːpə*] *n* busca *m*

blemish ['blɛmɪʃ] *n* marca, mancha; (*on reputation*) tacha

blend [blɛnd] *n* mezcla ♦ *vt* mezclar; (*colours etc*) combinar, mezclar ♦ *vi* (*colours etc: also:* ~ **in**) combinarse, mezclarse

bless [blɛs] (*pt, pp* **blessed** *or* **blest**) *vt* bendecir; ~ **you!** (*after sneeze*) ¡Jesús!; ~ing *n* (*approval*) aprobación *f*; (*godsend*) don *m* del cielo, bendición *f*; (*advantage*) beneficio, ventaja

blew [bluː] *pt of* **blow**

blight [blaɪt] *vt* (*hopes etc*) frustrar, arruinar

blimey ['blaɪmɪ] (*BRIT: inf*) *excl* ¡caray!

blind [blaɪnd] *adj* ciego, (*fig*): ~ (**to**) ciego (a) ♦ *n* (*for window*) persiana ♦ *vt* cegar; (*dazzle*) deslumbrar; (*deceive*): **to ~ sb to ...** cegar a uno a ...; **the ~** *npl* los ciegos; ~ **alley** *n* callejón *m* sin salida; ~ **corner** (*BRIT*) *n* esquina escondida; ~**fold** *n* venda ♦ *adv* con los ojos vendados ♦ *vt* vendar los ojos a; ~**ly** *adv* a ciegas, ciegamente; ~**ness** *n* ceguera *f*; ~ **spot** *n* (*AUT*) ángulo ciego

blink [blɪŋk] *vi* parpadear, pestañear; (*light*) oscilar; ~**ers** *npl* anteojeras *fpl*

bliss [blɪs] *n* felicidad *f*

blister ['blɪstə*] *n* ampolla ♦ *vi* (*paint*) ampollarse

blithely ['blaɪðlɪ] *adv* alegremente

blitz [blɪts] *n* (*MIL*) bombardeo aéreo

blizzard ['blɪzəd] *n* ventisca

bloated ['bləʊtɪd] *adj* hinchado; (*person: full*) ahíto

blob [blɔb] *n* (*drop*) gota; (*indistinct object*) bulto

bloc [blɔk] *n* (*POL*) bloque *m*

block [blɔk] *n* bloque *m*; (*in pipes*) obstáculo; (*of buildings*) manzana (*SP*), cuadra (*AM*) ♦ *vt* obstruir, cerrar; (*progress*) estorbar; ~ **of flats** (*BRIT*) bloque *m* de pisos; **mental ~** bloqueo mental; ~**ade** [-'keɪd] *n* bloqueo ♦ *vt* bloquear; ~**age** *n* estorbo, obstrucción *f*; ~**buster** *n* (*book*) bestseller *m*; (*film*) éxito de público; ~ **letters** *npl* letras *fpl* de molde

bloke [bləʊk] (*BRIT: inf*) *n* tipo, tío

blond(e) [blɔnd] *adj, n* rubio/a *m/f*

blood [blʌd] *n* sangre *f*; ~ **donor** *n* donante *m/f* de sangre; ~ **group** *n* grupo sanguíneo; ~**hound** *n* sabueso; ~ **poisoning** *n* envenenamiento de la sangre; ~ **pressure** *n* presión *f* sanguínea; ~**shed** *n* derramamiento de sangre; ~**shot** *adj* inyectado en sangre; ~**stream** *n* corriente *f* sanguínea; ~ **test** *n* análisis *m inv* de sangre; ~**thirsty** *adj* sanguinario; ~ **vessel** *n* vaso sanguíneo; ~**y** *adj* sangriento; (*nose etc*) lleno de sangre; (*BRIT: inf!*): **this ~y...** este condenado *o* puñetero ... (!) ♦ *adv*: ~**y**

strong/good (*BRIT: inf*) terriblemente fuerte/bueno; ~**y-minded** (*BRIT: inf*) *adj* puñetero (!)

bloom [bluːm] *n* flor *f* ♦ *vi* florecer

blossom ['blɔsəm] *n* flor *f* ♦ *vi* (*also fig*) florecer

blot [blɔt] *n* borrón *m*; (*fig*) mancha ♦ *vt* (*stain*) manchar; ~ **out** *vt* (*view*) tapar

blotchy ['blɔtʃɪ] *adj* (*complexion*) lleno de manchas

blotting paper ['blɔtɪŋ-] *n* papel *m* secante

blouse [blaʊz] *n* blusa

blow [bləʊ] (*pt* **blew**, *pp* **blown**) *n* golpe *m*; (*with sword*) espadazo ♦ *vi* (*dust, sand etc*) volar; (*fuse*) fundirse ♦ *vt* (*subj: wind*) llevarse; (*fuse*) quemar; (*instrument*) tocar; **to ~ one's nose** sonarse; ~ **away** *vt* llevarse, arrancar; ~ **down** *vt* derribar; ~ **off** *vt* arrebatar; ~ **out** *vi* apagarse; ~ **over** *vi* amainar; ~ **up** *vi* estallar ♦ *vt* volar; (*tyre*) inflar; (*PHOT*) ampliar; ~**-dry** *n* moldeado (con secador); ~**lamp** (*BRIT*) *n* soplete *m*, lámpara de soldar; ~**-out** *n* (*of tyre*) pinchazo; ~**torch** *n* = ~**lamp**

blue [bluː] *adj* azul; (*depressed*) deprimido; ~ **film/joke** película/chiste *m* verde; **out of the ~** (*fig*) de repente; ~**bell** *n* campanilla, campánula azul; ~**bottle** *n* moscarda, mosca azul; ~**print** *n* (*fig*) anteproyecto

bluff [blʌf] *vi* tirarse un farol, farolear ♦ *n* farol *m*; **to call sb's ~** coger a uno la palabra

blunder ['blʌndə*] *n* patinazo, metedura de pata ♦ *vi* cometer un error, meter la pata

blunt [blʌnt] *adj* (*pencil*) desafilado, romo; (*knife*) desafilado, romo; (*person*) franco, directo

blur [bləː*] *n* (*shape*): **to become a ~** hacerse borroso ♦ *vt* (*vision*) enturbiar; (*distinction*) borrar

blurb [bləːb] *n* comentario de sobrecubierta

blurt out [bləːt-] *vt* descolgarse con, dejar escapar

blush [blʌʃ] *vi* ruborizarse, ponerse colorado ♦ *n* rubor *m*

blustering ['blʌstərɪŋ] *adj* (*person*) fanfarrón/ona

blustery ['blʌstərɪ] *adj* (*weather*) tempestuoso, tormentoso

boar [bɔː*] *n* verraco, cerdo

board [bɔːd] *n* (*card~*) cartón *m*; (*wooden*) tabla, tablero; (*on wall*) tablón *m*; (*for chess etc*) tablero; (*committee*) junta, consejo; (*in firm*) mesa *or* junta directiva; (*NAUT, AVIAT*): **on ~** a bordo ♦ *vt* (*ship*) embarcarse en; (*train*) subir a; **full ~** (*BRIT*) pensión completa; **half ~** (*BRIT*) media pensión; **to go by the ~** (*fig*) ser abandonado *or* olvidado; ~ **up** *vt* (*door*) tapiar; ~ **and lodging** *n* casa y comida; ~**er** *n* (*SCOL*) interno/a; ~**ing card** (*BRIT*) *n* tarjeta de embarque; ~**ing house** *n* casa de huéspedes; ~**ing pass** (US) n = ~**ing card**; ~**ing school** n internado; ~ **room** n sala de juntas

boast [bəʊst] vi: **to** ~ **(about** or **of)** alardear (de)

boat [bəʊt] n barco, buque m; (small) barca, bote m; ~**er** n (hat) canotié m

bob [bɒb] vi (also: ~ **up and down**) menearse, balancearse; ~ **up** vi (re)aparecer de repente

bobby ['bɒbɪ] (BRIT: inf) n poli m

bobsleigh ['bɒbsleɪ] n bob m

bode [bəʊd] vi: **to** ~ **well/ill (for)** ser prometedor/poco prometedor (para)

bodily ['bɒdɪlɪ] adj corporal ♦ adv (move: person) en peso

body ['bɒdɪ] n cuerpo; (corpse) cadáver m; (of car) caja, carrocería; (fig: group) grupo; (: organization) organismo; ~**-building** n culturismo; ~**guard** n guardaespaldas m inv; ~**work** n carrocería

bog [bɒg] n pantano, ciénaga ♦ vt: **to get** ~**ged down** (fig) empantanarse, atascarse

boggle ['bɒgl] vi: **the mind** ~**s!** ¡no puedo creerlo!

bogus ['bəʊgəs] adj falso, fraudulento

boil [bɔɪl] vt (water) hervir; (eggs) pasar por agua, cocer ♦ vi hervir; (fig: with anger) estar furioso; (: with heat) asfixiarse ♦ n (MED) furúnculo, divieso; **to come to the** ~, **to come to a** ~ (US) comenzar a hervir; **to** ~ **down to** (fig) reducirse a; ~ **over** vi salirse, rebosar; (anger etc) llegar al colmo; ~**ed egg** n huevo cocido (SP) or pasado (AM); ~**ed potatoes** npl patatas fpl (SP) or papas fpl (AM) hervidas; ~**er** n caldera; ~**er suit** (BRIT) n mono; ~**ing point** n punto de ebullición

boisterous ['bɔɪstərəs] adj (noisy) bullicioso; (excitable) exuberante; (crowd) tumultuoso

bold [bəʊld] adj valiente, audaz; (pej) descarado; (colour) llamativo

Bolivia [bə'lɪvɪə] n Bolivia; ~**n** adj, n boliviano/a m/f

bollard ['bɒləd] (BRIT) n (AUT) poste m

bolster ['bəʊlstə*] vt: ~ **up** reforzar

bolt [bəʊlt] n (lock) cerrojo; (with nut) perno, tornillo ♦ adv: ~ **upright** rígido, erguido ♦ vt (door) echar el cerrojo a; (also: ~ **together**) sujetar con tornillos; (food) engullir ♦ vi fugarse; (horse) desbocarse

bomb [bɒm] n bomba ♦ vt bombardear; ~**ard** [-'bɑːd] vt bombardear; (fig): **to** ~**ard with questions** acribillar a preguntas; ~**ardment** [-'bɑːdmənt] n bombardeo

bombastic [bɒm'bæstɪk] adj rimbombante; (person) farolero

bomb: ~ **disposal** n desmontaje m de explosivos; ~**er** n (AVIAT) bombardero; ~**shell** n (fig) bomba

bona fide ['bəʊnə'faɪd] adj genuino, auténtico

bond [bɒnd] n (promise) fianza; (FINANCE) bono; (link) vínculo, lazo; (COMM): **in** ~ en depósito bajo fianza

bondage ['bɒndɪdʒ] n esclavitud f

bone [bəʊn] n hueso; (of fish) espina ♦ vt deshuesar; quitar las espinas a; ~ **idle** adj gandul

bonfire ['bɒnfaɪə*] n hoguera, fogata

bonnet ['bɒnɪt] n gorra; (BRIT: of car) capó m

bonus ['bəʊnəs] n (payment) paga extraordinaria, plus m; (fig) bendición f

bony ['bəʊnɪ] adj (arm, face) huesudo; (MED: tissue) óseo; (meat) lleno de huesos; (fish) lleno de espinas

boo [buː] excl ¡uh! ♦ vt abuchear, rechiflar

booby trap ['buːbɪ-] n trampa explosiva

book [bʊk] n libro; (of tickets) taco; (of stamps etc) librito ♦ vt (ticket) sacar; (seat, room) reservar; ~**s** npl (COMM) cuentas fpl, contabilidad f; ~**case** n librería, estante m para libros; ~**ing office** n (BRIT: RAIL) despacho de billetes (SP) or boletos (AM); (THEATRE) taquilla (SP), boletería (AM); ~**-keeping** n contabilidad f; ~**let** n folleto; ~**maker** n corredor m de apuestas; ~**seller** n librero; ~**shop**, ~ **store** n librería

boom [buːm] n (noise) trueno, estampido; (in prices etc) alza rápida; (ECON, in population) boom m ♦ vi (cannon) hacer gran estruendo, retumbar; (ECON) estar en alza

boon [buːn] n favor m, beneficio

boost [buːst] n estímulo, empuje m ♦ vt estimular, empujar; ~**er** n (MED) reinyección f

boot [buːt] n bota; (BRIT: of car) maleta, maletero ♦ vt (COMPUT) arrancar; **to** ~ (in addition) además, por añadidura

booth [buːð] n (at fair) barraca; (telephone ~, voting ~) cabina

booty ['buːtɪ] n botín m

booze [buːz] (inf) n bebida

border ['bɔːdə*] n borde m, margen m; (of a country) frontera; (for flowers) arriate m ♦ vt (road) bordear; (another country: also: ~ **on**) lindar con; **B~s** n: **the B~s** región fronteriza entre Escocia y Inglaterra; ~ **on** vt fus (insanity etc) rayar en; ~**line** n: **on the** ~**line** en el límite; ~**line case** n caso dudoso

bore [bɔː*] pt of **bear** ♦ vt (hole) hacer un agujero en; (well) perforar; (person) aburrir ♦ n (person) pelmazo, pesado; (of gun) calibre m; **to be** ~**d** estar aburrido; ~**dom** n aburrimiento

boring ['bɔːrɪŋ] adj aburrido

born [bɔːn] adj: **to be** ~ nacer; **I was** ~ **in 1960** nací en 1960

borne [bɔːn] pp of **bear**

borough ['bʌrə] n municipio

borrow ['bɔrəu] *vt*: **to ~ sth (from sb)** tomar algo prestado (a alguien)

bosom ['buzəm] *n* pecho; **~ friend** amigo íntimo

boss [bɔs] *n* jefe *m* ♦ *vt* (*also*: **~ about** *or* *around*) mangonear; **~y** *adj* mandón/ona

bosun ['bəusn] *n* contramaestre *m*

botany ['bɔtəni] *n* botánica

botch [bɔtʃ] *vt* (*also*: **~ up**) arruinar, estropear

both [bəuθ] *adj, pron* ambos/as, los/las dos; **~ of us went, we ~ went** fuimos los dos, ambos fuimos ♦ *adv*: **~ A and B** tanto A como B

bother ['bɔðə*] *vt* (*worry*) preocupar; (*disturb*) molestar, fastidiar ♦ *vi* (*also*: **~ o.s.**) molestarse ♦ *n* (*trouble*) dificultad *f*; (*nuisance*) molestia, lata; **to ~ doing** tomarse la molestia de hacer

bottle ['bɔtl] *n* botella; (*small*) frasco; (*baby's*) biberón *m* ♦ *vt* embotellar; **~ up** *vt* suprimir; **~ bank** *n* contenedor *m* de vidrio; **~neck** *n* (*AUT*) embotellamiento; (*in supply*) obstáculo *m inv*; **~-opener** *n* abrebotellas *m inv*

bottom ['bɔtəm] *n* (*of box, sea*) fondo *m*; (*buttocks*) trasero, culo; (*of page*) pie *m*; (*of list*) final *m*; (*of class*) último/a ♦ *adj* (*lowest*) más bajo; (*last*) último; **~less** *adj* sin fondo, inacabable

bough [bau] *n* rama

bought [bɔːt] *pt, pp of* buy

boulder ['bəuldə*] *n* canto rodado

bounce [bauns] *vi* (*ball*) (re)botar; (*cheque*) ser rechazado ♦ *vt* hacer (re)botar ♦ *n* (*rebound*) (re)bote *m*; **~r** (*inf*) *n* gorila *m*=(que echa a los alborotadores de un bar, club etc)

bound [baund] *pt, pp of* bind ♦ *n* (*leap*) salto; (*gen pl: limit*) límite *m* ♦ *vi* (*leap*) saltar ♦ *vt* (*border*) rodear ♦ *adj*: **~ by** rodeado de; **to be ~ to do sth** (*obliged*) tener el deber de hacer algo; **he's ~ to come** es seguro que vendrá; **out of ~s** prohibido el paso; **~ for** con destino a

boundary ['baundri] *n* límite *m*

boundless ['baundlis] *adj* ilimitado

bouquet ['bukei] *n* (*of flowers*) ramo

bourgeois ['buəʒwɑː] *adj* burgués/esa *m/f*

bout [baut] *n* (*of malaria etc*) ataque *m*; (*of activity*) período; (*BOXING etc*) combate *m*, encuentro

bow¹ [bəu] *n* (*knot*) lazo; (*weapon, MUS*) arco

bow² [bau] *n* (*of the head*) reverencia; (*NAUT: also*: **~s**) proa ♦ *vi* inclinarse, hacer una reverencia; (*yield*): **to ~ to** *or* **before** ceder ante, someterse a

bowels [bauəlz] *npl* intestinos *mpl*, vientre *m*; (*fig*) entrañas *fpl*

bowl [bəul] *n* tazón *m*, cuenco; (*ball*) bola ♦ *vi* (*CRICKET*) arrojar la pelota

bow-legged ['bəu'lɛgd] *adj* estevado

bowler ['bəulə*] *n* (*CRICKET*) lanzador *m* (de la pelota); (*BRIT: also*: **~ hat**) hongo, bombín *m*

bowling ['bəulɪŋ] *n* (*game*) bochas *fpl*, bolos *mpl*; **~ alley** *n* bolera; **~ green** *n* pista para bochas

bowls [bəulz] *n* juego de las bochas, bolos *mpl*

bow tie ['bəu-] *n* corbata de lazo, pajarita

box [bɔks] *n* (*also*: **cardboard ~**) caja, cajón *m*; (*THEATRE*) palco ♦ *vt* encajonar ♦ *vi* (*SPORT*) boxear; **~er** *n* (*person*) boxeador *m*; **~ing** *n* (*SPORT*) boxeo; **B~ing Day** (*BRIT*) *n* día en que se dan los aguinaldos, 26 de diciembre; **~ing gloves** *npl* guantes *mpl* de boxeo; **~ing ring** *n* ring *m*, cuadrilátero; **~ office** *n* taquilla (*SP*), boletería (*AM*); **~room** *n* trastero

boy [bɔi] *n* (*young*) niño; (*older*) muchacho, chico; (*son*) hijo

boycott ['bɔikɔt] *n* boicot *m* ♦ *vt* boicotear

boyfriend ['bɔifrɛnd] *n* novio

boyish ['bɔiiʃ] *adj* juvenil; (*girl*) con aspecto de muchacho

B.R. *n abbr* (= *British Rail*) ≈ RENFE *f* (*SP*)

bra [brɑː] *n* sostén *m*, sujetador *m*

brace [breis] *n* (*BRIT: also*: **~s: on teeth**) corrector *m*, aparato; (*tool*) berbiquí *m* ♦ *vt* (*knees, shoulders*) tensionar; **~s** *npl* (*BRIT*) tirantes *mpl*; **to ~ o.s.** (*fig*) prepararse

bracelet ['breislit] *n* pulsera, brazalete *m*

bracing ['breisiŋ] *adj* vigorizante, tónico

bracket ['brækit] *n* (*TECH*) soporte *m*, puntal *m*; (*group*) clase *f*, categoría; (*also*: **brace ~**) soporte *m*, abrazadera; (*also*: **round ~**) paréntesis *m inv*; (*also*: **square ~**) corchete *m* ♦ *vt* (*word etc*) poner entre paréntesis

brag [bræg] *vi* jactarse

braid [breid] *n* (*trimming*) galón *m*; (*of hair*) trenza

brain [brein] *n* cerebro; **~s** *npl* sesos *mpl*; **she's got ~s** es muy lista; **~child** *n* invento; **~wash** *vt* lavar el cerebro; **~wave** *n* idea luminosa; **~y** *adj* muy inteligente

braise [breiz] *vt* cocer a fuego lento

brake [breik] *n* (*on vehicle*) freno ♦ *vi* frenar; **~ fluid** *n* líquido de frenos; **~ light** *n* luz *f* de frenado

bran [bræn] *n* salvado

branch [brɑːntʃ] *n* rama; (*COMM*) sucursal *f*; **~ out** *vi* (*fig*) extenderse

brand [brænd] *n* marca; (*fig: type*) tipo ♦ *vt* (*cattle*) marcar con hierro candente

brandish ['brændiʃ] *vt* blandir

brand-new ['brænd'njuː] *adj* flamante, completamente nuevo

brandy ['brændi] *n* coñac *m*

brash [bræʃ] *adj* (*forward*) descarado

brass [brɑːs] *n* latón *m*; **the ~** (*MUS*) los cobres; **~ band** *n* banda de metal

brassière ['bræsiə*] *n* sostén *m*, sujetador *m*

brat [bræt] (pej) n mocoso/a

bravado [brə'vɑːdəu] n fanfarronería

brave [breɪv] adj valiente, valeroso ♦ vt (face up to) desafiar; ~ry n valor m, valentía

brawl [brɔːl] n pelea, reyerta

brawny ['brɔːnɪ] adj fornido, musculoso

bray [breɪ] vi rebuznar

brazen ['breɪzn] adj descarado, cínico ♦ vt: to ~ it out echarle cara

brazier ['breɪzɪə*] n brasero

Brazil [brə'zɪl] n (el) Brasil; ~ian adj, n brasileño/a m/f

breach [briːtʃ] vt abrir brecha en ♦ n (gap) brecha; (breaking): ~ of contract infracción f de contrato; ~ of the peace perturbación f del órden público

bread [brɛd] n pan m; ~ and butter n pan con mantequilla; (fig) pan (de cada día); ~bin (US ~box) n panera; ~crumbs npl migajas fpl; (CULIN) pan rallado; ~line n: on the ~line en la miseria

breadth [brɛtθ] n anchura; (fig) amplitud f

breadwinner ['brɛdwɪnə*] n sustento m de la familia

break [breɪk] (pt **broke**, pp **broken**) vt romper; (promise) faltar a; (law) violar, infringir; (record) batir ♦ vi romperse, quebrarse; (storm) estallar; (weather) cambiar; (dawn) despuntar; (news etc) darse a conocer ♦ n (gap) abertura; (fracture) fractura; (time) intervalo; (: at school) (período de) recreo; (chance) oportunidad f; to ~ the news to sb comunicar la noticia a uno; ~ down vt (figures, data) analizar, descomponer ♦ vi (machine) estropearse; (AUT) averiarse; (person) romper a llorar; (talks) fracasar; ~ even vi cubrir los gastos; ~ free or loose vi escaparse; ~ in vt (horse etc) domar ♦ vi (burglar) forzar una entrada; (interrupt) interrumpir; ~ into vt fus (house) forzar; ~ off vi (speaker) pararse, detenerse; (branch) partir; ~ open vt (door etc) abrir por la fuerza, forzar; ~ out vi estallar; (prisoner) escaparse; to ~ out in spots salirle a uno granos; ~ up vi (ship) hacerse pedazos; (crowd, meeting) disolverse; (marriage) deshacerse; (SCOL) terminar (el curso) ♦ vt (rocks etc) partir; (journey) partir; (fight etc) acabar con; ~age n rotura; ~down n (AUT) avería; (in communications) interrupción f; (MED: also: nervous ~down) colapso, crisis f nerviosa; (of marriage, talks) fracaso; (of statistics) análisis m inv; ~down van (BRIT) n (camión m) grúa; ~er n (ola) rompiente f

breakfast ['brɛkfəst] n desayuno

break: ~-in n robo con allanamiento de morada; ~ing and entering n (LAW) violación f de domicilio, allanamiento de morada; ~through n (also fig) avance m; ~water n rompeolas m inv

breast [brɛst] n (of woman) pecho, seno; (chest) pecho; (of bird) pechuga; ~-feed (irreg: like feed) vt, vi amamantar, criar a los pechos; ~-stroke n braza (de pecho)

breath [brɛθ] n aliento, respiración f; to take a deep ~ respirar hondo; out of ~ sin aliento, sofocado

Breathalyser ['brɛθəlaɪzə*] ® (BRIT) n alcoholímetro m

breathe [briːð] vt, vi respirar; ~ in vt, vi aspirar; ~ out vt, vi espirar; ~r n respiro; **breathing** n respiración f

breath: ~less adj sin aliento, jadeante; ~taking adj imponente, pasmoso

breed [briːd] (pt, pp **bred**) vt criar ♦ vi reproducirse, procrear ♦ n (ZOOL) raza, casta; (type) tipo; ~ing n (of person) educación f

breeze [briːz] n brisa

breezy ['briːzɪ] adj de mucho viento, ventoso; (person) despreocupado

brevity ['brɛvɪtɪ] n brevedad f

brew [bruː] vt (tea) hacer; (beer) elaborar ♦ vi (fig: trouble) prepararse; (storm) amenazar; ~ery n fábrica de cerveza, cervecería

bribe [braɪb] n soborno ♦ vt sobornar, cohechar; ~ry n soborno, cohecho

bric-a-brac ['brɪkəbræk] n inv baratijas fpl

brick [brɪk] n ladrillo; ~layer n albañil m

bridal ['braɪdl] adj nupcial

bride [braɪd] n novia; ~groom n novio; ~smaid n dama de honor

bridge [brɪdʒ] n puente m; (NAUT) puente m de mando; (of nose) caballete m; (CARDS) bridge m ♦ vt (fig): to ~ a gap llenar un vacío

bridle ['braɪdl] n brida, freno; ~ path n camino de herradura

brief [briːf] adj breve, corto ♦ n (LAW) escrito; (task) cometido, encargo ♦ vt informar; ~s npl (for men) calzoncillos mpl; (for women) bragas fpl; ~case n cartera (SP), portafolio (AM); ~ing n (PRESS) informe m; ~ly adv (glance) fugazmente; (say) en pocas palabras

brigadier [brɪgə'dɪə*] n general m de brigada

bright [braɪt] adj brillante; (room) luminoso; (day) de sol; (person: clever) listo, inteligente; (: lively) alegre; (colour) vivo; (future) prometedor(a); ~en (also: ~en up) vt (room) hacer más alegre; (event) alegrar ♦ vi (weather) despejarse; (person) animarse, alegrarse; (prospects) mejorar

brilliance ['brɪljəns] n brillo, brillantez f; (of talent etc) brillantez

brilliant ['brɪljənt] adj brillante; (inf) fenomenal

brim [brɪm] n borde m; (of hat) ala

brine [braɪn] n salmuera

bring [brɪŋ] (pt, pp **brought**) vt (thing, person: with you) traer; (: to sb) llevar, conducir; (trouble, satisfaction) causar; ~ about *vt* ocasionar, producir; ~ **back** *vt* volver a traer; (*return*) devolver; ~ **down** *vt* (*government, plane*) rebajar; (*price*) rebajar; ~ **forward** *vt* adelantar; ~ **off** *vt* (*task, plan*) lograr, conseguir; ~ **out** *vt* sacar; (*book etc*) publicar; (*meaning*) subrayar; ~ **round** *vt* (*unconscious person*) hacer volver en sí; ~ **up** *vt* subir; (*person*) educar, criar; (*question*) sacar a colación; (*food: vomit*) devolver, vomitar

brink [brɪŋk] *n* borde *m*

brisk [brɪsk] *adj* (*abrupt: tone*) brusco; (*person*) enérgico, vigoroso; (*pace*) rápido; (*trade*) activo

bristle ['brɪsl] *n* cerda ♦ *vi*: **to ~ in anger** temblar de rabia

Britain ['brɪtən] *n* (*also*: **Great ~**) Gran Bretaña

British ['brɪtɪʃ] *adj* británico ♦ *npl*: **the ~** los británicos; ~ **Isles** *npl*: **the ~ Isles** las Islas Británicas; ~ **Rail** *n* = RENFE *f* (*SP*)

Briton ['brɪtən] *n* británico/a

brittle ['brɪtl] *adj* quebradizo, frágil

broach [brəutʃ] *vt* (*subject*) abordar

broad [brɔːd] *adj* ancho; (*range*) amplio; (*smile*) abierto; (*general: outlines etc*) general; (*accent*) cerrado; **in ~ daylight** en pleno día; ~**cast** (*irreg: like cast*) *n* emisión *f* ♦ *vt* (*RADIO*) emitir; (*TV*) transmitir ♦ *vi* emitir; transmitir; ~**en** *vt* ampliar ♦ *vi* ensancharse; **to ~en one's mind** hacer más tolerante a uno; ~**ly** *adv* en general; ~**minded** *adj* tolerante, liberal

broccoli ['brɔkəlɪ] *n* brécol *m*

brochure ['brəuʃjuə*] *n* folleto

broil [brɔɪl] *vt* (*CULIN*) asar a la parrilla

broke [brəuk] *pt* de **break** ♦ *adj* (*inf*) pelado, sin blanca

broken ['brəukən] *pp* de **break** ♦ *adj* roto; (*machine: also*: ~ **down**) averiado; ~ **leg** pierna rota; **in ~ English** en un inglés imperfecto; ~**-hearted** *adj* con el corazón partido

broker ['brəukə*] *n* agente *m/f*, bolsista *m/f*; (*insurance* ~) agente *m* de seguros

brolly ['brɔlɪ] (*BRIT: inf*) *n* paraguas *m inv*

bronchitis [brɔŋ'kaɪtɪs] *n* bronquitis *f*

bronze [brɔnz] *n* bronce *m*

brooch [brəutʃ] *n* prendedor *m*, broche *m*

brood [bruːd] *n* camada, cría ♦ *vi* (*person*) dejarse obsesionar

broom [brum] *n* escoba; (*BOT*) retama; ~**stick** *n* palo de escoba

Bros. *abbr* (= *Brothers*) Hnos

broth [brɔθ] *n* caldo

brothel ['brɔθl] *n* burdel *m*

brother ['brʌðə*] *n* hermano; ~**-in-law** *n* cuñado

brought [brɔːt] *pt, pp* de **bring**

brow [brau] *n* (*forehead*) frente *m*; (*eye~*) ceja; (*of hill*) cumbre *f*

brown [braun] *adj* (*colour*) marrón; (*hair*)

castaño; (*tanned*) bronceado, moreno ♦ *n* (*colour*) color *m* marrón *or* pardo ♦ *vt* (*CULIN*) dorar; ~ **bread** *n* pan integral

brownie ['braunɪ] *n* niña exploradora; (*US: cake*) pastel de chocolate con nueces

brown paper *n* papel *m* de estraza

brown sugar *n* azúcar *m* terciado

browse [brauz] *vi* (*through book*) hojear; (*in shop*) mirar

bruise [bruːz] *n* cardenal *m* (*SP*), moretón *m* (*AM*) ♦ *vt* magullar

brunch [brʌntʃ] *n* desayuno-almuerzo

brunette [bruː'nɛt] *n* morena

brunt [brʌnt] *n*: **to bear the ~ of** llevar el peso de

brush [brʌʃ] *n* cepillo; (*for painting, shaving etc*) brocha; (*artist's*) pincel *m*; (*with police etc*) roce *m* ♦ *vt* (*sweep*) barrer; (*groom*) cepillar; (*also*: ~ **against**) rozar al pasar; ~ **aside** *vt* rechazar, no hacer caso a; ~ **up** *vt* (*knowledge*) repasar, refrescar; ~**wood** *n* (*sticks*) leña

brusque [bruːsk] *adj* brusco, áspero

Brussels ['brʌslz] *n* Bruselas; ~ **sprout** *n* col *f* de Bruselas

brute [bruːt] *n* bruto; (*person*) bestia ♦ *adj*: **by ~ force** a fuerza bruta

B.Sc. *abbr* (= *Bachelor of Science*) licenciado en Ciencias

bubble ['bʌbl] *n* burbuja ♦ *vi* burbujear, borbotar; ~ **bath** *n* espuma para el baño; ~ **gum** *n* chicle *m* de globo

buck [bʌk] *n* (*rabbit*) conejo macho; (*deer*) gamo; (*US: inf*) dólar *m* ♦ *vi* corcovear; **to pass the ~ (to sb)** echar (a uno) el muerto; ~ **up** *vi* (*cheer up*) animarse, cobrar ánimo

bucket ['bʌkɪt] *n* cubo, balde *m*

buckle ['bʌkl] *n* hebilla ♦ *vt* abrochar con hebilla ♦ *vi* combarse

bud [bʌd] *n* (*of plant*) brote *m*, yema; (*of flower*) capullo ♦ *vi* brotar, echar brotes

Buddhism ['budɪzm] *n* Budismo

budding ['bʌdɪŋ] *adj* en ciernes, en embrión

buddy ['bʌdɪ] (*US*) *n* compañero, compinche *m*

budge [bʌdʒ] *vt* mover; (*fig*) hacer ceder ♦ *vi* moverse, ceder

budgerigar ['bʌdʒərɪgɑː*] *n* periquito

budget ['bʌdʒɪt] *n* presupuesto ♦ *vi*: **to ~ for sth** presupuestar algo

budgie ['bʌdʒɪ] *n* = **budgerigar**

buff [bʌf] *adj* (*colour*) color de ante ♦ *n* (*inf: enthusiast*) entusiasta *m/f*

buffalo ['bʌfələu] (*pl* ~ *or* ~**es**) *n* (*BRIT*) búfalo; (*US: bison*) bisonte *m*

buffer ['bʌfə*] *n* (*COMPUT*) memoria intermedia; (*RAIL*) tope *m*

buffet[1] ['bufeɪ] *n* (*BRIT: in station*) bar *m*, cafetería; (*food*) buffet *m*; ~ **car** (*BRIT*) *n* (*RAIL*) coche-comedor *m*

buffet² ['bʌfɪt] vt golpear

bug [bʌg] n (esp US: insect) bicho, sabandija; (COMPUT) error m; (germ) microbio, bacilo; (spy device) micrófono oculto ♦ vt (inf: annoy) fastidiar; (room) poner micrófono oculto en

buggy ['bʌgɪ] n cochecito de niño

bugle ['bju:gl] n corneta, clarín m

build [bɪld] (pt, pp built) n (of person) tipo ♦ vt construir, edificar; ~ up vt (morale, forces, production) acrecentar; (stocks) acumular; ~er n (contractor) contratista m/f; ~ing n construcción f; (structure) edificio; ~ing society (BRIT) n sociedad f inmobiliaria, cooperativa de construcciones

built [bɪlt] pt, pp of build ♦ adj: ~-in (wardrobe etc) empotrado; ~-up area n zona urbanizada

bulb [bʌlb] n (BOT) bulbo; (ELEC) bombilla (SP), foco (AM)

Bulgaria [bʌl'gɛərɪə] n Bulgaria; ~n adj, n búlgaro/a m/f

bulge [bʌldʒ] n bulto, protuberancia ♦ vi bombearse, pandearse; (pocket etc): to ~ (with) rebosar (de)

bulk [bʌlk] n masa, mole f; in ~ (COMM) a granel; the ~ of la mayor parte de; ~y adj voluminoso, abultado

bull [bul] n toro; (male elephant, whale) macho; ~dog n dogo

bulldozer ['buldəuzə*] n bulldozer m

bullet ['bulɪt] n bala

bulletin ['bulɪtɪn] n anuncio, parte m; (journal) boletín m

bulletproof ['bulɪtpru:f] adj a prueba de balas

bullfight ['bulfaɪt] n corrida de toros; ~er n torero; ~ing n los toros, el toreo

bullion ['buljən] n oro (or plata) en barras

bullock ['bulək] n novillo

bullring ['bulrɪŋ] n plaza de toros

bull's-eye n centro del blanco

bully ['bulɪ] n valentón, matón m ♦ vt intimidar, tiranizar

bum [bʌm] n (inf: backside) culo; (esp US: tramp) vagabundo

bumblebee ['bʌmblbi:] n abejorro

bump [bʌmp] n (blow) tope m, choque m; (jolt) sacudida; (on road etc) bache m; (on head etc) chichón m ♦ vt (strike) chocar contra; ~ into vt fus chocar contra, tropezar con; (person) topar con; ~er n (AUT) parachoques m inv ♦ adj: ~er crop/harvest cosecha abundante; ~er cars npl coches mpl de choque

bumptious ['bʌmpʃəs] adj engreído, presuntuoso

bumpy ['bʌmpɪ] adj (road) lleno de baches

bun [bʌn] n (BRIT: cake) pastel m; (US: bread) bollo; (of hair) moño

bunch [bʌntʃ] n (of flowers) ramo, (of keys) manojo, (of bananas) piña; (of people) grupo; (pej) pandilla; ~es npl (in hair) coletas fpl

bundle ['bʌndl] n bulto, fardo, (of sticks) haz m; (of papers) legajo ♦ vt (also: ~ up) atar, envolver; to ~ sth/sb into meter algo/a alguien precipitadamente en

bungalow ['bʌŋgələu] n bungalow m, chalé m

bungle ['bʌŋgl] vt hacer mal

bunion ['bʌnjən] n juanete m

bunk [bʌŋk] n litera; ~ beds npl literas fpl

bunker ['bʌŋkə*] n (coal store) carbonera; (MIL) refugio; (GOLF) bunker m

bunny ['bʌnɪ] n (also: ~ rabbit) conejito

bunting ['bʌntɪŋ] n banderitas fpl

buoy [bɔɪ] n boya; ~ up vt (fig) animar; ~ant adj (ship) capaz de flotar; (economy) boyante; (person) optimista

burden ['bɜːdn] n carga ♦ vt cargar

bureau [bjuə'rəu] (pl bureaux) n (BRIT: writing desk) escritorio, buró m; (US: chest of drawers) cómoda; (office) oficina, agencia

bureaucracy [bjuə'rɔkrəsɪ] n burocracia

bureaux [bjuə'rəuz] npl of bureau

burglar ['bɜːglə*] n ladrón/ona m/f; ~ alarm n alarma f antirrobo; ~y n robo con allanamiento, robo de una casa

burial ['berɪəl] n entierro

burly ['bɜːlɪ] adj fornido, membrudo

Burma ['bɜːmə] n Birmania

burn [bɜːn] (pt, pp burned or burnt) vt quemar; (house) incendiar ♦ vi quemarse, arder; incendiarse; (sting) escocer ♦ n quemadura; ~ down vt incendiar; ~er n (on cooker etc) quemador m; ~ing adj (building etc) en llamas; (hot: sand etc) abrasador(a); (ambition) ardiente; ~t [bɜːnt] pt, pp of burn

burrow ['bʌrəu] n madriguera ♦ vi hacer una madriguera; (rummage) hurgar

bursary ['bɜːsərɪ] (BRIT) n beca

burst [bɜːst] (pt, pp burst) vt reventar; (subj: river: banks etc) romper ♦ vi reventarse; (tyre) pincharse ♦ n (of gunfire) ráfaga; (also: ~ pipe) reventón m; a ~ of energy/speed/enthusiasm una explosión de energía/un ímpetu de velocidad/un arranque de entusiasmo; to ~ into flames estallar en llamas; to ~ into tears deshacerse en lágrimas; to ~ out laughing soltar la carcajada; to ~ open abrirse de golpe; to be ~ing with (subj: container) estar lleno a rebosar de; (person) reventar por or de; ~ into vt fus (room etc) irrumpir en

bury ['berɪ] vt enterrar; (body) enterrar, sepultar

bus [bʌs] n autobús m

bush [buʃ] n arbusto; (scrub land) monte m; to beat about the ~ andar(se) con rodeos; ~y adj (thick) espeso, poblado

busily ['bɪzɪlɪ] adv afanosamente

business ['bɪznɪs] n (matter) asunto; (trad-

ing) comercio, negocios *mpl*; (*firm*) empresa, casa; (*occupation*) oficio; **to be away on ~** estar en viaje de negocios; **it's my ~ to ...** me toca *or* corresponde ...; **it's none of my ~** yo no tengo nada que ver; **he means ~** habla en serio; **~man** *n* hombre *m* de negocios; **~ trip** *n* viaje *m* de negocios; **~woman** *n* mujer *f* de negocios

busker ['bʌskə*] (*BRIT*) *n* músico/a ambulante

bus-stop ['bʌsstɔp] *n* parada de autobús

bust [bʌst] *n* (*ANAT*) pecho; (*sculpture*) busto ♦ *adj* (*inf: broken*) roto, estropeado; **to go ~** quebrar

bustle ['bʌsl] *n* bullicio, movimiento ♦ *vi* menearse, apresurarse; **bustling** *adj* (*town*) animado, bullicioso

busy ['bɪzɪ] *adj* ocupado, atareado; (*shop, street*) concurrido, animado; (*TEL: line*) comunicando ♦ *vt*: **to ~ o.s. with** ocuparse en; **~body** *n* entrometido/a; **~ signal** (*US*) *n* (*TEL*) señal *f* de comunicando

――――――― *KEYWORD* ―――――――

but [bʌt] *conj* **1** pero; **he's not very bright, ~ he's hard-working** no es muy inteligente, pero es trabajador

2 (*in direct contradiction*) sino; **he's not English ~ French** no es inglés sino francés; **he didn't sing ~ he shouted** no cantó sino que gritó

3 (*showing disagreement, surprise etc*): **~ that's far too expensive!** ¡pero eso es carísimo!; **~ it does work!** ¡(pero) sí que funciona!

♦ *prep* (*apart from, except*) menos, salvo; **we've had nothing ~ trouble** no hemos tenido más que problemas; **no-one ~ him can do it** nadie más que él puede hacerlo; **who ~ a lunatic would do such a thing?** ¡sólo un loco haría una cosa así!; **~ for you/your help** si no fuera por ti/tu ayuda; **anything ~ that** cualquier cosa menos eso

♦ *adv* (*just, only*): **she's ~ a child** no es más que una niña; **had I ~ known** si lo hubiera sabido; **I can ~ try** al menos lo puedo intentar; **it's all ~ finished** está casi acabado

butcher ['butʃə*] *n* carnicero ♦ *vt* hacer una carnicería con; (*cattle etc*) matar; **~'s (shop)** *n* carnicería

butler ['bʌtlə*] *n* mayordomo

butt [bʌt] *n* (*barrel*) tonel *m*; (*of gun*) culata; (*of cigarette*) colilla; (*BRIT: fig: target*) blanco ♦ *vt* dar cabezadas contra, top(et)ar; **~ in** *vi* (*interrupt*) interrumpir

butter ['bʌtə*] *n* mantequilla ♦ *vt* untar con mantequilla; **~cup** *n* botón *m* de oro

butterfly ['bʌtəflaɪ] *n* mariposa; (*SWIMMING: also*: **~ stroke**) braza de mariposa

buttocks ['bʌtəks] *npl* nalgas *fpl*

button ['bʌtn] *n* botón *m*; (*US*) placa, chapa ♦ *vt* (*also*: **~ up**) abotonar, abrochar ♦ *vi* abrocharse

buttress ['bʌtrɪs] *n* contrafuerte *m*

buxom ['bʌksəm] *adj* exuberante

buy [baɪ] (*pt, pp* **bought**) *vt* comprar ♦ *n* compra; **to ~ sb sth/sth from sb** comprarle algo a alguien; **to ~ sb a drink** invitar a alguien a tomar algo; **~er** *n* comprador(a) *m/f*

buzz [bʌz] *n* zumbido; (*inf: phone call*) llamada (por teléfono) ♦ *vi* zumbar; **~er** *n* timbre *m*; **~ word** *n* palabra que está de moda

――――――― *KEYWORD* ―――――――

by [baɪ] *prep* **1** (*referring to cause, agent*) por; de; **killed ~ lightning** muerto por un relámpago; **a painting ~ Picasso** un cuadro de Picasso

2 (*referring to method, manner, means*): **~ bus/car/train** en autobús/coche/tren; **to pay ~ cheque** pagar con un cheque; **~ moonlight/candlelight** a la luz de la luna/ una vela; **~ saving hard, he ...** ahorrando, ...

3 (*via, through*) por; **we came ~ Dover** vinimos por Dover

4 (*close to, past*): **the house ~ the river** la casa junto al río; **she rushed ~ me** pasó a mi lado como una exhalación; **I go ~ the post office every day** paso por delante de Correos todos los días

5 (*time: not later than*) para; (*: during*): **~ daylight** de día; **~ 4 o'clock** para las cuatro; **~ this time tomorrow** mañana a estas horas; **~ the time I got here it was too late** cuando llegué ya era demasiado tarde

6 (*amount*): **~ the metre/kilo** por metro/ kilo; **paid ~ the hour** pagado por hora

7 (*MATH, measure*): **to divide/multiply ~ 3** dividir/multiplicar por 3; **a room 3 metres ~ 4** una habitación de 3 metros por 4; **it's broader ~ a metre** es un metro más ancho

8 (*according to*) según, de acuerdo con; **it's 3 o'clock ~ my watch** según mi reloj, son las tres; **it's all right ~ me** por mí, está bien

9: (**all**) **~ oneself** *etc* todo solo; **he did it (all) ~ himself** lo hizo él solo; **he was standing (all) ~ himself in a corner** estaba de pie solo en un rincón

10: **~ the way** a propósito, por cierto; **this wasn't my idea, ~ the way** pues, no fue idea mía

♦ *adv* **1** *see* **go**; **pass** *etc*

2: **~ and ~** finalmente; **they'll come back ~ and ~** acabarán volviendo; **~ and large** en líneas generales, en general

bye(-bye) ['baɪ('baɪ)] *excl* adiós, hasta luego
by(e)-law *n* ordenanza municipal
by-election (*BRIT*) *n* elección *f* parcial
bygone ['baɪɡɒn] *adj* pasado, del pasado ♦ *n*: **let ~s be ~s** lo pasado, pasado está
bypass ['baɪpɑːs] *n* carretera de circunvalación; (*MED*) (operación *f* de) by-pass *m* ♦ *vt* evitar
by-product *n* subproducto, derivado; (*of situation*) consecuencia
bystander ['baɪstændə*] *n* espectador(a) *m/f*
byte [baɪt] *n* (*COMPUT*) byte *m*, octeto
byword ['baɪwəːd] *n*: **to be a ~ for** ser conocidísimo por
by-your-leave *n*: **without so much as a ~** sin decir nada, sin dar ningún tipo de explicación

C c

C [siː] *n* (*MUS*) do *m*
C.A. *abbr* = **chartered accountant**
cab [kæb] *n* taxi *m*; (*of truck*) cabina
cabbage ['kæbɪdʒ] *n* col *f*, berza
cabin ['kæbɪn] *n* cabaña; (*on ship*) camarote *m*; (*on plane*) cabina; ~ **cruiser** *n* yate *m* de motor
cabinet ['kæbɪnɪt] *n* (*POL*) consejo de ministros; (*furniture*) armario; (*also: display ~*) vitrina
cable ['keɪbl] *n* cable *m* ♦ *vt* cablegrafiar; **~-car** *n* teleférico; ~ **television** *n* televisión *f* por cable
cache [kæʃ] *n* (*of weapons, drugs etc*) alijo
cackle ['kækl] *vi* lanzar risotadas; (*hen*) cacarear
cacti ['kæktaɪ] *npl of* **cactus**
cactus ['kæktəs] (*pl* **cacti**) *n* cacto
cadge [kædʒ] (*inf*) *vt* gorronear
Caesarean [siːˈzɛərɪən] *adj*: ~ (**section**) cesárea
café ['kæfeɪ] *n* café *m*
cafeteria [kæfɪˈtɪərɪə] *n* cafetería
cage [keɪdʒ] *n* jaula
cagey ['keɪdʒɪ] (*inf*) *adj* cauteloso, reservado
cagoule [kəˈɡuːl] *n* chubasquero
cajole [kəˈdʒəul] *vt* engatusar
cake [keɪk] *n* (*CULIN: large*) tarta; (: *small*) pastel *m*; (*of soap*) pastilla; **~d** *adj*: **~d with** cubierto de

calculate ['kælkjuleɪt] *vt* calcular; **calculating** *adj* (*scheming*) calculador(a); **calculation** [-'leɪʃən] *n* cálculo, cómputo; **calculator** *n* calculadora
calendar ['kæləndə*] *n* calendario; ~ **month/year** *n* mes *m*/año civil
calf [kɑːf] (*pl* **calves**) *n* (*of cow*) ternero, becerro; (*of other animals*) cría; (*also: ~skin*) piel *f* de becerro; (*ANAT*) pantorrilla
calibre ['kælɪbə*] (*US* **caliber**) *n* calibre *m*
call [kɔːl] *vt* llamar; (*meeting*) convocar ♦ *vi* (*shout*) llamar; (*TEL*) llamar (por teléfono), telefonear (*esp AM*); (*visit: also*: ~ **in**, ~ **round**) hacer una visita ♦ *n* llamada; (*of bird*) canto; **to be ~ed** llamarse; **on** ~ (*nurse, doctor etc*) de guardia; ~ **back** *vi* (*return*) volver; (*TEL*) volver a llamar; ~ **for** *vt fus* (*demand*) pedir, exigir; (*fetch*) venir por (*SP*), pasar por (*AM*); ~ **off** *vt* (*cancel: meeting, race*) cancelar; (: *deal*) anular; (: *strike*) desconvocar; ~ **on** *vt fus* (*visit*) visitar; (*turn to*) acudir a; ~ **out** *vi* gritar, dar voces; ~ **up** *vt* (*MIL*) llamar al servicio militar; (*TEL*) llamar; **~box** (*BRIT*) *n* cabina telefónica; **~er** *n* visita; (*TEL*) usuario/a; ~ **girl** *n* prostituta; **~-in** (*US*) *n* (*programa m*) coloquio (por teléfono); **~ing** *n* vocación *f*; (*occupation*) profesión *f*; **~ing card** (*US*) *n* tarjeta comercial *or* de visita
callous ['kæləs] *adj* insensible, cruel
calm [kɑːm] *adj* tranquilo; (*sea*) liso, en calma ♦ *n* calma, tranquilidad *f* ♦ *vt* calmar, tranquilizar; ~ **down** *vi* calmarse, tranquilizarse ♦ *vt* calmar, tranquilizar
Calor gas ['kælə*-] ® *n* butano
calorie ['kælərɪ] *n* caloría
calves [kɑːvz] *npl of* **calf**
camber ['kæmbə*] *n* (*of road*) combadura, comba
Cambodia [kæmˈbəudjə] *n* Camboya
camcorder ['kæmkɔːdə*] *n* cámara de vídeo portátil
came [keɪm] *pt of* **come**
camel ['kæməl] *n* camello
cameo ['kæmɪəu] *n* camafeo
camera ['kæmərə] *n* máquina fotográfica; (*CINEMA, TV*) cámara; **in** ~ (*LAW*) a puerta cerrada; **~man** *n* cámara *m*
camouflage ['kæməflɑːʒ] *n* camuflaje *m* ♦ *vt* camuflar
camp [kæmp] *n* campamento, camping *m*; (*MIL*) campamento; (*for prisoners*) campo; (*fig: faction*) bando ♦ *vi* acampar ♦ *adj* afectado, afeminado
campaign [kæmˈpeɪn] *n* (*MIL, POL etc*) campaña ♦ *vi* hacer campaña
camp: ~bed (*BRIT*) *n* cama de campaña; **~er** *n* campista *m/f*; (*vehicle*) caravana; **~ing** *n* camping *m*; **to go ~ing** hacer camping; **~site** *n* camping *m*
campus ['kæmpəs] *n* ciudad *f* universitaria
can[1] [kæn] *n* (*of oil, water*) bidón *m*; (*tin*)

lata, bote m ♦ vt enlatar

can² (negative **cannot**, **can't**; conditional and pt **could**) aux vb **1** (be able to) poder; **you ~ do it if you try** puedes hacerlo si lo intentas; **I ~'t see you** no te veo **2** (know how to) saber; **I ~ swim/play tennis/drive** sé nadar/jugar al tenis/conducir; **~ you speak French?** ¿hablas or sabes hablar francés? **3** (may) poder; **~ I use your phone?** ¿me dejas or puedo usar tu teléfono? **4** (expressing disbelief, puzzlement etc): **it ~'t be true!** ¡no puede ser (verdad)!; **what CAN he want?** ¿qué querrá? **5** (expressing possibility, suggestion etc): **he could be in the library** podría estar en la biblioteca; **she could have been delayed** pudo haberse retrasado

─────────────────────────

Canada ['kænədə] n (el) Canadá; **Canadian** [kə'neɪdɪən] adj, n canadiense m/f
canal [kə'næl] n canal m
canary [kə'nɛərɪ] n canario; **C~ Islands** npl las (Islas) Canarias
cancel ['kænsəl] vt cancelar; (train) suprimir; (cross out) tachar, borrar; **~lation** [-'leɪʃən] n cancelación f; supresión f
cancer ['kænsə*] n cáncer m; **C~** (ASTROLOGY) Cáncer m
candid ['kændɪd] adj franco, abierto
candidate ['kændɪdeɪt] n candidato/a
candle ['kændl] n vela; (in church) cirio; **~light** n: **by ~light** a la luz de una vela; **~stick** n (single) candelero; (low) palmatoria; (bigger, ornate) candelabro
candour ['kændə*] (US **candor**) n franqueza
candy ['kændɪ] n azúcar m cande; (US) caramelo; **~-floss** (BRIT) n algodón m (azucarado)
cane [keɪn] n (BOT) caña; (stick) vara, palmeta; (for furniture) mimbre f ♦ (BRIT) vt (SCOL) castigar (con vara)
canister ['kænɪstə*] n bote m, lata; (of gas) bombona
cannabis ['kænəbɪs] n marijuana
canned [kænd] adj en lata, de lata
cannibal ['kænɪbəl] n caníbal m/f
cannon ['kænən] (pl ~ or ~s) n cañón m
cannot ['kænɔt] = **can not**
canoe [kə'nu:] n canoa; (SPORT) piragua
canon ['kænən] n (clergyman) canónigo; (standard) canon m
can opener n abrelatas m inv
canopy ['kænəpɪ] n dosel m; toldo
can't [kænt] = **can not**
cantankerous [kæn'tæŋkərəs] adj quisquilloso
canteen [kæn'ti:n] n (eating place) cantina; (BRIT: of cutlery) juego

canter ['kæntə*] vi ir a medio galope
canvas ['kænvəs] n (material) lona; (painting) lienzo; (NAUT) velas fpl
canvass ['kænvəs] vi (POL): **to ~ for** solicitar votos por ♦ vt (COMM) sondear
canyon ['kænjən] n cañón m
cap [kæp] n (hat) gorra; (of pen) capuchón m; (of bottle) tapa, tapón m; (contraceptive) diafragma m; (for toy gun) cápsula ♦ vt (outdo) superar; (limit) recortar
capability [keɪpə'bɪlɪtɪ] n capacidad f
capable ['keɪpəbl] adj capaz
capacity [kə'pæsɪtɪ] n capacidad f; (position) calidad f
cape [keɪp] n capa; (GEO) cabo
caper ['keɪpə*] n (CULIN: gen: ~s) alcaparra; (prank) broma
capital ['kæpɪtl] n (also: ~ city) capital f; (money) capital m; (also: ~ letter) mayúscula; **~ gains tax** n impuesto sobre las ganancias de capital; **~ism** n capitalismo; **~ist** adj, n capitalista m/f; **~ize on** vt fus aprovechar; **~ punishment** n pena de muerte
capitulate [kə'pɪtjuleɪt] vi capitular, rendirse
Capricorn ['kæprɪkɔ:n] n (ASTROLOGY) Capricornio
capsize [kæp'saɪz] vt volcar, hacer zozobrar ♦ vi volcarse, zozobrar
capsule ['kæpsju:l] n cápsula
captain ['kæptɪn] n capitán m
caption ['kæpʃən] n (heading) título; (to picture) leyenda
captive ['kæptɪv] adj, n cautivo/a m/f
capture ['kæptʃə*] vt prender, apresar; (animal, COMPUT) capturar; (place) tomar; (attention) captar, llamar ♦ n apresamiento; captura; toma; (data ~) formulación f de datos
car [kɑ:*] n coche m, carro (AM), automóvil m; (US: RAIL) vagón m
carafe [kə'ræf] n jarra
carat ['kærət] n quilate m
caravan ['kærəvæn] n (BRIT) caravana, ruló f; (in desert) caravana; **~ site** (BRIT) n camping m para caravanas
carbohydrate [kɑ:bəu'haɪdreɪt] n hidrato de carbono; (food) fécula
carbon ['kɑ:bən] n carbono; **~ paper** n papel m carbón
carburettor [kɑ:bju'retə*] (US **carburetor**) n carburador m
carcass ['kɑ:kəs] n cadáver m (de animal)
card [kɑ:d] n (material) cartulina; (index ~ etc) ficha; (playing ~) carta, naipe m; (visiting ~, greetings ~ etc) tarjeta; **~board** n cartón m
cardigan ['kɑ:dɪgən] n rebeca
cardinal ['kɑ:dɪnl] adj cardinal; (importance, principal) esencial ♦ n cardenal m
card index n fichero

care [kɛə*] *n* cuidado; (*worry*) inquietud *f*; (*charge*) cargo, custodia ♦ *vi*: **to ~ about** (*person, animal*) tener cariño a; (*thing, idea*) preocuparse por; **~ of** en casa de, al cuidado de; **in sb's ~** a cargo de uno; **to take ~ to** cuidarse de, tener cuidado de; **to take ~ of** cuidar; (*problem etc*) ocuparse de; **I don't ~** no me importa; **I couldn't ~ less** eso me trae sin cuidado; **~ for** *vt fus* cuidar a; (*like*) querer

career [kə'rɪə*] *n* profesión *f*; (*in work, school*) carrera ♦ *vi* (*also: ~ along*) correr a toda velocidad; **~ woman** *n* mujer *f* dedicada a su profesión

carefree ['kɛəfriː] *adj* despreocupado

careful ['kɛəful] *adj* cuidadoso; (*cautious*) cauteloso; **(be) ~!** ¡tenga cuidado!; **~ly** *adv* con cuidado, cuidadosamente; con cautela

careless ['kɛəlɪs] *adj* descuidado; (*heedless*) poco atento; **~ness** *n* descuido; falta de atención

carer ['kɛərə*] *n* enfermero/a *m/f* (*official*); (*unpaid*) *persona que cuida a un pariente o vecino*

caress [kə'rɛs] *n* caricia ♦ *vt* acariciar

caretaker ['kɛəteɪkə*] *n* portero/a, conserje *m/f*

car-ferry *n* transbordador *m* para coches

cargo ['kɑːgəu] (*pl* **~es**) *n* cargamento, carga

car hire *n* alquiler *m* de automóviles

Caribbean [kærɪ'biːən] *n*: **the ~ (Sea)** el (Mar) Caribe

caring ['kɛərɪŋ] *adj* humanitario; (*behaviour*) afectuoso

carnation [kɑː'neɪʃən] *n* clavel *m*

carnival ['kɑːnɪvəl] *n* carnaval *m*; (*US: funfair*) parque *m* de atracciones

carol ['kærəl] *n*: **(Christmas) ~** villancico

carp [kɑːp] *n* (*fish*) carpa; **~ at** *vt fus* quejarse de

car park (*BRIT*) *n* aparcamiento, parking *m*

carpenter ['kɑːpɪntə*] *n* carpintero/a.

carpet ['kɑːpɪt] *n* alfombra; (*fitted*) moqueta ♦ *vt* alfombrar; **~ slippers** *npl* zapatillas *fpl*; **~ sweeper** *n* aparato para barrer alfombras

car phone *n* teléfono movil

carriage ['kærɪdʒ] *n* (*BRIT: RAIL*) vagón *m*; (*horse-drawn*) coche *m*; (*of goods*) transporte *m*; (: *cost*) porte *m*, flete *m*; **~way** (*BRIT*) *n* (*part of road*) calzada

carrier ['kærɪə*] *n* (*transport company*) transportista, empresa de transportes; (*MED*) portador *m*; **~ bag** (*BRIT*) *n* bolsa de papel o plástico

carrot ['kærət] *n* zanahoria

carry ['kærɪ] *vt* (*subj: person*) llevar; (*transport*) transportar; (*involve: responsibilities etc*) entrañar, implicar; (*MED*) ser portador de ♦ *vi* (*sound*) oírse; **to get carried away** (*fig*) entusiasmarse; **~ on** *vi* (*continue*) seguir (adelante), continuar ♦ *vt* proseguir, continuar; **~ out** *vt* (*orders*) cumplir; (*investigation*) llevar a cabo, realizar; **~ cot** (*BRIT*) *n* cuna portátil; **~-on** (*inf*) *n* (*fuss*) lío

cart [kɑːt] *n* carro, carreta ♦ *vt* (*inf: transport*) acarrear

carton ['kɑːtən] *n* (*box*) caja (de cartón); (*of milk etc*) bote *m*; (*of yogurt*) tarrina

cartoon [kɑː'tuːn] *n* (*PRESS*) caricatura; (*comic strip*) tira cómica; (*film*) dibujos *mpl* animados

cartridge ['kɑːtrɪdʒ] *n* cartucho; (*of pen*) recambio; (*of record player*) cápsula

carve [kɑːv] *vt* (*meat*) trinchar; (*wood, stone*) cincelar, esculpir; (*initials etc*) grabar; **~ up** *vt* dividir, repartir; **carving** *n* (*object*) escultura; (*design*) talla; (*art*) tallado; **carving knife** *n* trinchante *m*

car wash *n* lavado de coches

case [keɪs] *n* (*container*) caja; (*MED*) caso; (*for jewels etc*) estuche *m*; (*LAW*) causa, proceso; (*BRIT: also: suit~*) maleta; **in ~ of** en caso de; **in any ~** en todo caso; **just in ~** por si acaso

cash [kæʃ] *n* dinero en efectivo, dinero contante ♦ *vt* cobrar, hacer efectivo; **to pay (in) ~** pagar al contado; **~ on delivery** cóbrese al entregar; **~book** *n* libro de caja; **~ card** *n* tarjeta *f* dinero; **~desk** (*BRIT*) *n* caja; **~ dispenser** *n* cajero automático

cashew [kæ'ʃuː] *n* (*also: ~ nut*) anacardo

cash flow *n* flujo de fondos, cash-flow *m*

cashier [kæ'ʃɪə*] *n* cajero/a

cashmere ['kæʃmɪə*] *n* cachemira

cash register *n* caja

casing ['keɪsɪŋ] *n* revestimiento

casino [kə'siːnəu] *n* casino

casket ['kɑːskɪt] *n* cofre *m*, estuche *m*; (*US: coffin*) ataúd *m*

casserole ['kæsərəul] *n* (*food, pot*) cazuela

cassette [kæ'sɛt] *n* cassette *f*; **~ player/ recorder** *n* tocacassettes *m inv*, cassette *m*

cast [kɑːst] (*pt, pp* **cast**) *vt* (*throw*) echar, arrojar, lanzar; (*glance, eyes*) dirigir; (*THEATRE*): **to ~ sb as Othello** dar a uno el papel de Otelo ♦ *vi* (*FISHING*) lanzar ♦ *n* (*THEATRE*) reparto; (*also: plaster ~*) vaciado; **to ~ one's vote** votar; **to ~ off** *vi* (*NAUT*) suscitar dudas acerca de; **~ off** *vi* (*NAUT*) desamarrar; (*KNITTING*) cerrar (los puntos); **~ on** *vi* (*KNITTING*) poner los puntos

castanets [kæstə'nɛts] *npl* castañuelas *fpl*

castaway ['kɑːstəwəɪ] *n* náufrago/a

caste [kɑːst] *n* casta

caster sugar ['kɑːstə*-] (*BRIT*) *n* azúcar *m* extrafino

Castile [kæs'tiːl] *n* Castilla; **Castilian** *adj* castellano/a *m/f*

casting vote ['kɑːstɪŋ-] (*BRIT*) *n* voto decisivo

cast iron n hierro fundido

castle ['kɑːsl] n castillo; (CHESS) torre f

castor ['kɑːstə*] n (wheel) ruedecilla; ~ **oil** n aceite m de ricino

casual ['kæʒjul] adj fortuito; (irregular: work etc) eventual, temporero; (unconcerned) despreocupado; (clothes) de sport; ~**ly** adv de manera despreocupada; (dress) de sport

casualty ['kæʒjultɪ] n víctima, herido; (dead) muerto; (MED: department) urgencias fpl

cat [kæt] n gato; (big ~) felino

Catalan ['kætələn] adj, n catalán/ana m/f

catalogue ['kætələg] (US **catalog**) n catálogo ♦ vt catalogar

Catalonia [kætə'ləʊnɪə] n Cataluña

catalyst ['kætəlɪst] n catalizador m

catalytic converter [kætə'lɪtɪk kən'vɜːtə*] n catalizador m

catapult ['kætəpʌlt] n tirachinas m inv

catarrh [kə'tɑː*] n catarro

catastrophe [kə'tæstrəfɪ] n catástrofe f

catch [kætʃ] (pt, pp **caught**) vt coger (SP), agarrar (AM); (arrest) detener; (grasp) asir; (breath) contener; (surprise: person) sorprender; (attract: attention) captar; (hear) oír; (MED) contagiarse de, coger; (also: ~ up) alcanzar ♦ vi (fire) encenderse; (in branches etc) enredarse ♦ n (fish etc) pesca; (act of catching) cogida; (hidden problem) dificultad f; (game) pilla-pilla; (of lock) pestillo, cerradura; **to ~ fire** encenderse; **to ~ sight of** divisar; ~ **on** vi (understand) caer en la cuenta; (grow popular) hacerse popular; ~ **up** vi (fig) ponerse al día

catching ['kætʃɪŋ] adj (MED) contagioso

catchment area ['kætʃmənt-] (BRIT) n zona de captación

catchphrase ['kætʃfreɪz] n lema m, eslogan m

catchy ['kætʃɪ] adj (tune) pegadizo

category ['kætɪgərɪ] n categoría, clase f

cater ['keɪtə*] vi: **to ~ for** (BRIT) abastecer a; (needs) atender a; (COMM: parties etc) proveer comida a; ~**er** n abastecedor(a) m/f, proveedor(a) m/f; ~**ing** n (trade) hostelería

caterpillar ['kætəpɪlə*] n oruga, gusano; ~ **track** n rodado de oruga

cathedral [kə'θiːdrəl] n catedral f

catholic ['kæθəlɪk] adj (tastes etc) amplio; **C~** adj, n (REL) católico/a m/f

cat's-eye (BRIT) n (AUT) catafoto

cattle ['kætl] npl ganado

catty ['kætɪ] adj malicioso, rencoroso

caucus ['kɔːkəs] n (POL) camarilla política; (: US: to elect candidates) comité m electoral

caught [kɔːt] pt, pp of **catch**

cauliflower ['kɒlɪflaʊə*] n coliflor f

cause [kɔːz] n causa, motivo, razón f; (principle: also: POL) causa ♦ vt causar

caustic ['kɔːstɪk] adj cáustico; (fig) mordaz

caution ['kɔːʃən] n cautela, prudencia; (warning) advertencia, amonestación f ♦ vt amonestar

cautious ['kɔːʃəs] adj cauteloso, prudente, precavido; ~**ly** adv con cautela

cavalier [kævə'lɪə*] adj arrogante, desdeñoso

cavalry ['kævəlrɪ] n caballería

cave [keɪv] n cueva, caverna; ~ **in** vi (roof etc) derrumbarse, hundirse; ~**man** n cavernícola m, troglodita m

cavity ['kævɪtɪ] n hueco, cavidad f; (in tooth) caries f inv

cavort [kə'vɔːt] vi dar brincos

CB n abbr (= Citizens' Band (Radio)) banda ciudadana

CBI n abbr (= Confederation of British Industry) ≈ C.E.O.E. f (SP)

cc abbr = cubic centimetres; = carbon copy

CD n abbr (= compact disc) DC m; (player) (reproductor m de) disco compacto; ~-**ROM** [siːdiːˈrɔm] n abbr CD-ROM m

cease [siːs] vt, vi cesar; ~-**fire** n alto m el fuego; ~**less** adj incesante

cedar ['siːdə*] n cedro

ceiling ['siːlɪŋ] n techo; (fig) límite m

celebrate ['sɛlɪbreɪt] vt celebrar ♦ vi divertirse; ~**d** adj célebre; **celebration** [-'breɪʃən] n fiesta, celebración f

celery ['sɛlərɪ] n apio

celibacy ['sɛlɪbəsɪ] n celibato

cell [sɛl] n celda; (BIOL) célula; (ELEC) elemento

cellar ['sɛlə*] n sótano; (for wine) bodega

'cello ['tʃɛləʊ] n violoncelo

cellophane ['sɛləfeɪn] n celofán m

cellphone ['sɛlfəʊn] n teléfono celular

Celt [kɛlt, sɛlt] adj, n celta m/f; ~**ic** adj celta

cement [sə'mɛnt] n cemento; ~ **mixer** n hormigonera

cemetery ['sɛmɪtrɪ] n cementerio

censor ['sɛnsə*] n censor m ♦ vt (cut) censurar; ~**ship** n censura

censure ['sɛnʃə*] vt censurar

census ['sɛnsəs] n censo

cent [sɛnt] n (US) (coin) centavo, céntimo; see also **per**

centenary [sɛn'tiːnərɪ] n centenario

center ['sɛntə*] (US) = **centre**

centi... [sɛntɪ] prefix: ~**grade** adj centígrado; ~**litre** (US ~**liter**) n centilitro; ~**metre** (US ~**meter**) n centímetro

centipede ['sɛntɪpiːd] n ciempiés m inv

central ['sɛntrəl] adj central; (of house etc) céntrico; **C~ America** n Centroamérica; ~ **heating** n calefacción f central; ~**ize** vt centralizar

centre ['sɛntə*] (US **center**) n centro; (fig) núcleo ♦ vt centrar; ~-**forward** n (SPORT) delantero centro; **~-half** *n* (*SPORT*) medio centro

century ['sɛntjuri] *n* siglo; **20th ~** siglo veinte

ceramic [sɪ'ræmɪk] *adj* cerámico; **~s** *n* cerámica

cereal ['siːrɪəl] *n* cereal *m*

cerebral ['sɛrɪbrəl] *adj* cerebral; intelectual

ceremony ['sɛrɪmənɪ] *n* ceremonia; **to stand on ~** hacer ceremonias, estar de cumplido

certain ['sɜːtən] *adj* seguro; (*person*): **a ~ Mr Smith** un tal Sr Smith; (*particular, some*) cierto; **for ~** a ciencia cierta; **~ly** *adv* (*undoubtedly*) ciertamente; (*of course*) desde luego, por supuesto; **~ty** *n* certeza, certidumbre *f*, seguridad *f*, (*inevitability*) certeza

certificate [sə'tɪfɪkɪt] *n* certificado

certified ['sɜːtɪfaɪd]: **~ mail** (*US*) *n* correo certificado; **~ public accountant** (*US*) *n* contable *m/f* diplomado/a

certify ['sɜːtɪfaɪ] *vt* certificar; (*award diploma to*) conceder un diploma a; (*declare insane*) declarar loco

cervical ['sɜːvɪkl] *adj* cervical

cervix ['sɜːvɪks] *n* cuello del útero

cf. *abbr* (= *compare*) cfr

CFC *n abbr* clorofluorocarbono

ch. *abbr* (= *chapter*) cap

chafe [tʃeɪf] *vt* rozar

chagrin ['ʃægrɪn] *n* (*annoyance*) disgusto; (*disappointment*) decepción *f*

chain [tʃeɪn] *n* cadena; (*of mountains*) cordillera; (*of events*) sucesión *f* ♦ *vt* (*also: ~ up*) encadenar; **~ reaction** *n* reacción *f* en cadena; **~-smoke** *vi* fumar un cigarrillo tras otro; **~ store** *n* tienda de una cadena, ≈ gran almacén

chair [tʃɛə*] *n* silla; (*armchair*) sillón *m*, butaca; (*of university*) cátedra; (*of meeting etc*) presidencia ♦ *vt* (*meeting*) presidir; **~lift** *n* telesilla; **~man** *n* presidente *m*

chalet ['ʃæleɪ] *n* chalet *m*

chalk [tʃɔːk] *n* (*GEO*) creta; (*for writing*) tiza (*SP*), gis *m* (*AM*)

challenge ['tʃælɪndʒ] *n* desafío, reto ♦ *vt* desafiar, retar; (*statement, right*) poner en duda; **to ~ sb to do sth** retar a uno a que haga algo; **challenging** *adj* exigente; (*tone*) de desafío

chamber ['tʃeɪmbə*] *n* cámara, sala; (*POL*) cámara; (*BRIT: LAW: gen pl*) despacho; **~ of commerce** cámara de comercio; **~maid** *n* camarera; **~ music** *n* música de cámara

chamois ['ʃæmwɑː] *n* gamuza

champagne [ʃæm'peɪn] *n* champaña *m*, champán *m*

champion ['tʃæmpɪən] *n* campeón/ona *m/f*; (*of cause*) defensor(a) *m/f*; **~ship** *n* campeonato

chance [tʃɑːns] *n* (*opportunity*) ocasión *f*,

oportunidad *f*; (*likelihood*) posibilidad *f*; (*risk*) riesgo ♦ *vt* arriesgar, probar ♦ *adj* fortuito, casual; **to ~ it** arriesgarse, intentarlo; **to take a ~** arriesgarse; **by ~** por casualidad

chancellor ['tʃɑːnsələ*] *n* canciller *m*; **C~ of the Exchequer** (*BRIT*) *n* Ministro de Hacienda

chandelier [ʃændə'lɪə*] *n* araña (de luces)

change [tʃeɪndʒ] *vt* cambiar; (*replace*) cambiar, reemplazar; (*gear, clothes, job*) cambiar de; (*transform*) transformar ♦ *vi* cambiar(se); (*trains*) hacer transbordo; (*traffic lights*) cambiar de color; (*be transformed*): **to ~ into** transformarse en ♦ *n* cambio; (*alteration*) modificación *f*, transformación *f*, (*of clothes*) muda; (*coins*) suelto, sencillo; (*money returned*) vuelta; **to ~ gear** (*AUT*) cambiar de marcha; **to ~ one's mind** cambiar de opinión *or* idea; **for a ~** para variar; **~able** *adj* (*weather*) cambiable; **~ machine** *n* máquina de cambio; **~over** *n* (*to new system*) cambio

changing ['tʃeɪndʒɪŋ] *adj* cambiante; **~ room** (*BRIT*) *n* vestuario

channel ['tʃænl] *n* (*TV*) canal *m*; (*of river*) cauce *m*; (*groove*) conducto; (*fig: medium*) medio ♦ *vt* (*river etc*) encauzar; **the (English) C~** el Canal (de la Mancha); **the C~ Islands** las Islas Normandas

chant [tʃɑːnt] *n* (*of crowd*) gritos *mpl*; (*REL*) canto ♦ *vt* (*slogan, word*) repetir a gritos

chaos ['keɪɔs] *n* caos *m*

chap [tʃæp] (*BRIT: inf*) *n* (*man*) tío, tipo

chapel ['tʃæpl] *n* capilla

chaperone ['ʃæpərəun] *n* carabina

chaplain ['tʃæplɪn] *n* capellán *m*

chapped [tʃæpt] *adj* agrietado

chapter ['tʃæptə*] *n* capítulo

char [tʃɑː*] *vt* (*burn*) carbonizar, chamuscar ♦ *n* (*BRIT*) = **charlady**

character ['kærɪktə*] *n* carácter *m*, naturaleza, índole *f*; (*moral strength, personality*) carácter; (*in novel, film*) personaje *m*; **~istic** [-'rɪstɪk] *adj* característico ♦ *n* característica; **~ize** *vt* caracterizar

charcoal ['tʃɑːkəul] *n* carbón *m* vegetal; (*ART*) carboncillo

charge [tʃɑːdʒ] *n* (*LAW*) cargo, acusación *f*, (*cost*) precio, coste *m*; (*responsibility*) cargo ♦ *vt* (*LAW*): **to ~ (with)** acusar (de); (*battery*) cargar; (*price*) pedir; (*customer*) cobrar ♦ *vi* precipitarse; (*MIL*) cargar, atacar; **~s** *npl*: **to reverse the ~s** (*BRIT: TEL*) revertir el cobro; **to take ~ of** hacerse cargo de, encargarse de; **to be in ~ of** estar encargado de; (*business*) mandar; **how much do you ~?** ¿cuánto cobra usted?; **to ~ an expense (up) to sb's account** cargar algo a cuenta de alguien; **~ card** *n* tarjeta de cuenta

charitable ['tʃærɪtəbl] *adj* benéfico

charity [ˈtʃærɪtɪ] n caridad f; (organization) sociedad f benéfica; (money, gifts) limosnas fpl

charlady [ˈtʃɑːleɪdɪ] (BRIT) n mujer f de la limpieza

charlatan [ˈʃɑːlətən] n farsante m/f

charm [tʃɑːm] n encanto, atractivo; (talisman) hechizo; (on bracelet) dije m ♦ vt encantar; ~**ing** adj encantador(a)

chart [tʃɑːt] n (diagram) cuadro; (graph) gráfica; (map) carta de navegación ♦ vt (course) trazar; (progress) seguir; ~**s** npl (Top 40): **the ~s** ≈ los 40 principales (SP)

charter [ˈtʃɑːtə*] vt (plane) alquilar; (ship) fletar ♦ n (document) carta; (of university, company) estatutos mpl; ~**ed accountant** (BRIT) n contable m/f diplomado/a; ~ **flight** n vuelo chárter

charwoman [ˈtʃɑːwumən] n = **charlady**

chase [tʃeɪs] vt (pursue) perseguir; (also: ~ away) ahuyentar ♦ n persecución f

chasm [ˈkæzəm] n sima

chassis [ˈʃæsɪ] n chasis m

chat [tʃæt] vi (also: have a ~) charlar ♦ n charla; ~ **show** (BRIT) n programa m de entrevistas

chatter [ˈtʃætə*] vi (person) charlar; (teeth) castañear ♦ n (of birds) parloteo; (of people) charla, cháchara; ~**box** (inf) n parlanchín/ina m/f

chatty [ˈtʃætɪ] adj (style) informal; (person) hablador(a)

chauffeur [ˈʃəufə*] n chófer m

chauvinist [ˈʃəuvɪnɪst] n (male ~) machista m; (nationalist) chovinista m/f

cheap [tʃiːp] adj barato; (joke) de mal gusto; (poor quality) de mala calidad ♦ adv barato; ~**er** adj más barato; ~**ly** adv barato, a bajo precio

cheat [tʃiːt] vi hacer trampa ♦ vt: **to ~ sb (out of sth)** estafar (algo) a uno ♦ n (person) tramposo/a

check [tʃɛk] vt (examine) controlar; (facts) comprobar; (halt) parar, detener; (restrain) refrenar, restringir ♦ n (inspection) control m, inspección f; (curb) freno; (US: bill) nota, cuenta; (US) = **cheque**; (pattern: gen pl) cuadro ♦ adj (also: ~ed: pattern, cloth) a cuadros; ~ **in** vi (at hotel) firmar el registro; (at airport) facturar el equipaje ♦ vt (luggage) facturar; ~ **out** vi (of hotel) marcharse; ~ **up** vi: **to ~ up on sth** comprobar algo; **to ~ up on sb** investigar a alguien; ~**ered** (US) adj = **chequered**; ~**ers** (US) n juego de damas; ~-**in (desk)** n mostrador m de facturación; ~**ing account** (US) n cuenta corriente; ~**mate** n jaque m mate; ~**out** n caja; ~**point** n (punto de) control m; ~**room** (US) n consigna; ~**up** n (MED) reconocimiento general

cheek [tʃiːk] n mejilla; (impudence) descaro; **what a ~!** ¡qué cara!; ~**bone** n pómulo; ~**y** adj fresco, descarado

cheep [tʃiːp] vi piar

cheer [tʃɪə*] vt vitorear, aplaudir; (gladden) alegrar, animar ♦ vi dar vivas ♦ n viva m; ~**s** npl aplausos mpl; ~**s!** ¡salud!; ~ **up** vi animarse ♦ vt alegrar, animar; ~**ful** adj alegre

cheerio [tʃɪərɪˈəu] (BRIT) excl ¡hasta luego!

cheese [tʃiːz] n queso; ~**board** n tabla de quesos

cheetah [ˈtʃiːtə] n leopardo cazador

chef [ʃɛf] n jefe/a m/f de cocina

chemical [ˈkɛmɪkəl] adj químico ♦ n producto químico

chemist [ˈkɛmɪst] n (BRIT: pharmacist) farmacéutico/a; (scientist) químico/a; ~**ry** n química; ~'**s (shop)** (BRIT) n farmacia

cheque [tʃɛk] (US **check**) n cheque m; ~**book** n talonario de cheques (SP), chequera (AM); ~ **card** n tarjeta de cheque

chequered [ˈtʃɛkəd] (US **checkered**) adj (fig) accidentado

cherish [ˈtʃɛrɪʃ] vt (love) querer, apreciar; (protect) cuidar; (hope etc) abrigar

cherry [ˈtʃɛrɪ] n cereza; (also: ~ tree) cerezo

chess [tʃɛs] n ajedrez m; ~**board** n tablero (de ajedrez)

chest [tʃɛst] n (ANAT) pecho; (box) cofre m, cajón m; ~ **of drawers** n cómoda

chestnut [ˈtʃɛsnʌt] n castaña; ~ **(tree)** n castaño

chew [tʃuː] vt mascar, masticar; ~**ing gum** n chicle m

chic [ʃiːk] adj elegante

chick [tʃɪk] n pollito, polluelo; (inf: girl) chica

chicken [ˈtʃɪkɪn] n gallina, pollo; (food) pollo; (inf: coward) gallina m/f; ~ **out** (inf) vi rajarse; ~**pox** n varicela

chicory [ˈtʃɪkərɪ] n (for coffee) achicoria; (salad) escarola

chief [tʃiːf] n jefe/a m/f ♦ adj principal; ~ **executive** n director(a) m/f general; ~**ly** adv principalmente

chiffon [ˈʃɪfɒn] n gasa

chilblain [ˈtʃɪlbleɪn] n sabañón m

child [tʃaɪld] (pl **children**) n niño/a; (offspring) hijo/a; ~**birth** n parto; ~**hood** n niñez f, infancia; ~**ish** adj pueril, aniñado; ~**like** adj de niño; ~ **minder** (BRIT) n niñera; ~**ren** [ˈtʃɪldrən] npl of **child**

Chile [ˈtʃɪlɪ] n Chile m; ~**an** adj, n chileno/a m/f

chill [tʃɪl] n frío; (MED) resfriado ♦ vt enfriar; (CULIN) congelar

chilli [ˈtʃɪlɪ] (BRIT) n chile m (SP), ají m (AM)

chilly [ˈtʃɪlɪ] adj frío

chime [tʃaɪm] n repique m; (of clock) campanada ♦ vi repicar; sonar

chimney ['tʃɪmnɪ] n chimenea; ~ **sweep** n deshollinador m

chimpanzee [tʃɪmpæn'ziː] n chimpancé m

chin [tʃɪn] n mentón m, barbilla

china ['tʃaɪnə] n porcelana; (crockery) loza

China ['tʃaɪnə] n China; **Chinese** [tʃaɪ'niːz] adj chino ♦ n inv chino/a; (LING) chino

chink [tʃɪŋk] n (opening) grieta, hendedura; (noise) tintineo

chip [tʃɪp] n (gen pl: CULIN: BRIT) patata (SP) or papa (AM) frita; (: US: also: potato ~) patata or papa frita; (of wood) astilla; (of glass, stone) lasca; (at poker) ficha; (COMPUT) chip m ♦ vt (cup, plate) desconchar; ~ **in** (inf) vi interrumpir; (contribute) compartir los gastos

chiropodist [kɪ'rɔpədɪst] (BRIT) n pedicuro/a, callista m/f

chirp [tʃɜːp] vi (bird) gorjear, piar

chisel ['tʃɪzl] n (for wood) escoplo; (for stone) cincel m

chit [tʃɪt] n nota

chitchat ['tʃɪttʃæt] n chismes mpl, habladurías fpl

chivalry ['ʃɪvəlrɪ] n caballerosidad f

chives [tʃaɪvz] npl cebollinos mpl

chlorine ['klɔːriːn] n cloro

chock-a-block ['tʃɔkə'blɔk] adj atestado

chockfull ['tʃɔk'ful] adj atestado

chocolate ['tʃɔklɪt] n chocolate m; (sweet) bombón m

choice [tʃɔɪs] n elección f, selección f; (option) opción f; (preference) preferencia ♦ adj escogido

choir ['kwaɪə*] n coro; ~**boy** n niño de coro

choke [tʃəuk] vi ahogarse; (on food) atragantarse ♦ vt estrangular, ahogar; (block): **to be ~d with** estar atascado de ♦ n (AUT) estárter m

cholesterol [kə'lestərɔl] n colesterol m

choose [tʃuːz] (pt **chose**, pp **chosen**) vt escoger, elegir; (team) seleccionar; **to ~ to do sth** optar por hacer algo

choosy ['tʃuːzɪ] adj delicado

chop [tʃɔp] vt (wood) cortar, tajar; (CULIN: also: ~ up) picar ♦ n (CULIN) chuleta; ~**s** npl (jaws) boca, labios mpl

chopper ['tʃɔpə*] n (helicopter) helicóptero

choppy ['tʃɔpɪ] adj (sea) picado, agitado

chopsticks ['tʃɔpstiks] npl palillos mpl

chord [kɔːd] n (MUS) acorde m

chore [tʃɔː*] n faena, tarea; (routine task) trabajo rutinario

chortle ['tʃɔːtl] vi reír entre dientes

chorus ['kɔːrəs] n coro; (repeated part of song) estribillo

chose [tʃəuz] pt of **choose**

chosen ['tʃəuzn] pp of **choose**

Christ [kraɪst] n Cristo

christen ['krɪsn] vt bautizar

Christian ['krɪstɪən] adj, n cristiano/a m/f;

~**ity** [-'ænɪtɪ] n cristianismo; ~ **name** n nombre m de pila

Christmas ['krɪsməs] n Navidad f; **Merry** ~! ¡Felices Pascuas!; ~ **card** n crismas m inv, tarjeta de Navidad; ~ **Day** n día m de Navidad; ~ **Eve** n Nochebuena; ~ **tree** n árbol m de Navidad

chrome [krəum] n cromo

chronic ['krɔnɪk] adj crónico

chronological [krɔnə'lɔdʒɪkəl] adj cronológico

chubby ['tʃʌbɪ] adj regordete

chuck [tʃʌk] (inf) vt lanzar, arrojar; (BRIT: also: ~ up) abandonar; ~ **out** vt (person) echar (fuera); (rubbish etc) tirar

chuckle ['tʃʌkl] vi reírse entre dientes

chug [tʃʌg] vi resoplar; (car, boat: also: ~ along) avanzar traqueteando

chum [tʃʌm] n compañero/a

chunk [tʃʌŋk] n pedazo, trozo

church [tʃɜːtʃ] n iglesia; ~**yard** n cementerio

churlish ['tʃɜːlɪʃ] adj grosero

churn [tʃɜːn] n (for butter) mantequera; (for milk) lechera; ~ **out** vt producir en serie

chute [ʃuːt] n (also: rubbish ~) vertedero; (for coal etc) rampa de caída

chutney ['tʃʌtnɪ] n condimento a base de frutas de la India

CIA (US) n abbr (= Central Intelligence Agency) CIA f

CID (BRIT) n abbr (= Criminal Investigation Department) ≈ B.I.C. f (SP)

cider ['saɪdə*] n sidra

cigar [sɪ'gɑː*] n puro

cigarette [sɪgə'ret] n cigarrillo (SP), cigarro (AM); pitillo; ~ **case** n pitillera; ~ **end** n colilla

Cinderella [sɪndə'relə] n Cenicienta

cinders ['sɪndəz] npl cenizas fpl

cine-camera ['sɪnɪ-] (BRIT) n cámara cinematográfica

cinema ['sɪnəmə] n cine m

cinnamon ['sɪnəmən] n canela

circle ['sɜːkl] n círculo; (in theatre) anfiteatro ♦ vi dar vueltas ♦ vt (surround) rodear, cercar; (move round) dar la vuelta a

circuit ['sɜːkɪt] n circuito; (tour) gira; (track) pista; (lap) vuelta; ~**ous** [sɜː'kjuːtəs] adj indirecto

circular ['sɜːkjulə*] adj circular ♦ n circular f

circulate ['sɜːkjuleɪt] vi circular; (person: at party etc) hablar con los invitados ♦ vt poner en circulación; **circulation** [-'leɪʃən] n circulación f; (of newspaper) tirada

circumcise ['sɜːkəmsaɪz] vt circuncidar

circumspect ['sɜːkəmspekt] adj prudente

circumstances ['sɜːkəmstənsɪz] npl circunstancias fpl; (financial condition) situación f económica

circumvent ['sɜːkəmvent] vt burlar

circus ['sɜːkəs] n circo

CIS n abbr (= Commonwealth of Independent States) CEI f

cistern ['sɪstən] n tanque m, depósito; (in toilet) cisterna

citizen ['sɪtɪzn] n (POL) ciudadano/a; (of city) vecino/a, habitante m/f; **~ship** n ciudadanía

citrus fruits ['sɪtrəs-] npl agrios mpl

city ['sɪtɪ] n ciudad f; **the C~** centro financiero de Londres

civic ['sɪvɪk] adj cívico; (authorities) municipal; ~ **centre** (BRIT) n centro público

civil ['sɪvɪl] adj civil; (polite) atento, cortés; ~ **engineer** n ingeniero de caminos (, canales y puertos); **~ian** [sɪ'vɪlɪən] adj civil (no military) ♦ n civil m/f, paisano/a

civilization [sɪvɪlaɪ'zeɪʃən] n civilización f

civilized ['sɪvɪlaɪzd] adj civilizado

civil: ~ **law** n derecho civil; ~ **servant** n funcionario/a del Estado; **C~ Service** n administración f pública; ~ **war** n guerra civil

clad [klæd] adj: ~ **(in)** vestido (de)

claim [kleɪm] vt exigir, reclamar; (rights etc) reivindicar; (assert) pretender ♦ vi (for insurance) reclamar ♦ n reclamación f, pretensión f; **~ant** n demandante m/f

clairvoyant [kleə'vɔɪənt] n clarividente m/f

clam [klæm] n almeja

clamber ['klæmbə*] vi trepar

clammy ['klæmɪ] adj frío y húmedo

clamour ['klæmə*] (US **clamor**) vi: **to ~ for** clamar por, pedir a voces

clamp [klæmp] n abrazadera, grapa ♦ vt (2 things together) cerrar fuertemente; (one thing on another) afianzar (con abrazadera); ~ **down on** vt fus (subj: government, police) reforzar la lucha contra

clang [klæŋ] vi sonar, hacer estruendo

clap [klæp] vi aplaudir; **~ping** n aplausos mpl

claret ['klærət] n clarete m

clarify ['klærɪfaɪ] vt aclarar

clarinet ['klærɪ'net] n clarinete m

clash [klæʃ] n enfrentamiento; choque m; desacuerdo; estruendo ♦ vi (fight) enfrentarse; (beliefs) chocar; (disagree) estar en desacuerdo; (colours) desentonar; (two events) coincidir

clasp [klɑːsp] n (hold) apretón m; (of necklace, bag) cierre m ♦ vt apretar; abrazar

class [klɑːs] n clase f ♦ vt clasificar

classic ['klæsɪk] adj, n clásico; **~al** adj clásico

classified ['klæsɪfaɪd] adj (information) reservado; ~ **advertisement** n anuncio por palabras

classify ['klæsɪfaɪ] vt clasificar

classmate ['klɑːsmeɪt] n compañero/a de clase

classroom ['klɑːsrum] n aula

clatter ['klætə*] n estrépito ♦ vi hacer ruido or estrépito

clause [klɔːz] n cláusula; (LING) oración f

claw [klɔː] n (of cat) uña; (of bird of prey) garra; (of lobster) pinza; ~ **at** vt fus arañar

clay [kleɪ] n arcilla

clean [kliːn] adj limpio; (record, reputation) bueno, intachable; (joke) decente ♦ vt limpiar; (hands etc) lavar; ~ **out** vt limpiar; ~ **up** vt limpiar, asear; **~-cut** adj (person) bien parecido; **~er** n (person) asistenta; (substance) producto para la limpieza; **~er's** n tintorería; **~ing** n limpieza; **cleanliness** ['klɛnlɪnɪs] n limpieza

cleanse [klɛnz] vt limpiar; **~r** n (for face) crema limpiadora

clean-shaven adj sin barba, afeitado

cleansing department (BRIT) n departamento de limpieza

clear [klɪə*] adj claro; (road, way) libre; (conscience) limpio, tranquilo; (skin) terso; (sky) despejado ♦ vt (space) despejar, limpiar; (LAW: suspect) absolver; (obstacle) salvar, saltar por encima de; (cheque) aceptar ♦ vi (fog etc) despejarse ♦ adv: ~ **of** a distancia de; **to ~ the table** recoger or levantar la mesa; ~ **up** vt limpiar; (mystery) aclarar, resolver; **~ance** n (removal) despeje m; (permission) acreditación f; **~-cut** adj bien definido, nítido; **~ing** n (in wood) claro; **~ing bank** (BRIT) n cámara de compensación; **~ly** adv claramente; (evidently) sin duda; **~way** (BRIT) n carretera donde no se puede parar

cleaver ['kliːvə] n cuchilla (de carnicero)

clef [klɛf] n (MUS) clave f

cleft [klɛft] n (in rock) grieta, hendedura

clench [klɛntʃ] vt apretar, cerrar

clergy ['klɜːdʒɪ] n clero; **~man** n clérigo

clerical ['klɛrɪkəl] adj de oficina; (REL) clerical

clerk [klɑːk, (US) klɜːrk] n (BRIT) oficinista m/f; (US) dependiente/a m/f, vendedor(a) m/f

clever ['klɛvə*] adj (intelligent) inteligente, listo; (skilful) hábil; (device, arrangement) ingenioso

click [klɪk] vt (tongue) chasquear; (heels) taconear

client ['klaɪənt] n cliente m/f

cliff [klɪf] n acantilado

climate ['klaɪmɪt] n clima m

climax ['klaɪmæks] n (of battle, career) apogeo; (of film, book) punto culminante; (sexual) orgasmo

climb [klaɪm] vi subir; (plant) trepar; (move with effort): **to ~ over a wall/into a car** trepar a una tapia/subir a un coche ♦ vt (stairs) subir; (tree) trepar a; (mountain) escalar ♦ n subida; **~-down** n vuelta atrás; **~er** n alpinista m/f (SP), andinista m/f (AM); **~ing** n alpinismo (SP), andinismo

(AM)

clinch [klɪntʃ] vt (deal) cerrar; (argument) remachar

cling [klɪŋ] (pt, pp **clung**) vi: **to ~ to** agarrarse a; (clothes) pegarse a

clinic ['klɪnɪk] n clínica; **~al** adj clínico; (fig) frío

clink [klɪŋk] vi tintinar

clip [klɪp] n (for hair) horquilla; (also: paper ~) sujetapapeles m inv, clip m; (TV, CINEMA) fragmento ♦ vt (cut) cortar; (also: ~ together) unir; **~pers** npl (for gardening) tijeras fpl; **~ping** n (newspaper) recorte m

clique [kliːk] n camarilla

cloak [kləuk] n (for hair) capa, manto ♦ vt (fig) encubrir, disimular; **~room** n guardarropa; (BRIT: WC) lavabo (SP), aseos mpl (SP), baño (AM)

clock [klɔk] n reloj m; **~ in or on** vi fichar, picar; **~ off or out** vi fichar or picar la salida; **~wise** adv en el sentido de las agujas del reloj; **~work** n aparato de relojería ♦ adj (toy) de cuerda

clog [klɔg] n zueco, chanclo ♦ vt atascar ♦ vi (also: ~ up) atascarse

cloister ['klɔɪstə*] n claustro

close¹ [kləus] adj (near): ~ **(to)** cerca (de); (friend) íntimo; (connection) estrecho; (examination) detallado, minucioso; (weather) bochornoso; **to have a ~ shave** (fig) escaparse por un pelo ♦ adv cerca; **~ by, ~ at hand** muy cerca; **~ to** prep cerca de

close² [kləuz] vt (shut) cerrar; (end) concluir, terminar ♦ vi (shop etc) cerrarse; (end) concluirse, terminarse ♦ n (end) fin m, final m, conclusión f; **~ down** vi cerrarse definitivamente; **~d** adj (shop etc) cerrado; **~d shop** n taller m gremial

close-knit [kləus'nɪt] adj (fig) muy unido

closely ['kləuslɪ] adv (study) con detalle; (watch) de cerca; (resemble) estrechamente

closet ['klɔzɪt] n armario

close-up ['kləusʌp] n primer plano

closure ['kləuʒə*] n cierre m

clot [klɔt] n (gen: blood ~) coágulo; (inf: idiot) imbécil m/f ♦ vi (blood) coagularse

cloth [klɔθ] n (material) tela, paño; (rag) trapo

clothe [kləuð] vt vestir; **~s** npl ropa; **~s brush** n cepillo (para la ropa); **~s line** n cuerda (para tender la ropa); **~s peg** (US **~s pin**) n pinza

clothing ['kləuðɪŋ] n = **clothes**

cloud [klaud] n nube f; **~burst** n aguacero; **~y** adj nublado, nebuloso; (liquid) turbio

clout [klaut] vt dar un tortazo a

clove [kləuv] n clavo; **~ of garlic** n diente m de ajo

clover ['kləuvə*] n trébol m

clown [klaun] n payaso ♦ vi (also: ~ about, ~ around) hacer el payaso

cloying ['klɔɪɪŋ] adj empalagoso

club [klʌb] n (society) club m; (weapon) porra, cachiporra; (also: golf ~) palo ♦ vt aporrear ♦ vi: **to ~ together** (for gift) comprar entre todos; **~s** npl (CARDS) tréboles mpl; **~ car** (US) n (RAIL) coche m sálon; **~house** n local social, sobre todo en clubs deportivos

cluck [klʌk] vi cloquear

clue [kluː] n pista; (in crosswords) indicación f; **I haven't a ~** no tengo ni idea

clump [klʌmp] n (of trees) grupo

clumsy ['klʌmzɪ] adj (person) torpe, desmañado; (tool) difícil de manejar; (movement) desgarbado

clung [klʌŋ] pt, pp of **cling**

cluster ['klʌstə*] n grupo ♦ vi agruparse, apiñarse

clutch [klʌtʃ] n (AUT) embrague m; (grasp): **~es** garras fpl ♦ vt asir; agarrar

clutter ['klʌtə*] vt atestar

cm abbr (= centimetre) cm

CND n abbr (= Campaign for Nuclear Disarmament) plataforma pro desarme nuclear

Co. abbr = **county**; **company**

c/o abbr (= care of) c/a, a/c

coach [kəutʃ] n autocar m (SP), coche m de línea; (horse-drawn) coche m; (of train) vagón m, coche m; (SPORT) entrenador(a) m/f, instructor(a) m/f; (tutor) profesor(a) m/f particular ♦ vt (SPORT) entrenar; (student) preparar, enseñar; **~ trip** n excursión f en autocar

coal [kəul] n carbón m; **~ face** n frente m de carbón; **~field** n yacimiento de carbón

coalition [kəuə'lɪʃən] n coalición f

coal: **~man** n carbonero; **~ merchant** n = **~man**; **~mine** ['kəulmaɪn] n mina de carbón

coarse [kɔːs] adj basto, burdo; (vulgar) grosero, ordinario

coast [kəust] n costa, litoral m ♦ vi (AUT) ir en punto muerto; **~al** adj costero, costanero; **~guard** n guardacostas m inv; **~line** n litoral m

coat [kəut] n abrigo; (of animal) pelaje m, lana; (of paint) mano f, capa ♦ vt cubrir, revestir; **~ of arms** n escudo de armas; **~ hanger** n percha (SP), gancho (AM); **~ing** n capa, baño

coax [kəuks] vt engatusar

cob [kɔb] n see **corn**

cobbler ['kɔblə] n zapatero (remendón)

cobbles ['kɔblz] npl, **cobblestones** ['kɔblstəunz] npl adoquines mpl

cobweb ['kɔbweb] n telaraña

cock [kɔk] n (rooster) gallo; (male bird) macho ♦ vt (gun) amartillar; **~erel** n gallito; **~eyed** adj (idea) disparatado

cockle ['kɔkl] n berberecho

cockney ['kɔknɪ] n habitante de ciertos barrios de Londres

cockpit ['kɔkpɪt] n cabina

cockroach ['kɔkrəʊtʃ] n cucaracha
cocktail ['kɔkteɪl] n coctel m, cóctel m; ~ **cabinet** n mueble-bar m; ~ **party** n coctel m, cóctel m
cocoa ['kəʊkəʊ] n cacao; (drink) chocolate m
coconut ['kəʊkənʌt] n coco
cocoon [kə'ku:n] n (ZOOL) capullo
cod [kɔd] n bacalao
C.O.D. abbr (= cash on delivery) C.A.E
code [kəʊd] n código; (cipher) clave f; (dialling ~) prefijo; (post ~) código postal
cod-liver oil ['kɔdlɪvə*-] n aceite m de hígado de bacalao
coercion [kəʊ'ɜ:ʃən] n coacción f
coffee ['kɔfɪ] n café m; ~ **bar** (BRIT) n cafetería; ~ **bean** n grano de café; ~ **break** n descanso (para tomar café); ~**pot** n cafetera; ~ **table** n mesita (para servir el café)
coffin ['kɔfɪn] n ataúd m
cog [kɔg] n (wheel) rueda dentada; (tooth) diente m
cogent ['kəʊdʒənt] adj convincente
cognac ['kɔnjæk] n coñac m
coil [kɔɪl] n rollo; (ELEC) bobina, carrete m; (contraceptive) espiral f ♦ vt enrollar
coin [kɔɪn] n moneda ♦ vt (word) inventar, idear; ~**age** n moneda; ~**box** (BRIT) n cabina telefónica
coincide [kəʊɪn'saɪd] vi coincidir; (agree) estar de acuerdo; **coincidence** [kəʊ'ɪnsɪdəns] n casualidad f
coke [kəʊk] n (coal) coque m
Coke [kəʊk] ® n Coca-Cola ®
colander ['kɔləndə*] n colador m, escurridor m
cold [kəʊld] adj frío ♦ n frío; (MED) resfriado; **it's** ~ hace frío; **to be** ~ (person) tener frío; **to catch** ~ enfriarse; **to catch a** ~ resfriarse, acatarrarse; **in** ~ **blood** a sangre fría; ~**shoulder** vt dar or volver la espalda a; ~ **sore** n herpes mpl or fpl
coleslaw ['kəʊlslɔ:] n especie de ensalada de col
colic ['kɔlɪk] n cólico
collapse [kə'læps] vi hundirse, derrumbarse; (MED) sufrir un colapso ♦ n hundimiento, derrumbamiento; (MED) colapso; **collapsible** adj plegable
collar ['kɔlə*] n (of coat, shirt) cuello; (of dog etc) collar; ~**bone** n clavícula
collateral [kɔ'lætərəl] n garantía colateral
colleague ['kɔli:g] n colega m/f
collect [kə'lekt] vt (litter, mail etc) recoger; (as a hobby) coleccionar; (BRIT: call and pick up) recoger; (debts, subscriptions etc) recaudar ♦ vi reunirse; (dust) acumularse; **to call** ~ (US: TEL) llamar a cobro revertido; ~**ion** [kə'lekʃən] n colección f; (of mail, for charity) recogida
collector [kə'lektə*] n coleccionista m/f
college ['kɔlɪdʒ] n colegio mayor; (of agri-

culture, technology) escuela universitaria
collide [kə'laɪd] vi chocar
collie ['kɔlɪ] n perro pastor escocés, collie m
colliery ['kɔlɪərɪ] (BRIT) n mina de carbón
collision [kə'lɪʒən] n choque m
colloquial [kə'ləʊkwɪəl] adj familiar, coloquial
collusion [kə'lu:ʒən] n confabulación f, connivencia
Colombia [kə'lɔmbɪə] n Colombia; ~**n** adj, n colombiano/a
colon ['kəʊlən] n (sign) dos puntos; (MED) colon m
colonel ['kɜ:nl] n coronel m
colonial [kə'ləʊnɪəl] adj colonial
colony ['kɔlənɪ] n colonia
colour ['kʌlə*] (US **color**) n color m ♦ vt color(e)ar; (dye) teñir; (fig: account) adornar; (: judgement) distorsionar ♦ vi (blush) sonrojarse; ~**s** npl (of party, club) colores mpl; **in** ~ en color; ~ **in** vt colorear; ~ **bar** n segregación f racial; ~**blind** adj daltónico; ~**ed** adj de color; (photo) en color; ~ **film** n película en color; ~**ful** adj lleno de color; (story) fantástico; (person) excéntrico; ~**ing** n (complexion) tez f; (in food) colorante m; ~ **scheme** n combinación f de colores; ~ **television** n televisión f en color
colt [kəʊlt] n potro
column ['kɔləm] n columna; ~**ist** ['kɔləmnɪst] n columnista m/f
coma ['kəʊmə] n coma m
comb [kəʊm] n peine m; (ornamental) peineta ♦ vt (hair) peinar; (area) registrar a fondo
combat ['kɔmbæt] n combate m ♦ vt combatir
combination [kɔmbɪ'neɪʃən] n combinación f
combine [vb kəm'baɪn, n 'kɔmbaɪn] vt combinar; (qualities) reunir ♦ vi combinarse ♦ n (ECON) cartel m; ~ (**harvester**) n cosechadora

---

KEYWORD

come [kʌm] (pt **came**, pp **come**) vi **1** (movement towards) venir; **to** ~ **running** venir corriendo
2 (arrive) llegar; **he's** ~ **here to work** ha venido aquí para trabajar; **to** ~ **home** volver a casa
3 (reach): **to** ~ **to** llegar a; **the bill came to £40** la cuenta ascendía a cuarenta libras
4 (occur): **an idea came to me** se me ocurrió una idea
5 (be, become): **to** ~ **loose/undone** etc aflojarse/desabrocharse, desatarse etc; **I've** ~ **to like him** por fin ha llegado a gustarme
come about vi suceder, ocurrir

come across vt fus (person) topar con; (thing) dar con
come away vi (leave) marcharse; (become detached) desprenderse
come back vi (return) volver
come by vt fus (acquire) conseguir
come down vi (price) bajar; (tree, building) ser derribado
come forward vi presentarse
come from vt fus (place, source) ser de
come in vi (visitor) entrar; (train, report) llegar; (fashion) ponerse de moda; (on deal etc) entrar
come in for vt fus (criticism etc) recibir
come into vt fus (money) heredar; (be involved) tener que ver con; **to ~ into fashion** ponerse de moda
come off vi (button) soltarse, desprenderse; (attempt) salir bien
come on vi (pupil) progresar; (work, project) desarrollarse; (lights) encenderse; (electricity) volver; **~ on!** ¡vamos!
come out vi (fact) salir a la luz; (book, sun) salir; (stain) quitarse
come round vi (after faint, operation) volver en sí
come to vi (wake) volver en sí
come up vi (sun) salir; (problem) surgir; (event) aproximarse; (in conversation) mencionarse
come up against vt fus (resistance etc) tropezar con
come up with vt fus (idea) sugerir; (money) conseguir
come upon vt fus (find) dar con

comeback ['kʌmbæk] n: **to make a ~** (THEATRE) volver a las tablas
comedian [kə'miːdɪən] n cómico; **comedienne** [-'ɛn] n cómica
comedy ['kɒmɪdɪ] n comedia; (humour) comicidad f
comet ['kɒmɪt] n cometa m
comeuppance [kʌm'ʌpəns] n: **to get one's ~** llevar su merecido
comfort ['kʌmfət] n bienestar m; (relief) alivio ♦ vt consolar; **~s** npl (of home etc) comodidades fpl; **~able** adj cómodo; (financially) acomodado; (easy) fácil; **~ably** adv (sit) cómodamente; (live) holgadamente; **~ station** (US) n servicios mpl
comic ['kɒmɪk] adj (also: ~al) cómico ♦ n (comedian) cómico; (BRIT: for children) tebeo; (BRIT: for adults) comic m; **~ strip** n tira cómica
coming ['kʌmɪŋ] n venida, llegada ♦ adj que viene; **~(s) and going(s)** n(pl) ir y venir m, ajetreo
comma ['kɒmə] n coma
command [kə'mɑːnd] n orden f, mandato; (MIL: authority) mando; (mastery) dominio ♦ vt (troops) mandar; (give orders to): **to ~**

sb to do mandar or ordenar a uno hacer; **~eer** [kɒmən'dɪə*] vt requisar; **~er** n (MIL) comandante m/f, jefe/a m/f; **~ment** n (REL) mandamiento
commemorate [kə'mɛməreɪt] vt conmemorar
commence [kə'mɛns] vt, vi comenzar, empezar
commend [kə'mɛnd] vt elogiar, alabar; (recommend) recomendar
commensurate [kə'mɛnsərɪt] adj: **~ with** en proporción a, que corresponde a
comment ['kɒmɛnt] n comentario ♦ vi: **to ~ on** hacer comentarios sobre; "no ~" (written) "sin comentarios"; (spoken) "no tengo nada que decir"; **~ary** ['kɒməntərɪ] n comentario; **~ator** ['kɒməntert ə*] n comentarista m/f
commerce ['kɒmɔːs] n comercio
commercial [kə'mɔːʃəl] adj comercial ♦ n (TV, RADIO) anuncio
commiserate [kə'mɪzəreɪt] vi: **to ~ with** compadecerse de, condolerse de
commission [kə'mɪʃən] n (committee, fee) comisión f ♦ vt (work of art) encargar; **out of ~** fuera de servicio; **~aire** [kəmɪʃə'nɛə*] (BRIT) n portero; **~er** n (POLICE) comisario de policía
commit [kə'mɪt] vt (act) cometer; (resources) dedicar; (to sb's care) entregar; **to ~ o.s. (to do)** comprometerse a hacer); **to ~ suicide** suicidarse; **~ment** n compromiso; (to ideology etc) entrega
committee [kə'mɪtɪ] n comité m
commodity [kə'mɒdɪtɪ] n mercancía
common ['kɒmən] adj común; (pej) ordinario ♦ n campo común; **the C~s** npl (BRIT) (la Cámara de) los Comunes mpl; **in ~** en común; **~er** n plebeyo; **~ law** n ley f consuetudinaria; **~ly** adv comúnmente; **C~ Market** n Mercado Común; **~place** adj de lo más común; **~room** n sala común; **~ sense** n sentido común; **the C~wealth** n la Commonwealth
commotion [kə'məuʃən] n tumulto, confusión f
commune [n 'kɒmjuːn, vb kə'mjuːn] n (group) comuna ♦ vi: **to ~ with** comulgar or conversar con
communicate [kə'mjuːnɪkeɪt] vt comunicar ♦ vi: **to ~ (with)** comunicarse (con); (in writing) estar en contacto (con)
communication [kəmjuːnɪ'keɪʃən] n comunicación f; **~ cord** (BRIT) n timbre m de alarma
communion [kə'mjuːnɪən] n (also: Holy C~) comunión f
communiqué [kə'mjuːnɪkeɪ] n comunicado, parte f
communism ['kɒmjunɪzəm] n comunismo; **communist** adj, n comunista m/f
community [kə'mjuːnɪtɪ] n comunidad f;

(large group) colectividad f; ~ **centre** n centro social; ~ **chest** *(US)* n arca comunitaria, fondo común; ~ **home** *(BRIT)* n correccional m

commutation ticket [kɔmjuːˈteɪʃən-] *(US)* n billete m de abono

commute [kəˈmjuːt] vi viajar a diario de la casa al trabajo ♦ vt conmutar; **~r** n persona (que ... *see vi*)

compact [adj kəmˈpækt, n ˈkɔmpækt] adj compacto ♦ n *(also: powder ~)* polvera; ~ **disc** n compact disc m; ~ **disc player** n reproductor m de disco compacto, compact disc m

companion [kəmˈpænɪən] n compañero/a; **~ship** n compañerismo

company [ˈkʌmpənɪ] n compañía; *(COMM)* sociedad f, compañía; **to keep sb** ~ acompañar a uno; ~ **secretary** *(BRIT)* n secretario/a de compañía

comparative [kəmˈpærətɪv] adj relativo; *(study)* comparativo; **~ly** adv *(relatively)* relativamente

compare [kəmˈpeə*] vt: **to** ~ **to** sth/sb **with/to** comparar algo/a uno con ♦ vi: **to** ~ **(with)** compararse (con); **comparison** [-ˈpærɪsn] n comparación f

compartment [kəmˈpɑːtmənt] n *(also: RAIL)* compartim(i)ento

compass [ˈkʌmpəs] n brújula; **~es** npl *(MATH)* compás m

compassion [kəmˈpæʃən] n compasión f; **~ate** adj compasivo

compatible [kəmˈpætɪbl] adj compatible

compel [kəmˈpel] vt obligar; **~ling** adj *(fig: argument)* convincente

compensate [ˈkɔmpənseɪt] vt compensar ♦ vi: **to** ~ **for** compensar; **compensation** [-ˈseɪʃən] n *(for loss)* indemnización f

compère [ˈkɔmpeə*] n presentador m

compete [kəmˈpiːt] vi *(take part)* tomar parte, concurrir; *(vie with)*: **to** ~ **with** competir con, hacer competencia a

competence [ˈkɔmpɪtəns] n capacidad f, aptitud f

competent [ˈkɔmpɪtənt] adj competente, capaz

competition [kɔmpɪˈtɪʃən] n *(contest)* concurso; *(rivalry)* competencia

competitive [kəmˈpetɪtɪv] adj *(ECON, SPORT)* competitivo

competitor [kəmˈpetɪtə*] n *(rival)* competidor(a) m/f; *(participant)* concursante m/f

compile [kəmˈpaɪl] vt compilar

complacency [kəmˈpleɪsnsɪ] n autosatisfacción f

complacent [kəmˈpleɪsənt] adj autocomplaciente

complain [kəmˈpleɪn] vi quejarse; *(COMM)* reclamar; **~t** n queja; reclamación f; *(MED)* enfermedad f

complement [n ˈkɔmplɪmənt, vb ˈkɔmplɪment] n complemento; *(esp of ship's crew)* dotación f ♦ vt *(enhance)* complementar; **~ary** [kɔmplɪˈmentərɪ] adj complementario

complete [kəmˈpliːt] adj *(full)* completo; *(finished)* acabado ♦ vt *(fulfil)* completar; *(finish)* acabar; *(a form)* llenar; **~ly** adv completamente; **completion** [-ˈpliːʃən] n terminación f; *(of contract)* realización f

complex [ˈkɔmpleks] adj, n complejo

complexion [kəmˈplekʃən] n *(of face)* tez f, cutis m

compliance [kəmˈplaɪəns] n *(submission)* sumisión f; *(agreement)* conformidad f; **in** ~ **with** de acuerdo con

complicate [ˈkɔmplɪkeɪt] vt complicar; **~d** adj complicado; **complication** [-ˈkeɪʃən] n complicación f

complicity [kəmˈplɪsɪtɪ] n complicidad f

compliment [ˈkɔmplɪmənt] n *(formal)* cumplido ♦ vt felicitar; **~s** npl *(regards)* saludos mpl; **to pay sb a** ~ hacer cumplidos a uno; **~ary** [-ˈmentərɪ] adj lisonjero; *(free)* de favor

comply [kəmˈplaɪ] vi: **to** ~ **with** cumplir con

component [kəmˈpəunənt] adj componente ♦ n *(TECH)* pieza

compose [kəmˈpəuz] vt: **to be ~d of** componerse de; *(music etc)* componer; **to** ~ **o.s.** tranquilizarse; **~d** adj sosegado; **~r** n *(MUS)* compositor(a) m/f; **composition** [kɔmpəˈzɪʃən] n composición f

compost [ˈkɔmpɔst] n abono (vegetal)

composure [kəmˈpəuʒə*] n serenidad f, calma

compound [ˈkɔmpaund] n *(CHEM)* compuesto; *(LING)* palabra compuesta; *(enclosure)* recinto ♦ adj compuesto; *(fracture)* complicado

comprehend [kɔmprɪˈhend] vt comprender; **comprehension** [-ˈhenʃən] n comprensión f

comprehensive [kɔmprɪˈhensɪv] adj exhaustivo; *(INSURANCE)* contra todo riesgo; ~ **(school)** n centro estatal de enseñanza secundaria; ≈ Instituto Nacional de Bachillerato *(SP)*

compress [vb kəmˈpres, n ˈkɔmpres] vt comprimir; *(information)* condensar ♦ n *(MED)* compresa

comprise [kəmˈpraɪz] vt *(also: be ~d of)* comprender, constar de; *(constitute)* constituir

compromise [ˈkɔmprəmaɪz] n *(agreement)* arreglo ♦ vt comprometer ♦ vi transigir

compulsion [kəmˈpʌlʃən] n compulsión f; *(force)* obligación f

compulsive [kəmˈpʌlsɪv] adj compulsivo; *(viewing, reading)* obligado

compulsory [kəmˈpʌlsərɪ] adj obligatorio

computer [kəmˈpjuːtə*] n ordenador m,

computador *m*, computadora; ~ **game** *n*
juego para ordenador; ~**ize** *vt* (*data*) computerizar; (*system*) informatizar; ~ **programmer** *n* programador(a) *m/f*; ~ **programming** *n* programación *f*; ~ **science**
n informática; **computing** [kəm'pjuːtɪŋ] *n*
(*activity, science*) informática
comrade [ˈkɔmrɪd] *n* (POL, MIL) camarada;
(*friend*) compañero/a; ~**ship** *n* camaradería, compañerismo
con [kɔn] *vt* (*deceive*) engañar; (*cheat*) estafar ♦ *n* estafa
conceal [kənˈsiːl] *vt* ocultar
conceit [kənˈsiːt] *n* presunción *f*, ~**ed** *adj*
presumido
conceivable [kənˈsiːvəbl] *adj* concebible
conceive [kənˈsiːv] *vt, vi* concebir
concentrate [ˈkɔnsəntreɪt] *vi* concentrarse
♦ *vt* concentrar
concentration [kɔnsənˈtreɪʃən] *n* concentración *f*
concept [ˈkɔnsept] *n* concepto
conception [kənˈsepʃən] *n* (*idea*) concepto,
idea; (BIOL) concepción *f*
concern [kənˈsəːn] *n* (*matter*) asunto;
(COMM) empresa; (*anxiety*) preocupación *f*
♦ *vt* (*worry*) preocupar; (*involve*) afectar;
(*relate*) tener que ver con; **to be** ~**ed**
(**about**) interesarse (por), preocuparse
(por); ~**ing** *prep* sobre, acerca de
concert [ˈkɔnsət] *n* concierto; ~**ed**
[kənˈsəːtəd] *adj* (*efforts etc*) concertado; ~
hall *n* sala de conciertos
concertina [kɔnsəˈtiːnə] *n* concertina
concerto [kənˈtʃəːtəu] *n* concierto
concession [kənˈseʃən] *n* concesión *f*; **tax**
~ privilegio fiscal
concise [kənˈsaɪs] *adj* conciso
conclude [kənˈkluːd] *vt* concluir; (*treaty
etc*) firmar; (*agreement*) llegar a; (*decide*)
llegar a la conclusión de; **conclusion**
[-ˈkluːʒən] *n* conclusión *f*; firma; **conclusive** [-ˈkluːsɪv] *adj* decisivo, concluyente
concoct [kənˈkɔkt] *vt* confeccionar; (*plot*)
tramar; ~**ion** [-ˈkɔkʃən] *n* mezcla
concourse [ˈkɔŋkɔːs] *n* vestíbulo
concrete [ˈkɔŋkriːt] *n* hormigón *m* ♦ *adj* de
hormigón; (*fig*) concreto
concur [kənˈkəː*] *vi* estar de acuerdo, asentir
concurrently [kənˈkʌrntlɪ] *adv* al mismo
tiempo
concussion [kənˈkʌʃən] *n* conmoción *f* cerebral
condemn [kənˈdem] *vt* condenar; (*building*)
declarar en ruina; ~**ation** [kɔndemˈneɪʃən]
n condena
condense [kənˈdens] *vi* condensarse ♦ *vt*
condensar, abreviar; ~**d milk** *n* leche *f*
condensada
condescending [kɔndɪˈsendɪŋ] *adj* condescendiente

condition [kənˈdɪʃən] *n* condición *f*, estado; (*requirement*) condición *f* ♦ *vt* condicionar; **on** ~ **that** la condición (de) que; ~**al**
adj condicional; ~**er** *n* suavizante
condolences [kənˈdəulənsɪz] *npl* pésame *m*
condom [ˈkɔndəm] *n* condón *m*
condone [kənˈdəun] *vt* condonar
conducive [kənˈdjuːsɪv] *adj*: ~ **to** conducente a
conduct [*n* ˈkɔndʌkt, *vb* kənˈdʌkt] *n* conducta, comportamiento ♦ *vt* (*lead*) conducir; (*manage*) llevar a cabo, dirigir; (MUS)
dirigir; **to** ~ **o.s.** comportarse; ~**ed tour**
(BRIT) *n* visita acompañada; ~**or** *n* (*of orchestra*) director *m*; (US: *on train*) revisor(a)
m/f; (*on bus*) cobrador *m*; (ELEC) conductor *m*; ~**ress** *n* (*on bus*) cobradora
cone [kəun] *n* cono; (*pine* ~) piña; (*on
road*) pivote *m*; (*for ice-cream*) cucurucho
confectioner [kənˈfekʃənə*] *n* repostero/a;
~'**s** (**shop**) *n* confitería; ~**y** *n* dulces *mpl*
confer [kənˈfəː*] *vt*: ~ **sth on** otorgar
algo a ♦ *vi* conferenciar
conference [ˈkɔnfərns] *n* (*meeting*) reunión
f; (*convention*) congreso
confess [kənˈfes] *vt* confesar ♦ *vi* admitir;
~**ion** [-ˈfeʃən] *n* confesión *f*
confetti [kənˈfetɪ] *n* confeti *m*
confide [kənˈfaɪd] *vi*: **to** ~ **in** confiar en
confidence [ˈkɔnfɪdns] *n* (*also: self* ~) confianza; (*secret*) confidencia; **in** ~ (*speak,
write*) en confianza; ~ **trick** *n* timo; **confident** *adj* seguro de sí mismo; (*certain*) seguro; **confidential** [kɔnfɪˈdenʃəl] *adj* confidencial
confine [kənˈfaɪn] *vt* (*limit*) limitar; (*shut
up*) encerrar; ~**d** *adj* (*space*) reducido;
~**ment** *n* (*prison*) prisión *f*; ~**s** [ˈkɔnfaɪnz]
npl confines *mpl*
confirm [kənˈfəːm] *vt* confirmar; ~**ation**
[kɔnfəˈmeɪʃən] *n* confirmación *f*; ~**ed** *adj*
empedernido
confiscate [ˈkɔnfɪskeɪt] *vt* confiscar
conflict [*n* ˈkɔnflɪkt, *vb* kənˈflɪkt] *n* conflicto
♦ *vi* (*opinions*) chocar; ~**ing** *adj* contradictorio
conform [kənˈfɔːm] *vi* conformarse; **to** ~
to ajustarse a
confound [kənˈfaund] *vt* confundir
confront [kənˈfrʌnt] *vt* (*problems*) hacer
frente a; (*enemy, danger*) enfrentarse con;
~**ation** [kɔnfrənˈteɪʃən] *n* enfrentamiento
confuse [kənˈfjuːz] *vt* (*perplex*) aturdir, desconcertar; (*mix up*) confundir; (*complicate*)
complicar; ~**d** *adj* confuso; (*person*) perplejo; **confusing** *adj* confuso; **confusion**
[-ˈfjuːʒən] *n* confusión *f*
congeal [kənˈdʒiːl] *vi* (*blood*) coagularse;
(*sauce etc*) cuajarse
congenial [kənˈdʒiːnɪəl] *adj* agradable
congenital [kənˈdʒenɪtl] *adj* congénito
congested [kənˈdʒestɪd] *adj* congestionado

congestion [kən'dʒestʃən] n congestión f
conglomerate [kən'glɒmərət] n (COMM, GEO) conglomerado
congratulate [kən'grætjuleɪt] vt: to ~ sb (on) felicitar a uno (por); **congratulations** [-'leɪʃənz] npl felicitaciones fpl; ~! ¡enhorabuena!
congregate ['kɒŋgrɪgeɪt] vi congregarse; **congregation** [-'geɪʃən] n (of a church) feligreses mpl
congress ['kɒŋgres] n congreso; (US): C~ Congreso; ~**man** (US) n miembro del Congreso
conifer ['kɒnɪfə*] n conífera
conjecture [kən'dʒektʃə*] n conjetura
conjugal ['kɒndʒugl] adj conyugal
conjugate ['kɒndʒugeɪt] vt conjugar
conjunctivitis [kəndʒʌŋktɪ'vaɪtɪs] n conjuntivitis f
conjure ['kʌndʒə*] vi hacer juegos de manos; ~ **up** vt (ghost, spirit) hacer aparecer; (memories) evocar; ~**r** n ilusionista m/f
conk out [kɒŋk-] (inf) vi averiarse
con man ['kɒn-] n estafador m
connect [kə'nekt] vt juntar, unir; (ELEC) conectar; (TEL: subscriber) poner; (TEL: caller) poner al habla; (fig) relacionar, asociar ♦ vi: to ~ with (train) enlazar con; to be ~ed with (associated) estar relacionado con; ~**ion** [-ʃən] n juntura, unión f; (ELEC) conexión f; (RAIL) enlace m; (TEL) comunicación f; (fig) relación f
connive [kə'naɪv] vi: to ~ at hacer la vista gorda a
connoisseur [kɒnɪ'sə*] n experto/a, entendido/a
conquer ['kɒŋkə*] vt (territory) conquistar; (enemy, feelings) vencer; ~**or** n conquistador m
conquest ['kɒŋkwest] n conquista
cons [kɒnz] npl see **convenience; pro**
conscience ['kɒnʃəns] n conciencia
conscientious [kɒnʃɪ'enʃəs] adj concienzudo; (objection) de conciencia
conscious ['kɒnʃəs] adj (deliberate) deliberado; (awake, aware) consciente; ~**ness** n conciencia; (MED) conocimiento
conscript ['kɒnskrɪpt] n recluta m; ~**ion** [kən'skrɪpʃən] n servicio militar (obligatorio)
consecrate ['kɒnsɪkreɪt] vt consagrar
consensus [kən'sensəs] n consenso
consent [kən'sent] n consentimiento ♦ vi: to ~ (to) consentir (en)
consequence ['kɒnsɪkwəns] n consecuencia; (significance) importancia
consequently ['kɒnsɪkwəntlɪ] adv por consiguiente
conservation [kɒnsə'veɪʃən] n conservación f
conservative [kən'sɔːvətɪv] adj conservador(a); (estimate etc) cauteloso; C~ (BRIT)

adj, n (POL) conservador(a) m/f
conservatory [kən'sɔːvətrɪ] n invernadero; (MUS) conservatorio
conserve [kən'sɔːv] vt conservar ♦ n conserva
consider [kən'sɪdə*] vt considerar; (take into account) tener en cuenta; (study) estudiar, examinar; to ~ doing sth pensar en (la posibilidad de) hacer algo; ~**able** adj considerable; ~**ably** adv notablemente
considerate [kən'sɪdərɪt] adj considerado; **consideration** [-'reɪʃən] n consideración f; (factor) factor m; to give sth further consideration estudiar algo más a fondo
considering [kən'sɪdərɪŋ] prep teniendo en cuenta
consign [kən'saɪn] vt: to ~ to (sth unwanted) relegar a; (person) destinar a; ~**ment** n envío
consist [kən'sɪst] vi: to ~ of consistir en
consistency [kən'sɪstənsɪ] n (of argument etc) coherencia; consecuencia; (thickness) consistencia
consistent [kən'sɪstənt] adj (person) consecuente; (argument etc) coherente
consolation [kɒnsə'leɪʃən] n consuelo
console[1] [kən'səul] vt consolar
console[2] ['kɒnsəul] n consola
consonant ['kɒnsənənt] n consonante f
consortium [kən'sɔːtɪəm] n consorcio
conspicuous [kən'spɪkjuəs] adj (visible) visible
conspiracy [kən'spɪrəsɪ] n conjura, complot m
conspire [kən'spaɪə*] vi conspirar; (events etc) unirse
constable ['kʌnstəbl] (BRIT) n policía m/f; chief ~ ≈ jefe m de policía
constabulary [kən'stæbjulərɪ] n ≈ policía
constant ['kɒnstənt] adj constante; ~**ly** adv constantemente
constipated ['kɒnstɪpeɪtəd] adj estreñido; **constipation** [kɒnstɪ'peɪʃən] n estreñimiento
constituency [kən'stɪtjuənsɪ] n (POL: area) distrito electoral; (: electors) electorado; **constituent** [-ənt] n (POL) elector(a) m/f; (part) componente m
constitute ['kɒnstɪtjuːt] vt constituir; (make up: whole) componer
constitution [kɒnstɪ'tjuːʃən] n constitución f; ~**al** adj constitucional
constraint [kən'streɪnt] n obligación f; (limit) restricción f
construct [kən'strʌkt] vt construir; ~**ion** [-ʃən] n construcción f; ~**ive** adj constructivo
construe [kən'struː] vt interpretar
consul ['kɒnsl] n cónsul m/f; ~**ate** ['kɒnsjulɪt] n consulado
consult [kən'sʌlt] vt consultar; ~**ant** n (BRIT: MED) especialista m/f; (other special-

ist) asesor(a) *m/f*; ~**ation** [kɔnsəl'teɪʃən] *n* consulta; ~**ing room** (*BRIT*) *n* consultorio

consume [kən'sju:m] *vt* (*eat*) comerse; (*drink*) beberse; (*fire etc, COMM*) consumir; ~**r** *n* consumidor(a) *m/f*; ~**r goods** *npl* bienes *mpl* de consumo; ~**rism** *n* consumismo

consummate ['kɔnsʌmeɪt] *vt* consumar

consumption [kən'sʌmpʃən] *n* consumo

cont. *abbr* (= *continued*) sigue

contact ['kɔntækt] *n* contacto; (*person*) contacto; (: *pej*) enchufe *m* ♦ *vt* ponerse en contacto con; ~ **lenses** lentes *fpl* de contacto

contagious [kən'teɪdʒəs] *adj* contagioso

contain [kən'teɪn] *vt* contener; **to** ~ **o.s.** contenerse; ~**er** *n* recipiente *m*; (*for shipping etc*) contenedor *m*

contaminate [kən'tæmɪneɪt] *vt* contaminar

cont'd *abbr* (= *continued*) sigue

contemplate ['kɔntəmpleɪt] *vt* contemplar; (*reflect upon*) considerar

contemporary [kən'tempərərɪ] *adj*, *n* contemporáneo/a *m/f*

contempt [kən'tempt] *n* desprecio; ~ **of court** (*LAW*) desacato (a los tribunales); ~**ible** *adj* despreciable; ~**uous** *adj* desdeñoso

contend [kən'tend] *vt* (*argue*) afirmar ♦ *vi*: **to** ~ **with/for** luchar contra/por; ~**er** *n* (*SPORT*) contendiente *m/f*

content [*adj*, *vb* kən'tent, *n* 'kɔntent] *adj* (*happy*) contento; (*satisfied*) satisfecho ♦ *vt* contentar; satisfacer ♦ *n* contenido; ~**s** *npl* contenido; (**table of**) ~**s** índice *m* de materias; ~**ed** *adj* contento; satisfecho

contention [kən'tenʃən] *n* (*assertion*) aseveración *f*; (*disagreement*) discusión *f*

contentment [kən'tentmənt] *n* contento

contest [*n* 'kɔntest, *vb* kən'test] *n* lucha; (*competition*) concurso ♦ *vt* (*dispute*) impugnar; (*POL*) presentarse como candidato/a en; ~**ant** [kən'testənt] *n* concursante *m/f*; (*in fight*) contendiente *m/f*

context ['kɔntekst] *n* contexto

continent ['kɔntɪnənt] *n* continente *m*; **the C~** (*BRIT*) el continente europeo; ~**al** [-'nentl] *adj* continental; ~**al quilt** (*BRIT*) *n* edredón *m*

contingency [kən'tɪndʒənsɪ] *n* contingencia

continual [kən'tɪnjuəl] *adj* continuo; ~**ly** *adv* constantemente

continuation [kəntɪnju'eɪʃən] *n* prolongación *f*; (*after interruption*) reanudación *f*

continue [kən'tɪnju:] *vi*, *vt* seguir, continuar

continuous [kən'tɪnjuəs] *adj* continuo; ~ **stationery** *n* papel *m* continuo

contort [kən'tɔ:t] *vt* retorcer; ~**ion** [-'tɔ:ʃən] *n* (*movement*) contorsión *f*

contour ['kɔntuə*] *n* contorno; (*also*: ~ *line*) curva de nivel

contraband ['kɔntrəbænd] *n* contrabando

contraception [kɔntrə'sepʃən] *n* contracepción *f*

contraceptive [kɔntrə'septɪv] *adj*, *n* anticonceptivo

contract [*n* 'kɔntrækt, *vb* kən'trækt] *n* contrato ♦ *vi* (*COMM*): **to** ~ **to do sth** comprometerse por contrato a hacer algo; (*become smaller*) contraerse, encogerse ♦ *vt* contraer; ~**ion** [kən'trækʃən] *n* contracción *f*; ~**or** *n* contratista *m/f*

contradict [kɔntrə'dɪkt] *vt* contradecir; ~**ion** [-ʃən] *n* contradicción *f*; ~**ory** *adj* contradictorio

contraption [kən'træpʃən] (*pej*) *n* artilugio *m*

contrary[1] ['kɔntrərɪ] *adj* contrario ♦ *n* lo contrario; **on the** ~ al contrario; **unless you hear to the** ~ a no ser que le digan lo contrario

contrary[2] [kən'trɛərɪ] *adj* (*perverse*) terco

contrast [*n* 'kɔntrɑ:st, *vt* kən'trɑ:st] *n* contraste *m* ♦ *vt* comparar; **in** ~ **to** en contraste con; ~**ing** (*opinions*) opuesto; (*colours*) que hace contraste

contravene [kɔntrə'vi:n] *vt* infringir

contribute [kən'trɪbju:t] *vi* contribuir ♦ *vt*: **to** ~ **£10/an article** to contribuir con 10 libras/un artículo a; **to** ~ **to** (*charity*) donar a; (*newspaper*) escribir para; (*discussion*) intervenir en; ~**ion** [kɔntrɪ'bju:ʃən] *n* (*donation*) donativo; (*BRIT: for social security*) cotización *f*; (*to debate*) intervención *f*; (*to journal*) colaboración *f*; **contributor** *n* contribuyente *m/f*; (*to newspaper*) colaborador(a) *m/f*

contrive [kən'traɪv] *vt* (*invent*) idear ♦ *vi*: **to** ~ **to do** lograr hacer

control [kən'trəul] *vt* controlar; (*process etc*) dirigir; (*machinery*) manejar; (*temper*) dominar; (*disease*) contener ♦ *n* control *m*; ~**s** *npl* (*of vehicle*) instrumentos *mpl* de mando; (*of radio*) controles *mpl*; (*governmental*) medidas *fpl* de control; **under** ~ bajo control; **to be in** ~ **of** tener el mando de; **the car went out of** ~ se perdió el control del coche; ~ **panel** *n* tablero de instrumentos; ~ **room** *n* sala de mando; ~ **tower** *n* (*AVIAT*) torre *f* de control

controversial [kɔntrə'vɔ:ʃl] *adj* polémico

controversy ['kɔntrəvɔ:sɪ] *n* polémica

conurbation [kɔnə:'beɪʃən] *n* urbanización *f*

convalesce [kɔnvə'les] *vi* convalecer

convector [kən'vektə*] *n* calentador *m* de aire

convene [kən'vi:n] *vt* convocar ♦ *vi* reunirse

convenience [kən'vi:nɪəns] *n* (*easiness*) comodidad *f*; (*suitability*) idoneidad *f*; (*advantage*) ventaja; **at your** ~ cuando le sea conveniente; **all modern** ~**s, all mod cons**

(*BRIT*) todo confort

convenient [kən'viːnɪənt] *adj* (*useful*) útil; (*place, time*) conveniente

convent ['kɔnvənt] *n* convento

convention [kən'venʃən] *n* convención *f*; (*meeting*) asamblea; (*agreement*) convenio; **~al** *adj* convencional

converge [kən'vɔːdʒ] *vi* convergir; (*people*): **to ~ on** dirigirse todos a

conversant [kən'vɔːsnt] *adj*: **to be ~ with** estar al tanto de

conversation [kɔnvə'seɪʃən] *n* conversación *f*; **~al** *adj* familiar; **~al skill** facilidad *f* de palabra

converse [*n* 'kɔnvɜːs, *vb* kən'vɜːs] *n* inversa ♦ *vi* conversar; **~ly** [-'vɜːslɪ] *adv* a la inversa

conversion [kən'vɔːʃən] *n* conversión *f*

convert [*vb* kən'vɔːt, *n* 'kɔnvɜːt] *vt* (*REL, COMM*) convertir; (*alter*): **to ~ sth into/to** transformar algo en/convertir algo a ♦ *n* converso/a; **~ible** *adj* convertible ♦ *n* descapotable *m*

convey [kən'veɪ] *vt* llevar; (*thanks*) comunicar; (*idea*) expresar; **~or belt** *n* cinta transportadora

convict [*vb* kən'vɪkt, *n* 'kɔnvɪkt] *vt* (*find guilty*) declarar culpable a ♦ *n* presidiario/a; **~ion** [-ʃən] *n* condena; (*belief, certainty*) convicción *f*

convince [kən'vɪns] *vt* convencer; **~d** *adj*: **~d of/that** convencido de/de que; **convincing** *adj* convincente

convoluted ['kɔnvəluːtɪd] *adj* (*argument etc*) enrevesado

convoy ['kɔnvɔɪ] *n* convoy *m*

convulse [kən'vʌls] *vt*: **to be ~d with laughter** desternillarse de risa; **convulsion** [-'vʌlʃən] *n* convulsión *f*

coo [kuː] *vi* arrullar

cook [kuk] *vt* (*stew etc*) guisar; (*meal*) preparar ♦ *vi* cocer; (*person*) cocinar ♦ *n* cocinero/a; **~ book** *n* libro de cocina; **~er** *n* cocina; **~ery** *n* cocina; **~ery book** (*BRIT*) *n* = **~ book**; **~ie** (*US*) *n* galleta; **~ing** *n* cocina

cool [kuːl] *adj* fresco; (*not afraid*) tranquilo; (*unfriendly*) frío ♦ *vt* enfriar ♦ *vi* enfriarse; **~ness** *n* frescura; tranquilidad *f*; (*indifference*) falta de entusiasmo

coop [kuːp] *n* gallinero ♦ *vt*: **to ~ up** (*fig*) encerrar

cooperate [kəu'ɔpəreɪt] *vi* cooperar, colaborar; **cooperation** [-'reɪʃən] *n* cooperación *f*, colaboración *f*; **cooperative** [-rətɪv] *adj* (*business*) cooperativo; (*person*) servicial ♦ *n* cooperativa

coordinate [*vb* kəu'ɔːdɪneɪt, *n* kəu'ɔːdɪnət] *vt* coordinar ♦ *n* (*MATH*) coordenada; **~s** *npl* (*clothes*) coordinados *mpl*; **coordination** [-'neɪʃən] *n* coordinación *f*

co-ownership [kəu'əunəʃɪp] *n* copropiedad *f*

cop [kɔp] (*inf*) *n* poli *m* (*SP*), tira *m* (*AM*)

cope [kəup] *vi*: **to ~ with** (*problem*) hacer frente a

copious ['kəupɪəs] *adj* copioso, abundante

copper ['kɔpə*] *n* (*metal*) cobre *m*; (*BRIT: inf*) poli *m*; **~s** *npl* (*money*) calderilla (*SP*), centavos *mpl* (*AM*)

coppice ['kɔpɪs] *n* bosquecillo

copulate ['kɔpjuleɪt] *vi* copularse

copy ['kɔpɪ] *n* copia; (*of book etc*) ejemplar *m* ♦ *vt* copiar; **~right** *n* derechos *mpl* de autor

coral ['kɔrəl] *n* coral *m*; **~ reef** *n* arrecife *m* (de coral)

cord [kɔːd] *n* cuerda; (*ELEC*) cable *m*; (*fabric*) pana

cordial ['kɔːdɪəl] *adj* cordial ♦ *n* cordial *m*

cordon ['kɔːdn] *n* cordón *m*; **~ off** *vt* acordonar

corduroy ['kɔːdərɔɪ] *n* pana

core [kɔː*] *n* centro, núcleo; (*of fruit*) corazón *m*; (*of problem*) meollo ♦ *vt* quitar el corazón de

coriander [kɔrɪ'ændə*] *n* culantro

cork [kɔːk] *n* corcho; (*tree*) alcornoque *m*; **~screw** *n* sacacorchos *m inv*

corn [kɔːn] *n* (*BRIT: cereal crop*) trigo; (*US: maize*) maíz *m*; (*on foot*) callo; **~ on the cob** (*CULIN*) maíz en la mazorca (*SP*), choclo (*AM*)

corned beef ['kɔːnd-] *n* carne *f* acecinada (en lata)

corner ['kɔːnə*] *n* (*outside*) esquina; (*inside*) rincón *m*; (*in road*) curva; (*FOOTBALL*) córner *m*; (*BOXING*) esquina ♦ *vt* (*trap*) arrinconar; (*COMM*) acaparar ♦ *vi* (*in car*) tomar las curvas; **~stone** *n* (*also fig*) piedra angular

cornet ['kɔːnɪt] *n* (*MUS*) corneta; (*BRIT: of ice-cream*) cucurucho

cornflakes ['kɔːnfleɪks] *npl* copos *mpl* de maíz, cornflakes *mpl*

cornflour ['kɔːnflauə*] (*BRIT*), **cornstarch** ['kɔːnstɑːtʃ] (*US*) *n* harina de maíz

Cornwall ['kɔːnwəl] *n* Cornualles *m*

corny ['kɔːnɪ] (*inf*) *adj* gastado

coronary ['kɔrənərɪ] *n* (*also*: **~ thrombosis**) infarto

coronation [kɔrə'neɪʃən] *n* coronación *f*

coroner ['kɔrənə*] *n* juez *m* (de instrucción)

corporal ['kɔːpərl] *n* cabo ♦ *adj*: **~ punishment** castigo corporal

corporate ['kɔːpərɪt] *adj* (*action, ownership*) colectivo; (*finance, image*) corporativo

corporation [kɔːpə'reɪʃən] *n* (*of town*) ayuntamiento; (*COMM*) corporación *f*

corps [kɔː*, *pl* kɔːz] *n inv* cuerpo; **diplomatic ~** cuerpo diplomático; **press ~** gabinete *m* de prensa

corpse [kɔːps] *n* cadáver *m*

corral [kə'rɑːl] *n* corral *m*

correct [kə'rɛkt] adj justo, exacto; (proper) correcto ♦ vt corregir; (exam) corregir, calificar; (in stance) rectificación f

correspond [kɔrɪs'pɔnd] vi (write): **to ~ (with)** escribirse (con); (be equivalent to): **to ~ (to)** corresponder (a); (be in accordance): **to ~ (with)** corresponder (con); **~ence** n correspondencia; **~ence course** n curso por correspondencia; **~ent** n corresponsal m/f

corridor ['kɔrɪdɔ:*] n pasillo

corroborate [kə'rɔbəreɪt] vt corroborar

corrode [kə'rəud] vt corroer ♦ vi corroerse; **corrosion** [-'rəuʒən] n corrosión f

corrugated ['kɔrəgeɪtɪd] adj ondulado; **~ iron** n chapa ondulada

corrupt [kə'rʌpt] adj (person) corrupto; (COMPUT) corrompido ♦ vt corromper; (COMPUT) degradar; **~ion** [-ʃən] n corrupción f

corset ['kɔ:sɪt] n faja

Corsica ['kɔ:sɪkə] n Córcega

cosmetic [kɔz'mɛtɪk] adj, n cosmético

cosmonaut ['kɔzmənɔ:t] n cosmonauta m/f

cosmopolitan [kɔzmə'pɔlɪtn] adj cosmopolita

cosset ['kɔsɪt] vt mimar

cost [kɔst] (pt, pp cost) n (price) precio; **~s** npl (COMM) costes mpl; (LAW) costas fpl ♦ vi costar, valer ♦ vt preparar el presupuesto de; **how much does it ~?** ¿cuánto cuesta?; **to ~ sb time/effort** costarle a uno tiempo/esfuerzo; **it ~ him his life** le costó la vida; **at all ~s** cueste lo que cueste

co-star ['kəustɑ:*] n coprotagonista m/f

Costa Rica ['kɔstə'ri:kə] n Costa Rica; **~n** adj, n costarriqueño/a m/f

cost-effective [kɔstɪ'fɛktɪv] adj rentable

costly ['kɔstlɪ] adj costoso

cost-of-living [kɔstəv'lɪvɪŋ] adj: **~ allowance** plus m de carestía de vida; **~ index** n índice m del costo de vida

cost price (BRIT) n precio de coste

costume ['kɔstjuːm] n traje m; (BRIT: also: **swimming ~**) traje de baño; **~ jewellery** n bisutería

cosy ['kəuzɪ] (US **cozy**) adj (person) cómodo; (room) acogedor(a)

cot [kɔt] n (BRIT: child's) cuna; (US: camp-bed) cama de campaña

cottage ['kɔtɪdʒ] n casita de campo; (rustic) barraca; **~ cheese** n requesón m

cotton ['kɔtn] n algodón m; (thread) hilo; **~ on to** (inf) vt fus caer en la cuenta de; **~ candy** (US) n algodón m (azucarado); **~ wool** (BRIT) n algodón m (hidrófilo)

couch [kautʃ] n sofá m; (doctor's etc) diván m

couchette [ku:'ʃɛt] n-litera

cough [kɔf] vi toser ♦ n tos f; **~ drop** n pastilla para la tos

could [kud] pt of **can²**; **~n't** = **could not**

council ['kaunsl] n consejo; **city or town ~** consejo municipal; **~ estate** (BRIT) n urbanización f de viviendas municipales de alquiler; **~ house** (BRIT) n vivienda municipal de alquiler; **~lor** n concejal(a) m/f

counsel ['kaunsl] n (advice) consejo; (lawyer) abogado/a ♦ vt aconsejar; **~lor** n consejero/a; **~or** (US) n abogado/a

count [kaunt] vt contar; (include) incluir ♦ vi contar ♦ n cuenta; (of votes) escrutinio; (level) nivel m; (nobleman) conde m; **~ on** vt fus contar con; **~down** n cuenta atrás

countenance ['kauntɪnəns] n semblante m, rostro ♦ vt (tolerate) aprobar, tolerar

counter ['kauntə*] n (in shop) mostrador m; (in games) ficha ♦ vt contrarrestar ♦ adv: **to run ~ to** ser contrario a, ir en contra de; **~act** vt contrarrestar

counterfeit ['kauntəfɪt] n falsificación f, simulación f ♦ vt falsificar ♦ adj falso, falsificado

counterfoil ['kauntəfɔɪl] n talón m

countermand ['kauntəmɑ:nd] vt revocar, cancelar

counterpart ['kauntəpɑ:t] n homólogo/a

counter-productive [kauntəprə'dʌktɪv] adj contraproducente

countersign ['kauntəsaɪn] vt refrendar

countess ['kauntɪs] n condesa

countless ['kauntlɪs] adj innumerable

country ['kʌntrɪ] n país m; (native land) patria; (as opposed to town) campo; (region) región f, tierra; **~ dancing** (BRIT) n baile m regional; **~ house** n casa de campo; **~man** (compatriot) compatriota m; (rural) campesino, paisano; **~side** n campo

county ['kauntɪ] n condado

coup [ku:] (pl **~s**) n (also: **~ d'état**) golpe m (de estado); (achievement) éxito

coupé ['ku:peɪ] n cupé m

couple ['kʌpl] n (of things) par m; (of people) pareja; (married ~) matrimonio; **a ~ of** un par de

coupon ['ku:pɔn] n cupón m; (voucher) valé m

courage ['kʌrɪdʒ] n valor m, valentía; **~ous** [kə'reɪdʒəs] adj valiente

courgette [kuə'ʒɛt] (BRIT) n calabacín m (SP), calabacita (AM)

courier ['kurɪə*] n mensajero/a; (for tourists) guía m/f (de turismo)

course [kɔ:s] n (direction) dirección f; (of river, SCOL) curso; (process) transcurso; (MED): **~ of treatment** tratamiento; (of ship) rumbo; (part of meal) plato; (GOLF) campo; **of ~** desde luego, naturalmente; **of ~!** ¡claro!

court [kɔ:t] n (royal) corte f; (LAW) tribunal m, juzgado; (TENNIS etc) pista, cancha ♦ vt (woman) cortejar a; **to take to ~** demandar

courteous ['kɔ:tɪəs] adj cortés

courtesan [kɔːtɪˈzæn] *n* cortesana
courtesy [ˈkɔːtəsɪ] *n* cortesía; **(by)** ~ **of** por cortesía de
court-house [ˈkɔːthaus] *(US) n* palacio de justicia
courtier [ˈkɔːtɪə*] *n* cortesano
court-martial *(pl* **courts-martial)** *n* consejo de guerra
courtroom [ˈkɔːtrum] *n* sala de justicia
courtyard [ˈkɔːtjɑːd] *n* patio
cousin [ˈkʌzn] *n* primo/a; **first** ~ primo/a carnal, primo/a hermano/a
cove [kəuv] *n* cala, ensenada
covenant [ˈkʌvənənt] *n* pacto
cover [ˈkʌvə*] *vt* cubrir; *(feelings, mistake)* ocultar; *(with lid)* tapar; *(book etc)* forrar; *(distance)* recorrer; *(include)* abarcar; *(protect: also: INSURANCE)* cubrir; *(PRESS)* investigar; *(discuss)* tratar ♦ *n* cubierta; *(lid)* tapa; *(for chair etc)* funda; *(envelope)* sobre *m*; *(for book)* forro; *(of magazine)* portada; *(shelter)* abrigo; *(INSURANCE)* cobertura; *(of spy)* cobertura; ~**s** *npl (on bed)* sábanas; mantas; **to take** ~ *(shelter)* protegerse, resguardarse; **under** ~ *(indoors)* bajo techo; **under** ~ **of darkness** al amparo de la oscuridad; **under separate** ~ *(COMM)* por separado; ~ **up** *vi*: **to** ~ **up for sb** encubrir a uno; ~**age** *n (TV, PRESS)* cobertura; ~**alls** *npl* mono; ~ **charge** *n* precio del cubierto; ~**ing** *n* capa; ~**ing letter** *(US* ~ **letter)** *n* carta de explicación; ~ **note** *n (INSURANCE)* póliza provisional
covert [ˈkʌvət] *adj* secreto, encubierto
cover-up *n* encubrimiento
covet [ˈkʌvɪt] *vt* codiciar
cow [kau] *n* vaca; *(inf!: woman)* bruja ♦ *vt* intimidar
coward [ˈkauəd] *n* cobarde *m/f*; ~**ice** [-ɪs] *n* cobardía; ~**ly** *adj* cobarde
cowboy [ˈkaubɔɪ] *n* vaquero
cower [ˈkauə*] *vi* encogerse (de miedo)
coy [kɔɪ] *adj* tímido
cozy [ˈkəuzɪ] *(US) adj* = **cosy**
CPA *(US) n abbr* = **certified public accountant**
crab [kræb] *n* cangrejo; ~ **apple** *n* manzana silvestre
crack [kræk] *n* grieta; *(noise)* crujido; *(drug)* crack *m* ♦ *vt* agrietar, romper; *(nut)* cascar; *(solve: problem)* resolver; *(: code)* descifrar; *(whip etc)* chasquear; *(knuckles)* crujir; *(joke)* contar ♦ *adj (expert)* de primera; ~ **down on** *vt fus* adoptar fuertes medidas contra; ~ **up** *vi (MED)* sufrir una crisis nerviosa; ~**er** *n (biscuit)* crácker *m*; *(Christmas* ~*er)* petardo sorpresa
crackle [ˈkrækl] *vi* crepitar
cradle [ˈkreɪdl] *n* cuna
craft [krɑːft] *n (skill)* arte *m*; *(trade)* oficio; *(cunning)* astucia; *(boat: pl inv)* barco; *(plane: pl inv)* avión *m*

craftsman [ˈkrɑːftsmən] *n* artesano; ~**ship** *n (quality)* destreza
crafty [ˈkrɑːftɪ] *adj* astuto
crag [kræg] *n* peñasco
cram [kræm] *vt (fill)*: **to** ~ **sth with** llenar algo (a reventar) de; *(put)*: **to** ~ **sth into** meter algo a la fuerza en ♦ *vi (for exams)* empollar
cramp [kræmp] *n (MED)* calambre *m*; ~**ed** *adj* apretado, estrecho
cranberry [ˈkrænbərɪ] *n* arándano agrio
crane [kreɪn] *n (TECH)* grúa; *(bird)* grulla
crank [kræŋk] *n* manivela; *(person)* chiflado; ~**shaft** *n* cigüeñal *m*
cranny [ˈkrænɪ] *n see* **nook**
crash [kræʃ] *n (noise)* estrépito; *(of cars etc)* choque *m*; *(of plane)* accidente *m* de aviación; *(COMM)* quiebra ♦ *vt (car, plane)* estrellar ♦ *vi (car, plane)* estrellarse; *(two cars)* chocar; *(COMM)* quebrar; ~ **course** *n* curso acelerado; ~ **helmet** *n* casco (protector); ~ **landing** *n* aterrizaje *m* forzado
crass [kræs] *adj* grosero, maleducado
crate [kreɪt] *n* cajón *m* de embalaje; *(for bottles)* caja
crater [ˈkreɪtə*] *n* cráter *m*
cravat(e) [krəˈvæt] *n* pañuelo
crave [kreɪv] *vt, vi*: **to** ~ **(for)** ansiar, anhelar
crawl [krɔːl] *vi (drag o.s.)* arrastrarse; *(child)* andar a gatas, gatear; *(vehicle)* avanzar (lentamente) ♦ *n (SWIMMING)* crol *m*
crayfish [ˈkreɪfɪʃ] *n inv (freshwater)* cangrejo de río; *(saltwater)* cigala
crayon [ˈkreɪən] *n* lápiz *m* de color
craze [kreɪz] *n (fashion)* moda
crazy [ˈkreɪzɪ] *adj (person)* loco; *(idea)* disparatado; *(inf: keen)*: ~ **about sb/sth** loco por uno/algo; ~ **paving** *(BRIT) n* pavimento de baldosas irregulares
creak [kriːk] *vi (floorboard)* crujir; *(hinge etc)* chirriar, rechinar
cream [kriːm] *n (of milk)* nata, crema; *(lotion)* crema; *(fig)* flor *f* y nata ♦ *adj (colour)* color crema; ~ **cake** *n* pastel *m* de nata; ~ **cheese** *n* queso blanco; ~**y** *adj* cremoso; *(colour)* color crema
crease [kriːs] *n (fold)* pliegue *m*; *(in trousers)* raya; *(wrinkle)* arruga ♦ *vt (wrinkle)* arrugar ♦ *vi (wrinkle up)* arrugarse
create [kriːˈeɪt] *vt* crear; **creation** [-ʃən] *n* creación *f*; **creative** *adj* creativo; **creator** *n* creador(a) *m/f*
creature [ˈkriːtʃə*] *n (animal)* animal *m*, bicho; *(person)* criatura
crèche [krɛʃ] *n* guardería (infantil)
credence [ˈkriːdəns] *n*: **to lend** *or* **give** ~ **to** creer en, dar crédito a
credentials [krɪˈdɛnʃlz] *npl (references)* referencias *fpl*; *(identity papers)* documentos *mpl* de identidad
credible [ˈkrɛdɪbl] *adj* creíble; *(trustworthy)*

digno de confianza

credit ['krɛdɪt] n crédito; (*merit*) honor m, mérito ♦ vt (COMM) abonar; (*believe: also:* give ~ *to*) creer, prestar fe a ♦ adj crediticio; **~s** npl (CINEMA) fichas fpl técnicas; **to be in ~** (*person*) tener saldo a favor; **to ~ sb with** (*fig*) reconocer a uno el mérito de; **~ card** n tarjeta de crédito; **~or** n acreedor(a) m/f

creed [kri:d] n credo

creek [kri:k] n cala, ensenada; (US) riachuelo

creep [kri:p] (*pt, pp* **crept**) vi arrastrarse; **~er** n enredadera; **~y** adj (*frightening*) horripilante

cremate [krɪ'meɪt] vt incinerar

crematorium [krɛmə'tɔ:rɪəm] (*pl* **crematoria**) n crematorio

crêpe [kreɪp] n (*fabric*) crespón m; (*also: ~ rubber*) crepé m; **~ bandage** (BRIT) n venda de crepé

crept [krɛpt] pt, pp of **creep**

crescent ['krɛsnt] n media luna; (*street*) calle f (en forma de semicírculo)

cress [krɛs] n berro

crest [krɛst] n (*of bird*) cresta; (*of hill*) cima, cumbre f; (*of coat of arms*) blasón m; **~fallen** adj alicaído

crevice ['krɛvɪs] n grieta, hendedura

crew [kru:] n (*of ship etc*) tripulación f; (TV, CINEMA) equipo; **~-cut** n corte m al rape; **~-neck** n cuello a la caja

crib [krɪb] n cuna ♦ vt (*inf*) plagiar

crick [krɪk] n (*in neck*) torticolis f

cricket ['krɪkɪt] n (*insect*) grillo; (*game*) críquet m

crime [kraɪm] n (*no pl: illegal activities*) crimen m; (*illegal action*) delito; **criminal** ['krɪmɪnl] n criminal m/f, delincuente m/f ♦ adj criminal; (*illegal*) delictivo; (*law*) penal

crimson ['krɪmzn] adj carmesí

cringe [krɪndʒ] vi agacharse, encogerse

crinkle ['krɪŋkl] vt arrugar

cripple ['krɪpl] n lisiado/a, cojo/a ♦ vt lisiar, mutilar

crises ['kraɪsi:z] npl of **crisis**

crisis ['kraɪsɪs] (*pl* **crises**) n crisis f inv

crisp [krɪsp] adj fresco; (*vegetables etc*) crujiente; (*manner*) seco; **~s** (BRIT) npl patatas fpl (SP) or papas fpl (AM) fritas

criss-cross ['krɪskrɔs] adj entrelazado

criterion [kraɪ'tɪərɪən] (*pl* **criteria**) n criterio

critic ['krɪtɪk] n crítico/a; **~al** adj crítico; (*illness*) grave; **~ally** adv (*speak etc*) en tono crítico; (*ill*) gravemente; **~ism** ['krɪtɪsɪzm] n crítica; **~ize** ['krɪtɪsaɪz] vt criticar

croak [krəuk] vi (*frog*) croar; (*raven*) graznar; (*person*) gruñir

Croatia [krəu'eɪʃə] n Croacia

crochet ['krəuʃeɪ] n ganchillo

crockery ['krɔkərɪ] n loza, vajilla

crocodile ['krɔkədaɪl] n cocodrilo

crocus ['krəukəs] n croco, crocus m

croft [krɔft] n granja pequeña

crony ['krəunɪ] (*inf: pej*) n compinche m/f

crook [kruk] n ladrón/ona m/f; (*of shepherd*) cayado; **~ed** ['krukɪd] adj torcido; (*dishonest*) nada honrado

crop [krɔp] n (*produce*) cultivo; (*amount produced*) cosecha; (*riding ~*) látigo de montar ♦ vt cortar, recortar; **~ up** vi surgir, presentarse

croquette [krə'kɛt] n croqueta

cross [krɔs] n cruz f; (*hybrid*) cruce m ♦ vt (*street etc*) cruzar, atravesar ♦ adj de mal humor, enojado; **~ out** vt tachar; **~ over** vi cruzar; **~bar** n travesaño; **~country (race)** n carrera a campo traviesa, cross m; **~-examine** vt interrogar; **~-eyed** adj bizco; **~fire** n fuego cruzado; **~ing** n (*sea passage*) travesía; (*also: pedestrian ~ing*) paso para peatones; **~ing guard** (US) n persona encargada de ayudar a los niños a cruzar la calle; **~ purposes** npl: **to be at ~ purposes** no comprender se una a otro; **~ reference** n referencia, llamada; **~roads** n cruce m, encrucijada; **~ section** n corte m transversal; (*of population*) muestra (representativa); **~walk** (US) n paso de peatones; **~wind** n viento de costado; **~word** n crucigrama m

crotch [krɔtʃ] n (ANAT, *of garment*) entrepierna

crotchet ['krɔtʃɪt] n (MUS) negra

crotchety ['krɔtʃɪtɪ] adj antipático

crouch [krautʃ] vi agacharse, acurrucarse

crow [krəu] n (*bird*) cuervo; (*of cock*) canto, cacareo ♦ vi (*cock*) cantar

crowbar ['krəuba:*] n palanca

crowd [kraud] n muchedumbre f, multitud f ♦ vt (*fill*) llenar ♦ vi (*gather*): **to ~ round** reunirse en torno a; (*cram*): **to ~ in** entrar en tropel; **~ed** adj (*full*) atestado; (*densely populated*) superpoblado

crown [kraun] n corona; (*of head*) coronilla; (*for tooth*) funda; (*of hill*) cumbre f ♦ vt coronar; (*fig*) completar, rematar; **~ jewels** npl joyas fpl reales; **~ prince** n príncipe m heredero

crow's feet npl patas fpl de gallo

crucial ['kru:ʃl] adj decisivo

crucifix ['kru:sɪfɪks] n crucifijo; **~ion** [-'fɪkʃən] n crucifixión f

crude [kru:d] adj (*materials*) bruto; (*fig: basic*) tosco; (: *vulgar*) ordinario; **~ (oil)** n (petróleo) crudo

cruel ['kruəl] adj cruel; **~ty** n crueldad f

cruise [kru:z] n crucero ♦ vi (*ship*) hacer un crucero; (*car*) ir a velocidad de crucero; **~r** n (*motorboat*) yate m de motor; (*warship*) crucero

crumb [krʌm] n miga, migaja

crumble ['krʌmbl] vt desmenuzar ♦ vi (*build-*

ing, also fig) desmoronarse; **crumbly** *adj*
que se desmigaja fácilmente

crumpet ['krʌmpɪt] *n* ≈ bollo para tostar

crumple ['krʌmpl] *vt* (*paper*) estrujar; (*material*) arrugar

crunch [krʌntʃ] *vt* (*with teeth*) mascar; (*underfoot*) hacer crujir ♦ *n* (*fig*) hora *or* momento de la verdad; ~**y** *adj* crujiente

crusade [kruː'seɪd] *n* cruzada

crush [krʌʃ] *n* (*crowd*) aglomeración *f*; (*infatuation*): **to have a ~ on sb** estar loco por uno; (*drink*): **lemon ~** limonada ♦ *vt* aplastar; (*paper*) estrujar; (*cloth*) arrugar; (*fruit*) exprimir; (*opposition*) aplastar; (*hopes*) destruir

crust [krʌst] *n* corteza; (*of snow, ice*) costra

cru:ch [krʌtʃ] *n* muleta

crux [krʌks] *n*: **the ~ of** lo esencial de, el quid de

cry [kraɪ] *vi* llorar; (*shout: also*: ~ **out**) gritar ♦ *n* (*shriek*) chillido; (*shout*) grito; ~ **off** *vi* echarse atrás

cryptic ['krɪptɪk] *adj* enigmático, secreto

crystal ['krɪstl] *n* cristal *m*; ~-**clear** *adj* claro como el agua

cub [kʌb] *n* cachorro; (*also*: ~ **scout**) niño explorador

Cuba ['kjuːbə] *n* Cuba; ~**n** *adj*, *n* cubano/a *m/f*

cubbyhole ['kʌbɪhəʊl] *n* cuchitril *m*

cube [kjuːb] *n* cubo ♦ *vt* (*MATH*) cubicar; **cubic** *adj* cúbico

cubicle ['kjuːbɪkl] *n* (*at pool*) caseta; (*for bed*) cubículo

cuckoo ['kukuː] *n* cuco; ~ **clock** *n* reloj *m* de cucú

cucumber ['kjuːkʌmbə*] *n* pepino

cuddle ['kʌdl] *vt* abrazar ♦ *vi* abrazarse

cue [kjuː] *n* (*snooker ~*) taco; (*THEATRE etc*) señal *f*

cuff [kʌf] *n* (*of sleeve*) puño; (*US: of trousers*) vuelta; (*blow*) bofetada; **off the ~** *adv* de improviso; ~**links** *npl* gemelos *mpl*

cuisine [kwɪ'ziːn] *n* cocina

cul-de-sac ['kʌldəsæk] *n* callejón *m* sin salida

cull [kʌl] *vt* (*idea*) sacar ♦ *n* (*of animals*) matanza selectiva

culminate ['kʌlmɪneɪt] *vi*: **to ~ in** terminar en; **culmination** [-'neɪʃən] *n* culminación *f*, colmo

culottes [kuː'lɒts] *npl* falda pantalón *f*

culprit ['kʌlprɪt] *n* culpable *m/f*

cult [kʌlt] *n* culto

cultivate ['kʌltɪveɪt] *vt* (*also fig*) cultivar; ~**d** *adj* culto; **cultivation** [-'veɪʃən] *n* cultivo

cultural ['kʌltʃərəl] *adj* cultural

culture ['kʌltʃə*] *n* (*also fig*) cultura; (*BIO*) cultivo; ~**d** *adj* culto

cumbersome ['kʌmbəsəm] *adj* de mucho bulto, voluminoso; (*process*) enrevesado

cunning ['kʌnɪŋ] *n* astucia ♦ *adj* astuto

cup [kʌp] *n* taza; (*as prize*) copa

cupboard ['kʌbəd] *n* armario; (*kitchen*) alacena

cup-tie ['kʌptaɪ] (*BRIT*) *n* partido de copa

curate ['kjuərɪt] *n* cura *m*

curator [kjuə'reɪtə*] *n* director(a) *m/f*

curb [kəːb] *vt* refrenar; (*person*) reprimir ♦ *n* freno; (*US*) bordillo

curdle ['kəːdl] *vi* cuajarse

cure [kjuə*] *vt* curar ♦ *n* cura, curación *f*; (*fig: solution*) remedio

curfew ['kəːfjuː] *n* toque *m* de queda

curio ['kjuərɪəu] *n* curiosidad *f*

curiosity [kjuərɪ'ɒsɪtɪ] *n* curiosidad *f*

curious ['kjuərɪəs] *adj* curioso; (*person: interested*): **to be ~** sentir curiosidad

curl [kəːl] *n* rizo ♦ *vt* (*hair*) rizar ♦ *vi* rizarse; ~ **up** *vi* (*person*) hacerse un ovillo; ~**er** *n* rulo; ~**y** *adj* rizado

currant ['kʌrnt] *n* pasa (de Corinto); (*black~, red~*) grosella

currency ['kʌrnsɪ] *n* moneda; **to gain ~** (*fig*) difundirse

current ['kʌrnt] *n* corriente *f* ♦ *adj* (*accepted*) corriente; (*present*) actual; ~ **account** (*BRIT*) *n* cuenta corriente; ~ **affairs** *npl* noticias *fpl* de actualidad; ~**ly** *adv* actualmente

curriculum [kə'rɪkjuləm] (*pl* ~**s** *or* **curricula**) *n* plan *m* de estudios; ~ **vitae** *n* currículum *m*

curry ['kʌrɪ] *n* curry *m* ♦ *vt*: **to ~ favour with** buscar favores con; ~ **powder** *n* curry *m* en polvo

curse [kəːs] *vi* soltar tacos ♦ *vt* maldecir ♦ *n* maldición *f*; (*swearword*) palabrota, taco

cursor ['kəːsə*] *n* (*COMPUT*) cursor *m*

cursory ['kəːsərɪ] *adj* rápido, superficial

curt [kəːt] *adj* corto, seco

curtail [kəː'teɪl] *vt* (*visit etc*) acortar; (*freedom*) restringir; (*expenses etc*) reducir

curtain ['kəːtn] *n* cortina; (*THEATRE*) telón *m*

curts(e)y ['kəːtsɪ] *vi* hacer una reverencia

curve [kəːv] *n* curva ♦ *vi* (*road*) hacer una curva; (*line etc*) curvarse

cushion ['kuʃən] *n* cojín *m*; (*of air*) colchón *m* ♦ *vt* (*shock*) amortiguar

custard ['kʌstəd] *n* natillas *fpl*

custody ['kʌstədɪ] *n* custodia; **to take into ~** detener

custom ['kʌstəm] *n* costumbre *f*; (*COMM*) clientela; ~**ary** *adj* acostumbrado

customer ['kʌstəmə*] *n* cliente *m/f*

customized ['kʌstəmaɪzd] *adj* (*car etc*) hecho a encargo

custom-made *adj* hecho a la medida

customs ['kʌstəmz] *npl* aduana; ~ **duty** *n* derechos *mpl* de aduana; ~ **officer** *n* aduanero/a

cut [kʌt] (*pt, pp* **cut**) *vt* cortar; (*price*) rebajar; (*text, programme*) acortar; (*reduce*) reducir ♦ *vi* cortar ♦ *n* (*of garment*) corte *m*; (*in skin*) cortadura; (*in salary etc*) rebaja; (*in spending*) reducción *f*, recorte *m*; (*slice of meat*) tajada; **to ~ a tooth** echar un diente; **~ down** *vt* (*tree*) derribar; (*reduce*) reducir; **~ off** *vt* cortar; (*person, place*) aislar; (*TEL*) desconectar; **~ out** *vt* (*shape*) recortar; (*stop: activity etc*) dejar; (*remove*) quitar; **~ up** *vt* cortar (en pedazos); **~back** *n* reducción *f*

cute [kjuːt] *adj* mono
cuticle ['kjuːtɪkl] *n* cutícula
cutlery ['kʌtlərɪ] *n* cubiertos *mpl*
cutlet ['kʌtlɪt] *n* chuleta; (*nut etc* ~) plato vegetariano hecho con nueces y verdura en forma de chuleta
cut: **~out** *n* (*switch*) dispositivo de seguridad, disyuntor *m*; (*cardboard* ~) recortable *m*; **~-price** (*US* **~-rate**) *adj* a precio reducido; **~throat** *n* asesino/a ♦ *adj* feroz
cutting ['kʌtɪŋ] *adj* (*remark*) mordaz ♦ *n* (*BRIT: from newspaper*) recorte *m*; (*from plant*) esqueje *m*
CV *n abbr* = **curriculum vitae**
cwt *abbr* = **hundredweight(s)**
cyanide ['saɪənaɪd] *n* cianuro
cycle ['saɪkl] *n* ciclo; (*bicycle*) bicicleta ♦ *vi* ir en bicicleta; **cycling** *n* ciclismo; **cyclist** *n* ciclista *m/f*
cyclone ['saɪkləun] *n* ciclón *m*
cygnet ['sɪgnɪt] *n* pollo de cisne
cylinder ['sɪlɪndə*] *n* cilindro; (*of gas*) bombona; **~-head gasket** *n* junta de culata
cymbals ['sɪmblz] *npl* platillos *mpl*
cynic ['sɪnɪk] *n* cínico/a; **~al** *adj* cínico; **~ism** ['sɪnɪsɪzəm] *n* cinismo
cypress ['saɪprɪs] *n* ciprés *m*
Cyprus ['saɪprəs] *n* Chipre *f*
cyst [sɪst] *n* quiste *m*; **~itis** [-'taɪtɪs] *n* cistitis *f*
czar [zɑː*] *n* zar *m*
Czech [tʃɛk] *adj*, *n* checo/a *m/f*
Czechoslovakia [tʃɛkəslə'vækɪə] *n* Checoslovaquia; **~n** *adj*, *n* checo/a *m/f*

D d

D [diː] *n* (*MUS*) re *m*
dab [dæb] *vt* (*eyes, wound*) tocar (ligeramente); (*paint, cream*) poner un poco de
dabble ['dæbl] *vi*: **to ~ in** ser algo aficionado a
dad [dæd] *n* = **daddy**
daddy ['dædɪ] *n* papá *m*
daffodil ['dæfədɪl] *n* narciso
daft [dɑːft] *adj* tonto
dagger ['dægə*] *n* puñal *m*, daga
daily ['deɪlɪ] *adj* diario, cotidiano ♦ *adv* todos los días, cada día
dainty ['deɪntɪ] *adj* delicado
dairy ['dɛərɪ] *n* (*shop*) lechería; (*on farm*) vaquería; **~ farm** *n* granja; **~ products** *npl* productos *mpl* lácteos; **~ store** (*US*) *n* lechería
dais ['deɪɪs] *n* estrado
daisy ['deɪzɪ] *n* margarita; **~ wheel** *n* margarita
dale [deɪl] *n* valle *m*
dam [dæm] *n* presa ♦ *vt* construir una presa sobre, represar
damage ['dæmɪdʒ] *n* lesión *f*; daño; (*dents etc*) desperfectos *mpl*; (*fig*) perjuicio ♦ *vt* dañar, perjudicar; (*spoil, break*) estropear; **~s** *npl* (*LAW*) daños *mpl* y perjuicios
damn [dæm] *vt* condenar; (*curse*) maldecir ♦ *n* (*inf*): **I don't give a ~** me importa un pito ♦ *adj* (*inf: also: ~ed*) maldito; **~ (it)!** ¡maldito sea!; **~ing** *adj* (*evidence*) irrecusable
damp [dæmp] *adj* húmedo, mojado ♦ *n* humedad *f* ♦ *vt* (*also: ~en: cloth, rag*) mojar; (*: enthusiasm*) enfriar
damson ['dæmzən] *n* ciruela damascena
dance [dɑːns] *n* baile *m* ♦ *vi* bailar; **~ hall** *n* salón *m* de baile; **dancer** *n* bailador(a) *m/f*; (*professional*) bailarín/ina *m/f*; **dancing** *n* baile *m*
dandelion ['dændɪlaɪən] *n* diente *m* de león
dandruff ['dændrəf] *n* caspa
Dane [deɪn] *n* danés/esa *m/f*
danger ['deɪndʒə*] *n* peligro; (*risk*) riesgo; **~!** (*on sign*) ¡peligro de muerte!; **to be in ~ of** correr riesgo de; **~ous** *adj* peligroso; **~ously** *adv* peligrosamente
dangle ['dæŋgl] *vt* colgar ♦ *vi* pender, colgar
Danish ['deɪnɪʃ] *adj* danés/esa ♦ *n* (*LING*)

danés *m*

dapper ['dæpə*] *adj* pulcro, apuesto

dare [dɛə*] *vt*: to ~ **sb to do** desafiar a
uno a hacer ♦ *vi*: **to ~ (to) do sth** atreverse a hacer algo; **I ~ say** (*I suppose*) puede
ser (que); ~**devil** *n* temerario/a, atrevido/
a; **daring** *adj* atrevido, osado ♦ *n* atrevimiento, osadía

dark [dɑːk] *adj* oscuro; (*hair, complexion*)
moreno ♦ *n*: **in the ~** a oscuras; **to be in
the ~ about** (*fig*) no saber nada de; **after
~** después del anochecer; ~**en** *vt* (*colour*)
hacer más oscuro ♦ *vi* oscurecerse; ~
glasses *npl* gafas *fpl* negras (*SP*), anteojos
mpl negros (*AM*); ~**ness** *n* oscuridad *f*;
~**room** *n* cuarto oscuro

darling ['dɑːlɪŋ] *adj, n* querido/a *m/f*

darn [dɑːn] *vt* zurcir

dart [dɑːt] *n* dardo; (*in sewing*) sisa ♦ *vi*
precipitarse; ~ **away/along** *vi* salir/
marchar disparado; ~**board** *n* diana; ~**s** *n*
dardos *mpl*

dash [dæʃ] *n* (*small quantity: of liquid*) gota,
chorrito; (: *of solid*) pizca; (*sign*) raya ♦ *vt*
(*throw*) tirar; (*hopes*) defraudar ♦ *vi* precipitarse, ir de prisa; ~ **away** *or* **off** *vi* marcharse apresuradamente

dashboard ['dæʃbɔːd] *n* (*AUT*) salpicadero

dashing ['dæʃɪŋ] *adj* gallardo

data ['deɪtə] *npl* datos *mpl*; ~**base** *n* base *f*
de datos; ~ **processing** *n* proceso de da-
tos

date [deɪt] *n* (*day*) fecha; (*with friend*) cita;
(*fruit*) dátil *m* ♦ *vt* fechar; (*person*) salir
con; ~ **of birth** fecha de nacimiento; **to ~**
adv hasta la fecha; ~**d** *adj* anticuado

daub [dɔːb] *vt* embadurnar

daughter ['dɔːtə*] *n* hija; ~**-in-law** *n* nuera, hija política

daunting ['dɔːntɪŋ] *adj* desalentador(a)

dawdle ['dɔːdl] *vi* (*go slowly*) andar muy
despacio

dawn [dɔːn] *n* alba, amanecer *m*; (*fig*) nacimiento ♦ *vi* (*day*) amanecer; (*fig*): **it ~ed
on him that** ... cayó en la cuenta de que
....

day [deɪ] *n* día *m*; (*working ~*) jornada;
(*hey~*) tiempos *mpl*, días *mpl*; **the ~
before/after** el día anterior/siguiente; **the
~ after tomorrow** pasado mañana; **the ~
before yesterday** anteayer; **the following
~** el día siguiente; **by ~** de día; ~**break** *n*
amanecer *m*; ~**dream** *vi* soñar despierto;
~**light** *n* luz *f* (del día); ~ **return** (*BRIT*) *n*
billete *m* de ida y vuelta (en un día);
~**time** *n* día *m*; ~**-to-~** *adj* cotidiano

daze [deɪz] *vt* (*stun*) aturdir ♦ *n*: **in a ~**
aturdido

dazzle ['dæzl] *vt* deslumbrar

DC *abbr* (= *direct current*) corriente *f* conti-
nua

dead [dɛd] *adj* muerto; (*limb*) dormido;
(*telephone*) cortado; (*battery*) agotado ♦ *adv*
(*completely*) totalmente; (*exactly*) exactamente; **to shoot sb ~** matar a uno a tiros;
~ **tired** muerto (de cansancio); **to stop ~**
parar en seco; **the ~** *npl* los muertos; **to be
a ~ loss** (*inf: person*) ser un inútil; ~ **en** *vt*
(*blow, sound*) amortiguar; (*pain etc*) aliviar;
~ **end** *n* callejón *m* sin salida; ~ **heat** *n*
(*SPORT*) empate *m*; ~**line** *n* fecha (*or*
hora) tope; ~**lock** *n*: **to reach ~lock** llegar
a un punto muerto; ~**ly** *adj* mortal, fatal;
~**pan** *adj* sin expresión; **the D~ Sea** *n* el
Mar Muerto

deaf [dɛf] *adj* sordo; ~**en** *vt* ensordecer;
~**ness** *n* sordera

deal [diːl] (*pt, pp* **dealt**) *n* (*agreement*) pacto, convenio; (*business ~*) trato ♦ *vt* dar;
(*card*) repartir; **a great ~ (of)** bastante, mucho; ~ **in** *vt fus* tratar en, comerciar en; ~
with *vt fus* (*people*) tratar con; (*problem*)
ocuparse de; (*subject*) tratar de; ~**ings** *npl*
(*COMM*) transacciones *fpl*; (*relations*) relaciones *fpl*

dealt [dɛlt] *pt, pp of* **deal**

dean [diːn] *n* (*REL*) deán *m*; (*SCOL: BRIT*)
decano; (: *US*) decano; rector *m*

dear [dɪə*] *adj* querido; (*expensive*) caro ♦
n: **my ~** mi querido/a ♦ *excl*: ~ **me!** ¡Dios
mío!; **D~ Sir/Madam** (*in letter*) Muy Señor
Mío, Estimado Señor/Estimada Señora; **D~
Mr/Mrs X** Estimado/a Señor(a) X; ~**ly** *adv*
(*love*) mucho; (*pay*) caro

death [dɛθ] *n* muerte *f*; ~ **certificate** *n*
partida de defunción; ~**ly** *adj* (*white*) como
un muerto; (*silence*) sepulcral; ~ **penalty**
n pena de muerte; ~ **rate** *n* mortalidad *f*;
~ **toll** *n* número de víctimas

debacle [deɪ'bɑːkl] *n* desastre *m*

debar [dɪ'bɑː*] *vt*: **to ~ sb from doing**
prohibir a uno hacer

debase [dɪ'beɪs] *vt* degradar

debatable [dɪ'beɪtəbl] *adj* discutible

debate [dɪ'beɪt] *n* debate *m* ♦ *vt* discutir

debauchery [dɪ'bɔːtʃərɪ] *n* libertinaje *m*

debilitating [dɪ'bɪlɪteɪtɪŋ] *adj* (*illness etc*)
debilitante

debit ['dɛbɪt] *n* debe *m* ♦ *vt*: **to ~ a sum
to sb** *or* **to sb's account** cargar una suma
en cuenta a alguien

debris ['dɛbriː] *n* escombros *mpl*

debt [dɛt] *n* deuda; **to be in ~** tener deudas; ~**or** *n* deudor(a) *m/f*

debunk [diː'bʌŋk] *vt* desprestigiar, desacreditar

début ['deɪbjuː] *n* presentación *f*

decade ['dɛkeɪd] *n* decenio, década

decadence ['dɛkədəns] *n* decadencia

decaffeinated [dɪ'kæfɪneɪtɪd] *adj* descafeinado

decanter [dɪ'kæntə*] *n* garrafa

decay [dɪ'keɪ] *n* (*of building*) desmorona-
miento; (*of tooth*) caries *f inv* ♦ *vi* (*rot*) pu-

drirse

deceased [dɪ'siːst] n: **the ~** el/la difunto/a
deceit [dɪ'siːt] n engaño; **~ful** adj engañoso; **deceive** [dɪ'siːv] vt engañar
December [dɪ'sɛmbə*] n diciembre m
decent ['diːsənt] adj (proper) decente; (person: kind) amable, bueno
deception [dɪ'sɛpʃən] n engaño
deceptive [dɪ'sɛptɪv] adj engañoso
decibel ['dɛsɪbel] n decibel(io) m
decide [dɪ'saɪd] vt (person) decidir; (question, argument) resolver ♦ vi decidir; **to ~ to do/that** decidir hacer/que; **to ~ on sth** decidirse por algo; **~d** adj (resolute) decidido; (clear, definite) indudable; **~dly** [-dɪdlɪ] adv (decidedly) decididamente; (emphatically) con resolución
deciduous [dɪ'sɪdjuəs] adj de hoja caduca
decimal ['dɛsɪməl] adj decimal ♦ n decimal m; **~ point** n coma decimal
decimate ['dɛsɪmeɪt] vt diezmar
decipher [dɪ'saɪfə*] vt descifrar
decision [dɪ'sɪʒən] n decisión f
decisive [dɪ'saɪsɪv] adj decisivo; (person) decidido
deck [dɛk] n (NAUT) cubierta; (of bus) piso; (record ~) platina; (of cards) baraja; **~chair** n tumbona
declaration [dɛklə'reɪʃən] n declaración f
declare [dɪ'klɛə*] vt declarar
decline [dɪ'klaɪn] n disminución f, descenso ♦ vt rehusar ♦ vi (person, business) decaer; (strength) disminuir
decode [diː'kəud] vt descifrar
decoder [diː'kəudə*] n (TV) decodificador m
decompose [diːkəm'pəuz] vi descomponerse
décor ['deɪkɔː*] n decoración f; (THEATRE) decorado
decorate ['dɛkəreɪt] vt (adorn): **to ~ (with)** adornar (de), decorar (de); (paint) pintar; (paper) empapelar; **decoration** [-'reɪʃən] n adorno; (act) decoración f; (medal) condecoración f; **decorative** ['dɛkərətɪv] adj decorativo; **decorator** n (workman) pintor m (decorador)
decorum [dɪ'kɔːrəm] n decoro
decoy ['diːkɔɪ] n señuelo
decrease [n 'diːkriːs, vb dɪ'kriːs] n: **~ (in)** disminución f (de) ♦ vt disminuir, reducir ♦ vi reducirse
decree [dɪ'kriː] n decreto; **~ nisi** n sentencia provisional de divorcio
dedicate ['dɛdɪkeɪt] vt dedicar; **dedication** [-'keɪʃən] n (devotion) dedicación f; (in book) dedicatoria
deduce [dɪ'djuːs] vt deducir
deduct [dɪ'dʌkt] vt restar; descontar; **~ion** [dɪ'dʌkʃən] n (amount deducted) descuento; (conclusion) deducción f, conclusión f
deed [diːd] n hecho, acto; (feat) hazaña;

(LAW) escritura
deem [diːm] vt juzgar
deep [diːp] adj profundo; (expressing measurements) de profundidad; (voice) bajo; (breath) profundo; (colour) intenso ♦ adv: **the spectators stood 20 ~** los espectadores se formaron de 20 en fondo; **to be 4 metres ~** tener 4 metros de profundidad; **~en** vt ahondar, profundizar ♦ vi aumentar, crecer; **~-freeze** n congelador m; **~-fry** vt freír en aceite abundante; **~ly** adv (breathe) a pleno pulmón; (interested, moved, grateful) profundamente, hondamente; **~-sea diving** n buceo de altura; **~-seated** adj (beliefs) (profundamente) arraigado
deer [dɪə*] n inv ciervo
deface [dɪ'feɪs] vt (wall, surface) estropear, pintarrajear
default [dɪ'fɔːlt] n: **by ~** (win) por incomparecencia ♦ adj (COMPUT) por defecto
defeat [dɪ'fiːt] n derrota ♦ vt derrotar, vencer; **~ist** adj, n derrotista m/f
defect [n 'diːfɛkt, vb dɪ'fɛkt] n defecto ♦ vi: **to ~ to the enemy** pasarse al enemigo; **~ive** [dɪ'fɛktɪv] adj defectuoso
defence [dɪ'fɛns] (US **defense**) n defensa; **~less** adj indefenso
defend [dɪ'fɛnd] vt defender; **~ant** n acusado/a; (in civil case) demandado/a; **~er** n defensor(a) m/f; (SPORT) defensa m/f
defense [dɪ'fɛns] (US) n = **defence**
defensive [dɪ'fɛnsɪv] adj defensivo ♦ n: **on the ~** a la defensiva
defer [dɪ'fɜː*] vt aplazar; **~ence** ['dɛfərəns] n deferencia, respeto
defiance [dɪ'faɪəns] n desafío; **in ~ of** en contra de; **defiant** [dɪ'faɪənt] adj (challenging) desafiante, retador(a)
deficiency [dɪ'fɪʃənsɪ] n (lack) falta; (defect) defecto; **deficient** [dɪ'fɪʃənt] adj deficiente
deficit ['dɛfɪsɪt] n déficit m
defile [dɪ'faɪl] vt manchar
define [dɪ'faɪn] vt (word etc) definir; (limits etc) determinar
definite ['dɛfɪnɪt] adj (fixed) determinado; (obvious) claro; (certain) indudable; **he was ~ about it** no dejó lugar a dudas (sobre ello); **~ly** adv desde luego, por supuesto
definition [dɛfɪ'nɪʃən] n definición f; (clearness) nitidez f
deflate [diː'fleɪt] vt desinflar
deflect [dɪ'flɛkt] vt desviar
defraud [dɪ'frɔːd] vt: **to ~ sb of sth** estafar algo a uno
defrost [diː'frɒst] vt descongelar; **~er** (US) n (demister) eliminador m de vaho
deft [dɛft] adj diestro, hábil
defunct [dɪ'fʌŋkt] adj difunto; (organization etc) ya que no existe
defuse [diː'fjuːz] vt desactivar; (situation)

calmar

defy [dɪ'faɪ] vt (resist) oponerse a; (challenge) desafiar; (fig): **it defies description** resulta imposible describirlo

degenerate [vb dɪ'dʒɛnəreɪt, adj dɪ'dʒɛn-ərɪt] vi degenerar ♦ adj degenerado

degree [dɪ'griː] n grado; (SCOL) título; **to have a ~ in maths** tener una licenciatura en matemáticas; **by ~s** (gradually) poco a poco, por etapas; **to some ~** hasta cierto punto

dehydrated [diːhaɪ'dreɪtɪd] adj deshidratado; (milk) en polvo

de-ice [diː'aɪs] vt deshelar

deign [deɪn] vi: **to ~ to do** dignarse hacer

deity [ˈdiːɪtɪ] n deidad f, divinidad f

dejected [dɪ'dʒɛktɪd] adj abatido, desanimado

delay [dɪ'leɪ] vt demorar, aplazar; (person) entretener; (train) retrasar ♦ vi tardar ♦ n demora, retraso; **to be ~ed** retrasarse; **without ~** en seguida, sin tardar

delectable [dɪ'lɛktəbl] adj (person) encantador(a); (food) delicioso

delegate [n 'dɛlɪgɪt, vb 'dɛlɪgeɪt] n delegado/a ♦ vt (person) delegar en; (task) delegar

delete [dɪ'liːt] vt suprimir, tachar

deliberate [adj dɪ'lɪbərɪt, vb dɪ'lɪbəreɪt] adj (intentional) intencionado; (slow) pausado, lento ♦ vi deliberar; **~ly** adv (on purpose) a propósito

delicacy [ˈdɛlɪkəsɪ] n delicadeza; (choice food) manjar m

delicate [ˈdɛlɪkɪt] adj delicado; (fragile) frágil

delicatessen [dɛlɪkə'tɛsn] n ultramarinos mpl finos

delicious [dɪ'lɪʃəs] adj delicioso

delight [dɪ'laɪt] n (feeling) placer m, deleite m; (person, experience etc) encanto, delicia ♦ vt encantar, deleitar; **to take ~ in** deleitarse en; **~ed** adj: **~ed (at or with/to do)** encantado (con/de hacer); **~ful** adj encantador(a), delicioso

delinquent [dɪ'lɪŋkwənt] adj, n delincuente m/f

delirious [dɪ'lɪrɪəs] adj: **to be ~** delirar, desvariar; **to be ~ with** estar loco de

deliver [dɪ'lɪvə*] vt (distribute) repartir; (hand over) entregar; (message) comunicar; (speech) pronunciar; (MED) asistir al parto de; **~y** n reparto; entrega; (of speaker) modo de expresarse; (MED) parto, alumbramiento; **to take ~y of** recibir

delude [dɪ'luːd] vt engañar

deluge [ˈdɛljuːdʒ] n diluvio

delusion [dɪ'luːʒən] n ilusión f, engaño

de luxe [də'lʌks] adj de lujo

delve [dɛlv] vi: **to ~ into** (subject) ahondar en; (cupboard etc) hurgar en

demand [dɪ'mɑːnd] vt (gen) exigir; (rights)

reclamar ♦ n exigencia; (claim) reclamación f; (ECON) demanda; **to be in ~** ser muy solicitado; **on ~** a solicitud; **~ing** adj (boss) exigente; (work) absorbente

demean [dɪ'miːn] vt: **to ~ o.s.** rebajarse

demeanour [dɪ'miːnə*] (US **demeanor**) n porte m, conducta

demented [dɪ'mɛntɪd] adj demente

demise [dɪ'maɪz] n (death) fallecimiento

demister [diː'mɪstə*] n (AUT) eliminador m de vaho

demo [ˈdɛməu] (inf) n abbr (= demonstration) manifestación f

democracy [dɪ'mɔkrəsɪ] n democracia; **democrat** [ˈdɛməkræt] n demócrata m/f; **democratic** [dɛmə'krætɪk] adj democrático; (US) demócrata

demolish [dɪ'mɔlɪʃ] vt derribar, demoler; (fig: argument) destruir; **demolition** [dɛmə'lɪʃən] n derribo, demolición f; destrucción f

demon [ˈdiːmən] n (evil spirit) demonio

demonstrate [ˈdɛmənstreɪt] vt demostrar; (skill, appliance) mostrar ♦ vi manifestarse; **demonstration** [-'streɪʃən] n (POL) manifestación f; (proof, exhibition) demostración f; **demonstrator** n (POL) manifestante m/f; (COMM) demostrador(a) m/f; vendedor(a) m/f

demoralize [dɪ'mɔrəlaɪz] vt desmoralizar

demote [dɪ'məut] vt degradar

demure [dɪ'mjuə*] adj recatado

den [dɛn] n (of animal) guarida; (room) habitación f

denatured alcohol [diː'neɪtʃəd-] (US) n alcohol m desnaturalizado

denial [dɪ'naɪəl] n (refusal) negativa; (of report etc) negación f

denim [ˈdɛnɪm] n tela vaquera; **~s** npl vaqueros mpl

Denmark [ˈdɛnmɑːk] n Dinamarca

denomination [dɪnɔmɪ'neɪʃən] n valor m; (REL) confesión f

denote [dɪ'nəut] vt indicar, significar

denounce [dɪ'nauns] vt denunciar

dense [dɛns] adj (crowd) denso; (thick) espeso; (: foliage etc) tupido; (inf: stupid) torpe; **~ly** adv: **~ly populated** con una alta densidad de población

density [ˈdɛnsɪtɪ] n densidad f; **single/double-~ disk** n (COMPUT) disco de densidad sencilla/doble densidad

dent [dɛnt] n abolladura ♦ vt (also: **make a ~ in**) abollar

dental [ˈdɛntl] adj dental; **~ surgeon** n odontólogo/a

dentist [ˈdɛntɪst] n dentista m/f; **~ry** n odontología

dentures [ˈdɛntʃəz] npl dentadura (postiza)

denunciation [dɪnʌnsɪ'eɪʃən] n denuncia, denunciación f

deny [dɪ'naɪ] vt negar; (charge) rechazar

deodorant [diːˈəudərənt] *n* desodorante *m*

depart [dɪˈpɑːt] *vi* irse, marcharse; *(train)* salir; **to ~ from** *(fig: differ from)* apartarse de

department [dɪˈpɑːtmənt] *n* *(COMM)* sección *f*; *(SCOL)* departamento; *(POL)* ministerio; **~ store** *n* gran almacén *m*

departure [dɪˈpɑːtʃə*] *n* partida, ida; *(of train)* salida; *(of employee)* marcha; **a new ~** un nuevo rumbo; **~ lounge** *n* *(at airport)* sala de embarque

depend [dɪˈpend] *vi*: **to ~ on** depender de; *(rely on)* contar con; **it ~s** depende, según; **~ing on the result** según el resultado; **~able** *adj (person)* formal, serio; *(watch)* exacto; *(car)* seguro; **~ant** *n* dependiente *m/f*; **~ence** *n* dependencia; **~ent** *adj*: **to be ~ent on** depender de ♦ *n* = **dependant**

depict [dɪˈpɪkt] *vt* *(in picture)* pintar; *(describe)* representar

depleted [dɪˈpliːtɪd] *adj* reducido

deplorable [dɪˈplɔːrəbl] *adj* deplorable

deploy [dɪˈplɔɪ] *vt* desplegar

depopulation [diːpɔpjuˈleɪʃən] *n* despoblación *f*

deport [dɪˈpɔːt] *vt* deportar

deportment [dɪˈpɔːtmənt] *n* comportamiento; *(way of walking)* porte *m*

depose [dɪˈpəuz] *vt* deponer

deposit [dɪˈpɔzɪt] *n* depósito; *(CHEM)* sedimento; *(of ore, oil)* yacimiento ♦ *vt (gen)* depositar; **~ account** *(BRIT)* *n* cuenta de ahorros

depot [ˈdepəu] *n* *(storehouse)* depósito; *(for vehicles)* parque *m*; *(US)* estación *f*

depreciate [dɪˈpriːʃɪeɪt] *vi* depreciarse, perder valor; **depreciation** [-ˈeɪʃən] *n* depreciación *f*

depress [dɪˈpres] *vt* deprimir; *(wages etc)* hacer bajar; *(press down)* apretar; **~ed** *adj* deprimido; **~ing** *adj* deprimente; **~ion** [dɪˈpreʃən] *n* depresión *f*

deprivation [deprɪˈveɪʃən] *n* privación *f*

deprive [dɪˈpraɪv] *vt*: **to ~ sb of** privar a uno de; **~d** *adj* necesitado

depth [depθ] *n* profundidad *f*; *(of cupboard)* fondo; **to be in the ~s of despair** sentir la mayor desesperación; **to be out of one's ~** *(in water)* no hacer pie; *(fig)* sentirse totalmente perdido

deputation [depjuˈteɪʃən] *n* delegación *f*

deputize [ˈdepjutaɪz] *vi*: **to ~ for sb** suplir a uno

deputy [ˈdepjutɪ] *adj*: **~ head** subdirector(a) *m/f* ♦ *n* sustituto/a, suplente *m/f*; *(US: POL)* diputado/a; *(US: also: ~ sheriff)* agente *m* (del sheriff)

derail [dɪˈreɪl] *vt*: **to be ~ed** descarrilarse; **~ment** *n* descarrilamiento

deranged [dɪˈreɪndʒd] *adj* trastornado

derby [ˈdɔːbɪ] *(US)* *n* *(hat)* hongo

derelict [ˈderɪlɪkt] *adj* abandonado

derisory [dɪˈraɪzərɪ] *adj* *(sum)* irrisorio

derivative [dɪˈrɪvətɪv] *n* derivado

derive [dɪˈraɪv] *vt* *(benefit etc)* obtener ♦ *vi*: **to ~ from** derivarse de

derogatory [dɪˈrɔgətərɪ] *adj* despectivo

descend [dɪˈsend] *vt, vi* descender, bajar; **to ~ from** descender de; **to ~ to** rebajarse a; **~ant** *n* descendiente *m/f*

descent [dɪˈsent] *n* descenso; *(origin)* descendencia

describe [dɪsˈkraɪb] *vt* describir; **description** [-ˈkrɪpʃən] *n* descripción *f*; *(sort)* clase *f*, género

desecrate [ˈdesɪkreɪt] *vt* profanar

desert [*n* ˈdezət, *vb* dɪˈzɜːt] *n* desierto ♦ *vt* abandonar ♦ *vi* *(MIL)* desertar; **~er** [dɪˈzɜːtə*] *n* desertor(a) *m/f*; **~ion** [dɪˈzɜːʃən] *n* deserción *f*; *(LAW)* abandono; **~ island** *n* isla desierta; **~s** [dɪˈzɜːts] *npl*: **to get one's just ~s** llevar su merecido

deserve [dɪˈzɜːv] *vt* merecer, ser digno de; **deserving** *adj (person)* digno; *(action, cause)* meritorio

design [dɪˈzaɪn] *n* *(sketch)* bosquejo; *(layout, shape)* diseño; *(pattern)* dibujo; *(intention)* intención *f* ♦ *vt* diseñar

designate [*vb* ˈdezɪgneɪt, *adj* ˈdezɪgnɪt] *vt* *(appoint)* nombrar; *(destine)* designar ♦ *adj* designado

designer [dɪˈzaɪnə*] *n* diseñador(a) *m/f*; *(fashion ~)* modisto/a, diseñador(a) *m/f* de moda

desirable [dɪˈzaɪərəbl] *adj (proper)* deseable; *(attractive)* atractivo

desire [dɪˈzaɪə*] *n* deseo ♦ *vt* desear

desk [desk] *n* *(in office)* escritorio; *(for pupil)* pupitre *m*; *(in hotel, at airport)* recepción *f*; *(BRIT: in shop, restaurant)* caja

desolate [ˈdesəlɪt] *adj (place)* desierto; *(person)* afligido; **desolation** [-ˈleɪʃən] *n (of place)* desolación *f*; *(of person)* aflicción *f*

despair [dɪsˈpɛə*] *n* desesperación *f* ♦ *vi*: **to ~ of** perder la esperanza de

despatch [dɪsˈpætʃ] *n, vt* = **dispatch**

desperate [ˈdespərɪt] *adj* desesperado; *(fugitive)* peligroso; **to be ~ for sth/to do** necesitar urgentemente algo/hacer; **~ly** *adv* desesperadamente; *(very)* terriblemente, gravemente

desperation [despəˈreɪʃən] *n* desesperación *f*; **in (sheer) ~** *(absolutamente)* desesperado

despicable [dɪsˈpɪkəbl] *adj* vil, despreciable

despise [dɪsˈpaɪz] *vt* despreciar

despite [dɪsˈpaɪt] *prep* a pesar de, pese a

despondent [dɪsˈpɔndənt] *adj* deprimido, abatido

dessert [dɪˈzɜːt] *n* postre *m*; **~spoon** *n* cuchara (de postre)

destination [destɪˈneɪʃən] *n* destino

destiny [ˈdestɪnɪ] *n* destino

destitute [ˈdestɪtjuːt] *adj* desamparado, in-

digente
destroy [dɪs'trɔɪ] vt destruir; (animal) sacrificar; **~er** n (NAUT) destructor m
destruction [dɪs'trʌkʃən] n destrucción f; **destructive** [dɪs'trʌktɪv] adj destructivo, destructor(a)
detach [dɪ'tætʃ] vt separar; (unstick) despegar; **~able** adj de quita y pon; **~ed** adj (attitude) objetivo, imparcial; **~ed house** n ≈ chalé m, ≈ chalet m; **~ment** n (aloofness) frialdad f; (MIL) destacamento
detail ['diːteɪl] n detalle m; (no pl: in picture etc) detalles mpl; (trifle) pequeñez f ♦ vt detallar; (MIL) destacar; **in ~** detalladamente; **~ed** adj detallado
detain [dɪ'teɪn] vt retener; (in captivity) detener
detect [dɪ'tekt] vt descubrir; (MED, POLICE) identificar; (MIL, RADAR, TECH) detectar; **~ion** [dɪ'tekʃən] n descubrimiento; identificación f; **~ive** n detective m/f; **~ive story** n novela policíaca; **~or** n detector m
détente [deɪ'taːnt] n distensión f
detention [dɪ'tenʃən] n detención f, arresto; (SCOL) castigo
deter [dɪ'təː*] vt (dissuade) disuadir
detergent [dɪ'təːdʒənt] n detergente m
deteriorate [dɪ'tɪərɪəreɪt] vi deteriorarse; **deterioration** [-'reɪʃən] n deterioro
determination [dɪtəːmɪ'neɪʃən] n resolución f; (establishment) establecimiento
determine [dɪ'təːmɪn] vt determinar; **~d** adj (person) resuelto, decidido; **~d to do** resuelto a hacer
deterrent [dɪ'terənt] n (MIL) fuerza de disuasión
detest [dɪ'test] vt aborrecer
detonate ['detəneɪt] vi estallar ♦ vt hacer detonar
detour ['diːtuə*] n (gen, US: AUT) desviación f
detract [dɪ'trækt] vt: **to ~ from** quitar mérito a, desvirtuar
detriment ['detrɪmənt] n: **to the ~ of** en perjuicio de; **~al** [detrɪ'mentl] adj: **~al (to)** perjudicial (a)
devaluation [dɪvælju'eɪʃən] n devaluación f
devalue [diː'vælju:] vt (currency) devaluar; (fig) quitar mérito a
devastate ['devəsteɪt] vt devastar; (fig): **to be ~d by** quedar destrozado por; **devastating** adj devastador(a); (fig) arrolladora)
develop [dɪ'veləp] vt desarrollar; (PHOT) revelar; (disease) coger; (habit) adquirir; (fault) empezar a tener ♦ vi desarrollarse; (advance) progresar; (facts, symptoms) aparecer; **~ing country** n país m en (vías de) desarrollo; **~er** n promotor m; **~ment** n desarrollo; (advance) progreso; (of affair, case) desenvolvimiento; (of land) urbanización f

deviate ['diːvɪeɪt] vi: **to ~ (from)** desviarse (de); **deviation** [-'eɪʃən] n desviación f
device [dɪ'vaɪs] n (apparatus) aparato, mecanismo
devil ['devl] n diablo, demonio; **~ish** adj diabólico
devious ['diːvɪəs] adj taimado
devise [dɪ'vaɪz] vt idear, inventar
devoid [dɪ'vɔɪd] adj: **~ of** desprovisto de
devolution [diːvə'luːʃən] n (POL) descentralización f
devote [dɪ'vəut] vt: **to ~ sth to** dedicar algo a; **~d** adj (loyal) leal, fiel; **to be ~d to sb** querer con devoción a alguien; **the book is ~d to politics** el libro trata de la política; **~e** [devəu'tiː] n entusiasta m/f; (REL) devoto/a
devotion [dɪ'vəuʃən] n dedicación f; (REL) devoción f
devour [dɪ'vauə*] vt devorar
devout [dɪ'vaut] adj devoto
dew [djuː] n rocío
dexterity [deks'terɪtɪ] n destreza
diabetes [daɪə'biːtiːz] n diabetes f; **diabetic** [-'betɪk] adj, n diabético/a m/f
diabolical [daɪə'bɒlɪkəl] (inf) adj (weather, behaviour) pésimo
diagnose [daɪəg'nəuz] vt diagnosticar; **diagnoses** [-'nəusiːz] npl of **diagnosis**; **diagnosis** [-'nəusɪs] (pl **-ses**) n diagnóstico
diagonal [daɪ'ægənl] adj, n diagonal f
diagram ['daɪəgræm] n diagrama m, esquema m
dial ['daɪəl] n esfera, cuadrante m, cara (AM); (on radio etc) selector m; (of phone) disco ♦ vt (number) marcar
dialling ['daɪəlɪŋ]: **~ code** (US **dial code**) n prefijo; **~ tone** (US **dial tone**) n (BRIT) señal f or tono de marcar
dialogue ['daɪəlɒg] (US **dialog**) n diálogo
diameter [daɪ'æmɪtə*] n diámetro
diamond ['daɪəmənd] n diamante m; (shape) rombo; **~s** npl (CARDS) diamantes mpl
diaper ['daɪəpə*] (US) n pañal m
diaphragm ['daɪəfræm] n diafragma m
diarrhoea [daɪə'riːə] (US **diarrhea**) n diarrea
diary ['daɪərɪ] n (daily account) diario; (book) agenda
dice [daɪs] n inv dados mpl ♦ vt (CULIN) cortar en cuadritos
dichotomy [daɪ'kɒtəmɪ] n dicotomía
Dictaphone ['dɪktəfəun] ® n dictáfono ®
dictate [dɪk'teɪt] vt dictar; (conditions) imponer; **dictation** [-'teɪʃən] n dictado; (giving of orders) órdenes fpl
dictator [dɪk'teɪtə*] n dictador m; **~ship** n dictadura
dictionary ['dɪkʃənrɪ] n diccionario
did [dɪd] pt of **do**
didn't ['dɪdənt] = **did not**
die [daɪ] vi morir; (fig: fade) desvanecerse,

desaparecer; **to be dying for sth/to do sth** morirse por algo/de ganas de hacer algo; ~ **away** vi (sound, light) perderse; ~ **down** vi apagarse; (wind) amainar; ~ **out** vi desaparecer

diehard ['daɪhɑːd] n reaccionario/a

diesel ['diːzəl] n vehículo con motor Diesel; ~ **engine** n motor m Diesel; ~ **(oil)** n gasoil m

diet ['daɪət] n dieta; (restricted food) régimen m ♦ vi (also: **be on a** ~) estar a dieta, hacer régimen

differ ['dɪfə*] vi: **to** ~ **(from)** (be different) ser distinto (a), diferenciarse (de); (disagree) discrepar (de); ~**ence** n diferencia; (disagreement) desacuerdo; ~**ent** adj diferente, distinto; ~**entiate** [-'renʃɪeɪt] vi: **to** ~**entiate (between)** distinguir (entre); ~**ently** adv de otro modo, en forma distinta

difficult ['dɪfɪkəlt] adj difícil; ~**y** n dificultad f

diffident ['dɪfɪdənt] adj tímido

diffuse [adj dɪ'fjuːs, vb dɪ'fjuːz] adj difuso ♦ vt difundir

dig [dɪg] (pt, pp **dug**) vt (hole, ground) cavar ♦ n (prod) empujón m; (archaeological) excavación f; (remark) indirecta; **to** ~ **one's nails into** clavar las uñas en; ~ **into** vt fus (savings) consumir; ~ **out** vt (hole) excavar; (fig) sacar; ~ **up** vt (information) desenterrar; (plant) desarraigar

digest [vb daɪ'dʒest, n 'daɪdʒest] vt (food) digerir; (facts) asimilar ♦ n resumen m; ~**ion** [dɪ'dʒestʃən] n digestión f

digit ['dɪdʒɪt] n (number) dígito; (finger) dedo; ~**al** adj digital

dignified ['dɪgnɪfaɪd] adj grave, solemne

dignity ['dɪgnɪtɪ] n dignidad f

digress [daɪ'gres] vi: **to** ~ **from** apartarse de

digs [dɪgz] (BRIT: inf) npl pensión f, alojamiento

dilapidated [dɪ'læpɪdeɪtɪd] adj desmoronado, ruinoso

dilemma [daɪ'lemə] n dilema m

diligent ['dɪlɪdʒənt] adj diligente

dilute [daɪ'luːt] vt diluir

dim [dɪm] adj (light) débil; (outline) indistinto; (room) oscuro; (inf: stupid) lerdo ♦ vt (light) bajar

dime [daɪm] (US) n moneda de diez centavos

dimension [dɪ'menʃən] n dimensión f

diminish [dɪ'mɪnɪʃ] vt, vi disminuir

diminutive [dɪ'mɪnjutɪv] adj diminuto ♦ n (LING) diminutivo

dimmers ['dɪməz] (US) npl (AUT: dipped headlights) luces fpl cortas; (: parking lights) luces fpl de posición

dimple ['dɪmpl] n hoyuelo

din [dɪn] n estruendo, estrépito

dine [daɪn] vi cenar; ~**r** n (person) comensal m/f; (US) restaurante m económico

dinghy ['dɪŋgɪ] n bote m; (also: **rubber** ~) lancha (neumática)

dingy ['dɪndʒɪ] adj (room) sombrío; (colour) sucio

dining car ['daɪnɪŋ-] (BRIT) n (RAIL) coche-comedor m

dining room n comedor m

dinner ['dɪnə*] n (evening meal) cena; (lunch) comida; (public) cena, banquete m; ~ **jacket** n smoking m; ~ **party** n cena; ~ **time** n (evening) hora de cenar; (midday) hora de comer

dinosaur ['daɪnəsɔː*] n dinosaurio

dint [dɪnt] n: **by** ~ **of** a fuerza de

diocese ['daɪəsɪs] n diócesis f inv

dip [dɪp] n (slope) pendiente m; (in sea) baño; (CULIN) salsa ♦ vt (in water) mojar; (ladle etc) meter; (BRIT: AUT): **to** ~ **one's lights** poner luces de cruce ♦ vi (road etc) descender, bajar

diphthong ['dɪfθɒŋ] n diptongo

diploma [dɪ'pləumə] n diploma m

diplomacy [dɪ'pləuməsɪ] n diplomacia

diplomat ['dɪpləmæt] n diplomático/a; ~**ic** [dɪplə'mætɪk] adj diplomático

diprod ['dɪprəd] (US) n = **dipstick**

dipstick ['dɪpstɪk] (BRIT) n (AUT) varilla de nivel (del aceite)

dipswitch ['dɪpswɪtʃ] (BRIT) n (AUT) interruptor m

dire [daɪə*] adj calamitoso

direct [daɪ'rekt] adj directo; (challenge) claro; (person) franco ♦ vt dirigir; (order): **to** ~ **sb to do sth** mandar a uno hacer algo ♦ adv derecho; **can you** ~ **me to...?** ¿puede indicarme dónde está...?; ~ **debit** (BRIT) n domiciliación f bancaria de recibos

direction [dɪ'rekʃən] n dirección f; **sense of** ~ sentido de la dirección; ~**s** npl (instructions) instrucciones fpl; ~**s for use** modo de empleo

directly [dɪ'rektlɪ] adv (in straight line) directamente; (at once) en seguida

director [dɪ'rektə*] n director(a) m/f

directory [dɪ'rektərɪ] n (TEL) guía (telefónica); (COMPUT) directorio

dirt [dɜːt] n suciedad f; (earth) tierra; ~-**cheap** adj baratísimo; ~**y** adj sucio; (joke) verde (SP), colorado (AM) ♦ vt ensuciar; (stain) manchar; ~**y trick** n juego sucio

disability [dɪsə'bɪlɪtɪ] n incapacidad f

disabled [dɪs'eɪbld] adj: **to be physically** ~ ser minusválido/a; **to be mentally** ~ ser deficiente mental

disadvantage [dɪsəd'vɑːntɪdʒ] n desventaja, inconveniente m

disaffection [dɪsə'fekʃən] n descontento

disagree [dɪsə'griː] vi (differ) discrepar; **to** ~ **(with)** no estar de acuerdo (con); ~**able** adj desagradable; (person) antipático;

~ment *n* desacuerdo
disallow [dɪsə'lau] *vt* (*goal*) anular; (*claim*) rechazar
disappear [dɪsə'pɪə*] *vi* desaparecer; **~ance** *n* desaparición *f*
disappoint [dɪsə'pɔɪnt] *vt* decepcionar, defraudar; **~ed** *adj* decepcionado; **~ing** *adj* decepcionante; **~ment** *n* decepción *f*
disapproval [dɪsə'pruːvəl] *n* desaprobación *f*
disapprove [dɪsə'pruːv] *vi*: **to ~ of** ver mal
disarm [dɪs'ɑːm] *vt* desarmar; **~ament** *n* desarme *m*; **~ing** *adj* (*smile etc*) que desarma
disarray [dɪsə'reɪ] *n*: **in ~** (*army, organization*) desorganizado; (*hair, clothes*) desarreglado
disaster [dɪ'zɑːstə*] *n* desastre *m*
disband [dɪs'bænd] *vt* disolver ♦ *vi* desbandarse
disbelief [dɪsbə'liːf] *n* incredulidad *f*
disc [dɪsk] *n* disco; (*COMPUT*) = **disk**
discard [dɪs'kɑːd] *vt* (*old things*) tirar; (*fig*) descartar
discern [dɪ'sɜːn] *vt* percibir, discernir; (*understand*) comprender; **~ing** *adj* perspicaz
discharge [*vb* dɪs'tʃɑːdʒ, *n* 'dɪstʃɑːdʒ] *vt* (*task, duty*) cumplir; (*waste*) verter; (*patient*) dar de alta; (*employee*) despedir; (*soldier*) licenciar; (*defendant*) poner en libertad ♦ *n* (*ELEC*) descarga; (*MED*) supuración *f*; (*dismissal*) despedida; (*of duty*) desempeño; (*of debt*) pago, descargo
disciple [dɪ'saɪpl] *n* discípulo
discipline ['dɪsɪplɪn] *n* disciplina ♦ *vt* disciplinar; (*punish*) castigar
disc jockey *n* pinchadiscos *m/f inv*
disclaim [dɪs'kleɪm] *vt* negar
disclose [dɪs'kləuz] *vt* revelar; **disclosure** [-'kləuʒə*] *n* revelación *f*
disco ['dɪskəu] *n abbr* = **discothèque**
discoloured [dɪs'kʌləd] (*US* **discolored**) *adj* descolorido
discomfort [dɪs'kʌmfət] *n* incomodidad *f*; (*unease*) inquietud *f*; (*physical*) malestar *m*
disconcert [dɪskən'sɜːt] *vt* desconcertar
disconnect [dɪskə'nɛkt] *vt* separar; (*ELEC etc*) desconectar
discontent [dɪskən'tɛnt] *n* descontento; **~ed** *adj* descontento
discontinue [dɪskən'tɪnjuː] *vt* interrumpir; (*payments*) suspender; **"~d"** (*COMM*) "ya no se fabrica"
discord ['dɪskɔːd] *n* discordia; (*MUS*) disonancia; **~ant** [dɪs'kɔːdənt] *adj* discorde
discothèque ['dɪskəutek] *n* discoteca
discount [*n* 'dɪskaunt, *vb* dɪs'kaunt] *n* descuento ♦ *vt* descontar
discourage [dɪs'kʌrɪdʒ] *vt* desalentar; (*advise against*): **to ~ sb from doing** disuadir a uno de hacer; **discouraging** *adj* desalentador(a)

discover [dɪs'kʌvə*] *vt* descubrir; (*error*) darse cuenta de; **~y** *n* descubrimiento
discredit [dɪs'krɛdɪt] *vt* desacreditar
discreet [dɪ'skriːt] *adj* (*tactful*) discreto; (*careful*) circunspecto, prudente
discrepancy [dɪ'skrɛpənsɪ] *n* diferencia
discretion [dɪ'skrɛʃən] *n* (*tact*) discreción *f*; **at the ~ of** a criterio de
discriminate [dɪ'skrɪmɪneɪt] *vi*: **to ~ between** distinguir entre; **to ~ against** discriminar contra; **discriminating** *adj* entendido; **discrimination** [-'neɪʃən] *n* (*discernment*) perspicacia; (*bias*) discriminación *f*
discuss [dɪ'skʌs] *vt* discutir; (*a theme*) tratar; **~ion** [dɪ'skʌʃən] *n* discusión *f*
disdain [dɪs'deɪn] *n* desdén *m*
disease [dɪ'ziːz] *n* enfermedad *f*
disembark [dɪsɪm'bɑːk] *vt, vi* desembarcar
disenchanted [dɪsɪn'tʃɑːntɪd] *adj*: **~ (with)** desilusionado (con)
disengage [dɪsɪn'geɪdʒ] *vt*: **to ~ the clutch** (*AUT*) desembragar
disentangle [dɪsɪn'tæŋgl] *vt* soltar; (*wire, thread*) desenredar
disfigure [dɪs'fɪgə*] *vt* (*person*) desfigurar; (*object*) afear
disgrace [dɪs'greɪs] *n* ignominia; (*shame*) vergüenza, escándalo ♦ *vt* deshonrar; **~ful** *adj* vergonzoso
disgruntled [dɪs'grʌntld] *adj* disgustado, descontento
disguise [dɪs'gaɪz] *n* disfraz *m* ♦ *vt* disfrazar; **in ~** disfrazado
disgust [dɪs'gʌst] *n* repugnancia ♦ *vt* repugnar, dar asco a; **~ing** *adj* repugnante, asqueroso; (*behaviour etc*) vergonzoso
dish [dɪʃ] *n* (*gen*) plato; **to do** *or* **wash the ~es** fregar los platos; **~ up** *vt* servir; **~ out** *vt* repartir; **~cloth** *n* estropajo
dishearten [dɪs'hɑːtn] *vt* desalentar
dishevelled [dɪ'ʃɛvəld] *adj* (*hair*) despeinado; (*appearance*) desarreglado
dishonest [dɪs'ɔnɪst] *adj* (*person*) poco honrado, tramposo; (*means*) fraudulento; **~y** *n* falta de honradez
dishonour [dɪs'ɔnə*] (*US* **dishonor**) *n* deshonra; **~able** *adj* deshonroso
dishtowel ['dɪʃtauəl] (*US*) *n* estropajo
dishwasher ['dɪʃwɔʃə*] *n* lavaplatos *m inv*
disillusion [dɪsɪ'luːʒən] *vt* desilusionar
disincentive [dɪsɪn'sɛntɪv] *n* desincentivo
disinfect [dɪsɪn'fɛkt] *vt* desinfectar; **~ant** *n* desinfectante *m*
disintegrate [dɪs'ɪntɪgreɪt] *vi* disgregarse, desintegrarse
disinterested [dɪs'ɪntrəstɪd] *adj* desinteresado
disjointed [dɪs'dʒɔɪntɪd] *adj* inconexo
disk [dɪsk] *n* (*esp US*) = **disc**; (*COMPUT*) disco, disquete *m*; **single-/double-sided ~** disco de una cara/dos caras; **~ drive** *n* disc drive *m*; **~ette** *n* = **disk**

dislike [dɪs'laɪk] *n* antipatía, aversión *f* ♦ *vt* tener antipatía a

dislocate ['dɪsləkeɪt] *vt* dislocar

dislodge [dɪs'lɔdʒ] *vt* sacar

disloyal [dɪs'lɔɪəl] *adj* desleal

dismal ['dɪzml] *adj* (*gloomy*) deprimente, triste; (*very bad*) malísimo, fatal

dismantle [dɪs'mæntl] *vt* desmontar, desarmar

dismay [dɪs'meɪ] *n* consternación *f* ♦ *vt* consternar

dismiss [dɪs'mɪs] *vt* (*worker*) despedir; (*pupils*) dejar marchar; (*soldiers*) dar permiso para irse; (*idea, LAW*) rechazar; (*possibility*) descartar; **~al** *n* despido

dismount [dɪs'maunt] *vi* apearse

disobedience [dɪsə'biːdɪəns] *n* desobediencia

disobedient [dɪsə'biːdɪənt] *adj* desobediente

disobey [dɪsə'beɪ] *vt* desobedecer

disorder [dɪs'ɔːdə*] *n* desorden *m*; (*rioting*) disturbios *mpl*; (*MED*) trastorno; **~ly** *adj* desordenado; (*meeting*) alborotado; (*conduct*) escandaloso

disorientated [dɪs'ɔːrɪɛnteɪtəd] *adj* desorientado

disown [dɪs'əun] *vt* (*action*) renegar de; (*person*) negar cualquier tipo de relación con

disparaging [dɪs'pærɪdʒɪŋ] *adj* despreciativo

disparate ['dɪspərɪt] *adj* dispar

disparity [dɪs'pærɪtɪ] *n* disparidad *f*

dispassionate [dɪs'pæʃənɪt] *adj* (*unbiased*) imparcial

dispatch [dɪs'pætʃ] *vt* enviar ♦ *n* (*sending*) envío; (*PRESS*) informe *m*; (*MIL*) parte *m*

dispel [dɪs'pɛl] *vt* disipar

dispense [dɪs'pɛns] *vt* (*medicines*) preparar; **~ with** *vt fus* prescindir de; **~r** *n* (*container*) distribuidor *m* automático; **dispensing chemist** (*BRIT*) *n* farmacia

disperse [dɪs'pɜːs] *vt* dispersar ♦ *vi* dispersarse

dispirited [dɪ'spɪrɪtɪd] *adj* desanimado, desalentado

displace [dɪs'pleɪs] *vt* desplazar, reemplazar; **~d person** *n* (*POL*) desplazado/a

display [dɪs'pleɪ] *n* (*in shop window*) escaparate *m*; (*exhibition*) exposición *f*; (*COMPUT*) visualización *f*; (*of feeling*) manifestación *f* ♦ *vt* exponer; manifestar; (*ostentatiously*) lucir

displease [dɪs'pliːz] *vt* (*offend*) ofender; (*annoy*) fastidiar; **~d** *adj*: **~d with** disgustado con; **displeasure** [-'plɛʒə*] *n* disgusto

disposable [dɪs'pəuzəbl] *adj* desechable; (*income*) disponible; **~ nappy** *n* pañal *m* desechable

disposal [dɪs'pəuzl] *n* (*of rubbish*) destrucción *f*; **at one's ~** a su disposición

dispose [dɪs'pəuz] *vi*: **to ~ of** (*unwanted goods*) deshacerse de; (*problem etc*) resolver; **~d** *adj*: **~d to do** dispuesto a hacer; **to be well-~d towards sb** estar bien dispuesto hacia uno; **disposition** [-'zɪʃən] *n* (*nature*) temperamento; (*inclination*) propensión *f*

disproportionate [dɪsprə'pɔːʃənət] *adj* desproporcionado

disprove [dɪs'pruːv] *vt* refutar

dispute [dɪs'pjuːt] *n* disputa; (*also: industrial ~*) conflicto (laboral) ♦ *vt* (*argue*) disputar, discutir; (*question*) cuestionar

disqualify [dɪs'kwɔlɪfaɪ] *vt* (*SPORT*) desclasificar; **to ~ sb for sth/from doing sth** incapacitar a alguien para algo/hacer algo

disquiet [dɪs'kwaɪət] *n* preocupación *f*, inquietud *f*

disregard [dɪsrɪ'gɑːd] *vt* (*ignore*) no hacer caso de

disrepair [dɪsrɪ'pɛə*] *n*: **to fall into ~** (*building*) desmoronarse

disreputable [dɪs'rɛpjutəbl] *adj* (*person*) de mala fama; (*behaviour*) vergonzoso

disrespectful [dɪsrɪ'spɛktful] *adj* irrespetuoso

disrupt [dɪs'rʌpt] *vt* (*plans*) desbaratar, trastornar; (*conversation*) interrumpir; **~ion** [-'rʌpʃən] *n* (*disturbance*) trastorno; (*interruption*) interrupción *f*

dissatisfaction [dɪssætɪs'fækʃən] *n* disgusto, descontento

dissect [dɪ'sɛkt] *vt* disecar

dissent [dɪ'sɛnt] *n* disensión *f*

dissertation [dɪsə'teɪʃən] *n* tesina

disservice [dɪs'sɜːvɪs] *n*: **to do sb a ~** perjudicar a alguien

dissident ['dɪsɪdənt] *adj, n* disidente *m/f*

dissimilar [dɪ'sɪmɪlə*] *adj* distinto

dissipate ['dɪsɪpeɪt] *vt* disipar; (*waste*) desperdiciar

dissociate [dɪ'səuʃɪeɪt] *vt* disociar

dissolute ['dɪsəluːt] *adj* disoluto

dissolution [dɪsə'luːʃən] *n* disolución *f*

dissolve [dɪ'zɔlv] *vt* disolver ♦ *vi* disolverse; **to ~ in(to) tears** deshacerse en lágrimas

dissuade [dɪ'sweɪd] *vt*: **to ~ sb (from)** disuadir a uno (de)

distance ['dɪstəns] *n* distancia; **in the ~** a lo lejos

distant ['dɪstənt] *adj* lejano; (*manner*) reservado, frío

distaste [dɪs'teɪst] *n* repugnancia; **~ful** *adj* repugnante, desagradable

distended [dɪ'stɛndɪd] *adj* (*stomach*) hinchado

distil [dɪs'tɪl] (*US* **distill**) *vt* destilar; **~lery** *n* destilería

distinct [dɪs'tɪŋkt] *adj* (*different*) distinto; (*clear*) claro; (*unmistakeable*) inequívoco; **as ~ from** a diferencia de; **~ion** [dɪs'tɪŋkʃən] *n* distinción *f*; (*honour*) honor *m*; (*in exam*)

sobresaliente *m*; **~ive** *adj* distintivo
distinguish [dɪs'tɪŋgwɪʃ] *vt* distinguir; **to ~
o.s.** destacarse; **~ed** *adj* (*eminent*) distinguido; **~ing** *adj* (*feature*) distintivo
distort [dɪs'tɔːt] *vt* distorsionar; (*shape,
image*) deformar; **~ion** [dɪs'tɔːʃən] *n* distor-
sión *f*; deformación *f*
distract [dɪs'trækt] *vt* distraer; **~ed** *adj* dis-
traído; (*confusion*) aturdimiento; **~ion** [dɪs'trækʃən] *n* distracción *f*;
(*confusion*) aturdimiento
distraught [dɪs'trɔːt] *adj* loco de inquietud
distress [dɪs'trɛs] *n* (*anguish*) angustia,
aflicción *f* ♦ *vt* afligir; **~ing** *adj* angustioso;
doloroso; **~ signal** *n* señal *f* de socorro
distribute [dɪs'trɪbjuːt] *vt* (*share
out*) repartir; **distribution** [-'bjuːʃən] *n* distribución *f*, reparto; **distributor** *n* (*AUT*)
distribuidor *m*; (*COMM*) distribuidora
district [dɪstrɪkt] *n* (*of country*) zona, región *f*; (*of town*) barrio; (*ADMIN*) distrito; **~
attorney** (*US*) *n* fiscal *m/f*; **~ nurse**
(*BRIT*) *n* enfermera que atiende a pacientes a
domicilio
distrust [dɪs'trʌst] *n* desconfianza ♦ *vt* desconfiar de
disturb [dɪs'tɜːb] *vt* (*person: bother, interrupt*) molestar; (: *upset*) perturbar, inquietar; (*disorganize*) alterar; **~ance** *n* (*upheaval*) perturbación *f*; (*political etc: gen pl*)
disturbio; (*of mind*) trastorno; **~ed** *adj*
(*worried, upset*) preocupado, angustiado;
emotionally ~ed trastornado; (*childhood*)
inseguro; **~ing** *adj* inquietante, perturba-
dor(a)
disuse [dɪs'juːs] *n*: **to fall into ~** caer en
desuso
disused [dɪs'juːzd] *adj* abandonado
ditch [dɪtʃ] *n* zanja; (*irrigation ~*) acequia ♦
vt (*inf: partner*) deshacerse de; (: *plan, car
etc*) abandonar
dither ['dɪðə*] (*pej*) *vi* vacilar
ditto ['dɪtəu] *adv* ídem, lo mismo
divan [dɪ'væn] *n* (*also: ~ bed*) cama tur-
ca
dive [daɪv] *n* (*from board*) salto; (*underwater*) buceo; (*of submarine*) sumersión *f* ♦ *vi*
(*swimmer: into water*) saltar; (: *under water*)
zambullirse, bucear; (*fish, submarine*) sumergirse; (*bird*) lanzarse en picado; **to ~
into** (*bag etc*) meter la mano en; (*place*)
meterse de prisa en; **~r** *n* (*underwater*)
buzo
diverge [daɪ'vɜːdʒ] *vi* divergir
diverse [daɪ'vɜːs] *adj* diversos/as, varios/as
diversion [daɪ'vɜːʃən] *n* (*BRIT: AUT*) desviación *f*; (*distraction, MIL*) diversión *f*; (*of
funds*) distracción *f*
divert [daɪ'vɜːt] *vt* (*turn aside*) desviar
divide [dɪ'vaɪd] *vt* dividir; (*separate*) separar ♦ *vi* dividirse; (*road*) bifurcarse; **~d
highway** (*US*) *n* carretera de doble calzada

dividend ['dɪvɪdɛnd] *n* dividendo; (*fig*): **to
pay ~s** proporcionar beneficios
divine [dɪ'vaɪn] *adj* (*also fig*) divino
diving ['daɪvɪŋ] *n* (*SPORT*) salto; (*underwater*) buceo; **~ board** *n* trampolín *m*
divinity [dɪ'vɪnɪtɪ] *n* divinidad *f*; (*SCOL*)
teología
division [dɪ'vɪʒən] *n* división *f*; (*sharing
out*) reparto; (*disagreement*) diferencias *fpl*;
(*COMM*) sección *f*
divorce [dɪ'vɔːs] *n* divorcio ♦ *vt* divorciarse
de; **~d** *adj* divorciado; **~e** [-'siː] *n*
divorciado/a
divulge [daɪ'vʌldʒ] *vt* divulgar, revelar
D.I.Y. (*BRIT*) *adj*, *n abbr* = **do-it- yourself**
dizzy ['dɪzɪ] *adj* (*spell*) de mareo; **to feel ~**
marearse
DJ *n abbr* = **disc jockey**

───────────────── *KEYWORD*

do [duː] (*pt* **did**, *pp* **done**) *n* (*inf: party etc*):
we're having a little ~ on Saturday da-
mos una fiestecita el sábado; **it was rather
a grand ~** fue un acontecimiento a lo
grande
♦ *aux vb* **1** (*in negative constructions: not
translated*) **I don't understand** no entiendo
2 (*to form questions: not translated*) **didn't
you know?** ¿no lo sabías?; **what ~ you
think?** ¿qué opinas?
3 (*for emphasis, in polite expressions*):
people ~ make mistakes sometimes sí
que se cometen errores a veces; **she does
seem rather late** a mí también me parece
que se ha retrasado; **~ sit down/help
yourself** siéntate/sírvete por favor; **~ take
care!** ¡ten cuidado(, te pido)!
4 (*used to avoid repeating vb*): **she sings
better than I ~** canta mejor que yo; **~ you
agree? — yes, I ~/no, I don't** ¿estás de
acuerdo? — sí (lo estoy)/no (lo estoy); **she
lives in Glasgow — so ~ I** vive en Glasgow — yo también; **he didn't like it and
neither did we** no le gustó y a nosotros
tampoco; **who made this mess? — I did**
¿quién hizo esta chapuza? — yo; **he asked
me to help him and I did** me pidió que le
ayudara y lo hice
5 (*in question tags*): **you like him, don't
you?** te gusta, ¿verdad? *or* ¿no?; **I don't
know him, ~ I?** creo que no le conozco
♦ *vt* **1** (*gen, carry out, perform etc*): **what
are you ~ing tonight?** ¿qué haces esta noche?; **what can I ~ for you?** ¿en qué puedo servirle?; **to ~ the washing-up/
cooking** fregar los platos/cocinar; **to ~
one's teeth/hair/nails** lavarse los dientes/
arreglarse el pelo/arreglarse las uñas
2 (*AUT etc*): **the car was ~ing 100** el coche iba a 100; **we've done 200 km already**
ya hemos hecho 200 km; **he can ~ 100 in
that car** puede dar los 100 en ese coche

♦ vi **1** (act, behave) hacer; ~ **as I** ~ haz como yo
2 (get on, fare): he's ~ing well/badly at school va bien/mal en la escuela; the firm is ~ing well la empresa anda or va bien; how ~ you ~? mucho gusto; (less formal) ¿qué tal?
3 (suit): will it ~? ¿sirve?, ¿está or va bien?
4 (be sufficient) bastar; will £10 ~? ¿será bastante con £10?; that'll ~ así está bien; that'll ~! (in annoyance) ¡ya está bien!, ¡basta ya!; to make ~ (with) arreglárselas (con)
do away with vt fus (kill, disease) eliminar; (abolish: law etc) abolir; (withdraw) retirar
do up vt (laces) atar; (zip, dress, shirt) abrochar; (renovate: room, house) renovar
do with vt fus (need): I could ~ with a drink/some help no me vendría mal un trago/un poco de ayuda; (be connected) tener que ver con; what has it got to ~ with you? ¿qué tiene que ver contigo?
do without vi: if you're late for tea then you'll ~ without si llegas tarde tendrás que quedarte sin cenar ♦ vt fus pasar sin; I can ~ without a car puedo pasar sin coche

dock [dɔk] n (NAUT) muelle m; (LAW) banquillo (de los acusados); ~s npl (NAUT) muelles mpl, puerto sg ♦ vi (enter ~) atracar (la) muelle; (SPACE) acoplarse; ~er n trabajador m portuario, estibador m; ~yard n astillero
doctor ['dɔktə*] n médico/a; (PhD etc) doctor(a) m/f ♦ vt (drink etc) adulterar; D~ of Philosophy n Doctor en Filosofía y Letras
doctrine ['dɔktrɪn] n doctrina
document ['dɔkjumənt] n documento; ~ary [-'mentərɪ] adj documental ♦ n documental m
dodge [dɔdʒ] n (fig) truco ♦ vt evadir; (blow) esquivar
dodgems ['dɔdʒəmz] (BRIT) npl coches mpl de choque
doe [dəu] n (deer) cierva, gama; (rabbit) coneja
does [dʌz] vb see do; ~n't = ~ not
dog [dɔg] n perro ♦ vt seguir los pasos de; (subj: bad luck) perseguir; ~ collar n collar m de perro; (of clergyman) alzacuellos m inv; ~-eared adj sobado
dogged ['dɔgɪd] adj tenaz, obstinado
dogsbody ['dɔgzbɔdɪ] (BRIT: inf) n burro de carga
doings ['duɪŋz] npl (activities) actividades fpl
do-it-yourself n bricolaje m
doldrums ['dɔldrəmz] npl: to be in the ~ (person) estar abatido; (business) estar estancado
dole [dəul] n (BRIT) (payment) subsidio de paro; on the ~ parado; ~ out vt repartir
doleful ['dəulful] adj triste, lúgubre
doll [dɔl] n muñeca; (US: inf: woman) muñeca, gachí f; ~ed-up (inf) adj arreglado
dollar ['dɔlə*] n dólar m
dolphin ['dɔlfɪn] n delfín m
domain [də'meɪn] n (fig) campo, competencia; (land) dominios mpl
dome [dəum] n (ARCH) cúpula
domestic [də'mestɪk] adj (animal, duty) doméstico; (flight, policy) nacional; ~ated adj domesticado; (home-loving) casero, hogareño
dominant ['dɔmɪnənt] adj dominante
dominate ['dɔmɪneɪt] vt dominar
domineering [dɔmɪ'nɪərɪŋ] adj dominante
dominion [də'mɪnɪən] n dominio
domino ['dɔmɪnəu] (pl ~es) n ficha de dominó; ~es n (game) dominó
don [dɔn] n (BRIT) n profesor(a) m/f universitario/a
donate [də'neɪt] vt donar; **donation** [də'neɪʃən] n donativo
done [dʌn] pp of do
donkey ['dɔŋkɪ] n burro
donor ['dəunə*] n donante m/f
don't [dəunt] = do not
doodle ['du:dl] vi hacer dibujitos or garabatos
doom [du:m] n (fate) suerte f ♦ vt: to be ~ed to failure estar condenado al fracaso; ~sday n día m del juicio final
door [dɔ:*] n puerta; ~bell n timbre m; ~handle n tirador m; (of car) manija; ~man n (in hotel) portero; ~mat n felpudo, estera; ~step n peldaño; ~-to-~ adj de puerta en puerta; ~way n entrada, puerta
dope [dəup] n (inf: illegal drug) droga; (: person) imbécil m/f ♦ vt (horse etc) drogar
dopey ['dəupɪ] (inf) adj (groggy) atontado; (stupid) imbécil
dormant ['dɔ:mənt] adj inactivo
dormice ['dɔ:maɪs] npl of dormouse
dormitory ['dɔ:mɪtrɪ] n (BRIT) dormitorio; (US) colegio mayor
dormouse ['dɔ:maus] (pl -mice) n lirón m
DOS n abbr = disk operating system) DOS m
dosage ['dəusɪdʒ] n dosis f inv
dose [dəus] n dósis f inv
doss house ['dɔss-] (BRIT) n pensión f de mala muerte
dossier ['dɔsɪeɪ] n expediente m, dosier m
dot [dɔt] n punto ♦ vi: ~ted with salpicado de; on the ~ en punto
dote [dəut]: to ~ on vt fus adorar, idolatrar
dot-matrix printer n impresora matricial (or de matriz) de puntos
double ['dʌbl] adj doble ♦ adv (twice): to

cost ~ costar el doble ♦ *n* doble *m* ♦ *vt* doblar ♦ *vi* doblarse; **on the ~, at the ~** (*BRIT*) corriendo; ~ **bass** *n* contrabajo; ~ **bed** *n* cama de matrimonio; ~ **bend** (*BRIT*) *n* doble curva; ~**-breasted** *adj* cruzado; ~**cross** *vt* (*trick*) engañar; (*betray*) traicionar; ~**decker** *n* autobús *m* de dos pisos; ~ **glazing** (*BRIT*) *n* doble acristalamiento; ~ **room** *n* habitación *f* doble; ~**s** *n* (*TENNIS*) juego de dobles; **doubly** *adv* doblemente

doubt [daut] *n* duda ♦ *vt* dudar; (*suspect*) dudar de; **to ~ that** dudar que; ~**ful** *adj* dudoso; (*person*): **to be ~ful about sth** tener dudas sobre algo; ~**less** *adv* sin duda

dough [dəu] *n* masa, pasta; ~**nut** *n* ≈ rosquilla

douse [daus] *vt* (*drench*) mojar; (*extinguish*) apagar

dove [dʌv] *n* paloma

dovetail ['dʌvteɪl] *vi* (*fig*) encajar

dowdy ['daudɪ] *adj* (*person*) mal vestido; (*clothes*) pasado de moda

down [daun] *n* (*feathers*) plumón *m*, flojel *m* ♦ *adv* (~*wards*) abajo, hacia abajo; (*on the ground*) por *or* en tierra ♦ *prep* abajo ♦ *vt* (*inf: drink*) beberse; ~ **with X!** ¡abajo X!; ~**-and-out** *n* vagabundo/a; ~**-at-heel** *adj* venido a menos; (*appearance*) desaliñado; ~**cast** *adj* abatido; ~**fall** *n* caída, ruina; ~**hearted** *adj* desanimado; ~**hill** *adv*: **to go ~hill** (*also fig*) ir cuesta abajo; ~ **payment** *n* entrada, pago al contado; ~**pour** *n* aguacero; ~**right** *adj* (*nonsense, lie*) manifiesto; (*refusal*) terminante

Down's syndrome ['daunz-] *n* síndrome *m* de Down

down: ~**stairs** *adv* (*below*) (en la casa de) abajo; (~*wards*) escaleras abajo; ~**stream** *adv* aguas *or* río abajo; ~**-to-earth** *adj* práctico; ~**town** *adv* en el centro de la ciudad; ~ **under** *adv* en Australia (*or* Nueva Zelanda); ~**ward** [-wəd] *adj, adv* hacia abajo; ~**wards** [-wədz] *adv* hacia abajo

dowry ['daurɪ] *n* dote *f*

doz. *abbr* = **dozen**

doze [dəuz] *vi* dormitar; ~ **off** *vi* quedarse medio dormido

dozen ['dʌzn] *n* docena; **a ~ books** una docena de libros; ~**s of** cantidad de

Dr. *abbr* = **doctor; drive**

drab [dræb] *adj* gris, monótono

draft [drɑːft] *n* (*first copy*) borrador *m*; (*POL: of bill*) anteproyecto; (*US: call-up*) quinta ♦ *vt* (*plan*) preparar; (*write roughly*) hacer un borrador de; *see also* **draught**

draftsman ['drɑːftsmən] (*US*) *n* = **draughtsman**

drag [dræg] *vt* arrastrar; (*river*) dragar, rastrear ♦ *vi* (*time*) pasar despacio; (*play, film etc*) hacerse pesado ♦ *n* (*inf*) lata; (*women's clothing*): **in ~** vestido de travesti; ~ **on** *vi* ser interminable

dragon ['drægən] *n* dragón *m*

dragonfly ['drægənflaɪ] *n* libélula

drain [dreɪn] *n* desaguadero; (*in street*) sumidero; (*source of loss*): **to be a ~ on** consumir, agotar ♦ *vt* (*land, marshes*) desaguar; (*reservoir*) desecar; (*vegetables*) escurrir ♦ *vi* escurrirse; ~**age** *n* (*act*) desagüe *m*; (*MED, AGR*) drenaje *m*; (*sewage*) alcantarillado; ~**board** ['dreɪnbɔːd] (*US*) *n* = ~**ing board**; ~**ing board** *n* escurridera, escurridor *m*; ~**pipe** *n* tubo de desagüe

drama ['drɑːmə] *n* (*art*) teatro; (*play*) drama *m*; (*excitement*) emoción *f*; ~**tic** [drə'mætɪk] *adj* dramático; (*sudden, marked*) espectacular; ~**tist** ['dræmətɪst] *n* dramaturgo/a; ~**tize** ['dræmətaɪz] *vt* (*events*) dramatizar; (*adapt: for TV, cinema*) adaptar a la televisión/al cine

drank [dræŋk] *pt of* **drink**

drape [dreɪp] *vt* (*cloth*) colocar; (*flag*) colgar; ~**s** (*US*) *npl* cortinas *fpl*

drastic ['dræstɪk] *adj* (*measure*) severo; (*change*) radical, drástico

draught [drɑːft] (*US* **draft**) *n* (*of air*) corriente *f* de aire; (*NAUT*) calado; **on ~** (*beer*) de barril; ~**board** (*BRIT*) *n* tablero de damas; ~**s** (*BRIT*) *n* (*game*) juego de damas

draughtsman ['drɑːftsmən] (*US* **draftsman**) *n* delineante *m*

draw [drɔː] (*pt* **drew**, *pp* **drawn**) *vt* (*picture*) dibujar; (*cart*) tirar de; (*curtain*) correr; (*take out*) sacar; (*attract*) atraer; (*money*) retirar; (*wages*) cobrar ♦ *vi* (*SPORT*) empatar ♦ *n* (*SPORT*) empate *m*; (*lottery*) sorteo; ~ **near** *vi* acercarse; ~ **out** *vi* (*lengthen*) alargarse ♦ *vt* sacar; ~ **up** *vi* (*stop*) pararse ♦ *vt* (*chair*) acercar; (*document*) redactar; ~**back** *n* inconveniente *m*, desventaja; ~**bridge** *n* puente *m* levadizo

drawer [drɔː*] *n* cajón *m*

drawing ['drɔːɪŋ] *n* dibujo; ~ **board** *n* tablero (de dibujante); ~ **pin** (*BRIT*) *n* chincheta; ~ **room** *n* salón *m*

drawl [drɔːl] *n* habla lenta y cansina

drawn [drɔːn] *pp of* **draw**

dread [dred] *n* pavor *m*, terror *m* ♦ *vt* temer, tener miedo *or* pavor a; ~**ful** *adj* horroroso

dream [driːm] (*pt, pp* **dreamed** *or* **dreamt**) *n* sueño ♦ *vt, vi* soñar; ~**er** *n* soñador(a) *m/f*; **dreamt** [dremt] *pt, pp of* **dream**; ~**y** *adj* (*distracted*) soñador(a), distraído; (*music*) suave

dreary ['drɪərɪ] *adj* monótono

dredge [dredʒ] *vt* dragar

dregs [dregz] *npl* posos *mpl*; (*of humanity*) hez *f*

drench [drentʃ] *vt* empapar

dress [dres] *n* vestido; (*clothing*) ropa ♦ *vt* vestir; (*wound*) vendar ♦ *vi* vestirse; **to get**

~ed vestirse; ~ up *vi* vestirse de etiqueta; (*in fancy dress*) disfrazarse; ~ circle (*BRIT*) *n* principal *m*; (: *US*) cómoda (con espejo); ~ing *n* (*MED*) vendaje *m*; (*CULIN*) aliño; ~ing gown (*BRIT*) *n* bata; ~ing room *n* (*THEATRE*) camarín *m*; (*SPORT*) vestuario; ~ing table *n* tocador *m*; ~maker *n* modista, costurera; ~ rehearsal *n* ensayo general

drew [dru:] *pt of* **draw**

dribble ['drɪbl] *vi* (*baby*) babear ♦ *vt* (*ball*) regatear

dried [draɪd] *adj* (*fruit*) seco; (*milk*) en polvo

drier ['draɪə*] *n* = **dryer**

drift [drɪft] *n* (*of current etc*) flujo; (*of snow*) ventisquero; (*meaning*) significado ♦ *vi* (*boat*) ir a la deriva; (*sand, snow*) amontonarse; ~**wood** *n* madera de deriva

drill [drɪl] *n* (~ *bit*) broca; (*tool for DIY etc*) taladro; (*of dentist*) fresa; (*for mining etc*) perforadora, barrena; (*MIL*) instrucción *f* ♦ *vt* perforar, taladrar; (*troops*) enseñar la instrucción a ♦ *vi* (*for oil*) perforar

drink [drɪŋk] (*pt* **drank**, *pp* **drunk**) *n* bebida; (*sip*) trago ♦ *vt, vi* beber; **to have a** ~ tomar algo; tomar una copa *or* un trago; **a** ~ **of water** un trago de agua; ~**er** *n* bebedor(a) *m/f*; ~**ing water** *n* agua potable

drip [drɪp] *n* (*act*) goteo; (*one* ~) gota; (*MED*) gota a gota *m* ♦ *vi* gotear; ~**-dry** *adj* (*shirt*) inarrugable; ~**ping** *n* (*animal fat*) pringue *m*

drive [draɪv] (*pt* **drove**, *pp* **driven**) *n* (*journey*) viaje *m* (en coche); (*also*: ~**way**) entrada; (*energy*) energía, vigor *m*; (*COMPUT*: *also*: *disk* ~) drive *m* ♦ *vt* (*car*) conducir (*SP*), manejar (*AM*); (*nail*) clavar; (*push*) empujar; (*TECH: motor*) impulsar ♦ *vi* (*AUT*: *at controls*) conducir; (: *travel*) pasearse en coche; **left-/right-hand** ~ conducción *f* a la izquierda/derecha; **to** ~ **sb mad** volverle loco a uno

drivel ['drɪvl] (*inf*) *n* tonterías *fpl*

driven ['drɪvn] *pp of* **drive**

driver ['draɪvə*] *n* conductor(a) *m/f* (*SP*), chofer *m* (*AM*); (*of taxi, bus*) chofer; ~**'s license** (*US*) *n* carnet *m* de conducir

driveway ['draɪvweɪ] *n* entrada

driving ['draɪvɪŋ] *n* el conducir (*SP*), el manejar (*AM*); ~ **instructor** *n* instructor(a) *m/f* de conducción *or* manejo; ~ **lesson** *n* clase *f* de conducción *or* manejo; ~ **licence** (*BRIT*) *n* permiso de conducir; ~ **school** *n* autoescuela; ~ **test** *n* examen *m* de conducción *or* manejo

drizzle ['drɪzl] *n* llovizna

drone [drəun] *n* (*noise*) zumbido; (*bee*) zángano

drool [dru:l] *vi* babear

droop [dru:p] *vi* (*flower*) marchitarse; (*shoulders*) encorvarse; (*head*) inclinarse

drop [drɔp] *n* (*of water*) gota; (*lessening*)

baja; (*fall*) caída ♦ *vt* dejar caer; (*voice, eyes, price*) bajar; (*passenger*) dejar; (*omit*) omitir ♦ *vi* (*object*) caer; (*wind*) amainar; ~**s** *npl* (*MED*) gotas *fpl*; ~ **off** *vi* (*sleep*) dormirse ♦ *vt* (*passenger*) dejar; ~ **out** *vi* (*withdraw*) retirarse; ~**-out** *n* marginado/a; (*SCOL*) estudiante que abandona los estudios; ~**per** *n* cuentagotas *m inv*; ~**pings** *npl* excremento

drought [draut] *n* sequía

drove [drəuv] *pt of* **drive**

drown [draun] *vt* ahogar ♦ *vi* ahogarse

drowsy ['drauzɪ] *adj* soñoliento; **to be** ~ tener sueño

drudgery ['drʌdʒərɪ] *n* trabajo monótono

drug [drʌg] *n* medicamento; (*narcotic*) droga ♦ *vt*. drogar; **to be on** ~**s** drogarse; ~ **addict** *n* drogadicto/a; ~**gist** (*US*) *n* farmacéutico; ~**store** (*US*) *n* farmacia

drum [drʌm] *n* tambor *m*; (*for oil, petrol*) bidón *m*; ~**s** *npl* batería; ~**mer** *n* tambor *m*

drunk [drʌŋk] *pp of* **drink** ♦ *adj* borracho ♦ *n* (*also*: ~*ard*) borracho/a; ~**en** *adj* borracho; (*laughter, party*) de borrachos

dry [draɪ] *adj* seco; (*day*) sin lluvia; (*climate*) árido, seco ♦ *vt* secar; (*tears*) enjugarse ♦ *vi* secarse; ~ **up** *vi* (*river*) secarse; ~-**cleaner's** *n* tintorería; ~-**cleaning** *n* lavado en seco; ~**er** *n* (*for hair*) secador *m*; (*US*: *for clothes*) secadora; ~**ness** *n* sequedad *f*; ~ **rot** *n* putrefacción *f* fungoide

DSS *n abbr* = **Department of Social Security**

dual ['djuəl] *adj* doble; ~ **carriageway** (*BRIT*) *n* carretera de doble calzada; ~ **nationality** *n* doble nacionalidad *f*; ~-**purpose** *adj* de doble uso

dubbed [dʌbd] *adj* (*CINEMA*) doblado

dubious ['dju:bɪəs] *adj* indeciso; (*reputation, company*) sospechoso

duchess ['dʌtʃɪs] *n* duquesa

duck [dʌk] *n* pato ♦ *vi* agacharse; ~**ling** *n* patito

duct [dʌkt] *n* conducto, canal *m*

dud [dʌd] *n* (*object, tool*) engaño, engañifa ♦ *adj*: ~ **cheque** (*BRIT*) cheque *m* sin fondos

due [dju:] *adj* (*owed*): **he is** ~ **£10** se le deben 10 libras; (*expected*: *event*): **the meeting is** ~ **on Wednesday** la reunión tendrá lugar el miércoles; (: *arrival*) **the train is** ~ **at 8am** el tren tiene su llegada para las 8; (*proper*) debido ♦ *n*: **to give sb his** (*or* **her**) ~ ser justo con alguien ♦ *adv*: ~ **north** derecho al norte; ~**s** *npl* (*for club, union*) cuota; (*in harbour*) derechos *mpl*; **in** ~ **course** a su debido tiempo; ~ **to** debido a; **to be** ~ **to** deberse a

duet [dju:'et] *n* dúo

duffel ['dʌfəl] *adj*: ~ **bag** *n* bolsa de lona; ~ **coat** *n* trenca, abrigo de tres cuartos

dug [dʌg] *pt, pp of* dig
duke [djuːk] *n* duque *m*
dull [dʌl] *adj* (*light*) débil; (*stupid*) torpe; (*boring*) pesado; (*sound, pain*) sordo; (*weather, day*) gris ♦ *vt* (*pain, grief*) aliviar; (*mind, senses*) entorpecer
duly ['djuːlɪ] *adv* debidamente; (*on time*) a su debido tiempo
dumb [dʌm] *adj* mudo; (*pej: stupid*) estúpido; ~**founded** [dʌm'faundɪd] *adj* pasmado
dummy ['dʌmɪ] *n* (*tailor's* ~) maniquí *m*; (*mock-up*) maqueta; (*BRIT: for baby*) chupete *m* ♦ *adj* falso, postizo
dump [dʌmp] *n* (*also: rubbish* ~) basurero, vertedero; (*inf: place*) cuchitril *m* ♦ *vt* (*put down*) dejar; (*get rid of*) deshacerse de; (*COMPUT: data*) transferir
dumpling ['dʌmplɪŋ] *n* bola de masa hervida
dumpy ['dʌmpɪ] *adj* regordete/a
dunce [dʌns] *n* zopenco
dung [dʌŋ] *n* estiércol *m*
dungarees [dʌŋgə'riːz] *npl* mono
dungeon ['dʌndʒən] *n* calabozo
duo ['djuːəu] *n* (*gen, MUS*) dúo
dupe [djuːp] *n* (*victim*) víctima ♦ *vt* engañar
duplex ['djuːplɛks] *n* dúplex *m*
duplicate [*n* 'djuːplɪkət, *vb* 'djuːplɪkeɪt] *n* duplicado ♦ *vt* duplicar; (*photocopy*) fotocopiar; (*repeat*) repetir; in ~ por duplicado
durable ['djuərəbl] *adj* duradero
duration [djuə'reɪʃən] *n* duración *f*
duress [djuə'rɛs] *n*: under ~ por compulsión
during ['djuərɪŋ] *prep* durante
dusk [dʌsk] *n* crepúsculo, anochecer *m*
dust [dʌst] *n* polvo ♦ *vt* quitar el polvo a, desempolvar; (*cake etc*): to ~ with espolvorear de; ~**bin** (*BRIT*) *n* cubo de la basura (*SP*), balde *m* (*AM*); ~**er** *n* paño, trapo; ~**man** (*BRIT*) *n* basurero; ~**y** *adj* polvoriento
Dutch [dʌtʃ] *adj* holandés/esa ♦ *n* (*LING*) holandés *m*; the ~ *npl* los holandeses; to go ~ (*inf*) pagar cada uno lo suyo; ~**man/woman** *n* holandés/esa *m/f*
dutiful ['djuːtɪful] *adj* obediente, sumiso
duty ['djuːtɪ] *n* deber *m*; (*tax*) derechos *mpl* de aduana; on ~ de servicio; (*at night etc*) de guardia; off ~ libre (de servicio); ~**free** *adj* libre de impuestos
duvet ['duːveɪ] (*BRIT*) *n* edredón *m*
dwarf [dwɔːf] (*pl* dwarves) *n* enano/a ♦ *vt* empequeñecer; **dwarves** [dwɔːvz] *npl* of dwarf
dwell [dwɛl] (*pt, pp* dwelt) *vi* morar; ~ on *vt fus* explayarse en; ~**ing** *n* vivienda
dwindle ['dwɪndl] *vi* menguar, disminuir
dye [daɪ] *n* tinte *m* ♦ *vt* teñir
dying ['daɪɪŋ] *adj* moribundo, agonizante
dyke [daɪk] (*BRIT*) *n* dique *m*
dynamic [daɪ'næmɪk] *adj* dinámico

dynamite ['daɪnəmaɪt] *n* dinamita
dynamo ['daɪnəməu] *n* dinamo *f*
dynasty ['dɪnəstɪ] *n* dinastía

E e

E [iː] *n* (*MUS*) mi *m*
each [iːtʃ] *adj* cada *inv* ♦ *pron* cada uno; ~ other el uno al otro; they hate ~ other se odian (entre ellos *or* mutuamente); they have 2 books ~ tienen 2 libros por persona
eager ['iːgə*] *adj* (*keen*) entusiasmado; to be ~ to do sth tener muchas ganas de hacer algo, impacientarse por hacer algo; to be ~ for tener muchas ganas de
eagle ['iːgl] *n* águila
ear [ɪə*] *n* oreja; oído; (*of corn*) espiga; ~**ache** *n* dolor *m* de oídos; ~**drum** *n* tímpano
earl [əːl] *n* conde *m*
earlier ['əːlɪə*] *adj* anterior ♦ *adv* antes
early ['əːlɪ] *adv* temprano; (*before time*) con tiempo, con anticipación ♦ *adj* temprano; (*settlers etc*) primitivo; (*death, departure*) prematuro; (*reply*) pronto; to have an ~ night acostarse temprano; in the ~ *or* ~ in the spring/19th century a principios de primavera/del siglo diecinueve; ~ retirement *n* jubilación *f* anticipada
earmark ['ɪəmɑːk] *vt*: to ~ (for) reservar (para), destinar (a)
earn [əːn] *vt* (*salary*) percibir; (*interest*) devengar; (*praise*) merecerse
earnest ['əːnɪst] *adj* (*wish*) fervoroso; (*person*) serio, formal; in ~ en serio
earnings ['əːnɪŋz] *npl* (*personal*) sueldo, ingresos *mpl*; (*company*) ganancias *fpl*
ear: ~**phones** *npl* auriculares *mpl*; ~**ring** *n* pendiente *m*, arete *m*; ~**shot** *n*: within ~shot al alcance del oído
earth [əːθ] *n* tierra; (*BRIT: ELEC*) cable *m* de toma de tierra ♦ *vt* (*BRIT: ELEC*) conectar a tierra; ~**enware** *n* loza (de barro); ~**quake** *n* terremoto; ~**y** *adj* (*fig: vulgar*) grosero
ease [iːz] *n* facilidad *f*; (*comfort*) comodidad *f* ♦ *vt* (*lessen: problem*) mitigar; (: *pain*) aliviar; (: *tension*) reducir; to ~ sth in/out meter/sacar algo con cuidado; at ~! (*MIL*) ¡descansen!; ~ off *or* ~ up *vi* (*wind, rain*) amainar; (*slow down*) aflojar la marcha
easel ['iːzl] *n* caballete *m*

easily ['iːzɪlɪ] *adv* fácilmente
east [iːst] *n* este *m* ♦ *adj* del este, oriental; (*wind*) este ♦ *adv* al este, hacia el este; **the E~** el Oriente; (*POL*) los países del Este
Easter ['iːstə*] *n* Pascua (de Resurrección); **~ egg** *n* huevo de Pascua
easterly ['iːstəlɪ] *adj* (*to the east*) al este; (*from the east*) del este
eastern ['iːstən] *adj* del este, oriental; (*oriental*) oriental; (*communist*) del este
East Germany *n* Alemania Oriental
eastward(s) ['iːstwəd(z)] *adv* hacia el este
easy ['iːzɪ] *adj* fácil; (*simple*) sencillo; (*comfortable*) holgado, cómodo; (*relaxed*) tranquilo ♦ *adv*: **to take it** *or* **things ~** (*not worry*) tomarlo con calma; (*rest*) descansar; **~ chair** *n* sillón *m*; **~-going** *adj* acomodadizo
eat [iːt] (*pt* **ate**, *pp* **eaten**) *vt* comer; **~ into** *vt fus* corroer; (*savings*) mermar; **~ away at** *vt fus* corroer; mermar
eau de Cologne [əudəkə'ləun] *n* (agua de) Colonia
eaves [iːvz] *npl* alero
eavesdrop ['iːvzdrɔp] *vi*: **to ~ (on)** escuchar a escondidas
ebb [ɛb] *n* reflujo ♦ *vi* bajar; (*fig: also*: **~ away**) decaer
ebony ['ɛbənɪ] *n* ébano
EC *n abbr* (= *European Community*) CE *f*
eccentric [ɪk'sɛntrɪk] *adj*, *n* excéntrico/a *m/f*
echo ['ɛkəu] (*pl* **~es**) *n* eco *m* ♦ *vt* (*sound*) repetir ♦ *vi* resonar, hacer eco
éclair [ɪ'klɛə*] *n* pastelillo relleno de crema y con chocolate por encima
eclipse [ɪ'klɪps] *n* eclipse *m*
ecology [ɪ'kɔlədʒɪ] *n* ecología
economic [iːkə'nɔmɪk] *adj* económico; (*business etc*) rentable; **~al** *adj* económico; **~s** *n* (*SCOL*) economía ♦ *npl* (*of project etc*) rentabilidad *f*
economize [ɪ'kɔnəmaɪz] *vi* economizar, ahorrar
economy [ɪ'kɔnəmɪ] *n* economía; **~ class** *n* (*AVIAT*) clase *f* económica; **~ size** *n* tamaño económico
ecstasy ['ɛkstəsɪ] *n* éxtasis *m inv*; **ecstatic** [-'tætɪk] *adj* extático
ECU ['eɪkjuː] *n* (= *European Currency Unit*) ECU *m*
Ecuador ['ekwədɔːr] *n* Ecuador *m*; **~ian** *adj*, *n* ecuatoriano/a *m/f*
eczema ['ɛksɪmə] *n* eczema *m*
edge [ɛdʒ] *n* (*of knife etc*) filo; (*of object*) borde *m*; (*of lake etc*) orilla ♦ *vt* (*SEWING*) ribetear; **on ~** (*fig*) = **edgy**; **to ~ away from** alejarse poco a poco de; **~ways** *adv*: **he couldn't get a word in ~ways** no pudo meter ni baza
edgy ['ɛdʒɪ] *adj* nervioso, inquieto
edible ['ɛdɪbl] *adj* comestible

Edinburgh ['ɛdɪnbərə] *n* Edimburgo
edit ['ɛdɪt] *vt* (*be editor of*) dirigir; (*text, report*) corregir, preparar; **~ion** [ɪ'dɪʃən] *n* edición *f*; **~or** *n* (*of newspaper*) director(a) *m/f*; (*of column*): **foreign/political ~or** encargado de la sección de extranjero/política; (*of book*) redactor(a) *m/f*; **~orial** [-'tɔːrɪəl] *adj* editorial ♦ *n* editorial *m*
educate ['ɛdjukeɪt] *vt* (*gen*) educar; (*instruct*) instruir
education [ɛdju'keɪʃən] *n* educación *f*; (*schooling*) enseñanza; (*SCOL*) pedagogía; **~al** *adj* (*policy etc*) educacional; (*experience*) docente; (*toy*) educativo
EEC *n abbr* (= *European Economic Community*) CEE *f*
eel [iːl] *n* anguila
eerie ['ɪərɪ] *adj* misterioso
effect [ɪ'fɛkt] *n* efecto ♦ *vt* efectuar, llevar a cabo; **to take ~** (*law*) entrar en vigor *or* vigencia; (*drug*) surtir efecto; **in ~** en realidad; **~ive** *adj* eficaz; (*actual*) verdadero; **~ively** *adv* eficazmente; (*in reality*) efectivamente; **~iveness** *n* eficacia
effeminate [ɪ'fɛmɪnɪt] *adj* afeminado
efficiency [ɪ'fɪʃənsɪ] *n* eficiencia; rendimiento
efficient [ɪ'fɪʃənt] *adj* eficiente; (*machine*) de buen rendimiento
effort ['ɛfət] *n* esfuerzo; **~less** *adj* sin ningún esfuerzo; (*style*) natural
effrontery [ɪ'frʌntərɪ] *n* descaro
effusive [ɪ'fjuːsɪv] *adj* efusivo
e.g. *adv abbr* (= *exempli gratia*) p. ej.
egg [ɛg] *n* huevo; **hard-boiled/soft-boiled ~** huevo duro/pasado por agua; **~ on** *vt* incitar; **~cup** *n* huevera; **~ plant** (*esp US*) *n* berenjena; **~shell** *n* cáscara de huevo
ego ['iːgəu] *n* ego; **~tism** *n* egoísmo; **~tist** *n* egoísta *m/f*
Egypt ['iːdʒɪpt] *n* Egipto; **~ian** [ɪ'dʒɪpʃən] *adj*, *n* egipcio/a *m/f*
eiderdown ['aɪdədaun] *n* edredón *m*
eight [eɪt] *num* ocho; **~een** *num* diez y ocho, dieciocho; **~h** [eɪtθ] *num* octavo; **~y** *num* ochenta
Eire ['ɛərə] *n* Eire *m*
either ['aɪðə*] *adj* cualquiera de los dos; (*both, each*) cada ♦ *pron*: **~ (of them)** cualquiera (de los dos) ♦ *adv* tampoco; **on ~ side** en ambos lados; **I don't like ~** no me gusta ninguno/a de los/las dos; **no, I don't ~** no, yo tampoco ♦ *conj*: **~ yes or no** o sí o no
eject [ɪ'dʒɛkt] *vt* echar, expulsar; (*tenant*) desahuciar; **~or seat** *n* asiento proyectable
eke [iːk]: **to ~ out** *vt* hacer que alcance
elaborate [*adj* ɪ'læbərɪt, *vb* ɪ'læbəreɪt] *adj* (*complex*) complejo ♦ *vt* (*expand*) ampliar; (*refine*) refinar ♦ *vi* explicar con más detalles
elapse [ɪ'læps] *vi* transcurrir

elastic [ɪ'læstɪk] n elástico ♦ adj elástico; (fig) flexible; ~ **band** (BRIT) n gomita
elated [ɪ'leɪtɪd] adj: **to be** ~ regocijarse
elbow ['ɛlbəʊ] n codo
elder ['ɛldə*] adj mayor ♦ n (tree) saúco; (person) mayor; ~**ly** adj de edad, mayor ♦ npl: **the** ~**ly** los mayores
eldest ['ɛldɪst] adj, n el/la mayor
elect [ɪ'lɛkt] vt elegir ♦ adj: **the president** ~ el presidente electo; **to** ~ **to do** optar por hacer; ~**ion** [ɪ'lɛkʃən] n elección f; ~**ioneering** [ɪlɛkʃə'nɪərɪŋ] n campaña electoral; ~**or** n elector(a) m/f; ~**oral** adj electoral; ~**orate** n electorado
electric [ɪ'lɛktrɪk] adj eléctrico; ~**al** adj eléctrico; ~ **blanket** n manta eléctrica; ~ **fire** n estufa eléctrica
electrician [ɪlɛk'trɪʃən] n electricista m/f
electricity [ɪlɛk'trɪsɪtɪ] n electricidad f
electrify [ɪ'lɛktrɪfaɪ] vt (RAIL) electrificar; (fig: audience) electrizar
electron [ɪ'lɛktrɒn] n electrón m
electronic [ɪlɛk'trɒnɪk] adj electrónico; ~ **mail** n correo electrónico; ~**s** n electrónica
elegant ['ɛlɪgənt] adj elegante
element ['ɛlɪmənt] n elemento; (of kettle etc) resistencia; ~**ary** [-'mɛntərɪ] adj elemental; (primitive) rudimentario; (school) primario
elephant ['ɛlɪfənt] n elefante m
elevation [ɛlɪ'veɪʃən] n elevación f; (height) altura
elevator ['ɛlɪveɪtə*] n (US) ascensor m; (in warehouse etc) montacargas m inv
eleven [ɪ'lɛvn] num once; ~**ses** (BRIT) npl café m de las once; ~**th** num undécimo
elf [ɛlf] (pl **elves**) n duende m
elicit [ɪ'lɪsɪt] vt: **to** ~ (**from**) sacar (de)
eligible ['ɛlɪdʒəbl] adj: **an** ~ **young man/woman** un buen partido; **to be** ~ **for sth** llenar los requisitos para algo
eliminate [ɪ'lɪmɪneɪt] vt (eradicate) suprimir; (opponent) eliminar
elm [ɛlm] n olmo
elongated ['iːlɒŋgeɪtɪd] adj alargado
elope [ɪ'ləʊp] vi fugarse (para casarse); ~**ment** n fuga
eloquent ['ɛləkwənt] adj elocuente
else [ɛls] adv: **something** ~ otra cosa; **somewhere** ~ en otra parte; **everywhere** ~ en todas partes menos aquí; **where** ~? ¿dónde más?, ¿en qué otra parte?; **there was little** ~ **to do** apenas quedaba otra cosa que hacer; **nobody** ~ **spoke** no habló nadie más; ~**where** adv (be) en otra parte; (go) a otra parte
elucidate [ɪ'luːsɪdeɪt] vt aclarar
elude [ɪ'luːd] vt (subj: idea etc) escaparse a; (capture) esquivar
elusive [ɪ'luːsɪv] adj esquivo; (quality) difícil de encontrar

emaciated [ɪ'meɪsɪeɪtɪd] adj demacrado
emanate ['ɛməneɪt] vi: **to** ~ **from** (idea) surgir de; (light, sound) proceder de
emancipate [ɪ'mænsɪpeɪt] vt emancipar
embankment [ɪm'bæŋkmənt] n terraplén m
embargo [ɪm'bɑːgəʊ] (pl ~**es**) n prohibición f, embargo
embark [ɪm'bɑːk] vi embarcarse ♦ vt embarcar; **to** ~ **on** (journey) emprender; (course of action) lanzarse a; ~**ation** [ɛmbɑː'keɪʃən] n (people) embarco; (goods) embarque m
embarrass [ɪm'bærəs] vt avergonzar; (government etc) dejar en mal lugar; ~**ed** adj (laugh, silence) embarazoso; ~**ing** adj (situation) violento; (question) embarazoso; ~**ment** n (shame) vergüenza; (problem): **to be an** ~**ment for sb** poner en un aprieto a uno
embassy ['ɛmbəsɪ] n embajada
embedded [ɪm'bɛdɪd] adj (object) empotrado; (thorn etc) clavado
embellish [ɪm'bɛlɪʃ] vt embellecer; (story) adornar
embers ['ɛmbəz] npl rescoldo, ascua
embezzle [ɪm'bɛzl] vt desfalcar, malversar
embitter [ɪm'bɪtə*] vt (fig: sour) amargar
embody [ɪm'bɒdɪ] vt (spirit) encarnar; (include) incorporar
embossed [ɪm'bɒst] adj realzado
embrace [ɪm'breɪs] vt abrazar, dar un abrazo a; (include) abarcar ♦ vi abrazarse ♦ n abrazo
embroider [ɪm'brɔɪdə*] vt bordar; ~**y** n bordado
embryo ['ɛmbrɪəʊ] n embrión m
emerald ['ɛmərəld] n esmeralda
emerge [ɪ'məːdʒ] vi salir; (arise) surgir
emergency [ɪ'məːdʒənsɪ] n crisis f inv; **in an** ~ en caso de urgencia; **state of** ~ estado de emergencia; ~ **cord** (US) n timbre m de alarma; ~ **exit** n salida de emergencia; ~ **landing** n aterrizaje m forzoso; ~ **services** npl (fire, police, ambulance) servicios mpl de urgencia or emergencia
emergent [ɪ'məːdʒənt] adj (nation) recién independizado; (group) recién aparecido
emery board ['ɛmərɪ-] n lima de uñas
emigrate ['ɛmɪgreɪt] vi emigrar
emissions [ɪ'mɪʃənz] npl emisión f
emit [ɪ'mɪt] vt emitir; (smoke) arrojar; (smell) despedir; (sound) producir
emotion [ɪ'məʊʃən] n emoción f; ~**al** adj (needs) emocional; (person) sentimental; (scene) conmovedor(a), emocionante; (speech) emocionado
emperor ['ɛmpərə*] n emperador m
emphases ['ɛmfəsiːz] npl of **emphasis**
emphasis ['ɛmfəsɪs] (pl -**ses**) n énfasis m inv
emphasize ['ɛmfəsaɪz] vt (word, point) sub-

rayar, recalcar; (*feature*) hacer resaltar
emphatic [ɛm'fætɪk] *adj* (*reply*) categórico;
(*person*) insistente; ~**ally** *adv* con énfasis;
(*certainly*) sin ningún género de dudas
empire ['ɛmpaɪə*] *n* (*also fig*) imperio
employ [ɪm'plɔɪ] *vt* emplear; ~**ee** [-'iː] *n*
empleado/a; ~**er** *n* patrón/ona *m/f*; empresario; ~**ment** *n* (*work*) trabajo; ~**ment
agency** *n* agencia de colocaciones
empower [ɪm'pauə*] *vt*: **to** ~ **sb to do sth**
autorizar a uno para hacer algo
empress ['ɛmprɪs] *n* emperatriz *f*
emptiness ['ɛmptɪnɪs] *n* vacío; (*of life etc*)
vaciedad *f*
empty ['ɛmptɪ] *adj* vacío; (*place*) desierto;
(*house*) desocupado; (*threat*) vano ♦ *vt* vaciar; (*place*) dejar vacío ♦ *vi* vaciarse;
(*house etc*) quedar desocupado; ~**-handed**
adj con las manos vacías
emulate ['ɛmjuleɪt] *vt* emular
emulsion [ɪ'mʌlʃən] *n* emulsión *f*; (*also*: ~
paint) pintura emulsión
enable [ɪ'neɪbl] *vt*: **to** ~ **sb to do sth** permitir a uno hacer algo
enact [ɪn'ækt] *vt* (*law*) promulgar; (*play*) representar; (*role*) hacer
enamel [ɪ'næməl] *n* esmalte *m*; (*also*: ~
paint) pintura esmaltada
enamoured [ɪ'næməd] *adj*: **to be** ~ **of**
(*person*) estar enamorado de; (*activity etc*)
tener gran afición a; (*idea*) aferrarse a
encased [ɪn'keɪst] *adj*: ~ **in** (*covered*) re-
vestido de
enchant [ɪn'tʃɑːnt] *vt* encantar; ~**ing** *adj*
encantador(a)
encircle [ɪn'sɜːkl] *vt* rodear
encl. *abbr* (= *enclosed*) *adj*
enclose [ɪn'kləuz] *vt* (*land*) cercar; (*letter
etc*) adjuntar; **please find** ~**d** le mandamos
adjunto
enclosure [ɪn'kləuʒə*] *n* cercado, recinto
encompass [ɪn'kʌmpəs] *vt* abarcar
encore [ɔŋ'kɔː*] *excl* ¡otra!, ¡bis! ♦ *n* bis *m*
encounter [ɪn'kauntə*] *n* encuentro ♦ *vt*
encontrar, encontrarse con; (*difficulty*) tropezar con
encourage [ɪn'kʌrɪdʒ] *vt* alentar, animar;
(*activity*) fomentar; (*growth*) estimular;
~**ment** *n* estímulo; (*of industry*) fomento
encroach [ɪn'krəutʃ] *vi*: **to** ~ **(up)on** invad-
dir; (*rights*) usurpar; (*time*) adueñarse de
encumber [ɪn'kʌmbə*] *vt*: **to be** ~**ed with**
(*baggage etc, debts*) estar cargado de
encyclop(a)edia [ɛnsaɪkləu'piːdɪə] *n* enci-
clopedia
end [ɛnd] *n* (*gen, also aim*) fin *m*; (*of table*)
extremo; (*of street*) final *m*; (*SPORT*) lado ♦
vt terminar, acabar; (*also*: **bring to an** ~, **put
an** ~ **to**) acabar con ♦ *vi* terminar, acabar;
in the ~ al fin; **on** ~ (*object*) de punta, de
cabeza; **to stand on** ~ (*hair*) erizarse; **for
hours on** ~ hora tras hora; ~ **up** *vi*: **to** ~

up in terminar en; (*place*) ir a parar en
endanger [ɪn'deɪndʒə*] *vt* poner en peligro
endearing [ɪn'dɪərɪŋ] *adj* simpático, atractivo
endeavour [ɪn'dɛvə*] (*US* **endeavor**) *n* esfuerzo; (*attempt*) tentativa ♦ *vi*: **to** ~ **to do**
esforzarse por hacer; (*try*) procurar hacer
ending ['ɛndɪŋ] *n* (*of book*) desenlace *m*;
(*LING*) terminación *f*
endive ['ɛndaɪv] *n* (*chicory*) endibia; (*curly*)
escarola
endless ['ɛndlɪs] *adj* interminable, inacabable
endorse [ɪn'dɔːs] *vt* (*cheque*) endosar; (*approve*) aprobar; ~**ment** *n* (*on driving licence*) nota de inhabilitación
endow [ɪn'dau] *vt* (*provide with money*): **to**
~ **(with)** dotar (de); **to be** ~**ed with** (*fig*)
estar dotado de
endurance [ɪn'djuərəns] *n* resistencia
endure [ɪn'djuə*] *vt* (*bear*) aguantar, soportar ♦ *vi* (*last*) durar
enemy ['ɛnəmɪ] *adj, n* enemigo/a *m/f*
energetic [ɛnə'dʒɛtɪk] *adj* enérgico
energy ['ɛnədʒɪ] *n* energía
enforce [ɪn'fɔːs] *vt* (*LAW*) hacer cumplir
engage [ɪn'geɪdʒ] *vt* (*attention*) llamar; (*interest*) ocupar; (*in conversation*) abordar;
(*worker*) contratar; (*AUT*): **to** ~ **the clutch**
embragar ♦ *vi* (*TECH*) engranar; **to** ~ **in** dedicarse a, ocuparse en; ~**d** *adj* (*BRIT*: *busy,
in use*) ocupado; (*betrothed*) prometido; **to
get** ~**d** prometerse; ~**d tone** (*BRIT*) *n*
(*TEL*) señal *f* de comunicando; ~**ment** *n*
(*appointment*) compromiso, cita; (*booking*)
contratación *f*; (*to marry*) compromiso;
(*period*) noviazgo; ~**ment ring** *n* anillo de
prometida
engaging [ɪn'geɪdʒɪŋ] *adj* atractivo
engender [ɪn'dʒɛndə*] *vt* engendrar
engine ['ɛndʒɪn] *n* (*AUT*) motor *m*; (*RAIL*)
locomotora; ~ **driver** *n* maquinista *m/f*
engineer [ɛndʒɪ'nɪə*] *n* ingeniero; (*BRIT*:
for repairs) mecánico; (*on ship, US*: *RAIL*)
maquinista *m*; ~**ing** *n* ingeniería
England ['ɪŋglənd] *n* Inglaterra
English ['ɪŋglɪʃ] *adj* inglés/esa ♦ *n* (*LING*)
inglés *m*; **the** ~ *npl* los ingleses *mpl*; **the** ~
Channel *n* (el Canal de) la Mancha;
~**man/woman** *n* inglés/esa *m/f*
engraving [ɪn'greɪvɪŋ] *n* grabado
engrossed [ɪn'grəust] *adj*: ~ **in** absorto en
engulf [ɪn'gʌlf] *vt* (*subj*: *water*) sumergir,
hundir; (: *fire*) prender; (: *fear*) apoderarse
de
enhance [ɪn'hɑːns] *vt* (*gen*) aumentar;
(*beauty*) realzar
enjoy [ɪn'dʒɔɪ] *vt* (*health, fortune*) disfrutar
de, gozar de; (*like*) gustarle a uno; **to** ~
o.s. divertirse; ~**able** *adj* agradable; (*amusing*) divertido; ~**ment** *n* (*joy*) placer *m*;
(*activity*) diversión *f*

enlarge [ɪn'lɑːdʒ] vt aumentar; (broaden) extender; (PHOT) ampliar ♦ vi: **to ~ on** (subject) tratar con más detalles; **~ment** n (PHOT) ampliación f

enlighten [ɪn'laɪtn] vt (inform) informar; **~ed** adj comprensivo; **the E~ment** n (HISTORY) ≈ la Ilustración, ≈ el Siglo de las Luces

enlist [ɪn'lɪst] vt alistar; (support) conseguir ♦ vi alistarse

enmity ['enmɪtɪ] n enemistad f

enormous [ɪ'nɔːməs] adj enorme

enough [ɪ'nʌf] adj: **~ time/books** bastante tiempo/bastantes libros ♦ pron bastante(s) ♦ adv: **big ~** bastante grande; **he has not worked ~** no ha trabajado bastante; **have you got ~?** ¿tiene usted bastante(s)?; **~ to eat** (lo) suficiente or (lo) bastante para comer; **~!** ¡basta ya!; **that's ~, thanks** con eso basta, gracias; **I've had ~ of him** estoy harto de él; ... **which, funnily or oddly ~** ... ... lo que, por extraño que parezca...

enquire [ɪn'kwaɪə*] vt, vi = **inquire**

enrage [ɪn'reɪdʒ] vt enfurecer

enrich [ɪn'rɪtʃ] vt enriquecer

enrol [ɪn'rəul] vt (members) inscribir; (SCOL) matricular ♦ vi inscribirse; matricularse; **~ment** n inscripción f; matriculación f

en route [ɔn'ruːt] adv durante el viaje

ensue [ɪn'sjuː] vi seguirse; (result) resultar

ensure [ɪn'ʃuə*] vt asegurar

entail [ɪn'teɪl] vt suponer

entangled [ɪn'tæŋgld] adj: **to become ~ (in)** quedarse enredado (en) or enmarañado (en)

enter ['entə*] vt (room) entrar en; (club) hacerse socio de; (army) alistarse en; (sb for a competition) inscribir; (write down) anotar, apuntar; (COMPUT) meter ♦ vi entrar; **~ for** vt fus presentarse para; **~ into** vt fus (discussion etc) entablar; (agreement) llegar a, firmar

enterprise ['entəpraɪz] n empresa; (spirit) iniciativa f; **free ~** la libre empresa; **private ~** la iniciativa privada; **enterprising** adj emprendedor(a)

entertain [entə'teɪn] vt (amuse) divertir; (invite: guest) invitar a (casa); (idea) abrigar; **~er** n artista m/f; **~ing** adj divertido, entretenido; **~ment** n (amusement) diversión f; (show) espectáculo

enthralled [ɪn'θrɔːld] adj encantado

enthusiasm [ɪn'θuːzɪæzm] n entusiasmo

enthusiast [ɪn'θuːzɪæst] n entusiasta m/f; **~ic** [-'æstɪk] adj entusiasta; **to be ~ic about** entusiasmarse por

entice [ɪn'taɪs] vt tentar

entire [ɪn'taɪə*] adj entero; **~ly** adv totalmente; **~ty** [ɪn'taɪərətɪ] n: **in its ~ty** en su totalidad

entitle [ɪn'taɪtl] vt: **to ~ sb to sth** dar a

uno derecho a algo; **~d** adj (book) titulado; **to be ~d to do** tener derecho a hacer

entourage [ɔntu'rɑːʒ] n séquito

entrails ['entreɪlz] npl entrañas fpl

entrance [n 'entrəns, vb ɪn'trɑːns] n entrada ♦ vt encantar, hechizar; **to gain ~ to** (university etc) ingresar en; **~ examination** n examen m de ingreso; **~ fee** n cuota; **~ ramp** (US) n (AUT) rampa de acceso

entrant ['entrənt] n (in race, competition) participante m/f; (in examination) candidato/a

entreat [en'triːt] vt rogar, suplicar

entrenched [en'trentʃd] adj inamovible

entrepreneur [ɔntrəprə'nəː] n empresario

entrust [ɪn'trʌst] vt: **to ~ sth to sb** confiar algo a uno

entry ['entrɪ] n entrada; (in competition) participación f; (in register) apunte m; (in account) partida; (in reference book) artículo; **"no ~"** "prohibido el paso"; (AUT) "dirección prohibida"; **~ form** n hoja de inscripción; **~ phone** n portero automático

enunciate [ɪ'nʌnsɪeɪt] vt pronunciar; (principle etc) enunciar

envelop [ɪn'veləp] vt envolver

envelope ['envələup] n sobre m

envious ['envɪəs] adj envidioso; (look) de envidia

environment [ɪn'vaɪərənmənt] n (surroundings) entorno; (natural world) el medio ambiente; **~al** [-'mentl] adj ambiental; medioambiental; **~-friendly** adj no perjudicial para el medio ambiente

envisage [ɪn'vɪzɪdʒ] vt prever

envoy ['envɔɪ] n enviado

envy ['envɪ] n envidia ♦ vt tener envidia a; **to ~ sb sth** envidiar algo a uno

epic ['epɪk] n épica ♦ adj épico

epidemic [epɪ'demɪk] n epidemia

epilepsy ['epɪlepsɪ] n epilepsia

episode ['epɪsəud] n episodio

epitome [ɪ'pɪtəmɪz] vt epitomar, resumir

equable ['ekwəbl] adj (climate) templado; (character) tranquilo, afable

equal ['iːkwl] adj; igual; (treatment) equitativo ♦ n igual m/f ♦ vt ser igual a; (fig) igualar; **to be ~ to** (task) estar a la altura de; **~ity** [iː'kwɔlɪtɪ] n igualdad f; **~ize** vi (SPORT) empatar; **~ly** adv igualmente; (share etc) a partes iguales

equate [ɪ'kweɪt] vt: **to ~ sth with** equiparar algo con; **equation** [ɪ'kweɪʒən] n (MATH) ecuación f

equator [ɪ'kweɪtə*] n ecuador m

equilibrium [iːkwɪ'lɪbrɪəm] n equilibrio

equip [ɪ'kwɪp] vt equipar; (person) proveer; **to be well ~ped** estar bien equipado; **~ment** n equipo; (tools) avíos mpl

equitable ['ekwɪtəbl] adj equitativo

equities ['ekwɪtɪz] (BRIT) npl (COMM) derechos mpl sobre or en el activo

equivalent [ɪˈkwɪvələnt] *adj*: ~ **(to)** equivalente (a) ♦ *n* equivalente *m*

equivocal [ɪˈkwɪvəkl] *adj* (*ambiguous*) ambiguo; (*open to suspicion*) equívoco

era [ˈɪərə] *n* era, época

eradicate [ɪˈrædɪkeɪt] *vt* erradicar

erase [ɪˈreɪz] *vt* borrar; ~**r** *n* goma de borrar

erect [ɪˈrɛkt] *adj* erguido ♦ *vt* erigir, levantar; (*assemble*) montar; ~**ion** [-ʃən] *n* construcción *f*; (*assembly*) montaje *m*; (PHYSIOL) erección *f*

ERM *n abbr* (= *Exchange Rate Mechanism*) *tipo de cambio europeo*

ermine [ˈəːmɪn] *n* armiño

erode [ɪˈrəud] *vt* (GEO) erosionar; (*metal*) corroer, desgastar; (*fig*) desgastar

erotic [ɪˈrɔtɪk] *adj* erótico

err [əː*] *vi* (*formal*) equivocarse

errand [ˈɛrnd] *n* recado (SP), mandado (AM)

erratic [ɪˈrætɪk] *adj* desigual, poco uniforme

erroneous [ɪˈrəunɪəs] *adj* erróneo

error [ˈɛrə*] *n* error *m*, equivocación *f*

erupt [ɪˈrʌpt] *vi* entrar en erupción; (*fig*) estallar; ~**ion** [ɪˈrʌpʃən] *n* erupción *f*; (*of war*) estallido

escalate [ˈɛskəleɪt] *vi* extenderse, intensificarse

escalator [ˈɛskəleɪtə*] *n* escalera móvil

escapade [ɛskəˈpeɪd] *n* travesura

escape [ɪˈskeɪp] *n* fuga ♦ *vi* escaparse; (*flee*) huir, evadirse; (*leak*) fugarse ♦ *vt* (*responsibility etc*) evitar, eludir; (*consequences*) escapar a; (*elude*): **his name ~s me** no me sale su nombre; **to ~ from** (*place*) escaparse de; (*person*) escaparse a

escort [*n* ˈɛskɔːt, *vb* ɪˈskɔːt] *n* acompañante *m/f*; (MIL) escolta ♦ *vt* acompañar

Eskimo [ˈɛskɪməu] *n* esquimal *m/f*

especially [ɪˈspɛʃlɪ] *adv* (*above all*) sobre todo; (*particularly*) en particular, especialmente

espionage [ˈɛspɪənɑːʒ] *n* espionaje *m*

esplanade [ɛspləˈneɪd] *n* (*by sea*) paseo marítimo

espouse [ɪˈspauz] *vt* adherirse a

Esquire [ɪˈskwaɪə] *n* (*abbr* **Esq.**) *n*: **J. Brown, ~ Sr. D. J. Brown**

essay [ˈɛseɪ] *n* (LITERATURE) ensayo; (SCOL: *short*) redacción *f*; (: *long*) trabajo

essence [ˈɛsns] *n* esencia

essential [ɪˈsɛnʃl] *adj* (*necessary*) imprescindible; (*basic*) esencial; ~**s** *npl* lo imprescindible, lo esencial; ~**ly** *adv* esencialmente

establish [ɪˈstæblɪʃ] *vt* establecer; (*prove*) demostrar; (*relations*) entablar; (*reputation*) ganarse; ~**ed** *adj* (*business*) conocido; (*practice*) arraigado; ~**ment** *n* establecimiento; **the E~ment** la clase dirigente

estate [ɪˈsteɪt] *n* (*land*) finca, hacienda; (*inheritance*) herencia; (BRIT: *also*: *housing* ~) urbanización *f*; ~ **agent** (BRIT) *n* agente *m/f* inmobiliario/a; ~ **car** (BRIT) *n* furgoneta

esteem [ɪˈstiːm] *n*: **to hold sb in high ~** estimar en mucho a uno

esthetic [ɪsˈθɛtɪk] (US) *adj* = **aesthetic**

estimate [*n* ˈɛstɪmət, *vb* ˈɛstɪmeɪt] *n* estimación *f*, apreciación *f*; (*assessment*) tasa, cálculo; (COMM) presupuesto ♦ *vt* estimar, tasar; calcular; **estimation** [-ˈmeɪʃən] *n* opinión *f*, juicio; cálculo

estranged [ɪˈstreɪndʒd] *adj* separado

estuary [ˈɛstjuərɪ] *n* estuario, ría

etc *abbr* (= *et cetera*) etc

etching [ˈɛtʃɪŋ] *n* aguafuerte *m or f*

eternal [ɪˈtəːnl] *adj* eterno

eternity [ɪˈtəːnɪtɪ] *n* eternidad *f*

ethical [ˈɛθɪkl] *adj* ético; **ethics** [ˈɛθɪks] *n* ética ♦ *npl* moralidad *f*

Ethiopia [iːθɪˈəupɪə] *n* Etiopía

ethnic [ˈɛθnɪk] *adj* étnico

ethos [ˈiːθɔs] *n* genio, carácter *m*

etiquette [ˈɛtɪkɛt] *n* etiqueta

Eurocheque [juərəutʃɛk] *n* Eurocheque *m*

Europe [ˈjuərəp] *n* Europa; ~**an** [-ˈpiːən] *adj*, *n* europeo/a *m/f*

evacuate [ɪˈvækjueɪt] *vt* (*people*) evacuar; (*place*) desocupar; **evacuation** [-ˈeɪʃən] *n* evacuación *f*

evade [ɪˈveɪd] *vt* evadir, eludir

evaluate [ɪˈvæljueɪt] *vt* evaluar

evaporate [ɪˈvæpəreɪt] *vi* evaporarse; (*fig*) desvanecerse; ~**d milk** *n* leche *f* evaporada

evasion [ɪˈveɪʒən] *n* evasión *f*

eve [iːv] *n*: **on the ~ of** en vísperas de

even [ˈiːvn] *adj* (*level*) llano; (*smooth*) liso; (*speed, temperature*) uniforme; (*number*) par ♦ *adv* hasta, incluso; (*introducing a comparison*) aún, todavía; ~ **if**, ~ **though** aunque + *sub*; ~ **more** aun más; ~ **so** aun así; **not** ~ ni siquiera; ~ **he was there** hasta él estuvo allí; ~ **on Sundays** incluso los domingos; **to get ~ with sb** ajustar cuentas con uno; ~ **out** *vi* nivelarse

evening [ˈiːvnɪŋ] *n* tarde *f*; (*late*) noche *f*; **in the ~** por la tarde; ~ **class** *n* clase *f* nocturna; ~ **dress** *n* (*no pl*: *formal clothes*) traje *m* de etiqueta; (*woman's*) traje *m* de noche

event [ɪˈvɛnt] *n* suceso, acontecimiento; (SPORT) prueba; **in the ~ of** en caso de; ~**ful** *adj* (*life*) activo; (*day*) ajetreado

eventual [ɪˈvɛntʃuəl] *adj* final; ~**ity** [-ˈælɪtɪ] *n* eventualidad *f*; ~**ly** *adv* (*finally*) finalmente; (*in time*) con el tiempo

ever [ˈɛvə*] *adv* (*at any time*) nunca, jamás; (*at all times*) siempre; (*in question*): **why not?** ¿y por qué no?; **the best ~** lo nunca visto; **have you ~ seen it?** ¿lo ha visto usted alguna vez?; **better than ~** mejor que nunca; ~ **since** *adv* desde entonces ♦ *conj* después de que; ~**green** n árbol m de hoja perenne; ~**lasting** adj eterno, perpetuo

──────── KEYWORD

every ['ɛvrɪ] adj **1** (each) cada; ~ **one of them** (persons) todos ellos/as; (objects) cada uno de ellos/as; ~ **shop in the town was closed** todas las tiendas de la ciudad estaban cerradas
2 (all possible) todo/a; **I gave you ~ assistance** te di toda la ayuda posible; **I have ~ confidence in him** tiene toda mi confianza; **we wish you ~ success** te deseamos toda suerte de éxitos
3 (showing recurrence) todo/a; ~ **day/ week** todos los días/todas las semanas; ~ **other car had been broken into** habían forzado uno de cada dos coches; **she visits me ~ other/third day** me visita cada dos/ tres días; ~ **now and then** de vez en cuando

everybody ['ɛvrɪbɔdɪ] pron = **everyone**
everyday ['ɛvrɪdeɪ] adj (daily) cotidiano, de todos los días; (usual) acostumbrado
everyone ['ɛvrɪwʌn] pron todos/as, todo el mundo
everything ['ɛvrɪθɪŋ] pron todo; **this shop sells ~** esta tienda vende de todo
everywhere ['ɛvrɪwɛə*] adv: **I've been looking for you ~** te he estado buscando por todas partes; ~ **you go you meet ...** en todas partes encuentras ...
evict [ɪ'vɪkt] vt desahuciar; ~**ion** [ɪ'vɪkʃən] n desahucio
evidence ['ɛvɪdəns] n (proof) prueba; (of witness) testimonio; (sign) indicios mpl; **to give ~** prestar declaración, dar testimonio
evident ['ɛvɪdənt] adj evidente, manifiesto; ~**ly** adv por lo visto
evil ['iːvl] adj malo; (influence) funesto ♦ n mal m
evocative [ɪ'vɔkətɪv] adj sugestivo, evocador(a)
evoke [ɪ'vəuk] vt evocar
evolution [iːvə'luːʃən] n evolución f
evolve [ɪ'vɔlv] vt desarrollar ♦ vi evolucionar, desarrollarse
ewe [juː] n oveja
ex- [ɛks] prefix ex
exact [ɪg'zækt] adj exacto; (person) meticuloso ♦ vt: **to ~ sth (from)** exigir algo (de); ~**ing** adj exigente; (conditions) arduo; ~**ly** adv exactamente; (indicating agreement) exacto
exaggerate [ɪg'zædʒəreɪt] vt, vi exagerar; **exaggeration** [-'reɪʃən] n exageración f
exalted [ɪg'zɔːltɪd] adj eminente
exam [ɪg'zæm] n abbr (SCOL) = **examination**
examination [ɪgzæmɪ'neɪʃən] n examen m; (MED) reconocimiento

examine [ɪg'zæmɪn] vt examinar; (inspect) inspeccionar, escudriñar; (MED) reconocer; ~**r** n examinador(a) m/f
example [ɪg'zɑːmpl] n ejemplo; **for ~** por ejemplo
exasperate [ɪg'zɑːspəreɪt] vt exasperar, irritar; **exasperation** [-ʃən] n exasperación f, irritación f
excavate ['ɛkskəveɪt] vt excavar
exceed [ɪk'siːd] vt (amount) exceder; (number) pasar de; (speed limit) sobrepasar; (powers) excederse en; (hopes) superar; ~**ingly** adv sumamente, sobremanera
excel [ɪk'sɛl] vi: **to ~ (at/in)** sobresalir (en)
excellent ['ɛksələnt] adj excelente
except [ɪk'sɛpt] prep (also: ~ **for**, ~**ing**) excepto, salvo ♦ vt exceptuar, excluir; ~ **if/ when** excepto si/cuando; ~ **that** salvo que; ~**ion** [ɪk'sɛpʃən] n excepción f; **to take ~ion to** ofenderse por, ~**ional** [ɪk'sɛpʃənl] adj excepcional
excerpt ['ɛksəːpt] n extracto
excess [ɪk'sɛs] n exceso; ~**es** npl (of cruelty etc) atrocidades fpl; ~ **baggage** n exceso de equipaje; ~ **fare** n suplemento; ~**ive** adj excesivo
exchange [ɪks'tʃeɪndʒ] n intercambio; (conversation) diálogo; (also: telephone ~) central f (telefónica) ♦ vt: **to ~ (for)** cambiar (por); ~ **rate** n tipo de cambio
exchequer [ɪks'tʃɛkə*] (BRIT) n: **the ~** la Hacienda del Fisco
excise ['ɛksaɪz] n impuestos mpl sobre el alcohol y el tabaco
excite [ɪk'saɪt] vt (stimulate) estimular; (arouse) excitar; ~**d** adj: **to get ~d** emocionarse; ~**ment** n (agitation) excitación f, (exhilaration) emoción f; **exciting** adj emocionante
exclaim [ɪk'skleɪm] vi exclamar; **exclamation** [ɛksklə'meɪʃən] n exclamación f; **exclamation mark** n punto de admiración
exclude [ɪk'skluːd] vt excluir; exceptuar
exclusive [ɪk'skluːsɪv] adj exclusivo; (club, district) selecto; ~ **of tax** excluyendo impuestos; ~**ly** adv únicamente
excommunicate [ɛkskə'mjuːnɪkeɪt] vt excomulgar
excruciating [ɪk'skruːʃɪeɪtɪŋ] adj (pain) agudísimo, atroz; (noise, embarrassment) horrible
excursion [ɪk'skəːʃən] n (tourist ~) excursión f
excuse [n ɪk'skjuːs, vb ɪk'skjuːz] n disculpa, excusa; (pretext) pretexto ♦ vt (justify) justificar; (forgive) disculpar, perdonar; **to ~ sb from doing sth** dispensar a uno de hacer algo; ~ **me!** (attracting attention) ¡por favor!; (apologizing) ¡perdón!; **if you will ~ me** con su permiso
ex-directory ['ɛksdɪ'rɛktərɪ] (BRIT) adj que no consta en la guía

execute ['eksɪkjuːt] vt (plan) realizar; (order) cumplir; (person) ajusticiar, ejecutar; **execution** [-'kjuːʃən] n realización f, cumplimiento; ejecución f; **executioner** [-'kjuːʃənə*] n verdugo

executive [ɪg'zekjutɪv] n (person, committee) ejecutivo; (POL: committee) poder m ejecutivo ♦ adj ejecutivo

executor [ɪg'zekjutə*] n albacea m, testamentario

exemplify [ɪg'zemplɪfaɪ] vt ejemplificar; (illustrate) ilustrar

exempt [ɪg'zempt] adj: ~ **from** exento de ♦ vt: **to** ~ **sb from** eximir a uno de; ~**ion** [-ʃən] n exención f

exercise ['eksəsaɪz] n ejercicio ♦ vt (patience) usar de; (right) valerse de; (dog) llevar de paseo; (mind) preocupar ♦ vi (also: **to take** ~) hacer ejercicio(s); ~ **bike** n ciclostátic ® m, bicicleta estática; ~ **book** n cuaderno

exert [ɪg'zəːt] vt ejercer; **to** ~ **o.s.** esforzarse; ~**ion** [-ʃən] n esfuerzo

exhale [eks'heɪl] vt despedir ♦ vi exhalar

exhaust [ɪg'zɔːst] n (AUT: also: ~ **pipe**) escape m; (: fumes) gases mpl de escape ♦ vt agotar; ~**ed** adj agotado; ~**ion** [ɪg'zɔːstʃən] n agotamiento; **nervous** ~**ion** postración f nerviosa; ~**ive** adj exhaustivo

exhibit [ɪg'zɪbɪt] n (ART) obra expuesta; (LAW) objeto expuesto ♦ vt (show: emotions) manifestar; (: courage, skill) demostrar; (paintings) exponer; ~ **ion** [eksɪ'bɪʃən] n exposición f; (of talent etc) demostración f

exhilarating [ɪg'zɪləreɪtɪŋ] adj estimulante, tónico

exile ['eksaɪl] n exilio; (person) exiliado/a ♦ vt desterrar, exiliar

exist [ɪg'zɪst] vi existir; (live) vivir; ~**ence** n existencia; ~**ing** adj existente, actual

exit ['eksɪt] n salida ♦ vi (THEATRE) hacer mutis; (COMPUT) salir (al sistema); ~ **ramp** (US) n (AUT) vía de acceso

exodus ['eksədəs] n éxodo

exonerate [ɪg'zɔnəreɪt] vt: **to** ~ **from** exculpar de

exotic [ɪg'zɔtɪk] adj exótico

expand [ɪk'spænd] vt ampliar; (number) aumentar ♦ vi (population) aumentar; (trade etc) expandirse; (gas, metal) dilatarse

expanse [ɪk'spæns] n extensión f

expansion [ɪk'spænʃən] n (of population) aumento; (of trade) expansión f

expect [ɪk'spekt] vt esperar; (require) contar con; (suppose) suponer ♦ vi: **to be** ~**ing** (pregnant woman) estar embarazada; ~**ancy** n (anticipation) esperanza; **life** ~**ancy** esperanza de vida; ~**ant mother** n futura madre f; ~**ation** [ekspek'teɪʃən] n (hope) esperanza; (belief) expectativa

expedient [ɪk'spiːdɪənt] adj conveniente,

oportuno ♦ n recurso, expediente m

expedition [ekspə'dɪʃən] n expedición f

expel [ɪk'spel] vt arrojar; (from place) expulsar

expend [ɪk'spend] vt (money) gastar; (time, energy) consumir; ~**able** adj prescindible; ~**iture** n gastos mpl, desembolso; consumo

expense [ɪk'spens] n gasto, gastos mpl; (high cost) costa; ~**s** npl (COMM) gastos mpl; **at the** ~ **of** a costa de; ~ **account** n cuenta de gastos

expensive [ɪk'spensɪv] adj caro, costoso

experience [ɪk'spɪərɪəns] n experiencia ♦ vt experimentar; (suffer) sufrir; ~**d** adj experimentado

experiment [ɪk'sperɪmənt] n experimento ♦ vi hacer experimentos; ~**al** [-'mentl] adj experimental

expert ['ekspəːt] adj experto, perito ♦ n experto/a, perito/a; (specialist) especialista m/f; ~**ise** [-'tiːz] n pericia

expire [ɪk'spaɪə*] vi caducar, vencer; **expiry** n vencimiento

explain [ɪk'spleɪn] vt explicar; **explanation** [eksplə'neɪʃən] n explicación f; **explanatory** [ɪk'splænətrɪ] adj explicativo; aclaratorio

explicit [ɪk'splɪsɪt] adj explícito

explode [ɪk'spləʊd] vi estallar, explotar; (population) crecer rápidamente; (with anger) reventar

exploit [n 'eksplɔɪt, vb ɪk'splɔɪt] n hazaña ♦ vt explotar; ~**ation** [-'teɪʃən] n explotación f

exploratory [ɪk'splɔrətrɪ] adj de exploración; (fig: talks) exploratorio, preliminar

explore [ɪk'splɔ:*] vt explorar; (fig) examinar; investigar; ~**r** n explorador(a) m/f

explosion [ɪk'spləʊʒən] n (also fig) explosión f; **explosive** [ɪks'pləʊsɪv] adj, n explosivo

exponent [ɪk'spəʊnənt] n (of theory etc) partidario/a; (of skill etc) exponente m/f

export [vb ek'spɔːt, n 'ekspɔːt] vt exportar ♦ n (process) exportación f; (product) producto de exportación ♦ cpd de exportación; ~**er** n exportador m

expose [ɪk'spəʊz] vt exponer; (unmask) desenmascarar; ~**d** adj expuesto

exposure [ɪk'spəʊʒə*] n exposición f; (publicity) publicidad f; (PHOT: speed) velocidad f de obturación; (: shot) fotografía; **to die from** ~ (MED) morir de frío; ~ **meter** n fotómetro

expound [ɪk'spaʊnd] vt exponer

express [ɪk'spres] adj (definite) expreso, explícito; (BRIT: letter etc) urgente ♦ n (train) rápido ♦ vt expresar; ~**ion** [-'spreʃən] n expresión f; (of actor etc) sentimiento; ~**ly** adv expresamente; ~**way** (US) n (urban motorway) autopista

exquisite [ek'skwɪzɪt] adj exquisito

extend [ɪk'stend] vt (visit, street) prolongar;

(*building*) ampliar; (*invitation*) ofrecer ♦ *vi* (*land*) extenderse; (*period of time*) prolongarse

extension [ɪkˈstɛnʃən] *n* extensión *f*; (*building*) ampliación *f*; (*of time*) prolongación *f*; (TEL: *in private house*) línea derivada; (: *in office*) extensión *f*

extensive [ɪkˈstɛnsɪv] *adj* extenso; (*damage*) importante; (*knowledge*) amplio; ~**ly** *adv*: **he's travelled** ~**ly** ha viajado por muchos países

extent [ɪkˈstɛnt] *n* (*breadth*) extensión *f*; (*scope*) alcance *m*; **to some** ~ hasta cierto punto; **to the ~ of...** hasta el punto de...; **to such an ~ that...** hasta tal punto que...; **to what ~?** ¿hasta qué punto?

extenuating [ɪkˈstɛnjueɪtɪŋ] *adj*: ~ **circumstances** circunstancias *fpl* atenuantes

exterior [ɛkˈstɪərɪə*] *adj* exterior, externo ♦ *n* exterior *m*

exterminate [ɪkˈstɜːmɪneɪt] *vt* exterminar

external [ɛkˈstɜːnl] *adj* externo

extinct [ɪkˈstɪŋkt] *adj* (*volcano*) extinguido; (*race*) extinto

extinguish [ɪkˈstɪŋgwɪʃ] *vt* extinguir, apagar; ~**er** *n* extintor *m*

extort [ɪkˈstɔːt] *vt* obtener por fuerza; ~**ion** [ɪkˈstɔːʃən] *n* extorsión *f*; ~**ionate** [ɪkˈstɔːʃnət] *adj* excesivo, exorbitante

extra [ˈɛkstrə] *adj* adicional ♦ *adv* (*in addition*) de más ♦ *n* (*luxury, addition*) extra *m*; (CINEMA, THEATRE) extra *m/f*, comparsa *m/f*

extra... [ˈɛkstrə] *prefix* extra....

extract [*vb* ɪkˈstrækt, *n* ˈɛkstrækt] *vt* sacar; (*tooth*) extraer; (*money, promise*) obtener ♦ *n* extracto

extracurricular [ɛkstrəkəˈrɪkjulə*] *adj* extraescolar, extra-académico

extradite [ˈɛkstrədaɪt] *vt* extraditar

extramarital [ɛkstrəˈmærɪtl] *adj* extramatrimonial

extramural [ɛkstrəˈmjuərl] *adj* extraescolar

extraordinary [ɪkˈstrɔːdnrɪ] *adj* extraordinario; (*odd*) raro

extravagance [ɪkˈstrævəgəns] *n* derroche *m*, despilfarro; (*thing bought*) extravagancia

extravagant [ɪkˈstrævəgənt] *adj* (*lavish: person*) pródigo; (: *gift*) (demasiado) caro; (*wasteful*) despilfarrador(a)

extreme [ɪkˈstriːm] *adj* extremo, extremado ♦ *n* extremo; ~**ly** *adv* sumamente, extremadamente

extremity [ɪkˈstrɛmɪtɪ] *n* extremidad *f*, punta; (*of situation*) extremo

extricate [ˈɛkstrɪkeɪt] *vt*: **to** ~ **sth/sb from** librar algo/a uno de

extrovert [ˈɛkstrəvɜːt] *n* extrovertido/a

exuberant [ɪgˈzjuːbərnt] *adj* (*person*) eufórico; (*imagination*) exuberante

exude [ɪgˈzjuːd] *vt* (*confidence*) rebosar; (*liquid, smell*) rezumar

eye [aɪ] *n* ojo ♦ *vt* mirar de soslayo, ojear; **to keep an** ~ **on** vigilar; ~**ball** *n* globo del ojo; ~**bath** *n* ojera; ~**brow** *n* ceja; ~**brow pencil** *n* lápiz *m* de cejas; ~**drops** *npl* gotas *fpl* para los ojos, colino; ~**lash** *n* pestaña; ~**lid** *n* párpado; ~**liner** *n* lápiz *m* de ojos; ~**opener** *n* revelación *f*, gran sorpresa; ~**shadow** *n* sombreador *m* de ojos; ~**sight** *n* vista; ~**sore** *n* monstruosidad *f*; ~ **witness** *n* testigo *m/f* presencial

F f

F [ɛf] *n* (MUS) fa *m*

F. *abbr* = **Fahrenheit**

fable [ˈfeɪbl] *n* fábula

fabric [ˈfæbrɪk] *n* tejido, tela

fabrication [fæbrɪˈkeɪʃən] *n* (*lie*) invención *f*; (*making*) fabricación *f*

fabulous [ˈfæbjuləs] *adj* fabuloso

façade [fəˈsɑːd] *n* fachada

face [feɪs] *n* (ANAT) cara, rostro; (*of clock*) esfera (SP), cara (AM); (*of mountain*) cara, ladera; (*of building*) fachada ♦ *vt* (*direction*) estar de cara a; (*situation*) hacer frente a; (*facts*) aceptar; ~ **down** (*person, card*) boca abajo; **to lose** ~ desprestigiarse; **to make** *or* **pull a** ~ hacer muecas; **in the** ~ **of** (*difficulties etc*) ante; **on the** ~ **of it** a primera vista; ~ **to** ~ cara a cara; ~ **up to** *vt fus* hacer frente a, arrostrar; ~ **cloth** (BRIT) *n* manopla; ~ **cream** *n* crema (de belleza); ~ **lift** *n* estirado facial; (*of building*) renovación *f*; ~ **powder** *n* polvos *mpl*; ~**-saving** *adj* para salvar las apariencias

facetious [fəˈsiːʃəs] *adj* gracioso

face value *n* (*of stamp*) valor *m* nominal; **to take sth at** ~ (*fig*) tomar algo en sentido literal

facile [ˈfæsaɪl] *adj* superficial

facilities [fəˈsɪlɪtɪz] *npl* (*buildings*) instalaciones *fpl*; (*equipment*) servicios *mpl*; **credit** ~ facilidades *fpl* de crédito

facing [ˈfeɪsɪŋ] *prep* frente a

facsimile [fækˈsɪmɪlɪ] *n* (*replica*) facsímil(e) *m*; (*machine*) telefax *m*; (*fax*) fax *m*

fact [fækt] *n* hecho; **in** ~ en realidad

factor [ˈfæktə*] *n* factor *m*

factory [ˈfæktərɪ] *n* fábrica

factual [ˈfæktjuəl] *adj* basado en los hechos

faculty [ˈfækəltɪ] *n* facultad *f*; (US: *teaching staff*) personal *m* docente

fad [fæd] n novedad f, moda
fade [feɪd] vi desteñirse; (sound, smile) desvanecerse; (light) apagarse; (flower) marchitarse; (hope, memory) perderse
fag [fæg] (BRIT: inf) n (cigarette) pitillo (SP), cigarro
fail [feɪl] vt (candidate) suspender; (exam) no aprobar (SP), reprobar (AM); (subj: memory etc) fallar a ♦ vi suspender; (be unsuccessful) fracasar; (strength, brakes) fallar; (light) acabarse; **to ~ to do sth** (neglect) dejar de hacer algo; (be unable) no poder hacer algo; **without ~** sin falta; **~ing** n falta, defecto ♦ prep a falta de; **~ure** ['feɪljə*] n fracaso; (person) fracasado/a; (mechanical etc) fallo
faint [feɪnt] adj débil; (recollection) vago; (mark) apenas visible ♦ n desmayo ♦ vi desmayarse; **to feel ~** estar mareado, marearse
fair [feə*] adj justo; (hair, person) rubio; (weather) bueno; (good enough) regular; (considerable) considerable ♦ adv (play) limpio ♦ n feria; (BRIT: funfair) parque m de atracciones; **~ly** adv (justly) con justicia; (quite) bastante; **~ness** n justicia, imparcialidad f; **~ play** n juego limpio
fairy ['feəri] n hada; **~ tale** n cuento de hadas
faith [feɪθ] n fe f; (trust) confianza; (sect) religión f; **~ful** adj (loyal: troops etc) leal; (spouse) fiel; (account) exacto; **~fully** adv fielmente; **yours ~fully** (BRIT: in letters) le saluda atentamente
fake [feɪk] n (painting etc) falsificación f; (person) impostor(a) m/f ♦ adj falso ♦ vt fingir; (painting etc) falsificar
falcon ['fɔːlkən] n halcón m
fall [fɔːl] (pt **fell**, pp **fallen**) n caída; (in price etc) descenso; (US) otoño ♦ vi caer(se); (price) bajar, descender; **~s** npl (water~) cascada, salto de agua; **to ~ flat** (on one's face) caerse (boca abajo); (plan) fracasar; (joke, story) no hacer gracia; **~ back** vi retroceder; **~ back on** vt fus (remedy etc) recurrir a; **~ behind** vi quedarse atrás; **~ down** vi (person) caerse; (building, hopes) derrumbarse; **~ for** vt fus (trick) dejarse engañar por; (person) enamorarse de; **~ in** vi (roof) hundirse; (MIL) alinearse; **~ off** vi caerse; (diminish) disminuir; **~ out** vi (friends etc) reñir; (hair, teeth) caerse; **~ through** vi (plan, project) fracasar
fallacy ['fæləsɪ] n error m
fallen ['fɔːlən] pp of **fall**
fallout ['fɔːlaut] n lluvia radioactiva; **~ shelter** n refugio antiatómico
fallow ['fæləu] adj en barbecho
false [fɔːls] adj falso; **under ~ pretences** con engaños; **~ alarm** n falsa alarma; **~ teeth** npl dentadura postiza
falter ['fɔːltə*] vi vacilar; (engine) fallar
fame [feɪm] n fama

familiar [fə'mɪlɪə*] adj conocido, familiar; (tone) de confianza; **to be ~ with** (subject) conocer (bien)
family ['fæmɪlɪ] n familia; **~ business** n negocio familiar; **~ doctor** n médico/a de cabecera
famine ['fæmɪn] n hambre f, hambruna
famished ['fæmɪʃt] adj hambriento
famous ['feɪməs] adj famoso, célebre; **~ly** adv (get on) estupendamente
fan [fæn] n abanico; (ELEC) ventilador m; (of pop star) fan m/f; (SPORT) hincha m/f ♦ vt abanicar; (fire, quarrel) atizar; **~ out** vi desparramarse
fanatic [fə'nætɪk] n fanático/a
fan belt n correa del ventilador
fanciful ['fænsɪful] adj (design, name) fantástico
fancy ['fænsɪ] n (whim) capricho, antojo; (imagination) imaginación f ♦ adj (luxury) lujoso, de lujo ♦ vt (feel like, want) tener ganas de; (imagine) imaginarse; (think) creer; **to take a ~ to sb** tomar cariño a uno; **he fancies her** (inf) le gusta (ella) mucho; **~ dress** n disfraz m; **~-dress ball** n baile m de disfraces
fanfare ['fænfeə*] n fanfarria (de trompeta)
fang [fæŋ] n colmillo
fantastic [fæn'tæstɪk] adj (enormous) enorme; (strange, wonderful) fantástico
fantasy ['fæntəzɪ] n (dream) sueño; (unreality) fantasía
far [fɑː*] adj (distant) lejano ♦ adv lejos; (much, greatly) mucho; **~ away, ~ off** (a lo) lejos; **~ better** mucho mejor; **~ from** lejos de; **by ~** con mucho; **go as ~ as the farm** vaya hasta la granja; **as ~ as I know** que yo sepa; **how ~?** ¿hasta dónde?; (fig) ¿hasta qué punto?; **~away** adj remoto; (look) distraído
farce [fɑːs] n farsa; **farcical** adj absurdo
fare [feə*] n (in trains, buses) precio (del billete); (in taxi: cost) tarifa; (food) comida; **half ~** medio pasaje m; **full ~** pasaje completo
Far East n: **the ~** el Extremo Oriente
farewell [feə'wel] excl, n adiós m
farm [fɑːm] n granja (SP), finca (AM), estancia (AM) ♦ vt cultivar; **~er** n granjero (SP), estanciero (AM); **~hand** n peón m; **~house** n granja, casa de hacienda (AM); **~ing** n agricultura; (of crops) cultivo; (of animals) cría; **~land** n tierra de cultivo; **~ worker** n = **~hand**; **~yard** n corral m
far-reaching [fɑː'riːtʃɪŋ] adj (reform, effect) de gran alcance
fart [fɑːt] (inf!) vi tirarse un pedo (!)
farther ['fɑːðə*] adv más lejos, más allá ♦ adj más lejano
farthest ['fɑːðɪst] superlative of **far**
fascinate ['fæsɪneɪt] vt fascinar; **fascination** [-'neɪʃən] n fascinación f

fascism ['fæʃɪzəm] n fascismo

fashion ['fæʃən] n moda; (~ *industry*) industria de la moda; (*manner*) manera ♦ vt formar; **in** ~ a la moda; **out of** ~ pasado de moda; **~able** adj de moda; **~ show** n desfile m de modelos

fast [fɑːst] adj rápido; (*dye, colour*) resistente; (*clock*): **to be** ~ estar adelantado ♦ adv rápidamente, de prisa; (*stuck, held*) firmemente ♦ n ayuno ♦ vi ayunar; ~ **asleep** profundamente dormido

fasten ['fɑːsn] vt atar, sujetar; (*coat, belt*) abrochar ♦ vi atarse; abrocharse; ~**er** n cierre m; (*of door etc*) cerrojo; ~**ing** n = ~**er**

fast food n comida rápida, platos mpl preparados

fastidious [fæs'tɪdɪəs] adj (*fussy*) quisquilloso

fat [fæt] adj gordo; (*book*) grueso; (*profit*) grande, pingüe ♦ n grasa; (*on person*) carnes fpl; (*lard*) manteca

fatal ['feɪtl] adj (*mistake*) fatal; (*injury*) mortal; ~**istic** [-'lɪstɪk] adj fatalista; ~**ity** [fə'tælɪtɪ] n (*road death etc*) víctima; ~**ly** adv fatalmente; mortalmente

fate [feɪt] n destino; (*of person*) suerte f; ~**ful** adj fatídico

father ['fɑːðə*] n padre m; ~**-in-law** n suegro; ~**ly** adj paternal

fathom ['fæðəm] n braza ♦ vt (*mystery*) desentrañar; (*understand*) lograr comprender

fatigue [fə'tiːg] n fatiga, cansancio

fatten ['fætn] vt, vi engordar

fatty ['fætɪ] adj (*food*) graso ♦ n (*inf*) gordito/a, gordinflón/ona m/f

fatuous ['fætjuəs] adj fatuo, necio

faucet ['fɔːsɪt] (*US*) n grifo (*SP*), llave f (*AM*)

fault [fɔːlt] n (*blame*) culpa; (*defect: in person, machine*) defecto; (*GEO*) falla ♦ vt criticar; **it's my** ~ es culpa mía; **to find** ~ **with** criticar, poner peros a; **at** ~ culpable; ~**y** adj defectuoso

fauna ['fɔːnə] n fauna

faux pas ['fəu'pɑː] n plancha

favour ['feɪvə*] (*US* **favor**) n favor m; (*approval*) aprobación f ♦ vt (*proposition*) estar a favor de ~, aprobar; (*assist*) ser propicio a; **to do sb a** ~ hacer un favor a uno; **to find** ~ **with sb** caer en gracia a uno; **in** ~ **of** a favor de; ~**able** adj favorable; ~**ite** [-rɪt] adj, n favorito, preferido

fawn [fɔːn] n cervato ♦ adj (*also*: ~-*coloured*) color de cervato, leonado ♦ vi: **to** ~ (**up)on** adular

fax [fæks] n (*document*) fax m; (*machine*) telefax m ♦ vt mandar por telefax

FBI (*US*) n abbr (= *Federal Bureau of Investigation*) ≈ BIC f (*SP*)

fear [fɪə*] n miedo, temor m ♦ vt tener mie-

do de, temer; **for** ~ **of** por si; ~**ful** adj temeroso, miedoso; (*awful*) terrible; ~**less** adj audaz

feasible ['fiːzəbl] adj factible

feast [fiːst] n banquete m; (*REL: also:* ~ *day*) fiesta ♦ vi festejar

feat [fiːt] n hazaña

feather ['feðə*] n pluma

feature ['fiːtʃə*] n característica; (*article*) artículo de fondo ♦ vt (*subj: film*) presentar ♦ vi: **to** ~ **in** tener un papel destacado en; ~**s** npl (*of face*) facciones fpl; ~ **film** n largometraje m

February ['fɛbruərɪ] n febrero

fed [fɛd] pt, pp of **feed**

federal ['fɛdərəl] adj federal

fed-up [fɛd'ʌp] adj: **to be** ~ (**with**) estar harto (de)

fee [fiː] n pago; (*professional*) derechos mpl, honorarios mpl; (*of club*) cuota; **school** ~**s** matrícula

feeble ['fiːbl] adj débil; (*joke*) flojo

feed [fiːd] (*pt, pp* **fed**) n comida; (*of animal*) pienso; (*on printer*) dispositivo de alimentación ♦ vt alimentar; (*BRIT: baby: breast*~) dar el pecho a; (*animal*) dar de comer a; (*data, information*): **to** ~ **into** meter en; ~ **on** vt fus alimentarse de; ~**back** n reacción f, feedback m; ~**ing bottle** (*BRIT*) n biberón m

feel [fiːl] (*pt, pp* **felt**) n (*sensation*) sensación f; (*sense of touch*) tacto; (*impression*): **to have the** ~ **of** parecerse a ♦ vt (*pain etc*) sentir; (*think, believe*) creer; **to** ~ **hungry/cold** tener hambre/frío; **to** ~ **lonely/better** sentirse solo/mejor; **I don't** ~ **well** no me siento bien; **it** ~**s soft** es suave al tacto; **to** ~ **like** (*want*) tener ganas de; ~ **about** *or* **around** vt tantear; ~**er** n (*of insect*) antena; **to put out a** ~**er** *or* ~**ers** (*fig*) sondear; ~**ing** n (*physical*) sensación f; (*foreboding*) presentimiento; (*emotion*) sentimiento

feet [fiːt] npl of **foot**

feign [feɪn] vt fingir

fell [fɛl] pt of **fall** ♦ vt (*tree*) talar

fellow ['fɛləu] n tipo, tío (*SP*); (*comrade*) compañero; (*of learned society*) socio/a ♦ cpd: ~ **citizen** n conciudadano/a; ~ **countryman** n compatriota m; ~ **men** npl semejantes mpl; ~**ship** n compañerismo; (*grant*) beca

felony ['fɛlənɪ] n crimen m

felt [fɛlt] pt, pp of **feel** ♦ n fieltro; ~**-tip pen** n rotulador m

female ['fiːmeɪl] n (*pej: woman*) mujer f, tía; (*ZOOL*) hembra ♦ adj femenino; hembra

feminine ['fɛmɪnɪn] adj femenino

feminist ['fɛmɪnɪst] n feminista

fence [fɛns] n valla, cerca ♦ vt (*also:* ~ **in**) cercar ♦ vi (*SPORT*) hacer esgrima; **fencing** n esgrima

fend [fɛnd] *vi*: **to ~ for o.s.** valerse por sí mismo; **~ off** *vt* (*attack*) rechazar; (*questions*) evadir

fender ['fɛndə*] *n* guardafuego; (*US: AUT*) parachoques *m inv*

ferment [*vb* fə'mɛnt, *n* 'fɛːmɛnt] *vi* fermentar ♦ *n* (*fig*) agitación *f*

fern [fəːn] *n* helecho

ferocious [fə'rəʊʃəs] *adj* feroz; **ferocity** [-'rɒsɪtɪ] *n* ferocidad *f*

ferret ['fɛrɪt] *n* hurón *m*; **~ out** *vt* desentrañar

ferry ['fɛrɪ] *n* (*small*) barca (de pasaje), balsa; (*large*: *also*: **~boat**) transbordador *m* (*SP*), embarcadero (*AM*) ♦ *vt* transportar

fertile ['fəːtaɪl] *adj* fértil, (*BIOL*) fecundo; **fertility** [fə'tɪlɪtɪ] *n* fertilidad *f*; fecundidad *f*; **fertilize** ['fəːtɪlaɪz] *vt* (*BIOL*) fecundar; (*AGR*) abonar; **fertilizer** *n* abono

fervent ['fəːvənt] *adj* ferviente, entusiasta

fervour ['fəːvə*] *n* fervor *m*, ardor *m*

fester ['fɛstə*] *vi* ulcerarse

festival ['fɛstɪvəl] *n* (*REL*) fiesta; (*ART, MUS*) festival *m*

festive ['fɛstɪv] *adj* festivo; **the ~ season** (*BRIT*: *Christmas*) las Navidades

festivities [fɛs'tɪvɪtɪz] *npl* fiestas *fpl*

festoon [fɛs'tuːn] *vt*: **to ~ with** engalanar de

fetch [fɛtʃ] *vt* ir a buscar; (*sell for*) venderse por

fetching ['fɛtʃɪŋ] *adj* atractivo

fête [feɪt] *n* fiesta

fetish ['fɛtɪʃ] *n* obsesión *f*

fetus ['fiːtəs] (*US*) *n* = **foetus**

feud [fjuːd] *n* (*hostility*) enemistad *f*; (*quarrel*) disputa

fever ['fiːvə*] *n* fiebre *f*; **~ish** *adj* febril

few [fjuː]; *adj* (*not many*) pocos; **a ~** *adj* unos pocos, algunos ♦ *pron* pocos; algunos; **~er** *adj* menos; **~est** *adj* los/las menos

fiancé [fɪ'ɑ̃ːŋseɪ] *n* novio, prometido; **~e** *n* novia, prometida

fiasco [fɪ'æskəʊ] *n* desastre *m*

fib [fɪb] *n* mentirilla

fibre ['faɪbə*] (*US* **fiber**) *n* fibra; **~-glass** *n* fibra de vidrio

fickle ['fɪkl] *adj* inconstante

fiction ['fɪkʃən] *n* ficción *f*; **~al** *adj* novelesco; **fictitious** [fɪk'tɪʃəs] *adj* ficticio

fiddle ['fɪdl] *n* (*MUS*) violín *m*; (*cheating*) trampa ♦ *vt* (*BRIT*: *accounts*) falsificar; **~ with** *vt fus* juguetear con

fidget ['fɪdʒɪt] *vi* enredar; **stop ~ing!** ¡estáte quieto!

field [fiːld] *n* campo; (*fig*) campo, esfera; (*SPORT*) campo, cancha (*AM*); **~ marshal** *n* mariscal *m*; **~work** *n* trabajo de campo

fiend [fiːnd] *n* demonio; **~ish** *adj* diabólico

fierce [fɪəs] *adj* feroz; (*wind, heat*) fuerte; (*fighting, enemy*) encarnizado

fiery ['faɪərɪ] *adj* (*burning*) ardiente; (*temperament*) apasionado

fifteen [fɪf'tiːn] *num* quince

fifth [fɪfθ] *num* quinto

fifty ['fɪftɪ] *num* cincuenta; **~-~** *adj* (*deal, split*) a medias ♦ *adv* a medias, mitad por mitad

fig [fɪg] *n* higo

fight [faɪt] (*pt, pp* **fought**) *n* (*gen*) pelea; (*MIL*) combate *m*; (*struggle*) lucha ♦ *vt* luchar contra; (*cancer, alcoholism*) combatir; (*election*) intentar ganar; (*emotion*) resistir ♦ *vi* pelear, luchar; **~er** *n* combatiente *m/f*; (*plane*) caza *m*; **~ing** *n* combate *m*, pelea

figment ['fɪgmənt] *n*: **a ~ of the imagination** una quimera

figurative ['fɪgjʊrətɪv] *adj* (*meaning*) figurado; (*style*) figurativo

figure ['fɪgə*] *n* (*DRAWING, GEOM*) figura, dibujo; (*number, cipher*) cifra; (*body, outline*) tipo; (*personality*) figura ♦ *vt* (*esp US*) imaginar ♦ *vi* (*appear*) figurar; **~ out** *vt* (*work out*) resolver; **~head** *n* (*NAUT*) mascarón *m* de proa; (*pej*: *leader*) figura decorativa; **~ of speech** *n* figura retórica

filch [fɪltʃ] (*inf*) *vt* hurtar, robar

file [faɪl] *n* (*tool*) lima; (*dossier*) expediente *m*; (*folder*) carpeta; (*COMPUT*) fichero; (*row*) fila ♦ *vt* limar; (*LAW*: *claim*) presentar; (*store*) archivar; **~ in/out** *vi* entrar/salir en fila; **filing cabinet** *n* fichero, archivador *m*

fill [fɪl] *vt* (*space*): **to ~ (with)** llenar (de); (*vacancy, need*) cubrir ♦ *n*: **to eat one's ~** llenarse; **~ in** *vt* rellenar; **~ up** *vt* llenar (hasta el borde) ♦ *vi* (*AUT*) poner gasolina

fillet ['fɪlɪt] *n* filete *m*; **~ steak** *n* filete *m* de ternera

filling ['fɪlɪŋ] *n* (*CULIN*) relleno; (*for tooth*) empaste *m*; **~ station** *n* estación *f* de servicio

film [fɪlm] *n* película ♦ *vt* (*scene*) filmar ♦ *vi* rodar (una película); **~ star** *n* astro, estrella de cine; **~strip** *n* tira de película

filter ['fɪltə*] *n* filtro ♦ *vt* filtrar; **~ lane** (*BRIT*) *n* carril *m* de selección; **~-tipped** *adj* con filtro

filth [fɪlθ] *n* suciedad *f*; **~y** *adj* sucio; (*language*) obsceno

fin [fɪn] *n* (*gen*) aleta

final ['faɪnl] *adj* (*last*) final, último; (*definitive*) definitivo, terminante ♦ *n* (*BRIT*: *SPORT*) final *f*; **~s** *npl* (*SCOL*) examen *m* final; (*US*: *SPORT*) final *f*

finale [fɪ'nɑːlɪ] *n* final *m*

final: **~ist** *n* (*SPORT*) finalista *m/f*; **~ize** *vt* concluir, completar; **~ly** *adv* (*lastly*) por último, finalmente; (*eventually*) por fin

finance [faɪ'næns] *n* (*money*) fondos *mpl*; **~s** *npl* finanzas *fpl*; (*personal ~s*) situación *f* económica ♦ *vt* financiar; **financial** [-'nænʃəl] *adj* financiero; **financier** *n* financiero/a

find [faɪnd] (*pt, pp* **found**) *vt* encontrar, hallar; (*come upon*) descubrir ♦ *n* hallazgo; descubrimiento; **to ~ sb guilty** (*LAW*) declarar culpable a uno; **~ out** *vt* averiguar; (*truth, secret*) descubrir; **to ~ out about** (*subject*) informarse sobre; (*by chance*) enterarse de; **~ings** *npl* (*LAW*) veredicto, fallo; (*of report*) recomendaciones *fpl*

fine [faɪn] *adj* excelente; (*thin*) fino ♦ *adv* (*well*) bien ♦ *n* (*LAW*) multa ♦ *vt* (*LAW*) multar; **to be ~** (*person*) estar bien; (*weather*) hacer buen tiempo; **~ arts** *npl* bellas artes *fpl*

finery ['faɪnərɪ] *n* adornos *mpl*

finesse [fɪ'nɛs] *n* sutileza

finger ['fɪŋɡə*] *n* dedo ♦ *vt* (*touch*) manosear; **little/index ~** (dedo) meñique *m*/índice *m*; **~nail** *n* uña; **~print** *n* huella dactilar; **~tip** *n* yema del dedo

finicky ['fɪnɪkɪ] *adj* delicado

finish ['fɪnɪʃ] *n* (*end*) fin *m*; (*SPORT*) meta; (*polish etc*) acabado ♦ *vt, vi* terminar; **to ~ doing sth** acabar de hacer algo; **to ~ third** llegar el tercero; **~ off** *vt* acabar, terminar; (*kill*) rematar; **~ up** *vt* acabar, terminar ♦ *vi* ir a parar, terminar; **~ing line** *n* línea de llegada *or* meta; **~ing school** *n* academia para señoritas

finite ['faɪnaɪt] *adj* finito; (*verb*) conjugado

Finland ['fɪnlənd] *n* Finlandia

Finn [fɪn] *n* finlandés/esa *m/f*; **~ish** *adj* finlandés/esa ♦ *n* (*LING*) finlandés *m*

fir [fə:*] *n* abeto

fire ['faɪə*] *n* fuego; (*in hearth*) lumbre *f*; (*accidental*) incendio; (*heater*) estufa ♦ *vt* (*gun*) disparar; (*interest*) despertar; (*inf: dismiss*) despedir ♦ *vi* (*shoot*) disparar; **on ~** ardiendo, en llamas; **~ alarm** *n* alarma de incendios; **~arm** *n* arma de fuego; **~ brigade** (*US* **~ department**) *n* (cuerpo de) bomberos *mpl*; **~ engine** *n* coche *m* de bomberos; **~ escape** *n* escalera de incendios; **~ extinguisher** *n* extintor *m* (de incendios); **~guard** *n* rejilla de protección; **~man** *n* bombero; **~place** *n* chimenea; **~side** *n*: **by the ~side** al lado de la chimenea; **~ station** *n* parque *m* de bomberos; **~wood** *n* leña; **~works** *npl* fuegos *mpl* artificiales

firing squad ['faɪrɪŋ-] *n* pelotón *m* de ejecución

firm [fə:m] *adj* firme; (*look, voice*) resuelto ♦ *n* firma, empresa; **~ly** *adv* firmemente; resueltamente

first [fə:st] *adj* primero ♦ *adv* (*before others*) primero; (*when listing reasons etc*) en primer lugar, primeramente ♦ *n* (*person: in race*) primero/a; (*AUT*) primera; (*BRIT: SCOL*) título de licenciado con calificación de sobresaliente; **at ~** al principio; **~ of all** ante todo; **~ aid** *n* primera ayuda, primeros auxilios *mpl*; **~-aid kit** *n* botiquín *m*; **~-class** *adj* (*excellent*) de primera (catego-

ría); (*ticket etc*) de primera clase; **~-hand** *adj* de primera mano; **F~ Lady** (*esp US*) *n* primera dama; **~ly** *adv* en primer lugar; **~ name** *n* nombre *m* (de pila); **~-rate** *adj* estupendo

fish [fɪʃ] *n inv* pez *m*; (*food*) pescado ♦ *vt, vi* pescar; **to go ~ing** ir de pesca; **~erman** *n* pescador *m*; **~ farm** *n* criadero de peces; **~ fingers** (*BRIT*) *npl* croquetas *fpl* de pescado; **~ing boat** *n* barca de pesca; **~ing line** *n* sedal *m*; **~ing rod** *n* caña (de pescar); **~monger's (shop)** (*BRIT*) *n* pescadería; **~ sticks** (*US*) *npl* = **~ fingers**; **~y** (*inf*) *adj* sospechoso

fist [fɪst] *n* puño

fit [fɪt] *adj* (*healthy*) en (buena) forma; (*proper*) adecuado, apropiado ♦ *vt* (*subj: clothes*) estar *or* sentar bien a; (*instal*) poner; (*equip*) proveer, dotar; (*facts*) cuadrar *or* corresponder con ♦ *vi* (*clothes*) sentar bien; (*in space, gap*) caber; (*facts*) coincidir ♦ *n* (*MED*) ataque *m*; **~ to** (*ready*) a punto de; **~ for** apropiado para; **a ~ of anger/pride** un arranque de cólera/orgullo; **this dress is a good ~** este vestido me sienta bien; **by ~s and starts** a rachas; **~ in** *vi* (*fig: person*) llevarse bien (con todos); **~ful** *adj* espasmódico, intermitente; **~ment** *n* módulo adosable; **~ness** *n* (*MED*) salud *f*; **~ted carpet** *n* moqueta; **~ted kitchen** *n* cocina amueblada; **~ter** *n* ajustador *m*; **~ting** *adj* apropiado ♦ *n* (*of dress*) prueba; (*of piece of equipment*) instalación *f*; **~ting room** *n* probador *m*; **~tings** *npl* instalaciones *fpl*

five [faɪv] *num* cinco; **~r** (*inf: BRIT*) *n* billete *m* de cinco libras; (: *US*) billete *m* de cinco dólares

fix [fɪks] *vt* (*secure*) fijar, asegurar; (*mend*) arreglar; (*prepare*) preparar ♦ *n*: **to be in a ~** estar en un aprieto; **~ up** *vt* (*meeting*) arreglar; **to ~ sb up with sth** proveer a uno de algo; **~ation** [fɪk'seɪʃən] *n* obsesión *f*; **~ed** [fɪkst] *adj* (*prices etc*) fijo; **~ture** ['fɪkstʃə*] *n* (*SPORT*) encuentro; **~tures** *npl* (*cupboards etc*) instalaciones *fpl* fijas

fizzle out ['fɪzl-] *vi* apagarse

fizzy ['fɪzɪ] *adj* (*drink*) gaseoso

fjord [fjɔ:d] *n* fiordo

flabbergasted ['flæbəɡɑ:stɪd] *adj* pasmado, alucinado

flabby ['flæbɪ] *adj* gordo

flag [flæɡ] *n* bandera; (*stone*) losa ♦ *vi* decaer; **to ~ down** hacer señas a uno para que se pare; **~pole** *n* asta de bandera; **~ship** *n* buque *m* insignia; (*fig*) bandera

flair [flɛə*] *n* aptitud *f* especial

flak [flæk] *n* (*MIL*) fuego antiaéreo; (*inf: criticism*) lluvia de críticas

flake [fleɪk] *n* (*of rust, paint*) escama; (*of snow, soap powder*) copo ♦ *vi* (*also:* **~ off**) desconcharse

flamboyant [flæm'bɔɪənt] *adj (dress)* vistoso; *(person)* extravagante

flame [fleɪm] *n* llama

flamingo [flə'mɪŋɡəʊ] *n* flamenco

flammable ['flæməbl] *adj* inflamable

flan [flæn] *(BRIT) n* tarta

flank [flæŋk] *n (of animal)* ijar *m; (of army)* flanco ♦ *vt* flanquear

flannel ['flænl] *n (BRIT: also: face* ~*)* manopla; *(fabric)* franela; ~**s** *npl (trousers)* pantalones *mpl* de franela

flap [flæp] *n (of pocket, envelope)* solapa ♦ *vt (wings, arms)* agitar ♦ *vi (sail, flag)* ondear

flare [flɛə*] *n* llamarada; *(MIL)* bengala; *(in skirt etc)* vuelo; ~ **up** *vi* encenderse; *(fig: person)* encolerizarse; *(: revolt)* estallar

flash [flæʃ] *n* relámpago; *(also: news* ~*)* noticias *fpl* de última hora; *(PHOT)* flash *m* ♦ *vt (light, headlights)* lanzar un destello con; *(news, message)* transmitir; *(smile)* lanzar ♦ *vi* brillar; *(hazard light etc)* lanzar destellos; **in a** ~ en un instante; **he** ~**ed by** *or* **past** pasó como un rayo; ~**back** *n (CINEMA)* flashback *m*; ~**bulb** *n* bombilla fusible; ~ **cube** *n* cubo de flash; ~**light** *n* linterna

flashy ['flæʃɪ] *(pej) adj* ostentoso

flask [flɑːsk] *n* frasco; *(also: vacuum* ~*)* termo

flat [flæt] *adj* llano; *(smooth)* liso; *(tyre)* desinflado; *(battery)* descargado; *(beer)* muerto; *(refusal etc)* rotundo; *(MUS)* desafinado; *(rate)* fijo ♦ *n (BRIT: apartment)* piso *(SP)*, departamento *(AM)*, apartamento; *(AUT)* pinchazo; *(MUS)* bemol *m;* **to work** ~ **out** trabajar a toda mecha; ~**ly** *adv* terminantemente, de plano; ~**ten** *vt (also:* ~**ten out)** allanar; *(smooth out)* alisar; *(building, plants)* arrasar

flatter ['flætə*] *vt* adular, halagar; ~**ing** *adj* halagüeño; *(dress)* que favorece; ~**y** *n* adulación *f*

flaunt [flɔːnt] *vt* ostentar, lucir

flavour ['fleɪvə*] *(US* **flavor)** *n* sabor *m,* gusto ♦ *vt* sazonar, condimentar; **strawberry** ~**ed** con sabor a fresa; ~**ing** *n (in product)* aromatizante *m*

flaw [flɔː] *n* defecto; ~**less** *adj* impecable

flax [flæks] *n* lino; ~**en** *adj* rubio

flea [fliː] *n* pulga

fleck [flɛk] *n (mark)* mota

flee [fliː] *(pt, pp* **fled)** *vt* huir de ♦ *vi* huir, fugarse

fleece [fliːs] *n* vellón *m; (wool)* lana ♦ *vt (inf)* desplumar

fleet [fliːt] *n* flota; *(of lorries etc)* escuadra

fleeting ['fliːtɪŋ] *adj* fugaz

Flemish ['flɛmɪʃ] *adj* flamenco

flesh [flɛʃ] *n* carne *f; (skin)* piel *f; (of fruit)* pulpa; ~ **wound** *n* herida superficial

flew [fluː] *pt of* **fly**

flex [flɛks] *n* cordón *m* ♦ *vt (muscles)* tensar; ~**ibility** [-ɪ'bɪlɪtɪ] *n* flexibilidad *f;* ~**ible** *adj* flexible

flick [flɪk] *n* capirotazo; chasquido ♦ *vt (with hand)* dar un capirotazo a; *(whip etc)* chasquear; *(switch)* accionar; ~ **through** *vt fus* hojear

flicker ['flɪkə*] *vi (light)* parpadear; *(flame)* vacilar

flier ['flaɪə*] *n* aviador(a) *m/f*

flight [flaɪt] *n* vuelo; *(escape)* huida, fuga; *(also:* ~ **of steps)** tramo (de escaleras); ~ **attendant** *(US) n* camarero/azafata; ~ **deck** *n (AVIAT)* cabina de mandos; *(NAUT)* cubierta de aterrizaje

flimsy ['flɪmzɪ] *adj (thin)* muy ligero; *(building)* endeble; *(excuse)* flojo

flinch [flɪntʃ] *vi* encogerse; **to** ~ **from** retroceder ante

fling [flɪŋ] *(pt, pp* **flung)** *vt* arrojar

flint [flɪnt] *n* pedernal *m; (in lighter)* piedra

flip [flɪp] *vt* dar la vuelta a; *(switch: turn on)* encender; *(: turn off)* apagar; *(coin)* echar a cara o cruz

flippant ['flɪpənt] *adj* poco serio

flipper ['flɪpə*] *n* aleta

flirt [flɜːt] *vi* coquetear, flirtear ♦ *n* coqueta

flit [flɪt] *vi* revolotear

float [fləʊt] *n* flotador *m; (in procession)* carroza; *(money)* reserva ♦ *vi* flotar; *(swimmer)* hacer la plancha

flock [flɒk] *n (of sheep)* rebaño; *(of birds)* bandada ♦ *vi:* **to** ~ **to** acudir en tropel a

flog [flɒɡ] *vt* azotar

flood [flʌd] *n* inundación *f; (of letters, imports etc)* avalancha ♦ *vt* inundar ♦ *vi (place)* inundarse; *(people):* **to** ~ **into** inundar; ~**ing** *n* inundaciones *fpl;* ~**light** *n* foco

floor [flɔː*] *n* suelo; *(storey)* piso; *(of sea)* fondo ♦ *vt (subj: question)* dejar sin respuesta; *(: blow)* derribar; **ground** ~, **first** ~ *(US)* planta baja; **first** ~, **second** ~ *(US)* primer piso; ~**board** *n* tabla; ~ **show** *n* cabaret *m*

flop [flɒp] *n* fracaso ♦ *vi (fail)* fracasar; *(fall)* derrumbarse

floppy ['flɒpɪ] *adj* flojo ♦ *n (COMPUT: also:* ~ **disk)** floppy *m*

flora ['flɔːrə] *n* flora

floral ['flɔːrl] *adj (pattern)* floreado

florid ['flɒrɪd] *adj* florido; *(complexion)* rubicundo

florist ['flɒrɪst] *n* florista *m/f;* ~'**s (shop)** *n* florería

flounce [flaʊns] *n* volante *m;* ~ **out** *vi* salir enfadado

flounder ['flaʊndə*] *vi (swimmer)* patalear; *(fig: economy)* estar en dificultades ♦ *n (ZOOL)* platija

flour [flaʊə*] *n* harina

flourish ['flʌrɪʃ] *vi* florecer ♦ *n* ademán *m,* movimiento (ostentoso); ~**ing** *adj* floreciente

flout [flaut] vt burlarse de

flow [fləu] n (movement) flujo; (of traffic) circulación f; (tide) corriente f ♦ vi (river, blood) fluir; (traffic) circular; **~ chart** n organigrama m

flower ['flauə*] n flor f ♦ vi florecer; **~ bed** n macizo; **~pot** n tiesto; **~y** adj (fragrance) floral; (pattern) floreado; (speech) florido

flown [fləun] pp of **fly**

flu [flu:] n: **to have ~** tener la gripe

fluctuate ['flʌktjueɪt] vi fluctuar

fluent ['flu:ənt] adj (linguist) que habla perfectamente; (speech) elocuente; **he speaks ~ French, he's ~ in French** domina el francés; **~ly** adv con fluidez

fluff [flʌf] n pelusa; **~y** adj de pelo suave

fluid ['flu:ɪd] adj (movement) fluido, líquido; (situation) inestable ♦ n fluido, líquido

fluke [flu:k] (inf) n chiripa

flung [flʌŋ] pt, pp of **fling**

fluoride ['fluəraɪd] n fluoruro

flurry ['flʌrɪ] n (of snow) temporal m; **~ of activity** frenesí m de actividad

flush [flʌʃ] n rubor m; (fig: of youth etc) resplandor m ♦ vt limpiar con agua ♦ vi ruborizarse ♦ adj: **~ with** a ras de; **to ~ the toilet** hacer funcionar la cisterna; **~ out** vt (game, birds) levantar; **~ed** adj ruborizado

flustered ['flʌstəd] adj aturdido

flute [flu:t] n flauta

flutter ['flʌtə*] n (of wings) revoloteo, aleteo; **a ~ of panic/excitement** una oleada de pánico/excitación ♦ vi revolotear

flux [flʌks] n: **to be in a state of ~** estar continuamente cambiando

fly [flaɪ] (pt **flew**, pp **flown**) n mosca; (on trousers: also: **flies**) bragueta ♦ vt (plane) pilot(e)ar; (cargo) transportar (en avión); (distances) recorrer (en avión) ♦ vi volar; (passengers) ir en avión; (escape) evadirse; (flag) ondear; **~ away** or **off** vi emprender el vuelo; **~ing** n (activity) (el) volar; (action) vuelo ♦ adj: **~ing visit** visita relámpago; **with ~ing colours** con lucimiento; **~ing saucer** n platillo volante; **~ing start** n: **to get off to a ~ing start** empezar con buen pie; **~over** (BRIT) n paso a desnivel or superior; **~sheet** n (for tent) doble techo

foal [fəul] n potro

foam [fəum] n espuma ♦ vi hacer espuma; **~ rubber** n goma espuma

fob [fɔb] vt: **to ~ sb off with sth** despachar a uno con algo

focal point ['fəukl-] n (fig) centro de atención

focus ['fəukəs] (pl **~es**) n foco; (centre) centro ♦ vt (field glasses etc) enfocar ♦ vi: **to ~ (on)** enfocar (a); (issue etc) centrarse en; **in/out of ~** enfocado/desenfocado

fodder ['fɔdə*] n pienso

foetus ['fi:təs] (US **fetus**) n feto

fog [fɔg] n niebla; **~gy** adj: **it's ~gy** hay niebla, está brumoso; **~ lamp** (US **~ light**) n (AUT) faro de niebla

foil [fɔɪl] vt frustrar ♦ n hoja; (kitchen ~) papel m (de) aluminio; (complement) complemento; (FENCING) florete m

fold [fəuld] n (bend, crease) pliegue m; (AGR) redil m ♦ vt doblar; (arms) cruzar; **~ up** vi plegarse, doblarse; (business) quebrar ♦ vt (map etc) plegar; **~er** n (for papers) carpeta; (ring-bind, bed) plegable

foliage ['fəulɪɪdʒ] n follaje m

folk [fəuk] npl gente f ♦ adj popular, folklórico; **~s** npl (family) familia sg, parientes mpl; **~lore** ['fəuklɔ:*] n folklore m; **~ song** n canción f popular or folklórica

follow ['fɔləu] vt seguir ♦ vi seguir; (result) resultar; **to ~ suit** hacer lo mismo; **~ up** vt (letter, offer) responder a; (case) investigar; **~er** n (of person, belief) partidario/a; **~ing** adj siguiente ♦ n afición f, partidarios mpl

folly ['fɔlɪ] n locura

fond [fɔnd] adj (memory, smile etc) cariñoso; (hopes) ilusorio; **to be ~ of** tener cariño a; (pastime, food) ser aficionado a

fondle ['fɔndl] vt acariciar

font [fɔnt] n pila bautismal; (TYP) fundición f

food [fu:d] n comida; **~ mixer** n batidora; **~ poisoning** n intoxicación f alimenticia; **~ processor** n robot m de cocina; **~stuffs** npl comestibles mpl

fool [fu:l] n tonto/a; (CULIN) puré m de frutas con nata ♦ vt engañar ♦ vi (gen: ~ around) bromear; **~hardy** adj temerario; **~ish** adj tonto; (careless) imprudente; **~proof** adj (plan etc) infalible

foot [fut] (pl **feet**) n pie m; (measure) pie m (= 304 mm); (of animal) pata ♦ vt (bill) pagar; **on ~** a pie; **~age** n (CINEMA) imágenes fpl; **~ball** n balón m; (game: BRIT) fútbol m; (: US) fútbol m americano; **~ball player** (BRIT: also: **~baller**) futbolista m; (US) jugador m de fútbol americano; **~brake** n freno de pie; **~bridge** n puente m para peatones; **~hills** npl estribaciones fpl; **~hold** n pie m firme; **~ing** n (fig) posición f; **to lose one's ~ing** perder el pie; **~lights** npl candilejas fpl; **~man** n lacayo; **~note** n nota (al pie de la página); **~path** n sendero; **~print** n huella, pisada; **~step** n paso; **~wear** n calzado

––––––––– **KEYWORD**

for [fɔ:] prep **1** (indicating destination, intention) para; **the train ~ London** el tren con destino a or de Londres; **he left ~ Rome** marchó para Roma; **he went ~ the paper** fue por el periódico; **is this ~ me?** ¿es esto para mí?; **it's time ~ lunch** es la hora

de comer
2 (*indicating purpose*) para; **what('s it)** ~?
¿para qué (es)?; **to pray ~ peace** rezar
por la paz
3 (*on behalf of, representing*): **the MP ~
Hove** el diputado por Hove; **he works ~
the government/a local firm** trabaja para
el gobierno/en una empresa local; **I'll ask
him ~ you** se lo pediré por ti; **G ~
George** G de Gerona
4 (*because of*) por esta razón; ~ **fear of
being criticized** por temor a ser criticado
5 (*with regard to*) para; **it's cold ~ July**
hace frío para julio; **he has a gift ~ languages** tiene don de lenguas
6 (*in exchange for*) por; **I sold it ~ £5** lo
vendí por £5; **to pay 50 pence ~ a ticket**
pagar 50 peniques por un billete
7 (*in favour of*): **are you ~ or against us?**
¿estás con nosotros o contra nosotros?;
I'm all ~ it estoy totalmente a favor; **vote
~ X** vote (a) X
8 (*referring to distance*): **there are road-
works ~ 5 km** hay obras en 5 km; **we
walked ~ miles** caminamos kilómetros y
kilómetros
9 (*referring to time*): **he was away ~ 2
years** estuvo fuera (durante) dos años; **it
hasn't rained ~ 3 weeks** no ha llovido
durante *or* en 3 semanas; **I have known
her ~ years** la conozco desde hace años;
can you do it ~ tomorrow? ¿lo podrás
hacer para mañana?
10 (*with infinitive clauses*): **it is not ~ me
to decide** la decisión no es cosa mía; **it
would be best ~ you to leave** sería mejor
que te fueras; **there is still time ~ you to
do it** todavía te queda tiempo para hacerlo;
~ this to be possible ... para que esto sea
posible ...
11 (*in spite of*) a pesar de; **~ all his com-
plaints** a pesar de sus quejas
♦ *conj* (*since, as: rather formal*) puesto que

forage ['forɪdʒ] *vi* (*animal*) forrajear; (*person*): **to ~ for** hurgar en busca de
foray ['foreɪ] *n* incursión *f*
forbad(e) [fə'bæd] *pt of* **forbid**
forbid [fə'bɪd] (*pt* **forbad(e)**, *pp* **forbidden**)
vt prohibir; **to ~ sb to do sth** prohibir a
uno hacer algo
force [fo:s] *n* fuerza ♦ *vt* forzar; (*push*) meter a la fuerza; **to ~ o.s. to do** hacer un
esfuerzo por hacer; **the F~s** *npl* (*BRIT*) las
Fuerzas Armadas; **in ~** en vigor; **~d** [fo:st]
adj forzado; **~-feed** *vt* alimentar a la fuerza; **~ful** *adj* enérgico
forcibly ['fo:sɪblɪ] *adv* a la fuerza; (*speak*)
enérgicamente
ford [fo:d] *n* vado
fore [fo:*] *n*: **to come to the ~** empezar a
destacar

forearm ['fo:rɑ:m] *n* antebrazo
foreboding [fo:'bəudɪŋ] *n* presentimiento
forecast ['fo:kɑ:st] *n* pronóstico ♦ *vt* (*irreg:
like cast*) pronosticar
forecourt ['fo:ko:t] *n* patio
forefathers ['fo:fɑ:ðəz] *npl* antepasados
mpl
forefinger ['fo:fɪŋgə*] *n* (dedo) índice *m*
forefront ['fo:frʌnt] *n*: **in the ~ of** en la
vanguardia de
forego *vt* = **forgo**
foregone ['fo:gon] *pp of* **forego** ♦ *adj*: **it's
a ~ conclusion** es una conclusión evidente
foreground ['fo:graund] *n* primer plano
forehead ['forɪd] *n* frente *f*
foreign ['forɪn] *adj* extranjero; (*trade*) exterior; (*object*) extraño; **~er** *n* extranjero/a;
~ exchange *n* divisas *fpl*; **F~ Office**
(*BRIT*) *n* Ministerio de Asuntos Exteriores;
F~ Secretary (*BRIT*) *n* Ministro de Asuntos Exteriores
foreleg ['fo:leg] *n* pata delantera
foreman ['fo:mən] *n* capataz *m*; (*in construction*) maestro de obras
foremost ['fo:məust] *adj* principal ♦ *adv*:
first and ~ ante todo
forensic [fə'rensɪk] *adj* forense
forerunner ['fo:rʌnə*] *n* precursor(a) *m/f*
foresaw [fo:'so:] *pt of* **foresee**
foresee [fo:'si:] (*pt* **foresaw**, *pp* **foreseen**)
vt prever; **~able** *adj* previsible
foreshadow [fo:'ʃædəu] *vt* prefigurar,
anunciar
foresight ['fo:saɪt] *n* previsión *f*
forest ['forɪst] *n* bosque *m*
forestall [fo:'sto:l] *vt* prevenir
forestry ['forɪstrɪ] *n* silvicultura
foretaste ['fo:teɪst] *n* muestra
foretell [fo:'tel] (*pt, pp* **foretold**) *vt* predecir, pronosticar
foretold [fo:'təuld] *pt, pp of* **foretell**
forever [fə'revə*] *adv* para siempre; (*end-
lessly*) constantemente
forewent [fo:'went] *pt of* **forego**
foreword ['fo:wə:d] *n* prefacio
forfeit ['fo:fɪt] *vt* perder
forgave [fə'geɪv] *pt of* **forgive**
forge [fo:dʒ] *n* herrería ♦ *vt* (*signature,
money*) falsificar; (*metal*) forjar; **~ ahead**
vi avanzar mucho; **~ry** *n* falsificación *f*
forget [fə'get] (*pt* **forgot**, *pp* **forgotten**) *vt*
olvidar ♦ *vi* olvidarse; **~ful** *adj* despistado;
~-me-not *n* nomeolvides *f inv*
forgive [fə'gɪv] (*pt* **forgave**, *pp* **forgiven**) *vt*
perdonar; **to ~ sb for sth** perdonar algo a
uno; **~ness** *n* perdón *m*
forgo [fo:'gəu] (*pt* **forwent**, *pp* **forgone**) *vt*
(*give up*) renunciar a; (*go without*) privarse
de
forgot [fə'got] *pt of* **forget**
forgotten [fə'gotn] *pp of* **forget**
fork [fo:k] *n* (*for eating*) tenedor *m*; (*for gar-*

dening) horca; (*of roads*) bifurcación *f* ♦ *vi* (*road*) bifurcarse; ~ **out** (*inf*) *vt* (*pay*) desembolsar; ~-**lift truck** *n* máquina elevadora

forlorn [fə'lɔ:n] *adj* (*person*) triste, melancólico; (*place*) abandonado; (*attempt, hope*) desesperado

form [fɔ:m] *n* forma; (*BRIT: SCOL*) clase *f*; (*document*) formulario ♦ *vt* formar; (*idea*) concebir; (*habit*) adquirir; **in top** ~ en plena forma; **to ~ a queue** hacer cola

formal [fɔ:məl] *adj* (*offer, receipt*) por escrito; (*person etc*) correcto; (*occasion, dinner*) de etiqueta; (*dress*) correcto; (*garden*) (de estilo) clásico; ~**ity** [-'mælɪtɪ] *n* (*procedure*) trámite *m*; corrección *f*; etiqueta; ~**ly** *adv* oficialmente

format ['fɔ:mæt] *n* formato ♦ *vt* (*COMPUT*) formatear

formative ['fɔ:mətɪv] *adj* (*years*) de formación; (*influence*) formativo

former ['fɔ:mə*] *adj* anterior; (*earlier*) antiguo; (*ex*) ex; **the** ~ ... **the latter** ... aquél ... éste ...; ~**ly** *adv* antes

formula ['fɔ:mjulə] *n* fórmula

forsake [fə'seɪk] (*pt* **forsook**, *pp* **forsaken**) *vt* (*gen*) abandonar; (*plan*) renunciar a

forsaken [fə'seɪkən] *pp of* **forsake**

fort [fɔ:t] *n* fuerte *m*

forte [fɔ:tɪ] *n* fuerte *m*

forth [fɔ:θ] *adv*: **back and** ~ de acá para allá; **and so** ~ y así sucesivamente; ~**coming** *adj* próximo, venidero; (*help, information*) disponible; (*character*) comunicativo; ~**right** *adj* franco; ~**with** *adv* en el acto

fortify ['fɔ:tɪfaɪ] *vt* (*city*) fortificar; (*person*) fortalecer

fortitude ['fɔ:tɪtju:d] *n* fortaleza

fortnight ['fɔ:tnaɪt] (*BRIT*) *n* quince días *mpl*; quincena; ~**ly** *adj* de cada quince días, quincenal ♦ *adv* cada quince días, quincenalmente

fortress ['fɔ:trɪs] *n* fortaleza

fortunate ['fɔ:tʃənɪt] *adj* afortunado; **it is** ~ **that** ... (es una) suerte que ...; ~**ly** *adv* afortunadamente

fortune ['fɔ:tʃən] *n* suerte *f*; (*wealth*) fortuna; ~-**teller** *n* adivino/a

forty ['fɔ:tɪ] *num* cuarenta

forum ['fɔ:rəm] *n* foro

forward ['fɔ:wəd] *adj* (*movement, position*) avanzado; (*front*) delantero; (*in time*) adelantado; (*not shy*) atrevido ♦ *n* (*SPORT*) delantero ♦ *vt* (*letter*) remitir; (*career*) promocionar; **to move** ~ avanzar; ~(**s**) *adv* (hacia) adelante

fossil ['fɔsl] *n* fósil *m*

foster ['fɔstə*] *vt* (*child*) acoger en una familia; fomentar; ~ **child** *n* hijo/a adoptivo/a

fought [fɔ:t] *pt, pp of* **fight**

foul [faul] *adj* sucio, puerco; (*weather, smell*

etc) asqueroso; (*language*) grosero; (*temper*) malísimo ♦ *n* (*SPORT*) falta ♦ *vt* (*dirty*) ensuciar; ~ **play** *n* (*LAW*) muerte *f* violenta

found [faund] *pt, pp of* **find** ♦ *vt* fundar; ~**ation** [-'deɪʃən] *n* (*act*) fundación *f*; (*basis*) base *f*; (*also*: ~**ation cream**) crema base; ~**ations** *npl* (*of building*) cimientos *mpl*

founder ['faundə*] *n* fundador(a) *m/f* ♦ *vi* hundirse

foundry ['faundrɪ] *n* fundición *f*

fountain ['fauntɪn] *n* fuente *f*; ~ **pen** *n* pluma (estilográfica) (*SP*), pluma-fuente *f* (*AM*)

four [fɔ:*] *num* cuatro; **on all** ~**s** a gatas; ~-**poster** (**bed**) *n* cama de dosel; ~**some** ['fɔ:səm] *n* grupo de cuatro personas; ~**teen** *num* catorce; ~**th** *num* cuarto

fowl [faul] *n* ave *f* (de corral)

fox [fɔks] *n* zorro ♦ *vt* confundir

foyer ['fɔɪeɪ] *n* vestíbulo

fraction ['frækʃən] *n* fracción *f*

fracture ['fræktʃə*] *n* fractura

fragile ['frædʒaɪl] *adj* frágil

fragment ['frægmənt] *n* fragmento

fragrant ['freɪgrənt] *adj* fragante, oloroso

frail [freɪl] *adj* frágil; (*person*) débil

frame [freɪm] *n* (*TECH*) armazón *m*; (*of person*) cuerpo; (*of picture, door etc*) marco; (*of spectacles: also*: ~**s**) montura ♦ *vt* enmarcar; ~ **of mind** *n* estado de ánimo; ~**work** *n* marco

France [fru:ns] *n* Francia

franchise ['fræntʃaɪz] *n* (*POL*) derecho de votar, sufragio; (*COMM*) licencia, concesión *f*

frank [fræŋk] *adj* franco ♦ *vt* (*letter*) franquear; ~**ly** *adv* francamente; ~**ness** *n* franqueza

frantic ['fræntɪk] *adj* (*distraught*) desesperado; (*hectic*) frenético

fraternity [frə'tə:nɪtɪ] *n* (*feeling*) fraternidad *f*; (*group of people*) círculos *mpl*

fraud [frɔ:d] *n* fraude *m*; (*person*) impostor(a) *m/f*

fraught [frɔ:t] *adj*: ~ **with** lleno de

fray [freɪ] *n* combate *m*, lucha ♦ *vi* deshilacharse; **tempers were** ~**ed** el ambiente se ponía tenso

freak [fri:k] *n* (*person*) fenómeno; (*event*) suceso anormal

freckle ['frɛkl] *n* peca

free [fri:] *adj* libre; (*gratis*) gratuito ♦ *vt* (*prisoner etc*) poner en libertad; (*jammed object*) soltar; ~ (**of charge**), **for** ~ gratis; ~**dom** ['fri:dəm] *n* libertad *f*; ~-**for-all** *n* riña general; ~ **gift** *n* prima; ~**hold** *n* propiedad *f* vitalicia; ~ **kick** *n* tiro libre; ~**lance** *adj* independiente ♦ *adv* por cuenta propia; ~**ly** *adv* libremente; (*liberally*) generosamente; **F**~**mason** *n* francmasón *m*; **F**~**post** *n* porte *m* pagado; ~-**range** *adj* (*hen, eggs*) de granja; ~ **trade** *n* libre

comercio; ~**way** (*US*) *n* autopista; ~ **will**
n libre albedrío; **of one's own** ~ **will** por
su propia voluntad
freeze [friːz] (*pt* **froze**, *pp* **frozen**) *vi* (*weath-er*) helar; (*liquid, pipe, person*) helarse, con-gelarse ♦ *vt* helar; (*food, prices, salaries*)
congelar ♦ *n* helada; (*on arms, wages*) con-gelación *f*; ~**-dried** *adj* liofilizado; ~**r** *n*
congelador *m* (*SP*), congeladora (*AM*)
freezing ['friːzɪŋ] *adj* helado; **3 degrees be-low** ~ tres grados bajo cero; ~ **point** *n*
punto de congelación
freight [freɪt] *n* (*goods*) carga; (*money charged*) flete *m*; ~ **train** (*US*) *n* tren *m* de
mercancías
French [frentʃ] *adj* francés/esa ♦ *n* (*LING*)
francés *m*; **the** ~ *npl* los franceses; ~ **bean**
n judía verde; ~ **fried potatoes** *npl* pata-tas *fpl* (*SP*) or papas *fpl* (*AM*) fritas; ~ **fries**
(*US*) *npl* = ~ **fried potatoes**; ~**man/woman** *n* francés/esa *m/f*; ~ **window** *n*
puerta de cristal
frenzy ['frenzɪ] *n* frenesí *m*
frequent [*adj* 'friːkwənt, *vb* frɪ'kwent] *adj*
frecuente ♦ *vt* frecuentar; ~**ly** [-əntlɪ] *adv*
frecuentemente, a menudo
fresh [freʃ] *adj* fresco; (*bread*) tierno; (*new*)
nuevo; ~**en** *vi* (*wind, air*) soplar más recio;
~**en up** *vi* (*person*) arreglarse, lavarse; ~**er**
(*BRIT: inf*) *n* (*SCOL*) estudiante *m/f* de pri-mer año; ~**ly** *adv* (*made, painted etc*) re-cién; ~**man** (*US*) *n* = ~**er**; ~**ness** *n* fres-cura; ~**water** *adj* (*fish*) de agua dulce
fret [fret] *vi* inquietarse
friar ['fraɪə*] *n* fraile *m*; (*before name*) fray
m
friction ['frɪkʃən] *n* fricción *f*
Friday ['fraɪdɪ] *n* viernes *m inv*
fridge [frɪdʒ] (*BRIT*) *n* nevera (*SP*), refrige-radora (*AM*)
fried [fraɪd] *adj* frito
friend [frend] *n* amigo/a; ~**ly** *adj* simpáti-co; (*government*) amigo; (*place*) acoge-dor(a); (*match*) amistoso; ~**ship** *n* amistad
f
frieze [friːz] *n* friso
frigate ['frɪgɪt] *n* fragata
fright [fraɪt] *n* (*terror*) terror *m*; (*scare*) sus-to; **to take** ~ asustarse; ~**en** *vt* asustar;
~**ened** *adj* asustado; ~**ening** *adj* espanto-so; ~**ful** *adj* espantoso, horrible
frigid ['frɪdʒɪd] *adj* (*MED*) frígido, frío
frill [frɪl] *n* volante *m*
fringe [frɪndʒ] *n* (*BRIT: of hair*) flequillo; (*on lampshade etc*) flecos *mpl*; (*of forest etc*)
borde *m*, margen *m*; ~ **benefits** *npl* be-neficios *mpl* marginales
frisk [frɪsk] *vt* cachear, registrar
frisky ['frɪskɪ] *adj* juguetón/ona
fritter ['frɪtə*] *n* buñuelo; ~ **away** *vt* des-perdiciar
frivolous ['frɪvələs] *adj* frívolo

frizzy ['frɪzɪ] *adj* rizado
fro [frəu] *see* **to**
frock [frɔk] *n* vestido
frog [frɔg] *n* rana; ~**man** *n* hombre-rana *m*
frolic ['frɔlɪk] *vi* juguetear

KEYWORD

from [frɔm] *prep* **1** (*indicating starting place*)
de, desde; **where do you come** ~? ¿de
dónde eres?; ~ **London to Glasgow** de
Londres a Glasgow; **to escape** ~ **sth/sb**
escaparse de algo/alguien
2 (*indicating origin etc*) de; **a letter/telephone call** ~ **my sister** una carta/llamada de mi hermana; **tell him** ~ **me that ...** dígale de mi parte que ...
3 (*indicating time*): ~ **one o'clock to** or **un-til** or **till two** de(sde) la una a or hasta las
dos; ~ **January** (**on**) a partir de enero
4 (*indicating distance*) de; **the hotel is 1
km** ~ **the beach** el hotel está a 1 km de la
playa
5 (*indicating price, number etc*) de; **prices
range** ~ **£10 to £50** los precios van desde
£10 a or hasta £50; **the interest rate was
increased** ~ **9% to 10%** el tipo de interés
fue incrementado de un 9% a un 10%
6 (*indicating difference*) de; **he can't tell
red** ~ **green** no sabe distinguir el rojo del
verde; **to be different** ~ **sb/sth** ser diferen-te a algo/alguien
7 (*because of, on the basis of*): ~ **what he
says** por lo que dice; **weak** ~ **hunger** de-bilitado por el hambre

---

front [frʌnt] *n* (*foremost part*) parte *f* delan-tera; (*of house*) fachada; (*of dress*) delante-ro; (*promenade: also: sea* ~) paseo maríti-mo; (*MIL, POL, METEOROLOGY*) frente *m*;
(*fig: appearances*) apariencias *fpl* ♦ *adj*
(*wheel, leg*) delantero; (*row, line*) primero;
in ~ (**of**) delante (de); ~**age** ['frʌntɪdʒ] *n*
(*of building*) fachada; ~ **door** *n* puerta
principal; ~**ier** ['frʌntɪə*] *n* frontera; ~
page *n* primera plana; ~ **room** (*BRIT*) *n*
salón *m*, sala; ~**-wheel drive** *n* tracción *f*
delantera
frost [frɔst] *n* helada; (*also: hoar*~) escar-cha; ~**bite** *n* congelación *f*; ~**ed** *adj*
(*glass*) deslustrado; ~**y** *adj* (*weather*) de he-lada; (*welcome etc*) glacial
froth [frɔθ] *n* espuma
frown [fraun] *vi* fruncir el ceño
froze [frəuz] *pt of* **freeze**
frozen ['frəuzn] *pp of* **freeze**
fruit [fruːt] *n inv* fruta; fruto; (*fig*) fruto; re-sultados *mpl*; ~**erer** *n* frutero/a; ~**erer's
(shop)** *n* frutería; ~**ful** *adj* provechoso;
~**ion** [fruː'ɪʃən] *n*: **to come to** ~**ion** reali-zarse; ~ **juice** *n* zumo (*SP*) or jugo (*AM*)
de fruta; ~ **machine** (*BRIT*) *n* máquina *f*
tragaperras; ~ **salad** *n* macedonia (*SP*) or

ensalada (*AM*) de frutas

frustrate [frʌs'treɪt] *vt* frustrar; **~d** *adj*
frustrado

fry [fraɪ] (*pt, pp* **fried**) *vt* freír; **small ~** gente *f* menuda; **~ing pan** *n* sartén *f*

ft. *abbr* = **foot; feet**

fuddy-duddy ['fʌdɪdʌdɪ] (*pej*) *n* carroza
m/f

fudge [fʌdʒ] *n* (*CULIN*) caramelo blando

fuel [fjuəl] *n* (*for heating*) combustible *m*;
(*coal*) carbón *m*; (*wood*) leña; (*for engine*)
carburante *m*; **~ oil** *n* fuel oil *m*; **~ tank**
n depósito (de combustible)

fugitive ['fjuːdʒɪtɪv] *n* fugitivo/a

fulfil [ful'fɪl] *vt* (*function*) cumplir con; (*condition*) satisfacer; (*wish, desire*) realizar;
~ment *n* satisfacción *f*; (*of promise, desire*)
realización *f*

full [ful] *adj* lleno; (*fig*) pleno; (*complete*)
completo; (*maximum*) máximo; (*informa-
tion*) detallado; (*price*) íntegro; (*skirt*) amplio ♦ *adv*: **to know ~ well that** saber perfectamente que; **I'm ~ (up)** no puedo más;
~ employment pleno empleo; **a ~ two
hours** dos horas completas; **at ~ speed** a
máxima velocidad; **in ~** (*reproduce, quote*)
íntegramente; **~-length** *adj* (*novel etc*) entero; (*coat*) largo; (*portrait*) de cuerpo entero; **~ moon** *n* luna llena; **~-scale** *adj* (*attack, war*) en gran escala; (*model*) de tamaño natural; **~ stop** *n* punto; **~-time** *adj*
(*work*) de tiempo completo ♦ *adv*: **to work
~-time** trabajar a tiempo completo; **~y**
adv completamente; (*at least*) por lo menos;
~y-fledged *adj* (*teacher, barrister*) diplomado

fulsome ['fulsəm] (*pej*) *adj* (*praise, gratitude*) excesivo, exagerado

fumble ['fʌmbl] *vi*: **to ~ with** manejar torpemente

fume [fjuːm] *vi* (*rage*) estar furioso; **~s** *npl*
humo, gases *mpl*

fun [fʌn] *n* (*amusement*) diversión *f*; **to
have ~** divertirse; **for ~** en broma; **make
~ of** *vt fus* burlarse de

function ['fʌŋkʃən] *n* función *f* ♦ *vi* funcionar; **~al** *adj* (*operational*) en buen estado;
(*practical*) funcional

fund [fʌnd] *n* fondo; (*reserve*) reserva; **~s**
npl (*money*) fondos *mpl*

fundamental [fʌndə'mentl] *adj* fundamental

funeral ['fjuːnərəl] *n* (*burial*) entierro; (*ceremony*) funerales *mpl*; **~ parlour** (*BRIT*)
n funeraria; **~ service** *n* misa de difuntos,
funeral *m*

funfair ['fʌnfɛə*] (*BRIT*) *n* parque *m* de
atracciones

fungi ['fʌngaɪ] *npl of* **fungus**

fungus ['fʌngəs] (*pl* **fungi**) *n* hongo;
(*mould*) moho

funnel ['fʌnl] *n* embudo; (*of ship*) chimenea

funny ['fʌnɪ] *adj* gracioso, divertido; (*strange*) curioso, raro

fur [fəː*] *n* piel *f*; (*BRIT*: *in kettle etc*) sarro;
~ coat *n* abrigo de pieles

furious ['fjuərɪəs] *adj* furioso; (*effort*) violento

furlong ['fəːlɔŋ] *n* octava parte de una milla,
= 201.17 m

furlough ['fəːləu] *n* (*MIL*) permiso

furnace ['fəːnɪs] *n* horno

furnish ['fəːnɪʃ] *vt* amueblar; (*supply*) suministrar; (*information*) facilitar; **~ings** *npl*
muebles *mpl*

furniture ['fəːnɪtʃə*] *n* muebles *mpl*; **piece
of ~** mueble *m*

furrow ['fʌrəu] *n* surco

furry ['fəːrɪ] *adj* peludo

further ['fəːðə*] *adj* (*new*) nuevo, adicional
♦ *adv* más lejos; (*more*) más; (*moreover*)
además ♦ *vt* promover, adelantar; **~ education** *n* educación *f* superior; **~more**
[fəːðə'mɔː*] *adv* además

furthest ['fəːðɪst] *superlative of* **far**

fury ['fjuərɪ] *n* furia

fuse [fjuːz] (*US* **fuze**) *n* fusible *m*; (*for bomb
etc*) mecha ♦ *vt* (*metal*) fundir; (*fig*) fusio-
nar ♦ *vi* fundirse; fusionarse; (*BRIT: ELEC*):
to ~ the lights fundir los plomos; **~ box**
n caja de fusibles

fuss [fʌs] *n* (*excitement*) conmoción *f*; (*trouble*) alboroto; **to make a ~** armar un lío or
jaleo; **to make a ~ of sb** mimar a uno; **~y**
adj (*person*) exigente; (*too ornate*) recargado

futile ['fjuːtaɪl] *adj* vano

future ['fjuːtʃə*] *adj* futuro; (*coming*) venidero ♦ *n* futuro; (*prospects*) porvenir; **in ~**
de ahora en adelante

fuze [fjuːz] (*US*) = **fuse**

fuzzy ['fʌzɪ] *adj* (*PHOT*) borroso; (*hair*) muy
rizado

G g

G [dʒiː] *n* (*MUS*) sol *m*

g. *abbr* (= **gram(s)**) gr

G7 *abbr* (= **Group of Seven**) el grupo de
los 7

gabble ['gæbl] *vi* hablar atropelladamente

gable ['geɪbl] *n* aguilón *m*

gadget ['gædʒɪt] *n* aparato

Gaelic ['geɪlɪk] *adj, n* (*LING*) gaélico

gaffe [gæf] *n* plancha

gag [gæg] *n* (*on mouth*) mordaza; (*joke*)

chiste *m* ♦ *vt* amordazar

gaiety ['geɪɪtɪ] *n* alegría

gaily ['geɪlɪ] *adv* alegremente

gain [geɪn] *n*: ~ **(in)** aumento (de); (*profit*) ganancia ♦ *vt* ganar ♦ *vi* (*watch*) adelantarse; **to** ~ **from/by sth** sacar provecho de algo; **to** ~ **on sb** ganar terreno a uno; **to** ~ **3 lbs (in weight)** engordar 3 libras

gait [geɪt] *n* (modo de) andar *m*

gal. *abbr* = **gallon**

gala ['gɑːlə] *n* fiesta

gale [geɪl] *n* (*wind*) vendaval *m*

gallant ['gælənt] *adj* valiente; (*towards ladies*) atento; ~**ry** *n* valentía; galantería

gall bladder ['gɔːl-] *n* vesícula biliar

gallery ['gælərɪ] *n* (*also: art* ~: *public*) pinacoteca; (: *private*) galería de arte; (*for spectators*) tribuna

galley ['gælɪ] *n* (*ship's kitchen*) cocina

gallon ['gælən] *n* galón *m* (BRIT = 4,546 *litros*, US = 3,785 *litros*)

gallop ['gæləp] *n* galope *m* ♦ *vi* galopar

gallows ['gæləuz] *n* horca

gallstone ['gɔːlstəun] *n* cálculo biliario

galore [gə'lɔː*] *adv* en cantidad, en abundancia

galvanize ['gælvənaɪz] *vt*: **to** ~ **sb into action** animar a uno para que haga algo

gambit ['gæmbɪt] *n* (*fig*): (*opening*) ~ estrategia (inicial)

gamble ['gæmbl] *n* (*risk*) riesgo ♦ *vt* jugar, apostar ♦ *vi* (*take a risk*) jugárselas; (*bet*) apostar; **to** ~ **on** apostar a; (*success etc*) contar con; ~**r** *n* jugador(a) *m/f*; **gambling** *n* juego

game [geɪm] *n* juego; (*match*) partido; (*of cards*) partida; (*HUNTING*) caza ♦ *adj* (*willing*): **to be** ~ **for anything** atreverse a todo; **big** ~ caza mayor; ~**keeper** *n* guardabosques *m inv*

gammon ['gæmən] *n* (*bacon*) tocino ahumado; (*ham*) jamón *m* ahumado

gamut ['gæmət] *n* gama

gang [gæŋ] *n* (*of criminals*) pandilla; (*of friends etc*) grupo; (*of workmen*) brigada; ~ **up** *vi*: **to** ~ **up on sb** aliarse contra uno

gangster ['gæŋstə*] *n* gángster *m*

gangway ['gæŋweɪ] *n* (*on ship*) pasarela; (BRIT: *in theatre, bus etc*) pasillo

gaol [dʒeɪl] (BRIT) *n*, *vt* = **jail**

gap [gæp] *n* vacío, hueco (AM); (*in trees, traffic*) claro; (*in time*) intervalo; (*difference*): ~ **(between)** diferencia (entre)

gape [geɪp] *vi* mirar boquiabierto; (*shirt etc*) abrirse (completamente); **gaping** *adj* (*completamente*) abierto

garage ['gærɑːʒ] *n* garaje *m*; (*for repairs*) taller *m*

garbage ['gɑːbɪdʒ] (US) *n* basura; (*inf: nonsense*) tonterías *fpl*; ~ **can** *n* cubo (SP) or bote *m* (AM) de la basura

garbled ['gɑːbld] *adj* (*distorted*) falsificado,

amañado

garden ['gɑːdn] *n* jardín *m*; ~**s** *npl* (*park*) parque *m*; ~**er** *n* jardinero/a; ~**ing** *n* jardinería

gargle ['gɑːgl] *vi* hacer gárgaras, gargarear (AM)

garish ['geərɪʃ] *adj* chillón/ona

garland ['gɑːlənd] *n* guirnalda

garlic ['gɑːlɪk] *n* ajo

garment ['gɑːmənt] *n* prenda (de vestir)

garnish ['gɑːnɪʃ] *vt* (CULIN) aderezar

garrison ['gærɪsn] *n* guarnición *f*

garrulous ['gærjuləs] *adj* charlatán/ana

garter ['gɑːtə*] *n* (*for sock*) liga; (US) liguero

gas [gæs] *n* gas *m*; (*fuel*) combustible *m*; (US: *gasoline*) gasolina ♦ *vt* asfixiar con gas; ~ **cooker** (BRIT) *n* cocina de gas; ~ **cylinder** *n* bombona de gas; ~ **fire** *n* estufa de gas

gash [gæʃ] *n* raja; (*wound*) cuchillada ♦ *vt* rajar; acuchillar

gasket ['gæskɪt] *n* (AUT) junta de culata

gas mask *n* careta antigás

gas meter *n* contador *m* de gas

gasoline ['gæsəliːn] (US) *n* gasolina

gasp [gɑːsp] *n* boqueada; (*of shock etc*) grito sofocado ♦ *vi* (*pant*) jadear; ~ **out** *vt* (*say*) decir con voz entrecortada

gas station (US) *n* gasolinera

gastric ['gæstrɪk] *adj* gástrico

gate [geɪt] *n* puerta; (*iron* ~) verja; ~**crash** (BRIT) *vt* colarse en; ~**way** *n* (*also fig*) puerta

gather ['gæðə*] *vt* (*flowers, fruit*) coger (SP), recoger; (*assemble*) reunir; (*pick up*) recoger; (SEWING) fruncir; (*understand*) entender ♦ *vi* (*assemble*) reunirse; **to** ~ **speed** ganar velocidad; ~**ing** *n* reunión *f*, asamblea

gauche [gəuʃ] *adj* torpe

gaudy ['gɔːdɪ] *adj* chillón/ona

gauge [geɪdʒ] *n* (*instrument*) indicador *m* ♦ *vt* medir; (*fig*) juzgar

gaunt [gɔːnt] *adj* (*haggard*) demacrado; (*stark*) desolado

gauntlet ['gɔːntlɪt] *n* guante *m*; (*fig*): **to run the** ~ **of** exponerse a; **to throw down the** ~ arrojar el guante

gauze [gɔːz] *n* gasa

gave [geɪv] *pt of* **give**

gay [geɪ] *adj* (*homosexual*) gay; (*joyful*) alegre; (*colour*) vivo

gaze [geɪz] *n* mirada fija ♦ *vi*: **to** ~ **at sth** mirar algo fijamente

gazelle [gə'zɛl] *n* gacela

gazetteer [gæzə'tɪə*] *n* diccionario geográfico

gazumping [gə'zʌmpɪŋ] (BRIT) *n* la subida del precio de una casa una vez que ya ha sido apalabrado

GB *abbr* = **Great Britain**

GCE n abbr (BRIT) = General Certificate of Education

GCSE (BRIT) n abbr (= General Certificate of Secondary Education) examen de reválida que se hace a los 16 años

gear [gɪə*] n equipo, herramientas fpl; (TECH) engranaje m; (AUT) velocidad f, marcha ♦ vt (fig: adapt): **to ~ sth to** adaptar or ajustar algo a; **top** or **high** (US)/**low ~** cuarta/primera velocidad; **in ~** en marcha; **~ box** n caja de cambios; **~ lever** n palanca de cambio; **~ shift** (US) n = **~ lever**

geese [giːs] npl of goose

gel [dʒɛl] n gel m

gem [dʒɛm] n piedra preciosa

Gemini ['dʒɛmɪnaɪ] n Géminis m, Gemelos mpl

gender ['dʒɛndə*] n género

gene [dʒiːn] n gen(e) m

general ['dʒɛnərl] n general m ♦ adj general; **in ~** en general; **~ delivery** (US) n lista de correos; **~ election** n elecciones fpl generales; **~ization** [-aɪ'zeɪʃən] n generalización f; **~ly** adv generalmente, en general; **~ practitioner** n médico general

generate ['dʒɛnəreɪt] vt (ELEC) generar; (jobs, profits) producir

generation [dʒɛnə'reɪʃən] n generación f

generator ['dʒɛnəreɪtə*] n generador m

generosity [dʒɛnə'rɒsɪtɪ] n generosidad f

generous ['dʒɛnərəs] adj generoso

genetic engineering [dʒɪ'nɛtɪkɛndʒɪ-'nɪərɪŋ] n ingeniería genética

Geneva [dʒɪ'niːvə] n Ginebra

genial ['dʒiːnɪəl] adj afable, simpático

genitals ['dʒɛnɪtlz] npl (órganos mpl) genitales mpl

genius ['dʒiːnɪəs] n genio

genteel [dʒɛn'tiːl] adj fino, elegante

gentle ['dʒɛntl] adj apacible, dulce; (animal) manso; (breeze, curve etc) suave

gentleman ['dʒɛntlmən] n señor m; (well-bred man) caballero

gentleness ['dʒɛntlnɪs] n apacibilidad f, dulzura; mansedumbre f; suavidad f

gently ['dʒɛntlɪ] adv dulcemente; suavemente

gentry ['dʒɛntrɪ] n alta burguesía

gents [dʒɛnts] n aseos mpl (de caballeros)

genuine ['dʒɛnjuɪn] adj auténtico; (person) sincero

geography [dʒɪ'ɒgrəfɪ] n geografía

geology [dʒɪ'ɒlədʒɪ] n geología

geometric(al) [dʒɪə'mɛtrɪk(l)] adj geométrico

geranium [dʒɪ'reɪnjəm] n geranio

geriatric [dʒɛrɪ'ætrɪk] adj, n geriátrico/a m/f

germ [dʒəːm] n (microbe) microbio, bacteria; (seed, fig) germen m

German ['dʒəːmən] adj alemán/ana ♦ n alemán/ana m/f; (LING) alemán m; **~ measles** n rubéola

Germany ['dʒəːmənɪ] n Alemania

gesture ['dʒɛstjə*] n gesto; (symbol) muestra

--- **KEYWORD** ---

get [gɛt] (pt, pp **got**, pp **gotten** (US)) vi **1** (become, be) ponerse, volverse; **to ~ old/ tired** envejecer/cansarse; **to ~ drunk** emborracharse; **to ~ dirty** ensuciarse; **to ~ married** casarse; **when do I ~ paid?** ¿cuándo me pagan or se me paga?; **it's ~ting late** se está haciendo tarde

2 (go): **to ~ to/from** llegar a/de; **to ~ home** llegar a casa

3 (begin) empezar a; **to ~ to know sb** (llegar a) conocer a uno; **I'm ~ting to like him** me está empezando a gustar; **let's ~ going** or **started** ¡vamos (a empezar)!

4 (modal aux vb): **you've got to do it** tienes que hacerlo

♦ vt **1**: **to ~ sth done** (finish) terminar algo; (have done) mandar hacer algo; **to ~ one's hair cut** cortarse el pelo; **to ~ the car going** or **to go** arrancar el coche; **to ~ sb to do sth** conseguir or hacer que alguien haga algo; **to ~ sth/sb ready** preparar algo/a alguien

2 (obtain: money, permission, results) conseguir; (find: job, flat) encontrar; (fetch: person, doctor) buscar; (object) ir a buscar, traer; **to ~ sth for sb** conseguir algo para alguien; **~ me Mr Jones, please** (TEL) póngame or comuníqueme (AM) con el Sr. Jones, por favor; **can I ~ you a drink?** ¿quieres algo de beber?

3 (receive: present, letter) recibir; (acquire: reputation) alcanzar; (: prize) ganar; **what did you ~ for your birthday?** ¿qué te regalaron por tu cumpleaños?; **how much did you ~ for the painting?** ¿cuánto sacaste por el cuadro?

4 (catch) coger (SP), agarrar (AM); (hit: target etc) dar en; **to ~ sb by the arm/throat** coger or agarrar a uno por el brazo/cuello; **~ him!** ¡cógelo! (SP), ¡atrápalo! (AM); **the bullet got him in the leg** la bala le dio en la pierna

5 (take, move) llevar; **to ~ sth to sb** hacer llegar algo a alguien; **do you think we'll ~ it through the door?** ¿crees que lo podremos meter por la puerta?

6 (catch, take: plane, bus etc) coger (SP), tomar (AM); **where do I ~ the train for Birmingham?** ¿dónde se coge or se toma el tren para Birmingham?

7 (understand) entender; (hear) oír; **I've got it!** ¡ya lo tengo!, ¡eureka!; **I don't ~ your meaning** no te entiendo; **I'm sorry, I didn't ~ your name** lo siento, no cogí tu nombre

8 (*have, possess*): **to have got** tener
get about *vi* salir mucho; (*news*) divulgarse
get along *vi* (*agree*) llevarse bien; (*depart*) marcharse; (*manage*) = **get by**
get at *vt fus* (*attack*) atacar; (*reach*) alcanzar
get away *vi* marcharse; (*escape*) escaparse
get away with *vt fus* hacer impunemente
get back *vi* (*return*) volver ♦ *vt* recobrar
get by *vi* (*pass*) (lograr) pasar; (*manage*) arreglárselas
get down *vi* bajarse ♦ *vt fus* bajar ♦ *vt* bajar; (*depress*) deprimir
get down to *vt fus* (*work*) ponerse a
get in *vi* entrar; (*train*) llegar; (*arrive home*) volver a casa, regresar
get into *vt fus* entrar en; (*vehicle*) subir a; **to ~ into a rage** enfadarse
get off *vi* (*from train etc*) bajar; (*depart: person, car*) marcharse ♦ *vt* (*remove*) quitar ♦ *vt fus* (*train, bus*) bajar de
get on *vi* (*at exam etc*): **how are you ~ting on?** ¿cómo te va?; (*agree*): **to ~ on (with)** llevarse bien (con) ♦ *vt fus* subir a
get out *vi* salir; (*of vehicle*) bajar ♦ *vt* sacar
get out of *vt fus* salir de; (*duty etc*) escaparse de
get over *vt fus* (*illness*) recobrarse de
get round *vt fus* rodear; (*fig: person*) engatusar a
get through *vi* (*TEL*) (lograr) comunicarse
get through to *vt fus* (*TEL*) comunicar con
get together *vi* reunirse ♦ *vt* reunir, juntar
get up *vi* (*rise*) levantarse ♦ *vt fus* subir
get up to *vt fus* (*reach*) llegar a; (*prank*) hacer

geyser ['gi:zə*] *n* (*water heater*) calentador *m* de agua; (*GEO*) géiser *m*
ghastly ['gɑ:stlɪ] *adj* horrible
gherkin ['gə:kɪn] *n* pepinillo
ghetto blaster ['getəublɑ:stə*] *n* cassette *m* portátil de gran tamaño
ghost [gəust] *n* fantasma *m*
giant ['dʒaɪənt] *n* gigante *m/f* ♦ *adj* gigantesco, gigante
gibberish ['dʒɪbərɪʃ] *n* galimatías *m*
gibe [dʒaɪb] *n* = **jibe**
giblets ['dʒɪblɪts] *npl* menudillos *mpl*
Gibraltar [dʒɪ'brɔ:ltə*] *n* Gibraltar *m*
giddy ['gɪdɪ] *adj* mareado
gift [gɪft] *n* regalo; (*ability*) talento; **~ed** *adj* dotado; **~ token** *or* **voucher** *n* vale *m* canjeable por un regalo
gigantic [dʒaɪ'gæntɪk] *adj* gigantesco
giggle ['gɪgl] *vi* reírse tontamente
gill [dʒɪl] *n* (*measure*) = 0.25 pints (*BRIT* = 0.148l, *US* = 0.118l)
gills [gɪlz] *npl* (*of fish*) branquias *fpl*, agallas

fpl
gilt [gɪlt] *adj, n* dorado; **~-edged** *adj* (*COMM*) de máxima garantía
gimmick ['gɪmɪk] *n* truco
gin [dʒɪn] *n* ginebra
ginger ['dʒɪndʒə*] *n* jengibre *m*; **~ ale** = **~ beer**; **~ beer** (*BRIT*) *n* gaseosa de jengibre; **~bread** *n* pan *m* (*or* galleta) de jengibre
gingerly ['dʒɪndʒəlɪ] *adv* con cautela
gipsy ['dʒɪpsɪ] *n* = **gypsy**
giraffe [dʒɪ'rɑ:f] *n* jirafa
girder ['gə:də*] *n* viga
girdle ['gə:dl] *n* (*corset*) faja
girl [gə:l] *n* (*small*) niña; (*young woman*) chica, joven *f*, muchacha; (*daughter*) hija; **an English ~** una (chica) inglesa; **~friend** *n* (*of girl*) amiga; (*of boy*) novia; **~ish** *adj* de niña
giro ['dʒaɪrəu] *n* (*BRIT: bank ~*) giro bancario; (*post office ~*) giro postal; (*state benefit*) cheque quincenal del subsidio de desempleo
girth [gə:θ] *n* circunferencia; (*of saddle*) cincha
gist [dʒɪst] *n* lo esencial
give [gɪv] (*pt* gave, *pp* given) *vt* dar; (*deliver*) entregar; (*as gift*) regalar ♦ *vi* (*break*) romperse; (*stretch: fabric*) dar de sí; **to ~ sb sth, ~ sth to sb** dar algo a uno; **~ away** *vt* (*give free*) regalar; (*betray*) traicionar; (*disclose*) revelar; **~ back** *vt* devolver; **~ in** *vi* ceder ♦ *vt* entregar; **~ off** *vt* despedir; **~ out** *vt* distribuir; **~ up** *vi* rendirse, darse por vencido ♦ *vt* renunciar a; **to ~ up smoking** dejar de fumar; **to ~ o.s. up** entregarse; **~ way** *vi* ceder; (*BRIT: AUT*) ceder el paso
glacier ['glæsɪə*] *n* glaciar *m*
glad [glæd] *adj* contento
gladly ['glædlɪ] *adv* con mucho gusto
glamorous ['glæmərəs] *adj* encantador(a), atractivo; **glamour** ['glæmə*] *n* encanto, atractivo
glance [glɑ:ns] *n* ojeada, mirada ♦ *vi*: **to ~ at** echar una ojeada a; **~ off** *vt* rebotar en; **glancing** *adj* (*blow*) oblicuo
gland [glænd] *n* glándula
glare [gleə*] *n* (*of anger*) mirada feroz; (*of light*) deslumbramiento, brillo; **to be in the ~ of publicity** ser el foco de la atención pública ♦ *vi* deslumbrar; **to ~ at** mirar con odio a; **glaring** *adj* (*mistake*) manifiesto
glass [glɑ:s] *n* vidrio, cristal *m*; (*for drinking*) vaso; (*: with stem*) copa; **~es** *npl* (*spectacles*) gafas *fpl*; **~house** *n* invernadero; **~ware** *n* cristalería; **~y** *adj* (*eyes*) vidrioso
glaze [gleɪz] *vt* (*window*) poner cristales a; (*pottery*) vidriar ♦ *n* vidriado; **glazier** ['gleɪzɪə*] *n* vidriero/a

gleam [gli:m] *vi* brillar
glean [gli:n] *vt* (*information*) recoger
glee [gli:] *n* alegría, regocijo
glen [glɛn] *n* cañada
glib [glɪb] *adj* de mucha labia; (*promise, response*) poco sincero
glide [glaɪd] *vi* deslizarse; (*AVIAT, birds*) planear; **~r** *n* (*AVIAT*) planeador *m*; **gliding** *n* (*AVIAT*) vuelo sin motor
glimmer ['glɪmə*] *n* luz *f* tenue; (*of interest*) muestra; (*of hope*) rayo
glimpse [glɪmps] *n* vislumbre *m* ♦ *vt* vislumbrar, entrever
glint [glɪnt] *vi* centellear
glisten ['glɪsn] *vi* relucir, brillar
glitter ['glɪtə*] *vi* relucir, brillar
gloat [gləut] *vi*: **to ~ over** recrearse en
global ['gləubl] *adj* mundial
globe [gləub] *n* globo; (*model*) globo terráqueo
gloom [glu:m] *n* tinieblas *fpl*, oscuridad *f*; (*sadness*) tristeza, melancolía; **~y** *adj* (*dark*) oscuro; (*sad*) triste; (*pessimistic*) pesimista
glorious ['glɔːrɪəs] *adj* glorioso; (*weather etc*) magnífico
glory ['glɔːrɪ] *n* gloria
gloss [glɔs] *n* (*shine*) brillo; (*paint*) pintura de aceite; **~ over** *vt fus* disimular
glossary ['glɔsərɪ] *n* glosario
glossy ['glɔsɪ] *adj* lustroso; (*magazine*) de lujo
glove [glʌv] *n* guante *m*; **~ compartment** *n* (*AUT*) guantera
glow [gləu] *vi* brillar
glower ['glauə*] *vi*: **to ~ at** mirar con ceño
glue [glu:] *n* goma (de pegar), cemento ♦ *vt* pegar
glum [glʌm] *adj* (*person, tone*) melancólico
glut [glʌt] *n* superabundancia
glutton ['glʌtn] *n* glotón/ona *m/f*; **a ~ for work** un(a) trabajador(a) incansable
gnarled [nɑːld] *adj* nudoso
gnat [næt] *n* mosquito
gnaw [nɔ:] *vt* roer
gnome [nəum] *n* gnomo
go [gəu] (*pt* went, *pp* gone; *pl* ~es) *vi* ir; (*travel*) viajar; (*depart*) irse, marcharse; (*work*) funcionar, marchar; (*be sold*) venderse; (*time*) pasar; (*fit, suit*): **to ~ with** hacer juego con; (*become*) ponerse; (*break etc*) estropearse, romperse ♦ *n*: **to have a ~ (at)** probar suerte (con); **to be on the ~** no parar; **whose ~ is it?** ¿a quién le toca?; **he's going to do it** va a hacerlo; **to ~ for a walk** ir de paseo; **to ~ dancing** ir a bailar; **how did it ~?** ¿qué tal salió *or* resultó?, ¿cómo ha ido?; **to ~ round the back** pasar por detrás; **~ about** *vi* (*rumour*) propagarse ♦ *vt fus*: **how do I ~ about this?** ¿cómo me las arreglo para hacer esto?; **~ ahead** *vi* seguir adelante; **~ along** *vi* ir ♦ *vt fus* bordear; **to ~ along**

with (*agree*) estar de acuerdo con; **~ away** *vi* irse, marcharse; **~ back** *vi* volver; **~ back on** *vt fus* (*promise*) faltar a; **~ by** *vi* (*time*) pasar ♦ *vt fus* guiarse por; **~ down** *vi* bajar; (*ship*) hundirse; (*sun*) ponerse ♦ *vt fus* bajar por; **~ for** *vt fus* (*fetch*) ir por; (*like*) gustar; (*attack*) atacar; **~ in** *vi* entrar; **~ in for** *vt fus* (*competition*) presentarse a; **~ into** *vt fus* entrar en; (*investigate*) investigar; (*embark on*) dedicarse a; **~ off** *vi* irse, marcharse; (*food*) pasarse; (*explode*) estallar; (*event*) realizarse ♦ *vt fus* dejar de gustar; **I'm going off him/the idea** ya no me gusta tanto él/la idea; **~ on** *vi* (*continue*) seguir, continuar; (*happen*) pasar, ocurrir; **to ~ on doing sth** seguir haciendo algo; **~ out** *vi* salir; (*fire, light*) apagarse; **~ over** *vi* (*ship*) zozobrar ♦ *vt fus* (*check*) revisar; **~ through** *vt fus* (*town etc*) atravesar; **~ up** *vi*, *vt fus* subir; **~ without** *vt fus* pasarse sin
goad [gəud] *vt* aguijonear
go-ahead *adj* (*person*) dinámico; (*firm*) innovador(a) ♦ *n* luz *f* verde
goal [gəul] *n* meta; (*score*) gol *m*; **~keeper** *n* portero; **~-post** *n* poste *m* (de la portería)
goat [gəut] *n* cabra
gobble ['gɔbl] *vt* (*also*: **~ down, ~ up**) tragarse, engullir
go-between *n* intermediario/a
god [gɔd] *n* dios *m*; **G~** *n* Dios *m*; **~child** *n* ahijado/a; **~daughter** *n* ahijada; **~dess** *n* diosa; **~father** *n* padrino; **~forsaken** *adj* dejado de la mano de Dios; **~mother** *n* madrina; **~send** *n* don *m* del cielo; **~son** *n* ahijado
goggles ['gɔglz] *npl* gafas *fpl*
going ['gəuɪŋ] *n* (*conditions*) estado del terreno ♦ *adj*: **the ~ rate** la tarifa corriente *or* en vigor
gold [gəuld] *n* oro ♦ *adj* de oro; **~en** *adj* (*made of ~*) de oro; (*~ in colour*) dorado; **~fish** *n* pez *m* de colores; **~mine** *n* (*also fig*) mina de oro; **~-plated** *adj* chapado en oro; **~smith** *n* orfebre *m/f*
golf [gɔlf] *n* golf *m*; **~ ball** *n* (*for game*) pelota de golf; (*on typewriter*) esfera; **~ club** *n* club *m* de golf; (*stick*) palo (de golf); **~ course** *n* campo de golf; **~er** *n* golfista *m/f*
gone [gɔn] *pp of* go
good [gud] *adj* bueno; (*pleasant*) agradable; (*kind*) bueno, amable; (*well-behaved*) educado ♦ *n* bien *m*, provecho; **~s** *npl* (*COMM*) mercancías *fpl*; **~!** ¡qué bien!; **to be ~ at** tener aptitud para; **to be ~ for** servir para; **it's ~ for you** te hace bien; **would you be ~ enough to ...?** ¿podría hacerme el favor de ...?, ¿sería tan amable de ...?; **a ~ deal (of)** mucho; **a ~ many** muchos; **to make ~** reparar; **it's no ~ complaining** no vale

la pena (de) quejarse; **for** ~ para siempre,
definitivamente; ~ **morning/afternoon**
¡buenos días/buenas tardes!; ~ **evening!**
¡buenas noches!; ~ **night!** ¡buenas noches!;
~**bye!** ¡adiós!; **to say** ~**bye** despedirse;
G~ Friday ['ɡʊːsfleʃ] *n* Santo; ~**-looking**
adj guapo; ~**-natured** *adj* amable, simpático; ~**ness** ·*n* (*of person*) bondad *f*; **for**
~**ness sake!** ¡por Dios!; ~**ness gracious!**
¡Dios mío!; ~**s train** (*BRIT*) *n* tren *m* de
mercancías; ~**will** *n* buena voluntad *f*
goose [ɡuːs] (*pl* **geese**) *n* ganso, oca
gooseberry ['ɡuzbəri] *n* grosella espinosa;
to play ~ hacer de carabina
gooseflesh ['ɡuːsfleʃ] *n* = **goose pimples**
goose pimples *npl* carne *f* de gallina
gore [ɡɔː*] *vt* cornear ♦ *n* sangre *f*
gorge [ɡɔːdʒ] *n* barranco ♦ *vr*: **to** ~ **o.s.**
(on) atracarse (de)
gorgeous ['ɡɔːdʒəs] *adj* (*thing*) precioso;
(*weather*) espléndido; (*person*) guapísimo
gorilla [ɡə'rɪlə] *n* gorila *m*
gorse [ɡɔːs] *n* tojo
gory ['ɡɔːrɪ] *adj* sangriento
go-slow (*BRIT*) *n* huelga de manos caídas
gospel ['ɡɔspl] *n* evangelio
gossip ['ɡɔsɪp] *n* (*scandal*) cotilleo, chismes
mpl; (*chat*) charla; (*scandalmonger*) cotilla
m/f, chismoso/a ♦ *vi* cotillear
got [ɡɔt] *pt, pp* of **get**; ~**ten** (*US*) *pp* of **get**
gout [ɡaut] *n* gota
govern ['ɡʌvən] *vt* gobernar; (*influence*) dominar
governess ['ɡʌvənɪs] *n* institutriz *f*
government ['ɡʌvnmənt] *n* gobierno
governor ['ɡʌvənə*] *n* gobernador(a) *m/f*;
(*of school etc*) miembro del consejo; (*of jail*)
director(a) *m/f*
gown [ɡaun] *n* traje *m*; (*of teacher, BRIT: of
judge*) toga
G.P. *n abbr* = **general practitioner**
grab [ɡræb] *vt* coger (*SP*) or agarrar (*AM*),
arrebatar ♦ *vi*: **to** ~ **at** intentar agarrar
grace [ɡreɪs] *n* gracia ♦ *vt* honrar; (*adorn*)
adornar; **5 days'** ~ un plazo de 5 días;
~**ful** *adj* grácil, ágil; (*style, shape*) elegante,
gracioso; **gracious** ['ɡreɪʃəs] *adj* amable
grade [ɡreɪd] *n* (*quality*) clase *f*, calidad *f*;
(*in hierarchy*) grado; (*SCOL: mark*) nota;
(*US: school class*) curso ♦ *vt* clasificar; ~
crossing (*US*) *n* paso a nivel; ~ **school**
(*US*) *n* escuela primaria
gradient ['ɡreɪdɪənt] *n* pendiente *f*
gradual ['ɡrædjuəl] *adj* paulatino; ~**ly** *adv*
paulatinamente
graduate [*n* 'ɡrædjuɪt, *vb* 'ɡrædjueɪt] *n* (*US:
of high school*) graduado/a; (*of university*)
licenciado/a ♦ *vi* graduarse; licenciarse;
graduation [-'eɪʃən] *n* (*ceremony*) entrega
del título
graffiti [ɡrə'fiːtɪ] *n* pintadas *fpl*
graft [ɡrɑːft] *n* (*AGR, MED*) injerto; (*BRIT:*

inf) trabajo duro; (*bribery*) corrupción *f* ♦ *vt*
injertar
grain [ɡreɪn] *n* (*single particle*) grano; (*corn*)
granos *mpl*, cereales *mpl*; (*of wood*) fibra
gram [ɡræm] (*US*) *n* gramo
grammar ['ɡræmə*] *n* gramática; ~ **school**
(*BRIT*) *n* ≈ instituto de segunda enseñanza,
liceo (*SP*)
grammatical [ɡrə'mætɪkl] *adj* gramatical
gramme [ɡræm] *n* = **gram**
gramophone ['ɡræməfəun] (*BRIT*) *n* tocadiscos *m inv*
grand [ɡrænd] *adj* magnífico, imponente;
(*wonderful*) estupendo; (*gesture etc*) grandioso; ~**children** *npl* nietos *mpl*; ~**dad**
(*inf*) *n* yayo, abuelito; ~**daughter** *n* nieta;
~**eur** ['ɡrændjə*] *n* magnificencia, lo grandioso; ~**father** *n* abuelo; ~**ma** (*inf*) *n*
yaya, abuelita; ~**mother** *n* abuela; ~**pa**
(*inf*) *n* = ~**dad**; ~**parents** *npl* abuelos *mpl*;
~ **piano** *n* piano de cola; ~**son** *n* nieto;
~**stand** *n* (*SPORT*) tribuna
granite ['ɡrænɪt] *n* granito
granny ['ɡrænɪ] (*inf*) *n* abuelita, yaya
grant [ɡrɑːnt] *vt* (*concede*) conceder; (*admit*) reconocer ♦ *n* (*SCOL*) beca; (*ADMIN*)
subvención *f*; **to take sth/sb for** ~**ed** dar
algo por sentado/no hacer ningún caso a
uno
granulated sugar ['ɡrænjuːleɪtɪd-] (*BRIT*)
n azúcar *m* blanquilla
granule ['ɡrænjuːl] *n* grano, gránulo
grape [ɡreɪp] *n* uva
grapefruit ['ɡreɪpfruːt] *n* pomelo (*SP*), toronja (*AM*)
graph [ɡrɑːf] *n* gráfica; ~**ic** *adj* gráfico;
~**ics** *n* artes *fpl* gráficas ♦ *npl* (*drawings*)
dibujos *mpl*
grapple ['ɡræpl] *vi*: **to** ~ **with sth/sb** agarrar a algo/uno
grasp [ɡrɑːsp] *vt* agarrar, asir; (*understand*)
comprender ♦ *n* (*grip*) asimiento; (*understanding*) comprensión *f*; ~**ing** *adj* (*mean*)
avaro
grass [ɡrɑːs] ·*n* hierba; (*lawn*) césped *m*;
~**hopper** *n* saltamontes *m inv*; ~**-roots**
adj (*fig*) popular
grate [ɡreɪt] *n* parrilla de chimenea ♦ *vi*: **to**
~ **(on)** chirriar (sobre) ♦ *vt* (*CULIN*) rallar
grateful ['ɡreɪtful] *adj* agradecido
grater ['ɡreɪtə*] *n* rallador *m*
gratifying ['ɡrætɪfaɪŋ] *adj* grato
grating ['ɡreɪtɪŋ] *n* (*iron bars*) reja ♦ *adj*
(*noise*) áspero
gratitude ['ɡrætɪtjuːd] *n* agradecimiento
gratuity [ɡrə'tjuːɪtɪ] *n* gratificación *f*
grave [ɡreɪv] *n* tumba ♦ *adj* serio, grave
gravel ['ɡrævl] *n* grava
gravestone ['ɡreɪvstəun] *n* lápida
graveyard ['ɡreɪvjɑːd] *n* cementerio
gravity ['ɡrævɪtɪ] *n* gravedad *f*
gravy ['ɡreɪvɪ] *n* salsa de carne

gray [greɪ] *adj* = **grey**

graze [greɪz] *vi* pacer ♦ *vt (touch lightly)* rozar; *(scrape)* raspar ♦ *n (MED)* abrasión *f*

grease [griːs] *n (fat)* grasa; *(lubricant)* lubricante *m* ♦ *vt* engrasar; lubrificar; ~**proof paper** *(BRIT)* *n* papel *m* apergaminado; **greasy** *adj* grasiento

great [greɪt] *adj* grande; *(inf)* magnífico, estupendo; **G~ Britain** *n* Gran Bretaña; ~**grandfather** *n* bisabuelo; ~**grandmother** *n* bisabuela; ~**ly** *adv* muy; *(with verb)* mucho; ~**ness** *n* grandeza

Greece [griːs] *n* Grecia

greed [griːd] *n (also:* ~**iness)** codicia, avaricia; *(for food)* gula; *(for power etc)* avidez *f*; ~**y** *adj* avaro; *(for food)* glotón/ona

Greek [griːk] *adj* griego ♦ *n* griego/a; *(LING)* griego

green [griːn] *adj (also POL)* verde; *(inexperienced)* novato ♦ *n* verde *m*; *(stretch of grass)* césped *m*; *(GOLF)* green *m*; ~**s** *npl (vegetables)* verduras *fpl*; ~ **belt** *n* zona verde; ~ **card** *n (AUT)* carta verde; *(US: work permit)* permiso de trabajo para los extranjeros en EE. UU;* ~**ery** *n* verdura, ~**grocer** *(BRIT)* *n* verdulero/a; ~**house** *n* invernadero; ~**house effect** *n* efecto invernadero; ~**house gas** *n* gases *mpl* de invernadero; ~**ish** *adj* verdoso

Greenland ['griːnlənd] *n* Groenlandia

greet [griːt] *vt (welcome)* dar la bienvenida a; *(receive: news)* recibir; ~**ing** *n (welcome)* bienvenida; ~**ing(s) card** *n* tarjeta de felicitación

grenade [grəˈneɪd] *n* granada

grew [gruː] *pt* of **grow**

grey [greɪ] *adj* gris; *(weather)* sombrío; ~**haired** *adj* canoso; ~**hound** *n* galgo

grid [grɪd] *n* reja; *(ELEC)* red *f*

grief [griːf] *n* dolor *m*, pena

grievance ['griːvəns] *n* motivo de queja, agravio

grieve [griːv] *vi* afligirse, acongojarse ♦ *vt* dar pena a; **to** ~ **for** llorar por

grievous ['griːvəs] *adj*: ~ **bodily harm** *(LAW)* daños *mpl* corporales graves

grill [grɪl] *n (on cooker)* parrilla; *(also: mixed* ~*)* parrillada ♦ *vt (BRIT)* asar a la parrilla; *(inf: question)* interrogar

grille [grɪl] *n* reja; *(AUT)* rejilla

grim [grɪm] *adj (place)* sombrío; *(situation)* triste; *(person)* ceñudo

grimace [grɪˈmeɪs] *n* mueca ♦ *vi* hacer muecas

grime [graɪm] *n* mugre *f*, suciedad *f*

grin [grɪn] *n* sonrisa abierta ♦ *vi* sonreír abiertamente

grind [graɪnd] *(pt, pp* **ground)** *vt (coffee, pepper etc)* moler; *(US: meat)* picar; *(make sharp)* afilar ♦ *n (work)* rutina

grip [grɪp] *n (hold)* asimiento; *(control)* control *m*, dominio; *(of tyre etc)*: **to have a**

good/bad ~ agarrarse bien/mal; *(handle)* asidero; *(holdall)* maletín *m* ♦ *vt* agarrar; *(viewer, reader)* fascinar; **to get to** ~**s with** enfrentarse con; ~**ping** *adj* absorbente

grisly ['grɪzlɪ] *adj* horripilante, horrible

gristle ['grɪsl] *n* ternilla

grit [grɪt] *n* gravilla; *(courage)* valor *m* ♦ *vt (road)* poner gravilla en; **to** ~ **one's teeth** apretar los dientes

groan [grəʊn] *n* gemido; quejido ♦ *vi* gemir, quejarse

grocer ['grəʊsə*] *n* tendero *(de ultramarinos (SP))*; ~**ies** *npl* comestibles *mpl*; ~'**s (shop)** *n* tienda de ultramarinos *or* de abarrotes *(AM)*

groggy ['grɒgɪ] *adj* atontado

groin [grɔɪn] *n* ingle *f*

groom [gruːm] *n* mozo/a de cuadra; *(also: bride~)* novio ♦ *vt (horse)* almohazar; *(fig)*: **to** ~ **sb for** preparar a uno para; **well-~ed** de buena presencia

groove [gruːv] *n* ranura, surco

grope [grəʊp] : **to** ~ **for** *vt fus* buscar a tientas

gross [grəʊs] *adj (neglect, injustice)* grave; *(vulgar: behaviour)* grosero; *(: appearance)* de mal gusto; *(COMM)* bruto; ~**ly** *adv (greatly)* enormemente

grotesque [grəˈtɛsk] *adj* grotesco

grotto ['grɒtəʊ] *n* gruta

grotty ['grɒtɪ] *(inf)* *adj* horrible

ground [graʊnd] *pt, pp* of **grind** ♦ *n* suelo; tierra; *(SPORT)* campo, terreno; *(reason: gen pl)* causa, razón *f*; *(US: also:* ~ **wire)** tierra ♦ *vt (plane)* mantener en tierra; *(US: ELEC)* conectar con tierra; ~**s** *npl (of coffee etc)* poso; *(gardens etc)* jardines *mpl*, parque *m*; **on the** ~ en el suelo; **to the** ~ al suelo; **to gain/lose** ~ ganar/perder terreno; ~ **cloth** *(US)* *n* = ~**sheet**; ~**ing** *n (in education)* conocimientos *mpl* básicos; ~**less** *adj* infundado; ~**sheet** *(BRIT)* *n* tela impermeable; suelo; ~ **staff** *n* personal *m* de tierra; ~**swell** *n (of opinion)* marejada; ~**work** *n* preparación *f*

group [gruːp] *n* grupo; *(musical)* conjunto ♦ *vt (also:* ~ **together)** agrupar ♦ *vi (also:* ~ **together)** agruparse

grouse [graʊs] *n inv (bird)* urogallo ♦ *vi (complain)* quejarse

grove [grəʊv] *n* arboleda

grovel ['grɒvl] *vi (fig)*: **to** ~ **before** humillarse ante

grow [grəʊ] *(pt* **grew,** *pp* **grown)** *vi* crecer; *(increase)* aumentar; *(expand)* desarrollarse; *(become)* volverse; **to** ~ **rich/weak** enriquecerse/debilitarse ♦ *vt* cultivar; *(hair, beard)* dejar crecer; ~ **up** *vi* crecer, hacerse hombre/mujer; ~**er** *n* cultivador(a) *m/f*, productor(a) *m/f*; ~**ing** *adj* creciente

growl [graʊl] *vi* gruñir

grown [grəʊn] *pp* of **grow**; ~**-up** *n* adulto,

mayor *m/f*
growth [grəuθ] *n* crecimiento, desarrollo; (*what has grown*) brote *m*; (*MED*) tumor *m*
grub [grʌb] *n* larva, gusano; (*inf: food*) comida
grubby ['grʌbɪ] *adj* sucio, mugriento
grudge [grʌdʒ] *n* (motivo de) rencor *m* ♦ *vt*: **to ~ sb sth** dar algo a uno de mala gana; **to bear sb a ~** guardar rencor a uno
gruelling ['gruəlɪŋ] *adj* penoso, duro
gruesome ['gru:səm] *adj* horrible
gruff [grʌf] *adj* (*voice*) ronco; (*manner*) brusco
grumble ['grʌmbl] *vi* refunfuñar, quejarse
grumpy ['grʌmpɪ] *adj* gruñón/ona
grunt [grʌnt] *vi* gruñir
G-string ['dʒi:strɪŋ] *n* taparrabo
guarantee [gærən'ti:] *n* garantía ♦ *vt* garantizar
guard [gɑ:d] *n* (*squad*) guardia; (*one man*) guardia *m*; (*BRIT: RAIL*) jefe *m* de tren; (*on machine*) dispositivo de seguridad; (*also: fire~*) rejilla de protección ♦ *vt* guardar; (*prisoner*) vigilar; **to be on one's ~** estar alerta; **~ against** *vt fus* (*prevent*) protegerse de; **~ed** *adj* (*fig*) cauteloso; **~ian** *n* guardián/ana *m/f*; (*of minor*) tutor(a) *m/f*; **~'s van** *n* (*BRIT: RAIL*) furgón *m*
Guatemala [gwætɪ'mɑ:lə] *n* Guatemala; **~n** *adj*, *n* guatemalteco/a *m/f*
guerrilla [gə'rɪlə] *n* guerrillero/a
guess [ges] *vi* adivinar; (*US*) suponer ♦ *vt* adivinar; suponer ♦ *n* suposición *f*, conjetura; **to take or have a ~** tratar de adivinar; **~work** *n* conjeturas *fpl*
guest [gest] *n* invitado/a, (*in hotel*) huésped(a) *m/f*; **~-house** *n* casa de huéspedes, pensión *f*; **~ room** *n* cuarto de huéspedes
guffaw [gʌ'fɔ:] *vi* reírse a carcajadas
guidance ['gaɪdəns] *n* (*advice*) consejos *mpl*
guide [gaɪd] *n* (*person*) guía *m/f*; (*book, fig*) guía ♦ *vt* (*round museum etc*) guiar; (*direct*) orientar; (*girl*) **~** *n* exploradora; **~book** *n* guía; **~ dog** *n* perro *m* guía; **~lines** *npl* (*advice*) directrices *fpl*
guild [gɪld] *n* gremio
guile [gaɪl] *n* astucia
guillotine ['gɪlətiːn] *n* guillotina
guilt [gɪlt] *n* culpabilidad *f*; **~y** *adj* culpable
guinea ['gɪnɪ] (*BRIT*) *n* (*old*) guinea (= 21 chelines)
guinea pig *n* cobaya; (*fig*) conejillo de Indias
guise [gaɪz] *n*: **in** *or* **under the ~ of** bajo apariencia de
guitar [gɪ'tɑ:*] *n* guitarra
gulf [gʌlf] *n* golfo; (*abyss*) abismo
gull [gʌl] *n* gaviota
gullet ['gʌlɪt] *n* esófago
gullible ['gʌlɪbl] *adj* crédulo
gully ['gʌlɪ] *n* barranco
gulp [gʌlp] *vi* tragar saliva ♦ *vt* (*also: ~*

down) tragarse
gum [gʌm] *n* (*ANAT*) encía; (*glue*) goma, cemento; (*sweet*) caramelo de goma; (*also: chewing-~*) chicle *m* ♦ *vt* pegar con goma; **~boots** (*BRIT*) *npl* botas *fpl* de goma
gumption ['gʌmpʃən] *n* sentido común
gun [gʌn] *n* (*small*) pistola, revólver *m*; (*shotgun*) escopeta; (*rifle*) fusil *m*; (*cannon*) cañón *m*; **~boat** *n* cañonero; **~fire** *n* disparos *mpl*; **~man** *n* pistolero; **~point** *n*: **at ~point** a mano armada; **~powder** *n* pólvora; **~shot** *n* escopetazo
gurgle ['gə:gl] *vi* (*baby*) gorgotear; (*water*) borbotear
gush [gʌʃ] *vi* salir a raudales; (*person*) deshacerse en efusiones
gust [gʌst] *n* (*of wind*) ráfaga
gusto ['gʌstəu] *n* entusiasmo
gut [gʌt] *n* intestino; **~s** *npl* (*ANAT*) tripas *fpl*; (*courage*) valor *m*
gutter ['gʌtə*] *n* (*of roof*) canalón *m*; (*in street*) cuneta
guy [gaɪ] *n* (*also: ~rope*) cuerda; (*inf: man*) tío (*SP*), tipo; (*also: G~ Fawkes*) monigote *m*
guzzle ['gʌzl] *vi* tragar ♦ *vt* engullir
gym [dʒɪm] *n* (*also: gymnasium*) gimnasio; (*also: gymnastics*) gimnasia; **~nast** *n* gimnasta *m/f*; **~ shoes** *npl* zapatillas *fpl* (de deporte); **~ slip** (*BRIT*) *n* túnica de colegiala
gynaecologist [gaɪnɪ'kɒlədʒɪst] (*US* **gynecologist**) *n* ginecólogo/a
gypsy ['dʒɪpsɪ] *n* gitano/a
gyrate [dʒaɪ'reɪt] *vi* girar

--- *H h*

haberdashery [hæbə'dæʃərɪ] (*BRIT*) *n* mercería
habit ['hæbɪt] *n* hábito, costumbre *f*; (*drug ~*) adicción *f*; (*costume*) hábito
habitual [hə'bɪtjuəl] *adj* acostumbrado, habitual; (*drinker, liar*) empedernido
hack [hæk] *vt* (*cut*) cortar; (*slice*) tajar ♦ *n* (*pej: writer*) escritor(a) *m/f* a sueldo; **~er** *n* (*COMPUT*) pirata *m/f* informático
hackneyed ['hæknɪd] *adj* trillado
had [hæd] *pt*, *pp* of **have**
haddock ['hædək] (*pl* **~** *or* **~s**) *n* especie de merluza
hadn't ['hædnt] = **had not**
haemorrhage ['hemərɪdʒ] (*US* **hemor-**

rhage) *n* hemorragia
haemorrhoids ['hemərɔɪdz] (*US* **hemorrhoids**) *npl* hemorroides *fpl*
haggard ['hægəd] *adj* ojeroso
haggle ['hægl] *vi* regatear
Hague [heɪg] *n*: **The ~** La Haya
hail [heɪl] *n* granizo; (*fig*) lluvia ♦ *vt* saludar; (*taxi*) llamar a; (*acclaim*) aclamar ♦ *vi* granizar; **~stone** *n* (piedra de) granizo
hair [heə*] *n* pelo, cabellos *mpl*; (*one ~*) pelo, cabello; (*on legs etc*) vello; **to do one's ~** arreglarse el pelo; **to have grey ~** tener canas *fpl*; **~brush** *n* cepillo (para el pelo); **~cut** *n* corte *m* (de pelo); **~do** *n* peinado; **~dresser** *n* peluquero/a; **~dresser's** *n* peluquería; **~dryer** *n* secador *m* de pelo; **~grip** *n* horquilla; **~net** *n* redecilla; **~piece** *n* postizo; **~pin** *n* horquilla; **~pin bend** (*US* **~pin curve**) *n* curva de horquilla; **~raising** *adj* espeluznante; **~ removing cream** *n* crema depilatoria; **~spray** *n* laca; **~style** *n* peinado; **~y** *adj* peludo; velludo; (*inf: frightening*) espeluznante
hake [heɪk] (*pl inv or* **~s**) *n* merluza
half [hɑːf] (*pl* **halves**) *n* mitad *f*; (*of beer*) ≈ caña (*SP*); media pinta; (*RAIL, BUS*) billete *m* de niño ♦ *adj* medio ♦ *adv* medio, a medias; **two and a ~** dos y media; **~ a dozen** media docena; **~ a pound** media libra; **to cut sth in ~** cortar algo por la mitad; **~-caste** *n* mestizo/a; **~-hearted** *adj* indiferente, poco entusiasta; **~-hour** *n* media hora; **~-mast** *n*: **at ~-mast** (*flag*) a media asta; **~-price** *adj, adv* a mitad de precio; **~ term** (*BRIT*) *n* (*SCOL*) vacaciones de mediados del trimestre; **~-time** *n* descanso; **~way** *adv* a medio camino; (*in period of time*) a mitad de
hall [hɔːl] *n* (*for concerts*) sala; (*entrance way*) hall *m*; vestíbulo; **~ of residence** (*BRIT*) *n* residencia
hallmark ['hɔːlmɑːk] *n* sello
hallo [hə'ləu] *excl* = **hello**
Hallowe'en [hæləu'iːn] *n* víspera de Todos los Santos
hallucination [həluːsɪ'neɪʃən] *n* alucinación *f*
hallway ['hɔːlweɪ] *n* vestíbulo
halo ['heɪləu] *n* (*of saint*) halo, aureola
halt [hɔːlt] *n* (*stop*) alto, parada ♦ *vt* parar; interrumpir ♦ *vi* pararse
halve [hɑːv] *vt* partir por la mitad
halves [hɑːvz] *npl of* **half**
ham [hæm] *n* jamón *m* (cocido)
hamburger ['hæmbə:gə*] *n* hamburguesa
hamlet ['hæmlɪt] *n* aldea
hammer ['hæmə*] *n* martillo ♦ *vt* (*nail*) clavar; (*force*): **to ~ an idea into sb/a message across** meter una idea en la cabeza a uno/machacar una idea ♦ *vi* dar golpes
hammock ['hæmək] *n* hamaca

hamper ['hæmpə*] *vt* estorbar ♦ *n* cesto
hand [hænd] *n* mano *f*; (*of clock*) aguja; (*writing*) letra; (*worker*) obrero ♦ *vt* dar, pasar; **to give** *or* **lend sb a ~** echar una mano a uno, ayudar a uno; **at ~** a mano; **in ~** (*time*) libre; (*job etc*) entre manos; **on ~** (*person, services*) a mano, al alcance; **to ~** (*information etc*) a mano; **on the one ~ ..., on the other ~ ...** por una parte ... por otra (parte) ...; **~ in** *vt* entregar; **~ out** *vt* distribuir; **~ over** *vt* (*deliver*) entregar; **~bag** *n* bolso (*SP*), cartera (*AM*); **~book** *n* manual *m*; **~brake** *n* freno de mano; **~cuffs** *npl* esposas *fpl*; **~ful** *n* puñado
handicap ['hændɪkæp] *n* minusvalía; (*disadvantage*) desventaja; (*SPORT*) handicap *m* ♦ *vt* estorbar; **mentally/physically ~ped** deficiente *m/f* (mental)/minusválido/a (físico/a)
handicraft ['hændɪkrɑːft] *n* artesanía; (*object*) objeto de artesanía
handiwork ['hændɪwəːk] *n* obra
handkerchief ['hæŋkətʃɪf] *n* pañuelo
handle ['hændl] *n* (*of door etc*) tirador *m*; (*of cup etc*) asa; (*of knife etc*) mango; (*for winding*) manivela ♦ *vt* (*touch*) tocar; (*deal with*) encargarse de; (*treat: people*) manejar; **"~ with care"** "(manéjele) con cuidado"; **to fly off the ~** perder los estribos; **~bar(s)** *n(pl)* manillar *m*
hand: **~luggage** *n* equipaje *m* de mano; **~made** ['hændmeɪd] *adj* hecho a mano; **~out** ['hændaut] *n* (*money etc*) limosna; (*leaflet*) folleto; **~rail** ['hændreɪl] *n* pasamanos *m inv*; **~shake** ['hændʃeɪk] *n* apretón *m* de manos
handsome ['hænsəm] *adj* guapo; (*building*) bello; (*fig: profit*) considerable
handwriting ['hændraɪtɪŋ] *n* letra
handy ['hændɪ] *adj* (*close at hand*) a la mano; (*tool etc*) práctico; (*skilful*) hábil, diestro; **~man** *n* manitas *m inv*
hang [hæŋ] (*pt, pp* **hung**) *vt* colgar; (*criminal: pt, pp* **hanged**) ahorcar ♦ *vi* (*painting, coat etc*) colgar; (*hair, drapery*) caer; **to get the ~ of sth** (*inf*) lograr dominar algo; **~ about** *or* **around** *vi* haraganear; **~ on** *vi* (*wait*) esperar; **~ up** *vi* (*TEL*) colgar ♦ *vt* colgar
hanger ['hæŋə*] *n* percha; **~-on** *n* parásito
hang-gliding ['-glaɪdɪŋ] *n* vuelo libre
hangover ['hæŋəuvə*] *n* (*after drinking*) resaca
hang-up *n* complejo
hanker ['hæŋkə*] *vi*: **to ~ after** añorar
hankie ['hæŋkɪ], **hanky** ['hæŋkɪ] *n abbr* = **handkerchief**
haphazard [hæp'hæzəd] *adj* fortuito
happen ['hæpən] *vi* suceder, ocurrir; (*chance*): **to ~ed to hear/see** dió la casualidad de que oyó/vió; **as it ~s** da la casualidad de que; **~ing** *n* suceso, acontecimiento

happily ['hæpɪlɪ] *adv* (*luckily*) afortunadamente; (*cheerfully*) alegremente

happiness ['hæpɪnɪs] *n* felicidad *f*; (*cheerfulness*) alegría

happy ['hæpɪ] *adj* feliz; (*cheerful*) alegre; **to be ~ (with)** estar contento (con); **to be ~ to do** estar encantado de hacer; **~ birthday!** ¡feliz cumpleaños!; **~-go-lucky** *adj* despreocupado

harass ['hærəs] *vt* acosar, hostigar; **~ment** *n* persecución *f*

harbour ['hɑːbə*] (*US* **harbor**) *n* puerto *m* ◆ *vt* (*fugitive*) dar abrigo a; (*hope etc*) abrigar

hard [hɑːd] *adj* duro; (*difficult*) difícil; (*work*) arduo; (*person*) severo; (*fact*) innegable ◆ *adv* (*work*) mucho, duro; (*think*) profundamente; **to look ~ at** clavar los ojos en; **to try ~** esforzarse; **no ~ feelings!** ¡sin rencor(es)!; **to be ~ of hearing** ser duro de oído; **to be ~ done by** ser tratado injustamente; **~back** *n* libro en cartoné; **~ cash** *n* dinero contante; **~ disk** *n* (*COMPUT*) disco duro *or* rígido; **~en** *vt* endurecer; (*fig*) curtir ◆ *vi* endurecerse; curtirse; **~-headed** *adj* realista; **~ labour** *n* trabajos *mpl* forzados

hardly ['hɑːdlɪ] *adv* apenas; **~ ever** casi nunca

hardship ['hɑːdʃɪp] *n* privación *f*

hard-up (*inf*) *adj* sin un duro (*SP*), sin plata (*AM*)

hardware ['hɑːdwɛə*] *n* ferretería; (*COMPUT*) hardware *m*; (*MIL*) armamento; **~ shop** *n* ferretería

hard-wearing *adj* resistente, duradero

hard-working *adj* trabajador(a)

hardy ['hɑːdɪ] *adj* fuerte; (*plant*) resistente

hare [hɛə*] *n* liebre *f*; **~-brained** *adj* descabellado

harem [hɑː'riːm] *n* harén *m*

harm [hɑːm] *n* daño, mal *m* ◆ *vt* (*person*) hacer daño a; (*health, interests*) perjudicar; (*thing*) dañar; **out of ~'s way** a salvo; **~ful** *adj* dañino; **~less** *adj* (*person*) inofensivo; (*joke etc*) inocente

harmony ['hɑːmənɪ] *n* armonía

harness ['hɑːnɪs] *n* arreos *mpl*; (*for child*) arnés *m*; (*safety ~*) arneses *mpl* ◆ *vt* (*horse*) enjaezar; (*resources*) aprovechar

harp [hɑːp] *n* arpa ◆ *vi*: **to ~ on (about)** machacar (con)

harpoon [hɑː'puːn] *n* arpón *m*

harrowing ['hærəʊɪŋ] *adj* angustioso

harsh [hɑːʃ] *adj* (*cruel*) duro, cruel; (*severe*) severo; (*sound*) áspero; (*light*) deslumbrador(a)

harvest ['hɑːvɪst] *n* (*~ time*) siega; (*of cereals etc*) cosecha; (*of grapes*) vendimia ◆ *vt* cosechar

has [hæz] *vb see* **have**

hash [hæʃ] *n* (*CULIN*) picadillo; (*fig: mess*) lío

hashish ['hæʃɪʃ] *n* hachís *m*

hasn't ['hæznt] = **has not**

hassle ['hæsl] (*inf*) *n* lata

haste [heɪst] *n* prisa; **~n** ['heɪsn] *vt* acelerar ◆ *vi* darse prisa; **hastily** *adv* de prisa; precipitadamente; **hasty** *adj* apresurado; (*rash*) precipitado

hat [hæt] *n* sombrero

hatch [hætʃ] *n* (*NAUT: also:* **~way**) escotilla; (*also: service ~*) ventanilla ◆ *vi* (*bird*) salir del cascarón ◆ *vt* incubar; (*plot*) tramar; **5 eggs have ~ed** han salido 5 pollos

hatchback ['hætʃbæk] *n* (*AUT*) tres *or* cinco puertas *m*

hatchet ['hætʃɪt] *n* hacha

hate [heɪt] *vt* odiar, aborrecer ◆ *n* odio; **~ful** *adj* odioso; **hatred** ['heɪtrɪd] *n* odio

haughty ['hɔːtɪ] *adj* altanero

haul [hɔːl] *vt* tirar ◆ *n* (*of fish*) redada; (*of stolen goods etc*) botín *m*; **~age** (*BRIT*) *n* transporte *m*; (*costs*) gastos *mpl* de transporte; **~ier** (*US* **~er**) *n* transportista *m/f*

haunch [hɔːntʃ] *n* anca; (*of meat*) pierna

haunt [hɔːnt] *vt* (*subj: ghost*) aparecerse en; (*obsess*) obsesionar ◆ *n* guarida

─────────────── **KEYWORD**

have [hæv] (*pt, pp* **had**) *aux vb* **1** (*gen*) haber; **to ~ arrived/eaten** haber llegado/comido; **having finished** *or* **when he had finished, he left** cuando hubo acabado, se fue

2 (*in tag questions*): **you've done it, ~n't you?** lo has hecho, ¿verdad? *or* ¿no?

3 (*in short answers and questions*): **I ~n't** no; **so I ~** pues, es verdad; **we ~n't paid — yes we ~!** no hemos pagado — ¡sí que hemos pagado!; **I've been there before, ~ you?** he estado allí antes, ¿y tú?

◆ *modal aux vb* (*be obliged*): **to ~ (got) to do sth** tener que hacer algo; **you ~n't to tell her** no hay *que* *or* no debes decírselo

◆ *vt* **1** (*possess*): **he has (got) blue eyes/dark hair** tiene los ojos azules/el pelo negro

2 (*referring to meals etc*): **to ~ breakfast/lunch/dinner** desayunar/comer/cenar; **to ~ a drink/a cigarette** tomar algo/fumar un cigarrillo

3 (*receive*) recibir; (*obtain*) obtener; **may I ~ your address?** ¿puedes darme tu dirección?; **you can ~ it for £5** te lo puedes quedar por £5; **I must ~ it by tomorrow** lo necesito para mañana; **to ~ a baby** tener un niño *or* bebé

4 (*maintain, allow*): **I won't ~ it/this nonsense!** ¡no lo permitiré!/¡no permitiré estas tonterías!; **we can't ~ that** no podemos permitir eso

5: **to ~ sth done** hacer *or* mandar hacer algo; **to ~ one's hair cut** cortarse el pelo; **to ~ sb do sth** hacer que alguien haga

algo
6 (*experience, suffer*): **to ~ a cold/flu** tener un resfriado/la gripe; **she had her bag stolen/her arm broken** le robaron el bolso/se rompió un brazo; **to ~ an operation** operarse
7 (*+ noun*): **to ~ a swim/walk/bath/rest** nadar/dar un paseo/darse un baño/descansar; **let's ~ a look** vamos a ver; **to ~ a meeting/party** celebrar una reunión/una fiesta; **let me ~ a try** déjame intentarlo
have out vt: **to ~ it out with sb** (*settle a problem etc*) dejar las cosas en claro con alguien

haven ['heɪvn] n puerto; (*fig*) refugio
haven't ['hævnt] = **have not**
haversack ['hævəsæk] n mochila
havoc ['hævək] n estragos mpl
hawk [hɔːk] n halcón m
hay [heɪ] n heno; **~ fever** n fiebre f del heno; **~stack** n almiar m
haywire ['heɪwaɪə*] (*inf*) adj: **to go ~** (*plan*) embrollarse
hazard ['hæzəd] n peligro ♦ vt aventurar; **~ous** adj peligroso; **~ warning lights** npl (*AUT*) señales fpl de emergencia
haze [heɪz] n neblina
hazelnut ['heɪzlnʌt] n avellana
hazy ['heɪzɪ] adj brumoso; (*idea*) vago
he [hiː] pron él; **~ who ...** él que ..., quien ...

head [hɛd] n cabeza; (*leader*) jefe/a m/f; (*of school*) director(a) m/f ♦ vt (*list*) encabezar; (*group*) capitanear; (*company*) dirigir; **~s (or tails)** cara (o cruz); **~ first** de cabeza; **~ over heels** (*in love*) perdidamente; **to ~ the ball** cabecear (la pelota); **~ for** vt fus dirigirse a; (*disaster*) ir camino de; **~ache** n dolor m de cabeza; **~dress** n tocado; **~ing** n título; **~lamp** (*BRIT*) n = **~light**; **~land** n promontorio; **~light** n faro; **~line** n titular m; **~long** adv (*fall*) de cabeza; (*rush*) precipitadamente; **~master/mistress** n director(a) m/f (de escuela); **~office** n oficina central, central f; **~-on** adj (*collision*) de frente; **~phones** npl auriculares mpl; **~quarters** npl sede f central; (*MIL*) cuartel m general; **~-rest** n reposacabezas m inv; **~room** n (*in car*) altura f interior; (*under bridge*) (límite m de) altura; **~scarf** n pañuelo; **~strong** adj testarudo; **~ waiter** n maître m; **~way** n: **to make ~way** (*fig*) hacer progresos; **~wind** n viento contrario; **~y** adj (*experience, period*) apasionante; (*wine*) cabezón; (*atmosphere*) embriagador(a)
heal [hiːl] vt curar ♦ vi cicatrizarse
health [hɛlθ] n salud f; **~ food** n alimentos mpl orgánicos; **the H~ Service** (*BRIT*) n el servicio de salud pública; ≈ el Insalud

(*SP*); **~y** adj sano, saludable
heap [hiːp] n montón m ♦ vt: **to ~ (up)** amontonar; **to ~ sth with** llenar algo hasta arriba de; **~s of** un montón de.
hear [hɪə*] (*pt, pp* heard) vt (*also LAW*) oír; (*news*) saber ♦ vi oír; **to ~ about** oír hablar de; **to ~ from sb** tener noticias de uno; **heard** [hɜːd] pt, pp of **hear**; **~ing** n (*sense*) oído; (*LAW*) vista; **~ing aid** n audífono; **~say** n rumores mpl, habladurías fpl
hearse [hɜːs] n coche m fúnebre
heart [hɑːt] n corazón m; (*fig*) valor m; (*of lettuce*) cogollo; **~s** npl (*CARDS*) corazones mpl; **to lose/take ~** descorazonarse/cobrar ánimo; **at ~** en el fondo; **by ~** (*learn, know*) de memoria; **~ attack** n infarto (de miocardio); **~beat** n latido (del corazón); **~breaking** adj desgarrador(a); **~broken** adj: **she was ~broken about it** esto le partió el corazón; **~burn** n acedía; **~ failure** n fallo cardíaco; **~felt** adj (*deeply felt*) más sentido
hearth [hɑːθ] n (*fireplace*) chimenea
heartless ['hɑːtlɪs] adj cruel
hearty ['hɑːtɪ] adj (*person*) campechano; (*laugh*) sano; (*dislike, support*) absoluto
heat [hiːt] n calor m; (*SPORT: also: qualifying ~*) prueba eliminatoria ♦ vt calentar; **~ up** vi calentarse ♦ vt calentar; **~ed** adj caliente; (*fig*) acalorado; **~er** n estufa; (*in car*) calefacción f
heath [hiːθ] (*BRIT*) n brezal m
heather ['hɛðə*] n brezo
heating ['hiːtɪŋ] n calefacción f
heatstroke ['hiːtstrəuk] n insolación f
heatwave ['hiːtweɪv] n ola de calor
heave [hiːv] vt (*pull*) tirar; (*push*) empujar con esfuerzo; (*lift*) levantar (con esfuerzo) ♦ vi (*chest*) palpitar; (*retch*) tener náuseas ♦ n tirón m; empujón m; **to ~ a sigh** suspirar
heaven ['hɛvn] n cielo; (*fig*) una maravilla; **~ly** adj (*fig*) maravilloso
heavily ['hɛvɪlɪ] adv pesadamente; (*drink, smoke*) con exceso; (*sleep, sigh*) profundamente; (*depend*) mucho
heavy ['hɛvɪ] adj pesado; (*work, blow*) duro; (*sea, rain, meal*) fuerte; (*drinker, smoker*) grande; (*responsibility*) grave; (*schedule*) ocupado; (*weather*) bochornoso; **~ goods vehicle** n vehículo pesado; **~weight** n (*SPORT*) peso pesado
Hebrew ['hiːbruː] adj, n (*LING*) hebreo
heckle ['hɛkl] vt interrumpir
hectic ['hɛktɪk] adj agitado
he'd [hiːd] = **he would**; **he had**
hedge [hɛdʒ] n seto ♦ vi contestar con evasivas; **to ~ one's bets** (*fig*) cubrirse
hedgehog ['hɛdʒhɒg] n erizo
heed [hiːd] vt (*also: take ~ of*) (*pay attention to*) hacer caso de; **~less** adj: **to be ~less (of)** no hacer caso de
heel [hiːl] n talón m; (*of shoe*) tacón m ♦ vt

(shoe) poner tacón a
hefty ['heftɪ] *adj (person)* fornido; *(parcel, profit)* gordo
heifer ['hefə*] *n* novilla, ternera
height [haɪt] *n (of person)* estatura; *(of building)* altura; *(high ground)* cerro; *(altitude)* altitud *f*; *(fig: of season)*: **at the ~ of winter** en pleno invierno; *(: of power etc)* cúspide *f*; *(: of stupidity etc)* colmo; **~en** *vt* elevar; *(fig)* aumentar
heir [ɛə*] *n* heredero; **~ess** *n* heredera; **~loom** *n* reliquia de familia
held [held] *pt, pp of* **hold**
helicopter ['helɪkɔptə*] *n* helicóptero
helium ['hiːlɪəm] *n* helio
hell [hel] *n* infierno; **~!** *(inf)* ¡demonios!
he'll [hiːl] = **he will; he shall**
hello [hə'ləʊ] *excl* ¡hola!; *(to attract attention)* ¡oiga!; *(surprise)* ¡caramba!
helm [helm] *n (NAUT)* timón *m*
helmet ['helmɪt] *n* casco
help [help] *n* ayuda; *(cleaner etc)* criada, asistenta ♦ *vt* ayudar; **~!** ¡socorro!; **~ yourself** sírvete; **he can't ~ it** no es culpa suya; **~er** *n* ayudante *m/f*; **~ful** *adj* útil; *(person)* servicial; *(advice)* útil; **~ing** *n* ración *f*; **~less** *adj (incapable)* incapaz; *(defenceless)* indefenso
hem [hem] *n* dobladillo ♦ *vt* poner *or* coser el dobladillo; **~ in** *vt* cercar
hemorrhage ['hemərɪdʒ] *(US)* *n* = **haemorrhage**
hemorrhoids ['hemərɔɪdz] *(US)* *npl* = **haemorrhoids**
hen [hen] *n* gallina; *(female bird)* hembra
hence [hens] *adv (therefore)* por lo tanto; **2 years ~** de aquí a 2 años; **~forth** *adv* de hoy en adelante
henchman ['hentʃmən] *(pej)* *n* secuaz *m*
hepatitis [hepə'taɪtɪs] *n* hepatitis *f*
her [həː*] *pron (direct)* la; *(indirect)* le; *(stressed, after prep)* ella ♦ *adj* su; *see also* **me, my**
herald ['herəld] *n* heraldo ♦ *vt* anunciar; **~ry** *n* heráldica
herb [həːb] *n* hierba
herd [həːd] *n* rebaño
here [hɪə*] *adv* aquí; *(at this point)* en este punto; **~!** *(present)* ¡presente!; **~ is/are** aquí está/están; **~ she is** aquí está; **~after** *adv* en el futuro; **~by** *adv (in letter)* por la presente
heredity [hɪ'redɪtɪ] *n* herencia
heritage ['herɪtɪdʒ] *n* patrimonio
hermit ['həːmɪt] *n* ermitaño/a
hernia ['həːnɪə] *n* hernia
hero ['hɪərəʊ] *(pl* **~es)** *n* héroe *m*; *(in book, film)* protagonista *m*; **~ic** [hɪ'rəʊɪk] *adj* heroico
heroin ['herəʊɪn] *n* heroína
heroine ['herəʊɪn] *n* heroína; *(in book, film)* protagonista

heron ['herən] *n* garza
herring ['herɪŋ] *n* arenque *m*
hers [həːz] *pron* (el) suyo/(la) suya *etc*; *see also* **mine**[1]
herself [həː'self] *pron (reflexive)* se; *(emphatic)* ella misma; *(after prep)* sí (misma); *see also* **oneself**
he's [hiːz] = **he is; he has**
hesitant ['hezɪtənt] *adj* vacilante
hesitate ['hezɪteɪt] *vi* vacilar; *(in speech)* titubear; *(be unwilling)* resistirse a; **hesitation** ['-teɪʃən] *n* indecisión *f*; titubeo; dudas *fpl*
heterosexual [hetərəʊ'seksjʊəl] *adj* heterosexual
hew [hjuː] *vt (stone, wood)* labrar
heyday ['heɪdeɪ] *n*: **the ~ of** el apogeo de
HGV *n abbr* = **heavy goods vehicle**
hi [haɪ] *excl* ¡hola!; *(to attract attention)* ¡oiga!
hiatus [haɪ'eɪtəs] *n* vacío
hibernate ['haɪbəneɪt] *vi* invernar
hiccough ['hɪkʌp] = **hiccup**
hiccup ['hɪkʌp] *vi* hipar; **~s** *npl* hipo
hide [haɪd] *(pt* **hid**, *pp* **hidden)** *n (skin)* piel *f* ♦ *vt* esconder, ocultar ♦ *vi*: **to ~ (from sb)** esconderse *or* ocultarse (de uno); **~- and-seek** *n* escondite *m*; **~away** *n* escondrijo
hideous ['hɪdɪəs] *adj* horrible
hiding ['haɪdɪŋ] *n (beating)* paliza; **to be in ~** *(concealed)* estar escondido
hierarchy ['haɪərɑːkɪ] *n* jerarquía
hi-fi ['haɪfaɪ] *n* estéreo, hifi *m* ♦ *adj* de alta fidelidad
high [haɪ] *adj* alto; *(speed, number)* grande; *(price)* elevado; *(wind)* fuerte; *(voice)* agudo ♦ *adv* alto, a gran altura; **it is 20 m ~** tiene 20 m de altura; **~ in the air** en las alturas; **~brow** *adj* intelectual; **~chair** *n* silla alta; **~er education** *n* educación *f or* enseñanza superior; **~-handed** *adj* despótico; **~-heeled** *adj* de tacón alto; **~ jump** *n (SPORT)* salto de altura; **the H~lands** *npl* las tierras altas de Escocia; **~light** *n (fig: of event)* punto culminante; *(in hair)* reflejo ♦ *vt* subrayar; **~ly** *adv (paid)* muy bien; *(critical, confidential)* sumamente; *(a lot)*: **to speak/think ~ly of** hablar muy bien de/tener en mucho a; **~ly strung** *adj* hipertenso; **~ness** *n* altura; **Her** *or* **His H~ness** Su Alteza; **~-pitched** *adj* agudo; **~-rise block** *n* torre *f* de pisos; **~ school** *n* ≈ Instituto Nacional de Bachillerato *(SP)*; **~ season** *(BRIT)* *n* temporada alta; **~ street** *(BRIT)* *n* calle *f* mayor; **~way** *n* carretera; *(US)* carretera nacional; autopista; **H~way Code** *(BRIT)* *n* código de la circulación
hijack ['haɪdʒæk] *vt* secuestrar; **~er** *n* secuestrador(a) *m/f*
hike [haɪk] *vi (go walking)* ir de excursión (a pie) ♦ *n* caminata; **~r** *n* excursionista

m/f
hilarious [hɪ'lɛərɪəs] *adj* divertidísimo
hill [hɪl] *n* colina; *(high)* montaña; *(slope)* cuesta; **~side** *n* ladera; **~y** *adj* montañoso
hilt [hɪlt] *n (of sword)* empuñadura; **to the ~** *(fig: support)* incondicionalmente
him [hɪm] *pron (direct)* le, lo; *(indirect)* le; *(stressed, after prep)* él; *see also* **me**; **~self** *pron (reflexive)* se; *(emphatic)* él mismo; *(after prep)* sí (mismo); *see also* **oneself**
hind [haɪnd] *adj* posterior
hinder ['hɪndə*] *vt* estorbar, impedir; **hindrance** ['hɪndrəns] *n* estorbo
hindsight ['haɪndsaɪt] *n*: **with ~** en retrospectiva
Hindu ['hɪndu:] *n* hindú *m/f*
hinge [hɪndʒ] *n* bisagra, gozne ♦ *vi (fig)*: **to ~ on** depender de
hint [hɪnt] *n* indirecta; *(advice)* consejo; *(sign)* dejo ♦ *vt*: **to ~ that** insinuar que ♦ *vi*: **to ~ at** hacer alusión a
hip [hɪp] *n* cadera
hippopotamus [hɪpə'pɔtəməs] *(pl* **~es** *or* **-mi)** *n* hipopótamo
hire ['haɪə*] *vt (BRIT: car, equipment)* alquilar; *(worker)* contratar ♦ *n* alquiler *m*; **for ~** se alquila; *(taxi)* libre; **~ purchase** *(BRIT) n* compra a plazos
his [hɪz] *pron* (el) suyo/(la) suya *etc* ♦ *adj* su; *see also* **my, mine**[1]
Hispanic [hɪs'pænɪk] *adj* hispánico
hiss [hɪs] *vi* silbar
historian [hɪ'stɔːrɪən] *n* historiador(a) *m/f*
historic(al) [hɪ'stɔrɪk(l)] *adj* histórico
history ['hɪstərɪ] *n* historia
hit [hɪt] *(pt, pp* **hit)** *vt (strike)* golpear, pegar; *(reach: target)* alcanzar; *(collide with: car)* chocar contra; *(fig: affect)* afectar ♦ *n* golpe *m*; *(success)* éxito; **to ~ it off with sb** llevarse bien con uno; **~-and-run driver** *n conductor(a) que atropella y huye*
hitch [hɪtʃ] *vt (fasten)* atar, amarrar; *(also: ~ up)* remangar ♦ *n (difficulty)* dificultad *f*; **to ~ a lift** hacer autostop
hitch-hike *vi* hacer autostop; **~r** *n* autostopista *m/f*
hi-tech [haɪ'tɛk] *adj* de alta tecnología
hitherto [hɪðə'tu:] *adv* hasta ahora
HIV *n abbr* (= human immunodeficiency virus) VIH *m*; **~-negative/positive** *adj* VIH negativo/positivo
hive [haɪv] *n* colmena; **~ off** *(inf) vt (privatize)* privatizar
HMS *abbr* = **His (Her) Majesty's Ship**
hoard [hɔːd] *n (treasure)* tesoro; *(stockpile)* provisión *f* ♦ *vt* acumular; *(goods in short supply)* acaparar; **~ing** *n (for posters)* cartelera
hoarse [hɔːs] *adj* ronco
hoax [həuks] *n* trampa
hob [hɔb] *n* quemador *m*
hobble ['hɔbl] *vi* cojear

hobby ['hɔbɪ] *n* pasatiempo, afición *f*; **~-horse** *n (fig)* caballo de batalla
hobo ['həubəu] *(US) n* vagabundo
hockey ['hɔkɪ] *n* hockey *m*
hog [hɔg] *n* cerdo, puerco ♦ *vt (fig)* acaparar; **to go the whole ~** poner toda la carne en el asador
hoist [hɔɪst] *n (crane)* grúa ♦ *vt* levantar, alzar; *(flag, sail)* izar
hold [həuld] *(pt, pp* **held)** *vt* sostener; *(contain)* contener; *(have: power, qualification)* tener; *(keep back)* retener; *(believe)* sostener; *(consider)* considerar; *(keep in position)*: **to ~ one's head up** mantener la cabeza alta; *(meeting)* celebrar ♦ *vi (withstand pressure)* resistir; *(be valid)* valer ♦ *n (grasp)* asimiento; *(fig)* dominio; **~ the line!** *(TEL)* ¡no cuelgue!; **to ~ one's own** *(fig)* defenderse; **to catch** *or* **get (a) ~ of** agarrarse *or* asirse de; **~ back** *vt* retener; *(secret)* ocultar; **~ down** *vt (person)* sujetar; *(job)* mantener; **~ off** *vt (enemy)* rechazar; **~ on** *vi* agarrarse bien; *(wait)* esperar; **~ on!** *(TEL)* ¡(espere) un momento!; **~ on to** *vt fus* agarrarse a; *(keep)* guardar; **~ out** *vt* ofrecer ♦ *vi (resist)* resistir; **~ up** *vt (raise)* levantar; *(support)* apoyar; *(delay)* retrasar; *(rob)* asaltar; **~all** *(BRIT) n* bolsa; **~er** *n (container)* receptáculo; *(of ticket, record)* poseedor(a) *m/f*; *(of office, title etc)* titular *m/f*; **~ing** *n (share)* interés *m*; *(farmland)* parcela; **~up** *n (robbery)* atraco; *(delay)* retraso; *(BRIT: in traffic)* embotellamiento
hole [həul] *n* agujero ♦ *vt* agujerear
holiday ['hɔlədɪ] *n* vacaciones *fpl*; *(public ~)* (día *m* de) fiesta, día *m* feriado; **on ~** de vacaciones; **~ camp** *n (BRIT: also: ~ centre)* centro de vacaciones; **~-maker** *(BRIT) n* turista *m/f*; **~ resort** *n* centro turístico
holiness ['həulɪnɪs] *n* santidad *f*
Holland ['hɔlənd] *n* Holanda
hollow ['hɔləu] *adj* hueco; *(claim)* vacío; *(eyes)* hundido; *(sound)* sordo ♦ *n* hueco; *(in ground)* hoyo ♦ *vt*: **to ~ out** excavar
holly ['hɔlɪ] *n* acebo
holocaust ['hɔləkɔːst] *n* holocausto
holy ['həulɪ] *adj* santo, sagrado; *(water)* bendito
homage ['hɔmɪdʒ] *n* homenaje *m*
home [həum] *n* casa; *(country)* patria; *(institution)* asilo ♦ *cpd (domestic)* casero, de casa; *(ECON, POL)* nacional ♦ *adv (direction)* a casa; *(right in: nail etc)* a fondo; **at ~** en casa; *(in country)* en el país; *(fig)* como pez en el agua; **to go/come ~** ir/volver a casa; **make yourself at ~** ¡estás en tu casa!; **~ address** *n* domicilio; **~land** *n* tierra natal; **~less** *adj* sin hogar, sin casa; **~ly** *adj (simple)* sencillo; **~-made** *adj* casero; **H~ Office** *(BRIT) n* Mi-

nisterio del Interior; ~ **rule** *n* autonomía;
H~ **Secretary** (*BRIT*) *n* Ministro del Interior; ~**sick** *adj*: **to be** ~**sick** tener morriña,
sentir nostalgia; ~ **town** *n* ciudad *f* natal;
~**ward** ['həumwəd] *adj* (*journey*) hacia
casa; ~**work** *n* deberes *mpl*
homicide ['hɔmɪsaɪd] (*US*) *n* homicidio
homosexual [hɔməu'sɛksjuəl] *adj, n* homosexual *m/f*
Honduran [hɔn'djuərən] *adj, n* hondureño/
a *m/f*
Honduras [hɔn'djuərəs] *n* Honduras *f*
honest ['ɔnɪst] *adj* honrado; (*sincere*) franco, sincero; ~**ly** *adv* honradamente; francamente; ~**y** *n* honradez *f*
honey ['hʌnɪ] *n* miel *f*; ~**comb** *n* panal *m*;
~**moon** *n* luna de miel; ~**suckle** *n* madreselva
honk [hɔŋk] *vi* (*AUT*) tocar el pito, pitar
honorary ['ɔnərərɪ] *adj* (*member, president*)
de honor; (*title*) honorífico; ~ **degree** doctorado honoris causa
honour ['ɔnə*] (*US* **honor**) *vt* honrar;
(*commitment, promise*) cumplir con ♦ *n* honor *m*, honra; ~**able** *adj* honorable; ~**s**
degree (*SCOL*) título de licenciado con calificación alta
hood [hud] *n* capucha; (*BRIT*: *AUT*) capota;
(*US*: *AUT*) capó *m*; (*of cooker*) campana de humos
hoodwink ['hudwɪŋk] (*BRIT*) *vt* timar
hoof [hu:f] (*pl* **hooves**) *n* pezuña
hook [huk] *n* gancho; (*on dress*) corchete
m, broche *m*; (*for fishing*) anzuelo ♦ *vt* enganchar; (*fish*) pescar
hooligan ['hu:lɪgən] *n* gamberro
hoop [hu:p] *n* aro
hooray [hu:'reɪ] *excl* = **hurray**
hoot [hu:t] (*BRIT*) *vi* (*AUT*) tocar el pito, pitar; (*siren*) sonar la sirena; (*owl*) ulular;
~**er** (*BRIT*) *n* (*AUT*) pito, claxon *m*; (*NAUT*) sirena
Hoover ['hu:və*] ® (*BRIT*) *n* aspiradora ♦
vt: **h~** pasar la aspiradora por
hooves [hu:vz] *npl of* **hoof**
hop [hɔp] *vi* saltar, brincar; (*on one foot*)
saltar con un pie
hope [həup] *vt, vi* esperar ♦ *n* esperanza; **I**
~ **so/not** espero que sí/no; ~**ful** *adj* (*person*) optimista; (*situation*) prometedor(a);
~**fully** *adv* con esperanza; (*one hopes*):
~**fully he will recover** esperamos que se
recupere; ~**less** *adj* desesperado; (*person*):
to be ~**less** ser un desastre
hops [hɔps] *npl* lúpulo
horde [hɔːd] *n* (*fig*) multitud *f*
horizon [hə'raɪzn] *n* horizonte *m*; ~**tal**
[hɔrɪ'zɔntl] *adj* horizontal
hormone ['hɔːməun] *n* hormona
horn [hɔːn] *n* cuerno; (*MUS*: *also*: French ~)
trompa; (*AUT*) pito, claxon *m*
hornet ['hɔːnɪt] *n* avispón *m*

horny ['hɔːnɪ] (*inf*) *adj* cachondo
horoscope ['hɔrəskəup] *n* horóscopo
horrible ['hɔrɪbl] *adj* horrible
horrid ['hɔrɪd] *adj* horrible, horroroso
horrify ['hɔrɪfaɪ] *vt* horrorizar
horror ['hɔrə*] *n* horror *m*; ~ **film** *n* película de horror
hors d'œuvre [ɔː'dəːvrə] *n* entremeses *mpl*
horse [hɔːs] *n* caballo; **on** ~**back** a caballo;
~ **chestnut** (*tree*) castaño de Indias;
(*nut*) castaña de Indias; ~**man/woman** *n*
jinete/a *m/f*; ~**power** *n* caballo (de fuerza); ~-**racing** *n* carreras *fpl* de caballos;
~**radish** *n* rábano picante; ~**shoe** *n* herradura
hose [həuz] *n* (*also*: ~**pipe**) manguera
hosiery ['həuzɪərɪ] *n* (*in shop*) (sección *f*
de) medias *fpl*
hospitable [hɔs'pɪtəbl] *adj* hospitalario
hospital ['hɔspɪtl] *n* hospital *m*
hospitality [hɔspɪ'tælɪtɪ] *n* hospitalidad *f*
host [həust] *n* anfitrión *m*; (*TV, RADIO*) presentador *m*; (*REL*) hostia; (*large number*): **a**
~ **of** multitud de
hostage ['hɔstɪdʒ] *n* rehén *m*
hostel ['hɔstl] *n* hostal *m*; (**youth**) ~ *n* albergue *m* juvenil
hostess ['həustɪs] *n* anfitriona; (*BRIT*: air ~)
azafata; (*TV, RADIO*) presentadora
hostile ['hɔstaɪl] *adj* hostil
hot [hɔt] *adj* caliente; (*weather*) caluroso, de
calor; (*as opposed to warm*) muy caliente;
(*spicy*) picante; (*fig*) ardiente, acalorado; **to
be** ~ (*person*) tener calor; (*object*) estar caliente; (*weather*) hacer calor; ~**bed** *n* (*fig*)
semillero; ~ **dog** *n* perro caliente
hotel [həu'tɛl] *n* hotel *m*; ~**ier** *n* hotelero;
(*manager*) director *m*
hot: ~**headed** *adj* exaltado; ~**house** *n* invernadero; ~ **line** *n* (*POL*) teléfono rojo;
~**ly** *adv* con pasión, apasionadamente;
~**plate** *n* (*on cooker*) placa calentadora;
~-**water bottle** *n* bolsa de agua caliente
hound [haund] *vt* acosar ♦ *n* perro (de
caza)
hour ['auə*] *n* hora; ~**ly** *adj* (de) cada hora
house [*n* haus, *pl* 'hauzɪz, *vb* hauz] *n* (*gen,
firm*) casa; (*POL*) cámara; (*THEATRE*) sala ♦
vt (*person*) alojar; (*collection*) albergar; **on
the** ~ (*fig*) la casa invita; ~ **arrest** *n* arresto domiciliario; ~**boat** *n* casa flotante;
~**bound** *adj* confinado en casa; ~**breaking** *n* allanamiento de morada; ~**coat** *n*
bata; ~**hold** *n* familia; (*home*) casa; ~**keeper** *n* ama de llaves; ~**keeping** *n*
(*work*) trabajos *mpl* domésticos; ~**keeping**
(*money*) *n* dinero para gastos domésticos;
~-**warming party** *n* fiesta de estreno de
una casa; ~**wife** *n* ama de casa; ~**work** *n*
faenas *fpl* de casa
housing ['hauzɪŋ] *n* (*act*) alojamiento;
(*houses*) viviendas *fpl*; ~ **development** *n*

urbanización f; ~ **estate** (*BRIT*) n = ~ **development**

hovel ['hɔvl] n casucha

hover ['hɔvə*] vi flotar (en el aire); ~**craft** n aerodeslizador m

how [hau] adv (*in what way*) cómo; ~ **are you?** ¿cómo estás?; ~ **much milk/many people?** ¿cuánta leche/gente?; ~ **much does it cost?** ¿cuánto cuesta?; ~ **long have you been here?** ¿cuánto hace que estás aquí?; ~ **old are you?** ¿cuántos años tienes?; ~ **tall is he?** ¿cómo es de alto?; ~ **is school?** ¿cómo (te) va (en) la escuela?; ~ **was the film?** ¿qué tal la película?; ~ **lovely/awful!** ¡qué bonito/horror!

howl [haul] n aullido ♦ vi aullar; (*person*) dar alaridos; (*wind*) ulular

H.P. n abbr = **hire purchase**

h.p. abbr = **horse power**

HQ n abbr = **headquarters**

hub [hʌb] n (*of wheel*) cubo; (*fig*) centro

hubbub ['hʌbʌb] n barahúnda

hubcap ['hʌbkæp] n tapacubos m inv

huddle ['hʌdl] vi: **to ~ together** acurrucarse

hue [hju:] n color m, matiz m; ~ **and cry** n clamor m

huff [hʌf] n: **in a ~** enojado

hug [hʌg] vt abrazar; (*thing*) apretar con los brazos

huge [hju:dʒ] adj enorme

hulk [hʌlk] n (*ship*) barco viejo; (*person, building etc*) mole f

hull [hʌl] n (*of ship*) casco

hullo [hə'ləu] excl = **hello**

hum [hʌm] vt tararear, canturrear ♦ vi tararear, canturrear; (*insect*) zumbar

human ['hju:mən] adj, n humano

humane [hju:'meɪn] adj humano, humanitario

humanitarian [hju:mænɪ'tɛərɪən] adj humanitario

humanity [hju:'mænɪtɪ] n humanidad f

humble ['hʌmbl] adj humilde ♦ vt humillar

humbug ['hʌmbʌg] n tonterías fpl; (*BRIT: sweet*) caramelo de menta

humdrum ['hʌmdrʌm] adj (*boring*) monótono, aburrido

humid ['hju:mɪd] adj húmedo

humiliate [hju:'mɪlɪeɪt] vt humillar

humor ['hju:mə*] (*US*) n = **humour**

humorous ['hju:mərəs] adj gracioso, divertido

humour ['hju:mə*] (*US* **humor**) n humorismo, sentido del humor; (*mood*) humor m ♦ vt (*person*) complacer

hump [hʌmp] n (*in ground*) montículo; (*camel's*) giba; ~**backed** adj: ~**backed bridge** puente m (*de fuerte pendiente*)

hunch [hʌntʃ] n (*premonition*) presentimiento; ~**back** n joroba m/f; ~**ed** adj jo-

robado

hundred ['hʌndrəd] num ciento; (*before n*) cien; ~**s of** centenares de; ~**weight** n (*BRIT*) = 50.8 kg; 112 lb; (*US*) = 45.3 kg; 100 lb

hung [hʌŋ] pt, pp of **hang**

Hungarian [hʌŋ'gɛərɪən] adj, n húngaro/a m/f

Hungary ['hʌŋgərɪ] n Hungría

hunger ['hʌŋgə*] n hambre f ♦ vi: **to ~ for** (*fig*) tener hambre de, anhelar; ~ **strike** n huelga de hambre

hungry ['hʌŋgrɪ] adj: ~ (**for**) hambriento (de); **to be ~** tener hambre

hunk [hʌŋk] n (*of bread etc*) trozo, pedazo

hunt [hʌnt] vt (*seek*) buscar; (*SPORT*) cazar ♦ vi (*search*): **to ~ (for)** buscar; (*SPORT*) cazar ♦ n búsqueda; caza, cacería; ~**er** n cazador(a) m/f; ~**ing** n caza

hurdle ['hə:dl] n (*SPORT*) valla; (*fig*) obstáculo

hurl [hə:l] vt lanzar, arrojar

hurrah [hu'rɑ:] excl = **hurray**

hurray [hu'reɪ] excl ¡viva!

hurricane ['hʌrɪkən] n huracán m

hurried ['hʌrɪd] adj (*rushed*) hecho de prisa; ~**ly** adv con prisa, apresuradamente

hurry ['hʌrɪ] n prisa ♦ vi (*also*: ~ **up**) apresurarse, darse prisa ♦ vt (*also*: ~ **up**: *person*) dar prisa a; (: *work*) apresurar, hacer de prisa; **to be in a ~** tener prisa

hurt [hə:t] (*pt, pp* **hurt**) vt hacer daño a ♦ vi doler ♦ adj lastimado; ~**ful** adj (*remark etc*) hiriente

hurtle ['hə:tl] vi: **to ~ past** pasar como un rayo; **to ~ down** ir a toda velocidad

husband ['hʌzbənd] n marido

hush [hʌʃ] n silencio ♦ vt hacer callar; ~**!** ¡chitón!, ¡cállate!; ~ **up** vt encubrir

husk [hʌsk] n (*of wheat*) cáscara

husky ['hʌskɪ] adj ronco ♦ n perro esquimal

hustle ['hʌsl] vt (*hurry*) dar prisa a ♦ n: ~ **and bustle** ajetreo

hut [hʌt] n cabaña; (*shed*) cobertizo

hutch [hʌtʃ] n conejera

hyacinth ['haɪəsɪnθ] n jacinto

hydrant ['haɪdrənt] n (*also*: **fire ~**) boca de incendios

hydraulic [haɪ'drɔ:lɪk] adj hidráulico

hydroelectric [haɪdrəu'lɛktrɪk] adj hidroeléctrico

hydrofoil ['haɪdrəfɔɪl] n aerodeslizador m

hydrogen ['haɪdrədʒən] n hidrógeno

hygiene ['haɪdʒi:n] n higiene f; **hygienic** [-'dʒi:nɪk] adj higiénico

hymn [hɪm] n himno

hype [haɪp] (*inf*) n bombardeo publicitario

hypermarket ['haɪpəmɑ:kɪt] n hipermercado

hyphen ['haɪfn] n guión m

hypnotize ['hɪpnətaɪz] vt hipnotizar

hypochondriac [haɪpəu'kɔndrɪæk] n hipocondríaco/a

hypocrisy [hɪ'pɔkrɪsɪ] *n* hipocresía; **hypocrite** ['hɪpəkrɪt] *n* hipócrita *m/f*; **hypocritical** [hɪpə'krɪtɪkl] *adj* hipócrita

hypothesis [haɪ'pɔθɪsɪs] (*pl n* hypotheses) hipótesis *f inv*

hysteria [hɪ'stɪərɪə] *n* histeria; **hysterical** [-'stɛrɪkl] *adj* histérico; (*funny*) para morirse de risa; **hysterics** [-'stɛrɪks] *npl* histeria; **to be in hysterics** (*fig*) morirse de risa

I i

I [aɪ] *pron* yo

ice [aɪs] *n* hielo; (~ *cream*) helado ♦ *vt* (*cake*) alcorzar ♦ *vi* (*also*: ~ *over*, ~ *up*) helarse; ~**berg** *n* iceberg *m*; ~**box** *n* (*BRIT*) congelador *m*; (*US*) nevera (*SP*), refrigeradora (*AM*); ~ **cream** *n* helado; ~ **cube** *n* cubito de hielo; ~**d** *adj* (*cake*) escarchado; (*drink*) helado; ~ **hockey** *n* hockey *m* sobre hielo

Iceland ['aɪslənd] *n* Islandia

ice: ~ **lolly** (*BRIT*) *n* polo; ~ **rink** *n* pista de hielo; ~ **skating** *n* patinaje *m* sobre hielo

icicle ['aɪsɪkl] *n* carámbano

icing ['aɪsɪŋ] *n* (*CULIN*) alcorza; ~ **sugar** (*BRIT*) *n* azúcar *m* glas(eado)

icy ['aɪsɪ] *adj* helado

I'd [aɪd] = **I would; I had**

idea [aɪ'dɪə] *n* idea

ideal [aɪ'dɪəl] *n* ideal *m* ♦ *adj* ideal; ~**ist** *n* idealista *m/f*

identical [aɪ'dɛntɪkl] *adj* idéntico

identification [aɪdɛntɪfɪ'keɪʃən] *n* identificación *f*; (**means of**) ~ documentos *mpl* personales

identify [aɪ'dɛntɪfaɪ] *vt* identificar

Identikit [aɪ'dɛntɪkɪt] ® *n*: ~ (**picture**) retrato-robot *m*

identity [aɪ'dɛntɪtɪ] *n* identidad *f*; ~ **card** *n* carnet *m* de identidad

ideology [aɪdɪ'ɔlədʒɪ] *n* ideología

idiom ['ɪdɪəm] *n* modismo; (*style of speaking*) lenguaje *m*; ~**atic** [-'mætɪk] *adj* idiomático

idiosyncrasy [ɪdɪəu'sɪŋkrəsɪ] *n* idiosincrasia

idiot ['ɪdɪət] *n* idiota *m/f*; ~**ic** [-'ɔtɪk] *adj* tonto

idle ['aɪdl] *adj* (*inactive*) ocioso; (*lazy*) holgazán/ana; (*unemployed*) parado, de-

socupado; (*machinery etc*) parado; (*talk etc*) frívolo ♦ *vi* (*machine*) marchar en vacío; ~ **away** *vt*: **to** ~ **away the time** malgastar el tiempo

idol ['aɪdl] *n* ídolo; ~**ize** *vt* idolatrar

idyllic [ɪ'dɪlɪk] *adj* idílico

i.e. *abbr* (= *that is*) esto es

if [ɪf] *conj* si; ~ **necessary** si fuera necesario, si hiciese falta; ~ **I were you** yo en tu lugar; ~ **so/not** de ser así/si no; ~ **only I could!** ¡ojalá pudiera!; *see also* **as; even**

igloo ['ɪɡluː] *n* iglú *m*

ignite [ɪɡ'naɪt] *vt* (*set fire to*) encender ♦ *vi* encenderse

ignition [ɪɡ'nɪʃən] *n* (*AUT*: *process*) ignición *f*; (*AUT*: *mechanism*) encendido; **to switch on/off the** ~ arrancar/apagar el motor; ~ **key** *n* (*AUT*) llave *f* de contacto

ignorance ['ɪɡnərəns] *n* ignorancia

ignorant ['ɪɡnərənt] *adj* ignorante; **to be** ~ **of** ignorar

ignore [ɪɡ'nɔː*] *vt* (*person, advice*) no hacer caso de; (*fact*) pasar por alto

ill [ɪl] *adj* enfermo, malo ♦ *adv* mal; **to be taken** ~ ponerse enfermo; ~-**advised** *adj* (*decision*) imprudente; ~-**at-ease** *adj* incómodo

I'll [aɪl] = **I will; I shall**

illegal [ɪ'liːɡl] *adj* ilegal

illegible [ɪ'lɛdʒɪbl] *adj* ilegible

illegitimate [ɪlɪ'dʒɪtɪmət] *adj* ilegítimo

ill-fated *adj* malogrado

ill feeling *n* rencor *m*

illicit [ɪ'lɪsɪt] *adj* ilícito

illiterate [ɪ'lɪtərət] *adj* analfabeto

ill-mannered *adj* mal educado

illness ['ɪlnɪs] *n* enfermedad *f*

ill-treat *vt* maltratar

illuminate [ɪ'luːmɪneɪt] *vt* (*room, street*) iluminar, alumbrar; **illumination** [-'neɪʃən] *n* alumbrado; **illuminations** *npl* (*decorative lights*) iluminaciones *fpl*, luces *fpl*

illusion [ɪ'luːʒən] *n* ilusión *f*; (*trick*) truco

illustrate ['ɪləstreɪt] *vt* ilustrar

illustration [ɪlə'streɪʃən] *n* (*act of illustrating*) ilustración *f*; (*example*) ejemplo, ilustración *f*; (*in book*) lámina

illustrious [ɪ'lʌstrɪəs] *adj* ilustre

ill will *n* rencor *m*

I'm [aɪm] = **I am**

image ['ɪmɪdʒ] *n* imagen *f*; ~**ry** [-ərɪ] *n* imágenes *fpl*

imaginary [ɪ'mædʒɪnərɪ] *adj* imaginario

imagination [ɪmædʒɪ'neɪʃən] *n* imaginación *f*; (*inventiveness*) inventiva

imaginative [ɪ'mædʒɪnətɪv] *adj* imaginativo

imagine [ɪ'mædʒɪn] *vt* imaginarse

imbalance [ɪm'bæləns] *n* desequilibrio

imbecile ['ɪmbəsiːl] *n* imbécil *m/f*

imitate ['ɪmɪteɪt] *vt* imitar; **imitation** [-'teɪʃən] *n* imitación *f*; (*copy*) copia

immaculate [ɪ'mækjulət] *adj* inmaculado

immaterial [ɪməˈtɪərɪəl] *adj* (*unimportant*) sin importancia

immature [ɪməˈtjuə*] *adj* (*person*) inmaduro

immediate [ɪˈmiːdɪət] *adj* inmediato; (*pressing*) urgente, apremiante; (*nearest: family*) próximo; (: *neighbourhood*) inmediato; ~**ly** *adv* (*at once*) en seguida; (*directly*) inmediatamente; ~**ly next to** muy junto a

immense [ɪˈmɛns] *adj* inmenso, enorme; (*importance*) enorme

immerse [ɪˈmɜːs] *vt* (*submerge*) sumergir; **to be** ~**d in** (*fig*) estar absorto en

immersion heater [ɪˈmɜːʃən-] (*BRIT*) *n* calentador *m* de inmersión

immigrant [ˈɪmɪɡrənt] *n* inmigrante *m/f*; **immigration** [ɪmɪˈɡreɪʃən] *n* inmigración *f*

imminent [ˈɪmɪnənt] *adj* inminente

immobile [ɪˈməʊbaɪl] *adj* inmóvil

immoral [ɪˈmɒrəl] *adj* inmoral

immortal [ɪˈmɔːtl] *adj* inmortal

immune [ɪˈmjuːn] *adj*: ~ (**to**) inmune (a); **immunity** *n* (*MED, of diplomat*) inmunidad *f*

immunize [ˈɪmjunaɪz] *vt* inmunizar

imp [ɪmp] *n* diablillo; (*child*) pícaro

impact [ˈɪmpækt] *n* impacto

impair [ɪmˈpɛə*] *vt* perjudicar

impale [ɪmˈpeɪl] *vt* empalar

impart [ɪmˈpɑːt] *vt* comunicar; (*flavour*) proporcionar

impartial [ɪmˈpɑːʃl] *adj* imparcial

impassable [ɪmˈpɑːsəbl] *adj* (*barrier*) infranqueable; (*river, road*) intransitable

impasse [æmˈpɑːs] *n* punto muerto

impassive [ɪmˈpæsɪv] *adj* impasible

impatience [ɪmˈpeɪʃəns] *n* impaciencia

impatient [ɪmˈpeɪʃənt] *adj* impaciente; **to get** *or* **grow** ~ impacientarse

impeccable [ɪmˈpɛkəbl] *adj* impecable

impede [ɪmˈpiːd] *vt* estorbar

impediment [ɪmˈpɛdɪmənt] *n* obstáculo, estorbo; (*also: speech* ~) defecto (del habla)

impending [ɪmˈpɛndɪŋ] *adj* inminente

impenetrable [ɪmˈpɛnɪtrəbl] *adj* impenetrable; (*fig*) insondable

imperative [ɪmˈpɛrətɪv] *adj* (*tone*) imperioso; (*need*) imprescindible ♦ *n* (*LING*) imperativo

imperfect [ɪmˈpɜːfɪkt] *adj* (*goods etc*) defectuoso ♦ *n* (*LING: also:* ~ *tense*) imperfecto; ~**ion** [-ˈfɛkʃən] *n* (*blemish*) desperfecto; (*fault*) defecto

imperial [ɪmˈpɪərɪəl] *adj* imperial; ~**ism** *n* imperialismo

impersonal [ɪmˈpɜːsənl] *adj* impersonal

impersonate [ɪmˈpɜːsəneɪt] *vt* hacerse pasar por; (*THEATRE*) imitar

impertinent [ɪmˈpɜːtɪnənt] *adj* impertinente, insolente

impervious [ɪmˈpɜːvɪəs] *adj* impermeable; (*fig*): ~ **to** insensible a

impetuous [ɪmˈpɛtjuəs] *adj* impetuoso

impetus [ˈɪmpətəs] *n* ímpetu *m*; (*fig*) impulso

impinge [ɪmˈpɪndʒ]: **to** ~ **on** *vt fus* (*affect*) afectar a

implacable [ɪmˈplækəbl] *adj* implacable

implement [*n* ˈɪmplɪmənt, *vb* ˈɪmplɪment] *n* herramienta; (*for cooking*) utensilio ♦ *vt* (*regulation*) hacer efectivo; (*plan*) realizar

implicate [ˈɪmplɪkeɪt] *vt* (*in crime etc*) involucrar; **implication** [-ˈkeɪʃən] *n* consecuencia; (*involvement*) implicación *f*

implicit [ɪmˈplɪsɪt] *adj* implícito; (*belief, trust*) absoluto

implore [ɪmˈplɔː*] *vt* (*person*) suplicar

imply [ɪmˈplaɪ] *vt* (*involve*) suponer; (*hint*) dar a entender que

impolite [ɪmpəˈlaɪt] *adj* mal educado

import [*vb* ɪmˈpɔːt, *n* ˈɪmpɔːt] *vt* importar ♦ *n* (*COMM*) importación *f*; (: *article*) producto importado; (*meaning*) significado, sentido

importance [ɪmˈpɔːtəns] *n* importancia

important [ɪmˈpɔːtənt] *adj* importante; **it's not** ~ no importa, no tiene importancia

importer [ɪmˈpɔːtə*] *n* importador(a) *m/f*

impose [ɪmˈpəʊz] *vt* imponer ♦ *vi*: **to** ~ **on sb** abusar de uno; **imposing** *adj* imponente, impresionante

imposition [ɪmpəˈzɪʃn] *n* (*of tax etc*) imposición *f*; **to be an** ~ **on** (*person*) molestar a

impossible [ɪmˈpɒsɪbl] *adj* imposible; (*person*) insoportable

impostor [ɪmˈpɒstə*] *n* impostor(a) *m/f*

impotent [ˈɪmpətənt] *adj* impotente

impound [ɪmˈpaʊnd] *vt* embargar

impoverished [ɪmˈpɒvərɪʃt] *adj* necesitado

impracticable [ɪmˈpræktɪkəbl] *adj* no factible, irrealizable

impractical [ɪmˈpræktɪkl] *adj* (*person, plan*) poco práctico

imprecise [ɪmprɪˈsaɪs] *adj* impreciso

impregnable [ɪmˈprɛgnəbl] *adj* (*castle*) inexpugnable

impregnate [ˈɪmprɛgneɪt] *vt* (*saturate*) impregnar

impress [ɪmˈprɛs] *vt* impresionar; (*mark*) estampar; **to** ~ **sth on sb** hacer entender algo a uno

impression [ɪmˈprɛʃən] *n* impresión *f*; (*imitation*) imitación *f*; **to be under the** ~ **that** tener la impresión de que; ~**able** *adj* impresionable; ~**ist** *n* impresionista *m/f*

impressive [ɪmˈprɛsɪv] *adj* impresionante

imprint [ˈɪmprɪnt] *n* (*outline*) huella; (*PUBLISHING*) pie *m* de imprenta

imprison [ɪmˈprɪzn] *vt* encarcelar; ~**ment** *n* encarcelamiento; (*term of* ~*ment*) cárcel *f*

improbable [ɪmˈprɒbəbl] *adj* improbable, inverosímil

impromptu [ɪmˈprɒmptjuː] *adj* improvisado

improper [ɪmˈprɔpə*] *adj* (*unsuitable*: *conduct etc*) incorrecto; (: *activities*) deshonesto

improve [ɪmˈpruːv] *vt* mejorar; (*foreign language*) perfeccionar ♦ *vi* mejorarse; **~ment** *n* mejoramiento; perfección *f*; progreso

improvise [ˈɪmprəvaɪz] *vt*, *vi* improvisar

impudent [ˈɪmpjudnt] *adj* descarado, insolente

impulse [ˈɪmpʌls] *n* impulso; **to act on ~** obrar sin reflexión; **impulsive** [-ˈpʌlsɪv] *adj* irreflexivo

impunity [ɪmˈpjuːnɪtɪ] *n*: **with ~** impunemente

impure [ɪmˈpjuə*] *adj* (*adulterated*) adulterado; (*morally*) impuro; **impurity** *n* impureza

───────────── *KEYWORD* ─────────────

in [ɪn] *prep* **1** (*indicating place, position, with place names*) en; **~ the house/garden** en (la) casa/el jardín; **~ here/there** aquí/ahí **or** allí dentro; **~ London/England** en Londres/Inglaterra

2 (*indicating time*) en; **~ spring** en (la) primavera; **~ the afternoon** por la tarde; **at 4 o'clock ~ the afternoon** a las 4 de la tarde; **I did it ~ 3 hours/days** lo hice en 3 horas/días; **I'll see you ~ 2 weeks or ~ 2 weeks' time** te veré dentro de 2 semanas

3 (*indicating manner etc*) en; **~ a loud/soft voice** en voz alta/baja; **~ pencil/ink** a lápiz/bolígrafo; **the boy ~ the blue shirt** el chico de la camisa azul

4 (*indicating circumstances*): **~ the sun/shade/rain** al sol/a la sombra/bajo la lluvia; **a change ~ policy** un cambio de política

5 (*indicating mood, state*): **~ tears** en lágrimas, llorando; **~ anger/despair** enfadado/desesperado; **to live ~ luxury** vivir lujosamente

6 (*with ratios, numbers*): **1 ~ 10 households, 1 household ~ 10** una de cada 10 familias; **20 pence ~ the pound** 20 peniques por libra; **they lined up ~ twos** se alinearon de dos en dos

7 (*referring to people, works*) en; entre; **the disease is common ~ children** la enfermedad es común entre los niños; **~ (the works of) Dickens** en (las obras de) Dickens

8 (*indicating profession etc*): **to be ~ teaching** estar en la enseñanza

9 (*after superlative*) de; **the best pupil ~ the class** el/la mejor alumno/a de la clase

10 (*with present participle*): **~ saying this** al decir esto

♦ *adv*: **to be ~** (*person: at home*) estar en casa; (*work*) estar; (*train, ship, plane*) haber llegado; (*in fashion*) estar de moda; **she'll be ~ later today** llegará más tarde hoy; **to ask sb ~** hacer pasar a uno; **to run/limp etc ~** entrar corriendo/cojeando etc

♦ *npl*: **the ~s and outs** (*of proposal, situation etc*) los detalles

in. *abbr* = **inch**

inability [ɪnəˈbɪlɪtɪ] *n*: **~ (to do)** incapacidad *f* (de hacer)

inaccessible [ɪnəkˈsɛsɪbl] *adj* (*also fig*) inaccesible

inaccurate [ɪnˈækjurət] *adj* inexacto, incorrecto

inactivity [ɪnækˈtɪvɪtɪ] *n* inactividad *f*

inadequate [ɪnˈædɪkwət] *adj* (*income, reply etc*) insuficiente; (*person*) incapaz

inadvertently [ɪnədˈvəːtntlɪ] *adv* por descuido

inadvisable [ɪnədˈvaɪzəbl] *adj* poco aconsejable

inane [ɪˈneɪn] *adj* necio, fatuo

inanimate [ɪnˈænɪmət] *adj* inanimado

inappropriate [ɪnəˈprəuprɪət] *adj* inadecuado; (*improper*) poco oportuno

inarticulate [ɪnɑːˈtɪkjulət] *adj* (*person*) incapaz de expresarse; (*speech*) mal pronunciado

inasmuch as [ɪnəzˈmʌtʃ-] *conj* puesto que, ya que

inaudible [ɪnˈɔːdɪbl] *adj* inaudible

inaugurate [ɪˈnɔːgjureɪt] *vt* inaugurar; **inauguration** [-ˈreɪʃən] *n* ceremonia de apertura

inborn [ɪnˈbɔːn] *adj* (*quality*) innato

inbred [ɪnˈbrɛd] *adj* innato; (*family*) engendrado por endogamia

Inc. *abbr* (*US*: = **incorporated**) S.A.

incapable [ɪnˈkeɪpəbl] *adj* incapaz

incapacitate [ɪnkəˈpæsɪteɪt] *vt*: **to ~ sb** incapacitar a uno

incarcerate [ɪnˈkɑːsəreɪt] *vt* encarcelar

incarnation [ɪnkɑːˈneɪʃən] *n* encarnación *f*

incendiary [ɪnˈsɛndɪərɪ] *adj* incendiario

incense [*n* ˈɪnsɛns, *vb* ɪnˈsɛns] *n* incienso ♦ *vt* (*anger*) indignar, encolerizar

incentive [ɪnˈsɛntɪv] *n* incentivo, estímulo

incessant [ɪnˈsɛsnt] *adj* incesante, continuo; **~ly** *adv* constantemente

incest [ˈɪnsɛst] *n* incesto

inch [ɪntʃ] *n* pulgada; **to be within an ~ of** estar a dos dedos de; **he didn't give an ~** no dio concesión alguna; **~ forward** *vi* avanzar palmo a palmo

incidence [ˈɪnsɪdns] *n* (*of crime, disease*) incidencia

incident [ˈɪnsɪdnt] *n* incidente *m*

incidental [ɪnsɪˈdɛntl] *adj* accesorio; **~ to** relacionado con; **~ly** [-ˈdɛntəlɪ] *adv* (*by the way*) a propósito

incinerator [ɪnˈsɪnəreɪtə*] *n* incinerador *m*

incisive [ɪnˈsaɪsɪv] *adj* (*remark etc*) incisivo

incite [ɪnˈsaɪt] *vt* provocar

inclination [ɪnklɪˈneɪʃən] *n* (*tendency*) tendencia, inclinación *f*; (*desire*) deseo; (*dispo-*

sition) propensión *f*

incline [*n* 'ɪnklaɪn, *vb* ɪn'klaɪn] *n* pendiente *m*, cuesta ♦ *vt* (*head*) poner de lado ♦ *vi* inclinarse; **to be ~d to** (*tend*) ser propenso a

include [ɪn'kluːd] *vt* (*incorporate*) incluir; (*in letter*) adjuntar; **including** *prep* incluso, inclusive

inclusion [ɪn'kluːʒən] *n* inclusión *f*

inclusive [ɪn'kluːsɪv] *adj* inclusivo; **~ of tax** incluidos los impuestos

incognito [ɪnkɔg'niːtəu] *adv* de incógnito

incoherent [ɪnkəu'hɪərənt] *adj* incoherente

income ['ɪnkʌm] *n* (*earned*) ingresos *mpl*; (*from property etc*) renta; (*from investment etc*) rédito; **~ tax** *n* impuesto sobre la renta

incoming ['ɪnkʌmɪŋ] *adj* (*flight, government etc*) entrante

incomparable [ɪn'kɔmpərəbl] *adj* incomparable, sin par

incompatible [ɪnkəm'pætɪbl] *adj* incompatible

incompetent [ɪn'kɔmpɪtənt] *adj* incompetente

incomplete [ɪnkəm'pliːt] *adj* (*partial: achievement etc*) incompleto; (*unfinished: painting etc*) inacabado

incomprehensible [ɪnkɔmprɪ'hensɪbl] *adj* incomprensible

inconceivable [ɪnkən'siːvəbl] *adj* inconcebible

incongruous [ɪn'kɔŋgruəs] *adj* (*strange*) discordante; (*inappropriate*) incongruente

inconsiderate [ɪnkən'sɪdərət] *adj* desconsiderado

inconsistent [ɪnkən'sɪstənt] *adj* inconsecuente; (*contradictory*) incongruente; **~ with** (que) no concuerda con

inconspicuous [ɪnkən'spɪkjuəs] *adj* (*colour, building etc*) discreto; (*person*) que llama poco la atención

inconvenience [ɪnkən'viːnjəns] *n* inconvenientes *mpl*; (*trouble*) molestia, incomodidad *f* ♦ *vt* incomodar

inconvenient [ɪnkən'viːnjənt] *adj* incómodo, poco práctico; (*time, place, visitor*) inoportuno

incorporate [ɪn'kɔːpəreɪt] *vt* incorporar; (*contain*) comprender; (*add*) agregar; **~d** *adj*: **~d company** (*US*) ≈ sociedad *f* anónima

incorrect [ɪnkə'rekt] *adj* incorrecto

incorrigible [ɪn'kɔrɪdʒəbl] *adj* incorregible

incorruptible [ɪnkə'rʌptɪbl] *adj* insobornable

increase [*n* 'ɪnkriːs, *vb* ɪn'kriːs] *n* aumento ♦ *vi* aumentar; (*grow*) crecer; (*price*) subir ♦ *vt* aumentar; (*price*) subir; **increasing** *adj* creciente; **increasingly** *adv* cada vez más, más y más

incredible [ɪn'kredɪbl] *adj* increíble

incredulous [ɪn'kredjuləs] *adj* incrédulo

incriminate [ɪn'krɪmɪneɪt] *vt* incriminar

incubator ['ɪnkjubeɪtə*] *n* incubadora

incumbent [ɪn'kʌmbənt] *n* titular *m/f* ♦ *adj*: **it is ~ on him to...** le incumbe...

incur [ɪn'kə:*] *vt* (*expenditure*) incurrir; (*loss*) sufrir; (*anger, disapproval*) provocar

incurable [ɪn'kjuərəbl] *adj* incurable

indebted [ɪn'detɪd] *adj*: **to be ~ to sb** estar agradecido a uno

indecent [ɪn'diːsnt] *adj* indecente; **~ assault** (*BRIT*) *n* atentado contra el pudor; **~ exposure** *n* exhibicionismo

indecisive [ɪndɪ'saɪsɪv] *adj* indeciso

indeed [ɪn'diːd] *adv* efectivamente, en realidad; (*in fact*) en efecto; (*furthermore*) es más; **yes ~!** ¡claro que sí!

indefinitely [ɪn'defɪnɪtlɪ] *adv* (*wait*) indefinidamente

indelible [ɪn'delɪbl] *adj* imborrable

indemnity [ɪn'demnɪtɪ] *n* (*insurance*) indemnidad *f*; (*compensation*) indemnización *f*

independence [ɪndɪ'pendns] *n* independencia

independent [ɪndɪ'pendənt] *adj* independiente

indestructible [ɪndɪs'trʌktəbl] *adj* indestructible

index ['ɪndeks] (*pl* **~es**) *n* (*in book*) índice *m*; (: *in library etc*) catálogo; (*pl* **indices**: *ratio, sign*) exponente *m*; **~ card** *n* ficha; **~ed** (*US*) *adj* = **~-linked**; **~ finger** *n* índice *m*; **~-linked** (*BRIT*) *adj* vinculado al índice del coste de la vida

India ['ɪndɪə] *n* la India; **~n** *adj, n* indio/a *m/f*; **Red ~n** piel roja *m/f*; **~n Ocean** *n*: **the ~n Ocean** el Océano Índico

indicate ['ɪndɪkeɪt] *vt* indicar; **indication** [-'keɪʃən] *n* indicio, señal *f*; **indicative** [ɪn'dɪkətɪv] *adj*: **to be indicative of** indicar ♦ *n* (*LING*) indicativo; **indicator** *n* indicador *m*; (*AUT*) intermitente *m*

indices ['ɪndɪsiːz] *npl of* **index**

indictment [ɪn'daɪtmənt] *n* acusación *f*

indifference [ɪn'dɪfrəns] *n* indiferencia

indifferent [ɪn'dɪfrənt] *adj* indiferente; (*mediocre*) regular

indigenous [ɪn'dɪdʒɪnəs] *adj* indígena

indigestion [ɪndɪ'dʒestʃən] *n* indigestión *f*

indignant [ɪn'dɪgnənt] *adj*: **to be ~ at sth/with sb** indignarse por algo/con uno

indigo ['ɪndɪgəu] *adj* de color añil ♦ *n* añil *m*

indirect [ɪndɪ'rekt] *adj* indirecto; **~ly** *adv* indirectamente

indiscreet [ɪndɪ'skriːt] *adj* indiscreto, imprudente

indiscriminate [ɪndɪ'skrɪmɪnət] *adj* indiscriminado

indispensable [ɪndɪ'spensəbl] *adj* indispensable, imprescindible

indisposed [ɪndɪ'spəuzd] *adj* (*unwell*) indis-

puesto
indisputable [ˌɪndɪˈspjuːtəbl] *adj* incontestable

indistinct [ˌɪndɪˈstɪŋkt] *adj* (*noise, memory etc*) confuso

individual [ˌɪndɪˈvɪdjuəl] *n* individuo ♦ *adj* individual; (*personal*) personal; (*particular*) particular; ~**ist** *n* individualista *m/f*; ~**ly** *adv* (*singly*) individualmente

indoctrinate [ɪnˈdɔktrɪneɪt] *vt* adoctrinar

indolent [ˈɪndələnt] *adj* indolente, perezoso

indoor [ˈɪndɔː*] *adj* (*swimming pool*) cubierto; (*plant*) de interior; (*sport*) bajo cubierta; ~**s** [ɪnˈdɔːz] *adv* dentro

induce [ɪnˈdjuːs] *vt* inducir, persuadir; (*bring about*) producir; (*birth*) provocar; ~**ment** *n* (*incentive*) incentivo; (*pej: bribe*) soborno

indulge [ɪnˈdʌldʒ] *vt* (*whim*) satisfacer; (*person*) complacer; (*child*) mimar ♦ *vi*: to ~ **in** darse el gusto de; ~**nce** *n* vicio; (*leniency*) indulgencia; ~**nt** *adj* indulgente

industrial [ɪnˈdʌstrɪəl] *adj* industrial; ~ **action** *n* huelga; ~ **estate** (*BRIT*) *n* polígono (*SP*) or zona (*AM*) industrial; ~**ist** *n* industrial *m/f*; ~**ize** *vt* industrializar; ~ **park** (*US*) *n* = ~ **estate**

industrious [ɪnˈdʌstrɪəs] *adj* trabajador(a); (*student*) aplicado

industry [ˈɪndəstrɪ] *n* industria; (*diligence*) aplicación *f*

inebriated [ɪˈniːbrɪeɪtɪd] *adj* borracho

inedible [ɪnˈedɪbl] *adj* incomible; (*poisonous*) no comestible

ineffective [ˌɪnɪˈfektɪv] *adj* ineficaz, inútil

ineffectual [ˌɪnɪˈfektjuəl] *adj* = **ineffective**

inefficiency [ˌɪnɪˈfɪʃənsɪ] *n* ineficacia

inefficient [ˌɪnɪˈfɪʃənt] *adj* ineficaz, ineficiente

inept [ɪˈnept] *adj* incompetente

inequality [ˌɪnɪˈkwɔlɪtɪ] *n* desigualdad *f*

inert [ɪˈnɜːt] *adj* inerte, inactivo; (*immobile*) inmóvil; ~**ia** [ɪˈnɜːʃə] *n* inercia; (*laziness*) pereza

inescapable [ˌɪnɪˈskeɪpəbl] *adj* ineludible

inevitable [ɪnˈevɪtəbl] *adj* inevitable; **inevitably** *adv* inevitablemente

inexcusable [ˌɪnɪksˈkjuːzəbl] *adj* imperdonable

inexhaustible [ˌɪnɪgˈzɔːstɪbl] *adj* inagotable

inexpensive [ˌɪnɪkˈspensɪv] *adj* económico

inexperience [ˌɪnɪkˈspɪərɪəns] *n* falta de experiencia; ~**d** *adj* inexperto

inextricably [ˌɪnɪksˈtrɪkəblɪ] *adv* indisolublemente

infallible [ɪnˈfælɪbl] *adj* infalible

infamous [ˈɪnfəməs] *adj* infame

infancy [ˈɪnfənsɪ] *n* infancia

infant [ˈɪnfənt] *n* niño/a; (*baby*) niño pequeño, bebé *m*; ~**ile** *adj* infantil; (*pej*) aniñado; ~ **school** (*BRIT*) *n* parvulario

infantry [ˈɪnfəntrɪ] *n* infantería

infatuated [ɪnˈfætjueɪtɪd] *adj*: ~ **with** (*in love*) loco por

infatuation [ɪnˌfætjuˈeɪʃən] *n* enamoramiento, pasión *f*

infect [ɪnˈfekt] *vt* (*wound*) infectar; (*food*) contaminar; (*person, animal*) contagiar; ~**ion** [ɪnˈfekʃən] *n* infección *f*; (*fig*) contagio; ~**ious** [ɪnˈfekʃəs] *adj* (*also fig*) contagioso

infer [ɪnˈfɜː*] *vt* deducir, inferir; ~**ence** [ˈɪnfərəns] *n* deducción *f*, inferencia

inferior [ɪnˈfɪərɪə*] *adj, n* inferior *m/f*; ~**ity** [-rɪˈɔrətɪ] *n* inferioridad *f*; ~**ity complex** *n* complejo de inferioridad

inferno [ɪnˈfɜːnəʊ] *n* (*fire*) hoguera

infertile [ɪnˈfɜːtaɪl] *adj* estéril; (*person*) infecundo; **infertility** [-ˈtɪlɪtɪ] *n* esterilidad *f*; infecundidad *f*

infested [ɪnˈfestɪd] *adj*: ~ **with** plagado de

in-fighting *n* (*fig*) lucha(s) *f(pl)* interna(s)

infiltrate [ˈɪnfɪltreɪt] *vt* infiltrar en

infinite [ˈɪnfɪnɪt] *adj* infinito

infinitive [ɪnˈfɪnɪtɪv] *n* infinitivo

infinity [ɪnˈfɪnɪtɪ] *n* infinito; (*an* ~) infinidad *f*

infirm [ɪnˈfɜːm] *adj* enfermo, débil; ~**ary** *n* hospital *m*; ~**ity** *n* debilidad *f*; (*illness*) enfermedad *f*, achaque *m*

inflamed [ɪnˈfleɪmd] *adj*: to become ~ inflamarse

inflammable [ɪnˈflæməbl] *adj* inflamable

inflammation [ˌɪnfləˈmeɪʃən] *n* inflamación *f*

inflatable [ɪnˈfleɪtəbl] *adj* (*ball, boat*) inflable

inflate [ɪnˈfleɪt] *vt* (*tyre, price etc*) inflar; (*fig*) hinchar; **inflation** [ɪnˈfleɪʃən] *n* (*ECON*) inflación *f*

inflexible [ɪnˈfleksəbl] *adj* (*rule*) rígido; (*person*) inflexible

inflict [ɪnˈflɪkt] *vt*: to ~ sth on sb infligir algo en uno

influence [ˈɪnfluəns] *n* influencia ♦ *vt* influir en, influenciar; **under the** ~ **of alcohol** en estado de embriaguez; **influential** [-ˈenʃl] *adj* influyente

influenza [ˌɪnfluˈenzə] *n* gripe *f*

influx [ˈɪnflʌks] *n* afluencia

inform [ɪnˈfɔːm] *vt*: to ~ sb of sth informar a uno sobre *or* de algo ♦ *vi*: to ~ on sb delatar a uno

informal [ɪnˈfɔːməl] *adj* (*manner, tone*) familiar; (*dress, interview, occasion*) informal; (*visit, meeting*) extraoficial; ~**ity** [-ˈmælɪtɪ] *n* informalidad *f*; sencillez *f*

informant [ɪnˈfɔːmənt] *n* informante *m/f*

information [ˌɪnfəˈmeɪʃən] *n* información *f*; (*knowledge*) conocimientos *mpl*; **a piece of** ~ un dato; ~ **office** *n* información *f*

informative [ɪnˈfɔːmətɪv] *adj* informativo

informer [ɪnˈfɔːmə*] *n* (*also: police* ~) soplón/ona *m/f*

infra-red [ɪnfrə'red] *adj* infrarrojo
infrastructure ['ɪnfrəstrʌktʃə*] *n (of system etc)* infraestructura
infringe [ɪn'frɪndʒ] *vt* infringir, violar ♦ *vi*: **to ~ on** abusar de; **~ment** *n* infracción *f*, *(of rights)* usurpación *f*
infuriating [ɪn'fjuərɪeɪtɪŋ] *adj (habit, noise)* enloquecedor(a)
ingenious [ɪn'dʒiːnjəs] *adj* ingenioso; **ingenuity** [-dʒɪ'njuːɪtɪ] *n* ingeniosidad *f*
ingenuous [ɪn'dʒenjuəs] *adj* ingenuo
ingot ['ɪŋgət] *n* lingote *m*, barra
ingrained [ɪn'greɪnd] *adj* arraigado
ingratiate [ɪn'greɪʃɪeɪt] *vt*: **to ~ o.s. with** congraciarse con
ingredient [ɪn'griːdɪənt] *n* ingrediente *m*
inhabit [ɪn'hæbɪt] *vt* vivir en; **~ant** *n* habitante *m/f*
inhale [ɪn'heɪl] *vt* inhalar ♦ *vi (breathe in)* aspirar; *(in smoking)* tragar
inherent [ɪn'hɪərənt] *adj*: **~ in** or **to** inherente a
inherit [ɪn'herɪt] *vt* heredar; **~ance** *n* herencia; *(fig)* patrimonio
inhibit [ɪn'hɪbɪt] *vt* inhibir, impedir; **~ed** *adj (PSYCH)* cohibido; **~ion** [-'bɪʃən] *n* cohibición *f*
inhospitable [ɪnhɔs'pɪtəbl] *adj (person)* inhospitalario; *(place)* inhóspito
inhuman [ɪn'hjuːmən] *adj* inhumano
iniquity [ɪ'nɪkwɪtɪ] *n* iniquidad *f*, *(injustice)* injusticia
initial [ɪ'nɪʃl] *adj* primero ♦ *n* inicial *f* ♦ *vt* firmar con las iniciales; **~s** *npl (as signature)* iniciales *fpl*; *(abbreviation)* siglas *fpl*; **~ly** *adv* al principio
initiate [ɪ'nɪʃɪeɪt] *vt* iniciar; **to ~ proceedings against sb** *(LAW)* entablar proceso contra uno; **initiation** [-'eɪʃən] *n (into secret etc)* iniciación *f*; *(beginning)* comienzo
initiative [ɪ'nɪʃətɪv] *n* iniciativa
inject [ɪn'dʒekt] *vt* inyectar; **to ~ sb with sth** inyectar algo a uno; **~ion** [ɪn'dʒekʃən] *n* inyección *f*
injunction [ɪn'dʒʌŋkʃən] *n* interdicto
injure ['ɪndʒə*] *vt (hurt)* herir, lastimar; *(fig: reputation etc)* perjudicar; **~d** *adj (person, arm)* herido, lastimado; **injury** *n* herida, lesión *f*; *(wrong)* perjuicio, daño; **injury time** *n (SPORT)* (tiempo de) descuento
injustice [ɪn'dʒʌstɪs] *n* injusticia
ink [ɪŋk] *n* tinta
inkling ['ɪŋklɪŋ] *n* sospecha; *(idea)* idea
inlaid ['ɪnleɪd] *adj (with wood, gems etc)* incrustado
inland [*adj* 'ɪnlənd, *adv* ɪn'lænd] *adj (waterway, port etc)* interior ♦ *adv* tierra adentro; **I~ Revenue** *(BRIT)* *n* departamento de impuestos; ≈ Hacienda *(SP)*
in-laws ['ɪnlɔːz] *npl* suegros *mpl*
inlet ['ɪnlet] *n (GEO)* ensenada, cala; *(TECH)* admisión *f*, entrada

inmate ['ɪnmeɪt] *n (in prison)* preso/a; presidiario/a; *(in asylum)* internado/a
inn [ɪn] *n* posada, mesón *m*
innate [ɪ'neɪt] *adj* innato
inner ['ɪnə*] *adj (courtyard, calm)* interior; *(feelings)* íntimo; **~ city** *n* barrios deprimidos del centro de una ciudad; **~ tube** *n (of tyre)* cámara *(SP)* or llanta *(AM)*
innings ['ɪnɪŋz] *n (CRICKET)* entrada, turno
innocence ['ɪnəsəns] *n* inocencia
innocent ['ɪnəsnt] *adj* inocente
innocuous [ɪ'nɔkjuəs] *adj* inocuo
innovation [ɪnəu'veɪʃən] *n* novedad *f*
innuendo [ɪnju'endəu] *(pl* **~es)** *n* indirecta
inoculation [ɪnɔkju'leɪʃən] *n* inoculación *f*
inopportune [ɪn'ɔpətjuːn] *adj* inoportuno
inordinately [ɪ'nɔːdɪnɪtlɪ] *adv* desmesuradamente
in-patient *n* paciente *m/f* interno/a
input ['ɪnput] *n* entrada; *(of resources)* inversión *f*, *(COMPUT)* entrada de datos
inquest ['ɪnkwest] *n (coroner's)* encuesta judicial
inquire [ɪn'kwaɪə*] *vi* preguntar ♦ *vt*: **to ~ whether** preguntar si; **to ~ about** *(person)* preguntar por, *(fact)* informarse de; **~ into** *vt fus* investigar, indagar; **inquiry** *n* pregunta; *(investigation)* investigación *f*, pesquisa; **inquiry office** *(BRIT)* *n* oficina de información
inquisitive [ɪn'kwɪzɪtɪv] *adj (curious)* curioso
inroads ['ɪnrəudz] *npl*: **to make ~ into** mermar
ins *abbr* = **inches**
insane [ɪn'seɪn] *adj* loco; *(MED)* demente
insanity [ɪn'sænɪtɪ] *n* demencia, locura
insatiable [ɪn'seɪʃəbl] *adj* insaciable
inscription [ɪn'skrɪpʃən] *n* inscripción *f*, *(in book)* dedicatoria
inscrutable [ɪn'skruːtəbl] *adj* inescrutable, insondable
insect ['ɪnsekt] *n* insecto; **~icide** [ɪn'sektɪsaɪd] *n* insecticida *m*
insecure [ɪnsɪ'kjuə*] *adj* inseguro
insemination [ɪnsemɪ'neɪʃn] *n*: **artificial ~** inseminación *f* artificial
insensitive [ɪn'sensɪtɪv] *adj* insensible
inseparable [ɪn'seprəbl] *adj* inseparable
insert [*vb* ɪn'sɔːt, *n* 'ɪnsɔːt] *vt (into sth)* introducir ♦ *n* encarte *m*; **~ion** [ɪn'sɔːʃən] *n* inserción *f*
in-service *adj (training, course)* a cargo de la empresa
inshore [ɪn'ʃɔː*] *adj* de bajura ♦ *adv (be)* cerca de la orilla; *(move)* hacia la orilla
inside ['ɪn'saɪd] *n* interior *m* ♦ *adj* interior, interno ♦ *adv (be)* (por) dentro; *(go)* hacia dentro ♦ *prep* dentro de; *(of time):* **~ 10 minutes** en menos de 10 minutos; **~s** *npl (inf: stomach)* tripas *fpl*; **~ information** *n* información *f* confidencial; **~ lane** *n (AUT:*

in Britain) carril *m* izquierdo; (*AUT: in US, Europe etc*) carril *m* derecho; ~ **out** (*turn*) al revés; (*know*) a fondo

insider dealing, insider trading *n* (*STOCK EXCHANGE*) abuso de información privilegiada

insidious [ɪn'sɪdɪəs] *adj* insidioso

insight ['ɪnsaɪt] *n* perspicacia

insignia [ɪn'sɪgnɪə] *npl* insignias *fpl*

insignificant [ɪnsɪg'nɪfɪkənt] *adj* insignificante

insincere [ɪnsɪn'sɪə*] *adj* poco sincero

insinuate [ɪn'sɪnjueɪt] *vt* insinuar

insipid [ɪn'sɪpɪd] *adj* soso, insulso

insist [ɪn'sɪst] *vi* insistir; **to ~ on** insistir en; **to ~ that** insistir en que; (*claim*) exigir que; **~ence** *n* (*determination*) empeño; **~ent** *adj* insistente; (*noise, action*) persistente

insole ['ɪnsəʊl] *n* plantilla

insolent ['ɪnsələnt] *adj* insolente, descarado

insoluble [ɪn'sɒljubl] *adj* insoluble

insomnia [ɪn'sɒmnɪə] *n* insomnio

inspect [ɪn'spɛkt] *vt* inspeccionar, examinar; (*troops*) pasar revista a; **~ion** [ɪn'spɛkʃən] *n* inspección *f*, examen *m*; (*of troops*) revista; **~or** *n* inspector(a) *m/f*; (*BRIT: on buses, trains*) revisor(a) *m*

inspiration [ɪnspə'reɪʃən] *n* inspiración *f*; **inspire** [ɪn'spaɪə*] *vt* inspirar

instability [ɪnstə'bɪlɪtɪ] *n* inestabilidad *f*

install [ɪn'stɔːl] *vt* instalar; (*official*) nombrar; **~ation** [ɪnstə'leɪʃən] *n* instalación *f*

instalment [ɪn'stɔːlmənt] (*US* **installment**) *n* plazo; (*of story*) entrega; (*of TV serial etc*) capítulo; **in ~s** (*pay, receive*) a plazos

instance ['ɪnstəns] *n* ejemplo, caso; **for ~** por ejemplo; **in the first ~** en primer lugar

instant ['ɪnstənt] *n* instante *m*, momento ♦ *adj* inmediato; (*coffee etc*) instantáneo; **~ly** *adv* en seguida

instead [ɪn'stɛd] *adv* en cambio; **~ of** en lugar de, en vez de

instep ['ɪnstɛp] *n* empeine *m*

instil [ɪn'stɪl] *vt*: **to ~ sth into** inculcar algo a

instinct ['ɪnstɪŋkt] *n* instinto; **~ive** [-'stɪŋktɪv] *adj* instintivo

institute ['ɪnstɪtjuːt] *n* instituto; (*professional body*) colegio ♦ *vt* (*begin*) iniciar, empezar; (*proceedings*) entablar; (*system, rule*) establecer

institution [ɪnstɪ'tjuːʃən] *n* institución *f*; (*MED: home*) asilo; (*: asylum*) manicomio; (*of system etc*) establecimiento, (*of custom*) iniciación *f*

instruct [ɪn'strʌkt] *vt*: **to ~ sb in sth** instruir a uno en *or* sobre algo; **to ~ sb to do sth** dar instrucciones a uno de hacer algo; **~ion** [ɪn'strʌkʃən] *n* (*teaching*) instrucción *f*; **~ions** *npl* (*orders*) órdenes *fpl*; **~ions (for use)** modo de empleo; **~ive** *adj* instructivo; **~or** *n* instructor(a) *m/f*

instrument ['ɪnstrəmənt] *n* instrumento; **~al** [-'mɛntl] *adj* (*MUS*) instrumental; **to be ~al in** ser (el) artífice de; **~ panel** *n* tablero (de instrumentos)

insubordination [ɪnsəbɔːdɪ'neɪʃən] *n* insubordinación *f*

insufferable [ɪn'sʌfrəbl] *adj* insoportable

insufficient [ɪnsə'fɪʃənt] *adj* insuficiente

insular ['ɪnsjulə*] *adj* insular; (*person*) estrecho de miras

insulate ['ɪnsjuleɪt] *vt* aislar; **insulating tape** *n* cinta aislante; **insulation** [-'leɪʃən] *n* aislamiento

insulin ['ɪnsjulɪn] *n* insulina

insult [*n* 'ɪnsʌlt, *vb* ɪn'sʌlt] *n* insulto ♦ *vt* insultar; **~ing** *adj* insultante

insurance [ɪn'ʃuərəns] *n* seguro; **fire/life ~** seguro contra incendios/sobre la vida; **~ agent** *n* agente *m/f* de seguros; **~ policy** *n* póliza (de seguros)

insure [ɪn'ʃuə*] *vt* asegurar

intact [ɪn'tækt] *adj* íntegro; (*unharmed*) intacto

intake ['ɪnteɪk] *n* (*of food*) ingestión *f*; (*of air*) consumo; (*BRIT: SCOL*): **an ~ of 200 a year** 200 matriculados al año

integral ['ɪntɪgrəl] *adj* (*whole*) íntegro; (*part*) integrante

integrate ['ɪntɪgreɪt] *vt* integrar ♦ *vi* integrarse

integrity [ɪn'tɛgrɪtɪ] *n* honradez *f*, rectitud *f*

intellect ['ɪntəlɛkt] *n* intelecto; **~ual** [-'lɛktjuəl] *adj*, *n* intelectual *m/f*

intelligence [ɪn'tɛlɪdʒəns] *n* inteligencia

intelligent [ɪn'tɛlɪdʒənt] *adj* inteligente; **~sia** [ɪn'tɛlɪ'dʒɛntsɪə] *n* intelectualidad *f*

intelligible [ɪn'tɛlɪdʒɪbl] *adj* inteligible, comprensible

intend [ɪn'tɛnd] *vt* (*gift etc*): **to ~ sth for** destinar algo a; **to ~ to do sth** tener intención de *or* pensar hacer algo; **~ed** *adj* intencionado

intense [ɪn'tɛns] *adj* intenso; **~ly** *adv* (*extremely*) sumamente

intensify [ɪn'tɛnsɪfaɪ] *vt* intensificar; (*increase*) aumentar

intensive [ɪn'tɛnsɪv] *adj* intensivo; **~ care unit** *n* unidad *f* de vigilancia intensiva

intent [ɪn'tɛnt] *n* propósito; (*LAW*) premeditación *f* ♦ *adj* (*absorbed*) absorto; (*attentive*) atento; **to all ~s and purposes** prácticamente; **to be ~ on doing sth** estar resuelto a hacer algo

intention [ɪn'tɛnʃən] *n* intención *f*, propósito; **~al** *adj* deliberado; **~ally** *adv* a propósito

intently [ɪn'tɛntlɪ] *adv* atentamente, fijamente

interact [ɪntər'ækt] *vi* influirse mutuamente; **~ion** [-'ækʃən] *n* interacción *f*; **~ive** *adj* (*COMPUT*) interactivo

intercede [ɪntəˈsiːd] vi: **to ~ (with)** interceder (con)

intercept [ɪntəˈsɛpt] vt interceptar

interchange [ˈɪntətʃeɪndʒ] n intercambio; (on motorway) intersección f; **~able** adj intercambiable

intercom [ˈɪntəkəm] n interfono

intercourse [ˈɪntəkɔːs] n (sexual) relaciones fpl sexuales

interest [ˈɪntrɪst] n (also COMM) interés m ♦ vt interesar; **to be ~ed in** interesarse por; **~ing** adj interesante; **~ rate** n tipo or tasa de interés

interface [ˈɪntəfeɪs] n (COMPUT) junción f

interfere [ɪntəˈfɪə*] vi: **to ~ in** (quarrel, other people's business) entrometerse en; **to ~ with** (hinder) estorbar; (damage) estropear

interference [ɪntəˈfɪərəns] n intromisión f; (RADIO, TV) interferencia

interim [ˈɪntərɪm] n: **in the ~** en el ínterin ♦ adj provisional

interior [ɪnˈtɪərɪə*] n interior m ♦ adj interior; **~ designer** n interiorista m/f

interjection [ɪntəˈdʒɛkʃən] n interposición f; (LING) interjección f

interlock [ɪntəˈlɔk] vi entrelazarse

interlude [ˈɪntəluːd] n intervalo; (THEATRE) intermedio

intermarry [ɪntəˈmærɪ] vi casarse personas de distintas razas (or religiones etc)

intermediary [ɪntəˈmiːdɪərɪ] n intermediario/a

intermediate [ɪntəˈmiːdɪət] adj intermedio

interminable [ɪnˈtəːmɪnəbl] adj inacabable

intermission [ɪntəˈmɪʃən] n intermisión f; (THEATRE) descanso

intermittent [ɪntəˈmɪtnt] adj intermitente

intern [vb ɪnˈtəːn, n ˈɪntəːn] vt internar ♦ n (US) interno/a

internal [ɪnˈtəːnl] adj (layout, pipes, security) interior; (injury, structure, memo) internal; **~ly** adv: **"not to be taken ~ly"** "uso externo"; **I~ Revenue Service** (US) n departamento de impuestos; ≈ Hacienda (SP)

international [ɪntəˈnæʃənl] adj internacional ♦ n (BRIT: match) partido internacional

interplay [ˈɪntəpleɪ] n interacción f

interpret [ɪnˈtəːprɪt] vt interpretar; (translate) traducir; (understand) entender ♦ vi hacer de intérprete; **~ation** [-ˈteɪʃən] n interpretación f; traducción f; entendimiento; **~er** n intérprete m/f

interrelated [ɪntərɪˈleɪtɪd] adj interrelacionado

interrogate [ɪnˈtɛrəugeɪt] vt interrogar; **interrogation** [-ˈgeɪʃən] n interrogatorio f; **interrogative** [ɪntəˈrɔgətɪv] adj (LING) interrogativo

interrupt [ɪntəˈrʌpt] vt, vi interrumpir; **~ion** [-ˈrʌpʃən] n interrupción f

intersect [ɪntəˈsɛkt] vi (roads) cruzarse;

~ion [-ˈsɛkʃən] n (of roads) cruce m

intersperse [ɪntəˈspəːs] vt: **to ~ with** salpicar de

intertwine [ɪntəˈtwaɪn] vt entrelazarse

interval [ˈɪntəvl] n intervalo; (BRIT: THEATRE, SPORT) descanso; (: SCOL) recreo; **at ~s** a ratos, de vez en cuando

intervene [ɪntəˈviːn] vi intervenir; (event) interponerse; (time) transcurrir; **intervention** [-ˈvɛnʃən] n intervención f

interview [ˈɪntəvjuː] n entrevista ♦ vt entrevistarse con; **~er** n entrevistador(a) m/f

intestine [ɪnˈtɛstɪn] n intestino

intimacy [ˈɪntɪməsɪ] n intimidad f

intimate [adj ˈɪntɪmət, vb ˈɪntɪmeɪt] adj íntimo; (friendship) estrecho; (knowledge) profundo ♦ vt dar a entender

intimidate [ɪnˈtɪmɪdeɪt] vt intimidar, amedrentar

into [ˈɪntuː] prep en; (towards) a; (inside) hacia el interior de; **~ 3 pieces/French** en 3 pedazos/al francés

intolerable [ɪnˈtɔlərəbl] adj intolerable, insoportable

intolerant [ɪnˈtɔlərənt] adj: **~ (of)** intolerante (con or para)

intonation [ɪntəuˈneɪʃən] n entonación f

intoxicated [ɪnˈtɔksɪkeɪtɪd] adj embriagado; **intoxication** [ɪntɔksɪˈkeɪʃən] n embriaguez f

intractable [ɪnˈtræktəbl] adj (person) intratable; (problem) espinoso

intransitive [ɪnˈtrænsɪtɪv] adj intransitivo

intravenous [ɪntrəˈviːnəs] adj intravenoso

in-tray n bandeja de entrada

intricate [ˈɪntrɪkət] adj (design, pattern) intrincado

intrigue [ɪnˈtriːg] n intriga ♦ vt fascinar; **intriguing** adj fascinante

intrinsic [ɪnˈtrɪnsɪk] adj intrínseco

introduce [ɪntrəˈdjuːs] vt introducir, meter; (speaker, TV show etc) presentar; **to ~ sb (to sb)** presentar uno (a otro); **to ~ sb to** (pastime, technique) introducir a uno a; **introduction** [-ˈdʌkʃən] n introducción f; (of person) presentación f; **introductory** [-ˈdʌktərɪ] adj introductorio; (lesson, offer) de introducción

introvert [ˈɪntrəvəːt] n introvertido/a ♦ adj (also: **~ed**) introvertido

intrude [ɪnˈtruːd] vi (person) entrometerse; **to ~ on** estorbar; **~r** n intruso/a; **intrusion** [-ʒən] n invasión f

intuition [ɪntjuːˈɪʃən] n intuición f

inundate [ˈɪnʌndeɪt] vt: **to ~ with** inundar de

invade [ɪnˈveɪd] vt invadir

invalid [n ˈɪnvəlɪd, adj ɪnˈvælɪd] n (MED) minusválido/a ♦ adj (not valid) inválido, nulo

invaluable [ɪnˈvæljuəbl] adj inestimable

invariable [ɪnˈvɛərɪəbl] adj invariable

invasion [ɪn'veɪʒən] *n* invasión *f*
invent [ɪn'vɛnt] *vt* inventar; **~ion** [ɪn'vɛnʃən] *n* invento; (*lie*) ficción *f*, mentira; **~ive** *adj* inventivo; **~or** *n* inventor(a) *m/f*
inventory ['ɪnvəntrɪ] *n* inventario
invert [ɪn'vɜːt] *vt* invertir
invertebrate [ɪn'vɜːtɪbrət] *n* invertebrado
inverted commas (BRIT) *npl* comillas *fpl*
invest [ɪn'vɛst] *vt* invertir ♦ *vi*: **to ~ in** (*company etc*) invertir dinero en; (*fig*: *sth useful*) comprar
investigate [ɪn'vɛstɪgeɪt] *vt* investigar; **investigation** [-'geɪʃən] *n* investigación *f*, pesquisa; **investigator** *n* investigador(a) *m/f*
investment [ɪn'vɛstmənt] *n* inversión *f*
investor [ɪn'vɛstə*] *n* inversionista *m/f*
inveterate [ɪn'vɛtərət] *adj* empedernido
invidious [ɪn'vɪdɪəs] *adj* odioso
invigilator [ɪn'vɪdʒɪleɪtə*] *n* persona que vigila en un examen
invigorating [ɪn'vɪgəreɪtɪŋ] *adj* vigorizante
invincible [ɪn'vɪnsɪbl] *adj* invencible
invisible [ɪn'vɪzɪbl] *adj* invisible
invitation [ɪnvɪ'teɪʃən] *n* invitación *f*
invite [ɪn'vaɪt] *vt* invitar; (*opinions etc*) solicitar, pedir; **inviting** *adj* atractivo; (*food*) apetitoso
invoice ['ɪnvɔɪs] *n* factura ♦ *vt* facturar
invoke [ɪn'vəuk] *vt* (*law, principle*) recurrir a
involuntary [ɪn'vɔləntrɪ] *adj* involuntario
involve [ɪn'vɔlv] *vt* suponer, implicar; tener que ver con; (*concern, affect*) corresponder; **to ~ sb (in sth)** comprometer a uno (con algo); **~d** *adj* complicado; **to be ~d in** (*take part*) tomar parte en; (*be engrossed*) estar muy metido en; **~ment** *n* participación *f*; dedicación *f*
inward ['ɪnwəd] *adj* (*movement*) interior, interno; (*thought, feeling*) íntimo; **~(s)** *adv* hacia adentro
I/O *abbr* (COMPUT = *input/output*) entrada/salida
iodine ['aɪəudiːn] *n* yodo
ion ['aɪən] *n* ion *m*
iota [aɪ'əutə] *n* jota, ápice *m*
IOU *n abbr* (= *I owe you*) pagaré *m*
IQ *n abbr* (= *intelligence quotient*) cociente *m* intelectual
IRA *n abbr* (= *Irish Republican Army*) IRA *m*
Iran [ɪ'rɑːn] *n* Irán *m*; **~ian** [ɪ'reɪnɪən] *adj, n* iraní *m/f*
Iraq [ɪ'rɑːk] *n* Iraq *m*; **~i** *adj, n* iraquí *m/f*
irascible [ɪ'ræsɪbl] *adj* irascible
irate [aɪ'reɪt] *adj* enojado, airado
Ireland ['aɪələnd] *n* Irlanda
iris ['aɪrɪs] (*pl* **~es**) *n* (ANAT) iris *m*; (BOT) lirio
Irish ['aɪrɪʃ] *adj* irlandés/esa ♦ *npl*: **the ~** los irlandeses; **~man/woman** *n* irlandés/

esa *m/f*; **~ Sea** *n*: **the ~ Sea** el mar de Irlanda
irksome ['ɜːksʌm] *adj* fastidioso
iron ['aɪən] *n* hierro; (*for clothes*) plancha ♦ *cpd* de hierro ♦ *vt* (*clothes*) planchar; **~ out** *vt* (*fig*) allanar; **I~ Curtain** *n*: **the I~ Curtain** el Telón de Acero
ironic(al) [aɪ'rɔnɪk(l)] *adj* irónico
ironing ['aɪənɪŋ] *n* (*activity*) planchado; (*clothes: ironed*) ropa planchada; (*: to be ironed*) ropa por planchar; **~ board** *n* tabla de planchar
ironmonger's (**shop**) ['aɪənmʌŋgə*z] (BRIT) *n* ferretería, quincallería
irony ['aɪrənɪ] *n* ironía
irrational [ɪ'ræʃənl] *adj* irracional
irreconcilable [ɪrɛkən'saɪləbl] *adj* (*ideas*) incompatible; (*enemies*) irreconciliable
irregular [ɪ'rɛgjulə*] *adj* irregular; (*surface*) desigual; (*action, event*) anómalo; (*behaviour*) poco ortodoxo
irrelevant [ɪ'rɛləvənt] *adj* fuera de lugar, inoportuno
irreplaceable [ɪrɪ'pleɪsəbl] *adj* irremplazable
irrepressible [ɪrɪ'prɛsəbl] *adj* incontenible
irresistible [ɪrɪ'zɪstɪbl] *adj* irresistible
irresolute [ɪ'rɛzəluːt] *adj* indeciso
irrespective [ɪrɪ'spɛktɪv]: **~ of** *prep* sin tener en cuenta, no importa
irresponsible [ɪrɪ'spɔnsɪbl] *adj* (*act*) irresponsable; (*person*) poco serio
irrigate ['ɪrɪgeɪt] *vt* regar; **irrigation** [-'geɪʃən] *n* riego
irritable ['ɪrɪtəbl] *adj* (*person*) de mal humor
irritate ['ɪrɪteɪt] *vt* fastidiar; (MED) picar; **irritating** *adj* fastidioso; **irritation** [-'teɪʃən] *n* fastidio; irritación; picazón *f*, picor *m*
IRS (US) *n abbr* = **Internal Revenue Service**
is [ɪz] *vb see* **be**
Islam ['ɪzlɑːm] *n* Islam *m*; **~ic** [ɪz'læmɪk] *adj* islámico
island ['aɪlənd] *n* isla; **~er** *n* isleño/a
isle [aɪl] *n* isla
isn't ['ɪznt] = **is not**
isolate ['aɪsəleɪt] *vt* aislar; **~d** *adj* aislado; **isolation** [-'leɪʃən] *n* aislamiento
Israel ['ɪzreɪl] *n* Israel *m*; **~i** [ɪz'reɪlɪ] *adj, n* israelí *m/f*
issue ['ɪʃuː] *n* (*problem, subject, most important part*) cuestión *f*; (*outcome*) resultado; (*of banknotes etc*) emisión *f*; (*of newspaper etc*) edición *f*; (*offspring*) sucesión *f*, descendencia ♦ *vt* (*rations, equipment*) distribuir, repartir; (*orders*) dar; (*certificate, passport*) expedir; (*decree*) promulgar; (*magazine*) publicar; (*cheques*) extender; (*banknotes, stamps*) emitir; **at ~** en cuestión; **to take ~ with sb (over)** estar en desacuerdo con uno (sobre); **to make an ~**

of sth hacer una cuestión de algo
Istanbul [ɪstæn'buːl] *n* Estambul *m*
isthmus ['ɪsməs] *n* istmo

──────── *KEYWORD*

it [ɪt] *pron* **1** (*specific*: *subject*: *not generally translated*) él/ella; (: *direct object*) lo, la; (: *indirect object*) le; (*after prep*) él/ella; (*abstract concept*) ello; ~'s **on the table** está en la mesa; **I can't find** ~ no lo (*or* la) encuentro; **give** ~ **to me** dámelo (*or* dámela); **I spoke to him about** ~ le hablé del asunto; **what did you learn from** ~? ¿qué aprendiste de él (*or* ella)?; **did you go to** ~? (*party, concert etc*) ¿fuiste?
2 (*impersonal*): ~'s **raining** llueve, está lloviendo; ~'s **6 o'clock/the 10th of August** son las 6/es el 10 de agosto; **how far is** ~? — ~'s **10 miles/2 hours on the train** ¿a qué distancia está? — a 10 millas/2 horas en tren; **who is** ~? — ~'s **me** ¿quién es? — soy yo

Italian [ɪ'tæljən] *adj* italiano ♦ *n* italiano/a; (*LING*) italiano
italics [ɪ'tælɪks] *npl* cursiva
Italy ['ɪtəlɪ] *n* Italia
itch [ɪtʃ] *n* picazón *f* ♦ *vi* (*part of body*) picar; **to** ~ **to do sth** rabiar por hacer algo; ~**y** *adj*: **my hand is** ~**y** me pica la mano
it'd ['ɪtd] = **it would; it had**
item ['aɪtəm] *n* artículo; (*on agenda*) asunto (a tratar); (*also*: **news** ~) noticia; ~**ize** *vt* detallar
itinerant [ɪ'tɪnərənt] *adj* ambulante
itinerary [aɪ'tɪnərərɪ] *n* itinerario
it'll ['ɪtl] = **it will; it shall**
its [ɪts] *adj* su; sus *pl*
it's [ɪts] = **it is; it has**
itself [ɪt'sɛlf] *pron* (*reflexive*) sí mismo/a; (*emphatic*) él mismo/ella misma
ITV *n abbr* (*BRIT*: = *Independent Television*) cadena de televisión comercial independiente del Estado
I.U.D. *n abbr* (= *intra-uterine device*) DIU *m*
I've [aɪv] = **I have**
ivory ['aɪvərɪ] *n* marfil *m*; (*colour*) (color) de marfil; ~ **tower** *n* torre *f* de marfil
ivy ['aɪvɪ] *n* (*BOT*) hiedra

J j

jab [dʒæb] *vt*: **to** ~ **sth into sth** clavar algo en algo ♦ *n* (*inf*) (*MED*) pinchazo
jack [dʒæk] *n* (*AUT*) gato; (*CARDS*) sota; ~ **up** *vt* (*AUT*) levantar con gato
jackal ['dʒækɔːl] *n* (*ZOOL*) chacal *m*
jacket ['dʒækɪt] *n* chaqueta, americana, saco (*AM*); (*of book*) sobrecubierta
jack-knife *vi* colear
jack plug *n* (*ELEC*) enchufe *m* de clavija
jackpot ['dʒækpɔt] *n* premio gordo
jaded ['dʒeɪdɪd] *adj* (*tired*) cansado; (*fed-up*) hastiado
jagged ['dʒægɪd] *adj* dentado
jail [dʒeɪl] *n* cárcel *f* ♦ *vt* encarcelar
jam [dʒæm] *n* mermelada; (*also*: **traffic** ~) embotellamiento; (*inf*: *difficulty*) apuro ♦ *vt* (*passage etc*) obstruir; (*mechanism, drawer etc*) atascar; (*RADIO*) interferir ♦ *vi* atascarse, trabarse; **to** ~ **sth into sth** meter algo a la fuerza en algo
Jamaica [dʒə'meɪkə] *n* Jamaica
jangle ['dʒæŋgl] *vi* entrechocar (ruidosamente)
janitor ['dʒænɪtə*] *n* (*caretaker*) portero, conserje *m*
January ['dʒænjuərɪ] *n* enero
Japan [dʒə'pæn] *n* (el) Japón; ~**ese** [dʒæpə'niːz] *adj* japonés/esa ♦ *n inv* japonés/esa *m/f*; (*LING*) japonés *m*
jar [dʒɑː*] *n* tarro, bote *m* ♦ *vi* (*sound*) chirriar; (*colours*) desentonar
jargon ['dʒɑːgən] *n* jerga
jasmine ['dʒæzmɪn] *n* jazmín *m*
jaundice ['dʒɔːndɪs] *n* ictericia; ~**d** *adj* desilusionado, poco entusiasta
jaunt [dʒɔːnt] *n* excursión *f*; ~**y** *adj* alegre
javelin ['dʒævlɪn] *n* jabalina
jaw [dʒɔː] *n* mandíbula
jay [dʒeɪ] *n* (*ZOOL*) arrendajo
jaywalker ['dʒeɪwɔːkə*] *n* peatón/ona *m/f* imprudente
jazz [dʒæz] *n* jazz *m*; ~ **up** *vt* (*liven up*) animar, avivar
jealous ['dʒɛləs] *adj* celoso; (*envious*) envidioso; ~**y** *n* celos *mpl*; envidia
jeans [dʒiːnz] *npl* vaqueros *mpl*, tejanos *mpl*
Jeep [dʒiːp] ® *n* jeep *m*
jeer [dʒɪə*] *vi*: **to** ~ **(at)** (*mock*) mofarse (de)
jelly ['dʒɛlɪ] *n* (*jam*) jalea; (*dessert etc*) gela-

tina; ~**fish** n inv medusa (SP), aguaviva (AM)

jeopardy ['dʒɛpədɪ] n: **to be in ~** estar en peligro

jerk [dʒɜːk] n (jolt) sacudida; (wrench) tirón m; (inf) imbécil m/f ♦ vt tirar bruscamente de ♦ vi (vehicle) traquetear

jerkin ['dʒɜːkɪn] n chaleco

jersey ['dʒɜːzɪ] n jersey m; (fabric) (tejido de) punto

jest [dʒɛst] n broma

Jesus ['dʒiːzəs] n Jesús m

jet [dʒɛt] n (of gas, liquid) chorro; (AVIAT) avión m a reacción; ~-**black** adj negro como el azabache; ~ **engine** n motor m a reacción; ~ **lag** n desorientación f después de un largo vuelo

jettison ['dʒɛtɪsn] vt desechar

jetty ['dʒɛtɪ] n muelle m, embarcadero

Jew [dʒuː] n judío

jewel ['dʒuːəl] n joya; (in watch) rubí m; ~**ler** n joyero/a; ~**ler's (shop)** (US ~**ry store**) n joyería; ~**lery** (US ~**ry**) n joyas fpl, alhajas fpl

Jewess ['dʒuːɪs] n judía

Jewish ['dʒuːɪʃ] adj judío

jibe [dʒaɪb] n mofa

jiffy ['dʒɪfɪ] (inf) n: **in a ~** en un santiamén

jig [dʒɪg] n giga

jigsaw ['dʒɪgsɔː] n (also: ~ **puzzle**) rompecabezas m inv, puzle m

jilt [dʒɪlt] vt dejar plantado a

jingle ['dʒɪŋgl] n musiquilla ♦ vi tintinear

jinx [dʒɪŋks] n: **there's a ~ on it** está gafado

jitters ['dʒɪtəz] (inf) npl: **to get the ~** ponerse nervioso

job [dʒɔb] n (task) tarea; (post) empleo; **it's not my ~** no me incumbe a mí; **it's a good ~ that ...** menos mal que ...; **just the ~!** ¡estupendo!; ~ **centre** (BRIT) n oficina estatal de colocaciones; ~**less** adj sin trabajo

jockey ['dʒɔkɪ] n jockey m/f ♦ vi: **to ~ for position** maniobrar para conseguir una posición

jocular ['dʒɔkjʊlə*] adj gracioso

jog [dʒɔg] vt empujar (ligeramente) ♦ vi (run) hacer footing; **to ~ sb's memory** refrescar la memoria a uno; ~ **along** vi (fig) ir tirando; ~**ging** n footing m

join [dʒɔɪn] vt (things) juntar, unir; (club) hacerse socio de; (POL: party) afiliarse a; (queue) ponerse en; (meet: people) reunirse con ♦ vi (roads) juntarse; (rivers) confluir ♦ n juntura; ~ **in** vi tomar parte, participar ♦ vt fus tomar parte or participar en; ~ **up** vi reunirse; (MIL) alistarse

joiner ['dʒɔɪnə*] (BRIT) n carpintero/a; ~**y** n carpintería

joint [dʒɔɪnt] n (TECH) junta, unión f; (ANAT) articulación f; (BRIT: CULIN) pieza

de carne (para asar); (inf: place) tugurio; (: of cannabis) porro ♦ adj (common) común; (combined) combinado; ~ **account** (with bank etc) cuenta común

joke [dʒəuk] n chiste m; (also: practical ~) broma ♦ vi bromear; **to play a ~ on** gastar una broma a; ~**r** n (CARDS) comodín m

jolly ['dʒɔlɪ] adj (merry) alegre; (enjoyable) divertido ♦ adv (BRIT: inf) muy, terriblemente

jolt [dʒəult] n (jerk) sacudida; (shock) susto ♦ vt (physically) sacudir; (emotionally) asustar

jostle ['dʒɔsl] vt dar empellones a, codear

jot [dʒɔt] n: **not one** ni jota, ni pizca; ~ **down** vt apuntar; ~**ter** n bloc m

journal ['dʒɜːnl] n (magazine) revista; (diary) periódico, diario; ~**ism** n periodismo; ~**ist** n periodista m/f, reportero/a

journey ['dʒɜːnɪ] n viaje m; (distance covered) trayecto

jovial ['dʒəuvɪəl] adj risueño, jovial

joy [dʒɔɪ] n alegría; ~**ful** adj alegre; ~**ous** adj alegre; ~ **ride** n (illegal) paseo en coche robado; ~**rider** n gamberro que roba un coche para dar una vuelta y luego abandonarlo; ~ **stick** n (AVIAT) palanca de mando; (COMPUT) palanca de control

J.P. n abbr = **Justice of the Peace**

Jr abbr = **junior**

jubilant ['dʒuːbɪlnt] adj jubiloso

jubilee ['dʒuːbɪliː] n aniversario

judge [dʒʌdʒ] n juez m/f; (fig: expert) perito ♦ vt juzgar; (consider) considerar; **judg(e)ment** n juicio

judiciary [dʒuː'dɪʃɪərɪ] n poder m judicial

judicious [dʒuː'dɪʃəs] adj juicioso

judo ['dʒuːdəu] n judo

jug [dʒʌg] n jarra

juggernaut ['dʒʌgənɔːt] (BRIT) n (huge truck) trailer m

juggle ['dʒʌgl] vi hacer juegos malabares; ~**r** n malabarista m/f

Jugoslav ['juːgəuslɑːv] etc = **Yugoslav** etc

juice [dʒuːs] n zumo, jugo (esp AM); **juicy** adj jugoso

jukebox ['dʒuːkbɔks] n tocadiscos m inv tragaperras m inv

July [dʒuː'laɪ] n julio

jumble ['dʒʌmbl] n revoltijo ♦ vt (also: ~ up) revolver; ~ **sale** (BRIT) n venta de objetos usados con fines benéficos

jumbo (jet) ['dʒʌmbəu-] n jumbo

jump [dʒʌmp] vi saltar, dar saltos; (with fear, surprise) pegar un bote; (increase) aumentar ♦ vt saltar ♦ n salto; aumento; **to ~ the queue** (BRIT) colarse; ~ **cables** (US) npl = **leads**

jumper ['dʒʌmpə*] n (BRIT: pullover) suéter m, jersey m; (US: dress) mandil m

jump leads (BRIT) npl cables mpl puente de batería

jumpy ['dʒʌmpɪ] (*inf*) *adj* nervioso
Jun. *abbr* = **junior**
junction ['dʒʌŋkʃən] *n* (*BRIT: of roads*) cruce *m*; (*RAIL*) empalme *m*
juncture ['dʒʌŋktʃə*] *n*: **at this ~** en este momento, en esta coyuntura
June [dʒuːn] *n* junio
jungle ['dʒʌŋgl] *n* selva, jungla
junior ['dʒuːnɪə*] *adj* (*in age*) menor, más joven; (*brother/sister etc*): **7 years her ~** siete años menor que ella; (*position*) subalterno ♦ *n* menor *m/f*, joven *m/f*; **~ school** (*BRIT*) *n* escuela primaria
junk [dʒʌŋk] *n* (*cheap goods*) baratijas *fpl*; (*rubbish*) basura; **~ food** *n* alimentos preparados y envasados de escaso valor nutritivo
junkie ['dʒʌŋkɪ] (*inf*) *n* drogadicto/a, yonqui *m/f*
junk mail *n* propaganda de buzón
junk shop *n* tienda de objetos usados
Junr *abbr* = **junior**
jurisdiction [dʒuərɪs'dɪkʃən] *n* jurisdicción *f*
juror ['dʒuərə*] *n* jurado
jury ['dʒuərɪ] *n* jurado
just [dʒʌst] *adj* justo ♦ *adv* (*exactly*) exactamente; (*only*) sólo, solamente; **he's ~ done it/left** acaba de hacerlo/irse; **~ right** perfecto; **~ two o'clock** las dos en punto; **she's ~ as clever as you** (ella) es tan lista como tú; **~ as well that ...** menos mal que ...; **~ as he was leaving** en el momento en que se marchaba; **~ before/enough** justo antes/lo suficiente; **~ here** aquí mismo; **he ~ missed** ha fallado por poco; **~ listen to this** escucha esto un momento
justice ['dʒʌstɪs] *n* justicia; (*US: judge*) juez *m*; **to do ~ to** (*fig*) hacer justicia a; **J~ of the Peace** *n* juez *m* de paz
justify ['dʒʌstɪfaɪ] *vt* justificar; (*text*) alinear
jut [dʒʌt] *vi* (*also:* ~ **out**) sobresalir
juvenile ['dʒuːvənaɪl] *adj* (*court*) de menores; (*humour, mentality*) infantil ♦ *n* menor *m* de edad
juxtapose ['dʒʌkstəpəuz] *vt* yuxtaponer

K k

K *abbr* (= *one thousand*) mil; (= *kilobyte*) kilobyte *m*, kiilocteto
kaleidoscope [kə'laɪdəskəup] *n* calidoscopio
kangaroo [kæŋgə'ruː] *n* canguro
karate [kə'rɑːtɪ] *n* karate *m*
kebab [kə'bæb] *n* pincho moruno
keel [kiːl] *n* quilla; **on an even ~** (*fig*) en equilibrio
keen [kiːn] *adj* (*interest, desire*) grande, vivo; (*eye, intelligence*) agudo; (*competition*) reñido; (*edge*) afilado; (*eager*) entusiasta; **to be ~ to do or on doing sth** tener muchas ganas de hacer algo; **to be ~ on sth/sb** interesarse por algo/uno
keep [kiːp] (*pt, pp* **kept**) *vt* (*preserve, store*) guardar; (*hold back*) quedarse con; (*maintain*) mantener; (*detain*) detener; (*shop*) ser propietario de; (*feed: family etc*) mantener; (*promise*) cumplir; (*chickens, bees etc*) criar; (*accounts*) llevar; (*diary*) escribir; (*prevent*): **to ~ sb from doing sth** impedir a uno hacer algo ♦ *vi* (*food*) conservarse; (*remain*) seguir, continuar ♦ *n* (*of castle*) torreón *m*; (*food etc*) comida, subsistencia; (*inf*): **for ~s** para siempre; **to ~ doing sth** seguir haciendo algo; **to ~ sb happy** tener a uno contento; **to ~ a place tidy** mantener un lugar limpio; **to ~ sth to o.s.** guardar algo para sí mismo; **to ~ sth (back) from sb** ocultar algo a uno; **to ~ time** (*clock*) mantener la hora exacta; **~ on** *vi*: **to ~ on doing** seguir *or* continuar haciendo; **to ~ on (about sth)** no parar de hablar (de algo); **~ out** *vi* (*stay out*) permanecer fuera; **"~ out"** "prohibida la entrada"; **~ up** *vt* mantener, conservar ♦ *vi* no retrasarse; **to ~ up with** (*pace*) ir al paso de; (*level*) mantenerse a la altura de; **~er** *n* guardián/ana *m/f*; **~-fit** *n* gimnasia (para mantenerse en forma); **~ing** *n* (*care*) cuidado; **in ~ing with** de acuerdo con; **~sake** *n* recuerdo
kennel ['kɛnl] *n* perrera; **~s** *npl* residencia canina
Kenya ['kɛnjə] *n* Kenia
kept [kɛpt] *pt, pp of* **keep**
kerb [kɜːb] (*BRIT*) *n* bordillo
kernel ['kɜːnl] *n* (*nut*) almendra; (*fig*) meollo

ketchup ['kɛtʃəp] *n* salsa de tomate, catsup *m*

kettle ['kɛtl] *n* hervidor *m* de agua; ~ **drum** *n* (MUS) timbal *m*

key [ki:] *n* llave *f*; (MUS) tono; (of piano, typewriter) tecla ♦ *adj* (issue etc) clave *inv* ♦ *vt* (also: ~ *in*) teclear; ~**board** *n* teclado; ~**ed up** *adj* (person) nervioso; ~**hole** *n* ojo (de la cerradura); ~**note** *n* (MUS) tónica; (of speech) punto principal *or* clave; ~**ring** *n* llavero

khaki ['kɑːkɪ] *n* caqui

kick [kɪk] *vt* dar una patada *or* un puntapié a; (inf: habit) quitarse de ♦ *vi* (horse) dar coces ♦ *n* patada; puntapié *m*; (of animal) coz *f*; (thrill): **he does it for ~s** lo hace por pura diversión; ~ **off** *vi* (SPORT) hacer el saque inicial

kid [kɪd] *n* (inf: child) chiquillo/a; (animal) cabrito; (leather) cabritilla ♦ *vi* (inf) bromear

kidnap ['kɪdnæp] *vt* secuestrar; ~**per** *n* secuestrador(a) *m/f*; ~**ping** *n* secuestro

kidney ['kɪdnɪ] *n* riñón *m*

kill [kɪl] *vt* matar; (murder) asesinar ♦ *n* matanza; **to ~ time** matar el tiempo; ~**er** *n* asesino/a; ~**ing** *n* (one) asesinato; (several) matanza; **to make a ~ing** (fig) hacer su agosto; ~**joy** (BRIT) *n* aguafiestas *m/f inv*

kiln [kɪln] *n* horno

kilo ['kiːləu] *n* kilo; ~**byte** *n* (COMPUT) kilobyte *m*, kilocteto; ~**gram(me)** ['kɪləugræm] *n* kilo, kilogramo; ~**metre** ['kɪləmiːtə*] (US ~**meter**) *n* kilómetro; ~**watt** ['kɪləuwɔt] *n* kilovatio

kilt [kɪlt] *n* falda escocesa

kin [kɪn] *n* see **kith**; **next**

kind [kaɪnd] *adj* amable, atento ♦ *n* clase *f*, especie *f*; (species) género; **in ~** (COMM) en especie; **a ~ of** una especie de; **to be two of a ~** ser tal para cual

kindergarten ['kɪndəgɑːtn] *n* jardín *m* de la infancia

kind-hearted *adj* bondadoso, de buen corazón

kindle ['kɪndl] *vt* encender; (arouse) despertar

kindly ['kaɪndlɪ] *adj* bondadoso; cariñoso ♦ *adv* bondadosamente, amablemente; **will you ~ ...** sea usted tan amable de ...

kindness ['kaɪndnɪs] *n* (quality) bondad *f*, amabilidad *f*; (act) favor *m*

kindred ['kɪndrɪd] *n* familia ♦ *adj*: ~ **spirits** almas *fpl* gemelas

kinetic [kɪ'nɛtɪk] *adj* cinético

king [kɪŋ] *n* rey *m*; ~**dom** *n* reino; ~**fisher** *n* martín *m* pescador; ~-**size** *adj* de tamaño extra

kinky ['kɪŋkɪ] *adj* (pej: person, behaviour) extraño; (: sexually) perverso

kiosk ['kiːɔsk] *n* quiosco; (BRIT: TEL) cabina

kipper ['kɪpə*] *n* arenque *m* ahumado

kiss [kɪs] *n* beso ♦ *vt* besar; **to ~ (each other)** besarse; ~ **of life** *n* respiración *f* boca a boca

kit [kɪt] *n* (equipment) equipo; (tools etc) (caja de) herramientas *fpl*; (assembly ~) juego de armar

kitchen ['kɪtʃɪn] *n* cocina; ~ **sink** *n* fregadero

kite [kaɪt] *n* (toy) cometa

kith [kɪθ] *n*: ~ **and kin** parientes *mpl* y allegados

kitten ['kɪtn] *n* gatito/a

kitty ['kɪtɪ] *n* (pool of money) fondo común

kleptomaniac [klɛptəu'meɪnɪæk] *n* cleptómano/a

km *abbr* (= kilometre) km

knack [næk] *n*: **to have the ~ of doing sth** tener el don de hacer algo

knapsack ['næpsæk] *n* mochila

knead [niːd] *vt* amasar

knee [niː] *n* rodilla; ~**cap** *n* rótula

kneel [niːl] (pt, pp **knelt**) *vi* (also: ~ **down**) arrodillarse

knell [nɛl] *n* toque *m* de difuntos

knelt [nɛlt] *pt, pp* of **kneel**

knew [njuː] *pt* of **know**

knickers ['nɪkəz] (BRIT) *npl* bragas *fpl*

knife [naɪf] (pl **knives**) *n* cuchillo ♦ *vt* acuchillar

knight [naɪt] *n* caballero; (CHESS) caballo; ~**hood** (BRIT) *n* (title): **to receive a** ~**hood** recibir el título de Sir

knit [nɪt] *vt* tejer, tricotar ♦ *vi* hacer punto, tricotar; (bones) soldarse; **to ~ one's brows** fruncir el ceño; ~**ting** *n* labor *f* de punto; ~**ting machine** *n* máquina de tricotar; ~**ting needle** *n* aguja de hacer punto; ~**wear** *n* prendas *fpl* de punto

knives [naɪvz] *npl* of **knife**

knob [nɔb] *n* (of door) tirador *m*; (of stick) puño; (on radio, TV) botón *m*

knock [nɔk] *vt* (strike) golpear; (bump into) chocar contra; (inf) criticar ♦ *vi* (at door etc): **to ~ at/on** llamar a ♦ *n* golpe *m*; (on door) llamada; ~ **down** *vt* atropellar; ~ **off** (inf) *vi* (finish) salir del trabajo ♦ *vt* (from price) descontar; (inf: steal) birlar; ~ **out** *vt* dejar sin sentido; (BOXING) poner fuera de combate, dejar K.O.; (in competition) eliminar; ~ **over** *vt* (object) tirar; (person) atropellar; ~**er** *n* (on door) aldabón *m*; ~**out** *n* (BOXING) K.O. *m*, knockout *m* ♦ *cpd* (competition etc) eliminatorio

knot [nɔt] *n* nudo ♦ *vt* anudar; ~**ty** *adj* (fig) complicado

know [nəu] (pt **knew**, pp **known**) *vt* (facts) saber; (be acquainted with) conocer; (recognize) reconocer, conocer; **to ~ how to swim** saber nadar; **to ~ about** *or* **of sb/sth** saber de uno/algo; ~-**all** *n* sabelotodo *m/f*; ~-**how** *n* conocimientos *mpl*; ~**ing**

adj (*look*) de complicidad; ~**ingly** adv (*purposely*) adrede; (*smile, look*) con complicidad

knowledge ['nɔlɪdʒ] n conocimiento; (*learning*) saber m, conocimientos mpl; ~**able** adj entendido

known [nəun] pp of **know**

knuckle ['nʌkl] n nudillo

K.O. n abbr = **knockout**

Koran [kɔ'rɑːn] n Corán m

Korea [kə'rɪə] n Corea

kosher ['kəuʃə*] adj autorizado por la ley judía

L l

L (*BRIT*) abbr = **learner driver**

l. abbr (= *litre*) l

lab [læb] n abbr = **laboratory**

label ['leɪbl] n etiqueta ♦ vt poner etiqueta a

labor etc ['leɪbə*] (*US*) = **labour**

laboratory [lə'bɔrətərɪ] n laboratorio

laborious [lə'bɔːrɪəs] adj penoso

labour ['leɪbə*] (*US* **labor**) n (*hard work*) trabajo; (~ *force*) mano f de obra; (*MED*): **to be in** ~ estar de parto ♦ vi: **to** ~ (**at sth**) trabajar (en algo) ♦ vt: **to** ~ **a point** insistir en un punto; **L~, the L~ party** (*BRIT*) el partido laborista, los laboristas mpl; ~**ed** adj (*breathing*) fatigoso; ~**er** n peón m; **farm** ~**er** peón m; (**day** ~**er**) jornalero

labyrinth ['læbɪrɪnθ] n laberinto

lace [leɪs] n encaje m; (*of shoe etc*) cordón m ♦ vt (*shoes: also:* ~ **up**) atarse (los zapatos)

lack [læk] n (*absence*) falta ♦ vt faltarle a uno, carecer de; **through** or **for** ~ **of** por falta de; **to be** ~**ing** faltar, no haber; **to be** ~**ing in sth** faltarle a uno algo

lacquer ['lækə*] n laca

lad [læd] n muchacho, chico

ladder ['lædə*] n escalera (de mano); (*BRIT: in tights*) carrera

laden ['leɪdn] adj: ~ (**with**) cargado (de)

ladle ['leɪdl] n cucharón m

lady ['leɪdɪ] n señora; (*dignified, graceful*) dama; "**ladies and gentlemen ...**" "señoras y caballeros ..."; **young** ~ señorita; **the ladies' (room)** los servicios de señoras; ~**bird** (*US* ~**bug**) n mariquita; ~**like** adj fino; **L~ship** n: **your L~ship** su Señoría

lag [læg] n retraso ♦ vi (*also:* ~ **behind**) retrasarse, quedarse atrás ♦ vt (*pipes*) revestir

lager ['lɑːgə*] n cerveza (rubia)

lagoon [lə'guːn] n laguna

laid [leɪd] pt, pp of **lay**; ~ **back** (*inf*) adj relajado; ~ **up** adj: **to be** ~ **up (with)** tener que guardar cama (a causa de)

lain [leɪn] pp of **lie**

lair [lɛə*] n guarida

lake [leɪk] n lago

lamb [læm] n cordero; (*meat*) (carne f de) cordero; ~ **chop** n chuleta de cordero; **lambswool** n lana de cordero

lame [leɪm] adj cojo; (*excuse*) poco convincente

lament [lə'mɛnt] n quejo ♦ vt lamentarse de

laminated ['læmɪneɪtɪd] adj (*metal*) laminado; (*wood*) contrachapado; (*surface*) plastificado

lamp [læmp] n lámpara

lampoon [læm'puːn] vt satirizar

lamp: ~**post** (*BRIT*) n (poste m de) farol m; ~**shade** n pantalla

lance [lɑːns] n lanza ♦ vt (*MED*) abrir con lanceta

land [lænd] n tierra; (*country*) país m; (*piece of* ~) terreno; (*estate*) tierras fpl, finca ♦ vi (*from ship*) desembarcar; (*AVIAT*) aterrizar; (*fig: fall*) caer, terminar ♦ vt (*passengers, goods*) desembarcar; **to** ~ **sb with sth** (*inf*) hacer cargar a uno con algo; ~ **up** vi: **to** ~ **up in/at** ir a parar a/en; ~**ing** n aterrizaje m; (*of staircase*) rellano; ~**ing gear** n (*AVIAT*) tren m de aterrizaje; ~**ing strip** n pista de aterrizaje; ~**lady** n (*of rented house, pub etc*) dueña; (*of pub etc*) patrón m; ~**lord** n propietario; (*of pub etc*) patrón m; ~**mark** n lugar m conocido; **to be a** ~**mark** (*fig*) marcar un hito histórico; ~**owner** n terrateniente m/f

landscape ['lænskeɪp] n paisaje m; ~ **gardener** n arquitecto de jardines

landslide ['lændslaɪd] n (*GEO*) corrimiento de tierras; (*fig: POL*) victoria arrolladora

lane [leɪn] n (*in country*) camino; (*AUT*) carril m; (*in race*) calle f

language ['læŋgwɪdʒ] n lenguaje m; (*national tongue*) idioma m, lengua; **bad** ~ palabrotas fpl; ~ **laboratory** n laboratorio de idiomas

languish ['læŋgwɪʃ] vi languidecer

lank [læŋk] adj (*hair*) lacio

lanky ['læŋkɪ] adj larguirucho

lantern ['læntn] n linterna, farol m

lap [læp] n (*of track*) vuelta; (*of body*) regazo; **to sit on sb's** ~ sentarse en las rodillas de uno ♦ vt (*also:* ~ **up**) beber a lengüetadas ♦ vi (*waves*) chapotear; ~ **up** vt (*fig*) tragarse

lapel [lə'pɛl] n solapa

Lapland ['læplænd] n Laponia

lapse [læps] n fallo; (*moral*) desliz m; (*of*

time) intervalo ♦ *vi (expire)* caducar; *(time)* pasar, transcurrir; **to ~ into bad habits** caer en malos hábitos

laptop (computer) ['læptɔp-] *n* ordenador *m* portátil

larceny ['lɑːsənɪ] *n* latrocinio

larch [lɑːtʃ] *n* alerce *m*

lard [lɑːd] *n* manteca (de cerdo)

larder ['lɑːdə*] *n* despensa

large [lɑːdʒ] *adj* grande; **at ~** *(free)* en libertad; *(generally)* en general; **~ly** *adv* *(mostly)* en su mayor parte; *(introducing reason)* en gran parte; **~-scale** *adj (map)* en gran escala; *(fig)* importante

largesse [lɑːˈʒes] *n* generosidad *f*

lark [lɑːk] *n (bird)* alondra; *(joke)* broma; **~ about** *vi* bromear, hacer el tonto

laryngitis [lærɪnˈdʒaɪtɪs] *n* laringitis *f*

larynx ['lærɪŋks] *n* laringe *f*

laser ['leɪzə*] *n* láser *m*; **~ printer** *n* impresora (por) láser

lash [læʃ] *n* latigazo; *(also: eye~)* pestaña ♦ *vt* azotar; *(tie)*: **to ~ to/together** atar a/ atar; **~ out** *vi*: **to ~ out (at sb)** *(hit)* arremeter (contra uno); **to ~ out against sb** lanzar invectivas contra uno

lass [læs] *(BRIT)* *n* chica

lasso [læˈsuː] *n* lazo

last [lɑːst] *adj* último; *(end: of series etc)* final ♦ *adv (most recently)* la última vez; *(finally)* por último ♦ *vi* durar; *(continue)* continuar, seguir; **~ night** anoche; **~ week** la semana pasada; **at ~** por fin; **but one** penúltimo; **~-ditch** *adj (attempt)* último, desesperado; **~ing** *adj* duradero; **~ly** *adv* por último, finalmente; **~-minute** *adj* de última hora

latch [lætʃ] *n* pestillo

late [leɪt] *adj (far on: in time, process etc)* al final de; *(not on time)* tarde, atrasado; *(dead)* fallecido ♦ *adv* tarde; *(behind time, schedule)* con retraso; **of ~** últimamente; **~ at night** a última hora de la noche; **in ~ May** hacia fines de mayo; **the ~ Mr X** el difunto Sr X; **~comer** *n* recién llegado/a; **~ly** *adv* últimamente

later ['leɪtə*] *adj (date etc)* posterior; *(version etc)* más reciente ♦ *adv* más tarde, después

lateral ['lætərl] *adj* lateral

latest ['leɪtɪst] *adj* último; **at the ~** a más tardar

lathe [leɪð] *n* torno

lather ['lɑːðə*] *n* espuma (de jabón) ♦ *vt* enjabonar

Latin ['lætɪn] *n* latín *m* ♦ *adj* latino; **~ America** *n* América latina; **~-American** *adj, n* latinoamericano/a

latitude ['lætɪtjuːd] *n* latitud *f*; *(fig)* libertad *f*

latrine [ləˈtriːn] *n* letrina

latter ['lætə*] *adj* último; *(of two)* segundo

♦ *n*: **the ~** el último, éste; **~ly** *adv* últimamente

lattice ['lætɪs] *n* enrejado

laudable ['lɔːdəbl] *adj* loable

laugh [lɑːf] *n* risa ♦ *vi* reír(se); **(to do sth) for a ~** (hacer algo) en broma; **~ at** *vt fus* reírse de; **~ off** *vt* tomar algo a risa; **~able** *adj* ridículo; **~ing stock** *n*: **the ~ing stock of** el hazmerreír de; **~ter** *n* risa

launch [lɔːntʃ] *n* lanzamiento; *(boat)* lancha ♦ *vt (ship)* botar; *(rocket etc)* lanzar; *(fig)* comenzar; **~(ing) pad** *n* plataforma de lanzamiento; **~ into** *vt fus* lanzarse a

launder ['lɔːndə*] *vt* lavar

Launderette [lɔːnˈdret] *(®:BRIT)* *n* lavandería (automática)

Laundromat ['lɔːndrəmæt] *(®:US)* *n* = **Launderette**

laundry ['lɔːndrɪ] *n (dirty)* ropa sucia; *(clean)* colada; *(room)* lavadero

laureate ['lɔːrɪət] *adj see* **poet**

lavatory ['lævətərɪ] *n* wáter *m*

lavender ['lævəndə*] *n* lavanda

lavish ['lævɪʃ] *adj (amount)* abundante; *(person)*: **~ with** pródigo en ♦ *vt*: **to ~ sth on sb** colmar a uno de algo

law [lɔː] *n* ley *f*; *(SCOL)* derecho; *(a rule)* regla; *(professions connected with ~)* jurisprudencia; **~-abiding** *adj* respetuoso de la ley; **~ and order** *n* orden *m* público; **~ court** *n* tribunal *m* (de justicia); **~ful** *adj* legítimo, lícito; **~less** *adj (action)* criminal

lawn [lɔːn] *n* césped *m*; **~mower** *n* cortacésped *m*; **~ tennis** *n* tenis *m* sobre hierba

law school *(US)* *n (SCOL)* facultad *f* de derecho

lawsuit ['lɔːsuːt] *n* pleito

lawyer ['lɔːjə*] *n* abogado/a; *(for sales, wills etc)* notario/a

lax [læks] *adj* laxo

laxative ['læksətɪv] *n* laxante *m*

lay [leɪ] *(pt, pp laid)* *pt of* **lie** ♦ *adj* laico; *(not expert)* lego ♦ *vt (place)* colocar; *(eggs, table)* poner; *(cable)* tender; *(carpet)* extender; **~ aside** *or* **by** *vt* dejar a un lado; **~ down** *vt (pen etc)* dejar; *(rules etc)* establecer; **to ~ down the law** *(pej)* imponer las normas; **~ off** *vt (workers)* despedir; **~ on** *vt (meal, facilities)* proveer; **~ out** *vt (spread out)* disponer, exponer; **~about** *(inf)* *n* vago/a; **~-by** *n (BRIT: AUT)* área de aparcamiento

layer ['leɪə*] *n* capa

layman ['leɪmən] *n* lego

layout ['leɪaut] *n (design)* plan *m*, trazado; *(PRESS)* composición *f*

laze [leɪz] *vi (also: ~ about)* holgazanear

laziness ['leɪzɪnɪs] *n* pereza

lazy ['leɪzɪ] *adj* perezoso, vago; *(movement)* lento

lb. *abbr* = **pound** *(weight)*

lead¹ [liːd] (pt, pp **led**) n (front position) delantera; (clue) pista; (ELEC) cable m; (for dog) correa; (THEATRE) papel m principal ♦ vt (walk etc in front of) ir a la cabeza de; (guide): **to ~ sb somewhere** conducir a uno a algún sitio; (be leader of) dirigir; (start, guide: activity) protagonizar ♦ vi (road, pipe etc) conducir a; (SPORT) ir primero; **to be in the ~** (SPORT) llevar la delantera; (fig) ir a la cabeza; **to ~ the way** (also fig) llevar la delantera; **~ away** vt llevar; **~ back** vt (person, route) llevar de vuelta; **~ on** vt (tease) engañar; **~ to** vt fus producir, provocar; **~ up to** vt fus (events) conducir a; (in conversation) preparar el terreno para

lead² [led] n (metal) plomo; (in pencil) mina

leader ['liːdə*] n jefe/a m/f, líder m; (SPORT) líder m; (~ship) n dirección f; (position) mando; (quality) iniciativa

leading ['liːdɪŋ] adj (main) principal; (first) primero; (front) delantero; **~ lady** n (THEATRE) primera actriz f; **~ light** n (person) figura principal; **~ man** n (THEATRE) primer galán m

lead singer n cantante m/f

leaf [liːf] (pl **leaves**) n hoja ♦ vi: **to ~ through** hojear; **to turn over a new ~** reformarse

leaflet ['liːflɪt] n folleto

league [liːg] n sociedad f; (FOOTBALL) liga; **to be in ~ with** haberse confabulado con

leak [liːk] n (of liquid, gas) escape m, fuga; (in pipe) agujero; (in roof) gotera; (in security) filtración f ♦ vi (shoes, ship) hacer agua; (pipe) tener (un) escape; (roof) gotear; (liquid, gas) escaparse, fugarse; (fig) divulgarse ♦ vt (fig) filtrar

lean [liːn] (pt, pp **leaned** or **leant**) adj (thin) flaco; (meat) magro ♦ vt: **to ~ sth on sth** apoyar algo en algo ♦ vi (slope) inclinarse; **to ~ against** apoyarse contra; **to ~ on** apoyarse en; **~ back/forward** vi inclinarse hacia atrás/adelante; **~ out** vi asomarse; **~ over** vi inclinarse; **~ing** n: **~ing (towards)** inclinación f (hacia); **leant** [lent] pt, pp of **lean**

leap [liːp] (pt, pp **leaped** or **leapt**) n salto ♦ vi saltar; **~frog** n pídola; **leapt** [lept] pt, pp of **leap**; **~ year** n año bisiesto

learn [ləːn] (pt, pp **learned** or **learnt**) vt aprender ♦ vi aprender; **to ~ about sth** enterarse de algo; **to ~ to do sth** aprender a hacer algo; **~ed** ['ləːnɪd] adj erudito; **~er** n (BRIT: also: ~er driver) principiante m/f; **~ing** n el saber m, conocimientos mpl; **learnt** [ləːnt] pt, pp of **learn**

lease [liːs] n arriendo ♦ vt arrendar

leash [liːʃ] n correa

least [liːst] adj: **the ~** (slightest) el menor, el más pequeño; (smallest amount of) mínimo ♦ adv (+vb) menos; (+adj): **the ~ ex-**pensive el/la menos costoso/a; **the ~ possible effort** el menor esfuerzo posible; **at ~** por lo menos, al menos; **you could at ~ have written** por lo menos podías haber escrito; **not in the ~** en absoluto

leather ['leðə*] n cuero

leave [liːv] (pt, pp **left**) vt dejar; (go away from) abandonar; (place etc: permanently) salir de ♦ vi irse; (train etc) salir ♦ n permiso; **to ~ sth to sb** (money etc) legar algo a uno; (responsibility) encargar a uno de algo; **to be left** quedar, sobrar; **there's some milk left over** sobra or queda algo de leche; **on ~** de permiso; **~ behind** vt (on purpose) dejar; (accidentally) dejarse; **~ out** vt omitir; **~ of absence** n permiso de ausentarse

leaves [liːvz] npl of **leaf**

Lebanon ['lebənən] n: **the ~** el Líbano

lecherous ['letʃərəs] (pej) adj lascivo

lecture ['lektʃə*] n conferencia; (SCOL) clase f ♦ vi dar una clase ♦ vt (scold): **to ~ sb on or about sth** echar una reprimenda a uno por algo; **to give a ~ on** dar una conferencia sobre; **~r** n conferenciante m/f; (BRIT: at university) profesor(a) m/f

led [led] pt, pp of **lead**

ledge [ledʒ] n repisa; (of window) alféizar m; (of mountain) saliente m

ledger ['ledʒə*] n libro mayor

leech [liːtʃ] n sanguijuela

leek [liːk] n puerro

leer [lɪə*] vi: **to ~ at sb** mirar de manera lasciva a uno

leeway ['liːweɪ] n (fig): **to have some ~** tener cierta libertad de acción

left [left] pt, pp of **leave** ♦ adj izquierdo; (remaining): **there are 2 ~** quedan dos ♦ n izquierda ♦ adv a la izquierda; **on or to the ~** a la izquierda; **the L~** (POL) la izquierda; **~-handed** adj zurdo; **the ~-hand side** n la izquierda; **~-luggage (office)** (BRIT) n consigna; **~-overs** npl sobras fpl; **~-wing** adj (POL) de izquierdas, izquierdista

leg [leg] n pierna; (of animal, chair) pata; (trouser ~) pernera; (CULIN: of lamb) pierna; (of chicken) pata; (of journey) etapa

legacy ['legəsɪ] n herencia

legal ['liːgl] adj (permitted by law) lícito; (of law) legal; **~ holiday** (US) n fiesta oficial; **~ize** vt legalizar; **~ly** adv legalmente; **~ tender** n moneda de curso legal

legend ['ledʒənd] n (also fig: person) leyenda

legislation [ledʒɪs'leɪʃən] n legislación f

legislature ['ledʒɪslətʃə*] n cuerpo legislativo

legitimate [lɪ'dʒɪtɪmət] adj legítimo

leg-room n espacio para las piernas

leisure ['leʒə*] n ocio, tiempo libre; **at ~** con tranquilidad; **~ centre** n centro de recreo; ~**ly** adj sin prisa; lento

lemon ['lɛmən] n limón m; ~**ade** [-'neɪd] n (fizzy) gaseosa; ~ **tea** n té m con limón

lend [lɛnd] (pt, pp **lent**) vt: **to** ~ **sth to sb** prestar algo a alguien; ~**ing library** n biblioteca de préstamo

length [lɛŋθ] n (size) largo, longitud f; (distance): **the** ~ **of** todo lo largo de; (of swimming pool, cloth) largo; (of wood, string) trozo; (amount of time) duración f; **at** ~ (at last) por fin, finalmente; (lengthily) largamente; ~**en** vt alargar ♦ vi alargarse; ~**ways** adv a lo largo; ~**y** adj largo, extenso

lenient ['liːnɪənt] adj indulgente

lens [lɛnz] n (of spectacles) lente f; (of camera) objetivo

lent [lɛnt] pt, pp of **lend**

Lent [lɛnt] n Cuaresma

lentil ['lɛntl] n lenteja

Leo ['liːəu] n Leo

leotard ['liːətɑːd] n mallas fpl

leprosy ['lɛprəsɪ] n lepra

lesbian ['lɛzbɪən] n lesbiana

less [lɛs] adj (in size, degree etc) menor; (in quality) menos ♦ pron, adv menos ♦ prep: ~ **tax/10% discount** menos impuestos/el 10 por ciento de descuento; ~ **than half** menos de la mitad; ~ **than ever** menos que nunca; ~ **and** ~ cada vez menos; **the** ~ **he works...** cuanto menos trabaja...

lessen ['lɛsn] vi disminuir, reducirse ♦ vt disminuir, reducir

lesser ['lɛsə*] adj menor; **to a** ~ **extent** en menor grado

lesson ['lɛsn] n clase f; (warning) lección f

lest [lɛst] conj para que

let [lɛt] (pt, pp **let**) vt (allow) dejar, permitir; (BRIT: lease) alquilar; **to** ~ **sb do sth** dejar que uno haga algo; **to** ~ **sb know sth** comunicar algo a uno; ~**'s go** ¡vamos!; ~ **him come** que venga; **"to** ~**"** "se alquila"; ~ **down** vt (tyre) desinflar; (disappoint) defraudar; ~ **go** vi, vt soltar; ~ **in** vt dejar entrar; (visitor etc) hacer pasar; ~ **off** vt (culprit) dejar escapar; (gun) disparar; (bomb) accionar; (firework) hacer estallar; ~ **on** (inf) vi divulgar; ~ **out** vt dejar salir; (sound) soltar; ~ **up** vi amainar, disminuir

lethal ['liːθl] adj (weapon) mortífero; (poison, wound) mortal

lethargic [lə'θɑːdʒɪk] adj letárgico

letter ['lɛtə*] n (of alphabet) letra; (correspondence) carta; ~ **bomb** n cartabomba; ~**box** (BRIT) n buzón m; ~**ing** n letras fpl

lettuce ['lɛtɪs] n lechuga

let-up n disminución f

leukaemia [luː'kiːmɪə] (US **leukemia**) n leucemia

level ['lɛvl] adj (flat) llano ♦ adv: **to draw** ~ **with** llegar a la altura de ♦ n nivel m; (height) altura ♦ vt nivelar; allanar; (destroy: building) derribar; (: forest) arrasar; **to be** ~ **with** estar a nivel de; **"A"** ~**s** (BRIT) npl ≈ exámenes mpl de bachillerato superior, B.U.P.; **"O"** ~**s** (BRIT) npl ≈ exámenes mpl de octavo de básica; **on the** ~ (fig: honest) serio; ~ **off** or **out** vi (prices etc) estabilizarse; ~ **crossing** (BRIT) n paso a nivel; ~**-headed** adj sensato

lever ['liːvə*] n (also fig) palanca ♦ vt: **to** ~ **up** levantar con palanca; ~**age** n (using bar etc) apalancamiento; (fig: influence) influencia

levity ['lɛvɪtɪ] n frivolidad f

levy ['lɛvɪ] n impuesto ♦ vt exigir, recaudar

lewd [luːd] adj lascivo; (joke) obsceno, colorado (AM)

liability [laɪə'bɪlɪtɪ] n (pej: person, thing) estorbo, lastre m; (JUR: responsibility) responsabilidad f; **liabilities** npl (COMM) pasivo

liable ['laɪəbl] adj (subject): ~ **to** sujeto a; (responsible): ~ **for** responsable de; (likely): ~ **to do** propenso a hacer

liaise [lɪ'eɪz] vi: **to** ~ **with** enlazar con; **liaison** [liː'eɪzɒn] n (coordination) enlace m; (affair) relaciones fpl amorosas

liar ['laɪə*] n mentiroso/a

libel ['laɪbl] n calumnia ♦ vt calumniar

liberal ['lɪbərəl] adj liberal; (offer, amount etc) generoso

liberate ['lɪbəreɪt] vt (people: from poverty etc) librar; (prisoner) libertar; (country) liberar

liberty ['lɪbətɪ] n libertad f; (criminal): **to be at** ~ estar en libertad; **to be at** ~ **to do** estar libre para hacer; **to take the** ~ **of doing sth** tomarse la libertad de hacer algo

Libra ['liːbrə] n Libra

librarian [laɪ'brɛərɪən] n bibliotecario/a

library ['laɪbrərɪ] n biblioteca

libretto [lɪ'brɛtəu] n libreto

Libya ['lɪbɪə] n Libia; ~**n** adj, n libio/a m/f

lice [laɪs] npl of **louse**

licence ['laɪsəns] (US **license**) n licencia; (permit) permiso; (also: driving ~, (US) driver's ~) carnet m de conducir (SP), permiso (AM)

license ['laɪsəns] n (US) = **licence** ♦ vt autorizar, dar permiso a; ~**d** adj (for alcohol) autorizado para vender bebidas alcohólicas; (car) matriculado; ~ **plate** (US) n placa (de matrícula)

lichen ['laɪkən] n liquen m

lick [lɪk] vt lamer; (inf: defeat) dar una paliza a; **to** ~ **one's lips** relamerse

licorice ['lɪkərɪs] (US) n = **liquorice**

lid [lɪd] n (of box, case) tapa; (of pan) tapadera

lido ['laɪdəu] n (BRIT) piscina

lie [laɪ] (pt **lay**, pp **lain**) vi (rest) estar echado, estar acostado; (of object: be situated) estar, encontrarse; (tell lies: pt, pp **lied**) mentir ♦ *n* mentira; **to ~ low** (*fig*) mantenerse a escondidas; **~ about** *or* **around** *vi* (*things*) estar tirado; (*BRIT: people*) estar tumbado; **~-down** (*BRIT*) *n*: **to have a ~-down** echarse (una siesta); **~-in** (*BRIT*) *n*: **to have a ~-in** quedarse en la cama

lieu [luː]: **in ~ of** *prep* en lugar de

lieutenant [lɛf'tɛnənt, (*US*) luː'tɛnənt] *n* (*MIL*) teniente *m*

life [laɪf] (*pl* **lives**) *n* vida; **to come to ~** animarse; **~ assurance** (*BRIT*) *n* seguro de vida; **~belt** (*BRIT*) *n* cinturón *m* salvavidas; **~boat** *n* lancha de socorro; **~guard** *n* vigilante *m/f*, socorrista *m/f*; **~ imprisonment** *n* cadena perpetua; **~ insurance** *n* = **~ assurance**; **~ jacket** *n* chaleco salvavidas; **~less** *adj* sin vida; (*dull*) soso; **~like** *adj* (*model etc*) que parece vivo; (*realistic*) realista; **~line** *n* (*fig*) cordón *m* umbilical; **~long** *adj* de toda la vida; **~ preserver** (*US*) *n* = **~belt**; **~ sentence** *n* cadena perpetua; **~-size** *adj* de tamaño natural; **~ span** *n* vida; **~ style** *n* estilo de vida; **~ support system** *n* (*MED*) sistema *m* de respiración asistida; **~time** *n* (*of person*) vida; (*of thing*) período de vida

lift [lɪft] *vt* levantar; (*end: ban, rule*) levantar, suprimir ♦ *vi* (*fog*) disiparse ♦ *n* (*BRIT: machine*) ascensor *m*; **to give sb a ~** (*BRIT*) llevar a uno en el coche; **~-off** *n* despegue *m*

light [laɪt] (*pt, pp* **lighted** *or* **lit**) *n* luz *f*; (*lamp*) luz *f*, lámpara; (*AUT*) faro; (*for cigarette etc*): **have you got a ~?** ¿tienes fuego? ♦ *vt* (*candle, cigarette, fire*) encender (*SP*), prender (*AM*); (*room*) alumbrar ♦ *adj* (*colour*) claro; (*not heavy, also fig*) ligero; (*room*) con mucha luz; (*gentle, graceful*) ágil; **~s** *npl* (*traffic ~s*) semáforos *mpl*; **to come to ~** salir a luz; **in the ~ of** (*new evidence etc*) a la luz de; **~ up** *vi* (*smoke*) encender un cigarrillo; (*face*) iluminarse ♦ *vt* (*illuminate*) iluminar, alumbrar; (*set fire to*) encender; **~ bulb** *n* bombilla (*SP*), foco (*AM*); **~en** *vt* (*make less heavy*) aligerar; **~er** *n* (*also: cigarette ~er*) encendedor *m*, mechero; **~-headed** *adj* (*dizzy*) mareado; (*excited*) exaltado; **~-hearted** *adj* (*person*) alegre; (*remark etc*) divertido; **~house** *n* faro; **~ing** *n* (*system*) alumbrado; **~ly** *adv* ligeramente; (*not seriously*) con poca seriedad; **to get off ~ly** ser castigado con poca severidad; **~ness** *n* (*in weight*) ligereza

lightning ['laɪtnɪŋ] *n* relámpago, rayo; **~ conductor** (*US* **~ rod**) *n* pararrayos *m inv*

light: **~ pen** *n* lápiz *m* óptico; **~weight** *adj* (*suit*) ligero ♦ *n* (*BOXING*) peso ligero; **~ year** *n* año luz

like [laɪk] *vt* gustarle a uno ♦ *prep* como ♦ *adj* parecido, semejante ♦ *n*: **and the ~** y otros por el estilo; **his ~s and dislikes** sus gustos y aversiones; **I would ~**, **I'd ~** me

gustaría; (*for purchase*) quisiera; **would you ~ a coffee?** ¿te apetece un café?; **I ~ swimming** me gusta nadar; **she ~s apples** le gustan las manzanas; **to be** *or* **look ~ sb/sth** parecerse a alguien/algo; **what does it look/taste/sound ~?** ¿cómo es/a qué sabe/cómo suena?; **that's just ~ him** es muy de él, es característico de él; **do it ~ this** hazlo así; **it is nothing ~ ...** no tiene parecido alguno con ...; **~able** *adj* simpático, agradable

likelihood ['laɪklɪhud] *n* probabilidad *f*

likely ['laɪklɪ] *adj* probable; **he's ~ to leave** es probable que se vaya; **not ~!** ¡ni hablar!

likeness ['laɪknɪs] *n* semejanza, parecido; **that's a good ~** se parece mucho

likewise ['laɪkwaɪz] *adv* igualmente; **to do ~** hacer lo mismo

liking ['laɪkɪŋ] *n*: **~ (for)** (*person*) cariño (a); (*thing*) afición (a); **to be to sb's ~** ser del gusto de uno

lilac ['laɪlək] *n* (*tree*) lilo; (*flower*) lila

lily ['lɪlɪ] *n* lirio, azucena; **~ of the valley** *n* lirio de los valles

limb [lɪm] *n* miembro

limber ['lɪmbə*]: **to ~ up** *vi* (*SPORT*) hacer ejercicios de calentamiento

limbo ['lɪmbəu] *n*: **to be in ~** (*fig*) quedar a la expectativa

lime [laɪm] *n* (*tree*) limero; (*fruit*) lima; (*GEO*) cal *f*

limelight ['laɪmlaɪt] *n*: **to be in the ~** (*fig*) ser el centro de atención

limerick ['lɪmərɪk] *n* especie de poema humorístico

limestone ['laɪmstəun] *n* piedra caliza

limit ['lɪmɪt] *n* límite *m* ♦ *vt* limitar; **limitation** *n* limitación *f*; (*weak point*) punto flaco; (*restriction*) restricción *f*; **~ed** *adj* limitado; **to be ~ed to** limitarse a; **~ed (liability) company** (*BRIT*) *n* sociedad *f* anónima

limousine ['lɪməziːn] *n* limusina

limp [lɪmp] *n*: **to have a ~** tener cojera ♦ *vi* cojear ♦ *adj* flojo; (*material*) fláccido

limpet ['lɪmpɪt] *n* lapa

line [laɪn] *n* línea; (*rope*) cuerda; (*for fishing*) sedal *m*; (*wire*) hilo; (*row, series*) fila, hilera; (*of writing*) renglón *m*, línea; (*of song*) verso; (*on face*) arruga; (*RAIL*) vía ♦ *vt* (*road etc*) llenar; (*SEWING*) forrar; **to ~ the streets** llenar las aceras; **in ~ with** alineado con; (*according to*) de acuerdo con; **~ up** *vi* hacer cola ♦ *vt* alinear; (*prepare*) preparar; organizar

linear ['lɪnɪə*] *adj* lineal

lined [laɪnd] *adj* (*face*) arrugado; (*paper*) rayado

linen ['lɪnɪn] *n* ropa blanca; (*cloth*) lino

liner ['laɪnə*] *n* vapor *m* de línea, transatlántico; (*for bin*) bolsa (de basura)

linesman ['laɪnzmən] *n* (*SPORT*) juez *m* de

línea
line-up n (US: *queue*) cola; (*SPORT*) alineación f
linger ['lɪŋgə*] vi retrasarse, tardar en marcharse; (*smell, tradition*) persistir
lingerie ['lænʒəriː] n lencería
lingo ['lɪŋgəu] (pl ~es) (inf) n jerga
linguist ['lɪŋgwɪst] n lingüista m/f; ~**ic** adj lingüístico; ~**ics** n lingüística
lining ['laɪnɪŋ] n forro; (*ANAT*) (membrana) mucosa
link [lɪŋk] n (of a chain) eslabón m; (relationship) relación f, vínculo ♦ vt vincular, unir; (associate): **to ~ with** or **to** relacionar con; ~**s** npl (*GOLF*) campo de golf; ~ **up** vt acoplar ♦ vi unirse
lino ['laɪnəu] n = **linoleum**
linoleum [lɪ'nəuliəm] n linóleo
lion ['laɪən] n león m; ~**ess** n leona
lip [lɪp] n labio; ~**read** vi leer los labios; ~**salve** n crema protectora para labios; ~**service** n: **to pay** ~ **service to sth** (pej) prometer algo de boquilla; ~**stick** n lápiz m de labios, carmín m
liqueur [lɪ'kjuə*] n licor m
liquid ['lɪkwɪd] adj, n líquido; ~**ize** [-aɪz] vt (*CULIN*) licuar; ~**izer** [-aɪzə*] n licuadora
liquor ['lɪkə*] n licor m, bebidas fpl alcohólicas
liquorice ['lɪkərɪs] (*BRIT*) n regaliz m
liquor store (US) n bodega, *tienda de vinos y bebidas alcohólicas*
Lisbon ['lɪzbən] n Lisboa
lisp [lɪsp] n ceceo ♦ vi cecear
list [lɪst] n lista ♦ vt (*mention*) enumerar; (*put on a list*) poner en una lista; ~**ed building** (*BRIT*) n *monumento declarado de interés histórico-artístico*
listen ['lɪsn] vi escuchar, oír; **to ~ to sb/sth** escuchar a uno/algo; ~**er** n oyente m/f; (*RADIO*) radioyente m/f
listless ['lɪstlɪs] adj apático, indiferente
lit [lɪt] pt, pp of **light**
litany ['lɪtənɪ] n letanía
liter ['liːtə*] (US) n = **litre**
literacy ['lɪtərəsɪ] n *capacidad f de leer y escribir*
literal ['lɪtərl] adj literal
literary ['lɪtərərɪ] adj literario
literate ['lɪtərət] adj *que sabe leer y escribir*; (*educated*) culto
literature ['lɪtərɪtʃə*] n literatura; (*brochures etc*) folletos mpl
lithe [laɪð] adj ágil
litigation [lɪtɪ'geɪʃən] n litigio
litre ['liːtə*] (US **liter**) n litro
litter ['lɪtə*] n (*rubbish*) basura; (*young animals*) camada, cría; ~ **bin** (*BRIT*) n papelera; ~**ed** adj: ~**ed with** (*scattered*) lleno de
little ['lɪtl] adj (*small*) pequeño; (*not much*) poco ♦ adv poco; **a ~** un poco (de); ~ **house/bird** casita/pajarito; **a ~ bit** un po-

quito; ~ **by** ~ poco a poco; ~ **finger** n dedo meñique
live [vi lɪv, adj laɪv] vi vivir ♦ adj (*animal*) vivo; (*wire*) conectado; (*broadcast*) en directo; (*shell*) cargado; ~ **down** vt hacer olvidar; ~ **on** vt fus (*food, salary*) vivir de; ~ **together** vi vivir juntos; ~ **up to** vt fus (*fulfil*) cumplir con
livelihood ['laɪvlɪhud] n sustento
lively ['laɪvlɪ] adj vivo; (*interesting: place, book etc*) animado
liven up ['laɪvn-] vt animar ♦ vi animarse
liver ['lɪvə*] n hígado
lives [laɪvz] npl of **life**
livestock ['laɪvstɔk] n ganado
livid ['lɪvɪd] adj lívido; (*furious*) furioso
living ['lɪvɪŋ] adj (*alive*) vivo ♦ n: **to earn** or **make a** ~ ganarse la vida; ~ **conditions** npl condiciones fpl de vida; ~ **room** n sala (de estar); ~ **standards** npl nivel m de vida; ~ **wage** n jornal m suficiente para vivir
lizard ['lɪzəd] n lagarto; (*small*) lagartija
load [ləud] n carga; (*weight*) peso ♦ vt (*COMPUT*) cargar; (*also:* ~ **up**): **to ~ (with)** cargar (con or de); **a ~ of rubbish** (inf) tonterías fpl; **a ~ of**, ~**s of** (fig) (gran) cantidad de, montones de; ~**ed** adj (*vehicle*): **to be ~ed with** estar cargado de; (*question*) intencionado; (*inf: rich*) forrado (de dinero)
loaf [ləuf] (pl **loaves**) n (barra de) pan m
loan [ləun] n préstamo ♦ vt prestar; **on** ~ prestado
loath [ləuθ] adj: **to be** ~ **to do sth** estar poco dispuesto a hacer algo
loathe [ləuð] vt aborrecer; (*person*) odiar; **loathing** n aversión f; odio
loaves [ləuvz] npl of **loaf**
lobby ['lɔbɪ] n vestíbulo, sala de espera; (*POL: pressure group*) grupo de presión ♦ vt presionar
lobe [ləub] n lóbulo
lobster ['lɔbstə*] n langosta
local ['ləukl] adj local ♦ n (*pub*) bar m; **the** ~**s** los vecinos, los del lugar; ~ **anaesthetic** n (*MED*) anestesia local; ~ **authority** n municipio, ayuntamiento (*SP*); ~ **call** n (*TEL*) llamada local; ~ **government** n gobierno municipal; ~**ity** [-'kælɪtɪ] n localidad f; ~**ly** [-kəlɪ] adv en la vecindad; por aquí
locate [ləu'keɪt] vt (*find*) localizar; (*situate*): **to be ~d in** estar situado en
location [ləu'keɪʃən] n situación f; **on** ~ (*CINEMA*) en exteriores
loch [lɔx] n lago
lock [lɔk] n (of door, box) cerradura; (of canal) esclusa; (of hair) mechón m ♦ vt (with key) cerrar (con llave) ♦ vi (door etc) cerrarse (con llave); (wheels) trabarse; ~ **in** vt encerrar; ~ **out** vt (*person*) cerrar la

puerta a; ~ **up** vt (*criminal*) meter en la cárcel; (*mental patient*) encerrar; (*house*) cerrar (con llave) ♦ vi echar la llave

locker ['lɔkə*] n casillero

locket ['lɔkɪt] n medallón m

locksmith ['lɔksmɪθ] n cerrajero/a

lockup ['lɔkʌp] n (*jail, cell*) cárcel f

locomotive [ləukə'məutɪv] n locomotora

locum ['ləukəm] n (MED) (médico/a) interino/a

locust ['ləukəst] n langosta

lodge [lɔdʒ] n casita (del guarda) ♦ vi (*person*): **to ~ (with)** alojarse (en casa de); (*bullet, bone*) incrustarse ♦ vt (*complaint*) presentar; **~r** n huésped(a) m/f

lodgings ['lɔdʒɪŋz] npl alojamiento

loft [lɔft] n desván m

lofty ['lɔftɪ] adj (*noble*) sublime; (*haughty*) altanero

log [lɔg] n (*of wood*) leño, tronco; (*written account*) diario ♦ vt anotar

logbook ['lɔgbuk] n (NAUT) diario de a bordo; (AVIAT) libro de vuelo; (*of car*) documentación f (del coche (SP) or carro (AM))

loggerheads ['lɔgəhɛdz] npl: **to be at ~ (with)** estar en desacuerdo (con)

logic ['lɔdʒɪk] n lógica; **~al** adj lógico

logo ['ləugəu] n logotipo

loin [lɔɪn] n (CULIN) lomo, solomillo

loiter ['lɔɪtə*] vi (*linger*) entretenerse

loll [lɔl] vi (*also:* ~ **about**) repantigarse

lollipop ['lɔlɪpɔp] n chupa-chup m ®, pirulí m; ~ **lady/man** (BRIT) n persona encargada de ayudar a los niños a cruzar la calle

London ['lʌndən] n Londres; **~er** n londinense m/f

lone [ləun] adj solitario

loneliness ['ləunlɪnɪs] n soledad f; aislamiento

lonely ['ləunlɪ] adj (*situation*) solitario; (*person*) solo; (*place*) aislado

long [lɔŋ] adj largo ♦ adv mucho tiempo, largamente ♦ vi: **to ~ for sth** anhelar algo; **so** or **as ~ as** mientras, con tal que; **don't be ~!** ¡no tardes!, ¡vuelve pronto!; **how ~ is the street?** ¿cuánto tiene la calle de largo?; **how ~ is the lesson?** ¿cuánto dura la clase?; **6 metres ~** que mide 6 metros, de 6 metros de largo; **6 months ~** que dura 6 meses, de 6 meses de duración; **all night ~** toda la noche; **he no ~er comes** ya no viene; **~ before** mucho antes; **before ~** (+ *future*) dentro de poco; (+ *past*) poco tiempo después; **at ~ last** al fin, por fin; **~-distance** adj (*race*) de larga distancia; (*call*) interurbano; **~-haired** adj de pelo largo; **~-hand** n escritura sin abreviaturas; **~ing** n anhelo, ansia; (*nostalgia*) nostalgia ♦ adj anhelante

longitude ['lɔŋgɪtjuːd] n longitud f

long: ~ **jump** n salto de longitud; **~-life**

adj (*batteries*) de larga duración; (*milk*) uperizado; **~-lost** adj desaparecido hace mucho tiempo; **~-playing record** n elepé m, disco de larga duración; **~-range** adj (*plan*) de gran alcance; (*missile*) de largo alcance; **~-sighted** (BRIT) adj présbita; **~-standing** adj de mucho tiempo; **~-suffering** adj sufrido; **~-term** adj a largo plazo; ~ **wave** n onda larga; **~-winded** adj prolijo

loo [luː] (BRIT: inf) n wáter m

look [luk] vi mirar; (*seem*) parecer; (*building etc*): **to ~ south/on to the sea** dar al sur/al mar ♦ n (*gen*): **to have a ~** mirar; (*glance*) mirada; (*appearance*) aire m, aspecto; **~s** npl (*good ~s*) belleza; ~ **(here)!** (*expressing annoyance etc*) ¡oye!; ~**!** (*expressing surprise*) ¡mira!; ~ **after** vt fus (*care for*) cuidar a; (*deal with*) encargarse de; ~ **at** vt fus mirar; (*read quickly*) echar un vistazo a; ~ **back** vi mirar hacia atrás; ~ **down on** vt fus (*fig*) despreciar, mirar con desprecio; ~ **for** vt fus buscar; ~ **forward to** vt fus esperar con ilusión; (*in letters*): **we ~ forward to hearing from you** quedamos a la espera de sus gratas noticias; ~ **into** vt investigar; ~ **on** vi mirar (como espectador); ~ **out** vi (*beware*) tener cuidado (de); ~ **out for** vt fus (*seek*) buscar; (*await*) esperar; ~ **round** vi volver la cabeza; ~ **through** vt fus (*examine*) examinar; ~ **to** vt fus (*rely on*) contar con; ~ **up** vi mirar hacia arriba; (*improve*) mejorar ♦ vt (*word*) buscar; ~ **up to** vt fus admirar; **~-out** n (*tower etc*) puesto de observación; (*person*) vigía m/f; **to be on the ~-out for sth** estar al acecho de algo

loom [luːm] vi: ~ **(up)** (*threaten*) surgir, amenazar; (*event: approach*) aproximarse

loony ['luːnɪ] (*inf*) n, adj loco/a m/f

loop [luːp] n lazo ♦ vt: **to ~ sth round sth** pasar algo alrededor de algo; **~hole** n escapatoria

loose [luːs] adj suelto; (*clothes*) ancho; (*morals, discipline*) relajado; **to be on the ~** estar en libertad; **to be at a ~ end** or **at ~ ends** (US) no saber qué hacer; ~ **change** n cambio; ~ **chippings** npl (*on road*) gravilla suelta; **~ly** adv libremente, aproximadamente; **~n** vt aflojar

loot [luːt] n botín m ♦ vt saquear

lop off [lɔp-] vt (*branches*) podar

lop-sided adj torcido

lord [lɔːd] n señor m; **L~ Smith** Lord Smith; **the L~** el Señor; **my ~** (*to bishop*) Ilustrísima; (*to noble etc*) Señor; **good L~!** ¡Dios mío!; **the (House of) L~s** (BRIT) la Cámara de los Lores; **~ship** n: **your L~ship** su Señoría

lore [lɔː*] n tradiciones fpl

lorry ['lɔrɪ] (BRIT) n camión m; ~ **driver** n camionero/a

lose [luːz] (*pt, pp* lost) *vt* perder ♦ *vi* perder, ser vencido; **to ~ (time)** (*clock*) atrasarse; **~r** *n* perdedor(a) *m/f*

loss [lɔs] *n* pérdida; **heavy ~es** (*MIL*) grandes pérdidas; **to be at a ~** no saber qué hacer; **to make a ~** sufrir pérdidas

lost [lɔst] *pt, pp* of **lose** ♦ *adj* perdido; **~ property** (*US* = **and found**) *n* objetos *mpl* perdidos

lot [lɔt] *n* (*group: of things*) grupo; (*at auctions*) lote *m*; **the ~** el todo, todos; **a ~** (*large number: of books etc*) muchos; (*a great deal*) mucho, bastante; **a ~ of, ~s of** mucho(s) (*pl*); **I read a ~** leo bastante; **to draw ~s (for sth)** echar suertes (para decidir algo)

lotion [ˈləʊʃən] *n* loción *f*

lottery [ˈlɔtərɪ] *n* lotería

loud [laud] *adj* (*voice, sound*) fuerte; (*laugh, shout*) estrepitoso; (*condemnation etc*) enérgico; (*gaudy*) chillón/ona ♦ *adv* (*speak etc*) fuerte; **out ~** en voz alta; **~hailer** (*BRIT*) *n* megáfono; **~ly** *adv* (*noisily*) fuerte; (*aloud*) en voz alta; **~speaker** *n* altavoz *m*

lounge [laundʒ] *n* salón *m*, sala (de estar); (*at airport etc*) sala; (*BRIT: also:* ~-**bar**) salón-bar *m* ♦ *vi* (*also:* ~ **about or around**) reposar, holgazanear; **~ suit** (*BRIT*) *n* traje *m* de calle

louse [laus] (*pl* **lice**) *n* piojo

lousy [ˈlauzɪ] (*inf*) *adj* (*bad quality*) malísimo, asqueroso; (*ill*) fatal

lout [laut] *n* gamberro/a

lovable [ˈlʌvəbl] *adj* amable, simpático

love [lʌv] *n* (*romantic, sexual*) amor *m*; (*kind, caring*) cariño ♦ *vt* amar, querer; (*thing, activity*) encantarle a uno; **"~ from Anne"** (*on letter*) "un abrazo (de) Anne"; **to ~ to do** encantarle a uno hacer; **to be/ fall in ~ with** estar enamorado/enamorarse de; **to make ~** hacer el amor; **for the ~ of** por amor de; **"15 ~"** (*TENNIS*) "15 a cero"; **I ~ paella** me encanta la paella; **~ affair** *n* aventura sentimental; **~ letter** *n* carta de amor; **~ life** *n* vida sentimental

lovely [ˈlʌvlɪ] *adj* (*delightful*) encantador(a); (*beautiful*) precioso

lover [ˈlʌvə*] *n* amante *m/f*; (*person in love*) enamorado; (*amateur*): **a ~ of** un(a) aficionado/a *or* un(a) amante de

loving [ˈlʌvɪŋ] *adj* amoroso, cariñoso; (*action*) tierno

low [ləʊ] *adj, adv* bajo ♦ *n* (*METEOROLOGY*) área de baja presión; **to be ~ on** (*supplies etc*) andar mal de; **to feel ~** sentirse deprimido; **to turn (down) ~** bajar; **~-alcohol** *adj* de bajo contenido en alcohol; **~-cut** *adj* (*dress*) escotado

lower [ˈləʊə*] *adj* más bajo; (*less important*) menos importante ♦ *vt* bajar; (*reduce*) reducir ♦ *vr*: **to ~ o.s. to** (*fig*) rebajarse a

low: ~-fat *adj* (*milk, yoghurt*) desnatado;

(*diet*) bajo en calorías; **~lands** *npl* (*GEO*) tierras *fpl* bajas; **~ly** *adj* humilde, inferior

loyal [ˈlɔɪəl] *adj* leal; **~ty** *n* lealtad *f*

lozenge [ˈlɔzɪndʒ] *n* (*MED*) pastilla

L.P. *n abbr* (= *long-playing record*) elepé *m*

L-plates [ˈɛl-] (*BRIT*) *npl* placas *fpl* de aprendiz de conductor

Ltd *abbr* (= *limited company*) S.A

lubricate [ˈluːbrɪkeɪt] *vt* lubricar, engrasar

lucid [ˈluːsɪd] *adj* lúcido

luck [lʌk] *n* suerte *f*; **bad ~** mala suerte; **good ~!** ¡que tengas suerte!, ¡suerte!; **bad or hard or tough ~!** ¡qué pena!; **~ily** *adv* afortunadamente; **~y** *adj* afortunado; (*at cards etc*) con suerte; (*object*) que trae suerte

ludicrous [ˈluːdɪkrəs] *adj* absurdo

lug [lʌg] *vt* (*drag*) arrastrar

luggage [ˈlʌgɪdʒ] *n* equipaje *m*; **~ rack** *n* (*on car*) baca, portaequipajes *m inv*

lukewarm [ˈluːkwɔːm] *adj* tibio

lull [lʌl] *n* tregua ♦ *vt*: **to ~ sb to sleep** arrullar a uno; **to ~ sb into a false sense of security** dar a alguien una falsa sensación de seguridad

lullaby [ˈlʌləbaɪ] *n* nana

lumbago [lʌmˈbeɪgəʊ] *n* lumbago

lumber [ˈlʌmbə*] *n* (*junk*) trastos *mpl* viejos; (*wood*) maderos *mpl*; **~ with** *vt*: **to be ~ed with** tener que cargar con algo; **~jack** *n* maderero

luminous [ˈluːmɪnəs] *adj* luminoso

lump [lʌmp] *n* terrón *m*; (*fragment*) trozo; (*swelling*) bulto ♦ *vt* (*also:* ~ **together**) juntar; **~ sum** *n* suma global; **~y** *adj* (*sauce*) lleno de grumos; (*mattress*) lleno de bultos

lunar [ˈluːnə*] *adj* lunar

lunatic [ˈluːnətɪk] *adj* loco

lunch [lʌntʃ] *n* almuerzo, comida ♦ *vi* almorzar

luncheon [ˈlʌntʃən] *n* almuerzo; **~ meat** *n* tipo de fiambre; **~ voucher** (*BRIT*) *n* vale *m* de comida

lunch time *n* hora de comer

lung [lʌŋ] *n* pulmón *m*

lunge [lʌndʒ] *vi* (*also:* ~ **forward**) abalanzarse; **to ~ at** arremeter contra

lurch [lɜːtʃ] *vi* dar sacudidas ♦ *n* sacudida; **to leave sb in the ~** dejar a uno plantado

lure [luə*] *n* (*attraction*) atracción *f* ♦ *vt* tentar

lurid [ˈluərɪd] *adj* (*colour*) chillón/ona; (*account*) espeluznante

lurk [lɜːk] *vi* (*person, animal*) estar al acecho; (*fig*) acechar

luscious [ˈlʌʃəs] *adj* (*attractive: person, thing*) precioso; (*food*) delicioso

lush [lʌʃ] *adj* exuberante

lust [lʌst] *n* lujuria; (*greed*) codicia; **~ after or for** *vt fus* codiciar

lustre [ˈlʌstə*] (*US* **luster**) *n* lustre *m*, brillo

lusty [ˈlʌstɪ] *adj* robusto, fuerte

Luxembourg ['lʌksəmbɔːg] *n* Luxemburgo
luxuriant [lʌg'zjuərɪənt] *adj* exuberante
luxurious [lʌg'zjuərɪəs] *adj* lujoso
luxury ['lʌkʃərɪ] *n* lujo ♦ *cpd* de lujo
lying ['laɪɪŋ] *n* mentiras *fpl* ♦ *adj* mentiroso
lyrical ['lɪrɪkl] *adj* lírico
lyrics ['lɪrɪks] *npl* (*of song*) letra

——— *M m*

m. *abbr* = **metre; mile; million**
M.A. *abbr* = **Master of Arts**
mac [mæk] (*BRIT*) *n* impermeable *m*
macaroni [mækə'rəʊnɪ] *n* macarrones *mpl*
machine [mə'ʃiːn] *n* máquina ♦ *vt* (*dress etc*) coser a máquina; (*TECH*) hacer a máquina; ~ **gun** *n* ametralladora; ~ **language** *n* (*COMPUT*) lenguaje *m* máquina; ~**ry** *n* maquinaria; (*fig*) mecanismo
macho ['mætʃəʊ] *adj* machista
mackerel ['mækrl] *n inv* caballa
mackintosh ['mækɪntɔʃ] (*BRIT*) *n* impermeable *m*
mad [mæd] *adj* loco; (*idea*) disparatado; (*angry*) furioso; (*keen*): **to be** ~ **about sth** volverle loco a uno algo
madam ['mædəm] *n* señora
madden ['mædn] *vt* volver loco
made [meɪd] *pt, pp of* **make**
Madeira [mə'dɪərə] *n* (*GEO*) Madera; (*wine*) vino de Madera
made-to-measure (*BRIT*) *adj* hecho a la medida
madly ['mædlɪ] *adv* locamente
madman ['mædmən] *n* loco
madness ['mædnɪs] *n* locura
Madrid [mə'drɪd] *n* Madrid
Mafia ['mæfɪə] *n* Mafia
magazine [mægə'ziːn] *n* revista; (*RADIO, TV*) programa *m* magazina
maggot ['mægət] *n* gusano
magic ['mædʒɪk] *n* magia ♦ *adj* mágico; ~**ian** [mə'dʒɪʃən] *n* mago/a; (*conjurer*) prestidigitador(a) *m/f*
magistrate ['mædʒɪstreɪt] *n* juez *m/f* (municipal)
magnet ['mægnɪt] *n* imán *m*; ~**ic** [-'nɛtɪk] *adj* magnético; (*personality*) atrayente; ~**ic tape** *n* cinta magnética
magnificent [mæg'nɪfɪsənt] *adj* magnífico
magnify ['mægnɪfaɪ] *vt* (*object*) ampliar; (*sound*) aumentar; ~**ing glass** *n* lupa
magpie ['mægpaɪ] *n* urraca

mahogany [mə'hɔgənɪ] *n* caoba
maid [meɪd] *n* criada; **old** ~ (*pej*) solterona
maiden ['meɪdn] *n* doncella ♦ *adj* (*aunt etc*) solterona; (*speech, voyage*) inaugural; ~ **name** *n* nombre *m* de soltera
mail [meɪl] *n* correo; (*letters*) cartas *fpl* ♦ *vt* echar al correo; (*US*) *n* buzón *m*; ~**ing list** *n* lista de direcciones; ~**-order** *n* pedido postal
maim [meɪm] *vt* mutilar, lisiar
main [meɪn] *adj* principal, mayor ♦ *n* (*pipe*) cañería maestra; (*US*) red *f* eléctrica; **the** ~**s** *npl* (*BRIT: ELEC*) la red eléctrica; **in the** ~ en general; ~**frame** *n* (*COMPUT*) ordenador *m* central; ~**land** *n* tierra firme; ~**ly** *adv* principalmente; ~**box** *n* carretera; ~**road** *n* carretera; ~**stay** *n* (*fig*) pilar *m*; ~**stream** *n* corriente *f* principal
maintain [meɪn'teɪn] *vt* mantener; **maintenance** ['meɪntənəns] *n* mantenimiento; (*LAW*) manutención *f*
maize [meɪz] (*BRIT*) *n* maíz *m* (*SP*), choclo (*AM*)
majestic [mə'dʒɛstɪk] *adj* majestuoso
majesty ['mædʒɪstɪ] *n* majestad *f*; (*title*): **Your M~** Su Majestad
major ['meɪdʒə*] *n* (*MIL*) comandante *m* ♦ *adj* principal; (*MUS*) mayor
Majorca [mə'jɔːkə] *n* Mallorca
majority [mə'dʒɔrɪtɪ] *n* mayoría
make [meɪk] (*pt, pp* **made**) *vt* hacer; (*manufacture*) fabricar; (*mistake*) cometer; (*speech*) pronunciar; (*cause to be*): **to** ~ **sb sad** poner triste a alguien; (*force*): **to** ~ **sb do sth** obligar a alguien a hacer algo; (*earn*) ganar; (*equal*): **2 and 2** ~ **4** 2 y 2 son 4 ♦ *n* marca; **to** ~ **the bed** hacer la cama; **to** ~ **a fool of sb** poner a alguien en ridículo; **to** ~ **a profit/loss** obtener ganancias/sufrir pérdidas; **to** ~ **it** (*arrive*) llegar; (*achieve sth*) tener éxito; **what time do you** ~ **it?** ¿qué hora tienes?; **to** ~ **do with** contentarse con; ~ **for** *vt fus* (*place*) dirigirse a; ~ **out** *vt* (*decipher*) descifrar; (*understand*) entender; (*see*) distinguir; (*cheque*) extender; ~ **up** *vt* (*invent*) inventar; (*prepare*) hacer; (*constitute*) constituir ♦ *vi* reconciliarse; (*with cosmetics*) maquillarse; ~ **up for** *vt fus* compensar; ~**-believe** *n* ficción *f*, invención *f*; ~**r** *n* fabricante *m/f*, (*of film, programme*) autor(a) *m/f*; ~**-shift** *adj* improvisado; ~**-up** *n* maquillaje *m*; ~**-up remover** *n* desmaquillador *m*
making ['meɪkɪŋ] *n* (*fig*): **in the** ~ en vías de formación; **to have the** ~**s of** (*person*) tener madera de
malaise [mæ'leɪz] *n* malestar *m*
Malaysia [mə'leɪzɪə] *n* Malasia, Malaysia
male [meɪl] *n* (*BIOL*) macho ♦ *adj* (*sex, attitude*) masculino; (*child etc*) varón
malfunction [mæl'fʌŋkʃən] *n* mal funcionamiento

malice ['mælɪs] *n* malicia; **malicious** [mə'lɪʃəs] *adj* malicioso; rencoroso

malign [mə'laɪn] *vt* difamar, calumniar

malignant [mə'lɪgnənt] *adj* (*MED*) maligno

mall [mɔːl] (*US*) *n* (*also: shopping* ~) centro comercial

mallet ['mælɪt] *n* mazo

malnutrition [mælnjuː'trɪʃən] *n* desnutrición *f*

malpractice [mæl'præktɪs] *n* negligencia profesional

malt [mɔːlt] *n* malta; (*whisky*) whisky *m* de malta

Malta ['mɔːltə] *n* Malta; **Maltese** *adj, n inv* maltés/esa *m/f*

mammal ['mæml] *n* mamífero

mammoth ['mæməθ] *n* mamut *m* ♦ *adj* gigantesco

man [mæn] (*pl* **men**) *n* hombre *m*; (~*kind*) el hombre ♦ *vt* (*NAUT*) tripular; (*MIL*) guarnecer; (*operate: machine*) manejar; **an old** ~ un viejo; ~ **and wife** marido y mujer

manage ['mænɪdʒ] *vi* arreglárselas, ir tirando ♦ *vt* (*be in charge of*) dirigir; (*control: person*) manejar; (: *ship*) gobernar; ~**able** *adj* manejable; ~**ment** *n* dirección *f*; ~**r** *n* director(a) *m/f*; (*of pop star*) mánayer *m/f*; (*SPORT*) entrenador(a) *m/f*; ~**ress** *n* directora; entrenadora; ~**rial** [-ə'dʒɪərɪəl] *adj* directivo; **managing director** *n* director(a) *m/f* general

mandarin ['mændərɪn] *n* (*also:* ~ *orange*) mandarina; (*person*) mandarín *m*

mandate ['mændeɪt] *n* mandato

mandatory ['mændətərɪ] *adj* obligatorio

mane [meɪn] *n* (*of horse*) crin *f*; (*of lion*) melena

maneuver [mə'nuːvə*] (*US*) = **manoeuvre**

manfully ['mænfəlɪ] *adv* valientemente

mangle ['mæŋgl] *vt* mutilar, destrozar

mangy ['meɪndʒɪ] *adj* (*animal*) sarnoso

manhandle ['mænhændl] *vt* maltratar

manhole ['mænhəʊl] *n* agujero de acceso

manhood ['mænhʊd] *n* edad *f* viril; (*state*) virilidad *f*

man-hour *n* hora-hombre *f*

manhunt ['mænhʌnt] *n* (*POLICE*) búsqueda y captura

mania ['meɪnɪə] *n* manía; ~**c** ['meɪnɪæk] *n* maníaco/a; (*fig*) maniático

manic ['mænɪk] *adj* frenético; ~-**depressive** *n* maníaco/a depressive/a

manicure ['mænɪkjʊə*] *n* manicura

manifest ['mænɪfɛst] *vt* manifestar, mostrar ♦ *adj* manifiesto

manifesto [mænɪ'fɛstəʊ] *n* manifiesto

manipulate [mə'nɪpjʊleɪt] *vt* manipular

mankind [mæn'kaɪnd] *n* humanidad *f*, género humano

manly ['mænlɪ] *adj* varonil

man-made *adj* artificial

manner ['mænə*] *n* manera, modo; (*be-*

haviour) conducta, manera de ser; (*type*): **all** ~ **of things** toda clase de cosas; ~**s** *npl* (*behaviour*) modales *mpl*; **bad** ~**s** mala educación; ~**ism** *n* peculiaridad *f* de lenguaje (*or* de comportamiento)

manoeuvre [mə'nuːvə*] (*US* **maneuver**) *vt, vi* maniobrar ♦ *n* maniobra

manor ['mænə*] *n* (*also:* ~ *house*) casa solariega

manpower ['mænpaʊə*] *n* mano *f* de obra

mansion ['mænʃən] *n* palacio, casa grande

manslaughter ['mænslɔːtə*] *n* homicidio no premeditado

mantelpiece ['mæntlpiːs] *n* repisa, chimenea

manual ['mænjʊəl] *adj* manual ♦ *n* manual *m*

manufacture [mænjʊ'fæktʃə*] *vt* fabricar ♦ *n* fabricación *f*; ~**r** *n* fabricante *m/f*

manure [mə'njʊə*] *n* estiércol *m*

manuscript ['mænjʊskrɪpt] *n* manuscrito

many ['mɛnɪ] *adj, pron* muchos/as; **a great** ~ muchísimos, un buen número de; ~ **a time** muchas veces

map [mæp] *n* mapa *m*; **to** ~ **out** *vt* proyectar

maple ['meɪpl] *n* arce *m* (*SP*), maple *m* (*AM*)

mar [mɑː*] *vt* estropear

marathon ['mærəθən] *n* maratón *m*

marauder [mə'rɔːdə*] *n* merodeador(a) *m/f*

marble ['mɑːbl] *n* mármol *m*; (*toy*) canica

March [mɑːtʃ] *n* marzo

march [mɑːtʃ] *vi* (*MIL*) marchar; (*demonstrators*) manifestarse ♦ *n* marcha; (*demonstration*) manifestación *f*

mare [mɛə*] *n* yegua

margarine [mɑːdʒə'riːn] *n* margarina

margin ['mɑːdʒɪn] *n* margen *m*; (*COMM: profit*: ~) margen *m* de beneficios; ~**al** *adj* marginal; ~**al seat** *n* (*POL*) escaño electoral difícil de asegurar

marigold ['mærɪgəʊld] *n* caléndula

marijuana [mærɪ'wɑːnə] *n* marijuana

marina [mə'riːnə] *n* puerto deportivo

marinate ['mærɪneɪt] *vt* marinar

marine [mə'riːn] *adj* marino ♦ *n* soldado de marina

marital ['mærɪtl] *adj* matrimonial; ~ **status** estado civil

marjoram ['mɑːdʒərəm] *n* mejorana

mark [mɑːk] *n* marca, señal *f*; (*in snow, mud etc*) huella; (*stain*) mancha; (*BRIT: SCOL*) nota; (*currency*) marco ♦ *vt* marcar; manchar; (*damage: furniture*) rayar; (*indicate: place etc*) señalar; (*BRIT: SCOL*) calificar, corregir; **to** ~ **time** marcar el paso; (*fig*) marcar(se) un ritmo; ~**ed** *adj* (*obvious*) marcado, acusado; ~**er** *n* (*sign*) marcador *m*; (*bookmark*) señal *f* (de libro)

market ['mɑːkɪt] *n* mercado ♦ *vt* (*COMM*) comercializar; ~ **garden** (*BRIT*) *n* huerto;

~**ing** n márketing m; ~**place** n mercado; ~ **research** n análisis m inv de mercados

marksman ['mɑːksmən] n tirador m

marmalade ['mɑːməleɪd] n mermelada de naranja

maroon [mə'ruːn] vt: **to be ~ed** quedar aislado; (fig) quedar abandonado

marquee [mɑː'kiː] n entoldado

marquess ['mɑːkwɪs] n marqués m

marquis ['mɑːkwɪs] n = **marquess**

marriage ['mærɪdʒ] n (relationship, institution) matrimonio; (wedding) boda; (act) casamiento; ~ **bureau** n agencia matrimonial; ~ **certificate** n partida de casamiento

married ['mærɪd] adj casado; (life, love) conyugal

marrow ['mærəu] n médula; (vegetable) calabacín m

marry ['mærɪ] vt casarse con; (subj: father, priest etc) casar ♦ vi (also: **get married**) casarse

Mars [mɑːz] n Marte m

marsh [mɑːʃ] n pantano; (salt ~) marisma

marshal ['mɑːʃl] n (MIL) mariscal m; (at sports meeting etc) oficial m; (US: of police, fire department) jefe/a m/f ♦ vt (thoughts etc) ordenar; (soldiers) formar

marshy ['mɑːʃɪ] adj pantanoso

martial ['mɑːʃl] adj marcial; ~ **law** n ley f marcial

martyr ['mɑːtə*] n mártir m/f; ~**dom** n martirio

marvel ['mɑːvl] n maravilla, prodigio ♦ vi: **to ~ (at)** maravillarse (de); ~**lous** (US ~**ous**) adj maravilloso

Marxist ['mɑːksɪst] adj, n marxista m/f

marzipan ['mɑːzɪpæn] n mazapán m

mascara [mæs'kɑːrə] n rímel m

masculine ['mæskjulɪn] adj masculino

mash [mæʃ] vt machacar; ~**ed potatoes** npl puré m de patatas (SP) or papas (AM)

mask [mɑːsk] n máscara ♦ vt (cover): **to ~ one's face** ocultarse la cara; (hide: feelings) esconder

masochist ['mæsəkɪst] n masoquista m/f

mason ['meɪsn] n (also: **stone~**) albañil m; (also: **free~**) masón m; ~**ry** n (in building) mampostería

masquerade [mæskə'reɪd] vi: **to ~ as** disfrazarse de, hacerse pasar por

mass [mæs] n (people) muchedumbre f; (of air, liquid etc) masa; (of detail, hair etc) gran cantidad f; (REL) misa ♦ cpd masivo ♦ vi reunirse; concentrarse; **the ~es** npl las masas; ~**es of** (inf) montones de

massacre ['mæsəkə*] n masacre f

massage ['mæsɑːʒ] n masaje m ♦ vt dar masaje en

masseur [mæ'sɜː*] n masajista m

masseuse [mæ'sɜːz] n masajista f

massive ['mæsɪv] adj enorme; (support, changes) masivo

mass media npl medios mpl de comunicación

mass-production n fabricación f en serie

mast [mɑːst] n (NAUT) mástil m; (RADIO etc) torre f

master ['mɑːstə*] n (of servant) amo; (of situation) dueño, maestro; (in primary school) maestro; (in secondary school) profesor m; (title for boys): **M~ X** Señorito X ♦ vt dominar; **M~ of Arts/Science** n licenciatura superior en Letras/Ciencias; ~**ly** adj magistral; ~**mind** n inteligencia superior ♦ vt dirigir, planear; ~**piece** n obra maestra; ~**y** n maestría

masturbate ['mæstəbeɪt] vi masturbarse

mat [mæt] n estera; (also: **door~**) felpudo; (also: **table ~**) salvamanteles m inv, posavasos m inv ♦ adj = **matt**

match [mætʃ] n cerilla, fósforo; (game) partido; (equal) igual m/f ♦ vt (go well with) hacer juego con; (equal) igualar; (correspond to) corresponderse con; (pair: also: ~ **up**) casar con ♦ vi hacer juego; **to be a good ~** hacer juego; ~**box** n caja de cerillas; ~**ing** adj que hace juego

mate [meɪt] n (work~) colega m/f; (inf: friend) amigo/a; (animal) macho m/hembra f; (in merchant navy) segundo de a bordo ♦ vi acoplarse, aparearse ♦ vt aparear

material [mə'tɪərɪəl] n (substance) materia; (information) material m; (cloth) tela, tejido ♦ adj material; (important) esencial; ~**s** npl materiales mpl; ~**istic** [-'lɪstɪk] adj materialista; ~**ize** vi materializarse

maternal [mə'tɜːnl] adj maternal

maternity [mə'tɜːnɪtɪ] n maternidad f; ~ **dress** n vestido premamá

math [mæθ] (US) n = **mathematics**

mathematical [mæθə'mætɪkl] adj matemático

mathematician [mæθəmə'tɪʃən] n matemático/a

mathematics [mæθə'mætɪks] n matemáticas fpl

maths [mæθs] (BRIT) n = **mathematics**

matinée ['mætɪneɪ] n sesión f de tarde

matrices ['meɪtrɪsiːz] npl of **matrix**

matriculation [mətrɪkju'leɪʃən] n (formalización f de) matrícula

matrimony ['mætrɪmənɪ] n matrimonio

matrix ['meɪtrɪks] (pl **matrices**) n matriz f

matron ['meɪtrən] n enfermera f jefe; (in school) ama de llaves

mat(t) [mæt] adj mate

matted ['mætɪd] adj enmarañado

matter ['mætə*] n cuestión f, asunto; (PHYSICS) sustancia, materia; (reading ~) material m; (MED: pus) pus m ♦ vi importar; ~**s** npl (affairs) asuntos mpl, temas mpl; **it doesn't ~** no importa; **what's the ~?** ¿qué pasa?; **no ~ what** pase lo que pase; **as a ~ of course** por rutina; **as a ~ of**

fact de hecho; **~-of-fact** *adj* prosaico, práctico

mattress ['mætrɪs] *n* colchón *m*

mature [mə'tjuə*] *adj* maduro ♦ *vi* madurar; **maturity** *n* madurez *f*

maul [mɔ:l] *vt* magullar

mauve [məuv] *adj* de color malva (*SP*) or guinda (*AM*)

maverick ['mævərɪk] *n* hombre/mujer *m/f* poco ortodoxo/a

maxim ['mæksɪm] *n* máxima

maximum ['mæksɪməm] (*pl* **maxima**) *adj* máximo ♦ *n* máximo

May [meɪ] *n* mayo

may [meɪ] (*conditional*: **might**) *vi* (*indicating possibility*): **he ~ come** puede que venga; (*be allowed to*): **~ I smoke?** ¿puedo fumar?; (*wishes*): **~ God bless you!** ¡que Dios le bendiga!; **you ~ as well go** bien puedes irte

maybe ['meɪbɪ] *adv* quizá(s)

May Day *n* el primero de Mayo

mayhem ['meɪhem] *n* caos *m* total

mayonnaise [meɪə'neɪz] *n* mayonesa

mayor [meə*] *n* alcalde *m*; **~ess** *n* alcaldesa

maze [meɪz] *n* laberinto

M.D. *abbr* = **Doctor of Medicine**

me [mi:] *pron* (*direct*) me; (*stressed, after pron*) mí; **can you hear ~?** ¿me oyes?; **he heard ME!** me oyó a mí; **it's ~** soy yo; **give them to ~** dámelos/las; **with/without ~** conmigo/sin mí

meadow ['medəu] *n* prado, pradera

meagre ['mi:gə*] (*US* **meager**) *adj* escaso, pobre

meal [mi:l] *n* comida; (*flour*) harina; **~time** *n* hora de comer

mean [mi:n] (*pt*, *pp* **meant**) *adj* (*with money*) tacaño; (*unkind*) mezquino, malo; (*shabby*) humilde; (*average*) medio ♦ *vt* (*signify*) querer decir, significar; (*refer to*) referirse a; (*intend*): **to ~ to do sth** pensar or pretender hacer algo ♦ *n* medio, término medio; **~s** *npl* (*way*) medio, manera; (*money*) recursos *mpl*, medios *mpl*; **by ~s of** mediante, por medio de; **by all ~s!** ¡naturalmente!, ¡claro que sí!; **do you ~ it?** ¿lo dices en serio?; **what do you ~?** ¿qué quiere decir?; **to be meant for sb/sth** ser para uno/algo

meander [mɪ'ændə*] *vi* (*river*) serpentear

meaning ['mi:nɪŋ] *n* significado, sentido; (*purpose*) sentido, propósito; **~ful** *adj* significativo; **~less** *adj* sin sentido

meanness ['mi:nnɪs] *n* (*with money*) tacañería; (*unkindness*) maldad *f*, mezquindad *f*; (*shabbiness*) humildad *f*

meant [ment] *pt*, *pp* of **mean**

meantime ['mi:ntaɪm] *adv* (*also*: **in the ~**) mientras tanto

meanwhile ['mi:nwaɪl] *adv* = **meantime**

measles ['mi:zlz] *n* sarampión *m*

measly ['mi:zlɪ] (*inf*) *adj* miserable

measure ['meʒə*] *vt*, *vi* medir ♦ *n* medida; (*ruler*) regla; **~d** *adj* (*tone*, *step*) comedido; **~ments** *npl* medidas *fpl*

meat [mi:t] *n* carne *f*; **cold ~** fiambre *m*; **~ball** *n* albóndiga; **~ pie** *n* pastel *m* de carne

Mecca ['mekə] *n* La Meca

mechanic [mɪ'kænɪk] *n* mecánico/a; **~s** *n* mecánica ♦ *npl* mecanismo; **~al** *adj* mecánico

mechanism ['mekənɪzəm] *n* mecanismo

medal ['medl] *n* medalla; **~lion** [mɪ'dælɪən] *n* medallón *m*; **~list** (*US* **~ist**) *n* (*SPORT*) medallista *m/f*

meddle ['medl] *vi*: **to ~ in** entrometerse en; **to ~ with sth** manosear algo

media ['mi:dɪə] *npl* medios *mpl* de comunicación ♦ *npl of* **medium**

mediaeval [medɪ'i:vl] *adj* = **medieval**

mediate ['mi:dɪeɪt] *vi* mediar; **mediator** *n* intermediario/a, mediador(a) *m/f*

Medicaid ['medɪkeɪd] (*US*) *n* programa de ayuda médica para los pobres

medical ['medɪkl] *adj* médico ♦ *n* reconocimiento médico

Medicare ['medɪkeə*] (*US*) *n* programa de ayuda médica para los ancianos

medication [medɪ'keɪʃən] *n* medicación *f*

medicine ['medsɪn] *n* medicina; (*drug*) medicamento

medieval [medɪ'i:vl] *adj* medieval

mediocre [mi:dɪ'əukə*] *adj* mediocre

meditate ['medɪteɪt] *vi* meditar

Mediterranean [medɪtə'reɪnɪən] *adj* mediterráneo; **the ~ (Sea)** el (Mar) Mediterráneo

medium ['mi:dɪəm] (*pl* **media**) *adj* mediano, regular ♦ *n* (*means*) medio; (*pl mediums*: *person*) médium *m/f*; **~ wave** *n* onda media

medley ['medlɪ] *n* mezcla; (*MUS*) popurrí *m*

meek [mi:k] *adj* manso, sumiso

meet [mi:t] (*pt*, *pp* **met**) *vt* encontrar; (*accidentally*) encontrarse con, tropezar con; (*by arrangement*) reunirse con; (*for the first time*) conocer; (*go and fetch*) ir a buscar; (*opponent*) enfrentarse con; (*obligations*) cumplir; (*problem*) hacer frente a; (*need*) satisfacer ♦ *vi* encontrarse; (*in session*) reunirse; (*join: objects*) unirse; (*for the first time*) conocerse; **~ with** *vt fus* (*difficulty*) tropezar con; **to ~ with success** tener éxito; **~ing** *n* encuentro; (*arranged*) cita, compromiso; (*business ~ing*) reunión *f*; (*POL*) mitin *m*

megabyte ['megəbaɪt] *n* (*COMPUT*) megabyte *m*, megaocteto

megaphone ['megəfəun] *n* megáfono

melancholy ['melənkəlɪ] *n* melancolía ♦

adj melancólico

mellow ['mɛləu] *adj (wine)* añejo; *(sound, colour)* suave ♦ *vi (person)* ablandar

melody ['mɛlədɪ] *n* melodía

melon ['mɛlən] *n* melón *m*

melt [mɛlt] *vi (metal)* fundirse; *(snow)* derretirse ♦ *vt* fundir; ~**down** *n (in nuclear reactor)* fusión *f* de un reactor (nuclear); ~**ing pot** *n (fig)* crisol *m*

member ['mɛmbə*] *n (gen, ANAT)* miembro; *(of club)* socio/a; **M~ of Parliament** *(BRIT)* diputado/a; **M~ of the European Parliament** *(BRIT)* eurodiputado/a; ~**ship** *n (members)* número de miembros; *(state)* filiación *f*; ~**ship card** *n* carnet *m* de socio

memento [mə'mɛntəu] *n* recuerdo

memo ['mɛməu] *n* apunte *m*, nota

memoirs ['mɛmwɑːz] *npl* memorias *fpl*

memorandum [mɛmə'rændəm] *(pl* **memoranda)** *n* apunte *m*, nota; *(official note)* acta

memorial [mɪ'mɔːrɪəl] *n* monumento conmemorativo ♦ *adj* conmemorativo

memorize ['mɛmɔraɪz] *vt* aprender de memoria

memory ['mɛmɔrɪ] *n (also: COMPUT)* memoria; *(instance)* recuerdo; *(of dead person)*: **in ~ of** a la memoria de

men [mɛn] *npl of* **man**

menace ['mɛnəs] *n* amenaza ♦ *vt* amenazar; **menacing** *adj* amenazador(a)

mend [mɛnd] *vt* reparar, arreglar; *(darn)* zurcir ♦ *vi* reponerse ♦ *n* arreglo, reparación *f*; zurcido ♦ *n*: **to be on the ~** ir mejorando; **to ~ one's ways** enmendarse; ~**ing** *n* reparación *f*; *(clothes)* ropa por remendar

menial ['miːnɪəl] *(often pej) adj* bajo

meningitis [mɛnɪn'dʒaɪtɪs] *n* meningitis *f*

menopause ['mɛnəupɔːz] *n* menopausia

menstruation [mɛnstru'eɪʃən] *n* menstruación *f*

mental ['mɛntl] *adj* mental; ~**ity** [-'tælɪtɪ] *n* mentalidad *f*

mention ['mɛnʃən] *n* mención *f* ♦ *vt* mencionar; *(speak of)* hablar de; **don't ~ it!** ¡de nada!

menu ['mɛnjuː] *n (set ~)* menú *m*; *(printed)* carta; *(COMPUT)* menú *m*

MEP *n abbr* = **Member of the European Parliament**

mercenary ['mɔːsɪnərɪ] *adj, n* mercenario/a *m/f*

merchandise ['mɔːtʃəndaɪz] *n* mercancías *fpl*

merchant ['mɔːtʃənt] *n* comerciante *m/f*; ~ **bank** *(BRIT)* *n* banco comercial; ~ **navy** *(US* = **marine)** *n* marina mercante

merciful ['mɔːsɪful] *adj* compasivo; *(fortunate)* afortunado

merciless ['mɔːsɪlɪs] *adj* despiadado

mercury ['mɔːkjurɪ] *n* mercurio

mercy ['mɔːsɪ] *n* compasión *f*; *(REL)* miseri-

cordia; **at the ~ of** a la merced de

mere [mɪə*] *adj* simple, mero; ~**ly** *adv* simplemente, sólo

merge [mɔːdʒ] *vt (join)* unir ♦ *vi* unirse; *(COMM)* fusionarse; *(colours etc)* fundirse; ~**r** *n (COMM)* fusión *f*

meringue [mə'ræŋ] *n* merengue *m*

merit ['mɛrɪt] *n* mérito ♦ *vt* merecer

mermaid ['mɔːmeɪd] *n* sirena

merry ['mɛrɪ] *adj* alegre; **M~ Christmas!** ¡Felices Pascuas!; ~**-go-round** *n* tiovivo

mesh [mɛʃ] *n* malla

mesmerize ['mɛzmɔraɪz] *vt* hipnotizar

mess [mɛs] *n (muddle: of situation)* confusión *f*; *(: of room)* revoltijo; *(dirt)* porquería; *(MIL)* comedor *m*; ~ **about** *or* **around** *(inf) vi* perder el tiempo; *(pass the time)* entretenerse; ~ **about** *or* **around with** *(inf) vt fus* divertirse con; ~ **up** *vt (spoil)* estropear; *(dirty)* ensuciar

message ['mɛsɪdʒ] *n* recado, mensaje *m*

messenger ['mɛsɪndʒə*] *n* mensajero/a

Messrs *abbr (on letters:* = *Messieurs)* Sres

messy ['mɛsɪ] *adj (dirty)* sucio; *(untidy)* desordenado

met [mɛt] *pt, pp of* **meet**

metabolism [mɛ'tæbəlɪzəm] *n* metabolismo

metal ['mɛtl] *n* metal *m*; ~**lic** [-'tælɪk] *adj* metálico

metaphor ['mɛtəfə*] *n* metáfora

mete [miːt]: **to ~ out** *vt (punishment)* imponer

meteor ['miːtɪə*] *n* meteoro; ~**ite** [-aɪt] *n* meteorito

meteorology [miːtɪə'rɔlədʒɪ] *n* meteorología

meter ['miːtə*] *n (instrument)* contador *m*; *(US: unit)* = **metre** ♦ *vt (US: POST)* franquear

method ['mɛθəd] *n* método

Methodist ['mɛθədɪst] *adj, n* metodista *m/f*

meths [mɛθs] *(BRIT) n* = **methylated spirit**

methylated spirit ['mɛθɪleɪtɪd-] *(BRIT) n* alcohol *m* metilado *or* desnaturalizado

metre ['miːtə*] *(US* **meter)** *n* metro

metric ['mɛtrɪk] *adj* métrico

metropolis [mɪ'trɔpəlɪs] *n* metrópoli *f*

metropolitan [mɛtrə'pɔlɪtən] *adj* metropolitano; **the M~ Police** *(BRIT) n* la policía londinense

mettle ['mɛtl] *n*: **to be on one's ~** estar dispuesto a mostrar todo lo que uno vale

mew [mjuː] *vi (cat)* maullar

mews [mjuːz] *n*: ~ **flat** *(BRIT)* piso acondicionado en antiguos establos *o* cocheras

Mexican ['mɛksɪkən] *adj, n* mejicano/a *m/f*, mexicano/a *f*

Mexico ['mɛksɪkəu] *n* Méjico *(SP)*, México *(AM)*; ~ **City** *n* Ciudad *f* de Méjico *or* México

miaow [miː'au] *vi* maullar

mice [maɪs] *npl of* **mouse**

micro... [maɪkrəʊ] *prefix* micro...; **~chip** *n* microplaqueta; **~(computer)** *n* microordenador *m*; **~phone** *n* micrófono; **~processor** *n* microprocesador *m*; **~scope** *n* microscopio; **~wave** *n* (*also:* ~wave oven) horno microondas

mid [mɪd] *adj*: **in ~ May** a mediados de mayo; **in ~ afternoon** a media tarde; **in ~ air** en el aire; **~day** *n* mediodía *m*

middle ['mɪdl] *n* centro; (*half-way point*) medio; (*waist*) cintura ♦ *adj* de en medio; (*course, way*) intermedio; **in the ~ of the night** en plena noche; **~-aged** *adj* de mediana edad; **the M~ Ages** *npl* la Edad Media; **~-class** *adj* de clase media; **the ~ class(es)** *n(pl)* la clase media; **M~ East** *n* Oriente *m* Medio; **~man** *n* intermediario; **~ name** *n* segundo nombre; **~-of-the-road** *adj* moderado; **~weight** *n* (*BOXING*) peso medio; **middling** *adj* mediano

midge [mɪdʒ] *n* mosquito

midget ['mɪdʒɪt] *n* enano/a

Midlands ['mɪdləndz] *npl*: **the ~** la región central de Inglaterra

midnight ['mɪdnaɪt] *n* medianoche *f*

midriff ['mɪdrɪf] *n* diafragma *m*

midst [mɪdst] *n*: **in the ~ of** (*crowd*) en medio de; (*situation, action*) en mitad de

midsummer [mɪd'sʌmə*] *n*: **in ~** en pleno verano

midway [mɪd'weɪ] *adj, adv*: **~ (between)** a medio camino (entre); **~ through** a la mitad (de)

midweek [mɪd'wiːk] *adv* entre semana

midwife ['mɪdwaɪf] (*pl* midwives) *n* comadrona, partera

midwinter [mɪd'wɪntə*] *n*: **in ~** en pleno invierno

might [maɪt] *vb see* **may** ♦ *n* fuerza, poder *m*; **~y** *adj* fuerte, poderoso

migraine ['miːgreɪn] *n* jaqueca

migrant ['maɪgrənt] *n adj* (*bird*) migratorio; (*worker*) emigrante

migrate [maɪ'greɪt] *vi* emigrar

mike [maɪk] *n abbr* (= microphone) micro

mild [maɪld] *adj* (*person*) apacible; (*climate*) templado; (*slight*) ligero; (*taste*) suave; (*illness*) leve

mildew ['mɪldjuː] *n* moho

mildly ['maɪldlɪ] *adv* ligeramente; suavemente; **to put it ~** para no decir más

mile [maɪl] *n* milla; **~age** *n* número de millas, ≈ kilometraje *m*; **~ometer** *n* ≈ cuentakilómetros *m inv*; **~stone** *n* mojón *m*

milieu ['miːljə:] *n* (medio) ambiente *m*

militant ['mɪlɪtnt] *adj, n* militante *m/f*

military ['mɪlɪtərɪ] *adj* militar

militate ['mɪlɪteɪt] *vi*: **to ~ against** ir en contra de, perjudicar

militia [mɪ'lɪʃə] *n* milicia

milk [mɪlk] *n* leche *f* ♦ *vt* (*cow*) ordeñar; (*fig*) chupar; **~ chocolate** *n* chocolate *m*

con leche; **~man** *n* lechero; **~ shake** *n* batido, malteada (*AM*); **~y** *adj* lechoso; **M~y Way** *n* Vía Láctea

mill [mɪl] *n* (*windmill etc*) molino; (*coffee* ~) molinillo; (*factory*) fábrica ♦ *vt* moler ♦ *vi* (*also:* ~ about) arremolinarse

millennium [mɪ'lɛnɪəm] (*pl* ~s *or* **millennia**) *n* milenio, milenario

miller ['mɪlə*] *n* molinero

milli... ['mɪlɪ] *prefix*: **~gram(me)** *n* miligramo; **~metre** (*US* **~meter**) *n* milímetro

millinery ['mɪlɪnrɪ] *n* sombrerería

million ['mɪljən] *n* millón *m*; **a ~ times** un millón de veces; **~aire** *n* millonario/a

milometer [maɪ'lɒmɪtə*] (*BRIT*) *n* = **mileometer**

mime [maɪm] *n* mímica; (*actor*) mimo/a ♦ *vt* remedar ♦ *vi* actuar de mimo

mimic ['mɪmɪk] *n* imitador(a) *m/f* ♦ *adj* mímico ♦ *vt* remedar, imitar

min. *abbr* = **minute(s)**; **minimum**

minaret [mɪnə'rɛt] *n* alminar *m*

mince [mɪns] *vt* picar ♦ *vi* (*in walking*) andar con pasos menudos ♦ *n* (*BRIT: CULIN*) carne *f* picada; **~meat** *n* conserva de fruta picada; (*US: meat*) carne *f* picada; **~ pie** *n* empanadilla rellena de fruta picada; **~r** *n* picadora de carne

mind [maɪnd] *n* mente *f*; (*intellect*) intelecto; (*contrasted with matter*) espíritu *m* ♦ *vt* (*attend to, look after*) ocuparse de, cuidar; (*be careful of*) tener cuidado con; (*object to*): **I don't ~ the noise** no me molesta el ruido; **it is on my ~** me preocupa; **to bear sth in ~** tomar or tener algo en cuenta; **to make up one's ~** decidirse; **I don't ~** me es igual; **~ you,** ... te advierto que ...; **never ~!** ¡es igual!, ¡no importa!; (*don't worry*) ¡no te preocupes!; **"~ the step"** "cuidado con el escalón"; **~er** *n* guardaespaldas *m inv*; (*child ~er*) ≈ niñera; **~ful** *adj*: **~ful of** consciente de; **~less** *adj* (*crime*) sin motivo; (*work*) de autómata

mine¹ [maɪn] *pron* el mío/la mía *etc*; **a friend of ~** un(a) amigo/a mío/mía ♦ *adj*: **this book is ~** este libro es mío

mine² [maɪn] *n* mina ♦ *vt* (*coal*) extraer; (*bomb: beach etc*) minar; **~field** *n* campo de minas; **miner** *n* minero/a

mineral ['mɪnərəl] *adj* mineral ♦ *n* mineral *m*; **~s** *npl* (*BRIT: soft drinks*) refrescos *mpl*; **~ water** *n* agua mineral

mingle ['mɪŋgl] *vi*: **to ~ with** mezclarse con

miniature ['mɪnətʃə*] *adj* (en) miniatura ♦ *n* miniatura

minibus ['mɪnɪbʌs] *n* microbús *m*

minim ['mɪnɪm] *n* (*MUS*) blanca

minimal ['mɪnɪml] *adj* mínimo

minimize ['mɪnɪmaɪz] *vt* minimizar; (*play down*) empequeñecer

minimum ['mɪnɪməm] (*pl* **minima**) *n, adj*

mínimo

mining ['maɪnɪŋ] n explotación f minera

miniskirt ['mɪnɪskɔːt] n minifalda

minister ['mɪnɪstə*] n (BRIT: POL) ministro/a (SP), secretario/a (AM); (REL) pastor m ♦ vi: to ~ to atender a

ministry ['mɪnɪstrɪ] n (BRIT: POL) ministerio (SP), secretaria (AM); (REL) sacerdocio

mink [mɪŋk] n visón m

minnow ['mɪnəu] n pececillo (de agua dulce)

minor ['maɪnə*] adj (repairs, injuries) leve; (poet, planet) menor; (MUS) menor ♦ n (LAW) menor m de edad

Minorca [mɪ'nɔːkə] n Menorca

minority [maɪ'nɔrɪtɪ] n minoría

mint [mɪnt] n (plant) menta, hierbabuena; (sweet) caramelo de menta ♦ vt (coins) acuñar; **the (Royal) M~, the (US) M~** la Casa de la Moneda; **in ~ condition** en perfecto estado

minus ['maɪnəs] n (also: ~ sign) signo de menos ♦ prep menos; **12 ~ 6 equals 6** 12 menos 6 son 6; **~ 24°C** menos 24 grados

minute [n 'mɪnɪt, adj maɪ'njuːt] n minuto; (fig) momento; ~s npl (of meeting) actas fpl ♦ adj diminuto, (search) minucioso; **at the last ~** a última hora

miracle ['mɪrəkl] n milagro

mirage ['mɪraːʒ] n espejismo

mirror ['mɪrə*] n espejo; (in car) retrovisor m

mirth [mɔːθ] n alegría

misadventure [mɪsəd'ventʃə*] n desgracia

misapprehension [mɪsæprɪ'henʃən] n equivocación f

misappropriate [mɪsə'prəuprɪeɪt] vt malversar

misbehave [mɪsbɪ'heɪv] vi portarse mal

miscalculate [mɪs'kælkjuleɪt] vt calcular mal

miscarriage ['mɪskærɪdʒ] n (MED) aborto; ~ **of justice** error m judicial

miscellaneous [mɪsɪ'leɪnɪəs] adj varios/as, diversos/as

mischief ['mɪstʃɪf] n travesuras fpl, diabluras fpl; (maliciousness) malicia; **mischievous** [-ʃɪvəs] adj travieso

misconception [mɪskən'sepʃən] n idea equivocada; equivocación f

misconduct [mɪs'kɔndʌkt] n mala conducta; **professional ~** falta profesional

misdemeanour [mɪsdɪ'miːnə*] (US **misdemeanor**) n delito, ofensa

miser ['maɪzə*] n avaro/a

miserable ['mɪzərəbl] adj (unhappy) triste, desgraciado; (unpleasant, contemptible) miserable

miserly ['maɪzəlɪ] adj avariento, tacaño

misery ['mɪzərɪ] n tristeza; (wretchedness) miseria, desdicha

misfire ['mɪsfaɪə*] vi fallar

misfit ['mɪsfɪt] n inadaptado/a

misfortune [mɪs'fɔːtʃən] n desgracia

misgiving [mɪs'gɪvɪŋ] n (apprehension) presentimiento; **to have ~s about sth** tener dudas acerca de algo

misguided [mɪs'gaɪdɪd] adj equivocado

mishandle [mɪs'hændl] vt (mismanage) manejar mal

mishap ['mɪshæp] n desgracia, contratiempo

misinform [mɪsɪn'fɔːm] vt informar mal

misinterpret [mɪsɪn'tɔːprɪt] vt interpretar mal

misjudge [mɪs'dʒʌdʒ] vt juzgar mal

mislay [mɪs'leɪ] (irreg) vt extraviar, perder

mislead [mɪs'liːd] (irreg) vt llevar a conclusiones erróneas; ~**ing** adj engañoso

mismanage [mɪs'mænɪdʒ] vt administrar mal

misnomer [mɪs'nəumə*] n término inapropiado or equivocado

misogynist [mɪ'sɔdʒɪnɪst] n misógino

misplace [mɪs'pleɪs] vt extraviar

misprint ['mɪsprɪnt] n errata, error m de imprenta

Miss [mɪs] n Señorita

miss [mɪs] vt (train etc) perder; (fail to hit: target) errar; (regret the absence of): **I ~ him** (yo) le echo de menos or a faltar; (fail to see): **you can't ~ it** no tiene pérdida ♦ vi fallar ♦ n (shot) tiro fallido or perdido; ~ **out** (BRIT) vt omitir

misshapen [mɪs'ʃeɪpən] adj deforme

missile ['mɪsaɪl] n (AVIAT) mísil m; (object thrown) proyectil m

missing ['mɪsɪŋ] adj (pupil) ausente; (thing) perdido; (MIL): ~ **in action** desaparecido en combate

mission ['mɪʃən] n misión f; (official representation) delegación f; ~**ary** n misionero/a

misspent ['mɪs'spent] adj: **his ~ youth** su juventud disipada

mist [mɪst] n (light) neblina; (heavy) niebla; (at sea) bruma ♦ vi (eyes: also: ~ over, ~ up) llenarse de lágrimas; (BRIT: windows: also: ~ over, ~ up) empañarse

mistake [mɪs'teɪk] (vt: irreg) n error m ♦ vt entender mal; **by ~** por equivocación; **to make a ~** equivocarse; **to ~ A for B** confundir A con B; **mistaken** pp of **mistake** ♦ adj equivocado; **to be mistaken** equivocarse, engañarse

mister ['mɪstə*] (inf) n señor m; see **Mr**

mistletoe ['mɪsltəu] n muérdago

mistook [mɪs'tuk] pt of **mistake**

mistress ['mɪstrɪs] n (lover) amante f; (of house) señora (de la casa); (BRIT: in primary school) maestra; (in secondary school) profesora; (of situation) dueña

mistrust [mɪs'trʌst] vt desconfiar de

misty ['mɪstɪ] adj (day) de niebla; (glasses)

etc) empañado

misunderstand [mɪsʌndə'stænd] *(irreg) vt,
vi* entender mal; **~ing** *n* malentendido

misuse [*n* mɪs'juːs, *vb* mɪs'juːz] *n* mal uso;
(of power) abuso; *(of funds)* malversación *f*
♦ *vt* abusar de; malversar

mitt(en) ['mɪt(n)] *n* manopla

mix [mɪks] *vt* mezclar; *(combine)* unir ♦ *vi*
mezclarse; *(people)* llevarse bien ♦ *n* mezcla; **~ up** *vt* mezclar; *(confuse)* confundir;
~ed *adj* mixto; *(feelings etc)* encontrado;
~ed-up *adj (confused)* confuso, revuelto;
~er *n (for food)* licuadora; *(for drinks)* coc-
telera; *(person)*: **he's a good ~er** tiene don
de gentes; **~ture** *n* mezcla; *(also: cough
~ture)* jarabe *m*; **~-up** *n* confusión *f*

mm *abbr* (= *millimetre*) mm

moan [məun] *n* gemido ♦ *vi* gemir; *(inf:
complain)*: **to ~ (about)** quejarse (de)

moat [məut] *n* foso

mob [mɔb] *n* multitud *f* ♦ *vt* acosar

mobile ['məubaɪl] *adj* móvil ♦ *n* móvil *m*;
~ home *n* caravana; **~ phone** *n* teléfono
portátil

mock [mɔk] *vt (ridicule)* ridiculizar; *(laugh
at)* burlarse de ♦ *adj* fingido; **~ exam** *examen* preparatorio antes de los exámenes ofi-
ciales; **~ery** *n* burla; **~-up** *n* maqueta

mod [mɔd] *adj see* **convenience**

mode [məud] *n* modo

model ['mɔdl] *n* modelo; *(fashion ~, artist's
~)* modelo *m/f* ♦ *adj* modelo ♦ *vt (with clay
etc)* modelar *(copy)*: **to ~ o.s. on** tomar
como modelo a ♦ *vi* ser modelo; **~ railway** *n* ferrocarril *m* de juguete; **to ~
clothes** pasar modelos, ser modelo

modem ['məudəm] *n* modem *m*

moderate [*adj* 'mɔdərət, *vb* 'mɔdəreɪt] *adj*
moderado/a ♦ *vi* moderarse, calmarse ♦ *vt*
moderar

modern ['mɔdən] *adj* moderno; **~ize** *vt*
modernizar

modest ['mɔdɪst] *adj* modesto; *(small)* módico; **~y** *n* modestia

modicum ['mɔdɪkəm] *n*: **a ~ of** un mínimo
de

modify ['mɔdɪfaɪ] *vt* modificar

mogul ['məugəl] *n (fig)* magnate *m*

mohair ['məuhɛə*] *n* mohair *m*

moist [mɔɪst] *adj* húmedo; **~en** ['mɔɪsn] *vt*
humedecer; **~ure** ['mɔɪstʃə*] *n* humedad *f*;
~urizer ['mɔɪstʃəraɪzə*] *n* crema hidratante

molar ['məulə*] *n* muela

mold [məuld] *(US) n, vt* = **mould**

mole [məul] *n (animal, spy)* topo; *(spot)* lunar *m*

molecule ['mɔlɪkjuːl] *n* molécula

molest [məu'lɛst] *vt* importunar; *(assault
sexually)* abusar sexualmente de

mollycoddle ['mɔlɪkɔdl] *vt* mimar

molt [məult] *(US) vi* = **moult**

molten ['məultən] *adj* fundido; *(lava)* líquido

mom [mɔm] *(US) n* = **mum**

moment ['məumənt] *n* momento; **at the ~**
de momento, por ahora; **~ary** *adj* momentáneo; **~ous** [-'mɛntəs] *adj* trascendental,
importante

momentum [məu'mɛntəm] *n* momento;
(fig) ímpetu *m*; **to gather ~** cobrar velocidad; *(fig)* ganar fuerza

mommy ['mɔmɪ] *(US) n* = **mummy**

Monaco ['mɔnəkəu] *n* Mónaco

monarch ['mɔnək] *n* monarca *m/f*; **~y** *n*
monarquía

monastery ['mɔnəstərɪ] *n* monasterio

Monday ['mʌndɪ] *n* lunes *m inv*

monetary ['mʌnɪtərɪ] *adj* monetario

money ['mʌnɪ] *n* dinero; *(currency)* moneda; **to make ~** ganar dinero; **~ order** *n*
giro; **~-spinner** *(inf) n*: **to be a ~-spinner**
dar mucho dinero

mongrel ['mʌŋgrəl] *n (dog)* perro mestizo

monitor ['mɔnɪtə*] *n (SCOL)* monitor *m*;
(also: television ~) receptor *m* de control;
(of computer) monitor *m* ♦ *vt* controlar

monk [mʌŋk] *n* monje *m*

monkey ['mʌŋkɪ] *n* mono; **~ nut** *(BRIT) n*
cacahuete *m (SP)*, maní *(AM)*; **~ wrench**
n llave *f* inglesa

mono ['mɔnəu] *adj (recording)* mono

monopoly [mə'nɔpəlɪ] *n* monopolio

monotone ['mɔnətəun] *n* voz *f* (or tono)
monocorde

monotonous [mə'nɔtənəs] *adj* monótono

monsoon [mɔn'suːn] *n* monzón *m*

monster ['mɔnstə*] *n* monstruo

monstrosity [mɔns'trɔsɪtɪ] *n* monstruosidad *f*

monstrous ['mɔnstrəs] *adj (huge)* enorme;
(atrocious, ugly) monstruoso

month [mʌnθ] *n* mes *m*; **~ly** *adj* mensual ♦
adv mensualmente

monument ['mɔnjumənt] *n* monumento;
~al [-'mɛntl] *adj* monumental

moo [muː] *vi* mugir

mood [muːd] *n* humor *m*; *(of crowd, group)*
clima *m*; **to be in a good/bad ~** estar de
buen/mal humor; **~y** *adj (changeable)* de
humor variable; *(sullen)* malhumorado

moon [muːn] *n* luna; **~light** *n* luz *f* de la
luna; **~lighting** *n* pluriempleo; **~lit** *adj*: **a
~lit night** una noche de luna

Moor [muə*] *n* moro/a

moor [muə*] *n* páramo ♦ *vt (ship)* amarrar
♦ *vi* echar las amarras

Moorish ['muərɪʃ] *adj* moro; *(architecture)*
árabe, morisco

moorland ['muələnd] *n* páramo, brezal *m*

moose [muːs] *n inv* alce *m*

mop [mɔp] *n* fregona; *(of hair)* greña, melena ♦ *vt* fregar; **~ up** *vt* limpiar

mope [məup] *vi* estar o andar deprimido

moped ['məupɛd] *n* ciclomotor *m*

moral ['mɔrl] adj moral ♦ n moraleja; ~s npl moralidad f, moral f
morale [mə'rɑːl] n moral f
morality [mə'ræliti] n moralidad f
morass [mə'ræs] n pantano
morbid ['mɔːbid] adj (interest) morboso

KEYWORD

---

more [mɔː*] adj **1** (greater in number etc) más; ~ **people/work than before** más gente/trabajo que antes
2 (additional) más; **do you want (some)** ~ **tea?** ¿quieres más té?; **is there any** ~ **wine?** ¿queda vino?; **it'll take a few** ~ **weeks** tardará unas semanas más; **it's 2 kms** ~ **to the house** faltan 2 kms para la casa; ~ **time/letters than we expected** más tiempo del que/más cartas de las que esperábamos
♦ pron (greater amount, additional amount) más; ~ **than 10** más de 10; **it cost** ~ **than the other one/than we expected** costó más que el otro/más de lo que esperábamos; **is there any** ~? ¿hay más?; **many/much** ~ muchos(as)/mucho(a) más
♦ adv más; ~ **dangerous/easily (than)** más peligroso/fácilmente (que); ~ **and** ~ **expensive** cada vez más caro; ~ **or less** más o menos; ~ **than ever** más que nunca

---

moreover [mɔː'rəuvə*] adv además, por otra parte
morgue [mɔːg] n depósito de cadáveres
Mormon ['mɔːmən] n mormón/ona m/f
morning ['mɔːnɪŋ] n mañana; (early ~) madrugada ♦ cpd matutino, de la mañana; **in the** ~ por la mañana; **7 o'clock in the** ~ las 7 de la mañana; ~ **sickness** n náuseas fpl matutinas
Morocco [mə'rɔkəu] n Marruecos m
moron ['mɔːrɔn] (inf) n imbécil m/f
morose [mə'rəus] adj hosco, malhumorado
morphine ['mɔːfiːn] n morfina
Morse [mɔːs] n (also: ~ code) (código) Morse
morsel ['mɔːsl] n (of food) bocado
mortar ['mɔːtə*] n argamasa; (implement) mortero
mortgage ['mɔːgɪdʒ] n hipoteca ♦ vt hipotecar; ~ **company** (US) n ≈ banco hipotecario
mortify ['mɔːtɪfaɪ] vt mortificar, humillar
mortuary ['mɔːtjuərɪ] n depósito de cadáveres
Moscow ['mɔskəu] n Moscú
Moslem ['mɔzləm] adj, n = **Muslim**
mosque [mɔsk] n mezquita
mosquito [mɔs'kiːtəu] (pl ~es) n mosquito (SP), zancudo (AM)
moss [mɔs] n musgo
most [məust] adj la mayor parte de, la mayoría de ♦ pron la mayor parte, la mayoría

♦ adv el más; (very) muy; **the** ~ (also: + adj) el más; ~ **of them** la mayor parte de ellos; **I saw the** ~ yo vi el que más; **at the (very)** ~ a lo sumo, todo lo más; **to make the** ~ **of** aprovechar (al máximo); **a** ~ **interesting book** un libro interesantísimo
mostly ['məustlɪ] adv en su mayor parte, principalmente
MOT (BRIT) n abbr (= Ministry of Transport): **the** ~ (test) inspección (anual) obligatoria de coches y camiones
motel [məu'tɛl] n motel m
moth [mɔθ] n mariposa nocturna; (clothes ~) polilla; ~**ball** n bola de naftalina
mother ['mʌðə*] n madre f ♦ adj materno ♦ vt (care for) cuidar (como una madre); ~**hood** n maternidad f; ~**-in-law** n suegra; ~**ly** adj maternal; ~**-of-pearl** n nácar m; ~**-to-be** n futura madre f; ~ **tongue** n lengua materna
motif [məu'tiːf] n motivo
motion ['məuʃən] n movimiento; (gesture) ademán m, señal f; (at meeting) moción f ♦ vt, vi: **to** ~ (**to**) **sb to do sth** hacer señas a uno para que haga algo; ~**less** adj inmóvil; ~ **picture** n película
motivated ['məutɪveɪtɪd] adj motivado
motive ['məutɪv] n motivo
motley ['mɔtlɪ] adj variado
motor ['məutə*] n motor m; (BRIT: inf: vehicle) coche m (SP), carro (AM), automóvil m ♦ adj motor (f: motora or motriz); ~**bike** n moto f; ~**boat** n lancha motora; ~**car** (BRIT) n coche m, carro, automóvil m; ~**cycle** n motocicleta; ~**cycle racing** n motociclismo; ~**cyclist** n motociclista m/f; ~**ing** (BRIT) n automovilismo; ~**ist** n conductor(a) m/f, automovilista m/f; ~ **racing** (BRIT) n carreras fpl de coches, automovilismo; ~ **vehicle** n automóvil m; ~**way** (BRIT) n autopista
mottled ['mɔtld] adj abigarrado, multicolor
motto ['mɔtəu] (pl ~es) n lema m; (watchword) consigna
mould [məuld] (US **mold**) n molde m; (mildew) moho ♦ vt moldear; (fig) formar; ~**y** adj enmohecido
moult [məult] (US **molt**) vi mudar la piel (or las plumas)
mound [maund] n montón m, montículo
mount [maunt] n monte m ♦ vt montar, subir a; (jewel) engarzar; (picture) enmarcar; (exhibition etc) organizar ♦ vi (increase) aumentar; ~ **up** vi aumentar
mountain ['mauntɪn] n montaña ♦ cpd de montaña; ~ **bike** n bicicleta de montaña; ~**eer** [-'nɪə*] n montañero/a (SP), andinista m/f (AM); ~**eering** [-'nɪərɪŋ] n montañismo, andinismo; ~**ous** adj montañoso; ~ **rescue team** n equipo de rescate de montaña; ~**side** n ladera de la montaña

mourn [mɔ:n] *vt* llorar, lamentar ♦ *vi*: **to ~ for** llorar la muerte de; **~er** *n* doliente *m/f*; dolorido/a; **~ful** *adj* triste, lúgubre; **~ing** *n* luto; **in ~ing** de luto

mouse [maus] *(pl* **mice)** *n* (ZOOL, COMPUT) ratón *m*; **~trap** *n* ratonera

mousse [mu:s] *n* (CULIN) crema batida; *(for hair)* espuma (moldeadora)

moustache [məsˈtɑ:ʃ] *(US* **mustache)** *n* bigote *m*

mousy [ˈmausɪ] *adj (hair)* pardusco

mouth [mauθ, *pl* mauðz] *n* boca; *(of river)* desembocadura; **~ful** *n* bocado; **~ organ** *n* armónica; **~piece** *n* *(of musical instrument)* boquilla; *(spokesman)* portavoz *m/f*; **~wash** *n* enjuague *m*; **~-watering** *adj* apetitoso

movable [ˈmu:vəbl] *adj* movible

move [mu:v] *n* *(movement)* movimiento; *(in game)* jugada; (: *turn to play)* turno; *(change: of house)* mudanza; (: *of job)* cambio de trabajo ♦ *vt* mover; *(emotionally)* conmover; *(POL: resolution etc)* proponer ♦ *vi* moverse; *(traffic)* circular; *(also: ~ house)* trasladarse, mudarse; **to ~ sb to do sth** mover a uno a hacer algo; **to get a ~ on** darse prisa; **~ about or around** *vi* moverse; *(travel)* viajar; **~ along** *vi* avanzar, adelantarse; **~ away** *vi* alejarse; **~ back** *vi* retroceder; **~ forward** *vi* avanzar; **~ in** *vi* *(to a house)* instalarse; *(police, soldiers)* intervenir; **~ on** *vi* ponerse en camino; **~ out** *vi* *(of house)* mudarse; **~ over** *vi* apartarse, hacer sitio; **~ up** *vi* *(employee)* ser ascendido

moveable [ˈmu:vəbl] *adj* = **movable**

movement [ˈmu:vmənt] *n* movimiento

movie [ˈmu:vɪ] *n* película; **to go to the ~s** ir al cine; **~ camera** *n* cámara cinematográfica

moving [ˈmu:vɪŋ] *adj (emotional)* conmovedor(a); *(that moves)* móvil

mow [məu] *(pt* **mowed** *or* **mown)** *vt (grass, corn)* cortar, segar; **~ down** *vt (shoot)* acribillar; **~er** *n* *(also: lawn~er)* cortacéspedes *m inv*, segadora

MP *n abbr* = **Member of Parliament**

m.p.h. *abbr* = **miles per hour** (60 m.p.h. = 96 k.p.h.)

Mr [ˈmɪstə*] *(US* **Mr.)** *n*: **~ Smith** (el) Sr. Smith

Mrs [ˈmɪsɪz] *(US* **Mrs.)** *n*: **~ Smith** (la) Sra. Smith

Ms [mɪz] *(US* **Ms.)** *n* (= **Miss** *or* **Mrs**): **~ Smith** (la) Sr(t)a. Smith

M.Sc. *abbr* = **Master of Science**

much [mʌtʃ] *adj* mucho ♦ *adv* mucho; *(before pp)* muy ♦ *n or pron* mucho; **how ~ is it?** ¿cuánto es?, ¿cuánto cuesta?; **too ~** es demasiado; **it's not ~** no es mucho; **as ~ as** tanto como; **however ~ he tries** por mucho que se esfuerce

muck [mʌk] *n* suciedad *f*; **~ about** *or*

~ around *(inf)* *vi* perder el tiempo; *(enjoy o.s.)* entretenerse; **~ up** *(inf)* *vt* arruinar, estropear

mud [mʌd] *n* barro, lodo

muddle [ˈmʌdl] *n* desorden *m*, confusión *f*; *(mix-up)* embrollo, lío ♦ *vt (also: ~ up)* embrollar, confundir; **~ through** *vi* salir del paso

muddy [ˈmʌdɪ] *adj* fangoso, cubierto de lodo

mudguard [ˈmʌdgɑ:d] *n* guardabarros *m inv*

muffin [ˈmʌfɪn] *n* panecillo dulce

muffle [ˈmʌfl] *vt (sound)* amortiguar; *(against cold)* embozar; **~d** *adj (noise etc)* amortiguado, apagado; **~r** *n* *(US)* *(AUT)* silenciador *m*

mug [mʌg] *n* taza grande *(sin platillo)*; *(for beer)* jarra; *(inf: face)* jeta; (: *fool)* bobo ♦ *vt (assault)* asaltar; **~ging** *n* asalto

muggy [ˈmʌgɪ] *adj* bochornoso

mule [mju:l] *n* mula

mull over [mʌl-] *vt* meditar sobre

multi... [ˈmʌltɪ] *prefix* multi...

multi-level [mʌltɪˈlevl] *(US)* *adj* = **multistorey**

multiple [ˈmʌltɪpl] *adj* múltiple ♦ *n* múltiplo; **~ sclerosis** *n* esclerosis *f* múltiple

multiplication [mʌltɪplɪˈkeɪʃən] *n* multiplicación *f*

multiply [ˈmʌltɪplaɪ] *vt* multiplicar ♦ *vi* multiplicarse

multistorey [mʌltɪˈstɔ:rɪ] *(BRIT)* *adj* de muchos pisos

multitude [ˈmʌltɪtju:d] *n* multitud *f*

mum [mʌm] *(BRIT: inf)* *n* mamá ♦ *adj*: **to keep ~** mantener la boca cerrada

mumble [ˈmʌmbl] *vt, vi* hablar entre dientes, refunfuñar

mummy [ˈmʌmɪ] *n* *(BRIT: mother)* mamá; *(embalmed)* momia

mumps [mʌmps] *n* paperas *fpl*

munch [mʌntʃ] *vt, vi* mascar

mundane [mʌnˈdeɪn] *adj* trivial

municipal [mju:ˈnɪsɪpl] *adj* municipal

munitions [mju:ˈnɪʃənz] *npl* munición *f*

murder [ˈmə:də*] *n* asesinato; *(in law)* homicidio ♦ *vt* asesinar, matar; **~er/ess** *n* asesino/a; **~ous** *adj* homicida

murky [ˈmə:kɪ] *adj (water)* turbio; *(street, night)* lóbrego

murmur [ˈmə:mə*] *n* murmullo ♦ *vt, vi* murmurar

muscle [ˈmʌsl] *n* músculo; *(fig: strength)* garra, fuerza; **~ in** *vi* entrometerse; **muscular** [ˈmʌskjulə*] *adj* muscular; *(person)* musculoso

muse [mju:z] *vi* meditar ♦ *n* musa

museum [mju:ˈzɪəm] *n* museo

mushroom [ˈmʌʃrum] *n* seta, hongo; *(CULIN)* champiñón *m* ♦ *vi* crecer de la noche a la mañana

music ['mju:zɪk] n música; ~**al** adj musical; (sound) melodioso; (person) con talento musical ♦ n (show) comedia musical; ~**al instrument** n instrumento musical; ~ **hall** n teatro de variedades; ~**ian** [-'zɪʃən] n músico/a

musk [mʌsk] n almizcle m

Muslim ['mʌzlɪm] adj, n musulmán/ana m/f

muslin ['mʌzlɪn] n muselina

mussel ['mʌsl] n mejillón m

must [mʌst] aux vb (obligation): **I** ~ **do it** debo hacerlo, tengo que hacerlo; (probability): **he** ~ **be there by now** ya debe (de) estar allí ♦ n: **it's a** ~ es imprescindible

mustache ['mʌstæʃ] (US) n = **moustache**

mustard ['mʌstəd] n mostaza

muster ['mʌstə*] vt juntar, reunir

mustn't ['mʌsnt] = **must not**

musty ['mʌstɪ] adj mohoso, que huele a humedad

mute [mju:t] adj, n mudo/a m/f

muted ['mju:tɪd] adj callado; (colour) apagado

mutilate ['mju:tɪleɪt] vt (person) mutilar; (thing) destrozar

mutiny ['mju:tɪnɪ] n motín m ♦ vi amotinarse

mutter ['mʌtə*] vt, vi murmurar

mutton ['mʌtn] n carne f de cordero

mutual ['mju:tʃuəl] adj mutuo; (interest) común; ~**ly** adv mutuamente

muzzle ['mʌzl] n hocico; (for dog) bozal m; (of gun) boca ♦ vt (dog) poner un bozal a

my [maɪ] adj mi(s); ~ **house/brother/ sisters** mi casa/mi hermano/mis hermanas; **I've washed** ~ **hair/cut** ~ **finger** me he lavado el pelo/cortado un dedo; **is this** ~ **pen or yours?** ¿es este bolígrafo mío o tuyo?

myopic [maɪ'ɔpɪk] adj miope

myself [maɪ'self] pron (reflexive) me; (emphatic) yo mismo; (after prep) mí (mismo); see also **oneself**

mysterious [mɪs'tɪərɪəs] adj misterioso

mystery ['mɪstərɪ] n misterio

mystify ['mɪstɪfaɪ] vt (perplex) dejar perplejo

mystique [mɪs'ti:k] n misterio (profesional etc)

myth [mɪθ] n mito

N n

n/a abbr (= not applicable) no interesa

nag [næg] vt (scold) regañar; ~**ging** adj (doubt) persistente; (pain) continuo

nail [neɪl] n (human) uña; (metal) clavo ♦ vt clavar; **to** ~ **sth to sth** clavar algo en algo; **to** ~ **sb down to doing sth** comprometer a uno a que haga algo; ~**brush** n cepillo para las uñas; ~**file** n lima para las uñas; ~ **polish** n esmalte m or laca para las uñas; ~ **polish remover** n quitaesmalte m; ~ **scissors** npl tijeras fpl para las uñas; ~ **varnish** (BRIT) n = ~ **polish**

naïve [naɪ'i:v] adj ingenuo

naked ['neɪkɪd] adj (nude) desnudo; (flame) expuesto al aire

name [neɪm] n nombre m; (surname) apellido; (reputation) fama, renombre m ♦ vt (child) poner nombre a; (criminal) identificar; (price, date etc) fijar; **what's your** ~? ¿cómo se llama?; **by** ~ de nombre; **in the** ~ **of** en nombre de; **to give one's** ~ **and address** dar sus señas; ~**less** adj (unknown) desconocido; (anonymous) anónimo, sin nombre; ~**ly** adv a saber; ~**sake** n tocayo/a

nanny ['nænɪ] n niñera

nap [næp] n (sleep) sueñecito, siesta; **to be caught** ~**ping** estar desprevenido

nape [neɪp] n: ~ **of the neck** nuca, cogote m

napkin ['næpkɪn] n (also: table ~) servilleta

nappy ['næpɪ] (BRIT) n pañal m; ~ **rash** n prurito

narcotic [nɑː'kɔtɪk] adj, n narcótico

narrow ['nærəu] adj estrecho, angosto; (fig: majority etc) corto; (: ideas etc) estrecho ♦ vi (road) estrecharse; (diminish) reducirse; **to have a** ~ **escape** escaparse por los pelos; **to** ~ **sth down** reducir algo; ~**ly** adv (miss) por poco; ~-**minded** adj de miras estrechas

nasty ['nɑːstɪ] adj (remark) feo; (person) antipático; (revolting: taste, smell) asqueroso; (wound, disease etc) peligroso, grave

nation ['neɪʃən] n nación f

national ['næʃənl] adj, n nacional m/f; ~ **dress** n vestido nacional; **N~ Health Service** (BRIT) n servicio nacional de salud pública; ≈ Insalud m (SP); **N~ Insurance** (BRIT) n seguro social nacional; ~**ism** n nacionalismo; **~ist** *adj, n* nacionalista *m/f*; **~ity** [-'næliti] *n* nacionalidad *f*; **~ize** *vt* nacionalizar; **~ly** *adv* (*nationwide*) en escala nacional; (*as a nation*) nacionalmente, como nación

nationwide ['neɪʃənwaɪd] *adj* en escala *or* a nivel nacional

native ['neɪtɪv] *n* (*local inhabitant*) natural *m/f*, nacional *m/f*; (*of tribe etc*) indígena *m/f*, nativo/a ♦ *adj* (*indigenous*) indígena; (*country*) natal; (*innate*)· natural, innato; **a ~ of Russia** un(a) natural *m/f* de Rusia; **a ~ speaker of French** un hablante nativo de francés; **~ language** *n* lengua materna

Nativity [nə'tɪvɪtɪ] *n*: **the ~** Navidad *f*

NATO ['neɪtəu] *n abbr* (= *North Atlantic Treaty Organization*) OTAN *f*

natural ['nætʃrəl] *adj* natural; **~ize** *vt*: **to become ~ized** (*person*) naturalizarse; (*plant*) aclimatarse; **~ly** *adv* (*speak etc*) naturalmente; (*of course*) desde luego, por supuesto

nature ['neɪtʃə*] *n* (*also*: *N~*) naturaleza; (*group, sort*) género, clase *f*; (*character*) carácter *m*, genio; **by ~** por *or* de naturaleza

naught [nɔːt] *n* = **nought**

naughty ['nɔːtɪ] *adj* (*child*) travieso

nausea ['nɔːsɪə] *n* náuseas *fpl*; **nauseate** [-sɪeɪt] *vt* dar náuseas a; (*fig*) dar asco a

nautical ['nɔːtɪkl] *adj* náutico, marítimo; (*mile*) marino

naval ['neɪvl] *adj* naval, de marina; **~ officer** *n* oficial *m/f* de marina

nave [neɪv] *n* nave *f*

navel ['neɪvl] *n* ombligo

navigate ['nævɪgeɪt] *vt* gobernar ♦ *vi* navegar; (*AUT*) ir de copiloto; **navigation** [-'geɪʃən] *n* (*action*) navegación *f*; (*science*) náutica; **navigator** *n* navegador(a) *m/f*, navegante *m/f*; (*AUT*) copiloto *m/f*

navvy ['nævɪ] (*BRIT*) *n* peón *m* caminero

navy ['neɪvɪ] *n* marina de guerra; (*ships*) armada, flota; **~(-blue)** *adj* azul marino

Nazi ['nɑːtsɪ] *n* nazi *m/f*

NB *abbr* (= *nota bene*) nótese

near [nɪə*] *adj* (*place, relation*) cercano; (*time*) próximo ♦ *adv* cerca ♦ *prep* (*also*: ~ **to**: *space*) cerca de, junto a; (: *time*) cerca de ♦ *vt* acercarse a, aproximarse a; **~by** [nɪə'baɪ] *adj* cercano, próximo ♦ *adv* cerca; **~ly** *adv* casi, por poco; **I ~ly fell** por poco me caigo; **~ miss** *n* tiro cercano; **~side** *n* (*AUT*: *in Britain*) lado izquierdo; (: *in US, Europe etc*) lado derecho; **~-sighted** *adj* miope, corto de vista

neat [niːt] *adj* (*place*) ordenado, bien cuidado; (*person*) pulcro; (*plan*) ingenioso; (*spirits*) solo; **~ly** *adv* (*tidily*) con esmero; (*skilfully*) ingeniosamente

necessarily ['nesɪsrɪlɪ] *adv* necesariamente

necessary ['nesɪsrɪ] *adj* necesario, preciso

necessitate [nɪ'sesɪteɪt] *vt* hacer necesario

necessity [nɪ'sesɪtɪ] *n* necesidad *f*; **necessities** *npl* artículos *mpl* de primera necesidad

neck [nek] *n* (*of person, garment, bottle*) cuello; (*of animal*) pescuezo ♦ *vi* (*inf*) besuquearse; **~ and ~** parejos; **~lace** ['neklɪs] *n* collar *m*; **~line** *n* escote *m*; **~tie** ['nektaɪ] *n* corbata

née [neɪ] *adj*: **~ Scott** de soltera Scott

need [niːd] *n* (*lack*) escasez *f*, falta; (*necessity*) necesidad *f* ♦ *vt* (*require*) necesitar; **I ~ to do it** tengo que *or* debo hacerlo; **you don't ~ to go** no hace falta que (te) vayas

needle ['niːdl] *n* aguja ♦ *vt* (*fig*: *inf*) picar, fastidiar

needless ['niːdlɪs] *adj* innecesario; **~ to say** huelga decir que

needlework ['niːdlwəːk] *n* (*activity*) costura, labor *f* de aguja

needn't ['niːdnt] = **need not**

needy ['niːdɪ] *adj* necesitado

negative ['negətɪv] *n* (*PHOT*) negativo; (*LING*) negación *f* ♦ *adj* negativo

neglect [nɪ'glekt] *vt* (*one's duty*) faltar a, no cumplir con; (*child*) descuidar, desatender ♦ *n* (*of house, garden etc*) abandono; (*of child*) desatención *f*; (*of duty*) incumplimiento

negligee ['neglɪʒeɪ] *n* (*nightgown*) salto de cama

negligence ['neglɪdʒəns] *n* negligencia, descuido

negligible ['neglɪdʒɪbl] *adj* insignificante, despreciable

negotiate [nɪ'gəuʃɪeɪt] *vt* (*treaty, loan*) negociar; (*obstacle*) franquear; (*bend in road*) tomar ♦ *vi*: **to ~ (with)** negociar (con); **negotiation** [-'eɪʃən] *n* negociación *f*, gestión *f*

Negress ['niːgrɪs] *n* negra

Negro ['niːgrəu] *adj, n* negro

neigh [neɪ] *vi* relinchar

neighbour ['neɪbə*] (*US* **neighbor**) *n* vecino/a; **~hood** *n* (*place*) vecindad *f*, barrio; (*people*) vecindario; **~ing** *adj* vecino; **~ly** *adj* (*person*) amable; (*attitude*) de buen vecino

neither ['naɪðə*] *adj* ni ♦ *conj*: **I didn't move and ~ did John** no me he movido, ni Juan tampoco ♦ *pron* ninguno; **~ is true** ninguno/a de los/las dos es cierto/a ♦ *adv*: **~ good nor bad** ni bueno ni malo

neon ['niːɔn] *n* neón *m*; **~ light** *n* lámpara de neón

nephew ['nevjuː] *n* sobrino

nerve [nəːv] *n* (*ANAT*) nervio; (*courage*) valor *m*; (*impudence*) descaro, frescura; **a fit of ~s** un ataque de nervios; **~-racking** *adj* desquiciante

nervous ['nəːvəs] *adj* (*anxious, ANAT*) nervioso; (*timid*) tímido, miedoso; **~ breakdown** *n* crisis *f* nerviosa

nest [nest] *n* (*of bird*) nido; (*wasps'* ~) avispero ♦ vi anidar; ~ **egg** n (fig) ahorros mpl

nestle ['nɛsl] vi: **to ~ down** acurrucarse

net [nɛt] n (gen) red f; (fabric) tul m ♦ adj (COMM) neto, líquido ♦ vt coger (SP) or agarrar (AM) con red; (SPORT) marcar; ~**ball** n básquet m; ~ **curtains** npl visillos mpl

Netherlands ['nɛðələndz] npl: **the ~** los Países Bajos

nett [nɛt] adj = **net**

netting ['nɛtɪŋ] n red f, redes fpl

nettle ['nɛtl] n ortiga

network ['nɛtwə:k] n red f

neurotic [njuə'rɔtɪk] adj, n neurótico/a m/f

neuter ['nju:tə*] adj (LING) neutro ♦ vt castrar, capar

neutral ['nju:trəl] adj (person) neutral; (colour etc, ELEC) neutro ♦ n (AUT) punto muerto; ~**ize** vt neutralizar

never ['nɛvə*] adv nunca, jamás; **I ~ went** no fui nunca; **~ in my life** jamás en la vida; see also **mind**; ~**-ending** adj interminable, sin fin; ~**theless** [nɛvəðə'lɛs] adv sin embargo, no obstante

new [nju:] adj nuevo; (brand new) a estrenar; (recent) reciente; ~**born** adj recién nacido; ~**comer** ['nju:kʌmə*] n recién venido/a or llegado/a; ~**fangled** (pej) adj modernísimo; ~**found** adj (friend) nuevo; (enthusiasm) recién adquirido; ~**ly** adv nuevamente, recién; ~**ly-weds** npl recién casados mpl

news [nju:z] n noticias fpl; **a piece of ~** una noticia; **the ~** (RADIO, TV) las noticias fpl; ~ **agency** n agencia de noticias; ~**agent** (BRIT) n vendedor(a) m/f de periódicos; ~**caster** n presentador(a) m/f, locutor(a) m/f; ~ **dealer** (US) n = ~**agent**; ~ **flash** n noticia de última hora; ~**letter** n hoja informativa, boletín m; ~**paper** n periódico, diario; ~**print** n papel m de periódico; ~**reader** n = ~**caster**; ~**reel** n noticiario; ~ **stand** n quiosco or puesto de periódicos

newt [nju:t] n tritón m

New Year n Año Nuevo; ~**'s Day** n Día m de Año Nuevo; ~**'s Eve** n Nochevieja

New York ['nju:'jɔ:k] n Nueva York

New Zealand [nju:'zi:lənd] n Nueva Zelanda; ~**er** n neozelandés/esa m/f

next [nɛkst] adj (house, room) vecino; (bus stop, meeting) próximo; (following: page etc) siguiente ♦ adv después; **the ~ day** el día siguiente; ~ **time** la próxima vez; ~ **year** el año próximo or que viene; ~ **to** junto a, al lado de; ~ **to nothing** casi nada; ~ **please!** ¡el siguiente! ~ **door** adv en la casa de al lado ♦ adj vecino, de al lado; ~**-of-kin** n pariente m más cercano

NHS n abbr = **National Health Service**

nib [nɪb] n plumilla

nibble ['nɪbl] vt mordisquear, mordiscar

Nicaragua [nɪkə'rægjuə] n Nicaragua; ~**n** adj, n nicaragüense m/f

nice [naɪs] adj (likeable) simpático; (kind) amable; (pleasant) agradable; (attractive) bonito, mono, lindo (AM); ~**ly** adv amablemente; bien

nick [nɪk] n (wound) rasguño; (cut, indentation) mella, muesca ♦ vt (inf) birlar, robar; **in the ~ of time** justo a tiempo

nickel ['nɪkl] n níquel m; (US) moneda de 5 centavos

nickname ['nɪkneɪm] n apodo, mote m ♦ vt apodar

nicotine ['nɪkəti:n] n nicotina

niece [ni:s] n sobrina

Nigeria [naɪ'dʒɪərɪə] n Nigeria; ~**n** adj, n nigeriano/a m/f

niggling ['nɪglɪŋ] adj (trifling) nimio, insignificante; (annoying) molesto

night [naɪt] n noche f; (evening) tarde f; **the ~ before last** anteanoche; **at ~**, **by ~** de noche, por la noche; ~**cap** n (drink) bebida que se toma antes de acostarse; ~ **club** n cabaret m; ~**dress** (BRIT) n camisón m; ~**fall** n anochecer m; ~**gown** n = ~**dress**; ~**ie** ['naɪtɪ] n = ~**dress**

nightingale ['naɪtɪŋgeɪl] n ruiseñor m

nightlife ['naɪtlaɪf] n vida nocturna

nightly ['naɪtlɪ] adj de todas las noches ♦ adv todas las noches, cada noche

nightmare ['naɪtmeə*] n pesadilla

night: ~ **porter** n portero de noche; ~ **school** n clase(s) f(pl) nocturna(s); ~ **shift** n turno nocturno or de noche; ~**-time** n noche f; ~ **watchman** n vigilante m nocturno

nil [nɪl] (BRIT) n (SPORT) cero, nada

Nile [naɪl] n: **the ~** el Nilo

nimble ['nɪmbl] adj (agile) ágil, ligero; (skilful) diestro

nine [naɪn] num nueve; ~**teen** num diecinueve, diez y nueve; ~**ty** num noventa

ninth [naɪnθ] adj noveno

nip [nɪp] vt (pinch) pellizcar; (bite) morder

nipple ['nɪpl] n (ANAT) pezón m

nitrogen ['naɪtrədʒən] n nitrógeno

─── **KEYWORD**

no [nəu] (pl ~**es**) adv (opposite of "yes") no; **are you coming? — ~ (I'm not)** ¿vienes? — no; **would you like some more? — ~ thank you** ¿quieres más? — no gracias

♦ adj (not any): **I have ~ money/time/ books** no tengo dinero/tiempo/libros; **~ other man would have done it** ningún otro lo hubiera hecho; **"~ entry"** "prohibido el paso"; **"~ smoking"** "prohibido fumar"

♦ n no m

nobility [nəu'bɪlɪtɪ] n nobleza
noble ['nəubl] adj noble
nobody ['nəubədɪ] pron nadie
nod [nɔd] vi saludar con la cabeza; (in agreement) decir que sí con la cabeza; (doze) dar cabezadas ♦ vt: to ~ one's head inclinar la cabeza ♦ n propuesta, inclinación f de cabeza; ~ off vi dar cabezadas
noise [nɔɪz] n ruido; (din) escándalo, estrépito; **noisy** adj ruidoso; (child) escandaloso
nominate ['nɔmɪneɪt] vt (propose) proponer; (appoint) nombrar; **nomination** [-'neɪʃən] n propuesta; nombramiento; **nominee** [-'niː] n candidato/a
non... [nɔn] prefix no, des..., in...; ~-**alcoholic** adj no alcohólico; ~-**aligned** adj no alineado
nonchalant ['nɔnʃələnt] adj indiferente
non-committal ['nɔnkə'mɪtl] adj evasivo
nondescript ['nɔndɪskrɪpt] adj soso
none [nʌn] pron ninguno/a ♦ adv de ninguna manera; ~ **of you** ninguno de vosotros; **I've ~ left** no me queda ninguno/a; **he's ~ the worse for it** no le ha hecho ningún mal
nonentity [nɔ'nentɪtɪ] n cero a la izquierda, nulidad f
nonetheless [nʌnðə'les] adv sin embargo, no obstante
non-existent adj inexistente
non-fiction n literatura no novelesca
nonplussed [nɔn'plʌst] adj perplejo
nonsense ['nɔnsəns] n tonterías fpl, disparates fpl; ~! ¡qué tonterías!
non: ~-**smoker** n no fumador(a) m/f; ~-**stick** adj (pan, surface) antiadherente; ~-**stop** adj continuo; (RAIL) directo ♦ adv sin parar
noodles ['nuːdlz] npl tallarines mpl
nook [nuk] n: ~**s and crannies** escondrijos mpl
noon [nuːn] n mediodía m
no-one pron = **nobody**
noose [nuːs] n (hangman's) dogal m
nor [nɔː*] conj = **neither** ♦ adv see **neither**
norm [nɔːm] n norma
normal ['nɔːml] adj normal; ~**ly** adv normalmente
north [nɔːθ] n norte m ♦ adj del norte, norteño ♦ adv al or hacia el norte; **N~ Africa** n África del Norte; **N~ America** n América del Norte; ~-**east** n nor(d)este m; ~**erly** ['nɔːðəlɪ] adj (point, direction) norteño; ~**ern** ['nɔːðən] adj norteño, del norte; **N~ern Ireland** n Irlanda del Norte; **N~ Pole** n Polo Norte; **N~ Sea** n Mar m del Norte; ~**ward(s)** ['nɔːθwəd(z)] adv hacia el norte; ~-**west** n nor(d)oeste m
Norway ['nɔːweɪ] n Noruega; **Norwegian** [-'wiːdʒən] adj noruego/a ♦ n noruego/a; (LING) noruego
nose [nəuz] n (ANAT) nariz f; (ZOOL) hoci-

co; (sense of smell) olfato ♦ vi: to ~ about curiosear; ~**bleed** n hemorragia nasal; ~-**dive** n (of plane: deliberate) picado vertical; (: involuntary) caída en picado; ~**y** (inf) adj curioso, fisgón/ona
nostalgia [nɔs'tældʒɪə] n nostalgia
nostril ['nɔstrɪl] n ventana de la nariz
nosy ['nəuzɪ] (inf) adj = **nosey**
not [nɔt] adv no; ~ **that ...** no es que ...; **it's too late, isn't it?** es demasiado tarde, ¿verdad or no?; ~ **yet/now** todavía/ahora no; **why ~?** ¿por qué no?; see also **all**; **only**
notably ['nəutəblɪ] adv especialmente
notary ['nəutərɪ] n notario/a
notch [nɔtʃ] n muesca, corte m
note [nəut] n (MUS, record, letter) nota; (banknote) billete m; (tone) tono ♦ vt (observe) notar, observar; (write down) apuntar, anotar; ~**book** n libreta, cuaderno; ~**d** ['nəutɪd] adj célebre, conocido; ~**pad** n bloc m; ~**paper** n papel m para cartas
nothing ['nʌθɪŋ] n nada; (zero) cero; **he does ~** no hace nada; ~ **new** nada nuevo; ~ **much** no mucho; **for ~** (free) gratis, sin pago; (in vain) en balde
notice ['nəutɪs] n (announcement) anuncio; (warning) aviso; (dismissal) despido; (resignation) dimisión f; (period of time) plazo ♦ vt (observe) notar, observar; **to bring sth to sb's ~** (attention) llamar la atención de uno sobre algo; **to take ~ of** tomar nota de, prestar atención a; **at short ~** con poca anticipación; **until further ~** hasta nuevo aviso; **to hand in one's ~** dimitir; ~**able** adj evidente, obvio; ~ **board** (BRIT) n tablón m de anuncios
notify ['nəutɪfaɪ] vt: to ~ **sb (of sth)** comunicar (algo) a uno
notion ['nəuʃən] n idea; (opinion) opinión f
notorious [nəu'tɔːrɪəs] adj notorio
notwithstanding [nɔtwɪθ'stændɪŋ] adv no obstante, sin embargo ♦ prep a pesar de
nougat ['nuːgɑː] n turrón m
nought [nɔːt] n cero
noun [naun] n nombre m, sustantivo
nourish ['nʌrɪʃ] vt nutrir; (fig) alimentar; ~**ing** adj nutritivo; ~**ment** n alimento, sustento
novel ['nɔvl] n novela ♦ adj (new) nuevo, original; (unexpected) insólito; ~**ist** n novelista m/f; ~**ty** n novedad f
November [nəu'vembə*] n noviembre m
novice ['nɔvɪs] n principiante m/f, novato/a; (REL) novicio/a
now [nau] adv (at the present time) ahora; (these days) actualmente, hoy día ♦ conj: ~ (that) ya que, ahora que; **right** ~ ahora mismo; **by** ~ ya; **just** ~ ahora mismo; ~ **and then,** ~ **and again** de vez en cuando; **from** ~ **on** de ahora en adelante; ~**adays** ['nauədeɪz] adv hoy (en) día, actualmente

nowhere ['nəuwɛə*] *adv* (*direction*) a ninguna parte; (*location*) en ninguna parte
nozzle ['nɔzl] *n* boquilla
nuance ['njuːɑːns] *n* matiz *m*
nuclear ['njuːklɪə*] *adj* nuclear
nuclei ['njuːklɪaɪ] *npl of* nucleus
nucleus ['njuːklɪəs] (*pl* **nuclei**) *n* núcleo
nude [njuːd] *adj, n* desnudo/a *m/f*; **in the ~** desnudo
nudge [nʌdʒ] *vt* dar un codazo a
nudist ['njuːdɪst] *n* nudista *m/f*
nuisance ['njuːsns] *n* molestia, fastidio; (*person*) pesado, latoso; **what a ~!** ¡qué lata!
nuke ['njuːk] (*inf*) *n* bomba atómica ♦ *vt* atacar con arma nuclear
null [nʌl] *adj*: **~ and void** nulo y sin efecto
numb [nʌm] *adj*: **~ with cold/fear** entumecido por el frío/paralizado de miedo
number ['nʌmbə*] *n* número; (*quantity*) cantidad *f* ♦ *vt* (*pages etc*) numerar, poner número a; (*amount to*) sumar, ascender a; **to be ~ed among** figurar entre; **a ~ of** varios, algunos; **they were ten in ~** eran diez; **~ plate** (*BRIT*) *n* matrícula, placa
numeral ['njuːmərəl] *n* número, cifra
numerate ['njuːmərɪt] *adj* competente en la aritmética
numerous ['njuːmərəs] *adj* numeroso
nun [nʌn] *n* monja, religiosa
nurse [nɜːs] *n* enfermero/a; (*also*: **~maid**) niñera ♦ *vt* (*patient*) cuidar, atender
nursery ['nɜːsərɪ] *n* (*institution*) guardería infantil; (*room*) cuarto de los niños; (*for plants*) criadero, semillero; **~ rhyme** *n* canción *f* infantil; **~ school** *n* parvulario, escuela de párvulos; **~ slope** (*BRIT*) *n* (*SKI*) cuesta para principiantes
nursing ['nɜːsɪŋ] *n* (*profession*) profesión *f* de enfermera; (*care*) asistencia, cuidado; **~ home** *n* clínica de reposo; **~ mother** *n* madre *f* lactante
nurture ['nɜːtʃə*] *vt* (*child, plant*) alimentar, nutrir
nut [nʌt] *n* (*TECH*) tuerca; (*BOT*) nuez *f*; **~crackers** *npl* cascanueces *m inv*
nutmeg ['nʌtmɛg] *n* nuez *f* moscada
nutritious [njuː'trɪʃəs] *adj* nutritivo, alimenticio
nuts [nʌts] (*inf*) *adj* loco
nutshell ['nʌtʃɛl] *n*: **in a ~** en resumidas cuentas.
nylon ['naɪlɔn] *n* nilón *m* ♦ *adj* de nilón

O o

oak [əuk] *n* roble *m* ♦ *adj* de roble
O.A.P. (*BRIT*) *n abbr* = **old-age pensioner**
oar [ɔː*] *n* remo
oases [əu'eɪsiːz] *npl of* **oasis**
oasis [əu'eɪsɪs] (*pl* **oases**) *n* oasis *m inv*
oath [əuθ] *n* juramento; (*swear word*) palabrota; **on** (*BRIT*) **or under ~** bajo juramento
oatmeal ['əutmiːl] *n* harina de avena
oats [əuts] *n* avena
obedience [ə'biːdɪəns] *n* obediencia
obedient [ə'biːdɪənt] *adj* obediente
obey [ə'beɪ] *vt* obedecer; (*instructions, regulations*) cumplir
obituary [ə'bɪtjuərɪ] *n* necrología
object [*n* 'ɔbdʒɪkt, *vb* əb'dʒɛkt] *n* objeto; (*purpose*) objeto, propósito; (*LING*) complemento ♦ *vi*: **to ~ to** estar en contra de; (*proposal*) oponerse a; **to ~ that** objetar que; **expense is no ~** no importa cuánto cuesta; **I ~!** ¡yo protesto!; **~ion** [əb'dʒɛkʃən] *n* protesta; **I have no ~ion to ...** no tengo inconveniente en que ...; **~ionable** [əb'dʒɛkʃənəbl] *adj* desagradable; (*conduct*) censurable; **~ive** *adj, n* objetivo
obligation [ɔblɪ'geɪʃən] *n* obligación *f*; (*debt*) deber *m*; **without ~** sin compromiso
oblige [ə'blaɪdʒ] *vt* (*do a favour for*) complacer, hacer un favor a; **to ~ sb to do sth** forzar *or* obligar a uno a hacer algo; **to be ~d to sb for sth** estarle agradecido a uno por algo; **obliging** *adj* servicial, atento
oblique [ə'bliːk] *adj* oblicuo; (*allusion*) indirecto
obliterate [ə'blɪtəreɪt] *vt* borrar
oblivion [ə'blɪvɪən] *n* olvido; **oblivious** [-ɪəs] *adj*: **oblivious of** inconsciente de
oblong ['ɔblɔŋ] *adj* rectangular ♦ *n* rectángulo
obnoxious [əb'nɔkʃəs] *adj* odioso, detestable; (*smell*) nauseabundo
oboe ['əubəu] *n* oboe *m*
obscene [əb'siːn] *adj* obsceno
obscure [əb'skjuə*] *adj* oscuro ♦ *vt* oscurecer; (*hide: sun*) esconder
obsequious [əb'siːkwɪəs] *adj* servil
observance [əb'zɔːvns] *n* observancia, cumplimiento
observant [əb'zɔːvnt] *adj* observador(a)
observation [ɔbzə'veɪʃən] *n* observación *f*;

(MED) examen m

observe [əb'zə:v] vt observar; (rule) cumplir; ~r n observador(a) m/f

obsess [əb'sɛs] vt obsesionar; ~**ive** adj obsesivo; obsesionante

obsolete ['ɔbsəli:t] adj: **to be** ~ estar en desuso

obstacle ['ɔbstəkl] n obstáculo; (nuisance) estorbo; ~ **race** n carrera de obstáculos

obstinate ['ɔbstɪnɪt] adj terco, porfiado; (determined) obstinado

obstruct [əb'strʌkt] vt obstruir; (hinder) estorbar, obstaculizar; ~**ion** [əb'strʌkʃən] n (action) obstrucción f; (object) estorbo, obstáculo

obtain [əb'teɪn] vt obtener; (achieve) conseguir; ~**able** adj asequible

obvious ['ɔbvɪəs] adj obvio, evidente; ~**ly** adv evidentemente, naturalmente; ~**ly not** por supuesto que no

occasion [ə'keɪʒən] n oportunidad f, ocasión f; (event) acontecimiento; ~**al** adj poco frecuente, ocasional; ~**ally** adv de vez en cuando

occult [ɔ'kʌlt] n: **the** ~ lo sobrenatural, lo oculto

occupant ['ɔkjupənt] n (of house) inquilino/a; (of car) ocupante m/f

occupation [ɔkju'peɪʃən] n ocupación f; (job) trabajo; (pastime) ocupaciones fpl; ~**al hazard** n riesgo profesional

occupier ['ɔkjupaɪə*] n inquilino/a

occupy ['ɔkjupaɪ] vt (seat, post, time) ocupar; (house) habitar; **to** ~ **o.s. in doing** pasar el tiempo haciendo

occur [ə'kə:*] vi pasar, suceder; **to** ~ **to sb** ocurrírsele a uno; ~**rence** [ə'kʌrəns] n acontecimiento; (existence) existencia

ocean ['əuʃən] n océano; ~-**going** adj de alta mar

ochre ['əukə*] (US **ocher**) n ocre m

o'clock [ə'klɔk] adv: **it is 5** ~ son las 5

OCR n abbr = **optical character recognition/reader**

octave ['ɔktɪv] n octava

October [ɔk'təubə*] n octubre m

octopus ['ɔktəpəs] n pulpo

odd [ɔd] adj extraño, raro; (number) impar; (sock, shoe etc) suelto; **60**~ **60** y pico; **at** ~ **times** de vez en cuando; **to be the** ~ **one out** estar de más; ~**ity** n rareza; (person) excéntrico; ~-**job man** n chico para todo; ~ **jobs** npl bricolaje m; ~**ly** adv curiosamente, extrañamente; see also **enough**; ~**ments** npl (COMM) retales mpl; ~**s** npl (in betting) puntos mpl de ventaja; **it makes no** ~**s** da lo mismo; **at** ~**s** reñidos/as; ~**s-and-ends** npl minucias fpl

ode [əud] n oda

odometer [ɔ'dɔmɪtə*] (US) n cuentakilómetros m inv

odour ['əudə*] (US **odor**) n olor m; (unpleasant) hedor m

of [ɔv, əv] prep **1** (gen) de; **a friend** ~ **ours** un amigo nuestro; **a boy** ~ **10** un chico de 10 años; **that was kind** ~ **you** eso fue muy amable por or de tu parte

2 (expressing quantity, amount, dates etc) de; **a kilo** ~ **flour** un kilo de harina; **there were 3** ~ **them** había tres; **3** ~ **us went** tres de nosotros fuimos; **the 5th** ~ **July** el 5 de julio

3 (from, out of) de; **made** ~ **wood** (hecho) de madera

off [ɔf] adj, adv (engine) desconectado; (light) apagado; (tap) cerrado; (BRIT: food: bad) pasado, malo; (: milk) cortado; (cancelled) cancelado ♦ prep de; **to be** ~ (to leave) irse, marcharse; **to be** ~ **sick** estar enfermo or de baja; **a day** ~ un día libre or sin trabajar; **to have an** ~ **day** tener un día malo; **he had his coat** ~ se había quitado el abrigo; **10%** ~ (COMM) (con el) 10% de descuento; **5 km** ~ (the road) a 5 km (de la carretera); ~ **the coast** frente a lá costa; **I'm** ~ **meat** (no longer eat/like it) paso de la carne; **on the** ~ **chance** por si acaso; ~ **and on** de vez en cuando

offal ['ɔfl] (BRIT) n (CULIN) menudencias fpl

off-colour [ɔf'kʌlə*] (BRIT) adj (ill) indispuesto

offence [ə'fɛns] (US **offense**) n (crime) delito; **to take** ~ **at** ofenderse por

offend [ə'fɛnd] vt (person) ofender; ~**er** n delincuente m/f

offensive [ə'fɛnsɪv] adj ofensivo; (smell etc) repugnante ♦ n (MIL) ofensiva

offer ['ɔfə*] n oferta, ofrecimiento; (proposal) propuesta ♦ vt ofrecer; (opportunity) facilitar; "**on** ~" (COMM) "en oferta"; ~**ing** n ofrenda

offhand [ɔf'hænd] adj informal ♦ adv de improviso

office ['ɔfɪs] n (place) oficina; (room) despacho; (position) carga, oficio; **doctor's** ~ (US) consultorio; **to take** ~ entrar en funciones; ~ **automation** n ofimática, buromática; ~ **block** (US ~ **building**) n bloque m de oficinas; ~ **hours** npl horas fpl de oficina; (US: MED) horas fpl de consulta

officer ['ɔfɪsə*] n (MIL etc) oficial m/f; (also: **police** ~) agente m/f de policía; (of organization) director(a) m/f

office worker n oficinista m/f

official [ə'fɪʃl] adj oficial, autorizado ♦ n funcionario, oficial m; ~**dom** n burocracia

offing ['ɔfɪŋ] n: **in the** ~ (fig) en perspectiva

off: ~-**licence** (BRIT) n (shop) bodega, tienda de vinos y bebidas alcohólicas; ~-**line** adj, adv (COMPUT) fuera de línea; ~-**peak**

adj (*electricity*) de banda económica; (*ticket*) billete de precio reducido por viajar fuera de las horas punta; **~-putting** (*BRIT*) *adj* (*person*) asqueroso; (*remark*) desalentador(a); **~-season** *adj, adv* fuera de temporada

offset ['ɔfsɛt] (*irreg*) *vt* contrarrestar, compensar

offshoot ['ɔfʃuːt] *n* (*fig*) ramificación *f*

offshore [ɔf'ʃɔː*] *adj* (*breeze, island*) costera; (*fishing*) de bajura

offside ['ɔf'saɪd] *adj* (*SPORT*) fuera de juego; (*AUT: in Britain*) del lado derecho; (: *in US, Europe etc*) del lado izquierdo

offspring ['ɔfsprɪŋ] *n inv* descendencia

off: **~stage** *adv* entre bastidores; **~-the-peg** (*US* **~-the-rack**) *adv* confeccionado; **~-white** *adj* blanco grisáceo

often ['ɔfn] *adv* a menudo, con frecuencia; **how ~ do you go?** ¿cada cuánto vas?

ogle ['əʊgl] *vt* comerse con los ojos a

oh [əʊ] *excl* ¡ah!

oil [ɔɪl] *n* aceite *m*; (*petroleum*) petróleo; (*for heating*) aceite *m* combustible ♦ *vt* engrasar; **~can** *n* lata de aceite; **~field** *n* campo petrolífero; **~ filter** *n* (*AUT*) filtro de aceite; **~ painting** *n* pintura al óleo; **~ rig** *n* torre *f* de perforación; **~skins** *npl* impermeables *mpl* de hule, chubasquero; **~ tanker** *n* petrolero; (*truck*) camión *m* cisterna; **~ well** *n* pozo (de petróleo); **~y** *adj* aceitoso; (*food*) grasiento

ointment ['ɔɪntmənt] *n* ungüento

O.K., okay ['əʊ'keɪ] *excl* O.K., ¡está bien!, ¡vale! (*SP*) ♦ *adj* bien ♦ *vt* dar el visto bueno a

old [əʊld] *adj* viejo; (*former*) antiguo; **how ~ are you?** ¿cuántos años tienes?, ¿qué edad tienes?; **he's 10 years ~** tiene 10 años; **~er brother** hermano mayor; **~ age** *n* vejez *f*; **~-age pensioner** (*BRIT*) *n* jubilado/a; **~-fashioned** *adj* anticuado, pasado de moda

olive ['ɔlɪv] *n* (*fruit*) aceituna; (*tree*) olivo ♦ *adj* (*also*: **~-green**) verde oliva; **~ oil** *n* aceite *m* de oliva

Olympic [əʊ'lɪmpɪk] *adj* olímpico; **the ~ Games** *npl* las Olimpíadas; **the ~s** *npl* las Olimpíadas

omelet(te) ['ɔmlɪt] *n* tortilla (*SP*), tortilla de huevo (*AM*)

omen ['əʊmən] *n* presagio

ominous ['ɔmɪnəs] *adj* de mal agüero, amenazador(a)

omit [əʊ'mɪt] *vt* omitir

───────── KEYWORD ─────────

on [ɔn] *prep* **1** (*indicating position*) en; sobre; **~ the wall** en la pared; **it's ~ the table** está sobre *or* en la mesa; **~ the left** a la izquierda

2 (*indicating means, method, condition etc*): **~ foot** a pie; **~ the train/plane** (*go*) en

tren/avión; (*be*) en el tren/el avión; **~ the radio/television/telephone** por *or* en la radio/televisión/al teléfono; **to be ~ drugs** drogarse; (*MED*) estar a tratamiento; **to be ~ holiday/business** estar de vacaciones/en viaje de negocios

3 (*referring to time*): **~ Friday** el viernes; **~ Fridays** los viernes; **~ June 20th** el 20 de junio; **a week ~ Friday** del viernes en una semana; **~ arrival** al llegar; **~ seeing this** al ver esto

4 (*about, concerning*) sobre, acerca de; **a book ~ physics** un libro de *or* sobre física

♦ *adv* **1** (*referring to dress*): **to have one's coat ~** tener *or* llevar el abrigo puesto; **she put her gloves ~** se puso los guantes

2 (*referring to covering*): **"screw the lid ~ tightly"** "cerrar bien la tapa"

3 (*further, continuously*): **to walk** *etc* **~** seguir caminando *etc*

♦ *adj* **1** (*functioning, in operation: machine, radio, TV, light*) encendido/a (*SP*), prendido/a (*AM*); (: *tap*) abierto/a; (: *brakes*) echado/a, puesto/a; **is the meeting still ~?** ¿todavía continúa la reunión?; (*not cancelled*) ¿va a haber reunión al fin?; **there's a good film ~ at the cinema** ponen una buena película en el cine

2: **that's not ~!** (*inf: not possible*) ¡eso ni hablar!; (: *not acceptable*) ¡eso no se hace!

once [wʌns] *adv* una vez; (*formerly*) antiguamente ♦ *conj* una vez que; **~ he had left/it was done** una vez que se había marchado/se hizo; **at ~** en seguida, inmediatamente; (*simultaneously*) a la vez; **~ a week** una vez por semana; **~ more** otra vez; **~ and for all** de una vez por todas; **~ upon a time** érase una vez

oncoming ['ɔnkʌmɪŋ] *adj* (*traffic*) que viene de frente

───────── KEYWORD ─────────

one [wʌn] *num* un(o)/una; **~ hundred and fifty** ciento cincuenta; **~ by ~** uno a uno

♦ *adj* **1** (*sole*) único; **the ~ book which** el único libro que; **the ~ man who** el único que

2 (*same*) mismo/a; **they came in the ~ car** vinieron en un solo coche

♦ *pron* **1**: **this ~** éste/ésta; **that ~** ése/ésa; (*more remote*) aquél/aquella; **I've already got (a red) ~** ya tengo uno/a (rojo/a); **~ by ~** uno/a por uno/a

2: **~ another** os (*SP*), se (+ *el uno al otro, unos a otros etc*); **do you two ever see ~ another?** ¿vosotros dos os veis alguna vez? (*SP*), ¿se ven ustedes dos alguna vez?; **the boys didn't dare look at ~ another** los chicos no se atrevieron a mirarse (el uno al otro); **they all kissed ~ another**

se besaron unos a otros
3 (*impers*): ~ **never knows** nunca se sabe;
to cut ~'s **finger** cortarse el dedo; ~
needs to eat hay que comer

one: ~-**day excursion** (*US*) *n* billete *m* de
ida y vuelta en un día; ~-**man** *adj* (*business*) individual; ~-**man band** *n* hombre-
orquesta *m*; ~-**off** (*BRIT*: *inf*) *n* (*event*)
acontecimiento único
oneself [wʌn'self] *pron* (*reflexive*) se; (*after
prep*) sí; (*emphatic*) uno/a mismo/a; **to
hurt** ~ hacerse daño; **to keep sth for** ~
guardarse algo; **to talk to** ~ hablar solo
one: ~-**sided** *adj* (*argument*) parcial; ~-
to-~ *adj* (*relationship*) de dos; ~-
upmanship *n* arte *m* de aventajar a los
demás; ~-**way** *adj* (*street*) de sentido único
ongoing ['ɒnɡəʊɪŋ] *adj* continuo
onion ['ʌnjən] *n* cebolla
on-line *adj*, *adv* (*COMPUT*) en línea
onlooker ['ɒnlʊkə*] *n* espectador(a) *m/f*
only ['əʊnlɪ] *adv* solamente, sólo ♦ *adj* único, solo ♦ *conj* solamente que, pero; **an** ~
child un hijo único; **not** ~ ... **but also** ...
no sólo ... sino también ...
onset ['ɒnsɛt] *n* comienzo
onshore ['ɒnʃɔ:*] *adj* (*wind*) que sopla del
mar hacia la tierra
onslaught ['ɒnslɔ:t] *n* ataque *m*, embestida
onto ['ɒntu] *prep* = **on to**
onus ['əʊnəs] *n* responsabilidad *f*
onward(s) ['ɒnwəd(z)] *adv* (*move*) (hacia)
adelante; **from that time** ~ desde entonces
en adelante
onyx ['ɒnɪks] *n* ónice *m*
ooze [u:z] *vi* rezumar
opaque [əʊ'peɪk] *adj* opaco
OPEC ['əʊpɛk] *n abbr* (= *Organization of
Petroleum-Exporting Countries*) OPEP *f*
open ['əʊpn] *adj* abierto; (*car*) descubierto;
(*road, view*) despejado; (*meeting*) público;
(*admiration*) manifiesto ♦ *vt* abrir ♦ *vi* abrirse; (*book etc*: *commence*) comenzar; **in the**
~ (**air**) al aire libre; ~ **on to** *vt fus* (*subj*:
room, door) dar a; ~ **up** *vt* abrir; (*blocked
road*) despejar ♦ *vi* abrirse, empezar; ~**ing**
n abertura; (*start*) comienzo; (*opportunity*)
oportunidad *f*; ~**ly** *adv* abiertamente; ~-
minded *adj* imparcial; ~-**necked** *adj*
(*shirt*) desabrochado; sin corbata; ~-**plan**
adj: ~-**plan office** gran oficina sin particio-
nes
opera ['ɒpərə] *n* ópera *f*; ~ **house** *n* teatro
de la ópera
operate ['ɒpəreɪt] *vt* (*machine*) hacer funcionar; (*company*) dirigir ♦ *vi* funcionar; **to**
~ **on sb** (*MED*) operar a uno
operatic [ɒpə'rætɪk] *adj* de ópera
operating table ['ɒpəreɪtɪŋ-] *n* mesa de
operaciones
operating theatre *n* sala de operaciones

operation [ɒpə'reɪʃən] *n* operación *f*; (*of
machine*) funcionamiento; **to be in** ~ estar
funcionando *or* en funcionamiento; **to
have an** ~ (*MED*) ser operado; ~**al** *adj*
operacional, en buen estado
operative ['ɒpərətɪv] *adj* en vigor
operator ['ɒpəreɪtə*] *n* (*of machine*) maquinista *m/f*, operario/a; (*TEL*) operador(a) *m/
f*, telefonista *m/f*
opinion [ə'pɪnɪən] *n* opinión *f*; **in my** ~ en
mi opinión, a mi juicio; ~**ated** *adj* testarudo; ~ **poll** *n* encuesta, sondeo
opponent [ə'pəʊnənt] *n* adversario/a, contrincante *m/f*
opportunist [ɒpə'tju:nɪst] *n* oportunista
m/f
opportunity [ɒpə'tju:nɪtɪ] *n* oportunidad *f*;
to take the ~ **of doing** aprovechar la ocasión para hacer
oppose [ə'pəʊz] *vt* oponerse a; **to be** ~**d
to sth** oponerse a algo; **as** ~**d to** a diferencia de; **opposing** *adj* opuesto, contrario
opposite ['ɒpəzɪt] *adj* opuesto, contrario a;
(*house etc*) de enfrente ♦ *adv* en frente ♦
prep en frente de, frente a ♦ *n* lo contrario
opposition [ɒpə'zɪʃən] *n* oposición *f*
oppress [ə'prɛs] *vt* oprimir; ~**ion**
[ə'prɛʃən] *n* opresión *f*; ~**ive** *adj* opresivo;
(*weather*) agobiante
opt [ɒpt] *vi*: **to** ~ **for** optar por; **to** ~ **to do**
optar por hacer; ~ **out** *vi*: **to** ~ **out of** optar por no hacer
optical ['ɒptɪkl] *adj* óptico
optician [ɒp'tɪʃən] *n* óptico *m/f*
optimist ['ɒptɪmɪst] *n* optimista *m/f*; ~**ic**
[-'mɪstɪk] *adj* optimista
optimum ['ɒptɪməm] *adj* óptimo
option ['ɒpʃən] *n* opción *f*; ~**al** *adj* facultativo, discrecional
or [ɔ:*] *conj* o; (*before o, ho*) u; (*with negative*): **he hasn't seen** ~ **heard anything**
no ha visto ni oído nada; ~ **else** si no
oracle ['ɒrəkl] *n* oráculo
oral ['ɔ:rəl] *adj* oral ♦ *n* examen *m* oral
orange ['ɒrɪndʒ] *n* (*fruit*) naranja ♦ *adj* color naranja
orator ['ɒrətə*] *n* orador(a) *m/f*
orbit ['ɔ:bɪt] *n* órbita ♦ *vt*, *vi* orbitar
orchard ['ɔ:tʃəd] *n* huerto
orchestra ['ɔ:kɪstrə] *n* orquesta; (*US*: *seat-
ing*) platea
orchid ['ɔ:kɪd] *n* orquídea
ordain [ɔ:'deɪn] *vt* (*REL*) ordenar, decretar
ordeal [ɔ:'di:l] *n* experiencia horrorosa
order ['ɔ:də*] *n* orden *m*; (*command*) orden
f; (*good* ~) buen estado; (*COMM*) pedido ♦
vt (*also*: *put in* ~) arreglar, poner en orden;
(*COMM*) pedir; (*command*) mandar, ordenar; **in** ~ en orden; (*of document*) en regla;
in (**working**) ~ en funcionamiento; **in** ~ **to
do/that** para hacer/que; **on** ~ (*COMM*) pedido; **to be out of** ~ estar desórdenado;

(*not working*) no funcionar; **to ~ sb to do sth** mandar a uno hacer algo; **~ form** *n* hoja de pedido; **~ly** *n* (*MIL*) ordenanza *m*; (*MED*) enfermero/a (auxiliar) ♦ *adj* ordenado

ordinary ['ɔːdnrɪ] *adj* corriente, normal; (*pej*) común y corriente; **out of the ~** fuera de lo común

Ordnance Survey ['ɔːdnəns-] (*BRIT*) *n* servicio oficial de topografía

ore [ɔː*] *n* mineral *m*

organ ['ɔːgən] *n* órgano; **~ic** [ɔː'gænɪk] *adj* orgánico; **~ism** *n* organismo

organization [ɔːgənaɪ'zeɪʃən] *n* organización *f*

organize ['ɔːgənaɪz] *vt* organizar; **~r** *n* organizador(a) *m/f*

orgasm ['ɔːgæzəm] *n* orgasmo

orgy ['ɔːdʒɪ] *n* orgía

Orient ['ɔːrɪənt] *n* Oriente *m*; **oriental** [-'entl] *adj* oriental

orientate ['ɔːrɪənteɪt] *vt*: **to ~ o.s.** orientarse

origin ['ɒrɪdʒɪn] *n* origen *m*

original [ə'rɪdʒɪnl] *adj* original; (*first*) primero; (*earlier*) primitivo ♦ *n* original *m*; **~ity** [-'nælɪtɪ] *n* originalidad *f*; **~ly** *adv* al principio

originate [ə'rɪdʒɪneɪt] *vi*: **to ~ from, to ~ in** surgir de, tener su origen en

Orkneys ['ɔːknɪz] *npl*: **the ~** (*also: the Orkney Islands*) las Orcadas

ornament ['ɔːnəmənt] *n* adorno; (*trinket*) chuchería; **~al** [-'mɛntl] *adj* decorativo, de adorno

ornate [ɔː'neɪt] *adj* muy ornado, vistoso

orphan ['ɔːfn] *n* huérfano/a; **~age** *n* orfanato

orthodox ['ɔːθədɔks] *adj* ortodoxo; **~y** *n* ortodoxia

orthopaedic [ɔːθə'piːdɪk] (*US* **orthopedic**) *adj* ortopédico

oscillate ['ɒsɪleɪt] *vi* oscilar; (*person*) vacilar

ostensibly [ɒs'tɛnsɪblɪ] *adv* aparentemente

ostentatious [ɒstɛn'teɪʃəs] *adj* ostentoso

osteopath ['ɒstɪəpæθ] *n* osteópata *m/f*

ostracize ['ɒstrəsaɪz] *vt* hacer el vacio a

ostrich ['ɒstrɪtʃ] *n* avestruz *m*

other ['ʌðə*] *adj* otro ♦ *pron*: **the ~ (one)** el/la otro/a ♦ *adv*: **~ than** aparte de; **~s** (*~ people*) otros; **the ~ day** el otro día; **~wise** *adv* de otra manera ♦ *conj* (*if not*) si no

otter ['ɒtə*] *n* nutria

ouch [autʃ] *excl* ¡ay!

ought [ɔːt] (*pt* **ought**) *aux vb*: **I ~ to do it** debería hacerlo; **this ~ to have been corrected** esto debiera haberse corregido; **he ~ to win** (*probability*) debe *or* debiera ganar

ounce [auns] *n* onza (*28.35g*)

our ['auə*] *adj* nuestro; *see also* **my**; **~s** *pron* (el) nuestro/(la) nuestra *etc*; *see also* **mine**[1]; **~selves** *pron pl* (*reflexive, after prep*) nosotros; (*emphatic*) nosotros mismos; *see also* **oneself**

oust [aust] *vt* desalojar

out [aut] *adv* fuera, afuera; (*not at home*) fuera (de casa); (*light, fire*) apagado; **~ there** allí (fuera); **he's ~** (*absent*) no está, ha salido; **to be ~ in one's calculations** equivocarse (en sus cálculos); **to run ~** salir corriendo; **~ loud** en alta voz; **~ of** (*outside*) fuera de; (*because of*: *anger etc*) por; **~ of petrol** sin gasolina; **"~ of order"** "no funciona"

out-and-out *adj* (*liar, thief etc*) redomado, empedernido

outback ['autbæk] *n* interior *m*

outboard ['autbɔːd] *adj*: **~ motor** (motor *m*) fuera borda *m*

outbreak ['autbreɪk] *n* (*of war*) comienzo; (*of disease*) epidemia; (*of violence etc*) ola

outburst ['autbɜːst] *n* explosión *f*, arranque *m*

outcast ['autkɑːst] *n* paria *m/f*

outcome ['autkʌm] *n* resultado

outcrop ['autkrɒp] *n* (*of rock*) afloramiento

outcry ['autkraɪ] *n* protestas *fpl*

outdated [aut'deɪtɪd] *adj* anticuado, fuera de moda

outdo [aut'duː] (*irreg*) *vt* superar

outdoor [aut'dɔː*] *adj* exterior, de aire libre; (*clothes*) de calle; **~s** *adv* al aire libre

outer ['autə*] *adj* exterior, externo; **~ space** *n* espacio exterior

outfit ['autfɪt] *n* (*clothes*) conjunto

outgoing ['autgəuɪŋ] *adj* (*character*) extrovertido; (*retiring*: *president etc*) saliente; **~s** (*BRIT*) *npl* gastos *mpl*

outgrow [aut'grəu] (*irreg*) *vt*: **he has ~n his clothes** su ropa le queda pequeña ya

outhouse ['authaus] *n* dependencia

outing ['autɪŋ] *n* excursión *f*, paseo

outlandish [aut'lændɪʃ] *adj* estrafalario

outlaw ['autlɔː] *n* proscrito ♦ *vt* proscribir

outlay ['autleɪ] *n* inversión *f*

outlet ['autlet] *n* salida; (*of pipe*) desagüe *m*; (*US*: *ELEC*) toma de corriente; (*also: retail ~*) punto de venta

outline ['autlaɪn] *n* (*shape*) contorno, perfil *m*; (*sketch, plan*) esbozo *m*; (*of plan etc*) esbozar; **in ~** (*fig*) a grandes rasgos

outlive [aut'lɪv] *vt* sobrevivir a

outlook ['autluk] *n* (*fig*: *prospects*) perspectivas *fpl*; (: *for weather*) pronóstico

outlying ['autlaɪɪŋ] *adj* remoto, aislado

outmoded [aut'məudɪd] *adj* anticuado, pasado de moda

outnumber [aut'nʌmbə*] *vt* superar en número

out-of-date *adj* (*passport*) caducado; (*clothes*) pasado de moda

out-of-the-way *adj* apartado

outpatient ['autpeɪʃənt] *n* paciente *m/f* externo/a

outpost ['autpəust] *n* puesto avanzado

output ['autput] *n* (volumen *m* de) producción *f*, rendimiento; (*COMPUT*) salida

outrage ['autreɪdʒ] *n* escándalo; (*atrocity*) atrocidad *f* ♦ *vt* ultrajar; **~ous** [-'reɪdʒəs] *adj* monstruoso

outright [*adv* aut'raɪt, *adj* 'autraɪt] *adv* (*ask, deny*) francamente; (*refuse*) rotundamente; (*win*) de manera absoluta; (*be killed*) en el acto ♦ *adj* franco; rotundo

outset ['autset] *n* principio

outside [aut'saɪd] *n* exterior *m* ♦ *adj* exterior, externo ♦ *adv* fuera ♦ *prep* fuera de; (*beyond*) más allá de; **at the ~** (*fig*) a lo sumo; **~ lane** *n* (*AUT: in Britain*) carril *m* de la derecha; (: *in US, Europe etc*) carril *m* de la izquierda; **~ line** *n* (*TEL*) línea (exterior); **~r** *n* (*stranger*) extraño, forastero

outsize ['autsaɪz] *adj* (*clothes*) de talla grande

outskirts ['autskəːts] *npl* alrededores *mpl*, afueras *fpl*

outspoken [aut'spəukən] *adj* muy franco

outstanding [aut'stændɪŋ] *adj* excepcional, destacado; (*remaining*) pendiente

outstay [aut'steɪ] *vt*: **to ~ one's welcome** quedarse más de la cuenta

outstretched [aut'stretʃt] *adj* (*hand*) extendido

outstrip [aut'strɪp] *vt* (*competitors, demand*) dejar atrás, aventajar

out-tray *n* bandeja de salida

outward ['autwəd] *adj* externo; (*journey*) de ida; **~ly** *adv* por fuera

outweigh [aut'weɪ] *vt* pesar más que

outwit [aut'wɪt] *vt* ser más listo que

oval ['əuvl] *adj* ovalado ♦ *n* óvalo

ovary ['əuvərɪ] *n* ovario

oven ['ʌvn] *n* horno; **~proof** *adj* resistente al horno

over ['əuvə*] *adv* encima, por encima ♦ *adj* (*or adv*) (*finished*) terminado; (*surplus*) de sobra ♦ *prep* (por) encima de; (*above*) sobre; (*on the other side of*) al otro lado de; (*more than*) más de; (*during*) durante; **~ here** (por) aquí; **~ there** (por) allí *or* allá; **all ~** (*everywhere*) por todas partes; **~ and ~ (again)** una y otra vez; **~ and above** además de; **to ask sb ~** invitar a uno a casa; **to bend ~** inclinarse

overall [*adj, n* 'əuvərɔːl, *adv* əuvər'ɔːl] *adj* (*length etc*) total; (*study*) de conjunto ♦ *adv* en conjunto ♦ *n* (*BRIT*) guardapolvo; **~s** *npl* mono (*SP*), overol *m* (*AM*)

overawe [əuvər'ɔː] *vt*: **to be ~d (by)** quedar impresionado (con)

overbalance [əuvə'bæləns] *vi* perder el equilibrio

overbearing [əuvə'bɛərɪŋ] *adj* autoritario,
imperioso

overboard ['əuvəbɔːd] *adv* (*NAUT*) por la borda

overbook [əuvə'buk] *vt* sobrereservar

overcast ['əuvəkɑːst] *adj* encapotado

overcharge [əuvə'tʃɑːdʒ] *vt*: **to ~ sb** cobrar un precio excesivo a uno

overcoat ['əuvəkəut] *n* abrigo, sobretodo

overcome [əuvə'kʌm] (*irreg*) *vt* vencer; (*difficulty*) superar

overcrowded [əuvə'kraudɪd] *adj* atestado de gente; (*city, country*) superpoblado

overdo [əuvə'duː] (*irreg*) *vt* exagerar; (*overcook*) cocer demasiado; **to ~ it** (*work etc*) pasarse

overdose ['əuvədəus] *n* sobredosis *f inv*

overdraft ['əuvədrɑːft] *n* saldo deudor

overdrawn [əuvə'drɔːn] *adj* (*account*) en descubierto

overdue [əuvə'djuː] *adj* retrasado

overestimate [əuvər'estɪmeɪt] *vt* sobreestimar

overflow [*vb* əuvə'fləu, *n* 'əuvəfləu] *vi* desbordarse ♦ *n* (*also*: **~ pipe**) (cañería de) desagüe *m*

overgrown [əuvə'grəun] *adj* (*garden*) invadido por la vegetación

overhaul [*vb* əuvə'hɔːl, *n* 'əuvəhɔːl] *vt* revisar, repasar ♦ *n* revisión *f*

overhead [*adv* əuvə'hed, *adj* 'əuvəhed] *adv* por arriba *or* encima ♦ *adj* (*cable*) aéreo ♦ *n* (*US*) = **~s**; **~s** *npl* (*expenses*) gastos *mpl* generales

overhear [əuvə'hɪə*] (*irreg*) *vt* oír por casualidad

overheat [əuvə'hiːt] *vi* (*engine*) recalentarse

overjoyed [əuvə'dʒɔɪd] *adj* encantado, lleno de alegría

overkill ['əuvəkɪl] *n* excesos *mpl*

overland ['əuvəlænd] *adj, adv* por tierra

overlap [əuvə'læp] *vi* traslaparse

overleaf [əuvə'liːf] *adv* al dorso

overload [əuvə'ləud] *vt* sobrecargar

overlook [əuvə'luk] *vt* (*have view of*) dar a, tener vistas a; (*miss: by mistake*) pasar por alto; (*excuse*) perdonar

overnight [əuvə'naɪt] *adv* durante la noche; (*fig*) de la noche a la mañana ♦ *adj* de noche; **to stay ~** pasar la noche

overpass ['əuvəpɑːs] (*US*) *n* paso superior

overpower [əuvə'pauə*] *vt* dominar; (*fig*) embargar; **~ing** *adj* (*heat*) agobiante; (*smell*) penetrante

overrate [əuvə'reɪt] *vt* sobreestimar

override [əuvə'raɪd] (*irreg*) *vt* no hacer caso de; **overriding** *adj* predominante

overrule [əuvə'ruːl] *vt* (*decision*) anular; (*claim*) denegar

overrun [əuvə'rʌn] (*irreg*) *vt* (*country*) invadir; (*time limit*) rebasar, exceder

overseas [əuvə'siːz] *adv* (*abroad: live*) en el extranjero; (: *travel*) al extranjero ♦ *adj*

(trade) exterior; *(visitor)* extranjero
overshadow [əuvə'ʃædəu] vt: **to be ~ed by** estar a la sombra de
overshoot [əuvə'ʃuːt] *(irreg)* vt excederse
oversight ['əuvəsaɪt] n descuido
oversleep [əuvə'sliːp] *(irreg)* vi quedarse dormido
overstate [əuvə'steɪt] vt exagerar
overstep [əuvə'stɛp] vt: **to ~ the mark** pasarse de la raya
overt [əu'vɜːt] adj abierto
overtake [əuvə'teɪk] *(irreg)* vt sobrepasar; *(BRIT: AUT)* adelantar
overthrow [əuvə'θrəu] *(irreg)* vt *(government)* derrocar
overtime ['əuvətaɪm] n horas fpl extraordinarias
overtone ['əuvətəun] n *(fig)* tono
overture ['əuvətʃuə*] n *(MUS)* obertura; *(fig)* preludio
overturn [əuvə'tɜːn] vt volcar; *(fig: plan)* desbaratar; *(: government)* derrocar ♦ vi volcar
overweight [əuvə'weɪt] adj demasiado gordo or pesado
overwhelm [əuvə'wɛlm] vt aplastar; *(subj: emotion)* sobrecoger; **~ing** adj *(victory, defeat)* arrollador(a); *(feeling)* irresistible
overwork [əuvə'wɜːk] n trabajo excesivo ♦ vi trabajar demasiado
overwrought [əuvə'rɔːt] adj sobreexcitado
owe [əu] vt: **to ~ sb sth, to ~ sth to sb** deber algo a uno; **owing to** prep debido a, por causa de
owl [aul] n búho, lechuza
own [əun] vt tener, poseer ♦ adj propio; **a room of my ~** una habitación propia; **to get one's ~ back** tomar revancha; **on one's ~** solo, a solas; **~ up** vi confesar; **~er** n dueño/a; **~ership** n posesión f
ox [ɔks] *(pl ~en)* n buey m; **~tail** n: **~tail soup** sopa de rabo de buey
oxygen ['ɔksɪdʒən] n oxígeno; **~ mask/tent** n máscara/tienda de oxígeno
oyster ['ɔɪstə*] n ostra
oz. abbr = **ounce(s)**
ozone hole ['əuzəun-] n agujero m de/en la capa de ozono
ozone layer ['əuzəun-] n capa f de ozono

P p

p [piː] abbr = **penny; pence**
P.A. n abbr = **personal assistant; public address system**
p.a. abbr = **per annum**
pa [pɑː] *(inf)* n papá m
pace [peɪs] n paso ♦ vi: **to ~ up and down** pasearse de un lado a otro; **to keep ~ with** llevar el mismo paso que; **~maker** n *(MED)* regulador m cardíaco, marcapasos m inv; *(SPORT: also: ~setter)* liebre f
Pacific [pə'sɪfɪk] n: **the ~ (Ocean)** el (Océano) Pacífico
pacify ['pæsɪfaɪ] vt apaciguar
pack [pæk] n *(packet)* paquete m; *(of hounds)* jauría; *(of people)* manada, bando; *(of cards)* baraja; *(bundle)* fardo; *(US: of cigarettes)* paquete m; *(back ~)* mochila ♦ vt *(fill)* llenar; *(in suitcase etc)* meter, poner; *(cram)* llenar, atestar; **to ~ (one's bags)** hacerse la maleta; **to ~ sb off** despachar a uno; **~ it in!** *(inf)* ¡déjalo!
package ['pækɪdʒ] n paquete m; *(bulky)* bulto; *(also: ~ deal)* acuerdo global; **~ holiday** n vacaciones fpl organizadas; **~ tour** n viaje m organizado
packed lunch n almuerzo frío
packet ['pækɪt] n paquete m
packing ['pækɪŋ] n embalaje m; **~ case** n cajón m de embalaje
pact [pækt] n pacto
pad [pæd] n *(of paper)* bloc m; *(cushion)* cojinete m; *(inf: home)* casa ♦ vt rellenar; **~ding** n *(material)* relleno
paddle ['pædl] n *(oar)* canalete m; *(US: for table tennis)* paleta ♦ vt impulsar con canalete ♦ vi *(with feet)* chapotear; **~ steamer** n vapor m de ruedas; **paddling pool** *(BRIT)* n estanque m de juegos
paddock ['pædək] n corral m
paddy field ['pædɪ-] n arrozal m
padlock ['pædlɔk] n candado
paediatrics [piːdɪ'ætrɪks] *(US pediatrics)* n pediatría
pagan ['peɪgən] adj, n pagano/a m/f
page [peɪdʒ] n *(of book)* página; *(of newspaper)* plana; *(also: ~ boy)* paje m ♦ vt *(in hotel etc)* llamar por altavoz a
pageant ['pædʒənt] n *(procession)* desfile m; *(show)* espectáculo; **~ry** n pompa
pager ['peɪdʒə*] n *(TEL)* busca m

paging device ['peɪdʒɪŋ-] n (TEL) busca m
paid [peɪd] pt, pp of **pay** ♦ adj (work) remunerado; (holiday) pagado; (official etc) a sueldo; **to put ~ to** (BRIT) acabar con
pail [peɪl] n cubo, balde m
pain [peɪn] n dolor m; **to be in ~** sufrir; **to take ~s to do sth** tomarse grandes molestias en hacer algo; **~ed** adj (expression) afligido; **~ful** adj doloroso; (difficult) penoso; (disagreeable) desagradable; **~fully** adv (fig: very) terriblemente; **~killer** n analgésico; **~less** adj que no causa dolor; **~staking** ['peɪnzteɪkɪŋ] adj (person) concienzudo, esmerado
paint [peɪnt] n pintura ♦ vt pintar; **to ~ the door blue** pintar la puerta de azul; **~brush** n (artist's) pincel m; (decorator's) brocha; **~er** n pintor(a) m/f; **~ing** n pintura; **~work** n pintura
pair [pɛə*] n (of shoes, gloves etc) par m; (of people) pareja; **a ~ of scissors** unas tijeras; **a ~ of trousers** unos pantalones, un pantalón
pajamas [pə'dʒɔ:məz] (US) npl pijama m
Pakistan [pɑ:kɪ'stɑ:n] n Paquistán m; **~i** adj, n paquistaní m/f
pal [pæl] (inf) n compinche m/f, compañero/a
palace ['pæləs] n palacio
palatable ['pælɪtəbl] adj sabroso
palate ['pælɪt] n paladar m
palatial [pə'leɪʃəl] adj suntuoso, espléndido
pale [peɪl] adj (gen) pálido; (colour) claro ♦ n: **to be beyond the ~** pasarse de la raya
Palestine ['pælɪstaɪn] n Palestina; **Palestinian** [-'tɪnɪən] adj, n palestino/a m/f
palette ['pælɪt] n paleta
pall [pɔ:l] n (of smoke) capa (de humo) ♦ vi perder el sabor
pallet ['pælɪt] n (for goods) pallet m
pallid ['pælɪd] adj pálido
pallor ['pælə*] n palidez f
palm [pɑ:m] n (ANAT) palma; (also: ~ tree) palmera, palma ♦ vt: **to ~ sth off on sb** (inf) encajar algo a uno; **P~ Sunday** n Domingo de Ramos
palpable ['pælpəbl] adj palpable
paltry ['pɔ:ltrɪ] adj irrisorio
pamper ['pæmpə*] vt mimar
pamphlet ['pæmflət] n folleto
pan [pæn] n (also: sauce~) cacerola, cazuela, olla; (also: frying-~) sartén f
panache [pə'næʃ] n: **with ~** con estilo
Panama ['pænəmɑ:] n Panamá m; **the ~ Canal** el Canal de Panamá
pancake ['pænkeɪk] n crepe f
panda ['pændə] n panda m; **~ car** (BRIT) n coche m Z (SP)
pandemonium [pændɪ'məʊnɪəm] n jaleo
pander ['pændə*] vi: **to ~ to** complacer a
pane [peɪn] n cristal m
panel ['pænl] n (of wood etc) panel m; (RA-DIO, TV) panel m de invitados; **~ling** (US ~ing) n paneles mpl
pang [pæŋ] n: **a ~ of regret** (una punzada de) remordimiento; **hunger ~s** dolores mpl del hambre
panic ['pænɪk] n (terror m) pánico ♦ vi dejarse llevar por el pánico; **~ky** adj (person) asustadizo; **~-stricken** adj preso de pánico
pansy ['pænzɪ] n (BOT) pensamiento; (inf: pej) maricón m
pant [pænt] vi jadear
panther ['pænθə*] n pantera
panties ['pæntɪz] npl bragas fpl, pantis fpl
pantihose ['pæntɪhəʊz] (US) n pantimedias fpl
pantomime ['pæntəmaɪm] (BRIT) n revista musical representada en Navidad, basada en cuentos de hadas
pantry ['pæntrɪ] n despensa
pants [pænts] n (BRIT: underwear: woman's) bragas fpl; (: man's) calzoncillos mpl; (US: trousers) pantalones mpl
paper ['peɪpə*] n papel m; (also: news~) periódico, diario; (academic essay) ensayo; (exam) examen m ♦ adj de papel ♦ vt empapelar (SP), tapizar (AM); **~s** npl (also: identity ~s) papeles mpl, documentos mpl; **~back** n libro en rústica; **~ bag** n bolsa de papel; **~ clip** n clip m; **~ hankie** n pañuelo de papel; **~weight** n pisapapeles m inv; **~work** n trabajo administrativo
papier-mâché ['pæpɪeɪ'mæʃeɪ] n cartón m piedra
paprika ['pæprɪkə] n pimentón m
par [pɑ:*] n par f; (GOLF) par m; **to be on a ~ with** estar a la par con
parable ['pærəbl] n parábola
parachute ['pærəʃu:t] n paracaídas m inv
parade [pə'reɪd] n desfile m ♦ vt (show off) hacer alarde de ♦ vi desfilar; (MIL) pasar revista
paradise ['pærədaɪs] n paraíso
paradox ['pærədɔks] n paradoja; **~ically** [-'dɔksɪklɪ] adv paradójicamente
paraffin ['pærəfɪn] (BRIT) n (also: ~ oil) parafina
paragon ['pærəgən] n modelo
paragraph ['pærəgrɑ:f] n párrafo
parallel ['pærəlɛl] adj en paralelo; (fig) semejante ♦ n (line) paralela; (fig, GEO) paralelo
paralyse ['pærəlaɪz] vt paralizar
paralysis [pə'rælɪsɪs] n parálisis f inv
paralyze ['pærəlaɪz] (US) vt = **paralyse**
paramount ['pærəmaunt] adj: **of ~ importance** de suma importancia
paranoid ['pærənɔɪd] adj (person, feeling) paranoico
paraphernalia [pærəfə'neɪlɪə] n (gear) avíos mpl
paraphrase ['pærəfreɪz] vt parafrasear
parasite ['pærəsaɪt] n parásito/a

parasol ['pærəsɔl] n sombrilla, quitasol m
paratrooper ['pærətru:pə*] n paracaidista m/f
parcel ['pɑ:sl] n paquete m ♦ vt (also: ~ up) empaquetar, embalar
parch [pɑ:tʃ] vt secar, resecar; **~ed** adj (person) muerto de sed
parchment ['pɑ:tʃmənt] n pergamino
pardon ['pɑ:dn] n (LAW) indulto ♦ vt perdonar; ~ **me!, I beg your** ~! (I'm sorry!) ¡perdone usted!; **(I beg your)** ~?, ~ **me?** (what did you say?) ¿cómo?
parent ['pɛərənt] n (mother) madre f; (father) padre m; ~**s** npl padres mpl; ~**al** [pə'rɛntl] adj paternal/maternal
parentheses [pə'rɛnθɪsi:z] npl of **parenthesis**
parenthesis [pə'rɛnθɪsɪs] (pl **parentheses**) n paréntesis m inv
Paris ['pærɪs] n París
parish ['pærɪʃ] n parroquia
Parisian [pə'rɪzɪən] adj, n parisiense m/f
parity ['pærɪtɪ] n paridad f, igualdad f
park [pɑ:k] n parque m ♦ vt aparcar, estacionar ♦ vi aparcar, estacionarse
parka ['pɑ:kə] n anorak m
parking ['pɑ:kɪŋ] n aparcamiento, estacionamiento; **"no ~"** "prohibido estacionarse"; ~ **lot** (US) n parking m; ~ **meter** n parquímetro; ~ **ticket** n multa de aparcamiento
parlance ['pɑ:ləns] n lenguaje m
parliament ['pɑ:ləmənt] n parlamento; (Spanish) Cortes fpl; ~**ary** [-'mɛntərɪ] adj parlamentario
parlour ['pɑ:lə*] (US **parlor**) n sala de recibo, salón m, living m (AM)
parochial [pə'rəukɪəl] (pej) adj de miras estrechas
parody ['pærədɪ] n parodia
parole [pə'rəul] n: **on** ~ libre bajo palabra
parquet ['pɑ:keɪ] n: ~ **floor(ing)** parquet m
parrot ['pærət] n loro, papagayo
parry ['pærɪ] vt parar
parsimonious [pɑ:sɪ'məunɪəs] adj tacaño
parsley ['pɑ:slɪ] n perejil m
parsnip ['pɑ:snɪp] n chirivía
parson ['pɑ:sn] n cura m
part [pɑ:t] n (gen, MUS) parte f; (bit) trozo; (of machine) pieza; (THEATRE etc) papel m; (of serial) entrega; (US: in hair) raya ♦ adv = **partly** ♦ vt separar ♦ vi (people) separarse; (crowd) apartarse; **to take** ~ **in** tomar parte or participar en; **to take sth in good** ~ tomar algo en buena parte; **to take sb's** ~ defender a uno; **for my** ~ por mi parte; **for the most** ~ en su mayor parte; **to one's hair** hacerse la raya; ~ **with** vt fus ceder, entregar; (money) pagar; ~ **exchange** (BRIT) n: **in** ~ **exchange** como parte del pago
partial ['pɑ:ʃl] adj parcial; **to be** ~ **to** ser

aficionado a
participant [pɑ:'tɪsɪpənt] n (in competition) concursante m/f; (in campaign etc) participante m/f
participate [pɑ:'tɪsɪpeɪt] vi: **to** ~ **in** participar en; **participation** [-'peɪʃən] n participación f
participle ['pɑ:tɪsɪpl] n participio
particle ['pɑ:tɪkl] n partícula; (of dust) grano
particular [pə'tɪkjulə*] adj (special) particular; (concrete) concreto; (given) determinado; (fussy) quisquilloso; (demanding) exigente; ~**s** npl (information) datos mpl; (details) pormenores mpl; **in** ~ en particular; ~**ly** adv (in particular) sobre todo; (difficult, good etc) especialmente
parting ['pɑ:tɪŋ] n (act of) separación f; (farewell) despedida; (BRIT: in hair) raya ♦ adj de despedida
partisan [pɑ:tɪ'zæn] adj partidista ♦ n partidario/a
partition [pɑ:'tɪʃən] n (POL) división f; (wall) tabique m
partly ['pɑ:tlɪ] adv en parte
partner ['pɑ:tnə*] n (COMM) socio/a; (SPORT, at dance) pareja; (spouse) cónyuge m/f; (boy/girlfriend etc) compañero/a; ~**ship** n asociación f; (COMM) sociedad f
partridge ['pɑ:trɪdʒ] n perdiz f
part-time adj, adv a tiempo parcial
party ['pɑ:tɪ] n (POL) partido; (celebration) fiesta; (group) grupo; (LAW) parte f interesada ♦ cpd (POL) de partido; ~ **dress** n vestido de fiesta; ~ **line** n (TEL) línea compartida
pass [pɑ:s] vt (time, object) pasar; (place) pasar por; (overtake) rebasar; (exam) aprobar; (approve) aprobar ♦ vi pasar; (SCOL) aprobar, ser aprobado ♦ n (permit) permiso; (membership card) carnet m; (in mountains) puerto, desfiladero; (SPORT) pase m; (SCOL: also: ~ mark): **to get a** ~ aprobar en; **to** ~ **sth through sth** pasar algo por algo; **to make a** ~ **at sb** (inf) hacer proposiciones a uno; ~ **away** vi fallecer; ~ **by** vi pasar ♦ vt (ignore) pasar por alto; ~ **for** vt fus pasar por; ~ **on** vt transmitir; ~ **out** vi desmayarse; ~ **up** vt (opportunity) renunciar a; ~**able** adj (road) transitable; (tolerable) pasable
passage ['pæsɪdʒ] n (also: ~way) pasillo; (act of passing) tránsito; (fare, in book) pasaje m; (by boat) travesía; (ANAT) tubo
passbook ['pɑ:sbuk] n libreta de banco
passenger ['pæsɪndʒə*] n pasajero/a, viajero/a
passer-by [pɑ:sə'baɪ] n transeúnte m/f
passing ['pɑ:sɪŋ] adj pasajero; **in** ~ de paso; ~ **place** n (AUT) apartadero
passion ['pæʃən] n pasión f; ~**ate** adj apasionado

passive ['pæsɪv] adj (gen, also LING) pasivo; ~ **smoker** n fumador(a) m/f pasivo

Passover ['pɑːsəʊvə*] n Pascua (de los judíos)

passport ['pɑːspɔːt] n pasaporte m; ~ **control** n control m de pasaporte

password ['pɑːswɜːd] n contraseña

past [pɑːst] prep (in front of) por delante de; (further than) más allá de; (later than) después de ♦ adj pasado; (president etc) antiguo ♦ n (time) pasado; (of person) antecedentes mpl; **he's ~ forty** tiene más de cuarenta años; **ten/quarter ~ eight** las ocho y diez/cuarto; **for the ~ few/3 days** durante los últimos días/últimos 3 días; **to run ~ sb** pasar a uno corriendo

pasta ['pæstə] n pasta

paste [peɪst] n pasta; (glue) engrudo ♦ vt pegar

pastel ['pæstl] adj pastel

pasteurized ['pæstəraɪzd] adj pasteurizado

pastille ['pæstl] n pastilla

pastime ['pɑːstaɪm] n pasatiempo

pastry ['peɪstrɪ] n (dough) pasta; (cake) pastel m

pasture ['pɑːstʃə*] n pasto

pasty¹ ['pæstɪ] n empanada

pasty² ['peɪstɪ] adj (complexion) pálido

pat [pæt] vt dar una palmadita a; (dog etc) acariciar

patch [pætʃ] n (of material, eye ~) parche m; (mended part) remiendo; (of land) terreno ♦ vt remendar; **(to go through) a bad ~** (pasar por) una mala racha; ~ **up** vt reparar; (quarrel) hacer las paces en; ~**work** n labor m de retazos; ~**y** adj desigual

pâté ['pæteɪ] n paté m

patent ['peɪtnt] n patente f ♦ vt patentar ♦ adj patente, evidente; ~ **leather** n charol m

paternal [pə'tɜːnl] adj paternal; (relation) paterno

path [pɑːθ] n camino, sendero; (trail, track) pista; (of missile) trayectoria

pathetic [pə'θetɪk] adj patético, lastimoso; (very bad) malísimo

pathological [pæθə'lɒdʒɪkəl] adj patológico

pathos ['peɪθɒs] n patetismo

pathway ['pɑːθweɪ] n sendero, vereda

patience ['peɪʃns] n paciencia; (BRIT: CARDS) solitario

patient ['peɪʃnt] n paciente m/f ♦ adj paciente, sufrido

patio ['pætɪəʊ] n patio

patriot ['peɪtrɪət] n patriota m/f; ~**ic** [pætrɪ'ɒtɪk] adj patriótico

patrol [pə'trəʊl] n patrulla ♦ vt patrullar por; ~ **car** n coche m patrulla; ~**man** (US) n policía m

patron ['peɪtrən] n (in shop) cliente m/f; (of charity) patrocinador(a) m/f; ~ **of the arts** mecenas m; ~**age** ['pætrənɪdʒ] n patroci-

nio; ~**ize** ['pætrənaɪz] vt (shop) ser cliente de; (artist etc) proteger; (look down on) condescender con; ~ **saint** n santo/a patrón/ona m/f

patter ['pætə*] n golpeteo; (sales talk) labia ♦ vi (rain) tamborilear

pattern ['pætən] n (SEWING) patrón m; (design) dibujo

paunch [pɔːntʃ] n panza, barriga

pauper ['pɔːpə*] n pobre m/f

pause [pɔːz] n pausa ♦ vi hacer una pausa

pave [peɪv] vt pavimentar; **to ~ the way for** preparar el terreno para

pavement ['peɪvmənt] (BRIT) n acera (SP), vereda (AM)

pavilion [pə'vɪlɪən] n (SPORT) caseta

paving ['peɪvɪŋ] n pavimento, enlosado; ~ **stone** n losa

paw [pɔː] n pata

pawn [pɔːn] n (CHESS) peón m; (fig) instrumento ♦ vt empeñar; ~ **broker** n prestamista m/f; ~**shop** n monte m de piedad

pay [peɪ] (pt, pp **paid**) n (wage etc) sueldo, salario ♦ vt pagar ♦ vi (be profitable) rendir; **to ~ attention (to)** prestar atención (a); **to ~ sb a visit** hacer una visita a uno; **to ~ one's respects to sb** presentar sus respetos a uno; ~ **back** vt (money) reembolsar; (person) pagar; ~ **for** vt fus pagar; ~ **in** vt ingresar; ~ **off** vt saldar ♦ vi (scheme, decision) dar resultado; ~ **up** vt pagar (de mala gana); ~**able** adj; ~**able to** pagadero a; ~ **day** n día m de paga; ~**ee** n portador(a) m/f; ~ **envelope** (US) n = ~ **packet**; ~**ment** n pago; **monthly ~ment** mensualidad f; ~ **packet** (BRIT) n sobre m (de paga); ~ **phone** n teléfono público; ~**roll** n nómina; ~ **slip** n recibo de sueldo; ~ **television** n televisión f de pago

PC n abbr = **personal computer**; (BRIT) = **police constable**

p.c. abbr = **per cent**

pea [piː] n guisante m (SP), chícharo (AM), arveja (AM)

peace [piːs] n paz f; (calm) paz f, tranquilidad f; ~**ful** adj (gentle) pacífico; (calm) tranquilo, sosegado

peach [piːtʃ] n melocotón m (SP), durazno (AM)

peacock ['piːkɒk] n pavo real

peak [piːk] n (of mountain) cumbre f, cima; (of cap) visera; (fig) cumbre f; ~ **hours** npl = ~ **period**; ~ **period** n horas fpl punta

peal [piːl] n (of bells) repique m; ~ **of laughter** carcajada

peanut ['piːnʌt] n cacahuete m (SP), maní m (AM); ~ **butter** manteca de cacahuete or maní

pear [pɛə*] n pera

pearl [pɜːl] n perla

peasant ['peznt] n campesino/a

peat [piːt] n turba

pebble ['pɛbl] n guijarro
peck [pɛk] vt (also: ~ at) picotear ♦ n picotazo; (kiss) besito; **~ing order** n orden m de jerarquía; **~ish** (BRIT: inf) adj: **I feel ~ish** tengo ganas de picar algo
peculiar [pɪ'kju:lɪə*] adj (odd) extraño, raro; (typical) propio, característico; ~ **to** propio de; **~ity** [pɪkju:lɪ'ærɪtɪ] n peculiaridad f, característica
pedal ['pɛdl] n pedal m ♦ vi pedalear
pedantic [pɪ'dæntɪk] adj pedante
peddler ['pɛdlə*] n: **drugs ~** traficante m/f; camello
pedestrian [pɪ'dɛstrɪən] n peatón/ona m/f ♦ adj pedestre; ~ **crossing** (BRIT) n paso de peatones
pediatrics [pi:dɪ'ætrɪks] (US) n = **paediatrics**
pedigree ['pɛdɪgri:] n genealogía; (of animal) raza, pedigrí m ♦ cpd (animal) de raza, de casta
pee [pi:] (inf) vi mear
peek [pi:k] vi mirar a hurtadillas
peel [pi:l] n piel f; (of orange, lemon) cáscara; (: removed) peladuras fpl ♦ vt pelar ♦ vi (paint etc) desconcharse; (wallpaper) despegarse, desprenderse; (skin) pelar
peep [pi:p] n (BRIT: look) mirada furtiva; (sound) pío ♦ vi (BRIT: look) mirar furtivamente; ~ **out** vi salir (un poco); **~hole** n mirilla
peer [pɪə*] vi: **to ~ at** esudriñar ♦ n (noble) par m; (equal) igual m; (contemporary) contemporáneo/a; **~age** n nobleza
peeved [pi:vd] adj enojado
peg [pɛg] n (for coat etc) gancho, colgadero; (BRIT: also: clothes ~) pinza
Pekingese [pi:kɪ'ni:z] n (dog) pequinés/esa m/f
pelican ['pɛlɪkən] n pelícano; ~ **crossing** (BRIT) n (AUT) paso de peatones señalizado
pellet ['pɛlɪt] n bolita; (bullet) perdigón m
pelt [pɛlt] vt: **to ~ sb with sth** arrojarle algo a uno ♦ vi (rain) llover a cántaros; (inf: run) correr ♦ n pellejo
pen [pɛn] n (fountain ~) pluma; (ballpoint ~) bolígrafo; (for sheep) redil m
penal ['pi:nl] adj penal; **~ize** vt castigar
penalty ['pɛnltɪ] n (gen) pena; (fine) multa; ~ **(kick)** n (FOOTBALL) penalty m; (RUGBY) golpe m de castigo
penance ['pɛnəns] n penitencia
pence [pɛns] npl of **penny**
pencil ['pɛnsl] n lápiz m, lapicero (AM); ~ **case** n estuche m; ~ **sharpener** n sacapuntas m inv
pendant ['pɛndnt] n pendiente m
pending ['pɛndɪŋ] prep antes de ♦ adj pendiente
pendulum ['pɛndjuləm] n péndulo
penetrate ['pɛnɪtreɪt] vt penetrar; **pen-**

etrating adj penetrante
penfriend ['pɛnfrɛnd] (BRIT) n amigo/a por carta
penguin ['pɛŋgwɪn] n pingüino
penicillin [pɛnɪ'sɪlɪn] n penicilina
peninsula [pə'nɪnsjulə] n península
penis ['pi:nɪs] n pene m
penitent ['pɛnɪtnt] adj arrepentido
penitentiary [pɛnɪ'tɛnʃərɪ] (US) n cárcel f, presidio
penknife ['pɛnnaɪf] n navaja
pen name n seudónimo
penniless ['pɛnɪlɪs] adj sin dinero
penny ['pɛnɪ] (pl pennies or (BRIT) pence) n penique m; (US) centavo
penpal ['pɛnpæl] n amigo/a por carta
pension ['pɛnʃən] n (state benefit) jubilación f; **~er** (BRIT) n jubilado/a; **~-fund** n caja or fondo de pensiones
pensive ['pɛnsɪv] adj pensativo; (withdrawn) preocupado
pentagon ['pɛntəgən] n: **the P~** (US: POL) el Pentágono
Pentecost ['pɛntɪkɔst] n Pentecostés m
penthouse ['pɛnthaus] n ático de lujo
pent-up ['pɛntʌp] adj reprimido
people ['pi:pl] npl gente f; (citizens) pueblo, ciudadanos mpl; (POL): **the ~** el pueblo ♦ n (nation, race) pueblo, nación f; **several ~ came** vinieron varias personas; ~ **say that ...** dice la gente que ...
pep [pɛp] (inf) n energía; ~ **up** vt animar
pepper ['pɛpə*] n (spice) pimienta; (vegetable) pimiento ♦ vt (fig) salpicar de; **~mint** n (sweet) pastilla de menta
peptalk ['pɛptɔ:k] n: **to give sb a ~** darle a uno una inyección de ánimo
per [pə:*] prep por; ~ **day/person** por día/persona; ~ **annum** al año; ~ **capita** adj, adv per cápita
perceive [pə'si:v] vt percibir; (realize) darse cuenta de
per cent n por ciento
percentage [pə'sɛntɪdʒ] n porcentaje m
perception [pə'sɛpʃən] n percepción f; (insight) perspicacia; (opinion etc) opinión f; **perceptive** [-'sɛptɪv] adj perspicaz
perch [pə:tʃ] n (fish) perca; (for bird) percha ♦ vi: **to ~ (on)** (bird) posarse (en); (person) encaramarse (en)
percolator ['pə:kəleɪtə*] n (also: coffee ~) cafetera de filtro
peremptory [pə'rɛmptərɪ] adj perentorio; (person) autoritario
perennial [pə'rɛnɪəl] adj perenne
perfect [adj, n 'pə:fɪkt, vb pə'fɛkt] adj perfecto ♦ n (also: ~ tense) perfecto ♦ vt perfeccionar; **~ly** [pə'fɪktlɪ] adv perfectamente
perforate ['pə:fəreɪt] vt perforar
perform [pə'fɔ:m] vt (carry out) realizar, llevar a cabo; (THEATRE) representar; (piece of music) interpretar ♦ vi (well, badly)

funcionar; ~ance n (of a play) representación f; (of actor, athlete etc) actuación f; (of car, engine, company) rendimiento; (of economy) resultados mpl; ~er n (actor) actor m, actriz f

perfume ['pə:fju:m] n perfume m

perfunctory [pə'fʌŋktərɪ] adj superficial

perhaps [pə'hæps] adv quizá(s), tal vez

peril ['perɪl] n peligro, riesgo

perimeter [pə'rɪmɪtə*] n perímetro

period ['pɪərɪəd] n período; (SCOL) clase f; (full stop) punto; (MED) regla ♦ adj (costume, furniture) de época; ~ic(al) [-'ɔdɪk(l)] adj periódico; ~ical [-'ɔdɪkl] n periódico; ~ically [-'ɔdɪklɪ] adv de vez en cuando, cada cierto tiempo

peripheral [pə'rɪfərəl] adj periférico ♦ n (COMPUT) periférico, unidad f periférica

perish ['perɪʃ] vi perecer; (decay) echarse a perder; ~able adj perecedero

perjury ['pə:dʒərɪ] n (LAW) perjurio

perk [pə:k] n extra m; ~ up vi (cheer up) animarse; ~y adj alegre, despabilado

perm [pə:m] n permanente f

permanent ['pə:mənənt] adj permanente

permeate ['pə:mɪeɪt] vi penetrar, trascender ♦ vt penetrar, trascender a

permissible [pə'mɪsɪbl] adj permisible, lícito

permission [pə'mɪʃən] n permiso

permissive [pə'mɪsɪv] adj permisivo

permit [n 'pə:mɪt, vt pə'mɪt] n permiso, licencia ♦ vt permitir

pernicious [pə:'nɪʃəs] adj nocivo; (MED) pernicioso

perpetrate ['pə:pɪtreɪt] vt cometer

perpetual [pə'petjuəl] adj perpetuo

perpetuate [pə'petjueɪt] vt perpetuar

perplex [pə'pleks] vt dejar perplejo

persecute ['pə:sɪkju:t] vt perseguir

perseverance [pə:sɪ'vɪərəns] n perseverancia

persevere [pə:sɪ'vɪə*] vi persistir

Persian ['pə:ʃən] adj, n persa m/f; **the ~ Gulf** n el Golfo Pérsico

persist [pə'sɪst] vi: **to ~ (in doing sth)** persistir (en hacer algo); ~ence n empeño; ~ent adj persistente; (determined) porfiado

person ['pə:sn] n persona; **in ~** en persona; ~al adj personal, individual; (visit) en persona; ~al assistant n ayudante m/f personal; ~al call n (TEL) llamada persona a persona; ~al column n anuncios mpl personales; ~al computer n ordenador m personal; ~ality [-'nælɪtɪ] n personalidad f; ~ally adv personalmente; (in person) en persona; **to take sth ~ally** tomarse algo a mal; ~al organizer n agenda; ~al stereo n walkman m ®; ~ify [-'sɔnɪfaɪ] vt encarnar

personnel [pə:sə'nel] n personal m

perspective [pə'spektɪv] n perspectiva

Perspex ['pə:speks] ® n plexiglás m

perspiration [pə:spɪ'reɪʃən] n transpiración f

persuade [pə'sweɪd] vt: **to ~ sb to do sth** persuadir a uno para que haga algo

pertaining [pə:'teɪnɪŋ]: ~ **to** prep relacionado con

pertinent ['pə:tɪnənt] adj pertinente, a propósito

Peru [pə'ru:] n el Perú

peruse [pə'ru:z] vt leer con detención, examinar

Peruvian [pə'ru:vɪən] adj, n peruano/a m/f

pervade [pə'veɪd] vt impregnar, infundirse en

perverse [pə'və:s] adj perverso; (wayward) travieso

pervert [n 'pə:və:t, vb pə'və:t] n pervertido/a ♦ vt pervertir; (truth, sb's words) tergiversar

pessimist ['pesɪmɪst] n pesimista m/f; ~ic [-'mɪstɪk] adj pesimista

pest [pest] n (insect) insecto nocivo; (fig) lata, molestia

pester ['pestə*] vt molestar, acosar

pesticide ['pestɪsaɪd] n pesticida m

pet [pet] n animal m doméstico ♦ cpd favorito ♦ vt acariciar ♦ vi (inf) besuquearse; **teacher's ~** favorito/a (del profesor); ~ **hate** manía

petal ['petl] n pétalo

peter ['pi:tə*]: **to ~ out** vi agotarse, acabarse

petite [pə'ti:t] adj chiquita

petition [pə'tɪʃən] n petición f

petrified ['petrɪfaɪd] adj horrorizado

petrol ['petrəl] (BRIT) n gasolina; **two/four-star ~** gasolina normal/súper; ~ **can** n bidón m de gasolina

petroleum [pə'trəulɪəm] n petróleo

petrol: ~ **pump** (BRIT) n (in garage) surtidor m de gasolina; ~ **station** (BRIT) n gasolinera; ~ **tank** (BRIT) n depósito (de gasolina)

petticoat ['petɪkəut] n enaguas fpl

petty ['petɪ] adj (mean) mezquino; (unimportant) insignificante; ~ **cash** n dinero para gastos menores; ~ **officer** n contramaestre m

petulant ['petjulənt] adj malhumorado

pew [pju:] n banco

pewter ['pju:tə*] n peltre m

phantom ['fæntəm] n fantasma m

pharmacist ['fɑ:məsɪst] n farmacéutico/a

pharmacy ['fɑ:məsɪ] n farmacia

phase [feɪz] n fase f ♦ vt: **to ~ sth in/out** introducir/retirar algo por etapas

Ph.D. abbr = **Doctor of Philosophy**

pheasant ['feznt] n faisán m

phenomenon [fə'nɔmɪnən] (pl phenomena) n fenómeno

philanthropist [fɪ'lænθrəpɪst] n filántropo/a

Philippines ['fɪlɪpiːnz] *npl*: the ~ las Filipinas

philosopher [fɪ'lɔsəfə*] *n* filósofo/a

philosophy [fɪ'lɔsəfɪ] *n* filosofía

phlegm [flɛm] *n* flema; **~atic** [flɛg'mætɪk] *adj* flemático

phobia ['fəubjə] *n* fobia

phone [fəun] *n* teléfono ♦ *vt* telefonear, llamar por teléfono; **to be on the ~** tener teléfono; (*be calling*) estar hablando por teléfono; ~ **back** *vt, vi* volver a llamar; ~ **up** *vt, vi* llamar por teléfono; ~ **book** *n* guía telefónica; ~ **booth** *n* cabina telefónica; ~ **box** (*BRIT*) *n* = ~ **booth**; ~ **call** *n* llamada (telefónica); **~card** *n* teletarjeta; **~-in** (*BRIT*) *n* (*RADIO, TV*) programa *m* de participación (telefónica)

phonetics [fə'nɛtɪks] *n* fonética

phoney ['fəunɪ] *adj* falso

photo ['fəutəu] *n* foto *f*

photo... ['fəutəu] *prefix*: **~copier** *n* fotocopiadora; **~copy** *n* fotocopia ♦ *vt* fotocopiar

photograph ['fəutəgrɑːf] *n* fotografía ♦ *vt* fotografiar; **~er** [fə'tɔgrəfə*] *n* fotógrafo; **~y** [fə'tɔgrəfɪ] *n* fotografía

phrase [freɪz] *n* frase *f* ♦ *vt* expresar; ~ **book** *n* libro de frases

physical ['fɪzɪkl] *adj* físico; ~ **education** *n* educación *f* física; **~ly** *adv* físicamente

physician [fɪ'zɪʃən] *n* médico/a

physicist ['fɪzɪsɪst] *n* físico/a

physics ['fɪzɪks] *n* física

physiotherapy [fɪzɪəu'θɛrəpɪ] *n* fisioterapia

physique [fɪ'ziːk] *n* físico

pianist ['piːənɪst] *n* pianista *m/f*

piano [pɪ'ænəu] *n* piano

piccolo ['pɪkələu] *n* (*MUS*) flautín *m*

pick [pɪk] *n* (*tool: also*: **~-axe**) pico, piqueta ♦ *vt* (*select*) elegir, escoger; (*gather*) coger (*SP*), recoger; (*remove, take out*) sacar, quitar; (*lock*) abrir con ganzúa; **take your ~** escoja lo que quiera; **the ~ of** lo mejor de; **to ~ one's nose/teeth** hurgarse las narices/limpiarse los dientes; **to ~ a quarrel with sb** meterse con alguien; ~ **at** *vt fus*: **to ~ at one's food** comer con poco apetito; ~ **on** *vt fus* (*person*) meterse con; ~ **out** *vt* escoger; (*distinguish*) identificar; ~ **up** *vi* (*improve: sales*) ir mejor; (: *patient*) reponerse; (: *FINANCE*) recobrarse ♦ *vt* recoger; (*learn*) aprender; (*POLICE: arrest*) detener; (*person: for sex*) ligar; (*RADIO*) captar; **to ~ up speed** acelerarse; **to ~ o.s. up** levantarse

picket ['pɪkɪt] *n* piquete *m* ♦ *vt* piquetear

pickle ['pɪkl] *n* (*also*: **~s**: *as condiment*) escabeche *m*; (*fig: mess*) apuro ♦ *vt* encurtir

pickpocket ['pɪkpɔkɪt] *n* carterista *m/f*

pickup ['pɪkʌp] *n* (*small truck*) furgoneta

picnic ['pɪknɪk] *n* merienda ♦ *vi* ir de merienda

picture ['pɪktʃə*] *n* cuadro; (*painting*) pintura; (*photograph*) fotografía; (*TV*) imagen *f*, (*film*) película; (*fig: description*) descripción *f*, (: *situation*) situación *f* ♦ *vt* (*imagine*) imaginar; **~s** *npl*: **the ~s** (*BRIT*) el cine; ~ **book** *n* libro de dibujos

picturesque [pɪktʃə'rɛsk] *adj* pintoresco

pie [paɪ] *n* pastel *m*; (*open*) tarta; (*small: of meat*) empanada

piece [piːs] *n* pedazo, trozo; (*of cake*) trozo; (*item*): **a ~ of clothing/furniture/advice** una prenda (de vestir)/un mueble/un consejo ♦ *vt*: **to ~ together** juntar; (*TECH*) armar; **to take to ~s** desmontar; **~meal** *adv* poco a poco; **~work** *n* trabajo a destajo

pie chart *n* gráfico de sectores *or* tarta

pier [pɪə*] *n* muelle *m*, embarcadero

pierce [pɪəs] *vt* perforar

piercing ['pɪəsɪŋ] *adj* penetrante

piety ['paɪətɪ] *n* piedad *f*

pig [pɪg] *n* cerdo (*SP*), puerco (*SP*), chancho (*AM*); (*pej: unkind person*) asqueroso; (: *greedy person*) glotón/ona *m/f*

pigeon ['pɪdʒən] *n* paloma; (*as food*) pichón *m*; **~hole** *n* casilla

piggy bank ['pɪgɪ-] *n* hucha (*en forma de cerdito*)

pig: ~headed ['pɪg'hɛdɪd] *adj* terco, testarudo; **~let** ['pɪglɪt] *n* cochinillo; **~skin** *n* piel *f* de cerdo; **~sty** ['pɪgstaɪ] *n* pocilga; **~tail** *n* (*girl's*) trenza; (*Chinese, TAUR*) coleta

pike [paɪk] *n* (*fish*) lucio

pilchard ['pɪltʃəd] *n* sardina

pile [paɪl] *n* montón *m*; (*of carpet, cloth*) pelo ♦ *vt* (*also*: ~ **up**) amontonar; (*fig*) acumular ♦ *vi* (*also*: ~ **up**) amontonarse; acumularse; ~ **into** *vt fus* (*car*) meterse en; **~s** [paɪlz] *npl* (*MED*) almorranas *fpl*, hemorroides *mpl*; **~-up** *n* (*AUT*) accidente *m* múltiple

pilfering ['pɪlfərɪŋ] *n* ratería

pilgrim ['pɪlgrɪm] *n* peregrino/a; **~age** *n* peregrinación *f*, romería

pill [pɪl] *n* píldora; **the ~** la píldora

pillage ['pɪlɪdʒ] *vt* pillar, saquear

pillar ['pɪlə*] *n* pilar *m*; ~ **box** (*BRIT*) *n* buzón *m*

pillion ['pɪljən] *n* (*of motorcycle*) asiento trasero

pillory ['pɪlərɪ] *vt* poner en la picota, criticar con dureza

pillow ['pɪləu] *n* almohada; **~case** *n* funda

pilot ['paɪlət] *n* piloto ♦ *cpd* (*scheme etc*) piloto ♦ *vt* pilotar; ~ **light** *n* piloto

pimp [pɪmp] *n* chulo (*SP*), cafiche *m* (*AM*)

pimple ['pɪmpl] *n* grano

PIN *n abbr* (= *personal identification number*) número personal

pin [pɪn] *n* alfiler *m* ♦ *vt* prender (con alfiler); **~s and needles** hormigueo; **to ~ sb down** (*fig*) hacer que uno concrete; **to ~ sth on sb** (*fig*) colgarle a uno el sambenito

de algo
pinafore ['pɪnəfɔ:*] n delantal m; ~ **dress** (BRIT) n mandil m
pinball ['pɪnbɔ:l] n mesa americana
pincers ['pɪnsəz] npl pinzas fpl, tenazas fpl
pinch [pɪntʃ] n (of salt etc) pizca ♦ vt pellizcar; (inf: steal) birlar; **at a** ~ en caso de apuro
pincushion ['pɪnkuʃən] n acerico
pine [paɪn] n (also: ~ tree, wood) pino ♦ vi: **to** ~ **for** suspirar por; ~ **away** vi morirse de pena
pineapple ['paɪnæpl] n piña, ananás m
ping [pɪŋ] n (noise) sonido agudo; ~**-pong** ® n pingpong m ®
pink [pɪŋk] adj rosado, (color de) rosa ♦ n (colour) rosa; (BOT) clavel m, clavellina f
pinnacle ['pɪnəkl] n cumbre f
pinpoint ['pɪnpɔɪnt] vt precisar
pint [paɪnt] n pinta (BRIT = 568cc; US = 473cc); (BRIT: inf: of beer) pinta de cerveza, ≈ jarra (SP)
pin-up n fotografía erótica
pioneer [paɪə'nɪə*] n pionero/a
pious ['paɪəs] adj piadoso, devoto
pip [pɪp] n (seed) pepita; **the** ~**s** (BRIT) la señal
pipe [paɪp] n tubo, caño; (for smoking) pipa ♦ vt conducir en cañerías; ~**s** npl (gen) cañería; (also: bag~s) gaita; ~ **down** (inf) vi callarse; ~ **cleaner** n limpiapipas m inv; ~ **dream** n sueño imposible; ~**line** n (for oil) oleoducto; (for gas) gasoducto; ~**r** n gaitero/a
piping ['paɪpɪŋ] adv: **to be** ~ **hot** estar que quema
piquant ['pi:kənt] adj picante; (fig) agudo
pique [pi:k] n pique m, resentimiento
pirate ['paɪərət] n pirata m/f ♦ vt (cassette, book) piratear; ~ **radio** (BRIT) n emisora pirata
pirouette [pɪru'ɛt] n pirueta
Pisces ['paɪsi:z] n Piscis m
piss [pɪs] (inf!) vi mear; ~**ed** (inf!) adj (drunk) borracho
pistol ['pɪstl] n pistola
piston ['pɪstən] n pistón m, émbolo
pit [pɪt] n hoyo; (also: coal ~) mina; (in garage) foso de inspección; (also: orchestra ~) platea ♦ vt: **to** ~ **one's wits against sb** medir fuerzas con uno; ~**s** npl (AUT) box m
pitch [pɪtʃ] n (MUS) tono; (BRIT: SPORT) campo, terreno; (fig) punto; (tar) brea ♦ vt (throw) arrojar, lanzar ♦ vi (fall) caer(se); **to** ~ **a tent** montar una tienda (de campaña); ~**-black** adj negro como boca de lobo; ~**ed battle** n batalla campal
piteous ['pɪtɪəs] adj lastimoso
pitfall ['pɪtfɔ:l] n riesgo
pith [pɪθ] n (of orange) médula
pithy ['pɪθɪ] adj (fig) jugoso

pitiful ['pɪtɪful] adj (touching) lastimoso, conmovedor(a)
pitiless ['pɪtɪlɪs] adj despiadado
pittance ['pɪtns] n miseria
pity ['pɪtɪ] n compasión f, piedad f ♦ vt compadecer(se de); **what a** ~**!** ¡qué pena!
pivot ['pɪvət] n eje m
pizza ['pi:tsə] n pizza
placard ['plækɑ:d] n letrero; (in march etc) pancarta
placate [plə'keɪt] vt apaciguar
place [pleɪs] n lugar m, sitio; (seat) plaza, asiento; (post) puesto; (home): **at/to his** ~ en/a su casa; (role: in society etc) papel m ♦ vt (object) poner, colocar; (identify) reconocer; **to take** ~ tener lugar; **to be** ~**d** (in race, exam) colocarse; **out of** ~ (not suitable) fuera de lugar; **in the first** ~ en primer lugar; **to change** ~**s with sb** cambiarse de sitio con uno; ~ **of birth** n lugar m de nacimiento
placid ['plæsɪd] adj apacible
plagiarism ['pleɪdʒɪərɪzəm] n plagio
plague [pleɪg] n plaga; (MED) peste f ♦ vt (fig) acosar, atormentar
plaice [pleɪs] n inv platija
plaid [plæd] n (material) tartán m
plain [pleɪn] adj (unpatterned) liso; (clear) claro, evidente; (simple) sencillo; (not handsome) poco atractivo ♦ adv claramente ♦ n llano, llanura; ~ **chocolate** n chocolate m amargo; ~**-clothes** adj (police) vestido de paisano; ~**ly** adv claramente
plaintiff ['pleɪntɪf] n demandante m/f
plaintive ['pleɪntɪv] adj lastimero
plait [plæt] n trenza
plan [plæn] n (drawing) plano; (scheme) plan m, proyecto ♦ vt proyectar, planificar ♦ vi hacer proyectos; **to** ~ **to do** pensar hacer
plane [pleɪn] n (AVIAT) avión m; (MATH, fig) plano; (also: ~ tree) plátano; (tool) cepillo
planet ['plænɪt] n planeta m
plank [plæŋk] n tabla
planner ['plænə*] n planificador(a) m/f
planning ['plænɪŋ] n planificación f; **family** ~ planificación familiar; ~ **permission** n permiso para realizar obras
plant [plɑ:nt] n planta; (machinery) maquinaria; (factory) fábrica ♦ vt plantar; (field) sembrar; (bomb) colocar
plaque [plæk] n placa
plaster ['plɑ:stə*] n (for walls) yeso; (also: ~ of Paris) yeso mate; (BRIT: also: sticking ~) tirita (SP), esparadrapo, curita (AM) ♦ vt enyesar; (cover): **to** ~ **with** llenar o cubrir de; ~**ed** (inf) adj borracho; ~**er** n yesero
plastic ['plæstɪk] n plástico ♦ adj de plástico; ~ **bag** n bolsa de plástico
plasticine ['plæstɪsi:n] ® (BRIT) n plastilina ®

plastic surgery n cirujía plástica
plate [pleɪt] n (dish) plato; (metal, in book) lámina; (dental ~) placa de dentadura postiza
plateau ['plætəu] (pl ~s or ~x) n meseta, altiplanicie f
plateaux ['plætəuz] npl of **plateau**
plate glass n vidrio cilindrado
platform ['plætfɔːm] n (RAIL) andén m; (stage, BRIT: on bus) plataforma; (at meeting) tribuna; (POL) programa m (electoral)
platinum ['plætɪnəm] adj, n platino
platitude ['plætɪtjuːd] n lugar m común, tópico
platoon [plə'tuːn] n pelotón m
platter ['plætə*] n fuente f
plausible ['plɔːzɪbl] adj verosímil; (person) convincente
play [pleɪ] n (THEATRE) obra, comedia ♦ vt (game) jugar; (compete against) jugar contra; (instrument) tocar; (part: in play etc) hacer el papel de; (tape, record) poner ♦ vi jugar; (band) tocar; (tape, record) sonar; **to ~ safe** ir a lo seguro; ~ **down** vt quitar importancia a; ~ **up** vi (cause trouble to) dar guerra; ~**boy** n playboy m; ~**er** n jugador(a) m/f; (THEATRE) actor/actriz m/f; (MUS) músico/a; ~**ful** adj juguetón/ona; ~**ground** n (in school) patio de recreo; (in park) parque m infantil; ~**group** n jardín m de niños; ~**ing card** n naipe m, carta; ~**ing field** n campo de deportes; ~**mate** n compañero/a de juego; ~**-off** n (SPORT) (partido de) desempate m; ~**pen** n corral m; ~**thing** n juguete m; ~**time** n (SCOL) recreo; ~**wright** n dramaturgo/a
plc abbr (= public limited company) ≈ S.A
plea [pliː] n súplica, petición f; (LAW) alegato, defensa
plead [pliːd] vt (LAW): **to ~ sb's case** defender a uno; (give as excuse) poner como pretexto ♦ vi (LAW) declararse; (beg): **to ~ with sb** suplicar or rogar a uno
pleasant ['plɛznt] adj agradable; ~**ries** npl cortesías fpl
please [pliːz] excl ¡por favor! ♦ vt (give pleasure to) dar gusto a, agradar ♦ vi (think fit): **do as you ~** haz lo que quieras; ~ **yourself!** (inf) ¡haz lo que quieras!, ¡como quieras!; ~**d** adj (happy) alegre, contento; ~**d (with)** satisfecho (de); ~**d to meet you** ¡encantado!, ¡tanto gusto!; **pleasing** adj agradable, grato
pleasure ['plɛʒə*] n placer m, gusto; "**it's a ~**" "el gusto es mío"; ~ **boat** n barco de recreo
pleat [pliːt] n pliegue m
pledge [plɛdʒ] n (promise) promesa, voto ♦ vt prometer
plentiful ['plɛntɪful] adj copioso, abundante
plenty ['plɛntɪ] n: ~ **of** mucho(s)/a(s)
pliable ['plaɪəbl] adj flexible

pliant ['plaɪənt] adj = **pliable**
pliers ['plaɪəz] npl alicates mpl, tenazas fpl
plight [plaɪt] n situación f difícil
plimsolls ['plɪmsəlz] (BRIT) npl zapatos mpl de tenis
plinth [plɪnθ] n plinto
plod [plɒd] vi caminar con paso pesado; (fig) trabajar laboriosamente
plonk [plɒŋk] (inf) n (BRIT: wine) vino peleón ♦ vt: **to ~ sth down** dejar caer algo
plot [plɒt] n (scheme) complot m, conjura; (of story, play) argumento; (of land) terreno, lote m (AM) ♦ vt (mark out) trazar; (conspire) tramar, urdir ♦ vi conspirar; ~**ter** n (instrument) trazador m de gráficos
plough [plau] (US **plow**) n arado ♦ vt (earth) arar; **to ~ money into** invertir dinero en; ~ **through** vt fus (crowd) abrirse paso por la fuerza por; ~**man's lunch** (BRIT) n almuerzo de pub a base de pan, queso y encurtidos
ploy [plɔɪ] n truco, estratagema
pluck [plʌk] vt (fruit) coger (SP), recoger (AM); (musical instrument) puntear; (bird) desplumar; (eyebrows) depilar ♦ n valor m, ánimo; **to ~ up courage** hacer de tripas corazón
plug [plʌg] n tapón m; (ELEC) enchufe m, clavija; (AUT: also: spark(ing) ~) bujía ♦ vt (hole) tapar; (inf: advertise) dar publicidad a; ~ **in** vt (ELEC) enchufar
plum [plʌm] n (fruit) ciruela ♦ cpd: ~ **job** (inf) puesto (de trabajo) muy codiciado
plumb [plʌm] n vt: **to ~ the depths of** alcanzar los mayores extremos de
plumber ['plʌmə*] n fontanero/a (SP), plomero/a (AM)
plumbing ['plʌmɪŋ] n (trade) fontanería, plomería; (piping) cañería
plume [pluːm] n pluma; (on helmet etc) penacho
plummet ['plʌmɪt] vi: **to ~ (down)** caer a plomo
plump [plʌmp] adj rechoncho, rollizo ♦ vi: **to ~ for** (inf: choose) optar por; ~ **up** vt mullir
plunder ['plʌndə*] n pillaje m; (loot) botín m ♦ vt pillar, saquear
plunge [plʌndʒ] n zambullida ♦ vt sumergir, hundir ♦ vi (fall) caer; (dive) saltar; (person) arrojarse; **to take the ~** lanzarse; ~**r** n (for drain) desatascador m; **plunging** adj: **plunging neckline** escote m pronunciado
pluperfect [pluː'pəːfɪkt] n pluscuamperfecto
plural ['pluərl] adj plural ♦ n plural m
plus [plʌs] n (also: ~ **sign**) signo más ♦ prep más, y, además de; **ten/twenty ~** más de diez/veinte
plush [plʌʃ] adj lujoso
plutonium [pluː'təunɪəm] n plutonio

ply [plaɪ] *vt* (*a trade*) ejercer ♦ *vi* (*ship*) ir y venir ♦ *n* (*of wool, rope*) cabo; **to ~ sb with drink** insistir en ofrecer a uno muchas copas; **~wood** *n* madera contrachapada

P.M. *n abbr* = **Prime Minister**

p.m. *adv abbr* (= *post meridiem*) de la tarde *or* noche

pneumatic [njuːˈmætɪk] *adj* neumático; **~ drill** *n* martillo neumático

pneumonia [njuːˈməʊnɪə] *n* pulmonía

poach [pəʊtʃ] *vt* (*cook*) escalfar; (*steal*) cazar (*or* pescar) en vedado ♦ *vi* cazar (*or* pescar) en vedado; **~ed** *adj* escalfado; **~er** *n* cazador(a) *m/f* furtivo/a

P.O. Box *n abbr* = **Post Office Box**

pocket [ˈpɔkɪt] *n* bolsillo; (*fig: small area*) bolsa ♦ *vt* meter en el bolsillo; (*steal*) embolsar; **to be out of ~** (*BRIT*) salir perdiendo; **~book** (*US*) *n* cartera; **~ calculator** *n* calculadora de bolsillo; **~ knife** *n* navaja; **~ money** *n* asignación *f*

pod [pɔd] *n* vaina

podgy [ˈpɔdʒɪ] *adj* gordinflón/ona

podiatrist [pɔˈdiːətrɪst] (*US*) *n* pedicuro/a

poem [ˈpəʊɪm] *n* poema *m*

poet [ˈpəʊɪt] *n* poeta *m/f*; **~ic** [-ˈɛtɪk] *adj* poético; **~ laureate** *n* poeta *m* laureado; **~ry** *n* poesía

poignant [ˈpɔɪnjənt] *adj* conmovedor(a)

point [pɔɪnt] *n* punto; (*tip*) punta; (*purpose*) fin *m*, propósito; (*use*) utilidad *f*; (*significant part*) lo significativo; (*moment*) momento; (*ELEC*) toma (de corriente); (*also: decimal ~*): **2 ~ 3 (2.3)** dos coma tres (2,3) ♦ *vt* señalar; (*gun etc*): **to ~ sth at sb** apuntar algo a uno ♦ *vi*: **to ~** señalar; **~s** *npl* (*AUT*) contactos *mpl*; (*RAIL*) agujas *fpl*; **to be on the ~ of doing sth** estar a punto de hacer algo; **to make a ~ of** poner empeño en; **to get/miss the ~** comprender/no comprender; **to come to the ~** ir al meollo; **there's no ~ (in doing)** no tiene sentido (hacer); **~ out** *vt* señalar; **~ to** *vt fus* (*fig*) indicar, señalar; **~-blank** *adv* (*say, refuse*) sin más hablar; (*also: at ~-blank range*) a quemarropa; **~ed** *adj* (*shape*) puntiagudo, afilado; (*remark*) intencionado; **~edly** *adv* intencionadamente; **~er** *n* (*needle*) aguja, indicador *m*; **~less** *adj* sin sentido; **~ of view** *n* punto de vista

poise [pɔɪz] *n* aplomo, elegancia

poison [ˈpɔɪzn] *n* veneno ♦ *vt* envenenar; **~ing** *n* envenenamiento; **~ous** *adj* venenoso; (*fumes etc*) tóxico

poke [pəʊk] *vt* (*jab with finger, stick etc*) empujar; (*put*): **to ~ sth in(to)** introducir algo en; **~ about** *vi* fisgonear

poker [ˈpəʊkə*] *n* atizador *m*; (*CARDS*) póker *m*; **~-faced** *adj* de cara impasible

poky [ˈpəʊkɪ] *adj* estrecho

Poland [ˈpəʊlənd] *n* Polonia

polar [ˈpəʊlə*] *adj* polar; **~ bear** *n* oso polar

Pole [pəʊl] *n* polaco/a

pole [pəʊl] *n* palo; (*fixed*) poste *m*; (*GEO*) polo; **~ bean** (*US*) *n* ≈ judía verde; **~ vault** *n* salto con pértiga

police [pəˈliːs] *n* policía ♦ *vt* vigilar; **~ car** *n* coche-patrulla *m*; **~man** *n* policía *m*, guardia *m*; **~ state** *n* estado policial; **~ station** *n* comisaría; **~woman** *n* mujer *f* policía

policy [ˈpɔlɪsɪ] *n* política; (*also: insurance ~*) póliza

polio [ˈpəʊlɪəʊ] *n* polio *f*

Polish [ˈpəʊlɪʃ] *adj* polaco ♦ *n* (*LING*) polaco

polish [ˈpɔlɪʃ] *n* (*for shoes*) betún *m*; (*for floor*) cera (de lustrar); (*shine*) brillo, lustre *m*; (*fig: refinement*) educación *f* ♦ *vt* (*shoes*) limpiar; (*make shiny*) pulir, sacar brillo a; **~ off** *vt* (*work*) terminar; (*food*) despachar; **~ed** *adj* (*fig: person*) elegante

polite [pəˈlaɪt] *adj* cortés, atentó; **~ness** *n* cortesía

political [pəˈlɪtɪkl] *adj* político

politician [pɔlɪˈtɪʃən] *n* político/a

politics [ˈpɔlɪtɪks] *n* política

poll [pəʊl] *n* (*election*) votación *f*; (*also: opinion ~*) sondeo, encuesta ♦ *vt* encuestar; (*votes*) obtener

pollen [ˈpɔlən] *n* polen *m*

polling day [ˈpəʊlɪŋ-] *n* día *m* de elecciones

polling station *n* centro electoral

pollute [pəˈluːt] *vt* contaminar

pollution [pəˈluːʃən] *n* polución *f*, contaminación *f* del medio ambiente

polo [ˈpəʊləʊ] *n* (*sport*) polo; **~-necked** *adj* de cuello vuelto; **~ shirt** *n* polo, niqui *m*

polyester [pɔlɪˈɛstə*] *n* poliéster *m*

polystyrene [pɔlɪˈstaɪriːn] *n* poliestireno

polytechnic [pɔlɪˈtɛknɪk] *n* politécnico

polythene [ˈpɔlɪθiːn] (*BRIT*) *n* politeno

pomegranate [ˈpɔmɪɡrænɪt] *n* granada

pomp [pɔmp] *n* pompa

pompom [ˈpɔmpɔm] *n* borla, pompón *m*

pompous [ˈpɔmpəs] *adj* pomposo

pond [pɔnd] *n* (*natural*) charca; (*artificial*) estanque *m*

ponder [ˈpɔndə*] *vt* meditar

ponderous [ˈpɔndərəs] *adj* pesado

pong [pɔŋ] (*BRIT: inf*) *n* hedor *m*

pontoon [pɔnˈtuːn] *n* pontón *m*

pony [ˈpəʊnɪ] *n* poney *m*, jaca, potro (*AM*); **~tail** *n* cola de caballo; **~ trekking** (*BRIT*) *n* excursión *f* a caballo

poodle [ˈpuːdl] *n* caniche *m*

pool [puːl] *n* (*natural*) charca; (*also: swimming ~*) piscina (*SP*), alberca (*AM*); (*fig: of light etc*) charco; (*SPORT*) chapolín *m* ♦ *vt* juntar; **~s** *npl* (*football ~s*) quinielas *fpl*;

typing ~ servicio de mecanografía
poor [puə*] *adj* pobre; (*bad*) de mala calidad ♦ *npl*: **the** ~ los pobres; **~ly** *adj* mal, enfermo ♦ *adv* mal
pop [pɔp] *n* (*sound*) ruido seco; (*MUS*) (música) pop *m*; (*inf: father*) papá *m*; (*drink*) gaseosa ♦ *vt* (*put quickly*) meter (de prisa) ♦ *vi* reventar; (*cork*) saltar; ~ **in/out** *vi* entrar/salir un momento; ~ **up** *vi* aparecer inesperadamente; **~corn** *n* palomitas *fpl*
pope [pəup] *n* papa *m*
poplar ['pɔplə*] *n* álamo
poplin ['pɔplɪn] *n* popelina
popper ['pɔpə*] (*BRIT*) *n* automático
poppy ['pɔpɪ] *n* amapola
popsicle ['pɔpsɪkl] (*US*) *n* polo
pop star *n* estrella del pop
populace ['pɔpjuləs] *n* pueblo, plebe *f*
popular ['pɔpjulə*] *adj* popular; **~ize** *vt* popularizar; (*disseminate*) vulgarizar
population [pɔpju'leɪʃən] *n* población *f*
porcelain ['pɔːslɪn] *n* porcelana
porch [pɔːtʃ] *n* pórtico, entrada; (*US*) veranda
porcupine ['pɔːkjupaɪn] *n* puerco *m* espín
pore [pɔː*] *n* poro ♦ *vi*: **to ~ over** engolfarse en
pork [pɔːk] *n* carne *f* de cerdo (*SP*) or chancho (*AM*)
pornography [pɔː'nɔgrəfɪ] *n* pornografía
porpoise ['pɔːpəs] *n* marsopa
porridge ['pɔrɪdʒ] *n* gachas *fpl* de avena
port [pɔːt] *n* puerto; (*NAUT: left side*) babor *m*; (*wine*) vino de Oporto; ~ **of call** puerto de escala
portable ['pɔːtəbl] *adj* portátil
porter ['pɔːtə*] *n* (*for luggage*) maletero; (*doorkeeper*) portero/a, conserje *m/f*
portfolio [pɔːt'fəuliəu] *n* cartera
porthole ['pɔːthəul] *n* portilla
portion ['pɔːʃən] *n* porción *f*; (*of food*) ración *f*
portly ['pɔːtlɪ] *adj* corpulento
portrait ['pɔːtreɪt] *n* retrato
portray [pɔː'treɪ] *vt* retratar; (*subj: actor*) representar; **~al** *n* retrato; representación *f*
Portugal ['pɔːtjugl] *n* Portugal *m*
Portuguese [pɔːtju'giːz] *adj* portugués/esa ♦ *n inv* portugués/esa *m/f*; (*LING*) portugués *m*
pose [pəuz] *n* postura, actitud *f* ♦ *vi* (*pretend*): **to ~ as** hacerse pasar por ♦ *vt* (*question*) plantear; **to ~ for** posar para
posh [pɔʃ] (*inf*) *adj* elegante, de lujo
position [pə'zɪʃən] *n* posición *f*; (*job*) puesto; (*situation*) situación *f* ♦ *vt* colocar
positive ['pɔzɪtɪv] *adj* positivo; (*certain*) seguro; (*definite*) definitivo
possess [pə'zɛs] *vt* poseer; **~ion** [pə'zɛʃən] *n* posesión *f*; **~ions** *npl* (*belongings*) pertenencias *fpl*

possibility [pɔsɪ'bɪlɪtɪ] *n* posibilidad *f*
possible ['pɔsɪbl] *adj* posible; **as big as** ~ lo más grande posible; **possibly** *adv* posiblemente; **I cannot possibly come** me es imposible venir
post [pəust] *n* (*BRIT: system*) correos *mpl*; (*BRIT: letters, delivery*) correo; (*job, situation*) puesto; (*pole*) poste *m* ♦ *vt* (*BRIT: send by post*) echar al correo; (*BRIT: appoint*): **to ~ to** enviar a; **~age** *n* porte *m*, franqueo; **~age stamp** *n* sello de correos; **~al** *adj* postal, de correos; **~al order** *n* giro postal; **~box** (*BRIT*) *n* buzón *m*; **~card** *n* tarjeta postal; **~code** (*BRIT*) *n* código postal
postdate [pəust'deɪt] *vt* (*cheque*) poner fecha adelantada a
poster ['pəustə*] *n* cartel *m*
poste restante [pəust'rɛstɔ̃nt] (*BRIT*) *n* lista de correos
postgraduate ['pəust'grædjuət] *n* posgraduado/a
posthumous ['pɔstjuməs] *adj* póstumo
postman ['pəustmən] *n* cartero
postmark ['pəustmaːk] *n* matasellos *m inv*
post-mortem [-'mɔːtəm] *n* autopsia
post office *n* (*building*) (oficina de) correos *m*; (*organization*): **the P~ O~** Administración *f* General de Correos; **P~ O~ Box** *n* apartado postal (*SP*), casilla de correos (*AM*)
postpone [pəs'pəun] *vt* aplazar
postscript ['pəustskrɪpt] *n* posdata
posture ['pɔstʃə*] *n* postura, actitud *f*
postwar [pəust'wɔː*] *adj* de la posguerra
posy ['pəuzɪ] *n* ramillete *m* (de flores)
pot [pɔt] *n* (*for cooking*) olla; (*tea~*) tetera; (*coffee~*) cafetera; (*for flowers*) maceta; (*for jam*) tarro, pote *m*; (*inf: marijuana*) chocolate *m* ♦ *vt* (*plant*) poner en tiesto; **to go to** ~ (*inf*) irse al traste
potato [pə'teɪtəu] (*pl* **~es**) *n* patata (*SP*), papa (*AM*); **~ peeler** *n* pelapatatas *m inv*
potent ['pəutnt] *adj* potente, poderoso; (*drink*) fuerte
potential [pə'tɛnʃl] *adj* potencial, posible ♦ *n* potencial *m*; **~ly** *adv* en potencia
pothole ['pɔthəul] *n* (*in road*) bache *m*; (*BRIT: underground*) gruta; **potholing** (*BRIT*) *n*: **to go potholing** dedicarse a la espeleología
potluck [pɔt'lʌk] *n*: **to take** ~ tomar lo que haya
potted ['pɔtɪd] *adj* (*food*) en conserva; (*plant*) en tiesto o maceta; (*shortened*) resumido
potter ['pɔtə*] *n* alfarero/a ♦ *vi*: **to ~ around**, ~ **about** (*BRIT*) hacer trabajitos; **~y** *n* cerámica; (*factory*) alfarería
potty ['pɔtɪ] *adj* (*inf: mad*) chiflado ♦ *n* orinal *m* de niño
pouch [pautʃ] *n* (*ZOOL*) bolsa; (*for tobacco*)

petaca
poultry ['pəultrı] *n* aves *fpl* de corral; (*meat*) pollo
pounce [pauns] *vi*: **to ~ on** precipitarse sobre
pound [paund] *n* libra (*weight = 453g or 16oz; money = 100 pence*) ♦ *vt* (*beat*) golpear; (*crush*) machacar ♦ *vi* (*heart*) latir; **~ sterling** *n* libra esterlina
pour [pɔː*] *vt* echar; (*tea etc*) servir ♦ *vi* correr, fluir; **to ~ sb a drink** servirle a uno una copa; **~ away** *or* **off** *vt* vaciar, verter; **~ in** *vi* (*people*) entrar en tropel; **~ out** *vi* salir en tropel ♦ *vt* (*drink*) echar, servir; (*fig*): **to ~ out one's feelings** desahogarse; **~ing** *adj*: **~ing rain** lluvia torrencial
pout [paut] *vi* hacer pucheros
poverty ['pɔvətı] *n* pobreza, miseria; **~-stricken** *adj* necesitado
powder ['paudə*] *n* polvo; (*face ~*) polvos *mpl* ♦ *vt* polvorear; **to ~ one's face** empolvarse la cara; **~ compact** *n* polvera; **~ed milk** *n* leche *f* en polvo; **~ puff** *n* borla; **~ room** *n* aseos *mpl*
power ['pauə*] *n* poder *m*; (*strength*) fuerza; (*nation, TECH*) potencia; (*drive*) empuje *m*; (*ELEC*) fuerza, energía ♦ *vt* impulsar; **to be in ~** (*POL*) estar en el poder; **~ cut** (*BRIT*) *n* apagón *m*; **~ed** *adj*: **~ed by** impulsado por; **~ failure** *n* = **~ cut**; **~ful** *adj* poderoso; (*engine*) potente; (*speech etc*) convincente; **~less** *adj*: **~less (to do)** incapaz (de hacer); **~ point** (*BRIT*) *n* enchufe *m*; **~ station** *n* central *f* eléctrica
p.p. *abbr* (= *per procurationem*): **~ J. Smith** p.p. (por poder de) J. Smith; (= *pages*) págs
PR *n abbr* = **public relations**
practicable ['præktıkəbl] *adj* factible
practical ['præktıkl] *adj* práctico; **~ity** [-'kælıtı] *n* factibilidad *f*; **~ joke** *n* broma pesada; **~ly** *adv* (*almost*) casi
practice ['præktıs] *n* (*habit*) costumbre *f*; (*exercise*) práctica, ejercicio; (*training*) adiestramiento; (*MED: of profession*) práctica, ejercicio; (*MED, LAW: business*) consulta *vt, vi* (*US*) = **practise**; **in ~** (*in reality*) en la práctica; **out of ~** desentrenado
practise ['præktıs] (*US* **practice**) *vt* (*carry out*) practicar; (*profession*) ejercer; (*train at*) practicar ♦ *vi* ejercer; (*train*) practicar; **practising** *adj* (*Christian etc*) practicante; (*lawyer*) en ejercicio
practitioner [præk'tıʃənə*] *n* (*MED*) médico/a
prairie ['preərı] *n* pampa
praise [preız] *n* alabanza(s) *f(pl)*, elogio(s) *m(pl)* ♦ *vt* alabar, elogiar; **~worthy** *adj* loable
pram [præm] (*BRIT*) *n* cochecito de niño
prance [prɑːns] *vi* (*person*) contonearse
prank [præŋk] *n* travesura

prawn [prɔːn] *n* gamba
pray [preı] *vi* rezar
prayer [preə*] *n* oración *f*, rezo; (*entreaty*) ruego, súplica
preach [priːtʃ] *vi* (*also fig*) predicar; **~er** *n* predicador(a) *m/f*
precaution [prı'kɔːʃən] *n* precaución *f*
precede [prı'siːd] *vt, vi* preceder
precedent ['presıdənt] *n* precedente *m*
preceding [prı'siːdıŋ] *adj* anterior
precinct ['priːsıŋkt] *n* recinto; **~s** *npl* contornos *mpl*; **pedestrian ~** (*BRIT*) zona peatonal; **shopping ~** (*BRIT*) centro comercial
precious ['preʃəs] *adj* precioso
precipice ['presıpıs] *n* precipicio
precipitate [prı'sıpıteıt] *vt* precipitar
precise [prı'saıs] *adj* preciso, exacto; **~ly** *adv* precisamente, exactamente
preclude [prı'kluːd] *vt* excluir
precocious [prı'kəuʃəs] *adj* precoz
preconceived [priːkən'siːvd] *adj* preconcebido
precondition [priːkən'dıʃən] *n* condición *f* previa
predator ['predətə*] *n* animal *m* de rapiña, depredador *m*
predecessor ['priːdısesə*] *n* antecesor(a) *m/f*
predicament [prı'dıkəmənt] *n* apuro
predict [prı'dıkt] *vt* pronosticar; **~able** *adj* previsible; **~ion** [-'dıkʃən] *n* predicción *f*
predominantly [prı'dɔmınəntlı] *adv* en su mayoría
predominate [prı'dɔmıneıt] *vi* predominar
pre-empt [priː'empt] *vt* adelantarse a
preen [priːn] *vt*: **to ~ itself** (*bird*) limpiarse (las plumas); **to ~ o.s.** pavonearse
prefab ['priːfæb] *n* casa prefabricada
preface ['prefəs] *n* prefacio
prefect ['priːfekt] (*BRIT*) *n* (*in school*) monitor(a) *m/f*
prefer [prı'fɜː*] *vt* preferir; **to ~ doing** *or* **to do** preferir hacer; **~able** *adj* preferible; **~ably** ['prefrəblı] *adv* de preferencia; **~ence** ['prefrəns] *n* preferencia; (*priority*) prioridad *f*; **~ential** [prefə'renʃəl] *adj* preferente
prefix ['priːfıks] *n* prefijo
pregnancy ['pregnənsı] *n* (*of woman*) embarazo; (*of animal*) preñez *f*
pregnant ['pregnənt] *adj* (*woman*) embarazada; (*animal*) preñada
prehistoric ['priːhıs'tɔrık] *adj* prehistórico
prejudice ['predʒudıs] *n* prejuicio; **~d** *adj* (*person*) predispuesto
preliminary [prı'lımınərı] *adj* preliminar
prelude ['preljuːd] *n* preludio
premarital ['priː'mærıtl] *adj* premarital
premature ['premətʃuə*] *adj* prematuro
premier ['premıə*] *adj* primero, principal ♦ *n* (*POL*) primer(a) ministro/a
première ['premıeə*] *n* estreno

premise ['prɛmɪs] n premisa; **~s** npl (of business etc) local m; **on the ~s** en el lugar mismo

premium ['priːmɪəm] n premio; (insurance) prima; **to be at a ~** ser muy solicitado; **~ bond** (BRIT) n bono del estado que participa en una lotería nacional

premonition [prɛmə'nɪʃən] n presentimiento

preoccupied [priː'ɔkjupaɪd] adj ensimismado

prep [prɛp] n (SCOL: study) deberes mpl

prepaid [priː'peɪd] adj porte pagado

preparation [prɛpə'reɪʃən] n preparación f, **~s** npl preparativos mpl

preparatory [prɪ'pærətərɪ] adj preparatorio, preliminar; **~ school** n escuela preparatoria

prepare [prɪ'pɛə*] vt preparar, disponer; (CULIN) preparar ♦ vi: **to ~ for** (action) prepararse or disponerse para; (event) hacer preparativos para; **~d to** dispuesto a; **~d for** listo para

preponderance [prɪ'pɔndərns] n predominio

preposition [prɛpə'zɪʃən] n preposición f

preposterous [prɪ'pɔstərəs] adj absurdo, ridículo

prep school n = **preparatory school**

prerequisite [priː'rɛkwɪzɪt] n requisito

prerogative [prɪ'rɔgətɪv] n prerrogativa

Presbyterian [prɛzbɪ'tɪərɪən] adj, n presbiteriano/a m/f

preschool [priː'skuːl] adj preescolar

prescribe [prɪ'skraɪb] vt (MED) recetar

prescription [prɪ'skrɪpʃən] n (MED) receta

presence ['prɛzns] n presencia; **in sb's ~** en presencia de uno; **~ of mind** aplomo

present [adj, n 'prɛznt, vb prɪ'zɛnt] adj (in attendance) presente; (current) actual ♦ n (gift) regalo; (actuality): **the ~** la actualidad, el presente ♦ vt (introduce, describe) presentar; (expound) exponer; (give) presentar, dar, ofrecer; (THEATRE) representar; **to give sb a ~** regalar algo a uno; **at ~** actualmente; **~able** [prɪ'zɛntəbl] adj: **to make o.s. ~able** arreglarse; **~ation** [-'teɪʃən] n presentación f; (of report etc) exposición f, (formal ceremony) entrega de un regalo; **~-day** adj actual; **~er** [prɪ'zɛntə*] n (RADIO, TV) locutor(a) m/f; **~ly** adv (soon) dentro de poco; (now) ahora

preservation [prɛzə'veɪʃən] n conservación f

preservative [prɪ'zɜːvətɪv] n conservante m

preserve [prɪ'zɜːv] vt (keep safe) preservar, proteger; (maintain) mantener; (food) conservar ♦ n (for game) coto, vedado; (often pl: jam) conserva, confitura

preside [prɪ'zaɪd] vi: **to ~ over** presidir

president ['prɛzɪdənt] n presidente m/f; **~ial** [-'dɛnʃl] adj presidencial

press [prɛs] n (newspapers): **the P~** la prensa; (printer's) imprenta; (of button) pulsación f ♦ vt empujar; (button etc) apretar; (clothes: iron) planchar; (put pressure on: person) presionar; (insist): **to ~ sth on sb** insistir en que uno acepte algo ♦ vi (squeeze) apretar; (pressurize): **to ~ for** presionar por; **we are ~ed for time/ money** estamos apurados de tiempo/ dinero; **~ on** vi avanzar; (hurry) apretar el paso; **~ agency** n agencia de prensa; **~ conference** n rueda de prensa; **~ing** adj apremiante; **~ stud** (BRIT) n botón m de presión; **~-up** (BRIT) n plancha

pressure ['prɛʃə*] n presión f; **to put ~ on sb** presionar a uno; **~ cooker** n olla a presión; **~ gauge** n manómetro; **~ group** n grupo de presión; **pressurized** adj (container) a presión

prestige [prɛs'tiːʒ] n prestigio

presumably [prɪ'zjuːməblɪ] adv es de suponer que, cabe presumir que

presume [prɪ'zjuːm] vt: **to ~ (that)** presumir (que), suponer (que)

presumption [prɪ'zʌmpʃən] n suposición f

presumptuous [prɪ'zʌmptjuəs] adj presumido

presuppose [priːsə'pəuz] vt presuponer

pretence [prɪ'tɛns] (US **pretense**) n fingimiento; **under false ~s** con engaños

pretend [prɪ'tɛnd] vt, vi (feign) fingir

pretense [prɪ'tɛns] (US) n = **pretence**

pretentious [prɪ'tɛnʃəs] adj presumido; (ostentatious) ostentoso, aparatoso

pretext ['priːtɛkst] n pretexto

pretty ['prɪtɪ] adj bonito (SP), lindo (AM) ♦ adv bastante

prevail [prɪ'veɪl] vi (gain mastery) prevalecer; (be current) predominar; **~ing** adj (dominant) predominante

prevalent ['prɛvələnt] adj (widespread) extendido

prevent [prɪ'vɛnt] vt: **to ~ sb from doing sth** impedir a uno hacer algo; **to ~ sth from happening** evitar que ocurra algo; **~ative** adj = **preventive**; **~ive** adj preventivo

preview ['priːvjuː] n (of film) preestreno

previous ['priːvɪəs] adj previo, anterior; **~ly** adv antes

prewar [priː'wɔː*] adj de antes de la guerra

prey [preɪ] n presa ♦ vi: **to ~ on** (feed on) alimentarse de; **it was ~ing on his mind** le preocupaba, le obsesionaba

price [praɪs] n precio ♦ vt (goods) fijar el precio de; **~less** adj que no tiene precio; **~ list** n tarifa

prick [prɪk] n (sting) picadura ♦ vt pinchar; (hurt) picar; **to ~ up one's ears** aguzar el oído

prickle ['prɪkl] n (sensation) picor m; (BOT) espina; **prickly** adj espinoso; (fig: person)

enojadizo; **prickly heat** n sarpullido causado por exceso de calor
pride [praɪd] n orgullo; (*pej*) soberbia ♦ vt: **to ~ o.s. on** enorgullecerse de
priest [priːst] n sacerdote m; **~ess** n sacerdotisa; **~hood** n sacerdocio
prig [prɪg] n gazmoño/a
prim [prɪm] adj (*demure*) remilgado; (*prudish*) gazmoño
primarily ['praɪmərɪlɪ] adv ante todo
primary ['praɪmərɪ] adj (*first in importance*) principal ♦ n (*US: POL*) (elección f) primaria; **~ school** (*BRIT*) n escuela primaria
primate ['praɪmeɪt] n (*ZOOL*) primate m
prime [praɪm] adj primero, principal; (*excellent*) selecto, de primera clase ♦ n: **in the ~ of life** en la flor de la vida ♦ vt (*wood, fig*) preparar; **~ example** ejemplo típico; **P~ Minister** n primer(a) ministro/a
primeval [praɪ'miːvəl] adj primitivo
primitive ['prɪmɪtɪv] adj primitivo; (*crude*) rudimentario
primrose ['prɪmrəʊz] n primavera, prímula
primus (stove) ['praɪməs-] ® (*BRIT*) n hornillo de camping
prince [prɪns] n príncipe m
princess [prɪn'ses] n princesa
principal ['prɪnsɪpl] adj principal, mayor ♦ n director(a) m/f; **~ity** [-'pælɪtɪ] n principado
principle ['prɪnsɪpl] n principio; **in ~** en principio; **on ~** por principio
print [prɪnt] n (*foot~*) huella; (*finger~*) huella dactilar; (*letters*) letra de molde; (*fabric*) estampado; (*ART*) grabado; (*PHOT*) impresión f ♦ vt imprimir; (*cloth*) estampar; (*write in capitals*) escribir en letras de molde; **out of ~** agotado; **~ed matter** n impresos mpl; **~er** n (*person*) impresor(a) m/f; (*machine*) impresora; **~ing** n (*art*) imprenta; (*act*) impresión f; **~out** n (*COMPUT*) impresión f
prior ['praɪə*] adj anterior, previo; (*more important*) más importante; **~ to** antes de
priority [praɪ'ɔrɪtɪ] n prioridad f; **to have ~ (over)** tener prioridad (sobre)
prise [praɪz] vt: **to ~ open** abrir con palanca
prison ['prɪzn] n cárcel f, prisión f ♦ cpd carcelario; **~er** n (*in prison*) preso/a; (*captured person*) prisionero/a; **~er-of-war** n prisionero de guerra
pristine ['prɪstiːn] adj inmaculado
privacy ['prɪvəsɪ] n intimidad f
private ['praɪvɪt] adj (*personal*) particular; (*property, industry, discussion etc*) privado; (*person*) reservado; (*place*) tranquilo ♦ n soldado raso; **"~"** (*on envelope*) "confidencial"; (*on door*) "prohibido el paso"; **in ~** en privado; **~ enterprise** n empresa privada; **~ eye** n detective m/f privado/a; **~ property** n propiedad f privada; **~ school**

n colegio particular
privet ['prɪvɪt] n alheña
privilege ['prɪvɪlɪdʒ] n privilegio; (*prerogative*) prerrogativa
privy ['prɪvɪ] adj: **to be ~ to** estar enterado de
prize [praɪz] n premio ♦ adj de primera clase ♦ vt apreciar, estimar; **~-giving** n distribución f de premios; **~winner** n premiado/a
pro [prəʊ] n (*SPORT*) profesional m/f ♦ prep a favor de; **the ~s and cons** los pros y los contras
probability [prɔbə'bɪlɪtɪ] n probabilidad f; **in all ~** con toda probabilidad
probable ['prɔbəbl] adj probable
probably ['prɔbəblɪ] adv probablemente
probation [prə'beɪʃən] n: **on ~** (*employee*) a prueba; (*LAW*) en libertad condicional
probe [prəʊb] n (*MED, SPACE*) sonda; (*enquiry*) encuesta, investigación f ♦ vt sondar; (*investigate*) investigar
problem ['prɔbləm] n problema m
procedure [prə'siːdʒə*] n procedimiento; (*bureaucratic*) trámites mpl
proceed [prə'siːd] vi (*do afterwards*): **to ~ to do sth** proceder a hacer algo; (*continue*): **to ~ (with)** continuar or seguir (con); **~ings** npl acto(s) (pl); (*LAW*) proceso; **~s** ['prəʊsiːdz] npl (*money*) ganancias fpl, ingresos mpl
process ['prəʊses] n proceso ♦ vt tratar, elaborar; **~ing** n tratamiento, elaboración f; (*PHOT*) revelado
procession [prə'seʃən] n desfile m; **funeral ~** cortejo fúnebre
proclaim [prə'kleɪm] vt (*announce*) anunciar; **proclamation** [prɔklə'meɪʃən] n proclamación f; (*written*) proclama
procrastinate [prəʊ'kræstɪneɪt] vi demorarse
procure [prə'kjʊə*] vt conseguir
prod [prɔd] vt empujar ♦ n empujón m
prodigal ['prɔdɪgl] adj pródigo
prodigy ['prɔdɪdʒɪ] n prodigio
produce [n 'prɔdjuːs, vt prə'djuːs] n (*AGR*) productos mpl agrícolas ♦ vt producir; (*play, film, programme*) presentar; **~r** n productor(a) m/f; (*of film, programme*) director(a) m/f; (*of record*) productor(a) m/f
product ['prɔdʌkt] n producto
production [prə'dʌkʃən] n producción f; (*THEATRE*) presentación f; **~ line** n línea de producción
productive [prə'dʌktɪv] adj productivo; **productivity** [prɔdʌk'tɪvɪtɪ] n productividad f
profane [prə'feɪn] adj profano
profession [prə'feʃən] n profesión f; **~al** adj profesional ♦ n profesional m/f; (*skilled person*) perito
professor [prə'fesə*] n (*BRIT*) catedrático/

a; (US, Canada) profesor(a) m/f
proficiency [prə'fɪʃənsɪ] n capacidad f, habilidad f
proficient [prə'fɪʃənt] adj experto, hábil
profile ['prəʊfaɪl] n perfil m
profit ['prɒfɪt] n (COMM) ganancia ♦ vi: to ~ by or from aprovechar or sacar provecho de; ~**ability** [-ə'bɪlɪtɪ] n rentabilidad f; ~**able** adj (ECON) rentable
profound [prə'faʊnd] adj profundo
profusely [prə'fjuːslɪ] adv profusamente
profusion [prə'fjuːʒən] n profusión f, abundancia
programme ['prəʊgræm] (US **program**) n programa m ♦ vt programar; ~**r** (US **programer**) n programador(a) m/f; **programming** (US **programing**) n programación f
progress [n 'prəʊgres, vi prə'gres] n progreso; (development) desarrollo ♦ vi progresar, avanzar; **in** ~ en curso; ~**ive** [-'gresɪv] adj progresivo; (person) progresista
prohibit [prə'hɪbɪt] vt prohibir; **to** ~ **sb from doing sth** prohibir a uno hacer algo; ~**ion** [-'bɪʃn] n prohibición f; (US): **P~ion Ley f Seca**
project [n 'prɒdʒekt, vb prə'dʒekt] n proyecto ♦ vt proyectar ♦ vi (stick out) salir, sobresalir; **projectile** [prə'dʒektaɪl] n proyectil m; **projection** [prə'dʒekʃən] n proyección f; (overhang) saliente m; **projector** [prə'dʒektə*] n proyector m
proletarian [prəʊlɪ'teərɪən] n proletario/a
proletariat [prəʊlɪ'teərɪət] n proletariado
prologue ['prəʊlɒg] n prólogo
prolong [prə'lɒŋ] vt prolongar, extender
prom [prɒm] n abbr = **promenade**; (US: ball) baile m de gala
promenade [prɒmə'nɑːd] n (by sea) paseo marítimo; ~ **concert** (BRIT) n concierto (en que parte del público permanece de pie)
prominence ['prɒmɪnəns] n importancia
prominent ['prɒmɪnənt] adj (standing out) saliente; (important) eminente, importante
promiscuous [prə'mɪskjʊəs] adj (sexually) promiscuo
promise ['prɒmɪs] n promesa ♦ vt, vi prometer; **promising** adj prometedor/a
promote [prə'məʊt] vt (employee) ascender; (product, pop star) hacer propaganda por; (ideas) fomentar; ~**r** n (of event) promotor(a) m/f; (of cause etc) impulsor(a) m/f, **promotion** [-'məʊʃən] n (advertising campaign) campaña de promoción f, (in rank) ascenso
prompt [prɒmpt] adj rápido ♦ adv: **at 6 o'clock** ~ a las seis en punto ♦ n (COMPUT) aviso ♦ vt (urge) mover, incitar; (when talking) instar; (THEATRE) apuntar; **to** ~ **sb to do sth** instar a uno a hacer algo; ~**ly** adv rápidamente; (exactly) puntualmente

prone [prəʊn] adj (lying) postrado; ~ **to** propenso a
prong [prɒŋ] n diente m, punta
pronoun ['prəʊnaʊn] n pronombre m
pronounce [prə'naʊns] vt pronunciar; ~**d** adj (marked) marcado
pronunciation [prənʌnsɪ'eɪʃən] n pronunciación f
proof [pruːf] n prueba ♦ adj: ~ **against** a prueba de
prop [prɒp] n apoyo; (fig) sostén m ♦ vt (also: ~ **up**) apoyar; (lean): **to** ~ **sth against** apoyar algo contra
propaganda [prɒpə'gændə] n propaganda
propagate ['prɒpəgeɪt] vt (idea, information) difundir
propel [prə'pel] vt impulsar, propulsar; ~**ler** n hélice f
propensity [prə'pensɪtɪ] n propensión f
proper ['prɒpə*] adj (suited, right) propio; (exact) justo; (seemly) correcto, decente; (authentic) verdadero; (referring to place): **the village** ~ el pueblo mismo; ~**ly** adv (adequately) correctamente; (decently) decentemente; ~ **noun** n nombre m propio
property ['prɒpətɪ] n propiedad f; (personal) bienes mpl muebles; ~ **owner** n dueño/a de propiedad
prophecy ['prɒfɪsɪ] n profecía
prophesy ['prɒfɪsaɪ] vt (fig) predecir
prophet ['prɒfɪt] n profeta m
proportion [prə'pɔːʃən] n proporción f; (share) parte f; ~**al** adj: ~**al** (**to**) en proporción (con); ~**al representation** n representación f proporcional; ~**ate** adj: ~**ate** (**to**) en proporción (con)
proposal [prə'pəʊzl] n (offer of marriage) oferta de matrimonio; (plan) proyecto
propose [prə'pəʊz] vt proponer ♦ vi declararse; **to** ~ **to do** tener intención de hacer
proposition [prɒpə'zɪʃən] n propuesta
proprietor [prə'praɪətə*] n propietario/a, dueño/a
propriety [prə'praɪətɪ] n decoro
pro rata [-'rɑːtə] adv a prorrateo
prose [prəʊz] n prosa
prosecute ['prɒsɪkjuːt] vt (LAW) procesar; **prosecution** [-'kjuːʃən] n proceso, causa; (accusing side) acusación f; **prosecutor** n acusador(a) m/f; (also: **public prosecutor**) fiscal m
prospect [n 'prɒspekt, vb prə'spekt] n (possibility) posibilidad f; (outlook) perspectiva ♦ vi: **to** ~ **for** buscar; ~**s** npl (for work etc) perspectivas fpl; ~**ing** n prospección f; ~**ive** [prə'spektɪv] adj futuro
prospectus [prə'spektəs] n prospecto
prosper ['prɒspə*] vi prosperar; ~**ity** [-'sperɪtɪ] n prosperidad f; ~**ous** adj próspero
prostitute ['prɒstɪtjuːt] n prostituta; (male) hombre que se dedica a la prostitución
prostrate ['prɒstreɪt] adj postrado

protagonist [prə'tægənɪst] *n* protagonista *m/f*

protect [prə'tɛkt] *vt* proteger; **~ion** [-'tɛkʃən] *n* protección *f*; **~ive** *adj* protector(a)

protégé ['prəuteʒeɪ] *n* protegido/a

protein ['prəutiːn] *n* proteína

protest [*n* 'prəutɛst, *vb* prə'tɛst] *n* protesta ♦ *vi*: **to ~ about** *or* **at/against** protestar de/contra ♦ *vt* (*insist*): **to ~ (that)** insistir en (que)

Protestant ['prɔtɪstənt] *adj, n* protestante *m/f*

protester [prə'tɛstə*] *n* manifestante *m/f*

protracted [prə'træktɪd] *adj* prolongado

protrude [prə'truːd] *vi* salir, sobresalir

proud [praud] *adj* orgulloso; (*pej*) soberbio, altanero

prove [pruːv] *vt* probar; (*show*) demostrar ♦ *vi*: **to ~ (to be) correct** resultar correcto; **to ~ o.s.** probar su valía

proverb ['prɔvəːb] *n* refrán *m*

provide [prə'vaɪd] *vt* proporcionar, dar; **to ~ sb with sth** proveer a uno de algo; **~d (that)** *conj* con tal de que, a condición de que; **~ for** *vt fus* (*person*) mantener a; (*problem etc*) tener en cuenta; **providing** [prə'vaɪdɪŋ] *conj*: **~ (that)** a condición de que, con tal de que

province ['prɔvɪns] *n* provincia; (*fig*) esfera; **provincial** [prə'vɪnʃəl] *adj* provincial; (*pej*) provinciano

provision [prə'vɪʒən] *n* (*supplying*) suministro, abastecimiento; (*of contract etc*) disposición *f*; **~s** *npl* (*food*) comestibles *mpl*; **~al** *adj* provisional

proviso [prə'vaɪzəu] *n* condición *f*, estipulación *f*

provocative [prə'vɔkətɪv] *adj* provocativo

provoke [prə'vəuk] *vt* (*cause*) provocar, incitar; (*anger*) enojar

prow [prau] *n* proa

prowess ['prauɪs] *n* destreza

prowl [praul] *vi* (*also*: **~ about, ~ around**) merodear ♦ *n*: **on the ~** de merodeo; **~er** *n* merodeador(a) *m/f*

proxy ['prɔksɪ] *n*: **by ~** por poderes

prude [pruːd] *n* remilgado/a

prudent ['pruːdənt] *adj* prudente

prune [pruːn] *n* ciruela pasa ♦ *vt* podar

pry [praɪ] *vi*: **to ~ (into)** entrometerse (en)

PS *n abbr* (= *postscript*) P.D.

psalm [sɑːm] *n* salmo

pseudo- [sjuː'dəu] *prefix* seudo-; **pseudonym** *n* seudónimo

psyche ['saɪkɪ] *n* psique *f*

psychiatric [saɪkɪ'ætrɪk] *adj* psiquiátrico

psychiatrist [saɪ'kaɪətrɪst] *n* psiquiatra *m/f*

psychic ['saɪkɪk] *adj* (*also*: **~al**) psíquico

psychoanalyse [saɪkəu'ænəlaɪz] *vt* psicoanalizar; **psychoanalysis** [-ə'nælɪsɪs] *n* psicoanálisis *m inv*

psychological [saɪkə'lɔdʒɪkl] *adj* psicológico

psychologist [saɪ'kɔlədʒɪst] *n* psicólogo/a

psychology [saɪ'kɔlədʒɪ] *n* psicología

PTO *abbr* (= *please turn over*) sigue

pub [pʌb] *n abbr* (= *public house*) pub *m*, taberna

puberty ['pjuːbətɪ] *n* pubertad *f*

public ['pʌblɪk] *adj* público ♦ *n*: **the ~** el público; **in ~** en público; **to make ~** hacer público; **~ address system** *n* megafonía

publican ['pʌblɪkən] *n* tabernero/a

publication [pʌblɪ'keɪʃən] *n* publicación *f*

public: **~ company** *n* sociedad *f* anónima; **~ convenience** (*BRIT*) *n* aseos *mpl* públicos (*SP*), sanitarios *mpl* (*AM*); **~ holiday** *n* día de fiesta (*SP*), (día) feriado (*AM*); **~ house** (*BRIT*) *n* bar *m*, pub *m*

publicity [pʌb'lɪsɪtɪ] *n* publicidad *f*

publicize ['pʌblɪsaɪz] *vt* publicitar

publicly ['pʌblɪklɪ] *adv* públicamente, en público

public: **~ opinion** *n* opinión *f* pública; **~ relations** *n* relaciones *fpl* públicas; **~ school** *n* (*BRIT*) escuela privada; (*US*) instituto; **~-spirited** *adj* que tiene sentido del deber ciudadano; **~ transport** *n* transporte *m* público

publish ['pʌblɪʃ] *vt* publicar; **~er** *n* (*person*) editor(a) *m/f*; (*firm*) editorial *f*; **~ing** *n* (*industry*) industria del libro

puce [pjuːs] *adj* de color pardo rojizo

pucker ['pʌkə*] *vt* (*pleat*) arrugar; (*brow etc*) fruncir

pudding ['pudɪŋ] *n* pudín *m*; (*BRIT*: *dessert*) postre *m*; **black ~** morcilla

puddle ['pʌdl] *n* charco

puff [pʌf] *n* soplo; (*of smoke, air*) bocanada; (*of breathing*) resoplido ♦ *vt*: **to ~ one's pipe** chupar la pipa ♦ *vi* (*pant*) jadear; **~ out** *vt* hinchar; **~ed** (*inf*) *adj* (*out of breath*) sin aliento; **~ pastry** *n* hojaldre *m*; **~y** *adj* hinchado

pull [pul] *n* (*tug*): **to give sth a ~** dar un tirón a algo ♦ *vt* tirar de; (*press*: *trigger*) apretar; (*haul*) tirar, arrastrar; (*close*: *curtain*) echar ♦ *vi* tirar; **to ~ to pieces** hacer pedazos; **to not ~ one's punches** no andarse con bromas; **to ~ one's weight** hacer su parte; **to ~ o.s. together** sobreponerse; **to ~ sb's leg** tomar el pelo a uno; **~ apart** *vt* (*break*) romper; **~ down** *vt* (*building*) derribar; **~ in** *vi* (*car etc*) parar (junto a la acera); (*train*) llegar a la estación; **~ off** *vt* (*deal etc*) cerrar; **~ out** *vi* (*car, train etc*) salir ♦ *vt* sacar, arrancar; **~ over** *vi* (*AUT*) hacerse a un lado; **~ through** *vi* (*MED*) reponerse; **~ up** *vi* (*stop*) parar ♦ *vt* (*raise*) levantar; (*uproot*) arrancar, desarraigar

pulley ['pulɪ] *n* polea

pullover ['puləuvə*] *n* jersey *m*, suéter *m*

pulp [pʌlp] n (of fruit) pulpa
pulpit ['pulpɪt] n púlpito
pulsate [pʌl'seɪt] vi pulsar, latir
pulse [pʌls] n (ANAT) pulso; (rhythm) pulsación f; (BOT) legumbre f
pummel ['pʌml] vt aporrear
pump [pʌmp] n bomba; (shoe) zapatilla ♦ vt sacar con una bomba; ~ **up** vt inflar
pumpkin ['pʌmpkɪn] n calabaza
pun [pʌn] n juego de palabras
punch [pʌntʃ] n (blow) golpe m, puñetazo; (tool) punzón m; (drink) ponche m ♦ vt (hit): **to ~ sb/sth** dar un puñetazo or golpear a uno/algo; ~**line** n palabras que rematan un chiste; ~**-up** (BRIT: inf) n riña
punctual ['pʌŋktjuəl] adj puntual
punctuation [pʌŋktju'eɪʃən] n puntuación f
puncture ['pʌŋktʃə*] (BRIT) n pinchazo ♦ vt pinchar
pundit ['pʌndɪt] n experto/a
pungent ['pʌndʒənt] adj acre
punish ['pʌnɪʃ] vt castigar; ~**ment** n castigo
punk [pʌŋk] n (also: ~ rocker) punki m/f; (also: ~ rock) música punk; (US: inf: hoodlum) rufián m
punt [pʌnt] n (boat) batea
punter ['pʌntə*] (BRIT) n (gambler) jugador(a) m/f; (: inf) cliente m/f
puny ['pjuːnɪ] adj débil
pup [pʌp] n cachorro
pupil ['pjuːpl] n alumno/a; (of eye) pupila
puppet ['pʌpɪt] n títere m
puppy ['pʌpɪ] n cachorro, perrito
purchase ['pɔːtʃɪs] n compra ♦ vt comprar; ~**r** n comprador/a m/f
pure [pjuə*] adj puro
purée ['pjuəreɪ] n puré m
purely ['pjuəlɪ] adv puramente
purge [pɔːdʒ] n (MED, POL) purga ♦ vt purgar
purify ['pjuərɪfaɪ] vt purificar, depurar
puritan ['pjuərɪtən] n puritano/a
purity ['pjuərɪtɪ] n pureza
purple ['pɔːpl] adj purpúreo; morado
purport [pɔː'pɔːt] vi: **to ~ to be/do** dar a entender que es/hace
purpose ['pɔːpəs] n propósito; **on** ~ a propósito, adrede; ~**ful** adj resuelto, determinado
purr [pɔː*] vi ronronear
purse [pɔːs] n monedero; (US) bolsa (SP), cartera (AM) ♦ vt fruncir
purser ['pɔːsə*] n (NAUT) comisario/a
pursue [pə'sjuː] vt seguir; ~**r** n perseguidor(a) m/f
pursuit [pə'sjuːt] n (chase) caza; (occupation) actividad f
push [puʃ] n empuje m, empujón m; (of button) presión f; (drive) empuje m ♦ vt empujar; (button) apretar; (promote) pro-

mover ♦ vi empujar; (demand): **to ~ for** luchar por; ~ **aside** vt apartar con la mano; ~ **off** (inf) vi largarse; ~ **on** vi seguir adelante; ~ **through** (crowd) abrirse paso a empujones ♦ vt (measure) despachar; ~ **up** vt (total, prices) hacer subir; ~**chair** (BRIT) n sillita de ruedas; ~**er** n (drug ~er) traficante m/f de drogas; ~**over** (inf) n: **it's a ~over** está tirado; ~**-up** (US) n plancha; ~**y** (pej) adj agresivo
puss [pus] (inf) n minino
pussy(-cat) ['pusɪ-] (inf) n = **puss**
put [put] (pt, pp **put**) vt (place) poner, colocar; (~ into) meter; (say) expresar; (a question) hacer; (estimate) estimar; ~ **about** or **around** vt (rumour) diseminar; ~ **across** vt (ideas etc) comunicar; ~ **away** vt (store) guardar; ~ **back** vt (replace) devolver a su lugar; (postpone) aplazar; ~ **by** vt (money) guardar; ~ **down** vt (on ground) poner en el suelo; (animal) sacrificar; (in writing) apuntar; (revolt etc) sofocar; (attribute): **to ~ sth down to** atribuir algo a; ~ **forward** vt (ideas) presentar, proponer; ~ **in** vt (complaint) presentar; (time) dedicar; ~ **off** vt (postpone) aplazar; (discourage) desanimar; ~ **on** vt ponerse; (light etc) encender; (play etc) presentar; (gain): **to ~ on weight** engordar; (brake) echar; (record, kettle etc) poner; (assume) adoptar; ~ **out** vt (fire, light) apagar; (rubbish etc) sacar; (cat etc) echar; (one's hand) alargar; (inf: person): **to be ~ out** alterarse; ~ **through** vt (TEL) poner; (plan etc) hacer aprobar; ~ **up** vt (raise) levantar, alzar; (hang) colgar; (build) construir; (increase) aumentar; (accommodate) alojar; ~ **up with** vt fus aguantar
putrid ['pjuːtrɪd] adj podrido
putt [pʌt] n putt m, golpe m corto; ~**ing green** n green m; minigolf m
putty ['pʌtɪ] n masilla
put-up ['put-] adj (BRIT): ~ **job** (BRIT) n amaño
puzzle ['pʌzl] n rompecabezas m inv; (also: crossword ~) crucigrama m; (mystery) misterio ♦ vt dejar perplejo, confundir ♦ vi: **to ~ over sth** devanarse los sesos con algo; **puzzling** adj misterioso, extraño
pyjamas [pɪ'dʒɑːməz] (BRIT) npl pijama m
pylon ['paɪlən] n torre f de conducción eléctrica
pyramid ['pɪrəmɪd] n pirámide f
Pyrenees [pɪrə'niːz] npl: **the ~** los Pirineos
python ['paɪθən] n pitón m

Q q

quack [kwæk] *n* graznido; (*pej: doctor*) curandero/a
quad [kwɔd] *n abbr* = **quadrangle**; **quadruplet**
quadrangle ['kwɔdrængl] *n* patio
quadruple [kwɔ'drupl] *vt, vi* cuadruplicar
quadruplets [kwɔ'dru:plɪts] *npl* cuatrillizos/as
quagmire ['kwægmaɪə*] *n* lodazal *m*, cenegal *m*
quail [kweɪl] *n* codorniz *f* ♦ *vi*: **to ~ at** or **before** amedrentarse ante
quaint [kweɪnt] *adj* extraño; (*picturesque*) pintoresco
quake [kweɪk] *vi* temblar ♦ *n abbr* = **earthquake**
Quaker ['kweɪkə*] *n* cuáquero/a
qualification [kwɔlɪfɪ'keɪʃən] *n* (*ability*) capacidad *f*; (*often pl: diploma etc*) título; (*reservation*) salvedad *f*
qualified ['kwɔlɪfaɪd] *adj* capacitado; (*professionally*) titulado; (*limited*) limitado
qualify ['kwɔlɪfaɪ] *vt* (*make competent*) capacitar; (*modify*) modificar ♦ *vi* (*in competition*): **to ~ (for)** calificarse (para); (*pass examination(s)*): **to ~ (as)** calificarse (de), graduarse (en); (*be eligible*): **to ~ (for)** reunir los requisitos (para)
quality ['kwɔlɪtɪ] *n* calidad *f*; (*of person*) cualidad *f*
qualm [kwɑːm] *n* escrúpulo
quandary ['kwɔndrɪ] *n*: **to be in a ~** tener dudas
quantity ['kwɔntɪtɪ] *n* cantidad *f*; **in ~** en grandes cantidades; **~ surveyor** *n* aparejador(a) *m/f*
quarantine ['kwɔrntiːn] *n* cuarentena
quarrel ['kwɔrl] *n* riña, pelea ♦ *vi* reñir, pelearse; **~some** *adj* pendenciero
quarry ['kwɔrɪ] *n* cantera; (*animal*) presa
quart [kwɔːt] *n* ≈ litro
quarter ['kwɔːtə*] *n* cuarto, cuarta parte *f*; (*US: coin*) moneda de 25 centavos; (*of year*) trimestre *m*; (*district*) barrio ♦ *vt* dividir en cuartos; (*MIL: lodge*) alojar; **~s** *npl* (*barracks*) cuartel *m*; (*living ~s*) alojamiento; **a ~ of an hour** un cuarto de hora; **~ final** *n* cuarto de final; **~ly** *adj* trimestral ♦ *adv* cada 3 meses, trimestralmente
quartet(te) [kwɔː'tɛt] *n* cuarteto

quartz [kwɔːts] *n* cuarzo
quash [kwɔʃ] *vt* (*verdict*) anular
quasi- ['kweɪzaɪ] *prefix* cuasi
quaver ['kweɪvə*] (*BRIT*) *n* (*MUS*) corchea ♦ *vi* temblar
quay [kiː] *n* (*also: ~side*) muelle *m*
queasy ['kwiːzɪ] *adj*: **to feel ~** tener náuseas
queen [kwiːn] *n* reina; (*CARDS etc*) dama; **~ mother** *n* reina madre
queer [kwɪə*] *adj* raro, extraño ♦ *n* (*inf: highly offensive*) maricón *m*
quell [kwɛl] *vt* (*feeling*) calmar; (*rebellion etc*) sofocar
quench [kwɛntʃ] *vt*: **to ~ one's thirst** apagar la sed
querulous ['kwerʊləs] *adj* quejumbroso
query ['kwɪərɪ] *n* (*question*) pregunta ♦ *vt* dudar de
quest [kwɛst] *n* busca, búsqueda
question ['kwɛstʃən] *n* pregunta; (*doubt*) duda; (*matter*) asunto, cuestión *f* ♦ *vt* (*doubt*) dudar de; (*interrogate*) interrogar, hacer preguntas a; **beyond ~** fuera de toda duda; **out of the ~** imposible; ni hablar; **~able** *adj* dudoso; **~ mark** *n* punto de interrogación; **~naire** [-'nɛə*] *n* cuestionario
queue [kjuː] (*BRIT*) *n* cola ♦ *vi* (*also: ~ up*) hacer cola
quibble ['kwɪbl] *vi* sutilizar
quick [kwɪk] *adj* rápido; (*agile*) ágil; (*mind*) listo ♦ *n*: **cut to the ~** (*fig*) herido en lo vivo; **be ~!** ¡date prisa!, **~en** *vt* apresurar ♦ *vi* apresurarse, darse prisa; **~ly** *adv* rápidamente, de prisa; **~sand** *n* arenas *fpl* movedizas; **~-witted** *adj* perspicaz
quid [kwɪd] (*BRIT: inf*) *n inv* libra
quiet ['kwaɪət] *adj* (*voice, music etc*) bajo; (*person, place*) tranquilo; (*ceremony*) íntimo ♦ *n* silencio; (*calm*) tranquilidad *f* ♦ *vt, vi* (*US*) = **~en**; **~en** (*also: ~en down*) *vi* calmarse; (*grow silent*) callarse ♦ *vt* calmar; hacer callar; **~ly** *adv* tranquilamente; (*silently*) silenciosamente; **~ness** *n* silencio, tranquilidad *f*
quilt [kwɪlt] *n* edredón *m*
quin [kwɪn] *n abbr* = **quintuplet**
quinine [kwɪ'niːn] *n* quinina
quintet(te) [kwɪn'tɛt] *n* quinteto
quintuplets [kwɪn'tjuːplɪts] *npl* quintillizos/as
quip [kwɪp] *n* pulla
quirk [kwɔːk] *n* peculiaridad *f*; (*accident*) capricho
quit [kwɪt] (*pt, pp* **quit** or **quitted**) *vt* dejar, abandonar; (*premises*) desocupar ♦ *vi* (*give up*) renunciar; (*resign*) dimitir
quite [kwaɪt] *adv* (*rather*) bastante; (*entirely*) completamente; **that's not ~ big enough** no acaba de ser lo bastante grande; **~ a few of them** un buen número de ellos; **~ (so)!** ¡así es!, ¡exactamente!

quits [kwɪts] *adj*: ~ **(with)** en paz (con); **let's call it** ~ dejémoslo en tablas

quiver ['kwɪvə*] *vi* estremecerse

quiz [kwɪz] *n* concurso ♦ *vt* interrogar; **~zical** *adj* burlón(ona)

quota ['kwəʊtə] *n* cuota

quotation [kwəʊ'teɪʃən] *n* cita; *(estimate)* presupuesto; ~ **marks** *npl* comillas *fpl*

quote [kwəʊt] *n* cita; *(estimate)* presupuesto ♦ *vt* citar; *(price)* cotizar ♦ *vi*: **to** ~ **from** citar de; ~**s** *npl* *(inverted commas)* comillas *fpl*

quotient ['kwəʊʃənt] *n* cociente *m*

R r

rabbi ['ræbaɪ] *n* rabino

rabbit ['ræbɪt] *n* conejo; ~ **hutch** *n* conejera

rabble ['ræbl] *(pej)* *n* chusma, populacho

rabies ['reɪbiːz] *n* rabia

RAC *(BRIT)* *n* *abbr* = **Royal Automobile Club**

rac(c)oon [rə'kuːn] *n* mapache *m*

race [reɪs] *n* carrera; *(species)* raza ♦ *vt* *(horse)* hacer correr; *(engine)* acelerar ♦ *vi* *(compete)* competir; *(run)* correr; *(pulse)* latir a ritmo acelerado; ~ **car** *(US)* *n* = **racing car**; ~ **car driver** *(US)* *n* = **racing driver**; ~**course** *n* hipódromo; ~**horse** *n* caballo de carreras; ~**track** *n* pista; *(for cars)* autódromo

racial ['reɪʃl] *adj* racial

racing ['reɪsɪŋ] *n* carreras *fpl*; ~ **car** *(BRIT)* *n* coche *m* de carreras; ~ **driver** *(BRIT)* *n* corredor(a) *m/f* de coches

racism ['reɪsɪzəm] *n* racismo; **racist** [-sɪst] *adj, n* racista *m/f*

rack [ræk] *n* *(also: luggage* ~*)* rejilla; *(shelf)* estante *m*; *(also: roof* ~*)* baca, portaequipajes *m inv*; *(dish* ~*)* escurreplatos *m inv*; *(clothes* ~*)* percha ♦ *vt* atormentar; **to** ~ **one's brains** devanarse los sesos

racket ['rækɪt] *n* *(for tennis)* raqueta; *(noise)* ruido, estrépito; *(swindle)* estafa, timo

racquet ['rækɪt] *n* raqueta

racy ['reɪsɪ] *adj* picante, salado

radar ['reɪdɑ:*] *n* radar *m*

radiance ['reɪdɪəns] *n* brillantez *f*, resplandor *m*

radiant ['reɪdɪənt] *adj* radiante (de felicidad)

radiate ['reɪdɪeɪt] *vt* *(heat)* radiar; *(emotion)*

irradiar ♦ *vi* *(lines)* extenderse

radiation [reɪdɪ'eɪʃən] *n* radiación *f*

radiator ['reɪdɪeɪtə*] *n* radiador *m*

radical ['rædɪkl] *adj* radical

radii ['reɪdɪaɪ] *npl of* **radius**

radio ['reɪdɪəʊ] *n* radio *f*; **on the** ~ por radio

radio... [reɪdɪəʊ] *prefix*: ~**active** *adj* radioactivo; **radiography** [-'ɔgrəfɪ] *n* radiografía; **radiology** [-'ɔlədʒɪ] *n* radiología

radio station *n* emisora

radiotherapy [-'θerəpɪ] *n* radioterapia

radish ['rædɪʃ] *n* rábano

radius ['reɪdɪəs] *(pl* **radii***)* *n* radio

RAF *n abbr* = **Royal Air Force**

raffle ['ræfl] *n* rifa, sorteo

raft [rɑːft] *n* balsa; *(also: life* ~*)* balsa salvavidas

rafter ['rɑːftə*] *n* viga

rag [ræg] *n* *(piece of cloth)* trapo; *(torn cloth)* harapo; *(pej: newspaper)* periodicucho; *(for charity)* actividades estudiantiles benéficas; ~**s** *npl* *(torn clothes)* harapos *mpl*; ~**-and-bone man** *(BRIT)* *n* = ~**man**; ~ **doll** *n* muñeca de trapo

rage [reɪdʒ] *n* rabia, furor *m* ♦ *vi* *(person)* rabiar, estar furioso; *(storm)* bramar; **it's all the** ~ *(very fashionable)* está muy de moda

ragged ['rægɪd] *adj* *(edge)* desigual, mellado; *(appearance)* andrajoso, harapiento

ragman ['rægmæn] *n* trapero

raid [reɪd] *n* *(MIL)* incursión *f*; *(criminal)* asalto; *(by police)* redada ♦ *vt* invadir, atacar; asaltar

rail [reɪl] *n* *(on stair)* barandilla, pasamanos *m inv*; *(on bridge, balcony)* pretil *m*; *(of ship)* barandilla; *(also: towel* ~*)* toallero; ~**s** *npl* *(RAIL)* vía; **by** ~ por ferrocarril; ~**ing(s)** *n(pl)* vallado; ~**road** *(US)* *n* = ~**way**; ~**way** *(BRIT)* *n* ferrocarril *m*, vía férrea; ~**way line** *(BRIT)* *n* línea (de ferrocarril); ~**wayman** *(BRIT)* *n* ferroviario; ~**way station** *(BRIT)* *n* estación *f* de ferrocarril

rain [reɪn] *n* lluvia ♦ *vi* llover; **in the** ~ bajo la lluvia; **it's** ~**ing** llueve, está lloviendo; ~**bow** *n* arco iris; ~**coat** *n* impermeable *m*; ~**drop** *n* gota de lluvia; ~**fall** *n* lluvia; ~**forest** *n* selvas *fpl* tropicales; ~**y** *adj* lluvioso

raise [reɪz] *n* aumento ♦ *vt* levantar; *(increase)* aumentar; *(improve: morale)* subir; *(: standards)* mejorar; *(doubts)* suscitar; *(a question)* plantear; *(cattle, family)* criar; *(crop)* cultivar; *(army)* reclutar; *(loan)* obtener; **to** ~ **one's voice** alzar la voz

raisin ['reɪzn] *n* pasa de Corinto

rake [reɪk] *n* *(tool)* rastrillo; *(person)* libertino ♦ *vt* *(garden)* rastrillar; *(with machine gun)* barrer

rally ['rælɪ] *n* *(POL etc)* reunión *f*, mitin *m*; *(AUT)* rallye *m*; *(TENNIS)* peloteo ♦ *vt* reu-

nir ♦ *vi* recuperarse; ~ **round** *vt fus* (*fig*)
dar apoyo a

RAM [ræm] *n abbr* (= *random access
memory*) RAM *f*

ram [ræm] *n* carnero; (*also: battering* ~)
ariete *m* ♦ *vt* (*crash into*) dar contra, chocar
con; (*push: fist etc*) empujar con fuerza

ramble ['ræmbl] *n* caminata, excursión *f* en
el campo ♦ *vi* (*pej: also:* ~ **on**) divagar; ~**r**
n excursionista *m/f*; (*BOT*) trepadora; **ram-
bling** *adj* (*speech*) inconexo; (*house*) labe-
ríntico; (*BOT*) trepador(a)

ramp [ræmp] *n* rampa; **on/off** ~ (*US: AUT*)
vía de acceso/salida

rampage [ræm'peɪdʒ] *n*: **to be on the** ~
desmandarse ♦ *vi*: **they went rampaging
through the town** recorrieron la ciudad
armando alboroto

rampant ['ræmpɔnt] *adj* (*disease etc*): **to be**
~ estar extendiéndose mucho

rampart ['ræmpɑːt] *n* (*fortification*) baluarte
m

ramshackle ['ræmʃækl] *adj* destartalado

ran [ræn] *pt of* **run**

ranch [rɑːntʃ] *n* hacienda, estancia; ~**er** *n*
ganadero

rancid ['rænsɪd] *adj* rancio

rancour ['ræŋkə*] (*US* **rancor**) *n* rencor *m*

random ['rændəm] *adj* fortuito, sin orden;
(*COMPUT, MATH*) aleatorio ♦ *n*: **at** ~ al
azar

randy ['rændɪ] (*BRIT: inf*) *adj* cachondo

rang [ræŋ] *pt of* **ring**

range [reɪndʒ] *n* (*of mountains*) cadena de
montañas, cordillera; (*of missile*) alcance
m; (*of voice*) registro; (*series*) serie *f*; (*of
products*) surtido; (*MIL: also: shooting* ~)
campo de tiro; (*also: kitchen* ~) fogón *m* ♦
vt (*place*) colocar; (*arrange*) arreglar ♦ *vi*: **to**
~ **over** (*extend*) extenderse por; **to** ~ **from**
... **to** ... oscilar entre ... y ...

ranger [reɪndʒə*] *n* guardabosques *m inv*

rank [ræŋk] *n* (*row*) fila; (*MIL*) rango; (*status*) categoría; (*BRIT: also: taxi* ~) parada
de taxis ♦ *vi*: **to** ~ **among** figurar entre ♦
adj fétido, rancio; **the** ~ **and file** (*fig*) la
base

rankle ['ræŋkl] *vi* doler

ransack ['rænsæk] *vt* (*search*) registrar;
(*plunder*) saquear

ransom ['rænsəm] *n* rescate *m*; **to hold to**
~ (*fig*) hacer chantaje a

rant [rænt] *vi* divagar, desvariar

rap [ræp] *vt* golpear, dar un golpecito en ♦
n (*music*) rap *m*

rape [reɪp] *n* violación *f*; (*BOT*) colza ♦ *vt*
violar; ~ (**seed**) **oil** *n* aceite *m* de colza

rapid ['ræpɪd] *adj* rápido; ~**ity** [rə'pɪdɪtɪ] *n*
rapidez *f*; ~**ly** *adv* rápidamente; ~**s** *npl*
(*GEO*) rápidos *mpl*

rapist ['reɪpɪst] *n* violador *m*

rapport [ræ'pɔː*] *n* simpatía

rapture ['ræptʃə*] *n* éxtasis *m*; **rapturous**
adj extático

rare [rɛə*] *adj* raro, poco común; (*CULIN:
steak*) poco hecho

rarely ['rɛəlɪ] *adv* pocas veces

raring ['rɛərɪŋ] *adj*: **to be** ~ **to go** (*inf*) tener muchas ganas de empezar

rarity ['rɛərɪtɪ] *n* rareza, escasez *f*

rascal ['rɑːskl] *n* pillo, pícaro

rash [ræʃ] *adj* imprudente, precipitado ♦ *n*
(*MED*) sarpullido, erupción *f* (cutánea); (*of
events*) serie *f*

rasher ['ræʃə*] *n* lonja

raspberry ['rɑːzbərɪ] *n* frambuesa

rasping ['rɑːspɪŋ] *adj*: **a** ~ **noise** un ruido
áspero

rat [ræt] *n* rata

rate [reɪt] *n* (*ratio*) razón *f*; (*price*) precio; (:
of hotel etc) tarifa; (*of interest*) tipo; (*speed*)
velocidad *f* ♦ *vt* (*value*) tasar; (*estimate*) estimar; ~**s** *npl* (*BRIT: property tax*) impuesto
municipal; (*fees*) tarifa; **to** ~ **sth/sb as**
considerar algo/a uno como; ~**able value**
(*BRIT*) *n* valor *m* impuesto; ~**payer** (*BRIT*)
n contribuyente *m/f*

rather ['rɑːðə*] *adv*: **it's** ~ **expensive** es
algo caro; (*too much*) es demasiado caro;
(*to some extent*) más bien; **there's** ~ **a lot**
hay bastante; **I would** *or* **I'd** ~ **go** preferiría
ir; **or** ~ mejor dicho

ratify ['rætɪfaɪ] *vt* ratificar

rating ['reɪtɪŋ] *n* tasación *f*; (*score*) índice
m; (*BRIT: NAUT: sailor*) marinero; (*of ship*)
clase *f*; ~**s** *npl* (*RADIO, TV*) niveles *mpl* de
audiencia

ratio ['reɪʃɪəʊ] *n* razón *f*; **in the** ~ **of 100
to 1** a razón de 100 a 1

ration ['ræʃən] *n* ración *f* ♦ *vt* racionar; ~**s**
npl víveres *mpl*

rational ['ræʃənl] *adj* (*solution, reasoning*)
lógico, razonable; (*person*) cuerdo, sensato;
~**e** [-'nɑːl] *n* razón *f* fundamental; ~**ize** *vt*
justificar

rationing ['ræʃnɪŋ] *n* racionamiento

rat race *n* lucha incesante por la supervivencia

rattle ['rætl] *n* golpeteo; (*of train etc*) traqueteo; (*for baby*) sonaja, sonajero ♦ *vi* castañetear; (*car, bus*): **to** ~ **along** traquetear
♦ *vt* hacer sonar agitando; ~**snake** *n* serpiente *f* de cascabel

raucous ['rɔːkəs] *adj* estridente, ronco

ravage ['rævɪdʒ] *vt* hacer estragos en, destrozar; ~**s** *npl* estragos *mpl*

rave [reɪv] *vi* (*in anger*) encolerizarse; (*with
enthusiasm*) entusiasmarse; (*MED*) delirar,
desvariar

raven ['reɪvən] *n* cuervo

ravenous ['rævənəs] *adj* hambriento

ravine [rə'viːn] *n* barranco

raving ['reɪvɪŋ] *adj*: ~ **lunatic** loco/a de
atar

ravishing ['rævɪʃɪŋ] adj encantador(a)

raw [rɔ:] adj crudo; (not processed) bruto; (sore) vivo; (inexperienced) novato, inexperto; ~ **deal** (inf) n injusticia; ~ **material** n materia prima

ray [reɪ] n rayo; ~ **of hope** (rayo de) esperanza

rayon ['reɪɔn] n rayón m

raze [reɪz] vt arrasar

razor ['reɪzə*] n (open) navaja; (safety ~) máquina de afeitar; (electric ~) máquina (eléctrica) de afeitar; ~ **blade** n hoja de afeitar

Rd abbr = **road**

re [ri:] prep con referencia a

reach [ri:tʃ] n alcance m; (of river etc) extensión f entre dos recodos ♦ vt alcanzar, llegar a; (achieve) lograr ♦ vi extenderse; **within** ~ al alcance (de la mano); **out of** ~ fuera del alcance; ~ **out** vt: (hand) tender ♦ vi: **to** ~ **out for sth** alargar or tender la mano para tomar algo

react [ri:'ækt] vi reaccionar; ~**ion** [-'ækʃən] n reacción f

reactor [ri:'æktə*] n (also: nuclear ~) reactor m (nuclear)

read [ri:d, pt, pp rɛd] (pt, pp **read**) vi leer ♦ vt leer; (understand) entender; (study) estudiar; ~ **out** vt leer en alta voz; ~**able** adj (writing) legible; (book) leíble; ~**er** n lector(a) m/f; (book) libro de lecturas; (BRIT: at university) profesor(a) m/f adjunto/a; ~**ership** n (of paper etc) (número de) lectores mpl

readily ['rɛdɪlɪ] adv (willingly) de buena gana; (easily) fácilmente; (quickly) en seguida

readiness ['rɛdɪnɪs] n buena voluntad f; (preparedness) preparación f; **in** ~ (prepared) listo, preparado

reading ['ri:dɪŋ] n lectura; (on instrument) indicación f

readjust [ri:ə'dʒʌst] vt reajustar ♦ vi (adapt): **to** ~ (**to**) reajustarse (a)

ready ['rɛdɪ] adj listo, preparado; (willing) dispuesto; (available) disponible ♦ adv: ~- **cooked** listo para comer ♦ n: **at the** ~ (MIL) listo para tirar; **to get** ~ vi prepararse ♦ vt preparar; ~**-made** adj confeccionado; ~ **money** n dinero contante; ~ **reckoner** n libro de cálculos hechos; ~**-to-wear** adj confeccionado

real [rɪəl] adj verdadero, auténtico; **in** ~ **terms** en términos reales; ~ **estate** n bienes mpl raíces; ~**istic** [-'lɪstɪk] adj realista

reality [ri:'ælɪtɪ] n realidad f

realization [rɪəlaɪ'zeɪʃən] n comprensión f; (fulfilment, COMM) realización f

realize ['rɪəlaɪz] vt (understand) darse cuenta de; (fulfil, COMM: asset) realizar

really ['rɪəlɪ] adv realmente; (for emphasis) verdaderamente: **what** ~ **hap-**

pened lo que pasó en realidad; ~**?** ¿de veras?; ~**!** (annoyance) ¡vamos!, ¡por favor!

realm [rɛlm] n reino; (fig) esfera

realtor ['rɪəltɔ:*] n (US) n corredor(a) m/f de bienes raíces

reap [ri:p] vt segar; (fig) cosechar, recoger

reappear [ri:ə'pɪə*] vi reaparecer

rear [rɪə*] adj trasero ♦ n parte f trasera ♦ vt (cattle, family) criar ♦ vi (also: ~ **up**) (animal) encabritarse; ~**guard** n retaguardia

rearmament [ri:'ɑ:məmənt] n rearme m

rearrange [ri:ə'reɪndʒ] vt ordenar or arreglar de nuevo

rear-view: ~ **mirror** n (AUT) (espejo) retrovisor m

reason ['ri:zn] n razón f ♦ vi: **to** ~ **with sb** tratar de que uno entre en razón; **it stands to** ~ **that** es lógico que; ~**able** adj razonable; (sensible) sensato; ~**ably** adv razonablemente; ~**ed** adj (argument) razonado; ~**ing** n razonamiento, argumentos mpl

reassurance [ri:ə'ʃuərəns] n consuelo

reassure [ri:ə'ʃuə*] vt tranquilizar, alentar; **to** ~ **sb that** tranquilizar a uno asegurando que; **reassuring** adj alentador(a)

rebate ['ri:beɪt] n (on tax etc) desgravación f

rebel [n 'rɛbl, vi rɪ'bɛl] n rebelde m/f ♦ vi rebelarse, sublevarse; ~**lion** [rɪ'bɛljən] n rebelión f, sublevación f; ~**lious** [rɪ'bɛljəs] adj rebelde; (child) revoltoso

rebirth ['ri:bə:θ] n renacimiento

rebound [vi rɪ'baund, n 'ri:baund] vi (ball) rebotar ♦ n rebote m; **on the** ~ (also fig) de rebote

rebuff [rɪ'bʌf] n desaire m, rechazo

rebuild [ri:'bɪld] (irreg) vt reconstruir

rebuke [rɪ'bju:k] n reprimenda ♦ vt reprender

rebut [rɪ'bʌt] vt rebatir

recall [rɪ'kɔ:l] vt (remember) recordar; (ambassador etc) retirar ♦ n recuerdo; retirada

recant [rɪ'kænt] vi retractarse

recap ['ri:kæp] vt, vi recapitular

recapitulate [ri:kə'pɪtjuleɪt] vt, vi = **recap**

recapture [ri:'kæptʃə*] vt recobrar

rec'd abbr (= received) rbdo

recede [rɪ'si:d] vi (memory) ir borrándose; (hair) retroceder; **receding** adj (forehead, chin) huidizo; (hair): **to have a receding hairline** tener entradas

receipt [rɪ'si:t] n (document) recibo; (for parcel etc) acuse m de recibo; (act of receiving) recepción f; ~**s** npl (COMM) ingresos mpl

receive [rɪ'si:v] vt recibir; (guest) acoger; (wound) sufrir; ~**r** n (TEL) auricular m; (RADIO) receptor m; (of stolen goods) perista m/f; (COMM) administrador m jurídico

recent ['ri:snt] adj reciente; ~**ly** adv recientemente; ~**ly arrived** recién llegado

receptacle [rɪ'sɛptɪkl] n receptáculo

reception [rɪ'sɛpʃən] *n* recepción *f*; (*welcome*) acogida; ~ **desk** *n* recepción *f*; ~**ist** *n* recepcionista *m/f*

recess [rɪ'sɛs] *n* (*in room*) hueco; (*for bed*) nicho; (*secret place*) escondrijo; (*POL etc: holiday*) clausura; ~**ion** [-'sɛʃən] *n* recesión *f*

recharge [riː'tʃɑːdʒ] *vt* (*battery*) recargar

recipe ['rɛsɪpɪ] *n* receta; (*for disaster, success*) fórmula

recipient [rɪ'sɪpɪənt] *n* recibidor(a) *m/f*; (*of letter*) destinatario/a

recital [rɪ'saɪtl] *n* recital *m*

recite [rɪ'saɪt] *vt* (*poem*) recitar

reckless ['rɛkləs] *adj* temerario, imprudente; (*driving, driver*) peligroso; ~**ly** *adv* imprudentemente; de modo peligroso

reckon ['rɛkən] *vt* calcular; (*consider*) considerar; (*think*): **I** ~ **that ... me** parece que ...; ~ **on** *vt fus* contar con; ~**ing** *n* cálculo

reclaim [rɪ'kleɪm] *vt* (*land, waste*) recuperar; (*land: from sea*) rescatar; (*demand back*) reclamar

reclamation [rɛklə'meɪʃən] *n* (*of land*) acondicionamiento de tierras

recline [rɪ'klaɪn] *vi* reclinarse; **reclining** *adj* (*seat*) reclinable

recluse [rɪ'kluːs] *n* recluso/a

recognition [rɛkəg'nɪʃən] *n* reconocimiento; **transformed beyond** ~ irreconocible

recognizable ['rɛkəgnaɪzəbl] *adj*: ~ (**by**) reconocible (por)

recognize ['rɛkəgnaɪz] *vt*: **to** ~ (**by/as**) reconocer (por/como)

recoil [*vi* rɪ'kɔɪl, *n* 'riːkɔɪl] *vi* (*person*): **to** ~ **from doing sth** retraerse de hacer algo ♦ *n* (*of gun*) retroceso

recollect [rɛkə'lɛkt] *vt* recordar, acordarse de; ~**ion** [-'lɛkʃən] *n* recuerdo

recommend [rɛkə'mɛnd] *vt* recomendar

reconcile ['rɛkənsaɪl] *vt* (*two people*) reconciliar; (*two facts*) compaginar; **to** ~ **o.s. to sth** conformarse a algo

recondition [riːkən'dɪʃən] *vt* (*machine*) reacondicionar

reconnaissance [rɪ'kɒnɪsns] *n* (*MIL*) reconocimiento

reconnoitre [rɛkə'nɔɪtə*] (*US* **reconnoiter**) *vt, vi* (*MIL*) reconocer

reconsider [riːkən'sɪdə*] *vt* repensar

reconstruct [riːkən'strʌkt] *vt* reconstruir

record [*n* 'rɛkɔːd, *vt* rɪ'kɔːd] *n* (*MUS*) disco; (*of meeting etc*) acta; (*register*) registro, partida; (*file*) archivo; (*also: criminal* ~) antecedentes *mpl*; (*written*) expediente *m*; (*SPORT, COMPUT*) récord *m* ♦ *vt* registrar; (*MUS: song etc*) grabar; **in** ~ **time** en un tiempo récord; **off the** ~ *adj* no oficial ♦ *adv* confidencialmente; ~ **card** *n* (*in file*) ficha; ~**ed delivery** (*BRIT*) *n* (*POST*) entrega con acuse de recibo; ~**er** *n* (*MUS*) flauta de pico; ~ **holder** *n* (*SPORT*) actual poseedor(a)

m/f del récord; ~**ing** *n* (*MUS*) grabación *f*; ~ **player** *n* tocadiscos *m inv*

recount [rɪ'kaʊnt] *vt* contar

re-count [*n* 'riːkaʊnt, *vb* riː'kaʊnt] *n* (*POL: of votes*) segundo escrutinio ♦ *vt* volver a contar

recoup [rɪ'kuːp] *vt*: **to** ~ **one's losses** recuperar las pérdidas

recourse [rɪ'kɔːs] *n*: **to have** ~ **to** recurrir a

recover [rɪ'kʌvə*] *vt* recuperar ♦ *vi* (*from illness, shock*) recuperarse; ~**y** *n* recuperación *f*

recreation [rɛkrɪ'eɪʃən] *n* recreo; ~**al** *adj* de recreo

recruit [rɪ'kruːt] *n* recluta *m/f* ♦ *vt* reclutar; (*staff*) contratar (personal); ~**ment** *n* reclutamiento

rectangle ['rɛktæŋgl] *n* rectángulo; **rectangular** [-'tæŋgjulə*] *adj* rectangular

rectify ['rɛktɪfaɪ] *vt* rectificar

rector ['rɛktə*] *n* (*REL*) párroco; ~**y** *n* casa del párroco

recuperate [rɪ'kuːpəreɪt] *vi* reponerse, restablecerse

recur [rɪ'kɜː*] *vi* repetirse; (*pain, illness*) producirse de nuevo; ~**rence** [rɪ'kʌrəns] *n* repetición *f*; ~**rent** [rɪ'kʌrənt] *adj* repetido

recycle [riː'saɪkl] *vt* reciclar

red [rɛd] *n* rojo ♦ *adj* rojo; (*hair*) pelirrojo; (*wine*) tinto; **to be in the** ~ (*account*) estar en números rojos; (*business*) tener un saldo negativo; **to give sb the** ~ **carpet treatment** recibir a uno con todos los honores; **R~ Cross** *n* Cruz *f* Roja; ~**currant** *n* grosella roja; ~**den** *vt* enrojecer ♦ *vi* enrojecerse; ~**dish** *adj* rojizo

redeem [rɪ'diːm] *vt* redimir; (*promises*) cumplir; (*sth in pawn*) desempeñar; (*fig, also REL*) rescatar; ~**ing** *adj*: ~**ing feature** rasgo bueno *or* favorable

redeploy [riːdɪ'plɔɪ] *vt* (*resources*) reorganizar

red: ~**-haired** *adj* pelirrojo; ~**-handed** *adj*: **to be caught** ~**-handed** cogerse (*SP*) *or* pillarse (*AM*) con las manos en la masa; ~**head** *n* pelirrojo/a; ~ **herring** *n* (*fig*) pista falsa; ~**-hot** *adj* candente

redirect [riːdaɪ'rɛkt] *vt* (*mail*) reexpedir

red light *n*: **to go through a** ~ (*AUT*) pasar la luz roja; **red-light district** *n* barrio chino

redo [riː'duː] (*irreg*) *vt* rehacer

redolent ['rɛdələnt] *adj*: ~ **of** (*smell*) con fragancia *q*; **to be** ~ **of** (*fig*) recordar

redouble [riː'dʌbl] *vt*: **to** ~ **one's efforts** intensificar los esfuerzos

redress [rɪ'drɛs] *n* reparación *f* ♦ *vt* reparar

Red Sea *n*: **the** ~ el mar Rojo

redskin ['rɛdskɪn] *n* piel roja *m/f*

red tape *n* (*fig*) trámites *mpl*

reduce [rɪ'djuːs] *vt* reducir; **to** ~ **sb to**

tears hacer llorar a uno; **to be ~d to begging** no quedarle a uno otro remedio que pedir limosna; *"~ speed now"* (AUT) "reduzca la velocidad"; **at a ~d price** (*of goods*) (a precio) rebajado; **reduction** [rɪ'dʌkʃən] *n* reducción *f*; (*of price*) rebaja; (*discount*) descuento; (*smaller-scale copy*) copia reducida

redundancy [rɪ'dʌndənsɪ] *n* (*dismissal*) despido; (*unemployment*) desempleo

redundant [rɪ'dʌndnt] *adj* (BRIT: *worker*) parado, sin trabajo; (*detail, object*) superfluo; **to be made ~** quedar(se) sin trabajo

reed [riːd] *n* (BOT) junco, caña; (MUS) lengüeta

reef [riːf] *n* (*at sea*) arrecife *m*

reek [riːk] *vi*: **to ~ (of)** apestar (a)

reel [riːl] *n* carrete *m*, bobina; (*of film*) rollo; (*dance*) baile *m* escocés ♦ *vt* (*also*: ~ *up*) devanar; (*also*: ~ *in*) sacar ♦ *vi* (*sway*) tambalear(se)

ref [ref] (*inf*) *n abbr* = **referee**

refectory [rɪ'fektərɪ] *n* comedor *m*

refer [rɪ'fɜː*] *vt* (*send*: *patient*) referir; (: *matter*) remitir ♦ *vi*: **to ~ to** (*allude to*) referirse a; (*apply to*) relacionarse con; (*consult*) consultar

referee [refə'riː] *n* árbitro; (BRIT: *for job application*): **to be a ~ for sb** proporcionar referencias a uno ♦ *vt* (*match*) arbitrar en

reference ['refrəns] *n* referencia; (*for job application*: *letter*) carta de recomendación; **with ~ to** (COMM: *in letter*) me remito a; **~ book** *n* libro de consulta; **~ number** *n* número de referencia

refill [*vt* riː'fɪl, *n* 'riːfɪl] *vt* rellenar ♦ *n* repuesto, recambio

refine [rɪ'faɪn] *vt* refinar; **~d** *adj* (*person*) fino; **~ment** *n* cultura, educación *f*; (*of system*) refinamiento

reflect [rɪ'flekt] *vt* reflejar ♦ *vi* (*think*) reflexionar, pensar; **it ~s badly/well on him** le perjudica/le hace honor; **~ion** [-'flekʃən] *n* (*act*) reflexión *f*; (*image*) reflejo; (*criticism*): **on ~ion** pensándolo bien; **~or** *n* (AUT) captafaros *m inv*; (*of light, heat*) reflector *m*

reflex ['riːfleks] *adj*, *n* reflejo; **~ive** [rɪ'fleksɪv] *adj* (LING) reflexivo

reform [rɪ'fɔːm] *n* reforma ♦ *vt* reformar; **the R~ation** [refə'meɪʃən] *n* la Reforma; **~atory** (US) *n* reformatorio

refrain [rɪ'freɪn] *vi*: **to ~ from doing** abstenerse de hacer ♦ *n* estribillo

refresh [rɪ'freʃ] *vt* refrescar; **~er course** (BRIT) *n* curso de repaso; **~ing** *adj* refrescante; **~ments** *npl* refrescos *mpl*

refrigerator [rɪ'frɪdʒəreɪtə*] *n* nevera (SP), refrigeradora (AM)

refuel [riː'fjuəl] *vi* repostar (combustible)

refuge ['refjuːdʒ] *n* refugio, asilo; **to take ~ in** refugiarse en

refugee [refjuˈdʒiː] *n* refugiado/a

refund [*n* 'riːfʌnd, *vb* rɪ'fʌnd] *n* reembolso ♦ *vt* devolver, reembolsar

refurbish [riːˈfɜːbɪʃ] *vt* restaurar, renovar

refusal [rɪ'fjuːzəl] *n* negativa; **to have first ~ on** tener la primera opción a

refuse [*n* 'refjuːs, *vb* rɪ'fjuːz] *n* basura ♦ *vt* rechazar; (*invitation*) declinar; (*permission*) denegar ♦ *vi*: **to ~ to do sth** negarse a hacer algo; (*horse*) rehusar; **~ collection** *n* recolección *f* de basuras

regain [rɪ'geɪn] *vt* recobrar, recuperar

regal ['riːgl] *adj* regio, real

regalia [rɪ'geɪlɪə] *n* insignias *fpl*

regard [rɪ'gɑːd] *n* mirada; (*esteem*) respeto; (*attention*) consideración *f* ♦ *vt* (*consider*) considerar; **to give one's ~s to** saludar de su parte a; *"with kindest ~s"* "con muchos recuerdos"; **~ing**, **as ~s**, **with ~ to** con respecto a, en cuanto a; **~less** *adv* a pesar de todo; **~less of** sin reparar en

régime [reɪ'ʒiːm] *n* régimen *m*

regiment ['redʒɪmənt] *n* regimiento; **~al** [-'mentl] *adj* militar

region ['riːdʒən] *n* región *f*; **in the ~ of** (*fig*) alrededor de; **~al** *adj* regional

register ['redʒɪstə*] *n* registro ♦ *vt* registrar; (*birth*) declarar; (*car*) matricular; (*letter*) certificar; (*subj*: *instrument*) marcar, indicar ♦ *vi* (*at hotel*) registrarse; (*as student*) matricularse; (*make impression*) producir impresión; **~ed** *adj* (*letter, parcel*) certificado; **~ed trademark** *n* marca registrada

registrar ['redʒɪstrɑː*] *n* secretario/a (del registro civil)

registration [redʒɪs'treɪʃən] *n* (*act*) declaración *f*; (AUT: also: **~ number**) matrícula

registry ['redʒɪstrɪ] *n* registro; **~ office** (BRIT) *n* registro civil; **to get married in a ~ office** casarse por lo civil

regret [rɪ'gret] *n* sentimiento, pesar *m* ♦ *vt* sentir, lamentar; **~fully** *adv* con pesar; **~table** *adj* lamentable

regular ['regjulə*] *adj* regular; (*soldier*) profesional; (*usual*) habitual; (: *doctor*) de cabecera ♦ *n* (*client etc*) cliente/a *m/f* habitual; **~ity** [-'lærɪtɪ] *n* regularidad *f*; **~ly** *adv* con regularidad; (*often*) repetidas veces

regulate ['regjuleɪt] *vt* controlar; **regulation** [-'leɪʃən] *n* (*rule*) regla, reglamento

rehearsal [rɪ'hɜːsəl] *n* ensayo

rehearse [rɪ'hɜːs] *vt* ensayar

reign [reɪn] *n* reinado; (*fig*) predominio ♦ *vi* reinar; (*fig*) imperar

reimburse [riːɪm'bɜːs] *vt* reembolsar

rein [reɪn] *n* (*for horse*) rienda

reindeer ['reɪndɪə*] *n inv* reno

reinforce [riːɪn'fɔːs] *vt* reforzar; **~d concrete** *n* hormigón *m* armado; **~ment** *n* (*action*) refuerzo; **~ments** *npl* (MIL) refuerzos *mpl*

reinstate [riːɪn'steɪt] *vt* reintegrar; (*tax, law*)

reinstaurar

reiterate [riː'ɪtəreɪt] *vt* reiterar, repetir

reject [*n* 'riːdʒekt, *vb* rɪ'dʒekt] *n* (*thing*) desecho ♦ *vt* rechazar; (*suggestion*) descartar; (*coin*) expulsar; **~ion** [rɪ'dʒekʃən] *n* rechazo

rejoice [rɪ'dʒɔɪs] *vi*: **to ~ at** *or* **over** regocijarse *or* alegrarse de

rejuvenate [rɪ'dʒuːvəneɪt] *vt* rejuvenecer

relapse [rɪ'læps] *n* recaída

relate [rɪ'leɪt] *vt* (*tell*) contar, relatar; (*connect*) relacionar ♦ *vi* relacionarse; **~d** *adj* afín; (*person*) emparentado; **~d to** (*subject*) relacionado con; **relating to** referente a

relation [rɪ'leɪʃən] *n* (*person*) familiar *m/f*, pariente/a *m/f*; (*link*) relación *f*; **~s** *npl* (*relatives*) familiares *mpl*; **~ship** *n* relación *f*; (*personal*) relaciones *fpl*; (*also:* family **~ship**) parentesco

relative ['relətɪv] *n* pariente/a *m/f*, familiar *m/f* ♦ *adj* relativo; **~ly** *adv* (*comparatively*) relativamente

relax [rɪ'læks] *vi* descansar; (*unwind*) relajarse ♦ *vt* (*one's grip*) soltar, aflojar; (*control*) relajar; (*mind, person*) descansar; **~ation** [riːlæk'seɪʃən] *n* descanso; (*of rule, control*) relajamiento; (*entertainment*) diversión *f*; **~ed** *adj* relajado; (*tranquil*) tranquilo; **~ing** *adj* relajante

relay ['riːleɪ] *n* (*race*) carrera de relevos ♦ *vt* (*RADIO, TV*) retransmitir

release [rɪ'liːs] *n* (*liberation*) liberación *f*; (*from prison*) puesta en libertad; (*of gas etc*) escape *m*; (*of film etc*) estreno; (*of record*) lanzamiento ♦ *vt* (*prisoner*) poner en libertad; (*gas*) despedir, arrojar; (*from wreckage*) soltar; (*catch, spring etc*) desenganchar; (*film*) estrenar; (*book*) publicar; (*news*) difundir

relegate ['relɪgeɪt] *vt* relegar; (*BRIT: SPORT*): **to be ~d to** bajar a

relent [rɪ'lent] *vi* ablandarse; **~less** *adj* implacable

relevant ['relɪvənt] *adj* (*fact*) pertinente; **~ to** relacionado con

reliability [rɪlaɪə'bɪlɪtɪ] *n* fiabilidad *f*; seguridad *f*; veracidad *f*

reliable [rɪ'laɪəbl] *adj* (*person, firm*) de confianza, de fiar; (*method, machine*) seguro; (*source*) fidedigno; **reliably** *adv*: **to be reliably informed that ...** saber de fuente fidedigna que ...

reliance [rɪ'laɪəns] *n*: **~ (on)** dependencia (de)

relic ['relɪk] *n* (*REL*) reliquia; (*of the past*) vestigio

relief [rɪ'liːf] *n* (*from pain, anxiety*) alivio; (*help, supplies*) socorro, ayuda; (*ART, GEO*) relieve *m*

relieve [rɪ'liːv] *vt* (*pain*) aliviar; (*bring help to*) ayudar, socorrer; (*take over from*) sustituir; (*: guard*) relevar; **to ~ sb of sth** quitar

algo a uno; **to ~ o.s.** hacer sus necesidades

religion [rɪ'lɪdʒən] *n* religión *f*; **religious** *adj* religioso

relinquish [rɪ'lɪŋkwɪʃ] *vt* abandonar; (*plan, habit*) renunciar a

relish ['relɪʃ] *n* (*CULIN*) salsa; (*enjoyment*) entusiasmo ♦ *vt* (*food etc*) saborear; (*enjoy*): **to ~ sth** hacerle mucha ilusión a uno algo

relocate [riːləu'keɪt] *vt* cambiar de lugar, mudar ♦ *vi* mudarse

reluctance [rɪ'lʌktəns] *n* renuencia; **reluctant** *adj* renuente; **reluctantly** *adv* de mala gana

rely on [rɪ'laɪ-] *vt fus* depender de; (*trust*) contar con

remain [rɪ'meɪn] *vi* (*survive*) quedar; (*be left*) sobrar; (*continue*) quedar(se), permanecer; **~der** *n* resto; **~ing** *adj* que queda(n); (*surviving*) restante(s); **~s** *npl* restos *mpl*

remand [rɪ'mɑːnd] *n*: **on ~** detenido (bajo custodia) ♦ *vt*: **to be ~ed in custody** quedar detenido bajo custodia; **~ home** (*BRIT*) *n* reformatorio

remark [rɪ'mɑːk] *n* comentario ♦ *vt* comentar; **~able** *adj* (*outstanding*) extraordinario

remarry [riː'mærɪ] *vi* volver a casarse

remedial [rɪ'miːdɪəl] *adj* de recuperación

remedy ['remədɪ] *n* remedio ♦ *vt* remediar, curar

remember [rɪ'membə*] *vt* recordar, acordarse de; (*bear in mind*) tener presente; (*send greetings to*): **~ me to him** dale recuerdos de mi parte; **remembrance** *n* recuerdo

remind [rɪ'maɪnd] *vt*: **to ~ sb to do sth** recordar a uno que haga algo; **to ~ sb of sth** (*of fact*) recordar algo a uno; **she ~s me of her mother** me recuerda a su madre; **~er** *n* notificación *f*; (*memento*) recuerdo

reminisce [remɪ'nɪs] *vi* recordar (viejas historias); **~nt** *adj*: **to be ~nt of sth** recordar algo

remiss [rɪ'mɪs] *adj* descuidado; **it was ~ of him** fue un descuido de su parte

remission [rɪ'mɪʃən] *n* remisión *f*; (*of prison sentence*) disminución *f* de pena; (*REL*) perdón *m*

remit [rɪ'mɪt] *vt* (*send: money*) remitir, enviar; **~tance** *n* remesa, envío

remnant ['remnənt] *n* resto; (*of cloth*) retal *m*; **~s** *npl* (*COMM*) restos *mpl* de serie

remorse [rɪ'mɔːs] *n* remordimientos *mpl*; **~ful** *adj* arrepentido; **~less** *adj* (*fig*) implacable, inexorable

remote [rɪ'məut] *adj* (*distant*) lejano; (*person*) distante; **~ control** *n* telecontrol *m*; **~ly** *adv* remotamente; (*slightly*) levemente

remould ['riːməuld] (*BRIT*) *n* (*tyre*) neumático *or* llanta (*AM*) recauchutado/a

removable [rɪ'muːvəbl] *adj (detachable)* separable

removal [rɪ'muːvəl] *n (taking away)* el quitar; *(BRIT: from house)* mudanza; *(from office: dismissal)* destitución *f*; *(MED)* extirpación *f*; **~ van** *(BRIT) n* camión *m* de mudanzas

remove [rɪ'muːv] *vt* quitar; *(employee)* destituir; *(name: from list)* tachar, borrar; *(doubt)* disipar; *(abuse)* suprimir, acabar con; *(MED)* extirpar; **~rs** *(BRIT) npl (company)* agencia de mudanzas

Renaissance [rɪ'neɪsɔ̃s] *n*: **the ~** el Renacimiento

render ['rɛndə*] *vt (thanks)* dar; *(aid)* proporcionar, prestar; *(make)*: **to ~ sth useless** hacer algo inútil; **~ing** *n (MUS etc)* interpretación *f*

rendez-vous ['rɔndɪvuː] *n* cita

renew [rɪ'njuː] *vt* renovar; *(resume)* reanudar; *(loan etc)* prorrogar; **~able** *adj* renovable; **~al** *n* reanudación *f*, prórroga

renounce [rɪ'naʊns] *vt* renunciar a; *(right, inheritance)* renunciar

renovate ['rɛnəveɪt] *vt* renovar

renown [rɪ'naʊn] *n* renombre *m*; **~ed** *adj* renombrado

rent [rɛnt] *n (for house)* arriendo, renta ♦ *vt* alquilar; **~al** *n (for television, car)* alquiler *m*

renunciation [rɪnʌnsɪ'eɪʃən] *n* renuncia

rep [rɛp] *n abbr* = **representative; repertory**

repair [rɪ'pɛə*] *n* reparación *f*, compostura ♦ *vt* reparar, componer; *(shoes)* remendar; **in good/bad ~** en buen/mal estado; **~ kit** *n* caja de herramientas

repatriate [riː'pætrɪeɪt] *vt* repatriar

repay [riː'peɪ] *(irreg) vt (money)* devolver, reembolsar; *(person)* pagar; *(debt)* liquidar; *(sb's efforts)* devolver, corresponder a; **~ment** *n* reembolso, devolución *f*; *(sum of money)* recompensa

repeal [rɪ'piːl] *n* revocación *f* ♦ *vt* revocar

repeat [rɪ'piːt] *n (RADIO, TV)* reposición *f* ♦ *vt* repetir ♦ *vi* repetirse; **~edly** *adv* repetidas veces

repel [rɪ'pɛl] *vt (drive away)* rechazar; *(disgust)* repugnar; **~lent** *adj* repugnante ♦ *n*: **insect ~lent** crema *(or* loción *f)* antiinsectos

repent [rɪ'pɛnt] *vi*: **to ~ (of)** arrepentirse (de); **~ance** *n* arrepentimiento

repercussions [riːpə'kʌʃənz] *npl* consecuencias *fpl*

repertoire ['rɛpətwɑː*] *n* repertorio

repertory ['rɛpətərɪ] *n (also: ~ theatre)* teatro de repertorio

repetition [rɛpɪ'tɪʃən] *n* repetición *f*

repetitive [rɪ'pɛtɪtɪv] *adj* repetitivo

replace [rɪ'pleɪs] *vt (put back)* devolver a su sitio; *(take the place of)* reemplazar, sustituir; **~ment** *n (act)* reposición *f*; *(thing)* recambio; *(person)* suplente *m/f*

replay ['riːpleɪ] *n (SPORT)* desempate *m*; *(of tape, film)* repetición *f*

replenish [rɪ'plɛnɪʃ] *vt* rellenar; *(stock etc)* reponer

replica ['rɛplɪkə] *n* copia, reproducción *f* (exacta)

reply [rɪ'plaɪ] *n* respuesta, contestación *f* ♦ *vi* contestar, responder; **~ coupon** *n* cupón-respuesta *m*

report [rɪ'pɔːt] *n* informe *m*; *(PRESS etc)* reportaje *m*; *(BRIT: also: school ~)* boletín *m* escolar; *(of gun)* estallido ♦ *vt* informar de; *(PRESS etc)* hacer un reportaje sobre; *(notify: accident, culprit)* denunciar ♦ *vi (make a report)* presentar un informe; *(present o.s.)*: **to ~ (to sb)** presentarse (ante uno); **~ card** *n (US, Scottish)* cartilla escolar; **~edly** *adv* según se dice; **~er** *n* periodista *m/f*

repose [rɪ'pəʊz] *n*: **in ~** *(face, mouth)* en reposo

reprehensible [rɛprɪ'hɛnsɪbl] *adj* reprensible, censurable

represent [rɛprɪ'zɛnt] *vt* representar; *(COMM)* ser agente de; *(describe)*: **to ~ sth as** describir algo como; **~ation** [-'teɪʃən] *n* representación *f*; **~ations** *npl (protest)* quejas *fpl*; **~ative** *n* representante *m/f*; *(US: POL)* diputado/a *m/f* ♦ *adj* representativo

repress [rɪ'prɛs] *vt* reprimir; **~ion** [-'prɛʃən] *n* represión *f*

reprieve [rɪ'priːv] *n (LAW)* indulto; *(fig)* alivio

reprimand ['rɛprɪmɑːnd] *n* reprimenda ♦ *vt* reprender

reprint ['riːprɪnt] *n* reimpresión *f* ♦ *vt* reimprimir

reprisals [rɪ'praɪzlz] *npl* represalias *fpl*

reproach [rɪ'prəʊtʃ] *n* reproche *m* ♦ *vt*: **to ~ sb for sth** reprochar algo a uno; **~ful** *adj* de reproche, de acusación

reproduce [riːprə'djuːs] *vt* reproducir ♦ *vi* reproducirse; **reproduction** [-'dʌkʃən] *n* reproducción *f*

reproof [rɪ'pruːf] *n* reproche *m*

reprove [rɪ'pruːv] *vt*: **to ~ sb for sth** reprochar algo a uno

reptile ['rɛptaɪl] *n* reptil *m*

republic [rɪ'pʌblɪk] *n* república; **~an** *adj*, *n* republicano/a *m/f*

repudiate [rɪ'pjuːdɪeɪt] *vt* rechazar; *(violence etc)* repudiar

repulse [rɪ'pʌls] *vt* rechazar; **repulsive** *adj* repulsivo

reputable ['rɛpjutəbl] *adj (make etc)* de renombre

reputation [rɛpju'teɪʃən] *n* reputación *f*

reputed [rɪ'pjuːtɪd] *adj* supuesto; **~ly** *adv* según dicen *or* se dice

request [rɪ'kwɛst] n petición f; (formal) solicitud f ♦ vt: **to ~ sth of** or **from sb** solicitar algo a uno; **~ stop** (BRIT) n parada discrecional

require [rɪ'kwaɪə*] vt (need: subj: person) necesitar, tener necesidad de; (: thing, situation) exigir; (want) pedir; **to ~ sb to do sth** pedir a uno que haga algo; **~ment** n requisito; (need) necesidad f

requisite ['rɛkwɪzɪt] n requisito ♦ adj necesario

requisition [rɛkwɪ'zɪʃən] n: **~ (for)** solicitud f (de) ♦ vt (MIL) requisar

resale ['riːseɪl] n reventa

rescind [rɪ'sɪnd] vt (law) abrogar; (contract, order etc) anular

rescue ['rɛskjuː] n rescate m ♦ vt rescatar; **~ party** n expedición f de salvamento; **~r** n salvador(a) m/f

research [rɪ'sɜːtʃ] n investigaciones fpl ♦ vt investigar; **~er** n investigador(a) m/f

resemblance [rɪ'zɛmbləns] n parecido

resemble [rɪ'zɛmbl] vt parecerse a

resent [rɪ'zɛnt] vt tomar a mal; **~ful** adj resentido; **~ment** n resentimiento

reservation [rɛzə'veɪʃən] n reserva

reserve [rɪ'zɜːv] n reserva; (SPORT) suplente m/f ♦ vt (seats etc) reservar; **~s** npl (MIL) reserva; **in ~** de reserva; **~d** adj reservado

reservoir ['rɛzəvwɑː*] n embalse m

reshuffle [riː'ʃʌfl] n: **Cabinet ~** (POL) remodelación f del gabinete

reside [rɪ'zaɪd] vi residir, vivir

residence ['rɛzɪdəns] n (formal: home) domicilio; (length of stay) permanencia; **~ permit** (BRIT) n permiso de permanencia

resident ['rɛzɪdənt] n (of area) vecino/a; (in hotel) huésped(a) m/f ♦ adj (population) permanente; (doctor) residente; **~ial** [-'dɛnʃəl] adj residencial

residue ['rɛzɪdjuː] n resto

resign [rɪ'zaɪn] vt renunciar a ♦ vi dimitir; **to ~ o.s. to** (situation) resignarse a; **~ation** [rɛzɪg'neɪʃən] n dimisión f; (state of mind) resignación f; **~ed** adj resignado

resilient [rɪ'zɪlɪənt] adj (material) elástico; (person) resistente

resin ['rɛzɪn] n resina

resist [rɪ'zɪst] vt resistir, oponerse a; **~ance** n resistencia

resolute ['rɛzəluːt] adj resuelto; (refusal) tajante

resolution [rɛzə'luːʃən] n (gen) resolución f

resolve [rɪ'zɔlv] n resolución f ♦ vt resolver ♦ vi: **to ~ to do** resolver hacer; **~d** adj resuelto

resort [rɪ'zɔːt] n (town) centro turístico; (recourse) recurso ♦ vi: **to ~ to** recurrir a; **in the last ~** como último recurso

resound [rɪ'zaund] vi: **to ~ (with)** resonar (con); **~ing** adj sonoro, (fig) clamoroso

resource [rɪ'sɔːs] n recurso; **~s** npl recursos mpl; **~ful** adj despabilado, ingenioso

respect [rɪs'pɛkt] n respeto ♦ vt respetar; **~s** npl recuerdos mpl, saludos mpl; **with ~ to** con respecto a; **in this ~** en cuanto a eso; **~able** adj respetable; (large: amount) apreciable; (passable) tolerable; **~ful** adj respetuoso

respective [rɪs'pɛktɪv] adj respectivo; **~ly** adv respectivamente

respite ['rɛspaɪt] n respiro

resplendent [rɪs'plɛndənt] adj resplandeciente

respond [rɪs'pɔnd] vi responder; (react) reaccionar; **response** [-'pɔns] n respuesta; reacción f

responsibility [rɪspɔnsɪ'bɪlɪtɪ] n responsabilidad f

responsible [rɪs'pɔnsɪbl] adj (character) serio, formal; (job) de confianza; (liable): **~ (for)** responsable (de)

responsive [rɪs'pɔnsɪv] adj sensible

rest [rɛst] n descanso, reposo; (MUS, pause) pausa, silencio; (support) apoyo; (remainder) resto ♦ vt (lean): **to ~ sth on/against** apoyar algo en or sobre/contra; **the ~ of them** (people, objects) los demás; **it ~s with him to ...** depende de él el que ....

restaurant ['rɛstərɔŋ] n restaurante m; **~ car** (BRIT) n (RAIL) coche-comedor m

restful ['rɛstful] adj descansado, tranquilo

rest home n residencia para jubilados

restive ['rɛstɪv] adj inquieto; (horse) rebelón(ona)

restless ['rɛstlɪs] adj inquieto

restoration [rɛstə'reɪʃən] n restauración f, devolución f

restore [rɪ'stɔː*] vt (building) restaurar; (sth stolen) devolver; (health) restablecer; (to power) volver a poner a

restrain [rɪs'treɪn] vt (feeling) contener, refrenar; (person): **to ~ (from doing)** disuadir (de hacer); **~ed** adj reservado; **~t** n (restriction) restricción f; (moderation) moderación f; (of manner) reserva

restrict [rɪs'trɪkt] vt restringir, limitar; **~ion** [-kʃən] n restricción f, limitación f; **~ive** adj restrictivo

rest room (US) n aseos mpl

result [rɪ'zʌlt] n resultado ♦ vi: **to ~ in** terminar en, tener por resultado; **as a ~ of** a consecuencia de

resume [rɪ'zjuːm] vt reanudar ♦ vi comenzar de nuevo

résumé ['reɪzjuːmeɪ] n resumen m; (US) currículum m

resumption [rɪ'zʌmpʃən] n reanudación f

resurgence [rɪ'sɜːdʒəns] n resurgimiento

resurrection [rɛzə'rɛkʃən] n resurrección f

resuscitate [rɪ'sʌsɪteɪt] vt (MED) resucitar

retail ['riːteɪl] *adj, adv* al por menor; ~**er** *n* detallista *m/f* ~ **price** *n* precio de venta al público

retain [rɪ'teɪn] *vt (keep)* retener, conservar; ~**er** *n (fee)* anticipo

retaliate [rɪ'tælɪeɪt] *vi:* **to** ~ **(against)** tomar represalias (contra); **retaliation** [-'eɪʃən] *n* represalias *fpl*

retarded [rɪ'tɑːdɪd] *adj* retrasado

retch [retʃ] *vi* dársele a uno arcadas

retentive [rɪ'tentɪv] *adj (memory)* retentivo

reticent ['retɪsnt] *adj* reservado

retire [rɪ'taɪə*] *vi (give up work)* jubilarse; *(withdraw)* retirarse; *(go to bed)* acostarse; ~**d** *adj (person)* jubilado; ~**ment** *n (giving up work: state)* retiro; *(: act)* jubilación *f*; **retiring** *adj (leaving)* saliente; *(shy)* retraído

retort [rɪ'tɔːt] *vi* contestar

retrace [riː'treɪs] *vt:* **to** ~ **one's steps** volver sobre sus pasos, desandar lo andado

retract [rɪ'trækt] *vt (statement)* retirar; *(claws)* retraer; *(undercarriage, aerial)* replegar

retrain [riː'treɪn] *vt* reciclar; ~**ing** *n* readaptación *f* profesional

retread ['riːtred] *n* neumático *(SP)* or llanta *(AM)* recauchutado/a

retreat [rɪ'triːt] *n (place)* retiro; *(MIL)* retirada ♦ *vi* retirarse

retribution [retrɪ'bjuːʃən] *n* desquite *m*

retrieval [rɪ'triːvəl] *n* recuperación *f*

retrieve [rɪ'triːv] *vt* recobrar; *(situation, honour)* salvar; *(COMPUT)* recuperar; *(error)* reparar; ~**r** *n* perro cobrador

retrograde ['retrəɡreɪd] *adj* retrógrado

retrospect ['retrəspekt] *n:* **in** ~ retrospectivamente; ~**ive** [-'spektɪv] *adj* retrospectivo; *(law)* retroactivo

return [rɪ'tɜːn] *n (going or coming back)* vuelta, regreso; *(of sth stolen etc)* devolución *f*; *(FINANCE: from land, shares)* ganancia, ingresos *mpl* ♦ *cpd (journey)* de regreso; *(BRIT: ticket)* de ida y vuelta; *(match)* de vuelta ♦ *vi (person etc: come or go back)* volver, regresar; *(symptoms etc)* reaparecer; *(regain):* **to** ~ **to** recuperar ♦ *vt* devolver; *(favour, love etc)* corresponder a; *(verdict)* pronunciar; *(POL: candidate)* elegir; ~**s** *npl (COMM)* ingresos *mpl*; **in** ~ **(for)** a cambio (de); **by** ~ **of post** a vuelta de correo; **many happy** ~**s (of the day)!** ¡feliz cumpleaños!

reunion [riː'juːnɪən] *n (of family)* reunión *f*; *(of two people, school)* reencuentro

reunite [riːjuː'naɪt] *vt* reunir; *(reconcile)* reconciliar

rev [rev] *(AUT) n abbr (= revolution)* revolución *f* ♦ *vt (also:* ~ **up)** acelerar

revamp [riː'væmp] *vt (company etc)* reorganizar

reveal [rɪ'viːl] *vt* revelar; ~**ing** *adj* revela-

dor(a)

reveille [rɪ'vælɪ] *n (MIL)* diana

revel ['revl] *vi:* **to** ~ **in sth/in doing sth** gozar de algo/con hacer algo

revelry ['revlrɪ] *n* jarana, juerga

revenge [rɪ'vendʒ] *n* venganza; **to take** ~ **on** vengarse de

revenue ['revənjuː] *n* ingresos *mpl*, rentas *fpl*

reverberate [rɪ'vɜːbəreɪt] *vi (sound)* resonar, retumbar; *(fig: shock)* repercutir; **reverberation** [-'reɪʃən] *n* retumbo, eco; repercusión *f*

revere [rɪ'vɪə*] *vt* venerar; ~**nce** ['revərəns] *n* reverencia

Reverend ['revərənd] *adj (in titles):* **the** ~ **John Smith** *(Anglican)* el Reverendo John Smith; *(Catholic)* el Padre John Smith; *(Protestant)* el Pastor John Smith

reversal [rɪ'vɜːsl] *n (of order)* inversión *f*; *(of direction, policy)* cambio; *(of decision)* revocación *f*

reverse [rɪ'vɜːs] *n (opposite)* contrario; *(back: of cloth)* revés m; *(: of coin)* reverso; *(: of paper)* dorso; *(AUT: also:* ~ **gear)** marcha atrás; *(setback)* revés m ♦ *adj (order)* inverso; *(direction)* contrario; *(process)* opuesto ♦ *vt (decision, AUT)* dar marcha atrás a; *(position, function)* invertir ♦ *vi (BRIT: AUT)* dar marcha atrás; ~-**charge call** *(BRIT) n* llamada a cobro revertido; **reversing lights** *(BRIT) npl (AUT)* luces *fpl* de retroceso

revert [rɪ'vɜːt] *vi:* **to** ~ **to** volver a

review [rɪ'vjuː] *n (magazine, MIL)* revista; *(of book, film)* reseña; *(US: examination)* repaso, examen m ♦ *vt* repasar, examinar; *(MIL)* pasar revista a; *(book, film)* reseñar; ~**er** *n* crítico/a

revile [rɪ'vaɪl] *vt* injuriar, vilipendiar

revise [rɪ'vaɪz] *vt (manuscript)* corregir; *(opinion)* modificar; *(price, procedure)* revisar ♦ *vi (study)* repasar; **revision** [rɪ'vɪʒən] *n* corrección *f*; modificación *f*; *(for exam)* repaso

revitalize [riː'vaɪtəlaɪz] *vt* revivificar

revival [rɪ'vaɪvl] *n (recovery)* reanimación *f*; *(of interest)* renacimiento; *(THEATRE)* reestreno; *(of faith)* despertar m

revive [rɪ'vaɪv] *vt* resucitar; *(custom)* restablecer; *(hope)* despertar; *(play)* reestrenar ♦ *vi (person)* volver en sí; *(business)* reactivarse

revolt [rɪ'vəult] *n* rebelión *f* ♦ *vi* rebelarse, sublevarse ♦ *vt* dar asco a, repugnar; ~**ing** *adj* asqueroso, repugnante

revolution [revə'luːʃən] *n* revolución *f*; ~**ary** *adj, n* revolucionario/a *m/f*; ~**ize** *vt* revolucionar

revolve [rɪ'vɒlv] *vi* dar vueltas, girar; *(life, discussion):* **to** ~ **(a)round** girar en torno a

revolver [rɪ'vɒlvə*] *n* revólver *m*

revolving [rɪ'vɒlvɪŋ] *adj* (*chair, door etc*) giratorio

revue [rɪ'vju:] *n* (*THEATRE*) revista

revulsion [rɪ'vʌlʃən] *n* asco, repugnancia

reward [rɪ'wɔ:d] *n* premio, recompensa ♦ *vt*: **to ~ (for)** recompensar *or* premiar (por); **~ing** *adj* (*fig*) valioso

rewind [ri:'waɪnd] (*irreg*) rebobinar

rewire [ri:'waɪə*] *vt* (*house*) renovar la instalación eléctrica de

rewrite [ri:'raɪt] (*irreg*) *vt* reescribir

rhapsody ['ræpsədɪ] *n* (*MUS*) rapsodia

rhetorical [rɪ'tɒrɪkl] *adj* retórico

rheumatism ['ru:mətɪzəm] *n* reumatismo, reúma *m*

Rhine [raɪn] *n*: **the ~** el (río) Rin

rhinoceros [raɪ'nɒsərəs] *n* rinoceronte *m*

rhododendron [rəʊdə'dɛndrn] *n* rododendro

Rhone [rəʊn] *n*: **the ~** el (río) Ródano

rhubarb ['ru:bɑ:b] *n* ruibarbo

rhyme [raɪm] *n* rima; (*verse*) poesía

rhythm ['rɪðm] *n* ritmo

rib [rɪb] *n* (*ANAT*) costilla ♦ *vt* (*mock*) tomar el pelo a

ribbon ['rɪbən] *n* cinta; **in ~s** (*torn*) hecho trizas

rice [raɪs] *n* arroz *m*; **~ pudding** *n* arroz *m* con leche

rich [rɪtʃ] *adj* rico; (*soil*) fértil; (*food*) pesado; (: *sweet*) empalagoso; (*abundant*): **~ in** (*minerals etc*) rico en; **the ~** *npl* los ricos; **~es** *npl* riqueza; **~ly** *adv* ricamente; (*deserved, earned*) bien

rickets ['rɪkɪts] *n* raquitismo

rickety ['rɪkɪtɪ] *adj* tambaleante

rickshaw ['rɪkʃɔ:] *n* carro de culi

ricochet ['rɪkəʃeɪ] *vi* rebotar

rid [rɪd] (*pt, pp* rid) *vt*: **to ~ sb of sth** librar a uno de algo; **to get ~ of** deshacerse *or* desembarazarse de

ridden ['rɪdn] *pp of* ride

riddle ['rɪdl] *n* (*puzzle*) acertijo; (*mystery*) enigma *m*, misterio ♦ *vt*: **to be ~d with** ser lleno *or* plagado de

ride [raɪd] (*pt* rode, *pp* ridden) *n* paseo; (*distance covered*) viaje *m*, recorrido ♦ *vi* (*as sport*) montar; (*go somewhere: on horse, bicycle*) dar un paseo, pasearse; (*travel: on bicycle, motorcycle, bus*) viajar ♦ *vt* (*a horse*) montar a; (*a bicycle, motorcycle*) andar en; (*distance*) recorrer; **to take sb for a ~** (*fig*) engañar a uno; **~r** *n* (*on horse*) jinete/a *m/f*; (*on bicycle*) ciclista *m/f*; (*on motorcycle*) motociclista *m/f*

ridge [rɪdʒ] *n* (*of hill*) cresta; (*of roof*) caballete *m*; (*wrinkle*) arruga

ridicule ['rɪdɪkju:l] *n* irrisión *f*, burla ♦ *vt* poner en ridículo, burlarse de; **ridiculous** [-'dɪkjʊləs] *adj* ridículo

riding ['raɪdɪŋ] *n* equitación *f*; **I like ~** me gusta montar a caballo; **~ school** *n* escuela de equitación

rife [raɪf] *adj*: **to be ~** ser muy común; **to be ~ with** abundar en

riffraff ['rɪfræf] *n* gentuza

rifle ['raɪfl] *n* rifle *m*, fusil *m* ♦ *vt* saquear; **~ through** *vt* (*papers*) registrar; **~ range** *n* campo de tiro; (*at fair*) tiro al blanco

rift [rɪft] *n* (*in clouds*) claro; (*fig: disagreement*) desavenencia

rig [rɪg] *n* (*also: oil ~: at sea*) plataforma petrolera ♦ *vt* (*election etc*) amañar; **~ out** (*BRIT*) *vt* disfrazar; **~ up** *vt* improvisar; **~ging** *n* (*NAUT*) aparejo

right [raɪt] *adj* (*correct*) correcto, exacto; (*suitable*) indicado, debido; (*proper*) apropiado; (*just*) justo; (*morally good*) bueno; (*not left*) derecho ♦ *n* bueno; (*title, claim*) derecho; (*not left*) derecha ♦ *adv* bien, correctamente; (*not left*) a la derecha; (*exactly*): **~ now** ahora mismo ♦ *vt* enderezar; (*correct*) corregir ♦ *excl* ¡bueno!, ¡está bien!; **to be ~** (*person*) tener razón; (*answer*) ser correcto; (*of clock*): **is that the ~ time?** ¿es esa la hora buena?; **by ~s** en justicia; **on the ~** a la derecha; **to be in the ~** tener razón; **~ away** en seguida; **~ in the middle** exactamente en el centro; **~ angle** *n* ángulo recto; **~eous** ['raɪtʃəs] *adj* justado, honrado; (*anger*) justificado; **~ful** *adj* legítimo; **~-handed** *adj* diestro; **~-hand man** *n* brazo derecho; **~-hand side** *n* derecha; **~ly** *adv* correctamente, debidamente; (*with reason*) con razón; **~ of way** *n* (*on path etc*) derecho de paso; (*AUT*) prioridad *f*; **~-wing** *adj* (*POL*) derechista

rigid ['rɪdʒɪd] *adj* rígido; (*person, ideas*) inflexible

rigmarole ['rɪgmərəʊl] *n* galimatías *m inv*

rigorous ['rɪgərəs] *adj* riguroso

rigour ['rɪgə*] (*US* **rigor**) *n* rigor *m*, severidad *f*

rile [raɪl] *vt* irritar

rim [rɪm] *n* borde *m*; (*of spectacles*) aro; (*of wheel*) llanta

rind [raɪnd] *n* (*of bacon*) corteza; (*of lemon etc*) cáscara; (*of cheese*) costra

ring [rɪŋ] (*pt* rang, *pp* rung) *n* (*of metal*) aro; (*on finger*) anillo; (*of people*) corro; (*of objects*) círculo; (*gang*) banda; (*for boxing*) cuadrilátero; (*of circus*) pista; (*bull ~*) ruedo, plaza; (*sound of bell*) toque *m* ♦ *vi* (*on telephone*) llamar por teléfono; (*bell*) repicar; (*doorbell, phone*) sonar; (*also: ~ out*) sonar; (*ears*) zumbar ♦ *vt* (*BRIT: TEL*) llamar, telefonear; (*bell etc*) hacer sonar; (*doorbell*) tocar; **to give sb a ~** (*BRIT: TEL*) llamar *or* telefonear a alguien; **~ back** (*BRIT*) *vt, vi* (*TEL*) devolver la llamada; **~ off** (*BRIT*) *vi* (*TEL*) colgar, cortar la comunicación; **~ up** (*BRIT*) *vt* (*TEL*) llamar, telefonear; **~ing** *n* (*of bell*) repique *m*; (*of phone*) el sonar; (*in ears*) zumbido; **~ing**

tone n (TEL) tono de llamada; **~leader** n (of gang) cabecilla m; **~lets** ['rɪŋlɪts] npl rizos mpl, bucles mpl; **~ road** (BRIT) n carretera periférica or de circunvalación

rink [rɪŋk] n (also: ice ~) pista de hielo

rinse [rɪns] n aclarado; (dye) tinte m ♦ vt aclarar; (mouth) enjuagar

riot ['raɪət] n motín m, disturbio ♦ vi amotinarse; **to run ~** desmandarse; **~ous** adj alborotado; (party) bullicioso

rip [rɪp] n rasgón m, rasgadura ♦ vt rasgar, desgarrar ♦ vi rasgarse, desgarrarse; **~cord** n cabo de desgarre

ripe [raɪp] adj maduro; **~n** vt madurar; (cheese) curar ♦ vi madurar

ripple ['rɪpl] n onda, rizo; (sound) murmullo ♦ vi rizarse

rise [raɪz] (pt rose, pp risen) n (slope) cuesta, pendiente f; (hill) altura; (BRIT: in wages) aumento; (in prices, temperature) subida; (fig: to power etc) ascenso ♦ vi subir; (waters) crecer; (sun, moon) salir; (person: from bed etc) levantarse; (also: ~ up: rebel) sublevarse; (in rank) ascender; **to give ~ to** dar lugar or origen a; **to ~ to the occasion** ponerse a la altura de las circunstancias; **risen** ['rɪzn] pp of rise; **rising** adj (increasing: number) creciente; (: prices) en aumento or alza; (tide) creciente; (sun, moon) naciente

risk [rɪsk] n riesgo, peligro ♦ vt arriesgar; (run the ~ of) exponerse a; **to take** or **run the ~ of doing** correr el riesgo de hacer; **at ~** en peligro; **at one's own ~** bajo su propia responsabilidad; **~y** adj arriesgado, peligroso

risqué ['riːskeɪ] adj verde

rissole ['rɪsəul] n croqueta

rite [raɪt] n rito; **last ~s** exequias fpl

ritual ['rɪtjuəl] adj ritual ♦ n ritual m, rito

rival ['raɪvl] n rival m/f; (in business) competidor(a) m/f ♦ adj rival, opuesto ♦ vt competir con; **~ry** n competencia

river ['rɪvə*] n río ♦ cpd (port) de río; (traffic) fluvial; **up/down** ~ río arriba/abajo; **~bank** n orilla (del río); **~bed** n lecho, cauce m

rivet ['rɪvɪt] n roblón m, remache m ♦ vt (fig) captar

Riviera [rɪvɪˈɛərə] n: **the (French)** ~ la Costa Azul (francesa)

road [rəud] n camino; (motorway etc) carretera; (in town) calle f ♦ cpd (accident) de tráfico; **major/minor** ~ carretera principal/secundaria; **~block** n barricada; **~hog** n loco/a del volante; **~ map** n mapa m de carreteras; **~ safety** n seguridad f vial; **~side** n borde m (del camino); **~sign** n señal f de tráfico; **~ user** n usuario/a de la vía pública; **~way** n calzada; **~works** npl obras fpl; **~worthy** adj (car) en buen estado para circular

roam [rəum] vi vagar

roar [rɔː*] n rugido; (of vehicle, storm) estruendo; (of laughter) carcajada ♦ vi rugir; hacer estruendo; **to ~ with laughter** reírse a carcajadas; **to do a ~ing trade** hacer buen negocio

roast [rəust] n carne f asada, asado ♦ vt asar; (coffee) tostar; **~ beef** n rosbif m

rob [rɔb] vt robar; **to ~ sb of sth** robar algo a uno; (fig: deprive) quitar algo a uno; **~ber** n ladrón/ona m/f; **~bery** n robo

robe [rəub] n (for ceremony etc) toga; (also: bath ~, US) albornoz m

robin ['rɔbɪn] n petirrojo

robot ['rəubɔt] n robot m

robust [rəuˈbʌst] adj robusto, fuerte

rock [rɔk] n roca; (boulder) peña, peñasco; (US: small stone) piedrecita; (BRIT: sweet) ≈ pirulí ♦ vt (swing gently: cradle) balancear, mecer; (: child) arrullar; (shake) sacudir ♦ vi mecerse, balancearse; sacudirse; **on the ~s** (drink) con hielo; (marriage etc) en ruinas; **~ and roll** n rocanrol m; **~-bottom** n (fig) punto más bajo; **~ery** n cuadro alpino

rocket ['rɔkɪt] n cohete m

rocking ['rɔkɪŋ]: **~ chair** n mecedora; **~ horse** n caballo de balancín

rocky ['rɔkɪ] adj rocoso

rod [rɔd] n vara, varilla; (also: fishing ~) caña

rode [rəud] pt of ride

rodent ['rəudnt] n roedor m

roe [rəu] n (species: also: ~ deer) corzo; (of fish): **hard/soft** ~ hueva/lecha

rogue [rəug] n pícaro, pillo

role [rəul] n papel m

roll [rəul] n rollo; (of bank notes) fajo; (also: bread ~) panecillo; (register, list) lista, nómina; (sound: of drums etc) redoble m ♦ vt hacer rodar; (also: ~ up: string) enrollar; (: sleeves) arremangar; (cigarette) liar; (also: ~ out: pastry) aplanar; (flatten: road, lawn) apisonar ♦ vi rodar; (drum) redoblar; (ship) balancearse; **~ about** or **around** vi (person) revolcarse; (object) rodar (por); **~ by** vi (time) pasar; **~ in** vi (mail, cash) entrar a raudales; **~ over** vi dar una vuelta; **~ up** vi (inf: arrive) aparecer ♦ vt (carpet) arrollar; **~ call** n: **to take a ~ call** pasar lista; **~er** n rodillo; (wheel) rueda; (for road) apisonadora; (for hair) rulo; **~er coaster** n montaña rusa; **~er skates** npl patines mpl de rueda

rolling ['rəulɪŋ] adj (landscape) ondulado; **~ pin** n rodillo (de cocina); **~ stock** n (RAIL) material m rodante

ROM [rɔm] n abbr (COMPUT: = read only memory) ROM f

Roman ['rəumən] adj romano/a; **~ Catholic** adj, n católico/a m/f (romano/a)

romance [rəˈmæns] n (love affair) amor m;

(*charm*) lo romántico; (*novel*) novela de amor

Romania [ruːˈmeɪnɪə] *n* = **Rumania**

Roman numeral *n* número romano

romantic [rəˈmæntɪk] *adj* romántico

Rome [rəum] *n* Roma

romp [rɔmp] *n* retozo, juego ♦ *vi* (*also*: ~ *about*) jugar, brincar

rompers [ˈrɔmpəz] *npl* pelele *m*

roof [ruːf] (*pl* ~**s**) *n* (*gen*) techo; (*of house*) techo, tejado ♦ *vt* techar, poner techo a; **the ~ of the mouth** el paladar; ~**ing** *n* techumbre *f*; ~ **rack** *n* (*AUT*) baca, portaequipajes *m inv*

rook [ruk] *n* (*bird*) graja; (*CHESS*) torre *f*

room [ruːm] *n* cuarto, habitación *f*, pieza (*esp AM*); (*also*: *bed*~) dormitorio; (*in school etc*) sala; (*space, scope*) sitio, cabida; ~**s** *npl* (*lodging*) alojamiento; "~**s to let**", "~**s for rent**" (*US*) "se alquilan cuartos"; **single/double** ~ habitación individual/doble *or* para dos personas; ~**ing house** (*US*) *n* pensión *f*; ~**mate** *n* compañero/a de cuarto; ~ **service** *n* servicio de habitaciones; ~**y** *adj* espacioso; (*garment*) amplio

roost [ruːst] *vi* pasar la noche

rooster [ˈruːstə*] *n* gallo

root [ruːt] *n* raíz *f* ♦ *vi* arraigarse; ~ **about** *vi* (*fig*) buscar y rebuscar; ~ **for** *vt fus* (*support*) apoyar a; ~ **out** *vt* desarraigar

rope [rəup] *n* cuerda; (*NAUT*) cable *m* ♦ *vt* (*tie*) atar *or* amarrar con (una) cuerda; (*climbers: also*: ~ *together*) encordarse; (*an area: also*: ~ *off*) acordonar; **to know the ~s** (*fig*) conocer los trucos (del oficio); ~ **in** *vt* (*fig*): **to** ~ **sb in** persuadir a uno a tomar parte; ~ **ladder** *n* escala de cuerda

rosary [ˈrəuzərɪ] *n* rosario

rose [rəuz] *pt of* **rise** ♦ *n* rosa; (*shrub*) rosal *m*; (*on watering can*) roseta

rosé [ˈrəuzeɪ] *n* vino rosado

rosebud [ˈrəuzbʌd] *n* capullo de rosa

rosebush [ˈrəuzbuʃ] *n* rosal *m*

rosemary [ˈrəuzmərɪ] *n* romero

rosette [rəuˈzɛt] *n* escarapela

roster [ˈrɔstə*] *n*: **duty** ~ lista de deberes

rostrum [ˈrɔstrəm] *n* tribuna

rosy [ˈrəuzɪ] *adj* rosado, sonrosado; **a** ~ **future** un futuro prometedor

rot [rɔt] *n* podredumbre *f*; (*fig: pej*) tonterías *fpl* ♦ *vt* pudrir ♦ *vi* pudrirse

rota [ˈrəutə] *n* (sistema *m* de) turnos *mpl*

rotary [ˈrəutərɪ] *adj* rotativo

rotate [rəuˈteɪt] *vt* (*revolve*) hacer girar, dar vueltas a; (*jobs*) alternar ♦ *vi* girar, dar vueltas; **rotating** *adj* rotativo; **rotation** [-ˈteɪʃən] *n* rotación *f*

rote [rəut] *n*: **by** ~ maquinalmente, de memoria

rotten [ˈrɔtn] *adj* podrido; (*dishonest*) corrompido; (*inf: bad*) pocho; **to feel** ~ (*ill*) sentirse fatal

rotund [rəuˈtʌnd] *adj* regordete

rouble [ˈruːbl] (*US* **ruble**) *n* rublo

rouge [ruːʒ] *n* colorete *m*

rough [rʌf] *adj* (*skin, surface*) áspero; (*terrain*) quebrado; (*road*) desigual; (*voice*) bronco; (*person, manner*) tosco, grosero; (*weather*) borrascoso; (*treatment*) brutal; (*sea*) picado; (*town, area*) peligroso; (*cloth*) basto; (*plan*) preliminar; (*guess*) aproximado ♦ *n* (*GOLF*): **in the** ~ en las hierbas altas; **to** ~ **it** vivir sin comodidades; **to sleep** ~ (*BRIT*) pasar la noche al raso; ~**age** *n* fibra(s) *f(pl)*; ~**-and-ready** *adj* improvisado; ~ **copy** *n* borrador *m*; ~ **draft** *n* = ~ **copy**; ~**en** *vt* (*a surface*) poner áspero; ~**ly** *adv* (*handle*) torpemente; (*make*) toscamente; (*speak*) groseramente; (*approximately*) aproximadamente; ~**ness** *n* (*of surface*) aspereza; (*of person*) rudeza

roulette [ruːˈlɛt] *n* ruleta

Roumania [ruːˈmeɪnɪə] *n* = **Rumania**

round [raund] *adj* redondo ♦ *n* círculo; (*BRIT: of toast*) rebanada; (*of policeman*) ronda; (*of milkman*) recorrido; (*of doctor*) visitas *fpl*; (*game: of cards, in competition*) partida; (*of ammunition*) cartucho; (*BOXING*) asalto; (*of talks*) ronda ♦ *vt* (*corner*) doblar ♦ *prep* alrededor de ♦ *prep* (*surrounding*): ~ **his neck/the table** en su cuello/alrededor de la mesa; (*in a circular movement*): **to move** ~ **the room/sail** ~ **the world** dar una vuelta a la habitación/circunnavegar el mundo; (*in various directions*): **to move** ~ **a room/house** moverse por toda la habitación/casa; (*approximately*): ~ **all** ~ por todos lados; **the long way** ~ por el camino menos directo; **all the year** ~ durante todo el año; **it's just** ~ **the corner** (*fig*) está a la vuelta de la esquina; ~ **the clock** *adv* las 24 horas; **to go** ~ **to sb's (house)** ir a casa de uno; **to go** ~ **the back** pasar por atrás; **to go** ~ **a house** visitar una casa; **enough to go** ~ bastante (para todos); **a** ~ **of applause** una salva de aplausos; **a** ~ **of drinks/sandwiches** una ronda de bebidas/bocadillos; ~ **off** *vt* (*speech etc*) acabar, poner término a; ~ **up** *vt* (*cattle*) acorralar; (*people*) reunir; (*price*) redondear; ~**about** (*BRIT*) *n* (*AUT*) isleta; (*at fair*) tiovivo ♦ *adj* (*route, means*) indirecto; ~**ers** *n* (*game*) juego similar al béisbol; ~**ly** *adv* (*fig*) rotundamente; ~**-shouldered** *adj* cargado de espaldas; ~ **trip** *n* viaje *m* de ida y vuelta; ~**up** *n* rodeo; (*of criminals*) redada; (*of news*) resumen *m*

rouse [rauz] *vt* (*wake up*) despertar; (*stir up*) suscitar; **rousing** *adj* (*cheer, welcome*) caluroso

rout [raut] *n* (*MIL*) derrota ♦ *vt* derrotar

route [ruːt] *n* ruta, camino; (*of bus*) recorrido; (*of shipping*) derrota; ~ **map** (*BRIT*) *(for journey)* mapa *m* de carreteras

routine [ru:'ti:n] *adj* rutinario ♦ *n* rutina; *(THEATRE)* número

rove [rəuv] *vt* vagar *or* errar por

row[1] [rəu] *n (line)* fila, hilera; *(KNITTING)* pasada ♦ *vi (in boat)* remar ♦ *vt* conducir remando; **4 days in a ~** 4 días seguidos

row[2] [rau] *n (racket)* escándalo; *(dispute)* bronca, pelea; *(scolding)* regaño ♦ *vi* pelear(se)

rowboat ['rəubəut] *(US) n* bote *m* de remos

rowdy ['raudɪ] *adj (person: noisy)* ruidoso; *(occasion)* alborotado

rowing ['rəuɪŋ] *n* remo; **~ boat** *(BRIT)* bote *m* de remos

royal ['rɔɪəl] *adj* real; **R~ Air Force** *n* Fuerzas *fpl* Aéreas Británicas; **~ty** *n (~ persons)* familia real; *(payment to author)* derechos *mpl* de autor

rpm *abbr = revs per minute)* r.p.m.

R.S.V.P. *abbr (= répondez s'il vous plaît)* SRC

Rt. Hon. *abbr (BRIT. = Right Honourable)* título honorífico de diputado

rub [rʌb] *vt* frotar; *(scrub)* restregar ♦ *n:* **to give sth a ~** frotar algo; **to ~ sb up** *or* **~ sb** *(US)* **the wrong way** entrarle uno por mal ojo; **~ off** *vi* borrarse; **~ off on** *vt fus* influir en; **~ out** *vt* borrar

rubber ['rʌbə*] *n* caucho, goma; *(BRIT: eraser)* goma de borrar; **~ band** *n* goma, gomita; **~ plant** *n* ficus *m;* **~y** *adj* elástico; *(meat)* gomoso

rubbish ['rʌbɪʃ] *n* basura; *(waste)* desperdicios *mpl; (fig: pej)* tonterías *fpl; (junk)* pacotilla; **~ bin** *(BRIT)* *n* cubo *(SP)* **or** bote *m* *(AM)* de la basura; **~ dump** *n* vertedero, basurero

rubble ['rʌbl] *n* escombros *mpl*

ruble ['ru:bl] *(US) n =* **rouble**

ruby ['ru:bɪ] *n* rubí *m*

rucksack ['rʌksæk] *n* mochila

rudder ['rʌdə*] *n* timón *m*

ruddy ['rʌdɪ] *adj (face)* rubicundo; *(inf: damned)* condenado

rude [ru:d] *adj (impolite: person)* mal educado; *(: word, manners)* grosero; *(crude)* crudo; *(indecent)* indecente; **~ness** *n* descortesía

rueful ['ru:ful] *adj* arrepentido

ruffian ['rʌfɪən] *n* matón *m,* criminal *m*

ruffle ['rʌfl] *vt (hair)* despeinar; *(clothes)* arrugar; **to get ~d** *(fig: person)* alterarse

rug [rʌg] *n* alfombra; *(BRIT: blanket)* manta

rugby ['rʌgbɪ] *n (also: ~ football)* rugby *m*

rugged ['rʌgɪd] *adj (landscape)* accidentado; *(features)* robusto

rugger ['rʌgə*] *(BRIT: inf) n* rugby *m*

ruin ['ru:ɪn] *n* ruina ♦ *vt* arruinar; *(spoil)* estropear; **~s** *npl* ruinas *fpl,* restos *mpl;* **~ous** *adj* desastroso

rule [ru:l] *n (norm)* norma, costumbre *f; (regulation, ruler)* regla; *(government)* dominio ♦ *vt (country, person)* gobernar ♦ *vi* gobernar; *(LAW)* fallar; **as a ~** por regla general; **~ out** *vt* excluir; **~d** *adj (paper)* rayado; **~r** *n (sovereign)* soberano; *(for measuring)* regla; **ruling** *adj (party)* gobernante; *(class)* dirigente ♦ *n (LAW)* fallo, decisión *f*

rum [rʌm] *n* ron *m*

Rumania [ru:'meɪnɪə] *n* Rumanía; **~n** *adj* rumano/a ♦ *n* rumano/a *m/f; (LING)* rumano

rumble ['rʌmbl] *n (noise)* ruido sordo ♦ *vi* retumbar, hacer un ruido sordo; *(stomach, pipe)* sonar

rummage ['rʌmɪdʒ] *vi (search)* hurgar

rumour ['ru:mə*] *(US* **rumor)** *n* rumor *m* ♦ *vt:* **it is ~ed that ...** se rumorea que ....

rump [rʌmp] *n (of animal)* ancas *fpl,* grupa; **~ steak** *n* filete *m* de lomo

rumpus ['rʌmpəs] *n* lío, jaleo

run [rʌn] *(pt* **ran,** *pp* **run)** *n (fast pace):* **at a ~** corriendo; *(SPORT, in tights)* carrera; *(outing)* paseo, excursión *f; (distance travelled)* trayecto; *(series)* serie *f; (THEATRE)* temporada; *(SKI)* pista ♦ *vt* correr; *(operate: business)* dirigir; *(: competition, course)* organizar; *(: hotel, house)* administrar, llevar; *(COMPUT)* ejecutar; *(pass: hand)* pasar; *(PRESS: feature)* publicar ♦ *vi* correr; *(work: machine)* funcionar, marchar; *(bus, train: operate)* circular, ir; *(: travel)* ir; *(continue: play)* seguir; *(: contract)* ser válido; *(flow: river)* fluir; *(colours, washing)* desteñirse; *(in election)* ser candidato; **there was a ~ on** *(meat, tickets)* hubo mucha demanda de; **in the long ~** a la larga; **on the ~** en fuga; **I'll ~ you to the station** te llevaré a la estación (en coche); **to ~ a risk** correr un riesgo; **to ~ a bath** llenar la bañera; **~ about** *or* **around** *vi (children)* correr por todos lados; **~ across** *vt fus (find)* dar *or* topar con; **~ away** *vi* huir; **~ down** *vt (production)* ir reduciendo; *(factory)* ir restringiendo la producción en; *(subj: car)* atropellar; *(criticize)* criticar; **to be ~ down** *(person: tired)* estar debilitado; **~ in** *(BRIT) vt (car)* rodar; **~ into** *vt fus (meet: person, trouble)* tropezar con; *(collide with)* chocar con; **~ off** *vt (water)* dejar correr; *(copies)* sacar ♦ *vi* huir corriendo; **~ out** *vi (person)* salir corriendo; *(liquid)* irse; *(lease)* caducar, vencer; *(money etc)* acabarse; **~ out of** *vt fus* quedar sin; **~ over** *vt (AUT)* atropellar ♦ *vt fus (revise)* repasar; **~ through** *vt fus (instructions)* repasar; **~ up** *vt (debt)* contraer; **to ~ up against** *(difficulties)* tropezar con; **~away** *adj (horse)* desbocado; *(truck)* sin frenos; *(child)* escapado de casa

rung [rʌŋ] *pp of* **ring** ♦ *n (of ladder)* escalón *m,* peldaño

runner ['rʌnə*] *n (in race: person)* corredor(a) *m/f*; (: *horse*) caballo; (*on sledge*) patín *m*; **~ bean** (*BRIT*) *n* ≈ judía verde; **~-up** *n* subcampeón/ona *m/f*

running ['rʌnɪŋ] *n* (*sport*) atletismo; (*business*) administración *f* ♦ *adj* (*water, costs*) corriente; (*commentary*) continuo; **to be in/out of the ~ for sth** tener/no tener posibilidades de ganar algo; **6 days ~** 6 días seguidos; **~ commentary** *n* (*TV, RADIO*) comentario en directo; (*on guided tour etc*) comentario detallado; **~ costs** *npl* gastos *mpl* corrientes

runny ['rʌnɪ] *adj* fluido; (*nose, eyes*) gastante

run-of-the-mill *adj* común y corriente

runt [rʌnt] *n* (*also pej*) redrojo, enano

run-up *n*: **~ to** (*election etc*) período previo a

runway ['rʌnweɪ] *n* (*AVIAT*) pista de aterrizaje

rupee [ruːˈpiː] *n* rupia

rupture ['rʌptʃə*] *n* (*MED*) hernia

rural ['ruərl] *adj* rural

ruse [ruːz] *n* ardid *m*

rush [rʌʃ] *n* ímpetu *m*; (*hurry*) prisa; (*COMM*) demanda repentina; (*current*) corriente *f* fuerte; (*of feeling*) torrente; (*BOT*) junco ♦ *vt* apresurar; (*work*) hacer de prisa ♦ *vi* correr, precipitarse; **~ hour** *n* horas *fpl* punta

rusk [rʌsk] *n* bizcocho tostado

Russia ['rʌʃə] *n* Rusia; **~n** *adj* ruso/a ♦ *n* ruso/a *m/f*; (*LING*) ruso

rust [rʌst] *n* herrumbre *f*, moho ♦ *vi* oxidarse

rustic ['rʌstɪk] *adj* rústico

rustle ['rʌsl] *vi* susurrar ♦ *vt* (*paper*) hacer crujir; (*US: cattle*) hurtar, robar

rustproof ['rʌstpruːf] *adj* inoxidable

rusty ['rʌstɪ] *adj* oxidado

rut [rʌt] *n* surco *m*; (*ZOOL*) celo; **to be in a ~** ser esclavo de la rutina

ruthless ['ruːθlɪs] *adj* despiadado

rye [raɪ] *n* centeno; **~ bread** *n* pan de centeno

S s

Sabbath ['sæbəθ] *n* domingo; (*Jewish*) sábado

sabotage ['sæbətɑːʒ] *n* sabotaje *m* ♦ *vt* sabotear

saccharin(e) ['sækərɪn] *n* sacarina

sachet ['sæʃeɪ] *n* sobrecito

sack [sæk] *n* (*bag*) saco, costal *m* ♦ *vt* (*dismiss*) despedir; (*plunder*) saquear; **to get the ~** ser despedido; **~ing** *n* despido; (*material*) arpillera

sacred ['seɪkrɪd] *adj* sagrado, santo

sacrifice ['sækrɪfaɪs] *n* sacrificio ♦ *vt* sacrificar

sacrilege ['sækrɪlɪdʒ] *n* sacrilegio

sad [sæd] *adj* (*unhappy*) triste; (*deplorable*) lamentable

saddle ['sædl] *n* silla (de montar); (*of cycle*) sillín *m* ♦ *vt* (*horse*) ensillar; **to be ~d with sth** (*inf*) quedar cargado con algo; **~bag** *n* alforja

sadistic [sə'dɪstɪk] *adj* sádico

sadly ['sædlɪ] *adv* lamentablemente; **to be ~ lacking in** estar por desgracia carente de

sadness ['sædnɪs] *n* tristeza

s.a.e. *abbr* (= *stamped addressed envelope*) *sobre con las propias señas de uno y con sello*

safari [sə'fɑːrɪ] *n* safari *m*

safe [seɪf] *adj* (*out of danger*) fuera de peligro; (*not dangerous, sure*) seguro; (*unharmed*) ileso ♦ *n* caja de caudales, caja fuerte; **~ and sound** sano y salvo; (*just*) **to be on the ~ side** para mayor seguridad; **~-conduct** *n* salvoconducto; **~-deposit** *n* (*vault*) cámara acorazada; (*box*) caja de seguridad; **~guard** *n* protección *f*, garantía ♦ *vt* proteger, defender; **~keeping** *n* custodia; **~ly** *adv* seguramente, con seguridad; **to arrive ~ly** llegar bien; **~ sex** *n* sexo seguro

safety ['seɪftɪ] *n* seguridad *f*; **~ belt** *n* cinturón *m* (de seguridad); **~ pin** *n* imperdible *m* (*SP*), seguro (*AM*); **~ valve** *n* válvula de seguridad

saffron ['sæfrən] *n* azafrán *m*

sag [sæg] *vi* aflojarse

sage [seɪdʒ] *n* (*herb*) salvia; (*man*) sabio

Sagittarius [sædʒɪ'tɛərɪəs] *n* Sagitario

Sahara [sə'hɑːrə] *n*: **the ~ (Desert)** el (desierto del) Sáhara

said [sed] *pt, pp of* **say**

sail [seɪl] *n* (*on boat*) vela; (*trip*): **to go for a ~** dar un paseo en barco ♦ *vt* (*boat*) gobernar ♦ *vi* (*travel: ship*) navegar; (*SPORT*) hacer vela; (*begin voyage*) salir; **they ~ed into Copenhagen** arribaron a Copenhague; **~ through** *vt fus* (*exam*) aprobar sin ningún problema; **~boat** *n* (*US*) *n* velero, barco de vela; **~ing** *n* (*SPORT*) vela; **to go ~ing** hacer vela; **~ing boat** *n* barco de vela; **~ing ship** *n* velero; **~or** *n* marinero, marino

saint [seɪnt] *n* santo; **~ly** *adj* santo

sake [seɪk] *n*: **for the ~ of** por

salad ['sæləd] *n* ensalada; **~ bowl** *n* ensaladera; **~ cream** (*BRIT*) *n* (especie *f* de) mayonesa; **~ dressing** *n* aliño

salary ['sælərɪ] n sueldo
sale [seɪl] n venta; (at reduced prices) liquidación f, saldo; (auction) subasta; ~s npl (total amount sold) ventas fpl, facturación f; **"for ~"** "se vende"; **on ~** en venta; **on ~ or return** (goods) venta por reposición; **~room** n sala de subastas; **~s assistant** (US ~s **clerk**) n dependiente/a m/f; **salesman/woman** n (in shop) dependiente/a m/f; (representative) viajante m/f
salient ['seɪlɪənt] adj sobresaliente
saliva [sə'laɪvə] n saliva
sallow ['sæləu] adj cetrino
salmon ['sæmən] n inv salmón m
salon ['sælɔn] n (hairdressing ~) peluquería; (beauty ~) salón m de belleza
saloon [sə'luːn] n (US) bar m, taberna; (BRIT: AUT) (coche m de) turismo; (ship's lounge) cámara, salón m
salt [sɔlt] n sal f ♦ vt salar; (put ~ on) poner sal en; ~ **away** (inf) vt (money) ahorrar; ~ **cellar** n salero; **~water** adj de agua salada; **~y** adj salado
salutary ['sæljutərɪ] adj saludable
salute [sə'luːt] n saludo; (of guns) salva ♦ vt saludar
salvage ['sælvɪdʒ] n (saving) salvamento, recuperación f, (things saved) objetos mpl salvados ♦ vt salvar
salvation [sæl'veɪʃən] n salvación f; **S~ Army** n Ejército de Salvación
salvo ['sælvəu] n (MIL) salva
same [seɪm] adj mismo ♦ pron: **the ~** el/la mismo/a, los/las mismos/as; **the ~ book as** el mismo libro que; **at the ~ time** (at the ~ moment) al mismo tiempo; (yet) sin embargo; **all** or **just the ~** sin embargo, aun así; **to do the ~** (as sb) hacer lo mismo (que uno); **the ~ to you!** ¡igualmente!
sample ['sɑːmpl] n muestra ♦ vt (food) probar; (wine) catar
sanatorium [sænə'tɔːrɪəm] (pl **sanatoria**) (BRIT) n sanatorio
sanctimonious [sæŋktɪ'məunɪəs] adj mojigato
sanction ['sæŋkʃən] n aprobación f ♦ vt sancionar; aprobar; **~s** npl (POL) sanciones fpl
sanctity ['sæŋktɪtɪ] n santidad f; (inviolability) inviolabilidad f
sanctuary ['sæŋktjuərɪ] n santuario; (refuge) asilo, refugio; (for wildlife) reserva
sand [sænd] n arena; (beach) playa ♦ vt (also: ~ **down**) lijar
sandal ['sændl] n sandalia
sand: ~**box** (US) n = ~**pit**; ~**castle** n castillo de arena; ~ **dune** n duna; ~**paper** n papel m de lija; ~**pit** n (for children) cajón m de arena; ~**stone** n piedra arenisca
sandwich ['sændwɪtʃ] n bocadillo (SP), sandwich m, emparedado (AM) ♦ vt inter-

calar; ~**ed between** apretujado entre; **cheese/ham ~** sandwich de queso/jamón; ~ **course** (BRIT) n curso de medio tiempo
sandy ['sændɪ] adj arenoso; (colour) rojizo
sane [seɪn] adj cuerdo; (sensible) sensato
sang [sæŋ] pt of **sing**
sanitarium [sænɪ'tɛərɪəm] (US) n = **sanatorium**
sanitary ['sænɪtərɪ] adj sanitario; (clean) higiénico; ~ **towel** (US ~ **napkin**) n paño higiénico, compresa
sanitation [sænɪ'teɪʃən] n (in house) servicios mpl higiénicos; (in town) servicio de desinfección; ~ **department** (US) n departamento de limpieza y recogida de basuras
sanity ['sænɪtɪ] n cordura; (of judgment) sensatez f
sank [sæŋk] pt of **sink**
Santa Claus [sæntə'klɔːz] n San Nicolás, Papá Noel
sap [sæp] n (of plants) savia ♦ vt (strength) minar, agotar
sapling ['sæplɪŋ] n árbol nuevo or joven
sapphire ['sæfaɪə*] n zafiro
sarcasm ['sɑːkæzm] n sarcasmo
sardine [sɑː'diːn] n sardina
Sardinia [sɑː'dɪnɪə] n Cerdeña
sash [sæʃ] n faja
sat [sæt] pt, pp of **sit**
Satan ['seɪtn] n Satanás m
satchel ['sætʃl] n (child's) cartera (SP), mochila (AM)
satellite ['sætəlaɪt] n satélite m; ~ **dish** n antena de televisión por satélite; ~ **television** n televisión f vía satélite
satin ['sætɪn] n raso ♦ adj de raso
satire ['sætaɪə*] n sátira
satisfaction [sætɪs'fækʃən] n satisfacción f
satisfactory [sætɪs'fæktərɪ] adj satisfactorio
satisfy ['sætɪsfaɪ] vt satisfacer; (convince) convencer; **~ing** adj satisfactorio
saturate ['sætʃəreɪt] vt: **to ~ (with)** empapar or saturar (de)
Saturday ['sætədɪ] n sábado
sauce [sɔːs] n salsa; (sweet) crema; jarabe m; ~**pan** n cacerola, olla
saucer ['sɔːsə*] n platillo
saucy ['sɔːsɪ] adj fresco, descarado
Saudi ['saudɪ]: ~ **Arabia** n Arabia Saudí or Saudita; ~ **(Arabian)** adj, n saudí m/f, saudita m/f
sauna ['sɔːnə] n sauna
saunter ['sɔːntə*] vi: **to ~ in/out** entrar/ salir sin prisa
sausage ['sɔsɪdʒ] n salchicha; ~ **roll** n empanadita de salchicha
sauté ['səuteɪ] adj salteado
savage ['sævɪdʒ] adj (cruel, fierce) feroz, furioso; (primitive) salvaje ♦ n salvaje m/f ♦ vt (attack) embestir; **~ry** n salvajismo, salvajería

save [seɪv] vt (*rescue*) salvar, rescatar; (*money, time*) ahorrar; (*put by, keep: seat*) guardar; (*COMPUT*) salvar (y guardar); (*avoid: trouble*) evitar; (*SPORT*) parar ♦ vi (*also: ~ up*) ahorrar ♦ n (*SPORT*) parada ♦ prep salvo, excepto

saving ['seɪvɪŋ] n (*on price etc*) economía ♦ adj: **the ~ grace of** el único mérito de; **~s** npl ahorros mpl; **~s account** n cuenta de ahorros; **~s bank** n caja de ahorros

saviour ['seɪvjə*] (*US* **savior**) n salvador(a) m/f

savour ['seɪvə*] (*US* **savor**) vt saborear; **~y** adj sabroso; (*dish: not sweet*) salado

saw [sɔ:] (*pt* **sawed**, *pp* **sawed** *or* **sawn**) *pt of* **see** ♦ n (*tool*) sierra ♦ vt serrar; **~dust** n (a)serrín m; **~mill** n aserradero; **~n-off shotgun** n escopeta de cañones recortados

saxophone ['sæksəfəʊn] n saxófono

say [seɪ] (*pt, pp* **said**) n: **to have one's ~** expresar su opinión; **to have a** *or* **some ~ in sth** tener voz *or* tener que ver en algo ♦ vt decir; **to ~ yes/no** decir que sí/no; **could you ~ that again?** ¿podría repetir eso?; **that is to ~** es decir; **that goes without ~ing** ni que decir tiene; **~ing** n dicho, refrán m

scab [skæb] n costra; (*pej*) esquirol m

scaffold ['skæfəʊld] n cadalso; **~ing** n andamio, andamiaje m

scald [skɔ:ld] n escaldadura ♦ vt escaldar

scale [skeɪl] n (*gen, MUS*) escala; (*of fish*) escama; (*of salaries, fees etc*) escalafón m ♦ vt (*mountain*) escalar; (*tree*) trepar; **~s** npl (*for weighing: small*) balanza; (: *large*) báscula; **on a large ~** en gran escala; **~ of charges** tarifa, lista de precios; **~ down** vt reducir a escala

scallop ['skɒləp] n (*ZOOL*) venera; (*SEWING*) festón m

scalp [skælp] n cabellera ♦ vt escalpar

scalpel ['skælpl] n bisturí m

scamper ['skæmpə*] vi: **to ~ away** *or* **off** irse corriendo

scampi ['skæmpɪ] npl gambas fpl

scan [skæn] vt (*examine*) escudriñar; (*glance at quickly*) dar un vistazo a; (*TV, RADAR*) explorar, registrar ♦ n (*MED*): **to have a ~** pasar por el escáner

scandal ['skændl] n escándalo; (*gossip*) chismes mpl

Scandinavia [skændɪ'neɪvɪə] n Escandinavia; **~n** adj, n escandinavo/a m/f

scant [skænt] adj escaso; **~y** adj (*meal*) insuficiente; (*clothes*) ligero

scapegoat ['skeɪpgəʊt] n cabeza de turco, chivo expiatorio

scar [skɑ:] n cicatriz f; (*fig*) señal f ♦ vt dejar señales en

scarce [skɛəs] adj escaso; **to make o.s. ~** (*inf*) esfumarse; **~ly** adv apenas; **scarcity** n escasez f

scare [skɛə*] n susto, sobresalto; (*panic*) pánico ♦ vt asustar, espantar; **to ~ sb stiff** dar a uno un susto de muerte; **bomb ~** amenaza de bomba; **~ off** *or* **away** vt ahuyentar; **~crow** n espantapájaros m inv; **~d** adj: **to be ~d** estar asustado

scarf [skɑ:f] (*pl* **~s** *or* **scarves**) n (*long*) bufanda; (*square*) pañuelo

scarlet ['skɑ:lɪt] adj escarlata; **~ fever** n escarlatina

scarves [skɑ:vz] npl of **scarf**

scary ['skɛərɪ] (*inf*) adj espeluznante

scathing ['skeɪðɪŋ] adj mordaz

scatter ['skætə*] vt (*spread*) esparcir, desparramar; (*put to flight*) dispersar ♦ vi desparramarse; dispersarse; **~brained** adj ligero de cascos

scavenger ['skævəndʒə*] n (*person*) basurero/a

scenario [sɪ'nɑ:rɪəʊ] n (*THEATRE*) argumento; (*CINEMA*) guión m; (*fig*) escenario

scene [si:n] n (*THEATRE, fig etc*) escena; (*of crime etc*) escenario; (*view*) panorama m; (*fuss*) escándalo; **~ry** n (*THEATRE*) decorado; (*landscape*) paisaje m; **scenic** adj pintoresco

scent [sent] n perfume m, olor m; (*fig: track*) rastro, pista

sceptic ['skeptɪk] (*US* **skeptic**) n escéptico/a; **~al** adj escéptico; **~ism** ['skeptɪsɪzm] n escepticismo

sceptre ['septə*] (*US* **scepter**) n cetro

schedule ['ʃedjuːl, (*US*) 'skedjuːl] n (*timetable*) horario; (*of events*) programa m; (*list*) lista ♦ vt (*visit*) fijar la hora de; **to arrive on ~** llegar a la hora debida; **to be ahead of/behind ~** estar adelantado/en retraso; **~d flight** n vuelo regular

schematic [skɪ'mætɪk] adj (*diagram etc*) esquemático

scheme [skiːm] n (*plan*) plan m, proyecto; (*plot*) intriga; (*arrangement*) disposición f; (*pension ~ etc*) sistema m ♦ vi (*intrigue*) intrigar; **scheming** adj intrigante ♦ n intrigas fpl

schism ['skɪzəm] n cisma m

schizophrenic [skɪtzə'frenɪk] adj esquizofrénico

scholar ['skɒlə*] n (*pupil*) alumno/a; (*learned person*) sabio/a, erudito/a; **~ly** adj erudito; **~ship** n erudición f; (*grant*) beca

school [skuːl] n escuela, colegio; (*in university*) facultad f ♦ cpd escolar; **~ age** n edad f escolar; **~book** n libro de texto; **~boy** n alumno; **~ children** npl alumnos mpl; **~days** npl años mpl del colegio; **~girl** n alumna; **~ing** n enseñanza; **~master/mistress** n (*primary*) maestro/a; (*secondary*) profesor(a) m/f; **~teacher** n (*primary*) maestro/a; (*secondary*) profesor(a) m/f

schooner ['skuːnə*] n (*ship*) goleta

sciatica [saɪ'ætɪkə] n ciática
science ['saɪəns] n ciencia; ~ **fiction** n
ciencia-ficción f; **scientific** [-'tɪfɪk] adj científico; **scientist** n científico/a
scintillating ['sɪntɪleɪtɪŋ] adj brillante, ingenioso
scissors ['sɪzəz] npl tijeras fpl; **a pair of ~**
unas tijeras
scoff [skɔf] vt (BRIT: inf: eat) engullir ♦ vi:
to ~ **(at)** (mock) mofarse (de)
scold [skəʊld] vt regañar
scone [skɒn] n pastel de pan
scoop [skuːp] n (for flour etc) pala; (PRESS)
exclusiva; ~ **out** vt excavar; ~ **up** vt recoger
scooter ['skuːtə*] n moto f; (toy) patinete
m
scope [skəʊp] n (of plan) ámbito; (of person) competencia; (opportunity) libertad f
(de acción)
scorch [skɔːtʃ] vt (clothes) chamuscar;
(earth, grass) quemar, secar
score [skɔː*] n (points etc) puntuación f;
(MUS) partitura; (twenty) veintena ♦ vt
(goal, point) ganar; (mark) rayar; (achieve:
success) conseguir ♦ vi marcar un tanto;
(FOOTBALL) marcar (un) gol; (keep score)
llevar el tanteo; ~**s of** (very many) decenas
de; **on that** ~ en lo que se refiere a eso; **to**
~ **6 out of 10** obtener una puntuación de
6 sobre 10; ~ **out** vt tachar; ~ **over** vt fus
obtener una victoria sobre; ~**board** n marcador m
scorn [skɔːn] n desprecio ♦ vt despreciar;
~**ful** adj desdeñoso, despreciativo
Scorpio ['skɔːpɪəʊ] n Escorpión m
scorpion ['skɔːpɪən] n alacrán m
Scot [skɒt] n escocés/esa m/f
scotch [skɒtʃ] vt (rumour) desmentir; (plan)
abandonar; **S~** n whisky m escocés
scot-free adv: **to get off** ~ (unpunished)
salir impune
Scotland ['skɒtlənd] n Escocia
Scots [skɒts] adj escocés/esa; ~**man/
woman** n escocés/esa m/f; **Scottish**
['skɒtɪʃ] adj escocés/esa
scoundrel ['skaʊndrl] n canalla m/f, sinvergüenza m/f
scour ['skaʊə*] vt (search) recorrer, registrar
scourge [skɜːdʒ] n azote m
scout [skaʊt] n (MIL, also: boy ~) explorador m; **girl** ~ (US) niña exploradora; ~
around vi reconocer el terreno
scowl [skaʊl] vi fruncir el ceño; **to** ~ **at sb**
mirar con ceño a uno
scrabble ['skræbl] vi (claw): **to** ~ **(at)** arañar; (also: **to** ~ **around:** search) revolver
todo buscando ♦ n; **S~** ® Scrabble m ®
scraggy ['skrægɪ] adj descarnado
scram [skræm] (inf) vi largarse
scramble ['skræmbl] n (climb) subida (difícil); (struggle) pelea ♦ vi: **to** ~ **through/**

out abrirse paso/salir con dificultad; **to** ~
for pelear por; ~**d eggs** npl huevos mpl
revueltos
scrap [skræp] n (bit) pedacito; (fig) pizca;
(fight) riña, bronca; (also: ~ **iron**) chatarra,
hierro viejo ♦ vt (discard) desechar, descartar ♦ vi reñir, armar (una) bronca; ~**s** npl
(waste) sobras fpl, desperdicios mpl;
~**book** n álbum m de recortes; ~ **dealer**
n chatarrero/a
scrape [skreɪp] n: **to get into a** ~ meterse
en un lío ♦ vt raspar; (skin etc) rasguñar;
(~ **against**) rozar ♦ vi: **to** ~ **through**
(exam) aprobar por los pelos; ~ **together**
vt (money) arañar, juntar
scrap: ~ **heap** n (fig): **to be on the** ~
heap estar acabado; ~ **merchant** (BRIT)
n chatarrero/a; ~ **paper** n pedazos mpl de
papel; ~**py** adj (work) imperfecto
scratch [skrætʃ] n rasguño; (from claw) arañazo ♦ cpd: ~ **team** equipo improvisado ♦
vt (paint, car) rayar; (with claw, nail) rasguñar, arañar; (rub: nose etc) rascarse ♦ vi
rascarse; **to start from** ~ partir de cero; **to**
be up to ~ cumplir con los requisitos
scrawl [skrɔːl] n garabatos mpl ♦ vi hacer
garabatos
scrawny ['skrɔːnɪ] adj flaco
scream [skriːm] n chillido ♦ vi chillar
screech [skriːtʃ] vi chirriar
screen [skriːn] n (CINEMA, TV) pantalla;
(movable barrier) biombo ♦ vt (conceal) tapar; (from the wind etc) proteger; (film) proyectar; (candidates etc) investigar a; ~**ing** n
(MED) investigación f médica; ~**play** n
guión m
screw [skruː] n tornillo ♦ vt (also: ~ **in**)
atornillar; ~ **up** vt (paper etc) arrugar; **to**
~ **up one's eyes** arrugar el entrecejo; ~
driver n destornillador m
scribble ['skrɪbl] n garabatos mpl ♦ vt, vi
garabatear
script [skrɪpt] n (CINEMA etc) guión m;
(writing) escritura, letra
scripture(s) ['skrɪptʃə*(z)] n(pl) Sagrada
Escritura
scroll [skrəʊl] n rollo
scrounge [skraʊndʒ] (inf) vt: **to** ~ **sth off**
or from sb obtener algo de uno de gorra ♦
n: **on the** ~ de gorra; ~**r** n gorrón/ona m/f
scrub [skrʌb] n (land) maleza ♦ vt fregar,
restregar; (inf: reject) cancelar, anular
scruff [skrʌf] n: **by the** ~ **of the neck** por
el pescuezo
scruffy ['skrʌfɪ] adj desaliñado, piojoso
scrum(mage) ['skrʌm(mɪdʒ)] n (RUGBY)
melée f
scruple ['skruːpl] n (gen pl) escrúpulo
scrutinize ['skruːtɪnaɪz] vt escudriñar;
(votes) escrutar; **scrutiny** ['skruːtɪnɪ] n escrutinio, examen m
scuff [skʌf] vt (shoes, floor) rayar

scuffle ['skʌfl] *n* refriega
sculptor ['skʌlptə*] *n* escultor(a) *m/f*
sculpture ['skʌlptʃə*] *n* escultura
scum [skʌm] *n* (*on liquid*) espuma; (*pej: people*) escoria
scupper ['skʌpə*] (*BRIT: inf*) *vt* (*plans*) dar al traste con
scurrilous ['skʌrɪləs] *adj* difamatorio, calumnioso
scurry ['skʌrɪ] *vi* correr; **to ~ off** escabullirse
scuttle ['skʌtl] *n* (*also: coal ~*) cubo, carbonera ♦ *vt* (*ship*) barrenar ♦ *vi* (*scamper*): **to ~ away, ~ off** escabullirse
scythe [saɪð] *n* guadaña
SDP (*BRIT*) *n abbr* = **Social Democratic Party**
sea [si:] *n* mar *m* ♦ *cpd* de mar, marítimo; **by ~** (*travel*) en barco; **on the ~** (*boat*) en el mar; (*town*) junto al mar; **to be all at ~** (*fig*) estar despistado; **out to ~, at ~** en alta mar; **~board** *n* litoral *m*; **~food** *n* mariscos *mpl*; **~ front** *n* paseo marítimo; **~-going** *adj* de altura; **~gull** *n* gaviota
seal [si:l] *n* (*animal*) foca; (*stamp*) sello ♦ *vt* (*close*) cerrar; **~ off** *vt* (*area*) acordonar
sea level *n* nivel *m* del mar
sea lion *n* león *m* marino
seam [si:m] *n* costura; (*of metal*) juntura; (*of coal*) veta, filón *m*
seaman ['si:mən] *n* marinero
seamy ['si:mɪ] *adj* sórdido
seance ['seɪɔns] *n* sesión *f* de espiritismo
seaplane ['si:pleɪn] *n* hidroavión *m*
seaport ['si:pɔ:t] *n* puerto de mar
search [sɔ:tʃ] *n* (*for person, thing*) busca, búsqueda; (*COMPUT*) búsqueda; (*inspection: of sb's home*) registro ♦ *vt* (*look in*) buscar en; (*examine*) examinar; (*person, place*) registrar ♦ *vi*: **to ~ for** buscar; **in ~ of** en busca de; **~ through** *vt fus* registrar; **~ing** *adj* penetrante; **~light** *n* reflector *m*; **~ party** *n* pelotón *m* de salvamento; **~ warrant** *n* mandamiento (judicial)
sea: **~shore** *n* playa, orilla del mar; **~sick** *adj* mareado; **~side** *n* playa, orilla del mar; **~side resort** *n* centro turístico costero
season ['si:zn] *n* (*of year*) estación *f*; (*sporting etc*) temporada; (*of films etc*) ciclo ♦ *vt* (*food*) sazonar; **in/out of ~** en sazón/fuera de temporada; **~al** *adj* estacional; **~ed** *adj* (*fig*) experimentado; **~ing** *n* condimento, aderezo; **~ ticket** *n* abono
seat [si:t] *n* (*in bus, train*) asiento; (*chair*) silla; (*PARLIAMENT*) escaño; (*buttocks*) culo, trasero; (*of trousers*) culera ♦ *vt* sentar; (*have room for*) tener cabida para; **to be ~ed** sentarse; **~ belt** *n* cinturón *m* de seguridad
sea: **~ water** *n* agua del mar; **~weed** *n* alga marina; **~worthy** *adj* en condiciones de navegar

sec. *abbr* = **second(s)**
secluded [sɪ'klu:dɪd] *adj* retirado
seclusion [sɪ'klu:ʒən] *n* reclusión *f*
second ['sɛkənd] *adj* segundo ♦ *adv* en segundo lugar ♦ *n* segundo; (*AUT: also: ~ gear*) segunda; (*COMM*) artículo con algún desperfecto; (*BRIT: SCOL: degree*) título de licenciado con calificación de notable ♦ *vt* (*motion*) apoyar; (*BRIT: worker*) transferir; **~ary** *adj* secundario; **~ary school** *n* escuela secundaria; **~-class** *adj* de segunda clase ♦ *adv* (*RAIL*) en segunda; **~-hand** *adj* de segunda mano, usado; **~ hand** *n* (*on clock*) segundero; **~ly** *adv* en segundo lugar; **~ment** [sɪ'kɔndmənt] (*BRIT*) *n* traslado temporal; **~-rate** *adj* de segunda categoría; **~ thoughts** *npl*: **to have ~ thoughts** cambiar de opinión; **on ~ thoughts** *or* **thought** (*US*) pensándolo bien
secrecy ['si:krəsɪ] *n* secreto
secret ['si:krɪt] *adj, n* secreto; **in ~** en secreto
secretarial [sɛkrɪ'tɛərɪəl] *adj* de secretario; (*course, staff*) de secretariado
secretariat [sɛkrɪ'tɛərɪət] *n* secretaría
secretary ['sɛkrətərɪ] *n* secretario/a; **S~ of State (for)** (*BRIT: POL*) Ministro (de)
secretive ['si:krətɪv] *adj* reservado, sigiloso
secretly ['si:krɪtlɪ] *adv* en secreto
sect [sɛkt] *n* secta; **~arian** [-'tɛərɪən] *adj* sectario
section ['sɛkʃən] *n* sección *f*; (*part*) parte *f*; (*of document*) artículo; (*of opinion*) sector *m*; (*cross-~*) corte *m* transversal
sector ['sɛktə*] *n* sector *m*
secular ['sɛkjulə*] *adj* secular, seglar
secure [sɪ'kjuə*] *adj* seguro; (*firmly fixed*) firme, fijo ♦ *vt* (*fix*) asegurar, afianzar; (*get*) conseguir
security [sɪ'kjuərɪtɪ] *n* seguridad *f*; (*for loan*) fianza; (: *object*) prenda
sedan [sɪ'dæn] (*US*) *n* (*AUT*) sedán *m*
sedate [sɪ'deɪt] *adj* tranquilo; ♦ *vt* tratar con sedantes
sedation [sɪ'deɪʃən] *n* (*MED*) sedación *f*
sedative ['sɛdɪtɪv] *n* sedante *m*, sedativo
seduce [sɪ'dju:s] *vt* seducir; **seduction** [-'dʌkʃən] *n* seducción *f*; **seductive** [-'dʌktɪv] *adj* seductor(a)
see [si:] (*pt* **saw**, *pp* **seen**) *vt* ver; (*accompany*): **to ~ sb to the door** acompañar a uno a la puerta; (*understand*) ver, comprender ♦ *vi* ver ♦ *n* (*arz*)obispado; **to ~ that** (*ensure*) asegurar que; **~ you soon!** ¡hasta pronto!; **~ about** *vt fus* atender a, encargarse de; **~ off** *vt* despedir; **~ through** *vt fus* (*fig*) calar ♦ *vt* (*plan*) llevar a cabo; **~ to** *vt fus* atender a, encargarse de
seed [si:d] *n* semilla; (*in fruit*) pepita; (*fig: gen pl*) germen *m*; (*TENNIS*) preseleccionado/a; **to go to ~** (*plant*) granar; (*fig*) descuidarse; **~ling** *n* planta de

seeing → separate

semillero; **~y** adj (shabby) desaseado, raído
seeing ['si:ıŋ] conj: **~ (that)** visto que, en vista de que
seek [si:k] (pt, pp sought) vt buscar; (post) solicitar
seem [si:m] vi parecer; **there ~s to be ...** parece que hay ...; **~ingly** adv aparentemente, según parece
seen [si:n] pp of **see**
seep [si:p] vi filtrarse
seesaw ['si:sɔ:] n subibaja
seethe [si:ð] vi hervir; **to ~ with anger** estar furioso
see-through adj transparente
segment ['segmənt] n (part) sección f; (of orange) gajo
segregate ['segrıgeıt] vt segregar
seismic ['saızmık] adj sísmico
seize [si:z] vt (grasp) agarrar, asir; (take possession of) secuestrar; (: territory) apoderarse de; (opportunity) aprovecharse de; **~ (up)on** vt fus aprovechar; **~ up** vi (TECH) agarrotarse
seizure ['si:ʒə*] n (MED) ataque m; (LAW, of power) incautación f
seldom ['seldəm] adv rara vez
select [sı'lekt] adj selecto, escogido ♦ vt escoger, elegir; (SPORT) seleccionar; **~ion** [-'lekʃən] n selección f, elección f; (COMM) surtido
self [self] (pl selves) n uno mismo; **the ~** el yo ♦ prefix auto...; **~-assured** adj seguro de sí mismo; **~-catering** (BRIT) adj (flat etc) con cocina; **~-centred** (US **~-centered**) adj egocéntrico; **~-confidence** n confianza en sí mismo; **~-conscious** adj cohibido; **~-contained** (BRIT) adj (flat) con entrada particular; **~-control** n autodominio; **~-defence** (US **~-defense**) n defensa propia; **~-discipline** n autodisciplina; **~-employed** adj que trabaja por cuenta propia; **~-evident** adj patente; **~-governing** adj autónomo; **~-indulgent** adj autocomplaciente; **~-interest** n egoísmo; **~-ish** adj egoísta; **~-ishness** n egoísmo; **~-less** adj desinteresado; **~-made** adj: **~-made man** hombre m que se ha hecho a sí mismo; **~-pity** n lástima de sí mismo; **~-portrait** n autorretrato; **~-possessed** adj sereno, dueño de sí mismo; **~-preservation** n propia conservación f; **~-respect** n amor m propio; **~-righteous** adj santurrón/ona; **~-sacrifice** n abnegación f; **~-satisfied** adj satisfecho de sí mismo; **~-service** adj de autoservicio; **~-sufficient** adj autosuficiente; **~-taught** adj autodidacta
sell [sel] (pt, pp sold) vt vender ♦ vi venderse; **to ~ at or for £10** venderse a 10 libras; **~ off** vt liquidar; **~ out** vi: **to ~ out of tickets/milk** vender todas las entradas/toda la leche; **~-by date** n fecha de caducidad;

~er n vendedor(a) m/f; **~ing price** n precio de venta
sellotape ['seləuteıp] ® (BRIT) n cinta adhesiva, celo (SP), scotch m (AM)
selves [selvz] npl of **self**
semaphore ['seməfɔ:*] n semáforo
semblance ['sembləns] n apariencia
semen ['si:mən] n semen m
semester [sı'mestə*] (US) n semestre m
semi... [semı] prefix semi..., medio...; **~circle** n semicírculo; **~colon** n punto y coma; **~conductor** n semiconductor m; **~detached (house)** n (casa) semiseparada; **~final** n semi-final m; **~skimmed milk** n leche semidesnatada
seminar ['semına:*] n seminario
seminary ['semınərı] n (REL) seminario
semiskilled ['semıskıld] adj (work, worker) semi-cualificado
senate ['senıt] n senado; **senator** n senador(a) m/f
send [send] (pt, pp sent) vt mandar, enviar; (signal) transmitir; **~ away** vt despachar; **~ away for** vt fus pedir; **~ back** vt devolver; **~ for** vt fus mandar traer; **~ off** vt (goods) despachar; (BRIT: SPORT: player) expulsar; **~ out** vt (invitation) emitir; (signal) emitir; **~ up** vt (person, price) hacer subir; (BRIT: parody) parodiar; **~er** n remitente m/f; **~-off** n: **a good ~-off** una buena despedida
senior ['si:nıə*] adj (older) mayor, más viejo; (: on staff) de más antigüedad; (of higher rank) superior; **~ citizen** n persona de la tercera edad; **~ity** [-'ɒrıtı] n antigüedad f
sensation [sen'seıʃən] n sensación f; **~al** adj sensacional
sense [sens] n (faculty, meaning) sentido; (feeling) sensación f; (good ~) sentido común, juicio ♦ vt sentir, percibir; **it makes ~** tiene sentido; **~less** adj estúpido, insensato; (unconscious) sin conocimiento; **~ of humour** n sentido del humor
sensible ['sensıbl] adj sensato; (reasonable) razonable, lógico
sensitive ['sensıtıv] adj sensible; (touchy) susceptible
sensual ['sensjuəl] adj sensual
sensuous ['sensjuəs] adj sensual
sent [sent] pt, pp of **send**
sentence ['sentns] n (LING) oración f; (LAW) sentencia, fallo ♦ vt: **to ~ sb to death/to 5 years (in prison)** condenar a uno a muerte/a 5 años de cárcel
sentiment ['sentımənt] n sentimiento; (opinion) opinión f; **~al** [-'mentl] adj sentimental
sentry ['sentrı] n centinela m
separate [adj 'seprıt, vb 'sepəreıt] adj separado; (distinct) distinto ♦ vt separar; dividir ♦ vi separarse; **~s** npl (clothes) coordinados mpl; **~ly** adv por separado;

separation [-'reɪʃən] *n* separación *f*

September [sɛp'tɛmbə*] *n* se(p)tiembre *m*

septic ['sɛptɪk] *adj* séptico; ~ **tank** *n* fosa séptica

sequel ['siːkwl] *n* consecuencia, resultado; (*of story*) continuación *f*

sequence ['siːkwəns] *n* sucesión *f*, serie *f*; (*CINEMA*) secuencia

sequin ['siːkwɪn] *n* lentejuela

serene [sɪ'riːn] *adj* sereno, tranquilo

sergeant ['saːdʒənt] *n* sargento

serial ['sɪərɪəl] *n* (*TV*) telenovela, serie *f* televisiva; (*BOOK*) serie *f*; ~**ize** *vt* emitir como serial; ~ **number** *n* número de serie

series ['sɪəriːs] *n inv* serie *f*

serious ['sɪərɪəs] *adj* serio; (*grave*) grave; ~**ly** *adv* en serio; (*ill, wounded etc*) gravemente; ~**ness** *n* seriedad *f*; gravedad *f*

sermon ['saːmən] *n* sermón *m*

serrated [sɪ'reɪtɪd] *adj* serrado, dentellado

serum ['sɪərəm] *n* suero

servant ['saːvənt] *n* servidor(a) *m/f*; (*house* ~) criado/a

serve [saːv] *vt* servir; (*customer*) atender; (*subj: train*) pasar por; (*apprenticeship*) hacer; (*prison term*) cumplir ♦ *vi* (*at table*) servir; (*car etc*) servir de/para/para hacer ♦ *n* (*TENNIS*) saque *m*; it ~s him right se lo tiene merecido; ~ out *vt* (*food*) servir; ~ up *vt* = ~ out

service ['saːvɪs] *n* servicio; (*RFL*) misa; (*AUT*) mantenimiento; (*dishes etc*) juego ♦ *vt* (*car etc*) revisar; (*: repair*) reparar; the S~s *npl* las fuerzas armadas; to be of ~ to sb ser útil a uno; ~**able** *adj* servible, utilizable; ~ **area** *n* (*on motorway*) área de servicio; ~ **charge** (*BRIT*) *n* servicio; ~**man** *n* militar *m*; ~ **station** *n* estación *f* de servicio

serviette [saːvɪ'ɛt] (*BRIT*) *n* servilleta

session ['sɛʃən] *n* sesión *f*; to be in ~ estar en sesión

set [sɛt] (*pt, pp* set) *n* juego; (*RADIO*) aparato; (*TV*) televisor *m*; (*of utensils*) batería; (*of cutlery*) cubierto; (*of books*) colección *f*; (*TENNIS*) set *m*; (*group of people*) grupo; (*CINEMA*) plató *m*; (*THEATRE*) decorado; (*HAIRDRESSING*) marcado ♦ *adj* (*fixed*) fijo; (*ready*) listo ♦ *vt* (*place*) poner, colocar; (*fix*) fijar; (*adjust*) ajustar, arreglar; (*decide: rules etc*) establecer, decidir ♦ *vi* (*sun*) ponerse; (*jam, jelly*) cuajarse; (*concrete*) fraguar; (*bone*) componerse; to be ~ on doing sth estar empeñado en hacer algo; to ~ to music poner música a; to ~ on fire incendiar, poner fuego a; to ~ free poner en libertad; to ~ sth going poner algo en marcha; to ~ sail zarpar, hacerse a la vela; ~ about *vt fus* ponerse a; ~ aside *vt* poner aparte, dejar de lado; (*money, time*) reservar; ~ back *vt* (*cost*): to ~ sb back £5 costar a uno cinco libras; (: *in*

time): to ~ back (by) retrasar (por); ~ off *vi* partir ♦ *vt* (*bomb*) hacer estallar; (*events*) poner en marcha; (*show up well*) hacer resaltar; ~ out *vi* partir ♦ *vt* (*arrange*) disponer; (*state*) exponer; to ~ out to do sth proponerse hacer algo; to ~ up *vt* establecer; ~**back** *n* revés *m*, contratiempo; ~ **menu** *n* menú *m*

settee [sɛ'tiː] *n* sofá *m*

setting ['sɛtɪŋ] *n* (*scenery*) marco; (*position*) disposición *f*; (*of sun*) puesta; (*of jewel*) engaste *m*, montadura

settle ['sɛtl] *vt* (*argument*) resolver; (*accounts*) ajustar, liquidar; (*MED: calm*) calmar, sosegar ♦ *vi* (*dust etc*) depositarse; (*weather*) serenarse; (*also*: ~ down) instalarse; tranquilizarse; to ~ for sth convenir en aceptar algo; to ~ in *vi* instalarse; ~ up *vi*: to ~ up with sb ajustar cuentas con uno; ~**ment** *n* (*payment*) liquidación *f*; (*agreement*) acuerdo, convenio; (*village etc*) pueblo; ~**r** *n* colono/a, colonizador(a) *m/f*

setup ['sɛtʌp] *n* sistema *m*; (*situation*) situación *f*

seven ['sɛvn] *num* siete; ~**teen** *num* diez y siete, diecisiete; ~**th** *num* séptimo; ~**ty** *num* setenta

sever ['sɛvə*] *vt* cortar; (*relations*) romper

several ['sɛvərl] *adj, pron* varios/as *m/fpl*, algunos/as *mpl/fpl*; ~ of us varios de nosotros

severance ['sɛvərəns] *n* (*of relations*) ruptura; ~ **pay** *n* indemnización *f* por despido

severe [sɪ'vɪə*] *adj* severo; (*serious*) grave; (*hard*) duro; (*pain*) intenso; **severity** [sɪ'vɛrɪtɪ] *n* severidad *f*; gravedad *f*; intensidad *f*

sew [səu] (*pt* sewed, *pp* sewn) *vt, vi* coser; ~ up *vt* coser, zurcir

sewage ['suːɪdʒ] *n* aguas *fpl* residuales

sewer ['suːə*] *n* alcantarilla, cloaca

sewing ['səuɪŋ] *n* costura; ~ **machine** *n* máquina de coser

sewn [səun] *pp of* sew

sex [sɛks] *n* sexo; (*lovemaking*): to have ~ hacer el amor; ~**ist** *adj, n* sexista *m/f*; **sexual** ['sɛksjuəl] *adj* sexual; **sexy** *adj* sexy

shabby ['ʃæbɪ] *adj* (*person*) desharrapado; (*clothes*) raído, gastado; (*behaviour*) ruin *inv*

shack [ʃæk] *n* choza, chabola

shackles ['ʃæklz] *npl* grillos *mpl*, grilletes *mpl*

shade [ʃeɪd] *n* sombra; (*for lamp*) pantalla; (*for eyes*) visera; (*of colour*) matiz *m*, tonalidad *f*; (*small quantity*): a ~ (too big/more) un poquitín (grande/más) ♦ *vt* dar sombra a; (*eyes*) proteger del sol; in the ~ en la sombra

shadow ['ʃædəu] *n* sombra ♦ *vt* (*follow*) seguir y vigilar; ~ **cabinet** (*BRIT*) *n* (*POL*) gabinete paralelo formado por el partido de oposición; **~y** adj oscuro; (dim) indistinto

shady ['ʃeɪdɪ] adj sombreado; (fig: dishonest) sospechoso; (: deal) turbio

shaft [ʃɑːft] n (of arrow, spear) astil m; (AUT, TECH) eje m, árbol m; (of mine) pozo; (of lift) hueco, caja; (of light) rayo

shaggy ['ʃægɪ] adj peludo

shake [ʃeɪk] (pt shook, pp shaken) vt sacudir; (building) hacer temblar; (bottle, cocktail) agitar ♦ vi (tremble) temblar; **to ~ one's head** (in refusal) negar con la cabeza; (in dismay) mover o menear la cabeza, incrédulo; **to ~ hands with sb** estrechar la mano a uno; **~ off** vt sacudirse; (fig) deshacerse de; **~ up** vt agitar; (fig) reorganizar; **shaky** adj (hand, voice) trémulo; (building) inestable

shall [ʃæl] aux vb: **~ I help you?** ¿quieres que te ayude?; **I'll buy three, ~ I?** compro tres, ¿no te parece?

shallow ['ʃæləʊ] adj poco profundo; (fig) superficial

sham [ʃæm] n fraude m, engaño ♦ vt fingir, simular

shambles ['ʃæmblz] n confusión f

shame [ʃeɪm] n vergüenza ♦ vt avergonzar; **it is a ~ that/to do** es una lástima que/ hacer; **what a ~!** ¡qué lástima!; **~faced** adj avergonzado; **~ful** adj vergonzoso; **~less** adj desvergonzado

shampoo [ʃæm'puː] n champú m ♦ vt lavar con champú; **~ and set** n lavado y marcado

shamrock ['ʃæmrɒk] n trébol m (emblema nacional irlandés)

shandy ['ʃændɪ] n mezcla de cerveza con gaseosa

shan't [ʃɑːnt] = shall not

shanty town ['ʃæntɪ-] n barrio de chabolas

shape [ʃeɪp] n forma ♦ vt formar, dar forma a; (sb's ideas) formar; (sb's life) determinar; **to take ~** tomar forma; **~ up** vi (events) desarrollarse; (person) formarse; **-~d** suffix: **heart-~d** en forma de corazón; **~less** adj informe, sin forma definida; **~ly** adj (body etc) esbelto

share [ʃɛə*] n (part) parte f, porción f; (contribution) cuota; (COMM) acción f ♦ vt dividir; (have in common) compartir; **to ~ out** (among o between) repartir (entre); **~holder** (BRIT) n accionista m/f

shark [ʃɑːk] n tiburón m

sharp [ʃɑːp] adj (blade, nose) afilado; (point) puntiagudo; (outline) definido; (pain) intenso; (MUS) desafinado; (contrast) marcado; (voice) agudo; (person: quick-witted) astuto; (: dishonest) poco escrupuloso ♦ n (MUS) sostenido ♦ adv: **at 2 o'clock ~** a las 2 en punto; **~en** vt afilar; (pencil) sacar punta a; (fig) agudizar; **~ener** n (also: pencil ~ener) sacapuntas m inv; **~-eyed** adj de vista aguda; **~ly** adv (turn, stop) bruscamente; (stand out, contrast) claramente; (criticize, retort) severamente

shatter ['ʃætə*] vt hacer añicos or pedazos; (fig: ruin) destruir, acabar con ♦ vi hacerse añicos

shave [ʃeɪv] vt afeitar, rasurar ♦ vi afeitarse, rasurarse; **to have a ~** afeitarse; **~r** n (also: electric ~r) máquina de afeitar (eléctrica)

shaving ['ʃeɪvɪŋ] n (action) el afeitarse, rasurado; **~s** npl (of wood etc) virutas fpl; **~ brush** n brocha (de afeitar); **~ cream** n crema de afeitar; **~ foam** n espuma de afeitar

shawl [ʃɔːl] n chal m

she [ʃiː] pron ella; **~-cat** n gata

sheaf [ʃiːf] (pl sheaves) n (of corn) gavilla; (of papers) fajo

shear [ʃɪə*] (pt sheared, pp sheared or shorn) vt esquilar, trasquilar; **~s** npl (for hedge) tijeras fpl de jardín; **~ off** vi romperse

sheath [ʃiːθ] n vaina; (contraceptive) preservativo

sheaves [ʃiːvz] npl of sheaf

shed [ʃed] (pt, pp shed) n cobertizo ♦ vt (skin) mudar; (tears, blood) derramar; (load) derramar; (workers) despedir

she'd [ʃiːd] = she had; she would

sheen [ʃiːn] n brillo, lustre m

sheep [ʃiːp] n inv oveja; **~dog** n perro pastor; **~ish** adj tímido, vergonzoso; **~skin** n piel f de carnero

sheer [ʃɪə*] adj (utter) puro, completo; (steep) escarpado; (material) diáfano ♦ adv verticalmente

sheet [ʃiːt] n (on bed) sábana; (of paper) hoja; (of glass, metal) lámina; (of ice) capa

sheik(h) [ʃeɪk] n jeque m

shelf [ʃelf] (pl shelves) n estante m

shell [ʃel] n (on beach) concha; (of egg, nut etc) cáscara; (explosive) proyectil m, obús m; (of building) armazón f ♦ vt (peas) desenvainar; (MIL) bombardear

she'll [ʃiːl] = she will; she shall

shellfish ['ʃelfɪʃ] n inv crustáceo; (as food) mariscos mpl

shell suit n chándal m de calle

shelter ['ʃeltə*] n abrigo, refugio ♦ vt (aid) amparar, proteger; (give lodging to) abrigar ♦ vi abrigarse, refugiarse; **~ed** adj (life) protegido; (spot) abrigado; **~ed housing** n viviendas vigiladas para ancianos y minusválidos

shelve [ʃelv] vt (fig) aplazar; **~s** npl of shelf

shepherd ['ʃepəd] n pastor m ♦ vt (guide) guiar, conducir; **~'s pie** (BRIT) n pastel de carne y patatas

sherry ['ʃerɪ] n jerez m

she's [ʃiːz] = she is; she has

Shetland ['ʃetlənd] n (also: the ~s, the ~ Isles) las Islas de Zetlandia

shield [ʃiːld] n escudo; (protection) blindaje m ♦ vt: to ~ (from) proteger (de)

shift [ʃɪft] n (change) cambio; (at work) turno ♦ vt trasladar; (remove) quitar ♦ vi moverse; ~**less** adj (person) perezoso; ~ **work** n trabajo a turnos; ~**y** adj tramposo; (eyes) furtivo

shilling ['ʃɪlɪŋ] (BRIT) n chelín m

shilly-shally ['ʃɪlɪʃælɪ] vi titubear, vacilar

shimmer ['ʃɪmə*] n reflejo trémulo

shin [ʃɪn] n espinilla

shine [ʃaɪn] (pt, pp **shone**) n brillo, lustre m ♦ vi brillar, relucir ♦ vt (shoes) lustrar, sacar brillo a; to ~ **a torch on sth** dirigir una linterna hacia algo

shingle ['ʃɪŋgl] n (on beach) guijarros mpl; ~s n (MED) herpes mpl or fpl

shiny ['ʃaɪnɪ] adj brillante, lustroso

ship [ʃɪp] n buque m, barco ♦ vt (goods) embarcar; (send) transportar or enviar por vía marítima; ~**building** n construcción f de buques; ~**ment** n (goods) envío; ~**per** n exportador(a) m/f; ~**ping** n (act) embarque m; (traffic) buques mpl; ~**wreck** n naufragio ♦ vt: to be ~**wrecked** naufragar; ~**yard** n astillero

shire ['ʃaɪə*] (BRIT) n condado

shirk [ʃɜːk] vt (obligations) faltar a

shirt [ʃɜːt] n camisa; in (one's) ~ **sleeves** en mangas de camisa

shit [ʃɪt] (inf!) excl ¡mierda! (!)

shiver ['ʃɪvə*] n escalofrío ♦ vi temblar, estremecerse; (with cold) tiritar

shoal [ʃəʊl] n (of fish) banco; (fig: also: ~s) tropel m

shock [ʃɔk] n (impact) choque m; (ELEC) descarga (eléctrica); (emotional) conmoción f; (start) sobresalto, susto; (MED) postración f nerviosa ♦ vt dar un susto a; (offend) escandalizar; ~ **absorber** n amortiguador m; ~**ing** adj (awful) espantoso; (outrageous) escandaloso

shod [ʃɔd] pt, pp of **shoe**

shoddy ['ʃɔdɪ] adj de pacotilla

shoe [ʃuː] (pt, pp **shod**) n zapato; (for horse) herradura ♦ vt (horse) herrar; ~**brush** n cepillo para zapatos; ~**lace** n cordón m; ~ **polish** n betún m; ~**shop** n zapatería; ~**string** n (fig): on a ~**string** con muy poco dinero

shone [ʃɔn] pt, pp of **shine**

shoo [ʃuː] excl ¡fuera!

shook [ʃʊk] pt of **shake**

shoot [ʃuːt] (pt, pp **shot**) n (on branch, seedling) retoño, vástago ♦ vt disparar; (kill) matar a tiros; (wound) pegar un tiro; (execute) fusilar; (film) rodar, filmar ♦ vi (FOOTBALL) chutar; ~ **down** vt (plane) derribar; ~ **in/out** vi entrar corriendo/salir

disparado; ~ **up** vi (prices) dispararse; ~**ing** n (shots) tiros mpl; (HUNTING) caza con escopeta; ~**ing star** n estrella fugaz

shop [ʃɔp] n tienda; (workshop) taller m ♦ vi (also: go ~ping) ir de compras; ~ **assistant** (BRIT) n dependiente/a m/f; ~ **floor** (BRIT) n (fig) taller m, fábrica; ~**keeper** n tendero/a; ~**lifting** n mechería; ~**per** n comprador(a) m/f; ~**ping** n (goods) compras fpl; ~**ping bag** n bolsa (de compras); ~**ping centre** (US ~**ping center**) n centro comercial; ~**soiled** adj usado; ~ **steward** (BRIT) n (INDUSTRY) enlace m sindical; ~ **window** n escaparate m (SP), vidriera (AM)

shore [ʃɔː*] n orilla ♦ vt: to ~ **(up)** reforzar; on ~ en tierra

shorn [ʃɔːn] pp of **shear**

short [ʃɔːt] adj corto; (in time) breve, de corta duración; (person) bajo; (curt) brusco, seco; (insufficient) insuficiente; to be ~ of sth estar falto de algo; in ~ en pocas palabras; ~ of doing ... fuera de hacer ...; it is ~ for es la forma abreviada de; to cut ~ (speech, visit) interrumpir, terminar inesperadamente; everything ~ of ... todo menos ...; to fall ~ of no alcanzar; to run ~ of quedarle a uno poco; to stop ~ parar en seco; to stop ~ of detenerse antes de; ~**age** n: a ~**age of** una falta de; ~**bread** n especie de mantecada; ~**change** vt no dar el cambio completo a; ~**circuit** n cortocircuito; ~**coming** n defecto, deficiencia; ~**(crust) pastry** (BRIT) n pasta quebradiza; ~**cut** n atajo; ~**en** vt acortar; (visit) interrumpir; ~**fall** n déficit m; ~**hand** (BRIT) n taquigrafía; ~**hand typist** (BRIT) n taquimecanógrafo/a; ~ **list** (BRIT) n (for job) lista de candidatos escogidos; ~**lived** adj efímero; ~**ly** adv en breve, dentro de poco; ~**sighted** (BRIT) adj miope; (fig) imprudente; ~**staffed** adj: to be ~**staffed** estar falto de personal; ~ **story** n cuento; ~**tempered** adj enojadizo; ~**term** adj (effect) a corto plazo; ~**wave** n (RADIO) onda corta

shot [ʃɔt] pt, pp of **shoot** ♦ n (sound) tiro, disparo; (try) tentativa; (injection) inyección f; (PHOT) toma, fotografía; to be a **good/ poor** ~ (person) tener buena/mala puntería; **like a** ~ (without any delay) como un rayo; ~**gun** n escopeta

should [ʃʊd] aux vb: I ~ **go now** debo irme ahora; he ~ **be there now** debe de haber llegado (ya); I ~ **go if I were you** yo en tu lugar me iría; I ~ **like to** me gustaría

shoulder ['ʃəʊldə*] n hombro ♦ vt (fig) cargar con; ~ **bag** n cartera de bandolera; ~ **blade** n omóplato; ~ **strap** n tirante m

shouldn't ['ʃʊdnt] = should not

shout [ʃaʊt] n grito ♦ vt gritar ♦ vi gritar, dar voces; ~ **down** vt acallar a gritos;

~ing n griterío
shove [ʃʌv] n empujón m ♦ vt empujar;
(inf: put): **to ~ sth in** meter algo a empellones; **~ off** (inf) vi largarse
shovel ['ʃʌvl] n pala; (mechanical) excavadora ♦ vt mover con pala
show [ʃəu] (pt **showed**, pp **shown**) n (of emotion) demostración f; (semblance) apariencia; (exhibition) exposición f; (THEATRE) función f, espectáculo; (TV) show m ♦ vt mostrar, enseñar; (courage etc) mostrar, manifestar; (exhibit) exponer; (film) proyectar ♦ vi mostrarse; (appear) aparecer; **for ~** para impresionar; **on ~** (exhibits etc) expuesto; **~ in** vt (person) hacer pasar; **~ off** (pej) vi presumir ♦ vt (display) lucir; **~ out** vt: **to ~ sb out** acompañar a uno a la puerta; **~ up** vi (stand out) destacar; (inf: turn up) aparecer ♦ vt (unmask) desenmascarar; **~ business** n mundo del espectáculo; **~down** n enfrentamiento (final)
shower ['ʃauə*] n (rain) chaparrón m, chubasco; (of stones etc) lluvia; (for bathing) ducha (SP), regadera (AM) ♦ vi llover ♦ vt (fig): **to ~ sb with** sth colmar a uno de algo; **to have a ~** ducharse; **~proof** adj impermeable
showing ['ʃəuɪŋ] n (of film) proyección f
show jumping n hípica
shown [ʃəun] pp of **show**
show: **~-off** n (person) presumido/a; **~piece** n (of exhibition etc) objeto cumbre; **~room** n sala de muestras
shrank [ʃræŋk] pt of **shrink**
shrapnel ['ʃræpnl] n metralla
shred [ʃrɛd] n (gen pl) triza, jirón m ♦ vt hacer trizas; (CULIN) desmenuzar; **~der** n (vegetable ~der) picadora; (document ~der) trituradora (de papel)
shrewd [ʃru:d] adj astuto
shriek [ʃri:k] n chillido ♦ vi chillar
shrill [ʃrɪl] adj agudo, estridente
shrimp [ʃrɪmp] n camarón m
shrine [ʃraɪn] n santuario, sepulcro
shrink [ʃrɪŋk] (pt **shrank**, pp **shrunk**) vi encogerse; (be reduced) reducirse; (also: **~ away**) retroceder ♦ vt encoger ♦ n (inf: pej) loquero/a; **to ~ from (doing) sth** no atreverse a hacer algo; **~age** n encogimiento; reducción f; **~-wrap** vt embalar con película de plástico
shrivel ['ʃrɪvl] (also: **~ up**) vt (dry) secar ♦ vi secarse
shroud [ʃraud] n sudario ♦ vt: **~ed in mystery** envuelto en el misterio
Shrove Tuesday ['ʃrəuv-] n martes m de carnaval
shrub [ʃrʌb] n arbusto; **~bery** n arbustos mpl
shrug [ʃrʌg] n encogimiento de hombros ♦ vt, vi: **to ~ (one's shoulders)** encogerse de hombros; **~ off** vt negar importancia a

shrunk [ʃrʌŋk] pp of **shrink**
shudder ['ʃʌdə*] n estremecimiento, escalofrío ♦ vi estremecerse
shuffle ['ʃʌfl] vt (cards) barajar ♦ vi: **to ~ (one's feet)** arrastrar los pies
shun [ʃʌn] vt rehuir, esquivar
shunt [ʃʌnt] vt (train) maniobrar; (object) empujar
shut [ʃʌt] (pt, pp **shut**) vt cerrar ♦ vi cerrarse; **~ down** vt, vi cerrar; **~ off** vt (supply etc) cortar; **~ up** vi (inf: keep quiet) callarse ♦ vt (close) cerrar; (silence) hacer callar; **~ter** n contraventana; (PHOT) obturador m
shuttle ['ʃʌtl] n lanzadera; (also: **~ service**) servicio rápido y continuo entre dos puntos: (: AER) puente m aéreo
shuttlecock ['ʃʌtlkɔk] n volante m
shy [ʃaɪ] adj tímido; **~ness** n timidez f
sibling ['sɪblɪŋ] n hermano/a
Sicily ['sɪsɪlɪ] n Sicilia
sick [sɪk] adj (ill) enfermo; (nauseated) mareado; (humour) negro; (vomiting): **to be ~** (BRIT) vomitar; **to feel ~** tener náuseas; **to be ~ of** (fig) estar harto de; **~ bay** n enfermería; **~en** vt dar asco a; **~ening** adj (fig) asqueroso
sickle ['sɪkl] n hoz f
sick: **~ leave** n baja por enfermedad; **~ly** adj enfermizo; (smell) nauseabundo; **~ness** n enfermedad f, mal m; (vomiting) náuseas fpl; **~ pay** n subsidio de enfermedad
side [saɪd] n (gen) lado; (of body) costado; (of lake) orilla; (of hill) ladera; (team) equipo; ♦ adj (door, entrance) lateral ♦ vi: **to ~ with sb** tomar el partido de uno; **by the ~ of** al lado de; **~ by ~** juntos/as; **from ~ to ~** de un lado para otro; **from all ~s** de todos lados; **to take ~s (with)** tomar partido (con); **~board** n aparador m; **~boards** (BRIT) npl = **~burns**; **~burns** npl patillas fpl; **~ drum** n tambor m; **~ effect** n efecto secundario; **~light** n (AUT) luz f lateral; **~line** n (SPORT) línea de banda; (fig) empleo suplementario; **~long** adj de soslayo; **~saddle** adv a mujeriegas, a la inglesa; **~ show** n (stall) caseta; **~step** vt (fig) esquivar; **~ street** n calle f lateral; **~track** vt (fig) desviar (de su propósito); **~walk** (US) n acera; **~ways** adv de lado
siding ['saɪdɪŋ] n (RAIL) apartadero, vía muerta
sidle ['saɪdl] vi: **to ~ up (to)** acercarse furtivamente (a)
siege [si:dʒ] n cerco, sitio
sieve [sɪv] n colador m ♦ vt cribar
sift [sɪft] vt cribar; (fig: information) escudriñar
sigh [saɪ] n suspiro ♦ vi suspirar
sight [saɪt] n (faculty) vista; (spectacle) espectáculo; (on gun) mira, alza ♦ vt divisar; **in ~** a la vista; **out of ~** fuera de (la) vista; **on ~** (shoot) sin previo aviso; **~seeing** n

excursionismo, turismo; **to go ~seeing** hacer turismo

sign [saɪn] n (with hand) señal f, seña; (trace) huella, rastro; (notice) letrero; (written) signo ♦ vt firmar; (SPORT) fichar; **to ~ sth over to sb** firmar el traspaso de algo a uno; **~ on** vi (MIL) alistarse; (BRIT: as unemployed) registrarse como desempleado; (for course) inscribirse ♦ vt (MIL) alistar; (employee) contratar; **~ up** vi (MIL) alistarse; (for course) inscribirse ♦ vt (player) fichar

signal ['sɪgnl] n señal f ♦ vi señalizar ♦ vt (person) hacer señas a; (message) comunicar por señales; **~man** n (RAIL) guardavía m

signature ['sɪgnətʃə*] n firma; **~ tune** n sintonía de apertura de un programa

signet ring ['sɪgnət-] n anillo de sello

significance [sɪg'nɪfɪkəns] n (importance) trascendencia

significant [sɪg'nɪfɪkənt] adj significativo; (important) trascendente

signify ['sɪgnɪfaɪ] vt significar

sign language n lenguaje m para sordomudos

signpost ['saɪnpəust] n indicador m

silence ['saɪlns] n silencio ♦ vt acallar; (guns) reducir al silencio; **~r** n (on gun, BRIT: AUT) silenciador m

silent ['saɪlnt] adj silencioso; (not speaking) callado; (film) mudo; **to remain ~** guardar silencio; **~ partner** n (COMM) socio/a comanditario/a

silhouette [sɪluːˈɛt] n silueta

silicon chip ['sɪlɪkən-] n plaqueta de silicio

silk [sɪlk] n seda ♦ adj de seda; **~y** adj sedoso

silly ['sɪlɪ] adj (person) tonto; (idea) absurdo

silt [sɪlt] n sedimento

silver ['sɪlvə*] n plata; (money) moneda suelta ♦ adj de plata; (colour) plateado; **~ paper** (BRIT) n papel m de plata; **~-plated** adj plateado; **~smith** n platero/a; **~ware** n plata; **~y** adj argentino

similar ['sɪmɪlə*] adj: **~ (to)** parecido or semejante (a); **~ity** [-'lærɪtɪ] n semejanza; **~ly** adv del mismo modo

simile ['sɪmɪlɪ] n símil m

simmer ['sɪmə*] vi hervir a fuego lento

simpering ['sɪmpərɪŋ] adj (foolish) bobo

simple ['sɪmpl] adj (easy) sencillo; (foolish, COMM: interest) simple; **simplicity** [-'plɪsɪtɪ] n sencillez f; **simplify** ['sɪmplɪfaɪ] vt simplificar

simply ['sɪmplɪ] adv (live, talk) sencillamente; (just, merely) sólo

simulate ['sɪmjuːleɪt] vt fingir, simular; **~d** adj simulado; (fur) de imitación

simultaneous [sɪmǝl'teɪnɪǝs] adj simultáneo; **~ly** adv simultáneamente

sin [sɪn] n pecado ♦ vi pecar

since [sɪns] adv desde entonces, después ♦ prep desde ♦ conj (time) desde que; (because) ya que, puesto que; **~ then, ever ~** desde entonces

sincere [sɪnˈsɪǝ*] adj sincero; **~ly** adv: **yours ~ly** (in letters) le saluda atentamente; **sincerity** [-'sɛrɪtɪ] n sinceridad f

sinew ['sɪnjuː] n tendón m

sinful ['sɪnful] adj (thought) pecaminoso; (person) pecador(a)

sing [sɪŋ] (pt sang, pp sung) vt, vi cantar

Singapore [sɪŋǝ'pɔː*] n Singapur m

singe [sɪndʒ] vt chamuscar

singer ['sɪŋǝ*] n cantante m/f

singing ['sɪŋɪŋ] n canto

single ['sɪŋgl] adj único, solo; (unmarried) soltero; (not double) simple, sencillo ♦ n (BRIT: also: ~ ticket) billete m sencillo; (record) sencillo, single m; **~s** npl (TENNIS) individual m; **~ bed** cama individual; **~ out** vt (choose) escoger; **~-breasted** adj recto; **~ file** n: **in ~ file** en fila de uno; **~-handed** adv sin ayuda; **~-minded** adj resuelto, firme; **~ room** n cuarto individual

singly ['sɪŋglɪ] adv uno por uno

singular ['sɪŋgjulə*] adj (odd) raro, extraño; (outstanding) excepcional; (LING) singular ♦ n (LING) singular m

sinister ['sɪnɪstə*] adj siniestro

sink [sɪŋk] (pt sank, pp sunk) n fregadero ♦ vt (ship) hundir, echar a pique; (foundations) excavar ♦ vi (gen) hundirse; **to ~ sth into** hundir algo en; **~ in** vi (fig) penetrar, calar

sinner ['sɪnə*] n pecador(a) m/f

sinus ['saɪnǝs] n (ANAT) seno

sip [sɪp] n sorbo ♦ vt sorber, beber a sorbitos

siphon ['saɪfǝn] n sifón m; **~ off** vt desviar

sir [sǝ*] n señor m; **S~ John Smith** Sir John Smith; **yes ~** sí, señor

siren ['saɪǝrn] n sirena

sirloin ['sǝːlɔɪn] n (also: **~ steak**) solomillo

sissy ['sɪsɪ] (inf) n marica m

sister ['sɪstǝ*] n hermana; (BRIT: nurse) enfermera jefe; **~-in-law** n cuñada

sit [sɪt] (pt, pp sat) vi sentarse; (be sitting) estar sentado; (assembly) reunirse; (for painter) posar ♦ vt (exam) presentarse a; **~ down** vi sentarse; **~ in on** vt fus asistir a; **~ up** vi incorporarse; (not go to bed) velar

sitcom ['sɪtkǝm] n abbr (= situation comedy) comedia de situación

site [saɪt] n sitio; (also: building ~) solar m ♦ vt situar

sit-in n (demonstration) sentada

sitting ['sɪtɪŋ] n (of assembly etc) sesión f; (in canteen) turno; **~ room** n sala de estar

situated ['sɪtjueɪtɪd] adj situado

situation [sɪtju'eɪʃǝn] n situación f, **"~s vacant"** (BRIT) "ofrecen trabajo"

six [sɪks] *num* seis; **~teen** *num* diez y seis, dieciséis; **~th** *num* sexto; **~ty** *num* sesenta

size [saɪz] *n* tamaño; *(extent)* extensión *f*; *(of clothing)* talla; *(of shoes)* número; ~ **up** *vt* formarse una idea de; **~able** *adj* importante, considerable

sizzle ['sɪzl] *vi* crepitar

skate [skeɪt] *n* patín *m*; *(fish: pl inv)* raya ♦ *vi* patinar; **~board** *n* monopatín *m*; **~r** *n* patinador(a) *m/f*; **skating** *n* patinaje *m*; **skating rink** *n* pista de patinaje

skeleton ['skɛlɪtn] *n* esqueleto; *(TECH)* armazón *f*; *(outline)* esquema *m*; ~ **staff** *n* personal *m* reducido

skeptic *etc* ['skɛptɪk] *(US)* = **sceptic**

sketch [skɛtʃ] *n* *(drawing)* dibujo; *(outline)* esbozo, bosquejo; *(THEATRE)* sketch *m* ♦ *vt* dibujar; *(plan etc: also:* ~ *out)* esbozar; **~ book** *n* libro de dibujos; **~y** *adj* incompleto

skewer ['skjuːə*] *n* broqueta

ski [skiː] *n* esquí *m* ♦ *vi* esquiar; ~ **boot** *n* bota de esquí

skid [skɪd] *n* patinazo ♦ *vi* patinar

ski: **~er** *n* esquiador(a) *m/f*; **~ing** *n* esquí *m*; ~ **jump** *n* salto con esquís

skilful ['skɪlful] *(BRIT) adj* diestro, experto

ski lift *n* telesilla *m*, telesquí *m*

skill [skɪl] *n* destreza, pericia; técnica; **~ed** *adj* hábil, diestro; *(worker)* cualificado; **~full** *(US) adj* = **skilful**

skim [skɪm] *vt* *(milk)* desnatar; *(glide over)* rozar, rasar ♦ *vi:* **to ~ through** *(book)* hojear; **~med milk** *n* leche *f* desnatada

skimp [skɪmp] *vt* *(also:* ~ *on: work)* chapucear; *(cloth etc)* escatimar; **~y** *adj* escaso; *(skirt)* muy corto

skin [skɪn] *n* piel *f*; *(complexion)* cutis *m* ♦ *vt* *(fruit etc)* pelar; *(animal)* despellejar; ~ **cancer** *n* cáncer *m* de piel; **~-deep** *adj* superficial; ~ **diving** *n* buceo; **~ny** *adj* flaco; **~tight** *adj (dress etc)* muy ajustado

skip [skɪp] *n* brinco, salto; *(BRIT: container)* contenedor *m* ♦ *vi* brincar; *(with rope)* saltar a la comba ♦ *vt* saltarse

ski pants *npl* pantalones *mpl* de esquí

ski pole *n* bastón *m* de esquiar

skipper ['skɪpə*] *n* *(NAUT, SPORT)* capitán *m*

skipping rope ['skɪpɪŋ-] *(BRIT) n* comba

skirmish ['skɜːmɪʃ] *n* escaramuza

skirt [skɜːt] *n* falda *(SP)*, pollera *(AM)* ♦ *vt* *(go round)* ladear; **~ing board** *(BRIT) n* rodapié *m*

ski slope *n* pista de esquí

ski suit *n* traje *m* de esquiar

skittle ['skɪtl] *n* bolo; **~s** *n* *(game)* boliche *m*

skive [skaɪv] *(BRIT: inf) vi* gandulear

skulk [skʌlk] *vi* esconderse

skull [skʌl] *n* calavera; *(ANAT)* cráneo

skunk [skʌŋk] *n* mofeta

sky [skaɪ] *n* cielo; **~light** *n* tragaluz *m*, claraboya; **~scraper** *n* rascacielos *m inv*

slab [slæb] *n* *(stone)* bloque *m*; *(flat)* losa; *(of cake)* trozo

slack [slæk] *adj* *(loose)* flojo; *(slow)* de poca actividad; *(careless)* descuidado; **~s** *npl* pantalones *mpl*; **~en** *(also:* ~*en off) vi* aflojarse ♦ *vt* aflojar; *(speed)* disminuir

slag heap ['slæg-] *n* escorial *m*, escombrera

slag off *(BRIT: inf) vt* poner como un trapo

slain [sleɪn] *pp of* **slay**

slam [slæm] *vt* *(throw)* arrojar (violentamente); *(criticize)* criticar duramente ♦ *vi* *(door)* cerrarse de golpe; **to ~ the door** dar un portazo

slander ['slɑːndə*] *n* calumnia, difamación *f*

slang [slæŋ] *n* argot *m*; *(jargon)* jerga

slant [slɑːnt] *n* sesgo, inclinación *f*; *(fig)* interpretación *f*; **~ed** *adj (fig)* parcial; **~ing** *adj* inclinado; *(eyes)* rasgado

slap [slæp] *n* palmada; *(in face)* bofetada ♦ *vt* dar una palmada *or* bofetada a; *(paint etc):* **to ~ sth on sth** embadurnar algo con algo ♦ *adv* *(directly)* exactamente, directamente; **~dash** *adj* descuidado; **~stick** *n* comedia de golpe y porrazo; **~-up** *adj:* **a ~-up meal** *(BRIT)* un banquetazo, una comilona

slash [slæʃ] *vt* acuchillar; *(fig: prices)* fulminar

slat [slæt] *n* tablilla, listón *m*

slate [sleɪt] *n* pizarra ♦ *vt* *(fig: criticize)* criticar duramente

slaughter ['slɔːtə*] *n* *(of animals)* matanza; *(of people)* carnicería ♦ *vt* matar; **~house** *n* matadero

Slav [slɑːv] *adj* eslavo

slave [sleɪv] *n* esclavo/a ♦ *vi* *(also:* ~ *away)* sudar tinta; **~ry** *n* esclavitud *f*

slay [sleɪ] *(pt* **slew**, *pp* **slain**) *vt* matar

sleazy ['sliːzɪ] *adj* de mala fama

sledge [slɛdʒ] *n* trineo; **~hammer** *n* mazo

sleek [sliːk] *adj* *(shiny)* lustroso; *(car etc)* elegante

sleep [sliːp] *(pt, pp* **slept**) *n* sueño ♦ *vi* dormir; **to go to ~** quedarse dormido; ~ **around** *vi* acostarse con cualquiera; ~ **in** *vi* *(oversleep)* quedarse dormido; **~er** *n* *(person)* durmiente *m/f*; *(BRIT: RAIL: on track)* traviesa; (: *train)* coche-cama *m*; **~ing bag** *n* saco de dormir; **~ing car** *n* coche-cama *m*; **~ing partner** *(BRIT) n* *(COMM)* socio comanditario; **~ing pill** *n* somnífero; **~less** *adj:* **a ~less night** una noche en blanco; **~walker** *n* sonámbulo/a; **~y** *adj* soñoliento; *(place)* soporífero

sleet [sliːt] *n* aguanieve *f*

sleeve [sliːv] *n* manga; *(TECH)* manguito; *(of record)* portada; **~less** *adj* sin mangas

sleigh [sleɪ] *n* trineo

sleight [slaɪt] *n:* ~ **of hand** escamoteo

slender ['slɛndə*] *adj* delgado; (*means*) escaso

slept [slɛpt] *pt, pp of* **sleep**

slew [sluː] *pt of* **slay** ♦ *vi* (*BRIT: veer*) torcerse

slice [slaɪs] *n* (*of meat*) tajada; (*of bread*) rebanada; (*of lemon*) rodaja; (*utensil*) pala ♦ *vt* cortar (en tajos); rebanar

slick [slɪk] *adj* (*skilful*) hábil, diestro; (*clever*) astuto ♦ *n* (*also: oil ~*) marea negra

slide [slaɪd] *n* (*movement*) descenso, desprendimiento; (*in playground*) tobogán *m*; (*PHOT*) diapositiva; (*BRIT: also: hair ~*) pasador *m* ♦ *vt* correr, deslizar ♦ *vi* (*slip*) resbalarse; (*glide*) deslizarse; **sliding** *adj* (*door*) corredizo; **sliding scale** *n* escala móvil

slight [slaɪt] *adj* (*slim*) delgado; (*frail*) delicado; (*pain etc*) leve; (*trivial*) insignificante; (*small*) pequeño ♦ *n* desaire *m* ♦ *vt* (*insult*) ofender, desairar; **not in the ~est** en absoluto; **~ly** *adv* ligeramente, un poco

slim [slɪm] *adj* delgado, esbelto; (*fig: chance*) remoto ♦ *vi* adelgazar

slime [slaɪm] *n* limo, cieno; **slimy** *adj* cenagoso

slimming ['slɪmɪŋ] *n* adelgazamiento

sling [slɪŋ] (*pt, pp* **slung**) *n* (*MED*) cabestrillo; (*weapon*) honda ♦ *vt* tirar, arrojar

slip [slɪp] *n* (*slide*) resbalón *m*; (*mistake*) descuido; (*underskirt*) combinación *f*; (*of paper*) papelito ♦ *vt* (*slide*) deslizar ♦ *vi* deslizarse; (*stumble*) resbalar(se); (*decline*) decaer; (*move smoothly*): **to ~ into/out of** (*room etc*) introducirse en/salirse de; **to give sb the ~** eludir a uno; **a ~ of the tongue** un lapsus; **to ~ sth on/off** ponerse/quitarse algo; **~ away** *vi* escabullirse; **~ in** *vt* meter ♦ *vi* meterse; **~ out** *vi* (*go out*) salir (un momento); **~ up** *vi* (*make mistake*) equivocarse; meter la pata; **~ped disc** *n* vértebra dislocada

slipper ['slɪpə*] *n* zapatilla, pantufla

slippery ['slɪpərɪ] *adj* resbaladizo

slip: **~ road** (*BRIT*) *n* carretera de acceso; **~shod** *adj* descuidado; **~-up** *n* (*error*) desliz *m*; **~way** *n* grada, gradas *fpl*

slit [slɪt] (*pt, pp* **slit**) *n* raja; (*cut*) corte *m* ♦ *vt* rajar; cortar

slither ['slɪðə*] *vi* deslizarse

sliver ['slɪvə*] *n* (*of glass, wood*) astilla; (*of cheese etc*) raja

slob [slɒb] (*inf*) *n* abandonado/a

slog [slɒg] (*BRIT*) *vi* sudar tinta; **it was a ~** costó trabajo (hacerlo)

slogan ['sləʊgən] *n* eslogan *m*, lema *m*

slop [slɒp] *vi* (*also: ~ over*) derramarse, desbordarse ♦ *vt* derramar, verter

slope [sləʊp] *n* (*up*) cuesta, pendiente *f*; (*down*) declive *m*; (*side of mountain*) falda, vertiente *m* ♦ *vi*: **to ~ down** estar en declive; **to ~ up** inclinarse; **sloping** *adj* en pen-

diente; en declive; (*writing*) inclinado

sloppy ['slɒpɪ] *adj* (*work*) descuidado; (*appearance*) desaliñado

slot [slɒt] *n* ranura ♦ *vt*: **to ~ into** encajar en

sloth [sləʊθ] *n* (*laziness*) pereza

slot machine *n* (*BRIT: vending machine*) distribuidor *m* automático; (*for gambling*) tragaperras *m inv*

slouch [slaʊtʃ] *vi* andar *etc* con los hombros caídos

Slovenia [sləʊˈviːnɪə] *n* Eslovenia

slovenly ['slʌvənlɪ] *adj* desaliñado, desaseado; (*careless*) descuidado

slow [sləʊ] *adj* lento; (*not clever*) lerdo; (*watch*): **to be ~** atrasar ♦ *adv* lentamente, despacio ♦ *vt, vi* (*also: ~ down, ~ up*) retardar; **"~"** (*road sign*) "disminuir velocidad"; **~down** (*US*) *n* huelga de manos caídas; **~ly** *adv* lentamente, despacio; **~ motion** *n*: **in ~ motion** a cámara lenta

sludge [slʌdʒ] *n* lodo, fango

slue [sluː] (*US*) *vi* = **slew**

slug [slʌg] *n* babosa; (*bullet*) posta; **~gish** *adj* lento; (*person*) perezoso

sluice [sluːs] *n* (*gate*) esclusa; (*channel*) canal *m*

slum [slʌm] *n* casucha

slump [slʌmp] *n* (*economic*) depresión *f* ♦ *vi* hundirse; (*prices*) caer en picado

slung [slʌŋ] *pt, pp of* **sling**

slur [sləː*] *n*: **to cast a ~ on** insultar ♦ *vt* (*speech*) pronunciar mal

slush [slʌʃ] *n* nieve *f* a medio derretir; **~ fund** *n* caja negra (*fondos para sobornar*)

slut [slʌt] *n* putona

sly [slaɪ] *adj* astuto; (*smile*) taimado

smack [smæk] *n* bofetada ♦ *vt* dar con la mano a; (*child, on face*) abofetear ♦ *vi*: **to ~ of** saber a, oler a

small [smɔːl] *adj* pequeño; **~ ads** (*BRIT*) *npl* anuncios *mpl* por palabras; **~ change** *n* suelto, cambio; **~ fry** *npl* gente *f* del montón; **~holder** (*BRIT*) *n* granjero/a, parcelero/a; **~ hours** *npl*: **in the ~ hours** a las altas horas (de la noche); **~pox** *n* viruela; **~ talk** *n* cháchara

smart [smɑːt] *adj* elegante; (*clever*) listo, inteligente; (*quick*) rápido, vivo ♦ *vi* escocer, picar; **~en up** *vi* arreglarse ♦ *vt* arreglar

smash [smæʃ] *n* (*also: ~-up*) choque *m*; (*MUS*) exitazo ♦ *vt* (*break*) hacer pedazos; (*car etc*) estrellar; (*SPORT: record*) batir ♦ *vi* hacerse pedazos; (*against wall etc*) estrellarse; **~ing** (*inf*) *adj* estupendo

smattering ['smætərɪŋ] *n*: **a ~ of** algo de

smear [smɪə*] *n* mancha; (*MED*) frotis *m inv* ♦ *vt* untar; **~ campaign** *n* campaña de desprestigio

smell [smɛl] (*pt, pp* **smelt** *or* **smelled**) *n* olor *m*; (*sense*) olfato ♦ *vt, vi* oler; **~y** *adj* maloliente

smile [smaɪl] n sonrisa ♦ vi sonreír
smirk [smɜːk] n sonrisa falsa or afectada
smith [smɪθ] n herrero; **~y** ['smɪðɪ] n herrería
smock [smɔk] n blusa; (children's) mandilón m; (US: overall) guardapolvo
smog [smɔg] n esmog m
smoke [sməuk] n humo ♦ vi fumar; (chimney) echar humo ♦ vt (cigarettes) fumar; **~d** adj (bacon, glass) ahumado; **~r** n fumador(a) m/f; (RAIL) coche m fumador; **~ screen** n cortina de humo; **~ shop** (US) n estanco (SP), tabaquería (AM); **smoking** n: **"no smoking"** "prohibido fumar"; **smoky** adj (room) lleno de humo; (taste) ahumado
smolder ['sməuldə*] (US) vi = smoulder
smooth [smuːð] adj liso; (sea) tranquilo; (flavour, movement) suave; (sauce) fino; (person: pej) meloso ♦ vt (also: ~ out) alisar; (creases, difficulties) allanar
smother ['smʌðə*] vt sofocar; (repress) contener
smoulder ['sməuldə*] (US smolder) vi arder sin llama
smudge [smʌdʒ] n mancha ♦ vt manchar
smug [smʌg] adj presumido; orondo
smuggle ['smʌgl] vt pasar de contrabando; **~r** n contrabandista m/f; **smuggling** n contrabando
smutty ['smʌtɪ] adj (fig) verde, obsceno
snack [snæk] n bocado; **~ bar** n cafetería
snag [snæg] n problema m
snail [sneɪl] n caracol m
snake [sneɪk] n serpiente f
snap [snæp] n (sound) chasquido; (photograph) foto f ♦ adj (decision) instantáneo ♦ vt (break) quebrar; (fingers) castañetear ♦ vi quebrarse; (fig: speak sharply) contestar bruscamente; **to ~ shut** cerrarse de golpe; **~ at** vt fus (subj: dog) intentar morder; **~ off** vi partirse; **~ up** vt agarrar; **~ fastener** (US) n botón m de presión; **~py** (inf) adj (answer) instantáneo; (slogan) conciso; **make it ~py!** (hurry up) ¡date prisa!; **~shot** n foto f (instantánea)
snare [snɛə*] n trampa
snarl [snɑːl] vi gruñir
snatch [snætʃ] n (small piece) fragmento ♦ vt (~ away) arrebatar; (fig) agarrar; **to ~ some sleep** encontrar tiempo para dormir
sneak [sniːk] (pt (US) snuck) vi: **to ~ in/out** entrar/salir a hurtadillas ♦ n (inf) soplón/ona m/f; **to ~ up on sb** aparecérsele de improviso a uno; **~ers** npl zapatos mpl de lona; **~y** adj furtivo
sneer [snɪə*] vi reír con sarcasmo; (mock): **to ~ at** burlarse de
sneeze [sniːz] vi estornudar
sniff [snɪf] vi sollozar ♦ vt husmear, oler; (drugs) esnifar
snigger ['snɪgə*] vi reírse con disimulo
snip [snɪp] n tijeretazo; (BRIT: inf: bargain)

ganga ♦ vt tijeretear
sniper ['snaɪpə*] n francotirador(a) m/f
snippet ['snɪpɪt] n retazo
snivelling ['snɪvlɪŋ] adj llorón/ona
snob [snɔb] n (e)snob m/f; **~bery** n (e)snobismo; **~bish** adj (e)snob
snooker ['snuːkə*] n especie de billar
snoop [snuːp] vi: **to ~ about** fisgonear
snooty ['snuːtɪ] adj (e)snob
snooze [snuːz] n siesta ♦ vi echar una siesta
snore [snɔː*] n ronquido ♦ vi roncar
snorkel ['snɔːkl] n (tubo) respirador m
snort [snɔːt] n bufido ♦ vi bufar
snout [snaut] n hocico, morro
snow [snəu] n nieve f ♦ vi nevar; **~ball** n bola de nieve ♦ vi (fig) agrandarse, ampliarse; **~bound** adj bloqueado por la nieve; **~drift** n ventisquero; **~drop** n campanilla; **~fall** n nevada; **~flake** n copo de nieve; **~man** n figura de nieve; **~plough** (US **~plow**) n quitanieves m inv; **~shoe** n raqueta (de nieve); **~storm** n nevada, nevasca
snub [snʌb] vt (person) desairar ♦ n desaire m, repulsa; **~-nosed** adj chato
snuff [snʌf] n rapé m
snug [snʌg] adj (cosy) cómodo; (fitted) ajustado
snuggle ['snʌgl] vi: **to ~ up to sb** arrimarse a uno

— **KEYWORD**

so [səu] adv **1** (thus, likewise) así, de este modo; **if ~** de ser así; **I like swimming — ~ do I** a mí me gusta nadar — a mí también; **I've got work to do — ~ has Paul** tengo trabajo que hacer — Paul también; **it's 5 o'clock — ~ it is!** son las cinco — ¡pues es verdad!; **I hope/think ~** espero/creo que sí; **~ far** hasta ahora; (in past) hasta este momento
2 (in comparisons etc: to such a degree) tan; **~ quickly (that)** tan rápido (que); **~ big (that)** tan grande (que); **she's not ~ clever as her brother** no es tan lista como su hermano; **we were ~ worried** estábamos preocupadísimos
3: **~ much** adj, adv tanto; **~ many** tantos/as
4 (phrases): **10 or ~** unos 10, 10 o así; **~ long!** (inf: goodbye) ¡hasta luego!
♦ conj **1** (expressing purpose): **~ as to do** para hacer; **~ (that)** para que + sub
2 (expressing result) así que; **~ you see, I could have gone** así que ya ves, (yo) podría haber ido

soak [səuk] vt (drench) empapar; (steep in water) remojar ♦ vi remojarse, estar a remojo; **~ in** vi penetrar; **~ up** vt absorber
soap [səup] n jabón m; **~flakes** npl esca-

mas *fpl* de jabón; ~ **opera** *n* telenovela; ~
powder *n* jabón *m* en polvo; ~**y** *adj* jabo-
noso

soar [sɔ:*] *vi* (*on wings*) remontarse; (*rocket, prices*) dispararse; (*building etc*) elevarse

sob [sɔb] *n* sollozo ♦ *vi* sollozar

sober ['səubə*] *adj* (*serious*) serio; (*not drunk*) sobrio; (*colour, style*) discreto; ~ **up** *vt* quitar la borrachera

so-called *adj* así llamado

soccer ['sɔkə*] *n* fútbol *m*

social ['səuʃl] *adj* social ♦ *n* velada, fiesta; ~ **club** *n* club *m*; ~**ism** *n* socialismo; ~**ist** *adj, n* socialista *m/f*; ~**ize** *vi*: to ~**ize** (**with**) alternar (con); ~**ly** *adv* socialmente; ~ **security** *n* seguridad *f* social; ~ **work** *n* asistencia social; ~ **worker** *n* asistente/a *m/f* social

society [sə'saɪətɪ] *n* sociedad *f*; (*club*) asociación *f*; (*also*: high ~) alta sociedad

sociology [səusɪ'ɔlədʒɪ] *n* sociología

sock [sɔk] *n* calcetín *m* (*SP*), media (*AM*)

socket ['sɔkɪt] *n* cavidad *f*; (*BRIT: ELEC*) enchufe *m*

sod [sɔd] *n* (*of earth*) césped *m*; (*BRIT: inf!*) cabrón/ona *m/f* (!)

soda ['səudə] *n* (*CHEM*) sosa; (*also*: ~ water) soda; (*US*: also: ~ pop) gaseosa

sodden ['sɔdn] *adj* empapado

sodium ['səudɪəm] *n* sodio

sofa ['səufə] *n* sofá *m*

soft [sɔft] *adj* (*lenient, not hard*) blando; (*gentle, not bright*) suave; ~ **drink** *n* bebida no alcohólica; ~**en** ['sɔfn] *vt* ablandar; sua-
vizar; (*effect*) amortiguar ♦ *vi* ablandarse; suavizarse; ~**ly** *adv* suavemente; (*gently*) delicadamente, con delicadeza; ~**ness** *n* blandura; suavidad *f*; ~ **spot** *n*: to have a ~ **spot for sb** tener debilidad por uno; ~**ware** *n* (*COMPUT*) software *m*

soggy ['sɔgɪ] *adj* empapado

soil [sɔɪl] *n* (*earth*) tierra, suelo ♦ *vt* ensuciar; ~**ed** *adj* sucio

solace ['sɔlɪs] *n* consuelo

solar ['səulə*] *adj*: ~ **energy** *n* energía solar; ~ **panel** *n* panel *m* solar

sold [səuld] *pt, pp* of **sell**; ~ **out** *adj* (*COMM*) agotado

solder ['səuldə*] *vt* soldar ♦ *n* soldadura

soldier ['səuldʒə*] *n* soldado; (*army man*) militar *m*

sole [səul] *n* (*of foot*) planta; (*of shoe*) suela; (*fish: pl inv*) lenguado ♦ *adj* único

solemn ['sɔləm] *adj* solemne

sole trader *n* (*COMM*) comerciante *m* exclusivo

solicit [sə'lɪsɪt] *vt* (*request*) solicitar ♦ *vi* (*prostitute*) importunar

solicitor [sə'lɪsɪtə*] (*BRIT*) *n* (*for wills etc*) ≈ notario/a; (*in court*) ≈ abogado/a

solid ['sɔlɪd] *adj* sólido; (*gold etc*) macizo ♦ *n* sólido; ~**s** *npl* (*food*) alimentos *mpl* sóli-

dos

solidarity [sɔlɪ'dærɪtɪ] *n* solidaridad *f*

solitaire [sɔlɪ'tɛə*] *n* (*game, gem*) solitario

solitary ['sɔlɪtərɪ] *adj* solitario, solo; ~ **confinement** *n* incomunicación *f*

solitude ['sɔlɪtjuːd] *n* soledad *f*

solo ['səuləu] *n* solo ♦ *adv* (*fly*) en solitario; ~**ist** *n* solista *m/f*

soluble ['sɔljuːbl] *adj* soluble

solution [sə'luːʃən] *n* solución *f*

solve [sɔlv] *vt* resolver, solucionar

solvent ['sɔlvənt] *adj* (*COMM*) solvente ♦ *n* (*CHEM*) solvente *m*

sombre ['sɔmbə*] (*US* **somber**) *adj* sombrío

────────── **KEYWORD**

some [sʌm] *adj* **1** (*a certain amount or num-
ber of*): ~ **tea/water/biscuits** té/agua/(unas) galletas; **there's** ~ **milk in the fridge** hay leche en el frigo; **there were** ~ **people outside** había algunas personas fuera; **I've got** ~ **money, but not much** tengo algo de dinero, pero no mucho

2 (*certain: in contrasts*) algunos/as; ~ **people say that ...** hay quien dice que ...; ~ **films were excellent, but most were mediocre** hubo películas excelentes, pero la mayoría fueron mediocres

3 (*unspecified*): ~ **woman was asking for you** una mujer estuvo preguntando por ti; **he was asking for** ~ **book (or other)** pe-
día un libro; ~ **day** algún día; ~ **day next week** un día de la semana que viene

♦ *pron* **1** (*a certain number*): **I've got** ~ (*books etc*) tengo algunos/as

2 (*a certain amount*) algo; **I've got** ~ (*mon-
ey, milk*) tengo algo; **could I have** ~ **of that cheese?** ¿me puede dar un poco de ese queso?; **I've read** ~ **of the book** he leído parte del libro

♦ *adv*: ~ **10 people** unas 10 personas, una decena de personas

somebody ['sʌmbədɪ] *pron* = **someone**

somehow ['sʌmhau] *adv* de alguna manera; (*for some reason*) por una u otra razón

someone ['sʌmwʌn] *pron* alguien

someplace ['sʌmpleɪs] (*US*) *adv* = **somewhere**

somersault ['sʌməsɔːlt] *n* (*deliberate*) salto mortal; (*accidental*) vuelco ♦ *vi* dar un salto mortal; dar vuelcos

something ['sʌmθɪŋ] *pron* algo; **would you like** ~ **to eat/drink?** ¿te gustaría cenar/tomar algo?

sometime ['sʌmtaɪm] *adv* (*in future*) algún día, en algún momento; (*in past*): ~ **last month** durante el mes pasado

sometimes ['sʌmtaɪmz] *adv* a veces

somewhat ['sʌmwɔt] *adv* algo

somewhere ['sʌmwɛə*] *adv* (*be*) en alguna

parte; (go) a alguna parte; ~ **else** (be) en otra parte; (go) a otra parte

son [sʌn] n hijo
song [sɔŋ] n canción f
son-in-law n yerno
sonnet ['sɔnɪt] n soneto
sonny ['sʌnɪ] (inf) n hijo
soon [suːn] adv pronto, dentro de poco; ~ **afterwards** poco después; see also as; ~**er** adv (time) antes, más temprano; (preference): **I would ~er do that** preferiría hacer eso; ~**er or later** tarde o temprano
soot [sut] n hollín m
soothe [suːð] vt tranquilizar; (pain) aliviar
sophisticated [sə'fɪstɪkeɪtɪd] adj sofisticado
sophomore ['sɔfəmɔː*] (US) n estudiante m/f de segundo año
sopping ['sɔpɪŋ] adj: ~ (**wet**) empapado
soppy ['sɔpɪ] (pej) adj tonto
soprano [sə'prɑːnəu] n soprano f
sorcerer ['sɔːsərə*] n hechicero
sore [sɔː*] adj (painful) doloroso, que duele ♦ n llaga; ~**ly** adv: **I am ~ly tempted to** estoy muy tentado a
sorrow ['sɔrəu] n pena, dolor m; ~**s** npl pesares mpl; ~**ful** adj triste
sorry ['sɔrɪ] adj (regretful) arrepentido; (condition, excuse) lastimoso; ~! ¡perdón!, ¡perdone!; ~? ¿cómo?; **to feel ~ for sb** tener lástima a uno; **I feel ~ for him** me da lástima
sort [sɔːt] n clase f, género, tipo ♦ vt (also: ~ out: papers) clasificar; (: problems) arreglar, solucionar; ~**ing office** n sala de batalla
SOS n abbr (= save our souls) SOS m
so-so adv regular, así así
soufflé ['suːfleɪ] n suflé m
sought [sɔːt] pt, pp of seek
soul [səul] n alma; ~**-destroying** adj (work) deprimente; ~**ful** adj lleno de sentimiento
sound [saund] n (noise) sonido, ruido; (volume: on TV etc) volumen m; (GEO) estrecho ♦ adj (healthy) sano; (safe, not damaged) en buen estado; (reliable: person) digno de confianza; (sensible) sensato, razonable; (secure: investment) seguro ♦ adv: ~ **asleep** profundamente dormido ♦ vt (alarm) sonar ♦ vi sonar, resonar; (fig: seem) parecer; **to ~ like** sonar a; ~ **out** vt sondear; ~ **barrier** n barrera del sonido; ~ **effects** npl efectos mpl sonoros; ~**ly** adv (sleep) profundamente; (beaten) completamente; ~**proof** adj insonorizado; ~**track** n (of film) banda sonora
soup [suːp] n (thick) sopa; (thin) caldo; **in the** ~ (fig) en apuros; ~ **plate** n plato sopero; ~**spoon** n cuchara sopera
sour ['sauə*] adj agrio; (milk) cortado; **it's ~ grapes** (fig) están verdes
source [sɔːs] n fuente f

south [sauθ] n sur m ♦ adj del sur, sureño ♦ adv al sur, hacia el sur; **S~ Africa** n África del Sur; **S~ African** adj, n sudafricano/a m/f; **S~ America** n América del Sur, Sudamérica; **S~ American** adj, n sudamericano/a m/f; ~**-east** n sudeste m; ~**erly** ['sʌðəlɪ] adj sur; (from the ~) del sur; ~**ern** ['sʌðən] adj del sur, meridional; **S~ Pole** n Polo Sur; ~**ward(s)** adv hacia el sur; ~**-west** n suroeste m
souvenir [suːvə'nɪə*] n recuerdo
sovereign ['sɔvrɪn] adj, n soberano/a m/f; ~**ty** n soberanía
soviet ['səuvɪət] adj soviético; **the S~ Union** la Unión Soviética
sow¹ [səu] (pt sowed, pp sown) ♦ vt sembrar
sow² [sau] n cerda (SP), puerca (SP), chancha (AM)
soy [sɔɪ] (US) n = soya
soya ['sɔɪə] (BRIT) n soja; ~ **bean** n haba de soja; ~ **sauce** n salsa de soja
spa [spɑː] n balneario
space [speɪs] n espacio; (room) sitio ♦ cpd espacial ♦ vt (also: ~ out) espaciar; ~**craft** n nave f espacial; ~**man/woman** n astronauta m/f, cosmonauta m/f; ~**ship** n = ~craft; **spacing** n espaciado
spacious ['speɪʃəs] adj amplio
spade [speɪd] n (tool) pala, laya; ~**s** npl (CARDS: British) picas fpl, (: Spanish) espadas fpl
spaghetti [spə'gɛtɪ] n espaguetis mpl, fideos mpl
Spain [speɪn] n España
span [spæn] n (of bird, plane) envergadura; (of arch) luz f; (in time) lapso ♦ vt extenderse sobre, cruzar; (fig) abarcar
Spaniard ['spænjəd] n español(a) m/f
spaniel ['spænjəl] n perro de aguas
Spanish ['spænɪʃ] adj español(a) ♦ n (LING) español m, castellano; **the** ~ npl los españoles
spank [spæŋk] vt zurrar
spanner ['spænə*] (BRIT) n llave f (inglesa)
spar [spɑː*] n palo, verga ♦ vi (BOXING) entrenarse
spare [spɛə*] adj de reserva; (surplus) sobrante, de más ♦ n = ~ **part** ♦ vt (do without) pasarse sin; (refrain from hurting) perdonar; **to** ~ (surplus) sobrante, de sobra; ~ **part** n pieza de repuesto; ~ **time** n tiempo libre; ~ **wheel** n (AUT) rueda de recambio
sparing ['spɛərɪŋ] adj: **to be ~ with** ser parco en; ~**ly** adv con moderación
spark [spɑːk] n chispa; (fig) chispazo; ~**(ing) plug** n bujía
sparkle ['spɑːkl] n centelleo, destello ♦ vi (shine) relucir, brillar; **sparkling** adj (eyes, conversation) brillante; (wine) espumoso; (mineral water) con gas

sparrow ['spærəu] *n* gorrión *m*
sparse [spɑːs] *adj* esparcido, escaso
spartan ['spɑːtən] *adj* (*fig*) espartano
spasm ['spæzəm] *n* (*MED*) espasmo
spastic ['spæstɪk] *n* espástico/a
spat [spæt] *pt*, *pp* of **spit**
spate [speɪt] *n* (*fig*): **a ~ of** un torrente de
spatter ['spætə*] *vt*: **to ~ with** salpicar de
spawn [spɔːn] *vi* desovar, frezar ♦ *n* huevas *fpl*
speak [spiːk] (*pt* **spoke**, *pp* **spoken**) *vt* (*language*) hablar; (*truth*) decir ♦ *vi* hablar; (*make a speech*) intervenir; **to ~ to sb/of** *or* **about sth** hablar con uno/de *or* sobre algo; **~ up!** ¡habla fuerte!; **~er** *n* (*in public*) · orador(a) *m/f*; (*also: loud~er*) altavoz *m*; (*for stereo etc*) bafle *m*; (*POL*): **the S~er** (*BRIT*) el Presidente de la Cámara de los Comunes; (*US*) el Presidente del Congreso
spear [spɪə*] *n* lanza ♦ *vt* alancear; **~head** *vt* (*attack etc*) encabezar
spec [spɛk] (*inf*) *n*: **on ~** como especulación
special ['spɛʃl] *adj* especial; (*edition etc*) extraordinario; (*delivery*) urgente; **~ist** *n* especialista *m/f*; **~ity** [spɛʃɪ'ælɪtɪ] (*BRIT*) *n* especialidad *f*; **~ize** *vi*: **to ~ize (in)** especializarse (en); **~ly** *adv* sobre todo, en particular; **~ty** (*US*) *n* = **~ity**
species ['spiːʃiːz] *n inv* especie *f*
specific [spə'sɪfɪk] *adj* específico; **~ally** *adv* específicamente
specify ['spɛsɪfaɪ] *vt*, *vi* especificar, precisar
specimen ['spɛsɪmən] *n* ejemplar *m*; (*MED*: *of urine*) espécimen *m* (: *of blood*) muestra
speck [spɛk] *n* grano, mota
speckled ['spɛkld] *adj* moteado
specs [spɛks] (*inf*) *npl* gafas *fpl* (*SP*), anteojos *mpl*
spectacle ['spɛktəkl] *n* espectáculo; **~s** *npl* (*BRIT*: *glasses*) gafas *fpl* (*SP*), anteojos *mpl*; **spectacular** [-'tækjulə*] *adj* espectacular; (*success*) impresionante
spectator [spɛk'teɪtə*] *n* espectador(a) *m/f*
spectre ['spɛktə*] (*US* **specter**) *n* espectro, fantasma *m*
spectrum ['spɛktrəm] (*pl* **spectra**) *n* espectro
speculate ['spɛkjuleɪt] *vi*: **to ~ (on)** especular (en)
speculation [spɛkju'leɪʃən] *n* especulación *f*
speech [spiːtʃ] *n* (*faculty*) habla; (*formal talk*) discurso; (*spoken language*) lenguaje *m*; **~less** *adj* mudo, estupefacto; **~ therapist** *n* especialista que corrige defectos de pronunciación en los niños
speed [spiːd] *n* velocidad *f*; (*haste*) prisa; (*promptness*) rapidez *f*; **at full** *or* **top ~** a máxima velocidad; **~ up** *vi* acelerarse ♦ *vt* acelerar; **~boat** *n* lancha motora; **~ily** *adv* rápido, rápidamente; **~ing** *n* (*AUT*) exceso

de velocidad; **~ limit** *n* límite *m* de velocidad, velocidad *f* máxima; **~ometer** [spɪ'dɔmɪtə*] *n* velocímetro; **~way** *n* (*sport*) pista de carrera; **~y** *adj* (*fast*) veloz, rápido; (*prompt*) pronto
spell [spɛl] (*pt*, *pp* **spelt** (*BRIT*) *or* **spelled**) *n* (*also: magic ~*) encanto, hechizo; (*period of time*) rato, período ♦ *vt* deletrear; (*fig*) anunciar, presagiar; **to cast a ~ on sb** hechizar a uno; **he can't ~** pone faltas de ortografía; **~bound** *adj* embelesado, hechizado; **~ing** *n* ortografía
spend [spɛnd] (*pt*, *pp* **spent**) *vt* (*money*) gastar; (*time*) pasar; (*life*) dedicar; **~thrift** *n* derrochador(a) *m/f*, pródigo/a
sperm [spɜːm] *n* esperma
spew [spjuː] *vt* vomitar, arrojar
sphere [sfɪə*] *n* esfera
sphinx [sfɪŋks] *n* esfinge *f*
spice [spaɪs] *n* especia ♦ *vt* condimentar
spick-and-span ['spɪkən'spæn] *adj* aseado, (bien) arreglado
spicy ['spaɪsɪ] *adj* picante
spider ['spaɪdə*] *n* araña
spike [spaɪk] *n* (*point*) punta; (*BOT*) espiga
spill [spɪl] (*pt*, *pp* **spilt** *or* **spilled**) *vt* derramar, verter ♦ *vi* derramarse; **to ~ over** desbordarse
spin [spɪn] (*pt*, *pp* **spun**) *n* (*AVIAT*) barrena; (*trip in car*) paseo (en coche); (*on ball*) efecto ♦ *vt* (*wool etc*) hilar; (*ball etc*) hacer girar ♦ *vi* girar, dar vueltas; **~ out** *vt* alargar, prolongar
spinach ['spɪnɪtʃ] *n* espinaca; (*as food*) espinacas *fpl*
spinal ['spaɪnl] *adj* espinal; **~ cord** *n* columna vertebral
spindly ['spɪndlɪ] *adj* (*leg*) zanquivano
spin-dryer (*BRIT*) *n* secador *m* centrífugo
spine [spaɪn] *n* espinazo, columna vertebral; (*thorn*) espina; **~less** *adj* (*fig*) débil, pusilánime
spinning ['spɪnɪŋ] *n* hilandería; **~ top** *n* peonza; **~ wheel** *n* torno de hilar
spin-off *n* derivado, producto secundario
spinster ['spɪnstə*] *n* solterona
spiral ['spaɪərl] *n* espiral *f* ♦ *vi* (*fig*: *prices*) subir desorbitadamente; **~ staircase** *n* escalera de caracol
spire ['spaɪə*] *n* aguja, chapitel *m*
spirit ['spɪrɪt] *n* (*soul*) alma *f*; (*ghost*) fantasma *m*; (*attitude*, *sense*) espíritu *m*; (*courage*) valor *m*, ánimo *m*; **~s** *npl* (*drink*) licor(es) *m(pl)*; **in good ~s** alegre, de buen ánimo; **~ed** *adj* enérgico, vigoroso; **~ level** *n* nivel *m* de aire
spiritual ['spɪrɪtjuəl] *adj* espiritual ♦ *n* espiritual *m*
spit [spɪt] (*pt*, *pp* **spat**) *n* (*for roasting*) asador *m*, espetón *m*; (*saliva*) saliva ♦ *vi* escupir; (*sound*) chisporrotear; (*rain*) lloviznar
spite [spaɪt] *n* rencor *m*, ojeriza ♦ *vt* causar

pena a, mortificar; **in** ~ **of** a pesar de, pese a; **~ful** adj rencoroso, malévolo

spittle ['spɪtl] n saliva, baba

splash [splæʃ] n (sound) chapoteo; (of colour) mancha ♦ vt salpicar ♦ vi (also: ~ about) chapotear

spleen [spliːn] n (ANAT) bazo

splendid ['splendɪd] adj espléndido

splint [splɪnt] n tablilla

splinter ['splɪntə*] n (of wood etc) astilla; (in finger) espigón m ♦ vi astillarse, hacer astillas

split [splɪt] (pt, pp **split**) n hendedura, raja; (fig) división f; (POL) escisión f ♦ vt partir, rajar; (party) dividir; (share) repartir ♦ vi dividirse, escindirse; ~ **up** vi (couple) separarse; (meeting) acabarse

splutter ['splʌtə*] vi chisporrotear; (person) balbucear

spoil [spɔɪl] (pt, pp **spoilt** or **spoiled**) vt (damage) dañar; (mar) estropear; (child) mimar, consentir; **~s** npl despojo, botín m; **~sport** n aguafiestas m inv

spoke [spəʊk] pt of **speak** ♦ n rayo, radio

spoken ['spəʊkn] pp of **speak**

spokesman ['spəʊksmən] n portavoz m; **spokeswoman** ['spəʊkswʊmən] n portavoz f

sponge [spʌndʒ] n esponja; (also: ~ **cake**) bizcocho ♦ vt (wash) lavar con esponja ♦ vi: **to ~ off** or **on sb** vivir a costa de uno; ~ **bag** (BRIT) n esponjera

sponsor ['spɒnsə*] n patrocinador(a) m/f ♦ vt (applicant, proposal etc) proponer; **~ship** n patrocinio

spontaneous [spɒn'teɪnɪəs] adj espontáneo

spooky ['spuːkɪ] (inf) adj espeluznante, horripilante

spool [spuːl] n carrete m

spoon [spuːn] n cuchara; **~-feed** vt dar de comer con cuchara a; (fig) tratar como un niño a; **~ful** n cucharada

sport [spɔːt] n deporte m; (person): **to be a good ~** ser muy majo ♦ vt (wear) lucir, ostentar; **~ing** adj deportivo; (generous) caballeroso; **to give sb a ~ing chance** darle a uno una (buena) oportunidad; ~ **jacket** (US) n = ~**s jacket**; **~s car** n coche m deportivo; **~s jacket** (BRIT) n chaqueta deportiva; **sportsman** n deportista m; **sportsmanship** n deportividad f; **sportswear** n trajes mpl de deporte or sport; **sportswoman** n deportista f; **~y** adj deportista

spot [spɒt] n sitio, lugar m; (dot: on pattern) punto, mancha; (pimple) grano; (RADIO) cuña publicitaria; (TV) espacio publicitario; (small amount): **a ~ of** un poquito de ♦ vt (notice) notar, observar; **on the ~** allí mismo; ~ **check** n reconocimiento rápido; **~less** adj perfectamente limpio; **~light** n foco, reflector m; (AUT) faro auxiliar; **~ted**

adj (pattern) de puntos; **~ty** adj (face) con granos

spouse [spauz] n cónyuge m/f

spout [spaut] n (of jug) pico; (of pipe) caño ♦ vi salir en chorro

sprain [spreɪn] n torcedura ♦ vt: **to ~ one's ankle/wrist** torcerse el tobillo/la muñeca

sprang [spræŋ] pt of **spring**

sprawl [sprɔːl] vi tumbarse

spray [spreɪ] n rociada; (of sea) espuma; (container) atomizador m; (for paint etc) pistola rociadora; (of flowers) ramita ♦ vt rociar; (crops) regar

spread [spred] (pt, pp **spread**) n extensión f; (for bread etc) pasta para untar; (inf: food) comilona ♦ vt extender; (butter) untar; (wings, sails) desplegar; (work, wealth) repartir; (scatter) esparcir ♦ vi (also: ~ **out**: stain) extenderse; (news) diseminarse; ~ **out** vi (move apart) separarse; **~-eagled** adj a pata tendida; **~sheet** n (COMPUT) hoja electrónica or de cálculo

spree [spriː] n: **to go on a ~** ir de juerga

sprightly ['spraɪtlɪ] adj vivo, enérgico

spring [sprɪŋ] (pt **sprang**, pp **sprung**) n (season) primavera; (leap) salto, brinco; (coiled metal) resorte m; (of water) fuente f, manantial m ♦ vi saltar, brincar; ~ **up** vi (thing: appear) aparecer; (problem) surgir; **~board** n trampolín m; **~-clean(ing)** n limpieza general; **~time** n primavera

sprinkle ['sprɪŋkl] vt (pour: liquid) rociar; (: salt, sugar) espolvorear; **to ~ water** etc **on**, ~ **with water** etc rociar or salpicar de agua etc; **~r** n (for lawn) rociadera; (to put out fire) aparato de rociadura automática

sprint [sprɪnt] n esprint m ♦ vi esprintar

sprout [spraut] vi brotar, retoñar; **(Brussels) ~s** npl coles fpl de Bruselas

spruce [spruːs] n inv (BOT) pícea ♦ adj aseado, pulcro

sprung [sprʌŋ] pp of **spring**

spry [spraɪ] adj ágil, activo

spun [spʌn] pt, pp of **spin**

spur [spəː*] n espuela; (fig) estímulo, aguijón m ♦ vt (also: ~ **on**) estimular, incitar; **on the ~ of the moment** de improviso

spurious ['spjʊərɪəs] adj falso

spurn [spəːn] vt desdeñar, rechazar

spurt [spəːt] n chorro; (of energy) arrebato ♦ vi chorrear

spy [spaɪ] n espía m/f ♦ vi: **to ~ on** espiar a ♦ vt (see) divisar, lograr ver; **~ing** n espionaje m

sq. abbr = **square**

squabble ['skwɔbl] vi reñir, pelear

squad [skwɔd] n (MIL) pelotón m; (POLICE) brigada; (SPORT) equipo

squadron ['skwɔdrn] n (MIL) escuadrón m; (AVIAT, NAUT) escuadra

squalid ['skwɔlɪd] adj vil; (fig: sordid) sórdido

squall [skwɔːl] n (storm) chubasco; (wind) ráfaga

squalor ['skwɔlə*] n miseria

squander ['skwɔndə*] vt (money) derrochar, despilfarrar; (chances) desperdiciar

square [skwɛə*] n cuadro; (in town) plaza; (inf: person) carca m/f ♦ adj cuadrado; (inf: ideas, tastes) trasnochado ♦ vt (arrange) arreglar; (MATH) cuadrar; (reconcile) compaginar; **all** ~ igual(es); **to have a** ~ **meal** comer caliente; **2 metres** ~ 2 metros en cuadro; **2** ~ **metres** 2 metros cuadrados; ~**ly** adv de lleno

squash [skwɔʃ] n (BRIT: drink): **lemon/ orange** ~ zumo (SP) or jugo (AM) de limón/naranja; (US: BOT) calabacín m; (SPORT) squash m, frontenis m ♦ vt aplastar

squat [skwɔt] adj achaparrado ♦ vi (also: ~ down) agacharse, sentarse en cuclillas; ~**ter** n persona que ocupa ilegalmente una casa

squawk [skwɔːk] vi graznar

squeak [skwiːk] vi (hinge) chirriar, rechinar; (mouse) chillar

squeal [skwiːl] vi chillar, dar gritos agudos

squeamish ['skwiːmɪʃ] adj delicado, remilgado

squeeze [skwiːz] n presión f; (of hand) apretón m; (COMM) restricción f ♦ vt (hand, arm) apretar; ~ **out** vt exprimir

squelch [skwɛltʃ] vi chapotear

squid [skwɪd] n inv calamar m; (CULIN) calamares mpl

squiggle ['skwɪgl] n garabato

squint [skwɪnt] vi bizquear, ser bizco ♦ n (MED) estrabismo

squire ['skwaɪə*] (BRIT) n terrateniente m

squirm [skwɜːm] vi retorcerse, revolverse

squirrel ['skwɪrəl] n ardilla

squirt [skwɜːt] vi salir a chorros ♦ vt chiscar

Sr abbr = **senior**

St abbr = **saint; street**

stab [stæb] n (with knife) puñalada; (of pain) pinchazo; (inf: try): **to have a** ~ **at (doing) sth** intentar (hacer) algo ♦ vt apuñalar

stable ['steɪbl] adj estable ♦ n cuadra, caballeriza

stack [stæk] n montón m, pila ♦ vt amontonar, apilar

stadium ['steɪdɪəm] n estadio

staff [stɑːf] n (work force) personal m, plantilla; (BRIT: SCOL) cuerpo docente ♦ vt proveer de personal

stag [stæg] n ciervo, venado

stage [steɪdʒ] n escena; (point) etapa; (platform) plataforma; (profession): **the** ~ el teatro ♦ vt (play) poner en escena, representar; (organize) montar, organizar; **in** ~**s** por etapas; ~**coach** n diligencia; ~ **manager** n director(a) m/f de escena

stagger ['stægə*] vi tambalearse ♦ vt (amaze) asombrar; (hours, holidays) escalonar; ~**ing** adj asombroso

stagnant ['stægnənt] adj estancado

stagnate [stæg'neɪt] vi estancarse

stag party n despedida de soltero

staid [steɪd] adj serio, formal

stain [steɪn] n mancha; (colouring) tintura ♦ vt manchar; (wood) teñir; ~**ed glass window** n vidriera de colores; ~**less steel** n acero inoxidable; ~ **remover** n quitamanchas m inv

stair [stɛə*] n (step) peldaño, escalón m; ~**s** npl escaleras fpl; ~**case** n = ~**way**; ~**way** n escalera

stake [steɪk] n estaca, poste m; (COMM) interés m; (BETTING) apuesta ♦ vt (money) apostar; (life) arriesgar; (reputation) poner en juego; (claim) presentar una reclamación; **to be at** ~ estar en juego

stale [steɪl] adj (bread) duro; (food) pasado; (smell) rancio; (beer) agrio

stalemate ['steɪlmeɪt] n tablas fpl (por ahogado); (fig) estancamiento

stalk [stɔːk] n tallo, caña ♦ vt acechar, cazar al acecho; ~ **off** vi irse airado

stall [stɔːl] n (in market) puesto; (in stable) casilla (de establo) ♦ vt (AUT) calar; (fig) dar largas a ♦ vi (AUT) calarse; (fig) andarse con rodeos; ~**s** npl (BRIT: in cinema, theatre) butacas fpl

stallion ['stælɪən] n semental m

stalwart ['stɔːlwət] n leal

stamina ['stæmɪnə] n resistencia

stammer ['stæmə*] n tartamudeo ♦ vi tartamudear

stamp [stæmp] n sello (SP), estampilla (AM); (mark, also fig) marca, huella; (on document) timbre m ♦ vi (also: ~ **one's foot**) patear ♦ vt (mark) marcar; (letter) poner sellos or estampillas en; (with rubber ~) sellar; ~ **album** n álbum m para sellos or estampillas; ~ **collecting** n filatelia

stampede [stæm'piːd] n estampida

stance [stæns] n postura

stand [stænd] (pt, pp **stood**) n (position) posición f, postura; (for taxis) parada; (hall ~) perchero; (music ~) atril m; (SPORT) tribuna; (at exhibition) stand m ♦ vi (be) estar, encontrarse; (be on foot) estar de pie; (rise) levantarse; (remain) quedar en pie; (in election) presentar candidatura ♦ vt (place) poner, colocar; (withstand) aguantar, soportar; (invite to) invitar; **to make a** ~ (fig) mantener una postura firme; **to** ~ **for parliament** (BRIT) presentarse (como candidato) a las elecciones; ~ **by** vi (be ready) estar listo ♦ vt fus (opinion) aferrarse a; (person) apoyar; ~ **down** vi (withdraw) ceder el puesto; ~ **for** vt fus (signify) significar; (tolerate) aguantar, permitir; ~ **in for** vt fus suplir a; ~ **out** vi destacarse; ~ **up** vi levantarse, ponerse de pie; ~ **up for** vt fus defender; ~ **up to** vt fus hacer frente a

standard ['stændəd] n patrón m, norma; (level) nivel m; (flag) estandarte m ♦ adj (size etc) normal, corriente; (text) básico; ~s npl (morals) valores mpl morales; ~**ize** vt normalizar; ~ **lamp** (BRIT) n lámpara de pie; ~ **of living** n nivel m de vida

stand-by ['stændbaɪ] n (reserve) recurso seguro; **to be on** ~ estar sobre aviso; ~ **ticket** n (AVIAT) (billete m) standby m

stand-in ['stændɪn] n suplente m/f

standing ['stændɪŋ] adj (on foot) de pie, en pie; (permanent) permanente ♦ n reputación f; **of many years'** ~ que lleva muchos años; ~ **joke** n broma permanente; ~ **order** (BRIT) n (at bank) orden f de pago permanente; ~ **room** n sitio para estar de pie

stand: ~**-offish** adj reservado, poco afable; ~**point** n punto de vista; ~**still** n: **at a** ~**still** (industry, traffic) paralizado; (car) parado; **to come to a** ~**still** quedar paralizado; pararse

stank [stæŋk] pt of **stink**

staple ['steɪpl] n (for papers) grapa ♦ adj (food etc) básico ♦ vt grapar; ~**r** n grapadora

star [stɑː*] n estrella; (celebrity) estrella, astro ♦ vt (THEATRE, CINEMA) ser el/la protagonista de; **the** ~**s** npl (ASTROLOGY) el horóscopo

starboard ['stɑːbəd] n estribor m

starch [stɑːtʃ] n almidón m

stardom ['stɑːdəm] n estrellato

stare [stɛə*] n mirada fija ♦ vi: **to** ~ **at** mirar fijo

starfish ['stɑːfɪʃ] n estrella de mar

stark [stɑːk] adj (bleak) severo, escueto ♦ adv: ~ **naked** en cueros

starling ['stɑːlɪŋ] n estornino

starry ['stɑːrɪ] adj estrellado; ~**-eyed** adj (innocent) inocentón/ona, ingenuo

start [stɑːt] n principio, comienzo; (departure) salida; (sudden movement) salto, sobresalto; (advantage) ventaja ♦ vt empezar, comenzar; (cause) causar; (found) fundar; (engine) poner en marcha ♦ vi comenzar, empezar; (with fright) asustarse; (train etc) salir; **to** ~ **doing** or **to do sth** empezar a hacer algo; ~ **off** vi empezar, comenzar; (leave) salir, ponerse en camino; ~ **up** vi comenzar; (car) ponerse en marcha ♦ vt comenzar; poner en marcha; ~**er** n (AUT) botón m de arranque; (SPORT: official) juez m/f de salida; (BRIT: CULIN) entrada; ~**ing point** n punto de partida

startle ['stɑːtl] vt asustar, sobrecoger; **startling** adj alarmante

starvation [stɑː'veɪʃən] n hambre f

starve [stɑːv] vi tener mucha hambre; (to death) morir de hambre ♦ vt hacer pasar hambre

state [steɪt] n estado ♦ vt (say, declare) afirmar; **the S~s** los Estados Unidos; **to be in a** ~ estar agitado; ~**ly** adj majestuoso, imponente; ~**ment** n afirmación f; **statesman** n estadista m

static ['stætɪk] n (RADIO) parásitos mpl ♦ adj estático; ~ **electricity** n estática

station ['steɪʃən] n (gen) estación f; (RADIO) emisora; (rank) posición f social ♦ vt colocar, situar; (MIL) apostar

stationary ['steɪʃnərɪ] adj estacionario, fijo

stationer ['steɪʃənə*] n papelero/a; ~**'s (shop)** (BRIT) n papelería; ~**y** [-nərɪ] n papel m de escribir, artículos mpl de escritorio

station master n (RAIL) jefe m de estación

station wagon (US) n ranchera

statistic [stə'tɪstɪk] n estadística; ~**al** adj estadístico; ~**s** n (science) estadística

statue ['stætjuː] n estatua

status ['steɪtəs] n estado; (reputation) estatus m; ~ **symbol** n símbolo de prestigio

statute ['stætjuːt] n estatuto, ley f; **statutory** adj estatutario

staunch [stɔːntʃ] adj leal, incondicional

stave [steɪv] vt: **to** ~ **off** (attack) rechazar; (threat) evitar

stay [steɪ] n estancia ♦ vi quedar(se); (as guest) hospedarse; **to** ~ **put** seguir en el mismo sitio; **to** ~ **the night/5 days** pasar la noche/estar 5 días; ~ **behind** vi quedar atrás; ~ **in** vi quedarse en casa; ~ **on** vi quedarse; ~ **out** vi (of house) no volver a casa; (on strike) permanecer en huelga; ~ **up** vi (at night) velar, no acostarse; ~**ing power** n aguante m

stead [stɛd] n: **in sb's** ~ en lugar de uno; **to stand sb in good** ~ ser muy útil a uno

steadfast ['stɛdfɑːst] adj firme, resuelto

steadily ['stɛdɪlɪ] adv constantemente; (firmly) firmemente; (work, walk) sin parar; (gaze) fijamente

steady ['stɛdɪ] adj (firm) firme; (regular) regular; (person, character) sensato, juicioso; (boyfriend) formal; (look, voice) tranquilo ♦ vt (stabilize) estabilizar; (nerves) calmar

steak [steɪk] n (gen) filete m; (beef) bistec m

steal [stiːl] (pt **stole**, pp **stolen**) vt robar ♦ vi robar; (move secretly) andar a hurtadillas

stealth [stɛlθ] n: **by** ~ a escondidas, sigilosamente; ~**y** adj cauteloso, sigiloso

steam [stiːm] n vapor m; (mist) vaho, humo ♦ vt (CULIN) cocer al vapor ♦ vi echar vapor; ~ **engine** n máquina de vapor; ~ **r** n (buque m de) vapor m; ~**roller** n apisonadora; ~**ship** n = ~**er**; ~**y** adj (room) lleno de vapor; (window) empañado; (heat, atmosphere) bochornoso

steel [stiːl] n acero ♦ adj de acero; ~**works** n acería

steep [sti:p] *adj* escarpado, abrupto; *(stair)* empinado; *(price)* exorbitante, excesivo ♦ *vt* empapar, remojar

steeple ['sti:pl] *n* aguja; **~chase** *n* carrera de obstáculos

steer [stɪə*] *vt (car)* conducir *(SP)*, manejar *(AM)*; *(person)* dirigir ♦ *vi* conducir, manejar; **~ing** *n (AUT)* dirección *f*; **~ing wheel** *n* volante *m*

stem [stɛm] *n (of plant)* tallo; *(of glass)* pie *m* ♦ *vt* detener; *(blood)* restañar; **~ from** *vt fus* ser consecuencia de

stench [stɛntʃ] *n* hedor *m*

stencil ['stɛnsl] *n (pattern)* plantilla ♦ *vt* hacer un cliché de

stenographer [stɛ'nɔgrəfə*] *(US)* *n* taquígrafo/a

step [stɛp] *n* paso; *(on stair)* peldaño, escalón *m* ♦ *vi*: **to ~ forward/back** dar un paso adelante/hacia atrás; **~s** *npl (BRIT)* = **ladder**; **in/out of ~ (with)** acorde/en disonancia (con); **~ down** *vi (fig)* retirarse; **~ on** *vt fus* pisar; **~ up** *vt (increase)* aumentar; **~brother** *n* hermanastro; **~daughter** *n* hijastra; **~father** *n* padrastro; **~ladder** *n* escalera doble *or* de tijera; **~mother** *n* madrastra; **~ping stone** *n* pasadera; **~sister** *n* hermanastra; **~son** *n* hijastro

stereo ['stɛrɪəu] *n* estéreo ♦ *adj (also:* **~phonic)** estéreo, estereofónico

sterile ['stɛraɪl] *adj* estéril; **sterilize** ['stɛrɪlaɪz] *vt* esterilizar

sterling ['stə:lɪŋ] *adj (silver)* de ley ♦ *n (ECON)* (libras *fpl)* esterlinas *fpl*; **one pound ~** una libra esterlina

stern [stə:n] *adj* severo, austero ♦ *n (NAUT)* popa

stethoscope ['stɛθəskəup] *n* estetoscopio

stew [stju:] *n* cocido *(SP)*, estofado *(SP)*, guisado *(AM)* ♦ *vt* estofar, guisar; *(fruit)* cocer

steward ['stju:əd] *n* camarero; **~ess** *n (esp on plane)* azafata

stick [stɪk] *(pt, pp* **stuck)** *n* palo; *(of dynamite)* barreno; *(as weapon)* porra; *(walking* **~)** bastón *m* ♦ *vt (glue)* pegar; *(inf: put)* meter; *(: tolerate)* aguantar, soportar; *(thrust)*: **to ~ sth into** clavar *or* hincar algo en ♦ *vi* pegarse; *(be unmoveable)* quedarse parado; *(in mind)* quedarse grabado; **~ out** *vi* sobresalir; **~ up** *vi* sobresalir; **~ up for** *vt fus* defender; **~er** *n (label)* etiqueta engomada; *(with slogan)* pegatina; **~ing plaster** *n* esparadrapo

stickler ['stɪklə*] *n*: **to be a ~ for** insistir mucho en

stick-up *(inf)* *n* asalto, atraco

sticky ['stɪkɪ] *adj* pegajoso; *(label)* engomado; *(fig)* difícil

stiff [stɪf] *adj* rígido, tieso; *(hard)* duro; *(manner)* estirado; *(difficult)* difícil; *(person)*

inflexible; *(price)* exorbitante ♦ *adv*: **scared/bored ~** muerto de miedo/aburrimiento; **~en** *vi (muscles etc)* agarrotarse; **~ neck** *n* tortícolis *m inv*; **~ness** *n* rigidez *f*, tiesura

stifle ['staɪfl] *vt* ahogar, sofocar; **stifling** *adj (heat)* sofocante, bochornoso

stigma ['stɪgmə] *n (fig)* estigma *m*

stile [staɪl] *n* portillo, portilla

stiletto [stɪ'lɛtəu] *(BRIT)* *n (also:* **~ heel)** tacón *m* de aguja

still [stɪl] *adj* inmóvil, quieto ♦ *adv* todavía; *(even)* aun; *(nonetheless)* sin embargo, aun así; **~born** *adj* nacido muerto; **~ life** *n* naturaleza muerta

stilt [stɪlt] *n* zanco; *(pile)* pilar *m*, soporte *m*

stilted ['stɪltɪd] *adj* afectado

stimulate ['stɪmjuleɪt] *vt* estimular

stimuli ['stɪmjuːlaɪ] *npl of* **stimulus**

stimulus ['stɪmjuləs] *(pl* **stimuli)** *n* estímulo, incentivo

sting [stɪŋ] *(pt, pp* **stung)** *n* picadura; *(pain)* escozor *m*, picazón *f*; *(organ)* aguijón *m* ♦ *vt, vi* picar

stingy ['stɪndʒɪ] *adj* tacaño

stink [stɪŋk] *(pt* **stank,** *pp* **stunk)** *n* hedor *m*, tufo ♦ *vi* heder, apestar; **~ing** *adj* hediondo, fétido; *(fig: inf)* horrible

stint [stɪnt] *n* tarea, trabajo ♦ *vi*: **to ~ on** escatimar

stir [stə:*] *n (fig: agitation)* conmoción *f* ♦ *vt (tea etc)* remover; *(fig: emotions)* provocar ♦ *vi* moverse; **~ up** *vt (trouble)* fomentar

stirrup ['stɪrəp] *n* estribo

stitch [stɪtʃ] *n (SEWING)* puntada; *(KNITTING)* punto; *(MED)* punto (de sutura); *(pain)* punzada ♦ *vt* coser; *(MED)* suturar

stoat [stəut] *n* armiño

stock [stɔk] *n (COMM: reserves)* existencias *fpl*, stock *m*; *(: selection)* surtido; *(AGR)* ganado, ganadería; *(CULIN)* caldo; *(descent)* raza, estirpe *f*; *(FINANCE)* capital *m* ♦ *adj (fig: reply etc)* clásico ♦ *vt (have in ~)* tener existencias de; **~s and shares** acciones y valores; **in ~** en existencia *or* almacén; **out of ~** agotado; **to take ~ of** *(fig)* asesorar, examinar; **~ up with** *vt fus* abastecerse de; **~broker** ['stɔkbrəukə*] *n* agente *m/f or* corredor(a) *m/f* de bolsa; **~ cube** *(BRIT)* *n* pastilla de caldo; **~ exchange** *n* bolsa

stocking ['stɔkɪŋ] *n* media

stock: ~ist *(BRIT)* *n* distribuidor(a) *m/f*; **~ market** *n* bolsa (de valores); **~ phrase** *n* cliché *m*; **~pile** *n* reserva ♦ *vt* acumular, almacenar; **~taking** *(BRIT)* *n (COMM)* inventario

stocky ['stɔkɪ] *adj (strong)* robusto; *(short)* achaparrado

stodgy ['stɔdʒɪ] *adj* indigesto, pesado

stoke [stəuk] *vt* atizar

stole [stəul] *pt of* **steal** ♦ *n* estola

stolen ['stəuln] *pp of* **steal**

stolid ['stɔlɪd] *adj* imperturbable, impasible

stomach ['stʌmək] *n (ANAT)* estómago; *(belly)* vientre *m* ♦ *vt* tragar, aguantar; **~ache** *n* dolor *m* de estómago

stone [stəun] *n* piedra; *(in fruit)* hueso; = *6.348kg; 14 libras* ♦ *adj* de piedra ♦ *vt* apedrear; *(fruit)* deshuesar; **~-cold** *adj* helado; **~-deaf** *adj* sordo como una tapia; **~work** *n (art)* cantería; **stony** *adj* pedregoso; *(fig)* frío

stood [stud] *pt, pp of* **stand**

stool [stu:l] *n* taburete *m*

stoop [stu:p] *vi (also: ~ down)* doblarse, agacharse; *(also: have a ~)* ser cargado de espaldas

stop [stɔp] *n* parada; *(in punctuation)* punto ♦ *vt* parar, detener; *(break off)* suspender; *(block: pay)* suspender; *(: cheque)* invalidar; *(also: put a ~ to)* poner término a ♦ *vi* pararse, detenerse; *(end)* acabarse; **to ~ doing sth** dejar de hacer algo; **~ dead** *vi* pararse en seco; **~ off** *vi* interrumpir el viaje; **~ up** *vt (hole)* tapar; **~gap** *n (person)* interino/a; *(thing)* recurso provisional; **~over** *n* parada; *(AVIAT)* escala

stoppage ['stɔpɪdʒ] *n (strike)* paro; *(blockage)* obstrucción *f*

stopper ['stɔpə*] *n* tapón *m*

stop press *n* noticias *fpl* de última hora

stopwatch ['stɔpwɔtʃ] *n* cronómetro

storage ['stɔ:rɪdʒ] *n* almacenaje *m*; **~ heater** *n* acumulador *m*

store [stɔ:*] *n (stock)* provisión *f*; *(depot: BRIT: large shop)* almacén *m*; *(US)* tienda; *(reserve)* reserva, repuesto ♦ *vt* almacenar; **~s** *npl* víveres *mpl*; **in ~** *(fig)*: **to be in ~ for sb** esperarle a uno; **~ up** *vt* acumular; **~room** *n* despensa

storey ['stɔ:rɪ] *(US* **story**) *n* piso

stork [stɔ:k] *n* cigüeña

storm [stɔ:m] *n* tormenta; *(fig: of applause)* salva; *(: of criticism)* nube *f* ♦ *vi (fig)* rabiar ♦ *vt* tomar por asalto; **~y** *adj* tempestuoso

story ['stɔ:rɪ] *n* historia; *(lie)* mentira; *(US)* = **storey**; **~book** *n* libro de cuentos

stout [staut] *adj (strong)* sólido; *(fat)* gordo, corpulento; *(resolute)* resuelto ♦ *n* cerveza negra

stove [stəuv] *n (for cooking)* cocina; *(for heating)* estufa

stow [stəu] *vt (also: ~ away)* meter, poner; *(NAUT)* estibar; **~away** *n* polizón/ona *m/f*

straddle ['strædl] *vt* montar a horcajadas; *(fig)* abarcar

straggle ['strægl] *vi (houses etc)* extenderse; *(lag behind)* rezagarse; **straggly** *adj (hair)* desordenado

straight [streɪt] *adj* recto, derecho; *(frank)* franco, directo; *(simple)* sencillo ♦ *adv* derecho, directamente; *(drink)* sin mezcla; **to put *or* get sth ~** dejar algo en claro; **~ away, ~ off** en seguida; **~en** *vt (also: ~en out)* enderezar, poner derecho; **~-faced** *adj* serio; **~forward** *adj (simple)* sencillo; *(honest)* honrado, franco

strain [streɪn] *n* tensión *f*; *(TECH)* presión *f*; *(MED)* torcedura; *(breed)* tipo, variedad *f* ♦ *vt (back etc)* torcerse; *(resources)* agotar; *(stretch)* estirar; *(food, tea)* colar; **~s** *npl (MUS)* son *m*; **~ed** *adj (muscle)* torcido; *(laugh)* forzado; *(relations)* tenso; **~er** *n* colador *m*

strait [streɪt] *n (GEO)* estrecho; **to be in dire ~s** pasar grandes apuros; **~-jacket** *n* camisa de fuerza; **~-laced** *adj* mojigato, gazmoño

strand [strænd] *n (of thread)* hebra; *(of hair)* trenza; *(of rope)* ramal *m*

stranded ['strændɪd] *adj (person: without money)* desamparado; *(: without transport)* colgado

strange [streɪndʒ] *adj (not known)* desconocido; *(odd)* extraño, raro; **~ly** *adv* de un modo raro; *see also* **enough**; **~r** *n* desconocido/a; *(from another area)* forastero/a

strangle ['stræŋgl] *vt* estrangular; **~hold** *n (fig)* dominio completo

strap [stræp] *n* correa; *(of slip, dress)* tirante *m*

strapping ['stræpɪŋ] *adj* robusto, fornido

strategic [strə'ti:dʒɪk] *adj* estratégico

strategy ['strætɪdʒɪ] *n* estrategia

straw [strɔ:] *n* paja; *(drinking ~)* caña, pajita; **that's the last ~!** ¡eso es el colmo!

strawberry ['strɔ:bərɪ] *n* fresa, *(SP)*, frutilla *(AM)*

stray [streɪ] *adj (animal)* extraviado; *(bullet)* perdido; *(scattered)* disperso ♦ *vi* extraviarse, perderse; *(thoughts)* vagar

streak [stri:k] *n* raya; *(in hair)* raya ♦ *vt* rayar ♦ *vi*: **to ~ past** pasar como un rayo

stream [stri:m] *n* riachuelo, arroyo; *(of people, vehicles)* riada, caravana; *(of smoke, insults etc)* chorro ♦ *vt (SCOL)* dividir en grupos por habilidad ♦ *vi* correr, fluir; **to ~ in/out** *(people)* entrar/salir en tropel

streamer ['stri:mə*] *n* serpentina

streamlined ['stri:mlaɪnd] *adj* aerodinámico

street [stri:t] *n* calle *f*; **~car** *(US)* *n* tranvía *m*; **~ lamp** *n* farol *m*; **~ plan** *n* plano; **~wise** *(inf)* *adj* que tiene mucha calle

strength [strɛŋθ] *n* fuerza; *(of girder, knot etc)* resistencia; *(fig: power)* poder *m*; **~en** *vt* fortalecer, reforzar

strenuous ['strɛnjuəs] *adj (energetic, determined)* enérgico

stress [strɛs] *n* presión *f*; *(mental strain)* estrés *m*; *(accent)* acento ♦ *vt* subrayar, recalcar; *(syllable)* acentuar

stretch [strɛtʃ] *n (of sand etc)* trecho ♦ *vi* estirarse; *(extend)*: **to ~ to *or* as far as** extenderse hasta ♦ *vt* extender, estirar; (*make demands of*) exigir el máximo esfuerzo a; **to ~ to** *or* **as far as** extenderse hasta; **~ out** *vi* tenderse ♦ *vt* (*arm etc*) extender; (*spread*) estirar

stretcher ['strɛtʃə*] *n* camilla

strewn [struːn] *adj*: **~ with** cubierto *or* sembrado de

stricken ['strɪkən] *adj* (*person*) herido; (*city, industry etc*) condenado; **~ with** (*disease*) afectado por

strict [strɪkt] *adj* severo; (*exact*) estricto; **~ly** *adv* severamente; estrictamente

stride [straɪd] (*pt* **strode**, *pp* **stridden**) *n* zancada, tranco ♦ *vi* dar zancadas, andar a trancos

strident ['straɪdnt] *adj* estridente

strife [straɪf] *n* lucha

strike [straɪk] (*pt*, *pp* **struck**) *n* huelga; (*of oil etc*) descubrimiento; (*attack*) ataque *m* ♦ *vt* golpear, pegar; (*oil etc*) descubrir; (*bargain, deal*) cerrar ♦ *vi* declarar la huelga; (*attack*) atacar; (*clock*) dar la hora; **on ~** (*workers*) en huelga; **to ~ a match** encender un fósforo; **~ down** *vt* derribar; **~ up** *vt* (*MUS*) empezar a tocar; (*conversation*) entablar; (*friendship*) trabar; **~r** *n* huelgista *m/f*; (*SPORT*) delantero; **striking** *adj* llamativo

string [strɪŋ] (*pt*, *pp* **strung**) *n* (*gen*) cuerda; (*row*) hilera ♦ *vt*: **to ~ together** ensartar; **to ~ out** extenderse; **the ~s** *npl* (*MUS*) los instrumentos de cuerda; **to pull ~s** (*fig*) mover palancas; **~ bean** *n* judía verde, habichuela; **~(ed) instrument** *n* (*MUS*) instrumento de cuerda

stringent ['strɪndʒənt] *adj* riguroso, severo

strip [strɪp] *n* tira; (*of land*) franja; (*of metal*) cinta, lámina ♦ *vt* desnudar; (*paint*) quitar; (*also*: **~ down**: *machine*) desmontar ♦ *vi* desnudarse; **~ cartoon** *n* tira cómica (*SP*), historieta (*AM*)

stripe [straɪp] *n* raya; (*MIL*) galón *m*; **~d** *adj* a rayas, rayado

strip lighting *n* alumbrado fluorescente

stripper ['strɪpə*] *n* artista *m/f* de striptease

strive [straɪv] (*pt* **strove**, *pp* **striven**) *vi*: **to ~ for sth/to do sth** luchar por conseguir/ hacer algo; **striven** ['strɪvn] *pp of* **strive**

strode [strəʊd] *pt of* **stride**

stroke [strəʊk] *n* (*blow*) golpe *m*; (*SWIMMING*) brazada; (*MED*) apoplejía; (*of paintbrush*) toque *m* ♦ *vt* acariciar; **at a ~** de un solo golpe

stroll [strəʊl] *n* paseo, vuelta ♦ *vi* dar un paseo *or* una vuelta; **~er** (*US*) *n* (*for child*) sillita de ruedas

strong [strɒŋ] *adj* fuerte; **they are 50 ~** son 50; **~hold** *n* fortaleza; (*fig*) baluarte *m*; **~ly** *adv* fuertemente, con fuerza; (*believe*) firmemente; **~room** *n* cámara acorazada

strove [strəʊv] *pt of* **strive**

struck [strʌk] *pt*, *pp of* **strike**

structure ['strʌktʃə*] *n* estructura; (*building*) construcción *f*

struggle ['strʌgl] *n* lucha ♦ *vi* luchar

strum [strʌm] *vt* (*guitar*) rasguear

strung [strʌŋ] *pt*, *pp of* **string**

strut [strʌt] *n* puntal *m* ♦ *vi* pavonearse

stub [stʌb] *n* (*of ticket etc*) talón *m*; (*of cigarette*) colilla; **to ~ one's toe on sth** dar con el dedo (del pie) contra algo; **~ out** *vt* apagar

stubble ['stʌbl] *n* rastrojo; (*on chin*) barba (incipiente)

stubborn ['stʌbən] *adj* terco, testarudo

stuck [stʌk] *pt*, *pp of* **stick** ♦ *adj* (*jammed*) atascado; **~-up** *adj* engreído, presumido

stud [stʌd] *n* (*shirt ~*) corchete *m*; (*of boot*) taco; (*earring*) pendiente *m* (de bolita); (*also*: **~ farm**) caballeriza; (*also*: **~ horse**) caballo semental ♦ *vt* (*fig*): **~ded with** salpicado de

student ['stjuːdənt] *n* estudiante *m/f* ♦ *adj* estudiantil; **~ driver** (*US*) *n* aprendiz(a) *m/f*

studio ['stjuːdɪəʊ] *n* estudio; (*artist's*) taller *m*; **~ flat** (*US* **~ apartment**) *n* estudio

studious ['stjuːdɪəs] *adj* estudioso; (*studied*) calculado; **~ly** *adv* (*carefully*) con esmero

study ['stʌdɪ] *n* estudio ♦ *vt* estudiar; (*examine*) examinar, investigar ♦ *vi* estudiar

stuff [stʌf] *n* materia; (*substance*) material *m*, sustancia; (*things*) cosas *fpl* ♦ *vt* llenar; (*CULIN*) rellenar; (*animals*) disecar; (*inf: push*) meter; **~ing** *n* relleno; **~y** *adj* (*room*) mal ventilado; (*person*) de miras estrechas

stumble ['stʌmbl] *vi* tropezar, dar un traspié; **to ~ across**, **~ on** (*fig*) tropezar con; **stumbling block** *n* tropiezo, obstáculo

stump [stʌmp] *n* (*of tree*) tocón *m*; (*of limb*) muñón *m* ♦ *vt*: **to be ~ed for an answer** no saber qué contestar

stun [stʌn] *vt* dejar sin sentido

stung [stʌŋ] *pt*, *pp of* **sting**

stunk [stʌŋk] *pp of* **stink**

stunning ['stʌnɪŋ] *adj* (*fig: news*) pasmoso; (: *outfit etc*) sensacional

stunt [stʌnt] *n* (*in film*) escena peligrosa; (*publicity ~*) truco publicitario; **~ed** *adj* enano, achaparrado; **~man** *n* doble *m*

stupefy ['stjuːpɪfaɪ] *vt* dejar estupefacto

stupendous [stjuː'pɛndəs] *adj* estupendo, asombroso

stupid ['stjuːpɪd] *adj* estúpido, tonto; **~ity** [-'pɪdɪtɪ] *n* estupidez *f*

sturdy ['stɜːdɪ] *adj* robusto, fuerte

stutter ['stʌtə*] *n* tartamudeo ♦ *vi* tartamudear

sty [staɪ] *n* (*for pigs*) pocilga

stye [staɪ] *n* (*MED*) orzuelo

style [staɪl] *n* estilo; **stylish** *adj* elegante, a la moda

stylus ['staɪləs] n aguja
suave [swɑːv] adj cortés
sub... [sʌb] prefix sub...; **~conscious** adj subconsciente; **~contract** vt subcontratar; **~divide** vt subdividir
subdue [səb'djuː] vt sojuzgar; (passions) dominar; **~d** adj (light) tenue; (person) sumiso, manso
subject [n 'sʌbdʒɪkt, vb səb'dʒɛkt] n súbdito; (SCOL) asignatura; (matter) tema m; (GRAMMAR) sujeto ♦ vt: **to ~ sb to sth** someter a uno a algo; **to be ~ to** (law) estar sujeto a; (subj: person) ser propenso a; **~ive** [-'dʒɛktɪv] adj subjetivo; **~ matter** n (content) contenido
subjunctive [səb'dʒʌŋktɪv] adj, n subjuntivo
sublet [sʌb'lɛt] vt subarrendar
submachine gun ['sʌbməʃiːn-] n metralleta
submarine [sʌbmə'riːn] n submarino
submerge [səb'məːdʒ] vt sumergir ♦ vi sumergirse
submissive [səb'mɪsɪv] adj sumiso
submit [səb'mɪt] vt someter ♦ vi: **to ~ to sth** someterse a algo
subnormal [sʌb'nɔːməl] adj anormal
subordinate [sə'bɔːdɪnət]   adj,   n subordinado/a m/f
subpoena [səb'piːnə] n (LAW) citación f
subscribe [səb'skraɪb] vi suscribir; **to ~ to** (opinion, fund) suscribir, aprobar; (newspaper) suscribirse a; **~r** n (to periodical) subscriptor(a) m/f; (to telephone) abonado/a
subscription [səb'skrɪpʃən] n abono; (to magazine) subscripción f
subsequent ['sʌbsɪkwənt] adj subsiguiente, posterior; **~ly** adv posteriormente, más tarde
subside [səb'saɪd] vi hundirse; (flood) bajar; (wind) amainar; **~nce** [-'saɪdns] n hundimiento; (in road) socavón m
subsidiary [səb'sɪdɪərɪ] adj secundario ♦ n (also: ~ company) sucursal f, filial f
subsidize ['sʌbsɪdaɪz] vt subvencionar
subsidy ['sʌbsɪdɪ] n subvención f
subsistence [səb'sɪstəns] n subsistencia; **~ allowance** n salario mínimo
substance ['sʌbstəns] n sustancia
substantial [səb'stænʃl] adj sustancial, sustancioso; (fig) importante
substantiate [səb'stænʃɪeɪt] vt comprobar
substitute ['sʌbstɪtjuːt] n (person) suplente m/f; (thing) sustituto ♦ vt: **to ~ A for B** sustituir A por B, reemplazar B por A
subtitle ['sʌbtaɪtl] n subtítulo
subtle ['sʌtl] adj sutil; **~ty** n sutileza
subtotal [sʌb'teutl] n total m parcial
subtract [səb'trækt] vt restar, sustraer; **~ion** [-'trækʃən] n resta, sustracción f
suburb ['sʌbəːb] n barrio residencial; **the**

~s las afueras (de la ciudad); **~an** [sə'bəːbən] adj suburbano; (train etc) de cercanías; **~ia** [sə'bəːbɪə] n barrios mpl residenciales
subway ['sʌbweɪ] n (BRIT) paso subterráneo or inferior; (US) metro
succeed [sək'siːd] vi (person) tener éxito; (plan) salir bien ♦ vt suceder a; **to ~ in doing** lograr hacer; **~ing** adj (following) sucesivo
success [sək'sɛs] n éxito; **~ful** adj exitoso; (business) próspero; **to be ~ful (in doing)** lograr (hacer); **~fully** adv con éxito
succession [sək'sɛʃən] n sucesión f, serie f
successive [sək'sɛsɪv] adj sucesivo, consecutivo
succinct [sək'sɪŋkt] adj sucinto
succumb [sə'kʌm] vi: **to ~** sucumbir a, (illness) ser víctima de
such [sʌtʃ] adj tal, semejante; (of that kind): **~ a book** tal libro; (so much): **~ courage** tanto valor ♦ adv tan; **a long trip** un viaje tan largo; **~ a lot of** tanto(s)/a(s); **~ as** (like) tal como; **as ~** como tal; **~-and-~** adj tal o cual
suck [sʌk] vt chupar; (bottle) sorber; (breast) mamar; **~er** n (ZOOL) ventosa; (inf) bobo, primo
suction ['sʌkʃən] n succión f
Sudan [su'dɑːn] n Sudán m
sudden ['sʌdn] adj (rapid) repentino, súbito; (unexpected) imprevisto; **all of a ~** de repente; **~ly** adv de repente
suds [sʌdz] npl espuma de jabón
sue [suː] vt demandar
suede [sweɪd] n ante m (SP), gamuza (AM)
suet ['suɪt] n sebo
Suez ['suːɪz] n: **the ~ Canal** el Canal de Suez
suffer ['sʌfə*] vt sufrir, padecer; (tolerate) aguantar, soportar ♦ vi sufrir; **to ~ from** (illness etc) padecer; **~er** n víctima, (MED) enfermo/a; **~ing** n sufrimiento
suffice [sə'faɪs] vi bastar, ser suficiente
sufficient [sə'fɪʃənt] adj suficiente, bastante; **~ly** ad suficientemente, bastante
suffix ['sʌfɪks] n sufijo
suffocate ['sʌfəkeɪt] vi ahogarse, asfixiarse; **suffocation** [-'keɪʃən] n asfixia
suffrage ['sʌfrɪdʒ] n sufragio
suffused [sə'fjuːzd] adj: **~ with** bañado de
sugar ['ʃugə*] n azúcar m ♦ vt echar azúcar a, azucarar; **~ beet** n remolacha; **~ cane** n caña de azúcar
suggest [sə'dʒɛst] vt sugerir; **~ion** [-'dʒɛstʃən] n sugerencia; **~ive** (pej) adj indecente
suicide ['suɪsaɪd] n suicidio; (person) suicida m/f; see also **commit**
suit [suːt] n (man's) traje m; (woman's) conjunto; (LAW) pleito; (CARDS) palo ♦ vt convenir; (clothes) sentar a, ir bien a; (adapt):

to ~ sth to adaptar *or* ajustar algo a; **well ~ed** (*well matched: couple*) hecho el uno para el otro; **~able** *adj* conveniente; (*apt*) indicado; **~ably** *adv* convenientemente; (*impressed*) apropiadamente

suitcase ['suːtkeɪs] *n* maleta (*SP*), valija (*AM*)

suite [swiːt] *n* (*of rooms, MUS*) suite *f*; (*furniture*): **bedroom/dining room ~** (juego de) dormitorio/comedor

suitor ['suːtə*] *n* pretendiente *m*

sulfur ['sʌlfə*] (*US*) *n* = **sulphur**

sulk [sʌlk] *vi* estar de mal humor; **~y** *adj* malhumorado

sullen ['sʌlən] *adj* hosco, malhumorado

sulphur ['sʌlfə*] (*US* **sulfur**) *n* azufre *m*

sultana [sʌl'tɑːnə] *n* (*fruit*) pasa de Esmirna

sultry ['sʌltrɪ] *adj* (*weather*) bochornoso

sum [sʌm] *n* suma; (*total*) total *m*; **~ up** *vt* resumir ♦ *vi* hacer un resumen

summarize ['sʌməraɪz] *vt* resumir

summary ['sʌmərɪ] *n* resumen *m* ♦ *adj* (*justice*) sumario

summer ['sʌmə*] *n* verano ♦ *cpd* de verano; **in ~** en verano; **~ holidays** *npl* vacaciones *fpl* de verano; **~house** *n* (*in garden*) cenador *m*, glorieta; **~time** *n* (*season*) verano; **~ time** *n* (*by clock*) hora de verano

summit ['sʌmɪt] *n* cima, cumbre *f*; (*also:* **~ conference**, **~ meeting**) (conferencia) cumbre *f*

summon ['sʌmən] *vt* (*person*) llamar; (*meeting*) convocar; (*LAW*) citar; **~ up** *vt* (*courage*) armarse de; **~s** *n* llamamiento, llamada ♦ *vt* (*LAW*) citar

sump [sʌmp] (*BRIT*) *n* (*AUT*) cárter *m*

sumptuous ['sʌmptjuəs] *adj* suntuoso

sun [sʌn] *n* sol *m*

sunbathe ['sʌnbeɪð] *vi* tomar el sol

sunburn ['sʌnbɜːn] *n* (*painful*) quemadura; (*tan*) bronceado

Sunday ['sʌndɪ] *n* domingo; **~ school** *n* catequesis *f* dominical

sundial ['sʌndaɪəl] *n* reloj *m* de sol

sundown ['sʌndaun] *n* anochecer *m*

sundry ['sʌndrɪ] *adj* varios/as, diversos/as; **all and ~** todos sin excepción; **sundries** *npl* géneros *mpl* diversos

sunflower ['sʌnflauə*] *n* girasol *m*

sung [sʌŋ] *pp* of **sing**

sunglasses ['sʌnglɑːsɪz] *npl* gafas *fpl* (*SP*) *or* anteojos *mpl* de sol

sunk [sʌŋk] *pp* of **sink**

sun: **~light** *n* luz *f* del sol; **~lit** *adj* iluminado por el sol; **~ny** *adj* soleado; (*day*) de sol; (*fig*) alegre; **~rise** *n* salida del sol; **~ roof** *n* (*AUT*) techo corredizo; **~set** *n* puesta del sol; **~shade** *n* (*over table*) sombrilla; **~shine** *n* sol *m*; **~stroke** *n* insolación *f*; **~tan** *n* bronceado; **~tan oil** *n* aceite *m* bronceador

super ['suːpə*] (*inf*) *adj* genial

superannuation [suːpərænju'eɪʃən] *n* cuota de jubilación

superb [suː'pɜːb] *adj* magnífico, espléndido

supercilious [suːpə'sɪlɪəs] *adj* altanero

superfluous [suː'pɜːfluəs] *adj* superfluo, de sobra

superhuman [suːpə'hjuːmən] *adj* sobrehumano

superimpose ['suːpərɪm'pəuz] *vt* sobreponer

superintendent [suːpərɪn'tɛndənt] *n* director(a) *m/f*; (*POLICE*) subjefe/a *m/f*

superior [suː'pɪərɪə*] *adj* superior; (*smug*) desdeñoso ♦ *n* superior *m*; **~ity** [-'ɔrɪtɪ] *n* superioridad *f*

superlative [suː'pɜːlətɪv] *n* superlativo

superman ['suːpəmæn] *n* superhombre *m*

supermarket ['suːpəmɑːkɪt] *n* supermercado

supernatural [suːpə'nætʃərəl] *adj* sobrenatural ♦ *n*: **the ~** lo sobrenatural

superpower ['suːpəpauə*] *n* (*POL*) superpotencia

supersede [suːpə'siːd] *vt* suplantar

superstar ['suːpəstɑː*] *n* gran estrella

superstitious [suːpə'stɪʃəs] *adj* supersticioso

supertanker ['suːpətæŋkə*] *n* superpetrolero

supervise ['suːpəvaɪz] *vt* supervisar; **supervision** [-'vɪʒən] *n* supervisión *f*; **supervisor** *n* supervisor(a) *m/f*

supper ['sʌpə*] *n* cena

supplant [sə'plɑːnt] *vt* suplantar

supple ['sʌpl] *adj* flexible

supplement [*n* 'sʌplɪmənt, *vb* sʌplɪ'mɛnt] *n* suplemento ♦ *vt* suplir; **~ary** [-'mɛntərɪ] *adj* suplementario; **~ary benefit** (*BRIT*) *n* subsidio suplementario de la seguridad social

supplier [sə'plaɪə*] *n* (*COMM*) distribuidor(a) *m/f*

supply [sə'plaɪ] *vt* (*provide*) suministrar; (*equip*): **to ~ (with)** proveer (de) ♦ *n* provisión *f*; (*gas, water etc*) suministro; **supplies** *npl* (*food*) víveres *mpl*; (*MIL*) pertrechos *mpl*; **~ teacher** *n* profesor/a *m/f* suplente

support [sə'pɔːt] *n* apoyo; (*TECH*) soporte *m* ♦ *vt* apoyar; (*financially*) mantener; (*uphold, TECH*) sostener; **~er** *n* (*POL etc*) partidario/a; (*SPORT*) aficionado/a

suppose [sə'pəuz] *vt* suponer; (*imagine*) imaginarse; (*duty*): **to be ~d to do sth** deber hacer algo; **~dly** [sə'pəuzɪdlɪ] *adv* según cabe suponer; **supposing** *conj* en caso de que

suppress [sə'prɛs] *vt* suprimir; (*yawn*) ahogar

supreme [suː'priːm] *adj* supremo

surcharge ['sɜːtʃɑːdʒ] *n* sobretasa, recargo

sure [ʃuə*] *adj* seguro, (*definite, convinced*) cierto; **to make ~ of sth/that** asegurarse de algo/asegurar que; **~!** (*of course*) ¡claro!,

¡por supuesto!; ~ **enough** efectivamente;
~**-footed** *adj* ágil y seguro; ~**ly** *adv* (*certainly*) seguramente

surety ['ʃuərətɪ] *n* fianza

surf [sɔːf] *n* olas *fpl*

surface ['sɔːfɪs] *n* superficie *f* ♦ *vt* (*road*) revestir ♦ *vi* (*also fig*) salir a la superficie; **by ~ mail** por vía terrestre

surfboard ['sɔːfbɔːd] *n* tabla (de surf)

surfeit ['sɔːfɪt] *n*: **a ~ of** un exceso de

surfing ['sɔːfɪŋ] *n* surf *m*

surge [sɔːdʒ] *n* oleada, oleaje *m* ♦ *vi* (*wave*) romper; (*people*) avanzar en tropel

surgeon ['sɔːdʒən] *n* cirujano/a

surgery ['sɔːdʒərɪ] *n* cirugía; (*BRIT: room*) consultorio; ~ **hours** (*BRIT*) *npl* horas *fpl* de consulta

surgical ['sɔːdʒɪkl] *adj* quirúrgico; ~ **spirit** (*BRIT*) *n* alcohol *m* de 90°

surly ['sɔːlɪ] *adj* hosco, malhumorado

surmount [sɔːˈmaunt] *vt* superar, vencer

surname ['sɔːneɪm] *n* apellido

surpass [sɔːˈpɑːs] *vt* superar, exceder

surplus ['sɔːpləs] *n* excedente *m*; (*COMM*) superávit *m* ♦ *adj* excedente, sobrante

surprise [səˈpraɪz] *n* sorpresa ♦ *vt* sorprender; **surprising** *adj* sorprendente; **surprisingly** *adv*: **it was surprisingly easy** me *etc* sorprendió lo fácil que fue

surrender [səˈrɛndə*] *n* rendición *f*, entrega *f* ♦ *vi* rendirse, entregarse

surreptitious [sʌrəpˈtɪʃəs] *adj* subrepticio

surrogate ['sʌrəgɪt] *n* sucedáneo; ~ **mother** *n* madre *f* portadora

surround [səˈraund] *vt* rodear, circundar; (*MIL etc*) cercar; ~**ing** *adj* circundante; ~**ings** *npl* alrededores *mpl*, cercanías *fpl*

surveillance [sɔːˈveɪləns] *n* vigilancia

survey [*n* 'sɔːveɪ, *vb* sɔːˈveɪ] *n* inspección *f*, reconocimiento; (*inquiry*) encuesta ♦ *vt* examinar, inspeccionar; (*look at*) mirar, contemplar; ~**or** *n* agrimensor(a) *m/f*

survival [səˈvaɪvl] *n* supervivencia

survive [səˈvaɪv] *vi* sobrevivir; (*custom etc*) perdurar ♦ *vt* sobrevivir a; **survivor** *n* superviviente *m/f*

susceptible [səˈsɛptəbl] *adj*: ~ **(to)** (*disease*) susceptible (a); (*flattery*) sensible (a)

suspect [*adj*, *n* 'sʌspɛkt, *vb* səsˈpɛkt] *adj*, *n* sospechoso/a *m/f* ♦ *vt* (*person*) sospechar de; (*think*) sospechar

suspend [səsˈpɛnd] *vt* suspender; ~**ed sentence** *n* (*LAW*) libertad *f* condicional; ~**er belt** *n* portaligas *m inv*; ~**ers** *npl* (*BRIT*) ligas *fpl*; (*US*) tirantes *mpl*

suspense [səsˈpɛns] *n* incertidumbre *f*, duda; (*in film etc*) suspense *m*; **to keep sb in ~** mantener a uno en suspense

suspension [səsˈpɛnʃən] *n* (*gen*, *AUT*) suspensión *f*; (*of driving licence*) privación *f*; ~ **bridge** *n* puente *m* colgante

suspicion [səsˈpɪʃən] *n* sospecha; (*distrust*)

recelo; **suspicious** [-ʃəs] *adj* receloso; (*causing suspicion*) sospechoso

sustain [səsˈteɪn] *vt* sostener, apoyar; (*suffer*) sufrir, padecer; ~**able** *adj* sostenible; ~**ed** *adj* (*effort*) sostenido

sustenance ['sʌstɪnəns] *n* sustento

swab [swɔb] *n* (*MED*) algodón *m*

swagger ['swægə*] *vi* pavonearse

swallow ['swɔləu] *n* (*bird*) golondrina ♦ *vt* tragar; (*fig*, *pride*) tragarse; ~ **up** *vt* (*savings etc*) consumir

swam [swæm] *pt of* **swim**

swamp [swɔmp] *n* pantano, ciénaga ♦ *vt* (*with water etc*) inundar; (*fig*) abrumar, agobiar; ~**y** *adj* pantanoso

swan [swɔn] *n* cisne *m*

swap [swɔp] *n* canje *m*, intercambio ♦ *vt*: **to ~ (for)** cambiar (por)

swarm [swɔːm] *n* (*of bees*) enjambre *m*; (*fig*) multitud *f* ♦ *vi* (*bees*) formar un enjambre; (*people*) pulular; **to be ~ing with** ser un hervidero de

swarthy ['swɔːðɪ] *adj* moreno

swastika ['swɔstɪkə] *n* esvástica

swat [swɔt] *vt* aplastar

sway [sweɪ] *vi* mecerse, balancearse ♦ *vt* (*influence*) mover, influir en

swear [swɛə*] (*pt* **swore**, *pp* **sworn**) *vi* (*curse*) maldecir; (*promise*) jurar ♦ *vt* jurar; ~**word** *n* taco, palabrota

sweat [swɛt] *n* sudor *m* ♦ *vi* sudar

sweater ['swɛtə*] *n* suéter *m*

sweatshirt ['swɛtʃɔːt] *n* suéter *m*

sweaty ['swɛtɪ] *adj* sudoroso

Swede [swiːd] *n* sueco/a

swede [swiːd] (*BRIT*) *n* nabo

Sweden ['swiːdn] *n* Suecia; **Swedish** ['swiːdɪʃ] *adj* sueco ♦ *n* (*LING*) sueco

sweep [swiːp] (*pt*, *pp* **swept**) *n* (*act*) barrido; (*also: chimney ~*) deshollinador(a) *m/f* ♦ *vt* barrer; (*with arm*) empujar; (*subj: current*) arrastrar ♦ *vi* barrer; (*arm etc*) moverse rápidamente; (*wind*) soplar con violencia; ~ **away** *vt* barrer; ~ **past** *vi* pasar majestuosamente; ~ **up** *vi* barrer; ~**ing** *adj* (*gesture*) dramático; (*generalized: statement*) generalizado

sweet [swiːt] *n* (*candy*) dulce *m*, caramelo; (*BRIT: pudding*) postre *m* ♦ *adj* dulce; (*fig: kind*) dulce, amable; (: *attractive*) mono; ~**corn** *n* maíz *m*; ~**en** *vt* (*add sugar to*) poner azúcar a; (*person*) endulzar; ~**heart** *n* novio/a; ~**ness** *n* dulzura; ~ **pea** *n* guisante *m* de olor

swell [swɛl] (*pt* **swelled**, *pp* **swollen** *or* **swelled**) *n* (*of sea*) marejada, oleaje *m* ♦ *adj* (*US: inf: excellent*) estupendo, fenomenal ♦ *vt* hinchar, inflar ♦ *vi* (*also:* ~ *up*) hincharse; (*numbers*) aumentar; (*sound, feeling*) ir aumentando; ~**ing** *n* (*MED*) hinchazón *f*

sweltering ['swɛltərɪŋ] *adj* sofocante, de

mucho calor
swept [swɛpt] *pt, pp of* **sweep**
swerve [swəːv] *vi* desviarse bruscamente
swift [swɪft] *n* (*bird*) vencejo ♦ *adj* rápido, veloz; **~ly** *adv* rápidamente
swig [swɪg] (*inf*) *n* (*drink*) trago
swill [swɪl] *vt* (*also*: ~ *out*, ~ *down*) lavar, limpiar con agua
swim [swɪm] (*pt* **swam**, *pp* **swum**) *n*: **to go for a** ~ ir a nadar *or* a bañarse ♦ *vi* nadar; (*head, room*) dar vueltas ♦ *vt* nadar; (*the Channel etc*) cruzar a nado; **~mer** *n* nadador(a) *m/f*; **~ming** *n* natación *f*; **~ming cap** *n* gorro de baño; **~ming costume** (*BRIT*) *n* bañador *m*, traje *m* de baño; **~ming pool** *n* piscina (*SP*), alberca (*AM*); **~ming trunks** *n* bañador *m* (de hombre); **~suit** *n* = **~ming costume**
swindle [ˈswɪndl] *n* estafa ♦ *vt* estafar
swine [swaɪn] (*inf!*) canalla (*!*)
swing [swɪŋ] (*pt, pp* **swung**) *n* (*in playground*) columpio; (*movement*) balanceo, vaivén *m*; (*change of direction*) viraje *m*; (*rhythm*) ritmo ♦ *vt* balancear; (*also*: ~ *round*) voltear, girar ♦ *vi* balancearse, columpiarse; (*also*: ~ *round*) dar media vuelta; **to be in full** ~ estar en plena marcha; ~ **bridge** *n* puente *m* giratorio; ~ **door** (*US* **~ing door**) *n* puerta giratoria
swingeing [ˈswɪndʒɪŋ] (*BRIT*) *adj* (*blow*) abrumador(a); (*cuts*) atroz
swipe [swaɪp] *vt* (*hit*) golpear fuerte; (*inf*: *steal*) guindar
swirl [swəːl] *vi* arremolinarse
swish [swɪʃ] *vi* chasquear
Swiss [swɪs] *adj, n inv* suizo/a *m/f*
switch [swɪtʃ] *n* (*for light etc*) interruptor *m*; (*change*) cambio ♦ *vt* (*change*) cambiar de; ~ **off** *vt* apagar; (*engine*) parar; ~ **on** *vt* encender (*SP*), prender (*AM*); (*engine, machine*) arrancar; **~board** *n* (*TEL*) centralita (de teléfonos) (*SP*), conmutador *m* (*AM*)
Switzerland [ˈswɪtsələnd] *n* Suiza
swivel [ˈswɪvl] *vi* (*also*: ~ *round*) girar
swollen [ˈswəulən] *pp of* **swell**
swoon [swuːn] *vi* desmayarse
swoop [swuːp] *n* (*by police etc*) redada ♦ *vi* (*also*: ~ *down*) calarse
swop [swɔp] = **swap**
sword [sɔːd] *n* espada; **~fish** *n* pez *m* espada
swore [swɔː*] *pt of* **swear**
sworn [swɔːn] *pp of* **swear** ♦ *adj* (*statement*) bajo juramento; (*enemy*) implacable
swot [swɔt] (*BRIT*) *vt, vi* empollar
swum [swʌm] *pp of* **swim**
swung [swʌŋ] *pt, pp of* **swing**
sycamore [ˈsɪkəmɔː*] *n* sicomoro
syllable [ˈsɪləbl] *n* sílaba
syllabus [ˈsɪləbəs] *n* programa *m* de estudios

symbol [ˈsɪmbl] *n* símbolo
symmetry [ˈsɪmɪtrɪ] *n* simetría
sympathetic [sɪmpəˈθɛtɪk] *adj* (*understanding*) comprensivo; (*likeable*) simpático; (*showing support*): ~ **to(wards)** bien dispuesto hacia
sympathize [ˈsɪmpəθaɪz] *vi*: **to** ~ **with** (*person*) compadecerse de; (*feelings*) comprender; (*cause*) apoyar; **~r** *n* (*POL*) simpatizante *m/f*
sympathy [ˈsɪmpəθɪ] *n* (*pity*) compasión *f*; **sympathies** *npl* (*tendencies*) tendencias *fpl*; **with our deepest** ~ nuestro más sentido pésame; **in** ~ en solidaridad
symphony [ˈsɪmfənɪ] *n* sinfonía
symptom [ˈsɪmptəm] *n* síntoma *m*, indicio
synagogue [ˈsɪnəgɔg] *n* sinagoga
syndicate [ˈsɪndɪkɪt] *n* (*gen*) sindicato; (*of newspapers*) agencia (de noticias)
syndrome [ˈsɪndrəum] *n* síndrome *m*
synonym [ˈsɪnənɪm] *n* sinónimo
synopses [sɪˈnɔpsiːz] *npl of* **synopsis**
synopsis [sɪˈnɔpsɪs] (*pl* **synopses**) *n* sinopsis *f inv*
syntax [ˈsɪntæks] *n* sintaxis *f inv*
syntheses [ˈsɪnθəsiːz] *npl of* **synthesis**
synthesis [ˈsɪnθəsɪs] (*pl* **syntheses**) *n* síntesis *f inv*
synthetic [sɪnˈθɛtɪk] *adj* sintético
syphilis [ˈsɪfɪlɪs] *n* sífilis *f*
syphon [ˈsaɪfən] = **siphon**
Syria [ˈsɪrɪə] *n* Siria; **~n** *adj, n* sirio/a
syringe [sɪˈrɪndʒ] *n* jeringa
syrup [ˈsɪrəp] *n* jarabe *m*; (*also*: *golden* ~) almíbar *m*
system [ˈsɪstəm] *n* sistema *m*; (*ANAT*) organismo; **~atic** [-ˈmætɪk] *adj* sistemático, metódico; ~ **disk** *n* (*COMPUT*) disco del sistema; **~s analyst** *n* analista *m/f* de sistemas

T t

ta [tɑː] (*BRIT*: *inf*) *excl* ¡gracias!
tab [tæb] *n* lengüeta; (*label*) etiqueta; **to keep ~s on** (*fig*) vigilar
tabby [ˈtæbɪ] *n* (*also*: ~ *cat*) gato atigrado
table [ˈteɪbl] *n* mesa; (*of statistics etc*) cuadro, tabla ♦ *vt* (*BRIT*: *motion etc*) presentar; **to lay** *or* **set the** ~ poner la mesa; **~cloth** *n* mantel *m*; ~ **of contents** *n* índice *m* de materias; ~ **d'hôte** [tɑːblˈdəut] *adj* del menú; ~ **lamp** *n* lámpara de mesa; **~mat** *n* (*for plate*) posaplatos *m inv*; (*for hot dish*)

salvamantel *m*; ~**spoon** *n* cuchara de servir; (*also:* ~*spoonful: as measurement*) cucharada

tablet ['tæblɪt] *n* (*MED*) pastilla, comprimido; (*of stone*) lápida

table tennis *n* ping-pong *m*, tenis *m* de mesa

table wine *n* vino de mesa

tabloid ['tæblɔɪd] *n* periódico popular sensacionalista

tabulate ['tæbjuleɪt] *vt* disponer en tablas

tack [tæk] *n* (*nail*) tachuela; (*fig*) rumbo ♦ *vt* (*nail*) clavar con tachuelas; (*stitch*) hilvanar ♦ *vi* virar

tackle ['tækl] *n* (*fishing* ~) aparejo (de pescar); (*for lifting*) aparejo ♦ *vt* (*difficulty*) enfrentarse con; (*challenge: person*) hacer frente a; (*grapple with*) agarrar; (*FOOTBALL*) cargar; (*RUGBY*) placar

tacky ['tækɪ] *adj* pegajoso; (*pej*) cutre

tact [tækt] *n* tacto, discreción *f*; ~**ful** *adj* discreto, diplomático

tactics ['tæktɪks] *n, npl* táctica

tactless ['tæktlɪs] *adj* indiscreto

tadpole ['tædpəul] *n* renacuajo

taffy ['tæfɪ] (*US*) *n* toffee *m*

tag [tæg] *n* (*label*) etiqueta; ~ **along** *vi* ir (*or* venir) también

tail [teɪl] *n* cola; (*of shirt, coat*) faldón *m* ♦ *vt* (*follow*) vigilar a; ~**s** *npl* (*formal suit*) levita; ~ **away** *vi* (*in size, quality etc*) ir disminuyendo; ~ **off** *vi* = ~ **away**; ~**back** (*BRIT*) *n* (*AUT*) cola; ~ **end** *n* cola, parte *f* final; ~**gate** *n* (*AUT*) puerta trasera

tailor ['teɪlə*] *n* sastre *m*; ~**ing** *n* (*cut*) corte *m*; (*craft*) sastrería; ~**-made** *adj* (*also fig*) hecho a la medida

tailwind ['teɪlwɪnd] *n* viento de cola

tainted ['teɪntɪd] *adj* (*food*) pasado; (*water, air*) contaminado; (*fig*) manchado

take [teɪk] (*pt* **took**, *pp* **taken**) *vt* tomar; (*grab*) coger (*SP*), agarrar (*AM*); (*gain: prize*) ganar; (*require: effort, courage*) exigir; (*tolerate: pain etc*) aguantar; (*hold: passengers etc*) tener cabida para; (*accompany, bring, carry*) llevar; (*exam*) presentarse a; ~ **sth from** (*drawer etc*) sacar algo de; (*person*) quitar algo a; **I** ~ **it that** ... supongo que ...; ~ **after** *vt fus* parecerse a; ~ **apart** *vt* desmontar; ~ **away** *vt* (*remove*) quitar; (*carry off*) llevar; (*MATH*) restar; ~ **back** *vt* (*return*) devolver; (*one's words*) retractarse de; ~ **down** *vt* (*building*) derribar; (*letter etc*) apuntar; ~ **in** *vt* (*deceive*) engañar; (*understand*) entender; (*include*) abarcar; (*lodger*) acoger, recibir; ~ **off** *vi* (*AVIAT*) despegar ♦ *vt* (*remove*) quitar; ~ **on** *vt* (*work*) aceptar; (*employee*) contratar; (*opponent*) desafiar; ~ **out** *vt* sacar; ~ **over** *vt* (*business*) tomar posesión de; (*country*) tomar el poder ♦ *vi*: **to** ~ **over from sb** reemplazar a uno; ~ **to** *vt fus* (*person*) co-

ger cariño a, encariñarse con; (*activity*) aficionarse a; ~ **up** *vt* (*a dress*) acortar; (*occupy: time, space*) ocupar; (*engage in: hobby etc*) dedicarse a; (*accept*): **to** ~ **sb up on** aceptar; ~**away** (*BRIT*) *adj* (*food*) para llevar ♦ *n* tienda (*or* restaurante *m*) de comida para llevar; ~**off** *n* (*AVIAT*) despegue *m*; ~**over** *n* (*COMM*) absorción *f*; ~**out** (*US*) *n* = ~**away**

takings ['teɪkɪŋz] *npl* (*COMM*) ingresos *mpl*

talc [tælk] *n* (*also:* ~*um powder*) (polvos de) talco

tale [teɪl] *n* (*story*) cuento; (*account*) relación *f*; **to tell** ~**s** (*fig*) chivarse

talent ['tælnt] *n* talento; ~**ed** *adj* de talento

talk [tɔ:k] *n* charla; (*conversation*) conversación *f*; (*gossip*) habladurías *fpl*, chismes *mpl* ♦ *vi* hablar; ~**s** *npl* (*POL etc*) conversaciones *fpl*; **to** ~ **about** hablar de; **to** ~ **sb into doing sth** convencer a uno para que haga algo; **to** ~ **sb out of doing sth** disuadir a uno de que haga algo; **to** ~ **shop** hablar del trabajo; ~ **over** *vt* discutir; ~**ative** *adj* hablador(a); ~ **show** *n* programa *m* de entrevistas

tall [tɔ:l] *adj* alto; (*object*) grande; **to be 6 feet** ~ (*person*) ≈ medir 1 metro 80

tally ['tælɪ] *n* cuenta ♦ *vi*: **to** ~ **(with)** corresponder (con)

talon ['tælən] *n* garra

tambourine [tæmbə'ri:n] *n* pandereta

tame [teɪm] *adj* domesticado; (*fig*) mediocre

tamper ['tæmpə*] *vi*: **to** ~ **with** tocar, andar con

tampon ['tæmpən] *n* tampón *m*

tan [tæn] *n* (*also: sun~*) bronceado ♦ *vi* ponerse moreno ♦ *adj* (*colour*) marrón

tang [tæŋ] *n* sabor *m* fuerte

tangent ['tændʒənt] *n* (*MATH*) tangente *f*; **to go off at a** ~ (*fig*) salirse por la tangente

tangerine [tændʒə'ri:n] *n* mandarina

tangle ['tæŋgl] *n* enredo; **to get in(to) a** ~ enredarse

tank [tæŋk] *n* (*water* ~) depósito, tanque *m*; (*for fish*) acuario; (*MIL*) tanque *m*

tanker ['tæŋkə*] *n* (*ship*) buque *m* cisterna; (*truck*) camión *m* cisterna

tanned [tænd] *adj* (*skin*) moreno

tantalizing ['tæntəlaɪzɪŋ] *adj* tentador(a)

tantamount ['tæntəmaunt] *adj*: ~ **to** equivalente a

tantrum ['tæntrəm] *n* rabieta

tap [tæp] *n* (*BRIT: on sink etc*) grifo (*SP*), canilla (*AM*); (*gas* ~) llave *f*; (*gentle blow*) golpecito ♦ *vt* (*hit gently*) dar golpecitos en; (*resources*) utilizar, explotar; (*telephone*) intervenir; **on** ~ (*fig: resources*) a mano; ~-**dancing** *n* claqué *m*

tape [teɪp] *n* (*also: magnetic* ~) cinta magnética; (*cassette*) cassette *f*, cinta; (*sticky* ~) cinta adhesiva; (*for tying*) cinta ♦ *vt* (*rec-*

ord) grabar (en cinta); (*stick with* ~) pegar con cinta adhesiva; ~ **deck** *n* grabadora; ~ **measure** *n* cinta métrica, metro

taper ['teɪpə*] *n* cirio ♦ *vi* afilarse

tape recorder *n* grabadora

tapestry ['tæpɪstrɪ] *n* (*object*) tapiz *m*; (*art*) tapicería

tar [tɑː] *n* alquitrán *m*, brea

target ['tɑːgɪt] *n* (*gen*) blanco

tariff ['tærɪf] *n* (*on goods*) arancel *m*; (*BRIT: in hotels etc*) tarifa

tarmac ['tɑːmæk] *n* (*BRIT: on road*) asfaltado; (*AVIAT*) pista (de aterrizaje)

tarnish ['tɑːnɪʃ] *vt* deslustrar

tarpaulin [tɑː'pɔːlɪn] *n* lona impermeabilizada

tarragon ['tærəgən] *n* estragón *m*

tart [tɑːt] *n* (*CULIN*) tarta; (*BRIT: inf: prostitute*) puta ♦ *adj* agrio, ácido; ~ **up** (*BRIT: inf*) *vt* (*building*) remozar; **to** ~ **o.s. up** acicalarse

tartan ['tɑːtn] *n* tejido escocés *m*

tartar ['tɑːtə*] *n* (*on teeth*) sarro; ~**(e) sauce** *n* salsa tártara

task [tɑːsk] *n* tarea; **to take to** ~ reprender; ~ **force** *n* (*MIL, POLICE*) grupo de operaciones

taste [teɪst] *n* (*sense*) gusto; (*flavour*) sabor *m*; (*also: after~*) sabor *m*, dejo; (*sample*): **have a** ~! ¡prueba un poquito!; (*fig*) muestra, idea ♦ *vt* (*also fig*) probar ♦ *vi*: **to** ~ **of** *or* **like** (*fish, garlic etc*) saber a; **you can** ~ **the garlic (in it)** se nota el sabor a ajo; **in good/bad** ~ de buen/mal gusto; ~**ful** *adj* de buen gusto; ~**less** *adj* (*food*) soso; (*remark etc*) de mal gusto; **tasty** *adj* sabroso, rico

tatters ['tætəz] *npl*: **in** ~ hecho jirones

tattoo [tə'tuː] *n* tatuaje *m*; (*spectacle*) espectáculo militar ♦ *vt* tatuar

tatty ['tætɪ] (*BRIT: inf*) *adj* cochambroso

taught [tɔːt] *pt, pp of* **teach**

taunt [tɔːnt] *n* burla ♦ *vt* burlarse de

Taurus ['tɔːrəs] *n* Tauro

taut [tɔːt] *adj* tirante, tenso

tax [tæks] *n* impuesto ♦ *vt* gravar (con un impuesto); (*fig: memory*) poner a prueba (: *patience*) agotar; ~**able** *adj* (*income*) gravable; ~**ation** [-'seɪʃən] *n* impuestos *mpl*; ~ **avoidance** *n* evasión f de impuestos; ~ **disc** (*BRIT*) *n* (*AUT*) pegatina del impuesto de circulación; ~ **evasion** *n* evasión f fiscal; ~**free** *adj* libre de impuestos

taxi ['tæksɪ] *n* taxi *m* ♦ *vi* (*AVIAT*) rodar por la pista; ~ **driver** *n* taxista *m/f*; ~ **rank** (*BRIT*) *n* = ~ **stand**; ~ **stand** *n* parada de taxis

tax: ~ **payer** *n* contribuyente *m/f*; ~ **relief** *n* desgravación f fiscal; ~ **return** *n* declaración f de ingresos

TB *n abbr* = **tuberculosis**

tea [tiː] *n* té *m*; (*BRIT: meal*) ≈ merienda

(*SP*); **cena**; **high** ~ (*BRIT*) merienda-cena (*SP*); ~ **bag** *n* bolsita de té; ~ **break** (*BRIT*) *n* descanso para el té

teach [tiːtʃ] (*pt, pp* **taught**) *vt*: **to** ~ **sb sth,** ~ **sth to sb** enseñar algo a uno ♦ *vi* (*be a teacher*) ser profesor(a), enseñar; ~**er** *n* (*in secondary school*) profesor(a) *m/f*; (*in primary school*) maestro/a, profesor(a) de EGB; ~**ing** *n* enseñanza

tea cosy *n* cubretetera *m*

teacup ['tiːkʌp] *n* taza para el té

teak [tiːk] *n* (*madera de*) teca

team [tiːm] *n* equipo; (*of horses*) tiro; ~**work** *n* trabajo en equipo

teapot ['tiːpɔt] *n* tetera

tear¹ [tɪə*] *n* lágrima; **in** ~**s** llorando

tear² [tɛə*] (*pt* **tore**, *pp* **torn**) *n* rasgón *m*, desgarrón *m* ♦ *vt* romper, rasgar ♦ *vi* rasgarse; ~ **along** *vi* (*rush*) precipitarse; ~ **up** *vt* (*sheet of paper etc*) romper

tearful ['tɪəfəl] *adj* lloroso

tear gas *n* gas *m* lacrimógeno

tearoom ['tiːruːm] *n* salón *m* de té

tease [tiːz] *vt* tomar el pelo a

tea: ~ **set** *n* servicio de té; ~**spoon** *n* cucharita; (*also: ~spoonful: as measurement*) cucharadita

teat [tiːt] *n* (*of bottle*) tetina

teatime ['tiːtaɪm] *n* hora del té

tea towel (*BRIT*) *n* paño de cocina

technical ['tɛknɪkl] *adj* técnico; ~ **college** (*BRIT*) *n* ≈ escuela de artes y oficios (*SP*); ~**ity** [-'kælɪtɪ] *n* (*point of law*) formalismo; (*detail*) detalle *m* técnico; ~**ly** *adv* en teoría; (*regarding technique*) técnicamente

technician [tɛk'nɪʃn] *n* técnico/a

technique [tɛk'niːk] *n* técnica

technology [tɛk'nɔlədʒɪ] *n* tecnología

teddy (bear) ['tɛdɪ-] *n* osito de felpa

tedious ['tiːdɪəs] *adj* pesado, aburrido

teem [tiːm] *vi*: **to** ~ **with** rebosar de; **it is** ~**ing (with rain)** llueve a cántaros

teenage ['tiːneɪdʒ] *adj* (*fashions etc*) juvenil; (*children*) quinceañero; ~**r** *n* quinceañero/a

teens [tiːnz] *npl*: **to be in one's** ~ ser adolescente

tee-shirt ['tiːʃəːt] *n* = **T-shirt**

teeter ['tiːtə*] *vi* balancearse; (*fig*): **to** ~ **on the edge of** ... estar al borde de ...'

teeth [tiːθ] *npl of* **tooth**

teethe [tiːð] *vi* echar los dientes

teething ['tiːðɪŋ]: ~ **ring** *n* mordedor *m*; ~ **troubles** *npl* (*fig*) dificultades *fpl* iniciales

teetotal ['tiː'təutl] *adj* abstemio

telegram ['tɛlɪgræm] *n* telegrama *m*

telegraph ['tɛlɪgrɑːf] *n* telégrafo; ~ **pole** *n* poste *m* telegráfico

telepathy [tə'lɛpəθɪ] *n* telepatía

telephone ['tɛlɪfəun] *n* teléfono ♦ *vt* llamar por teléfono, telefonear; (*message*) dar por teléfono; **to be on the ~** (*talking*) hablar por teléfono; (*possessing ~*) tener teléfono; **~ booth** *n* cabina telefónica; **~ box** (*BRIT*) *n* = **~ booth**; **~ call** *n* llamada (telefónica); **~ directory** *n* guía (telefónica); **~ number** *n* número de teléfono; **telephonist** [tə'lɛfənɪst] (*BRIT*) *n* telefonista *m/f*

telescope ['tɛlɪskəup] *n* telescopio

television ['tɛlɪvɪʒən] *n* televisión *f*; **on ~** en la televisión; **~ set** *n* televisor *m*

telex ['tɛlɛks] *n* télex *m* ♦ *vt* enviar un télex a

tell [tɛl] (*pt, pp* **told**) *vt* decir; (*relate: story*) contar; (*distinguish*): **to ~ sth from** distinguir algo de ♦ *vi* (*talk*): **to ~** (*of*) contar; (*have effect*) tener efecto; **to ~ sb to do sth** mandar a uno hacer algo; **~ off** *vt*: **to ~ sb off** regañar a uno; **~er** *n* (*in bank*) cajero/a; **~ing** *adj* (*remark, detail*) revelador(a); **~tale** *adj* (*sign*) indicador(a)

telly ['tɛlɪ] (*BRIT: inf*) *n abbr* (= *television*) tele *f*

temp [tɛmp] *n abbr* (*BRIT*: = *temporary*) temporero/a

temper ['tɛmpə*] *n* (*nature*) carácter *m*; (*mood*) humor *m*; (*bad ~*) (mal) genio; (*fit of anger*) acceso de ira ♦ *vt* (*moderate*) moderar; **to be in a ~** estar furioso; **to lose one's ~** enfadarse, enojarse

temperament ['tɛmprəmənt] *n* (*nature*) temperamento

temperate ['tɛmprət] *adj* (*climate etc*) templado

temperature ['tɛmprətʃə*] *n* temperatura; **to have** *or* **run a ~** tener fiebre

temple ['tɛmpl] *n* (*building*) templo; (*ANAT*) sien *f*

tempo ['tɛmpəu] (*pl* **tempos** *or* **tempi**) *n* (*MUS*) tempo, tiempo; (*fig*) ritmo

temporarily ['tɛmpərərɪlɪ] *adv* temporalmente

temporary ['tɛmpərərɪ] *adj* provisional; (*passing*) transitorio; (*worker*) temporero; (*job*) temporal

tempt [tɛmpt] *vt* tentar; **to ~ sb into doing sth** tentar *or* inducir a uno a hacer algo; **~ation** [-'teɪʃən] *n* tentación *f*; **~ing** *adj* tentador(a); (*food*) apetitoso/a

ten [tɛn] *num* diez

tenacity [tə'næsɪtɪ] *n* tenacidad *f*

tenancy ['tɛnənsɪ] *n* arrendamiento, alquiler *m*

tenant ['tɛnənt] *n* inquilino/a

tend [tɛnd] *vt* cuidar ♦ *vi*: **to ~ to do sth** tener tendencia a hacer algo

tendency ['tɛndənsɪ] *n* tendencia

tender ['tɛndə*] *adj* (*person, care*) tierno, cariñoso; (*meat*) tierno; (*sore*) sensible ♦ *n* (*COMM: offer*) oferta; (*money*): **legal ~** moneda de curso legal ♦ *vt* ofrecer; **~ness** *n* ternura; (*of meat*) blandura

tenement ['tɛnəmənt] *n* casa de pisos (*SP*)

tenet ['tɛnət] *n* principio

tennis ['tɛnɪs] *n* tenis *m*; **~ ball** *n* pelota de tenis; **~ court** *n* cancha de tenis; **~ player** *n* tenista *m/f*; **~ racket** *n* raqueta de tenis

tenor ['tɛnə*] *n* (*MUS*) tenor *m*

tenpin bowling ['tɛnpɪn-] *n* (juego de los) bolos

tense [tɛns] *adj* (*person*) nervioso; (*moment, atmosphere*) tenso; (*muscle*) tenso, en tensión ♦ *n* (*LING*) tiempo

tension ['tɛnʃən] *n* tensión *f*

tent [tɛnt] *n* tienda (de campaña) (*SP*), carpa (*AM*)

tentative ['tɛntətɪv] *adj* (*person, smile*) indeciso; (*conclusion, plans*) provisional

tenterhooks ['tɛntəhuks] *npl*: **on ~** sobre ascuas

tenth [tɛnθ] *num* décimo

tent peg *n* clavija, estaca

tent pole *n* mástil *m*

tenuous ['tɛnjuəs] *adj* tenue

tenure ['tɛnjuə*] *n* (*of land etc*) tenencia; (*of office*) ejercicio

tepid ['tɛpɪd] *adj* tibio

term [tə:m] *n* (*word*) término; (*period*) período; (*SCOL*) trimestre *m* ♦ *vt* llamar; **~s** *npl* (*conditions, COMM*) condiciones *fpl*; **in the short/long ~** a corto/largo plazo; **to be on good ~s with sb** llevarse bien con uno; **to come to ~s with** (*problem*) aceptar

terminal ['tə:mɪnl] *adj* (*disease*) mortal; (*patient*) terminal ♦ *n* (*ELEC*) borne *m*; (*COMPUT*) terminal *m*; (*also: air ~*) terminal *f*; (*BRIT: also: coach ~*) (estación *f*) terminal *f*

terminate ['tə:mɪneɪt] *vt* terminar

terminus ['tə:mɪnəs] (*pl* **termini**) *n* término, (estación *f*) terminal *f*

terrace ['tɛrəs] *n* terraza; (*BRIT: row of houses*) hilera de casas adosadas; **the ~s** (*BRIT: SPORT*) las gradas *fpl*; **~d** *adj* (*garden*) en terrazas; (*house*) adosado

terrain [tɛ'reɪn] *n* terreno

terrible ['tɛrɪbl] *adj* terrible, horrible; (*inf*) atroz; **terribly** *adv* terriblemente; (*very badly*) malísimamente

terrier ['tɛrɪə*] *n* terrier *m*

terrific [tə'rɪfɪk] *adj* (*very great*) tremendo; (*wonderful*) fantástico, fenomenal

terrify ['tɛrɪfaɪ] *vt* aterrorizar

territory ['tɛrɪtərɪ] *n* (*also fig*) territorio

terror ['tɛrə*] *n* terror *m*; **~ism** *n* terrorismo; **~ist** *n* terrorista *m/f*

terse [tə:s] *adj* brusco, lacónico

test [tɛst] *n* (*gen, CHEM*) prueba; (*MED*) examen *m*; (*SCOL*) examen *m*, test *m*; (*also: driving ~*) examen *m* de conducir ♦ *vt* probar, poner a prueba; (*MED, SCOL*) examinar

testament ['tɛstəmənt] *n* testamento; **the Old/New T~** el Antiguo/Nuevo Testamento

testicle ['tɛstɪkl] *n* testículo

testify ['tɛstɪfaɪ] *vi* (*LAW*) prestar declaración; **to ~ to sth** atestiguar algo

testimony ['tɛstɪmənɪ] *n* (*LAW*) testimonio

test: ~ **match** *n* (*CRICKET, RUGBY*) partido internacional; ~ **pilot** *n* piloto/mujer piloto *m/f* de pruebas; ~ **tube** *n* probeta

tetanus ['tɛtənəs] *n* tétano

tether ['tɛðə*] *vt* atar (con una cuerda) ♦ *n*: **to be at the end of one's ~** no aguantar más

text [tɛkst] *n* texto; ~**book** *n* libro de texto

textiles ['tɛkstaɪlz] *npl* textiles *mpl*; (*textile industry*) industria textil

texture ['tɛkstʃə*] *n* textura

Thailand ['taɪlænd] *n* Tailandia

Thames [tɛmz] *n*: **the ~** el (río) Támesis

than [ðæn] *conj* (*in comparisons*): **more ~ 10/once** más de 10/una vez; **I have more/less ~ you/Paul** tengo más/menos que tú/Paul; **she is older ~ you think** es mayor de lo que piensas

thank [θæŋk] *vt* dar las gracias a, agradecer; ~ **you (very much)** muchas gracias; ~ **God!** ¡gracias a Dios!; ~**s** *npl* gracias *fpl* ♦ *excl* (*also: many ~s, ~s a lot*) ¡gracias!; ~**s to** *prep* gracias a; ~**ful** *adj*: ~**ful (for)** agradecido (por); ~**less** *adj* ingrato; **T~sgiving (Day)** *n* día *m* de Acción de Gracias

─────────── **KEYWORD** ───────────

that [ðæt] (*pl* **those**) *adj* (*demonstrative*) ese/a, *pl* esos/as; (*more remote*) aquel/aquella, *pl* aquellos/as; **leave those books on the table** deja esos libros sobre la mesa; ~ **one** ése/ésa; (*more remote*) aquél/aquélla; ~ **one over there** ése/ésa de ahí; aquél/aquélla de allí

♦ *pron* **1** (*demonstrative*) ése/a, *pl* ésos/as; (*neuter*) eso; (*more remote*) aquél/aquélla, *pl* aquéllos/as; (*neuter*) aquello; **what's ~?** ¿qué es eso (*or* aquello)?; **who's ~?** ¿quién es ése/a (*or* aquél/aquélla)?; **is ~ you?** ¿eres tú?; **will you eat all ~?** ¿vas a comer todo eso?; ~**'s my house** ésa es mi casa; ~**'s what he said** eso es lo que dijo; ~ **is (to say)** es decir

2 (*relative: subject, object*) que; (*with preposition*) (el/la) que *etc*, el/la cual *etc*; **the book (~) I read** el libro que leí; **the books ~ are in the library** los libros que están en la biblioteca; **all (~) I have** todo lo que tengo; **the box (~) I put it in** la caja en la que *or* donde lo puse; **the people (~) I spoke to** la gente con la que hablé

3 (*relative: of time*) que; **the day (~) he came** el día (en) que vino

♦ *conj* que; **he thought ~ I was ill** creyó que yo estaba enfermo

♦ *adv* (*demonstrative*): **I can't work ~**

much no puedo trabajar tanto; **I didn't realise it was ~ bad** no creí que fuera tan malo; ~ **high** así de alto

─────────────────────────

thatched [θætʃt] *adj* (*roof*) de paja; (*cottage*) con tejado de paja

thaw [θɔː] *n* deshielo ♦ *vi* (*ice*) derretirse; (*food*) descongelarse ♦ *vt* (*food*) descongelar

─────────── **KEYWORD** ───────────

the [ðiː, ðə] *def art* **1** (*gen*) el, *f* la, *pl* los, *fpl* las (*NB* = **el** *immediately before f n beginning with stressed (h)a*; **a+el = al**; **de+el = del**); ~ **boy/girl** el chico/la chica; ~ **books/flowers** los libros/las flores; **to ~ postman/from ~ drawer** al cartero/del cajón; **I haven't ~ time/money** no tengo tiempo/dinero

2 (+ *adj* to form *n*) los; lo; ~ **rich and ~ poor** los ricos y los pobres; **to attempt ~ impossible** intentar lo imposible

3 (*in titles*): **Elizabeth ~ First** Isabel primera; **Peter ~ Great** Pedro el Grande

4 (*in comparisons*): ~ **more he works ~ more he earns** cuanto más trabaja más gana

─────────────────────────

theatre ['θɪətə*] (*US* **theater**) *n* teatro; (*also: lecture ~*) aula; (*MED: also: operating ~*) quirófano; ~**-goer** *n* aficionado/a al teatro

theatrical [θɪ'ætrɪkl] *adj* teatral

theft [θɛft] *n* robo

their [ðɛə*] *adj* su; ~**s** *pron* (el) suyo/(la) suya *etc*; see also **mine[1]**

them [ðɛm, ðəm] *pron* (*direct*) los/las; (*indirect*) les; (*stressed, after prep*) ellos/ellas; see also **me**

theme [θiːm] *n* tema *m*; ~ **park** *n* parque de atracciones (*en torno a un tema central*); ~ **song** *n* tema *m* (*musical*)

themselves [ðəm'sɛlvz] *pl pron* (*subject*) ellos mismos/ellas mismas; (*complement*) se; (*after prep*) sí (mismos/as); see also **oneself**

then [ðɛn] *adv* (*at that time*) entonces; (*next*) después; (*later*) luego, después; (*and also*) además ♦ *conj* (*therefore*) en ese caso, entonces ♦ *adj*: **the ~ president** el entonces presidente; **by ~** para entonces; **from ~ on** desde entonces

theology [θɪ'ɔlədʒɪ] *n* teología

theoretical [θɪə'rɛtɪkl] *adj* teórico

theory ['θɪərɪ] *n* teoría

therapist ['θɛrəpɪst] *n* terapeuta *m/f*

therapy [θɛrəpɪ] *n* terapia

─────────── **KEYWORD** ───────────

there ['ðɛə*] *adv* **1**: ~ **is**, ~ **are** hay; ~ **is no-one here/no bread left** no hay nadie aquí/no queda pan; ~ **has been an acci-**

dent ha habido un accidente
2 (*referring to place*) ahí; (*distant*) allí; **it's ~** está ahí; **put it in/on/up/down ~** ponlo ahí dentro/encima/arriba/abajo; **I want that book ~** quiero ese libro de ahí; **~ he is!** ¡ahí está!
3: ~, ~ (*esp to child*) ea, ea

there: ~abouts *adv* por ahí; **~after** *adv* después; **~by** *adv* así, de ese modo; **~fore** *adv* por lo tanto; **~'s** = **there is; there has**
thermal ['θəːml] *adj* termal; (*paper*) térmico
thermometer [θə'mɔmɪtə*] *n* termómetro
Thermos ['θəːmɔs] ® *n* (*also: ~ flask*) termo
thermostat ['θəːməustæt] *n* termostato
thesaurus [θɪ'sɔːrəs] *n* tesoro
these [ðiːz] *pl adj* estos/as ♦ *pl pron* éstos/as
theses ['θiːsiːz] *npl of* **thesis**
thesis ['θiːsɪs] (*pl* **theses**) *n* tesis *f inv*
they [ðeɪ] *pl pron* ellos/ellas; (*stressed*) ellos (mismos)/ellas (mismas); **~ say that...** (*it is said that*) se dice que...; **~'d** = **they had; they would; ~'ll** = **they shall; they will; ~'re** = **they are; ~'ve** = **they have**
thick [θɪk] *adj* (*in consistency*) espeso; (*in size*) grueso; (*stupid*) torpe ♦ *n*: **in the ~ of the battle** en lo más reñido de la batalla; **it's 20 cm ~** tiene 20 cm de espesor; **~en** *vi* espesarse ♦ *vt* (*sauce etc*) espesar; **~ness** *n* espesor *m*; grueso; **~set** *adj* fornido; **~skinned** *adj* (*fig*) insensible
thief [θiːf] (*pl* **thieves**) *n* ladrón/ona *m/f*
thieves [θiːvz] *npl of* **thief**
thigh [θaɪ] *n* muslo
thimble ['θɪmbl] *n* dedal *m*
thin [θɪn] *adj* (*person, animal*) flaco; (*in size*) delgado; (*in consistency*) poco espeso; (*hair, crowd*) escaso ♦ *vt*: **to ~ (down)** diluir
thing [θɪŋ] *n* cosa; (*object*) objeto, artículo; (*matter*) asunto; (*mania*): **to have a ~ about sb/sth** estar obsesionado con uno/algo; **~s** *npl* (*belongings*) efectos *mpl* (personales); **the best ~ would be to ...** lo mejor sería ...; **how are ~s?** ¿qué tal?
think [θɪŋk] (*pt, pp* **thought**) *vi* pensar ♦ *vt* pensar, creer; **what did you ~ of them?** ¿qué te parecieron?; **to ~ about sth/sb** pensar en algo/uno; **I'll ~ about it** lo pensaré; **to ~ of doing sth** pensar en hacer algo; **I ~ so/not** creo que sí/no; **to ~ well of sb** tener buen concepto de uno; **~ over** *vt* reflexionar sobre, meditar; **~ up** *vt* (*plan etc*) idear; **~ tank** *n* gabinete *m* de estrategia
thinly ['θɪnlɪ] *adv* (*cut*) fino; (*spread*) ligeramente
third [θəːd] *adj* (*before n*) tercer(a); (*following n*) tercero/a ♦ *n* tercero/a; (*fraction*) tercio; (*BRIT: SCOL: degree*) título de licenciado con calificación de aprobado; **~ly** *adv* en

tercer lugar; **~ party insurance** (*BRIT*) *n* seguro contra terceros; **~-rate** *adj* (*de calidad*) mediocre; **T~ World** *n* Tercer Mundo
thirst [θəːst] *n* sed *f*; **~y** *adj* (*person, animal*) sediento; (*work*) que da sed; **to be ~y** tener sed
thirteen ['θəː'tiːn] *num* trece
thirty ['θəːtɪ] *num* treinta

this [ðɪs] (*pl* **these**) *adj* (*demonstrative*) este/a; *pl* estos/as; (*neuter*) esto; **~ man/woman** este hombre/esta mujer; **these children/flowers** estos chicos/estas flores; **~ one** (*here*) éste/a, esto (de aquí)
♦ *pron* (*demonstrative*) éste/a; *pl* éstos/as; (*neuter*) esto; **who is ~?** ¿quién es éste/ésta?; **what is ~?** ¿qué es esto?; **~ is where I live** aquí vivo; **~ is what he said** esto es lo que dijo; **~ is Mr Brown** (*in introductions*) le presento al Sr. Brown; (*photo*) éste es el Sr. Brown; (*on telephone*) habla el Sr. Brown
♦ *adv* (*demonstrative*): **~ high/long etc** así de alto/largo *etc*; **~ far** hasta aquí

thistle ['θɪsl] *n* cardo
thorn [θɔːn] *n* espina
thorough ['θʌrə] *adj* (*search*) minucioso; (*wash*) a fondo; (*knowledge, research*) profundo; (*person*) meticuloso; **~bred** *adj* (*horse*) de pura sangre; **~fare** *n* calle *f*; **"no ~fare"** "prohibido el paso"; **~ly** *adv* (*search*) minuciosamente; (*study*) profundamente; (*wash*) a fondo; (*utterly: bad, wet etc*) completamente, totalmente
those [ðəuz] *pl adj* esos/esas; (*more remote*) aquellos/as
though [ðəu] *conj* aunque ♦ *adv* sin embargo
thought [θɔːt] *pt, pp of* **think** ♦ *n* pensamiento; (*opinion*) opinión *f*; **~ful** *adj* pensativo; (*serious*) serio; (*considerate*) atento; **~less** *adj* desconsiderado
thousand ['θauzənd] *num* mil; **two ~** dos mil; **~s of** miles de; **~th** *num* milésimo
thrash [θræʃ] *vt* azotar; (*defeat*) derrotar; **~ about** *or* **around** *vi* debatirse; **~ out** *vt* discutir a fondo
thread [θrɛd] *n* hilo; (*of screw*) rosca ♦ *vt* (*needle*) enhebrar; **~bare** *adj* raído
threat [θrɛt] *n* amenaza; **~en** *vi* amenazar ♦ *vt*: **to ~en sb with/to do** amenazar a uno con/con hacer
three [θriː] *num* tres; **~-dimensional** *adj* tridimensional; **~-piece suit** *n* traje *m* de tres piezas; **~-piece suite** *n* tresillo; **~-ply** *adj* (*wool*) de tres cabos
thresh [θrɛʃ] *vt* (*AGR*) trillar
threshold ['θrɛʃhəuld] *n* umbral *m*
threw [θruː] *pt of* **throw**
thrifty ['θrɪftɪ] *adj* económico

thrill [θrɪl] *n* (*excitement*) emoción *f*; (*shudder*) estremecimiento ♦ *vt* emocionar; **to be ~ed** (*with gift etc*) estar encantado; **~er** *n* novela (*or obra o película*) de suspense; **~ing** *adj* emocionante

thrive [θraɪv] (*pt* **thrived** *or* **throve**, *pp* **thrived** *or* **thriven**) *vi* (*grow*) crecer; (*do well*): **to ~ on sth** sentarle muy bien a uno algo; **thriven** [ˈθrɪvn] *pp of* **thrive**; **thriving** *adj* próspero

throat [θrəʊt] *n* garganta; **to have a sore ~** tener dolor de garganta

throb [θrɔb] *n* (*of heart*) latido; (*of wound*) punzada; (*of engine*) vibración *f* ♦ *vi* latir; dar punzadas; vibrar

throes [θrəʊz] *npl*: **in the ~ of** en medio de

throne [θrəʊn] *n* trono

throng [θrɔŋ] *n* multitud *f*, muchedumbre *f* ♦ *vt* agolparse en

throttle [ˈθrɔtl] *n* (*AUT*) acelerador *m* ♦ *vt* estrangular

through [θruː] *prep* por, a través de; (*time*) durante; (*by means of*) por medio de, mediante; (*owing to*) gracias a ♦ *adj* (*ticket, train*) directo ♦ *adv* completamente, de parte a parte; **de principio a fin**; **to put sb ~ to sb** (*TEL*) poner *or* pasar a uno con uno; **to be ~** (*TEL*) tener comunicación; (*have finished*) haber terminado; **"no ~ road"** (*BRIT*) "calle sin salida"; **~out** *prep* (*place*) por todas partes de, por todo; (*time*) durante todo ♦ *adv* por *or* en todas partes

throve [θrəʊv] *pt of* **thrive**

throw [θrəʊ] (*pt* **threw**, *pp* **thrown**) *n* tiro; (*SPORT*) lanzamiento ♦ *vt* tirar, echar; (*SPORT*) lanzar; (*rider*) derribar; (*fig*) desconcertar; **to ~ a party** dar una fiesta; **~ away** *vt* tirar; (*money*) derrochar; **~ off** *vt* deshacerse de; **~ out** *vt* tirar; (*person*) echar; expulsar; **~ up** *vi* vomitar; **~away** *adj* para tirar, desechable; (*remark*) hecho de paso; **~-in** *n* (*SPORT*) saque *m*

thru [θruː] (*US*) = **through**

thrush [θrʌʃ] *n* zorzal *m*, tordo

thrust [θrʌst] (*pt, pp* **thrust**) *n* (*TECH*) empuje *m* ♦ *vt* empujar (con fuerza)

thud [θʌd] *n* golpe *m* sordo

thug [θʌg] *n* gamberro/a

thumb [θʌm] *n* (*ANAT*) pulgar *m*; **to ~ a lift** hacer autostop; **~ through** *vt fus* (*book*) hojear; **~tack** (*US*) *n* chincheta (*SP*)

thump [θʌmp] *n* golpe *m*; (*sound*) ruido seco *or* sordo ♦ *vt* golpear ♦ *vi* (*heart etc*) palpitar

thunder [ˈθʌndəʳ] *n* trueno ♦ *vi* tronar; (*train etc*): **to ~ past** pasar como un trueno; **~bolt** *n* rayo; **~clap** *n* trueno; **~storm** *n* tormenta; **~y** *adj* tormentoso

Thursday [ˈθɜːzdɪ] *n* jueves *m inv*

thus [ðʌs] *adv* así, de este modo

thwart [θwɔːt] *vt* frustrar

thyme [taɪm] *n* tomillo

thyroid [ˈθaɪrɔɪd] *n* (*also:* **~ gland**) tiroides *m inv*

tic [tɪk] *n* tic *m*

tick [tɪk] *n* (*sound: of clock*) tictac *m*; (*mark*) palomita; (*ZOOL*) garrapata; (*BRIT: inf*): **in a ~** en un instante ♦ *vi* hacer tictac ♦ *vt* marcar; **~ off** *vt* marcar; (*person*) reñir; **~ over** *vi* (*engine*) girar en marcha lenta; (*fig*) ir tirando

ticket [ˈtɪkɪt] *n* billete *m* (*SP*), tíquet *m*, boleto (*AM*); (*for cinema etc*) entrada (*SP*), boleto (*AM*); (*in shop: on goods*) etiqueta; (*for raffle*) papeleta; (*for library*) tarjeta; (*parking ~*) multa por estacionamiento ilegal; **~ collector** *n* revisor(a) *m/f*; **~ office** *n* (*THEATRE*) taquilla (*SP*), boletería (*AM*); (*RAIL*) despacho de billetes (*SP*) *or* boletos (*AM*)

tickle [ˈtɪkl] *vt* hacer cosquillas a ♦ *vi* hacer cosquillas; **ticklish** *adj* (*person*) cosquilloso; (*problem*) delicado

tidal [ˈtaɪdl] *adj* de marea; **~ wave** *n* maremoto

tidbit [ˈtɪdbɪt] (*US*) *n* = **titbit**

tiddlywinks [ˈtɪdlɪwɪŋks] *n* juego infantil con fichas de plástico

tide [taɪd] *n* marea; (*fig: of events etc*) curso, marcha; **~ over** *vt* (*help out*) ayudar a salir del apuro

tidy [ˈtaɪdɪ] *adj* (*room etc*) ordenado; (*dress, work*) limpio; (*person*) (bien) arreglado ♦ *vt* (*also: ~ up*) poner en orden

tie [taɪ] *n* (*string etc*) atadura; (*BRIT: also: neck~*) corbata; (*fig: link*) vínculo, lazo; (*SPORT etc: draw*) empate *m* ♦ *vt* atar ♦ *vi* (*SPORT*) empatar; **to ~ in a bow** atar con un lazo; **to ~ a knot in sth** hacer un nudo en algo; **~ down** *vt* (*fig: person: restrict*) atar; (: *to price, date etc*) obligar a; **~ up** *vt* (*parcel*) envolver; (*dog, person*) atar; (*arrangements*) concluir; **to be ~d up** (*busy*) estar ocupado

tier [tɪəʳ] *n* grada; (*of cake*) piso

tiger [ˈtaɪgəʳ] *n* tigre *m*

tight [taɪt] *adj* (*rope*) tirante; (*money*) escaso; (*clothes*) ajustado; (*bend*) cerrado; (*shoes, schedule*) apretado; (*budget*) ajustado; (*security*) estricto; (*inf: drunk*) borracho ♦ *adv* (*squeeze*) muy fuerte; (*shut*) bien; **~s** (*BRIT*) *npl* panti *mpl*; **~en** *vt* (*rope*) estirar; (*screw, grip*) apretar; (*security*) reforzar ♦ *vi* estirarse; apretarse; **~-fisted** *adj* tacaño; **~ly** *adv* (*grasp*) muy fuerte; **~rope** *n* cuerda floja

tile [taɪl] *n* (*on roof*) teja; (*on floor*) baldosa; (*on wall*) azulejo; **~d** *adj* de tejas; embaldosado; (*wall*) alicatado

till [tɪl] *n* caja (registradora) ♦ *vt* (*land*) cultivar ♦ *prep, conj* = **until**

tilt [tɪlt] *vt* inclinar ♦ *vi* inclinarse

timber [ˈtɪmbəʳ] *n* (*material*) madera; (*trees*)

árboles *mpl*

time [taɪm] *n* tiempo; (*epoch: often pl*) época; (*by clock*) hora; (*moment*) momento; (*occasion*) vez *f*; (*MUS*) compás *m* ♦ *vt* calcular *or* medir el tiempo de; (*race*) cronometrar; (*remark, visit etc*) elegir el momento para; **a long ~** mucho tiempo; **4 at a ~** de 4 en 4; 4 a la vez; **for the ~ being** de momento, por ahora; **from ~ to ~** de vez en cuando; **at ~s** a veces; **in ~** (*soon enough*) a tiempo; (*after some time*) con el tiempo; (*MUS*) al compás; **in a week's ~** dentro de una semana; **in no ~** en un abrir y cerrar de ojos; **any ~** cuando sea; **on ~** a la hora; **5 ~s 5** 5 por 5; **what ~ is it?** ¿qué hora es?; **to have a good ~** pasarlo bien, divertirse; **~ bomb** *n* bomba de efecto retardado; **~less** *adj* eterno; **~ limit** *n* plazo; **~ly** *adj* oportuno; **~ off** *n* tiempo libre; **~r** *n* (*in kitchen etc*) programador *m* horario; **~ scale** (*BRIT*) *n* escala de tiempo; **~ share** *n* apartamento (*or* casa) a tiempo compartido; **~ switch** (*BRIT*) *n* interruptor *m* (horario); **~table** *n* horario; **~ zone** *n* huso horario

timid ['tɪmɪd] *adj* tímido

timing ['taɪmɪŋ] *n* (*SPORT*) cronometraje *m*; **the ~ of his resignation** el momento que eligió para dimitir

timpani ['tɪmpənɪ] *npl* tímpanos *mpl*

tin [tɪn] *n* estaño; (*also:* **~ plate**) hojalata; (*BRIT: can*) lata; **~foil** *n* papel *m* de estaño

tinge [tɪndʒ] *n* matiz *m* ♦ *vt*: **~d with** teñido de

tingle ['tɪŋgl] *vi* (*person*): **to ~ (with)** estremecerse (de); (*hands etc*) hormiguear

tinker ['tɪŋkə*]: **~ with** *vt fus* jugar con, tocar

tinned [tɪnd] (*BRIT*) *adj* (*food*) en lata, en conserva

tin opener [-əupnə*] (*BRIT*) *n* abrelatas *m inv*

tinsel ['tɪnsl] *n* (guirnalda de) espumillón *m*

tint [tɪnt] *n* matiz *m*; (*for hair*) tinte *m*; **~ed** *adj* (*hair*) teñido; (*glass, spectacles*) ahumado

tiny ['taɪnɪ] *adj* minúsculo, pequeñito

tip [tɪp] *n* (*end*) punta; (*gratuity*) propina; (*BRIT: for rubbish*) vertedero; (*advice*) consejo ♦ *vt* (*waiter*) dar una propina a; (*tilt*) inclinar; (*empty: also:* **~ out**) vaciar, echar; (*overturn: also:* **~ over**) volcar; **~-off** *n* (*hint*) advertencia; **~ped** (*BRIT*) *adj* (*cigarette*) con filtro

Tipp-Ex ['tɪpeks] ® *n* Tipp-Ex ® *m*

tipsy ['tɪpsɪ] (*inf*) *adj* alegre, mareado

tiptoe ['tɪptəu] *n*: **on ~** de puntillas

tiptop ['tɪp'tɒp] *adj*: **in ~ condition** en perfectas condiciones

tire ['taɪə*] *n* (*US*) = **tyre** ♦ *vt* cansar ♦ *vi* (*gen*) cansarse; (*become bored*) aburrirse; **~d** *adj* cansado; **to be ~d of sth** estar

harto de algo; **~less** *adj* incansable; **~some** *adj* aburrido; **tiring** *adj* cansado

tissue ['tɪʃuː] *n* tejido; (*paper handkerchief*) pañuelo de papel, kleenex ® *m*; **~ paper** *n* papel *m* de seda

tit [tɪt] *n* (*bird*) herrerillo común; **to give ~ for tat** dar ojo por ojo

titbit ['tɪtbɪt] (*US* **tidbit**) *n* (*food*) golosina; (*news*) noticia sabrosa

titillate ['tɪtɪleɪt] *vt* estimular, excitar

title ['taɪtl] *n* título; **~ deed** *n* (*LAW*) título de propiedad; **~ role** *n* papel *m* principal

titter ['tɪtə*] *vi* reírse entre dientes

TM *abbr* = **trademark**

────────────────── ***KEYWORD***

to [tuː, tə] *prep* **1** (*direction*) a; **to go ~ France/London/school/the station** ir a Francia/Londres/al colegio/a la estación; **to go ~ Claude's/the doctor's** ir a casa de Claude/al médico; **the road ~ Edinburgh** la carretera de Edimburgo

2 (*as far as*) hasta, a; **from here ~ London** de aquí a *or* hasta Londres; **to count ~ 10** contar hasta 10; **from 40 ~ 50 people** entre 40 y 50 personas

3 (*with expressions of time*): **a quarter/twenty ~ 5** las 5 menos cuarto/veinte

4 (*for, of*): **the key ~ the front door** la llave de la puerta principal; **she is secretary ~ the director** es la secretaria del director; **a letter ~ his wife** una carta a *or* para su mujer

5 (*expressing indirect object*) a; **to give sth ~ sb** darle algo a alguien; **to talk ~ sb** hablar con alguien; **to be a danger ~ sb** ser un peligro para alguien; **to carry out repairs ~ sth** hacer reparaciones en algo

6 (*in relation to*): **3 goals ~ 2** 3 goles a 2; **30 miles ~ the gallon** ≈ 9,4 litros a los cien (kms)

7 (*purpose, result*): **to come ~ sb's aid** venir en auxilio *or* ayuda de alguien; **to sentence sb ~ death** condenar a uno a muerte; **~ my great surprise** con gran sorpresa mía

♦ *with vb* **1** (*simple infin*): **~ go/eat** ir/comer

2 (*following another vb*): **to want/try/start ~ do** querer/intentar/empezar a hacer; *see also* **relevant vb**

3 (*with vb omitted*): **I don't want ~** no quiero

4 (*purpose, result*) para; **I did it ~ help you** lo hice para ayudarte; **he came ~ see you** vino a verte

5 (*equivalent to relative clause*): **I have things ~ do** tengo cosas que hacer; **the main thing is ~ try** lo principal es intentarlo

6 (*after adj etc*): **ready ~ go** listo para irse; **too old ~ ...** demasiado viejo (como)

para ...
♦ *adv*: **pull/push the door** ~ tirar de/
empujar la puerta

toad [təud] *n* sapo; ~**stool** *n* hongo venenoso

toast [təust] *n* (*CULIN*) tostada; (*drink,
speech*) brindis *m* ♦ *vt* (*CULIN*) tostar;
(*drink to*) brindar por; ~**er** *n* tostador *m*

tobacco [tə'bækəu] *n* tabaco; ~**nist** *n*
estanquero/a (*SP*), tabaquero/a (*AM*);
~**nist's (shop)** (*BRIT*) *n* estanco (*SP*), tabaquería (*AM*)

toboggan [tə'bɔgən] *n* tobogán *m*

today [tə'dei] *adv, n* (*also fig*) hoy *m*

toddler ['tɔdlə*] *n* niño/a (que empieza a
andar)

to-do *n* (*fuss*) lío

toe [təu] *n* dedo (del pie); (*of shoe*) punta;
to ~ **the line** (*fig*) conformarse; ~**nail** *n*
uña del pie

toffee ['tɔfi] *n* toffee *m*; ~ **apple** (*BRIT*) *n*
manzana acaramelada

together [tə'gɛðə*] *adv* juntos; (*at same
time*) al mismo tiempo, a la vez; ~ **with**
junto con

toil [tɔil] *n* trabajo duro, labor *f* ♦ *vi* trabajar duramente

toilet ['tɔilət] *n* retrete *m*; (*BRIT: room*) servicios *mpl* (*SP*), wáter *m* (*SP*), sanitario
(*AM*) ♦ *cpd* (*soap etc*) de aseo; ~ **paper** *n*
papel *m* higiénico; ~**ries** *npl* artículos *mpl*
de tocador; ~ **roll** *n* rollo de papel higiénico; ~ **water** *n* (agua de) colonia

token ['təukən] *n* (*sign*) señal *f*, muestra;
(*souvenir*) recuerdo; (*disc*) ficha ♦ *adj*
(*strike, payment etc*) simbólico; **book/
record/gift** ~ (*BRIT*) vale *m* para comprar
libros/discos/vale-regalo

Tokyo ['təukjəu] *n* Tokio, Tokío

told [təuld] *pt, pp of* **tell**

tolerable ['tɔlərəbl] *adj* (*bearable*) soportable; (*fairly good*) pasable

tolerant ['tɔlərnt] *adj*: ~ **of** tolerante con

tolerate ['tɔləreit] *vt* tolerar

toll [təul] *n* (*of casualties*) número de víctimas; (*tax, charge*) peaje *m* ♦ *vi* (*bell*) doblar

tomato [tə'mɑːtəu] (*pl* ~**es**) *n* tomate *m*

tomb [tuːm] *n* tumba

tomboy ['tɔmbɔi] *n* marimacho

tombstone ['tuːmstəun] *n* lápida

tomcat ['tɔmkæt] *n* gato (macho)

tomorrow [tə'mɔrəu] *adv, n* (*also: fig*) mañana; **the day after** ~ pasado mañana; ~
morning mañana por la mañana

ton [tʌn] *n* tonelada (*BRIT = 1016 kg*; *US =
907 kg*); (*metric* ~) tonelada métrica; ~**s** *pl*
(*inf*) montones *mpl*

tone [təun] *n* tono ♦ *vi* (*also*: ~ **in**) armonizar; ~ **down** *vt* (*criticism*) suavizar; (*colour*) atenuar; ~ **up** *vt* (*muscles*) tonificar;
~**-deaf** *adj* con mal oído

tongs [tɔŋz] *npl* (*for coal*) tenazas *fpl*;
(*curling* ~) tenacillas *fpl*

tongue [tʌŋ] *n* lengua; ~ **in cheek** irónica-
mente; ~**-tied** *adj* (*fig*) mudo; ~**-twister** *n*
trabalenguas *m inv*

tonic ['tɔnik] *n* (*MED, also fig*) tónico; (*also*:
~ *water*) (agua) tónica

tonight [tə'nait] *adv, n* esta noche; esta tarde

tonnage ['tʌnidʒ] *n* (*NAUT*) tonelaje *m*

tonsil ['tɔnsl] *n* amígdala; ~**litis** [-'laitis] *n*
amigdalitis *f*

too [tuː] *adv* (*excessively*) demasiado; (*also*)
también; ~ **much** demasiado; ~ **many**
demasiados/as

took [tuk] *pt of* **take**

tool [tuːl] *n* herramienta; ~ **box** *n* caja de
herramientas

toot [tuːt] *n* pitido ♦ *vi* tocar el pito

tooth [tuːθ] (*pl* **teeth**) *n* (*ANAT, TECH*)
diente *m*; (*molar*) muela; ~**ache** *n* dolor *m*
de muelas; ~**brush** *n* cepillo de dientes;
~**paste** *n* pasta de dientes; ~**pick** *n* palillo

top [tɔp] *n* (*of mountain*) cumbre *f*, cima;
(*of tree*) copa; (*of head*) coronilla; (*of ladder, page*) lo alto; (*of table*) superficie *f*; (*of
cupboard*) parte *f* de arriba; (*lid: of box*)
tapa; (*: of bottle, jar*) tapón *m*; (*of list etc*)
cabeza; (*toy*) peonza; (*garment*) blusa; camiseta ♦ *adj* de arriba; (*in rank*) principal,
primero; (*best*) mejor ♦ *vt* (*exceed*) exceder;
(*be first in*) encabezar; **on** ~ **of** (*above*) sobre, encima de; (*in addition to*) además de;
from ~ **to bottom** de pies a cabeza; ~ **off**
(*US*) *vt* = ~ **up**; ~ **up** *vt* llenar; ~ **floor** *n*
último piso; ~ **hat** *n* sombrero de copa;
~**-heavy** *adj* (*object*) mal equilibrado

topic ['tɔpik] *n* tema *m*; ~**al** *adj* actual

top: ~**less** *adj* (*bather, bikini*) topless *inv*;
~**-level** *adj* (*talks*) al más alto nivel;
~**most** *adj* más alto

topple ['tɔpl] *vt* derribar ♦ *vi* caerse

top-secret *adj* de alto secreto

topsy-turvy ['tɔpsi'təːvi] *adj* al revés ♦ *adv*
patas arriba

torch [tɔːtʃ] *n* antorcha; (*BRIT: electric*) linterna

tore [tɔː*] *pt of* **tear**

torment [*n* 'tɔːment, *vt* tɔː'ment] *n* tormento ♦ *vt* atormentar; (*fig: annoy*) fastidiar

torn [tɔːn] *pp of* **tear**

torrent ['tɔrnt] *n* torrente *m*

torrid ['tɔrid] *adj* (*fig*) apasionado

tortoise ['tɔːtəs] *n* tortuga; ~**shell**
['tɔːtəʃel] *adj* de carey

torture ['tɔːtʃə*] *n* tortura ♦ *vt* torturar;
(*fig*) atormentar

Tory ['tɔːri] (*BRIT*) *adj, n* (*POL*) conserva-
dor(a) *m/f*

toss [tɔs] *vt* tirar, echar; (*one's head*) sacudir; **to** ~ **a coin** echar a cara o cruz; **to** ~
up for sth jugar a cara o cruz algo; **to** ~

and turn (*in bed*) dar vueltas

tot [tɔt] *n* (*BRIT: drink*) copita; (*child*) nene/a *m/f*

total ['təutl] *adj* total, entero; (*emphatic: failure etc*) completo, total ♦ *n* total *m*, suma ♦ *vt* (*add up*) sumar; (*amount to*) ascender a

totalitarian [təutælɪ'tɛərɪən] *adj* totalitario

totally ['təutəlɪ] *adv* totalmente

totter ['tɔtə*] *vi* tambalearse

touch [tʌtʃ] *n* tacto; (*contact*) contacto ♦ *vt* tocar; (*emotionally*) conmover; **a ~ of** (*fig*) un poquito de; **to get in ~ with sb** ponerse en contacto con uno; **to lose ~** (*friends*) perder contacto; **~ on** *vt fus* (*topic*) aludir (brevemente) a; **~ up** *vt* (*paint*) retocar; **~-and-go** *adj* arriesgado; **~down** *n* aterrizaje *m*; (*on sea*) amerizaje *m*; (*US: FOOT-BALL*) ensayo *m*; **~ed** *adj* (*moved*) conmovido; **~ing** *adj* (*moving*) conmovedor(a); **~line** *n* (*SPORT*) línea de banda; **~y** *adj* (*person*) quisquilloso

tough [tʌf] *adj* (*material*) resistente; (*meat*) duro; (*problem etc*) difícil; (*policy, stance*) inflexible; (*person*) fuerte; **~en** *vt* endurecer

toupée ['tu:peɪ] *n* peluca

tour ['tuə*] *n* viaje *m*, vuelta; (*also: package ~*) viaje *m* todo comprendido; (*of town, museum*) visita; (*by band etc*) gira ♦ *vt* recorrer, visitar

tourism ['tuərɪzm] *n* turismo

tourist ['tuərɪst] *n* turista *m/f* ♦ *cpd* turístico; **~ office** *n* oficina de turismo

tournament ['tuənəmənt] *n* torneo

tousled ['tauzld] *adj* (*hair*) despeinado

tout [taut] *vi*: **to ~ for business** solicitar clientes ♦ *n* (*also: ticket ~*) revendedor(a) *m/f*

tow [təu] *vt* remolcar; "*on or* **in** (*US*) *~*" (*AUT*) "a remolque"

toward(s) [tə'wɔ:d(z)] *prep* hacia; (*attitude*) respecto a, con; (*purpose*) para

towel ['tauəl] *n* toalla; **~ling** *n* (*fabric*) felpa; **~ rail** (*US* **~ rack**) *n* toallero

tower ['tauə*] *n* torre *f*; **~ block** (*BRIT*) *n* torre *f* (de pisos); **~ing** *adj* muy alto, imponente

town [taun] *n* ciudad *f*; **to go to ~** ir a la ciudad; (*fig*) echar la casa por la ventana; **~ centre** *n* centro de la ciudad; **~ council** *n* ayuntamiento, consejo municipal; **~ hall** *n* ayuntamiento; **~ plan** *n* plano de la ciudad; **~ planning** *n* urbanismo

towrope ['təurəup] *n* cable *m* de remolque

tow truck *n* camión *m* grúa

toy [tɔɪ] *n* juguete *m*; **~ with** *vt fus* jugar con; (*idea*) acariciar; **~shop** *n* juguetería

trace [treɪs] *n* rastro ♦ *vt* (*draw*) trazar, delinear; (*locate*) encontrar; (*follow*) seguir la pista de; **tracing paper** *n* papel *m* de calco

track [træk] *n* (*mark*) huella, pista; (*path: gen*) camino, senda; (*: of bullet etc*) trayectoria; (*: of suspect, animal*) pista, rastro; (*RAIL*) vía; (*SPORT*) pista; (*on tape, record*) canción *f* ♦ *vt* seguir la pista de; **to keep ~ of** mantenerse al tanto de, seguir; **~ down** *vt* (*prey*) seguir el rastro de; (*sth lost*) encontrar; **~suit** *n* chandal *m*

tract [trækt] *n* (*GEO*) región *f*; (*pamphlet*) folleto

traction ['trækʃən] *n* (*power*) tracción *f*; **in ~** (*MED*) en tracción

tractor ['træktə*] *n* tractor *m*

trade [treɪd] *n* comercio; (*skill, job*) oficio ♦ *vi* negociar, comerciar ♦ *vt* (*exchange*): **to ~ sth (for sth)** cambiar algo (por algo); **~ in** *vt* (*old car etc*) ofrecer como parte del pago; **~ fair** *n* feria comercial; **~mark** *n* marca de fábrica; **~ name** *n* marca registrada; **~r** *n* comerciante *m/f*; **~sman** *n* (*shopkeeper*) tendero; **~ union** *n* sindicato; **~ unionist** *n* sindicalista *m/f*

tradition [trə'dɪʃən] *n* tradición *f*; **~al** *adj* tradicional

traffic ['træfɪk] *n* (*gen, AUT*) tráfico, circulación *f*, tránsito (*AM*) ♦ *vi*: **to ~ in** (*pej: liquor, drugs*) traficar en; **~ circle** (*US*) *n* isleta; **~ jam** *n* embotellamiento; **~ lights** *npl* semáforo; **~ warden** *n* guardia *m/f* de tráfico

tragedy ['trædʒədɪ] *n* tragedia

tragic ['trædʒɪk] *adj* trágico

trail [treɪl] *n* (*tracks*) rastro, pista; (*path*) camino, sendero; (*dust, smoke*) estela ♦ *vt* (*drag*) arrastrar; (*follow*) seguir la pista de ♦ *vi* arrastrar; (*in contest etc*) ir perdiendo; **~ behind** *vi* quedar a la zaga; **~er** *n* (*AUT*) remolque *m*; (*caravan*) caravana; (*CINEMA*) trailer *m*, avance *m*; **~er truck** (*US*) *n* trailer *m*

train [treɪn] *n* tren *m*; (*of dress*) cola; (*series*) serie *f* ♦ *vt* (*educate, teach skills to*) formar; (*sportsman*) entrenar; (*dog*) adiestrar; (*point: gun etc*): **to ~ on** apuntar a ♦ *vi* (*SPORT*) entrenarse; (*learn a skill*): **to ~ as a teacher** *etc* estudiar para profesor *etc*; **one's ~ of thought** el razonamiento de uno; **~ed** *adj* (*worker*) cualificado; (*animal*) amaestrado; **~ee** [treɪ'ni:] *n* aprendiz *m/f*; **~er** *n* (*SPORT: coach*) entrenador(a) *m/f*; (*: shoe*): **~ers** *npl* zapatillas *fpl* (de deporte); (*of animals*) domador(a) *m/f*; **~ing** *n* formación *f*; entrenamiento; **to be in ~ing** (*SPORT*) estar entrenando; **~ing college** *n* (*gen*) colegio de formación profesional; (*for teachers*) escuela de formación del profesorado; **~ing shoes** *npl* zapatillas *fpl* (de deporte)

traipse [treɪps] *vi* andar penosamente

trait [treɪt] *n* rasgo

traitor ['treɪtə*] *n* traidor(a) *m/f*

tram [træm] (*BRIT*) *n* (*also:* **~car**) tranvía *m*

tramp [træmp] n (*person*) vagabundo/a; (*inf: pej: woman*) puta ♦ vi andar con pasos pesados

trample ['træmpl] vt: **to ~ (underfoot)** pisotear

trampoline ['træmpəli:n] n trampolín m

tranquil ['træŋkwɪl] adj tranquilo; **~lizer** n (*MED*) tranquilizante m

transact [træn'zækt] vt (*business*) despachar; **~ion** [-'zækʃən] n transacción f, operación f

transcend [træn'send] vt rebasar

transcript ['trænskrɪpt] n copia

transfer [n 'trænsfə:*, vb træns'fə:*] n (*of employees*) traslado; (*of money, power*) transferencia; (*SPORT*) traspaso; (*picture, design*) calcomanía ♦ vt trasladar; transferir; **to ~ the charges** (*BRIT: TEL*) llamar a cobro revertido

transform [træns'fɔ:m] vt transformar

transfusion [træns'fju:ʒən] n transfusión f

transient ['trænzɪənt] adj transitorio

transistor [træn'zɪstə*] n (*ELEC*) transistor m; **~ radio** n transistor m

transit ['trænzɪt] n: **in ~** en tránsito

transitional [træn'zɪʃənl] adj de transición

transitive ['trænzɪtɪv] adj (*LING*) transitivo

transit lounge n sala de tránsito

translate [trænz'leɪt] vt traducir; **translation** [-'leɪʃən] n traducción f; **translator** n traductor(a) m/f

transmit [trænz'mɪt] vt transmitir; **~ter** n transmisor m

transparency [træns'pɛərnsɪ] n transparencia; (*BRIT: PHOT*) diapositiva

transparent [træns'pærnt] adj transparente

transpire [træns'paɪə*] vi (*turn out*) resultar; (*happen*) ocurrir, suceder; **it ~d that ...** se supo que ...

transplant [n 'trænsplɑ:nt] n (*MED*) transplante m

transport [n 'trænspɔ:t, vt træns'pɔ:t] n transporte m; (*car*) coche m (*SP*), carro (*AM*), automóvil m ♦ vt transportar; **~ation** [-'teɪʃən] n transporte m; **~ café** (*BRIT*) n bar-restaurant m de carretera

transvestite [trænz'vestaɪt] n travestí m/f

trap [træp] n (*snare, trick*) trampa; (*carriage*) cabriolé m ♦ vt coger (*SP*) or agarrar (*AM*) en una trampa; (*trick*) engañar; (*confine*) atrapar; **~ door** n escotilla

trapeze [trə'pi:z] n trapecio

trappings ['træpɪŋz] npl adornos mpl

trash [træʃ] n (*rubbish*) basura; (*pej*): **the book/film is ~** el libro/la película no vale nada; (*nonsense*) tonterías fpl; **~ can** (*US*) n cubo (*SP*) or balde m (*AM*) de la basura

travel ['trævl] n el viajar ♦ vi viajar ♦ vt (*distance*) recorrer; **~s** npl (*journeys*) viajes mpl; **~ agent** n agente m/f de viajes; **~ler** (*US ~er*) n viajero/a; **~ler's cheque** (*US ~er's check*) n cheque m de viajero; **~ling**

(*US ~ing*) n los viajes, el viajar; **~ sickness** n mareo

travesty ['trævəstɪ] n parodia

trawler ['trɔ:lə*] n pesquero de arrastre

tray [treɪ] n bandeja; (*on desk*) cajón m

treacherous ['tretʃərəs] adj traidor, traicionero; (*dangerous*) peligroso

treacle ['tri:kl] (*BRIT*) n melaza

tread [tred] n (*pt trod, pp trodden*) n (*step*) paso, pisada; (*sound*) ruido de pasos; (*of stair*) escalón m; (*of tyre*) banda de rodadura ♦ vi pisar; **~ on** vt fus pisar

treason ['tri:zn] n traición f

treasure ['treʒə*] n (*also fig*) tesoro ♦ vt (*value: object, friendship*) apreciar; (: *memory*) guardar

treasurer ['treʒərə*] n tesorero/a

treasury ['treʒərɪ] n: **the T~** el Ministerio de Hacienda

treat [tri:t] n (*present*) regalo ♦ vt tratar; **to ~ sb to sth** invitar a uno a algo

treatment ['tri:tmənt] n tratamiento

treaty ['tri:tɪ] n tratado

treble ['trebl] adj triple ♦ vt triplicar ♦ vi triplicarse; **~ clef** n (*MUS*) clave f de sol

tree [tri:] n árbol m; **~ trunk** tronco (de árbol)

trek [trek] n (*long journey*) viaje m largo y difícil; (*tiring walk*) caminata

trellis ['trelɪs] n enrejado

tremble ['trembl] vi temblar

tremendous [trɪ'mendəs] adj tremendo, enorme; (*excellent*) estupendo

tremor ['tremə*] n temblor m; (*also: earth ~*) temblor m de tierra

trench [trentʃ] n zanja

trend [trend] n (*tendency*) tendencia; (*of events*) curso; (*fashion*) moda; **~y** adj de moda

trepidation [trepɪ'deɪʃən] n inquietud f

trespass ['trespəs] vi: **to ~ on** entrar sin permiso en; **"no ~ing"** "prohibido el paso"

trestle ['tresl] n caballete m

trial ['traɪəl] n (*LAW*) juicio, proceso; (*test: of machine etc*) prueba; **~s** npl (*hardships*) dificultades fpl; **by ~ and error** a fuerza de probar

triangle ['traɪæŋgl] n (*MATH, MUS*) triángulo

tribe [traɪb] n tribu f

tribulations [trɪbju'leɪʃənz] npl dificultades fpl, sufrimientos

tribunal [traɪ'bju:nl] n tribunal m

tributary ['trɪbju:tərɪ] n (*river*) afluente m

tribute ['trɪbju:t] n homenaje m, tributo; **to pay ~ to** rendir homenaje a

trick [trɪk] n (*skill, knack*) tino, truco; (*conjuring ~*) truco; (*joke*) broma; (*CARDS*) baza ♦ vt engañar; **to play a ~ on sb** gastar una broma a uno; **that should do the ~** a ver si funciona así; **~ery** n engaño

trickle ['trɪkl] n (of water etc) goteo ♦ vi gotear

tricky ['trɪkɪ] adj difícil; delicado

tricycle ['traɪsɪkl] n triciclo

trifle ['traɪfl] n bagatela; (CULIN) dulce de bizcocho borracho, gelatina, fruta y natillas ♦ adv: a ~ long un poquito largo; **trifling** adj insignificante

trigger ['trɪgə*] n (of gun) gatillo; ~ **off** vt desencadenar

trill [trɪl] vi trinar, gorjear

trim [trɪm] adj (house, garden) en buen estado; (person, figure) esbelto ♦ n (haircut etc) recorte m; (on car) guarnición f ♦ vt (neaten) arreglar; (cut) recortar; (decorate) adornar; (NAUT: a sail) orientar; ~**mings** npl (CULIN) guarnición f

trinket ['trɪŋkɪt] n chuchería

trip [trɪp] n viaje m; (excursion) excursión f; (stumble) traspié m ♦ vi (stumble) tropezar; (go lightly) andar a paso ligero; **on a ~ de** viaje; ~ **up** vi tropezar, caerse ♦ vt hacer tropezar or caer

tripe [traɪp] n (CULIN) callos mpl; (pej: rubbish) tonterías fpl

triple ['trɪpl] adj triple; **triplets** ['trɪplɪts] npl trillizos/as mpl/fpl; **triplicate** ['trɪplɪkət] n: **in triplicate** por triplicado

trite [traɪt] adj trillado

triumph ['traɪʌmf] n triunfo ♦ vi: **to ~ (over)** vencer; ~**ant** [traɪ'ʌmfənt] adj (team etc) vencedor(a); (wave, return) triunfal

trivia ['trɪvɪə] npl trivialidades fpl

trivial ['trɪvɪəl] adj insignificante; (commonplace) banal

trod [trɒd] pt of tread

trodden ['trɒdn] pp of tread

trolley ['trɒlɪ] n carrito; (also: ~ bus) trolebús m

trombone [trɒm'bəun] n trombón m

troop [tru:p] n grupo, banda; ~**s** npl (MIL) tropas fpl; ~ **in/out** vi entrar/salir en tropel; ~**ing the colour** n (ceremony) presentación f de la bandera

trophy ['trəufɪ] n trofeo

tropical ['trɒpɪkl] adj tropical

trot [trɒt] n trote m ♦ vi trotar; **on the ~** (BRIT: fig) seguidos/as

trouble ['trʌbl] n problema m, dificultad f; (worry) preocupación f; (bother, effort) molestia, esfuerzo; (unrest) inquietud f; (MED): **stomach** etc ~ problemas mpl gástricos etc ♦ vt (disturb) molestar; (worry) preocupar, inquietar ♦ vi: **to ~ to do sth** molestarse en hacer algo; ~**s** npl (POL etc) conflictos mpl; (personal) problemas mpl; **to be in ~** estar en un apuro; **it's no ~!** ¡no es molestia (ninguna)!; **what's the ~?** (with broken TV etc) ¿cuál es el problema?; (doctor to patient) ¿qué pasa?; ~**d** adj (person) preocupado; (country, epoch, life) agitado; ~**maker** n agitador(a) m/f; (child) alborotador m; ~**shooter** n (in conflict) conciliador(a) m/f; ~**some** adj molesto

trough [trɒf] n (also: drinking ~) abrevadero; (also: feeding ~) comedero; (depression) depresión f

troupe [tru:p] n grupo

trousers ['trauzəz] npl pantalones mpl; **short ~** pantalones mpl cortos

trousseau ['tru:səu] (pl ~**x** or ~**s**) n ajuar m

trout [traut] n inv trucha

trowel ['trauəl] n (of gardener) palita; (of builder) paleta

truant ['truənt] n: **to play ~** (BRIT) hacer novillos

truce [tru:s] n tregua

truck [trʌk] n (lorry) camión m; (RAIL) vagón m; ~ **driver** n camionero; ~ **farm** (US) n huerto

trudge [trʌdʒ] vi (also: ~ along) caminar penosamente

true [tru:] adj verdadero; (accurate) exacto; (genuine) auténtico; (faithful) fiel; **to come ~** realizarse

truffle ['trʌfl] n trufa

truly ['tru:lɪ] adv (really) realmente; (truthfully) verdaderamente; (faithfully): **yours ~** (in letter) le saluda atentamente

trump [trʌmp] n triunfo; ~**ed-up** adj inventado

trumpet ['trʌmpɪt] n trompeta

truncheon ['trʌntʃən] n porra

trundle ['trʌndl] vt (pushchair etc) empujar; hacer rodar ♦ vi: **to ~ along** ir sin prisas

trunk [trʌŋk] n (of tree, person) tronco; (of elephant) trompa; (case) baúl m; (US: AUT) maletero; ~**s** npl (also: swimming ~s) bañador m (de hombre)

truss [trʌs] n (MED) braguero; ~ **(up)** vt atar

trust [trʌst] n confianza; (responsibility) responsabilidad f; (LAW) fideicomiso ♦ vt (rely on) tener confianza en; (hope) esperar; (entrust): **to ~ sth to sb** confiar algo a uno; **to take sth on ~** aceptar algo a ojos cerrados; ~**ed** adj de confianza; ~**ee** [trʌs'ti:] n (LAW) fideicomisario; (of school) administrador m; ~**ful** adj confiado; ~**ing** adj confiado; ~**worthy** adj digno de confianza

truth [tru:θ, pl tru:ðz] n verdad f; ~**ful** adj veraz

try [traɪ] n tentativa, intento; (RUGBY) ensayo ♦ vt (attempt) intentar; (test: also: ~ out) probar, someter a prueba; (LAW) juzgar, procesar; (strain: patience) hacer perder ♦ vi probar; **to have a ~** probar suerte; **to ~ to do sth** intentar hacer algo; ~ **again!** ¡vuelve a probar!; ~ **harder!** ¡esfuérzate más!; **well, I tried** al menos lo intenté; ~ **on** vt (clothes) probarse; ~**ing** adj (experience) cansado; (person) pesado

tsar [zɑ:*] n zar m

T-shirt ['tiːʃəːt] n camiseta
T-square n regla en T
tub [tʌb] n cubo (SP), balde m (AM); (bath) tina, bañera
tubby ['tʌbɪ] adj regordete
tube [tjuːb] n tubo; (BRIT: underground) metro; (for tyre) cámara de aire
tuberculosis [tjubəːkjuˈləʊsɪs] n tuberculosis f inv
tube station (BRIT) n estación f de metro
tubular ['tjuːbjʊlə*] adj tubular
TUC (BRIT) n abbr (= Trades Union Congress) federación nacional de sindicatos
tuck [tʌk] vt (put) poner; ~ **away** vt (money) guardar; (building): **to be ~ed away** esconderse, ocultarse; ~ **in** vt meter dentro; (child) arropar ♦ vi (eat) comer con apetito; ~ **up** vt (child) arropar; ~ **shop** n (SCOL) tienda; ≈ bar m (del colegio) (SP)
Tuesday ['tjuːzdɪ] n martes m inv
tuft [tʌft] n mechón m; (of grass etc) manojo
tug [tʌg] n (ship) remolcador m ♦ vt tirar de; ~-**of-war** n lucha de tiro de cuerda; (fig) tira y afloja m
tuition [tjuːˈɪʃən] n (BRIT) enseñanza; (: private ~) clases fpl particulares; (US: school fees) matrícula
tulip ['tjuːlɪp] n tulipán m
tumble ['tʌmbl] n (fall) caída ♦ vi caer; **to ~ to sth** (inf) caer en la cuenta de algo; ~**down** adj destartalado; ~ **dryer** (BRIT) n secadora
tumbler ['tʌmblə*] n (glass) vaso
tummy ['tʌmɪ] (inf) n barriga, tripa
tumour ['tjuːmə*] (US **tumor**) n tumor m
tuna ['tjuːnə] n inv (also: ~ **fish**) atún m
tune [tjuːn] n melodía ♦ vt (MUS) afinar; (RADIO, TV, AUT) sintonizar; **to be in/out of ~** (instrument) estar afinado/desafinado; (singer) cantar afinadamente/desafinar; **to be in/out of ~ with** (fig) estar de acuerdo/en desacuerdo con; ~ **in** vi: **to ~ in (to)** (RADIO, TV) sintonizar (con); ~ **up** vi (musician) afinar (su instrumento); ~**ful** adj melodioso; ~**r** n: **piano ~r** afinador(a) m/f de pianos
tunic ['tjuːnɪk] n túnica
Tunisia [tjuːˈnɪzɪə] n Túnez m
tunnel ['tʌnl] n túnel m; (in mine) galería ♦ vi construir un túnel/una galería
turban ['təːbən] n turbante m
turbine ['təːbaɪn] n turbina
turbulent ['təːbjʊlənt] adj turbulento
tureen [təˈriːn] n sopera
turf [təːf] n césped m; (clod) tepe m ♦ vt cubrir con césped; ~ **out** (inf) vt echar a la calle
turgid ['təːdʒɪd] adj (prose) pesado
Turk [təːk] n turco/a
Turkey ['təːkɪ] n Turquía
turkey ['təːkɪ] n pavo

Turkish ['təːkɪʃ] adj, n turco
turmoil ['təːmɔɪl] n desorden m, alboroto; **in ~** revuelto
turn [təːn] n turno; (in road) curva; (of mind, events) rumbo; (THEATRE) número; (MED) ataque m ♦ vt girar, volver; (collar, steak) dar la vuelta a; (page) pasar; (change): **to ~ sth into** convertir algo en ♦ vi volver; (person: look back) volverse; (reverse direction) dar la vuelta; (milk) cortarse; (become): **to ~ nasty/forty** ponerse feo/cumplir los cuarenta; **a good ~** un favor; **it gave me quite a ~** me dio un susto; **"no left ~"** (AUT) "prohibido girar a la izquierda"; **it's your ~** te toca a ti; **in ~** por turnos; **to take ~s (at)** turnarse (en); ~ **away** vi apartar la vista ♦ vi rechazar; ~ **back** vi volverse atrás ♦ vt hacer retroceder; (clock) retrasar; (reduce) bajar; (fold) doblar; ~ **in** vi (inf: go to bed) acostarse ♦ vt (fold) doblar hacia dentro; ~ **off** vi (from road) desviarse ♦ vt (light, radio etc) apagar; (tap) cerrar; (engine) parar; ~ **on** vt (light, radio etc) encender (SP), prender (AM); (tap) abrir; (engine) poner en marcha; ~ **out** vt (light, gas) apagar; (produce) producir ♦ vi (voters) concurrir; **to ~ out to be ...** resultar ser ...; ~ **over** vi (person) volverse ♦ vt (object) dar la vuelta a; (page) volver; ~ **round** vi volverse; (rotate) girar; ~ **up** vi (person) llegar, presentarse; (lost object) aparecer ♦ vt (gen) subir; ~**ing** n (in road) vuelta; ~**ing point** n (fig) momento decisivo
turnip ['təːnɪp] n nabo
turnout ['təːnaʊt] n concurrencia
turnover ['təːnəʊvə*] n (COMM: amount of money) volumen m de ventas; (: of goods) movimiento
turnpike ['təːnpaɪk] (US) n autopista de peaje
turnstile ['təːnstaɪl] n torniquete m
turntable ['təːnteɪbl] n plato
turn-up (BRIT) n (on trousers) vuelta
turpentine ['təːpəntaɪn] n (also: **turps**) trementina
turquoise ['təːkwɔɪz] n (stone) turquesa ♦ adj color turquesa
turret ['tʌrɪt] n torreón m
turtle ['təːtl] n galápago; ~**neck (sweater)** n jersey m de cuello vuelto
tusk [tʌsk] n colmillo
tussle ['tʌsl] n pelea
tutor ['tjuːtə*] n profesor(a) m/f; ~**ial** [-ˈtɔːrɪəl] n (SCOL) seminario
tuxedo [tʌkˈsiːdəʊ] (US) n smóking m, esmoquin m
TV [tiːˈviː] n abbr (= television) tele f
twang [twæŋ] n (of instrument) punteado; (of voice) timbre m nasal
tweezers ['twiːzəz] npl pinzas fpl (de depi-

lar)

twelfth [twɛlfθ] *num* duodécimo

twelve [twɛlv] *num* doce; **at ~ o'clock** (*midday*) a mediodía; (*midnight*) a media-noche

twentieth ['twɛntɪθ] *adj* vigésimo

twenty ['twɛntɪ] *num* veinte

twice [twaɪs] *adv* dos veces; **~ as much** dos veces más

twiddle ['twɪdl] *vt* juguetear con ♦ *vi*: **to ~ (with) sth** dar vueltas a algo; **to ~ one's thumbs** (*fig*) estar mano sobre mano

twig [twɪg] *n* ramita ♦ *vi* (*inf*) caer en la cuenta

twilight ['twaɪlaɪt] *n* crepúsculo

twin [twɪn] *adj, n* gemelo/a *m/f* ♦ *vt* hermanar; **~-bedded room** *n* habitación *f* doble

twine [twaɪn] *n* bramante *m* ♦ *vi* (*plant*) enroscarse

twinge [twɪndʒ] *n* (*of pain*) punzada; (*of conscience*) remordimiento

twinkle ['twɪŋkl] *vi* centellear; (*eyes*) brillar

twirl [twɔːl] *vt* dar vueltas a ♦ *vi* dar vueltas

twist [twɪst] *n* (*action*) torsión *f*; (*in road, coil*) vuelta; (*in wire, flex*) doblez *f*; (*in story*) giro ♦ *vt* torcer; (*weave*) trenzar; (*roll around*) enrollar; (*fig*) deformar ♦ *vi* serpentear

twit [twɪt] *n* (*inf*) tonto

twitch [twɪtʃ] *n* (*pull*) tirón *m*; (*nervous*) tic *m* ♦ *vi* crisparse

two [tuː] *num.* dos; **to put ~ and ~ together** (*fig*) atar cabos; **~-door** *adj* (*AUT*) de dos puertas; **~-faced** *adj* (*pej: person*) falso; **~fold** *adv*: **to increase ~fold** doblarse; **~-piece** (*suit*) *n* traje *m* de dos piezas; **~-piece** (*swimsuit*) *n* dos piezas *m inv*, bikini *m*; **~some** *n* (*people*) pareja; **~-way** *adj*: **~-way traffic** circulación *f* de dos sentidos

tycoon [taɪˈkuːn] *n*: **(business) ~ magnate** *m*

type [taɪp] *n* (*category*) tipo, género; (*model*) tipo; (*TYP*) tipo, letra ♦ *vt* (*letter etc*) escribir a máquina; **~-cast** *adj* (*actor*) encasillado; **~-face** *n* letra; **~-script** *n* texto mecanografiado; **~-writer** *n* máquina de escribir; **~-written** *adj* mecanografiado

typhoid ['taɪfɔɪd] *n* tifoidea

typical ['tɪpɪkl] *adj* típico

typing ['taɪpɪŋ] *n* mecanografía

typist ['taɪpɪst] *n* mecanógrafo/a

tyranny ['tɪrənɪ] *n* tiranía

tyrant ['taɪərnt] *n* tirano/a

tyre ['taɪə*] (*US* **tire**) *n* neumático (*SP*), llanta (*AM*); **~ pressure** *n* presión *f* de los neumáticos

tzar [zɑː*] *n* = **tsar**

U u

U-bend ['juːˈbɛnd] *n* (*AUT, in pipe*) recodo

udder ['ʌdə*] *n* ubre *f*

UFO ['juːfəʊ] *n abbr* = (*unidentified flying object*) OVNI *m*

ugh [əːh] *excl* ¡uf!

ugly ['ʌglɪ] *adj* feo; (*dangerous*) peligroso

UK *n abbr* = **United Kingdom**

ulcer ['ʌlsə*] *n* úlcera; (*mouth ~*) llaga

Ulster ['ʌlstə*] *n* Ulster *m*

ulterior [ʌlˈtɪərɪə*] *adj*: **~ motive** segundas intenciones *fpl*

ultimate ['ʌltɪmət] *adj* último, final; (*greatest*) máximo; **~ly** *adv* (*in the end*) por último, al final; (*fundamentally*) a *or* en fin de cuentas

umbilical cord [ʌmˈbɪlɪkl-] *n* cordón *m* umbilical

umbrella [ʌmˈbrɛlə] *n* paraguas *m inv*; (*for sun*) sombrilla

umpire ['ʌmpaɪə*] *n* árbitro

umpteen [ʌmpˈtiːn] *adj* enésimos/as; **~th** *adj*: **for the ~th time** por enésima vez

UN *n abbr* (= *United Nations*) NN. UU.

unable [ʌnˈeɪbl] *adj*: **to be ~ to do sth** no poder hacer algo

unaccompanied [ʌnəˈkʌmpənɪd] *adj* no acompañado; (*song*) sin acompañamiento

unaccountably [ʌnəˈkaʊntəblɪ] *adv* inexplicablemente

unaccustomed [ʌnəˈkʌstəmd] *adj*: **to be ~ to** no estar acostumbrado a

unanimous [juːˈnænɪməs] *adj* unánime

unarmed [ʌnˈɑːmd] *adj* (*defenceless*) inerme; (*without weapon*) desarmado

unashamed [ʌnəˈʃeɪmd] *adj* descarado

unassuming [ʌnəˈsjuːmɪŋ] *adj* modesto, sin pretensiones

unattached [ʌnəˈtætʃt] *adj* (*person*) soltero y sin compromiso; (*part etc*) suelto

unattended [ʌnəˈtɛndɪd] *adj* desatendido

unattractive [ʌnəˈtræktɪv] *adj* poco atractivo

unauthorized [ʌnˈɔːθəraɪzd] *adj* no autorizado

unavoidable [ʌnəˈvɔɪdəbl] *adj* inevitable

unaware [ʌnəˈwɛə*] *adj*: **to be ~ of** ignorar; **~s** *adv* de improviso

unbalanced [ʌnˈbælənst] *adj* (*report*) poco objetivo; (*mentally*) trastornado

unbearable [ʌnˈbɛərəbl] *adj* insoportable

unbeatable [ʌn'biːtəbl] *adj (team)* invencible; *(price)* inmejorable; *(quality)* insuperable

unbelievable [ʌnbɪ'liːvəbl] *adj* increíble

unbend [ʌn'bɛnd] *(irreg) vi (relax)* relajarse ♦ *vt (wire)* enderezar

unbiased [ʌn'baɪəst] *adj* imparcial

unborn [ʌn'bɔːn] *adj* que va a nacer

unbroken [ʌn'brəʊkən] *adj (seal)* intacto; *(series)* continuo; *(record)* no batido; *(spirit)* indómito

unbutton [ʌn'bʌtn] *vt* desabrochar

uncalled-for [ʌn'kɔːldfɔː*] *adj* gratuito, inmerecido

uncanny [ʌn'kænɪ] *adj* extraño

unceremonious ['ʌnsɛrɪ'məʊnɪəs] *adj (abrupt, rude)* brusco, hosco

uncertain [ʌn'sɜːtn] *adj* incierto; *(indecisive)* indeciso

unchanged [ʌn'tʃeɪndʒd] *adj* igual, sin cambios

unchecked [ʌn'tʃɛkt] *adv* sin estorbo, sin restricción

uncivilized [ʌn'sɪvɪlaɪzd] *adj* inculto; *(fig: behaviour etc)* bárbaro; *(hour)* inoportuno

uncle ['ʌŋkl] *n* tío

uncomfortable [ʌn'kʌmfətəbl] *adj* incómodo; *(uneasy)* inquieto

uncommon [ʌn'kɔmən] *adj* poco común, raro

uncompromising [ʌn'kɔmprəmaɪzɪŋ] *adj* intransigente

unconcerned [ʌnkən'sɜːnd] *adj* indiferente, despreocupado

unconditional [ʌnkən'dɪʃənl] *adj* incondicional

unconscious [ʌn'kɔnʃəs] *adj* sin sentido; *(unaware)*: **to be ~ of** no darse cuenta de ♦ *n*: **the ~** el inconsciente

uncontrollable [ʌnkən'trəʊləbl] *adj (child etc)* incontrolable; *(temper)* indomable; *(laughter)* incontenible

unconventional [ʌnkən'vɛnʃənl] *adj* poco convencional

uncouth [ʌn'kuːθ] *adj* grosero, inculto

uncover [ʌn'kʌvə*] *vt* descubrir; *(take lid off)* destapar

undecided [ʌndɪ'saɪdɪd] *adj (character)* indeciso; *(question)* no resuelto

under ['ʌndə*] *prep* debajo de; *(less than)* menos de; *(according to)* según, de acuerdo con; *(sb's leadership)* bajo ♦ *adv* debajo, abajo; ~ **there** allí abajo; ~ **repair** en reparación

under... ['ʌndə*] *prefix* sub; ~**-age** *adj* menor de edad; *(drinking etc)* de los menores de edad; ~**carriage** *(BRIT) n (AVIAT)* tren *m* de aterrizaje; ~**charge** *vt* cobrar menos de la cuenta; ~**clothes** *npl* ropa interior *(SP)* or íntima *(AM)*; ~**coat** *n (paint)* primera mano; ~**cover** *adj* clandestino; ~**current** *n (fig)* corriente *f* oculta; ~**cut**

vt irreg vender más barato que; ~**developed** *adj* subdesarrollado; ~**dog** *n* desvalido/a; ~**done** *adj (CULIN)* poco hecho; ~**estimate** *vt* subestimar; ~**exposed** *adj (PHOT)* subexpuesto; ~**fed** *adj* subalimentado; ~**foot** *adv* con los pies; ~**go** *vt irreg* sufrir; *(treatment)* recibir; ~**graduate** *n* estudiante *m/f*; ~**ground** *n (BRIT: railway)* metro; *(POL)* movimiento clandestino ♦ *adj (car park)* subterráneo ♦ *adv (work)* en la clandestinidad; ~**growth** *n* maleza; ~**hand(ed)** *adj (fig)* socarrón; ~**lie** *vt irreg (fig)* ser la razón fundamental de; ~**line** *vt* subrayar; ~**ling** ['ʌndəlɪŋ] *(pej) n* subalterno/a; ~**mine** *vt* socavar, minar; ~**neath** [ʌndə'niːθ] *adv* debajo ♦ *prep* debajo de, bajo; ~**paid** *adj* mal pagado; ~**pants** *npl* calzoncillos *mpl*; ~**pass** *(BRIT) n* paso subterráneo; ~**privileged** *adj* desposeído; ~**rate** *vt* menospreciar, subestimar; ~**shirt** *(US) n* camiseta; ~**shorts** *(US) npl* calzoncillos *mpl*; ~**side** *n* parte *f* inferior; ~**skirt** *(BRIT) n* enaguas *fpl*

understand [ʌndə'stænd] *(irreg) vt, vi* entender, comprender; *(assume)* tener entendido; ~**able** *adj* comprensible; ~**ing** *adj* comprensivo ♦ *n* comprensión *f*, entendimiento; *(agreement)* acuerdo

understatement ['ʌndəsteɪtmənt] *n* modestia *(excesiva)*; **that's an ~!** ¡eso es decir poco!

understood [ʌndə'stud] *pt, pp of* **understand** ♦ *adj (agreed)* acordado; *(implied)*: **it is ~ that** se sobreentiende que

understudy ['ʌndəstʌdɪ] *n* suplente *m/f*

undertake [ʌndə'teɪk] *(irreg) vt* emprender; **to ~ to do sth** comprometerse a hacer algo

undertaker ['ʌndəteɪkə*] *n* director(a) *m/f* de pompas fúnebres

undertaking ['ʌndəteɪkɪŋ] *n* empresa; *(promise)* promesa

undertone ['ʌndətəʊn] *n*: **in an ~** en voz baja

underwater [ʌndə'wɔːtə*] *adv* bajo el agua ♦ *adj* submarino

underwear ['ʌndəweə*] *n* ropa interior *(SP)* or íntima *(AM)*

underworld ['ʌndəwɜːld] *n (of crime)* hampa, inframundo

underwriter ['ʌndəraɪtə*] *n (INSURANCE)* asegurador(a) *m/f*

undesirable [ʌndɪ'zaɪrəbl] *adj (person)* indeseable; *(thing)* poco aconsejable

undies ['ʌndɪz] *(inf) npl* ropa interior *(SP)* or íntima *(AM)*

undo [ʌn'duː] *(irreg) vt (laces)* desatar; *(button etc)* desabrochar; *(spoil)* deshacer; ~**ing** *n* ruina, perdición *f*

undoubted [ʌn'daʊtɪd] *adj* indudable

undress [ʌn'drɛs] *vi* desnudarse

undulating ['ʌndjuleɪtɪŋ] *adj* ondulante

unduly [ʌn'dju:lɪ] adv excesivamente, demasiado

unearth [ʌn'ɔ:θ] vt desenterrar

unearthly [ʌn'ɔ:θlɪ] adj (hour) inverosímil

uneasy [ʌn'i:zɪ] adj intranquilo, preocupado; (feeling) desagradable; (peace) inseguro

uneducated [ʌn'edjukeɪtɪd] adj ignorante, inculto

unemployed [ʌnɪm'plɔɪd] adj parado, sin trabajo ♦ npl: **the ~** los parados

unemployment [ʌnɪm'plɔɪmənt] n paro, desempleo

unending [ʌn'endɪŋ] adj interminable

unerring [ʌn'ɔ:rɪŋ] adj infalible

uneven [ʌn'i:vn] adj desigual; (road etc) lleno de baches

unexpected [ʌnɪk'spɛktɪd] adj inesperado; **~ly** adv inesperadamente

unfailing [ʌn'feɪlɪŋ] adj (support) indefectible; (energy) inagotable

unfair [ʌn'fɛə*] adj: **~ (to sb)** injusto (con uno)

unfaithful [ʌn'feɪθful] adj infiel

unfamiliar [ʌnfə'mɪlɪə*] adj extraño, desconocido; **to be ~ with** desconocer

unfashionable [ʌn'fæʃnəbl] adj pasado or fuera de moda

unfasten [ʌn'fɑ:sn] vt (knot) desatar; (dress) desabrochar; (open) abrir

unfavourable [ʌn'feɪvərəbl] (US **unfavorable**) adj desfavorable

unfeeling [ʌn'fi:lɪŋ] adj insensible

unfinished [ʌn'fɪnɪʃt] adj inacabado, sin terminar

unfit [ʌn'fɪt] adj bajo de forma; (incompetent): **~ (for)** incapaz (de); **~ for work** no apto para trabajar

unfold [ʌn'fəuld] vt desdoblar ♦ vi abrirse

unforeseen [ʌnfɔ:'si:n] adj imprevisto

unforgettable [ʌnfə'gɛtəbl] adj inolvidable

unfortunate [ʌn'fɔ:tʃnət] adj desgraciado; (event, remark) inoportuno; **~ly** adv desgraciadamente

unfounded [ʌn'faundɪd] adj infundado

unfriendly [ʌn'frɛndlɪ] adj antipático; (behaviour, remark) hostil, poco amigable

ungainly [ʌn'geɪnlɪ] adj desgarbado

ungodly [ʌn'gɔdlɪ] adj: **at an ~ hour** a una hora inverosímil

ungrateful [ʌn'greɪtful] adj ingrato

unhappiness [ʌn'hæpɪnɪs] n tristeza, desdicha

unhappy [ʌn'hæpɪ] adj (sad) triste; (unfortunate) desgraciado; (childhood) infeliz; **~ about/with** (arrangements etc) poco contento con, descontento de

unharmed [ʌn'hɑ:md] adj ileso

unhealthy [ʌn'hɛlθɪ] adj (place) malsano; (person) enfermizo; (fig: interest) morboso

unheard-of [ʌn'hɔ:dɔv] adj inaudito, sin precedente

unhurt [ʌn'hɔ:t] adj ileso

unidentified [ʌnaɪ'dɛntɪfaɪd] adj no identificado, sin identificar; see also **UFO**

uniform ['ju:nɪfɔ:m] n uniforme m ♦ adj uniforme

unify ['ju:nɪfaɪ] vt unificar, unir

uninhabited [ʌnɪn'hæbɪtɪd] adj desierto

unintentional [ʌnɪn'tenʃənəl] adj involuntario

union ['ju:njən] n unión f; (also: **trade ~**) sindicato ♦ cpd sindical; **U~ Jack** n bandera del Reino Unido

unique [ju:'ni:k] adj único

unison ['ju:nɪsn] n: **in ~** (speak, reply, sing) al unísono

unit ['ju:nɪt] n unidad f; (section: of furniture etc) elemento; (team) grupo; **kitchen ~** módulo de cocina

unite [ju:'naɪt] vt unir ♦ vi unirse; **~d** adj unido; (effort) conjunto; **U~d Kingdom** n Reino Unido; **U~d Nations (Organization)** n Naciones fpl Unidas; **U~d States (of America)** n Estados mpl Unidos

unit trust (BRIT) n bono fiduciario

unity ['ju:nɪtɪ] n unidad f

universe ['ju:nɪvɔ:s] n universo

university [ju:nɪ'vɔ:sɪtɪ] n universidad f

unjust [ʌn'dʒʌst] adj injusto

unkempt [ʌn'kempt] adj (appearance) descuidado; (hair) despeinado

unkind [ʌn'kaɪnd] adj poco amable; (behaviour, comment) cruel

unknown [ʌn'nəun] adj desconocido

unlawful [ʌn'lɔ:ful] adj ilegal, ilícito

unleaded [ʌn'lɛdɪd] adj (petrol, fuel) sin plombo

unleash [ʌn'li:ʃ] vt desatar

unless [ʌn'les] conj a menos que; **~ he comes** a menos que venga; **~ otherwise stated** salvo indicación contraria

unlike [ʌn'laɪk] adj (not alike) distinto de or a; (not like) poco propio de ♦ prep a diferencia de

unlikely [ʌn'laɪklɪ] adj improbable; (unexpected) inverosímil

unlimited [ʌn'lɪmɪtɪd] adj ilimitado

unlisted [ʌn'lɪstɪd] (US) adj (TEL) que no consta en la guía

unload [ʌn'ləud] vt descargar

unlock [ʌn'lɔk] vt abrir (con llave)

unlucky [ʌn'lʌkɪ] adj desgraciado; (object, number) que da mala suerte; **to be ~** tener mala suerte

unmarried [ʌn'mærɪd] adj soltero

unmistakable [ʌnmɪs'teɪkəbl] adj inconfundible

unnatural [ʌn'nætʃrəl] adj (gen) antinatural; (manner) afectado; (habit) perverso

unnecessary [ʌn'nesəsərɪ] adj innecesario, inútil

unnoticed [ʌn'nəutɪst] adj: **to go** or **pass ~** pasar desapercibido

UNO ['ju:nəu] n abbr (= United Nations Organization) ONU f

unobtainable [ˌʌnəb'teɪnəbl] *adj* inconseguible; *(TEL)* inexistente

unobtrusive [ˌʌnəb'truːsɪv] *adj* discreto

unofficial [ˌʌnə'fɪʃl] *adj* no oficial; *(news)* sin confirmar

unorthodox [ʌn'ɔːθədɒks] *adj* poco ortodoxo; *(REL)* heterodoxo

unpack [ʌn'pæk] *vi* deshacer las maletas ♦ *vt* deshacer

unpalatable [ʌn'pælətəbl] *adj* incomible; *(truth)* desagradable

unparalleled [ʌn'pærəleld] *adj (unequalled)* incomparable

unpleasant [ʌn'plɛznt] *adj (disagreeable)* desagradable; *(person, manner)* antipático

unplug [ʌn'plʌg] *vt* desenchufar, desconectar

unpopular [ʌn'pɒpjulə*] *adj* impopular, poco popular

unprecedented [ʌn'prɛsɪdəntɪd] *adj* sin precedentes

unpredictable [ʌnprɪ'dɪktəbl] *adj* imprevisible

unprofessional [ʌnprə'fɛʃənl] *adj (attitude, conduct)* poco ético

unqualified [ʌn'kwɒlɪfaɪd] *adj* sin título, no cualificado; *(success)* total

unquestionably [ʌn'kwɛstʃənəblɪ] *adv* indiscutiblemente

unravel [ʌn'rævl] *vt* desenmarañar; *(mystery)* desentrañar

unreal [ʌn'rɪəl] *adj* irreal; *(extraordinary)* increíble

unrealistic [ʌnrɪə'lɪstɪk] *adj* poco realista

unreasonable [ʌn'riːznəbl] *adj* irrazonable; *(demand)* excesivo

unrelated [ʌnrɪ'leɪtɪd] *adj* sin relación; *(family)* no emparentado

unrelenting [ʌnrɪ'lɛntɪŋ] *adj* inexorable

unreliable [ʌnrɪ'laɪəbl] *adj (person)* informal; *(machine)* poco fiable

unremitting [ʌnrɪ'mɪtɪŋ] *adj* constante

unreservedly [ʌnrɪ'zɜːvɪdlɪ] *adv* sin reserva

unrest [ʌn'rɛst] *n* inquietud *f*, malestar *m*; *(POL)* disturbios *mpl*

unroll [ʌn'rəul] *vt* desenrollar

unruly [ʌn'ruːlɪ] *adj* indisciplinado

unsafe [ʌn'seɪf] *adj* peligroso

unsaid [ʌn'sɛd] *adj:* **to leave sth ~** dejar algo sin decir

unsatisfactory ['ʌnsætɪs'fæktərɪ] *adj* poco satisfactorio

unsavoury [ʌn'seɪvərɪ] *(US* **unsavory**) *adj (fig)* repugnante

unscathed [ʌn'skeɪðd] *adj* ileso

unscrew [ʌn'skruː] *vt* destornillar

unscrupulous [ʌn'skruːpjuləs] *adj* sin escrúpulos

unsettled [ʌn'sɛtld] *adj* inquieto, intranquilo; *(weather)* variable

unshaven [ʌn'ʃeɪvn] *adj* sin afeitar

unsightly [ʌn'saɪtlɪ] *adj* feo

unskilled [ʌn'skɪld] *adj (work)* no especializado; *(worker)* no cualificado

unspeakable [ʌn'spiːkəbl] *adj* indecible; *(awful)* incalificable

unstable [ʌn'steɪbl] *adj* inestable

unsteady [ʌn'stɛdɪ] *adj* inestable

unstuck [ʌn'stʌk] *adj:* **to come ~** despegarse; *(fig)* fracasar

unsuccessful [ʌnsək'sɛsful] *adj (attempt)* infructuoso; *(writer, proposal)* sin éxito; **to be ~** *(in attempting sth)* no tener éxito, fracasar; **~ly** *adv* en vano, sin éxito

unsuitable [ʌn'suːtəbl] *adj* inapropiado; *(time)* inoportuno

unsure [ʌn'ʃuə*] *adj* inseguro, poco seguro

unsuspecting ['ʌnsəs'pɛktɪŋ] *adj* desprevenido

unsympathetic [ʌnsɪmpə'θɛtɪk] *adj* poco comprensivo; *(unlikeable)* antipático

untapped [ʌn'tæpt] *adj (resources)* sin explotar

unthinkable [ʌn'θɪŋkəbl] *adj* inconcebible, impensable

untidy [ʌn'taɪdɪ] *adj (room)* desordenado; *(appearance)* desaliñado

untie [ʌn'taɪ] *vt* desatar

until [ən'tɪl] *prep* hasta ♦ *conj* hasta que; **~ he comes** hasta que venga; **~ now** hasta ahora; **~ then** hasta entonces

untimely [ʌn'taɪmlɪ] *adj* inoportuno; *(death)* prematuro

untold [ʌn'təuld] *adj (story)* nunca contado; *(suffering)* indecible; *(wealth)* incalculable

untoward [ʌntə'wɔːd] *adj* adverso

unused [ʌn'juːzd] *adj* sin usar

unusual [ʌn'juːʒuəl] *adj* insólito, poco común; *(exceptional)* inusitado

unveil [ʌn'veɪl] *vt (statue)* descubrir

unwanted [ʌn'wɒntɪd] *adj (clothing)* viejo; *(pregnancy)* no deseado

unwelcome [ʌn'wɛlkəm] *adj* inoportuno; *(news)* desagradable

unwell [ʌn'wɛl] *adj:* **to be/feel ~** estar indispuesto/sentirse mal

unwieldy [ʌn'wiːldɪ] *adj* difícil de manejar

unwilling [ʌn'wɪlɪŋ] *adj:* **to be ~ to do sth** estar poco dispuesto a hacer algo; **~ly** *adv* de mala gana

unwind [ʌn'waɪnd] *(irg: like* **wind**) *vt* desenvolver ♦ *vi (relax)* relajarse

unwise [ʌn'waɪz] *adj* imprudente

unwitting [ʌn'wɪtɪŋ] *adj* inconsciente

unworkable [ʌn'wɔːkəbl] *adj (plan)* impracticable

unworthy [ʌn'wɔːðɪ] *adj* indigno

unwrap [ʌn'ræp] *vt* desenvolver

unwritten [ʌn'rɪtn] *adj (agreement)* tácito; *(rules, law)* no escrito

─── KEYWORD

up [ʌp] *prep:* **to go/be ~ sth** subir/estar subido en algo; **he went ~ the stairs/the**

hill subió las escaleras/la colina; **we walked/climbed ~ the hill** subimos la colina; **they live further ~ the street** viven más arriba en la calle; **go ~ that road and turn left** sigue por esa calle y gira a la izquierda
♦ *adv* **1** (*upwards, higher*) más arriba; **~ in the mountains** en lo alto (de la montaña); **put it a bit higher ~** ponlo un poco más arriba *or* alto; **~ there** ahí *or* allí arriba; **~ above** en lo alto, por encima, arriba
2: **to be ~** (*out of bed*) estar levantado; (*prices, level*) haber subido
3: **~ to** (*as far as*) hasta; **~ to now** hasta ahora *or* la fecha
4: **to be ~ to** (*depending on*): **it's ~ to you** depende de ti; **he's not ~ to it** (*job, task etc*) no es capaz de hacerlo; **his work is not ~ to the required standard** su trabajo no da la talla; (*inf: be doing*): **what is he ~ to?** ¿que estará tramando?
♦ *n*: **~s and downs** altibajos *mpl*

upbringing [ˈʌpˌbrɪŋɪŋ] *n* educación *f*
update [ʌpˈdeɪt] *vt* poner al día
upgrade [ʌpˈgreɪd] *vt* (*house*) modernizar; (*employee*) ascender
upheaval [ʌpˈhiːvl] *n* trastornos *mpl*; (*POL*) agitación *f*
uphill [ʌpˈhɪl] *adj* cuesta arriba; (*fig: task*) penoso, difícil ♦ *adv*: **to go ~** ir cuesta arriba
uphold [ʌpˈhəʊld] (*irreg*) *vt* defender
upholstery [ʌpˈhəʊlstərɪ] *n* tapicería
upkeep [ˈʌpkiːp] *n* mantenimiento
upon [əˈpɒn] *prep* sobre
upper [ˈʌpə*] *adj* superior, de arriba ♦ *n* (*of shoe: also:* ~**s**) empeine *m*; ~**-class** *adj* de clase alta; **~ hand** *n*: **to have the ~ hand** tener la sartén por el mango; ~**most** *adj* el más alto; **what was ~most in my mind** lo que me preocupaba más
upright [ˈʌpraɪt] *adj* derecho; (*vertical*) vertical; (*fig*) honrado
uprising [ˈʌpraɪzɪŋ] *n* sublevación *f*
uproar [ˈʌprɔː*] *n* escándalo
uproot [ʌpˈruːt] *vt* (*also fig*) desarraigar
upset [*n* ˈʌpset, *vb, adj* ʌpˈset] *n* (*to plan etc*) revés *m*, contratiempo; (*MED*) trastorno ♦ (*irreg*) *vt* (*glass etc*) volcar; (*plan*) alterar; (*person*) molestar, disgustar ♦ *adj* molesto, disgustado; (*stomach*) revuelto
upshot [ˈʌpʃɒt] *n* resultado
upside-down *adv* al revés; **to turn a place ~** (*fig*) revolverlo todo
upstairs [ʌpˈstɛəz] *adv* arriba ♦ *adj* (*room*) de arriba ♦ *n* el piso superior
upstart [ˈʌpstɑːt] *n* advenedizo/a
upstream [ʌpˈstriːm] *adv* río arriba
uptake [ˈʌpteɪk] *n*: **to be quick/slow on the ~** ser muy listo/torpe
uptight [ʌpˈtaɪt] *adj* tenso, nervioso

up-to-date *adj* al día
upturn [ˈʌptɜːn] *n* (*in luck*) mejora; (*COMM: in market*) resurgimiento económico
upward [ˈʌpwəd] *adj* ascendente; ~**(s)** *adv* hacia arriba; (*more than*): ~**(s) of** más de
urban [ˈɜːbən] *adj* urbano
urchin [ˈɜːtʃɪn] *n* pilluelo, golfillo
urge [ɜːdʒ] *n* (*desire*) deseo ♦ *vt*: **to ~ sb to do sth** animar a uno a hacer algo
urgent [ˈɜːdʒənt] *adj* urgente; (*voice*) perentorio
urinate [ˈjʊərɪneɪt] *vi* orinar
urine [ˈjʊərɪn] *n* orina, orines *mpl*
urn [ɜːn] *n* urna; (*also: tea ~*) cacharro metálico grande para hacer té
Uruguay [ˈjʊərəgwaɪ] *n* (el) Uruguay; ~**an** *adj, n* uruguayo/a *m/f*
US *n abbr* (= *United States*) EE. UU.
us [ʌs] *pron* nos; (*after prep*) nosotros/as; *see also* **me**
USA *n abbr* (= *United States* (*of America*)) EE. UU
usage [ˈjuːzɪdʒ] *n* (*LING*) uso
use [*n* juːs, *vb* juːz] *n* uso, empleo; (*usefulness*) utilidad *f* ♦ *vt* usar, emplear; **she ~d to do it** (ella) solía *or* acostumbraba hacerlo; **in ~** en uso; **out of ~** en desuso; **to be of ~** servir; **it's no ~** (*pointless*) es inútil; (*not useful*) no sirve; **to be ~d to** estar acostumbrado a, acostumbrar; **~ up** *vt* (*food*) consumir; (*money*) gastar; ~**d** *adj* (*car*) usado; ~**ful** *adj* útil; ~**fulness** *n* utilidad *f*; ~**less** *adj* (*unusable*) inservible; (*pointless*) inútil; (*person*) inepto; ~**r** *n* usuario/a; ~**r-friendly** *adj* (*computer*) amistoso
usher [ˈʌʃə*] *n* (*at wedding*) ujier *m*; ~**ette** [-ˈrɛt] *n* (*in cinema*) acomodadora
USSR *n*: **the ~** la URSS
usual [ˈjuːʒʊəl] *adj* normal, corriente; **as ~** como de costumbre; ~**ly** *adv* normalmente
utensil [juːˈtɛnsl] *n* utensilio; **kitchen ~s** batería de cocina
uterus [ˈjuːtərəs] *n* útero
utility [juːˈtɪlɪtɪ] *n* utilidad *f*; (*public ~*) (empresa de) servicio público; **~ room** *n* ofis *m*
utilize [ˈjuːtɪlaɪz] *vt* utilizar
utmost [ˈʌtməʊst] *adj* mayor ♦ *n*: **to do one's ~** hacer todo lo posible
utter [ˈʌtə*] *adj* total, completo ♦ *vt* pronunciar, proferir; ~**ance** *n* palabras *fpl*, declaración *f*; ~**ly** *adv* completamente, totalmente
U-turn [ˈjuːˈtɜːn] *n* viraje *m* en redondo

V v

v. *abbr* = **verse; versus;** (= *volt*) v; (= *vide*) véase

vacancy ['veɪkənsɪ] *n* (BRIT: *job*) vacante *f*; (*room*) habitación *f* libre

vacant ['veɪkənt] *adj* desocupado, libre; (*expression*) distraído; ~ **lot** (US) n solar *m*

vacate [və'keɪt] *vt* (*house, room*) desocupar; (*job*) dejar (vacante)

vacation [və'keɪʃən] *n* vacaciones *fpl*

vaccinate ['væksɪneɪt] *vt* vacunar

vaccine ['væksiːn] *n* vacuna

vacuum ['vækjum] *n* vacío; ~ **cleaner** *n* aspiradora; ~**-packed** *adj* empaquetado al vacío

vagina [və'dʒaɪnə] *n* vagina

vagrant ['veɪɡrnt] *n* vagabundo/a

vague [veɪɡ] *adj* vago; (*blurred: memory*) borroso; (*ambiguous*) impreciso; (*person: absent-minded*) distraído; (: *evasive*): **to be** ~ no decir las cosas claramente; ~**ly** *adv* vagamente; (*distractedly*) con evasivas

vain [veɪn] *adj* (*conceited*) presumido; (*useless*) vano, inútil; **in** ~ en vano

valentine ['væləntaɪn] *n* (*also:* ~ *card*) tarjeta del Día de los Enamorados

valet ['væleɪ] *n* ayuda *m* de cámara

valid ['vælɪd] *adj* válido; (*ticket*) valedero; (*law*) vigente

valley ['vælɪ] *n* valle *m*

valuable ['væljuəbl] *adj* (*jewel*) de valor; (*time*) valioso; ~**s** *npl* objetos *mpl* de valor

valuation [vælju'eɪʃən] *n* tasación *f*, valuación *f*; (*judgement of quality*) valoración *f*

value ['vælju:] *n* valor *m*; (*importance*) importancia ♦ *vt* (*fix price of*) tasar, valorar; (*esteem*) apreciar; ~**s** *npl* (*principles*) principios *mpl*; ~ **added tax** (BRIT) *n* impuesto sobre el valor añadido; ~**d** *adj* (*appreciated*) apreciado

valve [vælv] *n* válvula

van [væn] *n* (AUT) furgoneta (SP), camioneta (AM)

vandal ['vændl] *n* vándalo/a; ~**ism** *n* vandalismo; ~**ize** *vt* dañar, destruir

vanilla [və'nɪlə] *n* vainilla

vanish ['vænɪʃ] *vi* desaparecer

vanity ['vænɪtɪ] *n* vanidad *f*

vantage point ['vɑːntɪdʒ-] *n* (*for views*) punto panorámico

vapour ['veɪpə*] (US **vapor**) *n* vapor *m*; (*on breath, window*) vaho

variable ['veərɪəbl] *adj* variable

variance ['veərɪəns] *n*: **to be at** ~ **(with)** estar en desacuerdo (con)

variation [veərɪ'eɪʃən] *n* variación *f*

varicose ['værɪkəus] *adj*: ~ **veins** varices *fpl*

varied ['veərɪd] *adj* variado

variety [və'raɪətɪ] *n* (*diversity*) diversidad *f*; (*type*) variedad *f*; ~ **show** *n* espectáculo de variedades

various ['veərɪəs] *adj* (*several: people*) varios/as; (*reasons*) diversos/as

varnish ['vɑːnɪʃ] *n* barniz *m*; (*nail* ~) esmalte *m* ♦ *vt* barnizar; (*nails*) pintar (con esmalte)

vary ['veərɪ] *vt* variar; (*change*) cambiar ♦ *vi* variar

vase [vɑːz] *n* florero

Vaseline ['væsɪliːn] ® *n* Vaselina ®

vast [vɑːst] *adj* enorme

VAT [væt] (BRIT) *n abbr* (= *Value Added Tax*) IVA *m*

vat [væt] *n* tina, tinaja

Vatican ['vætɪkən] *n*: **the** ~ el Vaticano

vault [vɔːlt] *n* (*of roof*) bóveda; (*tomb*) panteón *m*; (*in bank*) cámara acorazada ♦ *vt* (*also:* ~ *over*) saltar (por encima de)

vaunted ['vɔːntɪd] *adj*: **much** ~ cacareado, alardeado

VCR *n abbr* = **video cassette recorder**

VD *n abbr* = **venereal disease**

VDU *n abbr* (= *visual display unit*) UPV *f*

veal [viːl] *n* ternera

veer [vɪə*] *vi* (*vehicle*) virar; (*wind*) girar

vegetable ['vedʒtəbl] *n* (BOT) vegetal *m*; (*edible plant*) legumbre *f*, hortaliza ♦ *adj* vegetal; ~**s** *npl* (*cooked*) verduras *fpl*

vegetarian [vedʒɪ'teərɪən] *adj*, *n* vegetariano/a *m/f*

vehement ['viːɪmənt] *adj* vehemente, apasionado

vehicle ['viːɪkl] *n* vehículo; (*fig*) medio

veil [veɪl] *n* velo ♦ *vt* velar; ~**ed** *adj* (*fig*) velado

vein [veɪn] *n* vena; (*of ore etc*) veta

velocity [vɪ'lɔsɪtɪ] *n* velocidad *f*

velvet ['vɛlvɪt] *n* terciopelo

vending machine ['vɛndɪŋ-] *n* distribuidor *m* automático

vendor ['vɛndə*] *n* vendedor(a) *m/f*

veneer [və'nɪə*] *n* chapa, enchapado; (*fig*) barniz *m*

venereal disease [vɪ'nɪərɪəl-] *n* enfermedad *f* venérea

Venetian blind [vɪ'niːʃən-] *n* persiana

Venezuela [vɛnɪ'zweɪlə] *n* Venezuela; ~**n** *adj*, *n* venezolano/a *m/f*

vengeance ['vɛndʒəns] *n* venganza; **with a** ~ (*fig*) con creces

venison ['vɛnɪsn] *n* carne *f* de venado

venom ['vɛnəm] *n* veneno; (*bitterness*)

odio; **~ous** adj venenoso; lleno de odio
vent [vɛnt] n (in jacket) respiradero; (in wall) rejilla (de ventilación) ♦ vt (fig: feelings) desahogar
ventilator ['vɛntɪleɪtə*] n ventilador m
venture ['vɛntʃə*] n empresa ♦ vt (opinion) ofrecer ♦ vi arriesgarse, lanzarse; **business ~** empresa comercial
venue ['vɛnjuː] n lugar m
veranda(h) [və'rændə] n terraza
verb [vɜːb] n verbo; **~al** adj verbal
verbatim [vɜː'beɪtɪm] adj, adv palabra por palabra
verbose [vɜː'bəus] adj prolijo
verdict ['vɜːdɪkt] n veredicto, fallo; (fig) opinión f, juicio
verge [vɜːdʒ] (BRIT) n borde m; **"soft ~s"** (AUT) "arcén m no asfaltado"; **to be on the ~** of doing sth estar a punto de hacer algo; **~ on** vt fus rayar en
verify ['vɛrɪfaɪ] vt comprobar, verificar
veritable ['vɛrɪtəbl] adj verdadero, auténtico
vermin ['vɜːmɪn] npl (animals) alimañas fpl; (insects, fig) parásitos mpl
vermouth ['vɜːməθ] n vermut m
vernacular [və'nækjulə*] n lengua vernácula
versatile ['vɜːsətaɪl] adj (person) polifacético; (machine, tool etc) versátil
verse [vɜːs] n poesía; (stanza) estrofa; (in bible) versículo
versed [vɜːst] adj: **(well-)~ in** versado en
version ['vɜːʃən] n versión f
versus ['vɜːsəs] prep contra
vertebra ['vɜːtɪbrə] (pl ~e) n vértebra
vertical ['vɜːtɪkl] adj vertical
verve [vɜːv] n brío
very ['vɛrɪ] adv muy ♦ adj: **the ~ book which** el mismo libro que; **the ~ last** el último de todos; **at the ~ least** al menos; **~ much** muchísimo
vessel ['vɛsl] n (ship) barco; (container) vasija; see **blood**
vest [vɛst] n (BRIT) camiseta; (US: waistcoat) chaleco; **~ed interests** npl (COMM) intereses mpl creados
vestige ['vɛstɪdʒ] n vestigio, rastro
vet [vɛt] vt (candidate) investigar ♦ n abbr (BRIT) = **veterinary surgeon**
veteran ['vɛtərn] n veterano
veterinary surgeon ['vɛtrɪnərɪ] (US **veterinarian**) n veterinario/a m/f
veto ['viːtəu] (pl ~es) n veto ♦ vt prohibir, poner el veto a
vex [vɛks] vt fastidiar; **~ed** adj (question) controvertido
VHF abbr (= very high frequency) muy alta frecuencia
via ['vaɪə] prep por, por medio de
vibrant ['vaɪbrənt] adj (lively) animado; (bright) vivo; (voice) vibrante

vibrate [vaɪ'breɪt] vi vibrar
vicar ['vɪkə*] n párroco (de la Iglesia Anglicana); **~age** n parroquia
vice [vaɪs] n (evil) vicio; (TECH) torno de banco
vice- [vaɪs] prefix vice-; **~-chairman** n vicepresidente m
vice squad n brigada antivicio
vice versa ['vaɪsɪ'vɜːsə] adv viceversa
vicinity [vɪ'sɪnɪtɪ] n: **in the ~ (of)** cercano (a)
vicious ['vɪʃəs] adj (attack) violento; (words) cruel; (horse, dog) resabido; **~ circle** n círculo vicioso
victim ['vɪktɪm] n víctima; **~ize** vt tomar represalias contra
victor ['vɪktə*] n vencedor(a) m/f
victorious [vɪk'tɔːrɪəs] adj (team) vencedor(a)
victory ['vɪktərɪ] n victoria
video ['vɪdɪəu] cpd vídeo ♦ n (~ film) videofilm m; (also: ~ cassette) videocassette f; (also: ~ cassette recorder) magnetoscopio; **~ game** n videojuego; **~ tape** n cinta de vídeo
vie [vaɪ] vi: **to ~ (with sb for sth)** competir (con uno por algo)
Vienna [vɪ'ɛnə] n Viena
Vietnam [vjɛt'næm] n Vietnam m; **~ese** [-nə'miːz] n inv, adj vietnamita m/f
view [vjuː] n vista; (outlook) perspectiva; (opinion) opinión f, criterio ♦ vt (look at) mirar; (fig) considerar; **on ~** (in museum etc) expuesto; **in full ~ (of)** en plena vista (de); **in ~ of the weather/the fact that** en vista del tiempo/del hecho de que; **in my ~** en mi opinión; **~er** n espectador(a) m/f; (TV) telespectador(a) m/f; **~finder** n visor m de imagen; **~point** n (attitude) punto de vista; (place) mirador m
vigour ['vɪgə*] (US **vigor**) n energía, vigor m
vile [vaɪl] adj vil, infame; (smell) asqueroso; (temper) endemoniado
villa ['vɪlə] n (country house) casa de campo; (suburban house) chalet m
village ['vɪlɪdʒ] n aldea; **~r** n aldeano/a
villain ['vɪlən] n (scoundrel) malvado/a; (in novel) malo; (BRIT: criminal) maleante m/f
vindicate ['vɪndɪkeɪt] vt vindicar, justificar
vindictive [vɪn'dɪktɪv] adj vengativo
vine [vaɪn] n vid f
vinegar ['vɪnɪgə*] n vinagre m
vineyard ['vɪnjɑːd] n viña, viñedo
vintage ['vɪntɪdʒ] n (year) vendimia, cosecha ♦ cpd de época; **~ wine** n vino añejo
vinyl ['vaɪnl] n vinilo
viola [vɪ'əulə] n (MUS) viola
violate ['vaɪəleɪt] vt violar
violence ['vaɪələns] n violencia
violent ['vaɪələnt] adj violento; (intense) intenso

violet ['vaɪələt] *adj* violado, violeta ♦ *n* (*plant*) violeta

violin [vaɪə'lɪn] *n* violín *m*; ~**ist** *n* violinista *m/f*

VIP *n abbr* (= *very important person*) VIP *m*

virgin ['vɜːdʒɪn] *n* virgen *f*

Virgo ['vɜːɡəʊ] *n* Virgo

virtually ['vɜːtjʊəlɪ] *adv* prácticamente

virtual reality ['vɜːtjʊəl-] *n* (COMPUT) mundo virtual

virtue ['vɜːtjuː] *n* virtud *f*; (*advantage*) ventaja; **by** ~ **of** en virtud de

virtuous ['vɜːtjʊəs] *adj* virtuoso

virus ['vaɪərəs] *n* (*also:* COMPUT) virus *m*

visa ['viːzə] *n* visado (SP), visa (AM)

vis-à-vis [viːzə'viː] *prep* con respecto a

visible ['vɪzəbl] *adj* visible

vision ['vɪʒən] *n* (*sight*) vista; (*foresight, in dream*) visión *f*

visit ['vɪzɪt] *n* visita ♦ *vt* (*person: US: also*: ~ **with**) visitar, hacer una visita a; (*place*) ir a, (ir a) conocer; ~**ing hours** *npl* (*in hospital etc*) horas *fpl* de visita; ~**or** *n* (*in museum*) visitante *m/f*; (*invited to house*) visita; (*tourist*) turista *m/f*

visor ['vaɪzə*] *n* visera

vista ['vɪstə] *n* vista, panorama *m*

visual ['vɪzjʊəl] *adj* visual; ~ **aid** *n* medio visual; ~ **display unit** *n* unidad *f* de presentación visual; ~**ize** *vt* imaginarse

vital ['vaɪtl] *adj* (*essential*) esencial, imprescindible; (*dynamic*) dinámico; (*organ*) vital; ~**ly** *adv*: ~**ly important** de primera importancia; ~ **statistics** *npl* (*fig*) medidas *fpl* vitales

vitamin ['vɪtəmɪn] *n* vitamina

vivacious [vɪ'veɪʃəs] *adj* vivaz, alegre

vivid ['vɪvɪd] *adj* (*account*) gráfico; (*light*) intenso; (*imagination, memory*) vivo; ~**ly** *adv* gráficamente; (*remember*) como si fuera hoy

V-neck ['viːnɛk] *n* cuello de pico

vocabulary [vəʊ'kæbjʊlərɪ] *n* vocabulario

vocal ['vəʊkl] *adj* vocal; (*articulate*) elocuente; ~ **chords** *npl* cuerdas *fpl* vocales

vocation [vəʊ'keɪʃən] *n* vocación *f*; ~**al** *adj* profesional

vodka ['vɒdkə] *n* vodka *m*

vogue [vəʊg] *n*: **in** ~ en boga, de moda

voice [vɔɪs] *n* voz *f* ♦ *vt* expresar

void [vɔɪd] *n* vacío; (*hole*) hueco ♦ *adj* (*invalid*) nulo, inválido; (*empty*): ~ **of** carente *or* desprovisto de

volatile ['vɒlətaɪl] *adj* (*situation*) inestable; (*person*) voluble; (*liquid*) volátil

volcano [vɒl'keɪnəʊ] *n* (*pl* ~**es**) *n* volcán *m*

volition [və'lɪʃən] *n*: **of one's own** ~ de su propia voluntad

volley ['vɒlɪ] *n* (*of gunfire*) descarga; (*of stones etc*) lluvia; (*fig*) torrente *m*; (TENNIS etc) volea; ~**ball** *n* vol(e)ibol *m*

volt [vəʊlt] *n* voltio; ~**age** *n* voltaje *m*

volume ['vɒljuːm] *n* (*gen*) volumen *m*; (*book*) tomo

voluminous [və'luːmɪnəs] *adj* (*clothes*) amplio; (*notes*) prolijo

voluntary ['vɒləntərɪ] *adj* voluntario

volunteer [vɒlən'tɪə*] *n* voluntario/a ♦ *vt* (*information*) ofrecer ♦ *vi* ofrecerse (de voluntario); **to** ~ **to do** ofrecerse a hacer

vomit ['vɒmɪt] *n* vómito ♦ *vt, vi* vomitar

vote [vəʊt] *n* voto; (*votes cast*) votación *f*; (*right to* ~) derecho de votar; (*franchise*) sufragio ♦ *vt* (*chairman*) elegir; (*propose*): **to** ~ **that** proponer que ♦ *vi* votar, ir a votar; ~ **of thanks** voto de gracias; ~**r** *n* votante *m/f*; **voting** *n* votación *f*

vouch [vaʊtʃ]: **to** ~ **for** *vt fus* garantizar, responder de

voucher ['vaʊtʃə*] *n* (*for meal, petrol*) vale *m*

vow [vaʊ] *n* voto ♦ *vt*: **to** ~ **to do/that** jurar hacer/que

vowel ['vaʊəl] *n* vocal *f*

voyage ['vɔɪɪdʒ] *n* viaje *m*

V-sign (BRIT) *n* ≈ corte *m* de mangas

vulgar ['vʌlgə*] *adj* (*rude*) ordinario, grosero; (*in bad taste*) de mal gusto; ~**ity** [-'gærɪtɪ] *n* grosería; mal gusto

vulnerable ['vʌlnərəbl] *adj* vulnerable

vulture ['vʌltʃə*] *n* buitre *m*

wad [wɒd] *n* bolita; (*of banknotes etc*) fajo

waddle ['wɒdl] *vi* anadear

wade [weɪd] *vi*: **to** ~ **through** (*water*) vadear; (*fig: book*) leer con dificultad; **wading pool** (US) *n* piscina para niños

wafer ['weɪfə*] *n* galleta, barquillo

waffle ['wɒfl] *n* (CULIN) gofre *m* ♦ *vi* dar el rollo

waft [wɒft] *vt* llevar por el aire ♦ *vi* flotar

wag [wæg] *vt* menear, agitar ♦ *vi* moverse, menearse

wage [weɪdʒ] *n* (*also*: ~**s**) sueldo, salario ♦ *vt*: **to** ~ **war** hacer la guerra; ~ **earner** *n* asalariado/a; ~ **packet** *n* sobre *m* de paga

wager ['weɪdʒə*] *n* apuesta

waggle ['wægl] *vt* menear, mover

wag(g)on ['wægən] *n* (*horse-drawn*) carro; (BRIT: RAIL) vagón *m*

wail [weɪl] *n* gemido ♦ *vi* gemir

waist [weɪst] *n* cintura, talle *m*; ~**coat** (BRIT) *n* chaleco; ~**line** *n* talle *m*

wait [weɪt] n (*interval*) pausa ♦ vi esperar; **to lie in ~ for** acechar a; **I can't ~ to** (*fig*) estoy deseando; **to ~ for** esperar (a); **~ behind** vi quedarse; **~ on** vt fus servir a; **~er** n camarero; **~ing** n: "**no ~ing**" (*BRIT: AUT*) "prohibido estacionarse"; **~ing list** n lista de espera; **~ing room** n sala de espera; **~ress** n camarera

waive [weɪv] vt suspender

wake [weɪk] (*pt* **woke** *or* **waked**, *pp* **woken** *or* **waked**) vt (*also: ~ up*) despertar ♦ vi (*also: ~ up*) despertarse ♦ n (*for dead person*) vela, velatorio; (*NAUT*) estela; **waken** vt, vi = **wake**

Wales [weɪlz] n País m de Gales; **the Prince of ~** el príncipe de Gales

walk [wɔːk] n (*stroll*) paseo; (*hike*) excursión f a pie, caminata; (*gait*) paso, andar m; (*in park etc*) paseo, alameda ♦ vi andar, caminar; (*for pleasure, exercise*) pasear ♦ vt (*distance*) recorrer a pie, andar; (*dog*) pasear; **10 minutes' ~ from here** a 10 minutos de aquí andando; **people from all ~s of life** gente de todas las esferas; **~ out** vi (*audience*) salir; (*workers*) declararse en huelga; **~ out on** (*inf*) vt fus abandonar; **~er** n (*person*) paseante m/f, caminante m/f; **~ie-talkie** ['wɔːkɪ'tɔːkɪ] n walkie-talkie m; **~ing** n el andar; **~ing shoes** npl zapatos mpl para andar; **~ing stick** n bastón m; **~out** n huelga; **~over** (*inf*) n: **it was a ~over** fue pan comido; **~way** n paseo

wall [wɔːl] n pared f; (*exterior*) muro; (*city ~ etc*) muralla; **~ed** adj amurallado; (*garden*) con tapia

wallet ['wɒlɪt] n cartera (*SP*), billetera (*AM*)

wallflower ['wɔːlflaʊə*] n alhelí m; **to be a ~** (*fig*) comer pavo

wallop ['wɒləp] (*inf*) vt zurrar

wallow ['wɒləʊ] vi revolcarse

wallpaper ['wɔːlpeɪpə*] n papel m pintado ♦ vt empapelar

walnut ['wɔːlnʌt] n nuez f; (*tree*) nogal m

walrus ['wɔːlrəs] (*pl* ~ *or* ~**es**) n morsa

waltz [wɔːlts] n vals m ♦ vi bailar el vals

wan [wɒn] adj pálido

wand [wɒnd] n (*also: magic ~*) varita (mágica)

wander ['wɒndə*] vi (*person*) vagar; deambular; (*thoughts*) divagar ♦ vt recorrer, vagar por

wane [weɪn] vi menguar

wangle ['wæŋgl] (*BRIT: inf*) vt agenciarse

want [wɒnt] vt querer, desear; (*need*) necesitar ♦ n: **for ~ of** por falta de; **~s** npl (*needs*) necesidades fpl; **to ~ to do** querer hacer; **to ~ sb to do sth** querer que uno haga algo; **~ed** adj (*criminal*) buscado; "**~ed**" (*in advertisements*) "se busca"; **~ing** adj: **to be found ~ing** no estar a la altura de las circunstancias

wanton ['wɒntn] adj (*playful*) juguetón/ona; (*licentious*) lascivo

war [wɔː*] n guerra; **to make ~ (on)** (*also fig*) declarar la guerra (a)

ward [wɔːd] n (*in hospital*) sala; (*POL*) distrito electoral; (*LAW: child: also: ~ of court*) pupilo/a; **~ off** vt (*blow*) desviar, parar; (*attack*) rechazar

warden ['wɔːdn] n (*BRIT: of institution*) director(a) m/f; (*of park, game reserve*) guardián/ana m/f; (*BRIT: also: traffic ~*) guardia m/f

warder ['wɔːdə*] (*BRIT*) n guardián/ana m/f, carcelero/a

wardrobe ['wɔːdrəub] n armario, guardarropa, ropero (*esp LAm*)

warehouse ['wɛəhaʊs] n almacén m, depósito

wares [wɛəz] npl mercancías fpl

warfare ['wɔːfɛə*] n guerra

warhead ['wɔːhed] n cabeza armada

warily ['wɛərɪlɪ] adv con cautela, cautelosamente

warlike ['wɔːlaɪk] adj guerrero; (*appearance*) belicoso

warm [wɔːm] adj caliente; (*thanks*) efusivo; (*clothes etc*) abrigado; (*welcome, day*) caluroso; **it's ~** hace calor; **I'm ~** tengo calor; **~ up** vi (*room*) calentarse; (*person*) entrar en calor; (*athlete*) hacer ejercicios de calentamiento ♦ vt calentar; **~-hearted** adj afectuoso; **~ly** adv afectuosamente; **~th** n calor m

warn [wɔːn] vt avisar, advertir; **~ing** n aviso, advertencia; **~ing light** n luz f de advertencia; **~ing triangle** n (*AUT*) triángulo señalizador

warp [wɔːp] vi (*wood*) combarse ♦ vt combar; (*mind*) pervertir

warrant ['wɒrnt] n autorización f; (*LAW: to arrest*) orden f de detención; (*: to search*) mandamiento de registro

warranty ['wɒrəntɪ] n garantía

warren ['wɒrən] n (*of rabbits*) madriguera; (*fig*) laberinto

warrior ['wɒrɪə*] n guerrero/a

Warsaw ['wɔːsɔː] n Varsovia

warship ['wɔːʃɪp] n buque m o barco de guerra

wart [wɔːt] n verruga

wartime ['wɔːtaɪm] n: **in ~** en tiempos de guerra, en la guerra

wary ['wɛərɪ] adj cauteloso

was [wɒz] pt of **be**

wash [wɒʃ] vt lavar ♦ vi lavarse; (*sea etc*): **to ~ against/over sth** llegar hasta/cubrir algo ♦ n (*clothes etc*) lavado; (*of ship*) estela; **to have a ~** lavarse; **~ away** vt (*stain*) quitar lavando; (*subj: river etc*) llevarse; **~ off** vi quitarse (al lavar); **~ up** vi (*BRIT*) fregar los platos; (*US*) lavarse; **~able** adj lavable; **~basin** (*US* **~bowl**) n lavabo; **~**

cloth (*US*) *n* manopla; **~er** *n* (*TECH*) arandela; **~ing** *n* (*dirty*) ropa sucia; (*clean*) colada; **~ing machine** *n* lavadora; **~ing powder** (*BRIT*) *n* detergente *m* (en polvo)

Washington ['wɔʃɪŋtən] *n* Washington *m*

wash: ~ing-up *n* fregado, platos *mpl* (para fregar); **~ing-up liquid** *n* líquido lavavajillas; **~-out** (*inf*) *n* fracaso; **~room** (*US*) *n* servicios *mpl*

wasn't ['wɔznt] = **was not**

wasp [wɔsp] *n* avispa

wastage ['weɪstɪdʒ] *n* desgaste *m*; (*loss*) pérdida

waste [weɪst] *n* derroche *m*, despilfarro; (*of time*) pérdida; (*food*) sobras *fpl*; (*rubbish*) basura, desperdicios *mpl* ♦ *adj* (*material*) de desecho; (*left over*) sobrante; (*land*) baldío, descampado ♦ *vt* malgastar, derrochar; (*time*) perder; (*opportunity*) desperdiciar; **~s** *npl* (*area of land*) tierras *fpl* baldías; **~ away** *vi* consumirse; **~ disposal unit** (*BRIT*) *n* triturador *m* de basura; **~ful** *adj* derrochador(a); (*process*) antieconómico; **~ ground** (*BRIT*) *n* terreno baldío; **~paper basket** *n* papelera; **~ pipe** *n* tubo de desagüe

watch [wɔtʃ] *n* (*also*: **wrist ~**) reloj *m*; (*MIL*: *group of guards*) centinela *m*; (*act*) vigilancia; (*NAUT*: *spell of duty*) guardia ♦ *vt* (*look at*) mirar, observar; (: *match, programme*) ver; (*spy on, guard*) vigilar; (*be careful of*) cuidarse de, tener cuidado de ♦ *vi* ver, mirar; (*keep guard*) montar guardia; **~ out** *vi* cuidarse, tener cuidado; **~dog** *n* perro guardián; (*fig*) persona u organismo encargado de asegurarse de que las empresas actúan dentro de la legalidad; **~ful** *adj* vigilante, sobre aviso; **~maker** *n* relojero/a; **~man** *n see* **night**; **~ strap** *n* pulsera (de reloj)

water ['wɔːtə*] *n* agua ♦ *vt* (*plant*) regar ♦ *vi* (*eyes*) llorar; (*mouth*) hacerse la boca agua; **~ down** *vt* (*milk etc*) aguar; (*fig: story*) dulcificar, diluir; **~ closet** *n* wáter *m*; **~colour** *n* acuarela; **~cress** *n* berro; **~fall** *n* cascada, salto de agua; **~ heater** *n* calentador *m* de agua; **~ing can** *n* regadera; **~ lily** *n* nenúfar *m*; **~line** *n* (*NAUT*) línea de flotación; **~logged** *adj* (*ground*) inundado; **~ main** *n* cañería del agua; **~melon** *n* sandía; **~proof** *adj* impermeable; **~shed** *n* (*GEO*) cuenca; (*fig*) momento crítico; **~-skiing** *n* esquí *m* acuático; **~tight** *adj* hermético; **~way** *n* vía fluvial *or* navegable; **~works** *n* central *f* depuradora; **~y** *adj* (*coffee etc*) aguado; (*eyes*) lloroso

watt [wɔt] *n* vatio

wave [weɪv] *n* (*of hand*) señal *f* con la mano; (*on water*) ola; (*RADIO, in hair*) onda; (*fig*) oleada ♦ *vi* agitar la mano; (*flag etc*) ondear ♦ *vt* (*handkerchief, gun*) agitar;

~length *n* longitud *f* de onda

waver ['weɪvə*] *vi* (*voice, love etc*) flaquear; (*person*) vacilar

wavy ['weɪvɪ] *adj* ondulado

wax [wæks] *n* cera ♦ *vt* encerar ♦ *vi* (*moon*) crecer; **~ paper** (*US*) *n* papel *m* apergaminado; **~works** *n* museo de cera ♦ *npl* figuras *fpl* de cera

way [weɪ] *n* camino; (*distance*) trayecto, recorrido; (*direction*) dirección *f*, sentido; (*manner*) modo, manera; (*habit*) costumbre *f*; **which ~? − this ~** ¿por dónde?, ¿en qué dirección? − **por aquí**; **on the ~** (*en route*) en (el) camino; **to be on one's ~** estar en camino; **to be in the ~** bloquear el camino; (*fig*) estorbar; **to go out of one's ~ to do sth** desvivirse por hacer algo; **under ~** en marcha; **to lose one's ~** extraviarse; **in a ~** en cierto modo *or* sentido; **no ~!** (*inf*) ¡de eso nada!; **by the ~ ...** a propósito ...; **"~ in"** (*BRIT*) "entrada"; **"~ out"** (*BRIT*) "salida"; **the ~ back** camino de vuelta; **"give ~"** (*BRIT*: *AUT*) "ceda el paso"

waylay [weɪ'leɪ] (*irreg*) *vt* salir al paso a

wayward ['weɪwəd] *adj* díscolo

W.C. *n* (*BRIT*) wáter *m*

we [wiː] *pl pron* nosotros/as

weak [wiːk] *adj* débil, flojo; (*tea etc*) claro; **~en** *vi* debilitarse; (*give way*) ceder ♦ *vt* debilitar; **~ling** *n* debilucho/a; (*morally*) persona de poco carácter; **~ness** *n* debilidad *f*; (*fault*) punto débil; **to have a ~ness for** tener debilidad por

wealth [wɛlθ] *n* riqueza; (*of details*) abundancia; **~y** *adj* rico

wean [wiːn] *vt* destetar

weapon ['wɛpən] *n* arma

wear [wɛə*] (*pt* **wore**, *pp* **worn**) *n* (*use*) uso; (*deterioration through use*) desgaste *m*; (*clothing*): **sports/baby~** ropa de deportes/de niños; **evening ~** ropa de etiqueta ♦ *vt* (*clothes*) llevar; (*shoes*) calzar; (*damage: through use*) gastar, usar ♦ *vi* (*last*) durar; (*rub through etc*) desgastarse; **~ away** *vt* gastar ♦ *vi* desgastarse; **~ down** *vt* gastar; (*strength*) agotar; **~ off** *vi* (*pain etc*) pasar, desaparecer; **~ out** *vt* desgastar; (*person, strength*) agotar; **~ and tear** *n* desgaste *m*

weary ['wɪərɪ] *adj* cansado; (*dispirited*) abatido ♦ *vi*: **to ~ of** cansarse de

weasel ['wiːzl] *n* (*ZOOL*) comadreja

weather ['wɛðə*] *n* tiempo ♦ *vt* (*storm, crisis*) hacer frente a; **under the ~** (*fig: ill*) indispuesto, pachucho; **~-beaten** *adj* (*skin*) curtido; (*building*) deteriorado por la intemperie; **~cock** *n* veleta; **~ forecast** *n* boletín *m* meteorológico; **~man** (*inf*) *n* hombre *m* del tiempo; **~ vane** *n* = **~cock**

weave [wiːv] (*pt* **wove**, *pp* **woven**) *vt* (*cloth*) tejer; (*fig*) entretejer; **~r** *n* tejedor(a) *m/f*; **weaving** *n* tejeduría

web [wɛb] *n* (*of spider*) telaraña; (*on duck's foot*) membrana; (*network*) red *f*

wed [wɛd] (*pt, pp* **wedded**) *vt* casar ♦ *vi* casarse

we'd [wi:d] = **we had; we would**

wedding ['wɛdɪŋ] *n* boda, casamiento; **silver/golden ~ (anniversary)** bodas *fpl* de plata/de oro; **~ day** *n* día *m* de la boda; **~ dress** *n* traje *m* de novia; **~ present** *n* regalo de boda; **~ ring** *n* alianza

wedge [wɛdʒ] *n* (*of wood etc*) cuña; (*of cake*) trozo ♦ *vt* acuñar; (*push*) apretar

Wednesday ['wɛdnzdɪ] *n* miércoles *m inv*

wee [wi:] (*Scottish*) *adj* pequeñito

weed [wi:d] *n* mala hierba, maleza ♦ *vt* escardar, desherbar; **~killer** *n* herbicida *m*; **~y** *adj* (*person*) mequetréfico

week [wi:k] *n* semana; **a ~ today/on Friday** de hoy/del viernes en ocho días; **~day** *n* día *m* laborable; (*com*) día *m* de la semana; **~end** *n* fin *m* de semana; **~ly** *adv* semanalmente, cada semana ♦ *adj* semanal ♦ *n* semanario

weep [wi:p] (*pt, pp* **wept**) *vi, vt* llorar; **~ing willow** *n* sauce *m* llorón

weigh [weɪ] *vt, vi* pesar; **to ~ anchor** levar anclas; **~ down** *vt* sobrecargar; (*fig: with worry*) agobiar; **~ up** *vt* sopesar

weight [weɪt] *n* peso; (*metal ~*) pesa; **to lose/put on ~** adelgazar/engordar; **~ing** *n* (*allowance*): (**London**) **~ing** dietas (*por residir en Londres*); **~lifter** *n* levantador *m* de pesas; **~y** *adj* pesado; (*matters*) de relevancia *or* peso

weir [wɪə*] *n* presa

weird [wɪəd] *adj* raro, extraño

welcome ['wɛlkəm] *adj* bienvenido ♦ *n* bienvenida ♦ *vt* dar la bienvenida a; (*be glad of*) alegrarse de; **thank you — you're ~** gracias — de nada

weld [wɛld] *n* soldadura ♦ *vt* soldar

welfare ['wɛlfɛə*] *n* bienestar *m*; (*social aid*) asistencia social; **~ state** *n* estado del bienestar; **~ work** *n* asistencia social

well [wɛl] *n* fuente *f*, pozo ♦ *adv* bien ♦ *adj*: **to be ~** estar bien (*de salud*) ♦ *excl* ¡vaya!, ¡bueno!; **as ~** también; **as ~ as** además de; **~ done!** ¡bien hecho!; **get ~ soon!** ¡que te mejores pronto!; **to do ~** (*business*) ir bien; (*person*) tener éxito; **~ up** *vi* (*tears*) saltar

we'll [wi:l] = **we will; we shall**

well: **~-behaved** *adj* bueno; **~-being** *n* bienestar *m*; **~-built** *adj* (*person*) fornido; **~-deserved** *adj* merecido; **~-dressed** *adj* bien vestido; **~-groomed** *adj* de buena presencia; **~-heeled** (*inf*) *adj* (*wealthy*) rico

wellingtons ['wɛlɪŋtənz] *npl* (*also:* **wellington boots**) botas *fpl* de goma

well: **~-known** *adj* (*person*) conocido; **~-mannered** *adj* educado; **~-meaning** *adj* bienintencionado; **~-off** *adj* acomodado;

~-read *adj* leído; **~-to-do** *adj* acomodado; **~-wisher** *n* admirador(a) *m/f*

Welsh [wɛlʃ] *adj* galés/esa ♦ *n* (*LING*) galés *m*; **the ~** *npl* los galeses; **~man** *n* galés *m*; **~ rarebit** *n* pan *m* con queso tostado; **~woman** *n* galesa

went [wɛnt] *pt of* **go**

wept [wɛpt] *pt, pp of* **weep**

were [wə:*] *pt of* **be**

we're [wɪə*] = **we are**

weren't [wə:nt] = **were not**

west [wɛst] *n* oeste *m* ♦ *adj* occidental, del oeste ♦ *adv* al *or* hacia el oeste; **the W~** *n* el Oeste, el Occidente; **W~ Country** (*BRIT*) *n*: **the W~ Country** el suroeste de Inglaterra; **~erly** *adj* occidental; (*wind*) del oeste; **~ern** *adj* occidental ♦ *n* (*CINEMA*) película del oeste; **W~ Germany** *n* Alemania Occidental; **W~ Indian** *adj, n* antillano/a *m/f*; **W~ Indies** *npl* Antillas *fpl*; **~ward(s)** *adv* hacia el oeste

wet [wɛt] *adj* (*damp*) húmedo; (*~ through*) mojado; (*rainy*) lluvioso ♦ (*BRIT*) *n* (*POL*) conservador(a) *m/f* moderado/a; **to get ~** mojarse; **"~ paint"** "recién pintado"; **~ blanket** *n*: **to be a ~ blanket** (*fig*) ser un/una aguafiestas; **~suit** *n* traje *m* térmico

we've [wi:v] = **we have**

whack [wæk] *vt* dar un buen golpe a

whale [weɪl] *n* (*ZOOL*) ballena

wharf [wɔ:f] *n* muelle *m*; **wharves** [wɔ:vz] *npl of* **wharf**

--- KEYWORD

what [wɔt] *adj* **1** (*in direct/indirect questions*) qué; **~ size is he?** ¿qué talla usa?; **~ colour/shape is it?** ¿de qué color/forma es?

2 (*in exclamations*): **~ a mess!** ¡qué desastre!; **~ a fool I am!** ¡qué tonto soy!

♦ *pron* **1** (*interrogative*) qué; **~ are you doing?** ¿qué haces *or* estás haciendo?; **~ is happening?** ¿qué pasa *or* está pasando?; **~ is it called?** ¿cómo se llama?; **~ about me?** ¿y yo qué?; **~ about doing ...?** ¿qué tal si hacemos ...?

2 (*relative*) lo que; **I saw ~ you did/was on the table** vi lo que hiciste/había en la mesa

♦ *excl* (*disbelieving*) ¡cómo!; **~, no coffee!** ¡que no hay café!

whatever [wɔt'ɛvə*] *adj*: **~ book you choose** cualquier libro que elijas ♦ *pron*: **do ~ is necessary** haga lo que sea necesario; **~ happens** pase lo que pase; **no reason ~ *or* whatsoever** ninguna razón sea la que sea; **nothing ~** nada en absoluto

whatsoever [wɔtsəu'ɛvə*] *adj* = **whatever**

wheat [wi:t] *n* trigo

wheedle ['wi:dl] *vt*: **to ~ sb into doing**

sth engatusar a uno para que haga algo; **to ~ sth out of sb** sonsacar algo a uno

wheel [wiːl] *n* rueda; (*AUT: also:* **steering ~**) volante *m*; (*NAUT*) timón *m* ♦ *vt* (*pram etc*) empujar ♦ *vi* (*also:* **~ round**) dar la vuelta, girar; **~barrow** *n* carretilla; **~chair** *n* silla de ruedas; **~ clamp** *n* (*AUT*) cepo

wheeze [wiːz] *vi* resollar

────────────── KEYWORD ──────────────

when [wɛn] *adv* cuando; **~ did it happen?** ¿cuándo ocurrió?; **I know ~ it happened** sé cuándo ocurrió

♦ *conj* **1** (*at, during, after the time that*) cuando; **be careful ~ you cross the road** ten cuidado al cruzar la calle; **that was ~ I needed you** fue entonces que te necesité

2 (*on, at which*): **on the day ~ I met him** el día en qué le conocí

3 (*whereas*) cuando

whenever [wɛnˈɛvə*] *conj* cuando; (*every time that*) cada vez que ♦ *adv* cuando sea

where [wɛə*] *adv* dónde ♦ *conj* donde; **this is ~** aquí es donde; **~abouts** *adv* dónde ♦ *n*: **nobody knows his ~abouts** nadie conoce su paradero; **~as** *conj* visto que, mientras; **~by** *pron* por lo cual; **~upon** *conj* con lo cual, después de lo cual; **~ver** [-'ɛvə*] *conj* dondequiera que; (*interrogative*) dónde; **~withal** *n* recursos *mpl*

whet [wɛt] *vt* estimular

whether [ˈwɛðə*] *conj* si; **I don't know ~ to accept or not** no sé si aceptar o no; **~ you go or not** vayas o no vayas

────────────── KEYWORD ──────────────

which [wɪtʃ] *adj* **1** (*interrogative: direct, indirect*) qué; **~ picture(s) do you want?** ¿qué cuadro(s) quieres?; **~ one?** ¿cuál?

2: **in ~ case** en cuyo caso; **we got there at 8 pm, by ~ time the cinema was full** llegamos allí a las 8, cuando el cine estaba lleno

♦ *pron* **1** (*interrogative*) cual; **I don't mind ~** el/la que sea

2 (*relative: replacing noun*) que; (*: replacing clause*) lo que; (*: after preposition*) (el/la) que *etc*, el/la cual *etc*; **the apple ~ you ate/~ is on the table** la manzana que comiste/que está en la mesa; **the chair on ~ you are sitting** la silla en la que estás sentado; **he said he knew, ~ is true/I feared** dijo que lo sabía, lo cual *or* lo que es cierto/me temía

whichever [wɪtʃˈɛvə*] *adj*: **take ~ book you prefer** coja (*SP*) el libro que prefiera; **~ book you take** cualquier libro que coja

whiff [wɪf] *n* vaharada

while [waɪl] *n* rato, momento ♦ *conj* mientras; (*although*) aunque; **for a ~** durante algún tiempo; **~ away** *vt* pasar

whim [wɪm] *n* capricho

whimper [ˈwɪmpə*] *n* sollozo ♦ *vi* lloriquear

whimsical [ˈwɪmzɪkl] *adj* (*person*) caprichoso; (*look*) juguetón/ona

whine [waɪn] *n* (*of pain*) gemido; (*of engine*) zumbido; (*of siren*) aullido ♦ *vi* gemir; zumbar; (*fig: complain*) gimotear

whip [wɪp] *n* látigo; (*POL: person*) encargado de la disciplina partidaria en el parlamento ♦ *vt* azotar; (*CULIN*) batir; (*move quickly*): **to ~ sth out/off** sacar/quitar algo de un tirón; **~ped cream** *n* nata *or* crema montada; **~-round** (*BRIT*) *n* colecta

whirl [wɜːl] *vt* hacer girar, dar vueltas a ♦ *vi* girar, dar vueltas; (*leaves etc*) arremolinarse; **~pool** *n* remolino; **~wind** *n* torbellino

whirr [wɜː*] *vi* zumbar

whisk [wɪsk] *n* (*CULIN*) batidor *m* ♦ *vt* (*CULIN*) batir; **to ~ sb away** *or* **off** llevar volando a uno

whiskers [ˈwɪskəz] *npl* (*of animal*) bigotes *mpl*; (*of man*) patillas *fpl*

whiskey [ˈwɪskɪ] (*US, Ireland*) *n* = **whisky**

whisky [ˈwɪskɪ] *n* whisky *m*

whisper [ˈwɪspə*] *n* susurro ♦ *vi, vt* susurrar

whist [wɪst] (*BRIT*) *n* juego de naipes

whistle [ˈwɪsl] *n* (*sound*) silbido; (*object*) silbato ♦ *vi* silbar

white [waɪt] *adj* blanco; (*pale*) pálido ♦ *n* blanco; (*of egg*) clara; **~ coffee** (*BRIT*) *n* café *m* con leche; **~-collar worker** *n* oficinista *m/f*; **~ elephant** *n* (*fig*) maula; **~ lie** *n* mentirilla; **~ness** *n* blancura; **~ noise** *n* sonido blanco; **~ paper** *n* (*POL*) libro rojo; **~wash** *n* (*paint*) jalbegue *m*, cal *f* ♦ *vt* (*also fig*) blanquear

whiting [ˈwaɪtɪŋ] *n inv* (*fish*) pescadilla

Whitsun [ˈwɪtsn] *n* pentecostés *m*

whittle [ˈwɪtl] *vt*: **to ~ away, ~ down** ir reduciendo

whizz [wɪz] *vi*: **to ~ past** *or* **by** pasar a toda velocidad; **~ kid** (*inf*) *n* prodigio

────────────── KEYWORD ──────────────

who [huː] *pron* **1** (*interrogative*) quién; **~ is it?, ~'s there?** ¿quién es?; **~ are you looking for?** ¿a quién buscas?; **I told her ~ I was** le dije quién era yo

2 (*relative*) que; **the man/woman ~ spoke to me** el hombre/la mujer que habló conmigo; **those ~ can swim** los que saben *or* sepan nadar

whodun(n)it [huːˈdʌnɪt] (*inf*) *n* novela policíaca

whoever [huːˈɛvə*] *pron*: **~ finds it** cualquiera *or* quienquiera que lo encuentre; **ask ~ you like** pregunta a quien quieras;

~ **he marries** no importa con quién se case

whole [həʊl] *adj* (*entire*) todo, entero; (*not broken*) intacto ♦ *n* todo; (*all*): **the ~ of the town** toda la ciudad, la ciudad entera ♦ *n* (*total*) total *m*; (*sum*) conjunto; **on the ~, as a ~** en general; ~ **food(s)** *n(pl)* alimento(s) *m(pl)* integral(es); ~**hearted** *adj* sincero, cordial; ~**meal** *adj* integral; ~**sale** *n* venta al por mayor ♦ *adj* al por mayor; (*fig*: *destruction*) sistemático; ~**saler** *n* mayorista *m/f*; ~**some** *adj* sano; ~**wheat** *adj* = ~**meal**; **wholly** *adv* totalmente, enteramente

--------- KEYWORD ---------

whom [huːm] *pron* **1** (*interrogative*): ~ **did you see?** ¿a quién viste?; **to ~ did you give it?** ¿a quién se lo diste?; **tell me from ~ you received it** dígame de quién lo recibió

2 (*relative*) que; **to ~** a quien(es); **of ~** de quien(es), del/de la que *etc*; **the man ~ I saw/to ~ I wrote** el hombre que vi/a quien escribí; **the lady about/with ~ I was talking** la señora de (la) que/con quien *or* (la) que hablaba

----

whooping cough ['huːpɪŋ-] *n* tos *f* ferina
whore [hɔː*] (*inf*: *pej*) *n* puta

--------- KEYWORD ---------

whose [huːz] *adj* **1** (*possessive*: *interrogative*): ~ **book is this?**, ~ **is this book?** ¿de quién es este libro?; ~ **pencil have you taken?** ¿de quién es el lápiz que has cogido?; ~ **daughter are you?** ¿de quién eres hija?

2 (*possessive*: *relative*) cuyo/a, *pl* cuyos/as; **the man ~ son you rescued** el hombre cuyo hijo rescataste; **those ~ passports I have** aquellas personas cuyos pasaportes tengo; **the woman ~ car was stolen** la mujer a quien le robaron el coche
♦ *pron* de quién; ~ **is this?** ¿de quién es esto?; **I know ~ it is** sé de quién es

--------- KEYWORD ---------

why [waɪ] *adv* por qué; ~ **not?** ¿por qué no?; ~ **not do it now?** ¿por qué no lo haces (*or* hacemos *etc*) ahora?
♦ *conj*: **I wonder ~ he said that** me pregunto por qué dijo eso; **that's not ~ I'm here** no es por eso (por lo) que estoy aquí; **the reason ~** la razón por la que
♦ *excl* (*expressing surprise, shock, annoyance*) ¡hombre!, ¡vaya! (*explaining*): ~, **it's you!** ¡hombre, eres tú!; ~, **that's impossible!** ¡pero sí eso es impossible!

----

wicked ['wɪkɪd] *adj* malvado, cruel
wickerwork ['wɪkəwɜːk] *n* artículos *mpl* de

mimbre ♦ *adj* de mimbre
wicket ['wɪkɪt] *n* (CRICKET: *stumps*) palos *mpl*; (: *grass area*) terreno de juego
wide [waɪd] *adj* ancho; (*area, knowledge*) vasto, grande; (*choice*) amplio ♦ *adv*: **to open** ~ abrir de par en par; **to shoot** ~ errar el tiro; ~**-angle lens** *n* objetivo de gran angular; ~**-awake** *adj* bien despierto; ~**ly** *adv* (*travelled*) mucho; (*spaced*) muy; **it is ~ly believed/known that...** mucha gente piensa/sabe que...; ~**n** *vt* ensanchar; (*experience*) ampliar ♦ *vi* ensancharse; ~ **open** *adj* abierto de par en par; ~**spread** *adj* extendido, general
widow ['wɪdəʊ] *n* viuda; ~**ed** *adj* viudo; ~**er** *n* viudo
width [wɪdθ] *n* anchura; (*of cloth*) ancho
wield [wiːld] *vt* (*sword*) blandir; (*power*) ejercer
wife [waɪf] (*pl* **wives**) *n* mujer *f*, esposa
wig [wɪg] *n* peluca
wiggle ['wɪgl] *vt* menear
wild [waɪld] *adj* (*animal*) salvaje; (*plant*) silvestre; (*person*) furioso, violento; (*idea*) descabellado; (*rough*: *sea*) bravo; (: *land*) agreste; (: *weather*) muy revuelto; ~**s** *npl* regiones *fpl* salvajes, tierras *fpl* vírgenes; ~**erness** ['wɪldənɪs] *n* desierto; ~**-goose chase** *n* (*fig*) búsqueda inútil; ~**life** *n* fauna; ~**ly** *adv* (*behave*) locamente; (*lash out*) a diestro y siniestro; (*guess*) a lo loco; (*happy*) a más no poder
wilful ['wɪlfʊl] (*US* **willful**) *adj* (*action*) deliberado; (*obstinate*) testarudo

--------- KEYWORD ---------

will [wɪl] *aux vb* **1** (*forming future tense*): **I ~ finish it tomorrow** lo terminaré *or* voy a terminar mañana; **I ~ have finished it by tomorrow** lo habré terminado para mañana; ~ **you do it?** ¬ **yes I ~/no I won't** ¿lo harás? – sí/no
2 (*in conjectures, predictions*): **he ~** *or* **he'll be there by now** ya habrá *or* debe (de) haber llegado; **that ~ be the postman** será *or* debe ser el cartero
3 (*in commands, requests, offers*): ~ **you be quiet!** ¡quieres callarte?; ~ **you help me?** ¿quieres ayudarme?; ~ **you have a cup of tea?** ¿te apetece un té?; **I won't put up with it!** ¡no lo soporto!
♦ *vt* (*pt, pp* **willed**): **to ~ sb to do sth** desear que alguien haga algo; **he ~ed himself to go on** con gran fuerza de voluntad, continuó ♦ *n* voluntad *f*; (*testament*) testamento

----

willful ['wɪlfʊl] (*US*) *adj* = **wilful**
willing ['wɪlɪŋ] *adj* (*with goodwill*) de buena voluntad; (*enthusiastic*) entusiasta; **he's ~ to do it** está dispuesto a hacerlo; ~**ly** *adv* con mucho gusto; ~**ness** *n* buena volun-

tad
willow ['wɪləu] *n* sauce *m*
willpower ['wɪlpauə*] *n* fuerza de voluntad
willy-nilly [wɪlɪ'nɪlɪ] *adv* quiérase o no
wilt [wɪlt] *vi* marchitarse
wily ['waɪlɪ] *adj* astuto
win [wɪn] (*pt, pp* **won**) *n* victoria, triunfo ♦
vt ganar; (*obtain*) conseguir, lograr ♦ *vi* ganar; ~ **over** *vt* convencer a; ~ **round**
(*BRIT*) *vt* = ~ **over**
wince [wɪns] *vi* encogerse
winch [wɪntʃ] *n* torno
wind[1] [wɪnd] *n* viento; (*MED*) gases *mpl* ♦
vt (*take breath away from*) dejar sin aliento
a
wind[2] [waɪnd] (*pt, pp* **wound**) *vt* enrollar;
(*wrap*) envolver; (*clock, toy*) dar cuerda a ♦
vi (*road, river*) serpentear; ~ **up** *vt* (*clock*)
dar cuerda a; (*debate, meeting*) concluir,
terminar
windfall ['wɪndfɔːl] *n* golpe *m* de suerte
winding ['waɪndɪŋ] *adj* (*road*) tortuoso;
(*staircase*) de caracol
wind instrument [wɪnd-] *n* (*MUS*) instrumento de viento
windmill ['wɪndmɪl] *n* molino de viento
window ['wɪndəu] *n* ventana; (*in car, train*)
ventanilla; (*in shop etc*) escaparate *m* (*SP*),
vitrina (*AM*); ~ **box** *n* jardinera de ventana; ~ **cleaner** *n* (*person*) limpiador *m* de
cristales; ~ **ledge** *n* alféizar *m*, repisa; ~
pane *n* cristal *m*; ~**-shopping** *n*: **to go**
~**-shopping** ir de escaparates; ~**sill** *n* alféizar *m*, repisa
windpipe ['wɪndpaɪp] *n* tráquea
wind power *n* energía eólica
windscreen ['wɪndskriːn] (*US* **windshield**)
n parabrisas *m inv*; ~ **washer** *n* lavapara-
brisas *m inv*; ~ **wiper** *n* limpiaparabrisas
m inv
windswept ['wɪndswept] *adj* azotado por
el viento
windy ['wɪndɪ] *adj* de mucho viento; **it's** ~
hace viento
wine [waɪn] *n* vino; ~ **bar** *n* enoteca; ~
cellar *n* bodega; ~ **glass** *n* copa (para
vino); ~ **list** *n* lista de vinos; ~ **merchant**
n vinatero; ~ **waiter** *n* escanciador *m*
wing [wɪŋ] *n* ala; (*AUT*) aleta; ~**s** *npl*
(*THEATRE*) bastidores *mpl*; ~**er** *n* (*SPORT*)
extremo
wink [wɪŋk] *n* guiño, pestañeo ♦ *vi* guiñar,
pestañear
winner ['wɪnə*] *n* ganador(a) *m/f*
winning ['wɪnɪŋ] *adj* (*team*) ganador(a);
(*goal*) decisivo; (*smile*) encantador(a); ~**s**
npl ganancias *fpl*
winter ['wɪntə*] *n* invierno ♦ *vi* invernar;
wintry ['wɪntrɪ] *adj* invernal
wipe [waɪp] *n*: **to give sth a** ~ pasar un
trapo sobre algo ♦ *vt* limpiar; (*tape*) borrar;
~ **off** *vt* limpiar con un trapo; (*remove*)

quitar; ~ **out** *vt* (*debt*) liquidar; (*memory*)
borrar; (*destroy*) destruir; ~ **up** *vt* limpiar
wire ['waɪə*] *n* alambre *m*; (*ELEC*) cable *m*
(eléctrico); (*TEL*) telegrama *m* ♦ *vt* (*house*)
poner la instalación eléctrica en; (*also*: ~
up) conectar; (*person: telegram*) telegrafiar
wireless ['waɪəlɪs] (*BRIT*) *n* radio *f*
wiring ['waɪərɪŋ] *n* instalación *f* eléctrica
wiry ['waɪərɪ] *adj* (*person*) enjuto y fuerte;
(*hair*) crespo
wisdom ['wɪzdəm] *n* sabiduría, saber *m*;
(*good sense*) cordura; ~ **tooth** *n* muela
del juicio
wise [waɪz] *adj* sabio; (*sensible*) juicioso
...wise [waɪz] *suffix*: **time**~ en cuanto a *or*
respecto al tiempo
wisecrack ['waɪzkræk] *n* broma
wish [wɪʃ] *n* deseo ♦ *vt* querer; **best** ~**es**
(*on birthday etc*) felicidades *fpl*; **with best**
~**es** (*in letter*) saludos *mpl*, recuerdos *mpl*;
to ~ **sb goodbye** despedirse de uno; **he**
~**ed me well** me deseó mucha suerte; ~
to do/sb to do sth querer hacer/que alguien haga algo; **to** ~ **for** desear; ~**ful** *adj*:
it's ~**ful thinking** eso sería soñar
wishy-washy ['wɪʃɪwɒʃɪ] (*inf*) *adj* (*colour,*
ideas) desvaído
wisp [wɪsp] *n* mechón *m*; (*of smoke*) voluta
wistful ['wɪstful] *adj* pensativo
wit [wɪt] *n* ingenio, gracia; (*also*: ~**s**) inteligencia; (*person*) chistoso/a
witch [wɪtʃ] *n* bruja; ~**craft** *n* brujería; ~**-
hunt** *n* (*fig*) caza de brujas

────────────────── *KEYWORD*

with [wɪð, wɪθ] *prep* **1** (*accompanying, in
the company of*) con (*con+ mí, ti, sí = conmigo, contigo, consigo*); **I was** ~ **him** estaba con él; **we stayed** ~ **friends** nos hospe-
damos en casa de unos amigos; **I'm (not)**
~ **you** (*understand*) (no) te entiendo; **to be**
~ **it** (*inf: person: up-to-date*) estar al tanto;
(: *alert*) ser despabilado
2 (*descriptive, indicating manner etc*) con;
de; **a room** ~ **a view** una habitación con
vistas; **the man** ~ **the grey hat/blue eyes**
el hombre del sombrero gris/de los ojos
azules; **red** ~ **anger** rojo de ira; **to shake**
~ **fear** temblar de miedo; **to fill sth** ~ **water** llenar algo de agua

withdraw [wɪθ'drɔː] (*irreg*) *vt* retirar, sacar
♦ *vi* retirarse; **to** ~ **money (from the bank)**
retirar fondos (del banco); ~**al** *n* retirada;
(*of money*) reintegro; ~**al symptoms** *npl*
(*MED*) síndrome *m* de abstinencia; ~**n** *adj*
(*person*) reservado, introvertido
wither ['wɪðə*] *vi* marchitarse
withhold [wɪθ'həuld] (*irreg*) *vt* (*money*) retener; (*decision*) aplazar; (*permission*) negar; (*information*) ocultar
within [wɪð'ɪn] *prep* dentro de ♦ *adv* den-

tro; ~ **reach (of)** al alcance (de); ~ **sight (of)** a la vista (de); ~ **the week** antes de acabar la semana; ~ **a mile (of)** a menos de una milla (de)

without [wɪð'aut] *prep* sin; **to go ~ sth** pasar sin algo

withstand [wɪθ'stænd] *(irreg) vt* resistir a

witness ['wɪtnɪs] *n* testigo *m/f* ♦ *vt (event)* presenciar; *(document)* atestiguar la veracidad de; **to bear ~ to** *(fig)* ser testimonio de; ~ **box** *n* tribuna de los testigos; ~ **stand** *(US) n* = ~ **box**

witty ['wɪtɪ] *adj* ingenioso

wives [waɪvz] *npl of* **wife**

wizard ['wɪzəd] *n* hechicero

wk *abbr* = **week**

wobble ['wɔbl] *vi* temblar; *(chair)* cojear

woe [wəu] *n* desgracia

woke [wəuk] *pt of* **wake**

woken ['wəukən] *pp of* **wake**

wolf [wulf] *n* lobo; **wolves** [wulvz] *npl of* **wolf**

woman ['wumən] *(pl* **women)** *n* mujer *f;* ~ **doctor** *n* médica; **women's lib** *(inf: pej) n* liberación *f* de la mujer; ~**ly** *adj* femenino

womb [wu:m] *n* matriz *f,* útero

women ['wɪmɪn] *npl of* **woman**

won [wʌn] *pt, pp of* **win**

wonder ['wʌndə*] *n* maravilla, prodigio; *(feeling)* asombro ♦ *vi:* **to ~ whether/why** preguntarse si/por qué; **to ~ at** asombrarse de; **to ~ about** pensar sobre *or* en; **it's no ~ (that)** no es de extrañarse (que *+ subjun);* ~**ful** *adj* maravilloso; ~**fully** *adv* maravillosamente, estupendamente

won't [wəunt] = **will not**

woo [wu:] *vt (woman)* cortejar

wood [wud] *n (timber)* madera; *(forest)* bosque *m;* ~ **carving** *n (act)* tallado en madera; *(object)* talla en madera; ~**ed** *adj* arbolado; ~**en** *adj* de madera; *(fig)* inexpresivo; ~**pecker** *n* pájaro carpintero; ~**wind** *n (MUS)* instrumentos *mpl* de viento de madera; ~**work** *n* carpintería; ~**worm** *n* carcoma

wool [wul] *n* lana; **to pull the ~ over sb's eyes** *(fig)* engatusar a uno; ~**en** *(US) adj* = ~**len;** ~**len** *adj* de lana; ~**lens** *npl* géneros *mpl* de lana; ~**ly** *adj* lanudo, de lana; *(fig: ideas)* confuso; ~**y** *(US) adj* = ~**ly**

word [wə:d] *n* palabra; *(news)* noticia; *(promise)* palabra (de honor) ♦ *vt* redactar; **in other ~s** en otras palabras; **to break/keep one's ~** faltar a la palabra/cumplir la promesa; **to have ~s with sb** reñir con uno; ~**ing** *n* redacción *f;* ~ **processing** *n* proceso de textos; ~ **processor** *n* procesador *m* de textos

wore [wɔ:*] *pt of* **wear**

work [wə:k] *n* trabajo; *(job)* empleo, trabajo; *(ART, LITERATURE)* obra ♦ *vi* trabajar; *(mechanism)* funcionar, marchar; *(medicine)*

ser eficaz, surtir efecto ♦ *vt (shape)* trabajar; *(stone etc)* tallar; *(mine etc)* explotar; *(machine)* manejar, hacer funcionar; **to be out of ~** estar parado, no tener trabajo; ~**s** *n (BRIT: factory)* fábrica ♦ *npl (of clock, machine)* mecanismo; **to ~ loose** *(part)* desprenderse; *(knot)* aflojarse; ~ **on** *vt fus* trabajar en, dedicarse a; *(principle)* basarse en; ~ **out** *vi (plans etc)* salir bien, funcionar ♦ *vt (problem)* resolver; *(plan)* elaborar; **it ~s out at £100** suma 100 libras; ~ **up** *vt:* **to get ~ed up** excitarse; ~**able** *adj (solution)* práctico, factible; ~**aholic** *n* trabajador(a) obsesivo/a *m/f;* ~**er** *n* trabajador(a) *m/f,* obrero/a; ~**force** *n* mano *f* de obra; ~**ing class** *n* clase *f* obrera; ~**ing-class** *adj* obrero; ~**ing order** *n:* **in ~ing order** en funcionamiento; ~**man** *n* obrero; ~**manship** *n* habilidad *f,* trabajo; ~**sheet** *n* hoja de trabajo; ~**shop** *n* taller *m;* ~ **station** *n* puesto *or* estación *f* de trabajo; ~**-to-rule** *(BRIT) n* huelga de celo

world [wə:ld] *n* mundo ♦ *cpd (champion)* del mundo; *(power, war)* mundial; **to think the ~ of sb** *(fig)* tener un concepto muy alto de uno; ~**ly** *adj* mundano; ~**-wide** *adj* mundial, universal

worm [wə:m] *n (also: earth~)* lombriz *f*

worn [wɔ:n] *pp of* **wear** ♦ *adj* usado; ~**out** *adj (object)* gastado; *(person)* rendido, agotado

worried ['wʌrɪd] *adj* preocupado

worry ['wʌrɪ] *n* preocupación *f* ♦ *vt* preocupar, inquietar ♦ *vi* preocuparse; ~**ing** *adj* inquietante

worse [wə:s] *adj, adv* peor ♦ *n* lo peor; **a change for the ~** un empeoramiento; ~**n** *vt, vi* empeorar; ~ **off** *adj (financially):* **to be ~ off** tener menos dinero; *(fig):* **you'll be ~ off this way** de esta forma estarás peor que nunca

worship ['wə:ʃɪp] *n* adoración *f* ♦ *vt* adorar; **Your W~** *(BRIT: to mayor)* señor alcalde; (: *to judge)* señor juez

worst [wə:st] *adj, adv* peor ♦ *n* lo peor; **at ~** en lo peor de los casos

worth [wə:θ] *n* valor *m* ♦ *adj:* **to be ~** valer; **it's ~ it** vale *or* merece la pena; **to be ~ one's while (to do)** merecer la pena (hacer); ~**less** *adj* sin valor; *(useless)* inútil; ~**while** *adj (activity)* que merece la pena; *(cause)* loable

worthy ['wə:ðɪ] *adj* respetable; *(motive)* honesto; ~ **of** digno de

<hr>

KEYWORD

would [wud] *aux vb* **1** *(conditional tense):* **if you asked him he ~ do it** si se lo pidieras, lo haría; **if you had asked him he ~ have done it** si se lo hubieras pedido, lo habría *or* hubiera hecho
2 *(in offers, invitations, requests):* ~ **you**

like a biscuit? ¿quieres una galleta?; (*formal*) ¿querría una galleta?; **~ you ask him to come in?** ¿quiere hacerle pasar?; **~ you open the window please?** ¿quiere *or* podría abrir la ventana, por favor?
3 (*in indirect speech*): **I said I ~ do it** dije que lo haría
4 (*emphatic*): **it WOULD have to snow today!** ¡tenía que nevar precisamente hoy!
5 (*insistence*): **she ~n't behave** no quiso comportarse bien
6 (*conjecture*): **it ~ have been midnight** sería medianoche; **it ~ seem so** parece ser que sí
7 (*indicating habit*): **he ~ go there on Mondays** iba allí los lunes

would-be (*pej*) *adj* presunto
wouldn't ['wudnt] = **would not**
wound¹ [wu:nd] *n* herida ♦ *vt* herir
wound² [waund] *pt, pp of* **wind**
wove [wəuv] *pt of* **weave**
woven ['wəuvən] *pp of* **weave**
wrangle ['ræŋgl] *n* riña
wrap [ræp] *n* (*stole*) chal *m*; (*cape*) capa ♦ *vt* (*also*: **~ up**) envolver; **~per** *n* (*on chocolate*) papel *m*; (*BRIT: of book*) sobrecubierta; **~ping paper** *n* papel *m* de envolver; (*fancy*) papel *m* de regalo
wrath [rɔθ] *n* cólera
wreak [ri:k] *vt*: **to ~ havoc (on)** hacer estragos (en); **to ~ vengeance (on)** vengarse (de)
wreath [ri:θ, *pl* ri:ðz] *n* (*funeral ~*) corona
wreck [rɛk] *n* (*ship: destruction*) naufragio; (*: remains*) restos *mpl* del barco; (*pej: person*) ruina ♦ *vt* (*car etc*) destrozar; (*chances*) arruinar; **~age** *n* restos *mpl*; (*of building*) escombros *mpl*
wren [rɛn] *n* (*ZOOL*) reyezuelo
wrench [rɛntʃ] *n* (*TECH*) llave *f* inglesa; (*tug*) tirón *m*; (*fig*) dolor *m* ♦ *vt* arrancar; **to ~ sth from sb** arrebatar algo violentamente a uno
wrestle ['rɛsl] *vi*: **to ~ (with sb)** luchar (con *or* contra uno); **~r** *n* luchador(a) *m/f* (de lucha libre); **wrestling** *n* lucha libre
wretched ['rɛtʃɪd] *adj* miserable
wriggle ['rɪgl] *vi* (*also*: **~ about**) menearse, retorcerse
wring [rɪŋ] (*pt, pp* **wrung**) *vt* retorcer; (*wet clothes*) escurrir; (*fig*): **to ~ sth out of sb** sacar algo por la fuerza a uno
wrinkle ['rɪŋkl] *n* arruga ♦ *vt* arrugar ♦ *vi* arrugarse
wrist [rɪst] *n* muñeca; **~ watch** *n* reloj *m* de pulsera
writ [rɪt] *n* mandato judicial
write [raɪt] (*pt* **wrote**, *pp* **written**) *vt* escribir; (*cheque*) extender ♦ *vi* escribir; **~ down** *vt* escribir; (*note*) apuntar; **~ off** *vt* (*debt*) borrar (como incobrable); (*fig*) des-

echar por inútil; **~ out** *vt* escribir; **~ up** *vt* redactar; **~-off** *n* siniestro total; **~r** *n* escritor(a) *m/f*
writhe [raɪð] *vi* retorcerse
writing ['raɪtɪŋ] *n* escritura; (*hand-~*) letra; (*of author*) obras *fpl*; **in ~** por escrito; **~ paper** *n* papel *m* de escribir
written ['rɪtn] *pp of* **write**
wrong [rɔŋ] *adj* (*wicked*) malo; (*unfair*) injusto; (*incorrect*) equivocado, incorrecto; (*not suitable*) inoportuno, inconveniente; (*reverse*) del revés ♦ *adv* equivocadamente ♦ *n* injusticia ♦ *vt* ser injusto con; **you are ~ to do it** haces mal en hacerlo; **you are ~ about that, you've got it ~** en eso estás equivocado; **to be in the ~** no tener razón, tener la culpa; **what's ~?** ¿qué pasa?; **to go ~** (*person*) equivocarse; (*plan*) salir mal; (*machine*) estropearse; **~ful** *adj* injusto; **~ly** *adv* mal, incorrectamente; (*by mistake*) por error
wrote [raut] *pt of* **write**
wrought [rɔ:t] *adj*: **~ iron** hierro forjado
wrung [rʌŋ] *pt, pp of* **wring**
wry [raɪ] *adj* irónico
wt. *abbr* = **weight**

Xmas ['ɛksməs] *n abbr* = **Christmas**
X-ray [ɛks'reɪ] *n* radiografía ♦ *vt* radiografiar, sacar radiografías de
xylophone ['zaɪləfəun] *n* xilófono

yacht [jɔt] *n* yate *m*; **~ing** *n* (*sport*) balandrismo; **~sman/woman** *n* balandrista *m/f*
Yank [jæŋk] (*pej*) *n* yanqui *m/f*
Yankee ['jæŋkɪ] (*pej*) *n* = **Yank**
yap [jæp] *vi* (*dog*) aullar
yard [jɑ:d] *n* patio; (*measure*) yarda; **~stick** *n* (*fig*) criterio, norma
yarn [jɑ:n] *n* hilo; (*tale*) cuento, historia

yawn [jɔːn] *n* bostezo ♦ *vi* bostezar; **~ing**
  adj (*gap*) muy abierto
yd(s). *abbr* = **yard(s)**
yeah [jɛə] (*inf*) *adv* sí
year [jɪə*] *n* año; **to be 8 ~s old** tener 8
  años; **an eight-~-old child** un niño de
  ocho años (de edad); **~ly** *adj* anual ♦ *adv*
  anualmente, cada año
yearn [jɔːn] *vi*: **to ~ for sth** añorar algo,
  suspirar por algo; **~ing** *n* ansia, añoranza
yeast [jiːst] *n* levadura
yell [jɛl] *n* grito, alarido ♦ *vi* gritar
yellow ['jɛləu] *adj* amarillo
yelp [jɛlp] *n* aullido ♦ *vi* aullar
yeoman ['jəumən] *n*: **Y~ of the Guard** alabardero de la Casa Real
yes [jɛs] *adv* sí ♦ *n* sí *m*; **to say/answer ~**
  decir/contestar que sí
yesterday ['jɛstədɪ] *adv* ayer ♦ *n* ayer *m*; **~**
  morning/evening ayer por la mañana/
  tarde; **all day ~** todo el día de ayer
yet [jɛt] *adv* ya; (*negative*) todavía ♦ *conj*
  sin embargo, a pesar de todo; **it is not**
  finished ~ todavía no está acabado; **the**
  best ~ el/la mejor hasta ahora; **as ~** hasta
  ahora, todavía
yew [juː] *n* tejo
yield [jiːld] *n* (*AGR*) cosecha; (*COMM*) rendimiento ♦ *vt* ceder; (*results*) producir, dar;
  (*profit*) rendir ♦ *vi* rendirse, ceder; (*US:*
  AUT) ceder el paso
YMCA *n abbr* (= *Young Men's Christian As-*
  sociation) Asociación *f* de Jóvenes Cristia-
  nos
yog(h)ourt ['jəugət] *n* yogur *m*
yog(h)urt ['jəugət] *n* = **yog(h)ourt**
yoke [jəuk] *n* yugo
yolk [jəuk] *n* yema (de huevo)
yonder ['jɔndə*] *adv* allá (a lo lejos)

────────── *KEYWORD* ──────────

you [juː] *pron* **1** (*subject: familiar*) tú, *pl*
  vosotros/as (*SP*), ustedes (*AM*); (*polite*) usted, *pl* ustedes; **~ are very kind** eres/es *etc*
  muy amable; **~ French enjoy your food a**
  vosotros (*or* ustedes) los franceses os (*or*
  les) gusta la comida; **~ and I will go** ire-
  mos tú y yo
2 (*object: direct: familiar*) te, *pl* os (*SP*), les
  (*AM*); (*polite*) le, *pl* les, *f* la, *pl* las; **I know**
  ~ te/le *etc* conozco
3 (*object: indirect: familiar*) te, *pl* os (*SP*),
  les (*AM*); (*polite*) le, *pl* les; **I gave the letter**
  to ~ yesterday te/os *etc* di la carta ayer
4 (*stressed*): **I told you to do it** te dije a ti
  que lo hicieras, es a ti a quien dije que lo
  hicieras; *see also* **3, 5**
5 (*after prep: NB:* con+ *ti* = *contigo: famili-*
  ar) ti, *pl* vosotros/as (*SP*), ustedes (*AM*); (:
  polite) usted, *pl* ustedes; **it's for ~** es para
  ti/vosotros *etc*
6 (*comparisons: familiar*) tú, *pl* vosotros/as

(*SP*), ustedes (*AM*); (: *polite*) usted, *pl* ustedes;
  she's younger than ~ es más joven que tú/
  vosotros *etc*
7 (*impersonal: one*): **fresh air does ~ good**
  el aire puro (te) hace bien; **~ never know**
  nunca se sabe; **~ can't do that!** ¡eso no se
  hace!

you'd [juːd] = **you had**; **you would**
you'll [juːl] = **you will**; **you shall**
young [jʌŋ] *adj* joven ♦ *npl* (*of animal*) cría;
  (*people*): **the ~** los jóvenes, la juventud;
  ~er (*brother etc*) menor; **~ster** *n* joven
  m/f
your [jɔː*] *adj* tu; (*pl*) vuestro; (*formal*) su;
  see also **my**
you're [juə*] = **you are**
yours [jɔːz] *pron* tuyo; (*pl*) vuestro; (*formal*)
  suyo; *see also* **faithfully; mine**[1]; **sincerely**
yourself [jɔː'sɛlf] *pron* tú mismo; (*complement*) te; (*after prep*) tí (mismo); (*formal*)
  usted mismo; (: *complement*) se; (: *after*
  prep) sí (mismo); **yourselves** *pl pron* vosotros mismos; (*after prep*) vosotros (mismos);
  (*formal*) ustedes (mismos); (: *complement*)
  se; (: *after prep*) sí mismos; *see also* **oneself**
youth [juːθ, *pl* juːðz] *n* juventud *f*; (*young*
  man) joven *m*; **~ club** *n* club *m* juvenil;
  ~ful *adj* juvenil; **~ hostel** *n* albergue *m*
  de juventud
you've [juːv] = **you have**
Yugoslav ['juːgəuslɑːv] *adj*, *n*
  yugo(e)slavo/a *m/f*
Yugoslavia [juːgəu'slɑːvɪə] *n* Yugoslavia
yuppie ['jʌpɪ] (*inf*) *adj*, *n* yupi *m/f*, yupy
  m/f
YWCA *n abbr* (= *Young Women's Christian*
  Association) Asociación *f* de Jóvenes Cris-
  tianas

Z z

zany ['zeɪnɪ] *adj* estrafalario
zap [zæp] *vt* (*COMPUT*) borrar
zeal [ziːl] *n* celo, entusiasmo; **~ous** ['zɛl-
  adj celoso, entusiasta
zebra ['ziːbrə] *n* cebra; **~ crossing**
  n paso de peatones
zenith ['zɛnɪθ] *n* cénit *m*
zero ['zɪərəu] *n* cero
zest [zɛst] *n* ánimo, vivacidad
  piel *f*
zigzag ['zɪgzæg] *n* zigzag

guear, hacer eses

zinc [zɪŋk] *n* cinc *m*, zinc *m*

zip [zɪp] *n* (*also:* ~ *fastener,* (*US*) ~*per*) cremallera (*SP*), cierre *m* (*AM*) ♦ *vt* (*also:* ~ *up*) cerrar la cremallera de; ~ **code** (*US*) *n* código postal

zodiac ['zəudɪæk] *n* zodíaco

zone [zəun] *n* zona

zoo [zuː] *n* (jardín *m*) zoo *m*

zoology [zuːˈɔlədʒɪ] *n* zoología

zoom [zuːm] *vi*: **to ~ past** pasar zumbando; ~ **lens** *n* zoom *m*

zucchini [zuːˈkiːnɪ] (*US*) *n*(*pl*) calabacín(ines) *m*(*pl*)

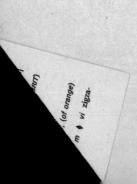